Fodor's 93
Canada

Fodor's Travel Publications, Inc.
New York • Toronto • London • Sydney • Auckland

Fodor's Canada

Editor: Conrad Little Paulus
Contributors: Josée Blanchette, Susan Brown, Marian Bruce, Craig Cabanis, Andrew Coe, Theodore Fischer, Allan Gould, Dorothy Guinan, Holly Hughes, Eve Johnson, Joanne Kates, Margaret Kearney, Danny Kucharsky, Caroline Liou, Patricia Lowe, Mac MacKay, Peter Oliver, Alice Oshins, Marcy Pritchard, Melissa Rivers, David Scott, Cathy Slota, Colleen Thompson, Paula Williams
Creative Director: Fabrizio La Rocca
Cartographer: David Lindroth
Illustrator: Karl Tanner
Cover Photograph: Peter Guttman

Design: Vignelli Associates

Special Sales

Contents

Maps and Plans

Foreword

We wish to express our gratitude to those who helped prepare this guide: the Canadian Consulate General office in New York, particularly Lois Gerber and Barbara Cartwright; the Montréal Convention and Tourism Bureau; the Québec Government Ministry of Tourism, particularly Brian LeCompte, Pauline Roy, and Manon Lefebvre; the Government of Newfoundland and Labrador Department of Development, especially Kay Coxworthy; Dana Ottman of Ontario House in New York; Helen–Jean Newman of the New Brunswick Department of Tourism; the Nova Scotia Department of Tourism, especially Randy Brooks and Lynn McGuinness; also Cathy Quesnelle; Lynda Hanscombe of the PEI Department of Tourism and Parks; the Metropolitan Toronto Convention & Visitors Association; Tourism Vancouver, especially Elvira Quarin; Whistler Resort Association; and the Alberta, Manitoba, and British Columbia Tourism bureaus.

While every care has been taken to ensure the accuracy of the information in this guide, the passage of time will always bring change, and consequently, the publisher cannot accept responsibility for errors that may occur.

All prices and opening times are based on information supplied to us at press time. Hours and admission fees may change, however, and the prudent traveler will avoid inconvenience by calling ahead.

Fodor's wants to hear about your travel experiences, both pleasant and unpleasant. When a hotel or restaurant fails to live up to its billing, let us know and we will investigate the complaint and revise our entries where the facts warrant it. Send your letters to the editors of Fodor's Travel Publications, 201 E. 50th Street, New York, NY 10022.

Highlights'93 and Fodor's Choice

Highlights '93

Efforts to hold together the Canadian union still look hopeful. The failure in 1990 of the Meech Lake Accord, a three-year attempt to grant the French-speaking province of Quebec special status under the Canadian Constitution, put Canada under a pressing deadline: According to law, if the federal and provincial governments couldn't reach an agreement before the end of 1992, the people of Quebec could hold a referendum on whether or not to remain in the union. A new **constitutional revision** proposed in February 1992, however, has the backing of all three major political parties—the Progressive Conservatives (Prime Minister Brian Mulroney's party), the Liberals, and the New Democrats. This proposal includes many steps toward a general decentralization of the federal government, to meet the demands not only of Quebec but also of the western provinces that resisted having special concessions for Quebec. It would also turn the Parliament's upper house, the Senate, into an elected body similar to the U.S. Senate, as opposed to the current Senate in which members are appointed to serve until age 75. While the current Senate has relatively little power, like the House of Lords in the United Kingdom, the elected Senate would have power equal to that of the lower house, the House of Commons. The new proposal has a good chance of being accepted, since it only requires ratification by seven of the country's 10 provinces (the Meech Lake Accord had to be ratified by all).

The 7% **Goods and Services Tax** that went into effect in 1991 imposed on virtually all goods and services, including restaurant meals, fast-food, hotel rooms, car rentals, and admission fees. In some provinces, the nationwide GST tax replaces former provincial taxes, but in others it is levied in addition to provincial taxes. It is refundable however, to tourists from other countries, provided they keep original receipts and apply for the refund. The refund system is complicated, so you may want to obtain information before you travel, by calling 613/991–3346 (outside Canada) or, from within Canada, 800/66–VISIT. You can also write to Revenue Canada, Customs and Excise Visitor's Rebate Program, Ottawa, Canada K1A 1J5, or pick up refund application forms and an explanatory booklet at airports, shops, hotels, and border crossing stations.

Toronto Busy **Pearson International Airport** has considerably expanded its facilities recently, and a face-lift at Terminal 2, which accommodates Air Canada, has just been completed. The city's skyline has a new addition at Yonge and Front streets: the twin towers of **BCE Place** (BC refers to Bell Canada), which will incorporate at ground level the restored 1885 **Bank of Montréal** building. When restoration is complete, the majestic former bank will house the new **Hockey Hall of Fame.**

Montréal In the wake of last year's 350th anniversary celebrations, Montréal has expanded its museum offerings. The annual Just for Laughs comedy festival held here each July spawned a new museum: the **International Museum of Humor,** situated in a former brewery. Exhibits will focus on cartoons, advertising, films, caricatures, and humor in literature. The **McCord Museum of Canadian History** doubled its exhibition space, renovating and expanding the historic building in which it is housed, the former McGill University Student Union Building. The new space gives the museum room to display more of its collection of Native Indian culture, historic Montréal photographs, decorative arts, costumes, and textiles. Exhibition space has tripled at the **Montréal Museum of Fine Arts,** with a new wing added directly across from the original structure on Rue Sherbrooke.

Montréal's vast **Underground City** has grown, too, with a connecting link built between Place Ville Marie to the Eaton Centre shopping mall. Travelers at the Voyageur bus terminals will find in front of it a new park, **Square Berri,** which features sculptures and public amenities, including a café and a stage.

Growth is upward as well as outward, with two noticeable additions to the skyline: the **IBM–Marathon Tower** on Boulevard René Lévesque and a skyscraper at **1000 rue de la Guachetière.** The latter features an indoor skating rink, open year-round, with an ice surface two-thirds that of the Montréal Forum. Both new buildings are as high as the top of Mont-Royal, the maximum height permitted by the city's new master plan for downtown development.

In the **Vieux-Port** (Old Port), the Lachine Canal has been reopened to pleasure craft, with moorings and recreational facilities along the banks. Archaeological ruins under Place Royale, site of the city's first settlement 351 years ago, are the central attraction of a new interpretation center at **Pointe à Callière** in the west end of Vieux-Montréal (Old Montréal).

Québec City The **Château Frontenac,** the city's landmark castle hotel, celebrates its 100th birthday this year with pomp and glitter, culminating in a big party on December 18. In preparation for this anniversary, the hotel renovated all guest rooms and built a new wing, adding more guest rooms, a health spa, and an indoor heated pool.

Rumor has it that another city landmark will be in the news this year. The **Capitol,** a turn-of-the-century theater just outside the St.-Jean Gate, may reopen after being closed for 20 years. Plans for the $12-million restoration include a 1,400-seat cabaret, a small European-style hotel, a bistro and terrace, and an interior garden.

British Columbia A new high-speed ferry service called **Sealink Express,** carrying passengers only, has begun running from downtown Vancouver to downtown Victoria, allowing visitors to take in both towns without the long trip to and from the regular car-ferry terminals. Another ferry company, Sea Containers, Ltd., is currently refurbishing its *Princess Marguerite* ferry with possible plans to put it to work on the Vancouver–Prince Rupert route along the Inside Passage. The plans for a new car ferry linking Victoria with Seattle, Washington, are still in the making.

Local Vancouver sightseeing has been improved, too, thanks to the **Vancouver Trolleys,** like old-fashioned streetcars, that take you on a guided tour of all the major attractions (Stanley Park, English Bay, Gastown, Robson Street, Granville Island, the Vancouver Museum, Queen Elizabeth Park, Chinatown, and Science World) for an all-day unlimited-stop ticket price of only $15 adults, $7 children.

British Columbia's High Country plays host to two big events in 1993: the **World Fly Fishing Tournament** outside Kamloops in early July, and the **Canada Summer Games,** also in Kamloops, in early August.

Canadian Rockies In the mountainous outback, an ongoing debate continues regarding trail usage. The **Canadian Parks Service** currently limits mountain biking, for the most part, to fire roads, while studying the use of bikes on backcountry trails. Park officials are concerned about encounters between bikers and wildlife (especially bears, who are easily surprised by swiftly approaching bikes) and about bikers having trouble getting out of the deep backcountry if their bikes break down.

Manitoba, Saskatchewan, Alberta Things are relatively quiet in the prairie provinces. A new Interpretive Centre will open in Cardston, Alberta, in 1993 to feature the **Remington Alberta Carriage Collection,** an assortment of restored horse-drawn carriages.

Ontario The possibility of a law permitting **casino gambling** has Ontario developers scurrying about looking for likely casino sites to buy. While no decision had been made at press time, general opinion in the province has changed over the past few years to favor such a law, largely because of the success of various lottery programs. The government would likely allow four or five casinos, possibly in Toronto, Sault Ste. Marie, Grand Bend, Ottawa, and Niagara Falls.

Quebec Province The ongoing constitutional debate, in Quebec and across Canada, finds Quebec still seeking special recognition of its French language and culture. A government policy paper requested that the province be recognized as a "sovereign state," although it could remain part of the Canadian Federation if granted certain conditions. If the federal and provincial governments do not reach an agreement, Quebec will hold a vote in November 1992, allowing the people of the province to decide their own future.

Nova Scotia The province's most recently opened national park, **Kekimkujik Seaside Adjunct,** a formerly private preserve, is still wild and remote, though hiking trails make it accessible to the public. To attract convention business, the province has been opening **meeting facilities** in places besides Halifax, which is still the major convention center. Inverary Lodge, in Baddeck, and White Point Beach Lodge, in Liverpool, now offer facilities for groups of 100 to 150.

Prince Edward Island A government announcement of a **causeway** to be built linking New Brunswick and Prince Edward Island has caused mixed reaction on the island. Although improved accessibility may increase tourism revenues and lower the cost of many goods currently shipped to the island, residents also fear disruption of their peaceful, unspoiled lifestyle, which is in itself a tourist draw. No construction date has been set—it may in fact be years away.

New Brunswick A 223-room Sheraton hotel opened in late spring 1992 in **Fredericton,** adding significantly to that city's supply of hotel rooms, although Saint John still offers more beds. About 11 miles west of Fredericton, the **Kings Clear Hotel and Resort** has opened—a new modern hotel, with an interesting history. It is operated by the Malicete Indian Band at Mactaquac, who received government help in building and running the motel as compensation for their voluntary surrender of their traditional net-fishing activity, which was endangering the Atlantic salmon.

The section of the **Trans-Canada Highway** that runs through New Brunswick is being upgraded, with the notable addition of signposts alerting travelers to the existence of special "scenic trails," off-the-beaten-track roads that motorists might otherwise miss.

Newfoundland and Labrador In 1993 the province will begin gearing up for the celebrations to come in 1997, celebrating John Cabot's landing in North America.

Wilderness Canada Parks Canada is moving toward opening visitor facilities in two new wilderness areas: **Northern Yukon National Park,** which contains one of the world's largest caribou herds, and **Ellesmere Island National Park,** with its extraordinary polar oasis of plant, animal, and bird life.

Fodor's Choice

No two people will agree on what makes a perfect vacation, but it's fun and helpful to know what others think. We hope you'll have a chance to experience some of Fodor's Choices yourself in Canada. For detailed information about each entry, refer to the appropriate chapter.

Toronto

Attractions Greektown, Toronto
Harbourfront, downtown Toronto
Ontario Science Centre, northeast Toronto
Royal Ontario Museum, Queen's Park

Shopping Eaton Centre
Kensington Market/Chinatown
Yorkville Avenue/Bloor Street area

Cultural Events Canadian Opera Company at the O'Keefe Centre
National Ballet of Canada at the O'Keefe Centre
Theater at the Royal Alexandra, St. Lawrence Centre, Elgin, and Winter Garden theaters

Restaurants Splendido (*Expensive*)
BamBoo (*Moderate*)
New World (*Moderate*)
Thai Magic (*Moderate*)
Pearl Court (*Inexpensive*)

Hotels Four Seasons Toronto (*Very Expensive*)
Chestnut Park Hotel (*Expensive*)
Journey's End Suites (*Moderate*)

Montréal

Attractions Montréal Botanical Garden
Montréal Museum of Fine Arts
La Ronde

Shopping Place Montréal Trust
Rue Faubourg Ste-Catherine
Notre-Dame Ouest for antiques
Marché aux puces (flea market), Vieux-Montréal
Les Promenades de la Cathédrale

Cultural Events L'Opéra de Montréal
L'Orchestre Symphonique de Montréal
Théâtre du Nouveau Monde

Restaurants Hostellerie Les Trois Tilleuls, Montérégie (*Very Expensive*)
Les Mignardises (*Very Expensive*)
Milos (*Expensive*)

Les Filles du Roy (*Moderate–Expensive*)

Hotels Le Quatre Saisons (*Very Expensive*)
Ritz-Carlton (*Very Expensive*)
Delta Montréal (*Expensive*)
Château Versailles (*Moderate*)

Québec City

Attractions Château Frontenac
Citadelle
Musée de la Civilisation

Shopping Marché du Vieux-Port
Place Québec
Quartier Petit-Champlain

Cultural Events Bibliothèque Gabrielle-Roy
Grand Théâtre de Québec

Restaurants À la Table de Serge Bruyère (*Very Expensive*)
Aux Anciens Canadiens (*Expensive*)
L'Echaudée (*Moderate*)
Chez Temporel (*Inexpensive*)

Hotels Hilton International Québec (*Very Expensive*)
Manoir d'Auteuil (*Expensive*)
L'Auberge du Quartier (*Moderate*)
Hôtel Maison Sainte-Ursule (*Inexpensive*)

Vancouver

Attractions Dr. Sun-yat Sen Classical Garden, Chinatown
Granville Public Market, Granville Island
Vancouver Aquarium

Shopping Fourth Avenue (between Burrard and Balsam streets)
Pacific Center Mall
Robson Street

Restaurants Tojo's (*Expensive*)
English Bay Café (*Moderate*)
The Raintree (*Moderate*)
Phnom Penh (*Inexpensive*)

Hotels Le Meridien (*Very Expensive*)
Wedgewood Hotel (*Expensive*)
Georgia Hotel (*Moderate*)
Sylvia Hotel (*Inexpensive*)

British Columbia

Attractions Butchart Gardens, Victoria
O'Keefe Historic Ranch, Okanagan Valley
Museum of Northern British Columbia, Prince Rupert
Native Heritage Center, Duncan

Shopping Government Street, Victoria
Market Square, Victoria

Great Outdoors Adams River Salmon Run, Okanagan Valley
Inside Passage
Pacific Rim National Park, Vancouver Island

Restaurants Sooke Harbour House, Sooke (*Very Expensive*)
The Aerie, Malahat (*Expensive*)
Les Deux Gros, Whistler (*Expensive*)
Old Mahle House, Nanaimo (*Moderate*)
Six-Mile-House, Victoria (*Inexpensive*)

Hotels The Aerie, Malahat (*Very Expensive*)
Hotel Grand Pacific, Victoria (*Very Expensive*)
Le Chamois, Whistler (*Very Expensive*)
Lake Okanagan Resort, Kelowna (*Expensive*)
The Kingfisher Inn, Courtenay (*Moderate*)
Lac le Jeune Resort, Kamloops (*Moderate*)
Craigmyle Guest House, Victoria (*Inexpensive–Moderate*)

Canadian Rockies

Sights The drive along the Icefields Parkway
The view from the Jasper Tramway
Lake Louise and Moraine Lake

Sporting Activities Mountaineering around the Columbia Icefields and the Bugaboos of the British Columbia Rockies
Horse-pack trips in Kananaskis Country
Skiing at Lake Louise, Nakiska, and Panorama
Heli-skiing in the British Columbia Rockies

Restaurants Le Beaujolais, Banff (*Very Expensive*)
Post Hotel, Lake Louise (*Very Expensive*)
One-Twelve, Revelstoke (*Expensive*)
Emerald Lake Lodge, Yoho (*Moderate–Expensive*)
Barbary Coast, Banff (*Inexpensive–Moderate*)

Hotels Chateau Lake Louise (*Very Expensive*)
Emerald Lake Lodge, Yoho (*Expensive*)
Storm Mountain Lodge, Banff (*Moderate–Expensive*)
Kilmorey Lodge, Waterton Lakes (*Moderate*)

Manitoba, Saskatchewan, Alberta

Attractions Alberta Science Centre/Planetarium, Calgary
Devonian Gardens, Calgary
Manitoba Museum of Man and Nature, Winnipeg
Muttart Conservatory, Edmonton
University of Saskatchewan, Saskatoon
Wascana Waterfowl Park Display Ponds, Regina

Shopping Centre Four, Calgary
Portage Place, Winnipeg
Strathdee Shoppes, Regina
West Edmonton Mall

Restaurants	Owl's Nest, Calgary (*Very Expensive*)
	Unheard of Dining Lounge, Edmonton (*Very Expensive*)
	Victor's, Winnipeg (*Very Expensive*)
	Mieka's, Regina (*Expensive*)
	Bistro Dansk, Winnipeg (*Moderate*)
	Adonis, Saskatoon (*Inexpensive*)
	Buzzards Café, Calgary (*Inexpensive*)
	Chianti, Edmonton (*Inexpensive*)
Hotels	Hilton International Edmonton (*Very Expensive*)
	Westin Hotel, Calgary (*Very Expensive*)
	Edmonton House (*Expensive*)
	Place Louis Riel, Winnipeg (*Expensive*)
	Sheraton Centre, Regina (*Expensive*)
	Prince Royal Inn, Calgary (*Moderate*)
	King George, Saskatoon (*Inexpensive*)
	Sandman Inn, Regina (*Inexpensive*)

Province of Ontario

Attractions	Old Fort William
	Maid of the Mist boats
	Sainte Marie Among the Hurons
	View of Niagara Falls by helicopter
Restaurants	Elora Mill, Elora (*Expensive*)
	Inn at the Falls, Bracebridge (*Expensive*)
	La Brassine, Goderich (*Moderate*)
Hotels	Château Laurier, Ottawa (*Very Expensive*)
	Langdon Hall, Cambridge (*Very Expensive*)
	Prince of Wales, Niagara-on-the-Lake (*Very Expensive*)
	Inn at the Falls, Bracebridge (*Expensive*)
	Albion Hotel, Bayfield (*Moderate*)
	Hartley House Hotel, Walkerton (*Inexpensive*)

Province of Québec

Sights	Basilica of Ste-Anne de Beaupre
	Bonaventure Island, the Gaspé Peninsula
Restaurants	L'Eau à la Bouche, Ste-Adèle (*Very Expensive*)
	Chatel Vienna, Ste-Agathe (*Moderate–Expensive*)
	Mouton Noir, Baie-St-Paul (*Inexpensive–Moderate*)
Hotels	Auberge la Pinsonnière, La Malbaie (*Very Expensive*)
	Hostellerie Les Trois Tilleuls, St. Marc sur Richelieu (*Very Expensive*)
	Auberge du Lac Saint-Piérre, Pointe duLac (*Expensive–Very Expensive*)
	Auberge la Maison Otis, Baie-St-Paul (*Expensive–Very Expensive*)
	Hôtel Cap-aux-Pierres, La Baleine (*Expensive*)
	Bishop's University, Lennoxville (*Inexpensive*)

Nova Scotia

Sights The Citadel, Halifax
Fortress Louisbourg, Cape Breton Island
Mabou Harbour, Cape Breton
Peggy's Cove

Restaurants Amherst Shore Country Inn, Amherst (*Expensive*)
Clipper Cay, Halifax (*Expensive*)
Daily Catch, Halifax (*Moderate*)

Hotels Delta Barrington, Halifax (*Very Expensive*)
Sheraton Halifax (*Very Expensive*)
Blomidon Inn, Wolfville (*Expensive*)
Normaway Inn, Margaree Valley (*Moderate*)
Heart of Hart's Tourist Farm, Northeast Margaree
(*Inexpensive*)

Prince Edward Island

Attractions Annual musical *Anne of Green Gables* at Confederation
Centre of the Arts, Charlottetown
Fort Amherst Port LaJoie National Historic Site, Rocky
Point
Green Gables, Cavendish
Province House, Charlottetown

Restaurants The Griffon Room, Charlottetown (*Very Expensive*)
Claddagh Room Restaurant, Charlottetown (*Expensive*)
Lobster suppers in New Glasgow, New London, and Hope
River (*Moderate*)

Hotels Dalvay-by-the-Sea, Grand Tracadie (*Very Expensive*)
Prince Edward Hotel and Convention Centre,
Charlottetown (*Very Expensive*)
Shaw's Hotel and Cottages, Brackley Beach (*Very
Expensive*)
Duchess of Kent Inn, Charlottetown (*Moderate*)
Sherwood Motel, Winslow (*Inexpensive*)
Southfort Motel, Charlottetown (*Inexpensive*)

New Brunswick

Attractions Acadian Village, Grande Anse, near Caraquet
Kings Landing Historical Settlement, Prince William,
near Fredericton

Shopping Craft and antiques shops of St. Andrews and Gagetown
Mulhouse Country Classics, Fredericton

Restaurants La Belle Vie, Saint John (*Expensive*)
Cy's, Moncton (*Moderate–Expensive*)
Goan's On Muffin Shop and Tearoom, Burton
(*Inexpensive*)

Hotels Hilton, Saint John (*Expensive*)
Sheraton Inn Fredericton, Fredericton (*Expensive*)

Oakley House, Jemseg (*Moderate–Expensive*)
Steamer Stop Inn, Jemseg (*Moderate*)

Newfoundland and Labrador

Attractions L' Anse aux Meadows, northern tip of Newfoundland
Signal Hill, St. John's
Gros Morne Mountain, Gros Morne National Park

Shopping NONIA, St. John's, for crafts

Restaurants The Cellar, Baird's Cove (*Very Expensive*)
Flake House, Quida Vida Village (*Expensive*)
Stone House, Kenna's Hill (*Moderate–Expensive*)

Hotels Hotel Newfoundland, St. John's (*Expensive*)
Compton House Bed-and-Breakfast, St. John's (*Moderate*)
Journey's End Motel, St. John's (*Moderate*)

Wilderness Canada

Attractions Klondike Gold Fields, Dawson City
Prince of Wales Northern Heritage Centre, Yellowknife
S. S. *Klondike*, Whitehorse
Virginia Falls, Nahanni National Park

Fishing Lodges Kluane Wilderness Lodge, Yukon
Plummer's Great Bear Lake Lodge, Northwest
Territories

Canada

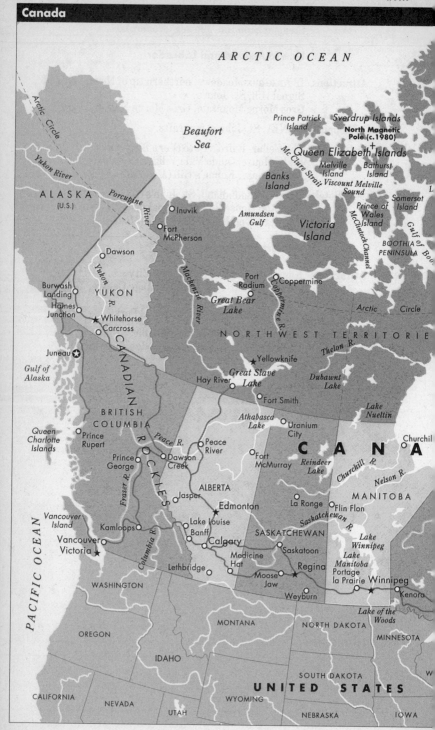

ARCTIC OCEAN

Arctic Circle

Yukon River

Beaufort Sea

Prince Patrick Island

Sverdrup Islands

North Magnetic Pole (c.1980) +

Queen Elizabeth Islands

Mc Clure Strait

Melville Island

Bathurst Island

Viscount Melville Sound

ALASKA (U.S.)

Porcupine River

Banks Island

Amundsen Gulf

Victoria Island

Prince of Wales Island

Somerset Island

L

McClintock Channel

BOOTHIA PENINSULA

Gulf of Boo

Inuvik

Fort McPherson

Dawson

Mackenzie River

Port Radium

Coppermine

Coppermine River

YUKON

Yukon R.

Burwash Landing

Haines Junction

Whitehorse

Carcross

Great Bear Lake

Arctic Circle

Juneau

CANADIAN

NORTHWEST TERRITORIE

Gulf of Alaska

Yellowknife

Thelon R.

Hay River

Great Slave Lake

Dubawnt Lake

Lake Nueltin

BRITISH COLUMBIA

ROCKIES

Fort Smith

Athabasca Lake

Uranium City

CANA

Churchill

Queen Charlotte Islands

Prince Rupert

Peace R.

Dawson Creek

Peace River

Fort McMurray

Reindeer Lake

Churchill R.

Nelson R.

Prince George

Fraser R.

Jasper

ALBERTA

MANITOBA

Vancouver Island

Kamloops

Lake Louise

Edmonton

La Ronge

Flin Flon

Saskatchewan R.

Banff

SASKATCHEWAN

Lake Winnipeg

PACIFIC OCEAN

Vancouver

Victoria

Columbia R.

Calgary

Medicine Hat

Saskatoon

Lake Manitoba

Portage la Prairie

Winnipeg

Lethbridge

Moose Jaw

Regina

Kenora

WASHINGTON

Weyburn

Lake of the Woods

OREGON

MONTANA

NORTH DAKOTA

MINNESOTA

IDAHO

SOUTH DAKOTA

UNITED STATES

CALIFORNIA

NEVADA

UTAH

WYOMING

NEBRASKA

IOWA

ICELAND

GREENLAND
(Denmark)

Denmark Strait

Ellesmere Island

Devon Island

Lancaster Sound

Baffin Bay

Baffin Island

Davis Strait

oothia

Prince Charles Island

Foxe Basin

ES

Southampton Island

Lake Amadjuak

Iqaluit

Lake Harbour

Hudson Strait

Cape Chidley

Labrador Sea

Coats Island *Mansel Island*

Ivujivik

Ungava Bay

Nain

Hudson Bay

hill

D   A

Belcher Islands

Fort Severn

NEWFOUNDLAND

LABRADOR

Battle Harbour

Schefferville

Goose Bay

Labrador City

Gander

Severn R.

Fort George

James Bay

Q U E B E C

Sept-Iles

Anticosti Island

Gulf of St. Lawrence

St. John's

Newfoundland

Lake Mistassini

GASPÉ PENINSULA

ST. PIERRE AND MIQUELON
(France)

O N T A R I O

Moosonee

Rimouski

River

PRINCE EDWARD ISLAND

Chicoutimi

NEW BRUNSWICK

Sydney

Lake Nipigon

Cochrane

Ste.-Agathe-Des-Monts

Québec City

Fredericton

Charlottetown

NOVA SCOTIA

Thunder Bay

Timmins

Trois-Rivières

Saint John

Halifax

Lake Superior

Sudbury

North Bay

Montréal

MAINE

Bay of Fundy

Sault Ste. Marie

Lake Huron

Ottawa

St. Lawrence

VT.

N.H.

N

ATLANTIC OCEAN

WISCONSIN

Lake Michigan

Toronto

Lake Ontario

NEW YORK

MASSACHUSETTS

R.I.

MICHIGAN

Niagara Falls

Lake Erie

CONN.

0   400 miles

ILLINOIS

INDIANA

OHIO

PENNSYLVANIA

N.J.

0   600 km

World Time Zones

MONDAY
SUNDAY

International Date Line

+12 +13

-9

-10

+12

-11

-10

+11

+12

1

2

3

4

5

6

7

-7

-8

8

9

-6

10

11

12

-5

13

14 **15**

16

17

18

-4

-5

19

20

-5

21

22

23

24

-4

-3

-3

-4

-3

-3

-4

-5

25

+11 +12 - -11 -10 -9 -8 -7 -6 -5 -4 -3 -2

Numbers below vertical bands relate each zone to Greenwich Mean Time (0 hrs.).
Local times frequently differ from these general indications,
as indicated by light-face numbers on map.

Algiers, **29**	Berlin, **34**	Delhi, **48**	Istanbul, **40**
Anchorage, **3**	Bogotá, **19**	Denver, **8**	Jerusalem, **42**
Athens, **41**	Budapest, **37**	Djakarta, **53**	Johannesburg, **44**
Auckland, **1**	Buenos Aires, **24**	Dublin, **26**	Lima, **20**
Baghdad, **46**	Caracas, **22**	Edmonton, **7**	Lisbon, **28**
Bangkok, **50**	Chicago, **9**	Hong Kong, **56**	London (Greenwich), **27**
Beijing, **54**	Copenhagen, **33**	Honolulu, **2**	Los Angeles, **6**
	Dallas, **10**		Madrid, **38**
			Manila, **57**

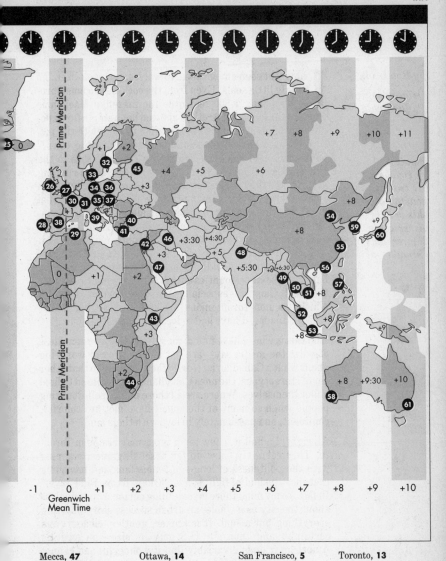

-1   0   +1   +2   +3   +4   +5   +6   +7   +8   +9   +10

Greenwich
Mean Time

Mecca, **47**	Ottawa, **14**	San Francisco, **5**	Toronto, **13**
Mexico City, **12**	Paris, **30**	Santiago, **21**	Vancouver, **4**
Miami, **18**	Perth, **58**	Seoul, **59**	Vienna, **35**
Montréal, **15**	Reykjavík, **25**	Shanghai, **55**	Warsaw, **36**
Moscow, **45**	Rio de Janeiro, **23**	Singapore, **52**	Washington, D.C., **17**
Nairobi, **43**	Rome, **39**	Stockholm, **32**	Yangon, **49**
New Orleans, **11**	Saigon (Ho Chi Minh City), **51**	Sydney, **61**	Zürich, **31**
New York City, **16**		Tokyo, **60**	

Introduction

by Bob Levin

Originally from Philadelphia, Pennsylvania, Maclean's *Foreign Editor Bob Levin moved to Toronto in October 1985. He traveled from coast to coast for this article on an American's impressions of Canada.*

I have not seen any moose. No wolves, no musk-oxen, no cuddly little seals. Even from the cockpit of a small propeller plane, 1,500 feet over the mazelike Mackenzie Delta in the icebound Arctic, I spotted not a single furry polar bear lumbering out of hibernation to complete the picture. "Foxes have been coming right up into the town," advised Ronald Knoller, who runs a general store in the tiny Arctic settlement of Aklavik. "You see them running around, and they've tangled with dog teams." But not when I was there. I did see an impressive elk in Banff National Park, trotting casually by the roadside, but for me Canada's wildlife has consisted mostly of squawking seagulls and mischievous raccoons in my Toronto neighborhood. And maybe that is just as well: It has forced an American, newly arrived, to avoid at least the "moose" half of the hated moose-and-Mounties cliché. While trying to discover the real Canada—especially the one beyond Toronto, which, as non-Torontonians are quick to argue, is not *really* Canada—I have had to focus on its people.

And this is what I have found: most Canadians—regardless of what the media say—are not sitting around worrying about what a Canadian is. Nor do they conform to that other set of stereotypes, the ones Canadians are supposed to hold about themselves. Where are all those pallid, self-doubting people when so many of the ones I have met are colorful, confident, and passionately in love with their land?

All right, I admit it, a few tepid types may reside in Toronto. They certainly show up for baseball games, clapping with the politeness of long-ago tennis fans and mouthing that most insipid of fight songs, "Okay, okay, Blue Jays." In fact, to my mind there is something curiously passionless about the city as a whole, an urban success story boasting everything but a soul. It is kinder, gentler, cleaner, and certainly safer than any U.S. city its size—my visiting American friends invariably find it wonderful and cannot understand its New York–like, love-to-hate-it place in the Canadian national consciousness. My own feelings fall closer to the American view. But "I love Toronto" could never be the city's slogan—no, I *like* Toronto sums it up perfectly.

It has been on trips outside the city, to the more far-flung sectors of this most resolutely regional of nations, that I have found Canada at its more extreme, independent, quirky—even romantic, as un-Canadian a word as that is supposed to be. One snow-swept morning in Pouch Cove, a fishing-village-turned-suburb north of St. John's, Newfoundland, I visited William Noseworthy in his white clapboard house high on Noseworthy's Hill. Blue-eyed and ruddy-cheeked, Noseworthy sat in the kitchen by a wood stove, distractedly smoking a cigarette. He was 66 and had just retired the year before after four decades of fishing, but he still stared out the window at the North Atlantic. "There's something that draws you to it," he said in the rich accent of "the Rock."

His son, 31-year-old Barry, sipping a Labatt's beer, recalled that once, when he was 13, his father caught him whistling in a boat. "He was going to throw me overboard," said Barry. "It's just bad luck." William explained: "You don't whistle on the water. You wouldn't dare. You wouldn't launch your boat on Friday either. They're just superstitions, maybe. But several years ago, someone launched a big fishing trawler on a Friday, and she was lost on a Friday, and all the crew members, too." A minute later, William pulled out a shiny red accordion and played a jig, tapping his foot, but his eyes never left the water.

Newfoundland was also a place to sample Canadian regionalism at its most craggy and entrenched. The province's inshore fishermen claim that their very way of life is endangered by declining cod catches, which they blame on offshore trawling, often by foreigners. And they blame Ottawa for not looking out for their interests—even 40 years after joining Confederation, the old refrain still comes quickly to some residents' lips: "A Newfoundlander first, a Canadian second." But in a Pouch Cove twine store, where four diehard fishermen repaired their cod traps while country music drawled from a tape player, Frank Noseworthy, a slim, mustachioed cousin of Barry, said that he rejected the Newfoundlanders-first sentiment—and would far rather be Canadian than American. "In the States," he said, "them that's got it, gets more; them that don't, gets less. The Canadian government's more generous toward people that don't have."

Noseworthy has met many American tourists and he has not been impressed. "They come in their flashy cars," he said, "putting on airs. They seem to think they're a superior race, but I haven't seen one that's superior to me yet." He poked at the broken twine with his knife. He had one more thing to say, a point of both resentment and pride. "Some of the worst are Newfoundlanders who moved to the States. They forget their roots. They're sort of looking down their noses, instead of appreciating that there are people here trying to maintain their heritage."

Canada has hardly cornered the market on regionalism. A divided United States fought a horrific civil war in the 1860s, and as a northerner who has lived down South, I can attest to the fact that, to some southerners, the old resentments have not gone with the wind. But the United States also has the Melting Pot, the American Dream, the Pledge of Allegiance, the Hollywood-enhanced legends of Davy Crockett and even Ronald Reagan—an ever-enlarging collection of nationalistic symbols, myths, and heroes that bind the country together. Like glue, they may sometimes seem sticky and malodorous, but they do the job.

On the other hand, Canadians, writes Toronto author June Callwood, "have never created a myth that would unify them into nationhood"—except for Québec francophones. The question of Québec nationalism, heating up again over Premier Robert Bourassa's decision last December to prohibit English on outdoor commercial signs, has arisen wherever I have gone in Canada. Much of the sentiment seems to reflect that of Pouch Cove's William Noseworthy, who said, "They're always looking for special treatment—if they want to get out of Canada, let 'em get out."

In Montréal, there is no missing the passion behind the sign law. But in the office of Daniel Latouche, a political scientist and a former adviser to René Lévesque, the separatist Québec premier who died in 1987, I asked whether Québecers had a special affinity for Americans—whether, as Callwood implies, the two share a romantic vision of themselves. "There is a belief here," he replied, "that there are only two kinds of North Americans—Americans and Québecers. Two kinds of people who tried to build what North America is all about. One is much bigger, the other one lost. But both have a dream.

That is the kind of language an American can understand. But it may be a sign of American myopia that few people south of the international border, I suspect, would immediately include Québecers in such a continent-wide club of dreams. In fact, the Québec issue is quite literally foreign to Americans. The closest U.S. equivalent is the current push by Spanish-speakers in some states for official bilingualism; English-speakers have reacted heatedly, and 17 states have now declared English to be their official language. But the Hispanics are mostly recent immigrants, not a cofounding people like Québec francophones—and no American can seriously imagine Florida trying to secede from the union.

In a 37th-floor Montréal office looking out toward the frozen St. Lawrence, I asked commercial lawyer Ronald Montcalm whether there was anything binding the English and French together, any mutual myths or heroes. Montcalm thought about it and smiled. "Our hockey teams—boy, that's Canada's game." I would recall that answer on a plane the next day, when the Edmonton Oilers were on board and a steady stream of young autograph-seekers were interrupting their card game, and center Craig MacTavish talked about how "we're not the biggest country population-wise but we produce the best hockey players." But in Montcalm's office, hockey seemed more than just a sport—it was the great unifier. "At one point," the lawyer said, "Québec ultranationalists were talking about having our own team. The argument against that is, 'Hey, you've got to have Mario Lemieux and Wayne Gretzky on the same team or the Russians will beat us.'"

No Canadian region has left a more indelible impression on me than the North. The frontier is among the most enduring of American symbols, and while the American West was settled long ago, the Canadian North still lies empty and alluring—a distant dreamscape reachable by Boeing 737. Last March, I visited Inuvik, Northwest Territories, a government-built town on the east side of the Mackenzie Delta. It is a place of fur-trimmed parkas and brightly colored houses, with a church shaped like an igloo and a bar called The Zoo.

But, more traditionally, it also has an RCMP detachment, a CBC office, and a Hudson's Bay Co. store. "Twelve hundred miles from anywhere," said Mayor John Hill, "and here's small-town Canada—at least the way the bureaucrats decided it would be." Which raises the question: How can a country whose government knows exactly what a Canadian town should look like—and can create one from scratch 200 kilometers (124 miles) north of the Arctic Circle—have such a famously chronic identity crisis?

For me, Inuvik aroused feelings of ambivalence as sharp as its -30°C (-22°F) cold. On the one hand, there is the exhilarating remoteness of the place and the upbeat attitudes of many immigrants to the area—prominent businesspeople who came originally from Scotland, Germany, Greece, even Lebanon. "You've got to have the balls to come and get started in business here," noted Hill, a British transplant. "But once you have, the competitiveness isn't as intense as it would be in, say, Edmonton." On the other hand, there is a local native population with profound problems. I am suspicious of snap impressions. I also know that Americans bear their own shame over their appalling treatment of natives, and I know that, for all the historic wrongs native people have suffered in Canada, they have now organized to elect legislators, fight for land claims, and combat social ills. But in the North, the despairing side of the picture is as obvious as stray beer cans. Inuvik's RCMP Cpl. John de Jong explained that at least 80% of local crimes are alcohol-related. "These are not what you'd call social drinkers," said de Jong. "They drink until the liquor is gone and then they search for more. Then we end up having to look after them one way or the other."

The natives' problems go beyond alcohol—the suicide rate among the Inuit of the Northwest Territories is four times the national average. "There's a lot of grief," confirmed Diane Nelson, a program coordinator with the Canadian Mental Health Association office in Inuvik. "This country is hard to live in, just trying to survive. People get drunk and wander off and die of hypothermia. They fall through the ice. There's a lot of tragedy in their lives." One Métis woman told me that her brother and sister had both died alcohol-related deaths—and that her father and several relatives had sexually abused her from the age of 6 to 17. "It puts you through hell," she said. However, she has managed to get on with her life—she is married and a college graduate.

The social workers and educators in town talked of culture shock—of native people thrust abruptly into the space age and paying the price emotionally; of old amusements like berry-picking and sliding and new ones like watching ever-present videos. In some places the old ways are still evident. One day I traveled the ice road, a slick, winter-only passage on the frozen Mackenzie, more than four feet thick, lined with scrubby bush and spindly black spruce—and speed-limit signs. The Richardson Mountains gleamed in the distance. The buzz of snowmobiles announced the onset of a town. Aklavik, a largely native settlement on the delta's west side, is a motley collection of wood houses, prone to erosion and flooding. Inuvik was designed to replace it, but many residents simply refused to leave. "This was supposed to be a ghost town," recalled Dorothy McLeod, a 59-year-old Métis. "But it's such a good place for hunting and trapping and fishing—you can almost live off the land. In Inuvik, you live out of the stores."

Maybe I was just seizing on hopeful signs; or maybe, like many whites, I tend to romanticize natives and their intense ties to the land. But later, when I thought of Aklavik, I thought also of the Newfoundland fishermen, clinging to a dwindling life in the boats, and of the French nationalists, fighting to preserve their language and culture—and I thought how they would have understood Dorothy McLeod, trying to hold on to the old ways.

Canadians share a collective guilt over the plight of the natives, but they take an often-justified pride in their treatment of other minorities. To an American, Canada's vaunted multiculturalism is, like Québec nationalism, simply a foreign concept. It is also an attractive one, although the gap between theory and practice is sometimes hard to ignore.

What is happening in Vancouver is a case in point. The trouble in Canada's Pacific paradise surrounds home-buyers from Hong Kong, which will become part of mainland China in 1997. The newcomers have cash on hand and have helped to drive up housing prices beyond the range of many Vancouverites, touching off a frenzied real estate boom. Never mind that the overwhelming majority of new British Columbians come not from Hong Kong but from such foreign locales as Alberta and Ontario—public perception has focused on the Asians. "There's always an element of anxiety about change," said Mayor Gordon Campbell. "But with a certain percentage there's clearly an element of racism as well."

Vancouver is undergoing a kind of tolerance test—one that, to some residents, lies at the very core of what it means to be Canadian. "I think Canada is developing some uniqueness," said Saintfield Wong, program coordinator of the Chinese Cultural Centre in Vancouver's Chinatown. "We're more receptive to new ideas—Canada's culture *is* multiculturalism." In his gift shop down the street, however, Harry Con expressed some doubts. The national president of Chinese Freemasons in Canada, Con maintained that multiculturalism keeps Canadians too tied to their old countries. "Everybody sends money home," he said. "Italians, Chinese. Whatever happens over there, people volunteer to help. But if the government here wants to raise taxes, we give them hell. So who loves Canada?"

Dwight Chan plainly does. Chan emigrated from Hong Kong in 1974 and now, at 39, he is a successful Vancouver real estate broker who understands the city's attractions to foreigners—the ocean and mountains, the mild climate, the patently laid-back lifestyle. I asked him, though, whether there is anything to tie newcomers to the country at large; even if current fears dissipate and the latest immigrants end up feeling as welcome as he does, is there, in American terms, such a thing as the Canadian Dream? After a moment's reflection, Chan said, "The Canadian Dream is probably a healthy, stable, and secure way of living, rather than the American Dream of big money. It's to have time to enjoy your life, to play, to travel. This country allows me to do all that, and that feels good to me."

Canada continues to defy easy definition. I have crossed and recrossed time zones, sampled caribou and cod's tongue, and gathered a startling variety of mental images that, like the country itself, may not add up to a coherent whole but certainly make a pretty picture. Canada is *not* the United States—that much is abundantly clear, even if Arctic-dwellers *can* watch Detroit news on television—and its ingrained regionalism is one of its most telling traits. Travel anywhere outside of Ontario, it seems, and over and over people say, as Vancouver's Mayor Campbell did: "We're very proud to be Canadians. But there is a strong sense that the central government does not recognize we're here." Americans say nasty things about Washington, too, but when their government launches an invasion of Grenada, they swiftly rally around.

In general, Canadians also strike me as more outward-looking than Americans. They did not, after all, grow up being told that they already live in the greatest country on earth. "Americans are like TV evangelists," maintained Roger Bill, an Indiana native who is now the Newfoundland-based Atlantic field producer for CBC Radio's *Sunday Morning* show. "They really believe theirs is the best way and everyone else should follow. Canadians aren't nearly so arrogant." They do, however, take a palpable pride in place, with a decided prejudice toward the small, friendly, and re-laxed. "I wouldn't live in the States, or in Toronto or Mont-réal," said Richard Harvey, a high-school principal from Upper Gullies, Newfoundland. "You couldn't pay me enough." I have heard Inuvik people say the same about Yellowknife—and Aklavik people say the same about Inuvik.

I only wish Canadians would say it louder, that they would boast—with the kind of cheerful cockiness I saw at the Calgary Olympics—of a nation vast, varied, scenic, wealthy, safe, fair-minded, and infinitely appealing. I wish they would make an epic movie or two about it, one with endless prairies and dazzling mountains and heroic characters hell-bent on, say, building a railroad clear to the Pacific. I wish they would brag about the CBC and national health insur-ance, too, and I wish, if they really want to dispel the moose-and-Mounties image, that they would stop making that ubiquitous line of postcards picturing furry seals and polar bears and saying simply, "Canada." But then, I am afraid I sound very much like an American. Only a Canadi-an can really sum it all up. As Montréal lawyer Montcalm put it, "Funny country, eh?"

1 Essential Information

Before You Go

Government Tourist Offices

United States In the United States, the Canadian Embassy and Consulates no longer provide general tourism information. American visitors should contact the tourism department of the province or territory that they plan to visit: Tourism British Columbia, Parliament Buildings, Victoria, BC V8V 1X4, tel. 800/663–6000; Alberta Tourism, 10025 Jasper Ave., 15th floor, Edmonton, AB T5J 3Z3, tel. 800/661–8888; Tourism Saskatchewan, 1919 Saskatchewan Dr., Regina, SK S4P 3V7, tel. 800/667–7191; Travel Manitoba, Dept. 20, 155 Carlton St., 7th floor, Winnipeg, MB R3C 3H8, tel. 800/665–0040, ext. 20; Ontario Travel, Queen's Park, Toronto, ON M7A 2E5, tel. 800/668–2746; Tourisme Québec, C.P. 20 000, Québec City, PQ G1K 7X2, tel. 800/363–7777; Tourism New Brunswick, Box 12345, Fredericton, NB E3B 5C3, tel. 800/561–0123; Nova Scotia Dept. of Tourism and Culture, Box 456, Halifax, NS B3J 2R5, tel. 800/341–6096; Prince Edward Island: Dept. of Tourism and Parks, Visitor Services Division, Box 940, Charlottetown, PEI C1A 7M5, tel. 800/565–0267; Newfoundland and Labrador: Dept. of Development, Box 8700, Saint John's, NF A1B 4J6, tel. 800/563–6353; Tourism Yukon, Box 2703, Whitehorse, YK Y1A 2C6, tel. 403/667–5340; Northwest Territories: TravelArctic, Yellowknife, NWT X1A 2L9, tel. 800/661–0788.

United Kingdom Canada House, Trafalgar Sq., London SW1Y 5BJ, England, tel. 44–71/629–9492.

If you know which province or city you plan to visit, contact its tourism office directly. The staff can offer more extensive information about special events, historic sites, and local accommodations. All except the Yukon office have toll-free numbers (*see* above).

Tour Groups

With such an incredible number and variety of package tours to Canada, the only possible drawback is deciding how and when to go. You can take a group tour, create your own itinerary or follow a prearranged one, go on a fly/drive package or a train tour, explore one city, or all of the above. Each option has advantages. To see as much as possible in a limited amount of time, think about a group tour. If freedom and flexibility are of primary importance, consider an independent package.

When evaluating any tour, be sure to find out (1) exactly what expenses are included—particularly tips, taxes, service charges, side trips, additional meals, and entertainment; (2) the ratings of all hotels on the itinerary and the facilities they offer; (3) the additional cost of single, rather than double, accommodations if you are traveling alone; and (4) the number of travelers in your group. Note if the operator reserves the right to change hotels, routes, or even prices after you've booked, and check out the operator's policy regarding cancellations, complaints, and trip-interruption insurance. Many tour operators request that packages be booked through a travel agent; there is generally no additional charge for doing so. Reduced rates are often available May/June and September/October shoulder seasons, and the weather and scenery are often as good as in the peak summer season.

General-interest Tours *From the United States* **Domenico Tours** (751 Broadway, Bayonne, NJ 07002, tel. 201/823–8687 or 800/554–8687) runs a wide selection of escorted motorcoach tours and cruises to eastern Canada destinations. **Maupintour** (Box 807, Lawrence, KS 66044, tel. 913/843–1211 or 800/255–4266) offers a choice of 11 tours, some of which combine rail, cruise, and helicopter flightseeing excursions. **Globus-Gateway** (95–25 Queens Blvd. Rego Park, NY 11374, tel. 718/268–7000 or 800/221–0090) and its budget-oriented affiliate, **Cosmos,** both offer motorcoach tours to eastern and western Canada. **Tauck Tours** (11 Wilton Rd., Westport, CT 06881, tel. 203/226–6911 or 800/468–2825) has motorcoach tours to Atlantic Canada, Ontario and Québec, and the Canadian Rockies. **Brennan Tours** (1402 3rd Ave., Suite 717, Seattle, WA 98101–2118, tel. 206/622–9155) specializes in tours of the Canadian Rockies, and runs two trips to eastern Canada. **Delta Dream Vacations** (tel. 305/522–1440 or 800/872–7786) offers "Canadian Adventure Circle" and "Heart of the Rockies" motorcoach tours. **Princess Tours** (2815 2nd Ave., Suite 400, Seattle, WA 98121, tel. 206/728–4202) has western Canada tours that connect with Alaska cruises and tours to eastern Canada. **Gadabout Tours** (700 E. Tahquitz Canyon Way, Palm Springs, CA 92262–6761, tel. 619/325–5556 or 800/952–5068) offers a 10-day western Canada rail tour and a 12-day French Canada tour.

From Canada **Atlantic Tours** (Box 3596, Halifax, NS B3J 3J2, tel. 902/423–6242 or 800/565–7173) has motorcoach tours to Nova Scotia, Prince Edward Island, New Brunswick, and Newfoundland, and a rail tour into Labrador; **Atlas Tours** (609 W. Hastings St., 5th floor, Vancouver, BC V6B 4W4, tel. 604/682–5820) features 30 tours in Yukon and Alaska, the Canadian Rockies, Ontario, Québec, and the Atlantic provinces. **Brewster Tours** (Box 1140, Banff, AB TOL OCO, tel. 403/762–6700) specializes in motorcoach and rail tours of the Canadian Rockies, transcontinental rail packages, and tours by rail through Ontario and Québec. **Horizon Holidays** (160 John St., Toronto, ON M5V 2X8, tel. 416/585–9911 or 800/387–2977) runs tours to all parts of Canada, including the Arctic, a rail journey across Canada, an Inside Passage cruise, and one of the few motorcoach tours to Newfoundland and Labrador.

From the United Kingdom **Albany Travel** (Central Buildings, 211 Deansgate, Manchester, M3 3NW, tel. 061/839–2244) has a good range of escorted coach tours to all areas of the country, as well as ski packages, adventure tours, car rentals and city hotel packages, and a three-day package to the Calgary Stampede (rodeo). **All Canada Travel & Holidays** (90 High St., Lowestoft, Suffolk NR32 1XN, tel. 0502/585825) runs scheduled tours and independent packages to all parts of Canada. **Bales Tours'** (Bales House, Junction Rd., Dorking, Surrey RH4 3HB, tel. 0306/76881) offerings include a 15-day escorted tour of Canada from Vancouver to Toronto, with a daylight crossing of the Rockies by rail; a 12-day tour of British Columbia and the Rockies; and a five-day trip to Toronto and Niagara Falls. **Canada Air Holidays** (50 Sauchiehall St., Glasgow, Strathclyde, Scotland G2 3AG, tel. 041/332–1511) offers a wide variety of packages. **Kuoni Travel** (Kuoni House, Dorking, Surrey RH4 4AZ, tel. 0306/742222) has a wide variety of tours in Canada, including tours of the eastern and western regions of the Rockies; a 17-night transcontinental tour;

and "City Stay" holidays in major Canadian cities and resorts. **National Holidays** (Clarendon House, Clarendon Rd., Eccles M30 9AA, tel. 061/707–4404) can arrange two- to seven-day tours of the Rockies if you want to spend most of your holiday traveling independently but also want an overview of the region's spectacular scenery. It runs a number of city tours, rail and coach tours, and motorhome and fly/drive packages as well. **Thomson Worldwide's** (Greater London House, Hampstead Rd., London NW1 7SD, tel. 081/200–8733) offers a 14-day "Canadian Wonderland" tour featuring the Rockies and western region, and a 12-day "Trans-Canadian" tour from Toronto to Vancouver.

Special-interest Tours

Adventure Opportunities for rugged outdoor activities, such as camping, fishing, backpacking, guided canoe trips, white-water rafting, and backcountry skiing, are excellent in Canada. **American Wilderness Experience** (Box 1486, Boulder, CO 80306, tel. 303/494–2992 or 800/444–0099) hooks travelers up with Canadian outfitters for backcountry canoe adventures along the Minnesota–Ontario Boundary Waters, the route followed by the French Canadian voyageurs in birch-bark canoes. **Arctic Odysseys** (3430 Evergreen Point Rd., Box 37, Medina, WA 98039, tel. 206/455–1960) offers tours to the Canadian Arctic that highlight the culture and history as well as the scenery and wildlife. **Brewster Rocky Mountain Adventures** (Box 964, Caribou St., Banff, AB TOL OCO, tel. 403/762–5454) offers pack trips, rafting trips, and other adventure packages in the Canadian Rockies. **Cline Marine** (Richardson Wharf, Deer Island, NB, tel. 506/529–4188) offers whale-watching tours in the Bay of Fundy. **Fundy Marine** (Brunswick Square, Saint John, NB, tel. 506/634–1530) offers kayaking and canoeing in New Brunswick. **Joseph Van Os Photo Safaris** (Box 655, Vashon Island, WA 98070, tel. 206/463–5383) allows you to travel with and learn from top nature photographers and see such events as the polar-bear migration in Churchill, Manitoba. **Tauck Tours** (*see* General-interest Tours, above) has five-day journeys by helicopter through the Canadian Rockies. **Worldwide Adventures** (920 Yonge St., Suite 747, Toronto, Ont. M4W 3C7, tel. 416/963–9163) leads wilderness expeditions throughout Canada and parts north, including a photo expedition near Churchill, Manitoba, in what's known as Polar Bear Country.

Cruises Ships of the **Commodore Cruise Line** (800 Douglas Rd., Suite 600, Coral Gables, FL 33134, tel. 305/529–3000 or 800/237–5361) cruise the waters around Nova Scotia and Prince Edward Island and down the St. Lawrence, with stays in Montréal and Québec City. **Royal Viking Line** (95 Merrick Way, Coral Gables, FL 33134, tel. 305/447–9660 or 800/442–8000) tours Canada's eastern coast, calling at Charlottetown (Prince Edward Island), Halifax (Nova Scotia), St. John (New Brunswick), and Montréal. **Holland America Line** (300 Elliott Ave. W, Seattle, WA 98119, tel. 206/281–3535) and **Princess Cruises** (Box 60010, Los Angeles, CA 90060, tel. 800/421–5522) operate Inside Passage cruises between Vancouver, B.C., and Alaska. Both schedule cruises to connect with land tours in Alaska/Yukon and the Canadian Rockies; **St. Lawrence Cruise Lines** (253 Ontario St., Kingston, ON K7L 2Z4, tel. 800/267–7868) has two replica steamships that cruise the St. Lawrence and Saguenay rivers.

Fall Foliage During the peak season **Domenico Tours** (*see* General-interest Tours, above) heads to Montréal and the Laurentians, Nova Scotia, and Toronto. **Parker Tours** (218–14 Northern Blvd., Bayside, NY 11361, tel. 718/428–7800 or 800/833–9600) leads weekend and week-long tours through Québec and Ontario.

Package Deals for Independent Travelers

American Airlines Fly AAway Vacations (tel. 800/433–7300) has three-, four-, and five-day packages in Vancouver, as well as a fly/drive program in Alberta. **SuperCities** (7855 Haskell Ave., 3rd floor, Van Nuys, CA 91406, tel. 818/988–7844 or 800/556–5660) offers hotel packages in Montréal, Québec City, Toronto, Niagara Falls, Vancouver, and Victoria. **Delta Dream Vacations** (tel. 800/872–7786) offers three-night packages to Vancouver, Montréal and Toronto, and Calgary, including round-trip air transportation, car rental, and hotel accommodations. **Go Vacations** (129 Carlingview Dr., Etobicoke, ON M9W 5E7, tel. 416/674–1880) rents recreational vehicles in Vancouver, Calgary, Edmonton, Winnipeg, Toronto, and Montréal.

When to Go

The sheer size of Canada—about half the area of the former Soviet Union and larger than China—makes it difficult to generalize about the weather. When to go will depend on which part of the country you're visiting and what your interests are. In eastern Canada—which includes the maritime provinces of **Nova Scotia, New Brunswick,** and **Prince Edward Island**—the weather is milder than it is inland. Winters, tempered by the Atlantic Ocean, are kinder here than in the rest of the country, though snow can remain on the ground well into spring. Summers, too, benefit from the Atlantic air. Heavy sea fog is common much of the year. In the other Atlantic province of **Newfoundland** and **Labrador** temperatures vary widely, as the province extends more than 1,200 kilometers (750 miles) north to south. While winter days in Saint John are about 32 degrees Fahrenheit (0°C), in Labrador and on the west coast, temperatures can be as low as –50°F (–45°C). If you like your summers steamy and hot, head for the southern portions of **Québec** and **Ontario,** which border the Great Lakes and the United States. Winters can be severe, with snow lasting from mid-December to mid-March. Farther west along Canada's southern border are the Canadian prairies that take in **Manitoba, Saskatchewan,** and **Alberta.** This is wheat-growing country. The summers are short but sunny, and marked by an occasional heavy shower. Winter snowfall in this area is light, but winter temperatures can dip very low for most of the season. Unlike eastern Canada, which experiences blooming springs and brilliant autumns, the Canadian prairies move abruptly from summer to winter weather. For warmer winters and mild summers, head for western Canada, which includes the southern part of **British Columbia** and the western part of **Alberta,** within the Rocky Mountains. Though the weather fluctuates because of the mountain ranges—the Coast Mountains and the eastern chain of the Rockies—generally, the coastal region has the country's mildest winters, with rainfall almost inevitable. Summers here are fairly sunny, but not as oppressively hot as in parts of the prairie region. The best time to visit northern Canada is during its short but surprisingly warm summer. The area—which includes the northern parts of the provinces of **British Columbia, Alberta, Saskatchewan, Manitoba, Ontario,** and **Québec,** as well as the **Yukon** and **Northwest Territories**—is marked by coniferous forest and Arctic tundra and makes up almost two-thirds of Canada. In winter, however, the weather in the north resembles that of Siberia, with devastating cold and dangerous windchills.

Climate The following are average daily maximum and minimum temperatures for a number of Canada's major cities.

Calgary	Jan.	23F	− 5C	May	61F	16C	Sept.	63F	17C
		2	−17		37	3		39	4
	Feb.	29F	− 2C	June	67F	19C	Oct.	54F	12C
		8	−13		44	7		30	− 1
	Mar.	34F	1C	July	74F	23C	Nov.	38F	3C
		14	−10		49	9		17	− 8
	Apr.	49F	9C	Aug.	72F	22C	Dec.	29F	− 2C
		27	− 3		47	8		8	−13

Edmonton	Jan.	14F	−10C	May	63F	17C	Sept.	62F	17C
		-3	−19		41	5		41	5
	Feb.	22F	− 6C	June	69F	21C	Oct.	52F	11C
		4	−16		48	9		32	0
	Mar.	31F	− 1C	July	74F	23C	Nov.	32F	0C
		13	−11		53	12		17	− 8
	Apr.	49F	9C	Aug.	71F	22C	Dec.	21F	− 6C
		29	− 2		50	10		5	−15

Halifax	Jan.	33F	1C	May	58F	14C	Sept.	67F	19C
		20	-7		41	5		53	12
	Feb.	33F	1C	June	67F	19C	Oct.	58F	14C
		19	-7		50	10		44	7
	Mar.	39F	4C	July	73F	23C	Nov.	48F	9C
		26	-3		57	14		36	2
	Apr.	48F	9C	Aug.	73F	24C	Dec.	37F	3C
		33	1		58	13		25	− 4

Montréal	Jan.	23F	− 5C	May	65F	18C	Sept.	68F	20C
		9	−13		48	9		53	12
	Feb.	25F	− 4C	June	74F	23C	Oct.	57F	14C
		12	−11		58	14		43	6
	Mar.	36F	2C	July	79F	26C	Nov.	42F	6C
		23	− 5		63	17		32	0
	Apr.	52F	11C	Aug.	76F	24C	Dec.	27F	− 3C
		36	2		61	16		16	− 9

Ottawa	Jan.	20F	− 7C	May	65F	18C	Sept.	68F	20C
		4	−16		44	7		49	9
	Feb.	23F	− 5C	June	75F	24C	Oct.	57F	14C
		6	−14		54	12		39	4
	Mar.	34F	1C	July	80F	27C	Nov.	41F	5C
		18	− 8		58	14		29	− 2
	Apr.	51F	11C	Aug.	77F	25C	Dec.	25F	− 4C
		33	1		56	13		12	−11

Québec City								
Jan.	20F	− 7C	**May**	62F	17C	**Sept.**	66F	19C
	6	−14		43	6		49	9
Feb.	23F	− 5C	**June**	72F	22C	**Oct.**	53F	12C
	8	−13		53	12		39	4
Mar.	33F	1C	**July**	78F	26C	**Nov.**	39F	4C
	19	− 7		58	14		28	− 2
Apr.	47F	8C	**Aug.**	75F	24C	**Dec.**	24F	− 4C
	32	0		56	13		12	−11

Toronto								
Jan.	30F	− 1C	**May**	64F	18C	**Sept.**	71F	22C
	18	− 8		47	8		54	12
Feb.	32F	0C	**June**	76F	24C	**Oct.**	60F	16C
	19	− 7		57	14		45	7
Mar.	40F	4C	**July**	80F	27C	**Nov.**	46F	8C
	27	− 3		62	17		35	2
Apr.	53F	12C	**Aug.**	79F	26C	**Dec.**	34F	1C
	38	3		61	16		23	− 5

Vancouver								
Jan.	42F	6C	**May**	60F	16C	**Sept.**	65F	18C
	33	1		47	8		52	11
Feb.	45F	7C	**June**	65F	18C	**Oct.**	56F	13C
	36	2		52	11		45	7
Mar.	48F	9C	**July**	70F	21C	**Nov.**	48F	9C
	37	3		55	13		39	4
Apr.	54F	12C	**Aug.**	70F	21C	**Dec.**	43F	6C
	41	5		55	13		35	2

By calling the Weather Channel Connection at 900/WEATHER from a touch-tone phone, you can get current weather information for foreign and domestic cities, local time and travel tips, as well as hurricane, foliage, and snow reports. The call costs 95¢ per minute.

National Holidays

Though banks, schools, and government offices close for national holidays, many stores remain open. As in the United States, the move has been to observe certain holidays on the Monday nearest to the actual date, making for a long weekend.

National holidays for 1993 are: New Year's Day (January 1), Good Friday (April 9), Easter Monday (April 12), Victoria Day (May 24), Canada Day (July 1), Labor Day (September 6), Thanksgiving (October 11), Remembrance Day (November 11), Christmas (December 25), and Boxing Day (December 26).

Provincial Holidays **Alberta:** Heritage Day (August 2).

British Columbia: British Columbia Day (August 2).

New Brunswick: New Brunswick Day (August 2).

Manitoba, Northwest Territories, Ontario, Saskatchewan, and **Nova Scotia:** Civic Holiday (August 2).

Newfoundland and **Labrador:** St. Patrick's Day (March 15), St. George's Day (April 26), Discovery Day (June 21), Memorial Day (July 1), Orangeman's Day (July 12).

Québec: St. Jean Baptiste Day (June 24). January 2 is also treated as a provincial holiday.

Yukon: Discovery Day (August 16).

Festivals and Seasonal Events

No matter where or when you travel in Canada, you're likely to be traveling around the time of a festival or special event. Provincial holidays are usually accompanied by local events. Victoria Day and Canada Day are celebrated in most places around the country. Winter is as active a time for Canadian celebrations as the summer. It's a good idea to pick up a local paper as soon as you arrive in a town. Listed below are only a select few of the provincial events. Some festivals, especially the music and dance festivals, may require tickets or reservations. It's best to contact the provincial tourist boards in advance for a complete listing of events and further details.

Alberta **January:** Jasper Winter Festival in Jasper and Marmot Basin features dogsledding, skating, ice sculpting, and other events. **February:** Calgary Winter Festival, with more than 200 events. **April:** Silver Buckle Rodeo at Red Deer attracts cowboys from all over North America. **May:** Edmonton International Children's Festival draws professional musicians, mimes, jugglers, clowns, puppeteers, and singers worldwide; there's also Red Deer Annual Westerner Spring Quarter Horse Show, where horses compete from western Canada and the United States. **June:** Jazz City International Festival in Edmonton features 10 days of jazz concerts, workshops, club dates, and free outdoor events; Ponoka 56th Annual Stampede professional rodeo attracts participants from across the continent. **July:** Canadian Showcase of Ukrainian Culture in Vegreville celebrates with costumes, traditional singing and dancing; Calgary Exhibition and Stampede is one of the most popular Canadian events and includes 10 days of Western showmanship, hot-air balloon races, chuck-wagon races, agricultural shows, crafts exhibits, and Indian dancing; Edmonton's Klondike Days celebrate the town's early frontier community with pancake breakfasts, gambling casinos, gold panning, and raft races. **August:** Fringe Theatre Festival, in Edmonton, is regarded as one of the largest festivals for alternative theater in North America. **September:** Spruce Meadows Masters' Tournament, Calgary, is an international horse-jumping competition at one of North America's leading equestrian centers.

British Columbia **January–February:** The Polar Bear Swim on New Year's Day in Vancouver is said to bring good luck all year. Skiing competitions take place at most alpine ski resorts throughout the province. **March–April:** Pacific Rim Whale Festival celebrates the spring migration of gray whales with guided tours by whale experts and accompanying music and dancing. The Vancouver International Wine Festival is held; Terrifvic Jazz Party, in Victoria, has 20 top international Dixieland bands. **May:** Cloverdale Rodeo in Surrey is rated sixth in the world by the Pro Rodeo Association; Vancouver Children's Festival features free open-air stage performances by more than 20 companies. **June:** Canadian International Dragon Boat Festival, in Vancouver, includes entertainment, exotic foods, and the ancient "awakening the dragons" ritual of long, slender boats decorated with huge dragon heads. **July:** Each year, Harrison Festival of the Arts focuses on different ethnic music, dance, and theater, such as African, Caribbean, and Central American; Vancouver Sea Festival celebrates the city's nautical heritage with the World Championship Bathtub Race, sailing regattas, and windsurfing races, Peach Festivals in Penticton. **August:** Squamish Days Loggers Sports Festival features loggers from around the world competing in a series of incredible logging feats; the Abbotsford International Airshow is three days of flight performances and a large-aircraft display; Pacific National Exhibition in Vancouver has parades, exhibits, sports, entertainment, and logging contests. **September:** The Vancouver International Film Festival is held; **October:** Okanagan Wine Festivals occur in the Okanagan-Similkameen area. Cars race through downtown Vancouver in the PGA Indy Car World Series. **December:** The Carol Ships, sailboats full of carollers, decorated with coloured lights ply the waters of the Vancouver harbor.

Manitoba **February:** Festival du Voyageur, in St. Boniface, Winnipeg, celebrates the history of the region's early fur traders. **March:** Royal Manitoba Winter Fair in Brandon. **June:** Red River Exhibition, in Winnipeg, features lumberjack contests, body-building shows, and an international band festival. **July:** Winnipeg Folk Festival takes place in Birds Hill Park, 24 kilometers (15 miles) northeast of Winnipeg, and features performers singing country, bluegrass, folk, Acadian music, and jazz on 10 stages scattered throughout the park; Threshermen's Reunion, in Austin, features antique tractor races, sheep tying, and threshing contests; Northwest Roundup and Exhibition, in Swan River, includes professional rodeo events, chuck-wagon races, and stage shows. **August:** Folklorama is the largest multicultural festival in the world, with more than 40 pavilions throughout Winnipeg; National Ukrainian Festival, in Dauphin, offers costumes, artifacts, exhibits, fiddling contests, dancing, and workshops; Icelandic Festival, in Gimli, gathers the largest Icelandic community outside of Iceland; Pioneer Days, in Steinbach, celebrates the heritage of the Mennonites with demonstrations of threshing and baking, a parade, a horse show, a barbecue, and Mennonite foods.

New Brunswick **June:** Covered Bridge Spud and Spoke Days, in Hartland, features truck-tractor rodeos, beauty pageants, and sporting events. **July:** Loyalist Days, in Saint John, celebrates the town's founding with parades, dancing, and sidewalk festivities; the Shediac Lobster Festival takes place in the town that calls itself the Lobster Capital of the World; there's an Irish festival in Chatham. **August:** Mirimachi Folk Song Festival, in Newcastle, features fiddling competitions, casinos, beer gardens, and a parade; Foire Brayonne, in Edmundston, is the largest French festival outside of Québec; Festival By the Sea, in Saint John, attracts more than 200 entertainers from across Canada and includes cultural and ethnic performances; Acadian Festival, at Caraquet, celebrates the region's Acadian heritage with folk singing and indigenous food; the Chocolate Festival in St. Stephen includes suppers, displays, and children's events.

Newfoundland and Labrador **June:** Opening of rainbow trout and salmon fishing seasons; St. John's Day celebrations in St. John's. **July:** Codroy Valley Folk Festival; Stephenville Festival of the Arts; the Hangashore Folk Festival in Corner Brook; The Exploits Valley Salmon Festival in the Grand Falls area; The Fish, Fun and Folk Festival in Twillingate; the Conception Bay Folk Festival in Carbonear; Signal Hill Tattoo in St. John's. **August:** The Festival of Flight in Gander; Une Longue Veillée in Cape St. George; The St. John's Regatta, St. John's; The Newfoundland and Labrador Folk Festival in St. John's; The Labrador Straits Bakeapple Folk Festival in southern Labrador. **September:** Humber Valley Agricultural Home and Handicraft Exhibition in Deer Lake. **October:** Halloween Mardi Gras in St. John's. **December:** First Night is a nonalcoholic New Year's Eve celebration featuring dozens of activities and concerts in Fredericton.

Nova Scotia **May/June:** Apple Blossom Festival, in Annapolis Valley, includes dancing, parades, and entertainment. **July:** Antigonish Highland Games; Nova Scotia International Tattoo in Halifax has entertainment and competitions; Nova Scotia Bluegrass and Oldtime Music Festival at Ardoise. **August:** Mahone Bay Wooden Boat Festival; Lunenburg Folk Harbour Festival; the Nova Scotia Gaelic Mod in Baddeck is a festival of Scottish culture; Scallop Days in Digby. **September:** Nova Scotia Fisheries Exhibition and Fishermen's Reunion in Lunenburg; Shearwater International Air Show.

Ontario **February:** Ontario Winter Carnival Bon Soo in Sault Ste. Marie. Winterlude-Bal de Neige, Ottawa, encourages icesculpting, snowshoe races, ice-boating, and other wintertime activities. **April:** Maple Syrup Festival in Elmira; Stratford Festival, in Stratford, features performances of many of Shakespeare's plays through beginning of November; Shaw Festival in Niagara-on-the-Lake (through November) presents plays by George Bernard Shaw and his contemporaries. **May:** Folk Arts Festival, in St. Catharines; the Canadian Tulip Festival, in Ottawa, heralds the season with 3 million blossoming tulips. **June:** Metro International Caravan is an ethnic fair in Toronto; International Festival of Native Arts features dancers, crafts booths, and entertainment in Toronto; Changing of the Guard begins at Ottawa's Parliament Buildings (through August). **July:** Canada Day celebrations in Ottawa have entertainment and fireworks; Queen's Plate Thoroughbred horse race takes place in Toronto; Blueberry Festival in Sudbury; Molson CART race in Toronto; Caribana draws on the riches of Toronto's West Indian community for this Caribbean festival. **August:** Glengarry Highland Games, in Maxville, is North America's largest Highland Gathering; Six Nations Native Pageant is an Iroquois celebration and exhibit of the tribe's culture and history in Brantford; Royal Canadian Henley Regatta, in St. Catharines, is the largest rowing regatta in North America; Canadian National Exhibition, in Toronto, features air shows, entertainment, and exhibits. **September:** The Canadian Open Golf Championship is in Oakville; Festival of Festivals is an international film festival in Toronto; Niagara Grape and Wine Festival, in St. Catharines, celebrates this fruit. **October:** Oktoberfest, in Kitchener–Waterloo, attracts more than half a million enthusiasts to its many beer halls and tents. **November:** the Royal Agricultural Winter Fair, in Toronto, is the largest indoor agricultural fair and equestrian competition in the world.

Prince Edward **June:** Irish Moss Festival in Tignish; Charlottetown Festival
Island Theatre (through September) offers a series of concerts and musicals. **July:** Rollo Bay Fiddle Festival; Summerside Lobster Carnival, in Summerside, is a week-long feast of lobster. **August:** Highland Games, in Eldon, is a gathering of Scotsmen for

games and celebrations; Annual Community Harvest Festival in Kensington; Old Home Week in Charlottetown.

Québec **January:** La Fete des Neiges winter carnival in Montréal. **February:** Winter Carnival, in Québec City, is an 11-day festival of winter sports competitions, ice-sculpture contests, and parades. **April:** Sugaring-off parties throughout the province celebrate the beginning of the maple syrup season. **May:** Festival des Cantons, in Sherbrooke, has hayrides, dancing, and contests. **June:** Molson Grand Prix, with some of the world's best drivers, takes place on the Gilles-Villeneuve Race Track, in Montréal; Festival Orford features international artists performing at Orford Park's music center (through August); International Jazz Festival in Québec; International Children's Folklore Festival takes place in Beauport, Québec. **July:** Festival International de Jazz de Montréal features more than 1,000 jazz musicians from all over the world for this 10-day series; Québec International Summer Festival offers entertainment in the streets and parks of old Québec City. Juste pour Rire (Just for Laughs) comedy festival features comics from around the world, in French and English. **August:** Montréal World Film Festival; Plein-Art (Arts and Crafts) Show in Québec City; Festival Gastronomique, in Granby, attracts more than 10,000 foodies to sample the cuisine at participating restaurants. **September:** Québec International Film Festival in Québec City. **October:** Festival of Colors, throughout the province.

Saskatchewan **March:** Winter Festival in Meadow Lake is a three-day festival with a minor hockey tournament, family snowmobile rally, dance, children's events, Jam Can curling, and sled races. **May:** International Band and Choral Festival, in Moose Jaw, attracts 7,000 musicians, 100 bands, and 25 choral groups. **June:** Vesna Festival, in Saskatoon, is the world's largest Ukrainian cabaret, with traditional Ukrainian food and crafts; Yellowhead Arabian Horse Show in Yorkton; Frontier Days, in Swift Current, is a community fair and exhibit with parades, horse show, and rodeo. **July–August:** Buffalo Days Exhibition, in Regina, features rides, a grandstand show, dancing, livestock judging, and horse racing; Big Valley Jamboree, in Regina, is a four-day country-music festival; Shakespeare on the Saskatchewan Festival, in Saskatoon, has productions in tents on the banks of the South Saskatchewan River.

Wilderness Canada **February:** The Yukon Sourdough Rendezvous, in Whitehorse, features dog-team races, leg wrestling, log sawing, snowshoe races, local arts and crafts, and talent contests. **March:** Caribou Carnival, in Yellowknife, features the Canadian Championship Dog Derby, and ice-sculptures and tea-making competitions. **June:** An annual Midnight Sun Golf Tournament in Yellowknife tees off at midnight on the first day of summer. **August:** Dawson City commemorates the Klondike gold strike with the Discovery Days festival, with parades, raft and canoe races, baseball tournaments, and dances.

What to Pack

Clothing How you pack for travel to Canada will depend more on the season in which you're traveling than on any Canadian customs. Layering is the best defense against Canada's cold, long winters; a hat, scarf, and gloves are essential. For summer travel, loose-fitting natural-fiber clothes are best. If you're planning to spend time in Canada's larger cities, pack both casual clothes for day touring and more formal wear for evenings out. If your visit includes a stay at a large city hotel, bring a bathing suit in any season to take advantage of the indoor pool.

Miscellaneous Like the United States, Canada has 110-volt, 60-cycle electric power. British visitors should bring an adaptor for their electric hair dryers, irons, razors, etc. An extra pair of glasses, contact lenses, or prescription sunglasses is always a good idea; pack any prescription medicines you use regularly and a copy of the prescription, as well as any allergy medication you may need. Zip-closing bags are useful for many things, and transparent tape is, too. Take a 75- or 100-watt light bulb to exchange temporarily for the often low-wattage reading lamp, and a pocket flashlight. A pocket calculator comes in handy to convert kilometers to miles, Celsius to Fahrenheit, and Canadian dollars to American dollars. If you plan on camping or hiking in the deep woods during the summer, especially in northern Canada, insect repellent is a must, especially in June, which is blackfly season.

Carry-on Luggage Airlines generally allow each passenger one piece of carry-on luggage on international flights from the United States. The bag cannot exceed 45 inches (length + width + height) and must fit under the seat or in the overhead luggage compartment.

Checked Luggage Passengers are generally allowed to check two pieces of luggage, neither of which can exceed 62 inches (length + width + height) or weigh more than 70 pounds. Baggage allowances vary slightly among airlines, so check with the carrier or your travel agent before departure.

Taking Money Abroad

Currency Exchange American money is readily accepted in much of Canada (especially in communities near the border), and traveler's checks and major U.S. credit cards are accepted in larger cities and resorts, but in smaller towns and rural areas, you may need cash. You won't get as good an exchange rate at home as abroad, but it's wise to change a small amount of money before you go; lines at airport currency-exchange booths can be very long. If your local bank can't change your currency, you can exchange money through **Thomas Cook Currency Services.** To find the office nearest you, write or call 630 5th Avenue, New York, NY 10111 (tel. 212/757–6915). **Deak International** (630 5th Ave., New York, NY 10011, tel. 212/635–0515) has offices throughout the United States; **Ruesch International** (tel. 800/424–2923) has offices in New York, Chicago, Washington, and Los Angeles but can arrange for overnight delivery of funds or traveler's checks to other cities and rural areas.

Credit Cards and Traveler's Checks For safety and convenience, it's always best to take traveler's checks. The most recognized traveler's checks are **American Express, Barclay's, Thomas Cook,** and those issued through major commercial banks, such as **Citibank** and **Bank of America.** Some banks issue the checks free to established customers, but most charge a 1% commission. Buying your traveler's checks in Canadian dollars will probably save you money. Remember to take the addresses of offices where you can get refunds for lost or stolen traveler's checks. Buy part of the traveler's checks in small denominations to cash toward the end of your trip. This will save you from having to cash a large check and ending up with more foreign money than you need. (Hold on to your receipts after exchanging your traveler's checks; it's easier to convert foreign currency back into dollars if you have the receipts.)

Getting Money from Home

There are at least three ways to get money from home: (1) Have it sent through a large commercial bank that has a branch where you are staying. The only drawback is that you must have an account with the bank; if not, you'll have to go through your own bank, and the process will be slower and more costly. (2) Have it sent through American Express. If you are a cardholder, you can cash a personal check or a counter check at an American Express office for up to $1,000 ($5,000 for gold cardholders, $10,000 for platinum) in cash and traveler's checks. There is a 1% commission on the traveler's checks. You can also receive money through an American Express MoneyGram, which enables you to obtain up to $10,000 in cash. It works this way: You call home and ask someone to go to an American Express office—or an American Express Money-Gram agent located in a retail outlet—and fill out an American Express MoneyGram. The amount sent must be paid for with cash (if more than $1,000) or the Optima card. The American Express MoneyGram agent authorizes the transfer of funds to an American Express office in the town where you're staying. You'll need to show identification when picking up the money. Depending on where you are, the money will be available in 15 minutes to 48 hours. Fees vary according to the amount of money sent and where it's sent from (sometimes there are local promotions). For sending $500, the usual fee is $39; for $1,000, $49. For the American Express MoneyGram location nearest your home and a list of Canadian locations, call 800/666–3947 or 800/543–4080. You do not have to be a cardholder to use this service. (3) Have money sent through Western Union, whose U.S. number is 800/325–6000. If you have a MasterCard or Visa, you can have money sent for any amount up to your credit limit. If not, have someone take cash or a certified cashier's check to a Western Union office. The money will be delivered to a Western Union office where you are staying, and will be available almost immediately. Fees vary with the amount of money sent; the standard fee for sending $1,000 is $50; for $500, $90.

Cash Machines　Virtually all U.S. and Canadian banks belong to a network of ATMs (Automated Teller Machines), which dispense cash 24 hours a day in cities throughout the country. There are some eight major networks in the United States, the largest of which are Cirrus, owned by MasterCard, and Plus, affiliated with Visa. Some banks belong to more than one network. To receive a card for one of these systems you must apply for it. Cards issued by Visa and MasterCard also may be used in the ATMs, but the fees are usually higher than the fees on bank cards. There is also a daily interest charge on credit card "loans," even if monthly bills are paid on time. Each network has a toll-free number you can call to locate machines in a given city. The Cirrus number is 800/4–CIRRUS; the Plus number is 800/THE-PLUS. Check with your bank for information on fees and on the amount of cash you can withdraw on any given day. **Express**

Cash allows American Express cardholders to withdraw up to $1,000 in a seven-day period (21 days overseas) from their personal checking accounts at ATMs worldwide. Gold cardmembers can receive up to $5,000 in a seven-day period (21 days overseas); platinum cardmembers, $10,000. Express Cash is not a cash advance service; only money already in the linked checking account can be withdrawn. Every transaction carries a 2% fee with a minimum charge of $2 and a maximum of $6. Apply for a PIN (personal identification number) and to link your accounts at least two to three weeks before departure. Call 800/CASH–NOW to receive an application or to locate the nearest Express Cash machine.

Canadian Currency

The units of currency in Canada are the Canadian dollar (C$) and the cent, in almost the same denominations as U.S. currency—the $1 bill is no longer used; instead it has been replaced by a $1 coin ($2, $5, $10, $20, 1¢, 5¢, 10¢, 25¢, etc.). The use of $2 paper currency is common here although rare in the United States. At press time (September 1992), the exchange rate was C$1.20 to U.S.$1 and C$2.14 to £1.

What It Will Cost

Note: Throughout this guide, unless otherwise stated, prices are quoted in Canadian dollars.

Food prices are higher in Canada than in the United States, but lower than in much of Western Europe. The biggest expense of the trip will be accommodations, but a range of choices, from economy to deluxe, is available in metropolitan areas, the country, and in resort areas.

Sample Prices 1993   The following prices are for Toronto; other cities and regions are often less expensive: Dinner at an Expensive restaurant, without tax, tip, or drinks, will cost $30–$40; Moderate, $20–$30; Inexpensive, under $20. A double room at an Expensive hotel costs $130–$200 or more; Moderate, $90–$130; Inexpensive, $65–$90, with suburban motels being cheaper. A soda (pop) costs $1–$1.25; a glass of beer, $3–$6; a sandwich, $3.50–$6; a taxi, as soon as the meter is turned on, $2.20, and $1 for every kilometer; a movie, about $8. (*See* Staying in Canada, GST and Sales Tax, below).

Passports and Visas

Americans   Because of the volume of border traffic between Canada and the United States (for example, many people live in Windsor, Ontario, and work in Detroit), entry requirements are fairly simple. Citizens and legal residents of the United States do not need a passport or a visa to enter Canada, but proof of citizenship (a birth certificate, valid passport, or voter registration card) and identity may be requested. U.S. citizens entering Canada from a third country must have a valid passport or an official U.S. travel document. If you return to the United States by air, possession of a passport can save a long wait in line. Naturalized U.S. citizens should carry a naturalization certificate or some other evidence of citizenship. Resident aliens should be in possession of their U.S. Alien Registration or "green" card. Children not accompanied by a parent should carry a letter from a parent or guardian giving them permission to travel to Canada. For more information, contact the Canadian Embassy (501 Pennsylvania Ave. NW, Washington, DC 20001, tel. 202/682–1740) or the Canadian Consulate General in Boston, New York, Atlanta, Detroit, Cleveland, Buffalo, Dallas, Minneapolis, Chicago, Seattle, San Francisco, or Los Angeles.

Britons All British citizens require a valid 10-year passport to enter Canada. The one-year British Visitors' Passports are not valid. Application forms are available from most travel agents and major post offices, or contact the **Passport Office** (Clive House, 70 Petty France, London SW1H 9BR, tel. 071/279–3434). Cost is £15 for a standard 32-page passport, £30 for a 94-page passport. All applications must be countersigned by your bank manager, or by a solicitor, a barrister, a doctor, a clergyman, or a justice of the peace, and must be accompanied by two photographs. British citizens do not need a visa or any inoculations to enter Canada but their stay cannot exceed six months without authorization from Canadian Immigration.

Customs and Duties

On Arrival Clothing and personal items may be brought in without charge
Americans and or restriction. American and British visitors may bring in the
Britons following items duty-free: 200 cigarettes, 50 cigars, and two pounds of tobacco; personal cars (for less than six months); boats or canoes; rifles, shotguns (but no handguns or automatic weapons), and 200 rounds of ammunition, providing they are for sporting or competition use and are declared (failure to declare them could mean seizure and forfeiture and possible criminal charges); cameras, radios, sports equipment, and typewriters. A deposit is sometimes required for trailers and household equipment (refunded upon return). If you are driving a rented car, be sure to keep the contract with you. Cats and dogs must have a certificate issued by a licensed veterinarian that clearly identifies the animal and certifies that it has been vaccinated against rabies during the preceding 36 months. Plant material must be declared and inspected.

On Departure If you have brought any foreign-made equipment from home,
Americans such as cameras, it's wise to carry the original receipt with you or to register it with U.S. Customs before you leave home (Form 4457). Otherwise, you may end up having to pay duty on your return. You may bring home duty-free up to $400 in foreign goods, as long as you have been out of the country for at least 48 hours and you haven't made an international trip in 30 days. Each member of the family is entitled to the same exemption, regardless of age, and exemptions may be pooled. For the next $1,000 worth of goods, a flat 5% rate is assessed; above $1,400, duties vary with the merchandise. Travelers 21 or older may bring home one liter of alcohol, 100 cigars (non-Cuban), and 200 cigarettes. Only one bottle of perfume trademarked in the United States may be imported. There is no duty on antiques or art over 100 years old. Anything exceeding these limits will be taxed at the port of entry, and may be taxed additionally in the traveler's home state. Gifts valued at less than $50 may be mailed to friends or relatives at home duty-free, but you may not send more than one package per day to any one addressee, and packages may not include tobacco, liquor, or perfumes costing more than $5.

Britons On your return to Great Britain you may bring home: (1) 200 cigarettes or 100 cigarillos or 50 cigars or 250 grams of tobacco; (2) two liters of table wine and, in addition, (a) one liter of alcohol over 22% by volume (most spirits), (b) two liters of alcohol under 22% by volume (fortified or sparkling wine), or (c) two more liters of table wine; (3) 60 milliliters of perfume and 250 milliliters of toilet water; and (4) other goods up to a value of £32, but not more than 50 liters of beer and 25 lighters.

For further information, contact **HM Customs and Excise** (Dorset House, Stamford St., London SE1 9PS, tel. 071/928–0533).

Traveling with Film

If your camera is new, shoot and develop a few rolls of film before leaving home. Pack some lens tissue and an extra battery for your built-in light meter. Film doesn't like hot weather, so if you're driving in summer, don't store film in the glove compartment or on the shelf under the rear window. Put it behind the front seat on the floor, on the side opposite the exhaust pipe.

On a plane trip, never pack unprocessed film in check-in luggage; if your bags get X-rayed, your film could be ruined. Always carry undeveloped film with you through security and ask to have it inspected by hand. (It helps to keep your film in a plastic bag, ready for quick inspection.) Inspectors at American airports are required by law to honor requests for hand inspection; abroad, you'll have to depend on the kindness of strangers. The newer airport scanning machines used in all U.S. airports are safe for varying numbers of scans, depending on the speed of your film, but the effects are cumulative; after five scans, you're asking for trouble.

Language

Canada's two official languages are English and French. Though English is widely spoken, it may be useful to learn a few French phrases if you plan to travel to the province of Québec or to the French Canadian communities in the maritime provinces (Nova Scotia, New Brunswick, and Prince Edward Island), northern Manitoba, and Ontario. Canadian French, known as Québecois or *joual*, is a colorful language often quite different from that spoken in Paris.

Canada, like the United States, has been settled by successive influxes of immigrants, from the British, Scottish, Irish, and French to the Germans, Scandinavians, Ukrainians, and Chinese. Many of these groups maintain their cultural identity through their native language, and ethnic daily and weekly newspapers are common. Immigration since the 1960s accounts for Asians, Arabs, East Indians, Italians, Hispanics, and Caribbean blacks. The native population of Canada now comprises less than 1% of the population, yet it is possible to hear the languages of Indians and Inuits where these groups reside.

Staying Healthy

Shots and No special shots are required for entry into Canada. If you have
Medications a health problem that may require purchase of prescription drugs, ask your doctor to write a spare prescription for you

using the drug's generic name, because brand names vary from country to country.

There has been an increased number of cases of meningococcal disease in several parts of eastern Canada: the Ottawa-Carlton area, the Laurentides and Lanaudière regions, near Montréal, the Outaouais area in West Québec, and Prince Edward Island. Although the risk for travelers is very low, visitors may wish to have their children between ages 2 and 19 vaccinated if they expect to have social or physical contact with school-age children. For further information, contact the Centers for Disease Control's international hotline at 404/332–4559.

Dangers Mosquitoes and blackflies are notorious pests in the northern backwoods of much of Canada. Take along insect repellent on hiking trips, especially in June—the height of blackfly season.

Doctors The **International Association for Medical Assistance to Travelers (IAMAT)** is a worldwide organization offering a list of approved English-speaking doctors whose training meets British and American standards. Contact IAMAT for a list of physicians and clinics in Canada that belong to this network. **In the United States:** 417 Center St., Lewiston, NY 14092, tel. 716/754–4883. **In Canada:** 40 Regal Rd., Guelph, Ont. N1K 1B5. **In Europe:** 57 Voirets, 1212 Grand-Lancy, Geneva, Switzerland. Membership is free.

Insurance

Travelers may seek insurance coverage in four areas: health and accident, lost luggage, trip cancellation, and flight. Your first step is to review your existing health and home-owner policies; some health insurance plans cover health expenses incurred while traveling, some major medical plans cover emergency transportation, and some home-owner policies cover the theft of luggage.

Health and Accident Several companies offer coverage designed to supplement existing health insurance for travelers:

Americans **Carefree Travel Insurance** (Box 310, 120 Mineola Blvd., Mineola, NY 11501, tel. 516/294–0220 or 800/323–3149) provides coverage for emergency medical evacuation and accidental death and dismemberment. It also offers 24-hour medical phone advice.

International SOS Assistance (Box 11568, Philadelphia, PA 19116, tel. 215/244–1500 or 800/523–8930), a medical assistance company, provides emergency evacuation services, worldwide medical referrals, and optional medical insurance.

Travel Assistance International (1133 15th St. NW, Suite 400, Washington, DC 20005, tel. 202/331–1609 or 800/821–2828) provides emergency evacuation services, medical insurance, and 24-hour medical referrals.

Travel Guard International, underwritten by Transamerica Occidental Life Companies (1145 Clark St., Stevens Point, WI 54481, tel. 715/345–0505 or 800/782–5151), offers reimbursement for medical expenses with no deductibles or daily limits and emergency evacuation services.

Wallach and Company, Inc. (Box 480, Middleburg, VA 22117–0480, tel. 703/687–3166 or 800/237–6615) offers comprehensive medical coverage, including emergency evacuation services worldwide.

Britons We recommend strongly that you purchase adequate insurance to guard against health problems, motoring mishaps, theft, flight cancellation, and loss of luggage. Most major tour operators offer holiday insurance, and details are given in brochures. For free general advice on all aspects of holiday insurance, contact the **Association of British Insurers** (51 Gresham St., London EC2V 7HQ, tel. 071/600–3333). A proven leader in the holiday insurance field is **Europ Assistance** (252 High St., Croydon, Surrey CR0 1NF, tel. 081/680–1234), and travel insurance can also be obtained from **Our Way Travel Ltd.** (Atlas House, Station Approach, Hayes, Kent BR2 7EQ, tel. 081/462–7746).

Lost Luggage On international flights, airlines are responsible for lost or damaged property of up to $9.07 per pound (or $20 per kilo) for checked baggage, and up to $400 per passenger for unchecked baggage. If you're carrying valuables, either take them with you on the plane or purchase additional insurance for lost luggage. Some airlines will issue extra luggage insurance when you check in, but many do not. Insurance for lost, damaged, or stolen luggage is available through travel agents or directly through various insurance companies. Luggage loss coverage is usually part of a comprehensive travel insurance package that includes personal accident, trip cancellation, and sometimes default and bankruptcy.

Two companies that issue luggage insurance are **Tele-Trip** (Box 31685, 3201 Farnam St., Omaha, NE 68131–0618, tel. 800/228–9792), a subsidiary of Mutual of Omaha, and **The Travelers Insurance Corporation** (Ticket and Travel Dept., 1 Tower Sq., Hartford, CT 06183–5040, tel. 203/277–0111 or 800/243–3174). Tele-Trip operates sales booths at airports, and also issues insurance through travel agents. Tele-Trip will insure checked luggage for up to 180 days; rates vary according to the length of the trip. The Travelers Insurance Corporation will insure checked or hand luggage for $500 to $2,000 valuation per person, also for a maximum of 180 days. Rates for one to five days for $500 valuation are $10; for 180 days, $85. Other companies with comprehensive policies include **Access America, Inc.,** a subsidiary of Blue Cross-Blue Shield (Box 11188, Richmond, VA 23230, tel. 800/334–7525 or 800/284–8300); **Near Services** (450 Prairie Ave., Suite 101, Calumet City, IL 60409, tel. 708/868–6700 or 800/654–6700); **Travel Guard International** and **Carefree Travel Insurance** (*see* Health and Accident Insurance, above).

Before you go, itemize the contents of each bag in case you need to file an insurance claim. Be certain to put your home or business address on each piece of luggage, including carry-on bags. If your luggage is lost or stolen and later recovered, the airline will deliver the luggage to your home free of charge.

Trip Cancellation Consider purchasing trip-cancellation insurance if you are
and Flight traveling on a promotional or discounted ticket that does not
Americans allow changes or cancellations. You are then covered if an emergency causes you to cancel or postpone your trip. Trip-cancellation insurance is usually included in combination travel insurance packages available from most tour operators, travel agents, and insurance agents. Flight insurance, which covers passengers in the case of death or dismemberment, is often in-

cluded in the price of a ticket when paid for with a major credit card.

Britons *See* Health and Accident Insurance, above.

Renting and Leasing Cars

If you're flying into a major city or arriving by train and plan to spend a few days there before exploring the rest of the province, you can save money by touring the city on foot and by public transportation and also by arranging to pick up your car in the city when you're ready to head out. However, you could waste precious hours trying to locate a cut-rate rental company in return for only a small financial savings. If you're arriving and departing from different airports, look for a one-way car rental with no return fees. Rental rates vary widely, depending on car size and model, number of days you use the car, insurance coverage, and whether drop-off fees are imposed. In most cases, rates quoted include unlimited free mileage and standard liability protection. Not included are the Collision Damage Waiver (CDW), which eliminates your deductible payment should you have an accident; personal accident insurance; gasoline; and sales tax.

Driver's licenses issued in the United States and in most other countries are valid in Canada. You must be at least 21 to rent a car.

To make sure you get the type of car you want, it's best to arrange a car rental before you leave home. Rental companies usually charge according to the exchange rate of the U.S. dollar at the time the car is returned or when the credit card payment is processed. **Avis** (tel. 800/331-1212), **Budget Rent-a-Car** (tel. 800/527-0700), and **Hertz** (tel. 800/654-3131) all have offices at major airports in Canada. You can try **Tilden Rent-a-Car,** 1485 Stanley St., Montréal, Québec H3A 1P6, tel. 514/842-9445, or in the U.S., call Tilden's affiliate, **National Rent-a-Car** (tel. 800/328-4567 for reservations throughout Canada.)

Rail Passes

Although **VIA Rail,** Canada's major passenger carrier, has made considerable cuts in its services—specifically, dropping all of its special rail tours—it is still possible to travel coast to coast using VIA Rail. The railroad offers a Canrailpass to independent travelers of any age, and discount fares to senior citizens and students; a Canrailpass for eastern Canada routes only is also available. Tickets must be purchased prior to arrival in Canada. VIA Rail information is available in the United States by calling 800/665-0200; in Great Britain contact Compass Travel (3rd floor, Priest Gate House, 5-7 Priest Gate, Peterborough PE1 1LE, tel. 0733/53-809).

Student and Youth Travel

The **International Student Identity Card** (ISIC) entitles full-time students to rail passes, special fares on local transportation, student charter flights, and discounts at museums, theaters, sports events, and many other attractions. If the ISIC card is purchased in the United States, the $14 cost also includes $3,000 in emergency medical coverage, $100 a day for up to 60 days of hospital coverage, as well as a collect phone number to call in case of emergency. Apply to the **Council on International Educational Exchange** (CIEE, 205 E. 42nd St., New York, NY 10017, tel. 212/661–1414). In Canada, the ISIC is available for C$13 from **Travel Cuts** (187 College St., Toronto, Ont. M5T 1P7, tel. 416/979–2406).

Travelers under age 26 can apply for a **Youth International Educational Exchange Card** (YIEE) issued by the **Federation of International Youth Travel Organizations** (FIYTO, 81 Islands Brugge, DK-2300 Copenhagen S, Denmark). It provides services and benefits similar to those provided by the ISIC card. The YIEE card is available in the United States from CIEE (*see* above) and in Canada from the **Canadian Hostelling Association** (CHA, 333 River Rd., Ottawa, Ont. K1L 8H9, tel. 613/ 476–3844).

An **International Youth Hostel Federation** (IYHF) membership card is the key to inexpensive dormitory-style accommodations at thousands of youth hostels around the world. Hostels aren't only for young travelers on a budget, though; many have family accommodations. Hostels provide separate sleeping quarters for men and women at rates ranging from $7 to $20 a night per person and are situated in a variety of facilities, including converted farmhouses, villas, restored castles, and even lighthouses, as well as specially constructed modern buildings. There are more than 5,000 hostel locations in 75 countries around the world. IYHF memberships, which are valid for 12 months from the time of purchase, are available in the United States through **American Youth Hostels** (AYH, Box 37613, Washington, DC 20013, tel. 202/783–6161) and in Canada through the Canadian Hostelling Association (*see* above). The cost for a first-year membership is $25 for adults 18 to 54. Renewal thereafter is $20. For youths (17 and under), the rate is $10; for senior citizens (55 and older), the rate is $15. Family membership is available for two adults traveling with up to two children for $35. Every national hostel association arranges special reductions for members visiting their country, such as discounted rail fare or free bus travel, so be sure to ask for an international concessions list when you buy your membership.

Council Travel, a CIEE subsidiary, is the foremost U.S. student travel agency, specializing in low-cost charters and serving as the exclusive U.S. agent for many student airfare bargains and student tours. CIEE's 72-page Student Travel catalog and "Council Charter" brochures are available free from any Council Travel office in the United States (enclose $1 postage if ordering by mail). In addition to the CIEE headquarters (205 E. 42nd St.) and branch office (35 W. 8th St.) in New York City, there are Council Travel offices in Tempe, AZ; Berkeley, La Jolla, Long Beach, Los Angeles, San Diego, San Francisco, and Sherman Oaks, CA; Boulder, CO; New Haven, CT; Washington, DC; Atlanta, GA; Chicago and Evanston, IL; New Orleans, LA; Amherst, Boston, and Cambridge, MA; Ann Arbor, MI; Minneapolis, MN; Durham, NC; Columbus, OH; Portland, OR; Providence, RI; Austin and Dallas, TX; Seattle, WA; and Milwaukee, WI.

Students who would like to work abroad should contact CIEE's **Work Abroad Department** (205 E. 42nd St., New York, NY 10017, tel. 212/661–1414, ext. 1130). The council arranges various types of paid and voluntary work experiences overseas for up to six months. CIEE also sponsors study programs in Europe, Latin America, Asia, and Australia, and publishes many books of interest to the student traveler. These include *Work, Study, Travel Abroad: The Whole World Handbook* ($12.95 plus $1.50 book-rate postage or $3 first-class postage) and *Volunteer! The Comprehensive Guide to Voluntary Service in the U.S. and Abroad* ($8.95 plus $1.50 book-rate postage or $3 first-class postage). The Information Center at the **Institute of International Education** (IIE) has reference books, foreign-university catalogs, study-abroad brochures, and other materials, which may be consulted by students and nonstudents alike, free of charge. The Information Center is located on 1st Avenue between 45th and 46th streets in New York City (809 UN Plaza, New York, NY 10017, tel. 212/883–8200). It's open weekdays 10–4; closed on holidays. **Canadian University Travel Service Ltd.** (CUTS), sister organization of CIEE, serves as Canada's student travel bureau. CUTS has offices in about 28 locations throughout Canada, including Halifax, Montréal, Québec City, Ottawa, Toronto, Saskatoon, Edmonton, Victoria, and Vancouver. They are usually located on a university campus. To use CUTS services, you'll need an International card, available at CUTS offices (with proper ID) or at the addresses already mentioned above. CUTS helps you find student discount fares, sells European train passes for further travel, and can arrange working holidays and set up language courses. In addition, CUTS arranges tours and canoe trips and can help you with domestic flights. The company's "Discount Handbook" lists more than 1,000 stores and service establishments that offer bargains to ISIC card carriers.

Traveling with Children

Publications — *Family Travel Times* is a newsletter published 10 times a year by Travel With Your Children (TWYCH, 45 W. 18th St., 7th floor, New York, NY 10011, tel. 212/206–0688). A one-year subscription costs $35 and includes access to back issues and twice-weekly opportunities to call in for specific advice.

Hotels — Although most major hotels in Canada welcome children, the policies and programs they offer are usually limited to a free stay for children under a certain age when rooming with their parents. For example, the Sheraton Hotels worldwide offer a free stay to children under the age of 17. At Best Westerns, the age limit ranges from 12 to 16, depending on the hotel, because each Best Western operates independently. Baby-sitting services can often be arranged at the front desk of most hotels. In addition, priority for connecting rooms is often given to families. Inquire about programs and discounts when you make your reservation.

Home Exchange — Exchanging homes is a surprisingly low-cost way to enjoy a vacation abroad, especially a long one. The largest home-exchange service, **Intervac U.S. International Home Exchange Service** (Box 590504, San Francisco, CA 94159, tel. 415/435–3497) publishes three directories a year. Membership ($45) entitles you to one listing in all three directories. Photos of your property cost an additional $11, and listing a second home costs $10. **Vacation Exchange Club** (Box 820, Haleiwa, HI 96712, tel. 800/638–3841) specializes in both international and domestic home exchanges. The club publishes four directories a year and updated late listings. Annual membership, which includes your listing in one book, a newsletter, and copies of all publications, is $50. **Loan-a-Home** (2 Park La., 6E, Mount Vernon, NY 10552, tel. 914/664–7640) is popular with the academic community on sabbatical and businesspeople on temporary assignment. There's no annual membership fee or charge for listing your home; however, one directory and a supplement costs $35. Loan-a-Home publishes two directories (in December and June) and two supplements (in March and September) each year. All four books cost $45 per year.

Getting There On international flights, children under 2 not occupying a seat pay 10% of adult fare. Various discounts apply to children from age 2 to 12, so check with your airline when booking. Reserve a seat behind the bulkhead of the plane, because there's usually more leg room and enough space to fit a bassinet, which the airlines will supply. At the same time, ask about special children's meals or snacks; most airlines offer them. For more information about the children's services offered by 46 airlines, see TWYCH's "Airline Guide," published in the February 1990 and 1992 issues of *Family Travel Times*.

Ask the airline in advance if you can bring aboard your child's car seat. For the booklet *Child/Infant Safety Seats Acceptable for Use in Aircraft,* write to the Federal Aviation Administration (APA-200, 800 Independence Ave. SW, Washington, DC 20591, tel. 202/267–3479).

Hints for Disabled Travelers

The **Information Center for Individuals with Disabilities** (Fort Point Pl., 1st floor, 27–43 Wormwood St., Boston, MA 02217, tel., and TDD, 11–4, 617/727–5540) offers useful problem-solving assistance, including lists of travel agents who specialize in tours for the disabled. For a small fee, **Moss Rehabilitation Hospital Travel Information Service** (200 W. Tabor Rd., Philadelphia, PA 19941–3099, tel. 215/329–5715; TDD 215/456–9602) provides information on tourist sights, transportation, and accommodations in destinations around the world. **Travel Industry and Disabled Exchange** (TIDE, 5435 Donna Ave., Tarzana, CA 91356, tel. 818/368–5648), for a $15 per-person annual-membership fee, provides a quarterly newsletter and a directory of travel agencies and tours to Europe, Canada, Great Britain, New Zealand, and Australia—all specializing in travel for the disabled. **Evergreen Travel/Wings on Wheels** (4114 198th St. SW, Lynnwood, WA 98036, tel. 206/776–1184) is a well-recognized tour operator specializing in travel for the disabled.

Mobility International USA (Box 3551, Eugene, OR 97403, tel. 503/343–1284) is an internationally affiliated organization with 500 members. For a $20 annual fee, it coordinates exchange programs for disabled people around the world and offers information on accommodations and organized study programs. **VIA Rail Canada** (tel. 800/665–0200) will arrange for preboarding of trains for people in wheelchairs or with other special needs if given at least 24 hours' notice. **Canadian Paraplegic Association** (780 W. Marine Dr., Vancouver, BC V6P 5Y7, tel. 604/324–3611) provides information to the disabled about touring in Canada.

Hints for Older Travelers

The **American Association of Retired Persons** (AARP, 601 E St. NW, Washington, DC 20049, tel. 202/434–2277) has two programs for independent travelers: (1) the Purchase Privilege Program, which offers discounts on hotels, airfare, car rentals, RV rentals, and sightseeing; and (2) the AARP Motoring Plan provided by Amoco, which furnishes emergency aid (road service) and trip-routing information for an annual fee of $33.95 per person or couple. (Both programs include the member and member's spouse or the member and another person who shares the household.) The AARP also arranges group tours, including apartment living in Europe and Australia, through **AARP Travel Experience from American Express** (400 Pinnacle Way, Suite 450, Norcross, GA 30071, tel. 800/927–0111 or, in GA, 800/637–6200). AARP members must be 50 or older; annual dues are $5 per person or per couple.

When using an AARP or other discount identification card, ask for reduced hotel rates at the time you make your reservation, not when you check out. At participating restaurants, show your card to the maître d' before being seated, since discounts may be limited to certain set menus, days, or hours. When renting a car, be sure to ask about special promotional rates, which may offer greater savings than the available discount.

Elderhostel (80 Boylston St., Suite 400, Boston, MA 02116, tel. 617/426–7788) is an innovative educational program for people 60 and older. Participants live in dorms on some 1,600 campuses around the world. Mornings are devoted to lectures and seminars; afternoons to sightseeing and field trips. Fees for two- to three-week international trips, including room, board, tuition, and round-trip transportation, range from $1,800 to $4,500.

Saga International Holidays (120 Boylston St., Boston, MA 02116, tel. 800/343–0273) specializes in group travel for people over 60. A selection of variously priced tours allows you to choose the package that meets your needs.

National Council of Senior Citizens (1331 F St. NW, Washington, DC 20004, tel. 202/347–8800) is a nonprofit advocacy group with some 5,000 local clubs across the country. Annual membership is $12 per person or per couple. Members receive a monthly newspaper with travel information and an ID card for reduced-rate hotels and car rentals.

Mature Outlook (6001 N. Clark St., Chicago, IL 60660, tel. 800/336–6330), a subsidiary of Sears Roebuck & Co., is a travel club for people over 50, with hotel and motel discounts and a bimonthly newsletter. Annual membership is $9.95; there are currently 800,000 members. Instant membership is available at participating Holiday Inns.

VIA Rail Canada (tel. 800/665–0200) offers senior citizens (60 and over) a 10% discount on basic transportation for travel any time and with no advance-purchase requirement. This 10% discount can also apply to off-peak reduced fares that have advance-purchase requirements.

Further Reading

Fiction Mordecai Richler is well known as the author of *The Apprenticeship of Duddy Kravitz*, a novel set in Montréal, which was made into a movie. His various collections of essays are also worth exploring. Margaret Atwood, a prolific poet and novelist, is also regarded as a stateswoman of sorts in her native Canada. Her most recent novel, *The Cat's Eye*, is set in northern Canada and Toronto. Alice Munro writes about small-town life in Ontario in *The Progress of Love*. *Northern Lights*, by Howard Norman, focuses on a child's experiences growing up in Manitoba and, later, Toronto. Howard Engel's mystery series features the adventures of Bennie Cooperman, a Toronto-based detective. *The Suicide Murders* is an especially compelling novel from the series. Jack Hodgin's *Spit Delaney's Island* is peopled with loggers, construction workers and other rural Canadians. *Peace Shall Destroy Many* is Rudy Wiebe's account of a Mennonite community in Manitoba. Joy Kogawa's first novel, *Obasan*, tells about the Japanese community of Canada during World War II. *Medicine River* is a collection of short stories by Native American writer Thomas King, who was one of the authors, along with Cheryl Calver and Helen Hoy, of *The Native in Literature*, about the image of Native Americans in literature. For an excellent view of New Brunswick, especially the famed salmon fishing region called the Miramichi, look for the humorous books *The Americans Are Coming* and *The Last Tasmanian* by local author Herb Curtis.

Nonfiction   *Canada North* is by Farley Mowat, as is *Never Cry Wolf*, his humorous account of a naturalist who goes to a remote part of Canada to commune with wolves. Andrew Malcolm gives a cultural and historical overview of the country in *The Canadians*. Stephen Brook's *The Maple Leaf Rag* is a collection of idiosyncratic travel essays. *My Country*, by Pierre Burton, is one of many of Burton's books about Canada worth reading for a personal look at Canada. *Short History of Canada*, by Desmond Morton, is a recent historical account of the country.

Arriving and Departing

From the U.S. by Plane

Be certain to distinguish among (1) nonstop flights—no changes, no stops; (2) direct flights—no changes but one or more stops; and (3) connecting flights—two or more planes, one or more stops.

Airports and Airlines   Every major U.S. airline has nonstop flights to Canada. The major international hubs are Montréal, Toronto, and Vancouver, but international flights also fly into Halifax, Calgary, and Edmonton. From the United States, nonstop service to Canada is available from New York, Hartford, Boston, Philadelphia, Pittsburgh, Washington, Baltimore, Atlanta, Miami, Tampa, Denver, Minneapolis-St. Paul, Indianapolis, Chicago, Cleveland, Columbus, Dayton, Seattle, San Francisco, Los Angeles, and Honolulu.

Flying Time To Montréal   From New York: 1½ hours; from Chicago: 2 hours; from Los Angeles: 6 hours; from London: 6½ hours.

To Toronto   From New York: 1½ hours; from Chicago: 1½ hours; from Los Angeles: 4½ hours.

To Calgary   From New York: 5½ hours; from Toronto: 3½ hours; from Los Angeles: 4 hours.

To Vancouver   From Montréal: 6½ hours; from Chicago: 4 hours; from Los Angeles: 2½ hours.

Discount Flights   The major airlines offer a range of tickets whose prices can vary by more than 300%, depending on the day of purchase. As a rule, the further in advance you buy the ticket, the less expensive it is and the greater the penalty (up to 100%) for canceling. Check with airlines for details. APEX (advance purchase) tickets on the major airlines not only must be bought in advance (usually 21 days); they restrict your travel, usually with a minimum stay of seven days and a maximum of 90; and also penalize you for changes—voluntary or not—in your travel plans. But if you can work around these drawbacks (and most travelers can), they are among the best-value fares available.

Consolidators   Other discounted fares—up to 50% below the cost of APEX tickets—can be found through consolidators, companies that buy blocks of tickets on scheduled airlines and sell them at wholesale prices. Tickets are subject to availability, so passengers must have flexible travel schedules. Here again, you may lose all or most of your money if you change plans, but at least you will be on a regularly scheduled flight with less risk of cancellation than on a charter. As an added precaution, you may want to purchase trip-cancellation insurance. Once you've made your reservation, call the airline to confirm it. Many consolidators advertise in newspaper travel sections.

Travel Clubs   Another option is to join a travel club that offers special discounts to its members. Several such organizations are **Discount Travel International** (114 Forrest Ave., Narberth, PA 19072, tel. 215/668–7184 or 800/334–9294); **Moment's Notice** (425 Madison Ave., New York, NY 10017, tel. 212/486–0500); **Travelers Advantage,** (CUC Travel Service, 49 Music Square W, Nashville, TN 37203, tel. 800/548–1116); and **Worldwide Discount Travel Club** (1674 Meridian Ave., Miami Beach, FL 33139, tel. 305/534–2082). These cut-rate tickets should be compared with APEX tickets on the major airlines.

Air Couriers   Travelers willing to put up with some restrictions and inconvenience, in exchange for a substantially reduced airfare, may be interested in flying as an air courier. A person who agrees to be a courier must accompany shipments between designated points. There are several sources of information on courier deals: For a telephone directory listing courier companies by the cities to which they fly, send $5 and a self-addressed, stamped business-size envelope to **Pacific Data Sales Publishing**, 2554 Lincoln Boulevard, Suite 275-I, Marina del Rey, CA 90291. *A Simple Guide to Courier Travel* is available for $15.95 postpaid by writing to Box 2394, Lake Oswego, OR 97035. For more information, call 800/344–9375. A $35 membership in the International Association of Air Travel Couriers will bring you six issues of its newsletter "Shoestring Traveler" and of its Air Courier Bulletin directory. Write IAATC, Box 1349, Lake Worth, FL 33460, tel. 407/582–8320.

Smoking   If a U.S. airline tells you there are no seats available in the nonsmoking section, insist on one: Department of Transportation regulations require carriers to find seats for all nonsmokers, provided they meet check-in time restrictions. These regulations apply to all international flights on U.S. domestic carriers. Smoking is also banned on all Canadian commercial carriers on North American routes.

From the U.S. by Car

Drivers must have proper owner registration and proof of insurance coverage, which is compulsory in Canada. U.S. motorists are advised to obtain a Canadian Non-Resident Inter-Provincial Motor Vehicle Liability Insurance Card, which is accepted as evidence of financial responsibility anywhere in Canada. It is available from any U.S. insurance company. You won't need an international driver's license; any valid one will do. If you are driving a rented car, be sure to have the vehicle registration forms, along with a copy of the rental contract, to indicate that use in Canada is authorized by the rental agency. If you are driving a car that is not registered in your name, you should carry a letter from the owner that authorizes your use of the vehicle. The use of seat belts (and approved infant seats) is mandatory for drivers and passengers in Canada, except in the Yukon Territory.

The U.S. Interstate Highway System leads directly into Canada at 12 points: I–95 from Maine to New Brunswick; I–91 and I–89 from Vermont to Québec; I–87 from New York to Québec; I–81 and a spur off I–90 from New York to Ontario; I–94, I–96, and I–75 from Michigan to Ontario; I–29 from North Dakota to Manitoba; I–15 from Montana to Alberta; and I–5 from Washington state to British Columbia. Most of these connections hook up with the Trans-Canada Highway within a few miles. There are many smaller highway crossings between the two countries as well.

From Alaska, take the Alaska Highway (from Fairbanks), the Klondike Highway (from Skagway), and the Top of the World Highway (to Dawson City).

From the U.S. by Train, Bus, and Ship

By Train **Amtrak** (tel. 800/872–7245) has service from New York to Montréal, New York and Buffalo to Toronto, and Chicago to Toronto. Amtrak's *Montrealer* departs from New York's Pennsylvania Station at 8:20 PM and arrives in Montréal the next day at about 10:45 AM. Sleepers are highly recommended for the overnight trip but must be booked well in advance. The *Montrealer* is the only Amtrak train to Canada that requires reservations.

A second Amtrak train to Montréal leaves New York City from Pennsylvania Station in the morning and takes 9½ hours; New York to Toronto (passing through Buffalo) takes 11 hours and 45 minutes; Chicago to Toronto takes 12 hours. In addition to these direct routes, there are connections from many major cities. On the west coast, Amtrak offers frequent service to Seattle. From there, buses are available to Vancouver and other Canadian destinations.

By Bus **Greyhound** has the most widespread bus service to Canada, but you can get from almost any point in the United States to any point in Canada on its extensive network. One of the longest routes, from New York City to Vancouver via Seattle, takes about 3½ days.

By Ship You can take a car ferry between Seattle and Victoria (British Columbia) or Maine and Nova Scotia (*see* Essential Information in individual chapters). Many Canadian cities are also accessible by water on private yachts and boats. Local marine authorities can advise you about the necessary documentation and procedure.

From the U.K. by Plane

Airlines   The major carriers between Great Britain and Canada are **Air Canada** (tel. 081/759–2636), **British Airways** (tel. 081/897–4000), and **Canadian Airlines International** (tel. 081/667–0666 in the London area, 0345/616–767 elsewhere). Air Canada has the most flights and serves the most cities, with at least one flight a day to Toronto, Vancouver, and Montréal from Heathrow, and considerably more at peak periods. Air Canada also flies to Calgary, Edmonton, Halifax, and St. John's from Heathrow; to Toronto from Birmingham and Manchester; and to Calgary, Halifax, Toronto, and Vancouver from Prestwick (Glasgow). British Airways has as many as 23 flights a week to Canada from Heathrow, serving Montréal, Toronto, and Vancouver. Canadian Airlines International serves Calgary, Edmonton, Ottawa, and Vancouver from London Gatwick, has at least one flight a day to Toronto, and has service from Manchester to Toronto.

Charters   The leading charter company, **Globespan International** (tel. 0293/562–690) offers daily flights from Gatwick to Toronto, as well as less frequent flights to Calgary, Edmonton, Halifax, Montréal, Ottawa, and Vancouver. It also offers weekly service from Birmingham, Cardiff, Manchester, Prestwick, and Stanstead to Toronto; and from Manchester and Prestwick to Vancouver. Fares are competitive. **Uni jet** (tel. 0444/459–100) also has charter flights from Britain to Canada. Specialist ticket companies such as **Travel Cuts** (tel. 071/637–3161) sometimes have even lower fares, though not at peak periods and with absolutely no frills. Check the advertisements in *Time Out* and the Sunday newspapers for other inexpensive fares.

From the U.K. by Ship

Gray Dawes Travel (Dugard House, Peartree Rd., Stanway, Colchester, Essex CO3 5UL, tel. 0206/762241) arranges passages on freighters to three Canadian cities: Halifax, Montréal, and Vancouver. The sailing to Halifax leaves from Bremerhaven every week and can take 8 to 12 passengers; fares begin at £475 one way and the trip takes 8 to 9 days. The sailing to Montréal leaves from Antwerp every 10 to 14 days and can take 10 to 12 passengers; the voyage takes about two weeks. The sailing to Vancouver leaves from Fleixstowe or Hamburg once a month and goes through the Panama Canal, then on to Los Angeles, Oakland, Portland, and Seattle. It can take 10 to 12 passengers, and the trip takes nearly a month. The demand for all these sailings is considerable, and you may have to book many months, even a year, in advance.

Staying in Canada

Getting Around

By Plane   **Air Canada** (tel. 800/776–3000) operates in every province. The other major domestic carrier is **Canadian Airlines International** (tel. 800/426–7000). Regularly scheduled flights to every major city and to most smaller cities are available on Air Canada or Canadian Airlines International or the domestic carriers associated with them: **Air Alliance** serves Québec; **Air Atlantic** flies in the Atlantic region; **Air BC** serves British Columbia with new extended service out of Portland and Seattle; **Air Nova** serves Atlantic Canada; **Air Ontario** serves the Ontario region; and **First Air** includes a flight from Ottawa to New York. These airlines can be contacted at local numbers within each of the many cities they serve. Check with the territorial tourist agencies for charter companies and with the District Controller of Air Services in the territorial (and provincial) capitals for the locations of air bases that allow private flights and for regulations.

Smoking   Smoking has been prohibited on Canadian commercial planes on North American routes since September 1988. The ban was extended to all Canadian flights, including flights to Europe and the Far East, on July 1, 1990.

By Train   Transcontinental rail service is provided by **VIA Rail Canada** (tel. 800/665–0200). If you're planning on traveling to several major cities in Canada, the train may be your best bet. Routes run across the country as well as within individual provinces, with the exception of the Northwest Territories and the Yukon, Newfoundland and Prince Edward Island.

You can choose either sleeping-car or coach accommodations on most trains. Both classes allow access to dining cars. Sleeping-car passengers can enjoy comfortable parlor cars, drawing rooms, bedrooms, and roomettes. First-class seats, sleeping-car accommodations, and Dayniter seats between Ontario, Québec, and the maritime provinces require reservations. Train information is available from the United States. (*See* From the U.S. by Train and Rail Passes, above).

By Bus   The bus is an essential form of transportation in Canada, especially if you want to visit out-of-the-way towns that do not have airports or rail lines. Two major bus companies, **Greyhound** (222 1st Ave. SW, Calgary, Alb. T2P 0A6, tel. 403/265–9111) and **Voyageur** (265 Catherine St., Ottawa, Ont. K1R 7S5, tel. 613/238–5900), offer interprovincial service.

By Car   Canada's highway system is excellent. It includes the Trans-Canada Highway, the longest in the world, which runs about 5,000 miles from Victoria, British Columbia, to St. John's, Newfoundland, using ferries to bridge coastal waters at each end. The second-largest Canadian highway, the Yellowhead Highway, follows the old Indian route from the Pacific Coast and over the Rockies to the prairie. North of the population centers, roads become fewer and less developed.

Speed limits vary from province to province, but they are usually within the 90–100 kph (50–60 mph) range outside the cities. The price of gasoline varies more than the speed limit, from 40¢ to 67¢ a liter. (There are 3.8 liters in a U.S. gallon, 4.5 liters in a Canadian Imperial gallon.) Distances are now always shown in kilometers, and gasoline is always sold in liters. The Imperial gallon is seldom used.

Foreign driver's licenses are valid in Canada. Members of the **Automobile Association of America** (AAA) can contact the **Canadian Automobile Association** (1775 Courtwood Crescent, Ottawa, Ont. K2C 3J2, tel. 613/226–7631) for travel information, itineraries, maps, and tour books. If you are a member of the AAA, you can also dial 800/336–4357 for emergency road service in Canada.

By Ferry Car ferries provide essential transportation on both the east and west coasts of Canada. **Marine Atlantic** (Box 250, North Sydney, NS B2A 3M3, tel. 902/794–5700 or 800/341–7981) operates ferries between Nova Scotia and Newfoundland; New Brunswick and Prince Edward Island; New Brunswick and Nova Scotia; and also between Portland, Maine, and Nova Scotia. On the west coast, the **British Columbia Ferry Corporation** (1112 Fort St., Victoria, BC V8V 4V2, tel. 604/656–0757) operates 38 ships among 42 ports of call. Other ferries also operate between the state of Washington and British Columbia's Vancouver Island.

Telephones

Phones work as they do in the United States. Drop 25¢ in the slot (pay phones eagerly accept American coins, unlike U.S. phones, which spit out Canadian money) and dial the number. There are no problems dialing direct to the United States; U.S. telephone credit cards are accepted. For directory assistance, dial 1, the area code, and 555–1212. To place calls outside Canada and the United States, dial "0" and ask for the overseas operator.

Mail

Postal Rates In Canada you can buy stamps at the post office or from automatic vending machines in most hotel lobbies, railway stations, airports, bus terminals, many retail outlets, and some newsstands. Within Canada, postcards and letters up to 30 grams cost 42¢. Letters and postcards to the United States cost 48¢ for up to 30 grams, 70¢ for up to 50 grams, $1.08 for up to 100 grams.

International mail and postcards run 84¢ for up to 20 grams, $1.26 for 20–50 grams.

Telepost is a fast "next day or sooner" service that combines the CN/CP Telecommunications network with letter-carrier delivery service. Messages may be telephoned to the nearest CN/CP Public Message Centre for delivery anywhere in Canada or the United States. Telepost service is available 24 hours a day, seven days a week, and billing arrangements may be made at the time the message is called in. **Intelpost** allows you to send documents or photographs via satellite to many Canadian, American, and European destinations. This service is available at main postal facilities in Canada, and is paid for in cash.

Visitors may have mail sent to them c/o General Delivery in the town they are visiting, for pickup in person within 15 days, after which it will be returned to the sender.

Tipping

Tips and service charges are not usually added to a bill in Canada. In general, tip 15% of the total bill. This goes for waiters, waitresses, barbers and hairdressers, taxi drivers, etc. Porters and doormen should get about 50¢ a bag ($1 or more in a luxury hotel). For maid service, $1 a day is sufficient ($2 in luxury hotels).

Opening and Closing Times

Stores, shops, and supermarkets are usually open Monday through Saturday from 9 to 6—although in major cities, supermarkets are often open from 7:30 AM until 9 PM. Blue laws are in effect in much of Canada, but a growing number of provinces have stores with limited Sunday hours (usually from noon to 5). Retail stores are generally open on Thursday and Friday evenings, most shopping malls until 9 PM. Most banks in Canada are open Monday through Thursday from 10 to 3, and from 10 to 5 or 6 on Friday. Some banks are open longer hours and are also open on Saturday morning. Many banks offer automated tellers at any hour. All banks are closed on national holidays. Drugstores in major cities are often open until 11 PM, and convenience stores are often open 24 hours a day, seven days a week.

GST and Sales Tax

A countrywide goods and services tax of 7% (GST) is applicable to virtually every transaction in Canada except for basic groceries. Nonresidents can get a full refund of the GST, on any merchandise they purchase and take with them out of the country, and on short-term accommodations, by submitting a rebate form within 60 days of leaving Canada. Forms may be obtained from certain retailers, duty-free shops, and customs officials or by writing to Revenue Canada, Visitor's Rebate Program, Ottawa, Ont. K1A 1J5. Instant rebates can be obtained at some duty-free shops when leaving Canada, and most provinces do not tax goods that are shipped directly by the vendor to the nonresident's home. Invoices must be attached for any goods or services for which a rebate is being claimed. All provinces, except Alberta, the Northwest Territories, and the Yukon, levy a sales tax from 4% to 12% on most items purchased in shops, on meals in restaurants, and, sometimes, on hotel accommodations. Alberta and Ontario charge 5% tax on hotel rooms, for example; British Columbia adds 8%; and New Brunswick, 11%. Some provinces offer a sales-tax rebate system similar to the federal one (call the various provincial toll-free information lines for details).

Shopping

A few years ago, the exchange rate so favored the U.S. dollar that you were always ensured a 25% discount. These days, though, Canadian prices don't exactly mirror those in the United States. With the current exchange rate, you can expect only a small "discount." In fact, the GST, combined with provincial taxes in some cases, has made the cost of some everyday items, such as cigarettes, prohibitive for Canadians.

In some of Canada's provinces, a sales tax refund is available when goods are exported from Canada (or, in some cases, from the province). Ontario has a particularly good system for such refunds, provided that the tax you are claiming back equals at least C$7. Ask about tax refunds at the time of your purchase, inquire at your hotel before setting out to shop, or call the toll-free provincial information lines.

Antiques   On the whole, prices for antiques are lower in Canada than in the United States. Along Montréal's rue Sherbrooke Ouest, the shops feature everything from ancient maps to fine crystal. For funkier finds, stroll through Vieux-Montréal and the rue Notre-Dame, where antiques and collectibles range from Napoleonic-period furniture to 1950s bric-a-brac. Toronto's offerings are equally eclectic, although priced higher than elsewhere in Canada. (But for comparison's sake, consider that many Toronto antiques dealers send their wares to New York City, where the price is doubled before it goes on the sales floor.) The Yorkville area caters to interior designers, with its European collections, although the antiques markets at Lansdowne and Harbourfront are livelier and have wider selections. Antiques shopping is a respectable pastime in Vancouver as well, and Victoria offers some of the best buys in antique silver in its shops clustered on Fort Street.

Arts and Crafts   Sweaters, silver objects, pottery, and Acadian crafts can be found in abundance in New Brunswick. For pewter, head for Fredericton. For woven items, visit the village of St. Andrews. In Québec, check out the wood carvings. The Mennonite communities of Ontario sell their handmade quilts each May at the Mennonite Relief sale. Prices can run to $2,000 for a large quilt.

Fur   You can buy a fur in any big city, but for the best prices, head to Toronto and Montréal, the wholesale fur districts of Canada. Mink is a good buy in Canada. You can also find fox coats, but fox is not a specialty of Canada. January is a particularly good time to shop for fur, since it is sale season. In the United States, fur garments must be labeled to distinguish farmed from trapped pelts. Canada's trapping business is legal and profitable, and the industry has resisted pressure from the United States to enforce a similar labeling system. If you are concerned about whether the animal was farmed or trapped, you'll have to ask the salesperson.

Indian Art   Interest has grown for the highly collectible Inuit art and sculpture, usually rendered in stone. For the best price and a guarantee of authenticity, purchase Inuit and other native crafts in the province where they originate. Many styles are now attributed to certain tribes and are mass-produced for sale in galleries and shops miles away from their regions of origin. At the very top galleries you can be assured of getting pieces done by individual artists, though the prices will be higher than in the provinces of origin. The Canadian government has registered the symbol of an igloo as a mark of a work's authenticity. Be sure this Canadian government sticker or tag is attached before you make your purchase. Many galleries and shops in the west also carry work done by the Indians of the Northwest, who have revived their ancient art. They are known for their highly stylized masks, totem poles, and canoes. Themes and images from nature, such as whales, bears, wolves, and eagles, are prominent in their work. Bright colors and geometric patterns distinguish their woven products: blankets, wall hangings, and clothing.

In and around Calgary you can find ceremonial headdresses, clothing, and tools made by the nomadic Plains Indians. Algonkian and Iroquoian art survives mainly in the museums of eastern Canada and in the gift shops of some of the reservations in Ontario.

Maple Syrup Eastern Canada is famous for its sugar maples. The trees are tapped in March, and the sap is collected in buckets to be boiled down into maple syrup. This natural confection is sold all year. Avoid the tourist shops and department stores; for the best prices and information, stop at the many farm stands and markets in the provinces of Québec, Ontario, and New Brunswick. A small can of syrup costs about $6.

National Parks

Banff, the country's first national park, was established in 1885, and since then the national park system has grown to encompass 34 national parks and 112 national historic sites (for day use only). Because of Canada's eagerness to preserve its environment, new lands are continually being added to this network. Almost every park offers camping—either primitive camping or campsites with various facilities that can accommodate recreational vehicles. Hiking trails weave their way through each of the parks. Among the most popular parks are Fundy National Park in New Brunswick and the several Rocky Mountain parks. Environment Canada publishes two pamphlets: *Canada's National Parks* lists each of the parks and any activities and facilities available, and *Canada's National Historic Sites* provides descriptions of each of these parks and sites, including opening and closing times and some background information. Write to Inquiry Center, Environment Canada, Ottawa, Ont. K1A 0H3, tel. 819/997–2800.

Participant Sports and Outdoor Activities

Biking Eastern and western Canada offer some of the best bicycling terrain. In the east, bikers favor the Gaspé Peninsula in Québec and the surrounding Atlantic provinces. The terrain varies from very hilly around the Gaspé to flat on Prince Edward Island, and varied in New Brunswick and Nova Scotia. A western tour might include the area around the Rocky Mountains and on through British Columbia. Some cities, such as Vancouver and Ottawa, have bike trails marked throughout town. Write to the provincial tourist boards for road maps (which are more detailed than the maps available at gas stations) and information on local cycling associations.

Boating With so much coastline—on the Atlantic and Pacific, the Great Lakes, major rivers, and thousands of smaller lakes—boating is extremely popular throughout Canada. Boat rentals are widely available, and provincial tourism departments can provide lists of companies.

Camping Canada's 2,000-plus campgrounds range from simple roadside turnoffs with sweeping mountain vistas to fully equipped facilities with groomed sites, trailer hookups, recreational facilities, and vacation village atmosphere. Many of the best sites are in Canada's national and provincial parks, with nominal overnight fees. Commercial campgrounds offer more amenities, such as electrical and water hookups, showers, and even game rooms and grocery stores. They cost more and somehow defeat the point of camping: getting a little closer to nature. For listings of private and public campgrounds, contact the tourist office of the province you plan to visit.

Canoeing and Kayaking   Your degree of expertise and experience will dictate where you will canoe. Beginners will look for waterways in more settled areas; the pros will head north to the streams and rivers that flow into the Arctic Ocean. Provincial tourist offices and the federal Department of Northern Development and Indian Affairs (Ottawa, Ont. K1A OH4, tel. 819/997–0002) can be of assistance, especially in locating an outfitter to suit your needs. You can also contact the **Canadian Recreational Canoeing Association** (5–1029 Hyde Park Rd., London, Ont. N0M 1Z0, tel. 519/473–2109).

Fishing   Anglers can find their catch in virtually any region of the country, though restrictions, seasons, license requirements, and bag limits vary from province to province. You should inquire at provincial tourist offices (*see* Essential Information in individual chapters for tourist office addresses and telephone numbers). In addition, a special fishing permit is required to fish in all national parks; it can be obtained at any national park site, for a nominal fee. **Prince Edward Island** offers cod, mackerel, salmon, and sea trout in the Atlantic and speckled trout and rainbow trout in its other waters. The waters surrounding Prince Edward Island have some of the best deep-sea tuna fishing. **Nova Scotia** has some of the most stringent freshwater restrictions in Canada, but the availability of Atlantic salmon, speckled trout, and striped bass makes the effort worthwhile. Salmon, trout, and black bass are abundant in the waters of **New Brunswick**, and although many salmon pools in the streams and rivers are leased to private freeholders, either individuals or clubs, fly fishing is still readily available for visitors. The lakes of **Québec** hold trout, bass, pike, and landlocked salmon, called ouananiche (pronounced *Wah*-nah-nish). Just about every kind of North American freshwater game fish is available in some part of **Ontario. Manitoba** and **Saskatchewan** offer lake trout, brook trout, pike, grayling, walleye, Hudson Bay salmon, and smallmouth bass. They also offer a winter fishing season, but some areas require a guide. **Alberta** is considered a paradise for sportfishers, with its trout in streams; its pike, walleye, and perch in lakes; and its grayling, goldeye, and whitefish in rivers. **British Columbia** is unparalleled for salmon, but only two of the five species may be taken in nontidal waters. **Northwest Territories** offers Arctic char, lake trout, and grayling in the Great Bear and Great Slave lakes.

Golf   Every province has something for the duffer, but British Columbia and Ontario dominate the golf scene. Ontario has nearly 400 golf courses. British Columbia also has many golf courses, and Victoria's mild weather makes it especially appealing to golfers. Because public courses are often overcrowded, if you are a member of a golf club, check to see if it has a reciprocal playing arrangement with any of the private clubs in the areas that you will be visiting.

Hiking   Miles and miles of trails weave through all of Canada's national and provincial parks. Write to the individual provincial tourist offices (*see* Essential Information in individual chapters) or the Inquiry Center for the National Parks Department (*see* National Parks, above).

Horseback Riding   This sport is popular out West, especially in places like Banff National Park in Alberta, which has many outfitters that can arrange week-long trips on the park's trails. Contact the park's information center for more details (tel. 403/762–3324) or the Alberta Tourism Department.

Hunting Canada is rich with a variety of game, including deer, black bear, moose, caribou, elk, and wild goose. As with fishing, hunting is governed by federal, provincial, and territorial laws. You will need a hunting license from each province or territory in which you plan to hunt. A federal permit is required for hunting migratory game birds and is available at most Canadian post offices. Weapons of any type are prohibited in many of Canada's provincial parks and reserves and adjacent areas, and no hunting is permitted in Canada's national parks. Guides are required in many places and are available almost everywhere. Provincial tourist offices can provide specific information.

Mountain Climbing Offering mountain climbers a challenge are the summits of Banff and Jasper national parks in Alberta and the provincial park of Mt. Robson and Yoho National Park in British Columbia. Mountain climbing should not be undertaken lightly. Write to the Inquiry Center (*see* National Parks, above) for more information about these parks, or contact mountaineering organizations listed in individual chapters.

Scuba Diving More than 3,000 shipwrecks lie off the coast of Nova Scotia, making it particularly attractive to divers. The provincial Department of Tourism can provide details on the location of wrecks and where to buy or rent equipment. A wealth of sea life makes diving in coastal areas of British Columbia particularly attractive. Contact **Dive B.C.** (707 Westminster Ave., Powell River, BC V8A 1C5, tel. 604/485–6267).

Skiing Skiing is probably the most popular winter sport in Canada. For downhill skiing there are slopes in every province, but those in Québec, Alberta, and British Columbia are the best. Alberta and British Columbia also offer heli-skiing trips. For cross-country skiing, almost any provincial or national park will do. *See* the individual chapters.

Whale Watching The shores off British Columbia are some of the best places to observe whales, seals, and other natural wildlife. Day-long and sometimes week-long boat trips are offered. In the Pacific Ocean, along Vancouver Island, migrating whales pass on their way to California breeding grounds in the fall and come back in the spring. On the Atlantic coast, the waters around Newfoundland offer excellent whale-watching, and giant humpback, right whales, finback and minke whales can be seen in the Bay of Fundy. Boat trips are available from New Brunswick and Nova Scotia.

White-water Rafting There are opportunities for rafting in almost every province, but the white waters of Ontario and British Columbia are especially inviting for thrill seekers. Commercial rafting companies offer a variety of trip packages.

Winter Sports Canadians flourish in winter, as the range of winter sports attests. In addition to the sports already mentioned, at the first drop of a snowflake Canadians will head outside to ice-skate, toboggan, snowmobile, dogsled, snowshoe, and ice-fish.

Spectator Sports

Baseball If you're missing a bit of Americana, don't fret. Baseball has been a favorite in Canada since the major leagues expanded into Montréal in 1969 with the Montréal Expos, and the Toronto Blue Jays formed a World Series–caliber club. Minor league teams compete in Vancouver, Edmonton, Calgary, Lethbridge, and Medicine Hat.

Curling For a true taste of Canadian sportsmanship you might want to watch a curling match, which is not unlike a bowling match on ice. Two teams of four players each compete by sliding large stones toward a mark in the center of a circle, or "house."

Football The Canadian Football League plays the game its own way, allowing three downs, a 110-yard field, and 12 players per side. Teams are located in Toronto, Ottawa, Hamilton, Winnipeg, Regina, Calgary, Edmonton, and Vancouver.

Hockey Officially, Canada's national sport is lacrosse, but tell that to Wayne Gretzky, who was a national hero until he defected to play hockey in Los Angeles. Ice hockey is played by children and professionals alike, with leagues and teams organized everywhere. The National Hockey League teams in Canada include the Vancouver Canucks, Calgary Flames, Winnipeg Jets, Edmonton Oilers, Toronto Maple Leafs, Ottawa Senators, Montréal Canadiens, and Québec Nordiques. The season runs from October to April.

Rodeos and Horse Racing Alberta is rodeo country. Thoroughbred racing during the spring, summer, and fall takes place in Ontario, Manitoba, Saskatchewan, Alberta, and British Columbia.

Dining

The earliest European settlers of Canada—the British and the French—bequeathed a rather bland diet of meat and potatoes. But though there are few really distinct national dishes here, except in Québec, the strong ethnic presence in Canada makes it difficult not to have a good meal, especially in the larger cities, where Greek, Italian, Chinese, Indian, and other immigrants operate restaurants. In addition, each province is well known for various specialties. **Ontario** is famous for its cheeses. Seafood usually heads the menu at restaurants in **British Columbia, Nova Scotia, New Brunswick,** and **Prince Edward Island.** Fiddleheads, curled young fern fronds picked in the spring, often accompany dishes in the maritime provinces of New Brunswick, Nova Scotia, and Prince Edward Island. Leave your vegetarian tendencies at home when visiting **Alberta** and **Saskatchewan,** where the meals invariably center on thick steaks and roasts. In some areas of Canada, especially in the plains, you may be lucky enough to find some native Indian treats, such as venison, pheasant, and buffalo meat accompanied by fiddlehead ferns in the spring or wild rice. And vestiges of what the European settlers learned from the Indians is evident in the hearty ingredients that make up the French Canadian cuisine, which thrives in **Québec.** To enjoy the best of the province's hearty meat pies and pâtés, head to Québec City; Montréal dining tends to be more classic French than French Canadian.

Lodging

Aside from the quaint hotels of Québec, Canada's range of accommodations more closely resembles that of the United States than Europe. In the cities you'll have a choice of luxury hotels, moderately priced modern properties, and smaller older hotels with perhaps fewer conveniences but a bit more charm. Options in smaller towns and in the country include large full-service resorts; small, privately owned hotels; roadside motels; and bed-and-breakfast establishments. Canada's answer to the small European family-run hotel is the mom-and-pop motel, but even though Canada is as attuned to automobile travel as the United States, you won't find these motels as frequently. Even here you'll need to make reservations at least on the day on which you're planning to pull into town.

Chain Hotels There are two advantages to staying at a chain hotel. The first is that you'll be assured of standard accommodations, your own bathroom, and a range of services at the front desk. The second is the ease with which you can get information and make or change reservations, since most chains have toll-free booking numbers.

The major hotel chains in Canada include:

Best Western International: tel. 800/528–1234
CP (Canadian Pacific) Hotels & Resorts: tel. 800/828–7447
Delta Hotels: tel. 800/877–1133
Four Seasons Hotels: tel. 800/332–3442
Holiday Inns: tel. 800/465–4329
Howard Johnson Hotels: tel. 800/654–2000
Radisson Hotels: tel. 800/333–3333
Ramada: tel. 800/228–2828
Sheraton Hotels: tel. 800/325–3535
Travelodge: tel. 800/255–3050
Westin Hotels: tel. 800/228–3000

Room Rates Expect accommodations to cost more during the heavy, summer tourism season than off-season. But don't be afraid to ask about special deals and packages when making your reservations. Big city hotels that cater to the business traveler often offer a special weekend package on Friday and Saturday nights, and many city hotels offer rooms at up to 50% off in winter. If you're planning to visit a major city or resort area during the high season, make your reservations well in advance. Also be aware of any special events or festivals that may coincide with your visit and block every room for miles around. For resorts and lodges, consider the winter ski season high as well and plan accordingly (*See* GST and Sales Tax, above).

Bed-and-Breakfasts and Country Inns One way to save on lodging and spend some time with a native Canadian is to stay at a bed-and-breakfast establishment. They are gaining in popularity and are located in both the country and the cities. Every provincial tourist board either has a listing of B&Bs or can refer you to an association that will help you secure reservations. Rates range from $20 to $70 a night and include a Continental or a full breakfast. Because most bed-and-breakfasts are in private homes, you might not have your own bathroom. And some B&B hosts lock up early. Be sure to ask about your host's policies. Room quality varies from home to home as well, so don't be bashful about asking to see a room before making a choice. **Fodor's** new guide *Canada's Great*

Country Inns lists great places to stay from coast to coast—from unpretentious houses with something special to the elegant Relais & Châteaux (*see* below). You can buy it in most bookstores or ask to have it ordered.

Farm Vacations Farm vacations are one way to enjoy the Canadian countryside. Depending on the size of the farm and the farmers' preferences, you'll be able to observe and/or participate in the daily activities of a working farm. These stays include breakfast and some offer other meals and special family rates. For more information about farm vacations, *see* individual chapters.

Dorms and Hostels There are a few alternatives to camping for those on a budget. Among them are hostels, which are open to young and old, families, and singles (**Canadian Hostelling Association,** 1600 James Naismith Dr., Suite 608, Gloucester, Ont. K1B 5N4, tel. 613/748–5638); the YM-YWCA (**YMCA Canada,** 2160 Yonge St., Toronto, Ont. M4S 2A9, tel. 416/485–9447); or the university campuses, which open their dorms to travelers for overnight stays from May through August.

Relais & Châteaux This prestigious association of small hotels and inns has 11 members in Canada. Many once served as private estates to the Canadian wealthy. One property is set in a wildlife preserve in the Algonquin Park in Ontario; another is in the countryside, just 30 minutes from Montréal. Reservations must be made directly with each property, though a list of the properties and other information about a Relais & Châteaux stay is available from **Relais & Châteaux Information** (tel. 800/743–8033; 800/677–3524 for reservations). Expect to spend anywhere from $150 to $450 a night.

Provincial Ratings There is no national government rating system for hotels, but many provinces rate their accommodations. For example, in British Columbia and Alberta, a blue Approved Accommodation decal on the window or door of a hotel or motel indicates that it has met provincial hotel association standards for courtesy, comfort, and cleanliness. Ontario's voluntary rating system boasts about 1,000 Ontario properties.

Credit Cards

The following credit card abbreviations are used throughout this guide: AE, American Express; D, Discover; DC, Diners Club; MC, MasterCard; V, Visa. It's a good idea to call ahead to check current credit card policies.

2 Portraits of Canada

A Great Northern Paradox

by Robert
Fulford

*Longtime Toronto
journalist and
broadcaster,
Robert Fulford
was editor of*
Saturday Night,
*the leading
Canadian
monthly for 19
years. His
specialty is the
arts and
literature.*

A character in an early play by Robertson Davies, who was a playwright long before he became a novelist of international renown, remarks sadly that Canada is not really a country you love: "It is a country you worry about." As it happens, I do love Canada, and most Canadians I know share this love; but it remains as true now as it was when Davies wrote it 40 years ago, that Canada is first of all a country you worry about, puzzle over, diagnose. It is a country whose citizens are more or less incessantly taking its temperature, always expecting the worst. Publicly and privately, in English and in French, in Parliament and in the newspapers and universities, we worry about Canada's identity, its future, its place in the world, and above all, its chance of surviving as a political entity in its present form. In the minds of Canadians—those nervous, cautious people who joined the Organization of American States after considering it for 79 years—the most striking fact about our country is that at almost any given moment it seems, if you follow the rhetoric of its leaders, to be on the verge of ceasing to exist.

For as long as any of us can remember, Canada has lived a peculiar contradiction—it is boundlessly promising and simultaneously fearful of the future. To describe it is to sound as if you are describing a talented but troubled adolescent. In fact, we often speak of Canada as a young country, and it is common for visitors or newcomers to remark on the newness, the freshness, and sometimes the innocence of it. Taken literally, this is nonsense—Canada has been in business for a long time. French immigrants, a mixture of peasants and priests and nobles, created New France on the banks of the St. Lawrence River (now the province of Québec) in the 17th century; even earlier there were fishing villages in Newfoundland, the island province out in the Atlantic. In 1867, before Germany and Italy were countries, Canada came together as a new kind of nation, a "dominion" from the Atlantic to the Pacific that was linked to Britain and loyal to the British crown but was understood to be moving toward independence. That event, Confederation, defined the political shape of the country; it was completed in 1949 when Newfoundland became the tenth province.

But "completed" is probably the wrong word to use about any element of Canadian history—Canada is a place that is always in a state of becoming, always transforming itself, always redefining its goals and its nature. Everything is contingent, and nothing is ever thought to be completed. Other countries—the United States being the leading example—may work out a constitution and set of values and then spend centuries living by that constitution and those values, doing the job well or badly as the occasion permits. Canada, on the other hand, changes not just the circumstances of national life, but the very philosophical underpinnings of that life. In a few decades we change our national beliefs, ideals, and emotional connections.

In 1867 Canada was proud to call itself "a British Dominion," even though a large fraction of its population was French-speaking. For a long time Canadian statesmen paid elaborate homage to England and the English monarch. But in the 20th century that connection began to appear to most Canadians as both unnecessary and dangerous. In both world wars Canadians fought as part of the British Empire or, as it was called later, the British Commonwealth. A great many French Canadians resented the fact that they, a minority within Canada, were drawn into war by the English-speaking and British-descended majority.

Before the 20th century was half over, there arose the idea that Québec was in some ways a distinct part of Canada, requiring its own status and privileges within the Confederation. Although only a quarter of Canadians were French-speaking, they asserted their belief that they deserved separate rights. By the 1960s, there was a popular movement within Québec to withdraw from Canada and form a separate state. That movement is still very much alive and remains a major reason why Canadians worry about their country's survival. Were Québec to separate it would still be the major trading partner of Canadians on either side of it; but they would *be* on either side of it—two chunks of Canada, separated as Pakistan was at its birth with such tragic results. This is why the constitutional discussions that became a more or less permanent part of Canadian life in the 1980s are crucial. The federal government and the governments of the 10 provinces are engaged once more, as Canadian leaders so often are, in saving Canada from falling apart.

The federal government has been working hard to satisfy Québec for the last 40 years or so, sometimes with the enthusiastic support of English-speaking Canada, and sometimes against the wishes of those English-speakers who have traditionally been suspicious of French Canadians' demands. In this process, the country has changed fundamentally. In 1950, a French-speaking Québecker would feel a foreigner when visiting the national capital in Ottawa. Even though that city is poised on a river between Ontario and Québec, it was then still a British city, and if you phoned the House of Commons the telephone operator answered only in English. Today Ottawa is bilingual, in keeping with the federal law that Canada has two official languages of equal status; elsewhere in Canada you can find bilingualism in everything from customs offices to federally owned broadcasting stations.

While making these changes, the federal government slowly began eliminating the signs of British influence. Canada stayed within the British Commonwealth, and to this minute Queen Elizabeth is still, constitutionally, our head of state. But to placate French Canada, Ottawa reorganized Canadian symbolism. In the 1950s the word "dominion" was quietly dropped, not because it was British in origin—in fact, Canada was the first country to use it as a national designation—but because British monarchs had taken to speaking of *their* "dominion beyond the seas."

In the 1960s Canada stopped using as its flag the Canadian ensign, which featured a British Union Jack, and got its own design: a simple maple leaf that betrayed no ancient allegiances, British or French. In the 1970s most other British symbols just faded away, usually without much announcement or mourning—the royal coat of arms disappeared off the mailboxes, for instance. A few decades ago Canadians were legally entitled to live and work in Britain at will, and the reverse was also true; today a Canadian is a foreigner in Britain, with less status than a Belgian or a citizen of any other EEC country. And in Canada, someone from Britain is treated like any other foreigner.

These symbols, these connections, are the outward signs of an inner progress toward a nationhood that always turns out to be something of a surprise. With each generation we reimagine ourselves in unpredictable ways. We may feel secure at any given moment in our identity—whether it is based on a region, a city, an ethnic group, or a pan-Canadian appreciation of the whole country—but is our sense of identity the same one that our grandparents understood? Is it in any way similar to the one our grandchildren will experience? In the United States, many can answer both of those questions with a confident "yes." Similarly, many people in France today can say that, yes, fulfilling the goals of the French Revolution will likely seem as important to their grandchildren as it does to them. But Canadians can't answer with anything like that kind of confidence.

This lack of a firm ideological mooring is not purely negative by any means. For many people it is altogether positive. Last year, when the United States twisted and writhed over a Supreme Court decision that seemed to permit desecration of the Stars and Stripes, Canadians watched in astonishment. No Canadian could imagine for a moment getting excited about the fate of a piece of cloth or any other secular symbol; but then, we have no symbols going back to the 18th century, and even if we did, we wouldn't know what they signified. It would be impossible to imagine a Committee on UnCanadian Activities, because first it would have to determine what a Canadian activity is—and that argument would never end. For the same reasons, a

Canadian Pledge of Allegiance, recited by schoolchildren across the country, is an impossibility.

What this means is that no political form is imposed on Canadians, and—for some of us at least—the cultural air therefore is easier to breathe. Outsiders are sometimes bemused by the fact that, in Canada, citizenship does not even require adherence to the idea of Canada itself. Citizens in Alberta or Québec or Newfoundland may openly declare themselves in favor of withdrawing their provinces from Canada or may publicly regret that they ever joined—even today there are many Newfoundlanders who frankly state that it was a mistake for Newfoundland to become a province of Canada in 1949. But these people, far from being shunned or exiled, are treated as perfectly good Canadians and may even find themselves filling certain jobs in the federal government. The late René Lévesque, a Québec premier who spent the last two decades of his life trying to uncouple Québec from the rest of Canada, was mourned as a national hero from sea to sea when he died. Why? Because he was honest and forthright, he represented his people as best he could, and he pursued his goals by democratic means. Certainly no one ever said Lévesque was unpatriotic just because he wanted to break up the country. No one in Canada says, "My country right or wrong." Canadians say, "My country, maybe" or "My country, if."

Even so, the late 1980s, as well as bringing us a constitutional crisis over the status of Québec, also produced the most passionate outburst of patriotism since the Second World War. This patriotism largely emerged in negative terms, specifically as anti-Americanism, but it is also true that the passion behind it was generated as a defense of Canada and its values.

The United States, of course, is perceived as the major external threat to Canadian independence, whether it recognizes itself in that role or not. The last time the United States and Canada actually went to war was in June 1812, the same month Napoleon attacked Russia. Britain, while conducting its war against Napoleon, had searched U.S. ships and partially blocked certain U.S. ports. In response, President James Madison attacked the British colonies to the north, which were still in the process of turning into Canada. The war eventually reached from the Atlantic provinces to what is now southwestern Ontario. Part of Toronto was burned, Montréal was attacked, and British troops defending Canada eventually penetrated as far south as Washington, D.C. After a peace treaty was negotiated in 1814, all territory was returned and both sides claimed victory. They have done so ever since, and to this day you can find quite different versions of the outcome given in the school textbooks used in Niagara Falls, New York, and, a hundred yards away, Niagara Falls, Ontario.

In the United States, save for a few border towns and some isolated university courses, Canada does not exist as a political and cultural entity: It is a source of evil weather, it is a large piece of geography, and for many it is a wonderful place for vacations. But neither the politics of Canada— which are entirely different from U.S. politics, being parliamentary—nor the culture of Canada, can even be glimpsed in the U.S. media or in U.S. education. The U.S. public was taken by surprise when the Free Trade Agreement (FTA) signed by the Reagan and Mulroney administrations in 1988 became the most important political issue in Canada in recent years. To some, the FTA seemed an entirely logical extension of a process that has been going on for more than half a century, the economic integration of North America. From the standpoint of the Mulroney government, the FTA was a way of ensuring markets for Canadian goods in the United States. But to a great many Canadians—including the Liberal Party, the New Democratic Party, and the majority of artists and intellectuals— the FTA looked like a way of allowing U.S. culture to swamp culture produced in this country.

I t touched a national nerve—*the* national nerve, in fact— the fear of U.S. domination. As it turned out, Mulroney's forces rallied, the FTA was ratified, and so far Canada remains an independent country. But 1988 reminded everyone that Canadian feelings about the United States run deep. Canadians watch U.S. TV and movies, read U.S. magazines, enjoy U.S. baseball, eat at McDonald's, and yet believe in themselves as a separate nation with a history worth remembering and traditions worth preserving.

Of course, there are still those who say that "Canadian culture" is an oxymoron, that the country lacks anything but highly derivative forms of artistic expression. Arthur Erickson, who is often regarded as the best of Canadian architects, once said, "I am fortunate that I can stand in Canada, a country without a culture, and look at the world." Canadians, in other words, being culture-free as well as ideology-free, can glory in the spiritual mobility this gives them. In truth, they have been working for a long time on building a culture, or cultures, and with notable success.

French Canada has found it easier, in a way, because of the comparative isolation that language provides—Québec poetry, novels, plays, TV shows, and movies speak directly to their intended audience (and often to faraway audiences in France, as well) in a way that no other art can. In English-speaking Canada, on the other hand, the majority of culture—mass movies, TV, music, fiction—traditionally has been imported from the United States; in a sense, the Canadian audience for popular culture is an overflow basin for U.S. products.

This means that Canadians must fight for an audience in these fields; even when government-backed, our movies and TV shows rarely capture huge audiences. Canadian artists, for the most part, have shifted to the higher ground of painting, poetry, serious fiction, and nonfiction, and in these spheres have done well. Canada produces a good many artists who find mass audiences, but usually the audiences are found in the United States, and in the rest of the world via the United States. "America's Sweetheart" in silent movie days, Mary Pickford, was a Toronto girl, and Lorne Greene, the star of what for years was the most popular TV drama, "Bonanza," was from Ottawa. The man who created Superman and the woman who played the superhero's girlfriend in the movies, Margot Kidder, are both Canadians. The writer who dreamt up Rambo, the macho hero of the 1980s, is a professor from a small city in Ontario. Regularly, Canada sends a stream of stars and producers across the border—Michael J. Fox; Donald Sutherland in one generation and his son, Kiefer, in the next; the creators of SCTV and of "Saturday Night Live." In the United States these personalities are seen as near-natives, which in a sense they are, since most of them grew up watching U.S. TV. Quickly, the successful Canadians are lost in the great ocean of life in the United States, and only their fellow citizens back home remember that once they were considered part of "Canadian culture."

To outsiders, Canada must seem a paradox: the second-largest country in the world, thinly populated, rich in natural resources and arable land, next door to the best market on the planet—yet insecure, internally conflicted, and altogether uncertain about how to approach the future. We are a country with problems as large and as varied as our geography. And yet they are the problems of a lucky people, and of a people who, for the most part, understand how lucky they are to be born in Canada, or to end up here. I cherish a story that emerged from Ottawa in 1950, when the Chancellor of the Exchequer in Britain's Labour Government, Hugh Gaitskell, was visiting Canada. At that time, his opposite number in Canada, Finance Minister Douglas Abbott, was bedeviled by many problems typically Canadian, involving the sharing of tax revenues between the federal and provincial governments. Gaitskell's England, on the other hand, was still devastated by the Second World War bombing, everything from sugar to clothing was rationed, the British pound was the subject of laughter in the money markets of the world, and the Labour Government was widely regarded as a gigantic failure. When Gaitskell arrived in Ottawa, Abbott described the excruciating political problems of the Canadian federal system and then asked, "What would you do if you had my problems?"

Gaitskell looked at him for a moment. "Well," he said, "first thing, I'd get down on my knees and thank God."

3 Toronto

by Allan Gould

Author of 17 books, including The New Entrepreneurs: 75 Canadian Success Stories *and* First Stage—The Making of the Stratford Festival, *Allan Gould has also written for many Canadian magazines and written and performed political satire and biographical sketches for radio and TV.*

A joke popular in the neighboring province of Québec between the wars went "First prize, one week in Toronto. Second prize, two weeks in Toronto. Third prize, three weeks in Toronto." Toronto was a deadly city, right into the 1950s, at which time its half-million citizens used to rush off to Detroit (a four-hour drive to the southwest) and Buffalo (90 minutes to the south, around Lake Ontario) for a good time. Today, of course, the rushing is in the opposite direction, except for Toronto shoppers eager to take advantage of far cheaper prices in the United States.

Like many cities around the world, Toronto encountered some tough times in 1992: Unemployment is up, upscale restaurants are shutting their doors faster than you can cry "waiter!", and the new, brutal 7% federal goods and services tax, alias GST, has shaken businesses and tourism to the core. (In many cases, that 7% is tacked on to the already steep 8% provincial [Ontario] sales tax.) Indeed, a major study taken in Geneva in 1991 rated Toronto as "the most expensive city in the Western Hemisphere, and the 23rd most expensive worldwide." But though Toronto may be expensive for those who live here, it need not be oppressively so for visitors, who can benefit from the city's numerous free events, special hotel packages, and the rebate of much of the GST.

Much of Toronto's excitement is explained by its ethnic diversity. Nearly two-thirds of the 3.2 million people who now live in the metropolitan area were born and raised somewhere else. Half a million Italians live here, as does the largest Chinese community in Canada and the biggest Portuguese colony in North America. What this has meant to Toronto is the rather rapid creation of a vibrant mix of cultures that has echoes of turn-of-the-century New York City—but without the slums, crowding, disease, and tensions.

Still, to give to its burgeoning ethnic population all, or even most, of the credit for Toronto's becoming a cosmopolitan, world-class city in just a few decades would be a kind of reverse racism, and not totally correct, either. Much of the thanks must be given to the so-called dour Scots who set up the banks, built the churches, and created the kind of solid base for community that would come to such a healthy fruition in the three-plus decades following World War II. Toronto is clearly this country's center of culture, commerce, and communications—"New York run by the Swiss," according to Peter Ustinov.

Toronto has gained the nickname Hollywood North, because literally dozens of major films have been made in this city, especially over the past decade, from *The Black Stallion* to *Three Men and a Baby*, and from David Cronenberg's *Dead Ringers* and *Naked Lunch* to such TV series as *Degrassi Junior High*, *Night Heat*, and many more. Indeed, it is hard to walk about the city nowadays without tripping over a movie crew and a number of famous people. But since this is Canada—and Toronto—you'll probably all apologize sweetly.

The city looks forward to the opening in 1993 of the **North York Performing Arts Centre,** which will house a theater, a recital hall, a studio, and a two-story art gallery. The complex, in North York, is 20 minutes up Yonge Street from midtown. Also scheduled for 1993 is a **2,000-seat theater,** built from scratch by Ed and David Mirvish across the street from their Royal Alex-

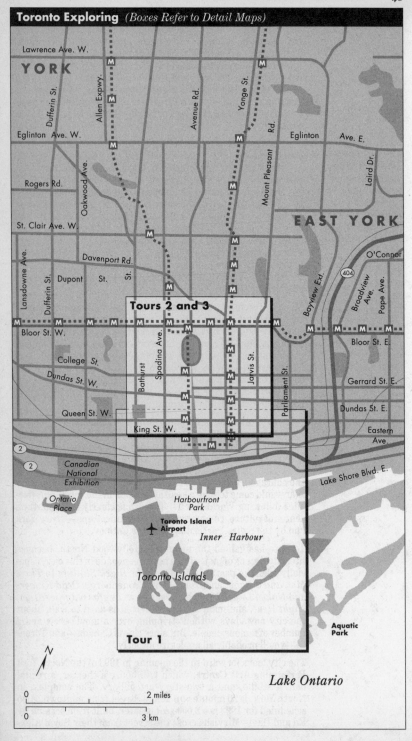

Toronto Exploring *(Boxes Refer to Detail Maps)*

andra Theatre. It's to open in May with *Miss Saigon*, that international hit.

Essential Information

Arriving and Departing by Plane

Airports and Airlines
Flights into Toronto land at the **Lester B. Pearson International Airport,** so named in 1984 to honor Canada's Nobel Peace Prize–winning prime minister of a quarter-century ago. It's commonly called "the Toronto airport" or "Malton" (after the once-small town where it was built, just northwest of the city), but it's just as often called "impossible," since its terminals are inadequate for the number of travelers who use it. Waits for bags are often lengthy—although the free carts are a human touch—and Pearson can be dreadfully overcrowded, both coming and going. Terminal 1, which opened in 1964 to handle 3 million passengers, handled more than *10 million* in 1990. The sorely needed Terminal 3 opened in February 1991, after many delays. And, thank heavens, the ugly and uncomfortable Terminal 2 has undergone a $52 million renovation.

Toronto is served by **Alaska Airlines** (flying only between Los Angeles, San Francisco and Toronto, tel. 800/426–0333), **American** (tel. 800/433–7300), **Delta** (tel. 800/843–9378), **Northwest** (tel. 800/225–2525), **United** (tel. 800/241–6522), **U.S. Air** (tel. 800/428–4322), **Air Canada** (tel. 800/422–6232), and **Canadian Airlines International** (tel. 800/387–2737). **Air Ontario,** affiliated with Air Canada (tel. 416/925–2311), flies from the Island Airport to and from Ottawa, Montréal, and London, Ontario. It is a good alternative to Pearson International for those staying downtown and making trips to these other Canadian cities.

Between the Airport and Center City
Although Pearson is not far from the downtown area (about 32 kilometers, or 18 miles), the drive can take well over an hour during Toronto's weekday rush hours (7–9 AM and 3:30–6:30 PM). Taxis and limos to a hotel or attraction near the lake can cost $30 or more. You may negotiate a fare, but the meter *must* be used, and the passenger pays whichever is less. Many airport and downtown hotels offer free buses from each of Toronto's three terminals. Travelers on a budget should consider the express coaches offered by **Grey Coach** (tel. 416/393–7911), which link the airport to three subway stops in the southwest and north-central areas of the city. Buses depart several times each hour, from 8 AM to 11:30 PM. Fares average $6–$7. Even better is the service to and from several downtown hotels, which operates every 30 minutes from 6 AM to midnight daily and costs approximately $11.

Should you be renting a car at the airport, be sure to ask for a street map of the city. Highway 427 runs south, some 5.8 kilometers (3.6 miles) to the lakeshore. Here you pick up the Queen Elizabeth Way (QEW or Queen E) east to the Gardiner Expressway, which runs east into the heart of downtown. If you take the QEW *west*, you'll find yourself swinging around Lake Ontario, toward Hamilton, Niagara-on-the-Lake, and Niagara Falls.

Arriving and Departing by Train, Bus, and Car

By Train **Amtrak** (tel. 800/872–7245) runs a daily train to Toronto from Chicago (a 12-hour trip), and another from New York City (11 hours). From Union Station you can walk underground to many hotels—a real boon in inclement weather.

By Bus **Greyhound** (no 800 number; check with local information) and **Grey Coach** (tel. 416/393–7911) both have regular bus service into Toronto from all over the United States. From Detroit, the trip takes five hours; from Buffalo, two to three hours; from Chicago and New York City, 11 hours. Buses arrive at 610 Bay Street, just above Dundas Street.

By Car Drivers should have proper owner registration and proof of insurance coverage. There is no need for an international driver's license; any valid one will do. You may be asked several questions at the border crossing, none of them terribly personal or offensive: your place of birth; your citizenship; your expected length of stay. Every fourth or fifth car may be searched, and this can increase the wait at peak visiting times to 30 minutes. A recent explosion of cross-border shopping finds thousands of Canadians shuttling across the border every month to take advantage of lower gas, food, and even appliance prices, so expect those Detroit–Windsor and Buffalo–Fort Erie crossings to take even longer, especially on weekends and holidays.

The wonderfully wide Highway 401—it reaches up to 16 lanes as it slashes across Metro Toronto from the airport on the west almost as far as the zoo on the east—is the major link between Windsor, Ontario (and Detroit), and Montréal, Québec. It's also known as the Macdonald-Cartier Freeway but is really never called anything other than "401." There are no tolls, but be warned: in weekday rushhours the 401 can become dreadfully crowded, even stop-and-go. Plan your trips to avoid these times.

Those who are driving from Buffalo, New York, or Niagara Falls should take the Queen Elizabeth Way, which curves up along the western shore of Lake Ontario, eventually turns into the Gardiner Expressway, and flows right into the downtown core.

Yonge Street, which begins at the Lakefront, is called Highway 11 once you get north of Toronto and continues all the way to the Ontario-Minnesota border, at Rainy River. At 1,896.2 kilometers (1,178.3 miles), it is the longest street in the world (as noted in the *Guinness Book of World Records*). We trust that you are duly impressed.

Getting Around

Most of Toronto is laid out on a grid pattern. The key street to remember is Yonge Street (pronounced "young"), which is the main north–south artery. Most major cross streets are numbered east and west of Yonge Street. In other words, if you are looking for 180 St. Clair Avenue West, you want a building a few blocks *west* of Yonge Street; 75 Queen Street East is a block or so *east* of Yonge Street.

At press time, the fare for buses, streetcars, and trolleys was $2 in exact change, but 10 adult tickets/tokens cost $11, which lowers the price per journey a bit. All fares will undoubtedly

rise at least a nickel during the first week of 1993; they invariably do. Children (2–13) pay only 50¢ in exact change, and may
purchase eight tickets for $2.50. Two-fare tickets are available
for $3 for adults. Visitors who plan to stay in Toronto for more
than a month should consider the **Metropass**, a photo-identity
card that costs $56.50 for adults plus $2.50 extra for the photo.
(And, yes, probably a few dollars more than that, as of January
1993.)

Families should take advantage of the so-called **Day Pass**. It
costs $5 and is good for unlimited travel for one person, Mon-
day–Friday after 9:30 AM, and all day Saturday. On Sunday and
holidays, it's good for up to 6 persons (maximum 2 adults) for unlimited travel. For information on how to take public transit to any
street or attraction in the city call 416/393–INFO from 7 AM to
11:30 PM. A very useful **Ride Guide** is published by the Toronto
Transit Commission each year. It shows nearly every major
place of interest and how to reach it by public transit. These
guides are available in most subways and many other places
around the city. The subways stop at 2 AM, but the Toronto
Transit Commission runs bus service from 1 to 5:30 AM on most
major streets, including King, Queen, College, Bloor, Yonge, and
as far north as Sheppard, Finch, and Steeles.

By Subway   The Toronto Transit Commission runs one of the safest,
cleanest, most trustworthy systems of its kind anywhere.
There are two major subway lines, with 60 stations along the
way: the **Bloor/Danforth Line,** which crosses Toronto about 4.8
kilometers (3 miles) north of the Lakefront, from east to west,
and the **Yonge/University/Spadina Line,** which loops north and
south, like a giant "U," with the bottom of the "U" at Union
Station. Tokens and tickets are sold in each subway station and
at hundreds of convenience stores along the many routes of the
TTC. Get your transfers just after you pay your fare and enter
the subway; you'll find them in machines on your way down to
the trains.

By Bus   All buses and streetcars accept exact change, tickets, or tokens. Paper transfers are free; pick one up at the time that you
pay your fare.

By Taxi   The meter begins at $2.20, and includes the first .2 kilometer.
Each additional .2 kilometer is 20¢—as is each additional passenger in excess of four. The waiting time "while under engage-
ment" is 20¢ for every 33 seconds—and in one of the horrible
traffic jams, this could add up. Still, it's possible to take a cab
across downtown Toronto for little more than $5. The largest
companies are **Beck** (tel. 416/467–0067), **Co-op** (tel. 416/364–
8161), **Diamond** (tel. 416/366–6868), and **Metro** (tel. 416/363–
5611). For more information, call the Metro Licensing Commission (tel. 416/392–3000).

By Car   Pedestrian crosswalks are sprinkled throughout the city; they
are marked clearly by overhead signs and very large painted
Xs. All a pedestrian has to do is stick out a hand, and cars
screech to a halt in both directions. Right turns on red lights
are nearly always permitted, except where otherwise posted.
You must come to a complete stop before making the turn.

Important Addresses and Numbers

Tourist Information The **Metropolitan Toronto Convention & Visitors Association** has its office at Queen's Quay Terminal (207 Queen's Quay W, Suite 509, M5J LA7, tel. 416/368–9821). Booths providing brochures and pamphlets about the city and its attractions, as well as accommodations, are set up in the summer outside the Eaton Centre, on Yonge Street just below Dundas Street, and outside the Royal Ontario Museum.

The **Traveller's Aid Society** is not just for the down-and-out. This is a nonprofit group whose 130 volunteers can recommend restaurants and hotels, and distribute subway maps, tourist publications, and Ontario sales tax rebate forms. *In Union Station, Room B23 on the basement level and also on the Arrivals level; tel. 416/366–7788. Open daily 9 AM–9 PM. In Terminal I at Pearson Airport, Arrivals level, past Customs, near Area B; tel. 416/676–2868. Open daily 9 AM–10 PM. In Terminal II, between International and Domestic Arrivals, tel. 416/676–2869. Open daily 9 AM–10 PM. In Terminal III, Arrivals level, near the International side; tel. 416/612–5890. Open daily 9 AM–10 PM.*

Embassies The **Consulate General of the United States** (360 University Ave., just north of Queen St., M56 1S4, tel. 416/595–1700).

The **Consulate General of Britain** (777 Bay St., at the corner of College St., M56 2G2, tel. 416/593–1267).

For all other consulates—there are dozens of countries represented in Toronto—look up "Consulate Generals" in the white pages of the phone book.

Emergencies Dial 911 for **police** and **ambulance.**

Doctors and Dentists. Check the Yellow Pages or ask at your hotel desk. Also, call **Dial-a-Doctor** (tel. 416/492–4713), or the **Dental Emergency Service** (tel. 416/924–8041).

24-Hour Pharmacies. Pharma Plus Drugmart (Church St. and Wellesley Ave., tel. 416/924–7760). **Lucliff Place,** (700 Bay and Gerrard, tel. 416/979–2424). **Shoppers Drug Mart** (2500 Hurontario St., Mississauga, tel. 416/277–3665).

Road Emergencies. The **CAA** (the Canadian version of AAA) has 24-hour road service (tel. 416/966–3000).

24-Hour Gas Stations and Auto Repairs. Texaco Stations, at 153 Dundas St. West, behind New City Hall; 333 Davenport, just south of Casa Loma; and 601 Eglinton Ave. East, west of the Ontario Science Center. **Cross Town Service Center,** 1467 Bathurst Street, at St. Clair Ave. West, is well known and respected for both gas and repairs. **Jim McCormack Esso,** 2901 Sheppard Ave. East, in the Scarborough area, heading toward the Metro Zoo. **Guido's Esso,** 1104 Albion Road, not far from the airport.

Guided Tours

Orientation **Toronto Harbour and Islands Boat Tours** are provided by **Gray Line** (tel. 416/364–2412) on attractive, sleek, Amsterdam-style touring boats, with competent tour guides. The hourly tour visits the Toronto Islands, with lovely views of the Toronto cityscape. Boats leave from the Queen's Quay Terminal daily from early May through mid-October noon–5. Tours leave as late as 7:15 PM during the summer. Other boats depart from the

Harbour Castle Westin. Prices are $9.95 adults, $7.95 students and senior citizens, $5.95 children ages 4–14.

Toronto Tours (tel. 416/869–1372 or 416/868–0400) also provides one-hour boat tours of the Toronto harborfront for similar prices from mid-May through October. It also runs an informative 90-minute tour aboard a restored 1920s trolley car, which goes by both city halls, and through the financial district and the historic St. Lawrence area. **Insight Planners** (tel. 416/868–6565) has been providing creative and reliable tours, particularly to art galleries, since 1974. **Reception Ontario** (tel. 416/636–0082) provides complete tour-planning services, including sightseeing tours, entertainment packages, hotel accommodations, and even guides in various languages. **Happy Day Tours** (tel. 416/593–6220) runs half-day tours of Toronto for about $30 per person, which include admission to Black Creek Pioneer Village and visits to the mansions of Forest Hills, Casa Loma, Chinatown, Queen's Park, Yorkville, and Harbourfront. Book ahead.

Gray Line Sightseeing Bus Tours (tel. 416/393–7911) runs tours during the high season that leave from the Bus Terminal (Bay and Dundas Sts.) and spend 2½ hours visiting such places as Eaton Centre, both city halls, Queen's Park, the University of Toronto, Yorkville, Ontario Place, and Casa Loma—the latter, for a full hour. Costs run about $17 for adults, $11 for children under 12.

Special-interest **Antours** (tel. 416/481–2862) provides several tours of Niagara-on-the-Lake, which include lunch and major performances at the Shaw Festival. **Art Tours of Toronto** (tel. 416/845–4044) offers a series of fall and spring gallery and walking tours. Most tours include lunch, and range from $40 to $50 per person. The **Toronto Stock Exchange** (tel. 416/947–4676) has tours of its exciting new facilities weekdays at 2 PM. The **Bruce Trail Association** (tel. 416/690–4453) arranges day and overnight hikes around Toronto and environs.

Exploring Toronto

Well, now you're in Toronto, and probably in the downtown area. It's rather confusing, isn't it? But once you establish that Lake Ontario runs along the south of the city, and that the fabulous Harbourfront complex is there, as well as the ferry to the lovely Toronto Islands, you are well on your way to orienting yourself.

Imagine the downtown area of Toronto as a large rectangle. The southern boundary is, as you already know, Lake Ontario. The western edge, shooting north to Bloor Street (the northern edge) and beyond, is Spadina Avenue, near the foot of which stands the CN Tower, Harbourfront, and the spectacular new SkyDome Stadium. Just west of the rectangle along the waterfront are the Canadian National Exhibition grounds, site of the enormous annual fair, and Ontario Place, an amusement park built on man-made islands. On the east side of downtown, running from the lakefront north for hundreds of miles (believe it or not), is Yonge Street, which divides the city in half. University Avenue, a major road that parallels Yonge Street, for some reason changes its name to Avenue Road at the corner of Bloor Street, next to the Royal Ontario Museum. A further note: College Street, legitimately named, since many of the University of Toronto's buildings run along it, becomes Carlton Street where it intersects Yonge Street, then heads east.

Highlights for First-time Visitors

Casa Loma, Tour 3: Academia, Culture, Commercialism, Crassness

CN Tower, Tour 1: Waterfront, the Financial District, and the Underground City

Eaton Centre, Tour 2: From Eaton Centre to the City Halls and the Far and Middle East

Harbourfront and Toronto Islands, Tour 1: Waterfront, the Financial District, and the Underground City

Metro Toronto Zoo, *see* What to See and Do with Children

Ontario Science Centre, *see* What to See and Do with Children

Royal Ontario Museum, Tour 3: Academia, Culture, etc.

Tour 1: Waterfront, the Financial District, and the Underground City

Numbers in the margin correspond to points of interest on the Tour 1 map.

Since, as we noted, Toronto has a waterfront as its southernmost border, it seems logical that we begin there. And it shouldn't be too hard to get there, since it's just south of Union Station, which is the terminus of both the University Avenue/Spadina Avenue and Yonge Street subways. Until quite recently, Toronto was notoriously negligent about its waterfront. The Gardiner Expressway, Lakeshore Boulevard, and a network of rusty rail yards stood as hideous barriers to the natural beauty of Lake Ontario.

Just over a decade ago the various levels of government—city, Metro, provincial (Ontario), and federal (Ottawa)—began a struggle to change this unfortunate situation. By that time, most of the area just south of the Gardiner Expressway and Lakeshore Boulevard was overflowing with grain silos, various warehouses, and unattractive (and unsweet-smelling) towers of malt, used by local breweries.

Part of the answer was the building of a very handsome hotel, the Harbour Castle Westin, and an attractive tower of condominiums at the foot of Yonge Street on Harbourfront. The hotel has an exterior, glassed-in elevator that offers guests a view of the waterfront and the Toronto Islands.

Toronto Islands
❶

Just behind the giant Harbour Castle Westin is the debarkation point for ferries to the **Toronto Islands,** surely one of the highlights of any trip to the city—especially from May to October. It takes only eight minutes for the quaint little ferries to chug across the tiny bay. The islands make up one of the world's great parks.

The four thin, curved, tree-lined islands—Centre, Ward's, Algonquin, and Hanlan's Point—have been attracting visitors since 1833, four years before Victoria became queen and just a year before the town of York changed its name to Toronto. And the more than 550 acres of parkland are irresistible, especially during the hot summer months.

The beaches on Ward's tend to be the least crowded. They're also the cleanest, although there have been problems with the cleanliness of Lake Ontario's water over the past decade. Except for the hottest days in August, the Great Lake tends to be uncomfortably chilly, so bring appropriate clothing. You'll be wise to rent a bike for an hour or more and work your way across the interconnected islands.

If you are traveling with children, Centre Island is certainly the one to check out first. A few hundred yards from the ferry docks lies **Centreville,** an amusement park that's supposed to be a turn-of-the-century children's village. The concept works wondrously well: True, the pizza, fries, and hot dogs are barely edible—pack a lunch!—but on the little Main Street there are charming shops, a town hall, a little railroad station, and more than a dozen rides, including a restored 1890s merry-go-round with more than four dozen hand-carved animals. And there's no entrance fee to the modest, 14-acre amusement park, although you'll have to pay a nominal charge for each ride or buy an all-day pass. Perhaps most enjoyable for children is the free **Far Enough Farm,** which is near enough to walk to. It has all kinds of animals to pet and feed, ranging from piglets to geese, cows to birds. *Tel. 416/363–1112. Centreville is open 10:30–8 weekends only Apr. 30–May 15; daily Victoria Day (mid-May)–Labor Day; weekends again Sept. 10–25.*

All transportation on these islands comes to you compliments of your feet: No cars are allowed anywhere. Your nostrils will wonder at the lack of exhaust fumes, while your feet will wonder why you walked all the way along the boardwalk from Centre to Ward's Island (2½ kilometers, or 1½ miles).

There you'll find **Gibraltar Lighthouse,** built back in 1808, making it the oldest monument in the city that is still standing on its original site. Right next to it is a pond stocked with rainbow trout, and a concession for buying bait and renting rods.

Sandy beaches circle the islands, the best ones being those on the southeast tip of Ward's, the southernmost edge of Centre, and the west side of Hanlan's. There are free changing rooms near each of these areas, but no facilities for checking your clothes. Swimming in the various lagoons and channels is prohibited. The winter can be bitter cold on the island, but snowshoeing and cross-country skiing, with downtown Toronto over your shoulder, will be irresistible to many. In the summer, there are rowboat and canoe rentals, tennis courts, gardens, playgrounds, and a wildlife sanctuary.

The ferries run irregularly during the winter: every half hour or so until 10 or 11 AM, and then every hour or so thereafter. In the summer, the ferries leave three times an hour at the foot of Bay Street. The cost is $2.50 adults, $1.25 students and senior citizens, 75¢ children under 15. For a recording giving the schedule and prices, call 416/392–8193; for other information, call 416/392–8186.

Harbourfront Back at the ferry docks on the mainland, your next move should
❷ be to **Harbourfront.** This is a trip that is well worth planning for—check *Now, eye,* and *Toronto Life* magazines, as well as daily newspaper listings, to see what concerts, dances, art shows, festivals, etc., are taking place there, and build your visit around them.

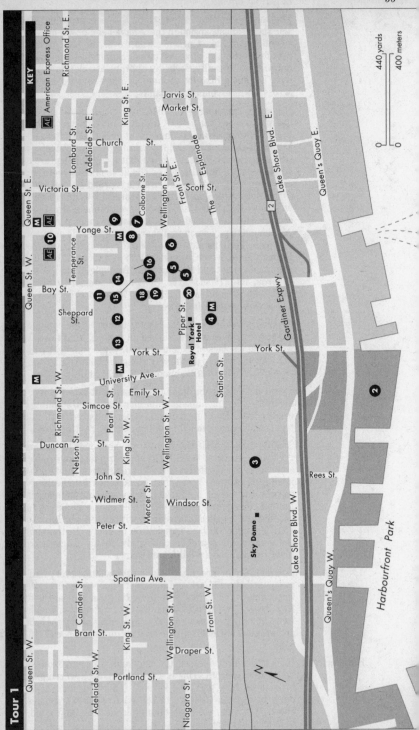

Tour 1

KEY

AE American Express Office

Richmond St. E.

Jarvis St.

Market St.

Lombard St.

Adelaide St. E.

King St. E.

Church St.

Queen St. E.

Victoria St.

Wellington St. E.

Front St. E.

Scott St.

The Esplanade

Colborne St.

9

7

Yonge St.

M

8

10

AE

AE

Temperance St.

6

Queen St. W.

Bay St.

17 16

5

5

14

Sheppard St.

11

15

18 19

20

12

Piper St.

4 M

13

Royal York Hotel

York St.

M

Station St.

York St.

M

University Ave.

Richmond St. W.

Emily St.

Simcoe St.

Pearl St.

Wellington St. W.

Duncan St.

Nelson St.

King St. W.

Lake Shore Blvd. E.

Queen's Quay E.

Gardiner Expwy.

2

John St.

Rees St.

Widmer St.

Mercer St.

Windsor St.

3

Peter St.

Sky Dome ■

2

Spadina Ave.

Wellington St. W.

Front St. W.

Lake Shore Blvd. W.

Camden St.

King St. W.

Queen's Quay W.

Harbourfront Park

Brant St.

Queen St. W.

Adelaide St. W.

Draper St.

Portland St.

Niagara St.

N

440 yards

400 meters

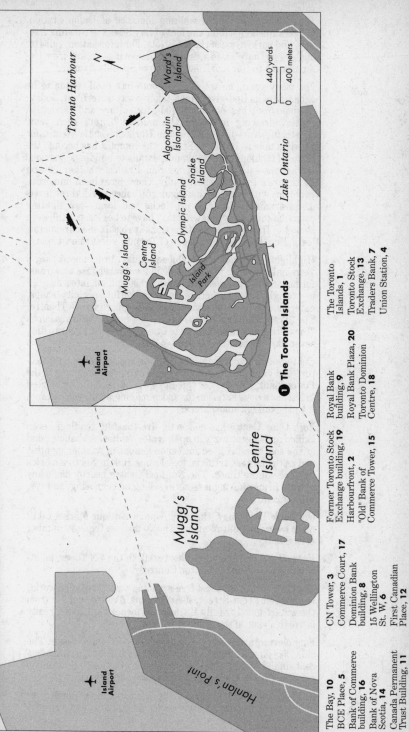

1 The Toronto Islands

Toronto Harbour

Ward's Island

Algonquin Island

Snake Island

Olympic Island

Mugg's Island

Centre Island

Island Park

Lake Ontario

Island Airport

N

0   440 yards
0   400 meters

The Bay, **10**
BCE Place, **5**
Bank of Commerce
building, **16**
Bank of Nova
Scotia, **14**
Canada Permanent
Trust Building, **11**

CN Tower, **3**
Commerce Court, **17**
Dominion Bank
building, **8**
15 Wellington
St. W, **6**
First Canadian
Place, **12**

Former Toronto Stock
Exchange building, **19**
Harbourfront, **2**
"Old" Bank of
Commerce Tower, **15**

Royal Bank
building, **9**
Royal Bank Plaza, **20**
Toronto Dominion
Centre, **18**

The Toronto
Islands, **1**
Toronto Stock
Exchange, **13**
Traders Bank, **7**
Union Station, **4**

Centre Island

Mugg's Island

Island Airport

Hanlan's Point

Harbourfront is within walking distance of Union Station.
Drivers should head for the foot of Bay Street or Spadina Avenue, and park in one of the many lots. For information, call 416/
364–5665. There's also a streetcar that swings around from Union Station to Harbourfront, and on to Spadina Avenue.

For many years, as we said, Toronto had good reason to be
ashamed of its God-given, man-taken-away waterfront. Today,
Harbourfront has become a 100-acre culture and recreation
center, drawing more than 3 million visitors each year.
Stretching from just west of the Harbour Castle Westin for
nearly a mile to Bathurst Street, the complex has become the
scene of fabulous entertainment, exquisite buildings, glorious
attractions—a true match for San Francisco's Pier 39 and
Baltimore's Inner Harbor. Sadly, there have been numerous
problems with funding this wonderful concept: All three levels
of government—federal, provincial and local—are fighting
over who should pay and what may have to be closed. Still, even
if some of Harbourfront's attractions are lost in the bureaucratic flip-flop, this will remain one of Toronto's best tourist spots.

Highlights are many. The **Queen's Quay** (pronounced "key")
Terminal is a must: The 57-year-old food warehouse was transformed in 1983, at a cost of more than $60 million, into a magnificent eight-story structure with delightful specialty shops,
eateries, and the handsome 450-seat Premiere Dance Theatre.
The "Traffic Hotline" will even give you current information on
"the fastest and easiest route to Queen's Quay," 24 hours a day,
seven days a week (tel. 416/363–4411).

Contemporary art exhibits of painting and sculpture, architecture and video, photography and design now take place at the
Power Plant, just west of Queen's Quay. (The building started
in 1927 as a power station for an ice-making plant; you can spot
it by the tall red smokestack.)

York Quay Centre has concerts, live theater, readings, even
skilled artisans at work in open crafts studios. A shallow pond
at the south end is used for canoe lessons in warmer months,
and as the largest artificial ice-skating rink in North America
in more wintry times. The Nautical Centre nearby has many
private firms offering lessons in sailing and canoeing, and vessels for rent.

On **Maple Leaf Quay,** the very popular **Antique Market** takes
place every day but Monday. The 70 dealers triple in number
each Sunday.

❸ From Harbourfront, it's a short walk to the **CN Tower,** an attraction second only to Eaton Centre.

The CN Tower, the tallest free-standing structure in the world,
is found on Front Street, near Spadina Avenue, not far from
the waterfront. It's fully 1,815 feet, 5 inches high, and it really
is worth a visit, if the weather is clear.

Four elevators zoom up the outside of the $57 million tower. The
ride takes but a minute, going at 20 feet a second, a rate of ascent similar to that of a jet-plane takeoff. But each elevator has
only one floor-to-ceiling glass wall, preventing vertigo.

The **Skypod,** about two-thirds up the tower, is seven stories
high and has two observation decks, a nightclub, and a revolv-

ing restaurant. It also has oodles of microwave equipment that is not open to the public but is its true raison d'être.

Level 2 is the **outdoor observation deck,** with an enclosed promenade, and an outdoor balcony for looking straight down at the ground. Level 3 of the Skypod, the **indoor observation deck,** has not only conventional telescopes, but also high-powered peritelescopes that almost simulate flight. Also here is a unique Tour Wand System, which provides an audio tour of the City of Toronto. A minitheater shows a presentation on the CN Tower.

The **Space Deck,** which is 33 stories higher, costs $2.35 extra; at an elevation of 1,465 feet, it is the world's highest public observation gallery. But even from the Skypod below, you can often see Lake Simcoe to the north, and the mist rising from Niagara Falls to the south. All the decks provide spectacular panoramic views of Toronto, Lake Ontario, and the Toronto Islands. *CN Tower, 301 Front St. W, tel. 416/360–8500. Observation deck: $10.95 adults, $5.35 senior citizens and children 13–16, $4.25 children 12 and under. The Audio Tour Wand is included in the price. Peak visiting hours: 11–4, especially on weekends. Open summers, daily 10 AM–midnight; the rest of the year, opening and closing times vary up to an hour, depending on season; call ahead.*

Tour of the Universe, located at the base of the CN Tower, is a charming one-hour simulated space shuttle journey to Jupiter in the year 2019, with everything from a 64-screen Multivision Wall that briefs you on your upcoming flight, laser "inoculation," an InterPlanetary Passport souvenir, and a too-brief ride in a flight simulator that provides physical motion to match the spectacular special-effects film. It's very well done and a pleasant break before or after the CN Tower visit. *Tel. 416/360–8500. Admission: $7 adults, $6.50 seniors citizens and children 13–16, $5.35 children 5–12.*

Financial District One doesn't always recommend visits to a train station, but **❹** **Union Station** is special. On the south side of Front Street, between Bay and York streets (and across from the handsome Royal York Hotel), Union Station is a most historic building, though it is of this century. It was designed back in 1907, when trains were still as exciting as space shuttles are today, and it was opened in 1927 by the Prince of Wales. Try to imagine the awe of the immigrants who poured into Toronto between the wars by the tens of thousands, staring up at the towering ceiling of Italian tile or leaning against one of the 22 pillars, each one 40 feet tall and weighing 75 tons. Walk along the lengthy concourse and study the mellow reflection in its walls. Get a sense of the beauty of the light flooding through the high, arched windows at each end of the mammoth hall.

As you come out of Union Station, walk back to Yonge Street and the beautiful **Bank of Montreal** building, at the northwest corner of Front Street. Built around the old bank is one of the **❺** two towers of the striking new **BCE Place,** with its exquisite, huge Galleria, completed in mid-1992, which, as one architectural critic wrote, "brings a new level of sophistication to the interior spaces of the city's core." Just steps north is a shabby row of shops, which are among the oldest surviving commercial buildings in the city. Many of the original Georgian facades have been drastically altered, but the one- and two-story buildings give you a sense of the scale of buildings from the 1850s and are the last remnants of the early business community of the then–brand-new city of Toronto.

Make a left turn at the first intersection, which is Wellington **(6)** Street West. **Number 15** is the oldest building on this walk, an elegant stone bank designed in the Greek Revival style.

Head back a few steps to Yonge Street and go north again. On the northeast corner of Yonge and Colborne streets, at 67 **(7)** Yonge Street, is **Traders Bank,** the first "skyscraper" of the city when it went up in 1905–06, complete with an observation deck. The next building to the north, built in 1913, helped make this among the tallest buildings in North America. It is still owned by **Canadian Pacific,** the largest private employer in Canada (planes, trains, hotels, and more).

At the southwest corner of King and Yonge streets is the **(8)** **Dominion Bank building,** erected in 1913 by the same architects who designed the voluptuous Bank of Montreal. It's a classic Chicago-style skyscraper and is well worth a visit inside. Climb the marble and bronze stairway to the opulent banking hall on the second floor, and enjoy the marble floor, marble walls, and the ornate plaster ceiling, which features the coats of arms of the then nine Canadian provinces.

(9) On the northeast corner is the original **Royal Bank building,** also put up in 1913. Note the distinctive cornice, the overhanging roof, the decorative pattern of sculpted ox skulls above the ground-floor windows, and the classically detailed leaves at the top of the Corinthian columns.

Farther north along Yonge Street, at Richmond Street West, is **(10)** the original Simpsons department store, now **The Bay.** Built in 1895, it was one of the city's first buildings with a steel-frame construction. There are attractive terra-cotta decorations in the section closest to Yonge Street, which went up in 1908; the part along Richmond Street, near Bay Street, added in 1928, is a fine example of the art deco style, popular between the two world wars.

Continue a few steps west to Bay Street, a name synonymous with finance and power in Canada, as Wall Street is in the United States. Head south (left), back toward the lakefront. Just south of Adelaide Street, on the west side of Bay Street, is **(11)** the **Canada Permanent Trust Building** (320 Bay St.). Built in the very year of the stock market crash (and we don't mean the 1987 one), it's a skyscraper in the New York wedding-cake style. Look up at the ornate stone carvings both on the lower stories and on the top, where carved, stylized faces peer down to the street below. Walk through the imposing vaulted entrance, with its polished brass doors, and note that even the elevator doors in the foyer are embossed brass. The spacious banking hall has a vaulted ceiling, marble walls and pillars, and a marble floor with mosaic borders.

Turn right (west) along King Street, and on your right is the first of the towering bank buildings that have defined Toronto's **(12)** skyline over the past two decades. This is **First Canadian Place** (100 King St. W), built in the early 1970s. Its 72 stories were deliberately faced with white marble to contrast with the black of the Toronto-Dominion Centre, to the south, and with the silver of the Commerce Court Tower.

(13) Farther along you come to the second phase of the project, opened in 1983, which houses the ultramodern **Toronto Stock Exchange (TSE).** The Exchange Tower (2 First Canadian Pl.) has a Visitor's Center, where visitors can learn about the securities industry through colorful displays, or even join in daily presentations. The attractions are many: a 100-foot public gallery, a 140-seat auditorium, recorded tours, and a mini slide show of the TSE 300 Composite Index (an echo of the Dow Jones Average). *Tel. 416/947–4670. Admission free. Open weekdays 9:30–4. Public tour daily at 2.*

(14) On the northeast corner of King and Bay streets (44 King St. W) is the **Bank of Nova Scotia.** Built between 1949 and 1951, and partially replaced by the recently completed Scotia Tower just to the east, it has sculptural panels inspired by Greek mythology above the large, exterior windows. In the lobby, there are reliefs symbolizing four regions of Canada and a brightly colored gilded plaster ceiling. The original stainless steel and glass stairway with marine motifs is attractive, as are the marble counters and floors. The north wall relief depicts some of the industries and enterprises financed by the bank.

(15) On the southeast corner of King and Bay streets is the **"Old" Bank of Commerce Tower,** which for a third of a century was the tallest building in the British Commonwealth. Its base has bas-relief carvings, and marvelous animal and floral ornamentation around the vaulted entrance. Because the top is set back, you must look up to see the huge, carved human heads on all four sides of the building.

(16) The **Bank of Commerce building** (25 King St. W) was built in the two years following the stock market crash of 1929, but the hard times didn't prevent the creation of a stunning interior of marble floors, limestone walls, and bronze vestibule doors decorated with masks, owls, and animals. In the alcoves on each side of the entrance are murals that trace the history of transportation. The bronze elevator doors are richly decorated, the vaulted banking hall is lit by period chandeliers, and each desk has its own lamp.

(17) Just south of the "old tower," at 243 Bay Street, is **Commerce Court,** the bank's 57-story stainless-steel sister. And due west, just across Bay Street, also on the south side of King Street, (18) are the two black towers of the **Toronto-Dominion Centre,** the first International Style skyscrapers built in Toronto, thanks to the "less is more" man, Mies van der Rohe. The two towers went up in the mid-1960s, and they are starkly plain and stripped of ornament. The only decoration consists of geometric repetition, and the only extravagance is the use of rich materials, such as marble counters and leather-covered furniture.

(19) Immediately south of the T-D Centre towers, at 232 Bay Street, is the **former Toronto Stock Exchange building,** which, for close to half a century, was the financial hub of Toronto. Built in 1937 of polished pink granite and smooth buff limestone, it's a delightful example of art deco design. The stainless-steel doors are a wonder, as is the wise and witty stone frieze carved above them. Don't miss the hilarious social commentary up there—the banker with the top hat marching behind the laborer, his hand sneaking into the worker's pocket.

(20) Walk south another block to the northwest corner of Bay and Front streets: There, in all its golden glory, is the **Royal Bank**

Plaza, built only in 1976 but already a classic of its kind. Be sure to go into the 120-foot-high banking hall and admire the lovely hanging sculpture by Jesus Raphael Soto.

Underground City The origins of Toronto's **Underground City**—purportedly the largest pedestrian walkway in the world, and more than four times the size of Montréal's—go back over a generation. One can walk—and shop, eat, browse, etc.—without ever seeing the light of day, from beneath Union Station to the Royal York Hotel, the Toronto-Dominion Centre, First Canadian Place, the Sheraton Centre, the Eaton Centre, and the Atrium. Altogether, it extends through nearly three miles of tunnels and seven subway stops.

Enter the subterranean community from anywhere between Dundas Street on the north and Union Station on the south, and you'll encounter everything from art exhibitions to buskers (the city actually auditions young musicians and licenses the best to perform throughout its subway system and elsewhere) to walkways, fountains, and trees growing as much as two stories high. Because up to 50% of the complex lies underneath Toronto's multibillion-dollar Financial District, you will keep bumping into men and women in business suits, browsing or on lunch breaks.

Tour 2: From Eaton Centre to the City Halls and the Far and Middle East

Numbers in the margin correspond to points of interest on the Tours 2 and 3 map.

From the corners of Yonge and Queen streets, one can begin a tour that will include several of this city's most popular attractions, as well as some of its most interesting neighborhoods. Alas, one of these, Eaton Centre, is closed on Sunday, while others thrive on what is still considered the Lord's Day in the province of Ontario. Still, the following walking/driving tour should make for a very pleasant day in the central and western portions of Toronto's downtown.

Eaton Centre   **Eaton Centre,** a 3-million-square-foot building that extends
and City Hall   along the west side of Yonge Street all the way from Queen
㉑   Street up to Dundas Street (with subway stops at each end), has quickly become the number-one tourist attraction of Toronto. Even people who rank shopping with the flu will still be charmed, even dazzled, for this is a very beautiful environment indeed. From its graceful glass roof, arching 127 feet above the lowest of the mall levels, to Michael Snow's exquisite flock of fiberglass Canada geese floating poetically in the open space of the Galleria, to the glass-enclosed elevators, porthole windows, and nearly two dozen long and graceful escalators, there are plenty of good reasons for visiting Eaton Centre.

Galleria Level 1 contains two food courts; popularly priced fashions; photo, electronics, and record stores; and much "convenience" merchandise. Level 2 is directed to the middle-income shopper, while Level 3, suitably, has the highest elevation, fashion, and prices. **Eaton's,** one of Canada's classic department-store chains, has a nine-floor branch here. At the southern end of Level 3 is a skywalk that connects the Centre to the seven-floor **The Bay** department store across Queen Street.

Dozens of restaurants, from snack to full-service, can be found here. A 17-theater cinema complex—the initial unit of the now worldwide Cineplex chain—is located at the Dundas Street entrance. *Eaton Centre open weekdays 10–9, Sat. 9:30–6.*

Exit the Eaton Centre at Queen Street and walk just one long block west to Toronto's city halls. Yes, the plural is correct.

㉒ **Old City Hall** is the very beautiful building at the northeast corner of Queen and Bay streets, sweetly coexisting with the fu-
㉓ turistic **New City Hall,** just across the street, on the west side. The creator of the old one, which opened in 1899, was none other than E.J. Lennox, who would later design Casa Loma. It was considered one of North America's most impressive municipal halls in its heyday, and since the opening of its younger sister, it has been the site for the provincial courts, county offices, and thousands of low-cost marriages. Do note the hideous gargoyles above the front steps, which were apparently the architect's witty way of mocking certain politicians of the time. The great stained-glass window as you enter is attractive, and the handsome old structure stands in delightful contrast to its daring and unique sibling.

The New City Hall was the result of a massive international competition in 1958. The winning presentation by Finnish architect Viljo Revell was very controversial: two towers of differing height, and curved! But there was and is a logic to it all: An aerial view of the New City Hall shows a circular council chamber sitting like an eye between the two tower "eyelids." Within months of its opening in 1965, the New City Hall became a symbol of a thriving city.

Annual events at the New City Hall include the Spring Flower Show in late March; the Toronto Outdoor Art Exhibition early each July, and the Cavalcade of Lights from late November through Christmas each year, when more than 100,000 sparkling lights are illuminated across both city halls. *Tel. 416/392–7341; TDD 416/392–7354. Underground garage for 2,400 cars. Open weekdays 8:30–4:30. Free 30-minute guided tours. Cafeteria open daily 7:30–4.*

Chinatown and the Museums Just north of the New City Hall begins Toronto's main **Chinatown,** which is the largest in all of North America. There are more than 100,000 Chinese living in the city, which is not bad, considering that just over a century ago there was only one— Sam Ching, who ran a hand laundry on Adelaide Street. Today, Chinatown covers much of the area around Spadina Avenue from Queen Street to College Street, running along Dundas Street nearly as far east as Bay Street.

One of the best times to explore Chinatown is on a Sunday, when, up and down Spadina Avenue and along Dundas Street, Chinese music blasts from storefronts, cash registers ring, abacuses clack, and bakeries, markets, herbalists, and restaurants do their best business of the week. But whatever day you wander, we recommend that you start on Elizabeth Street, just north of the New City Hall, and walk north to Dundas Street, east toward Bay Street, then turn back and walk west to Spadina Avenue. You will be thrilled by the diversity, the excitement, the liveliness—the sheer foreignness of it all.

㉔ The **Shing Wah Daily News,** on Hagerman Street, near Bay Street (tel. 416/977–3745) will show you some of the 10,000 Chi-

Tour 2
Art Gallery of
Ontario, **29**
Eaton Centre, **21**
52nd Division Police
Station, **26**
Kensington
Market, **30**
Mon Kuo, **25**
New City Hall, **23**
Old City Hall, **22**
Ontario College
of Art, **27**
Shing Wah Daily
News, **24**
Village by the
Grange, **28**

Tour 3
Bloor and Yorkville, **45**
Campbell House, **31**
Casa Loma, **49**
The Colonnade, **46**
George R. Gardiner
Museum of Ceramic
Art, **42**
Hart House, **33**
Hazelton Lanes, **48**
Knox College, **35**
McLaughlin
Planetarium, **43**
Medical Sciences
Building, **36**
Metropolitan Toronto
Library, **47**
Ontario Legislative
Bulding, **39**
Parliament
Buildings, **40**
Public and Community
Relations Office, **37**
Queen's Park, **38**
Royal Ontario
Museum, **41**
Sigmund Samuel
Canadiana
Collection, **44**
University College, **34**
University of
Toronto, **32**

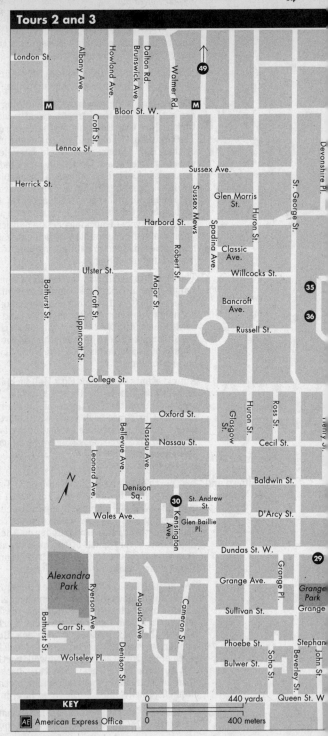

Tours 2 and 3

KEY

AE American Express Office

0   440 yards

0   400 meters

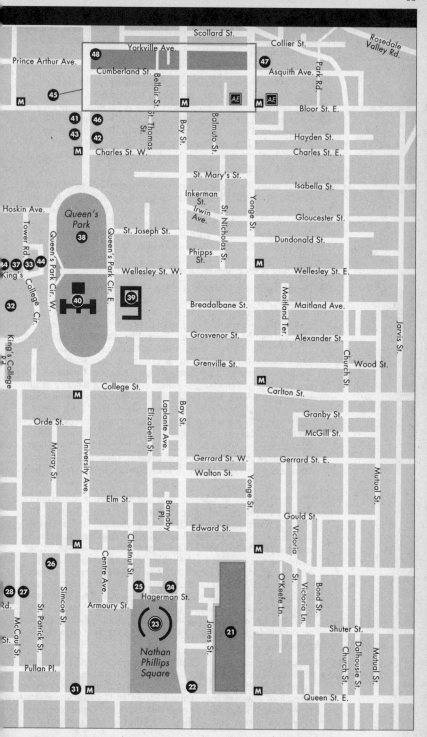

nese characters being typeset and printed, plus samples of
㉕ Blondie and Dagwood speaking Cantonese. **Mon Kuo Trading
Co. Ltd.** (120 Elizabeth St.) cultivates tens of thousands of bean
sprouts under a sprinkler system in the basement, on their one-
week growth to maturity.

On Dundas Street, you'll pass shops selling reasonably priced
silk blouses and antique porcelain, silk kimonos for less than
half the price elsewhere, lovely sake sets, and women's silk
㉖ suits. Huge Chinese characters hang over the **52nd Division police station,** a large building on the west side of Simcoe Street,
just south of Dundas Street. Many of the banks still have abacuses, for those who prefer the 4,000-year-old "hand-held cal-
culators" to modern ones.

㉗ Turn south off Dundas Street to the **Ontario College of Art** (100
McCaul St.), one of the major colleges of animation, design, advertising art, tapestry, glassblowing, sculpture, and painting
㉘ in Canada. Directly across the street is **Village by the Grange**
(89 McCaul St.), an apartment and shopping complex with
more than a hundred shops selling everything from ethnic fast
food to serious art. It's a perfect example of wise, careful
blending of the commercial and the residential.

㉙ Return to Dundas Street and head west to the **Art Gallery of
Ontario,** which has been slowly but steadily evolving into one of
the better art museums in North America. From extremely
modest beginnings in 1900, the AGO is now in the big league in
terms of exhibits and support. Recent international exhibits of
King Tut, Van Gogh, Turner, Judy Chicago, William Blake,
and Picasso will give you an idea of the gallery's importance,
image, and profile. The **Henry Moore Sculpture Centre** on the
second floor has the largest public collection of Moore's sculpture in the world. Also on the second floor is the **Samuel and
Ayala Zacks Wing,** with its fine collection of 20th-century
sculpture. The **Canadian Wing** includes major works by such
northern lights as Emily Carr, Cornelius Krieghoff, David
Milne, and Homer Watson. On the lower level is a "hands-on"
room where children are invited to paint, make slides, and otherwise creatively muck about (open Sunday, summers, and holidays).

The Art Gallery of Ontario also has a growing collection of
Rembrandt, Hals, Van Dyck, Hogarth, Reynolds, Chardin, Re-
noir, de Kooning, Rothko, Oldenburg, Picasso, Rodin, Degas,
Matisse, and many others. And it also has **The Grange,** a historic house just behind the AGO, a perfect place to browse, either
before or after a visit to the art gallery. *317 Dundas St. W, 3
blocks west of the St. Patrick station of the University subway
line; tel. 416/977–0414. Admission: $4.50 adults, $2.50 children 12–18 and senior citizens, $10 families. Free Wed. after
5:30 PM; free Fri. for senior citizens. Open Tues.–Sun. 11–5:30,
Wed. until 9; also late-May–Labor Day, Mon. 11–5:30. Closed
major holidays. Prices are approximate because of ongoing construction.*

Spadina and the   Toronto's widest street, **Spadina Avenue,** has been pronounced
Marketplaces   "Spa-*dye*-nah" for a century and a half, and we are too polite to
point out that it really should be called "Spa-*dee*-na." The
stretch of Spadina from Queen Street to College Street has
never been fashionable, or even worth a visit by most tourists.
Way back, it was just a collection of inexpensive stores, facto-

ries that sold to you wholesale if you had connections, ethnic food and fruit stores, and eateries that gave you your two cents' worth, usually plain.

And so it remains, with the exception of some often first-class, if modest-looking, Chinese restaurants sprinkled throughout the area. Each new wave of immigrants—Jewish, Chinese, Portuguese, East and West Indian, South American—added its own flavor to the mix, but Spadina-Kensington's basic bill of fare is still "bargains galore." Here you'll find gourmet cheeses at gourmet prices, fresh (no, not fresh-frozen) ocean fish, fine European kitchenware at half the price of that in stores in the Yorkville area, yards of remnants piled high in bins, designer clothes minus the labels, and the occasional rock-and-roll night spot and interesting greasy spoon.

For any visitor who plans to be in Toronto for more than four or five days, a few hours exploring the ins and outs of Spadina's garment district, between College and Queen, could bring great pleasure—and even greater bargains. Park your car at the lot just west of Spadina Avenue on St. Andrew's Street (a long block north of Dundas Street), or take the College or Queen streetcar to Spadina Avenue. (Also, *see* Shopping, below.)

㉚ Kensington Market is a delightful side tour off Spadina Avenue. Here, the bargains are of the more edible kind. All your senses will be titillated by this old, steamy, smelly, raucous, colorful, European-style marketplace. Come and explore, especially during warmer weather, when the goods pour out into the narrow streets: Russian rye breads, barrels of dill pickles, fresh fish on ice, mountains of cheese, bushels of ripe fruit, and crates of chickens and rabbits that will have your children both giggling and horrified. Jewish and Eastern European stores sit side by side with Portuguese, Caribbean, Latin American, and East Indian stores—with Vietnamese, Japanese, and Chinese establishments sprinkled throughout. Most shops are open every day except Sunday, from as early as 6 AM.

Afterward, you can rest in **Bellevue Square** (corner of Denison Square and Augusta Place), a lovely little park with shady trees, benches, and a wading pool and playground for children.

Tour 3: Academia, Culture, Commercialism, Crassness

University Avenue, running from Front Street for about three miles north to Bloor Street, where it changes its name to Avenue Road and continues north, is one of Toronto's few mistakes. It's horribly boring, with hospital after office building after insurance company after office building. Yet it is still an interesting start for a healthy walk, because it does have lovely flower beds and fountains in a well-maintained strip along its middle. Still, you may wish to drive this part of the tour.

㉛ One highlight is **Campbell House** (northwest corner of Queen Street and University Avenue), the stately Georgian mansion of Sir William Campbell, the sixth chief justice of Upper Canada. Built in 1822 and tastefully restored with elegant 18th- and early-19th-century furniture, it is one of Toronto's most charming "living museums." Costumed hostesses will tell you about the social life of the upper class. *Tel. 416/597-0227. Admission:*

$2.50 adults, $1.25 students and senior citizens. Guided tours available. Open Oct.–mid May, weekdays 9:30–11:30 and 2:30–4:30; summers, weekdays 9:30–11:30 and 2:30–4:30, weekends noon–4:30.

㉜ College Street is the southern boundary of the **University of Toronto.** It goes back to 1827, when King George IV signed a charter for a "King's College in the Town of York, Capital of Upper Canada." The Church of England had control then, but by 1850 the college was proclaimed nondenominational, renamed the University of Toronto, and put under the control of the province. And then, in a spirit of good Christian competition, the Anglicans started Trinity College, the Methodists began Victoria, and the Roman Catholics begat St. Michael's; by the time the Presbyterians founded Knox College, the whole thing was almost out of hand.

But not really: The 17 schools and faculties are now united, and they welcome anyone who can pass the entrance exams and afford the tuition. The architecture is interesting, if uneven. We recommend a walking tour. Enter the campus just behind the Parliament buildings, where Wellesley Street ends. Go under the bridge, past the guardhouse (whose keeper will not let you pass if you are encased in an automobile), and turn right, around King's College Circle.

㉝ At the top of the circle is **Hart House,** a Gothic-style student center built during the teens of this century by the Masseys— the folks who brought us Massey-Ferguson farm equipment, Massey Hall, Vincent Massey (a governor-general of Canada), and Raymond Massey, the actor. It was once an all-male enclave; today, anyone may visit the Great Hall and the library, both self-conscious imitations of Oxford and Cambridge. Check out the dining hall for its amazing stained-glass windows as well as its food, which is cheap and rather good.

As you continue around King's College Circle, you'll see on **㉞** your right the Romanesque **University College,** built in 1859. **㉟** Next is **Knox College,** whose Scottish origins are evident in the bagpipe music that escapes from the building at odd hours. It's been training ministers since 1844, although the building went up only yesterday—1915.

㊱ You may well wish to tip your hat to the **Medical Sciences Building,** which is no beauty but is where, in 1921, Drs. Banting, Best, and others discovered the insulin that has saved the lives of tens of millions of diabetics around the world.

There is lots more to see and do around the main campus of the **㊲** University of Toronto. Visit the **Public and Community Relations Office** (Room 133S, 27 King's College Circle, tel. 416/978–2021), across the field from Hart House, and pick up free maps of the school grounds. Guided one-hour walking tours are held on summer weekdays, setting out from the map room of Hart House at 10:30, 12:30, and 2:30 (tel. 416/978–5000).

Back at College Street and University Avenue, you can see the Victorian structure of the Parliament buildings to the north, with Queen's Park just north of them.

Queen's Park There are a number of meanings to **Queen's Park,** for the native **㊳** Torontonian as well as the visitor. The term can refer to the charming circular park just a few hundred yards south of the Royal Ontario Museum (on University Avenue, just below

Bloor Street). This is a grand place to rest your feet after a long day of shopping or visiting the Royal Ontario Museum. But **39** Queen's Park also refers to the **Ontario Legislative Building,** which is the home of the provincial parliament. The mammoth building was opened back in 1893, a century ago, and is really quite extraordinary, with its rectangular towers, triangular roofs, and circular and oval glass.

40 The **Parliament Buildings** look grotesque to some, with their pink exterior and heavy, almost Romanesque quality. But a close look will show the beautifully complex detail carved in the stone, and on the inside there are huge, lovely halls that echo half a millennium of English architecture. The long hallways are hung with hundreds of oils by Canadian artists, most of which capture scenes of the province's natural beauty. Should you choose to take one of the frequent (and free) tours, you will see the chamber where the 130 elected representatives from across Ontario, called MPPs (Members of Provincial Parliament), meet on a regular basis. There are two heritage rooms—one each for the parliamentary histories of Great Britain and Ontario—filled with old newspapers, periodicals, and pictures. And the lobby holds a fine collection of minerals and rocks of the province. On the lawn in front of the Parliament buildings, facing College Street, are many statues, including one of Queen Victoria and one of Canada's first prime minister, Sir John A. Macdonald. *Tel. 416/965-4028. Guided tours from mid-May to Labor Day, daily on the hour 9-4, weekends every half hour 9-11:30 and 1:30-4; frequent tours the rest of the year; also at 6:45 PM when evening sessions are held. University Ave. subway, College St. stop. There are parking lots in the area and metered parking around Queen's Park Circle.*

41 Just to the north of Queen's Park is the world-class **Royal Ontario Museum.** Once labeled "Canada's single greatest cultural asset" by the Canada Council, the museum floundered throughout much of its existence, which began in 1912 (the same day the *Titanic* sank). It never stopped collecting—always with brilliance—reaching more than 6 million items altogether. But by the 1970s, the monstrous building had leaky roofs, no climate control, and little space to display its glorious treasures. Today, thanks to a major fund-raising effort that brought in $80 million, the museum has the space it needs, and when expansion is completed sometime in the 1990s, the ROM will be the second-largest museum in North America, after New York's Metropolitan Museum of Art.

What makes the ROM unique is the fact that science, art, and archaeology exhibits are all under one roof. The **Dinosaur Collection** will stun children and adults alike. The **Evolution Gallery** has an ongoing audiovisual program on Darwin's theories of evolution. The **Roman Gallery** has the most extensive collection of Roman artifacts in Canada. And the **European Musical Instruments Gallery** has a revolutionary audio system and more than 1,200 instruments dating back to the late 16th century. The **Discovery Gallery** allows children (over age 6) to handle objects from the ROM's collections and to study them, using microscopes, ultraviolet light, and magnifying glasses.

The **Bat Cave,** opened in early 1988, contains 4,000 freeze-dried and artificial bats in a lifelike presentation. Piped-in narration directs visitors on a 15-minute walk through a dimly lit replica of an 8-foot-high limestone tunnel in Jamaica, filled with sounds of dripping water and bat squeaks. In early 1992, the brilliant **Ancient Egypt Gallery** reopened, joined with a brand-new **Nubia Gallery**—the only one in North America. *110 Queens Park, tel. 416/586–5549. Admission: $6 adults; $3.25 students and senior citizens; children 4 and under free; $13 family of 5. Senior citizens free Tues. (including Gardiner Museum and planetarium shows); all others free Tues. after 4:30. Open daily 10–6 (Tues. and Thurs. until 8). Closed Mon. from Labor Day to mid–May and New Year's Day. Discovery Gallery hours vary; please phone ahead. Take the University subway to the Museum stop; parking is expensive.*

42 The **George R. Gardiner Museum of Ceramic Art** has now merged with the ROM, meaning that it costs not a penny more to visit a magnificent $25 million collection of rare European ceramics. The collection features 17th-century English delftware and 18th-century yellow European porcelain. *Across University Ave. from the ROM, Open Tues.–Sun. 10–5.*

43 Just south of the ROM is the **McLaughlin Planetarium,** which attracts some 250,000 visitors a year. There are four new 45-minute star shows each year. Open since 1986 is the **Astrocentre,** which has hands-on exhibits, computer terminals designed for both adults and children, and an animated model of the star system. *Tel. 416/586–5736. Admission: $5 adults, $3 senior citizens, students, and children. Senior citizens free on Tues. Open same hours as the ROM, plus evening hours for the star shows. Tel. 416/586–5751 for a taped description of the current night sky.*

44 A five-minute walk south of the planetarium will bring you to the **Sigmund Samuel Canadiana Collection** (part of the ROM) of early Canadian furnishings, glassware, silver, and six room settings of 18th- and 19th-century furniture. *14 Queen's Park Crescent W, on the northwest corner of University Ave. and College St. Open Tues.–Sat. 10–5, Sun. 1–5.*

45 After so much culture, you may wish to enjoy one of the most dynamic and expensive areas of Toronto—**Bloor and Yorkville.** Some call it Toronto's Rodeo Drive; others call it Toronto's Fifth Avenue. One thing is certain: These blocks are packed with specialty shops, ritzy restaurants, and high-price stores specializing in designer clothes, furs, and jewels.

46 The **Colonnade,** on the south side of Bloor Street, a few doors east of University Avenue, has recently undergone a $10 million face-lift. In addition to several levels of luxury residential apartments and private offices, it also has more than two floors of stores selling quality leather goods, perfumes, jewelry, and European apparel.

47 A block north of Bloor and Yonge streets is the magnificent **Metropolitan Toronto Library.** Arranged around a tall and wide interior atrium, the library gives a fabulous sense of open space. It was designed by one of Canada's most admired architects, Raymond Moriyama, who also created the Ontario Science Centre. Browsers will appreciate that fully one-third of the more than 1.3 million books—spread across 28 miles of shelves—are open to the public. In the many audio carrels, with headphones, you may listen to any one of more than 10,000 albums. The **Arthur Conan Doyle Room** houses the finest public collection of Holmesiana anywhere, with records, films, photos, books, manuscripts, and letters. *789 Yonge St., just steps* *north of Bloor St., tel. 416/393-7000. Open May-Sept., Mon.-Thurs. 9-9, Fri. 9-6, Sat. 9-5; Oct.-Apr., Sun. 1:30-5. To get an answer to any question, on any subject, tel. 416/393-7131.*

㊽ On the east side of Avenue Road, two blocks north of Bloor Street, is a don't-miss shopping area—**Hazelton Lanes** (416/968-8600). Offering everything from Swiss chocolates to Hermès silks and Giorgio Armani's latest fashions, this is a wonderful, magical paean to capitalism. And in 1989 it doubled, in size and glory, with the addition of some 80 new stores.

㊾ **Casa Loma** (1 Austin Terr.; on Spadina Ave., south of St. Clair Ave. W and the St. Clair subway stop), is an honest-to-goodness 20th-century castle, with 98 rooms; two towers; secret panels; long, creepy passageways; and some of the best views of Toronto—all just a short distance from the heart of the city. The medieval-style castle was built shortly before World War I by Sir Henry Pellatt, a soldier and financier who spent more than $3 million to construct his dream. The architect E.J. Lennox, who also designed Toronto's Old City Hall and King Edward Hotel, created a remarkable structure; Toronto's "house on the hill" is a real treat. There are no more guided tours of Casa Loma—you now get automatic tape recordings. That's all for the best, because you can drift through at your own speed while the children rush off to the stables or towers. You'll have walked a good mile by the time you're done, so wear sensible shoes. *Tel. 416/923-1171. Admission: $8 adults, $4.50 senior citizens and children 6-16. Open daily 10-4. Closed Christmas Day and New Year's.*

What to See and Do with Children

Free Attractions The **ferry boat** to the **Toronto Islands** and **Far Enough Farm** (*see* Tour 1, above). The **David Dunlap Observatory** in Richmond Hill, just north of Metro Toronto, and the **McLaughlin Planetarium** (*see* Tour 3, above). **Harbourfront** nearly always has free events and activities, from painting and sculpting to concerts and plays. **Ontario Place,** just west of Harbourfront, is a waterfront entertainment complex built on three man-made islands that contains something for everyone: the **Cinesphere,** a dome with a six-story movie screen that shows Imax and 70mm films; several shows in pods that float above the water; the *Haida,* a World War II destroyer that's fun to explore; the outdoor **Forum,** where nightly concerts take place; various eateries; and **Children's Village,** with water games, slides, puppet shows, clowns, magicians, and a children's theater. *South of Lakeshore Blvd. across from CNE grounds. Tel. 416/965-7711. Open daily mid-May-mid-Sept. Admission free. Bumper boats, pedal boats, Cinesphere, and concerts have nominal admission fees.*

Modestly Priced Attractions **Apple, strawberry,** and **raspberry picking** are available within a short drive of downtown Toronto. Our favorite place is **Al Ferri's** (15 minutes west of the airport, near the corner of Mississauga Road and Steeles Avenue; tel. 416/455-8202). Please check out Ferri's astonishingly wonderful Macoun apples—like Red Delicious merged with MacIntosh. Glorious! For a free list of places to pick fruits and vegetables in the vicinity of Toronto, call 416/965-7701. The **Art Gallery of Ontario's** hands-on room and Henry Moore sculpture that children love to climb; and the fascinating, historic **Grange** house (*see* Tour 2, above). **Casa Loma** (*see* Tour 3, above).

More Expensive The **Ontario Science Centre** has free movies and thrilling space,
Attractions communications, laser, and electricity exhibits, and an irresistible new exhibit called Challenger. *770 Don Mills Rd.,
about 11 km (7 mi) from downtown. Take the Yonge St. subway
from downtown to the Eglinton station and Eglinton E bus to
the Don Mills Parkway stop. Tel. 416/696–3127 or 416/429–
4100. Admission: $5.89 adults, $4.82 children 13–17, $2.14
children 5–12, senior citizens and children under 5 free, $14.98
families (up to 2 adults and 6 children). Free after 5 PM Fri.
Parking $2. Open Sun.–Thur. and Sat. 10–6, Fri. 10–9.*

The **Young People's Theatre** (tel. 416/864–9732) often has excellent fare, as do **Roy Thomson Hall** (tel. 416/593–4828) and the
Minkler Auditorium (tel. 416/491–8877).

The Metro Toronto Zoo was built for animals, not people. The
Rouge Valley, just east of Toronto, was an inspired choice of
site when it was built in the 1960s, with its varied terrain, from
river valley to dense forest, where mammals, birds, reptiles,
and fish have been grouped according to where they live in the
wild. In most of the regions, you'll find remarkable botanical
exhibits in enclosed, climate-controlled pavilions. Don't miss
the three-ton banyan tree in the Indo-Malayan Pavilion, the
fan-shaped traveler's palm from Madagascar in the African Pavilion, or the perfumed flowers of the jasmine vines in the
Eurasian Pavilion. The "round-the-world tour" takes some
three hours and is suitable for any kind of weather, because
most of the time is spent inside pavilions. It's been estimated
that it would take four full days to see everything in the Metro
Zoo, so study the map you'll get at the zoo entrance and decide
in advance what you wish to see most.

For the younger children, there is the delightful Littlefootland,
a special area that allows contact with tame animals, such as
rabbits and sheep. In the winter, cross-country skiers follow
groomed trails that skirt the animal exhibits. Lessons and rentals are available. There is an electrically powered train that
moves silently among the animals without frightening them. It
can accommodate wheelchairs (available for free, inside the
main gate), and all pavilions have ramp access. *Meadowvale
Rd., just north of Highway 401, in Scarborough, a 30-minute
drive from downtown. Or take Bus 86A from the Kennedy subway station. Tel. 416/392–5900. Admission: $9 adults, $6 senior citizens and children 12–17, $4 children 5–11. Family rates
available. Free parking in winter; parking Mar.–Oct. $4. Open
daily except Christmas. Summer, daily 9:30–7; winter, daily
9:30–4:30.*

Off the Beaten Track

Watching the Italian promenade. St. Clair Avenue West, running from Bathurst Street to Dufferin Street and beyond, remains the heart of this city's vibrant Italian community. On
many evenings, especially Sunday, the street is filled with
thousands of men and women promenading between *gelaterie*,
eyeing each other, and generally enjoying their neighbors.

Greektown on a Sunday. The Danforth (Bloor Street east of the
Don Valley Parkway) has great Greek restaurants, gift shops,
and hundreds of Greek Canadians promenading. Welcome to
the Mediterranean!

There's no hotel more romantic than the **Guild Inn** (2010 Guildwood Pkwy., tel. 416/261–3331), and no view of Toronto more wonderful than from **Centre Island at sunset.**

Shopping

Toronto prides itself on having some of the finest shopping in North America; and, indeed, most of the world's name boutiques can be found here. There's also a large artistic and crafts community, with many art galleries, custom jewelers, clothing designers, and artisans. Selling everything from sophisticated glass sculpture to native art, traditional crafts, antiques, quilts, wood carvings, and pine furniture.

Local food items include wild rice, available in bulk or in gift packages, and maple syrup in jars or cans.

The biggest sale day of the year is Boxing Day, the first business day after Christmas, when nearly everything in the city, including furs, is half-price. In fact, clothing prices tend to drop even further as winter fades. Summer sales start in late June and continue through August.

Bargaining Shoppers can haggle at flea markets, including the Harbourfront Antique Market, and perhaps in the Chinatown and Kensington Market/Spadina Avenue areas.

Refund Information Visitors, including Canadians from other provinces, can receive a refund on the GST and on the 8% Ontario sales tax for purchases over $100 (*see* Staying in Canada, GST and Sales Tax, above).

Shopping Districts

The **Yorkville Avenue/Bloor Street area** is where you'll find the big fashion names, fine leather goods, important jewelers, some of the top private art galleries, upscale shoe stores, and discount china and glassware. Streets to explore include Yorkville Avenue, Cumberland Street, and Scollard Street, all running parallel to Bloor Street, and Hazelton Avenue, running north from Yorkville Avenue near Avenue Road. Hazelton Lanes, between Hazelton Avenue and Avenue Road, and the adjacent York Square are among the most chichi shopping areas in Canada, and they are headquarters for café society during the brief annual spell of warm weather.

On **Bloor Street** you'll find such wonderful stores as **Zoe,** with haute couture designs; **The Bay,** a department store with elegant, high-fashion designer clothes for men and women; **Holt Renfrew,** possibly the most stunning store in Toronto, with marble, chrome, glass, and glittering fashions for both sexes; **Eddie Bauer,** selling sturdily made and cleverly designed clothing, equipment, and accessories for all sports; **Harry Rosen** for men, **Georg Jensen,** and shoe shops like **Boutique Quinto** and **David's.** Très expensive, and très good.

The **Eaton Centre** is a very large galleria-style shopping center downtown, on Yonge Street between Queen and Dundas streets. With scores of large and small stores and restaurants, all sheltered from the weather, it's one of the city's major tourist attractions. Generally speaking, the lower levels are lower priced and the higher levels are more expensive.

Queen Street West, starting just west of University Avenue and continuing past Spadina Avenue, creeping ever westward past Bathurst Street, is a trendy area near the Ontario College of Art. Here, you'll find young, hip designers; new and used-book bookstores; vintage clothes; two comic-book stores, including the biggest in North America (**Silver Snail,** No. 367; see also Dragon Lady Comic Shop at No. 200); and the more progressive private galleries.

Harbourfront includes an antiques market that's Canada's biggest on Sunday, when there are about 200 dealers (390 Queen's Quay W, tel. 416/340–8377. Open Tues.–Fri. 11–6, Sat. 10–6, Sun. 8–6.). The **Queen's Quay Terminal** is a renovated warehouse that now houses a collection of unique boutiques, craft stalls, patisseries, and so on; it's a great place to buy gifts. There's a free shuttle bus from Union Station, or it's a fairly easy walk. Parking is expensive.

Spadina Avenue, from Wellington Street north to College Street, has plenty of low-price clothing for the whole family, as well as fur and leather factory outlets. **Winner's,** south of King Street, is a good discount outlet for women and children. **Evex Luggage Centre,** 369 Spadina Avenue, south of College, has good discount luggage, handbags, and leather accessories.

Downtown Toronto has a vast underground maze of shopping warrens that burrow in between and underneath the office towers. The tenants of the **Underground City** are mostly the usual assortment of chain stores, and the shopping is rather dull; also, directions are poorly marked. The network runs roughly from the Royal York Hotel near Union Station north to the Eaton Centre.

Department Stores

The major department stores have branches around the city and flagship stores downtown. They accept major credit cards and have liberal return policies. However, service tends to be very slow and uninformed compared with that of boutiques, and the stores generally lack the cachet of American stores like Bloomingdale's or Macy's. The big names are **Eaton's,** in the Eaton Centre, and **The Bay** (The Hudson's Bay Company), on Yonge Street between Queen and Richmond streets and at Yonge and Bloor streets.

Specialty Shops

Antiques and Galleries Yorkville is the headquarters of the establishment antiques dealers, including **Navarro Gallery** (33 Hazelton Ave., tel. 416/ 921–0031). There are several other pockets around town, including a strip along Queen Street East, roughly between Sherbourne and George streets.

The Allery (322½ Queen St. W, tel. 416/593–0853) specializes in antique prints and maps. **Art Metropole** (788 King St. W, tel. 416/367–2304) specializes in limited-edition, small-press, or self-published artists' books from around the world. **Ballenford Architectural Books** (98 Scollard St., tel. 416/960–0055) has Canada's largest selection of architectural titles and a gallery with usually interesting exhibits of architectural drawings and related work. **Jane Corkin Gallery** (179 John St., north of Queen St.; tel. 416/979–1980) specializes in photography. In the same building is **Isaacs Gallery,** owned by Av Isaacs, godfather of many of the established Canadian artists. The more avant-garde galleries include **Cold City** (30 Duncan St.), **YYZ** (1087 Queen St. W), and **Mercer Union** (333 Adelaide St. W). Also check out **Toronto Photographers Workshop** and the other galleries at 80 Spadina Avenue, where you'll usually find at least one opening on a Saturday afternoon. **Prime Canadian Crafts** (229 Queen St. W, tel. 416/593–5750) has an ever-changing array of merchandise. **Quasi Modo** (789 Queen St. W, next door to Dufflet Pastries; tel. 416/366–8370) has a quirky collection of 20th-century furniture and design. You never know what will be on display: vintage bicycles, Noguchi lamps, a corrugated cardboard table by Frank Gehry. **20th Century** (23 Beverley St., just north of Queen St.; tel. 416/598–2172) is for serious collectors of 20th-century design, particularly furniture, lamps, jewelry, and decorative arts. Many of the pieces are museum quality, and the owners are extremely erudite.

Books Toronto is rich in bookstores selling new books, used books, best-sellers, and remainders. If you just need a current magazine or a paperback for the plane, there are the ubiquitous chains—Coles, Classic Bookshops, and W.H. Smith. Otherwise, we recommend:

The **Albert Britnell Book Shop** (765 Yonge St., just north of Bloor St.; tel. 416/924–3321) has been a Toronto legend since 1893, with a marvelous, British ambience and great browsing.

The **Book Cellar** (1560 Yonge St., above St. Clair Ave., tel. 416/967–5577; 142 Yorkville Ave., near Avenue Rd., tel. 416/925–9955) offers a fine choice of classical records, as well as international political and intellectual journals.

Book City has three locations (501 Bloor St. W, near Honest Ed's, tel. 416/961–4496; Carrot Common, 348 Danforth Ave., near Chester Station, tel. 416/469–9997; and 2350 Bloor St. W., tel. 416/766–9412). It's strong on good remaindered books and has a knowledgeable staff.

Edward's Books and Art, one of the loveliest minichains in the city, now at four locations (356 Queen St. W, near Spadina Ave., tel. 416/593–0126; 2179 Queen St. E, in The Beaches, tel. 416/698–1442; 170 Bloor St. W, in the Park Plaza Hotel, tel. 416/961–2428; and 2200 Yonge St., south of Eglinton Ave., tel. 416/487–5431), advertises huge discounts on bestsellers and remainders in every Saturday's *Globe and Mail.* All are open Sunday.

Longhouse Book Shop (recently relocated to 497 Bloor St. W, just west of Bathurst St.; tel. 416/921–9995) stocks only Canadian titles, handsomely shelved or piled high on pine tables: more than 20,000 back titles and new publications.

Bob Miller Book Room (180 Bloor St. W, just northwest of the ROM; tel. 416/922–3557) has the best literature section in the city and a staff that has been with Bob for decades.

Pages Books and Magazines (256 Queen St. W, tel. 416/598–1447) has a wide selection of international and small-press literature; fashion and design books and magazines; and books on film, art, and literary criticism. This is one astoundingly intellectual bookstore!

This Ain't the Rosedale Library (483 Church St., south of Wellesley Ave.; tel. 416/929–9912) stocks the largest selection of baseball books in Canada, as well as a good selection of fiction, poetry, photography, design, rock, and jazz books.

Writers & Co. (2005 Yonge Street near Davisville, a few blocks south of Eglinton; tel. 416/481–8432) is arguably Canada's finest literary bookstore, with hard-to-find poets, essayists, and world novelists. If you have been looking for a rare Caribbean poetry collection, a Swedish play in translation, or an Asian novella, this is the one to visit. It's a marvelous place, and they'll be happy to order any book for you.

Clothing **Atomic Age** (350 Queen St. W, tel. 416/977–1296) features the hottest young Toronto designers. (Also in the neighborhood are other stores for the young and zany: **Fab,** at No. 274; **290 Ion,** at No. 290; **B Scene,** at No. 352; **Fashion Crimes,** at No. 395; **Strange,** at No. 319; **Boomer,** for men at No. 309; **Metropolis,** at No. 265; and **I.X.L.,** at No. 198.)

Brown's (1975 Avenue Rd., south of Hwy. 401; tel. 416/489–1975) provides classic clothing for short men and women. There's also a store for men only (545 Queen St. W, tel. 416/368–5937). An offshoot is **Muskat & Brown** (2528 Yonge St., tel. 416/489–4005) for petite women.

Fetoun (97 Scollard St., tel. 416/923–3434) is one of the latest high-fashion emporiums for the nouveau riche. If you go to a lot of charity balls, this is the place to shop.

La Mode de Vija (601 Markham St., in Mirvish Village; tel. 416/534–6711) sells discount designer clothing with names like Anne Klein at good prices.

Sportables (Queen's Quay Terminal, tel. 416/360–6540) offers a good assortment of well-made casual wear in natural fibers.

Vintage Furs (39a Charles St. W, at Bloor and Bay Sts.; tel. 416/960–5020) sells secondhand furs for men and women.

Food Markets **Kensington Market** (northwest of Dundas St. and Spadina Ave.) is an outdoor market with a vibrant ethnic mix. Saturday is the best day to go, preferably by public transit, because parking is difficult.

St. Lawrence Market (Front St. and Jarvis St., tel. 416/392–7219) is best early on Saturday, when, in addition to the permanent indoor market on the south side of Front Street, there's a farmer's market in the building on the north side. The historic south market was once Toronto's city hall, and it fronted the lake before extensive landfill projects were undertaken.

Gift Ideas **The Back Store** (2111 Yonge St., tel. 416/482–0426) has everything for a friend with an aching spine.

Bragg (446 Queen St., west of Spadina Ave.; tel. 416/366–6717) has an amusing assortment of vintage bric-a-brac, china, cards, and jewelry.

Early Learning (387 Queen St. W, tel. 416/598–2135) sells European and Japanese playthings.

Filigree (1210 Yonge St., tel. 415/961–5223) has a good assortment of linens, as well as drawer liners, silver frames, and other Victorian pleasures. In the neighborhood are other gift shops selling fine glass and antiques.

Jewelry **Secrett Jewel Salon** (150 Bloor St. W, tel. 416/967–7500) is a reputable source of unusual gemstones and fine new and estate jewelry; local gemologists consider it the best in town.

Sports and Fitness

Participant Sports

Contact the Ministry of Tourism and Recreation (Queen's Park, Toronto, Ont. M7A 2R2) for pamphlets on various activities. For information on sports activities in the province, call tel. 800/268–3735 from anywhere in the continental United States and Canada (except the Northwest Territories and the Yukon). In Toronto, contact Ontario Travel (tel. 416/965–4008).

A number of fine **conservation areas** circle Metro Toronto, many less than a half-hour from downtown. Most have large swimming areas, sledding, and cross-country skiing, as well as skating, fishing, and boating. Contact the Metro Conservation Authority (tel. 416/661–6600) and ask for a pamphlet.

Bicycling There are more than 18 miles of street bike routes cutting across the city and dozens more along safer paths through Toronto's many parks. Bikes can be rented on the Toronto Islands. The **Martin Goodman Trail** is a 12-mile strip that runs along the waterfront all the way from the Balmy Beach Club in the east end out past the western beaches southwest of High Park. Call the *Toronto Star* (tel. 416/367–2000) for a map.

Metro Parks Department (tel. 416/392–8186) has maps that show bike (and jogging) routes that run through Toronto parkland. **Ontario Cycling** (tel. 416/495–4141) has maps, booklets, and information.

Boating Grenadier Pond, in High Park, Centre Island, Ontario Place, Harbourfront, and most of the Conservation Areas surrounding Metro Toronto rent canoes, punts, and/or sailboats.

Fishing One does not have to go very far from downtown Toronto to catch trout, perch, bass, walleye, salmon, muskie, pike, and whitefish. Contact Communication Services, Wildlife Information, Ministry of Natural Resources (Queen's Park, Toronto M7A 1W3, tel. 416/965–4251).

Within Metro Toronto itself, fishing is permitted in the trout pond at Hanlon's Point on Toronto Island, as well as in Grenadier Pond in High Park. And the salmon fishing just off the Scarborough Bluffs, in Toronto's east end, is extraordinary.

There are more than 100 charter boats on Lake Ontario (about $60 for a half-day). Contact **Ontario Travel** (tel. 416/965–4008). Be warned, though: Some fish caught in this province have such high levels of mercury in them that you can take your temperature at the same time that you eat them. It's sad, but water pollution (including acid rain) has taken its toll upon the edibility of many fish in Ontario.

Golf The season lasts only from April to late October. The top course is **Glen Abbey** (tel. 416/844–1800), where the Canadian Open Championships is held. Cart and greens fees will cost up to $75 on weekends, but this course is a real beauty.

Less challenging courses—and much closer to the heart of the city—include the **Don Valley Golf Course,** just south of Highway 401 (Yonge St., tel. 416/392–2465); the **Flemingdon Park Golf Club** (Don Mills Rd. and Eglinton Ave., tel. 416/429–1740). For other courses, contact Metro Parks (tel. 416/367–8186) or Ontario Travel (tel. 416/965–4008).

Horseback Riding There are two stables within the city limits. **Central Don Stables,** in Sunnybrook Park (Leslie St. and Eglinton Ave.; tel. 416/444–4044), has an indoor arena, an outdoor ring, and nearly 12 miles of bridle trails through the Don Valley. **Eglinton Equestrian Club** (near Don Mills Rd. and John St., tel. 416/889–6375) has two indoor arenas.

Hotel Health Facilities Nearly every major hotel in the Metro Toronto area has a decent indoor swimming pool; some even have indoor/outdoor swimming pools. The best include the **Sheraton Centre,** at Queen and Bay streets, and the **Inn on the Park,** at Eglinton Avenue near Leslie Street. Many also have health clubs, with saunas and Nautilus equipment.

Ice Skating Toronto operates some 30 outdoor artificial rinks and 100 natural-ice rinks—and all are free! Among the most popular are in Nathan Phillips Square, in front of the New City Hall, at Queen and Bay streets; down at Harbourfront, which has Canada's largest outdoor artificial ice rink; College Park, at Yonge and College streets; Grenadier Pond, within High Park, at Bloor and Keele streets; and inside Hazelton Lanes, that classy shopping mall on the edge of Yorkville, on Avenue Road, just above Bloor Street. For details on any city rink, call 416/392–1111.

Jogging The **Martin Goodman Trail** (*see* Bicycling, above) is ideal. Also try the boardwalk of The Beaches in the east end, High Park in the west end, the Toronto Islands, or any of Toronto's parks.

Sailing This can be a breeze, especially between April and October. Contact the **Ontario Sailing Association** (tel. 416/495–4240).

Skiing
Cross-country Try Toronto's parks and ravines; High Park; the lakefront along the southern edge of the city; Tommy Thompson Park; Toronto Islands; and, perhaps best of all, the inspired concept of Zooski, out at the stunning Metro Toronto Zoo, where one can ski past lions, leopards, and other furry friends. Check the yellow pages for ski equipment rentals; there are many places. Only Zooski charges a fee; all other places are free.

Downhill Although there are a few places where one can get a taste of this sport within Metro Toronto, such as **Earl Bales Park,** on Bathurst Street, just south of Sheppard Avenue, and **Centennial Park Ski Hill,** in Etobicoke (tel. 416/394–8754), the *best* alpine hills are a good 30–60 minutes north of the city. These include **Blue Mountain Resorts** (tel. 416/869–3799) in Collingwood, the **Caledon Ski Club** (tel. 416/453–7404) in Caledon, **Glen Eden Ski Area** (tel. 416/878–5011) in Milton, **Hidden Valley** (tel. 705/789–2301) in Huntsville, **Hockley Valley Resort** (tel. 519/942–0754) in Orangeville, **Horseshoe Valley** (tel. 705/835–2790) in Barrie, and **Snow Valley Ski Resort,** just outside Barrie (tel. 416/283–2439). Call 416/963–2992 for daily reports on lifts and surface conditions.

Sleigh Riding and Tobogganing **Black Creek Pioneer Village** (tel. 416/661–6610 or 416/661–6600), north of 401 along Highway 400, at Steeles Avenue, is open winter weekends 10–4 for skating, tobogganing, and horse-drawn sleigh rides. The best parks for tobogganing include **High Park,** in the west end, and our favorite, **Winston Churchill Park,** at Spadina and St. Clair avenues, just two blocks from Casa Loma. It is sheer terror.

Tennis The city provides dozens of courts, all free, and many of them floodlighted. Parks with courts open from 7 AM to 11 PM, in season, include the famous High Park in the west end; Stanley Park, on King Street West, three blocks west of Bathurst Street; and Eglinton Park, on Eglinton Avenue West, just east of Avenue Road. Call the **Ontario Tennis Association** (tel. 416/495–4215).

Spectator Sports

Auto Racing For the past several years, the **Molson Indy** (tel. 416/595–5445) has been roaring around the Canadian National Exhibition grounds, including the major thoroughfare of Lakeshore Boulevard, for three days in mid-July. You'll pay more than $85 for a three-day "red" reserved seat, but general admission for the qualification rounds, the practice rounds, and the Indy itself can be as cheap as $10–$20, depending upon the day.

Less than a half-hour drive away is the **Cayuga International Speedway** (tel. 416/765–4461), where international stock-car races are held from May through September.

Baseball The **Toronto Blue Jays,** whose home is the SkyDome, have developed into one of baseball's most dynamic teams. The Jays have the most costly tickets in the major leagues, ranging from rotten $4 seats up to $13.50 and $17.50 seats. And they usually sell out every single home game, so plan way ahead of your Toronto visit. We hate to give the greedy little capitalists the publicity, but there are nearly always dozens of scalpers hawking tickets just outside the SkyDome to that day's game. *A hot tip:* Arrive a bit late, in the second or third inning or so, and they will often unload their tickets at a fraction of what they asked a half hour earlier. *For ticket information, tel. 416/341–1111; to charge tickets, tel. 416/595–1362.*

Canoeing and Rowing The world's largest **canoeing and rowing regatta** is held every July 1, as it has been for more than a century, on Toronto Island's Long Pond. *Canoe Ontario, tel. 416/495–4180.*

Football Although the Canadian Football League has been teetering on the brink of dissolution, the **Toronto Argonauts** have, in recent years, developed into annual contenders. Americans might find the three downs and 110-yard field to be rather quaint, but the game is much like their own. Since the Argos were bought in 1991, by a consortium (including Canadian hockey star Wayne Gretzky and Canadian comic actor John Candy), the team has gone from strength to strength. *Tel. 416/595–1131 for tickets and information.*

Golf The permanent site of the **Canadian Open** golf championship is Glen Abbey, a course designed by Jack Nicklaus. This tournament is one of golf's Big Five and is always played in late summer. *Less than a 45-min drive west, along the Queen Elizabeth Way (QEW). Tel. 416/844–1800.*

Hockey The **Toronto Maple Leafs** play 40 home games each season (Oct.–Apr.), usually on Wednesday and Saturday nights, in the big, ugly Maple Leaf Gardens. There are always tickets available at each game—at least from scalpers in front of the stadium on Carlton Street, a half-block east of the corner of Yonge and College streets. Call the office (tel. 416/977–1641) at 9 AM sharp on the day of the game you wish to see.

Horse Racing
Harness Racing

The **Greenwood** track, built in 1874, is where the best trotters and pacers do their stuff at three annual meetings. *Tel. 416/ 675–6110. Spring gathering runs Jan.–mid-Mar.; summer meeting, late May–Sept.; the brief winter meeting, the last two weeks in Dec.*

Thoroughbred Racing

There are four major racetracks handled by the Ontario Jockey Club (tel. 416/675–6110).

Greenwood Race Track is one of the premier harness tracks in North America and is the home of many of Canada's greatest trotting and pacing events, including the North American Cup. It is located in the city's east end, a 10-minute streetcar ride from downtown, at Woodbine Avenue and Queen Street East, near the lakeshore. *Tel. 416/698–3131. Winter meeting runs late Oct.–early Dec.; spring meeting runs mid-Mar.–late Apr.*

Woodbine Race Track is the showplace of Thoroughbred racing in Canada. *Located 30-min northeast of downtown Toronto, not far from the airport, at Hwy. 27 and Rexdale Blvd.; tel. 416/ 675–6110. Horses run late Apr.–late Oct.*

Mohawk is in the heart of Ontario's Standardbred breeding country, and it features a glass-enclosed, climate-controlled grandstand and other attractive facilities. *A 30-min drive west of Toronto, along Hwy. 401, past the town of Milton; tel. 416/ 854–2255.*

Fort Erie, in the Niagara tourist region, is one of the most picturesque racetracks in the world, with willows, manicured hedges, and flower-bordered infield lakes. It has racing on the dirt as well as on grass, with the year's highlight being the Prince of Wales Stakes, the second jewel in Canada's Triple Crown of Racing. *Tel. 416/871–3200 from Toronto, 716/856– 0293 from Buffalo.*

Royal Horse Show

This highlight of Canada's equestrian season is part of the Royal Winter Fair each November. *The CNE grounds, Dufferin St., by the waterfront. Tel. 416/393–6400.*

Soccer

Although Toronto keeps getting and losing and getting a professional soccer team, one can catch this exciting sport, as well as collegiate football, in the very handy **Varsity Stadium.** *Bloor St. W at Bedford, a block west of the Royal Ontario Museum and University Ave. Tel. 416/979–2186.*

Dining

by Joanne Kates

Restaurant critic for the Toronto Globe and Mail, *Joanne Kates is the author of four books, including her own cookbook and a Toronto restaurant guide.*

A decade ago visitors to Toronto enjoyed a varied mix of ethnic restaurants, but good food could not be found in the middle ground of gastronomy—between the Italian sandwiches and the Dover sole. Today, Toronto is a city of bistros.

The "bistroization" of Toronto is due in part to a new generation of chefs, the first wave of young people who are just now fanning out across the city, opening neighborhood restaurants that are a little cheaper, slightly less ambitious, and thus more accessible than those of their teachers.

What the bistros serve is another matter. That old tired imitation Continental menu, which Toronto's upper crust dined out on since before the Beatles, is finally dead. We are no longer stuck eating less than perfect imitations of what they do in Paris and Rome. The new bistros are eclectic, as likely to borrow from Bangkok as they are from Los Angeles. Furthermore, their clever mentors have taught the new generation of young chefs to do things that have heretofore been forbidden in kitchens—think for themselves, create dishes based on what dazzles them in the morning market, and use local ingredients and spontaneity of approach.

Highly recommended restaurants in each category are indicated with a star ★.

Category	Cost*
Very Expensive	over $40
Expensive	$30–$40
Moderate	$20–$30
Inexpensive	under $20

per person without tax, tip, or drinks

Bistros

Expensive
★ **Brownes Bistro.** In one night, you can count a dozen mink coats. Full-length dark ranch. What does a person who spends $17,000 on a coat want in a restaurant? Apparently she wants an impeccable bistro that avoids the tarted-up Paris look. Everything at Brownes is breathtakingly simple, from the white paper on the tables to the small black and white ceramic tiles. The monochromatic room is colored only by dark wood paneling and one fuchsia azalea at the bar. Lack of pretension is elevated to an art. Brownes's pizza may be the best in Toronto. The *gnocchi* are unexceptional. The bouillabaisse has perfect, sweet little fresh scallops, but a blandness of broth. There are seven main courses, and three of them are lamb. Brownes gives full glory to lamb's heretofore neglected parts, such as lamb shanks (braised till they soften like butter and served in their own heartwarming broth, slightly thickened, with fennel, potatoes, and carrots). A lemon curd and a darkly dense chocolate cake, served with crème fraîche and chocolate sauce, are both very fine. The price of under $70 for two, with wine—a real bargain—makes Brownes the hottest show in town. *4 Woodlawn Ave. E, tel. 416/924–8132. Reservations advised. Dress: casual. AE, DC, MC, V. Closed Sun. lunch.*

Moderate
★ **Avocado Club.** This sun-splashed fun spot serves casual food that is also of the highest quality. The Avocado Club is lighthearted from the minute you walk through the door. Bright and sassy colors are everywhere. The devil's avocado, the restaurant's most popular starter, is warmed avocado with scallops and shrimps in a black bean chili sauce with Japanese cooking sake. Other appetizers refer, but always with chef Bob Bermann's light touch, to Thailand, Vietnam, and India, such as satay skewers, sweet/hot curried mussel salad. These days this type of cooking is as common as mosquitoes in a swamp, but rarely are so many culinary influences collected with such a gentle touch. *165 John St., tel. 416/598–4656. Reservations advised. Dress: casual. AE, MC, V. Closed Sat. lunch, Sun.*

Avocado Club, **16**
BamBoo, **12**
Brownes Bistro, **3**
Camarra's, **1**
Centro, **2**
China Blues, **19**
Grano, **5**
Jerusalem, **6**
Kensington
Kitchen, **10**
La Fenice, **17**
Le Bistingo, **13**
L'Express Café, **14**
New World, **24**
North 44, **4**
Pearl Court, **20**
Renaissance Cafe, **8**
Rivoli, **11**
Sante Fe
Bar and Grill, **15**
Southern Accent, **7**
Splendido, **9**
Studio Café, **23**
Thai Magic, **25**
The Vegetarian
Restaurant, **22**
Young Lok, **18**
Young Thailand, **21**

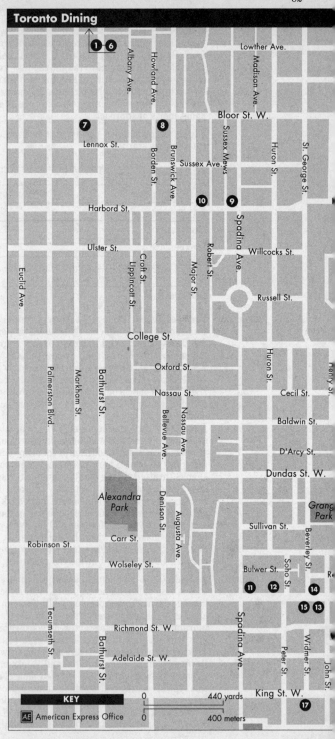

Toronto Dining

KEY

AE American Express Office

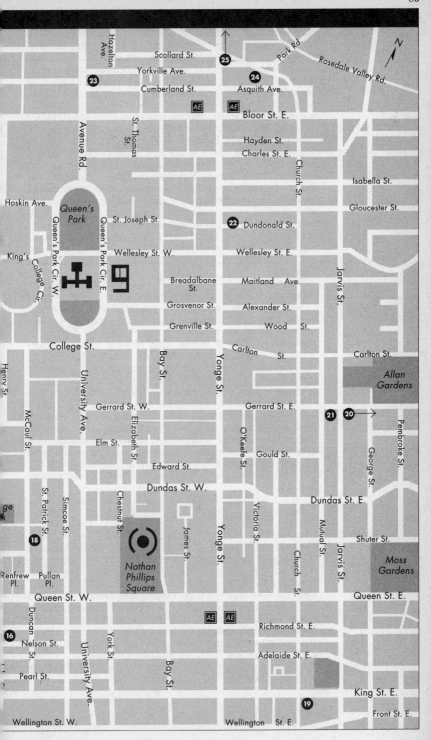

★ **BamBoo.** Inside a funky little inner courtyard decorated by a bohemian hand—fishnets on the walls, a stand of Muskoka bamboo, fading signs, all bordered by a thatched roof, à la South Pacific—is a relentlessly low-tech club-cum-restaurant that rebukes glitz-crazed Toronto with a smile up its sleeve. More and more ordinary people are going to the BamBoo for one purpose only: to eat food that jumps up joyously on the tongue. You can eat in the club area (240 seats, barnlike but warm) or in the small, funky dining room off to the right. On weekends guests line up for both the food and the live reggae, African, funk, and Latin music, which starts at 10 PM (*see* Nightlife, below). Much of the food is spicy. The callaloo, a creamed spinach and coconut soup, is the very weapon that blocked sinuses require. BamBoo's single most popular dish, Thai spicy noodles, comes in three modes—mild, medium, and wow! Mild is a superlative ungreasy wok-fry of rice noodles with peanuts, bean sprouts, chicken, shrimp, tofu, egg, Vietnamese fish sauce, chilies, sugar, garlic, and fresh lime juice. *312 Queen St. W, tel. 416/593–5771. No reservations. Dress: casual. AE, MC, V. Closed Sun.*

Brunch

Moderate **Kensington Kitchen.** Its clientele is the self-consciously unchic
★ University of Toronto people who live in the area and appreciate the ask-nothing ambience. The reigning sensibility belongs to Said Mukhayesh, who leans heavily toward the healthy, so his interpretation of Middle East cooking includes wholewheat pita; and if there's rice, it's brown. But none of this prevents Mukhayesh from serving wickedly wonderful spinach-and-cheese ravioli in a dense cream sauce. Ingredients are fresh and always prepared with affection and care. Where else do you get velvety *baba ghannoush, lubya* (green beans in a thick sauce of cinnamon and cardamom), divinely garlicky fried eggplant, and assertive cream soups? The tabbouleh (cracked wheat salad with parsley, tomato, and cucumber) is delicate, and the falafel in pita is a class act. Two people could lunch splendidly for $10. *124 Harbord St., south of Bloor St., tel. 416/961–3404. Reservations not necessary. Dress: casual. MC, V.*

Cafés

Inexpensive **L'Express Café.** Just across from the charming Parrot bistro on Queen Street West is a café that since the fall of 1987 has been serving good casual food with some dispatch. For under $6, they take the ordinary (chicken salad, ham and cheese) and anoint it with goat cheese or roasted red peppers in oil, laid lovingly between slices of impeccable Italian bread. The pizzas and savory tarts are enough to justify its existence. (The former is simple and robust; the latter, a texture of gossamer, thanks to the 35% cream.) The leek and *chèvre* tart with a touch of curry is one of the most inventive dishes. *254 Queen St. W, in walking distance of New City Hall; tel. 416/596–0205. No reservations. Dress: informal. V, for orders over $10. Open for brunch only on Sun.*

Cajun

Moderate **Southern Accent.** When these cooks blacken something, it comes out spiced and seared, melting in the middle and with a sensual surrender ensured by lemony beurre blanc on top. The appetizers are dazzling—light but tasty daily soups, often sweet and hot-and-sour. There are crunchy hush puppies (deep-fried corn fritters), and lovely greens with toasted pecans and citrus-scented vinaigrette. The gumbo, that Cajun classic based on a dark roux, is a dream from the bayou—highly flavored pork sausage (called *andouille*) and other meats in a strong broth based on roux with okra, and topped with a snowy hill of rice. Jambalaya, the major staple of Louisiana cooking, is rice-based with andouille, smoked ham, beef, chicken, bacon, vegetables, and shrimp, in Cajun spices. Southern Accent does it proud. *595 Markham St., tel. 416/536–3211. Dress: casual. Reservations advised. AE, DC, MC, V. Closed lunch.*

Chinese

Moderate **New World.** There is probably very little that could induce you
★ to penetrate the wilds of Scarborough on a wintry night, but this place can. Again and again and again. Do not miss the New World's *shui kow* soup—a sea of fine stock afloat with freshly made dumplings of chopped shrimp, Chinese mushrooms, and barbecued pork—and the fresh abalone that comes in its shell accompanied by one pristine broccoli floret in a translucent sauce made from beef stock reduced with oyster sauce. It's not on the menu, but the password is "Kam Wong said we could have it." New World is frankly Cantonese. There is a lick and a promise in the direction of Szechuan, but the cook's heart is on the sea. Big, fat, indelicate West Coast oysters come properly (barely) cooked in their own shells, dressed up with black beans, fresh coriander, and chives. Chicken cubes and scallops in phoenix nest are not to be missed. And I have never tasted fish so fresh in hot pots, nor eaten a hot pot crowned with soft-shell crab and oyster. No reservations are taken for the hot-pot tables, so go early. This place is a treasure. *3600 Victoria Park Ave., tel. 416/498–1818. Reservations advised on weekends. Dress: casual. AE, MC, V.*

Young Lok. Upwardly mobile and still delicious, this is a handsome restaurant in the very attractive Village by the Grange. The menu is biblical in scope, ranging from tired old Cantonese clichés to the fiery stars of the Szechuan kitchen. The clear soups are great; the panfried pancakes with scallions are a bargain appetizer and wonderful: cheap, greasy, and oniony. The main courses are almost all terrific: Sautéed shrimp with ginger and scallion is crunchy on the outside, sweetly juicy on the inside. Fresh lobster in black bean sauce is a perfect juxtaposition of sweet flesh and salty beans. Vegetarians' hodgepodge, a Young Lok classic, has a variety of crunchy vegetables. Mandarin crispy duck is for all unrepentant grease lovers. *122 St. Patrick St., at Dundas St., just south of the Art Gallery; tel. 416/593–9819. Reservations advised. Dress: casual. AE, MC, V. Dim sum weekends 10:30 AM–3 PM. Summer outdoor dining.*

Inexpensive **Pearl Court.** In 1991 Pearl Court made a lot of Sinophiles happy:
★ It moved from cramped and dingy quarters to a two-story postmodern dusty-rose and pale-green Chinese heaven. And the quality of the food suffered not a whit. The lobsters in gin-

ger and green onion are still seductive, and the scallops in black bean sauce are fat and fresh. There are also barely cooked, fat, fresh oysters sizzling on a hot iron plate with black pepper and green onion. Or fresh kiwi clams, each one steamed with a half-teaspoon of minced garlic. Garlic is a central theme here. So is fresh coriander. Lemon grass accents the oxtail in a fine citrusy stew pot. Chicken in paper is a platter of little paper packets, each holding a little morsel of pink tender chicken steamed in soy with five-spice powder. Skip the soups, which are bland, and consider the oysters. *663 Gerrard St. E, tel. 416/463–8773. Dress: casual. V.*

French

Expensive–Moderate
★
Le Bistingo. Certain gifts from chef Claude Bouillet's kitchen are among the finest flavors Toronto can offer: His open ravioli filled with shrimp and scallops are astonishing—toothsome pasta sheets laid over and under with soft, sweet seafood, all bathed in the lightest of *blancs* thinned with fish stock. The house signature appetizer, duck liver sautéed until just pink and soft and napped in a very tart raisin sauce, is fabulous. Among main courses, the fish dishes shine. A perfectly cooked fat red snapper sits on a wondrously astringent bed of stewed endive, surrounded by beurre blanc cleverly thinned with vermouth. Those in the know order a hot dessert with dinner, and are thus seduced by fresh-from-the-oven buttery puff pastry cradling caramelized apples, then bathed in a foam of Calvados sabayon. As if that were not enough, there are sauternes by the glass (or real champagne) to wash it all down. *349 Queen St. W, tel. 416/598–3490. Reservations required. Dress: casual. AE, DC, MC. V.*

Italian

Expensive
★
Centro. Franco Prevedello spent blood, sweat, and $2 million on dreamlike art deco lighting, etched glass, 18-foot ceilings with fat white columns, oxblood leather armchairs, Rosenthal china worth $45 a plate, and the most exciting Italian wine cellar in Toronto. The food can be heavy and overcomplicated—*agnolotti* with too much cream; overcooked poached salmon—but every day it moves closer to inspired Italian country style, with such specialties as poached skate in a mustardy coriander vinaigrette, and a fat, juicy roasted capon breast garnished with fresh pecans and lemon-pepper garlic mayonnaise. *2472 Yonge St., tel. 416/483–2211. Reservations advised. Dress: casual. AE, DC, MC, V. Closed lunch, Sun.*

★
La Fenice. This is the most authentic Italian restaurant in Toronto. Luigi Orgera is a ballerina in the kitchen, the Nureyev of the grill. Who else in Toronto has fresh porcini in October? Who else grates heavenly slivers of fresh white truffle on pasta? The antipasto trolley is more Rome than Toronto: mint-scented grilled eggplant; roasted zucchini; tangy salad of shrimps and squid; roasted sweet red peppers anointed in extra-virgin olive oil; and more. His *risotto al mare* is a tiny perfect stew of clams and mussels; the spaghetti is tossed with sweet chunks of sun-dried tomatoes, southern Italy incarnate. In fish, one can expect red and white snapper, yellowtail, and porgy, all as fresh as fish can be in this city. In 1990 La Fenice added a basement pasta bar. It's small and noisy and the chairs are uncomfortable, but for an inexpensive version of the Orgera alchemy, it's

worth it. *319 King St. W, near John St.; tel. 416/585–2377. Reservations required. Dress: casual. AE, DC, MC, V. Closed Sat. lunch, Sun.*

★ **Splendido.** Thanks to lighting as fun sculpture, glorious huge painted flowers, and a kitchen full of chefs in painters' hats, all behind a glass wall splashed with colors, Splendido is sophisticated fun. It is Toronto's answer to the Cal/Ital aesthetic: Homemade lamb sausage with silken polenta and a fresh rosemary sauce. Perfectly cooked juicy quails with pasta in tomato sauce. Competent pizzas with the usual new-age toppings. Nice light gnocchi. Rich strong soups with nary a hint of powdered base. The wood-roasted chicken on sourdough bread salad, Italian-style, via Zuni in San Francisco, is wondrously crisp. Rabbit is served in classic Italian style, with creamy porcini fettuccine, kale, and rapini. Avoid the nouvelle items: They sink like stones. Splendido is so fashionable and pretty that the true nature and strength of the food are obscured; it's the ultimate trattoria. *88 Harbord St., tel. 416/929–7788. Reservations advised. Dress: casual but chic. AE, MC, V. Closed lunch.*

Inexpensive **Camarra's.** Pizza heaven, in northwest Toronto. The dough has always been high and soft, with the delightful bite of a leavened dough. And on top are only good ingredients—real Italian plum tomatoes, not the canned tomato sauce of too many Toronto pizzerias. Very casual. *2899 Dufferin St., 1 mi south of Hwy. 401; tel. 416/789–3222. No reservations. Dress: casual. AE, MC, V. Closed Sun. lunch, Tues.*

Mexican

Moderate
★ **Santa Fe Bar & Grill.** You wouldn't be able to find Santa Fe if you didn't know it was there. The only clue to its presence is a big turquoise lizard on the roof. The interior has all the southwestern elements—adobe walls, cowhide tub chairs, wooden chairs painted with a Georgia O'Keeffe palette, southwestern rugs on the walls. The kitchen has troubled itself to stock the staples of casual Mexican cuisine: *chipotles* (smoked jalapeños), *jicamas* (sweet crunchy white tubers), blue corn chips, corn husks, flour tortillas, and black beans. It's fun food. Sip a blue margarita in a huge highball glass with a little pizza or a platter of blue and gold corn chips. The more proper Mexican cooking is done with the right chilies and generosity of spirit. *129 Peter St., tel. 416/345–9345. Reservations advised. Dress: casual. AE, DC, MC, V. Closed Sun.*

Nouvelle

Expensive **China Blues.** Chef Greg Couillard, Toronto's spicemeister, has moved on, but many of his signature dishes, with seasonings of India, Thailand, and the Caribbean, are still on the menu. You'll find tandoori salmon (baked with coconut, lime leaf, and coriander butter) and the popular "jump-up" soup, which is an artful balance on the knife's edge of sweet and hot, thanks to hot and sweet peppers, coconut, allspice, ginger, lime, and jerk chicken fragments. When you order salad, it's so long romaine and bibb, hello organic greens, Chinese vegetables, green mango, and passion fruit–honey vinaigrette. A number of the dishes are spicy, and you may not recognize some of the ingredients, but others are more conventional. This generally satisfying menu is a globe-trotter from Italy to the Far East. *125 King St. E, tel. 416/366–2556. Reservations required. Dress: informal. AE, MC, V. Closed Sat. lunch, Sun.*

★ **North 44.** Mark McEwan (formerly of Pronto) opened the most visually arresting dining room in Toronto in 1990. North 44, Toronto's longitude, is the restaurant's logo and an oft repeated visual refrain. Everywhere you look there is another design statement. The message is metallic and modern; even the washrooms have the designer touch. One of the five best cooks in Toronto, McEwan specializes in Southwest cuisine with a southeast Asian undertone, all afloat on a sea of beurre blanc and executed with finesse. McEwan dips fresh oysters in cornmeal, fries them crisp on the outside, melting on the inside, and sits them on a chili cream sauce. He pats together corn, potato and shrimp fragments into a pancake and fries it. Order the huge barely roasted scallops, and you get grilled bok choy and creamed peppers. The fried rock snapper comes with gingered plum tomatoes and a McEwan introduction—french-fried leeks, sophisticated kissin' cousin to onion rings. *2537 Yonge St., tel. 416/487–4897. Reservations advised. Dress: casual. AE, DC, MC, V. Closed lunch; brunch only Sun.*

Quick Meals

Moderate **Studio Café.** This is the coffee shop of the Four Seasons Hotel, but it's no ordinary coffee shop. The decor is eye-catchingly chic, with lots of chrome, designer furniture, and designer fabrics. There's art everywhere—paintings by Canadian artists and handmade glass beautifully displayed in illuminated showcases (the glass is for sale). The breakfast menu includes traditional fare as well as a Japanese breakfast of miso soup, grilled salmon, and rice. The lunch and dinner menu offers a wide selection, from pizzas and pastas to halibut burger and "crunchy whole quail," which tastes much better than it sounds. *21 Avenue Rd., just north of Bloor St., tel. 416/964–0411. Reservations not required. Jacket optional. AE, DC, MC, V.*

Inexpensive **Grano.** Franco Prevedello has served as godfather to a winner, helping a young couple, the Martellas, create a basic café—southern Italian style—the prettiest all-day café in Toronto. You order your meal at the bar, and Robert brings it. The soups and antipasti are dreams come true, the soups thick and strong, with fresh thyme and good stock. And some of the antipasti are as good as what you'd get in Bologna: Strips of zucchini are marinated with sweet oregano; a hint of caraway flavors the thin chewy strips of eggplant in oil. Grano's pizzas are so attractive because bread is the secret love at Grano (which means grain). All day the baker toils in the cellar under the café, and all day the breads come upstairs, fragrant and warm: The two most wonderful are the *foccaccia* and the oatmeal buttermilk bread. Avoid the steam-table stuff. *2035 Yonge St., below Eglinton Ave., tel. 416/440–1986. Dress: casual. MC, V. Closed Sun.*

★ **Jerusalem.** This is the ultimate family restaurant: The broadloom is dark red with a brown pattern, so accidents by children can go practically unnoticed. Service is fast. The bustle and noise are enough to camouflage the most unruly youngsters. And the food will not deliver a crisis to the taste buds. Jerusalem serves a rich variety of wonderful Middle Eastern foods—

the most tender falafel in town, rich fried tomatoes with garlic, *sam bousek* (a deep-fried dough packet of ground meat and pine nuts), very sweet charcoal-grilled shish kebab, and ungooey baklava. *955 Eglinton Ave. W, tel. 416/783-6494. Dress: casual. AE, MC, V.*

Thai

Moderate
★ **Thai Magic.** Consistency and competence are the bywords here; the food is neither greasy nor too sweet. But chiliphobes, beware: The divine Thai Magic mussels, steamed with curry sauce and unctuous coconut cream, are mouthburners, as is the otherwise lovely chicken coconut soup, Thailand's national soup, which is an amalgam of smooth (coconut) and sharp (kha, a gingerlike root). Barbecued foods, a piece of Thai magic served with a sweet/spicy peanut sauce, are short on chilies and long on charm. Even the satay is very good, as far as satay goes (which is not very far, considering the relative banality of meat on a stick). *1118 Yonge St., tel. 416/968-7366. Reservations advised on weekends. Dress: casual. AE, MC, V. Closed Sun. and for lunch.*

Inexpensive **Young Thailand.** This modest-looking restaurant in a slightly offbeat location is worth searching out. The dining room is open and airy, its plainness tempered with a few decorative touches to suggest Thai connections. Chef and owner Wandee Young, well known from her days at the Bamboo, here displays her skills at combining the herbs and flavors that are characteristically Thai. The food is fresh and varied and includes the popular *phad thai*, a noodle dish with shrimp, slivers of chicken, egg, bean sprouts, and a squeeze of lime. The delightful green mango salad has shrimp, chicken and red onion. Some of the dishes have a sweetness reminiscent of Cantonese food, and some can be searing, most notably the *tom yum goong* soup, which includes a few tiger shrimp, lemon grass, lime juice, mushrooms and some vicious red chilies. *111 Gerrard St. E, tel. 416/599-9099. Reservations recommended. Dress: informal. MC, V. Closed lunch Sat. and Sun.*

Vegetarian

Inexpensive **Renaissance Cafe.** A modest restaurant with a limited but cosmopolitan menu—the likes of ratatouille and curries. The daily buffet lunches are pleasant. *509 Bloor St. W, near Bathurst St.; tel. 416/968-6639. Dress: casual. Reservations advised. AE, DC, MC, V.*
The Vegetarian Restaurant. For the uninitiated, there are lovely soups and salads; for the adventuresome, soyburgers and tofu bourguignon. It's in a cheerfully renovated Victorian house, with cafeteria-style service. *4 Dundonald St., just east of Yonge St.; tel. 416/961-9522. Dress: casual. No reservations. DC, MC, V. Closed Sun. lunch.*

Lodging

Places to stay in this cosmopolitan city range, as one might expect, from luxurious hotels to budget motels to a handful of bed-and-breakfasts. Prices are cut nearly in half over weekends and during special times of the year (many Toronto hotels drop their rates a full 50% in January and February).

Accommodation Toronto (tel. 416/596–7117), a service of the Hotel Association of Toronto, is an excellent source of finding the room and price you want. Don't forget to ask about family deals and special packages. You might also try the **Metropolitan Bed & Breakfast** registry service (615 Mt. Pleasant Rd., Suite 269, Toronto M4S 3C5, tel. 416/964–2566, fax 416/537–0233).

Highly recommended properties in each category are indicated by a star ★.

Category	Cost*
Very Expensive	over $175
Expensive	$125–$175
Moderate	$70–$125
Inexpensive	under $70

All prices are for a standard double room, excluding optional service charge.

Very Expensive

★ **Four Seasons Toronto.** It's hard to imagine a lovelier or more exclusive hotel than the Four Seasons, which is usually rated among the top two dozen hotels in the world and one of the top three in North America. The location is ideal: on the edge of Yorkville, a few meters from the Royal Ontario Museum. The 380 units are tastefully appointed. Maids come twice a day, and there are comfortable bathrobes, oversize towels, fresh flowers, and a fine indoor/outdoor pool. Even the special family rates, however, will not drop the cost much below $200 a night. Yet during such slow months as January through March, sometimes into April, rooms on weekends have been offered for less than $150 per night (per person), and there is reason to believe that this tradition will continue in 1993. Its restaurants include the Studio Café, the Lobby Bar, La Serre, for dinner only, and the formal dining room, Truffles. *21 Avenue Rd., M5R 2G1, a block north of Bloor St.; tel. 416/964–0411 or 800/332–3442. AE, DC, MC, V.*

Harbour Castle Westin. This was a Hilton International hotel until 1987, when Westin and Hilton suddenly switched ownership of their major downtown Toronto hotels. A favorite with conventioneers, it's located just steps from Harbourfront and the Toronto Islands ferry. It's a bit inconvenient to the city's amenities except for those directly on the lakeshore, but it enjoys the best views of any hotel in the city. There's a shuttle bus service to downtown business and shopping, and the swimming pool, squash courts, and health club are among the best in town. Its 900 rooms are well appointed and tastefully modern, and the frequent family and weekend rates help bring its regular price down by as much as a third. Its Regatta restaurant is open all day, and the revolving Lighthouse restaurant, atop the 37th floor, is open for lunch and dinner. And what a view! *1 Harbour Sq., M5J 1A6, tel. 416/869–1600 or 800/228–3000. AE, DC, MC, V.*

Park Plaza Hotel. It may lack a pool, but it has one of the best locations in the city: a short distance from the Royal Ontario Museum, Queen's Park, and the Yorkville shopping area. The 350 units are well appointed in a plush, old-fashioned way, and they seem to coast by on their old-shoe familiarity to regular Toronto visitors who have been staying in them since the days when there was much less choice. The Roof Restaurant was once described by novelist Mordecai Richler as "the only civilized place in Toronto," and the Prince Arthur Room is open for good (business) breakfasts and lunch. Additions now include a 550-seat ballroom, a business center, a palm court, and a restaurant in the lobby, all designed by Zeidler Roberts Partnership, the same architects who were responsible for the Eaton Centre and Ontario Place. Through 1992, double rooms on weekends cost $99, including breakfast. *4 Avenue Rd., M5R 2E8, at the corner of Bloor St. W; tel. 416/924–5471 or 800/268–4927. AE, DC, MC, V.*

Expensive

★ **Best Western Chestnut Park Hotel.** One of the newest—and biggest—additions to Toronto's hotel scene, this handsome 16-floor hotel with glass-enclosed atrium lobby could hardly be more convenient: just steps behind City Hall and a few short blocks from Eaton Centre. The 522 guest rooms, which include 21 for the disabled, are all well decorated, with finely crafted furniture and desks; many have queen- and king-size beds. Recreational facilities include a large heated indoor pool, sauna, Jacuzzi, health club and gymnasium, and a children's creative center. Its restaurant, The Tapestry, is open for all meals. In addition, the Chestnut Park is now connected by a walkway from the mezzanine level to a Museum of Textiles, where some 15,000 textiles from around the world are displayed—the only museum of its kind in Canada. *108 Chestnut St., M5G 1R3, just north of Nathan Phillips Sq.; tel. 416/977–5000. AE, DC, MC, V.*

Novotel Toronto Centre. This moderately priced hotel—part of a popular French chain—opened in December 1987. There are 266 modest, modern rooms on nine floors in the heart of downtown, within walking distance of Harbourfront and the CN Tower. Facilities include an indoor pool, whirlpool, exercise room, and sauna, and its Café Nicole is open all day. *45 The Esplanade, M5E 1W2, tel. 416/367–8900 or 800/221–4542. AE, DC, MC, V.*

Sheraton Centre. This 1,430-room conventioneer's tower is across from the New City Hall, just a block from Eaton Centre. The below-ground level is part of Toronto's labyrinth of shop-lined corridors, and there are more shops on the ground and second floors. The restaurants' reach seems to exceed their grasp, but the Long Bar, overlooking Nathan Phillips Square, is a great place to meet friends for a drink. There's a nonsmoking floor and various special rates and packages. Facilities include a huge indoor/outdoor pool, hot tub, sauna, and workout room. As of 1992, $47 million had been spent on marvelous renovations, with completely refurbished guest rooms and bathrooms, six new floors in the exclusive Sheraton Towers, and 15 new, automated check-in and cashier stations. *123 Queen St. W, M5H 2M9, tel. 416/361–1000 or 800/325–3535. AE, DC, MC, V.*

Toronto Hilton International. This hotel, in the financial district, recently switched ownership with the Westin. The 600 rooms are newly renovated, and its nearness to New City Hall, major businesses, and more makes it a convenient base for most

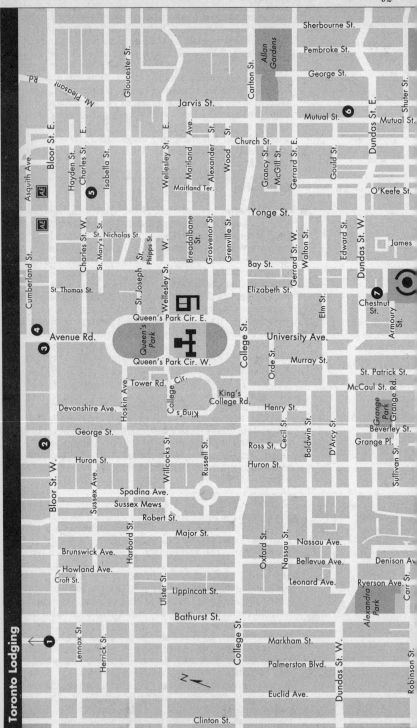

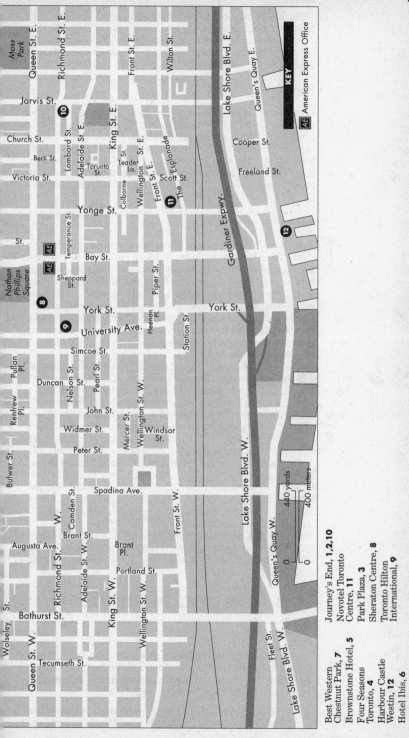

Best Western,
Chestnut Park, **7**
Brownstone Hotel, **5**
Four Seasons
Toronto, **4**
Harbour Castle
Westin, **12**
Hotel Ibis, **6**

Journey's End, **1**,**2**,**10**
Novotel Toronto
Centre, **11**
Park Plaza, **3**
Sheraton Centre, **8**
Toronto Hilton
International, **9**

KEY

AE American Express Office

visitors. The indoor/outdoor pool is modest, but the view of the city from the glass-enclosed elevators is a thrill. It has the Garden Court lobby restaurant and Trader Vic's, which is open for lunch and dinner. *145 Richmond St. W and University Ave., M5H 3M6, tel. 416/869–3456. AE, DC, MC, V.*

Moderate

Brownstone Hotel. This intimate hotel—110 units—has some of the charm of a private club. Though it's close to the center of town, you still get a quiet night's sleep. Ask for one of the recently renovated rooms. There were $90 double rooms in summer '92, and $70 ones in the winter. Children under 14 free. Some rates include Continental breakfast; the restaurant Pralines is open all day. *15 Charles St. E, M4Y 1S1, tel. 416/924–6631 or 800/263–8967. AE, DC, MC, V.*

Inexpensive

Hotel Ibis. This recent hotel belongs to one of Europe's leading chains. It is located just a few blocks from the New City Hall and Eaton Centre. As it proudly declares, "No bellhops, doormen, or concierges. No gushing fountains. And no room service with fancy silver trays." What it does have are 294 comfortable rooms with bare necessities (as well as 10 others specially designed and equipped for the disabled). There's no pool, but a lounge called The Bar and a restaurant called Le Restaurant take care of your generic needs. *240 Jarvis St., M5B 2B8, tel. 416/593–9400. AE, DC, MC, V.*

Journey's End Hotels. This is a rapidly growing chain that offers three convenient Toronto locations. A suite at Journey's End at the airport in the winter of '92 cost in the low $80s a night for as many as four. The two downtown locations actually charged less than $60 per night on weekends during the winter of 1992! These are an easy walk from many of the sights. Don't expect original antiques here, but all rooms are spotlessly clean and quite pleasant, and some locations have restaurants. No pools or saunas or convention rooms, but the prices are so low, how can you complain? *262 Carlingview Dr., M9W 5G1 near Hwy 427 (airport), 258 suites; 280 Bloor St. W. M5S 1V8, a few blocks west of Avenue/University, 214 rooms; 111 Lombard St., M5C 2T9 near Queen and Jarvis, 196 rooms; tel. 800/668–4200; in Toronto, 416/624–8200. AE, DC, MC, V.*

Toronto Bed & Breakfast. More than two dozen private homes are affiliated with this service, most of them scattered across Metro Toronto. Rooms cost as little as $50 a night and include breakfast. *Tel. 416/961–3676.*

The Arts and Nightlife

The Arts

Toronto is the capital of the lively arts in Canada. True, Winnipeg has a very fine ballet, and Montréal's orchestra is superb. But in nearly every aspect of music, opera, dance, and theater, Toronto is truly the New York City of the North.

The best places to get information on cultural happenings are in the Thursday editions of the *Toronto Star*, the Saturday *Globe and Mail*, the free weeklies *Now* and *eye*, and *Toronto Life*. For half-price tickets on the day of a performance, don't forget the **Five Star Tickets booth,** located in the Royal Ontario Museum lobby during the winter and, at other times, at the corner of Yonge and Dundas streets, outside the Eaton Centre. The museum booth is open daily 10–7, the Yonge and Dundas booth is open—in good weather—Monday–Saturday noon–7:30, and Sunday 11–3. Tickets are sold for cash only, all sales are final, and a small service charge is added to the price of each ticket. The booth outside the Eaton Centre also gives out piles of superb brochures and pamphlets on the city.

Concert Halls and Theaters   The **Roy Thomson Hall** (just below the CN Tower) has become since 1982 the most important concert hall in Toronto. It is the home today of the Toronto Symphony and the Toronto Mendelssohn Choir, one of the world's finest choral groups. It also hosts orchestras from around the world and popular entertainers from Liza Minnelli to Anne Murray. *60 Simcoe St., at the corner of King Street W, a block west of University Ave.; tel. 416/593–4828. Tickets $20–$60 (best rows H and J in the orchestra and row L upstairs). Rush seats are sold the day of a performance, two hours before show time. Tours of the stunning structure take place Mon.–Sat. 12:30 PM (cost: $3, but do call; it is subject to cancellation. Tel. 416/593–4822, ext. 363. On Wed. at 12:30 you can tour the impressive organ for $5.)*

Massey Hall has always been cramped and dingy, but its near-perfect acoustics and its handsome, U-shape tiers sloping down to the stage have made it a happy place to hear the Toronto Symphony, or almost anyone else in the world of music, for almost a century. The nearly 2,800 seats are not terribly comfortable, but it remains a venerable place to catch the greats and near-greats. *178 Victoria St. at Shuster, a few feet east of the Eaton Centre; tel. 416/593–4828. Best seats are rows G–M, center, and in the balcony, rows 32–50.*

The **O'Keefe Centre** has become the home of the Canadian Opera Company and the National Ballet of Canada. It is also home to visiting comedians, pre-Broadway musicals, rock stars, and almost anyone else who can fill it. When it was built in 1960, its 3,167 seats made it the largest concert hall on the continent. *1 Front St. E, a block east of Union Station; tel. 416/872–2262. Tickets $20–$50. Try for seats close to A47–48; avoid the very front rows, such as AA, BB, etc.*

About 50 yards east of the O'Keefe is the **St. Lawrence Centre for the Arts.** Since 1970, it has been presenting everything from live theater to string quartets and forums on city issues. The main hall, the luxuriously appointed **Bluma Appel Theatre,** hosts the often brilliant productions of the **Canadian Stage Company** and **Theater Plus.** Classical and contemporary plays are often on a level with the best of Broadway and London's West End. *Front St. at the corner of Scott St., tel. 416/366–7723. Tickets $20–$45. Try for rows E–N, seats 1–10.*

The other important theater in the city is the **Royal Alexandra,** which has been the place to be seen in Toronto since its opening in 1907. The plush red seats, gold brocade, and baroque swirls and curlicues all make theater-going a refined experience. It's astonishing to recall that all this magnificence was about to be torn down in the 1960s, but was rescued by none other than "Honest Ed" Mirvish of discount-store fame. He not only re-

stored the theater to its former glory but also made it profitable. *260 King St. W, tel. 416/872–3333. Tickets $35–$75 (more
for major musicals). Student tickets as low as $15. Avoid rows
A and B; try for rows C–L center. For musicals, try the first
rows of the first balcony.*

Classical Concerts **The Toronto Symphony,** now over 65 years old, is not about to
retire. Since 1922, with conductors of the quality of Seiji
Ozawa, Walter Susskind, Sir Thomas Beecham, and Andrew
Davis, it has achieved world acclaim. Its music director is
Maestro Gunther Herbig. When the TS is home, it presents
about three concerts weekly from September to May in Roy
Thomson Hall (*see* above) and a miniseason each summer at On-
tario Place. Tickets $16–$35.

The **Toronto Mendelssohn Choir** often guests with the Toronto
Symphony. This 180-singer group, going since 1894, has been
applauded worldwide, and its *Messiah* is handeled well every
Christmas (no, we couldn't resist that). *For program information, tel. 416/598–0422; for tickets, Roy Thomson Hall.*

Opera Since its founding in 1950, the **Canadian Opera Company** has
grown into the largest producer of opera in Canada. Each year,
at Toronto's O'Keefe Centre, more than 150,000 people attend
the season of seven operas, with such world-class performers as
Joan Sutherland, Grace Bumbry, Martina Arroyo, Marilyn
Horne, and Canada's own Louis Quilico and Maureen Forrest-
er. The COC also performs mini-operas in a tent during the
summer, at Harbourfront. *Tel. 416/363–8231 or 416/393–7469.*

Dance **National Ballet of Canada** made its official debut in 1951. In less
than four decades, the company has done some extraordinary
things, with such principal dancers as Karen Kain, Frank
Augustyn, Kevin Pugh, and Owen Montague all wowing the
Russians at the Moscow competitions. *Performances Nov.,
Feb., and May at the O'Keefe Centre (see above); in summer at
Ontario Pl. Office, tel. 416/362–1041, 416/872–1111 or 416/872–
2277. Tickets $15–$55.*

Toronto Dance Theatre, its roots in the Martha Graham tradi-
tion, tours Canada and has played major festivals in England,
Europe, and the United States. *Most performances are in the
Premiere Dance Theatre, at Harbourfront, 235 Queen's Quay
W; tel. 416/869–8444.*

Theater There are more than four dozen performing spaces in Toronto;
we will mention only a handful of the most prominent.

The **Young People's Theatre,** the only theater center in the
country devoted solely to children, does not condescend or com-
promise its dramatic integrity. *165 Front St. E, near Sherbourne, tel. 416/864–9732.*

The **Elgin** and **Winter Garden Theaters** are two recently renovated old vaudeville places, stacked upon each other (The
Elgin, downstairs, has about 1,500 seats; the Winter Garden is
some 500 seats smaller; both are stunningly attractive.) *189
Yonge St., just north of Queen, tel. 416/872–5555.*

Second City, just east of the heart of downtown, has been providing some of the best comedy in North America since its owner Andrew Alexander bought the rights to the name for one
dollar. Among those who have cut their teeth on the Toronto
stage are the late Gilda Radner, Dan Aykroyd, Martin Short,

Andrea Martin, Catherine O'Hara, and John Candy. Shows can be seen alone or in a dinner-theater package. *Old Firehall Theatre, 110 Lombard St., corner of Jarvis St., tel. 416/863–1111.*

Next to Second City, **Yuk-Yuk's Komedy Kabaret** has always been the major place for comedy in Toronto. This is where the zany comedian Howie Mandel and the inspired impressionist Jim Carrey got their starts, and where such comic luminaries as George Carlin, Rodney Dangerfield, Robin Williams, and Mort Sahl have presented their best routines. *1280 Bay St., just above Bloor St., 2335 Yonge St., just above Eglinton Ave. and 5165 Dixie, just above Eglinton; tel. 416/967–6425. Cover charge: $7 and up. Yonge St. location closed Sun.*

Mysteriously Yours . . . should be of special interest to murder-mystery buffs. On Thursday, Friday, and Saturday evenings, a "despicable crime" is perpetrated at the Royal York Hotel. The mystery begins to unravel during dinner (cocktails at 6:30) and is solved after dinner, by 10. The complete dinner and mystery costs $50–$60 per person, including tax and tip. Call Brian Caws at 416/486–7469 or 800/NOT–DEAD.

Film Every September since 1976, Toronto has been holding a world-class film festival, called—with no great modesty—**The Festival of Festivals** (tel. 416/967–7371). Whether retrospectives of the films of Marguerite Duras, Jean-Luc Godard, and Max Ophuls, or tributes to the careers of Martin Scorsese, Robert Duvall, and John Schlesinger, this is the time for lovers of film.

Toronto is one of the film capitals of the world, and you can often catch a movie here that is not showing anywhere else—or even available on video.

Carlton Cinemas, part of the Cineplex chain, shows rare, important films from around the world in nearly a dozen screening rooms. *20 Carlton St., just steps east of the College St. subway; tel. 416/296–FILM.*

Nightlife

Jazz Clubs **Bermuda Onion Restaurant and Jazz Club,** just southeast of the hot corner of Bloor and University, provides endless neon, aluminum tables, and some of the best jazz in Toronto. There's even a Sunday jazz brunch! *131 Bloor St. W, tel. 416/925–1470.*

A few blocks east of Eaton Centre is **George's Spaghetti House** (290 Dundas St. E, corner of Sherbourne St.; tel. 416/923–9887), the oldest jazz club in the city. The music starts at 8:30 PM, with the world-famous Moe Koffman (of "Swinging Shepherd Blues" fame) performing one week each month. (For Moe, and on weekends, you'll need reservations.) George's has a modest cover charge and a decent Italian menu. *Closed Sun.*

Chick 'n Deli has long been one of the great jazz places in Toronto. A casual atmosphere prevails, and the lack of dress code helps with the neighborhood-bar ambience. There's a dance floor and dark wood everywhere, giving it a publike feel. It's also famous for wings and live music; the former half-price, Mon.–Tues. until 9, the latter playing at 9 PM most nights, and 7:30 on Sundays. Check out the occasional jazz shows, and Sunday brunch—all you can eat for less than $10. *744 Mount Pleasant Rd., near Eglinton Ave.; tel. 416/489–3363 or 489–7931.*

Top O' The Senator, this city's first club exclusively for jazz, has the atmosphere of a between-the-wars lounge. With its long wooden bar and towering dark-blue ceilings, this is one fabulous place. *249 Victoria St., tel. 416/364–7517.*

Rock and Popular Music Most major international recording companies have offices in Toronto, so the city is a regular stop for top musical performers of today, whether Frank Sinatra, Billy Joel, Whitney Houston, Sting, Michael Jackson, or Bruce Springsteen. Tickets ($15–$40) can usually be booked through **Ticketmaster** (tel. 416/872–1111).

Major venues include the **SkyDome,** on Front Street, tel. 416/963–3513; **Maple Leaf Gardens,** 60 Carlton Street, a block east of Yonge Street and the College Street subway stop, tel. 416/977–1641; the **O'Keefe Centre,** Yonge and Front streets, tel. BASS, 416/872–2262; and **Exhibition Stadium,** at the CNE grounds, tel. 416/393–6000. **Ontario Place** (tel. 416/965–7711) has pop, rock, and jazz concerts all summer at a nominal cost. We say "nominal" because you may pay around $10 to see/hear a fabulous singer or group (or orchestra or ballet corps) that would cost you $25–$50 elsewhere. This is one of the loveliest and least expensive places for concerts in all of Toronto.

Kingswood Music Theatre, next to Canada's Wonderland, also has important rock and pop concerts during the warmer months. *Hwy. 400, 10 min north of Hwy. 401; tel. 416/832–8131. Admission usually less than $10 above the cost of Canada's Wonderland.*

Since May 1989, **Superstars Niteclub** has been packing 1,700 people nightly into its giant room. Monday through Wednesday, it has professional acts, on the line of The Fixx, Jerry Seinfeld, and the late Sam Kineson, with prices ranging $10–$25. Thursday to Saturday is for dancing, with a cover of about $9. Hamburgers, chicken fingers, etc., provide the fuel. Laws banning liquor from being served on Sunday have freed the owners to use the place for children's and teen's concerts, featuring rap groups. *6487 Dixie Rd., 1 mi north of Hwy 401; tel. 416/670–2211. Open Mon.–Sat. 7 PM–2 AM.*

A major showcase for more daring arts in Toronto has long been **The Rivoli,** along the Queen Street "mall." A place for new, local artists not yet established enough to have their own gallery showings, the back room functions as a club, with theater happenings, "new music" (progressive rock and jazz), comedy troupes with very funny improvisations twice a month, and more. *332 Queen St. W, just west of University Ave.; tel. 416/597–0794. No dress code. Cover charge: $5–$10. Closed Sun.*

Caribbean and More **BamBoo** is listed in our restaurant section because its Thai/Caribbean food is remarkably delicious and just as remarkably reasonably priced. But this crazy old building, a one-time commercial laundry hidden behind the popular Queen Street strip, is also the place to find everything from reggae to calypso, Caribbean to African, and even jazz. The sightlines can be terrible, it's no place for a quiet conversation, but it's wildly popular: great eating, and great music. *312 Queen St. W, tel. 416/593–5771.*

Rhythm and Blues The undisputed champion of R&B in Toronto is **Club Bluenote,** a few blocks north of the Yorkville area. It's quite unique, with many world-class musicians and singers frequenting it, and occasionally getting up and doing their stuff. A small dance floor, the age range is 25–50, and the clientele is upper-class. And this is no hit bar; people come here to listen to music in a serious way. When Whitney Houston, Sugar Ray Leonard, et al., are in town, this is where they go. *128 Pears Ave., tel. 416/924–8244. Usually closed Sun. Cover charge: $8–$10.*

Right next door is **Network,** an entertainment lounge specializing in name acts of the quality of The Stylistics, Junior Walker, and Goodman and Brown. It's a supper club and show, with the cover and buffet combined at a reasonable $20 or so. The only dress code is "No Jeans," and there is a dance floor. The clientele is urban professionals in their early thirties; the decor is modern—brass, black, polished oak. *138 Pears Ave., near Davenport Rd.; tel. 416/924–1768.*

Albert's Hall has been called one of the top 25 bars in all of North America, in spite of its shabby decor. It features top blues bands. The crowd is older and more laid-back than downstairs, in the Brunswick, but it's still noisy and friendly—and loud. *481 Bloor St. W, near Spadina Ave., tel. 416/964–2242. Cover charge on weekends; closed Sun.*

Dancing **Berlin** quickly became one of the most popular spots in Toronto, within a year of its opening in early 1987. There's no dress code, but people dress up for this upscale, European-style multilevel club. There is a Continental menu for dining and a seven-piece band for jazz, pop, and R&B. The crowd is 25–35 and very rich, and the club radiates a feeling of exclusivity. *2335 Yonge St., north of Eglinton Ave.; tel. 416/489–7777. Open Tues. and Thur. 6–2; Fri. and Sat. 6–3. Cover charge: $6–$12.*

DJs play '60s music (downstairs) and '90s music (upstairs) in a four-story century-old funhouse named **Big Bop.** Thursday nights are Ladies' Nights, with no cover for women. In rebellion against the New York School of Glitzy, there is no chrome or mirrors—just a deliberate effort to be campy, vibrant, and unpretentious. The clientele is 18–25. It's a true meat market, but it doesn't pretend to be otherwise. Capacity is 800, and jeans are de rigueur. Many international stars walk in, but the owner insists that it's no big deal. (No big deal? Jack Nicholson. William Hurt. Matt Dillon!) *651 Queen St. W, tel. 416/366–6699. Open weekends to 3 AM.*

In the heart of Yorkville is **The Copa,** which has to be seen to be believed. The former warehouse is gigantic, with a capacity of 1,100! The crowd is in the 20–25 range and on the prowl. There's a zillion-dollar light show, with lasers and video screens. Tina Turner played for its grand opening; B.B. King and Ray Parker, Jr., have also performed here. The music is Top-40; on Sunday nights, it gets funkier. *21 Scollard St., entrance off Yorkville Ave.; tel. 416/922–6500. Cover charge: $10.*

Heartbreak Hotel is all concrete and steel, and was known as the **Boom Boom Room,** one of Toronto's best rock-and-roll dance places, until the late 1980s. Here you can hear and dance to heavy metal or more trendy beats, with the worst sexism showing in the prices: "Guys, $5, Girls, $3." Ages range from 19 to 30, so beware. *650½ Queen St. W, 2 blocks west of Bathurst, tel. 416/368–6468. Open Wed.–Sat., 9 PM–2 AM.*

Back on Yorkville Avenue is **P.W.D. Dinkel's,** which has been attracting the trendies of the area for many years. The age range is 20–40, and regulars make up much of the crowd. The ratio of men to women is 50/50; the two stand-up bars are where the action is. A black and white dance floor has the usual mirrored ball and flashing disco lights nearby. Live bands play top-40–style, yet original, music. There's finger food and dinner at about $50 for two, with wine. *88 Yorkville Ave., tel. 416/923–9689. Open Mon.–Sun to 2 AM. Cover charge: about $9 on weekends.*

A bar/club called **StiLife** recently opened downtown and is very popular. It caters to an older (25–35) crowd and to rapidly aging 40-year-olds. The decor is metallic and modular, with all the furnishings custom-made. The art is aided by sophisticated lighting. No jeans or sneakers. A DJ provides dance music, and the clientele is Yorkville-ish, with many clothing designers, other restaurant owners, etc. Check out the bathrooms—you'll find out why. *217 Richmond St. W, tel. 416/593–6116. Closed Sun. Cover charge: $6–$15.*

Rockit has been described as "the mainstream dance crowd's terrestrial equivalent to rock-and-roll heaven." The pizza is dynamite, the wood-and-brass bar is gorgeous, and upstairs are the college kids in uniform (cool ties and designer jeans), dancing away to the Big Hits. *120 Church St., just east of Yonge Street, tel. 416/947–9555.*

Lounges Up on the 51st floor of the ManuLife Centre, **The Aquarius Lounge** is the highest piano lounge in the city. The busy time in the summer is Thursday–Saturday after 8:30 PM, but there's a high turnover, so the wait is never too long. In the winter, the lines begin as early as 8 PM. Its romantic atmosphere makes this a marvelous place for a date. No shorts, but jeans are allowed. *55 Bloor St. W, at Bay St.; tel. 416/967–5225.*

In the Brownstone Hotel is **Notes,** an intimate bar/restaurant with a grand piano and a grand bar around it. It's done up in pink and beige tones, with black-lacquer furniture and antiques. You'll find no windows here, and the lighting is dim, but it's a good, quiet place to get to know someone. Dinner for two runs about $40–$50, including wine (their fresh sole is fine). A fine pianist entertains Tuesday–Saturday. *15 Charles St. E, tel. 416/924–7381.*

In the classy Four Seasons Hotel is **La Serre,** which looks like a library in a mansion: plush and green, with lots of brass and dark wood. It has a stand-up piano bar and a pianist worth standing for. Drinks, coffees, and teas are all expensive, but what can you expect in one of the costliest hotels in the country? Weekdays attract a business crowd, weekends bring out the couples. *Avenue Rd. and Yorkville Ave., tel. 416/964–0411.*

The **Park Plaza Roof Lounge** has been used as a setting in the writings of such Canadian literary luminaries as Margaret Atwood and Mordecai Richler. The decor used to be plush, in an older European style, with chandelier, marble tables, and waiters in red jackets. It remains an important hangout for the upper-middle class, businesspeople, professional, and, *bien sur*, literary types. It was renovated in 1990, but it's still gorgeous and tasteful. *In the Park Plaza Hotel, Avenue Rd. and Bloor St.; tel. 416/924–5471.*

4 Montréal

by Patricia Lowe

Updated by Danny Kucharsky

"Plus ça change, plus c'est la même chose," like other travel clichés, no longer applies to Montréal, which marked its 350th anniversary last year. For years, as Québec's largest city and the world's third-largest French-speaking metropolis, Montréal clung to an international reputation attained in the heyday of former Mayor Jean Drapeau, who brought his beloved hometown the 1967 World's Fair (Expo '67), the Métro subway, its Underground City, and the 1976 Summer Olympics. During his nearly three decades in power, Drapeau's entrepreneurial spirit added pizzazz to this transportation and financial capital at the gateway to the St. Lawrence Seaway.

But with the arrival of a nationalist provincial government in 1976, the mayor and Montréal were forced to rest on their laurels as the province agonized over its place in Canada. Separation from the rest of the country was seriously considered. The provincial government passed Bill 101, a controversial language act (still in force) making French the official language of business and public communication. For the city it was a wrenching ideological change; the only difference that visitors saw was that English or bilingual billboards and public signs were replaced by French ones.

Nearly 60% of the province's population opted in 1980 to remain in the federal family, but a decade later, French-speaking Québeckers' (Québécois') old animosities regarding English Canada were rekindled when Prime Minister Mulroney attempted to unite all 10 provinces through a constitutional agreement called the Meech Lake accord. However, the legislatures of two provinces did not ratify the accord, thus setting off a constitutional debate that continues today.

The melding of old and new architecture that characterizes this city is no more apparent than in the flamboyant office tower of La Maison des Coopérants. Even though the design of this 35-story pink glass structure imitates the Gothic-style Christ Church Cathedral it overshadows, it was not what the earnest French missionaries who founded Montréal envisioned. What today is a metropolis of 2.9 million—some 20% of English mother tongue—began as 54 dedicated souls from France who landed on Montréal island in 1642 to convert the Indians to Christianity.

For nearly 200 years, city life was confined to a 95-acre walled community, today's Vieux-Montréal and a protected historic site. Ville-Marie became a fur-trading center, the chief embarkation point for the voyageurs setting off on discovery and trapping expeditions. This business quickly usurped religion as the settlement's raison d'être, along with its role as a major port at the confluence of the St. Lawrence and Ottawa rivers.

The Old Montréal of the French regime lasted until 1759, when during one of the battles of the Seven Years' War, British troops easily forced the poorly fortified and demoralized city to surrender. The Treaty of Paris ended the war in 1763, and Québec became one of Great Britain's most valuable colonies. British and Scottish settlers poured in to take advantage of Montréal's geography and economic potential. When it was incorporated as a city in 1832, it was a leading colonial capital of business, finance, and transportation.

Montréal is still Canada's transport hub: It is home to the national railway and airline, the largest private rail company (Canadian Pacific), the International Air Transport Association (IATA), and the United Nations' International Civil Aviation Organization (ICAO) on Sherbrooke.

Solidly established by the late-19th century, downtown today still reminds visitors of its grand old days, particularly along rue Sherbrooke, the lifeline of chic Montréal. The busy flower-lined stretch between rues Guy and University takes in the de la Montagne–Crescent–Bishop–Mackay sector, where sophis-ticated restaurants, cafés, and bars share canopied facades with haute-couture salons, antiques shops, and art galleries.

Rue Peel, between rue Sherbrooke and Place du Canada, rolls through the Montréal most tourists visit. The recently reno-vated Dominion Square Building is the art deco home of tour-ism offices and information bureaus. Bus tours, taxi guides, and *calèches* (horse-drawn carriages) all depart from some point around this public park.

To the east, rue St-Denis and the surrounding Latin Quarter attract Francophiles; a more ethnic flavor characterizes the Chinese, Greek, Portuguese, and other districts around Prince Arthur's pedestrian mall, boulevard St-Laurent, and avenue du Parc.

A bohemian atmosphere pervades rue Prince Arthur, blocked off to traffic between boulevard St-Laurent and Carré St-Lou-is. What the mall's many restaurants sometimes lack in quality they make up for in ethnic diversity—Chinese, Greek, Italian, Polish, Québecois, and Vietnamese—and price, especially at establishments where you supply the liquor (BYO). Some 12,000 Portuguese residents live in the area's St-Louis district, and their bright pastel houses and lush front gardens have con-tributed to the neighborhood's renaissance.

Early in this century, rue St-Denis cut through a bourgeois neighborhood of large, comfortable residences. After a period of decline, it revived in the early 1970s, and then boomed, largely as a result of the 1979 opening of Université du Québec's Montréal campus and the launch of the International Jazz Fes-tival in the summer of 1980. Rows of French and ethnic restau-rants, charming bistros, even hangouts for chess masters cater to Franco- and Anglo-academics, and stylish intellectuals prowl the Québec designer boutiques, antiques shops, and art galleries.

Activity reaches its peak during the 10 days in late June and early July, when some 500,000 jazz buffs descend upon the city to hear the likes of Dizzy Gillespie, Montréal-born Oscar Peter-son, and Pat Metheny. Theaters hosting the 1,000 or so per-formers range from sidewalk stages to Place des Arts, the main performing arts center in downtown Montréal.

The popularity of the jazz festival is rivaled only by August's World Film Festival, also featured near this area at Place des Arts and Cinéma Le Parisien on rue Ste-Catherine, among oth-er venues.

Place des Arts and the adjacent Complexe Desjardins consti-tute another intriguing hive of activity. Now joined by the new home of the Musée d'Art Contemporain, which opened in 1992, Place des Arts is really three separate halls built around a sweeping plaza overlooking rue Ste-Catherine.

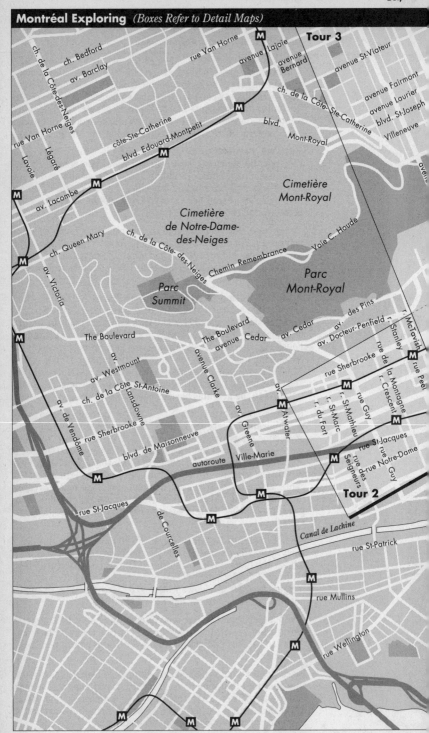

Montréal Exploring *(Boxes Refer to Detail Maps)*

Tour 3

Tour 2

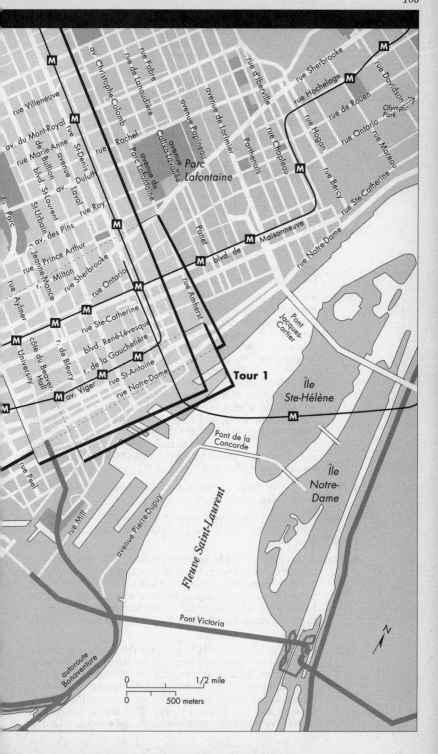

rue Villeneuve

av. du Mont-Royal

rue Marie-Anne

de Bullion

blvd. St-Laurent

St-Urbain

av. des Pins

r. Jeanne-Mance

rue Aylmer

University

côte du Beaver-Hall

r. de Bleury

av. Viger

rue Peel

rue Mill

rue Fabre

rue de Lanaudière

av. Christophe-Colomb

rue Rachel

avenue du Parc Lafontaine

avenue Calixa-Lavallée

avenue Papineau

avenue de Lorimier

rue d'Iberville

rue Sherbrooke

rue Hochelaga

rue Davidson

Olympic Park

Parc Lafontaine

Panet

Parthenais

rue Chapleau

rue Hogan

rue de Rouen

rue Bercy

rue Ontario

rue Moreau

rue Ste-Catherine

rue Roy

av. St-Denis

avenue Laval

avenue Duluth

Prince Arthur

Milton

rue Sherbrooke

r. Milton

rue Ontario

rue Amherst

blvd. de Maisonneuve

rue Notre-Dame

rue Ste-Catherine

blvd. René-Lévesque

r. de la Gauchetière

rue St-Antoine

rue Notre-Dame

Tour 1

Pont Jacques-Cartier

Île Ste-Hélène

Pont de la Concorde

Île Notre-Dame

avenue Pierre-Dupuy

Fleuve Saint-Laurent

Pont Victoria

autoroute Bonaventure

0   1/2 mile

0   500 meters

One often-overlooked sector of the city requires a Métro ride but is worth the fare for a varied tour of Olympic and de Maisonneuve parks, the Château Dufresne Decorative Arts Museum, the Botanical Garden, and the Biodome—all located at or near the corner of boulevard Pie-IX (Métro station of the same name) and rue Sherbrooke Est.

This triangle in the east end is distinguished by the flying-saucer design of the Olympic Stadium, completed by the world's "tallest inclined tower." The stadium's latest attraction is the funicular cable car that speeds sightseers to its observation deck for a spectacular view of the island of Montréal.

Essential Information

Arriving and Departing by Plane

Airports Montréal is served by two airports: **Dorval International,** 22½ kilometers (14 miles) west of the city, handles domestic and most U.S. flights; **Mirabel International,** 54½ kilometers (34 miles) northwest of the city, is a hub for the rest of the international trade.

Airlines From the United States: **Air Canada** (tel. 800/422–6232) has nonstop service from New York, Miami, and Tampa; nonstop from Boston via Air Canada's connector airline, Air Alliance; direct service is available from Chicago, Los Angeles, and San Francisco. **American Airlines** (tel. 800/433–7300) has nonstop service from Chicago and New York's La Guardia Airport with connections from the rest of the United States. **British Airways** (tel. 800/247–9297) has nonstop service from Detroit to Montréal. **Canadian Airlines International,** formerly CP Air (tel. 800/426–7000), has a nonstop charter from Miami and direct or connecting service from Hawaii, Los Angeles, and Pittsburgh. **Delta Air Lines** (tel. 800/221–1212) has nonstops from Boston; Hartford, Connecticut; and Miami and connecting service from most major U.S. cities. **US Air** (tel. 800/428–4322) has nonstop service from Buffalo and Syracuse, NY, and from Pittsburgh.

Flying Time From New York, 1½ hours; from Chicago, 2 hours; from Los Angeles, 6½ hours (with a connection).

Between the Airports and Center City Dorval Airport is about a 20- to 30-minute drive from downtown Montréal, and Mirabel International is about a 45-minute drive away.

By Taxi A taxi from Dorval to downtown will cost $23. The taxi rates from Mirabel to the center of Montréal are $50, and you can count on about the same cost for a taxi between the two airports. All taxi companies in Montréal must charge the same rates by law. It is best to have Canadian money with you, because the exchange rate for U.S. dollars is at the driver's discretion.

By Bus Aéroplus (tel. 514/476–1100) provides a much cheaper alternative into town from both airports. For $8.50 from Dorval or $11.75 from Mirabel, an Aéroplus van will take you into the city, with stops at Le Reine Elizabeth (Queen Elizabeth)—next to Gare Centrale—and the Voyageur bus station. Service between the two airports is $11.75. Aéroplus buses leave Dorval every 20 minutes on weekdays and every half hour on

weekends. From Mirabel, buses leave hourly or every half hour
between 2 PM and 8 PM.

Arriving and Departing by Train, Bus, and Car

By Train The Gare Centrale (Central Station), on rue de la Gauchetière
between rues University and Mansfield (behind Le Reine Elizabeth—Queen Elizabeth Hotel—on boulevard René-Lévesque
Ouest), is the rail terminus for all trains from the United States
and from other Canadian provinces. It is connected by underground passageway to the Métro's Bonaventure stop (schedule
information, tel. 514/871–1331).

Amtrak (tel. 800/USA–RAIL) reinstated the all-reserved overnight *Montrealer* in 1989, giving travelers in the Northeast the
option of day or night transportation. It has a dining car with
snacks, full dinners, and evening entertainment. Sleepers are
available and advised because the reclining seat-footrest combination is not conducive to a good night's sleep. Make sleeper
reservations well in advance, since they book early. The unre-
served *Adirondack* departs New York's Penn Station every
morning and takes 9½ hours to reach Montréal. It has a snack
car but no dinner service or sleepers. A round-trip ticket on either train is cheaper than two one-way fares, except during major holidays.

VIA Rail (tel. 800/361–3677 or 514/871–1331) connects Montréal by train with all the major cities of Canada, including Québec
City, Halifax, Ottawa, Toronto, Winnipeg, Calgary, and Vancouver.

By Bus **Greyhound** has coast-to-coast service and serves Montréal with
buses arriving from and departing for various cities in North
America. **Voyageur** and **Voyageur-Colonial** service primarily
destinations within Québec and Ontario. **Vermont Transit** (tel.
800/451–3292) also serves Montréal, by way of Boston, New
York, and other points in New England. Both lines use the
city's downtown bus terminal, Terminus Voyageur (tel. 514/
842–2281), which connects with the Berri-UQAM Métro station in downtown.

By Car Travelers can reach Montréal by a number of highways. It is
accessible from the rest of Canada via Trans-Canada Highway
401, which connects from the east and west via Highways 20
and 40. The New York State Thruway (I-87) becomes Highway
15 at the Canadian border, and then it's 47 kilometers (30 miles)
to the outskirts of Montréal. U.S. I-89 becomes two-lane Route
133 at the border, which is Highway 10 at St-Jean. From I-91
from Boston, you must take Highways 55 and 10 to reach Montréal. At the border you clear Canadian Customs, so be prepared with proof of citizenship and your vehicle's ownership
papers. On holidays and during the peak summer season, expect waits of a half hour or more at the major crossings.

Once you're in Québec, the road signs will be in French, but
they're designed so you shouldn't have much trouble under-
standing them. The speed limit is posted in kilometers; on highways the limit is 100 kph (about 62 mph). There are extremely
heavy penalties for driving while intoxicated, and drivers and
front-seat passengers must wear over-the-shoulder seat belts.
Gasoline is sold in liters (3.75 liters equal 1 U.S. gallon), and
lead-free is called *sans plomb*. If you're traveling in the depths

of winter, remember that your car may not start on extra-cold mornings unless it has been kept in a heated garage. All Montréal parking signs are in French, so brush up on your *gauche* (left) and *droit* (right).

You should be aware that Montréal police have a diligent tow-away and fine system for cars double-parked or stopped in no-stopping zones in downtown Montréal during rush hours and business hours. Penalties include a $35 ticket. If your car is towed away while illegally parked, it will cost an additional $35 to retrieve it. New York State residents should drive with extra care in Québec. Traffic violations in the province are now entered on their New York State driving record (and vice versa), since the passage of a traffic accord in July 1988.

Getting Around

By Métro and Bus   Armed with a few maps, you don't need a car to see Montréal; public transit will do quite well, thank you. The Métro is clean, quiet (it runs on rubber wheels), and relatively safe, and it's heated in winter and cooled in summer. Métro hours are from 5:30 AM to 12:30 AM (11 PM on the Blue Line), and the trains run as often as every three minutes on the most crowded lines. It's also connected to the 15 kilometers (9.3 miles) of the Underground City, so you may not need to go outside during bad weather. Each of the 65 Métro stops has been individually designed and decorated; Berri-UQAM has stained glass, and at Place d'Armes a small collection of archaeological artifacts is exhibited. The recently opened stations between Snowdon and Jean-Talon on the Blue Line are worth a visit, particularly Outremont, with its glass-block design. Each station connects with one or more bus routes, which cover the rest of the island. The STCUM (Société de Transport de la Communauté Urbaine de Montréal) administers both the Métro and the buses, so the same tickets and transfers are valid on either service. You should be able to go within a few blocks of anywhere in the city on one fare. The 1992–93 rates are: adults, $1.60; six tickets, $6.50; monthly pass, $41; children, 80¢; six tickets, $2.70; monthly pass, $15.50.

Free maps may be obtained at Métro ticket booths. Try to get the *Carte Réseau* (system map); it's the most complete. Transfers from Métro to buses are available from the dispenser just beyond the ticket booth inside the station. Bus-to-bus and bus-to-Métro transfers may be obtained from the bus driver. Information on reaching your destination can be had by dialing 514/AU-TOBUS (288–6287).

By Taxi   Taxis in Montréal all run on the same rate: $2.50 minimum and 96¢ a kilometer (at press time). They're usually prompt and reliable, although they may be hard to find on rainy nights after the Métro has closed. Each carries on its roof a white or orange plastic sign that is lit when available and off when occupied.

Important Addresses and Numbers

Tourist   **Greater Montreal Convention and Tourism Bureau,** 1555 rue
Information   Peel, Suite 600, Montréal, Québec H3A 1X6 (tel. 514/844–5400 or 800/363–7777) or **Tourisme-Québec** (tel. 514/873–2015).

Stop by the new downtown headquarters for Info-Touriste, the new home of Tourisme-Québec, on the north side of Square Dorchester. Run by the Greater Montreal Convention and

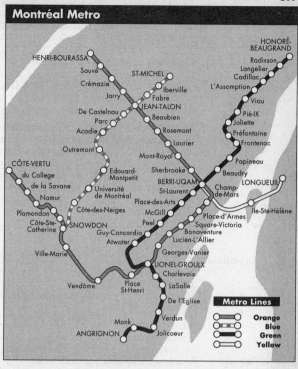

Montréal Metro

HENRI-BOURASSA

Sauvé
ST-MICHEL
Crémazie
Iberville
Jarry
Fabre
De Castelnau
JEAN-TALON
Parc
Beaubien
Acadie
Rosemont
Outremont
Laurier

CÔTE-VERTU
du College
de la Savane
Namur
Plamondon
Côte-Ste-
Catherine
SNOWDON

HONORÉ-
BEAUGRAND
Radisson
Langelier
Cadillac
L'Assomption
Viau
Pié-IX
Joliette
Préfontaine
Frontenac
Papineau
Beaudry
LONGUEUIL

Mont-Royal
Sherbrooke
BERRI-UQAM
St-Laurent
Place-des-Arts
McGill
Peel
Guy-Concordia
Atwater

Edouard-
Montpetit
Université
de Montréal
Côte-des-Neiges

Champ-
de-Mars
Place-d'Armes
Square-Victoria
Bonaventure
Lucien-L'Allier
Ile-Ste-Hélène

Georges-Vanier
LIONEL-GROULX
Charlevoix
LaSalle

Ville-Marie
Vendôme
Place
St-Henri
De l'Eglise
Verdun
Monk
Jolicoeur
ANGRIGNON

Metro Lines

Orange
Blue
Green
Yellow

Tourism Bureau, it is open daily, April–mid-May, 9–7; mid-May–Labor Day, 8–7; Labor Day to Canadian Thanksgiving (second Monday in October) 9–7; mid-October to Easter, 9–6; and Easter to June 9–6. Tel. 800/443–7000, eastern United States; 514/873–2015, Montréal; 800/361–5405, Québec Province. Info-Touriste also operates two smaller tourist information centers at 174 rue Notre-Dame Est in Vieux-Montréal (corner of Place Jacques-Cartier; September–May, weekdays 9–1 and 2:15–5, weekends 9–5; June–August, daily 9–6) and at Dorval Airport (September–May, daily 1–8; June–August, daily 10–8). Tel. 514/873–2015 for both locations.

Consulates **United States** (1155 St-Alexandre, Métro Place des Arts, tel. 514/398–9695).

United Kingdom (635 boul. René-Lévesque O, Métro Bonaventure, tel. 514/866–5863).

Emergencies Dialing 911 will put you through to the **police, fire,** and **ambulance.**

Doctors and The U.S. Consulate cannot recommend specific doctors and
Dentists dentists but does provide a list of various specialists in the Montréal area. Call in advance (tel. 514/398–9695) to make sure the consulate is open.

Dental clinic (tel. 514/342–4444) open 24 hours, Sun. emergency appointments only; **Montréal General Hospital** (tel. 514/937–6011); the **Québec Poison Control Centre** (800/463–5060); **Touring Club de Montréal-AAA, CAA, RAC** (514/861–7111).

Travel Agencies **American Express** (1141 boul. de Maisonneuve O, tel. 514/284–3300). **Thomas Cook** (1155 rue University, Suite 314, tel. 514/398–0555).

Opening and Closing Times

Banks are open weekdays from 10 to 4, with some banks open until 5 on weekdays and on Saturday morning. Many Montréal banks also have 24-hour banking-machine services.

Shops are open generally from 9 to 6 Monday to Wednesday, 9 to 9 Thursday and Friday, and 9 to 5 on Saturday. Some stores are open until 9 on Wednesday. You'll find many retail stores closed on Sunday and many specialty service shops closed on Monday, particularly in predominantly French neighborhoods. However, recent legislation allows stores in designated tourist zones, such as Vieux-Montréal, to remain open on Sunday.

Guided Tours

Orientation **Gray Line** (tel. 514/934–1222) has eight different tours of Montréal and its environs, including Île Ste-Hélène, the Laurentians, and the Underground City. It offers pickup service at the major hotels, or you may board the buses at Info-Touriste (1001 Square Dorchester).

Amphi Tour Ltée (tel. 514/386–1298) offers a unique tour of Vieux-Montréal (Old Montréal) and the Vieux-Port (Old Port) on both land and water in an amphibious bus. The one-hour tours run from May 1 to October 31.

Boat Tours **Montreal Harbour Cruises** (tel. 514/842–3871) offers 1½-hour tours of the harbor on the MV *Concordia*, a 27-meter (88-foot) ship with a restaurant, two decks, and room for 290 passengers. Boats leave as often as five times a day from Victoria Pier at the foot of rue Berri in the Vieux-Port next to Vieux-Montréal (Métro Champs de Mars).

Calèche Rides Open horse-drawn carriages—fleece-lined in winter—leave from rue Notre-Dame between rue Bonsecours and rue Gosford, Square Dorchester, Place d'Armes and rue de la Commune. An hour-long ride is $40 (tel. 514/653–0751).

Exploring Montréal

by Andrew Coe

Andrew Coe has written for the San Francisco Examiner *and other publications.*

When exploring Montréal, there's very little to remind you that it's an island. It lies in the St. Lawrence River roughly equidistant (256 kilometers, or 160 miles) from Lake Ontario and the point where the river widens into a bay. For its entire length, the St. Lawrence is flanked by flat, rich bottomland for 48 kilometers (30 miles) or more on each side. The only rise in the landscape is the 233-meter (764-foot) Mont Royal, which gave Montréal its name. The island itself is 51 kilometers (32 miles) long and 14 kilometers (9 miles) wide and is bounded on the north by the narrow Rivière des Prairies and on the south by the St. Lawrence. Aside from Mont Royal, the island is relatively flat, and because the majority of attractions are clustered around this hill, most tourists don't visit the rest of the island.

Head to the Mont Royal Belvedere (lookout) for a panoramic view of the city. You can drive most of the way, park, and walk ½ kilometer (¼ mile) or hike all the way up from avenues Côte-des-Neiges or Côte des Pins. If you look directly out—southeast—from the belvedere, at the foot of the hill will be the McGill University campus and, surrounding it, the skyscrapers of downtown Montréal. Just beyond, along the banks of the St. Lawrence, are the stone houses of Vieux-Montréal. Hugging the opposite banks are the Îles Ste-Hélène and Notre-Dame (St. Helen's and Notre-Dame islands), sites of La Ronde amusement park, the Biosphere, the Palais de la Civilisation exhibition center, acres of parkland, and the Lac de l'Île Notre-Dame public beach.

There are a host of attractions that you can see on all-day and half-day trips. The most popular are the amusement park complex on Île St-Hélène and the Olympic Stadium and its neighbor, the Botanical Garden. The 500 forested acres of Parc Mont-Royal are busy with joggers, strollers, and skaters all year. Beyond the city limits are the Eastern Townships and the Laurentians for day trips or weekends in the country.

Montréal is easy to explore. Street signs, subways, and bus lines are clearly marked. The city is divided by a grid of streets roughly aligned east–west and north–south. (This grid is tilted about 40 degrees off—to the left of—true north, so west is actually southwest and so on.) North–south street numbers begin at the Fleuve St-Laurent (St. Lawrence River) and increase as you head north. East–west street numbers begin at boulevard St-Laurent, which divides Montréal into east and west halves. The city is not so large that seasoned walkers can't see all the districts around the base of Mont Royal on foot.

Highlights for First-time Visitors

Botanical Garden/Olympic Park complex (*see* Parks and Gardens, below)
Historic Montréal, Tour 1: Vieux-Montréal
Mont Royal (*see* Parks and Gardens, below)
Rue St-Denis, Tour 3: St-Denis, Prince Arthur, and North
Rue Sherbrooke Ouest, Tour 2: Downtown Montréal

Tour 1: Vieux-Montréal (Old Montréal)

Numbers in the margin correspond to points of interest on the Tour 1: Vieux-Montréal map.

The Fleuve St-Laurent was the highway on which the first settlers arrived in 1642. Just past the island of Montréal are the Lachine Rapids, a series of violent falls over which the French colonists' boats could not safely travel. It was natural for them to build their houses just above the rapids, near the site of an old Iroquois settlement on the bank of the river nearest Mont Royal. In the mid-17th century Montréal consisted of a handful of wood houses clustered around a pair of stone buildings, the whole flimsily fortified by a wood stockade. For the next three centuries this district—bounded by rues McGill and Berri on the east and west, rue St-Antoine on the north, and the river to the south—was the financial and political heart of the city. Government buildings, the largest church, the stock exchange, the main market, and the port were there. The narrow but relatively straight streets were cobblestone and lined with solid, occasionally elegant houses, office buildings, and warehouses—also made of stone. Exiting the city meant using one of four gates through the thick stone wall that protected against Indians and marauding European powers. Montréal quickly grew past the bounds of its fortifications, however, and by World War I the center of the city had moved toward Mont Royal. The new heart of Montréal became Dominion Square (now Square Dorchester). For the next two decades Vieux-Montréal, as it became known, was gradually abandoned, the warehouses and offices emptied. In 1962 the city began studying ways to revitalize Vieux-Montréal, and a decade of renovations and restorations began.

Today, Vieux-Montréal is a center of cultural life and municipal government, if not of commerce and politics. Most of the summer activities revolve around Place Jacques-Cartier, which becomes a pedestrian mall with street performers and outdoor cafés spilling out of restaurants. This lovely square is a good place to view the fireworks festival, and it's adjacent to the Vieux-Port exhibition grounds and the docks for the harbor cruises. Classical music concerts are staged all year long at the Notre-Dame Basilica, which possesses one of the finest organs in North America, and plays are staged in English by the Centaur Theatre in the old stock-exchange building. This district has six museums devoted to history, religion, and decorative and fine arts.

To begin your tour of Vieux-Montréal, take the Métro to the Place d'Armes station, beneath the Palais des Congrès convention center, and walk 1½ blocks south on rue St-Urbain to **Place d'Armes.** In the 1600s, Place d'Armes was the site of battles with the Iroquois and later became the center of Montréal's "Upper Town." In the middle of the square is a statue of Paul de Chomedey, Sieur de Maisonneuve, the founder of Montréal. In 1644 he was wounded here in a battle with 200 Indians. Historians recently uncovered a network of tunnels beneath the square; they connected the various buildings, and one tunnel ran down to the river. These precursors of the Underground City protected the colonists from the extremes of winter weather and provided an escape route should the city be overrun. Unfortunately, the tunnels are too small and dangerous to visit. Calèches are available at the south end of the square.

❷ The north side of the square is dominated by the **Bank of Montréal,** an impressive building with Corinthian columns (remodeled by renowned architects McKim, Mead & White in 1905) that houses a small, interesting numismatics museum. *129 rue St-Jacques. Admission free. Open weekdays 10–4.*

The office building to the west of the square is the site of the old Café Dillon, a famous gourmet restaurant frequented by members of the fur traders' Beaver Club (*see* Dining, below). Two extremely important edifices form the south end of Place d'Armes: the Sulpician Seminary, the oldest building in Montréal, and the imposing Notre-Dame Basilica.

The first church called Notre-Dame was a bark-covered structure built within the fort in 1642, the year the first settlers arrived. Three times it was torn down and rebuilt, each time in a different spot, each time larger and more ornate. The enormous (3,800-seat) neo-Gothic **Notre-Dame Basilica,** which

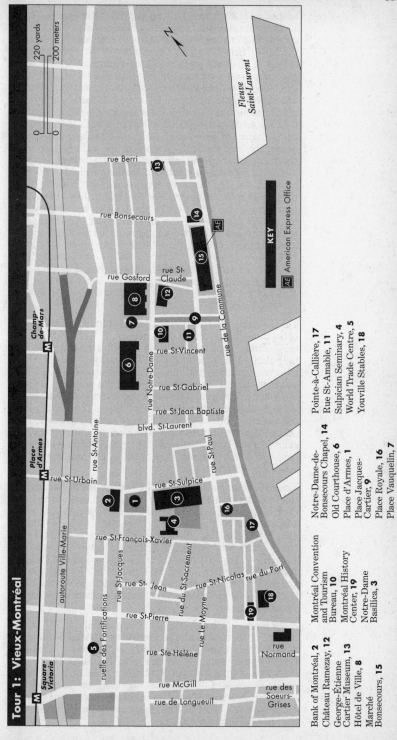

Tour 1: Vieux-Montréal

220 yards
200 meters

N

Fleuve Saint-Laurent

KEY

AE American Express Office

Square-Victoria

Place-d'Armes

Champ-de-Mars

rue Berri
rue Bonsecours
rue Gosford
rue St-Claude
rue de la Commune
rue St-Vincent
rue St-Gabriel
rue St-Jean Baptiste
blvd. St-Laurent
rue Notre-Dame
rue St-Antoine
rue St-Urbain
rue St-Sulpice
rue St-Paul
rue St-François-Xavier
autoroute Ville-Marie
rue St-Jacques
rue St- Jean
rue du St-Sacrement
rue St-Nicolas
rue du Port
rue St-Pierre
rue Le Moyne
ruelle des Fortifications
rue Ste-Hélène
rue Normand
rue McGill
rue de Longueuil
rue des Soeurs-Grises

Bank of Montréal, **2**
Château Ramezay, **12**
George-Étienne
Cartier Museum, **13**
Hôtel de Ville, **8**
Marché
Bonsecours, **15**

Montréal Convention
and Tourism
Bureau, **10**
Montréal History
Center, **19**
Notre-Dame
Basilica, **3**

Notre-Dame-de-
Bonsecours Chapel, **14**
Old Courthouse, **6**
Place d'Armes, **1**
Place Jacques-
Cartier, **9**
Place Royale, **16**
Place Vauquelin, **7**

Pointe-à-Callière, **17**
Rue St-Amable, **11**
Sulpician Seminary, **4**
World Trade Centre, **5**
Youville Stables, **18**

opened in 1829, is the most recent. The twin towers, named Temperance and Perseverance, are 227 meters (69 feet) high, and the western one holds one of North America's largest bells, the 12-ton Gros Bourdon. The interior of the church was designed in medieval style by Victor Bourgeau, with stained-glass windows, a stunning blue vault ceiling with gold stars, and pine and walnut wood carving in traditional Québec style. The church has many unique features: It is rectangular rather than cruciform in shape; it faces south rather than east; the floor slopes down 4 meters (1¼ feet) from back to front; and it has twin rows of balconies on each side. The Casavants, a Québec family, built the 5,722-pipe organ, one of the largest on the continent. Notre-Dame has particularly excellent acoustics and is often the site of Montréal Symphony (tel. 514/842–9951) concerts, notably, Handel's *Messiah* during the week before Christmas and the Mozart Plus Festival in July. Behind the main altar is the Sacré-Coeur Chapel, which was destroyed by fire in 1978 and rebuilt in five different styles. Also in the back of the church is a small museum of religious paintings and historical objects. *116 rue Notre-Dame O. Basilica: tel. 514/849–1070. Open Labor Day–June 24, daily 7–6; June 25–Labor Day, daily 7 AM–8 PM. Guided tours weekdays, mid-May–June 24, 9–4; June 24–Labor Day, 9–4:30; Labor Day–mid-Oct., 9–4. Museum: tel. 514/842–2925. Admission: $1 adults, 50¢ children. Open weekends 9:30–4.*

4 The low, more retiring stone building behind a wall to the west of the basilica is the **Sulpician Seminary**. This is Montréal's oldest building, built in 1685, and is still a residence for the Sulpician order (unfortunately, it's closed to the public). For almost two centuries, until 1854, the Sulpicians were *the* political power in the city, because they owned the property rights to the island of Montréal. They were also instrumental in recruiting and equipping colonists for New France. The building itself is considered the finest, most elegant example of rustic 17th-century Québec architecture. The clock on the roof over the main doorway is the oldest (pre-1701) public timepiece in North America. Behind the seminary building is a small garden, another Montréal first.

The street that runs alongside the basilica, **rue St-Sulpice,** was the first street in Montréal. On the eastern side of the street there's a plaque marking where the Hôtel-Dieu, the city's first hospital, was built in 1644. Now cross rue St-Sulpice—the art deco **Aldred Building** sits on the far left corner—and take rue Notre-Dame Est. One block farther, just past boulevard St-Laurent, on the left, rises the black-glass–sheathed **Palais de Justice** (1971), which houses the higher courts for both the city and the province. (Québec's legal system is based on the Napoléonic Code for civil cases and on British common law for criminal cases.)

5 A few blocks northwest on rue St-Jacques and rue St-Pierre is the site of the new **Centre de Commerce Mondial de Montréal** (World Trade Centre of Montréal), an ambitious block-long complex that combines old and new. It's home to the new Inter-Continental Hotel in Montréal, a retail mall, and office space. Developers of this innovative complex have gambled that they can attract businesses back from downtown to rue St-Jacques, which, when it was known as St. James Street, was the financial center of Canada.

⑥ In the direction of rue Notre-Dame, the large domed building at 155 rue Notre-Dame Est is the classic revival–style **Old Courthouse** (1857), now municipal offices. Across the street, at 160 rue Notre-Dame Est, is the **Maison de la Sauvegarde** (1811), one of the oldest houses in the city and now home to the European sausage restaurant, Chez Better (*see* Dining, below). The **⑦** Old Courthouse abuts the small **Place Vauquelin,** named after the 18th-century naval hero who is memorialized by a statue in its center. North of this square is **Champs de Mars,** the former site of a colonial military parade ground, for years a parking lot, and since a year of landscaping, completely transformed into a public park more in keeping with its origins. The ornate building on the east side of Place Vauquelin is the Second **⑧** Empire–style **Hôtel de Ville** (City Hall, 1878). On July 24, 1967, French President Charles de Gaulle stood on the central balcony of the hotel and made his famous *"Vive le Québec libre"* speech.

⑨ You are in a perfect spot to explore **Place Jacques-Cartier,** the heart of Vieux-Montréal. This two-block-long square opened in 1804 as a municipal market, and every summer it is transformed into a flower market. The 1809 monument at the top of the place celebrates Lord Nelson's victory at Trafalgar. At the western corner of rue Notre-Dame is a small building (1811), site of the old Silver Dollar Saloon, so named because there were 350 silver dollars nailed to the floor. Today it's the home of **⑩** the **Montreal Convention and Tourism Bureau** (*see* Important Addresses and Numbers, above). Both sides of the place are lined with two- and three-story stone buildings that were originally homes or hotels.

Time Out **Le St-Amable** (188 rue St-Amable, tel. 514/866–3471) features a Businessmen's Lunch weekdays from noon to 3 PM, but you don't have to be an executive or even be dressed like one to sample such classics as fresh poached salmon or grilled New Zealand lamb chops.

⑪ In the summer, the one-block **rue St-Amable** becomes a marketplace for local jewelers, artists, and craftspeople. From the bottom of Place Jacques-Cartier you can stroll out into the **Port of Montreal Exhibition Ground,** where from Winter Carnival through summer there is always something going on. At the foot of boulevard St-Laurent and rue de la Commune are the port's major exhibitions: **Images du Futur, IMAX Super Cinema,** and **Expotec.**

Retrace your steps to the north end of Place Jacques-Cartier, then continue east on rue Notre-Dame. At the corner of rue St-**⑫** Claude on the right is **Château Ramezay** (1705), built as the residence of the 11th governor of Montréal, Claude de Ramezay. In 1775–76 it was the headquarters for American troops seeking to conquer Canada. Benjamin Franklin stayed here during that winter occupation. One of the most elegant colonial buildings still standing in Montréal, the château is now a museum, and it has been restored to the style of Governor de Ramezay's day. The ground floor is furnished like a gentleman's residence of New France, with dining room, bedroom, and office. *280 rue Notre-Dame E, tel. 514/861-3708. Admission: $2 adults, $1 senior citizens, students, and children under 14. Wheelchair visitors are advised to reserve 1 day in advance. Open Tues.– Sun. 10–4:30. Open Mon. from mid-June through Aug.*

At the end of rue Notre-Dame are two houses built by Sir George-Étienne Cartier, a 19th-century Canadian statesman.
⑬ They recently have been opened as the **George-Étienne Cartier Museum.** Downstairs displays focus on the political career of this Québec-born Father of Canadian Confederation. Upstairs rooms are furnished as they would have been in the 1850s and 1860s when the Cartiers lived here. *458 rue Notre-Dame E, tel. 514/283–2282. Admission free. Open in summer, daily 9–5; rest of the year, Wed.–Sun. 10–5.*

One block back on rue Notre-Dame is rue Bonsecours, one of the oldest streets in the city. At the end of rue Bonsecours is
⑭ the small but beautiful **Notre-Dame-de-Bonsecours Chapel.** Marguerite de Bourgeoys, who was canonized in 1983, helped found Montréal and dedicated this chapel to the Virgin Mary in 1657. It became known as a sailor's church, and small wood models of sailing ships are suspended from the ceiling just above the congregation. In the basement there is a small, strange museum honoring the saint that includes a story of her life modeled by little dolls in a series of dioramas. A gift shop sells Marguerite de Bourgeoys souvenirs. From the museum you can climb to the rather precarious bell tower (beware of the slippery metal steps in winter) for a fine view of Vieux-Montréal and the port. *400 rue St-Paul E, tel. 514/845–9991. Admission: $2 adults, 50¢ children. Chapel and museum open May–Oct., 9–4:30, Nov.–April, 10:30–4:30. Closed Mon.*

At the corner of St-Paul and Bonsecours is the historic **Maison du Calvet,** now a charming café. Double back and head west on rue St-Paul. The long, large, domed building to the left is the
⑮ **Marché Bonsecours** (1845), for many years Montréal's main produce, meat, and fish market and now municipal offices. The market has been transformed into a permanent cultural center with temporary exhibits on Montreal.

Rue St-Paul is the most fashionable street in Vieux-Montréal. For almost 20 blocks it is lined with fine restaurants, shops, and even a few nightclubs. Québecois handcrafts are a specialty here, with shops at 88, 136, and 272 rue St-Paul Est. **L'Air du Temps,** at 191 rue St-Paul Ouest, is one of the city's top jazz clubs. Nightly shows usually feature local talent, with occasional international name bands. Take rue St-Paul eight short blocks west of Place Jacques-Cartier, and you will come to
⑯ **Place Royale,** the site of the first permanent settlement in Montréal.

⑰ Behind the Old Customs House you will find **Pointe-à-Callière,** a small park that commemorates the settlers' first landing. A small stream used to flow into the St. Lawrence here, and it was on the point of land between the two waters that the colonists landed their four boats at its mouth on May 17, 1642. After they built the stockade and the first buildings at this site, the settlement was almost washed away the next Christmas by a flood. When it was spared, de Maisonneuve placed a cross on top of Mont Royal as thanks to God. A 1½-block walk down rue
⑱ William takes you to the **Youville Stables** on the left. These low stone buildings enclosing a garden were originally built as warehouses in 1825 (they never were stables). A group of businesspeople renovated them in 1968, and the buildings now house offices, shops, and restaurants.

19 Across rue William from the stables is the **Montreal History Centre.** Visitors to this high-tech museum are led through a series of audiovisual environments depicting the life and history of Montréal. *335 Place d'Youville, tel. 514/872–3207. Admission: $2 adults, $1 senior citizens and students, 50¢ children 12 and under. Open mid-May–mid-Sept., 10–6; mid-Sept.–mid-May, 11–4:30. Closed Mon.*

Tour 2: Downtown

Numbers in the margin correspond to points of interest on the Tour 2: Downtown Montréal map.

Downtown is a sprawling 30- by 8-block area bounded by avenue Atwater and boulevard St-Laurent on the west and east, respectively, avenue des Pins on the north, and rue St-Antoine on the south.

After 1700, Vieux-Montréal wasn't big enough for the rapidly expanding city. In 1701 the French administration signed a peace treaty with the Iroquois, and the colonists began to feel safe about building outside Montréal's fortifications. The city inched northward, toward Mont Royal, particularly after the English conquest in 1760. By the end of the 19th century, rue Ste-Catherine was the main commercial thoroughfare, and the city's elite built mansions on the slope of the mountain. Since 1960 city planners have made a concerted effort to move the focus eastward. With the opening of Place des Arts (1963) and the Complexe Desjardins (1976), the city center shifted in that direction. It hasn't landed on any one corner yet, although some Montréalers will tell you it's at the intersection of avenue McGill College and rue Ste-Catherine.

A major development of the past 30 years is the inauguration of the **Underground City,** an enormous network of passages linking various shopping and office complexes. These have served to keep the retail trade in the downtown area, as well as to make shoppers and workers immune to the hardships of the Canadian winter.

Our tour of downtown—unless you are hale of limb you may not be able to do all of it in a day—begins at the McGill Métro station. The corner of rue University and boulevard de Maisonneuve has recently been the center of intensive development. Two huge office buildings, **2020 University** and **Galleries 2001,** with malls at street and basement levels, rise from the north side of the intersection. The southwest corner, indeed **20** the entire block, is taken up by **Eaton** (*see* Shopping, below), one of the Big Three department stores in the city. Aside from many floors of mid-priced clothing and other merchandise, the real attraction of Eaton is the ninth-floor art deco dining room.

Time Out **Eaton le 9e** was modeled after the dining room of the luxury liner *Ile-de-France,* Lady Eaton's favorite cruise ship. Elegant marble columns hold up the ceiling, and the walls are decorated with two art deco murals featuring willowy ladies at leisure. The patrons are usually shoppers, of course, dining on pasta, fish, and meat dishes. The service is practical and fast; the decor's the thing. *677 rue Ste-Catherine O, tel. 514/284–8421. AE, MC, V. Open Mon.–Wed. 11:30–3, Thurs. and Fri. 11:30–3 and 5–7, Sat. 11:30–3. Closed Sun.*

Tour 2: Downtown Montréal

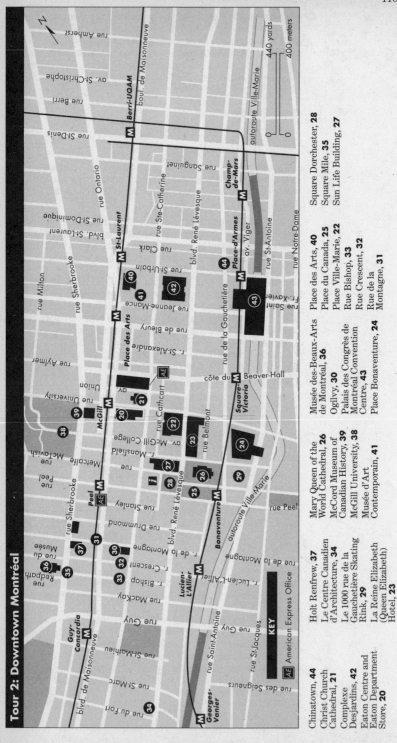

Chinatown, **44**
Christ Church
Cathedral, **21**
Complexe
Desjardins, **42**
Eaton Centre and
Eaton Department
Store, **20**

Holt Renfrew, **37**
Le Centre Canadien
d'Architecture, **34**
Le 1000 rue de la
Gauchetière Skating
Rink, **29**
La Reine Elizabeth
(Queen Elizabeth)
Hotel, **23**

Mary Queen of the
World Cathedral, **26**
McCord Museum of
Canadian History, **39**
McGill University, **38**
Musée d'Art
Contemporain, **41**

Musée des-Beaux-Arts
de Montréal, **36**
Ogilvy, **30**
Palais des Congrès de
Montréal Convention
Centre, **43**
Place Bonaventure, **24**

Place des Arts, **40**
Place du Canada, **25**
Place Ville-Marie, **22**
Rue Bishop, **33**
Rue Crescent, **32**
Rue de la
Montagne, **31**

Square Dorchester, **28**
Square Mile, **35**
Sun Life Building, **27**

Eaton is connected to the **Eaton Centre** shopping complex via passageways; it is connected as well to the McGill Métro and Les Promenades de la Cathédrale and La Baie (The Bay) eastward and Place Montréal Trust westward.

㉑ Across rue University from Eaton stands **Christ Church Cathedral** (1859), the main church of the Anglican Diocese of Montréal. In early 1988 this building was a sight. Plagued by years of high maintenance costs and declining membership, the church fathers leased their land and air rights to a consortium of developers for 99 years. All the land beneath and surrounding the cathedral was removed, and the structure was supported solely by a number of huge steel stilts. The glass 34-story office tower behind the cathedral, **La Maison des Coopérants,** and Les Promenades de la Cathédrale retail complex beneath it, are the products of that agreement.

㉒ **Place Ville-Marie** is an office, retail, and mall complex that signaled a new era for Montréal when it opened in 1962. It was the first link in the huge chain of the Underground City, which meant that people could have access to all the services of the city without setting foot outside. It was also the first step Montréal took to claiming its place as an international city. The labyrinth that is the Underground City now includes six hotels, thousands of offices, 30 movie theaters, more than 1,000 boutiques, hundreds of restaurants, and almost 15 kilometers (9.3 miles) of passageways.

From Place Ville-Marie head south via the passageways to-
㉓ ward **La Reine Elizabeth (Queen Elizabeth)** hotel. You can reach the **Gare Centrale (Central Railway Station)** just behind the hotel. Trains from the United States and the rest of Canada arrive here. Then follow the signs marked "Métro/Place Bona-
㉔ venture" to **Place Bonaventure,** the largest commercial building in Canada. On the lower floors there are shops and restaurants, then come exposition halls and offices, and finally the whole thing is topped by the Bonaventure Hilton International (*see* Lodging, below) and 2½ acres of gardens. From here take the route marked "Place du Canada," which will bring you to the mall in the base of the **Hôtel Château Champlain.** This building is known as the Cheesegrater because of its rows and rows of half-moon–shape windows (*see* Lodging, below). Our exploration of this leg of the Underground City will end at **Windsor Station** (follow the signs). This was the second railway station built in Montréal by the Canadian Pacific Railway Company. Windsor Station was designed in 1889 by George Price, a New York architect, with a massive rustic stone exterior holding up an amazing steel-and-glass roof over an arcade.

It's time for a bit of fresh air now, so exit at the north end of Windsor Station and cross the street to the park known as
㉕ **Place du Canada.** In the center of the park there is a statue to Sir John A. MacDonald, Canada's first prime minister. Then
㉖ cross the park and rue de la Cathédrale to the **Mary Queen of the World Cathedral** (1894), which you enter on boulevard René-Lévesque. This church is modeled after St. Peter's Basilica in Rome. Victor Bourgeau, the same architect who did the interior of Notre-Dame in Vieux-Montréal, thought the idea of the cathedral's design terrible but completed it after the original architect proved incompetent. Inside there is even a canopy over the altar that is a miniature copy of Bernini's *baldacchino* in St. Peter's. The massive gray granite edifice across boule-

㉗ vard René-Lévesque from the cathedral is the **Sun Life Building** (1914), at one time the largest building in the British Commonwealth. During World War II much of England's financial reserves and national treasures were stored in Sun Life's vaults. The park that faces the Sun Life building just north of

㉘ boulevard René-Lévesque is **Square Dorchester,** for many years the heart of Montréal. Until 1870 a Catholic burial ground occupied this block (and there are still bodies buried beneath the grass), but with the rapid development of the area, the city fathers decided to turn it into a park. The statuary of Square Dorchester includes a monument to the Boer War in the center and a statue of the Scottish poet Robert Burns near rue Peel.

In the large skyscraper just south of Square Dorchester is an
㉙ indoor skating rink, **Le 1000 rue de la Gauchetière,** that is open year-round. Located in the 1000 rue de la Gauchetière office tower, the $5 million rink is bathed in natural light and surrounded by a host of amenities, such as cafés, a food court, and a winter garden. It's open to all levels of skaters, and skate rentals and lockers are available. There are also a regular program of ice shows, Saturday-night skating to rock music, and skating lessons. *1000 rue de la Gauchetière, tel. 514/499–2001.*

A block north of Square Dorchester is rue Ste-Catherine, the main retail shopping street of Montréal. Three blocks west, at 1307 rue Ste-Catherine Ouest and rue de la Montagne, is
㉚ **Ogilvy,** the last of the Big Three department stores. The store has been divided into individual name boutiques that sell generally pricier lines than does La Baie or Eaton. Most days at noon a bagpiper plays Scottish airs as he circumnavigates the
㉛ ㉜ ground floor. **Rue de la Montagne (Mountain),** and **rues Cres-**
㉝ **cent** and **Bishop,** the two streets just west of it, constitute the heart of Montréal's downtown nightlife and restaurant scene. This area once formed the playing fields of the Montréal Lacrosse and Cricket Grounds, and later it became an exclusive suburb lined with millionaires' row houses. Since then these three streets between rues Sherbrooke and Ste-Catherine have become fertile ground for trendy bars, restaurants, and shops ensconced in those old row houses.

While you're in the vicinity, take in one of downtown's newest
㉞ attractions, **Le Centre Canadien d'Architecture (Canadian Centre for Architecture),** just four blocks west at rue St-Marc on rue Baile. The lifelong dream of its founding director, Phyllis Lambert (of the Bronfman fortune), the CCA opened in May 1989 and houses one of the world's premier architectural collections. *1920 rue Baile, tel. 514/939–7000. Admission free to children under 12 and Thurs. eve. to adults; otherwise, $3 adults, $2 senior citizens and students. Open Wed. and Fri. 11–6, Thurs. 11–8, weekends 11–5. Group rates available. Reservations required.*

Now that you're in the mood for historic pursuits, backtrack to rues Ste-Catherine and Bishop. By walking two blocks north on rue Bishop to rue Sherbrooke, you enter a very different en-
㉟ vironment: the exclusive neighborhood known as the **Square Mile.**

Directly across the street from the end of rue Bishop is the
㊱ **Musée des Beaux-Arts de Montréal (Montreal Museum of Fine Arts),** the oldest established museum in Canada (1860). The present building was completed in 1912 and holds a large collec-

tion of European and North American fine and decorative art; ancient treasures from Europe, the Near East, Asia, Africa, and America; art from Québec and Canada; and Indian and Eskimo artifacts. From June through October there is usually one world-class exhibition, such as the inventions of Leonardo da Vinci or the works of Marc Chagall.

The Museum of Fine Arts has undergone a major expansion, with a new wing opened in 1991. The museum has a gift shop, an art-book store, a restaurant and cafeteria, and a gallery from which you can buy or rent original paintings by local artists. *1379 rue Sherbrooke O, tel. 514/285–1600. Admission: permanent collection, \$5 adults, \$3 students, \$1 children 12 and under and senior citizens; visiting exhibitions, \$10 adults, \$5 students and senior citizens, \$2 children 12 and under; audio guides, \$3.50. Open Tues.–Sun., permanent collection 10–5, visiting exhibitions 10–5 and Sat. 10–8.*

Walking east on rue Sherbrooke brings you to the small and exclusive **Holt Renfrew** department store, perhaps the city's fanciest, at the corner of boulevard de la Montagne (*see* Shopping, below). A few blocks farther east along rue Drummond stands the **Ritz-Carlton,** the grande dame of Montréal hotels. It was built in 1912 so the local millionaires' European friends would have a suitable place to stay. Take a peek in the elegant Café de Paris restaurant. It's Montréal's biggest power dining spot, and you just might see the prime minister dining there. (For more on the Ritz-Carlton and its restaurants, *see* Lodging and Dining sections, below.) The Ritz-Carlton's only real competition in town is the modern and elegant **Hôtel Quatre Saisons (Four Seasons),** two blocks west at rues Sherbrooke and Peel. Just beyond this hotel on the other side of the street begins the grassy **McGill University** campus. James McGill, a wealthy Scottish fur trader, bequeathed the money and the land for this institution, which opened in 1828 and is perhaps the finest English-language school of higher education in the nation. The student body numbers 15,000, and the university is best known for its medical and engineering schools.

Just across rue Sherbrooke from the campus is the **McCord Museum of Canadian History,** which has reopened after undergoing expansion and renovation work for two years. The quality and extent of the McCord collections, which date primarily from the 18th century, make it one of the best history museums in Canada. The collections document the environment of Canadian native peoples and feature costumes and textiles, decorative arts, paintings, prints and drawings, and the 700,000-print-and-negative Notman Photographic Archives, which highlights 19th-century life in Montréal. The McCord is the only museum in Canada with a permanent costume gallery. There are guided tours (call for times), a reading room and documentation center, a gift shop and bookstore, and a tearoom. *690 rue Sherbrooke O, tel. 514/398–7100. Open Tues., Wed., and Fri. 10–6; Thurs. 10–9; Sat. and Sun. 10–5. Closed Mon., except on statutory holidays. Admission: \$5 adults, \$3 senior citizens, \$2 students, \$8 families, \$3 per person in groups, children under 12 free.*

Turn right on rue University and walk a block to the McGill Métro station. Take the train one stop in the direction of Honoré-Beaugrand to the Place des Arts station.

Montréal's Métro opened in 1966 with well-designed stations—
many decorated with works of art—and modern trains running
on quiet pneumatic wheels. Today there are 65 stations on four
lines with 65 kilometers (40 miles) of track. The 759 train cars
carry more than 700,000 passengers a day. When you exit at
40 **Place des Arts,** follow the signs to the theater complex of the
same name. From here you can walk the five blocks to Vieux-
Montréal totally underground. Place des Arts, which opened in
1963, is reminiscent of New York's Lincoln Center in that it is a
government-subsidized complex of three very modern theaters. The largest, Salle Wilfrid Pelletier, is the home of the
Orchestre Symphonique de Montréal (Montréal Symphony Orchestra), which has won international raves under the baton of
Charles Dutoit. The Orchestre Métropolitain de Montréal,
Grands Ballets Canadiens, and the Opéra du Québec also stage
productions here.

41 The complex also houses the **Musée d'Art Contemporain,** the
city's modern art museum, which moved here from Cité du
Havre in 1991. The museum's large permanent collection represents works by Québecois, Canadian, and international artists in every medium. The museum often features weekend
programs, with many child-oriented activities, and almost all
are free. There are guided tours, though hours vary and
groups of more than 15 are asked to make a reservation. *185 rue
Ste-Catherine Ouest, tel. 514/847–6226. Open Tues.–Sun. 10–6
and Wed. until 9. Admission: $5 adults, $4 seniors, $3 stu-
dents, children under 12 free.*

42 While still in Place des Arts, follow the signs to the **Complexe
Desjardins.** Built in 1976, this is another office building, hotel,
and mall development along the lines of Place Ville-Marie. The
luxurious Meridien Hotel (*see* Lodging, below) rises from its
northwest corner. The large galleria space is the scene of all
types of performances, from lectures on Japanese massage
techniques to pop music, as well as avid shopping in the dozens
of stores. The next development south is the **Complexe Guy-
Favreau,** a huge federal office building named after the Canadian Minister of Justice in the early '60s. If you continue in a
43 straight line, you will hit the **Palais des Congrès de Montréal
Convention Centre** above the Place d'Armes Métro stop. But if
you take a left out of Guy-Favreau onto rue de la Gauchetière,
44 you will be in **Chinatown,** a relief after all that artificially enclosed retail space.

The Chinese first came to Montréal in large numbers after
1880, following the construction of the transcontinental railroad. They settled in an 18-block area between boulevard René-
Lévesque and avenue Viger to the north and south, and near
rues Hôtel de Ville and Bleury on the east and west, an area
that became known as Chinatown, where there are many restaurants, food stores, and gift shops.

Tour 3: St-Denis, Prince Arthur, and North

*Numbers in the margin correspond to points of interest on the
Tour 3: St-Denis, Prince Arthur, and North map.*

After a long day of fulfilling your touristic obligations at the
historical sites and museums of downtown and Vieux-Montréal, it's good to relax and indulge in some primal pleasures, such
as eating, shopping, and nightlife. For these and other diver-

sions, head to the neighborhoods east and north of downtown. Our tour begins in the Latin Quarter, the main student district, then wends its way north.

The southern section of this area, around the base of rue St-Denis, was one of the city's first residential neighborhoods, built in the 19th century as the city burst the bounds of Vieux-Montréal. Then known as Faubourg St-Laurent, it was the home of many wealthy families. The lands to the north of present-day rue Sherbrooke were mostly farms and limestone quarries.

Our tour begins at the **Berri-UQAM** Métro stop, perhaps the most important in the whole city, because three lines intersect here. This area, particularly along **rue St-Denis** on each side of boulevard de Maisonneuve, is known as the **Latin Quarter** and is the site of the **Université du Québec à Montréal** and a number of other educational institutions. Rue St-Denis is lined with cafés, bistros, and restaurants that attract the academic crowd. On rue Ste-Catherine there are a number of low-rent nightclubs popular with avant-garde rock-and-roll types. Just **㊺** west of rue St-Denis you find the **Cinémathèque Québecoise**, a museum and repertory movie house. For $3 you can visit the permanent exhibition on the history of filmmaking equipment and see two movies. The museum also houses one of the largest cinematic reference libraries in the world. *335 boul. de Maisonneuve O, tel. 514/842–9763. Admission free; movies $3. Library open June–Aug., weekdays 12:30–4:30; Sept.–May, weekdays 12:30–5; museum and theater open Tues.–Sun. 5–8:30.*

Around the corner and half a block north on rue St-Denis **㊻** stands the 2,500-seat **Théâtre St-Denis,** the second-largest auditorium in Montréal (after Salle Wilfrid Pelletier in Place des Arts). Sarah Bernhardt and numerous other famous actors have graced its stage. It currently is the main site for the summertime concerts of the Montréal International Jazz Festival. On the next block north you see the Beaux Arts **Bibliothèque Nationale du Québec** (1915), a library that houses Québec's official archives (1700 rue St-Denis; open Tues.–Sat. 9–5). If you have a lot of money and some hours set aside for dining, try **Les Mignardises** at 2035–37 rue St-Denis just south of rue Sherbrooke (*see* Dining, below).

Continue north on rue St-Denis past rue Sherbrooke. On the right, above the Sherbrooke Métro station, is the **Hôtel de l'Institut,** the hands-on training academy of the government *hô-* **㊼** *telier* school. To the left is the small **Square St-Louis**, once considered among the most beautiful in Montréal. Unfortunately, now it is a haven for neighborhood panhandlers and the growing numbers of homeless in the city; as a result, the ambience has changed. In its heyday, this was the focal point of the community, and the surrounding neighborhood takes its name from the once grand square. Originally a reservoir, these blocks became a park in 1879 and attracted upper-middle-class families and artists to the area. French Canadian poets were among the most famous creative people to occupy the houses back then, and the neighborhood is the home today for Montréal painters, filmmakers, musicians, and writers. On the wall of 336 Square St-Louis you can see—and read, if your French is good—a long poem by Michel Bujold.

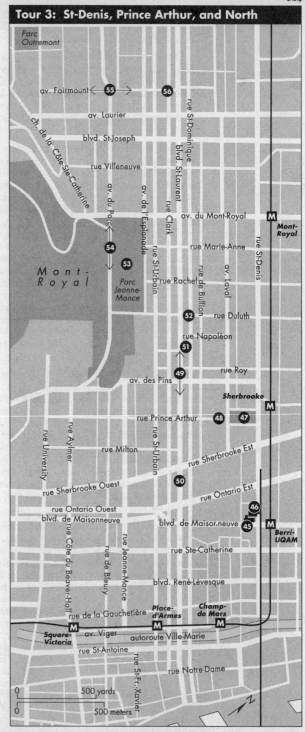

Tour 3: St-Denis, Prince Arthur, and North

48 **Rue Prince Arthur** begins at the western end of Square St-Louis. In the '60s the young people moving to the neighborhood transformed the next few blocks into a small hippie bazaar of clothing, leather, and smoke shops. It remains a center of youth culture, although it's much tamer and more commercial. In 1981 the city turned the blocks between avenue Laval and boulevard St-Laurent into a pedestrian mall. Hippie shops live on today as inexpensive Greek, Vietnamese, Italian, Polish, and Chinese restaurants and boîtes of the singles-bar variety.

49 When you reach **boulevard St-Laurent,** take a left and stroll south on the street that cuts through Montréal life in a number of ways. First, this is the east–west dividing street; like the Greenwich meridian, boulevard St-Laurent is where all the numbers begin. The street is also lined with shops and restaurants that represent the incredible ethnic diversity of Montréal. Until the late 19th century this was a neighborhood first of farms and then of middle-class Anglophone residences. It was on boulevard St-Laurent in 1892 that the first electric tramway was installed that could climb the slope to Plâteau Mont-Royal. Working-class families, who couldn't afford a horse and buggy to pull them up the hill, began to move in. In the 1880s the first of many waves of Russian-Jewish immigrants escaping the pogroms arrived and settled here. Boulevard St-Laurent became known as The Main, as in "main street," and Yiddish was the primary language spoken along some stretches. The Russian Jews were followed by Greeks, Eastern Europeans, Portuguese, and, most recently, Latin Americans.

50 Just north of rue Sherbrooke is the new **International Museum of Humor.** An offshoot of the highly successful Just for Laughs comedy festival, the multimedia museum celebrates humor in all its forms—from advertising and political cartoons to film and television. Visitors to the museum are first handed headphones and introduced to the "scientific" theory of humor; they are then guided through temporary exhibitions, which change annually. There is also Le Panthéon de l'Humour (The Humor Hall of Fame), which honors comics who have made thier mark in the world of comedy. The museum supports new talent with a cabaret open to stand-up comics. Located in the former Ekers Brewery, the museum is home to a production center for the École Nationale de l'Humour, a school that trains budding comics. There's a restaurant, as well as a boutique that sells anything related to the world of humor. *2101 boul. St-Laurent, tel. 514/845–3155.* Leaving the museum, turn right. The next 10 blocks are filled with delis, junk stores, restaurants, luncheonettes, and clothing stores, as well as fashionable boutiques, bistros, cafés, bars, nightclubs, bookstores, and galleries exhibiting the work of the latest wave of "immigrants" to the area—gentrifiers and artists. The block between rues Roy and Napoléon is particularly rich in delights. Just east at 74 rue Roy is **Waldman's Fish Market,** reputed to be the largest wholesale/retail fish market in North America. **Warshaw's Supermarket** at 3863 boulevard St-Laurent is a huge Eastern European–style emporium that sells all sorts of delicacies.

51 A few doors up the street from Warshaw's is **Schwartz's Delicatessen.** Among the many contenders for the smoked-meat king title in Montréal, Schwartz's is most frequently at the top. Smoked meat is just about all it serves, but the meat comes in lean, medium, or fatty cuts. The waiters give you your food and take your money, and that's that.

A block north is **Moishe's** (*see* Dining, below), home of the best, but priciest, steaks in Montréal as well as the noisiest atmos-

52 phere. The next corner is **rue Duluth,** where merchants are seeking to re-create rue Prince Arthur. If you take a walk to the right all the way to rue St-Denis, you will find Greek and Vietnamese restaurants and boutiques and art galleries on either side of the street. A left turn on rue Duluth and a three-

53 block walk brings you to **Parc Jeanne-Mance,** a flat, open field that's a perfect spot for a picnic of delicacies purchased on The Main. The park segues into the 2 wooded, hilly square kilometers (494 acres) of **Parc Mont-Royal.**

54 **Avenue du Parc** forms the western border of Parc Jeanne-Mance. To get there either cut through the park or take a left on avenue du Mont-Royal at the north end. No. 93 avenue du Mont-Royal Ouest is the home of **Beauty's,** a restaurant specializing in bagels, lox, pancakes, and omelets. Expect a line weekend mornings. Turn right and head north to **avenue Laurier.** All along this avenue, from Côte Ste-Catherine to boulevard St-Laurent, are some of the fanciest fur stores, boutiques, pastry shops, and jewelers in the city. For a quick chocolate eclair bracer or two, go to **Lenôtre Paris,** at 1050 avenue Laurier, a branch of the Parisian shop of the same name.

Time Out **La Petite Ardoise** is a casual, slightly arty café that serves soups, quiches, sandwiches, and more-expensive daily specials. The onion soup is lovingly overdosed with cheese, bread, and onions. Whether it's breakfast, lunch, or dinner, the best accompaniment for your meal is a big, steamy bowl of creamy café au lait. This café is a perfect place to take a breather from shopping. *222 av. Laurier O, tel. 514/495–4961. AE, DC, MC, V. Open 8 AM–midnight, later on weekends.*

The next three blocks of avenue du Parc form the heart of the Greek district. Try **Symposium,** at No. 5334, or the neighboring **Milos** at 5357 avenue du Parc (*see* Dining, below) for some of the best Greek appetizers, grilled seafood, and atmosphere you'll find in this hemisphere.

55 **Avenue Fairmount,** a block north of avenue Laurier, is the site of two small but internationally known culinary landmarks. The **Fairmount Bagel Factory,** at 74 avenue Fairmount Ouest, claims to make the best bagels in the world.

Half a block east, on the corner of avenue Fairmount and rue

56 Clark, stands the famous **Wilensky's Light Lunch** (*see* Dining, below). Moviegoers will recognize this Montréal institution from *The Apprenticeship of Duddy Kravitz,* based on the Mordecai Richler novel of the same name. Lunch is all that's served here, and it certainly is light on the wallet. A couple of dollars will get you a hot dog or a bologna, salami, and mustard pretzel-roll sandwich with a strawberry soda. Books are available for perusing. The atmosphere is free.

Parks and Gardens

Numbers in the margin correspond to points of interest on the Olympic Park and Botanical Garden map.

Of Montréal's three major parks, **Lafontaine** is the smallest (the other two are Parc Mont-Royal and Île Ste-Hélène). Parc Lafontaine, founded in 1867, is divided into eastern and western halves. The eastern half is French style; the paths, gardens, and lawns are laid out in rigid geometric shapes. There are two public swimming pools on the north end, along rue Rachel. In the winter the park is open for ice-skating. The western half is designed on the English system, in which the meandering paths and irregularly shaped ponds follow the natural contours of the topography. Pedal boats can be rented for a paddle around one of two man-made lakes. Its band shell is the site of many free outdoor summertime concerts, performances by dance and theater groups, and film screenings. Take the Métro to the Sherbrooke station and walk five blocks east along rue Cherrier. *4000 Calixa-Lavallée, tel. 514/872–6211. Open 9 AM–10 PM.*

The giant, mollusk-shape **Olympic Stadium** and the tilted tower that supports the roof are probably the preeminent symbols of modern Montréal. Planning for the Olympic Stadium complex began in 1972, and construction in the old Parc Maisonneuve started soon afterward. The Olympics took place in 1976, but the construction of the stadium's roof and tower was not completed until 1989. Many Montréalers were proud of what they had—at least until the summer of 1991, when a 55-ton concrete beam in the stadium came crashing to the ground. The stadium was forced to close for several months, forcing the Montréal Expos major-league baseball team to play its home games on the road. The stadium's retractable roof has never worked properly, and Montréal homeowners and cigarette smokers are still paying the bill for the $1 billion–plus stadium. Disgruntled Montréalers have nicknamed the Olympic Stadium the Big Owe and the Big Uh-Oh! The Olympic Park includes the 70,000-seat **57** **58** **Olympic Stadium,** the **Olympic Tower,** six swimming pools, the **59** **Aréna Maurice-Richard,** and the Olympic Village. Tours of the entire complex leave from Tourist Hall at 12:30 and 3:30 in the off-season, more often from June to August (tel. 514/252–8687). Perhaps the most popular visitor activity is a ride up to the tilted tower's observatory on the Funicular, the exterior cable car. The two-level cable car holds 90 people and takes two minutes to climb the 270 meters (890 feet) to the observatory, from which you can see up to 80 kilometers (50 miles) on clear days.

60 The **Biodôme,** in the former Olympic Park Velodrome, opened in June of 1992. This natural sciences museum combines four ecosystems—the boreal forest, tropical forest, polar world, and St. Lawrence River—under one climate-controlled dome. Visitors follow protected pathways through each environment, observing indigenous flora and fauna of each of the ecosystems. Animals from the former zoo at Angrignon Park and the now closed aquarium on Île Ste-Hélène have been incorporated into this new center. *For information on rates and hours, tel. 514/872–3034.*

If you've brought your swimsuit and towels, take a dip at the **61** **Aquatic Center** (tel. 514/252–4622 for hours). There are also a cafeteria and a souvenir shop on the grounds. You can reach the **Olympic Park** via the Pie-IX or Viau Métro stations (the latter is nearer the stadium entrance).

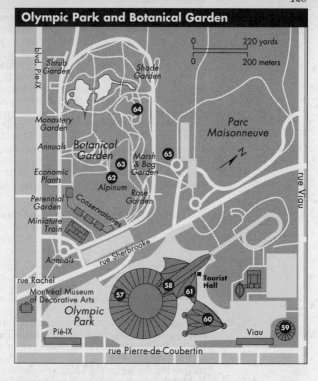

Olympic Park and Botanical Garden

Continuing your back-to-nature experience, cross rue Sherbrooke to the north of the Olympic Park (or take the free shuttle bus) to reach the **Botanical Garden** (closest Métro stop is Pie-IX). Founded in 1931, this garden is said to be one of the largest in the world. During the summer you can visit the 73 hectares (181 acres) of outdoor gardens—a favorite is the poisonous-plants garden; the 10 exhibition greenhouses are open year-round. There are more than 26,000 species of plants here. When the 5-acre **Montréal-Shanghai "Dream Lake" Garden** opened here in June 1991, it became the site of the largest Chinese garden outside Asia. The authentic Ming-style garden has seven elegant pavilions, including a large exhibition hall featuring periodic shows and a 30-foot rockery around a central reflecting pool. There is also an impressive collection of penjings or Chinese bonsais (miniature trees). A **Japanese garden** and its pavilion, where guests may join a formal tea ceremony, are next to the "Dream Lake." The **Insectarium**, a bug-shaped building, houses more than 250,000 insect specimens collected by Montréal entomologist Georges Brossard. *4101 rue Sherbrooke E, tel. 514/872–1400. Admission each to the greenhouses and the Insectarium: May 15–Oct. 15, $6 adults; Oct. 16–May 14, $4 adults.*

Île Ste-Hélène (along with Île Notre-Dame, the former site of the Expo '67 World's Fair), opposite Vieux-Montréal in the middle of the St. Lawrence River, draws big crowds, particularly during the warm months. You can reach it via either the Victoria or Jacques-Cartier bridges, via the Métro to the Île Ste-Hélène station, or by city bus (summer only) from downtown. Île Ste-Hélène is a wooded, rolling park perfect for picnicking in the summer and cross-country skiing and ice-skating during the snow season. The former 1967 World's Fair site on the island has been upgraded. Buckminster Fuller's biosphere (the world's largest geodesic dome when the famous architect and engineer built it for Expo '67, but since ravaged by fire) is scheduled to reopen this summer as a permanent water and environment interpretation center.

La Ronde was created as part of the Expo celebration. This world-class amusement park boasts a huge new roller coaster (the second-highest in the world), water slides with incredible drops, an international circus, Ferris wheels, boat rides, and rides, rides, rides. The **Aqua Park** shares the island with La Ronde and has 20 of its own thrilling slides and pools. A combined family pass is $41; admission for individuals is $18.50 for adults and $8.50 for children. Passes are good for a day at the amusement park as well as the water slides. Both parks have the same schedule. There are also haunted houses, musical cabarets, Wild West shows, restaurants, snack bars, and the obligatory monorail and cable-car rides. La Ronde is also the site of the annual Benson & Hedges International Fireworks Competition, running from the last week in May to mid-June on Wednesday and Saturday nights. *Île Ste-Hélène, tel. 514/872-6222 or 800/361-7178. Admission includes all rides and entertainment, family and special Wed. rates available. Open May and early June, weekends only; mid-June–Labor Day, Sun.–Thurs. 11 AM–midnight, Fri.–Sat. 11 AM–1 AM.*

A stroll back along the north side of the island brings you to the **Old Fort** just under the Jacques-Cartier Bridge. This former British arsenal has been turned into the **David M. Stewart Museum** and a dinner theater called **Le Festin du Gouverneur.** The latter is a re-creation of a 17th-century banquet, complete with balladeers and comedy skits. In the military museum are displays of old firearms, maps, scientific instruments, uniforms, and documents of colonial times. During the summer the parade ground is the scene of mock battles—cannons and all—by the Compagnie Franche de la Marine and bagpipe concerts by the 78th Fraser Highlanders. *Tel. 514/861-6701. Admission to museum: $2 adults, $1.50 children and senior citizens. Admission to museum and summer shows: $3 adults; $2 seniors, students, and children. Open summer, 10–6, closed Tues.; winter, 10–5, closed Tues.*

In mid-June, **Île Notre-Dame** is the site of the Molson Grand Prix du Canada, a top Formula I international circuit auto race at the Gilles Villeneuve Race Track.

Île Notre-Dame is also site of the city's only natural beach on **Lac de l'Île Notre-Dame.** Opened in the summer of 1990, it was an immediate success and is now packed on every hot, sunny day. Just a Métro stop away (Île Ste-Hélène Métro) from downtown, the beach is an oasis, with clear lake water filtered by a treatment system that relies on aquatic plants, and an inviting stretch of lawn and trees rimmed with sand. Lifeguards are on duty; there is a shop that rents swimming and boating accessories, and there are picnic areas and a restaurant on the premises. There is also a moderate admission fee.

The **Parc Mont-Royal,** the finest in the city, is not easy to overlook. These 494 acres of forest and paths at the heart of the city were designed by Frederick Law Olmsted, the celebrated architect of New York's Central Park. He believed that communion with nature could cure body and soul. The park is designed following the natural topography and accentuating its features, as in the English mode. You can go skating on Beaver Lake in the winter, visit one of the two lookouts and scan the horizon, or study the park interpretation center in the chalet at the Mont Royal belvedere. Horse-drawn transport is popular year-round: sleigh rides in winter and calèche rides in summer. On the eastern side of the hill stands the 30-meter (100-foot) steel cross that is the symbol of the city.

Shrines

St. Joseph's Oratory, on the northwest side of Mont Royal, is a Catholic shrine on a par with Lourdes or Fatima. Take the blue Métro line to the Côte-des-Neiges station, then walk three blocks uphill on the chemin de la Côte-des-Neiges. You can't miss the enormous church up on the hillside. Brother André, a member of the Society of the Brothers of the Holy Cross, constructed a small chapel to St. Joseph, Canada's patron saint, in 1904. Brother André was credited with a number of miracles and was beatified in 1982. His chapel became a pilgrimage site, the only one to St. Joseph in the world (St. Joseph is the patron saint of healing). The dome is among the world's largest, and while the interior is of little aesthetic interest, there is a small museum dedicated to the life of the Holy Family and containing many displays, including thousands of crutches discarded by the formerly crippled faithful. From early December through February the museum features a display of crèches (nativity scenes) from all over the world. Carillon, choral, and organ concerts are held weekly at the oratory during the summer, and you can still visit Brother André's original chapel and tomb at the side of the massive basilica. *3800 chemin Queen Mary, tel. 514/733–8211. Open summer, daily 6:30 AM–9:30 PM; fall and spring, 8 AM–8:30 PM; winter, 8–5.*

Montréal for Free

The Saidye Bronfman Centre hands-on fine arts school's open-house activities, gallery exhibitions, and public affairs lectures (*see* Off the Beaten Track, below).

Musée d'Art Contemporain. A donation is suggested (*see* Tour 2, above).

Classical and pop concerts, dance performances, and theater at **Parc de Lafontaine,** rue Rachel.

Picnic in **Parc Mont-Royal,** sail miniature boats in its Beaver Lake during the summer, and skate on it during the winter (*see* Parks and Gardens, above).

Bicycle along Montréal's waterfront to the Lachine Canal, atop its mountain, or through the Vieux-Port (*see* Participant Sports, below).

Le Centre Canadien d'Architecture, Thursday evening (*see* Tour 2, above).

What to See and Do with Children

La Ronde's Amusement Park (*see* Parks and Gardens, above).

Images du Futur offers futuristic, interactive exhibitions. *Vieux-Port at boul. St-Laurent and rue de la Commune, tel. 514/849–1612. June–Sept., daily noon–11 PM.*

IMAX Super Cinema offers films on a seven-story-tall screen. *Vieux-Port, Shed no. 7, tel. 514/496–IMAX for information, 514/522–1245 for tickets.* Next to Images du Futur is **Expotec**, a hands-on scientific exhibition. *Open daily 10–10, tel. 514/496–4629.*

Olympic Tower. Zoom up the "tallest-inclined-tower-in-the-world" on the funicular for a 50-mile panorama of Montréal and its environs. *4545 Pierre-de-Coubertin (Métro Pie-IX), tel. 514/252–8687, 10–10. Closed mid-Jan. to mid-Feb.*

The Botanical Garden's **Insectarium** (*see* Parks and Gardens, above).

Indoor skating year-round at the *1000 rue de La Gauchetière* (*see* Tour 2, above).

Biodôme de Montréal at Olympic Park (*See* Parks and Gardens, above).

Dow Planetarium. The heavens are reproduced with the aid of a giant Zeiss projector on the inside of the planetarium's vaulted dome. *1000 rue St-Antoine, tel. 514/872–4530. Open Tues.–Sun. 12:30–8:30.*

At the Old Fort on Île Ste-Hélène, now the site of the **David M. Stewart Museum,** mock battles, military drills, military-history exhibitions, and bagpipe concerts take place all summer long (*see* Parks and Gardens, above).

Off the Beaten Track

Just two blocks west of Victoria and the Métro Côte-Ste-Catherine station is the **Saidye Bronfman Centre.** This multidisciplinary institution has long been recognized as a focus of cultural activity for the Jewish community in particular and for Montréal as a whole. The center was a gift from the children of Saidye Bronfman in honor of their mother's lifelong commitment to the arts. In fact, the Mies van der Rohe–inspired building was originally designed by Mrs. Bronfman's daughter, Montréal architect Phyllis Lambert. Accessible by car, just one block east of the Décarie Expressway and about four blocks north of chemin Queen Mary, the center is well worth the trip.

Many of its activities, such as gallery exhibits, lectures on public and Jewish affairs, performances, and concerts, are offered free to the public. The center, open year-round, is home to the Yiddish Theatre Group, one of the few Yiddish companies performing today in North America. The theater also presents English works, often by local playwrights. Many an artist has passed through the doors of the center's School of Fine Arts. *5170 Côte Ste-Catherine, tel. 514/739–2301; box office 514/739–7944. Closed Fri. from 2 PM, Sat., and Jewish holidays. Call for information and program schedule.*

Accessible by metro and bus, **Maison Saint-Gabriel** dates back to 1668, when it served as a boarding school for Les Filles du

Roy—the young women, many of them orphans, who were brought over to New France to marry the predominantly male settlers. Here Montréal's first teacher (and Canada's first female saint), Marguerite Bourgeoys, patiently trained the "King's wards" to take on their duties as wives and mothers. The house was renovated in 1960. A typical "habitant" farmhouse, it displays furnishings and household objects from the 17th, 18th, and 19th centuries, as well as a kitchen much like the one Les Filles would have learned to bake in before setting off for their new homes. Guided tours are offered from mid-April to mid-December. It is advisable to call beforehand. *2146 Place Dublin (Square-Victoria Métro, then transfer to No. 61 bus), tel. 514/935–8136. Admission by donation. Tours Tues.–Sat., 1:30 and 3; Sun. 1:30, 2:30, and 3:30.*

Shopping

by Patricia Lowe

Montréalers *magasinent* (go shopping) with a vengeance, so it's no surprise that the city has 160 multifaceted retail areas encompassing some 6,200 stores. Between 1990 and 1992, some 800 new boutiques and retail outlets were added to this rough estimate.

Visitors usually reserve at least one day to hunt for either exclusive fashions along rue Sherbrooke or bargains at the Vieux-Montréal flea market. But there are specific items that the wise shopper seeks out in Montréal.

Montréal is one of the fur capitals of the world. Close to 85% of Canada's fur manufacturers are based in the city, as are many of their retail outlets: **Alexandor** (2015 rue de la Montagne), **Shuchat** (2015 rue de la Montagne); **Grosvenor** (400 boulevard de Maisonneuve O), **McComber** (440 boulevard de Maisonneuve O), and **Birger Christensen at Holt Renfrew** (1300 rue Sherbrooke O) are a few of the better showrooms.

Fine English bone china, crystal, and woolens are more readily available and cheaper in metropolitan stores than in their U.S. equivalents, thanks to Canada's tariff status as a Commonwealth country. There are three **Jaeger** boutiques (Ogilvy downtown, Centre Rockland in the town of Mount Royal, and Centre Fairview in the West Island) selling traditional woolen sweaters, along with $700 pure-wool suits. Collectors of china and crystal will do well at any of the **Birks Jewellers** on Square Phillips or in shopping complexes and suburban shopping centers. With lower price tags, **Caplan Duval** (Côte-St-Luc's Cavendish Mall and Montréal's Plaza Côte-des-Neiges) offers an overwhelming variety of patterns.

Today, only dedicated connoisseurs can uncover real treasures in traditional pine Canadiana, but scouting around for Québec *antiquités* and art can be fun and rewarding, especially along increasingly gentrified rue Notre-Dame Ouest.

The Montréal area has six major retail districts: the city center (or downtown), Vieux-Montréal, rue Notre-Dame Ouest, the Plâteau Mont-Royal–St-Denis area, the upper St-Laurent–Laurier Ouest areas of Outremont, and the city of Westmount.

Montréal stores, boutiques, and department stores are generally open from 9 or 9:30 to 6 Monday, Tuesday, and Wednesday. On Thursday and often on Friday, stores close at 9, Saturday at

5. Many stores downtown and in suburban shopping malls are open Wednesday until 9. A number of pharmacies are open six days a week until 11 PM or midnight; a few are 24-hour operations. An increasing number of retail outlets, particularly in designated tourist zones like Vieux-Montréal, are open on Sunday. Just about all stores, with the exception of some bargain outlets and a few selective art and antiques galleries, accept major credit cards. Buy your Canadian money at a bank or exchange bureau beforehand to take advantage of the latest rates on the dollar. Most purchases are subject to a federal goods and services tax of 7% as well as a provincial tax of 8%.

If you think you might be buying fur, it is wise to check with your country's customs officials before leaving to find out which animals are considered endangered and cannot be imported. Do the same if you think you might be buying Eskimo carvings, many of which are made of whalebone and ivory and cannot be brought into the United States.

City Center

Central downtown is Montréal's largest retail district. It takes in rue Sherbrooke, boulevard de Maisonneuve, rue Ste-Catherine, and the side streets between them. Because of the proximity and variety of shops, it's the best shopping bet for visitors in town overnight or over a weekend.

Faubourg Ste-Catherine Several new or soon-to-open complexes have added glamour to the city center shopping scene. A good place to start is the **Faubourg Ste-Catherine,** Montréal's answer to Boston's Quincy Market. At the corner of rues Ste-Catherine Ouest and Guy, it is a vast bazaar housed in a former parking and auto-body garage abutting the Grey Nuns' convent grounds. Three levels of clothing and crafts boutiques, as well as food counters selling fruits and vegetables, pastry, baked goods, and meats, surround the central atrium of tiered fountains and islands of café tables and chairs where food fair kiosks sell snacks such as egg rolls, pizza, souvlaki, and sushi. This is the place to pick up Québec maple syrup and maple candy, at the pine-decorated boutique at street level, or a fine French wine, about $30, at the government-run **Société d'Alcools du Québec.** Prices at most stores are generally reasonable here, especially if you're sampling the varied ethnic cuisine at any of the snack counters.

Les Cours Mont-Royal Continuing east on Ste-Catherine, the *très élégant* **Les Cours Mont-Royal** dominates the east side of rue Peel between this main shopping thoroughfare and boulevard de Maisonneuve. This mall caters to expensive tastes, but even bargain hunters find it an intriguing spot for window shopping.

Place Montréal Trust Just two blocks away, **Place Montréal Trust** at McGill College is the lively entrance to an imposing glass office tower. Shoppers, fooled by the aqua and pastel decor, may think they have stumbled into a California mall. Prices at the 120 outlets range from hundreds (for designs by **Alfred Sung,** haute couture at **Gigi** or **Rodier,** or men's high fashion at **Bally**) to mere dollars (for sensible cotton boys' T-shirts, or beef-and-kidney pies or minced tarts at the British dry goods and food store **Marks & Spencer**). These imported goodies share the floor space with moderately ticketed ladies' suits, menswear, lingerie, and children's clothing. Marks & Spencer is a far cry from neighboring **Abercrombie and Fitch,** which stocks the offbeat and the outrageous, such as a fold-up, miniature billiards table or a $5,995 toy sports car.

Les Cours Mont-Royal and this complex have competition from the **Centre Eaton** and **Les Promenades de la Cathédrale.** All four of these centers are linked to the Underground City retail network. Always a favorite with visitors, the nearly 15-kilometer (9-mile) "city below" draws large crowds to its shop-lined corridors honeycombing between Les Promenades de la Cathédrale, Place Ville-Marie, Place Bonaventure, and Complexe Desjardins.

Les Promenades de la Cathédrale   Nestled between Eaton and La Baie department stores, this underground retail complex is already proving popular with Montréalers. Its unusual location makes it a sightseeing adventure as well: It's connected to the McGill Métro and located directly beneath the stately and historic Christ Church Cathedral. A highlight (some say a travesty) of the retail mall's design is the replication of architectural details found in the cathedral above. Among its 150 boutiques and chain stores, Les Promenades boasts Canada's largest "Linen Chest" outlet, with hundreds of bedspreads and duvets draped over revolving racks plus aisles of china, crystal, linen, and silver.

Place Ville-Marie   Weatherproof shopping began in 1962 beneath the 42-story cruciform towers of Place Ville-Marie on boulevard René-Lévesque (formerly Dorchester Boulevard) at rue University. A recent renovation has opened Place Ville-Marie up to the light, creating a more cheerful ambience as well as adding stores.

Stylish women head to Place Ville-Marie's 125-plus retail outlets for the clothes: haute couture at **Lalla Fucci, Jacnel, Marie-Claire,** and **Cactus,** as well as **Holt Renfrew's** branch store. Traditionalists will love **Heritage House** and **Aquascutum.** More affordable clothes shops include **Dalmy's, Gazebo, Reitman's,** and, for shoes, **Mayfair, Brown's, François Villon,** and **French.**

Place Bonaventure   From here it's an easy underground trip through Gare Centrale (the train station) to Place Bonaventure's mall beneath one of Canada's largest commercial buildings. It houses some 120 stores, ranging from the trendy (**Au Coton** and **Bikini Village**) to the exclusive (**Armand Boudrias** boutique). There are also a number of fun shops: **Au Masculin** for men's gifts and games; **Au Coin des Petits** for children's clothes and toys; **Aldo** for trendy leather wear; and **Ici-Bas** for outrageous hose.

Complexe Desjardins   Still in the downtown area but a bit farther east on boulevard René-Lévesque is Complexe Desjardins. It's a fast ride via the Métro at Bonaventure station; just get off at Place des Arts and follow the tunnels to Desjardins' multitiered atrium mall. Filled with splashing fountains and exotic plants, Desjardins exudes a Mediterranean joie de vivre, even when it's below freezing outside. Roughly 80 stores include budget outlets like **Le Château** for fashion and **Sarosi** for shoes, as well as the exclusive **Rodier of Paris,** where wool and jersey-knit ensembles start at about $150.

Department Stores   **Eaton** is the city's leading department store and part of Canada's largest chain. Founded in Toronto by Timothy Eaton, the first Montréal outlet appeared in 1925. It now sells everything—from the art decorating the top-floor restaurant entrance to zucchini loaves in the basement bakery. The main restaurant is an unusual art deco replica of the dining room aboard the old *Île de France* ocean liner, once Lady Eaton's favorite cruise ship.

The nearby sandstone building housing **La Baie** opened in 1891, although the original Henry Morgan Company that founded it moved to Montréal in 1843. Morgan's was purchased in 1960 by the Hudson Bay Company, which was founded in 1670 by famous Montréal voyageurs and trappers Radisson and Grosseilliers. La Baie is known for its Hudson Bay red-, green-, and white-striped blankets and duffel coats. It also sells the typical department store fare.

Exclusive **Holt Renfrew,** at 1300 rue Sherbrooke Ouest, is known for its furs. The city's oldest store, it was established in 1837 as Henderson, Holt and Renfrew Furriers and made its name supplying coats to four generations of British royalty. When Queen Elizabeth II married Prince Phillip in 1947, Holt's created a priceless Labrador mink as a wedding gift. Commoners, however, must be content with a brown-dyed blue fox for $14,750. Holt's also now carries the exclusive and pricey line of furs by Denmark's Birger Christensen, as well as the haute-couture and prêt-à-porter collections of Yves St-Laurent.

Around the corner and two blocks down rue de la Montagne, at **Ogilvy** (1307 rue Ste-Catherine O), a kilted piper regales shoppers every day at noon. An institution with Montréalers since 1865, the once-homey department store has undergone a miraculous face-lift. Fortunately, it has preserved its delicate pink glass chandeliers and still stocks traditional apparel—Aquascutum, Jaeger, tweeds for men, and smocked dresses for little girls.

This area—bounded by rues Sherbrooke and Ste-Catherine, and rues de la Montagne and Crescent—also boasts antiques and art galleries as well as designer salons. Rue Sherbrooke is lined with an array of art and antiques galleries as well as tony clothing stores. Rue Crescent is a tempting blend of antiques, fashions, and jewelry boutiques displayed beneath colorful awnings.

Vieux-Montréal

The second major shopping district, historic Vieux-Montréal, can be a tourist trap, but a shopping spree there can be a lot less expensive and more relaxing than shopping downtown. Both rues Notre-Dame and St-Jacques, from rue McGill to Place Jacques-Cartier, are lined with low to moderately priced fashion boutiques, garish souvenir shops slung with thousands of Montréal T-shirts, and shoe stores.

Along the edge of Vieux-Montréal is Montréal's rejuvenated waterfront, the Vieux-Port, which hosts a sprawling flea market, the **Marché aux Puces,** on Quai King Edward (King Edward Pier). Dealers and pickers search for secondhand steals and antique treasures as they prowl through the huge hangar that is open Wednesday through Sunday from spring through early fall.

Notre-Dame Ouest

The place for antiquing is the city's third shopping sector, beginning at rue Guy and continuing west to avenue Atwater (a five-minute walk south from the Lionel-Groulx Métro station). Once a shabby strip of run-down secondhand stores, this area has blossomed beyond its former nickname of Attic Row. It now has the highest concentration of antiques, collectibles, and curiosity shops in Montréal. Collectors can find Canadian pine furniture—armoires, cabinets, spinning wheels, rocking chairs—for reasonable prices here. Consider a Sunday tour, beginning with brunch at **Salon de Thé Ambiance,** a charming restaurant that also sells antiques (No. 1874).

Plateau Mont-Royal and St-Denis

Popular with students, academics, and journalists, this easterly neighborhood embraces boulevard St-Laurent, the longtime student ghetto surrounding the Prince Arthur mall, St-Denis and its Latin Quarter near the Université du Québec à Montréal campus, and the Plateau district. Plateau Mont-Royal and St-Denis attracts a trendier, more avant-garde crowd than the determined antiquers along Notre-Dame.

Boulevard St-Laurent—dubbed "The Main" because it divides the island of Montréal into east and west—has always been a lively commercial artery. It was first developed by Jewish merchants who set up shop here in the early 1900s. Cutting a broad swath across the island's center, this long boulevard has an international flavor, with its mélange of stores run by Chinese, Greek, Latin American, Portuguese, Slav, and Vietnamese immigrants. Lower boulevard St-Laurent is lined with discount clothing and bric-a-brac stores, secondhand shops, electronics outlets, and groceries selling kosher meats, Hungarian pastries, Peking duck, and natural foods. Fashionable clothing shops join this colorful bazaar, though none has been as successful as the now international **Parachute Boutique** (No. 3526), which began its career in Montréal.

While boulevard St-Laurent's personality is multiethnic, rue St-Denis's is distinctly French. (Both are lengthy arteries, so make use of Bus 55 for boulevard St-Laurent, Bus 31 and 30 along rue St-Denis.) More academic in makeup, the boulevard has awnings that shelter bookstores (mostly French), art galleries, antiques stores, and a range of boutiques.

Upper St-Laurent and Laurier Ouest

Upper boulevard St-Laurent (for our purposes, roughly from avenue du Mont-Royal north to rue St-Viateur), intersecting with avenue Laurier Ouest and climbing the mountain to rue Bernard, has blossomed into one of Montréal's chicest *quartiers* in recent years. It's not entirely surprising, given that much of this area lies within or adjacent to Outremont, traditionally the enclave for wealthy Francophone Montréalers, with restaurants, boutiques, nightclubs, and bistros catering to the upscale visitor. In addition, the influx of a new generation of multiethnic professionals, artists, and entrepreneurs is making its mark on the area. It now rivals St-Denis, downtown, and Laurier Ouest as a cultural hot spot, and it is reminiscent of New York City's SoHo.

Avenue Laurier Ouest, from boulevard St-Laurent to chemin de la Côte-Ste-Catherine, is roughly an eight-block stretch; you'll crisscross it many times as you explore its Québec-style shops, which carry everything from crafts and clothing to books and paintings.

Square Westmount and Avenue Greene

Visitors with time to shop or friends in the elegant residential neighborhood of Westmount, a separate municipality in the middle of the island of Montréal, should explore Square Westmount and adjacent avenue Greene. Next door to downtown, these malls are on the Angrignon Métro line, easily accessible via the Atwater station, which has an exit at Square Westmount. Just follow the tunnel to this mall's 90 or so exclusive shops.

The square's plaza opens onto avenue Greene's two-block shopping area, which is lined with trees and flowers. Its redbrick row houses and even the renovated old post office are home to a wealth of boutiques and shops.

Sports and Fitness

The range of sporting activities available in Montréal is testament to Montréalers' love of the outdoors. With world-class skiing in the Laurentiens less than an hour away and dozens of skating rinks within the city limits, they revel in winter. When the last snowflake has melted, they store away skis, poles, and skates and dust off their bikes, tennis rackets, and fishing poles. And year-round they watch the pros at hockey matches, baseball games, car races, and tennis tournaments.

Participant Sports

Bicycling The island of Montréal—except for Mont Royal itself—is quite flat, and there are more than 20 cycling paths around the metropolitan area. Among the most popular are those on Île Ste-Hélène, along the Lachine Canal, and in Angrignon and Vieux-Port parks. You can rent 10-speed bicycles at **Cycle Peel** (6665 rue St-Jacques, tel. 514/486–1148) and at **Cyclo-Touriste** at the Centre Info-Touriste (1001 Dorchester Sq., tel. 514/393–1528).

Parks Canada conducts guided cycling tours along the historic **Lachine Canal** (1825) every summer weekend. Tours leave from the corner of rues McGill and de la Commune at 10:30 AM, in English on Saturday, in French on Sunday. For more details, call 514/283–6054 or 514/872–6211.

Golf For a complete listing of the many golf courses in the Montréal area, call **Tourisme-Québec** at 514/873–2015.

Hunting and Fishing Québec's rich waters and forests are filled with fish and wildlife. Before you begin the chase, you need to purchase the appropriate license from the Ministère des Loisirs, de la Chasse et de la Pêche or from an authorized agent. The lakes and rivers around Montréal team with fish, and a number of guides offer day trips. For hunting you'll have to go farther afield, to the Laurentians or l'Estrie (*see* Chapter 11). For complete information, call **Tourisme-Québec** (tel. 514/873–2015).

Ice Skating There are at least 195 outdoor and 21 indoor rinks in the city. You'll probably find one in the nearest park. Call parks and recreation (tel. 514/872–6211).

Jogging Montréal became a runner's city following the 1976 Olympics. There are paths in most city parks, but for running with a panoramic view, head to the dirt track in **Parc du Mont-Royal** (take rue Peel, then the steps up to the track).

Rafting Montréal is the only city in the world where you can step off a downtown dock and minutes later be crashing through Class V white water in a sturdy aluminum jet boat. The Lachine Rapids, just south of Vieux-Montréal, were responsible for the founding of Montréal. The roiling waves were too treacherous for the first settlers to maneuver, so they founded Ville-Marie, the forerunner of Vieux-Montréal. Modern voyageurs suit up for the 45-minute jet-boat trip in multiple layers of wool and rain gear, but it's nearly impossible to stay dry—or to have a bad time. *Lachine Rapids Tours Ltd., 105 rue de la Commune, Vieux-Montréal, tel. 514/284–9607. 5 trips daily, departing from Quai Victoria May–Sept., 10, noon, 2, 4, and 6. Trips are narrated in French and English and reservations are necessary. Rates: $40 adults, $35 senior citizens, $30 children 13–18, $20 children 6–12. Special group and family rates are available.*

Skiing
Downhill For the big slopes you'll have to go northwest to the Laurentians or south to the Eastern Townships, an hour or two away by car. There is a small slope in Parc du Mont-Royal. Pick up the Ski-Québec brochure at one of the Tourisme-Québec offices.

Cross-country Trails crisscross most of the city's parks, including Notre-Dame and Île Ste-Hélène, Angrignon, Maisonneuve, and Mont-Royal.

Squash You can reserve court time for this fast-paced racquet sport at **Nautilus Centre St-Laurent Côte-de-Liesse Racquet Club** (8305 chemin Côte-de-Liesse, tel. 514/739–3654).

Swimming There is a large indoor pool at the **Olympic Park** (Métro Viau, tel. 514/252–4622) and another at the **Centre Sportif et des Loisirs Claude-Robillard** (1000 av. Emile Journault, tel. 514/872–6900). The outdoor pool on Île Ste-Hélène is an extremely popular (and crowded) summer gathering place, open June–Labor Day. The new city-run beach at Île Notre-Dame is the only natural swimming hole in Montréal (tel. 514/872–6211).

Tennis There are public courts in the Jeanne-Mance, Kent, LaFontaine, and Somerled parks. For details, call Montreal Sports and Recreation (tel. 514/872–6211).

Windsurfing and Sailing Sailboards and small sailboats can be rented at **L'École de Voile de Lachine** (2105 boul. St-Joseph, Lachine, tel. 514/634–4326) and the **Société de l'Île Notre-Dame** (Île Notre-Dame, tel. 514/872–6093).

Spectator Sports

Baseball The National League **Montreal Expos** play at the Olympic Stadium from April through September. For information, call 514/253–3434 or 800/361–4595; for credit card reservations, call 514/253–0700.

Cycling **La Classique Cycliste de Montréal** is a professional cycling competition through the LaFontaine, Mont-Royal, and Olympic
parks held in early June (tel. 514/847–8687).

Le Tour de l'Île de Montréal has made the *Guinness Book of
World Records* for attracting the greatest number of participants. More than 30,000 amateur cyclists participate in "North
America's most important amateur cycling event" each June,
wending their way 70 kilometers (38 miles) through the streets
and parks of Montréal (514/847–8687).

In October, the Grand Prix Cycliste des Amériques brings together professional cyclists from around the world to compete
in this 224-kilometer (139-mile) cycling competition (tel. 514/
879–1027).

Grand Prix The annual **Molson Grand Prix du Canada,** which draws top
Formula 1 racers from around the world, takes place every June
at the Gilles Villeneuve Race Track on Île Notre-Dame (tel.
514/392–0000 for tickets, tel. 514/392–4731 for information).

Hockey The **Montréal Canadiens,** winners of 23 Stanley Cups, meet
National Hockey League rivals at the Forum (2313 rue Ste-
Catherine O, tel. 514/932–2582) from October to April.

Dining

The promise of a good meal is easily satisfied in Montréal. Les
Montréalais don't "eat out"; they "dine." And they are passionate about dining. The city has more than 7,000 restaurants of
every price representing more than 35 ethnic groups. It has culinary institutions like Les Mignardises, Le Paris, and the Beaver Club, which emphasize classic cuisine and tradition.
Delicatessens such as Briskets, Schwartz's, and Wilensky's are
mainstays for budget dining. In between there are ethnic
eateries featuring the foods of China, Greece, India, Morocco,
and Italy. Then there are the ubiquitous inexpensive fast-food
outlets and coffee shops. But above all, Montréal is distinguished by the European ambience of its restaurants. Catch a
glimpse of the eateries' terraces from midday to 2 PM for a look
at the hours that Montréal diners take most seriously. Each of the
city's well-known bistros is more Parisian than the last. The challenge to dining in Montréal is choosing from among the thousands
of restaurants and the varieties of inexpensive fast-food outlets
and coffee shops.

Many expensive French and Continental restaurants offer two
options, which can be a blessing or a burden to your wallet. Either
choice guarantees you a great meal. Instead of ordering à la
carte—you select each dish—you can opt for the table d'hôte or
the *menu de dégustation*. The table d'hôte is a complete two- to
four-course meal chosen by the chef. It is less expensive than a
complete meal ordered à la carte and often offers interesting
special dishes. It also may take less time to prepare. If you
want to splurge with your time and money, indulge yourself
with the *menu de dégustation*, a five- to seven-course dinner
executed by the chef. It usually includes, in this order, salad,
soup, a fish dish, sherbet, a meat dish, dessert, and coffee or
tea. At the city's finest restaurants, this menu for two and a
good bottle of wine can cost $170 and last three or four hours.
But it's worth every cent and every second.

Montréal restaurants are refreshingly relaxed. Although many of the hotel restaurants require a jacket and tie, neatness (no torn T-shirts and scruffy jeans) is appreciated in most of the other restaurants. Lunch hour is generally from noon to 2:30 and dinner from 6 to 11 or midnight. (Montréalers like to dine late, particularly on summer weekends.) Some restaurants are closed on Sunday or Monday. Because there is no consistent annual closing among Montréal eateries—some will take time off in August, while others will close around Christmas and January—call ahead to avoid disappointment.

Highly recommended restaurants in each price category are indicated by a star ★.

Category	Cost*
Very Expensive	over $30
Expensive	$20–$30
Moderate	$10–$20
Inexpensive	$5–$10

per person without tax (combined GST of 7% and provincial tax of 8% on all meals), service, or drinks

Chinese

Moderate **Cathay Restaurant.** Hong Kong investors, fearful of their city's future, are pouring money into Montréal's and other Chinatowns in North America. Among other businesses, they're opening slick, Hong Kong–style restaurants and competing with the older Chinese eateries. The consumer wins in these restaurant wars. The 15-year-old Cathay was remodeled and expanded in 1985, and is now the most popular and largest dim sum restaurant in the city. The two floors are both huge rooms with institutional dropped ceilings and the usual red and gold Chinese stage decorations. From 11 AM to 2:30 PM, waitresses emerge from the kitchen pushing carts laden with steaming beef dumplings in bamboo steamers, spicy cuttlefish, shrimp rice noodles, bean-curd rolls, and on and on. *73 rue de la Gauchetière O, Chinatown, tel. 514/866–3131. No reservations on weekends, so be prepared to wait on Sun. morning. Dress: casual. AE, DC, MC, V.*

Inexpensive **Tai Kim Lung.** This small restaurant along the Chinatown pedestrian mall serves one of the better deals in the area: a Cantonese selection of wonton soup, one egg roll, diced chicken with cashews, fried rice and crisp vegetables, tea, and an almond cookie for $3.25 (excluding taxes). The table d'hôte offerings here are always wholesome and filling, though sometimes bland, for example the beef with broccoli. There are four or five selections each of either spicy Szechuan dishes, such as hot General Tao chicken, or milder Cantonese offerings like the fillet of *Doré* (walleyed pike) in a garlic sauce. There is also an extensive, more complicated (and in many cases, more expensive) menu to choose from. The decor—muted, toasted wheat-colored walls, mirrors, and soft lighting—is restful, even during the noontime rush. To keep the meal authentic, some regulars order Great Wall Chinese wine, but the bar also carries French wine as well as a decent house label that may be had by the glass. *74 rue de la Lagauchetière O (Place d'Armes Métro), tel. 514/861–7556. Reservations not required. Dress: casual. AE, MC, V. Closed Sun. lunch.*

Continental

Inexpensive **La Charade.** A short walk east from City Hall on rue Notre-Dame Est, this storefront restaurant is a gathering place for civil servants and some of the more budget-minded city councillors. Pink and white tablecloths, maroon draperies, and African violets lined up along the window sills make for a cozy atmosphere. The food, although not gourmet fare, is plentiful and varied, served up by a pleasant staff. The menu features Italian and French dishes, with a sprinkling of other choices like paella with a tangy tomato sauce, and chicken or shrimp brochettes. The accent is definitely on pasta, offering five or six different linguine selections, for example, and there are a hearty veal Parmesan, one of the tastier dishes, and *coq au vin*, a hefty portion of chicken stewed in a thick wine sauce with onions and mushrooms. Lighter eaters may sample seafood stews of *moules* (mussels) and shrimp or a Caesar or shrimp salad. The table d'hôte offers a choice of meals with soup, a main course, and coffee, many of which come to less than $10 (excluding taxes). Every week the restaurant features three-course dinner specials at $10.50. Of course, ordering up a carafe of house wine or a bottle of imported beer adds to the bill. *358 rue Notre-Dame E (Champ-de-Mars Métro), tel. 514/861–8756. Reservations not required. Dress: casual. MC, V.*

Delicatessens

Inexpensive **Bens.** On the menu of this large, efficient deli, all the items with "Bens" in the name are red or are covered in red: "Bens Cheesecake" is smothered in strawberries; "Bens Ice Cold Drink" is the color of electric cherry juice; and the specialty, the "Big Ben Sandwich," is two slices of rye bread enclosing a seductive, pink pile of juicy smoked meat (Montréal's version of corned beef). According to Bens lore, the founder, Ben Kravitz, brought the first smoked-meat sandwich to Montréal in 1908. The rest, as they say, is history. A number of the walls are devoted to photos of celebrities who have visited Bens. The decor is strictly '50s, with yellow and green walls and vaguely art deco, institutional furniture. The waiters are often wisecracking characters but are nonetheless incredibly efficient. Beer, wine, and cocktails are served. *990 boul. de Maisonneuve O, downtown, tel. 514/844–1000. Reservations accepted. Dress: casual. MC, V. Closed Sun.*

Wilensky's Light Lunch. Since 1932 the Wilensky family has served up its special: Italian-American salami on a Jewish roll, generously slathered with mustard. Served hot, it's a meal in itself. You can also get hot dogs or a grilled sandwich, which comes with a marinated pickle and an old-fashioned sparkling beverage. The regulars at the counter are among the most colorful in Montréal. A visit here is a must. This neighborhood haunt was the setting for the film *The Apprenticeship of Duddy Kravitz*, from the novel by Mordecai Richler. The service, which is not very friendly, does not prompt one to linger, but the prices make up for it. *5167 rue Clark, tel. 514/271–0247. Dress: informal. No credit cards. No liquor license. Closed weekends.*

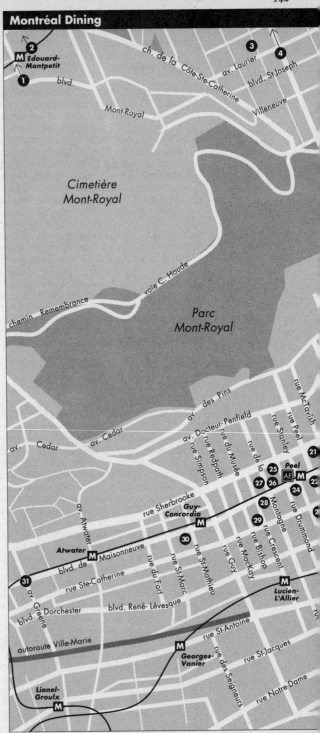

Montréal Dining

KEY

AE American Express Office

French

Very Expensive **The Beaver Club.** Early fur traders started the Beaver Club in a shack during Montréal's colonial days. In the 19th century it became a social club for the city's business and political elite. It still has the august atmosphere of a men's club devoted to those who trap: Pelts of bear, buffalo, and beaver still line the walls with members' engraved copper plates. The Beaver Club is a gourmet French restaurant open to anyone with a reservation who arrives in the proper attire. Master chef Edward Merard was among the first to introduce nouvelle cuisine to Montréal, and he has a large and devoted following. The luncheon table d'hôte includes such dishes as terrine of duckling with pistachios and onion, and cranberry compote. For more mundane tastes, the restaurant also specializes in meaty dishes like roast prime rib of beef au jus. The Beaver Club always offers one or two low-fat, low-salt, low-calorie plates. The waiters are veteran (Charles, the maître d', has worked here for more than 20 years), and the service is as excellent as the food. *La Reine Elizabeth, 900 boul. René-Lévesque O, downtown, tel. 514/861–3511. Reservations required. Jacket and tie required. AE, DC, MC, V.*

Le Café de Paris. This restaurant is a masterpiece of atmosphere. You sit at large, well-spaced tables in a room ablaze with flowers and with light streaming through the French windows. Renovated in 1991, the Ritz garden, with its picturesque duck pond, is open for summer dining alfresco. Inside or outside the waiters provide perfect, unobtrusive service. The menu opens with a selection of fresh caviar flown in from Petrossian in New York City. Then you turn to the seven-course *menu de dégustation*, a meal of small, exquisite dishes, such as quail salad with grapes, that adds up to a sumptuous repast. If you can't spend a couple of hours over dinner, you can choose from classics like calf sweetbreads with a slightly bitter endive sauce or the flambéed fillet of buffalo with green peppercorns. At meal's end the waiter will trundle over the dessert cart; the crème brûlée with raisins is a favorite. The wine list includes everything from reasonably priced bottles to extremely expensive vintages. The table to the right rear of the dining room as you enter is where the prime minister dines when in town. If the prime minister is not there, you are likely to see other national political and financial figures supping or schmoozing among the tables. *Hôtel Ritz-Carlton, 1228 rue Sherbrooke O, tel. 514/842–4212. Reservations required. Jacket required at lunch and dinner. AE, MC, V.*

Le Lutetia. This magnificent restaurant is worth a little detour, if only for the piano bar happy hour. The plethora of styles—rococo, renaissance, empire, fin de siècle, and baroque—is a spectacle in itself. This outrageously romantic restaurant is the perfect choice for a tête-à-tête by candlelight. The French cuisine, sometimes nouvelle, sometimes classic, is always served under a silver cover. Behind their glass partition, the cooks busy themselves and give the clientele an appetizing show, even at the busiest moments. The *menu gastronomique* changes each week according to the market and the seasons. À la carte half portions are available—which enables the diners to taste many dishes in one meal. Shrimp with fennel in puff pastry, ballotine of pheasant in a brioche dough, noisettes of veal *périgourdine* (with truffles), or medallions of beef with coarse mustard precede the cheese or the dessert cart. There is a very good wine list and champagne. *1430 rue de la Montagne, tel. 514/288–5656. Reservations advised. Dress: neat but casual. Terrace on the roof in summer. AE, DC, MC, V.*

★ **Les Halles.** Definitely French, this restaurant took its name from the celebrated Parisian market. Its old-France character, enhanced by mirrors and typical bistro inscriptions, will give you the feeling of having gone from busy rue Crescent to even busier rue Montorgueil. However, dependable cuisine and tradition make Les Halles very efficient. The fussy waiters, with their white aprons and towels on their arms, seem to come straight out of a '40s French film. The wine cellar is exceptional and contains about 250 different bottles, from $11 for half a bottle to $475. The menu shows a lot of imagination without ignoring the classics: Terrine of venison with a walnut sauce, fish stew with croutons, snails in all kinds of sauces, *plaice* (lemon sole) in cider, chicken *forestière*, and duck with foie gras in port sauce sit comfortably beside the chef's ventures into nouvelle cuisine, such as his lobster with ginger and coconut. The desserts are classic, delicious, and remarkably fresh. The Paris-Brest, a puff pastry with praline cream inside, is one of the best in town. *1450 rue Crescent, tel. 514/844–2328. Reservations advised. Dress: neat but casual. AE, DC, MC, V. Closed Sun.–Mon., Sat. lunch.*

★ **Les Mignardises.** Chef Jean-Pierre Monnet used to run the kitchen at Les Halles. Now that he has his own place, his talents are given free range. Les Mignardises is considered the finest and certainly the most expensive restaurant in town. You enter via the bar and climb up one flight to the simple, elegant dining room decorated with copper pans hanging from the exposed-brick walls. The dining area holds only about 20 tables, so reservations are a must. If your wallet is full, you can choose the seven-course *menu de dégustation* ($62.50). But if you're on a budget, it's still possible to enjoy a full meal. The three-course table d'hôte lunch menu allows you to sample delicious dishes like fish salad on gazpacho or marinated duck breast with vinegar sauce. Delicious potatoes sautéed with bouillon and onions in a little copper pot accompany the dishes. One of the house-special desserts is crepes with honey ice cream. The presentation always takes a back seat to the taste. As you would expect, the wine list is large and pricey. The waiters and waitresses are prompt, knowledgeable, and friendly. *2035–37 rue St-Denis, near Berri and Sherbrooke métros, tel. 514/842–1151. Reservations required. Dress: casual, but no jeans or T-shirts. AE, DC, MC, V. Closed Sun. and Mon.*

Expensive–Very Expensive **Le Cercle.** Le Quatre Saisons' management claims to have invented Montréal's version of power dining here. (The competition with the Ritz-Carlton continues.) Le Cercle certainly has the power look. The choicest seats are on a raised circular platform, encircled by a white Hellenistic colonnade. In these impressive surroundings Québec's political and business leaders dine on first-class nouvelle cuisine. Many must suffer from high blood pressure, because the menu features "alternative cuisine" dishes with reduced salt, cholesterol, and calories. The fricassee of sweetbreads and prawns with lobster butter is not on this list. If you suffer from chronic low wallet weight, you can stop in for lunch and have the onion soup with a ham and cheese sandwich on French bread. Power breakfasts start at 7 AM. The standard of service here, as in the rest of the hotel, is high. The wine list is expensive and excellent, of course. *Le Quatre Saisons, 1050 rue Sherbrooke O, tel. 514/284–1110. Reservations required. AE, DC, MC, V.*

Expensive **Auberge le Vieux St-Gabriel.** Established in a big stone house in 1754, this restaurant claims to be the oldest in America. The interior is lined with rough stone walls, and enormous old beams hold up the ceilings. In late 1987 it reopened with new owners who plan to expand both the menu and the dining space. At this writing the fare was hearty yet unadventurous French, with a bit of local Québecois flavor. The pea soup à la Canadienne is yellow and chunky rather than the American-style bland green puree. The perch fillets sautéed in dill butter are morsels of tender fish on top of mushy, overly rich creamed mushrooms. Other entrées include beef tenderloin with morels in a brandy and cream sauce and a terrine of rabbit with prunes and apples in a honey cream. If you're worried about your cholesterol, watch out. The restaurant seats close to 500 people, but you'd never guess it because there are so many separate dining rooms. *426 rue St-Gabriel, Vieux-Montréal, tel. 514/878–3561. Reservations advised. Dress: casual. AE, DC, MC, V. Closed Sun. except in summer.*

Moderate– **L'Express.** The crowd is elbow to elbow, and the animated at-
Expensive mosphere is reminiscent of a Paris train station at this earnest
★ establishment. L'Express has earned the title "best bistro in town." It is also the best stocked. Popular media figures come here to be seen, a task made easier by the mirrored walls. The atmosphere is smoky, and the noise level at its peak on weekend evenings. The cuisine is always impeccable, the service is fast, and the prices are very good. L'Express has one of the best and most original wine cellars in town. Wine and champagne are available by the glass as well as by the bottle. The steak tartare with french fries, the salmon with sorrel, the calves' liver with tarragon, the first course of chicken livers with pistachios, or even the modest smoked salmon are all marvelous year-round. There are specials of the day to give the many regulars a change of pace. Jars of gherkins and fresh *baguettes*, cheeses aged to perfection, and quality eaux-de-vie make the pleasure last longer. *3927 rue St-Denis, tel. 514/845–5333. Reservations required. Dress: neat but casual. AE, DC, MC, V.*

Greek

Expensive **Milos.** Nets, ropes, floats, and lanterns—the usual cliché sym-
★ bols of the sea—hang from Milos's walls and ceilings. The real display, however, is in the refrigerated cases and on the beds of ice in the back by the kitchen: fresh fish from all over the world; octopus, squid, and shrimp; crabs, oysters, and sea urchins; lamb chops, steaks, and chicken; and vegetables, cheese, and olives. The seafood is flown in from wholesalers in Nova Scotia, New York, Florida, and Athens. A meal can start out with chewy, tender, and hot octopus, or, if you're adventurous, you might try the cool and creamy roe scooped from raw sea urchins. The main dish at Milos is usually fish—pick whatever looks freshest—grilled over charcoal and seasoned with parsley, capers, and lemon juice. It's done to a turn and is achingly delicious. The fish are priced by the pound, and you can order one large fish to serve two or more. The bountiful Greek salad (enough for two) is a perfect side dish or can be a meal itself. For dessert you might try a *loukoumad* (honey ball), a deep-fried

puff of dough doused in honey, chopped nuts, and cinnamon. The waiters are professional but not always knowledgeable about the array of exotic seafood available. Milos is a healthy walk from Métro Laurier. You can also take Bus 51 from the same Métro stop and ask the driver to let you off at avenue du Parc; Milos is halfway up the block to the right. *5357 av. du Parc, tel. 514/272–3522. Reservations required. Dress: casual. AE, MC, V.*

Indian

Expensive **Le Taj.** One of the rare Indian restaurants in town in which the decor and the music are appropriate. The cuisine of the north of India is honored here, less spicy and more refined than that of the south. The tandoori ovens seal in the flavors of the grilled meat and fish, the *nan* bread comes piping hot to the table, and behind a glass partition the cook retrieves the skewers with his bare hands from the hot coals just like an experienced fakir. There are a few vegetarian specialties on the menu; for example, the *taj-thali,* consisting of lentils, chili *pakoras, basmati* rice, and *saag panir*—spicy white cheese with spinach. The tandoori quail and the nan stuffed with meat go well together, as does a whole series of dry curries, from lamb to chicken and beef with aromatic rice. The desserts, coconut ice cream, or mangoes (canned) are sometimes decorated with pure silver leaves if the patron so desires. Other cultures, other mores! The tea scented with cloves is delicious; it cleans the palate, warms in winter, and cools in summer. *2077 rue Stanley, tel. 514/845–9015. Weekend reservations advised. Dress: neat but casual. AE, MC, V. Closed Sat. lunch.*

Italian

Expensive ★ **Prego.** European chic lives at Prego. So does excellent nouvelle Italian cuisine. The clientele looks old and wealthy and is outfitted in the latest fashions. They sit on *faux* zebra-skin chairs or black banquettes and watch the flames in the high-tech black kitchen (if they aren't watching themselves in the mirror). Every dish is relatively light and absolutely fresh. The *insalata caprese* is a simple, satisfying salad of tomatoes, basil, olive oil, and bocconcini cheese. Between courses you are given a small serving of sorbet; if you're lucky, it will be the tarragon sorbet with poppy seeds sprinkled in it. The linguine with tuna, tomatoes, and capers is warm, light, and redolent of summer, even on a winter night. An excellent main dish is *medaglione di vitello ai pistacchi* (veal with cream; pistachios; fresh fruits; and Frangelico, a hazelnut liqueur). Keep some room for dessert, because Prego serves a tiramisu that should be in a hall of fame somewhere. The service and wine list are first-rate. *5142 boul. St-Laurent, 5 blocks from Métro Laurier, tel. 514/271–3234. Reservations required. Dress: neat but casual. AE, DC, MC, V. Closed lunch.*

Moderate– Expensive **Bocca d'Oro.** This Italian restaurant next to Métro Guy has a huge menu offering a wide variety of appetizers, pastas, and veal and vegetarian dishes. One pasta specialty is *tritico di pasta,* which is one helping each of spinach ravioli with salmon and caviar, shell-fish marinara, and spaghetti primavera. A good choice from the dozen or so veal dishes is scaloppine *zingara* (with tomatoes, mushrooms, pickles, and olives). With the dessert and coffee, the waiters bring out a big bowl of walnuts for you to crack at your table (nutcrackers provided). The two floors of dining rooms are decorated with brass rails, wood paneling, and paintings, and Italian pop songs play in the background. The staff is extremely friendly and professional; if you're in a hurry, they'll serve your meal in record time. *1448 rue St-Mathieu, downtown, tel. 514/933–8414. Reservations advised. Dress: neat but casual. AE, DC, MC, V. Closed Sun.*

Moderate **Pizzaiole.** The wood-fired oven pizzas have had no respite since they started to appear in Montréal in the beginning of the 1980s. Pizzaiole, the pioneer in the field, is still by far the best. The two branches have somewhat adopted the same fresh decor emphasizing the brick oven, but the clientele and the ambience of the rue Crescent location are a bit younger. In both places, there are about 20 possible combinations, without counting the toppings and extras that personalize a pizza in no time at all. Whether you choose a simple tomato-cheese or a ratatouille on a whole-wheat crust, you'll find that all the pizzas are made to order and brought immediately to the table. The calzone, a turnover filled with a variety of meats and cheeses, is worth the trip. Try the thirst-quenching Massawipi beer from a local brewery. *Two locations: 1446-A rue Crescent, tel. 514/845–4158; 5100 rue Hutchison, tel. 514/274–9349. AE, MC, V.*

Japanese

Expensive– Very Expensive **Katsura.** This cool, elegant Japanese restaurant introduced sushi to Montréal and is the haunt of businesspeople who equate raw food with power. If you're with a group or just want privacy, you can reserve a tatami room closed off from the rest of the restaurant by rice-paper screens. The sushi chefs create an assortment of raw seafood delicacies, as well as their own delicious invention, the Canada roll (smoked salmon and salmon caviar) at the sushi bar at the rear. Sushi connoisseurs may find some offerings less than top quality. The service is excellent, but if you sample all the sushi, the tab can be exorbitant. *2170 rue de la Montagne, downtown between Peel and Guy métros, tel. 514/849–1172. Reservations required, but you might get a seat at the sushi bar without them. Dress: neat but casual. AE, DC, MC, V. Closed weekend lunch.*

Jewish

Moderate **Friday Night at Bubby's.** Spending Friday night at grandmother's is a tradition carried out by Jews around the world. This Jewish-style (but not kosher) restaurant attempts to bring back memories for many by matching that atmosphere, with home-style non-deli cooking. Friday nights, of course, are special at the restaurant, with sittings at 6 PM and 8 PM; music with strolling *klezmer* musicians who play the clarinet, guitar, and violin; and loaves of fresh challah (egg) bread. Worth trying are the chicken-based soup with matzo balls and the chopped liver. The brisket, which is marinated for 24 hours, and the chopped, broiled veal are first-rate. All main dishes come with coleslaw, pickles, chicken wings, and latkes. The service is efficient and low-key. *1336 Greene Ave., Westmount, tel. 514/989–2225. Reservations advised, especially for Friday. Dress: casual. AE, MC, V. Open daily.*

Lebanese

Inexpensive **Basha.** The neon lights along gawdy rue Ste-Catherine and the ebb and flow of the crowd make this fast-food restaurant an entertaining spot for a quick evening bite. Bistro chairs and bare tables make up the utilitarian decor, and diners pick up plastic trays and choose their kebabs and falafels from the cafeteria-style counter. The menu, with prices as low as $2 and $3, includes beef and lamb shish-kebab sandwiches and platters, chicken brochettes, a daily falafel special, and a "Basha" grill platter. Open until 3 AM on weekends and until midnight during the week, this is one of the city's night-owl meccas; Montréalers stop by after a late movie for sticky, sweet Arab pastries and coffee. *930 rue Ste-Catherine O, level 2 (McGill or Peel Métro), tel. 514/866–4272. There is another downtown location at 2140 rue Guy, tel. 514/932–6682. Reservations not necessary. Dress: casual. No credit cards.*

Québécois

Moderate–
Expensive
★
Les Filles du Roy. This restaurant serves fine Québecois cuisine, a blend of 17th-century French recipes, North American produce and game, and some culinary tips picked up from Native Americans . . . with a lot of maple syrup poured over everything. The Trottier family opened Les Filles du Roy (the name refers to the women brought over to New France by Louis XIV to marry settlers) in an 18th-century stone mansion in 1964. A traditional Québecois meal starts with an appetizer like Canadian-style pork and beans or pea soup. If you like sweet meat dishes, try the ham with maple syrup. More refined dishes using local game and produce include wild lake duck with blueberries and *cipaille du Lac St-Jean*, which is a combination of six different meats, some wild, in a pie crust with vegetables. A large variety of maple syrup desserts are available: *trempette au sirop d'érable* (pieces of bread that have been dipped in boiling maple syrup in a bowl of heavy cream), sugar pie, and *oeuf cuit dans le sirop d'érable* (an egg poached in maple syrup). The popular Sunday brunch, served from 11 to 3, attracts groups of Japanese tourists wolfing down the ham and maple-syrup dishes. The interior of Les Filles du Roy is all stone and wood, and the furniture looks authentic; the staff wears the usual colonial-era dress. The service is knowledgeable and friendly. *415 rue Bonsecours, 3 blocks from Métro Champs-de-Mars in Vieux-Montréal, tel. 514/849–3535. Reservations required. Dress: neat but casual. AE, DC, MC, V.*

Sausages

Inexpensive **Chez Better.** The rustic fieldstone walls of historic Maison Sauvegarde create a fitting ambience for this North American branch of a popular European sausage house. Although the atmosphere—exposed stone walls, casement windows, dimmed lighting—is upscale, the limited nature of the menu keeps prices down, to only $2.95 (excluding taxes) in the case of the "Better Special," a satisfying sandwich of one mild sausage on freshly baked bread. It's a convenient refueling stop for visitors touring Vieux-Montréal, only a few steps from Place Jacques-Cartier and the Info-Touriste center on rue Notre-Dame Est. This Notre-Dame restaurant is the most elegant of the four "Betters," although all serve the same wide variety of sausages, imported beers, and rich desserts. Service is politely efficient and the noontime crowd lively; dining is more subdued in the evenings. *160 rue Notre-Dame E (Champ-de-Mars Mé-tro), 5400 chemin Côte-des-Neiges, 1310 boul. de Maisonneuve, 4382 boul. St-Laurent, and 1430 rue Stanley; tel. 514/861–2617. Reservations not necessary. Dress: casual. AE, MC, V.*

Seafood

Expensive **Chez Delmo.** This stretch of rue Notre-Dame is halfway be-
★ tween the courts and the stock exchange, and at lunchtime Chez Delmo is filled with professionals gobbling oysters and fish. The first room as you enter is lined with two long, dark, wood bars, which are preferred by those wishing a fast lunch. Above one is a mural depicting a medieval feast. The back room is a more sedate and cheerful dining room. In either room the dining is excellent and the seafood fresh. A good first course, or perhaps a light lunch, is the seafood salad, a delicious mix of shrimp, lobster, crab, and artichoke hearts on a bed of Boston lettuce, sprinkled with a scalliony vinaigrette. The poached salmon with hollandaise is a nice slab of perfectly cooked fish with potatoes and broccoli. The lobsters and oysters are priced according to market rates. Chez Delmo was founded at the same address in 1910. The service is efficient and low-key. *211–215 rue Notre-Dame O, Vieux-Montréal, tel. 514/849–4061. Dinner reservations advised. Dress: neat but casual. AE, DC, MC, V. Closed Mon. dinner, Sat. lunch, Sun.*

Steaks

Expensive **Moishe's.** A paradise for carnivores, Moishe's is the last place to
★ receive dietetic advice. The meat portions are as large as a pound, which will no doubt send your cholesterol level way up. Rib steak, T-bone, and filet Mignon are all grilled on wood and presented with dill-scented pickles, cole slaw, and french fries or baked potato. The meat, imported from western Canada, is juicy and tender, marbled and delectable, and aged 21 days in the restaurant's cold chambers. Moishe's grouchy service, its white aluminum-siding exterior and dark interior (reminiscent of an all-male private club), and its tasteless desserts don't seem to frighten away the real meat eaters. For those with a smaller appetite, the portions can be shared, but it will cost you an additional $4 and the waiter's reproachful look. *3961 boul. St-Laurent, tel. 514/845–1696. Reservations required for par-ties of 3 or more. Dress: casual. AE, MC, V.*

Inexpensive **Le Tramway.** The cheery, fire-engine-red facade of this steak and burger restaurant draws diners off rue Ste-Catherine, es-pecially in winter, when the lanterns inside glow a warm wel-come. Once you're aboard, the Tramway is a trip back some 50 years to a time when streetcars, not the Métro, ferried people around downtown Montréal. Interior decorations are refash-ioned memorabilia: old lamp fixtures, former fare boxes that now hold plants, and overhead racks now used as shelves above the shiny, red banquettes. A reasonably priced menu concen-trates on juicy hamburgers, although there is a "jumbo" smoked-meat sandwich with dill pickle and fries and a great thick Polish sausage garnished with sauerkraut and salad, all under $10. There are a few, more expensive selections, such as the charbroiled, prime-rib steak and filet Mignon, so this streetcar is a desirable choice for family diners with varying tastes and appetites. *1122 rue Ste-Catherine O, tel. 514/875–6300. No reservations. Dress: informal. Closed Sun. AE, DC, MC, V.*

Vietnamese

Moderate **Xuan.** Near the pedestrian zone of rue Prince Arthur, this lit-
★ tle restaurant strives to perpetuate real Vietnamese cuisine beyond the brochettes formula so popular with competitors. The owners lived in France for many years before settling in the province of Québec. They have included on the menu typical dishes, such as the Vietnamese crepe with vegetables and mint, the five-flavor stuffed quail, honey and citronella pork, and numerous soups at noontime that are hearty enough to be meals. The cold spring rolls in Hoisin sauce are particularly filling. For dessert, there is a delicious *assiette maison* (house plate) consisting of fruit puffs and rice-alcohol-scented ice cream, decorated with little Chinese umbrellas and flambéed in the French style. *26 rue Prince Arthur O, tel. 514/849–4923. AE, MC, V. Closed Mon.*

Tearooms

Inexpensive **La Chartreuse.** This tiny tearoom, in the Viennese tradition, has big surprises in store. On the counter are exhibited heavy and filling cakes, sparsely decorated but mouth-watering— *Nusstorte* with hazelnut butter cream, *Dobostorte* with chocolate layers and carmel icing, Sacher torte garnished with apricot jam, and Rigo Jancsi with chocolate ganache, fresh nuts, and coffee syrup make your time at La Chartreuse well spent. One moment on the lips, forever on the hips! The coffee (there is no espresso or cappuccino for lack of the appropriate equipment) is served with liqueurs, chocolate, cinnamon, or cream (whipped or not). Mozart is played discreetly in the background. *3439 rue St-Denis, tel. 514/842–0793. Dress: casual. No credit cards. Open 4 PM–midnight. Closed Mon.*

Restaurants near Montréal

Very Expensive **Le Mitoyen.** North of the city, in the small village of Ste-Dorothée (today part of the city of Laval), this great French restaurant leans resolutely in favor of nouvelle cuisine. People come from everywhere (mostly from Montréal) to taste the inventions of the self-taught chef. Meticulously decorated, this old house with the red roof is a haven for gourmands. Try the galette of smoked salmon, sweetbreads ragout with artichoke hearts, Guinea hen with sherry wine vinegar, or quail with juniper berries in puff pastry. All are heavenly. For dessert, the maple nougat glacé or the poached pears in red wine and pepper end the meal elegantly. *Place publique Ste-Dorothée, Laval (Rte. 15 N), tel. 514/689–2977. Reservations required. Dress: neat but casual. Closed Mon. and lunch daily (except for parties).*

★ **Les Trois Tilleuls.** In Saint Marc sur Richelieu, 20 minutes southeast of town, you can lunch or dine on delectable food right on the Rivière Richelieu. This romantic small inn, one of the Relais et Chateau chain, has a terrace on the river and a large, airy dining room. Chef Roger Robin is generous with his recipes, too. You can even stay overnight in one of the two dozen rooms or in the palatial royal suite if you really want to splurge. *290 rue Richelieu, Saint Marc sur Richelieu, tel. 514/584–2231, fax 514/584–3146. Reservations required. Dress: neat but casual.*

Expensive **La Sucrerie de la Montagne.** On the road to Rigaud in the direc-
★ tion of Ottawa, maple syrup flows from carafes year-round and seasons the plates of pork and beans, *tourtière,* maple-glazed ham, omelet soufflés, and crepes cooked over wood fires at this old-fashioned sugar hut. Even the bread is baked on the premises in the old brick ovens fired with maple wood. Everything in this young maple grove is intended to re-create the atmosphere of the sugar season: from the sap flowing in the snow (in season) to the workhorses to men collecting the sap bucket by bucket. Pierre Faucher, the owner of this immense sugar cabin, who looks more like a lumberjack than a restaurateur, greets the Sunday passersby as well as the buses overflowing with Japanese tourists in the middle of July. An old-fashioned general store sells Québec handcrafts and maple syrup. *Complete meal: $25 adults, half-price children under 12 (sleigh ride included in season). 300 rang St-Georges, Rigaud (Rte. 40, exit 17), tel. 514/451–5204. Reservations a must. Dress: informal. V.*

Lodging

On the island of Montréal alone there are 29,000 rooms available in every type of accommodation, from world-class luxury hotels to youth hostels, from student dormitories to budget executive motels. Keep in mind that during peak season (May–August), it may be difficult to find a bed without reserving, and most, but not all, hotels raise their prices. Prices often drop from mid-November to early April. Throughout the year a number of the better hotels have two-night, three-day, double-occupancy packages that offer substantial discounts.

If you arrive in Montréal without a hotel reservation, the tourism information booths at either airport can provide you with a list of hotels and room availability. You must, however, make the reservation yourself. There are no information booths at the Voyageur bus terminal, but the Gare Centrale is directly behind Le Reine Elizabeth hotel.

The following list is composed of recommended lodgings in Montréal for various budgets. The rates quoted are for a standard double room in May 1992; off-season rates are almost always lower.

Highly recommended hotels in each price category are indicated by a star ★.

Category	Cost*
Very Expensive	over $160
Expensive	$120–$160
Moderate	$85–$120
Inexpensive	under $85

*All prices are for a standard double room, excluding an optional service charge.

Downtown

Very Expensive **Bonaventure Hilton International.** This 394-room Hilton—situ-
★ ated atop a Métro station, the Place Bonaventure exhibition
center, and a mall crowded with shops and restaurants—is,
first and foremost, a resort hotel, and it's 17 floors above the
street. When you exit the elevator, you find yourself in a spacious reception area flanked by an outdoor swimming pool
(heated year-round) and 2½ acres of gardens, complete with
ducks. Also on this floor is a complex of three restaurants and a
nightclub that features well-known international entertainers.
Le Castillon is the flagship restaurant, known for its three-
course, 55-minute businessman's lunch. On Sunday, there's a
special theme menu. All rooms have fully stocked minibars and
black-and-white TVs in the bathrooms. The Bonaventure has
excellent access to the Métro station of the same name beneath
it and to all the shops at Place Ville-Marie through the Underground City. *1 Place Bonaventure, H5A 1E4, tel. 514/878–2332
or 800/445–8667. 394 rooms. Facilities: 3 restaurants, nightclub, health club with sauna, outdoor pool, rooftop garden, gift
shop (hotel is located in a building with a shopping mall), and
24-hr room service. AE, DC, MC, V.*

★ **Hôtel de la Montagne.** The reception area of the Hôtel de la
Montagne greets you with a naked, butterfly-winged nymph
rising out of a fountain. An enormous crystal chandelier hangs
from the ceiling and tinkles to the beat of disco music played a
little too loudly. The decor says Versailles rebuilt with a dash of
art nouveau by a discothèque architect circa 1975. The rooms
are tamer but large and comfortable. Another reason to stay in
or visit this hotel is the food. The main restaurant, Le Lutetia,
is known as one of the best and most innovative gourmet
eateries in Montréal (*see* Dining, above). Tea and cocktails are
served in the two lobby bars on each side of the hall, and a tunnel connects the hotel to Thursday's/Les Beaux Jeudis, a popular singles bar, restaurant, and dance club all rolled into one.
Clientele is a truly bilingual mixture of French-speaking Montréalers stopping by for a drink and Torontonians in town on
business. If you're staying elsewhere, the reception area is at
least worth a visit. *1430 rue de la Montagne, H3G 1Z5, tel. 514/
288–5656 or 800/361–6262. 136 rooms. Facilities: 2 restaurants, disco-bar, and outdoor pool. AE, D, DC, MC, V.*

Hotel Inter-Continental Montréal. This first Inter-Continental
property in Montréal, built in 1991, brings hotel luxury to
Vieux-Montréal for the first time in decades. The 24-story hotel is linked to the World Trade Centre, the block-long retail
and office development that combines old and new in the former
financial heart of the city, close to Vieux-Montréal attractions
and the Palais des Congrès convention center. The La Voûte
restaurants are housed in the 19th-century Nordheimer Building on rue St-Jacques, which has been restored to its original
Victorian splendor, with decorative plaster ceilings and cast-
iron columns. The restaurants are an oyster bar and wine-
tasting room and a steak and seafood restaurant. There are also
two bars, including the Peacock, at ground level. Matching the
Victorian flavor of the Nordheimer, the hotel rooms are designed in soft pastel colors. The interior of the hotel makes rich
use of granite and wood paneling. Other facilities include
minibars and refrigerators in rooms, computer and fax hookups, 12 meeting rooms, twice-daily maid service, complimentary shoe shine, a daily newspaper, and a ballroom once

Montréal Lodging

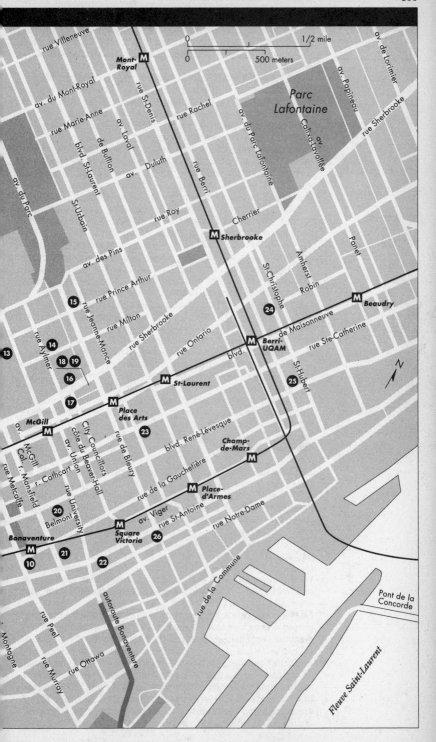

155

frequented by actress Sarah Bernhardt. *360 rue St-Antoine O, H2Y 3X4, tel. 514/987–9900 or 800/327–0200. 359 rooms, 22 suites. Facilities: restaurant, oyster bar, health club with sauna, indoor pool, cable TV, and 24-hour room service. AE, DC, MC, V.*

Hôtel Vogue. One of Montréal's newest and most elegant hotels, the Vogue opened in late 1990, happily surprising everyone who remembered this building as a drab office tower. Now beautifully transformed, with tall windows and a facade of polished rose granite and deep aqua trim, this hotel is chic, sophisticated, and in the heart of downtown, right across rue de la Montagne from Ogilvy department store. The lobby's focal point, the L'Opéra Bar, boasts an expansive bay window. Room furnishings are decorated in striped silk, and double, queen- and king-size beds are draped with satiny duvets. Fax machines and multiline telephones in rooms appeal to business travelers. Bathrooms come with Jacuzzis, televisions, and phones. The Société Café on the lobby level is already a favorite among downtowners. *1425 rue de la Montagne, H3G 1Z3, tel. 514/285–5555 or 800/243–1166. 149 rooms, 30 suites. Facilities: restaurant, bar, and exercise room. AE, D, MC, V.*

Le Centre Sheraton. In a huge 37-story complex well placed between the downtown business district and the restaurant streets of Crescent and Bishop, this Sheraton offers a wide variety of services to both the business and tourist crowds. It's also a favorite with international entertainment celebrities. There are three restaurants, five lounges, a nightclub, an indoor pool, a health club, and indoor parking for 600 cars. The elite, five-story Towers section is geared toward business travelers. The Sheraton caters to conventions, so expect to encounter such groups when you stay here. Though the decor is beige and unremarkable (once inside you could be in any large, modern hotel in any North American metropolis), the location's the thing. *1201 boul. René-Lévesque O, H3B 2L7, tel. 514/878–2000 or 800/325–3535. 878 rooms. Facilities: 3 restaurants, 5 lounges, nightclub, health club with whirlpool and sauna, indoor pool, unisex beauty parlor, and gift shop. AE, DC, MC, V.*

Le Château Champlain. In the heart of downtown Montréal, at the southern end of Place du Canada, Le Château Champlain is a 36-floor skyscraper with distinctive half-moon–shape windows. The decor of this hotel is formal, and there are only 20 rooms per floor. A number of floors are reserved for nonsmokers. Underground passageways connect the Champlain with the Bonaventure Métro station, the Bonaventure Hilton International, and Place Ville-Marie. *1 Place du Canada, H3B 4C9, tel. 514/878–9000 or 800/828–7447. 614 rooms. Facilities: 3 restaurants, lounge with entertainment, health club with sauna and whirlpool, large indoor pool, movie theater, and gift shops. AE, DC, MC, V.*

Le Meridien. This Air France property rises 12 stories from the center of the Complexe Desjardins, a boutique-rich mall in the center of the plushest stretch of the Underground City. The hotel caters to businesspeople and tourists who want ultramodern European style and convenience. Le Meridien is designed on a plan of circles of privilege within these already-exclusive surroundings. For instance, within Le Café Fleuri French restaurant there's a chicer, pricier enclave called Le Club. There are no-smoking floors and an indoor pool, sauna, and whirlpool facility. And if the atmosphere ever seems too confining, you can always burst out the door and go to Chinatown, a five-minute walk away. *4 Complexe Desjardins, H5B 1E5, tel. 514/285–1450 or 800/543–4300. 601 rooms. Facilities: 3 restaurants, business center, piano bar, indoor pool, sauna, whirlpool, guest passes to nearby YMCA and YWCA, and baby-sitting services; located in complex with shops and boutiques. AE, DC, MC, V.*

★ **Le Quatre Saisons.** The "Square Mile" of rue Sherbrooke Ouest—Montréal's Fifth Avenue—is decorated by the city's two best hotels. The Ritz-Carlton and this property are engaged in a constant battle to see which can give its clients the best and most in services. Even the least expensive room, known as a "Superior," has amenities galore: three phones, bathrobes, silk hangers, a minibar, a hair dryer, a clock-radio, and a safe. The more expensive suites have even more phones, and some are graced with marble bathtubs, like the one Michael Jackson presumably floated in when he was a guest. Le Quatre Saisons is renovated frequently, and the latest decor is at the same time slickly modern and filled with "stately English manor" furnishings. The white-column Le Cercle is known as one of Montréal's best places for nouvelle cuisine (*see* Dining, above). Le Quatre Saisons is one block from Métro Peel in the heart of Montréal's fanciest shopping district. *1050 rue Sherbrooke O, H3A 2R6, tel. 514/284–1110 or 800/332–3442. 302 rooms. Facilities: 1 restaurant, lounge, health club with whirlpool and sauna, outdoor pool, and 24-hr room service. AE, DC, MC, V.*

★ **Le Reine Elizabeth.** If the Ritz-Carlton is a stately old cruise ship, then the Queen Elizabeth, also called Le Reine Elizabeth, is a battleship. Massive and gray, this Canadian Pacific hotel sits on top of the Gare Centrale train station in the very heart of the city, beside Mary Queen of the World Catholic Cathedral and across the street from Place Ville-Marie. The lobby is a bit too much like a railway station—hordes march this way and that—to be attractive and personal, but upstairs the rooms are modern, spacious, and spotless, especially in the more expensive Entrée Gold section. All the latest gadgets and other trappings of luxury are present. The Beaver Club (*see* Dining, above), the flagship restaurant, is such an institution that there is a small museum devoted to it on the lobby level. There's a cheaper restaurant, too, as well as four lounges. Conventions are a specialty here. *900 boul. René-Lévesque, H3B 4A5, tel. 514/861–3511 or 800/268–9143. 1,045 rooms. Facilities: 4 restaurants, 2 bars/lounges, beauty salon, boutiques, and gift shops. AE, D, DC, MC, V.*

Le Shangrila Best Western. If you're a frequent traveler to Montréal, you may want to try something different: an Oriental-style hotel. The hotel's decor from reception to restaurant to rooms is modern, with an amalgam of Korean, Chinese, Japanese, and Indian motifs and artwork. In addition to special corporate-class extras, such as a lounge for buffet breakfasts and snacks, there are also pluses for the fitness fanatic: 12 to 15 "health rooms," private rooms with exercise facilities. There is a large Szechuan-style restaurant, Dynastie de Ming, on the lobby level. During the week the clientele is corporate; on weekends most of the guests are tourists from the United States and Ontario. Le Shangrila is situated across the street from Le Quatre Saisons on rue Sherbrooke, one block from Métro Peel. *3407 rue Peel, H3A 1W7, tel. 514/288–4141 or 800/528–*

1234. 162 rooms. Facilities: café, restaurant, bar, business lounge, gift shop, and salon. AE, DC, MC, V.

Ramada Renaissance du Parc. The Ramada chain bought the old Hôtel du Parc in 1987 and has made it the most luxurious of its four Montréal properties. Half a block away from the acres of greenery in Parc Mont-Royal, this Ramada's locale is prime. The hotel itself aims its services mainly at a corporate clientele. The rooms are large, and the decor is modern and well maintained. From the lobby you can descend to a shopping mall with many stores and movie theaters. The nightlife of rue Prince Arthur is six blocks away. *3625 av. du Parc, H2X 3P8, tel. 514/288–6666 or 800/228–9898. 455 rooms. Facilities: 2 restaurants, café-bar, business lounge, health club, squash courts, 2 swimming pools, tennis court, nonsmoking floors, and gift shop. AE, DC, MC, V.*

★ **Ritz-Carlton.** This property floats like a stately old luxury liner along rue Sherbrooke. It was opened in 1912 by a consortium of local investors who wanted a hotel in which their rich European friends could stay and indulge their champagne-and-caviar tastes. Since then many earth-shaking events have occurred here, including the marriage of Elizabeth Taylor and Richard Burton. Power breakfasts, lunches, and dinners are the rule at the elegant Café de Paris, and the prime minister and others in the national government are frequently sighted eating here. A less heady atmosphere prevails at the Ritz-Carlton's two other excellent restaurants. Guest rooms are a successful blend of Edwardian style—some suites have working fireplaces—with such modern accessories as electronic safes. Careful and personal attention are hallmarks of the Ritz-Carlton's service. Even if you're not a guest, stop by the Ritz's Hotel Courtyard during the summer for afternoon tea and to see the duck pond, a Ritz tradition since 1912. *1228 rue Sherbrooke O, H3A 2R6, tel. 514/842–4212 or 800/223–9868. 240 rooms. Facilities: 4 restaurants, piano bar, gift shop, beauty salon, barber shop, and 24-hour room service. AE, DC, MC, V.*

Expensive **Delta Montréal.** The French-style Delta is making a bid to break into the ranks of Montréal's world-class hotels. Many of the spacious guest rooms have balconies and excellent views of the city. The Le Bouquet restaurant and the piano lounge are designed like 19th-century Parisian establishments, with dark wood paneling and brass chandeliers. The cuisine is Continental and not above trendy touches like grilling over mesquite. The Delta has the most complete exercise and pool facility in Montréal. There are indoor and outdoor pools, two international squash courts, an exercise room, a sauna, and a whirlpool. The innovative Children's Creative Centre lets your children play (under supervision) while you gallivant around town. *450 rue Sherbrooke O, H3A 2T4 (entrance off av. du President-Kennedy), tel. 514/286–1986 or 800/268–1133. 453 rooms. Facilities: restaurant; jazz bar (which also serves lunch Mon.–Fri.); indoor and outdoor pools; health club with whirlpool, sauna; squash courts; aerobics classes; children's center; gift shop; and pinball and video-game rooms. AE, DC, MC, V.*

Holiday Inn Crowne Plaza. The flagship of the Holiday Inn chain's downtown Montréal hotels, the Crowne Plaza could just as well have been plopped down in Las Vegas or Atlanta. On the other hand, one doesn't stay in Holiday Inns for originality of design. This hotel *does* sparkle: It was recently renovated from top to bottom and has the largest indoor pool of the city's hotels, in addition to a health club, café-restaurant, and two bars. It has two suites, a penthouse, and two business floors. Popular for conventions, this hotel is near Métro McGill, rue Sherbrooke shopping, and downtown. *420 rue Sherbrooke O, H3A 1B4, tel. 514/842–6111 or 800/465–4329. 487 rooms. Facilities: 24-hour room service, café-restaurant, 2 bars, indoor pool, health club with sauna and whirlpool, unisex beauty parlor, and gift shop. AE, DC, MC, V.*

La Citadelle. There's a small pack of hotels on rue Sherbrooke, all of them convenient to Place des Arts, shopping, and the financial district; La Citadelle, a Clarion Hotel property, is one of them. This relatively small business hotel offers both four-star elegance in a low-key atmosphere and service, along with all the features of its better-known brethren: minibars, in-room movies, a small health club with an indoor pool, etc. There's also a passable French restaurant, C'est La Vie. *410 rue Sherbrooke O, H3A 1B3, tel. 514/844–8851 or 800/263–8967. 180 rooms. Facilities: restaurant; lounge with entertainment; health club with Nautilus, sauna, and steam room; indoor pool; and gift shop. AE, DC, MC, V.*

★ **Le Grand Hôtel.** Le Grand abuts the stock exchange; Place Bonaventure is half a block one way, the western fringe of Vieux-Montréal one block the other, and the Métro Square Victoria can be reached via an underground passage. In the midst of all this, Le Grand, a Hôtel des Gouverneurs property, rises above a stunning three-story atrium-reception area. It's yet another large, modern hotel attractive to meeting planners. Le Grand offers the usual health club and pool facilities, a more exclusive floor for higher-paying guests, and a shopping arcade on the underground level. Its most outstanding feature: the restaurants. The Tour de Ville on the top floor is the city's only revolving restaurant, and its bar has live jazz nightly. Chez Antoine is an art nouveau–style bistro with grilled meats a specialty. *777 rue University, H3C 3Z7, tel. 514/879–1370 or 800/361–8155. 707 rooms. Facilities: 2 restaurants, bar, health club with spa and steam room, aerobics classes, indoor pool, and gift shop. AE, DC, MC, V.*

Moderate **Château Versailles.** This small, charming hotel occupies a row of
★ four converted mansions in an excellent location on rue Sherbrooke Ouest. The owners have decorated it with many antique paintings, tapestries, and furnishings; some rooms have ornate moldings and plaster decorations on the walls and ceilings. Each room also has a full bath, TV, and air-conditioning. The reception area is designed to look like a European pension. Across the street, at 1808 rue Sherbrooke, the Villeneuve family has added a former apartment hotel as an annex to the original town houses. Called La Tour Versailles, it offers 107 larger, more Spartan rooms, at the same reasonable price, and a restaurant run by Christien Lévêque, former chef at the Ritz. It's aptly called the Champs-Élysées. The staff is extremely helpful and friendly. The Versailles is unassuming, not too expensive, and classy. *1659 rue Sherbrooke O (near Métro Guy-Concordia), H3H 1E3, tel. 514/933–3611 or 800/361–3664. 177 rooms. Facilities: breakfast and tearoom in the Château, restaurant in the Tour. AE, MC, V.*

Howard Johnson Hôtel Plaza. Completely renovated in 1988, this medium-size, medium-price hotel, next to the McGill campus, caters to the business trade and families. Exercise machines and a spa with sauna have been added, and the lobby was redone. The decor of the restaurant is Italianate, with lots of brass and marble and with bay windows overlooking the street. There's also a terrace for summer dining outdoors. The Hôtel Plaza is handy to downtown business and shopping areas. *475 rue Sherbrooke O, H3A 2L9, tel. 514/842–3961 or 800/654– 2000. 200 rooms. Facilities: restaurant and café. AE, DC, MC, V.*

Le Nouvel Hôtel. The Nouvel Hôtel is what hotel managers like to call a "new concept"—in its four towers it has studios, suites, and 2½-room apartments. It's not very classy, but it's all new, brightly colored, and functional. Le Nouvel Hôtel is near the restaurant district, five or six blocks from the heart of downtown and two blocks from the Guy-Concordia Métro station. *1740 boul. René-Lévesque O, H3H 1R3, tel. 514/931–8841 or 800/567–2737. 257 rooms. Facilities: restaurant, bar, gift shop, and outdoor pool. AE, DC, MC, V.*

Inexpensive **Le Royal Roussillon.** This hotel is adjacent to the Terminus Voyageur bus station (buses park directly beneath one wing of the hotel), and some of the bus station aura seems to rub off on the Roussillon; it's a little dingy. But if you're stumbling after a long bus ride and want somewhere to stay, *now*, the Rousillon's rooms are large and clean, the service is friendly, and the price is right. It's also handy to the Berri-UQAM Métro station. *1610 rue St-Hubert, H2L 3Z3, tel. 514/849–3214. 104 rooms. Facilities: restaurant. AE, DC, MC, V.*

Lord Berri. Next to the Université du Québec à Montréal, the Lord Berri is a new, moderately priced hotel convenient to the restaurants and nightlife of rue St-Denis. It offers some of the services of its more expensive competition: minibars, in-room movies, and nonsmoking floors. The De La Muse restaurant serves good bistro food and is popular with a local clientele. The Berri-UQAM Métro stop is a block away. *1199 rue Berri, H2L 4C6, tel. 514/845–9236 or 800/363–0363. 154 rooms. Facilities: restaurant and gift shop. AE, DC, MC, V.*

YMCA. This clean Y is downtown, next to Peel Métro station. Book at least two days in advance. Women should book seven days ahead—there are fewer rooms with showers for women. Anyone staying summer weekends must book a week ahead. *1450 rue Stanley, H3A 2W6, tel. 514/849–8393. 331 rooms, 429 beds. MC, V.*

YWCA. Very close to dozens of restaurants, the Y is right downtown, one block from rue Ste-Catherine. *1355 boul. René-Lévesque, H3G 1P3, tel. 514/866–9941. 107 rooms. Facilities: recently renovated hotel and fitness facilities. Accepts women only. Men may use café. Rooms with sink or bath available. (Reserve for best choice.) Oct.–May, stay 7 nights, pay for 6. Café open 7:30 AM–7 PM. Pool, sauna, whirlpool, weight room, fitness classes—no extra charge for hotel guests. MC, V.*

McGill University Area

Inexpensive **Auberge de Jeunesse Internationale de Montréal.** The youth hostel near the McGill campus in the student ghetto charges $9.50 for members, $12.50 for nonmembers, per night per person. Reserve early during the summer tourist season. *3541 rue Aylmer, H2X 2B9, tel. 514/843–3317. 112 beds. Facilities: rooms for 4–12 people (same sex); a few rooms available for couples and families. No credit cards.*

McGill Student Apartments. From mid-May to mid-August, when McGill is on summer recess, you can stay in its dorms on the grassy, quiet campus in the heart of the city. Nightly rates: $21 students; $28.50 nonstudents (single rooms only). *3935 rue University, H3A 2B4, tel. 514/398–6367. 1,000 rooms. Facilities: campus swimming pool and health facilities (visitors must pay to use them).*

Université de Montréal Area

Inexpensive **Université de Montréal Residence.** The university's student housing accepts visitors from May 9 to August 22. It's on the other side of Mont Royal, a long walk from downtown and Vieux-Montréal, but there's the new Université de Montréal Métro stop right next to the campus. Nightly rates: $17 students; $27 nonstudents. *2350 boul. Édouard-Montpetit, H3C 3J7, tel. 514/343–6531. 1,171 rooms. Facilities: campus sports center with pool and gym (visitors must pay to use it). AE, MC, V.*

Bed-and-Breakfasts

Bed and Breakfast à Montréal. Most of the more than 50 homes are downtown or in the elegant neighborhoods of Westmount and Outremont. Some of them can be quite ritzy. Others are less expensive, but all provide breakfast and a wealth of information about the city. *Contact: Marian Kahn, Box 575, Snowdon Station, Montréal H3X 3T8, tel. 514/738–9410. Single $30–$50, double $50–$100. "Unhosted" apartments also available, minimum 4-night stay, rates $90 and up. AE, MC, V accepted for deposits only; the balance must be paid with cash or traveler's checks.*

Downtown B & B Network. This organization will put you in touch with 75 homes and apartments, mostly around the downtown core and along rue Sherbrooke, that have one or more rooms available for visitors. These homes generally are clean, lovingly kept up, and filled with antiques. Even during the height of the tourist season, this organization has rooms open. *Contact: Bob Finkelstein, 3458 av. Laval (at rue Sherbrooke), Montréal H2X 3C8, tel. 514/289–9749. Single $25–$40, double $35–$55. AE, MC, V.*

The Arts and Nightlife

When it comes to entertainment, Montréal has a superiority complex. It can boast of serious culture—symphony orchestras, opera, and dance companies. At the pinnacle of the High Art scene stands the Orchestre Symphonique de Montréal, led by Charles Dutoit, and l'Opéra de Montréal. The city is known for its adventurous theatrical companies; unfortunately for the English-speaking visitor, most presentations are in French. Montréal is also the home of a small group of filmmakers and the National Film Board, who regularly bring home accolades from international festivals. On the low-life side of the tracks, the city is filled with all types of bars and clubs, including jazz and rock clubs, discos, cabarets, singles bars, and strip clubs. Puritanism is definitely not in fashion here. There are also a number of larger halls where international pop and rock stars regularly perform. Summer is the time for the most action—

more events, bigger crowds, later hours—but if you visit during the off-season there's sure to be something going on.

The entertainment section of the *Gazette*, the English-language daily paper, is a good place to find out about upcoming events. The Friday weekend guide has an especially good list of all events at the city's concert halls, theaters, clubs, dance spaces, and movie houses.

For tickets to major pop and rock concerts, shows, festivals, and hockey and baseball games, go to the individual box offices or call Admission (tel. 514/522–1245). Ticketron outlets are located in La Baie department store and in all Provigo supermarkets. Place des Arts tickets may be purchased at its box office underneath the Salle Wilfrid-Pelletier, next to the Métro station.

The Arts

Music   The **Orchestre Symphonique de Montréal** has gained world renown under the baton of Charles Dutoit. When not on tour its regular venue is the Salle Wilfrid-Pelletier at the Place des Arts. The orchestra also gives Christmas and summer concerts in the Notre-Dame Basilica and pop concerts at the Arena Maurice Richard in the Olympic Park. For tickets and program information, call 514/842–3402. Also check the *Gazette* listings for its free summertime concerts in Montréal's city parks. Montréal's other orchestra, the **Orchestre Métropolitain de Montréal** (tel. 514/598–0870), also stars at Place des Arts most weeks during the October–May season. McGill University, at Pollack Concert Hall (tel. 514/398–4547) and Redpath Hall (tel. 514/398–4539 or 514/398–4547), is also the site of many classical concerts. The most notable are given by the **McGill Chamber Orchestra,** which also occasionally plays at Place des Arts with guest artists. **L'Opéra de Montréal,** founded in 1980, stages four productions a year at Place des Arts (tel. 514/985–2222).

The 20,000-seat **Montréal Forum** (tel. 514/932–6131) and the much larger Olympic Stadium are where rock and pop concerts are staged. More intimate concert halls include the **Théâtre St-Denis** (1594 rue St-Denis, tel. 514/849–4211) and the **Spectrum** (318 rue Ste-Catherine O, tel. 514/861–5851).

Theater   French-speaking theater lovers will find a wealth of dramatic productions. There are at least 10 major companies in town, some of which have an international reputation. Best bets are productions at **Théâtre d'Aujourd'hui** (1297 rue Papineau, tel. 514/523–1211), **Théâtre du Nouveau Monde** (84 rue Ste-Catherine E, tel. 514/861–0563), and **Théâtre du Rideau Vert** (4664 rue St-Denis, tel. 514/844–1793). Anglophones have less to choose from, unless they want to chance the language barrier. **Centaur Theatre,** the best-known English theatrical company, stages productions in the Beaux Arts–style former stock exchange building at 453 rue St-François-Xavier in Vieux-Montréal (tel. 514/288–3161). English-language plays can also be seen at the **Saidye Bronfman Centre** at 5170 chemin de la Côte Ste-Catherine (tel. 514/739–7944). Michel Tremblay is Montréal's premier playwright, and all of his plays are worth seeing, even if in the English translation. Touring companies of Broadway productions can often be seen at the completely renovated and expanded **Théâtre St-Denis** on rue St-Denis (tel.

514/849–4211), as well as at Place des Arts (tel. 514/842–2112)—especially during the summer months.

Dance Traditional and contemporary dance companies thrive in Montréal, though many take to the road or are on hiatus in the summer. Among the best known are **Ballets Classiques de Montréal** (tel. 514/866–1771); **Les Grands Ballets Canadiens,** the leading Québec company (tel. 514/849–8681); **O Vertigo Danse** (tel. 514/251–9177); **Montréal Danse** (tel. 514/845–2031); **LaLaLa Human Steps** (tel. 514/288–8266); **Les Ballets Jazz de Montréal** (tel. 514/875–9640); **Margie Gillis Fondation de Danse** (tel. 514/845–3115); and **Tangente** (tel. 514/842–3532)—a nucleus for many of the more avant-garde dance troupes. When not on tour, many of these artists can be seen at Place des Arts or at any of the Maisons de la Culture (tel. 514/872–6211) performance spaces around town. Montréal's dancers have a brand-new downtown performance and rehearsal space, the Agora Dance Theatre, affiliated with the Université de Montréal dance faculty (840 rue Chérrier E, tel. 514/525–1500). Check newspaper listings for details. Every other September (that is, in the odd-numbered years, such as 1993), the **Festival International de Nouvelle Danse** brings "new" dance to various venues around town. Tickets for this event always sell quickly.

Nightlife

Bars and Clubs Elegant dinner-theater productions have revitalized Montréal's English theater. Prices range from about $12 for the show alone to more than $50 for the show and dinner (not including drinks—which can run up to about $6.50 each—tips, or tax). Small, cabaret-type shows can be found at a few major hotels. **Le Caf' Conc',** at the Château Champlain (tel. 514/878–9000), is a 19th-century French period piece, reminiscent of the theaters painted by Toulouse-Lautrec, which serves up a supper with a saucy can-can show and performances by guest artists. **La Diligence** (tel. 514/731–7771) has two dinner theaters and a solid reputation for presenting polished performances of popular productions—usually Broadway hits, as well as light musical comedies and plays in English. **The Csarda Restaurant** (3479 boul. St-Laurent) features Hungarian music Saturday and Sunday nights (tel. 514/843–4346). **Le Festin du Gouverneur,** at the old fort on Île Ste-Hélène (tel. 514/879–1141), offers a unique dinner-theater experience. Light operatic airs, beautifully rendered as a merry 17th-century frolic in the military barracks mess hall, are served up with copious amounts of food and drinks. Great for group outings. **The Foolhouse Theater Company** (tel. 514/483–5426) stages musical comedies, such as its local hit *Let's Go to the Ritz,* at various venues around town. Call for its latest show times and places.

Aside from full-fledged cabarets and dinner theaters, most of the big hotels offer some kind of live entertainment, including music and dancing to live music between shows. The Ritz-Carlton (tel. 514/842–4212) has a ground-floor bar (*très élégant*), with a pianist in evening dress, at which you can nibble on smoked salmon. There are music and slow dancing at **Puzzle's Jazz Bar** in the Ramada Renaissance (tel. 514/288–3733), the Sheraton's **L'Impromptu** (tel. 514/878–2000), and the **Tour de Ville,** atop Le Grand Hôtel (tel. 514/879–1370).

Jazz   Montréal has a very active local jazz scene. The best-known club is Vieux-Montréal's **L'Air du Temps** (191 rue St-Paul O, tel. 514/842–2003). This small, smoky club presents 90% local talent and 10% international acts from 5 PM on into the night. There's a cover charge Thursday through Saturday. Downtown, duck into **Biddle's** (tel. 514/842–8656), at 2060 rue Aylmer, where bassist Charles Biddle holds forth most evenings when he's not appearing at a local hotel. Bernard Primeau's Trio are weekend regulars. This upscale club is also a restaurant that serves ribs and chicken. There's a cover charge for the big acts. You also might try **Jazz Elda-James** (tel. 514/499–9403), at 408 rue St-François-Xavier, or **Le Grand Café** (tel. 514/849–6955), at 1720 rue St-Denis. **Le Bijou** (tel. 514/288–5508), at 300 rue Lemoyne, is another sure bet.

Rock   Rock clubs seem to spring up, flourish, then fizzle out overnight. **Club Soda** (tel. 514/270–7848), at 5240 avenue du Parc, the granddaddy of them all, sports a neon martini glass complete with neon effervescence outside. Inside it's a small hall with a stage, three bars, and room for about 400 people. International rock acts play here, as does local talent. It's also a venue for the comedy and jazz festivals. Open seven nights from 8 PM to 3 AM; admission ranges from nothing up to $20, depending. **Foufounes Électriques** (tel. 514/845–5484)—which translates as "electric buttocks"—at 97 rue Ste-Catherine Est in the Latin Quarter is the downscale, more avant-garde competitor of Club Soda. Foufounes is the center for the local band scene and also attracts up-and-coming acts from the United States. There's a "quiet" section for conversation and a "loud" section for music and dancing. Open weekdays 1 PM–3 AM, weekends 7 PM–3 AM; admission varies. Other clubs include **Studebaker's** (1255 rue Crescent, tel. 514/866–1101), **Déjà Vu** (1224 rue Bishop, tel. 514/866–0512), **Station 10** (2071 rue Ste-Catherine O, tel. 514/934–0484), **Terminal** (1635 rue Ste-Catherine, tel. 514/937–7401), and **Back Street Rock Bar** (382 rue Mayor, tel. 514/987–7671).

Discos   Montréalers are as into discos as you could imagine. The newest and the glitziest is **Metropolis** (tel. 514/288–5559), at 59 rue Ste-Catherine Est. The crowd is young, primarily French-speaking, and clad in black. It's open Thursday through Sunday, and the admission is $5 unless a band is appearing. The more popular discothèques are **Hard Rock Café** (1458 rue Crescent, tel. 514/987–1420) and the **Crocodile** (636 rue Cathcart, tel. 514/866–4979).

Singles Bars   Singles bars center on rues Crescent, Bishop, and de la Montagne. The two mainstays are **Thursday's**—the city's best known—and the **Sir Winston Churchill Pub** at Nos. 1449 and 1459 rue Crescent. The athletic set unwinds at **La Cage aux Sports**, not too far from the Forum, at 2250 rue Guy. Another bar scene takes place on rue Prince Arthur. The French-flavored **Vol de Nuit**, at No. 14, and **Du Côté de Chez Swann**, at No. 54, are the *classiest* joints there. Nearby, on boulevard St-Laurent, is **Lola's Paradise** (No. 3604)—a trendy, lively all-night hideaway conveying the glitz and glamour of the '30s. Bar service until 3 AM; it also serves dinner daily 5 PM–6 AM. **Le Keg** (25 rue St-Paul E) is known as a place for raucous carousing in Vieux-Montréal.

5 Québec City

by Alice H. Oshins

A New York–based
freelance writer,
Alice H. Oshins
has written
extensively on
French Canada.

Updated by
Dorothy Guinan

An excursion to French-speaking Canada is incomplete without a visit to Québec City, located in one of the most beautiful natural settings in North America. Don't be fooled by the fact that the area called la Vieille Ville (Old City) is only 1 square mile; it actually has a lot of ground to cover. This well-preserved part of town is a small and dense place, steeped in four centuries of history and French tradition. Once you begin to explore first hand the 17th- and 18th-century buildings, the ramparts that once protected the city, and the numerous parks and monuments, you will soon realize how much there is to see.

The oldest municipality in Québec province, Québec City was the first settlement of French explorers, fur trappers, and missionaries in the 17th century, who came here to establish the colony of New France. Today it still resembles a French provincial town in many ways, with its family-oriented residents with strong ties to their past. More than 95% of its metropolitan population of 600,000 are French-speaking. Québec City is also a fortified city, the only one in North America, an attribute that led UNESCO to declare it a world heritage treasure.

Québec City is huddled on a cliff above the St. Lawrence River, at a point where the body of water narrows; this strategic location forged its historic destiny as a military stronghold. When Winston Churchill visited Québec City in the early 1940s, he named it "Gibraltar of North America" because of its position at the gateway to the continent. The city's military prominence paved the way for its leading political role, first as the French colony's administrative center and eventually as the capital of Québec province.

In 1535, French explorer Jacques Cartier first came upon what the Algonquin Indians called "Kebec," meaning "where the river narrows." New France, however, was not actually founded in the area of what is now Québec City until 1608, when another French explorer, Samuel de Champlain, recognized the military advantages of the location and set up a fort. Along the banks of the St. Lawrence, on the spot now called Place Royale, this fort developed into an economic center for fur trade and shipbuilding. Twelve years later, de Champlain realized the French colony's vulnerability to attacks from above and expanded its boundaries to the top of the cliff, where he built the fort Château St-Louis on the site of the present-day Château Frontenac.

During the early days of New France, the French and British fought for the control of the area. In 1690, when an expedition led by Admiral Sir William Phipps arrived from England, Comte de Frontenac, New France's most illustrious governor, issued his famous statement, "Tell your lord that I will reply with the mouth of my cannons."

England was determined to conquer New France. The French constructed walls and other military structures and had the advantage of the defensive position on top of the cliff, but they still had to contend with Britain's naval supremacy. On September 13, 1759, the British army, led by General James Wolfe, scaled the colony's cliff and took the French troops led by Général Louis-Joseph Montcalm by surprise. The British defeated the French in a 20-minute battle on the Plains of Abraham, and New France came under English rule.

The British brought their mastery of trade to the region. In the 18th century, Québec City's economy prospered because of the success of the fishing, fur trading, shipbuilding, and timber industries. In order to further protect the city from invasion, the British continued to expand upon the fortifications left by the French. Defensive structures that were built included a wall encircling the city and a star-shaped citadel, both of which still enhance the city's urban landscape. The city remained under British rule until 1867, when the Act of Confederation united several Canadian provinces (Québec, Ontario, New Brunswick, and Nova Scotia) and designated Québec City the capital of the province of Québec.

During the mid-19th century, the economic center of eastern Canada shifted west from Québec City to Montréal and Toronto. Today government is Québec City's main business: More than 30,000 civil-service employees work and live in the area. Office complexes continue to appear outside the older portion of town; modern malls, convention centers, and imposing hotels now cater to an established business clientele.

Despite the period of British rule, Québec City has remained a center of French Canadian culture. It is home to Université Laval (Laval University), a large Catholic institution that grew out of Séminaire de Québec (Québec Seminary), founded in 1663 by French bishop François de Montmorency Laval; today Laval has a sprawling campus in the suburb of Sainte-Foy. Québec City also has several theaters, including the Grand Théâtre de Québec, where local artists perform plays that deal directly with French Canadian culture. The Québec government has completely restored many of the centuries-old buildings of Place Royale, one of the oldest districts on the continent. The city's ancient stone churches and homes, as well as its cultural institutions, such as Musée de Québec and Musée de la Civilisation, are firmly rooted in French Canadian society.

Québec City is a wonderful place in which to wander on foot. Its natural beauty is world renowned. You're bound to enjoy the view from Parc Montmorency (Montmorency Park), where the Laurentian Mountains jut majestically over the St. Lawrence River. Even more impressive vistas may be gazed upon if you walk along the walls or climb to the city's highest point, Cap Diamant (Cape Diamond). Several blissful days may be spent investigating the narrow cobblestone streets of the historic Old City, browsing for local arts and crafts in the boutiques of quartier Petit-Champlain, or strolling the Terrasse Dufferin promenade along the river. When you've worked up an appetite, you can stop to indulge in one of the many reliable cafés and restaurants, with a choice of French, Québecois, and international fare. If you've had enough of the past, another vibrant, modern part of town beckons beyond the city gates. And if you're tired of walking you can always board a calèche (horse-drawn carriage) near the city gates or hop on the ferry across the St. Lawrence River to Lévis for a thrilling view of the Québec City skyline. What follows will help you uncover some of the secrets of this exuberant romantic place.

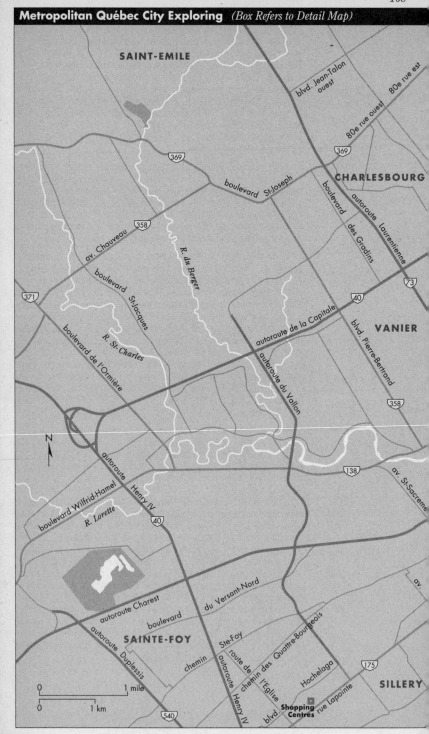

Metropolitan Québec City Exploring *(Box Refers to Detail Map)*

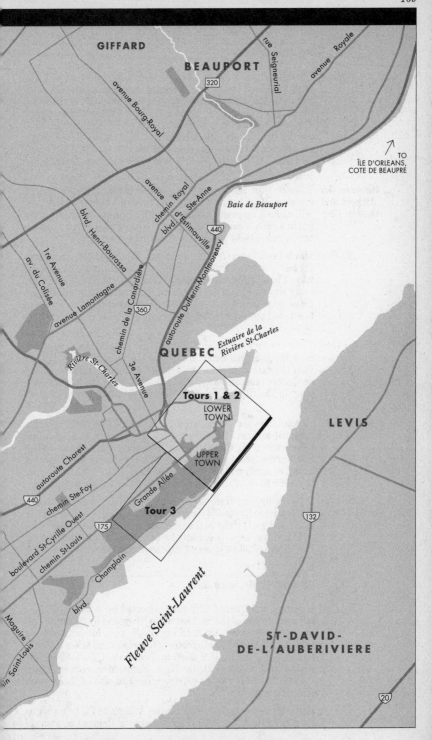

Arriving and Departing

By Plane

Airports/Airlines Québec City has one airport, **Quebec City International Airport,** located in the suburb of Sainte-Foy, approximately 19 kilometers (12 miles) from downtown. Few U.S. airlines fly directly to Québec City. You usually have to stop in Montréal or Toronto and take one of the regional and commuter airlines, such as Air Canada's **Air Alliance** (tel. 418/692–0770) or **Canadian Airlines International** (tel. 418/692–1031). Air Alliance offers a direct flight between Newark, New Jersey, and Québec City six days a week.

Between the Airport and Québec City The ride from the airport into town should be no longer than 30 minutes. Most hotels do not have an airport shuttle, but they will make a reservation for you with a bus company. If you're not in a rush, a shuttle bus offered by Maple Leaf Tours (*see* below) is convenient and only half the price of a taxi.

By Bus **Maple Leaf Tours** (240 3ième rue, tel. 418/649–9226) has a shuttle bus that runs from the airport to hotels and costs $9 one way. The shuttle makes about six trips to and from the airport every day except on weekends, when it makes four trips to and three trips from the airport. Stops include the major hotels in town, and any other hotel upon request. Reservations are necessary.

By Taxi Taxis are always available immediately outside the airport exit near the baggage claim area. Some local taxi companies are **Taxi Québec** (975 8ième av., tel. 418/522–2001) and **Taxi Coop de Québec** (496 2ième av., tel. 418/525–5191), the largest company in the city. A ride into the city will cost approximately $25.

By Limousine Private limo service is expensive, starting at $47 for the ride from the airport into Québec City. Try **Service de Limousines** (30 chemin de la Cornière, Lac Beauport, tel. 418/849–7473). Some of the local tour companies offer car service to the airport or act as a referral service. **Maple Leaf Tours** (240 3ième rue, tel. 418/649–9226) has a private car service for about $53.

By Car If you're driving from the airport, take Route 540 (Autoroute Duplessis) to Route 175 (boul. Laurier), which becomes Grande Allée and leads right to the Old City. The ride is about 30 minutes and may be only slightly longer (45 minutes or so) during rush hours (7:30 AM–8:30 AM into town, and 4 PM–5:30 PM leaving town).

By Car, Train, and Bus

By Car Montréal and Québec City are connected by Autoroute 20 on the south shore of the St. Lawrence River and by Autoroute 40 on the north shore. On both highways, the ride between the two cities is about 240 kilometers (150 miles) and takes approximately three hours. U.S. I–87 in New York, U.S. I–89 in Vermont, and U.S. I–91 in New Hampshire connect with Autoroute 20. Highway 401 from Toronto also connects with Autoroute 20.

Driving northeast from Montréal on Autoroute 20, follow signs for Pont Pierre-Laporte (Pierre-Laporte Bridge) as you approach Québec City. After you've crossed the bridge, turn right onto boulevard Laurier (Route 175), which becomes the Grande Allée leading into Québec City.

It is necessary to have a car only if you are planning to visit outlying areas. The narrow streets of the Old City leave few two-hour metered parking spaces available. However, there are several parking garages at central locations in town, with rates running approximately $10 a day. Main garages are located at City Hall, Place d'Youville, Complex G, Place Québec, Château Frontenac, Québec Seminary, rue St-Paul, and the Old Port.

Rental Cars *See* Renting and Leasing Cars in Chapter 1.

By Train **VIA Rail,** Canada's passenger rail service, travels three times daily (morning, afternoon, and evening) from Montréal to Québec City along the south shore of the St. Lawrence River. The trip takes about three hours. The train makes a stop in Sainte-Foy and has first-class service available. Tickets must be purchased in advance at any VIA Rail office or travel agent. The basic price is $42 each way. A limited number of seats are available for $25 each way. Reservations must be made at least five days in advance. The discount is not offered on Friday, Sunday, or holidays. First-class service is $68 each way. *Tel. 418/692–3940 or 800/361–5390 in Québec City and in Sainte-Foy; in Québec province, tel. 800/361–5390.*

The train arrives in Québec City at the 19th-century **Gare du Palais** (450 rue de la Gare du Palais, tel. 418/524–6452), in the heart of the Old City. Take a taxi to your hotel or walk, depending on how much luggage you have and on where your hotel is located.

By Bus **Voyageur Inc.** provides regular service from Montréal to Québec City daily, departing hourly 6 AM–11 PM. On Friday and Sunday there are two additional departures, at midnight and 1 AM. The cost of the three-hour ride is $35 one way. A round-trip costs $48 if you return within 10 days and do not travel on Friday. Senior citizens travel for $23 each way. The only way to buy tickets is at the terminal; tickets are not sold on the bus.

Bus Terminals **Montréal:** Voyageur Terminal (505 boul. de Maisonneuve E, tel. 514/842–2281).

Québec: Downtown Terminal (225 boul. Charest E, tel. 418/524–4692); Sainte-Foy Terminal (2700 boul. Laurier, tel. 418/651–7015).

Staying in Québec City

Getting Around

Walking is the best way to explore Québec City. The Old City measures only 1 square mile, so most historic sites, hotels, and restaurants are located within the walls or a short distance outside. City maps are available at tourist information offices.

By Bus The public transportation system in Québec City is dependable, and buses run frequently. You can get to anywhere in Québec City and the outlying areas, although you may be required to transfer. The city's transit system, **Commission de Transport de la Communauté Urbaine de Québec (CTCUQ)** (tel. 418/627–2511) runs buses approximately every 15 or 20 minutes that stop at major points around town. The cost is $1.75 for adults, $1.20 for children; you'll need exact change. All buses stop in Lower Town at Place Jacques-Cartier or outside St-Jean Gate at Place d'Youville in Upper Town. Transportation maps are available at tourist information offices.

By Taxi Taxis are stationed in front of major hotels, including the Château Frontenac, Hilton International, Loews Le Concorde, and Hôtel des Gouverneurs, as well as in front of Hôtel de Ville (City Hall) along rue des Jardins and Place d'Youville outside St-Jean Gate. For radio-dispatched cars, try **Taxi Coop de Québec** (tel. 418/525–5191) and **Taxi Québec** (tel. 418/522–2001). Passengers are charged an initial $2.15, plus 96¢ for each kilometer.

By Limousine **Service de Limousines de la Capitale** (1400 ave. St-Jean-Baptiste, Suite 140, tel. 418/872–2664) and **Service de Limousines Québec** (30 chemin de la Cornière, Lac Beauport, tel. 418/849–7473) have 24-hour service.

Important Addresses and Numbers

Tourist Information **Québec City Region Tourism and Convention Bureau** has two tourist information centers:

Québec City: 60 rue d'Auteuil, tel. 418/692–2471. Open June–Aug., daily 8:30 AM–8 PM; Sept.–mid-Oct., daily 8:30–5:30; mid-Oct.–mid-Apr., weekdays 9–5; mid-Apr.–May, weekdays 8:30–5:30.

Sainte-Foy: 3005 boul. Laurier (near the Québec and Pierre-Laporte bridges), tel. 418/651–2882. Open June–Aug., daily 8:30 AM–8 PM; Sept.–mid-Oct., daily 8:30–6; mid-Oct.–mid Apr., daily 9–5; mid-Apr.–May, daily 8:30–6.

Québec Government Tourism Department: 12 rue Ste-Anne (Place d'Armes), tel. 418/643–2280 or 800/363–7777. Open 9–5; summer open 8:30–7:30.

U.S. Consulate The consulate (2 Place Terrasse Dufferin, tel. 418/692–2095) faces the Governors Park near the Château Frontenac.

Emergencies **Police** and **fire,** tel. 418/691–6911; **provincial police,** tel. 418/623–6262.

Medical Care **Hôtel-Dieu Hospital** (11 côte du Palais, tel. 418/691–5042) is the main hospital inside the Old City; **Jeffrey Hale Hospital** (1250 chemin Sainte-Foy, tel. 418/683–4471) is opposite St. Sacrament Church.

24-hour Medical Service (tel. 418/687–9915).

Distress Center (tel. 418/683–2153).

24-hour Poison Center (tel. 418/656–8090).

Dental Service 1175 rue Lavigerie, Room 100, Sainte-Foy, tel. 418/653–5412; weekends, tel. 418/656–6060. Open Mon.–Tues. 8–8, Wed.–Thurs. 8–5, Fri. 8–4.

Pharmacy **Pharmacie Lippens** (Les Galeries Charlesbourg, 4266 Lière av., north of Québec City in Charlesbourg, tel. 418/623–1571) is open Mon.–Sat. 8 AM–midnight, Sun. 10 AM–midnight.

Road Conditions Tel. 418/643–6830.

Weather Tel. 418/877–8787.

English-language Bookstore	**La Maison Anglaise** (Place de la Cité, Sainte-Foy, tel. 418/654–9523).
Travel Agencies	**Inter-Voyage** (1155 rue Claire-Fontaine, tel. 418/524–1414), located on the first floor of the Édifice la Laurentienne (Laurentian Building) behind the Parliament, is open weekdays 8:30–5.

Opening and Closing Times

Most banks are open Monday through Wednesday 10–3 and close later on Thursday and Friday. **Bank of Montreal** (Place Laurier, 2700 boul. Laurier, Sainte-Foy, tel. 418/525–3786) is open on Saturday 10–3. For currency exchange, **Banque d'Amérique** (24 côte de la Fabrique, tel. 418/694–1937) is open June 24–Aug., weekdays 9–6, weekends 9–5; Sept.–June 23, weekdays 9–5, weekends 10–4.

Museum hours are typically 10–5, with longer evening hours during summer months. Most are closed on Monday.

Shopping hours are Monday through Wednesday 9:30–5:30, Thursday and Friday 9:30–9, and Saturday 9:30–5. Stores tend to stay open later during summer months.

During the winter, many attractions and shops change their hours; visitors are advised to call ahead.

Guided Tours

Orientation Tours *By Bus*	The three major touring companies—Gray Line, Maple Leaf, and Visite Touristique de Québec—offer similar full- and half-day guided tours in English in a motorbus. Tours cover such sights as Québec City, Montmorency Falls, and Sainte-Anne-de-Beaupré; combination city and harbor cruise tours are also available. Québec City tours operate year-round; other excursions to outlying areas may operate only in the summer.

Gray Line offers guided bus tours. Tickets can be purchased at most major hotels or at the kiosk at Terrasse Dufferin at Place d'Armes. Prices are $20–$45, children 4–12 half price. *720 rue des Rocailles, tel. 418/622–7420. Tours May 18–Oct. 14.*

Maple Leaf Sightseeing Tours (240 3ième rue, tel. 418/649–9226) offers guided tours in a minibus. Call for a reservation, and the company will pick you up at your hotel. Prices are $19–$56, with reduced rates for children.

Visite Touristique de Québec (C.P. 174, Sillery, tel. 418/653–9722) gives tours in a panoramic bus, costing $10–$38, with reduced rates for children.

Smaller companies offering tours include **La Tournée du Québec Inc.** (tel. 418/831–1385), open in summer only; **Fleur de Lys** (418/831–0188); and **Group Voyages Québec Inc.** (tel. 418/525–4585), open year-round.

By Ferry The Québec-Lévis ferry offers a 15-minute crossing of the St. Lawrence River to the town of Lévis. It leaves daily from the pier at rue Dalhousie across from Place Royale every half hour from 6:30 AM until 6:30 PM, then hourly until 2:30 AM, with a final crossing at 3:45 AM. *Tel. 418/644–3704. Cost: $1.25 adults, 75¢ children 5–11 and senior citizens.*

By Horse-drawn Carriage Hire a calèche (horse-drawn carriage) on rue d'Auteuil between the St-Louis and Kent gates from **André Beaurivage** (tel.

418/687–9797). The cost is about $60 for a 45-minute tour of the Old City.

Special-interest Tours
Boat Trips

Beau Temps, Mauvais Temps (991 rte. Prévost, Île d'Orléans, tel. 418/828–2275) offers three river cruises that stop to tour neighboring islands. Boats depart from piers at Saint-Laurent on Île d'Orleans, and Pier 19 at Vieux-Port, in Québec. The boat trip to Île-aux-Grues, costs $75 for adults, with reduced rates for children. The boat trip to Grosse-Île, costs $67 for adults; children under 12 are not accepted. Both trips include a light lunch. The boat trip to Île d'Orléans leaves from Pier 19. The cost is $23.

Croisières AML Inc. (Pier Chouinard, 10 rue Dalhousie, tel. 418/692–1159) runs cruises on the St. Lawrence River aboard the MV *Louis-Jolliet*. One- to three-hour cruises from May through mid-October cost $13–$24 for adults, $7–$12 for children 5 and over, $12–$22 for senior citizens.

Île d'Orléans

Beau Temps, Mauvais Temps (991 rte. Prévost, Île d'Orléans, 418/828–2275) has guided tours of Île d'Orléans by bus, walking tours of the island's historic manors and churches, and trips to a maple-sugar hut.

Walking Tours

Baillairgé Cultural Tours, Inc. (2216 chemin du Foulon, Sillery, tel. 418/658–4799) has a 2½-hour walking tour, "Québec on Foot," from late June through September at 9:30 AM and 2 PM daily. The tour begins at the Musée du Fort and includes sights in both the Upper and Lower towns. The cost is $13 for adults, children under 12 free.

Exploring Québec City

Québec City's split-level landscape is notable for having one part on the cape (Upper Town) and the other along the shores of the St. Lawrence (Lower Town). If you look out from the Terrasse Dufferin boardwalk in Upper Town, you will see the rooftops of Lower Town buildings directly below. Separating these two sections of the city is steep and precipitous rock, against which were built the city's more than 25 *escaliers* (staircases). Today you can also take the *funiculaire* (funicular), a cable car that climbs and descends the cliff between Terrasse Dufferin and the Maison Jolliet in Lower Town.

With the exception of some of the outlying suburbs, most of Québec City's historic area will interest tourists. The first two tours offered here remain primarily in the oldest sections of town, while the third tour strays off the beaten path to provide a glimpse of the modern part of the city.

Tour 1: Upper Town

Numbers in the margin correspond to points of interest on the Tours 1 and 2: Upper and Lower Towns map.

This tour takes you to the most prominent buildings of its earliest inhabitants, who came from Europe in the 17th century to set up political, educational, and religious institutions. Upper Town became the political capital of the colony of New France and, later, of British North America. It was also the place where the religious orders first set down their roots: The Jesuits founded the first school for priests in 1635; the Ursuline nuns, a school for girls in 1639; and the Augustine nuns, the first hospital in 1639. Historic buildings, with thick stone walls, large wood doors, glimmering copper roofs, and majestic steeples, compose the heart of the city.

Begin this tour where rue St-Louis meets rue du Fort at Upper Town's most central location, **Place d'Armes.** For centuries, this square seated on a cliff has been a meeting place for parades and military events. It is bordered by government buildings; at its west side, the majestic **Ancien Palais de Justice** (Old Courthouse), a Renaissance building from 1887, replaced the original 1650 courthouse, which was smaller and situated farther from the square. The present courthouse stands on land that was occupied by a church and convent of the Recollet missionaries (Franciscan monks), who in 1615 were the first order of priests to arrive in New France. The Gothic fountain at the center of Place d'Armes pays tribute to their arrival.

The colony's former treasury building, **Maison Maillou,** at the south end at 17 rue St-Louis, possesses architectural traits typical of New France: a sharply slanted roof, dormer windows, concrete chimneys, shutters with iron hinges, and limestone walls. Built between 1736 and 1753, it marks the end of rue du Trésor, the road colonists took on their way to pay rent to the king's officials. Maison Maillou is not open to tourists and is now used as the location for the Québec City Chamber of Commerce offices.

You are now within a few steps east of Québec City's most celebrated landmark, **Château Frontenac** (1 rue des Carrières, tel. 418/692–3861), once the administrative and military headquarters of New France. The imposing green-turreted castle with its slanting copper roof owes its name to the Comte de Frontenac, governor of the French colony between 1672 and 1698. Looking at the magnificence of the château, you can see why Frontenac said, "For me, there is no site more beautiful nor more grandiose than that of Québec City."

Samuel de Champlain, who founded Québec City in 1608, was responsible for Château St-Louis, the first structure to appear on the site of the Frontenac; it was built between 1620 and 1624 as a residence for colonial governors. In 1784, Château Haldimand was constructed here, but it was demolished in 1892 to make way for Château Frontenac. The latter was built as a hotel in 1893, and it was considered to be remarkably luxurious at that time: Guest rooms contained fireplaces, private bathrooms, and marble fixtures, and a special commissioner traveled to England and France in search of antiques for the establishment. The hotel was designed by New York architect Bruce Price, who also worked on Québec City's **Gare du Palais** (Rail Station) and other Canadian landmarks, such as Montréal's Windsor Station. The Frontenac was completed in 1925 with the addition of a 20-story central tower. Owned by Canadian Pacific Hotels, it has accumulated a star-studded guest roster, including Queen Elizabeth, Madame Chiang Kai-shek, Ronald Reagan, and François Mitterrand, as well as Franklin Roosevelt and Winston Churchill, who convened here in 1943 and 1944 for two wartime conferences.

As you head to the boardwalk behind the Frontenac, notice the glorious bronze statue of Samuel de Champlain, situated where he built his residence. The statue's steps are made of des

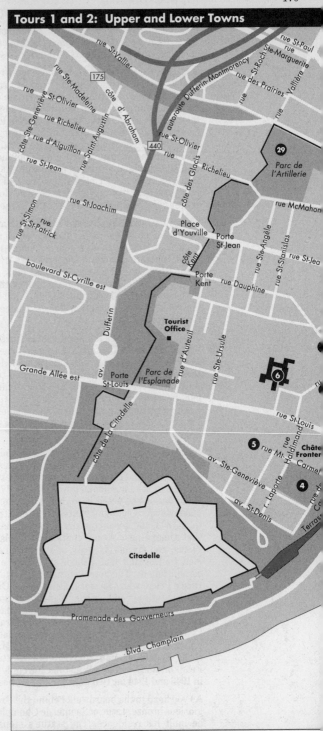

Tours 1 and 2: Upper and Lower Towns

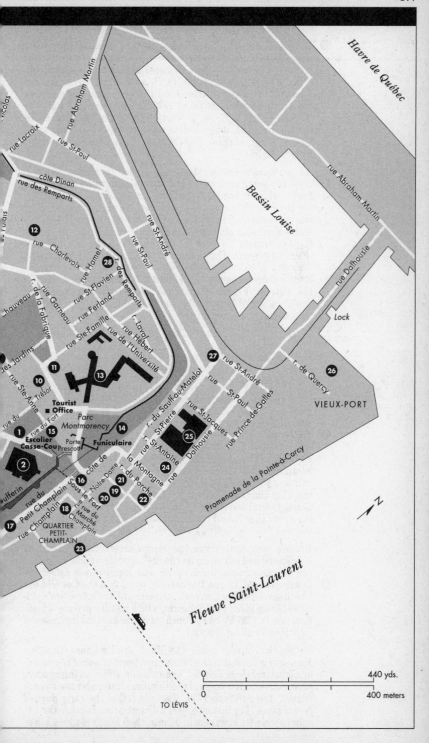

Havre de Québec

rue Abraham Martin

rue Abraham Martin

rue Lacroix

rue St-Paul

côte Dinan

rue des Remparts

Nicolas

12

rue Charlevoix

28

rue Hamel

F. des Remparts

rue St-Flavien

rue St-André

rue St-Paul

Bassin Louise

rue Dalhousie

Lock

Chauveau

rue de la Fabrique

rue Garneau

rue Ferland

rue Ste-Famille

rue Laval

rue Hébert

rue de l'Université

les Jardins

11

13

27

rue St-André

26

rue St-Paul

r. du Sault-au-Matelot

r. de Quercy

VIEUX-PORT

10

rue Ste-Anne

rue Trésor

Tourist Office

Parc Montmorency

rue du Fort

1

15

14

rue St-Pierre

rue St-Jacques

rue Prince-de-Galles

Escalier Cassa-Cou

Porte Prescott

Funiculaire

25

rue Dalhousie

2

16

côte de la Montagne

rue St-Antoine

24

ufferin

rue du Petit Champlain

Notre Dame

21

r. du Porche

rue Sous le Fort

20

19

22

Promenade de la Pointe-à-Carcy

18

rue du Marché Champlain

17

rue Champlain

QUARTIER PETIT-CHAMPLAIN

23

N

Fleuve Saint-Laurent

| 0 | | | 440 yds. |
| 0 | | | 400 meters |

TO LÉVIS

Vosges granite, and the pedestal consists of Château-Landon stone, the same material used for the Arc de Triomphe in Paris.

3 Walk south along the boardwalk called the **Terrasse Dufferin** for a panoramic view of the St. Lawrence River, the town of Lévis on the opposite shore, Île d'Orléans, and the Laurentian Mountains. The wide boardwalk, with an intricate wrought-iron guardrail, was named after Lord Dufferin, who was governor of Canada between 1872 and 1878 and who had this walkway constructed in 1878. At its western tip begins the **Promenade des Gouverneurs,** which skirts along the cliff and leads up to Québec's highest point, Cap Diamant (Cape Diamond), and also to the Citadel.

As you pass to the southern side of the Frontenac, you will
4 come to a small park called **Jardin des Gouverneurs** (Governors' Park), which is bordered by three streets of old manors. During the French regime, the public area served as a garden for the governors who resided in Château St-Louis. The park's Wolfe-Montcalm Monument, a 50-foot obelisk, is unique in that it pays tribute to both a winning (English) and a losing (French) general. The monument recalls the 1759 battle on the Plains of Abraham, which ended French rule of New France. British General James Wolfe lived only long enough to hear of his victory; French Général Louis-Joseph Montcalm died shortly after Wolfe with the knowledge that the city was lost. *Admission free. Open daily.*

On the southeast corner of the park is the **U.S. Consulate** (2 Place Terrasse Dufferin). On the south side of the park is **avenue Ste-Geneviève,** lined with well-preserved Victorian homes dating from 1850 to 1900 that have been converted to quaint old-fashioned inns.

Once you've stopped admiring the view from the park, make your way to the north side and follow rue Mont Carmel until you come to another small park landscaped with footpaths and
5 flower beds, **Cavalier du Moulin.** The former stone windmill, which became part of the French fortifications, was considered during the 17th century to be located on the outskirts of town because most of the city was situated below the cliff. The windmill was strategically placed so that its cannons could destroy the Cap-Diamant Redoubt (situated near Promenade des Gouverneurs) and the St-Louis Bastion (near St-Louis Gate) in the event that New France was captured by the British. *Admission free. Open May–Nov., daily 7 AM–9 PM.*

Retrace your steps down rue Mont Carmel, turn left on rue Haldimand and left again on rue St-Louis; then make a right on rue du Parloir until it intersects with a tiny street called rue
6 Donnacona. At 12 rue Donnacona, you'll find the **Couvent des Ursulines** (Ursuline Convent), the site of North America's oldest teaching institution for girls, which is still a private school. Founded in 1639 by two French nuns, the convent has many of its original walls still intact.

Within the convent walls, the **Musée des Ursulines** (Ursuline Museum) is housed in the former residence of one of the founders, Madame de la Peltrie. The museum offers an informative perspective on 120 years of the Ursulines' life under the French regime, from 1639 to 1759. Exhibits tell of the early days of New France. For instance, you'll discover that because the Ursulines were without heat in winter, their heavy clothing sometimes weighed as much as 20 pounds. You'll also see why it took an Ursuline nun nine years of training to attain the level of a professional embroiderer; the museum contains magnificent pieces of ornate embroidery, such as altar frontals having gold and silver threads intertwined with precious jewels. *12 rue Donnacona, tel. 418/694–0694. Admission: $2.50 adults, $1.25 students, $1.50 senior citizens, 75¢ children under 12. Open Jan.–Nov., Tues.–Sat. 9:30–noon and 1:30–4:30, Sun. 12:30–5:15.*

At the same address is the **Chapelle des Ursulines** (Ursuline Chapel), where French Général Montcalm was buried after he died in the 1759 battle. The chapel's exterior was rebuilt in 1902, but the interior contains the original chapel, which is the work of sculptor Pierre-Noël Levasseur, accomplished between 1726 and 1736. The votive lamp here was lit in 1717 and has never been extinguished. *12 rue Donnacona. Admission free. Open May–Oct., same hours as Ursuline Museum.*

Next to the museum at the **Centre Marie-de-l'Incarnation** are a bookstore and an exhibit on the life of the Ursulines' first superior, who came from France and cofounded the convent. *10 rue Donnacona, tel. 418/692–1569. Admission free. Open Tues.–Sat. 10–11:30 and 2–4:30, Sun. 2–4:30.*

Time Out The neon-lit **Café Taste-Vin,** on the corner of rue des Jardins and rue St-Louis, shares a kitchen with the gourmet restaurant next door. The two eateries also share chefs when it comes to salads, pastries, and desserts, making the café an ideal stop for the weary tourist. *32 rue St-Louis, tel. 418/692–4191. AE, DC, MC, V. Open Mar.–Nov., daily 7:30 AM–11 PM; Dec.–Feb., daily 11–11.*

From rue Donnacona, walk north to rue des Jardins. Within a few yards you'll see the **Holy Trinity Anglican Cathedral.** This stone church dates to 1804 and is the first Anglican cathedral outside the British Isles. Its simple and dignified facade is reminiscent of London's St. Martin-in-the-Fields. The cathedral's land was originally given to the Recollet fathers (Franciscan monks from France) in 1681 by the king of France for a church and monastery. When Québec came under British rule, the Recollets made the church available to the Anglicans for services. Later, King George III of England ordered construction of the present cathedral, the requirement being that an area be set aside for members of the royal family. A portion of the north balcony still remains exclusively for the use of the reigning sovereign or her representative. The church houses precious objects donated by George III. The oak benches were imported from the Royal Forest at Windsor. The cathedral's impressive rear organ has more than 2,500 pipes. *31 rue des Jardins, tel. 418/692–2193. Admission free. Open June–Aug., daily 9–9; Sept.–mid-Oct., weekdays 9–3.*

The building on the corner of rue des Jardins and rue Ste-Anne is one of Québec City's finest art deco structures. Geometric patterns of stone and wrought iron decorate the interior of the **Hôtel Clarendon** (57 rue Ste-Anne, tel. 418/692–2480). Although the Clarendon dates back to 1866, it was reconstructed with its current art deco decor in 1930.

More art deco design can be found next door at 65 rue Ste-Anne, the 15-story **Édifice Price** (Price Building). The city's first skyscraper was built in 1929 and served as the headquarters of the Price Brothers Company, the lumber company founded in Canada by Sir William Price. Today it is owned by the provincial government and houses the offices of Québec City's mayor. Don't miss the interior: Exquisite copper plaques depict scenes of the company's early pulp and paper activities, while the two artfully carved maple-wood elevators are '30s classics.

Head back on rue Ste-Anne past the Holy Trinity Anglican Cathedral and continue straight on this street until it becomes a narrow, cobblestone thoroughfare lined with boutiques and restaurants. During the summer, the activity here starts buzzing early in the morning and continues until late at night. Stores stay open, artists paint, and street musicians perform as long as there is an audience, even if it's one o'clock in the morning.

🔟 Turn left into a narrow alley called **rue du Trésor,** where hundreds of colorful prints, paintings, and other artworks are on display. You won't necessarily find masterpieces here, but this walkway is a good stop for a souvenir sketch or two. During the French regime people came to this street to pay rent to the crown; the royal treasury stood at the end of the street, at Maison Maillou.

At the bottom of rue du Trésor, turn left on rue Buade. When you reach the corner of côte de la Fabrique, you'll see the ⑪ **Basilique Notre-Dame-de-Québec** (Our Lady of Québec Basilica), with the oldest parish in North America, dating to 1647. The basilica has been rebuilt on three separate occasions: in the early 1700s, when François de Montmorency Laval was the first bishop; in 1759, when cannons at Lévis aimed fire at it during the siege of Québec, and in 1922, after a fire. This basilica has a somber ambience despite its ornate interior, which includes a canopy dais over the episcopal throne, a ceiling of clouds decorated with gold leaf, richly colored stained-glass windows, and a chancel lamp that was a gift of Louis XIV. Perhaps the solemn mood here may be attributed to the basilica's large and famous crypt, which was Québec City's first cemetery; more than 900 people are interred here, including 20 bishops and four governors of New France. The founder of Québec City, Samuel de Champlain, is believed to be buried somewhere near the basilica. Archaeologists have been searching for his tomb for more than 40 years. *16 rue Buade, tel. 418/692–2533. Admission free. Open daily 9–noon and 11:30–4:30.*

The basilica marks the beginning of Québec City's Latin Quarter, which extends to the streets northwest of Québec Seminary (rue Buade, rue des Remparts, côte de la Fabrique, and côte du Palais) as far as rue St-Jean. This district was deemed the Latin Quarter because Latin was once a required language course at the seminary and was spoken among the students. Although Latin is no longer compulsory and Québec Seminary–Laval University has moved out to a larger campus in Sainte-Foy, students still cling to this neighborhood.

Head down côte de la Fabrique and turn right when it meets rue Collins. The cluster of old stone buildings sequestered at ⑫ the end of the street is the **Monastère des Augustines de l'Hôtel-Dieu de Québec** (Augustine Monastery). Augustine nuns arrived from Dieppe, France, in 1639 with a mission to care for the sick in the new colony, and they established the first hospital north of Mexico, the **Hôtel-Dieu Hospital,** which is the large building west of the monastery. The **Musée des Augustines** (Augustine Museum) is housed in hospitallike quarters with large sterile corridors leading into a ward that features a small exhibit of antique medical instruments used by the Augustines, such as an 1850 microscope and a pill-making device from the 17th century.

Upon request, the Augustines also offer guided tours of the chapel (1800) and the cellars used by the nuns as a hiding place beginning in 1659, during bombardments from the British. *32 rue Charlevoix, tel. 418/692–2492. Admission free. Open Tues.–Sat. 9:30–11:30 and 1:30–5, Sun. 1:30–5.*

Time Out For a crusty white or whole-wheat croissant, try **Croissant Plus** (50 rue Garneau, tel. 418/692–4215).

Retrace your steps on Collins Street and côte de la Fabrique. When you reach rue Ste-Famille on the left, you will find the
⓭ wrought-iron entrance gates of the **Séminaire de Québec** (Québec Seminary). Behind these gates lies a tranquil courtyard surrounded by austere stone buildings with rising steeples; these structures have housed classrooms and student residences since 1663. The seminary was founded by François de Montmorency Laval, the first bishop of New France, to train priests of the new colony. In 1852 the seminary became Université Laval (Laval University), the first Catholic university in North America. The university eventually outgrew these cramped quarters; in 1946, Laval moved to a larger, modern campus in the suburb of Sainte-Foy. The Musée du Seminaire (*see* below) offers guided tours of the seminary during the summer. *1 côte de la Fabrique.*

Head north across the courtyard to the **Musée du Séminaire** (Seminary Museum). Housed in a former student residence, the museum focuses on the three centuries of the seminary's existence, until 1940. It emphasizes European secular and religious works of art; there are more than 400 landscape and still-life paintings dating as far back as the 15th century. The museum also houses a showcase of scientific instruments that were acquired through the centuries for the purposes of research and teaching. A former chapel has been renovated and now holds an exhibit of elegant religious and secular antique silver. The museum also has a rare collection of Canadian money that was used in colonial times. *9 rue de l'Université, tel. 418/692–2843. Admission: $3 adults, $1.50 students, $1 children under 16, $2 senior citizens, $6 families. Open June–Sept., Tues.–Sun. 10:30–5:30; Oct.–May, Tues.–Sun. 10:30–5. Closed Mon. year-round.*

Then visit the Québec Seminary's **Chapelle Extérieure** (Outer Chapel), at the seminary's west entrance. The small Roman-style chapel was built in 1888, after the fire destroyed the first chapel, built in 1750. In 1950 a memorial crypt of Laval was added here. Admission and hours at the chapel are the same as those of the musuem (*see* above).

⓮ Now exit the seminary from the east at rue de l'Université and head south to côte de la Montagne, where **Parc Montmorency** (Montmorency Park) straddles the hill between Upper Town and Lower Town. This park marks the spot where Canada's first wheat was grown in 1618 and where the nation's first legislation was passed in 1694. A monument stands in tribute to Louis Herbert, a former apothecary and the first Canadian farmer, who cleared and tilled this area's land.

In 1688, Monseigneur de Saint-Vallier, the second bishop of New France, had his residence, the first episcopal palace, built here. In 1792 the palace's chapel became the seat of the first parliament of Lower Canada. The chapel was demolished in 1833, and a new legislative building was constructed that served as Québec's parliament until 1883, when it was destroyed by fire. A park monument commemorates Georges-Étienne Cartier, a French Canadian political leader and a father of the 1867 Confederation.

Take the **Escalier Frontenac** (Frontenac Stairway) up to the north end of the Terrasse Dufferin. You may be out of breath, but the climb is worth it for the 30-minute recap on the six **15** sieges of Québec City at the **Musée du Fort** (Fort Museum). This museum's sole exhibit is a sound-and-light show with a model of 18th-century Québec that reenacts the region's most important battles, including the Battle of the Plains of Abraham and the 1775 attack by American generals Arnold and Montgomery. *10 rue Ste-Anne, tel. 418/692–2175. Admission: $4.50 adults, $3 students and senior citizens. Open Jan. and Nov., Mon.–Fri. 11–3, Sat. 10–5, Sun. noon–5; Feb. 1–Feb. 13, Apr.–June, and Sept.–Oct., daily 10–5; Feb. 14–Mar., Mon.–Fri. 11–12:30 and 2–4, Sat. 10–5, Sun. noon–5; July–Aug., daily 10–6.*

As you exit from the museum, head southeast to the funicular booth along Terrasse Dufferin. Ride the funicular ($1) to Lower Town to begin Tour 2.

Tour 2: Lower Town

New France began to flourish in the streets of Lower Town along the banks of the St. Lawrence River. These streets became the colony's economic crossroads, where furs were traded, ships came in, and merchants established their residences.

Despite the status of Lower Town as the oldest neighborhood in North America, its narrow and time-worn thoroughfares have a new and polished look. In the '60s, after a century of decay as the commercial boom moved west and left Lower Town an abandoned district, the Québec government committed millions of dollars to restore the area to the way it had been during the days of New France. Today modern boutiques, restaurants, galleries, and shops catering to tourists occupy the former warehouses and residences.

Begin this tour on the northern tip of rue du Petit-Champlain **16** at **Maison Louis-Jolliet** (16 rue du Petit-Champlain, tel. 418/ 692–1132), which houses the lower station of the funicular and a souvenir shop. Built in 1683, this home was used by the first settlers of New France as a base for further westward explorations. The first Canadian born in Québec to make history, Louis Jolliet discovered the Mississippi River in 1672. A monument commemorating this discovery stands in the park next to the house.

At the north side of the house is **Escalier Casse-Cou** (Breakneck Steps), the city's first iron stairway. Its steepness is ample evidence of how it got its name. Its ambitious 1893 design was by Charles Baillairgé, a city architect and engineer, and it was built on the site of the original 17th-century stairway that linked Upper Town and Lower Town during the French regime. Today tourist shops, quaint boutiques, and restaurants are situated at various levels.

⑰ Heading south on **rue du Petit-Champlain,** the city's oldest street, you'll notice the cliff on the right that borders this narrow thoroughfare, with Upper Town situated on the heights above. Rue du Petit-Champlain retains its size from when it was the main street of a harbor village, replete with trading posts and the homes of rich merchants. In 1977 artists, craftsmen, and private investors decided to initiate a revival of the street; today it consists of pleasant boutiques and cafés. The best buys here are found in the ceramics, wood carvings, and jewelry done by local artists. Natural-fiber weaving, Inuit carvings, hand-painted silks, and enameled copper crafts are some of the local specialties for sale.

At the point where rue du Petit-Champlain intersects with boulevard Champlain, make a U-turn to head back north. One block farther, at the corner of rue du Marché-Champlain, you'll
⑱ find **Maison Chevalier,** an annex of the ethnographic Civilization Museum. This old stone house was built in 1752 for shipowner Jean-Baptiste Chevalier. It was restored in 1959, adding two 17th-century buildings to the original structure. Inside you will find the original wood beams and stone fireplaces, and an exhibit of 18th-century furniture. *60 rue du Marché-Champlain, tel. 418/643–9689. Admission free. Open mid-June–Sept., daily 10–5.*

East of Maison Chevalier, take rue Notre-Dame, which leads
⑲ directly to **Place Royale,** formerly the heart of New France. This cobblestone square is encircled by buildings with steep Normandy-style roofs, dormer windows, and several chimneys. These were once the homes of wealthy merchants. Until 1686 the area was called Place du Marché, but its name was changed when a bust of Louis XIV, *"le Roi Soleil"* (the Sun King), was erected at its center.

During the late 1600s and early 1700s, when Place Royale was continually under threat of attacks from the British, the colonists progressively moved to higher and safer quarters atop the cliff in Upper Town. Yet after the French colony fell to British rule in 1759, Place Royale flourished again with shipbuilding, logging, fishing, and fur trading.

The small stone church at the south side of the Place Royale is
⑳ the **Église Notre-Dame-des-Victoires** (Our Lady of Victory Church), the oldest church in Québec, dating to 1688. It was built on the site of Samuel de Champlain's first residence, which also served as a fort and trading post. However, the church had to be completely restored on two occasions: after a fire in 1759 and more recently in 1969. It got its name from two French victories against the British: one in 1690 against Admiral William Phipps and another in 1711 against Sir Hovendon Walker. The interior contains copies of such European masters as Van Dyck, Rubens, and Boyermans; its altar resembles the shape of a fort. A scale model suspended from the ceiling represents *Le Brezé*, the boat that transported French soldiers to New France in 1664. The side chapel is dedicated to Sainte-

Geneviève, the guardian saint of Paris. Mass is offered on Sunday mornings at 8:30, 9:45, 11, and noon. *Place Royale, tel. 418/692-1650. Admission free. Open May 15–Sept., daily 9–4:30, except during mass, marriages, and funerals; Oct.–May 14, Tues.–Sat. 9–11:30.*

㉑ Turn to the northwest corner of the square to the cool, dark, and musty cellars of the **Maison des Vins,** a former warehouse dating to 1689; here the Québec Société des Alcools sells more than 1,000 kinds of rare and vintage wines, which range in price from $7 to $1,000. *1 Place Royale, tel. 418/643–1214. Admission free. Open Tues.–Wed. 9:30–5:30, Thurs.–Fri. 9:30–9, Sat. 9:30–5. Closed Sun. and Mon.*

㉒ On the east side of Place Royale, take rue de la Place, which leads to an open square, **Place de Paris,** a newcomer to these historic quarters. Looming at its center is a black-and-white geometric sculpture, *Dialogue avec l'Histoire* (Dialogue with History), a gift from France positioned on the site where the first French settlers landed. Paris Mayor Jacques Chirac inaugurated the square in August 1987 with Québec City's Mayor Jean Pelletier. Its French counterpart is the Place du Québec, inaugurated in 1984 at St-Germain-des-Prés in Paris.

㉓ At this point of the tour you may conveniently catch the 15-minute **Lévis-Québec ferry** on the opposite shore of the St. Lawrence River. The boat docks a block south on rue Dalhousie; we recommend that you take the ferry for the opportunity of an unprecedented view of Québec City's skyline, with the Château Frontenac and the Québec Seminary high above the cliff. The view is even more impressive at night. *Ferry departs every half hour 6:00 AM–6:00 PM, then every hour until 2:00 AM, with a final crossing at 3:15 AM. Cost: $1.25 adults, 75¢ children and senior citizens.*

Time Out **Café Loft,** located in a converted garage on rue Dalhousie between Place de Paris and the Civilization Museum, offers delectable desserts, such as a pyramid-shape chocolate cake. Grab an inviting *baguette* sandwich and equally scrumptious quiches and salads. *49 rue Dalhousie, tel. 418/692–4864. AE, MC, V. Open Mon.–Fri. 11–midnight, Sat.–Sun. 9 AM–midnight.*

㉔ Next door to the Café Loft you will notice the new diorama, **Explore.** This 30-minute sound-and-light show works on the same principle as the one at the Musée du Fort (*see* Tour 1) except that it uses more-modern diorama technology. The show tells the story of Québec and the age of exploration, opening with the native Indians and leading up to Cartier's entrance into the St. Lawrence River. *Cor. rue Dalhousie and rue St-Antoine, tel. 418/692–2175. Admission: $4.25 adults, $2.75 children and senior citizens. Telephone for schedule.*

㉕ Continue north on the rue Dalhousie until you come to the **Musée de la Civilisation** (Civilization Museum). Wedged into the foot of the cliff, this spacious museum, with its striking limestone and glass facade, has been artfully designed to blend into the city landscape. Architect Moshe Safdie skillfully incorporated three historic buildings into the museum's modern structure: the house Estèbe, the site of the First Bank of Québec, and the Maison Pagé-Quercy. Many of the materials that were used to construct the newer portions of the museum are native to Québec province. The building's campanile echoes the shape of church steeples throughout the city.

The museum, which opened officially in 1988, houses innovative, entertaining, and sometimes playful exhibits devoted to aspects of Québec's culture and civilization. Several of the shows, with their imaginative use of artwork, video screens, computers, and sound, will appeal to both adults and children. Also featured are several temporary shows a year; an excellent permanent exhibition, "Memoires" ("Memories"), considers both Québec's history and French Canadian society today. In addition, there are dance, music, and theater performances and a good boutique for high-quality souvenirs. Guides are available in the exhibition rooms. *85 rue Dalhousie, tel. 418/ 643–2158. Admission: $5 adults, $4 senior citizens, $3 students; children under 16 free. Tuesday free. Open June 24– Sept. 6, daily 10–7; Sept. 7–June 23, Tues., Thurs.–Sun. 10–5, Wed. 10–9. Closed Mon.*

26 From rue Dalhousie, head east toward the river to the **Vieux-Port de Québec** (Old Port of Québec). The breezes here from the St. Lawrence provide a cool reprieve on a hot summer's day. The old harbor dates to the 17th century, when ships first arrived from Europe bringing supplies and settlers to the new colony. At one time this port was among the busiest on the continent: Between 1797 and 1897, Québec shipyards turned out more than 2,500 ships, many of which passed the 1,000-ton mark. Yet Québec City's port saw a rapid decline after steel replaced wood and the channel to Montréal was deepened to allow larger boats to reach a good port upstream.

In 1984, the 72-acre port was restored with a $100 million grant from the federal government; today it encompasses several parks and the **Agora**, the city's largest open-air theater. You can stroll along the riverside promenade, where merchant and cruise ships are docked. At its northern end, where the St. Charles meets the St. Lawrence, a lock protects the marina in the Louise basin from the generous tides of the St. Lawrence. Because Québec City is close to the Atlantic Ocean, it is susceptible to tides, which can range from 9 to 16 feet. At the northwest area of the port, an exhibition center, **Port de Québec in the 19th Century,** presents the history of the port in relation to the lumber trade and shipbuilding. *100 rue St-André, tel. 418/ 648–3300.*

The port's northwestern tip features the **Marché du Vieux-Port** (Farmer's Market), where farmers come from the countryside to sell their fresh produce. *Admission free. Open May–Oct., daily 8–8.*

27 You are now in the ideal spot to explore Québec City's **antiques district.** One block south from rue St-André, antiques boutiques cluster along rue St-Pierre and rue St-Paul (*see* Shopping, below). Rue St-Paul was formerly part of a business district where warehouses, stores, and businesses once abounded. After World War I, when shipping and commercial activities plummeted, the street consisted mainly of empty warehouses and offices. In 1964, the low rent and commercial nature of the area attracted several antiques dealers, who set up shops along rue St-Paul. Today numerous cafés, restaurants, and art galleries have turned this area into one of the town's more fashionable sections.

Walk west along rue St-Paul and turn left onto a steep brick incline called côte Dambourges; when you reach côte de la Cantonerie, take the stairs back on the cliff to rue des Remparts. Continue approximately a block west along rue des Remparts until you come to the last building in a row of purple houses. **Maison Montcalm** was the home of French Général Louis-Joseph Montcalm from 1758 until the capitulation of New France. A plaque dedicated to the general is situated on the right side of the house.

Continue west on rue des Remparts and turn left on rue de l'Arsenal, which brings you to the **Parc de l'Artillerie** (Artillery Park). This National Historic Park is a complex of 20 military, industrial, and civilian buildings, so situated to guard the St. Charles River and the Old Port. Its earliest buildings served as headquarters for the French garrison and were taken over in 1759 by the British Royal Artillery soldiers. The defense complex was used as a fortress, barracks, and cartridge factory during the American siege of Québec in 1775 and 1776. The area was converted to an industrial complex providing ammunition for the Canadian army from 1879 until 1964, when it became a historic park. *2 rue d'Auteil, tel. 418/648–4205. Admission: $2.50 adults, $1.50 senior citizens, $1.25 children 6–16, $6.25 families. Open June 24–Sept. 7.*

One of the three buildings you may visit is a former **powder house,** which in 1903 became a shell foundry. The building houses a detailed model of Québec City in 1808, rendered by two surveyors in the office of the Royal Engineers Corps, Jean-Baptiste Duberger of Québec and John By of England. Carved from wood, the model was intended to show British officials the strategic importance of Québec (it was sent to England in 1813) so that more money would be provided to expand the city's fortifications. The model offers the most accurate picture of the city during the early 19th century, detailing its houses, buildings, streets, and military structures. *Open Jan. 11–Apr., Sept. 8–Dec. 20, daily 1–5; May–Sept. 7, daily 10–5. Closed Dec. 21–Jan. 10.*

The **Dauphine Redoubt** (*dauphine* in French means "heir apparent") was named after the son of Louis XIV and was constructed from 1712 to 1748. It served as a barracks for the French garrison until 1760, when it became an officers' mess for the Royal Artillery Regiment. When the British called their soldiers back to England in 1871, it became a residence for the Canadian Arsenal superintendent. *Open June 24–Sept. 7, daily 10–5.*

The **Officers' Quarters** building, a dwelling for Royal Artillery officers until 1871 when the British army departed, is now a museum for children, with shows on military life during the British regime. *Open June 24–Sept. 7, daily 10–5.*

Tour 3: Outside the City Walls

Numbers in the margin correspond to points of interest on the Tour 3: Outside the City Walls map.

In the 20th century, Québec City grew into a modern metropolis outside the city walls and its historic confines. In this tour, you will see a glimpse of modern-day Québec City and explore neighborhoods typically left off the tourist track.

㉚ Start close to St-Louis Gate at **Parc de l'Esplanade** (Esplanade Park), the site of a former military drill and parade ground. In the 19th century, this area was a clear and uncluttered space surrounded by a picket fence and poplar trees. Today you'll find the completely renovated **Poudrière de l'Esplanade** (Powder Magazine), which the British constructed in 1820; it houses a model depicting the evolution of the wall surrounding the Old City. *100 rue St-Louis, tel. 418/648–7016. Admission free. Telephone for schedule.*

Esplanade Park is also the starting point to walk the city's 4.6 kilometers (3 miles) of walls; in the summer, guided tours begin here. The French began building ramparts along the city's natural cliff as early as 1690 to protect themselves from British invaders. But by 1759, when the British gained control of New France, the walls were still incomplete; the British took a century to finish them.

From the Powder Magazine, head south on côte de la Citadelle, ㉛ which leads directly to the **Citadelle** (Citadel). Built at the city's highest point, the Citadel is the largest fortified base in North America still occupied by troops. The 25-building fortress was intended to protect the port, prevent the enemy from taking up a position on the Plains of Abraham, and provide a last refuge in case of an attack. The French had constructed previous structures on this site based on plans of Québec engineer Gaspard Chaussegros de Léry, who came to the region in 1716.

Having inherited incomplete fortifications, the British sought to complete the Citadel to protect themselves against retaliations from the French. As fate would have it, by the time the Citadel was completed in 1832, the invasions and attacks against Québec City had ended.

Since 1920 the Citadel has served as a base for the Royal 22nd Regiment. A collection of firearms, uniforms, and decorations from the 17th century is housed in the **Royal 22nd Regiment Museum,** located in the former powder house, built in 1750. If weather permits, you may witness the Changing of the Guard, an elaborate ceremony in which the troops parade before the Citadel in the customary red coats and black fur hats. *1 côte de la Citadelle, tel. 418/648–3563. Guided tours only. Admission: $4 adults, $1.50 students; disabled persons free. Open Mar.–Apr. and Oct., weekdays 9–4; May–mid-June and Sept., daily 9–5; mid-June–Aug., daily 9–7; Nov., weekdays 9–2; Dec.–Feb., groups only; reservations are necessary. Changing of the Guard, mid-June–Labor Day, daily 10. Tattoo, July–Aug., Tues., Thurs., Sat., and Sun. 7 PM. Cannon fire from the Prince-de-Galles Bastion (Prince of Wales Bastion), daily noon and 9:30 PM.*

Retrace your steps back down côte de la Citadelle to Grande Allée. Continue west until you come to the Renaissance-style ㉜ **Parliament Buildings,** which mark the area known as **Parliament Hill,** headquarters of the provincial government. The constitution of 1791 designated Québec City the capital of Lower Canada until the 1840 Act of Union that united both Upper and Lower Canada and made Montréal the capital. In 1867, the Act of Confederation, uniting Québec, Ontario, New Brunswick, and Nova Scotia, made Québec City the capital of Québec province. Today the government is the biggest employer in Québec

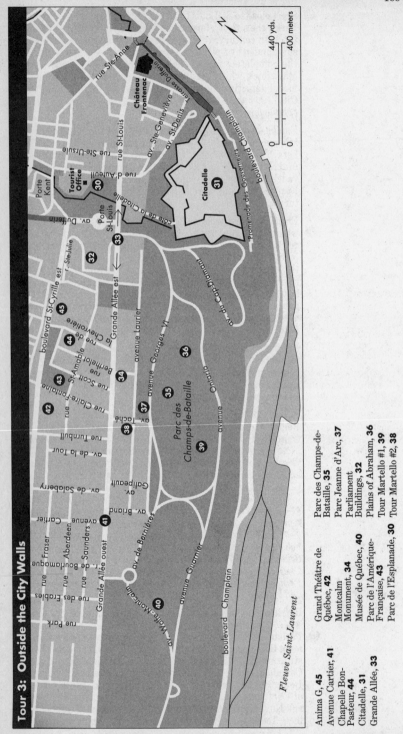

Tour 3: Outside the City Walls

188

Anima G, **45**
Avenue Cartier, **41**
Chapelle Bon-Pasteur, **44**
Citadelle, **31**
Grande Allée, **33**

Grand Théâtre de Québec, **42**
Montcalm Monument, **34**
Musée de Québec, **40**
Parc de l'Amérique-Française, **43**
Parc de l'Esplanade, **30**

Parc des Champs-de-Bataille, **35**
Parc Jeanne d'Arc, **37**
Parliament Buildings, **32**
Plains of Abraham, **36**
Tour Martello #1, **39**
Tour Martello #2, **38**

440 yds.
400 meters

Château Frontenac

Citadelle **31**

Parc des Champs-de-Bataille

Fleuve Saint-Laurent

City, with more than 30,000 civil servants working and living in the area.

The Parliament Buildings, erected between 1877 and 1884, are the seat of **L'Assemblée Nationale** (the National Assembly) of 125 provincial representatives. Québec architect Eugène-Étienne Taché designed the classic and stately buildings in the late-17th-century Renaissance style of Louis XIV, with four wings set in a square around an interior court. In front of the Parliament, statues pay tribute to important figures of Québec history: Cartier, de Champlain, de Frontenac, Wolfe, and Montcalm.

The Parliament offers a 30-minute tour (in English or French) of the President's Gallery, the National Assembly Chamber, and the Legislative Council Chamber. The chamber of the 125-member National Assembly is decorated in green, white, and gold, colors that correspond to the House of Commons in both London and in Ottawa. *Corner of av. Dufferin and Grande Allée E, door 3, tel. 418/643–7239. Admission free. Guided tours Jan.–May and Sept.–Nov., weekdays 9–4:30; June 24–Aug., daily 9–5. Closed Dec. and June 1–23.*

Across from the Parliament on the south side of Grande Allée is the **Manège Militaire,** a turreted granite armory built in 1888, four years after the Parliament Buildings. It was also designed by Taché. It is still a drill hall for the 22nd Regiment.

㉝ Continue along **Grande Allée,** Québec City's version of the Champs-Élysées, with its array of trendy cafés, clubs, and restaurants. One of the oldest streets, Grande Allée was the route people took from outlying areas to sell their furs in Québec City. The street actually has four names: in the old city, it is rue St-Louis; outside the walls, Grande Allée; farther west, chemin St-Louis; and farther still, boulevard Laurier.

One block after the armory, on your left (the south side of Grande Allée) you'll come to Place Montcalm. If you turn left, **㉞** you'll be facing the **Montcalm Monument.** France and Canada joined together to erect this monument honoring Louis-Joseph Montcalm, who claimed his fame by winning four major battles in North America—but his most famous battle was the one he lost, when the British conquered New France on September 13, 1759. Montcalm was north of Québec City at Beauport when he learned that the British attack was imminent. He quickly assembled his troops to meet the enemy and was wounded in battle in the leg and stomach. Montcalm was carried into the walled city, where he died the next morning.

Continue south on Place Montcalm to one of North America's **㉟** largest and most scenic parks, **Parc des Champs-de-Bataille** (Battlefields Park). This 250-acre area of gently rolling slopes offers unparalleled views of the St. Lawrence River. West of **㊱** the citadel are the **Plains of Abraham,** the site of the famous 1759 battle that decided the fate of New France. The Plains of Abraham were named after the river pilot Abraham Martin, who arrived in 1620 and owned several acres here. *A free shuttle bus circles the Plains of Abraham, with 11 stops. Also, an hour-long free, guided bus tour of the Plains of Abraham is offered, leaving from the Battlefield Park Interpretation Center (Pavillon Baillargé, Musée de Québec, tel. 418/648–4071), June 24–Sept. 7. Departures at noon, 1, 3, and 4.*

Take avenue Laurier, which runs parallel to Battlefields Park, a block west until you come to a neatly tended garden called
37 **Parc Jeanne d'Arc** (Joan of Arc Park); it is abundant with colorful flowers and is centered on an equestrian statue of Jeanne d'Arc. A symbol of courage, this statue stands in tribute to the heroes of 1759 near the place where New France was lost to the British. The park also commemorates the Canadian national anthem *Oh Canada;* it was played here for the first time on June 24, 1880.

If you continue west on avenue Laurier, you'll see a stone oval
38 defense tower, **Tour Martello #2** (Martello Tower), on the north corner of avenue Taché and avenue Laurier. This is the second of four Martello towers built in the early 19th century around Québec City to slow the enemy's approach to the city. At the
39 left, toward the south end of the park, stands **Tour Martello #1,** which was built between 1802 and 1810.

Of the 16 Martello towers in all of Canada, four were built in Québec City because the British government feared an invasion after the American Revolution. Tour #3 was located near Jeffery Hale Hospital in order to guard westward entry to the city, but it was demolished in 1904. Tour #4 is located on rue Lavigueur overlooking rivière St-Charles (St. Charles River). Towers 1 and 2 were formerly open to the public; now all three are closed.

Continue a block west on rue de Bernières and then follow avenue George V along the outskirts of Battlefields Park until it intersects with avenue Wolfe-Montcalm. You'll come to the tall **Wolfe Monument,** which marks the place where the British general died. Wolfe landed his troops less than 2 miles from the city's walls; the 4,500 English soldiers scaled the cliff and opened fire on the Plains of Abraham. Wolfe was mortally wounded in battle and was carried behind the lines to this spot.

Turn left on avenue Wolfe-Montcalm for a leisurely stroll
40 through the **Musée de Québec** (Québec Museum). This neoclassical beaux-arts showcase houses the finest collection of Québec art. With one of the largest acquisition budgets of Canada's museums, it possesses more than 15,000 traditional and contemporary pieces. The portraits done by artists well known in the area, such as Ozias Leduc (1864–1955) and Horatio Walker (1858–1938), are particularly notable; some locals find paintings of their relatives on the walls here.

The museum's very formal and dignified building in Battlefields Park was designed by Wilfrid Lacroix and erected in 1933 to commemorate the tricentennial anniversary of the founding of Québec. The museum recently received $22.4 million from the provincial government to renovate the original building, incorporating the space of a nearby, abandoned prison dating to 1867. A hallway of cells, with the iron bars and courtyard still intact, has been preserved as part of a permanent exhibition portraying the prison's history. *1 av. Wolfe-Montcalm, tel. 418/643–2150. Admission: $5 adults, $4 students and senior citizens, children under 16 free. Open June 15–Sept. 14, daily 10–8:45; Sept. 15–June 14, Tues., Thurs.–Sun. 10–5:45, Wed. 10–9:45. Closed Mon.*

From the museum head north on avenue Wolfe-Montcalm, turning right on Grande Allée and walking a block until you reach avenue Cartier. At 115 Grande Allée Ouest is the **Krieg-**

hoff House. This typical Québec home with its bell-shape roof and dormer windows is closed to tourists, but it's worth noting for its former owner, Cornelius Krieghoff, who lived there from 1858 to 1860. One of Canada's most famous landscape painters, Krieghoff was among the first to depict Québec scenery. Born in Amsterdam in 1815, he served in the American army, married a French Canadian in 1839, and settled in Québec in 1852.

④ Head north on **avenue Cartier** to indulge in the pleasures offered by the many good restaurants, clubs, and cafés lining the block. On the east side, stroll through the food mall, **Alimentation Petit-Cartier** (1191 avenue Cartier, tel. 418/688–1630). Here you'll find a supermarket and shops that sell French delicacies—cheeses, pastries, breads, and candies. Some of the better stores are **Boulangerie La Mère-Michele,** for breads and pastries such as petit fours, and **Le Vrac du Quartier,** where you can buy just about anything from spices to cookies in amounts you measure yourself. The mall also houses three restaurants: Café Rousseau, Le Piazetta, and Le Graffiti (*see* Dining, below).

Time Out On the east side of avenue Cartier is **Café Krieghoff,** named after the 19th-century painter who lived nearby. Grab a newspaper, play a game of chess, drink some of the best coffee in town, and complement it with a quiche, a croissant, or a dessert. *1089 av. Cartier, tel. 418/522–3711. V. Open Sun.–Wed. 7 AM–midnight, Thurs.–Sat. 7 AM–1 AM.*

If you continue north along avenue Cartier, the first major intersection is boulevard St-Cyrille Est. Turn right and walk two **④** blocks to the concrete modern building of the **Grand Théâtre de Québec,** a center for the city's performing arts and home of the music school, La Conservatoire de Musique de Québec. Opened in 1971, the theater incorporates two main halls, both named after 19th-century Canadian poets. The "Grande Salle" of Louis-Frechette, named after the first Québec poet and writer to be honored by the French Academy, holds 1,800 seats and is used for concerts, opera, and theater. The "Petite Salle" of Octave-Crémazie, used for experimental theater and variety shows, derives its name from the poet who stirred the rise of Québec nationalism in the mid-19th century.

As the complex was being constructed, Montréal architect Victor Prus commissioned Jordi Bonet, a Québec sculptor, to work simultaneously on a three-wall mural. The themes depicted in the three sections are death, life, and liberty. Bonet wrote "La Liberté" on one wall to symbolize the Québecois' struggle for freedom and cultural distinction. The theater has a full repertoire in the winter, but no shows in the summer. *269 boul. St-Cyrille E, tel. 418/646–0609. Guided tours offered daily 9–5. Telephone for reservations.*

High-waving flags east of the Grand Théâtre are displayed in **④** the **Parc de l'Amérique-Française,** dedicated to places in North America with a French-speaking population. Québec's own Fleur de Lys leads the way. The colors of blue and white, an emblem of Sun King Louis XIV, constitute a reminder of Québec's French origins, culture, and language. Inaugurated in 1985 by Québec Prime Minister Réne Lévesque, the park also has flags from Acadia, British Columbia, Louisiana, Manitoba, Saskatchewan, and Ontario.

Take rue Claire-Fontaine a block south, turn left on rue St-Amable, and then left again on rue de la Chevrotière. On the

(44) west side of the street you'll see the **Chapelle Bon-Pasteur** (Bon-Pasteur Chapel), which is surrounded by modern office complexes. This slender church with a steep sloping roof was designed by Charles Baillargé in 1868. Its ornate interior in a baroque style has carved wood designs painted elaborately in gold leaf. The chapel houses 32 religious paintings done by the Sisters of the community from 1868 to 1910. *1080 rue de la Chevrotière, tel. 418/641–1069. Admission free. Open May–Sept., Tues.–Sun. 1–4; Oct.–Apr., by reservation only; musical artists' Mass Sun. at 10:45.*

Across rue de la Chevrotière is the entrance of a large, gray

(45) concrete modern office tower called **Anima G** (Complex G), Québec's tallest office building. The structure, 31 stories high, has by far the best view of the city and the environs. An express elevator ascends to the observation gallery on top. *1037 rue de la Chevrotière, tel. 418/644–9841. Admission free. Open Mon.–Fri. 10–4, weekends and holidays 1–5; observation gallery may close later during summer. Closed mid-Dec.–mid-Jan.*

What to See and Do with Children

Aquarium du Québec (Québec Aquarium). Situated above the St. Lawrence River, the aquarium houses more than 300 species of marine life, including reptiles, exotic fish, and seals from the lower St. Lawrence River. A wooded picnic area makes this spot ideal for a family outing. The Québec City transit system, Commission de Transport de la Communauté Urbaine de Québec (CTCUQ) (tel. 418/627–2511), runs buses here. *1675 av. du Parc, Sainte-Foy, tel. 418/659–5266. Admission: Apr.–Oct., $4.75 adults, $2.50 students and senior citizens, children under 6 free, $9.25 families; Nov.–Mar., $2.50 adults, $1.50 students and senior citizens, children under 6 free, $4.75 families. Open daily 9–5.*

Jardin Zoologique du Québec (Québec Zoological Gardens). Children usually enjoy going to zoos, but this one is especially scenic because of the DuBerger River, which traverses the grounds. About 250 animal species reside here, including bears, wildcats, primates, and birds of prey. Children will enjoy the farm and the horse-drawn carriage rides. The zoo is situated 11 kilometers (7 miles) west of Québec City on Route 73. Québec Urban Community Transit (tel. 418/627–2511) operates buses here. *8191 av. du Zoo, Charlesbourg, tel. 418/622–0312. Admission: $7 adults, $3.25 students and senior citizens, children under 6 free; Nov.–Apr.: admission free weekdays, half price weekends. Open May–Oct., daily 9:30–6; Nov.–Apr., daily 9:30–5.*

Parc Cartier-Brébeuf. Stretched along the north bank of the St. Charles River, this national historic park commemorates the area where French explorer Jacques Cartier spent his first winter in Canada (1535–36); it also pays tribute to Father Jean de Brébeuf, founder of the Jesuit Order in New France. A replica of the *Grande Hermine*, the ship Cartier used on his second expedition to America, is stationed here. Playgrounds and 9 kilometers (5½ miles) of walking paths are available. *175 rue de l'Espinay, tel. 418/648–4038. Admission free. Open mid-May–Sept. 7, Mon. 1–5, Tues.–Sun. 10–5; Sept. 8–Nov.,*

Feb.–mid-May, Tues.–Fri., 10–noon and 1–4, Sat.–Mon., 1–4; Dec.–Jan. by reservation only.

Parc de l'Artillerie (Artillery Park). This 20-building complex near St-Jean Gate has for centuries played an important part in the city's defense structures. The Officers' Quarters, barracks for Royal Artillery officers until 1871, has a special program for children designed to show how the military lived when Québec was a British colony, from 1759 to 1867. Children's toys and educational games are also available. *2 rue d'Auteil, tel. 418/648–4205. Admission: $2.50 adults, $1.50 senior citizens, $1.25 children 6–16, $6.25 families, children under 6 free. Open June 24–Sept. 7.*

Parc du Porche. This playground has ladders and swings in a historic setting just outside Place Royale (between rue du Porche and rue de l'Union). *Admission free. Open daily.*

Shopping

Shopping is European-style along the fashionable streets of Québec City. The boutiques and specialty shops clustered along narrow streets (such as rue du Petit-Champlain, or rue Buade and rue St-Jean in the Latin Quarter) are located within one of the most striking historic settings on the continent.

Prices in Québec City tend to be on a par for the most part with those in Montréal and other North American cities, so you won't have much luck hunting bargains. When sales occur, they are usually listed in the French daily newspaper, *Le Soleil.*

Stores are generally open Monday through Wednesday 9:30–5:30, Thursday and Friday until 9, and Saturday until 5. During the summer, shops may be open seven days a week, and most have later evening hours.

Shopping Centers

The mall situated closest to the Old City is **Place Québec** (5 Place Québec, tel. 418/529–0551), near the National Assembly. This multilevel shopping complex and convention center with 65 stores is connected to the Hilton International. **Alimentation Petit-Cartier** (1191 av. Cartier, tel. 418/524–3682), located off Grande Allée and a 15-minute walk from St-Louis Gate, is a food mall for gourmets, with everything from utensils to petits fours.

Other shopping centers are approximately a 15-minute drive west along Grande Allée. **Place Sainte-Foy** (2450 boul. Laurier, Sainte-Foy, tel. 418/653–4184) has 120 specialty stores. Next door is **Place Belle Coeur** (2600 boul. Laurier, Sainte-Foy, tel. 418/653–4169), with 34 boutiques. Directly behind this mall you'll find the new **Place de la Cité** (2635 boul. Hochelaga, Sainte-Foy, tel. 418/657–6920), with 63 shops. And finally there is the massive **Place Laurier** (2700 boul. Laurier, Sainte-Foy, tel. 418/653–9318), with more than 350 stores.

Quartier Petit-Champlain (tel. 418/692–2613) in Lower Town is a pedestrian mall with some 50 boutiques, local businesses, and restaurants. This popular district is the best area to find native Québec arts and crafts, such as wood sculptures, weaving, ceramics, and jewelry. Recommended stores in the area are

Poten-Ciel (27 rue du Petit-Champlain, tel. 418/692–1743) for ceramics and **Pauline Pelletier** (38 rue du Petit-Champlain, tel. 418/692–4871) for porcelain.

Department Stores

Large department stores can be found in the malls of the suburb of Sainte-Foy, but most of them have outlets inside Québec City's walls.

Holt & Renfrew & Co., Ltd. (Place Sainte-Foy, Sainte-Foy, tel. 418/656–6783), one of the city's more exclusive stores, carries furs, perfume, and tailored designer collections for men and women.

La Baie (Place Laurier, Sainte-Foy, tel. 418/627–5959) is Québec's version of the Canadian Hudson's Bay Company conglomerate, founded in 1670 by Montréal trappers Pierre Radisson and Medard de Groseillers; the company established the first network of stores in the Canadian frontier. Today, La Baie carries both men's and women's clothing and household wares.

Simons (20 côte de la Fabrique, tel. 418/692–3630), one of Québec City's oldest family stores, used to be the city's only source for fine British woolens and tweeds, and now the store has added a large selection of designer clothing, linens, and other household items.

Food and Flea Markets

Marché du Vieux-Port enables farmers from the Québec countryside to sell their fresh produce in the Old Port near rue St-André, from May through October, 8 AM–8 PM.

Rue du Trésor offers a flea market near the Place d'Armes that features sketches, paintings, and etchings by local artists. Fine portraits of the Québec City landscape and region are plentiful. Good, inexpensive souvenirs also may be purchased here (*see* Exploring, Tour 1, above).

Specialty Stores

Antiques Québec City's antiques district is located in the area of rue St-Paul and rue St-Pierre, across from the Old Port. French Canadian, Victorian, and art deco furniture, along with clocks, silverware, and porcelain, are some of the rare collectibles that can be found here. Authentic Québec pine furniture, characterized by simple forms and lines, is becoming increasingly rare and costly.

L'Héritage Antiquités (109 rue St-Paul, tel. 418/692–1681) specializes in precious Québecois furniture from the 18th century. **Louis Zaor** (112 rue St-Paul, tel. 418/692–0581), the oldest store on rue St-Paul, is still the best place in the area to find excellent English, French, and Canadian antiques. The floor upstairs houses a fine collection of Québec wood furniture.

Art **Aux Multiples Collections** (69 rue Ste-Anne, tel. 418/692–1230) and **Galerie Brousseau et Brousseau** (Château Frontenac, 1 rue des Carrières, tel. 418/694–1828) feature a good selection of Inuit art done by Canada's native people, as well as antique furniture and accessories such as sculpted wood ducks.
Galerie Madeleine Lacerte (1 côte Dinan, tel. 418/692–1566),

situated in Lower Town, features contemporary art and sculpture for sale.

Books English-language books are difficult to find in Québec. One of the city's first bookstores, **Librarie Garneau** (24 côte de la Fabrique, tel. 418/692–4262), is centrally located near City Hall and carries mostly volumes in French. Other popular bookstores in the city include **La Maison Anglaise** (Place de la Cité, Sainte-Foy, tel. 418/654–9523), with the best selection of English-language titles in the area, and **Classic Bookshop** (Place Laurier, boul. Laurier, tel. 418/653–8683).

Clothing **François and Hélène Cote** (20 Cul de Sac, tel. 418/692–3395) is a chic boutique with fashions for men and women.
La Maison Darlington (7 rue Buade, tel. 418/692–2268) carries well-made woolens, dresses, and suits for women by fine names in couture.
Louis Laflamme (Place Québec, tel. 418/523–6633) has a large selection of stylish men's clothes.

Crafts **Les Trois Colombes Inc.** (46 rue St-Louis, tel. 418/694–1114) offers only items made by hand. You will find two floors filled with such goods as clothing made from hand-spun fabric, Indian and Inuit carvings, jewelry, pottery, and paintings.

Fur Fur trade has been an important industry for centuries in the area. Québec City is a good place to purchase high-quality furs at fairly reasonable prices. Since 1894, one of the best furriers in town has been **Jos Robitaille** (700 rue Richelieu, tel. 418/522–3288). The department store **J.B. Laliberté** (Mail Centre-Ville, tel. 418/525–4841) also carries furs.

Gifts **Collection Lazuli** (774 rue St-Jean, tel. 418/525–6528) features a tasteful selection of unusual art objects, gifts, and jewelry from around the world.

Jewelry **Les Bijoux Décade** (48 rue du Petit-Champlain, tel. 418/692–4425) has Québec-made and imported jewelry. Exclusive jewelry can also be found at **Zimmermann** (46 côte de la Fabrique, tel. 418/692–2672).

Sports and Fitness

Two parks are central to Québec City: the 250-acre Battlefields Park, with its panoramic views of the St. Lawrence River, and Cartier-Brébeuf Park, which runs along the St. Charles River. Both are favorite spots for outdoor sports, such as jogging, biking, and cross-country skiing. Scenic rivers and mountains close by (no more than 30 minutes by car) make this city ideal for the sporting life. For information about sports and fitness, contact **Quebec City Region and Convention Bureau** (60 rue d'Auteuil, Québec G1R 4C4, tel. 418/692–2471) or **Québec City Bureau of Parks and Recreation** (1595 Monseigneur-Plessis, Québec G1M 1A2, tel. 418/691–6017).

Participant Sports

Bicycling Short bike paths with rolling hills are found in Battlefields Park, located at the south side of the city. The best bet for a longer ride over flat terrain is the path north of the city skirting the St. Charles River; this route can be reached from Third Avenue near the Marie de l'Incarnation Bridge. Paths along the côte de Beaupré, beginning at the union of the St. Charles and St. Lawrence rivers, are especially scenic. They begin northeast of the city at rue de la Verandrye and boulevard Montmorency and continue 10 kilometers (6 miles) along the coast to Montmorency Falls.

Bicycles can be rented at **Location Petit Champlain** (94 rue du Petit-Champlain, tel. 418/692–2817).

Boating Lakes around the Québec City area have facilities for boating and canoeing. Take Route 73 north of the city to Saint-Dunstan de Lac Beauport, then take Exit 157, boulevard du Lac, to **Lac Beauport** (tel. 418/849–2821), one of the best nearby resorts. Boats and boards can be rented at **Campex** (8 chemin de l'Orrée, Lac Beauport, tel. 418/849–2236) for canoeing, kayaking, and windsurfing. You can also rent boats in **Lac St-Joseph**, 40 kilometers (25 miles) northwest of Québec City, at **La Vigie** (tel. 418/875–2727).

Fishing Permits are needed for hunting and fishing in Québec. They are available from the **Ministry of Recreation, Hunting, and Fishing** (Place de la Capitale, 150 boul. St-Cyrille E, tel. 418/643–3127). The ministry also publishes a pamphlet on fishing regulations that is available at tourist information offices.

Réserve Faunique des Laurentides (tel. 418/848–2422) is a wildlife reserve with good lakes for fishing approximately 48 kilometers (30 miles) north of Québec City via Route 73. Trout may be fished in stocked ponds, one of which is on the Île d'Orléans off Chemin Royal (the main road) in Sainte-Famille.

Golf The Québec City region has 18 golf courses, and several are open to the public. Reservations during summer months are essential. **Club de Golf de Cap Rouge** (4600 rue St-Felix, tel. 418/653–9381) in Cap Rouge, with 18 holes, is one of the closest courses to Québec City. **Club de Golf de Beauport** (3233 rue Clemenceau, tel. 418/663–1578), a nine-hole course, is 20 minutes by car via Route 73 N. **Parc du Mont Sainte-Anne** (Rte. 360, C.P. 653 Beaupré, G0A 3R0, tel. 418/827–3778), a half-hour drive north of Québec, has one of the best 18-hole courses in the region.

Health and Fitness Clubs One of the city's most popular health clubs is **Club Entrain** (Place Belle Cour, 2600 boul. Laurier, tel. 418/658–7771). Facilities include a weight room with Nautilus; a sauna; a whirlpool; aerobics classes; and racquetball and squash courts.

Nonguests at **Hôtel des Gouverneurs** (690 boul. St-Cyrille E, tel. 418/647–1717) can use the health club facilities, which include weights, a sauna, a whirlpool, and an outdoor heated pool, for a $12 fee.

Hilton International Québec (3 Place Québec, tel. 418/647–2411) has a smaller health club with weights, a sauna, and an outdoor pool available to nonguests for an $11 fee.

Pool facilities cost $2 at the **YMCA** (855 av. Holland, tel. 418/683–2155).

Hiking/Jogging The Parc Cartier-Brébeuf, north of the Old City along the banks of the St. Charles River, has about 13 kilometers (8 miles) of hiking trails. For more mountainous terrain, head 19 kilometers (12 miles) north via Route 73 to Lac Beauport. **Villages des Sports** (1860 boul. Valcartier, Val Cartier, tel. 418/

844–3725), a man-made sports complex 24 kilometers (15 miles) from downtown on Route 371, has 16 kilometers (10 miles) of trails. For jogging, Battlefields Park and Parc Cartier-Brébeuf are the most popular places in the area.

Rafting Jacques Cartier River, about 48 kilometers (30 miles) north-west of Québec City, provides good rafting; the waterway flows south from Laurentian Park 56 kilometers (35 miles) from Québec City into the St. Lawrence River.

Jacques Cartier Excursions (978 av. Jacques Cartier N, Tewkesbury, G0A 4P0, tel. 418/848–7238) offers rafting trips on the Jacques Cartier River. Tours originate from Tewkesbury, a half-hour drive from Québec City, from May through September. A half-day tour costs $53 on weekends, $42 on weekdays. A full day costs $72 on weekends, $59 on weekdays. **Nouveau Monde, Expeditions en Rivière** (C.P. 100, chemin de la Rivière Rouge, Calumet, J0V 1B0, tel. 800/361–5033) has excursions on the Jacques Cartier River from mid-May through September, and on the Rivière Rouge (Red River) from mid-April through September. Jacques Cartier half day: weekdays $44, weekends $56. A second trip down the river costs $21. Rivière Rouge full day: weekdays $66, weekends $85. Reserve one month in advance for weekends, two weeks in advance for weekdays.

Skating The skating season runs December through March. There is a 3.8-kilometer (2.4-mile) stretch for skating along the St. Charles River, between the Samson and Marie de l'Incarnation bridges, January through March, depending on the ice. Rentals and changing rooms are nearby. *Skating hours: weekdays noon–10, weekends 10–10.*

Place d'Youville, just outside St-Jean Gate, has an outdoor skating rink that has been recently renovated, with heated facilities from November to April. Nighttime skating can be done at **Villages des Sports** (1860 boul. Valcartier, Val Cartier, tel. 418/844–3725).

Skiing Numerous trails exist for cross-country skiing enthusiasts. *Cross-country* Battlefields Park on Québec City's south side, which you can access on Place Montcalm, has scenic marked trails (for information, call **Quebec City Bureau of Parks and Recreation**, tel. 418/691–6017). Lac Beauport, 19 kilometers (12 miles) north of the city, has more than 30 marked trails (250 kilometers; 155 miles). Contact **Les Sentiers du Moulin** (99 chemin du Moulin, tel. 418/849–2778) or **Le Saisonnier** (78 chemin du Brûlé, tel. 418/849–2821). **Parc du Mont Sainte-Anne** (Rte. 360, C.P. 400 Beaupré, G0A 1E0, tel. 418/827–4561), which is 40 kilometers (25 miles) northeast of Québec City, has 214 kilometers (128 miles) of cross-country trails. Contact **Rang Saint-Julien** (tel. 418/827–4561, ext. 408).

Downhill Four alpine ski resorts, all with night skiing, are located within a 30-minute drive of Québec City. **Parc du Mont Sainte-Anne** (Rte. 360, C.P. 400 Beaupré, G0A 1E0, tel. 418/827–4561) is the largest resort in eastern Canada, with 50 downhill trails, 12 lifts, and a gondola. **Stoneham** (1420 av. Hibou, Stoneham, Québec, G0A 4P0, tel. 418/848–2411) is known for its long, easy slopes with 25 downhill runs and 10 lifts. Two smaller alpine centers can be found at Lac Beauport: 14 trails at **Mont St-Castin** (82 chemin le Tour du Lac, Box 1129, Lac Beauport, Québec G0A 2C0, tel. 418/849–6776) and 24 trails at **Le Relais**

(1084 boul. du Lac, Box 280, Lac Beauport, Québec G0A 2C0, tel. 418/849–1851). Upon request, most major hotels arrange skibus service for guests for a fee.

A municipal bus service, **Skibus** (tel. 418/627–2511), is offered on Saturday and Sunday. It leaves from Place Laurier (2700 boul. Laurier, Sainte-Foy) at 8 AM for Stoneham and returns once a day at 4:15. The cost is $4 each way.

Visite Touristique de Québec (tel. 418/653–9722) offers a bus service to Mont Sainte-Anne and Stoneham. For Mont Sainte-Anne, it leaves from major hotels in Québec and Sainte-Foy daily between 7:30 AM and 8:30 AM and returns at 4:30 PM. For Stoneham, it leaves from major hotels on Wednesday, Thursday, and Friday nights between 5:30 and 6, and it returns at 10:30. Return trip costs $14. Telephone for reservations.

A brochure entitled "Ski Greater Quebec Area" is available at Quebec Tourism and Convention Bureaus or by telephoning 800/363–7777.

Tennis At **Montcalm Tennis Club** (901 boul. Champlain, Sillery, tel. 418/687–1250), south of Québec City in Sillery, four indoor and seven outdoor courts are open daily from 7 AM to 11 PM. Twelve indoor courts are also available at **Tennisport** (6280 boul. Hammel, Ancienne Lorette, tel. 418/872–0111).

Spectator Sports

Tickets for sporting events can be purchased at **Colisée de Québec** (Québec Coliseum; 2205 av. du Colisée, tel. 418/523–3333 or 800/463–3333) or through Billetech, whose main outlet is at the **Grand Théâtre de Québec** (269 boul. St-Cyrille E, tel. 418/643–8131). Other outlets are situated at Bibliothèque Gabrielle-Roy, Palais Montcalm, La Baie department store (Place Laurier, Sainte-Foy, tel. 418/627–5959), and Provigo supermarkets. The outlet hours vary depending on the location.

Harness Racing Horse racing is on view at the racetrack **Hippodrome de Québec.** *C.P. 2053, Parc de l'Exposition, tel. 418/524–5283. Admission: $2.50 adults, $1.50 children under 10 and senior citizens.*

Hockey A National Hockey League team, the Québec Nordiques, plays at the **Colisée de Québec** (Québec Coliseum). *2205 av. du Colisée, Parc de l'Exposition, tel. 418/523–3333 or 800/463–3333. Open Oct.–Mar.*

Dining

Québec City reveals its French heritage most obviously in its cuisine. You'll discover a French touch in the city's numerous cafés and brasseries and in the artful presentation of dishes at local restaurants. Most dining establishments usually have a selection of dishes à la carte, but you'll usually find more creative specialties by opting for the table d'hôte, a two- to four-course meal chosen daily by the chef. At dinner, most restaurants will offer a *menu de dégustation*, a five- to seven-course dinner of the chef's finest creations.

Although most visitors will find a gourmet meal in their price range, budget-conscious diners may want to try out the more expensive establishments during lunchtime. Lunch usually costs about 30% less than dinner, and many of the same dishes are available. Lunch is usually served 11:30 AM through 2:30 PM; dinner, 6:30 until about 11 PM. You should tip about 15% of the bill.

Québec City is the best place in the province to sample French Canadian cuisine, composed of robust, uncomplicated dishes that make use of the region's bounty of foods, including fowl and wild game (caribou, quail, venison), maple syrup, and various berries and nuts. Because Québec has a cold climate for a good portion of the year, it has a traditionally heavy cuisine, with such specialties as *cretons* (pâtés), *tourtière* (meat pie), and *tarte au sucre* (maple-syrup pie).

Highly recommended restaurants in each price category are indicated by a star ★.

Category	Cost*
Very Expensive	over $30
Expensive	$20–$30
Moderate	$10–$20
Inexpensive	under $10

*per person, excluding drinks, service, 7% federal sales tax, and 7% provincial sales tax

Very Expensive

★ **À la Table de Serge Bruyère.** This restaurant has put Québec on the map of great gastronomic cities. The city's most famous culinary institution serves classic French cuisine presented with plenty of crystal, silver, and fresh flowers and with relentless attention to detail. Only one sitting is offered each night. Chef Serge Bruyère came to Québec City from Lyons, France, and worked at various restaurants until he opened his own in 1980. The *menu gourmand* is a five-course meal for $47. The extensive wine list starts at $25 and goes up to $450. Specialties include scampi in puff pastry with fresh tomatoes, scallop stew with watercress, and duckling supreme with blueberry sauce. (In 1984, Bruyère expanded inside the restaurant's old 1843 Livernois building and created a minimall with a European-style tearoom, a contemporary piano bar, and a food store—all serving gourmet treats from his celebrated kitchen. If À la Table de Serge Bruyère is out of your price range, **À la Petite Table** in the food mall is less formal and less expensive, with such dishes as seafood terrine and pork with estragon sauce.) *1200 rue St-Jean, tel. 418/694–0618. Reservations required. Jacket required. AE, MC, V. No lunch weekends.*

Café de la Paix. An evening spent at this local favorite takes you back to a dining experience in Paris circa 1930. The tables could not get closer nor the lights dimmer amid the art deco extravagance of lamps in Venetian glass, wood sculpted in geometric patterns, and stained-glass windows. The food is on a par with other fine restaurants in the city, but there are hints that the chefs are relying on their reputations (the restaurant dates back from 1952). The table d'hôte includes such tasty dishes as pheasant with peaches. Salmon comes with four sauces: raspberry vinegar, hollandaise, tarragon, or mustard. The meat entrées, including filet Mignon and leg of lamb, are also recom-

Québec City Dining and Lodging

mended. You choose your dessert from a cart; try the fresh fruit and the chocolate truffle cake. The service is prompt and attentive. Private dining rooms are available on the second floor. *44 rue des Jardins, tel. 418/692–1430. Reservations advised. Dress: neat but casual. AE, DC, MC, V. No lunch Sun. in winter.*

★ **Gambrinus.** This comfortable restaurant offers excellent Continental cuisine in two elegant, mahogany-paneled, plant-filled dining rooms with windows facing the street. Its reliable menu features a range of meat, fish, and pasta entrées, with such specialties as pheasant supreme with fruit, seafood in puff pastry with saffron, and rack of lamb with basil. The table d'hôte is a good bet and provides generous portions and delectable desserts. Service here is unrushed and thoroughly professional. A talented singer-guitarist may accompany your meal; don't be surprised if one of the waiters also bursts into song. Gambrinus is conveniently located near rue du Trésor and the Château Frontenac. *15 rue du Fort, tel. 418/692–5144. Reservations advised. Dress: neat but casual. AE, DC, MC, V. No lunch weekends.*

Le Marie Clarisse. Wood-beam ceilings, stone walls, sea-blue decor, and a lit fireplace make this dining spot one of the coziest in town. Housed in an ancient building on the bottom of the Breakneck Steps near Place Royale, Le Marie Clarisse is well known for its unique seafood dishes, such as halibut with nuts and honey and scallops with port and paprika. Occasionally, the menu includes a good game dish such as caribou with curry. The *menu du jour* has about seven entrées to choose from; dinner includes soup, salad, dessert, and coffee. Wines are served from the restaurant's cellar. *12 rue du Petit-Champlain, tel. 418/692–0857. Reservations required. Dress: neat but casual. AE, DC, MC, V. Closed lunch Sat. and all day Sun.*

★ **Le Saint-Amour.** This restaurant has all the makings of a true haute-cuisine establishment without having a pretentious atmosphere. A light and airy atrium, with a retractable roof used for outdoor dining in summer, creates a relaxed dining ambience. Chef Jean-Luc Boulay continues to educate himself by taking various courses in France; his studies pay off in the creation of such specialties as stuffed quails in port sauce and salmon with light chive mousse. Sauces here are light, with no flour or butter. The *menu de dégustation* has nine courses, and the *menu gastronomique* has seven courses. If you plan to order one of these two menus, it's a good idea to mention this when making your reservation. Wines can be ordered by the glass to complement courses. The chef's true expertise shines when it comes to his diverse dessert menu. Try the nougat ice cream with fresh figs or the three-chocolate cake. Better yet, order the Saint-Amour assortment of desserts. *48 rue Ste-Ursule, tel. 418/694–0667. Reservations advised. Dress: neat but casual. AE, DC, MC, V.*

Expensive

★ **Aux Anciens Canadiens.** This establishment is named after a book by Philippe-Aubert de Gaspé, who once resided here. The place is worth trying for the experience of tasting authentic French Canadian cooking. The house dates back to 1675 and has four dining rooms with different themes. The *vaisselier* (dish room) is bright and cheerful, with colorful antique dishes, a fireplace, and an antique stove. Another room displays guns from the French regime. The hearty specialties include duck in maple glaze and lamb with blueberry wine sauce. The restaurant also serves the best caribou drink in town. (Caribou is a local beverage made with sweet red wine and whiskey; it is known for its kick.) *34 rue St-Louis, tel. 418/692–1627. Reservations advised. Dress: casual. AE, MC, V.*

L'Astral. This circular restaurant on the 29th floor of the Hôtel Loews Le Concorde revolves high above Battlefields Park and the Old City. The food, while showing signs of improvement, is not the best in town, but the views are excellent. The modern and uninspired decor does not detract from the view, either; there's no room for anything besides the dining tables next to large windows and the vast buffet of salads, meat, and poultry dishes. Sunday brunch offers more than 45 items for $21.75; children under 12, $6. *1225 Place Montcalm, tel. 418/647–2222. Reservations advised. Dress: neat but casual. AE, DC, MC, V.*

Le Graffiti. A good alternative to Old City dining, this restaurant, housed in a modern gourmet food mall, serves the cuisine of Provence. Gray tablecloths contrast with dark mahogany-paneled walls to contribute to the romantic setting, while large bay windows look out onto the passersby along avenue Cartier. The distinctive menu typically includes a choice of chicken, beef, and seafood dishes such as scampi spiced with basil and red pepper, and chicken liver mousse with pistachios. The reasonably priced table d'hôte comes with soup, appetizer, entrée, dessert, and coffee. Desserts are made fresh each day. *1191 av. Cartier, tel. 418/529–4949. Reservations advised. Dress: neat but casual. AE, DC, MC, V.*

★ **Le Paris Brest.** This busy restaurant on Grande Allée serves a gregarious crowd attracted to its tastefully presented French dishes. Its new look, with angular halogen lighting, a glassed-in wine cabinet, and soft yellow walls, adds a fresh, modern touch to this historic building. Traditional fare such as *escargots au Pernod* (snails with Pernod) and steak tartare are offered with special touches such as a tomato carved in the shape of a rose. Popular dishes served here include lamb with herbs from Provence and beef Wellington. À la carte and main-course dishes are accompanied by a generous side platter of vegetables. Wine prices range from $22 to $250. *590 Grande Allée E, tel. 418/529–2243. Reservations advised. Dress: neat but casual. AE, DC, MC, V.*

Restaurant au Parmesan. From the red-and-white checkered tablecloths to its standard pasta offerings, this restaurant has everything you expect in an Italian establishment and then some. Thousands of bottles with unusual shapes line the walls, and an accordion player will serenade you over typical dishes such as *gnocchi* (potato dumplings) with tomato sauce and tortellini with cream sauce. The service can be slow and inattentive, but with the jovial, boisterous crowd, you might not mind the wait. *38 rue St-Louis, tel. 418/692–0341. Reservations advised. Dress: casual. AE, DC, MC, V.*

Moderate

Chalet Suisse. This large chalet close to Place d'Armes serves Swiss cuisine. Fondues are a mainstay, and there are 25 different ones to choose from, with the Gruyère and the chocolate fondues being two of the tastiest house specialties. Another popular dish is *raclette*, a Swiss dish with melted cheese, served with bread and potatoes as well as diverse flavorings such as onions, pickles, and ham. The spacious chalet looms three stories high with clichéd murals of alpine scenes. In the summer, there are umbrella-shaded café tables outside. *32 rue Ste-Anne, tel. 418/694–1320. Reservations accepted. Dress: informal. AE, DC, MC, V.*

L'Apsara. Near St-Louis Gate, this restaurant serves innovative dishes from Vietnam, Thailand, and Cambodia. The Cambodian family that owns the restaurant excels at using both subtle and tangy spices to create unique flavors that are ideal for those seeking a reprieve from French fare. The decor combines Western and Eastern motifs, with flowered wallpaper, Oriental art, and small fountains. Good starters are *fleur de pailin* (a rice paste roll filled with fresh vegetables, meat, and shrimp) or *mou sati* (pork kebabs with peanut sauce and coconut milk). The assorted miniature Cambodian pastries are delicious with tea served from a little elephant container. *71 rue d'Auteuil, tel. 418/694–0232. Reservations accepted. Dress: casual. AE, MC, V.*

Le Café de la Terrasse. This restaurant, housed in the landmark Château Frontenac, does not share the hotel's opulence, but it does offer a view along Terrasse Dufferin and the St. Lawrence River. You can try the businessman's breakfast buffet of fruits, omelets, and croissants and an à la carte lunch menu of salads and sandwiches. Standard but dependable Continental dishes are served during the lunch and dinner buffets. *Château Frontenac, 1 rue Carrières, tel. 418/692–3861. Reservations accepted. Dress: neat but casual. AE, DC, MC, V.*

★ **L'Echaudée** (Whitewash). This chic black-and-white bistro attracts a mix of business and tourist clientele because of its location between the financial and antiques districts in Lower Town. The modern decor features a stark dining area with a mirrored wall and a stainless-steel bar where you dine atop high stools. Lunch offerings include *cuisse de canard confit* (duck confit) with french fries and fresh seafood salad. The three-course brunch for Sunday antiques shoppers includes giant croissants and a tantalizing array of desserts. *73 Sault-au-Matelot, tel. 418/692–1299. Weekend reservations advised. Dress: casual. AE, DC, MC, V. Closed Sun. night in winter.*

Inexpensive

Casse-Crêpe Breton. Crepes in generous proportions are served in this small, square, diner-style restaurant on rue St-Jean. From a menu of 15 ingredients, pick your own chocolate or fruit combinations, or design a larger meal with cheese, ham, and vegetables. The tables surround three round hot plates at which you watch your creations being made. Crepes made with two to five ingredients cost under $5. *1136 rue St-Jean. tel. 418/692–0438. No reservations. Dress: casual. No credit cards. Open 7:30 AM–1 AM.*

★ **Chez Temporel.** Tucked behind rue St-Jean and côte de la Fabrique, this homey café is an experience *très français*. The aroma of fresh coffee fills the air. The rustic decor incorporates wooden tables, chairs, and benches, while a tiny staircase winds to an upper level. Croissants are made in-house; the staff will fill them with Gruyère and ham or anything else you want. Try the equally delicious croque-monsieur and quiche Lorraine. *25 rue Couillard, tel. 418/694–1813. No reservations. Dress: casual. No credit cards. Open 7:30 AM–1:30 AM.*

Le Cochon Dingue (The Crazy Pig). Across the street from the ferry in Lower Town, this cheerful café with sidewalk tables and indoor dining rooms has artfully blended the chic and the antique. Black-and-white checkerboard floors contrast with ancient stone walls that are typical of the oldest sections of town. Café fare includes dependably tasty homemade quiches, thick soups, and such desserts as fresh raspberry tarte and maple-sugar pie. *46 boul. Champlain, tel. 418/692–2013. Reservations accepted. Dress: informal. AE, MC, V. Open 7:30 AM–11 PM.*

Mille Feuille. In the heart of the Latin Quarter, this vegetarian restaurant in a well-preserved, historic building dates to 1782. The daily menu offers three or four creative dishes, such as cabbage leaves stuffed with brown rice and vegetables, topped with rich tomato sauce and fresh Parmesan cheese, and or Greek-style pizza with black olives. All dishes are served with soup and salad. On Saturday and Sunday a "health brunch" is served from 8 AM to 3 PM for under $6. *32 rue Sainte-Angèle, tel. 418/692–2147. Reservations accepted. Dress: informal. MC, V.*

Pizzeria d'Youville. This restaurant located in the lively Latin Quarter has a pizza for everyone, with more than 25 combinations. Tasty pies are cooked in a wood oven and then heated by fire at your table. You can go beyond tomato sauce and cheese here and try the Hawaiian pizza, with ham, cheese, and pineapple, or L'Amalfitana, which combines tomato sauce, cheese, shrimp, and garlic. Meat dishes, pasta, and salads are also on offer. *1014 rue St-Jean, tel. 418/694–0299. Reservations accepted. Dress: informal. AE, DC, MC, V.*

Lodging

With more than 35 hotels within its 1-square-mile radius, Québec City has a range of lodging options. Landmark hotels stand as prominent as the city's most historic sites. Modern high rises outside the ramparts offer spectacular views of the Old City. Or visitors can immerse themselves in the city's historic charm by staying in one of the many old-fashioned inns where no two rooms are alike.

Whichever kind of accommodations you choose, during peak season, from May through September, be sure to make a reservation. If you are planning to visit during the summer or at the time of the Winter Carnival in February, you may have trouble finding a room without one. During busy times, hotel rates are usually 30% above prices at other times of the year. From November through April, many of the city's lodging places offer discount weekend packages and other promotions.

Highly recommended properties in each price category are indicated by a star ★.

Category	Cost*
Very Expensive	over $140
Expensive	$85–$140

Moderate	$50–$85
Inexpensive	under $50

All prices are for a standard double room, excluding 7% federal sales tax, 7% provincial sales tax, and an optional service charge.

Very Expensive

Château Bonne Entente. If you have a car, you may want to stay at this sprawling resort located 10 minutes from the airport and 20 minutes from the walled city. The hotel is more commonly called "The Other Château," the country cousin of the urban Frontenac. It was a private mansion until 1940, when it became a hotel; after a $7 million renovation in 1989, this establishment has become a popular spot for the well-heeled. Rooms are decorated in contemporary style with fine wood, plush carpeting, and all the modern amenities. The property encompasses 11 acres of land with a main complex as well as separate cottage rooms in back. *3400 chemin Ste-Foy, Sainte Foy G1X 1S6, tel. 418/653–5221 or 800/463–4390. 168 rooms. Facilities: bar, 2 restaurants, outdoor pool, tennis court, trout fishing in back pond, full day care. AE, DC, MC, V.*

★ **Château Frontenac.** Towering above the St. Lawrence River, the Château Frontenac is indisputably Québec City's most renowned landmark. Although the Frontenac can no longer claim to be the city's top-rated hotel, the mystique of staying at "the château" endures. Its public rooms, from the intimate piano bar to its 700-seat ballroom, which is reminiscent of the Versailles Hall of Mirrors, have all the opulence of years gone by, and almost all the guest rooms offer excellent views. You must make a reservation in advance, as the average booking rate is 80% a year. A five-year, $60 million renovation has been completed for 1993, in time to celebrate the hotel's 100th birthday. A new wing of rooms was added, as was a long-awaited health spa. The Frontenac has one of the finer restaurants in town, Le Champlain, where classic French cuisine is served by waiters dressed in traditional French costumes. The ground floor has several luxury shops and a restaurant, Le Café de la Terrasse (*see* Dining, above). *1 rue des Carrières, G1R 4P5, tel. 418/692–3861 or 800/268–9420. 610 rooms. Facilities: 3 restaurants, 2 bars, health spa, indoor pool. AE, DC, MC, V.*

★ **Hilton International Québec.** Just outside St-Jean Gate, the Hilton rises from the shadow of Parliament Hill as the city's finest luxury hotel. It has such spacious facilities and efficient services that it could easily cater exclusively to the convention crowd. Instead, it has adapted its renowned comfort and dependable service to tourists. The sprawling atrium lobby is flanked with a bar and an open-air restaurant, and it offers the added convenience of being connected with the mall, Place Québec, which offers 65 shops and boutiques. Ultramodern rooms with pine furniture feature tall windows so that rooms on upper floors give fine views of the Old City. *3 Place Québec, G1K 7M9, tel. 418/647–2411 or 800/268–9275. 565 rooms, 35 suites. Facilities: outdoor pool, health club, sauna, whirlpool, 2 restaurants, piano bar. AE, DC, MC, V.*

Hôtel des Gouverneurs. Opposite the Parliament Buildings, this large, full-service establishment is part of a Québec chain with 12 hotels in the province. Formerly called Auberge des Gouverneurs when it opened in 1975, the hotel has upgraded its light and spacious rooms by furnishing them with luminous pastel decor, wood furniture, and marble bathrooms. The recently added VIP floors were designed to lure the business traveler, but there is also plenty of room for tourists. Although it is part of a tall office complex, the hotel occupies only the first six floors, so views of the Old City are limited. The hotel does boast, however, a year-round outdoor swimming pool, perfect for use even when the weather is most frigid. *690 boul. St-Cyrille E, G1R 5A8, tel. 418/647–1717 or 800/463–2820. 377 rooms with private bath. Facilities: health club, heated indoor-outdoor pool, sauna, whirlpool, piano bar, restaurant. AE, DC, MC, V.*

★ **Hôtel Loews Le Concorde.** When Le Concorde was built in 1974, the shockingly tall concrete structure went up with controversy because it was taking the place of 19th-century Victorian homes. Yet of all the modern hotels outside the city gates, tourists will probably find that Le Concorde occupies one of the most convenient locations for city touring and nightlife. Inside the hotel there's almost as much going on as at the cafés and restaurants along the nearby Grande Allée; Le Concorde offers the revolving restaurant L'Astral, a sidewalk café, a bar, and a disco. Rooms have good views of Battlefields Park, and nearly all have been redone in modern decor combined with traditional furnishings. Amenities for business travelers have expanded; one of the new VIP floors is reserved for female executives. *1225 Place Montcalm, G1R 4W6, tel. 418/647–2222 or 800/463–5256; in the U.S., tel. 800/223–0888. 424 rooms. Facilities: heated outdoor pool, sauna, whirlpool, health club, bar, disco, 2 restaurants (L'Astral on the 28th floor and a sidewalk café). AE, DC, MC, V.*

Expensive

Le Château de Pierre. Built in 1853 and converted from a private residence in 1960, this tidy Victorian manor on a picturesque street has kept its English origins alive. The high-ceilinged halls have ornate chandeliers. The rooms are imaginatively decorated with floral themes, and each usually has some special added feature—a balcony, fireplace, or vanity room—to lend some extra charm. Rooms in the front face imposing old stone buildings across the way that date from the English regime. *17 av. Ste-Geneviève, G1R 4A8, tel. 418/694–0429. 15 rooms with private bath and air-conditioning. MC, V.*

L'Hôtel du Vieux Québec. Located on a secluded street in the Latin Quarter, this hotel has a brick exterior that gets lost amid the more striking historic structures around it. The establishment was once an apartment building and has the long-term visitor in mind. The interior design is also nondescript, featuring sparsely decorated but comfortable rooms done in earth tones. Most rooms have a full kitchenette with a stove, cabinets, a sink, and a refrigerator; all have cable TV. *8 rue Collins, G1R 4J2, tel. 418/692–1850. 27 units with private bath. AE, MC, V.*

★ **Manoir d'Auteuil.** Originally a private home, this lodging is one of the more lavish manors in town, artfully revamped at great expense. An ornate sculpted iron banister wraps around four floors. Guest rooms feature lavish trimmings in mahogany and marble and blend modern design with the art deco structure.

Each room differs in shape and design; one room was formerly the residence's chapel, while another has become a duplex with a luxurious marble bathroom on the second floor. Some rooms look out onto the wall between the St-Louis and St-Jean gates. *49 rue d'Auteuil, G1R 4C2, tel. 418/694–1173. 16 rooms with private bath. AE, MC, V.*

Manoir Sainte-Geneviève. This quaint and elaborately decorated hotel dating from 1880 stands near the Château Frontenac, on the southwest corner of the Jardin des Governeurs. A plush Victorian ambience is created with fanciful wallpaper and rooms decorated with precious stately English manor furnishings, such as marble lamps, large wooden bedposts, and velvet upholstery; you'll feel as if you are staying in a secluded country inn. A hidden porch facing the Citadel is perfect for relaxing and soaking in the atmosphere of Upper Town. Service here is personal and genteel. One suite on the ground floor has a private entrance. *13 av. Ste-Geneviève, G1R 4A7, tel. 418/694–1666. 9 rooms with private bath; 7 rooms have air-conditioning, color TV. V.*

Manoir Victoria. This promising new hotel is located in the heart of the Latin Quarter, off rue St-Jean. Since the hotel opened its doors in 1988, it has undergone extensive renovations, transforming the original turn-of-the-century Hotel Victoria into a modern-day manor. Don't be fooled by its conservative exterior: The hotel is larger and more elaborate than it appears. A popular downtown pub, the Saint-James, is connected to the hotel. The spacious lobby, with Greco-Roman pillars, is furnished with blue and pink sofas, and the walls feature an exhibit of Québec art. The brightly decorated rooms are clean and comfortable but lack the view offered by some other hotels. *44 côte du Palais, G1R 4H8, tel. 418/692–1030 or 800/463–6283. 143 rooms with private bath, 4 with whirlpool bath. Facilities: bar, 2 restaurants, health club, indoor pool, beauty salon, parking. AE, DC, MC, V.*

Moderate

Château de la Terrasse. Although this four-story inn may not have the same charm as others in the city, it does have something that the others are lacking: This is the sole inn within the area that has a view of the St. Lawrence River. However, only half of the rooms face the river; others in the rear look out onto the backs of buildings. While the interior hints at having once possessed a refined and elegant decor because of its high ceilings and stained glass lining the large bay windows, the furnishings these days are plain and unremarkable. *6 Place Terrasse Dufferin, G1R 4N5, tel. 418/694–9472. 18 rooms with private bath. V.*

Hôtel Château Laurier. This medium-size hotel closely resembles a dormitory, which may explain why it attracts a youthful clientele. Located at one of the louder intersections in town, it has front doors that open up to the nightlife on Grande Allée. The lobby consists of couches clustered around a central television. Guest rooms are spacious, but some of the no-frills furnishings appear worn. Some rooms look out onto Parliament Hill; others, facing Grande Allée, may be noisy at night. *695 Grande Allée E, G1R 2K4, tel. 418/522–8108. 55 rooms with private bath. Free parking. AE, DC, MC, V.*

★ **L'Auberge du Quartier.** This small, amiable inn, situated in a house dating from 1852, will please those seeking moderately priced lodging with a personal touch. Proprietors Lise Provost and Pierre Couture are highly attentive to their guests' needs. The cheerful rooms, without phones or televisions, are modestly furnished but well maintained; two of them have fireplaces. Rooms 5 and 8 are recommended to couples. A suite of rooms on the third floor can accommodate a family at a reasonable cost. This is one of the few inns in the area that offers a tasty Continental breakfast of warm croissants, homemade banana bread and preserves, strong coffee, and fresh fruits. A 20-minute walk west from the Old City, L'Auberge du Quartier is convenient to avenue Cartier and Grande Allée nightlife; joggers can use Battlefields Park across the street. *170 Grande Allée O, G1R 2G9, tel. 418/525–9726. 11 rooms with private bath. Free parking. AE, MC, V.*

L'Auberge Saint-Louis. This hotel is perfect for the traveler with convenience in mind; its central location on the main street of the city can't be beat. The inn features small rooms, tall staircases, and a lobby resembling a European pension. The newly decorated guest rooms contain comfortable but bare-bones furniture. The ultrabudget room on the fourth floor is just big enough for a bed. The service here is friendly and hospitable. Most guest rooms share floor bathrooms or have a semibathroom. *48 rue St-Louis, G1R 3Z3, tel. 418/692–2424. 22 rooms, 8 with private bath. MC, V.*

Inexpensive

★ **Hôtel Maison Sainte-Ursule.** Situated on a tiny street west of the Ursuline Convent, this well-kept hotel is a boon for the sophisticated yet economical traveler, offering both historic charm and reasonable prices. The building, constructed in 1780, is typical of the architecture of New France, with dormer windows, small doors, and a slanting roof. Immaculate accommodations contain the old-fashioned basics, with sturdy and simple wood furniture; some rooms even have the original pint-size doors. Seven rooms are located in an annex in a private rear courtyard that becomes a garden in the summer. The amiable staff is eager to see that you are comfortable. *40 rue Ste-Ursule, G1R 4E2, tel. 418/694–9794; in Québec, Ontario, and the maritime provinces, 800/267–1720. 15 rooms, 12 with private bath. MC, V.*

Manoir des Remparts. There's nothing fancy about this hotel, which is on a residential street bordering the north side of Québec City's natural cliff. But this manor offers just enough to attract the budget-conscious traveler: spacious and clean rooms with back-to-basics old-time furnishings. The halls are well lighted and considered large for a residence in the Old City. Guest rooms have private bath or share a bath on the floor but don't have telephones or televisions. *3½ rue des Remparts, G1R 3R4, tel. 418/692–2056. AE, MC, V.*

Bed-and-Breakfasts

Québec City has a large number of bed-and-breakfast and hostel accommodations. To guarantee a room during peak season, be sure to reserve in advance. **Quebec City Tourist Information** (60 rue d'Auteuil, G1R 4C4, tel. 418/692–2471) has B&B listings. **Bed and Breakfast–Bonjour Québec** (3765 boul. Monaco, G1P 3J3, tel. 418/527–1465) has several B&Bs to choose from in or close to the Old City. Reserve in advance in the summer.

Prices range from $35 for a single room to $60 for a double. Apartments are available for $85–$95.

Hostels

Centre International de Séjour (19 rue Ste-Ursule, G1R 4E1, tel. 418/694–0755). In the Old City, the center has 300 beds in rooms accommodating 2–30 beds. The cost is $11–$18 for one person. All meals are available in the cafeteria. *AE*, *MC*, *V*.

Service des Résidences de l'Université Laval (Pavillon Alphonse-Marie-Parent, Université Laval, Sainte-Foy, Québec G1K 7P4, tel. 418/656–5632). From May through August, rooms are available in the dormitories of the Laval University campus, located west of the Old City in suburban Sainte-Foy. Prices are $24 for a single; $32 for a double. Reserve at least two days in advance. Meals are served in the cafeteria. *MC*, *V*.

YWCA (855 av. Holland, G1S 3S5, tel. 418/683–2155). Near Jeffrey-Hale Hospital, this women's organization offers 42 rooms. A single costs $30 a night and a double costs $50 a night. Rooms are open to men during the summer only. Reservations are suggested. Meals are available in the cafeteria.

The Arts and Nightlife

For a place its size, Québec City boasts a wide variety of cultural events, from the reputable Québec Symphony Orchestra to several small theater companies. The arts scene changes significantly depending on the season. From September to May, a steady repertoire of concerts, plays, and performances is presented in theaters and halls around town. In summer, indoor theaters close to make room for several outdoor stages.

For arts and entertainment listings in English, consult the *Québec Chronicle-Telegraph,* published on Wednesday. Each day in the French-language daily newspaper, *Le Soleil,* listings appear on a page called "Où Aller à Québec" ("Where to Go in Québec"). *Voilà Québec* and *Hospitalité Québec* are bilingual quarterly entertainment guides distributed free in tourist information areas.

Tickets for most shows can be purchased through **Billetech,** whose main outlet is the Grand Théâtre de Québec (269 boul. St-Cyrille E, tel. 418/643–8131). Other outlets are located at Bibliothèque Gabrielle-Roy, Colisée, Implanthéâtre, Palais Montcalm, Salle Albert-Rousseau, La Baie department store (Place Laurier, tel. 418/627–5959), and Provigo supermarkets. Outlet hours vary, depending on the location.

The Arts

Dance   **Grand Théâtre de Québec** (269 boul. St-Cyrille E, tel. 418/643–8131) presents a dance series with both Canadian and international companies. Dancers also appear at Bibliothèque Gabrielle-Roy, Salle Albert-Rousseau, and the Palais Montcalm (*see* Theater, below, for more information).

Film   Most theaters present French films and American films dubbed into French. Two popular theaters are **Cinéma de Paris** (966 rue St-Jean, tel. 418/694–0891) and **Cinéma Place Charest** (500 rue du Pont, tel. 418/529–9745). **Cinéma Place Québec** (5

Place Québec, tel. 418/525–4524) almost always features films in English.

Music L'Orchestre Symphonique de Québec (Québec Symphony Orchestra) is Canada's oldest. It performs at Louis-Frechette Hall in the **Grand Théâtre de Québec** (269 boul. St-Cyrille E, tel. 418/643–8131).

Bibliothèque Gabrielle-Roy (350 rue St-Joseph E, tel. 418/529–0924). Classical concerts are offered at the Auditorium Joseph Lavergne. Tickets must be purchased in advance at the library.

Colisée de Québec (2205 av. du Colisée, Parc de l'Exposition, tel. 418/691–7211). Popular music concerts are often booked here.

Theater All theater productions are in French. The following theaters schedule shows from September through April:

Grand Théâtre de Québec (269 boul. St-Cyrille E, tel. 418/643–8131). Classic and contemporary plays are staged by the leading local theater company, le Théâtre du Trident (tel. 418/643–5873).

Palais Montcalm (995 Place d'Youville, tel. 418/670–9011). This municipal theater outside St-Jean Gate features a broad range of productions.

Salle Albert-Rousseau (2410 chemin Ste-Foy, Sainte-Foy, tel. 418/659–6710). A diverse repertoire, from classical to comedy, is offered here.

Théâtre de la Bordée (1143 rue St-Jean, tel. 418/694–9631). This local company presents small-scale productions.

Théâtre du Petit-Champlain (68 rue du Petit-Champlain, tel. 418/692–2631). On Québec City's smallest and oldest street, this theater's performances are staged in a café atmosphere.

Théâtre Périscope (2 rue Crémazie E, tel. 418/529–2183). This multipurpose, experimental theater offers about 200 presentations a year, including performances for children.

Summer Theater **Agora** (120 rue Dalhousie; for tickets and information, contact Billetech, tel. 418/643–8131). The largest open-air amphitheater in the Old Port, between the river and the customs building, features variety shows, plays, and classical and contemporary music concerts.

Place d'Youville (tel. 418/670–9011). During the summer, open-air concerts are presented here, just outside St-Jean Gate. Recent renovations have made this spot quite enjoyable.

Théâtre du Bois du Coulonge (office: 81 rue St-Pierre, tel. 418/692–3064). One of the most delightful theater settings in town is situated in Battlefields Park (1215 chemin St-Louis, Sillery), near the Québec Museum.

Nightlife

Nightlife in Québec City is centered on the clubs and cafés of rue St-Jean, avenue Cartier, and Grande Allée. In the winter, evening activity is livelier toward the end of the week, beginning on Wednesday. But as the warmer temperatures set in, the café-terrace crowd emerges, and bars stay open seven days a week. Most bars and clubs stay open until 3 AM.

Faculté de la Bière (595 Grande Allée E, tel. 418/529–0592). This pub offers an international menu, with beers from around the world to accompany each meal.

Bars and Lounges **Le Central** (1200 rue St-Jean, tel. 418/694–0618). At this stylish piano bar at Serge Bruyère's restaurant complex, you can order from the restaurant's sophisticated haute-cuisine menu.
Le Pub Saint-Alexandre (1087 rue St-Jean, tel. 418/694–0015). This popular English-style pub, formerly a men-only tavern, is a good place to look for your favorite brand of beer. There are approximately 135 different kinds.
Vogue and **Sherlock Holmes** (1170 d'Artigny, tel. 418/529–9973). You'll find mainly Yuppies at these two bars stacked one on top of the other. Sherlock Holmes is a pub-restaurant downstairs; for dancing, try Vogue upstairs.

Disco **Chez Dagobert** (600 Grande Allée E, tel. 418/522–0393). You'll find a little bit of everything—live rock bands to loud disco—at this large and popular club.
Le Dancing (1225 Place Montcalm, tel. 414/647–2222). Music videos and a loud stereo blare from this night spot on the lower level of the Hôtel Loews Le Concorde.
Merlin (1179 av. Cartier, tel. 418/529–9567). This one-room pub-style disco is a favorite Québecois hangout.

Folk, Jazz, **Chez Son Père** (24 St-Stanislas, tel. 418/692–5308). French Ca-
and Blues nadian folk songs fill this smoke-filled pub on the second floor of an old building in the Latin Quarter. Singers perform every night of the week.
Le d'Auteuil (35 rue d'Auteuil, tel. 418/692–2263). Rhythm and blues, jazz, and blues emanate from this converted church across from Kent Gate.
L'Emprise at Hôtel Clarendon (57 rue Ste-Anne, tel. 418/692–2480). The first jazz bar in Québec City is the preferred spot for enthusiasts. The art deco decor sets the mood for the Jazz Age rhythms.

Excursion 1: Côte de Beaupré

As legend tells it, when explorer Jacques Cartier first gained sight of the north shore of the St. Lawrence River in 1535, he exclaimed, *"Quel beau pré!"* ("What a lovely meadow!"), because the area was the first inviting piece of land he had spotted since leaving France. Today this fertile meadow, first settled by French farmers, is known as Côte de Beaupré (Beaupré Coast), stretching 40 kilometers (25 miles) from Québec City to the famous pilgrimage site of Sainte-Anne-de-Beaupré. The impressive Montmorency Falls are located midway between these two points.

Tourist Information

Beaupré Coast Interpretation Center, housed in the old mill Petit-Pré, built in 1695, features displays on the history and development of the region. *7007 av. Royale, Château-Richer, tel. 418/824–3677. Admission free. Open June–Aug., daily 9–noon and 1–5.*

Beau Temps, Mauvais Temps, offers guided bus tours and walking tours of the Côte de Beaupré. *991 rte. Prévost, Île d'Orléans, tel. 418/828–2275.*

The offices of the **Quebec City Region Tourism and Convention Bureau** (418/692–2471) can provide information on tours of the Côte de Beaupré (*see* Staying in Québec City, above).

Guided Tours

Québec City touring companies, such as **Gray Line** (tel. 418/622–7420) and **Maple Leaf Sightseeing Tours** (tel. 418/649–9226), offer day excursions along the Côte de Beaupré, with stops at Montmorency Falls and the Sainte-Anne-de-Beaupré Basilica.

Arriving and Departing

By Car To reach Montmorency Falls, take Route 440 (Dufferin-Montmorency Autoroute) northeast from Québec City. Approximately 9.6 kilometers (6 miles) east of the city is the exit for Montmorency Falls. To drive directly to Sainte-Anne-de Beaupré, continue northeast on Route 440 for approximately 29 kilometers (18 miles) and exit at Sainte-Anne-de-Beaupré.

An alternative way to reach Sainte-Anne-de-Beaupré is to take Route 360 or avenue Royale. Take Route 440 from Québec City, turn left at d'Estimauville, and right on boulevard des Chutes until it intersects with Route 360. Also called "le chemin du Roi" (the King's Road), this panoramic route is one of the oldest in North America, winding 30 kilometers (18.8 miles) along the steep ridge of the Côte de Beaupré. The road borders 17th- and 18th-century farmhouses, historic churches, and Normandy-style homes with half-buried root cellars. Route 360 goes past the Sainte-Anne-de-Beaupré Basilica.

Montmorency Falls

Begin this excursion with a visit to **Montmorency Falls.** The Montmorency River, named after Charles de Montmorency, who was a governor of New France, cascades over a coastal cliff and offers one of the most beautiful sights in the province. The falls, which are actually 50% higher than the wider Niagara Falls, measure 83 meters (274 feet) in height. During very cold weather conditions, the falls' heavy spray freezes and forms a giant loaf-shape ice cone known to Québecois as the Pain du Sucre (Sugarloaf); this phenomenon attracts sledders and sliders from Québec City. In the warmer months, a park in the river's gorge leads to an observation terrace that is continuously sprayed by a fine drizzle from water pounding onto the cliff rocks. The top of the falls can be observed from avenue Royale. *Admission free. Open daily.*

Time Out **Restaurant Baker** (8790 av. Royale, Château-Richer, tel. 418/824–4478), on the way to Sainte-Anne-de Beaupré on Route 360, is a good, old-fashioned rustic restaurant that serves such hearty, traditional French Canadian dishes as meat pie, pea soup, pâtés, and maple-sugar pie.

Basilique Sainte-Anne-de-Beaupré

The monumental and inspiring **Basilique Sainte-Anne-de-Beaupré** (Sainte-Anne-de-Beaupré Basilica) is located in a small town with the same name. The basilica has become a popular attraction as well as an important shrine: More than half a million people visit the site each year.

The French brought their devotion to Saint Anne with them when they sailed across the Atlantic to New France. In 1650, Breton sailors caught in a storm vowed to erect a chapel in honor of this patron saint at the exact spot where they would land. The present-day neo-Roman basilica constructed in 1923 was the fifth to be built on the site where the sailors first touched ground.

According to local legend, Saint Anne was responsible over the years for saving voyagers from shipwrecks in the harsh waters of the St. Lawrence. Tributes to her miraculous powers can be seen in the shrine's various mosaics, murals, altars, and church ceilings. A bas-relief at the entrance depicts Saint Anne welcoming her pilgrims, and ceiling mosaics represent details from her life. Numerous crutches and braces posted on the back pillars have been left by those who have felt the healing powers of Saint Anne.

The basilica, which is in the shape of a Latin cross, has two granite steeples jutting from its gigantic structure. Its interior has 22 chapels and 18 altars, as well as round arches and numerous ornaments in the Romanesque style. The 214 stained-glass windows by Frenchmen Auguste Labouret and Pierre Chaudière, finished in 1949, tell a story of salvation through personages who were believed to be instruments of God over the centuries. Other features of the shrine include intricately carved wood pews decorated with various animals and several smaller altars (behind the main altar) that are dedicated to different saints.

The original wood chapel built in the village of Sainte-Anne-de-Beaupré in the 17th century was situated too close to the St. Lawrence and was swept away by flooding of the river. In 1676, the chapel was replaced by a stone church that was visited by pilgrims for more than a century, but this structure was also demolished in 1872. The first basilica, which replaced the stone church, was destroyed by a fire in 1922. The following year architects Maxime Rosin from Paris and Louis-N. Audet from Québec province designed the basilica that now stands. *10,018 av. Royale, Sainte-Anne-de-Beaupré, tel. 418/827–3781. Admission free. Open year-round. Reception booth open May 15–July 16, 8:30–5:30; July 17–July 26, 8:30–7; July 27–Oct. 15, 8:30–5:30. Tours daily in summer at 1 PM start at the information booth at the southwest corner of the courtyard outside the basilica. Guided tours during the off-season (Oct. 16–May 14) can be arranged by phoning in advance.*

Across the street from the basilica on avenue Royale is the **Commemorative Chapel,** designed by Claude Bailiff and built in 1878. The memorial chapel was constructed on the location of the transept of a stone church built in 1676 and contains the old building's foundations. Among the remnants housed here are the old church's bell, dating from 1696; an early 18th-century altar designed by Vezina; a crucifix sculpted by François-Noël Levaseur in 1775; and a pulpit designed by François Baillargé in 1807.

Excursion 2: Île d'Orléans

Île d'Orléans, an island slightly downstream in a northeasterly direction from Québec City, exemplifies the historic charm of rural Québec province with its quiet, traditional lifestyle. A drive around the island will take you past stone churches that are among the oldest in the region and centuries-old houses amid acres of lush orchards and cultivated farmland. Horse-drawn carriages are still a means of transport. Île d'Orléans is also an important marketplace that provides fresh produce daily for Québec City; roadside stands on the island sell a variety of local products, such as crocheted blankets, woven articles, maple syrup, homemade bread and jams, and fruits and vegetables.

The island was discovered at about the same time as Québec City in 1535. Explorer Jacques Cartier noticed an abundance of vines on the island and called it the "Island of Bacchus," after the Greek god of wine. In 1536, Cartier renamed the island in honor of the duke of Orléans, son of the king of France, François I. Long considered part of the domain of Côte de Beaupré, the island was not given its seignorial autonomy until 1636, when it was bought by La Compagne des Cents Associés, a group formed by Louis XIII to promote settlement in New France.

The island, about 9 kilometers (5 miles) wide and 34 kilometers (21 miles) long, is now composed of six small villages. These villages have sought over the years to remain relatively private residential and agricultural communities; the island's bridge to the mainland was built only in 1935.

Important Addresses and Numbers

Tourist Information **Beau Temps, Mauvais Temps** has a tourist office located in Saint-Pierre (991 rte. Prévost, tel. 418/828–2275). *Open Feb.–May, 8:30–4; June–Sept., daily 8:30 AM–9 PM; Oct.–Jan., will respond to messages left on answering machine.*

The island's Chamber of Commerce operates a tourist information kiosk situated at the west corner of côte du Pont and chemin Royal. *490 côte du Pont, Saint-Pierre, tel. 418/828–9411. Open mid-May–Oct., daily 8:30–6; Nov.–mid-May, Mon.–Fri. 8:30–noon and 1–4:30.*

Medical Clinic **Centre Médical** (1015 rte. Prévost, Saint-Pierre, tel. 418/828–2213) is the only medical clinic on the island.

Guided Tours

Beau Temps, Mauvais Temps (991 rte. Prévost, Saint-Pierre, Île d'Orléans, tel. 418/828–2275) offers guided tours of all six villages year-long and river excursions that depart from Saint-Laurent mid-May–mid-September. The company is also a referral service for lodging.

The Québec City touring companies **Maple Leaf Sightseeing Tours** (tel. 418/649–9226), **Gray Line** (tel. 418/622–7420), and **Visite Touristiques de Québec** (tel. 418/653–9722) offer full- and half-day bus tours of the western tip of the island combined with sightseeing along the Côte de Beaupré.

Any of the offices of the **Québec City Region Tourism and Convention Bureau** can also provide information on tours and accommodations on the island (*see* Staying in Québec City, above).

Arriving and Departing

By Car Île d'Orléans has no public transportation; cars are the only way to get to and around the island, unless you take a guided tour (*see* Guided Tours, above). Parking on the island is never a problem; you can always stop and explore certain villages on foot. The main road, chemin Royal (Route 368), extends 67 kilometers (40 miles) through the island's six villages; street numbers along chemin Royal begin at No. 1 for each municipality.

From Québec City, take Route 440 (Dufferin-Montmorency Autoroute) northeast. After a drive of approximately 10 kilometers (7 miles) take the bridge, Pont de l'Île d'Orléans, to reach the island. Before you get to the island's only traffic light, turn right heading west on chemin Royal to begin the exploring tour below.

Exploring Île d'Orléans

Numbers in the margin correspond to points of interest on the Île d'Orléans map.

Start your tour heading west on chemin Royal to **Sainte-Pétronille,** the first village to be settled on the island. Founded in 1648, the community was chosen in 1759 by British General James Wolfe for his headquarters. With 40,000 soldiers and a hundred ships, the English bombarded French-occupied Québec City and Côte de Beaupré.

During the late-19th century, the English population of Québec developed Sainte-Pétronille into a resort village. This section is considered by many to be the island's most beautiful area, not only because of the spectacular views it offers of Montmorency Falls and Québec City but also for the stylish English villas and exquisitely tended gardens that can be seen from the roadside.

On the left at 20 chemin Royal is the **Plante family farm,** where you can stop to pick apples (in season) or buy some of the island's fresh fruits and vegetables.

➊ Farther along on the right is the **Maison Gourdeau de Beaulieu House** (137 chemin Royal), the island's first home, built in 1648 for Jacques Gourdeau de Beaulieu, who was the first seigneur of Sainte-Pétronille. Today this white building with blue shutters is still owned by his descendants. Over the years, the house has been remodeled so that it incorporates both French and Québecois styles. Its thick walls and dormer windows are characteristic of Breton architecture, but its sloping bell-shape roof, designed to protect buildings from large amounts of snow, is typically Québecois.

➋ After you descend an incline, turn right beside the river on the tiny street called **rue Horatio-Walker,** named after the 19th-century painter known for his landscapes of the island. Walker lived on this street from 1904 until his death in 1938. Around the corner are his home and studio, where exhibits of his paint-

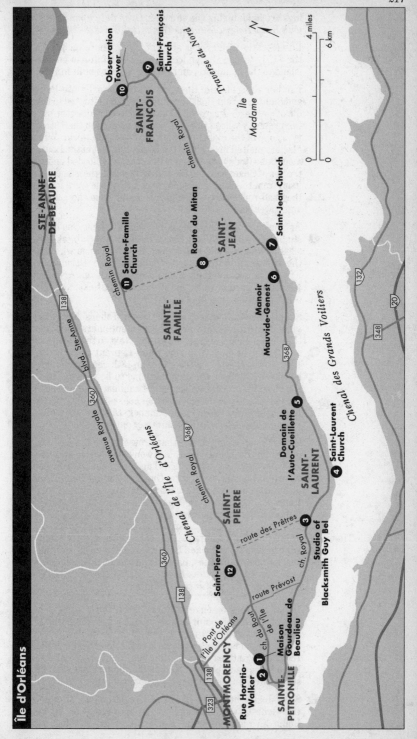

Île d'Orléans

217

STE-ANNE-
DE-BEAUPRE

MONTMORENCY

SAINTE-
PETRONILLE

Rue Horatio-
Walker

Maison
Gourdeau de
Beaulieu

Studio of
Blacksmith Guy Bel

Saint-Pierre

SAINT-
PIERRE

SAINT-
LAURENT

Saint-Laurent
Church

Domain de
l'Auto-Cueillette

Manoir
Mauvide-Genest

SAINTE-
FAMILLE

Sainte-Famille
Church

SAINT-
JEAN

Route du Mitan

Saint-Jean Church

SAINT-
FRANÇOIS

Saint-François
Church

Observation
Tower

Île
Madame

Traverse du Nord

Chenal des Grands Voiliers

Chenal de l'île d'Orléans

Pont de
l'île d'Orléans

ch. du Bout
de l'île

ch. Royal

route Prévost

route des Prêtres

chemin Royal

avenue Royale

blvd Ste-Anne

chemin Royal

chemin Royal

138

360

368

368

368

132

20

348

323

4 miles
6 km

ings are held during the summer. *Open only upon reservation with Beau Temps, Mauvais Temps (tel. 418/828–2275).*

Rue Horatio-Walker was also the place where people crossed the St. Lawrence by an ice path in the winter to go from the island to the mainland before the bridge was built in 1935.

Farther along chemin Royal, at the border of Sainte-Pétronille and Saint-Laurent, look for a large boulder situated in the middle of nowhere. The **roche à Maranda,** named after the owner of the property where the rock was discovered in the 19th century, is one of the oldest rock formations in the world. When the glaciers melted in 9000 BC, the land at the foot of the Laurentian mountains (today the Côte de Beaupré) was flooded and formed the Sea of Champlain. As the waters receded, the island detached itself from the land, and such rocks as this one were found after they had rolled down with glacial water from the Laurentians onto lower land.

❸ As you approach the village of Saint-Laurent, you'll find the **studio of blacksmith Guy Bel** (2200 chemin Royal, tel. 418/828–9300), a talented and well-known local craftsman who has done the ironwork restoration for Québec City. Born in Lyons, France, he studied there at the École des Beaux Arts. You can watch him hard at work; his stylish candlesticks, mantels, and other ironworks are for sale.

Saint-Laurent, founded in 1679, is one of the island's maritime villages. Until as late as 1935, residents here used boats as their main means of transportation. Next to the village's mari-
❹ na stands the tall, inspiring **Saint-Laurent Church.** Built in 1860, it was erected on the site of an 18th-century church that, because of its poor construction, had to be torn down. One of the church's procession chapels is a miniature stone replica of the church; the other wood chapel houses a gallery where artists display their work in the summer. *1532 chemin Royal. Admission free. Open daily in summer only.*

Generally speaking, crops that grow close to the earth tend to be among the island's best. You won't find better strawberries anywhere else in the province. There are about two dozen spots
❺ where you can pick your own. One of the larger fields, **Domaine de l'Auto-Cueillette** (211 chemin Royal), is located in Saint-Laurent. You can buy an empty basket here for less than 50¢; a full basket of strawberries will cost about $5.

Time Out | **Moulin de Saint-Laurent** is an early 18th-century stone mill. Dine here in the herb and flower garden out back. Scrumptious snacks, such as quiches, bagels, and salads, are available at the café-terrace. *754 chemin Royal, tel. 418/829–3888. AE, MC, V. Open May–Oct. for lunch and dinner.*

If you continue on chemin Royal, you'll come to the southern side of the island, **Saint-Jean,** a village whose inhabitants were once river pilots and navigators. Most of its small, homogeneous row homes were built close to the river between 1840 and 1860. Being at sea most of the time, the sailors did not need large homes and plots of land as did the farmers. The island's sudden drop in elevation is most noticeable in Saint-Jean.

❻ Saint-Jean's beautiful Normandy-style manor, **Manoir Mauvide-Genest,** was built in 1734 for Jean Mauvide, surgeon to Louis XV, and his wife, Marie-Anne Genest. Most notable about this house, which still has its original thick walls, ceiling beams, and fireplaces, is the degree to which it has held up over the years, in spite of being targeted by English guns during the 1759 siege of Québec City. The home is a pleasure to roam; all rooms are furnished with original antiques from the 18th and 19th centuries. It also offers an exhibit on French architecture and a downstairs restaurant that serves French cuisine. *1451 chemin Royal, tel. 418/829–2630. Open June–Aug., daily 10–5; Sept.–mid-Oct., Tues.–Sun. 10–5.*

North of the manor stands **Théâtre Paul-Hébert,** an indoor summer theater founded five years ago by an actor who lives on the island.

7 At the opposite end of the village, you'll see **Saint-Jean Church,** a massive granite structure with large red doors and a towering steeple built in 1749. The church bears a remarkable resemblance to a ship; it is big and round and appears to be sitting right on the St. Lawrence River. Paintings of the patron saints of seamen line the interior walls. The church's cemetery is also intriguing, especially if you can read French. Back in the 18th century, piloting the St. Lawrence was a dangerous profession; the boats could not easily handle the rough currents. The cemetery tombstones recall the tragedies of lost life in these harsh waters. *2001 chemin Royal. Admission free. Open daily.*

As you leave Saint-Jean, chemin Royal mounts the incline and

8 crosses **route du Mitan.** In old French, *mitan* means "halfway." This road, dividing the island in half, is the most direct route from north to south. It is also the most beautiful on the island, with acres of tended farmland, apple orchards, and maple groves. If you're running out of time and want to end the tour here, take route du Mitan, which brings you to Saint-Pierre and the bridge to the mainland.

When you come to 17th-century farmhouses separated by sprawling open fields, you know you've reached the island's least-toured and most rustic village, **Saint-François.** At the eastern tip of the island, this community is the one situated farthest from the St. Lawrence River and was originally settled mainly by farmers. Saint-François is also the perfect place to visit one of the island's *cabanes à sucre* (maple-sugaring huts) found along chemin Royal. Stop at a hut for a tasting tour; sap is gathered from the maple groves and boiled until it turns to a syrup. When it is poured on ice, it tastes like a delicious toffee. The maple season is late March through April, but these huts stay open year-round.

9 Straight on chemin Royal is **Saint-François Church,** built in 1734 and one of eight provincial churches dating from the French regime. At the time the English seized Québec in 1759, General Wolfe knew Saint-François to be among the better strategic points along the St. Lawrence. Consequently, he stationed the British troops here and used the church as a military hospital. In May 1988, a fatal car crash set the church on fire. Although it is in the process of being rebuilt, most of the interior treasures were lost.

About a mile down the road is a picnic area with a wood

10 **observation tower** situated for perfect viewing of the majestic St. Lawrence at its widest point, 10 times as wide as it is near Québec City. During the spring and autumn months, you can observe wild Canada geese here.

Heading north on chemin Royal, you'll come to one of the island's earliest villages, Sainte-Famille, which was founded in 1661. The scenery is exquisite here; there are abundant apple orchards and strawberry fields with a view of Côte de Beaupré and Mont Sainte-Anne in the distance. But the village also has plenty of man-made historic charm; it has the area's highest concentration of stone houses dating from the French regime.

⑪ Take a quick look at **Sainte-Famille Church,** which was constructed in 1749, later than some of the others on the island. This impressive structure is the only church in the province to have three bell towers at the front. Its ceiling was redone in the mid-19th century with elaborate designs in wood and gold. The church also holds a famous painting, *L'Enfant Jésus Voyant la Croix,* done in 1670 by Frère Luc (Father Luc), who was sent from France to decorate churches in the area. *3915 chemin Royal. Admission free. Open daily in summer.*

The next village situated on the north side of the island, **Saint-Pierre,** was established a bit later than Sainte-Famille, in 1679. Its church, though, is older, dates back to 1717, and is officially ⑫ the oldest on the island. **Saint-Pierre Church** is no longer open for worship, but it was restored during the 1960s and is open to tourists. Many of its original components are still intact, such as benches with compartments below, where hot bricks and stones were placed to keep people warm during winter services. *1243 chemin Royal. Admission free. Open daily in summer.*

Because Saint-Pierre is situated on a plateau with the island's most fertile land, the village has long been the center of traditional farming industries. The best products grown here are potatoes, asparagus, and corn, and the many dairy farms have given the village a renowned reputation for butter and other dairy products. At 2370 chemin Royal is the former home of Felix Leclerc, one of the many artists who have made the island their home. Leclerc, the father of Québecois folksinging, lived here until he died in August 1988.

If you continue west on chemin Royal, just up ahead are the bridge back to the mainland and Route 440.

Dining and Lodging

For price categories, *see* Québec City Dining and Lodging.

Dining **La Goéliche.** Although this rustic inn has a romantic dining
Expensive room with windows overlooking the St. Lawrence River and a view of Québec City, the main reason to dine here is the good food. The first rule of the kitchen is that only the freshest ingredients from the island's farms can be used. The menu is classic French and depends upon the fruits and vegetables in season. Lunch is a more moderately priced à la carte selection of salads, quiches, and omelets. The evening's menu features such specialties as quail with red vermouth and chicken with pistachio mousseline. The desserts, such as maple syrup mousse with strawberry syrup, have a regional flavor. *22 chemin du Quai, Sainte-Pétronille, tel. 418/828–2248. Reservations advised. Dress: neat but casual. MC, V.*

L'Atre. After you park your car, you'll take a horse-drawn carriage to a 17th-century Normandy-style house furnished with Québecois pine antiques. True to the establishment's name, which means "hearth," all the traditional dishes are cooked and served from a fireplace. The menu emphasizes hearty fare, such as beef Bourguignon and *tourtière* (meat pie), with maple-sugar pie for dessert. *4403 chemin Royal, Sainte-Famille, tel. 418/829–2474. Reservations required. Dress: neat but casual. AE, MC, V. Open mid-June–Labor Day.*

Manoir Mauvide-Genest. The dining room in one of the island's most beautiful and well-maintained homes (*see* Exploring, above) serves both elegant and home-style French cuisine. Specialties include such dishes as snails in Armagnac; the chef here excels at both traditional fowl dishes, such as *confit de canard* (duck confit), and more exotic creations, such as quail with a sweet white wine sauce. *1451 chemin Royal, Saint-Jean, tel. 418/829–2915. Reservations required. Dress: neat but casual. AE, MC, V. Open June–mid-Oct.*

Lodging
Moderate

Auberge le Chaumonot. This medium-size hotel in rural Saint-François is right near the St. Lawrence River at its widest point. The inn's large bay windows capitalize on the view of the river and neighboring islands, but otherwise the decor is uninspired, with simple wood furniture of the island. The service here is efficient and friendly. The restaurant serves Continental cuisine, with table d'hôte and à la carte menus. *425 chemin Royal, Saint-François, G0A 3S0, tel. 418/829–2735. 8 rooms with private bath and air-conditioning. Facilities: outdoor swimming pool, restaurant. AE, MC, V. Closed Oct.–Apr.*

La Goéliche. This 1890 Victorian country inn stands just steps away from the St. Lawrence River in the village of Sainte-Pétronille. Québecois antiques decorate light and spacious rooms with their original wood floors. Rooms are on the second and third floors, and half of them look out across the river to Québec City. The rooms have no television, but they do have phones. *22 chemin du Quai, Sainte-Pétronille, G0A 4C0, tel. 418/828–2248. 25 rooms, 18 with private bath. Facilities: 2 restaurants. MC, V.*

You can get to know the island by staying at one of its 30 bed-and-breakfasts. Reservations are necessary. The price for a room, double occupancy, runs about $40–$85. **Beau Temps, Mauvais Temps** (tel. 418/828–2275) is a referral service for these accommodations.

6 Vancouver

by Terri Wershler

Terri Wershler, publisher of Brighouse Press, a regional book publisher, is also the author of The Vancouver Guide.

Vancouver is a young city, even by North American standards. While three to four hundred years of settlement may make cities like Québec and Halifax historically interesting to travelers, Vancouver's youthful vigor attracts visitors with powerful elements not yet ground down by time. Vancouver is just over a hundred years old; it was not yet a town in 1870, when British Columbia became part of the Canadian confederation.

Vancouver's history, such as it is, remains visible to the naked eye. Eras are stacked east to west along the waterfront like some horizontal, century-old archaeological dig—from cobbled, late-Victorian Gastown to shiny postmodern glass cathedrals of commerce grazing the sunset.

The Chinese were among the first to recognize the possibilities of Vancouver's setting. They came to British Columbia during the 1850s seeking the gold that inspired them to name the province *Gum-shan,* or Gold Mountain. They built the Canadian Pacific Railway that gave Vancouver's original townsite a purpose—one beyond the natural splendor that Royal Navy Capt. George Vancouver admired during his lunchtime cruise around its harbor on June 13, 1792. The transcontinental railway, along with its Great White Fleet of clipper ships, gave Vancouver a full week's edge over the California ports in shipping tea and silk to New York at the dawn of the 20th century.

Vancouver's natural charms are less scattered than in other cities. On clear days, the mountains appear close enough to touch. Two 1,000-acre wilderness parks lie within the city limits. The salt water of the Pacific and fresh water direct from the Rocky Mountain Trench form the city's northern and southern boundaries.

Bring a healthy sense of reverence when you visit: Vancouver is a spiritual place. For its original inhabitants, the Coast Salish peoples, it was the sacred spot where the mythical Thunderbird and Killer Whale flung wind and rain all about the heavens during their epic battles—how else to explain the coast's occasional climatic fits of temper? Devotees of a later religious tradition might worship in the sepulchre of Stanley Park or in the polished, incense-filled quiet of St. James Anglican Church, designed by English architect Sir Adrian Gilbert Scott and perhaps Vancouver's finest building.

Vancouver has a level of nightlife possible only in a place where the finer things in life have never been driven out to the suburbs and where sidewalks have never rolled up at 5 PM. There is no shortage of excellent hotels and restaurants here either. But you can find good theater, accommodations, and dining almost anywhere these days. Vancouver's *real* culture consists in its tall fir trees practically downtown and its towering rock spires close by, the ocean at your doorstep, and people from every corner of the earth all around you.

Essential Information

Arriving and Departing by Plane

Airport and Airlines
International Airports

Vancouver International Airport is on an island about 14 kilometers (9 miles) south of downtown. The main terminal building has three levels: departures, international arrivals, and domestic arrivals; a small south terminal building services flights to secondary destinations within the province. **American Airlines** (tel. 800/433–7300), **Continental** (tel. 800/525–0280), **Delta** (tel. 604/221–1212), **Horizon Air** (800/547–9308), and **United** (tel. 800/241–6522) fly into the airport. The two major domestic airlines are **Air Canada** (tel. 604/688–5515) and **Canadian Airlines** (tel. 604/279–6611).

Other Facilities

Air BC (tel. 604/278–3800) offers 30-minute harbor-to-harbor service (downtown Vancouver to downtown Victoria) several times a day. Planes leave from near the Bayshore Hotel. Harbor-to-harbor service (Seattle to Vancouver) is run by **Lake Union Air** (tel. 800/826–1890). **Helijet Airways** (tel. 604/273–1414) has helicopter service from downtown Vancouver to downtown Victoria and Whistler. The heliport is near Vancouver's Pan Pacific Hotel.

Between the Airport and Downtown

The drive from the airport to downtown is 20–45 minutes, depending on the time of day. Airport hotels offer free shuttle service to and from the airport.

By Bus

The **Airport Express** (tel. 604/273–9023) bus leaves the domestic arrivals level of the terminal building every 15 minutes in summer and every 30 minutes in winter, stopping at major downtown hotels and the bus depot. It operates from 5:30 AM until 12:30 AM. The fare is $8.25.

By Taxi

Taxi stands are in front of the terminal building on domestic and international arrivals levels. Taxi fare to downtown is about $23. Area cab companies are **Yellow** (tel. 604/681–3311), **Black Top** (tel. 604/731–1111), and **MacLures** (tel. 604/731–9211).

By Limousine

Limousine service from **Airlimo** (tel. 604/273–1331) costs about the same as a taxi to downtown: The current rate is about $26.

Arriving and Departing

By Car

From the south, I–5 from Seattle becomes **Highway 99** at the U.S.–Canada border. Vancouver is a three-hour drive from Seattle. Avoid border crossings during peak times: holidays and weekends.

Highway 1, the **Trans-Canada Highway,** enters Vancouver from the east. If you enter the city after rush hour (8:30 AM), you should not have a problem with traffic.

By Ferry

BC Ferries operates two major ferry terminals outside Vancouver. From Tsawwassen to the south (an hour's drive from downtown), ferries sail to Victoria and Nanaimo on Vancouver Island and through the Gulf Islands (the small islands between the mainland and Vancouver Island). From Horseshoe Bay (30 minutes north from downtown), ferries sail a short distance up the coast and to Nanaimo on Vancouver Island. Call (tel. 604/685–1021) for departure and arrival times.

Sealink Express (tel. 604/687–6925) is a new service that takes passengers by high-speed catamaran from downtown Vancouver to downtown Victoria in 2½ hours. The two boats each seat 302 people and have such airplane-type amenities as movies, work tables, and headphones for music; there are also fax machines, telephones, two snack bars, a children's playroom, and a newsstand on board. At press time fares had not be firmly established, but for May–June 1992 one-way fares were: adult $28, senior citizens $24, and children $15; round-trips cost $48, $42, and $26.

By Train The **VIA Rail** (tel. 800/561–8630) station is at Main Street and Terminal Avenue. VIA provides service through the Rockies to Banff. Passenger trains leave the **BC Rail** (tel. 604/631–3500) station in North Vancouver for Whistler and the interior of British Columbia. There is no Amtrak service from Seattle.

By Bus **Greyhound** (tel. 604/662–3222) is the biggest bus line servicing Vancouver. The **Vancouver bus depot** is at the corner of Dunsmuir and Cambie streets, a 10-minute walk from Georgia and Granville streets. **Quick Shuttle** (tel. 604/526–2836) bus service runs between Vancouver and Seattle six times a day.

Getting Around

By Car Although no freeways cross Vancouver, rush-hour traffic is not yet horrendous. The worst rush-hour bottlenecks are the North Shore bridges, the George Massey Tunnel on Highway 99 south of Vancouver, and Highway 1 through Coquitlam and Surrey.

By Subway Vancouver has a one-line, 25-kilometer (15-mile) rapid transit system called **SkyTrain,** which travels underground downtown and is elevated for the rest of its route to New Westminster and Surrey. Trains leave about every five minutes. Tickets must be carried with you as proof of payment. They are sold at each station from machines; correct change is not necessary. You may use transfers from SkyTrain to SeaBus and BC Transit buses (*see* below) and vice versa.

By Bus Exact change is needed to ride the buses: $1.35 adults, 70¢ for senior citizens and children 5–13. Books of 25 tickets are sold at convenience stores and newsstands; look for a red, white, and blue "Fare Dealer" sign. Day passes, good for unlimited travel after 9:30 AM, cost $4 for adults. They are available from fare dealers and any SeaBus or SkyTrain station. Transfers are valid for 90 minutes and allow travel in both directions.

By Taxi It is difficult to hail a cab in Vancouver; unless you're near a hotel, you'd have better luck calling a taxi service. Try **Yellow** (tel. 604/681–3311), **Black Top** (tel. 604/731–1111), or **MacLures** (tel. 604/731–9211).

By SeaBus The **SeaBus** is a 400-passenger commuter ferry that crosses Burrard Inlet from the foot of Lonsdale (North Vancouver) to downtown. The ride takes 13 minutes and costs the same as the transit bus. With a transfer, connection can be made with any BC Transit bus or SkyTrain.

Important Addresses and Numbers

Tourist Information **Vancouver Travel Infocentre** (1055 Dunsmuir St., tel. 604/683–2000) provides maps and information about the city and is open

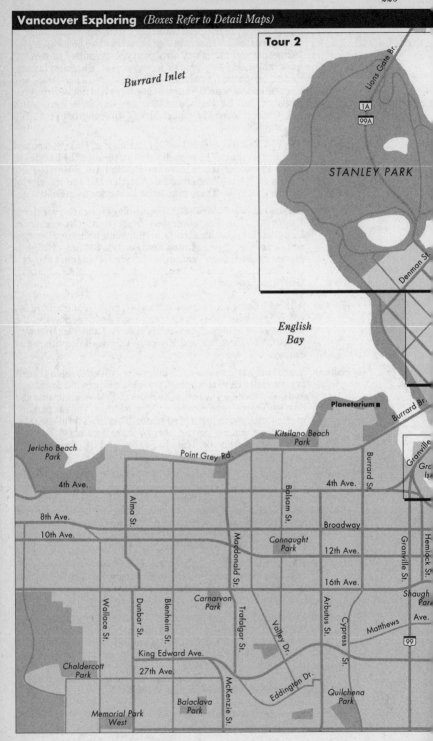

Tour 2

Burrard Inlet

1A
99A

STANLEY PARK

Lions Gate Br.

Denman St.

English Bay

Planetarium ■

Burrard Br.

Kitsilano Beach Park

Jericho Beach Park

Point Grey Rd.

Granville

Gra
Isl

4th Ave.

4th Ave.

Burrard St.

Alma St.

8th Ave.

10th Ave.

Broadway

Balsam St.

Connaught Park

12th Ave.

Granville St.

Hemlock St.

Macdonald St.

16th Ave.

Carnarvon Park

Shaugh
Park

Wallace St.

Dunbar St.

Blenheim St.

Trafalgar St.

Valley Dr.

Arbutus St.

Cypress St.

Matthews

Ave.

99

King Edward Ave.

Chaldercott Park

27th Ave.

McKenzie St.

Eddington Dr.

Quilchena Park

Memorial Park West

Balaclava Park

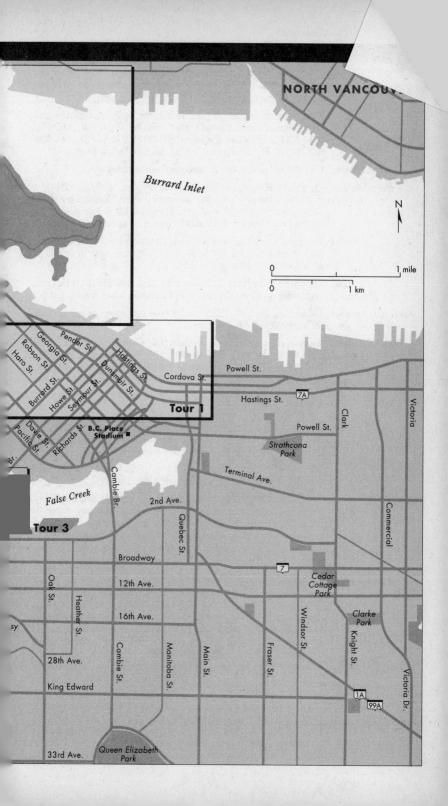

NORTH VANCOUV

Burrard Inlet

N

0   1 mile

0   1 km

Pender St.
Georgia St.
Robson St.
Haro St.
Hastings St.
Dunsmuir St.
Cordova St.
Powell St.
Burrard St.
Howe St.
Seymour St.
Hastings St.
7A
Powell St.
Davie St.
Richards St.
B.C. Place Stadium
Strathcona Park
Pacific St.
Tour 1
Clark
Victoria

Terminal Ave.

False Creek

Cambie Br.

Tour 3

2nd Ave.

Quebec St.

Broadway

7

Cedar Cottage Park

Commercial

Oak St.

Heather St.

12th Ave.

16th Ave.

Clarke Park

Cambie St.

Manitoba St.

Main St.

Fraser St.

Windsor St.

Knight St.

sy

28th Ave.

King Edward

1A

99A

Victoria Dr.

33rd Ave.

Queen Elizabeth Park

in summer, daily 8–6; in winter, Monday–Saturday 9–5. A kiosk in Pacific Centre Mall is open daily in summer, Monday–Saturday 9:30–5, Sunday noon–5; in winter, Monday–Saturday 9–5. Eaton's department store downtown also has a tourist information counter that is open all year.

Embassies There are no embassies in Vancouver, only consulates and trade commissions: **United States** (1075 W. Pender St., tel. 604/685–4311) and **United Kingdom** (800–1111 Melville St., tel. 604/683–4421). For a complete listing, see the Yellow Pages.

Emergencies Call 911 for **police, fire department,** and **ambulance.**

Hospitals and **St. Paul's Hospital** (1081 Burrard St., tel. 604/682–2344), a
Clinics downtown hospital, has an emergency ward. **Medicentre** (1055 Dunsmuir St., lower level, tel. 604/683–8138), a drop-in clinic on the lower level of the Bentall Centre, is open weekdays.

Dentist The counterpart to Medicentre is **Dentacentre** (1055 Dunsmuir St., lower level, tel. 604/669–6700), which is next door and is also open weekdays.

Late-night **Shopper's Drug Mart** (1125 Davie St., tel. 604/685–6445) is open
Pharmacy until midnight every night except Sunday, when it closes at 9.

Road Emergencies **BCAA** (tel. 604/293–2222) has 24-hour emergency road service for members of AAA or CAA.

Travel Agencies **American Express Travel Service** (1040 W. Georgia St., tel. 604/669–2813), **Hagen's Travel** (201–850 W. Hastings St., tel. 604/684–2448), and **P. Lawson Travel** (409 Granville St., tel. 604/682–4272).

Opening and Closing Times

Banks traditionally are open Monday–Thursday 10–3 and Friday 10–6, but many banks have extended hours and are open on Saturday, particularly outside of downtown.

Museums are generally open 10–5, including Saturday and Sunday. Most are open one evening a week as well.

Department store hours are Monday–Wednesday and Saturday 9:30–6, Thursday and Friday 9:30–9, and Sunday noon–5. Many smaller stores are also open Sunday. Robson Street and Chinatown are particularly good for Sunday shopping.

Guided Tours

Orientation **Gray Line** (tel. 604/681–8687), the largest tour operator, offers the 3½-hour Grand City bus tour year-round. Departing from the Hotel Vancouver, the tour includes Stanley Park, Chinatown, Gastown, English Bay, and Queen Elizabeth Park and costs about $31. **Westcoast City and Nature Sightseeing** (tel. 604/255–2444) accommodates up to 24 people in vans that run a 3½-hour City Highlights Tour for $27 (pickup available from any downtown location). A short city tour (2½ hours) is offered by **Vance Tours** (tel. 604/222–1966) in minibuses and costs $24.

The **Vancouver Trolley Company** (tel. 604/255–2444) runs turn-of-the-century–style trolleys through Vancouver from April to October on a 1½-hour narrated tour of Stanley Park, Gastown, English Bay, the Vancouver Museum, Granville Island, Queen Elizabeth Park, Science World, and Chinatown, among other sights. A day pass allows you to complete one full circuit, getting off and on as often as you like. Start the trip at any of the sights and buy a ticket on board. It's a perfect way to deal with a rainy day in Vancouver. Adult fare is $15, children's $7.

North Shore tours usually include any or several of the following: a gondola ride up Grouse Mountain, a walk across the Capilano Suspension Bridge, a stop at a salmon hatchery, the Lonsdale Quay Market, and a ride back to town on the SeaBus. Half-day tours cost about $45 and are offered by **Landsea Tours** (tel. 604/255–7272), **Harbour Ferries** (tel. 604/687–9558), **Gray Line** (tel. 604/681–8687), **City and Nature** (tel. 604/255–2444), and **Pacific Coach Lines** (tel. 604/662–7575).

Air Tours Tour the mountains and fjords of the North Shore by helicopter for $165 for 45 minutes: **Vancouver Helicopters** (tel. 604/683–4354) flies from the Harbour Heliport downtown. Or see Vancouver from the air for $60 for 20 minutes: **Harbour Air's** (tel. 604/688–1277) seaplanes leave from beside the Bayshore Hotel.

Boat Tours The Royal Hudson, Canada's only functioning steam train, heads along the mountainous coast up Howe Sound to the logging town of Squamish. After a break to explore, you sail back to Vancouver via the MV *Britannia*. This highly recommended excursion costs $45, takes 6½ hours, and is organized by **Harbour Ferries** (tel. 604/687–9558). Reservations are necessary.

The **SS *Beaver*** (tel. 604/682–7284), a replica of a Hudson Bay fur-trading vessel that ran aground here in 1888, offers two trips. One is the Harbour Sunset Dinner Cruise, a four-hour trip with a barbecued dinner; the other is a five-hour daytime trip up Indian Arm with salmon for lunch. Each is about $50. Reservations are necessary.

Harbour Ferries (tel. 604/687–9558) takes a 1½-hour tour of Burrard Inlet in a paddle wheeler. The cost is $18.

Fraser River Tours (tel. 604/250–3458 or 604/584–5517) will take you on a four-hour tour of a fascinating working river— past log booms, tugs, and houseboats. The cruiser *Atria Star* leaves from Westminster Quay Market (a handy destination from downtown via SkyTrain) and costs $25.

Personal Guides **Fridge's Early Motion Tours** (tel. 604/687–5088) covers Vancouver in a Model-A Ford convertible comfortably seating four or five people. Minimum charge is $60 for an hour-long trip around downtown, Chinatown, and Stanley Park.

AAA Horse & Carriage (tel. 604/681–5115) has a 50-minute tour of Stanley Park, along the waterfront, and through a cedar forest and a rose garden for $10.

Exploring Vancouver

The heart of Vancouver—which includes the downtown area, Stanley Park, and the West End high-rise residential neighborhood—sits on a peninsula bordered by English Bay and the Pacific Ocean to the west; by False Creek, an inlet on which you will find Granville Island, to the south; and to the north by Burrard Inlet, the working port of the city, past which loom the North Shore mountains. The oldest part of the city—Gastown and Chinatown—lies at the edge of Burrard Inlet, around Main Street, which runs north–south and is roughly the dividing line between the east side and the west side. All the avenues, which are numbered, have east and west designations.

Highlights for First-time Visitors

Chinatown, Tour 1: Downtown Vancouver
English Bay, Tour 2: Stanley Park
Granville Island, Tour 3: Granville Island
Robson Street (*see* Shopping, below)
Stanley Park, Tour 2: Stanley Park

Tour 1: Downtown Vancouver

Numbers in the margin correspond to points of interest on the Tour 1: Downtown Vancouver map.

1 You can logically begin your downtown tour in either of two ways. If you're in for a day of shopping, amble down **Robson Street** (*see* Shopping, below), where you'll find any item from souvenirs to high fashions, from espresso to sushi.

2 If you opt otherwise, start at **Robson Square,** built in 1975 and designed by architect Arthur Erickson to be the gathering place of downtown Vancouver. The complex, which functions from the outside as a park, encompasses the Vancouver Art Gallery and government offices and courts that have been built under landscaped walkways, a block-long glass canopy, and a waterfall that helps mask traffic noise. An ice-skating rink and restaurants occupy the below-street level.

3 The **Vancouver Art Gallery** that heads the Square was a neoclassical-style 1912 courthouse until Erickson converted it in 1980. Notice some original details: Lions that guard the majestic front steps and the use of columns and domes are features borrowed from ancient Roman architecture. In back of the old courthouse, a more modest staircase now serves as a speakers' corner. *750 Hornby St., tel. 604/682–5621. Admission: $4.25 adults, $2.50 students and senior citizens; free Thurs. eve. Open Mon.–Wed., Fri., and Sat. 10–5; Thurs. 10–9; Sun. noon–5.*

4 Adjacent to the art gallery, on Hornby Street, is the **Hotel Vancouver** (1939), one of the last of the railway-built hotels. (The last one built was the Chateau Whistler, in 1989.) Reminiscent of a medieval French castle, this château style has been incorporated into hotels throughout every major Canadian city. With the onset of the Depression, construction was halted here, and the hotel was finished only in time for the visit of King George VI in 1939. It has been renovated twice: During the 1960s it was unfortunately modernized, but the more recent refurbishment is more in keeping with the spirit of what is the most recognizable roof on Vancouver's skyline. The exterior of the building has carvings of malevolent gargoyles at the corners, an ornate chimney, Indian chiefs on the Hornby Street side, and an assortment of grotesque mythological figures.

5 **Christ Church Cathedral** (1895), across the street from the Hotel Vancouver, is the oldest church in Vancouver. The tiny church was built in a Gothic style with buttresses and pointed arched windows and looks like the parish church of an English village. By contrast, the cathedral's rough-hewn interior is that of a frontier town, with Douglas-fir beams and carpenter woodwork that offers excellent acoustics for the frequent vespers, carol services, and Gregorian chants presented here. *690 Burrard St., tel. 604/682–3848.*

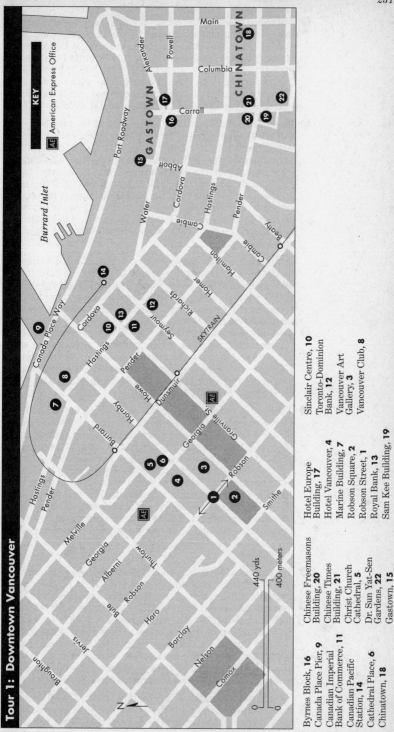

Tour 1: Downtown Vancouver

KEY

AE American Express Office

Burrard Inlet

GASTOWN

CHINATOWN

Main
Alexander
Powell
Columbia
Carrall
Port Roadway
Abbott
Water
Cordova
Hastings
Pender
Cambie
Hamilton
Homer
Richards
SKYTRAIN
Beatty
Canada Place Way
Cordova
Hastings
Pender
Seymour
Howe
Dunsmuir
Burrard
Hornby
Granville St.
Georgia
Robson
Smithe
Hastings
Pender
Melville
Georgia
Alberni
Thurlow
Robson
Haro
Bute
Barclay
Nelson
Comox
Jervis
Broughton

N

440 yds
400 meters

Byrnes Block, **16**
Canada Place Pier, **9**
Canadian Imperial
Bank of Commerce, **11**
Canadian Pacific
Station, **14**
Cathedral Place, **6**
Chinatown, **18**

Chinese Freemasons
Building, **20**
Chinese Times
Building, **21**
Christ Church
Cathedral, **5**
Dr. Sun Yat-Sen
Gardens, **22**
Gastown, **15**

Hotel Europe
Building, **17**
Hotel Vancouver, **4**
Marine Building, **7**
Robson Square, **2**
Robson Street, **1**
Royal Bank, **13**
Sam Kee Building, **19**

Sinclair Centre, **10**
Toronto-Dominion
Bank, **12**
Vancouver Art
Gallery, **3**
Vancouver Club, **8**

6 **Cathedral Place,** on the corner of Hornby and Georgia streets, is a spectacular new office tower adjacent to Christ Church Cathedral. The three large sculptures of nurses at the corners of the building are replicas of the statues that graced the previous structure on the site, an art deco office building beloved by Vancouverites. The restful courtyard, with access from Hornby Street, is a good spot to take a break, and it leads to the entrance of the **Canadian Craft Museum** (tel. 603/687–8266).

7 The **Marine Building** (1931), at the foot of Burrard Street, is Canada's best example of art deco style. Terra-cotta basreliefs depict the history of transportation: Airships, biplanes, steamships, locomotives, and submarines are figured. These motifs were once considered radical and modernistic adornments, because most buildings were still using classical or Gothic ornamentation. From the east, the Marine Building is reflected in bronze by 999 West Hastings, and in silver from the southeast by the Canadian Imperial Bank of Commerce. Stand on the corner of Hastings and Hornby streets for the best view of the Marine Building.

A nice walk is along Hastings Street—the old financial district. Until the 1966–1972 period, when the first of the bank towers and underground malls on West Georgia Street were developed, this was Canada's westernmost business terminus. The temple-style banks, businessmen's clubs, and investment houses survive as evidence of the city's sophisticated architec-

8 tural advances prior to World War I. The **Vancouver Club,** built between 1912 and 1914, was a gathering place for the city's elite. Its architectural design is reminiscent of private clubs in England that were inspired by Italian Renaissance palaces. The Vancouver Club is still a private businessmen's club. *915 W. Hastings St., tel. 604/685–9321.*

9 The foot of Howe Street, north of Hastings, is **Canada Place Pier.** Converted into Vancouver's Trade and Convention Center after Expo 86, Canada Place was originally built on an old cargo pier to be the off-site Canadian pavilion. It is dominated at the shore end by the luxurious Pan Pacific Hotel (*see* Lodging, below), with its spectacular three-story lobby and waterfall. The convention space is covered by a fabric roof shaped like 10 sails, which has become a landmark of Vancouver's skyline. Below is a cruise-ship facility, and at the north end are an Imax theater, a restaurant, and an outdoor performance space. A promenade runs along the pier's west side with views of the Burrard Inlet harbor and Stanley Park. *999 Canada Pl., tel. 604/688–8687.*

10 Walk back up to Hastings and Howe streets to the **Sinclair Centre.** Vancouver's outstanding architect, Richard Henriquez, has knitted four government office buildings (built 1905–1939) into an office-retail complex. The two Hastings Street buildings—the 1905 post office with the elegant clock tower and the 1913 Winch Building—are linked with the Post Office Extension and Customs Examining Warehouse to the north. Painstaking and very costly restoration involved finding master masons—the original terrazzo suppliers in Europe—and uncovering and refurbishing the pressed-metal ceilings.

Canada has a handful of old chartered banks. The oldest and

11 most impressive of these is the former **Canadian Imperial Bank of Commerce** headquarters (1906–1908) at Hastings and Gran-

ville streets; the columns, arches, and details are of typically
⑫ Roman influence. The **Toronto-Dominion Bank,** one block east,
is of the same style but was built in 1920.

Backtracking directly across from the CIBC on Hastings
⑬ Street is the more Gothic **Royal Bank.** It was intended to be half
of a symmetrical building that was never completed, due to the
Depression. Striking, though, is the magnificent hall, ecclesi-
astical in style, reminiscent of a European cathedral.

⑭ At the foot of Seymour Street is the **Canadian Pacific Station,**
the third and most pretentious of three Canadian Pacific Railway passenger terminals. Built 1912–1914, this terminal replaced the other two as the western terminus for Canada's
transcontinental railway. After Canada's railways merged, the
station became obsolete until a 1978 renovation turned it into
an office-retail complex and SeaBus terminal. Murals in the
waiting rooms show passengers what kind of scenery to expect
on their journeys across Canada.

From Seymour Street, pick up Water Street, on your way to
⑮ **Gastown.** Named after the original townsite saloon keeper,
"Gassy" Jack Deighton, Gastown is where Vancouver originated. Deighton arrived at Burrard Inlet in 1867 with his Indian wife, a barrel of whiskey, and few amenities. A statue of
Gassy Jack stands on the north side of Maple Tree Square, the
intersection of five streets, where he built his first saloon.

When the transcontinental train arrived in 1887, Gastown became the transfer point for trade with the Orient and was soon
crowded with hotels and warehouses. The Klondike gold rush
encouraged further development until 1912, when the "Golden
Years" ended. The 1930s–1950s saw hotels being converted
into rooming houses and the warehouse district shifting elsewhere. The area gradually became unattended and run-down.
However, both Gastown and Chinatown were declared historic
areas and have been revitalized.

⑯ The **Byrnes Block** building was constructed on the corner of
Water and Carrall streets (the site of Gassy Jack's second saloon) after the 1886 Great Fire. The date is just visible at the
top of the building above the door where it says "Herman
Block," which was its name for a short time. The extravagantly
detailed Alhambra Hotel that was situated here was luxury
class for the time, at a cost of a dollar a night.

Tucked behind 2 Water Street are **Blood Alley** and **Gaoler's
Mews.** Once the site of the city's first civic buildings—the con-
stable's cabin and courthouse, and a two-cell log jail—today
the cobblestone street with antique streetlighting is the home
of architectural offices.

⑰ The **Hotel Europe** (1908–1909), a flatiron building at Powell and
Alexander streets, was billed as the best hotel in the city and
was Vancouver's first reinforced concrete structure. Designed
as a functional commercial building, the hotel lacks ornamentation and fine detail, a style unusually utilitarian for the time.

From Maple Tree Square, walk three blocks up Carrall Street
⑱ to Pender Street, where **Chinatown** begins. There was already
a sizable Chinese community in British Columbia because of
the 1858 Cariboo gold rush in central British Columbia, but
the biggest influx from China occurred in the 1880s, during
construction of the Canadian Pacific Railway, when 15,000

laborers were imported. The Chinese were among the first inhabitants of Vancouver, and some of the oldest buildings in the city are in Chinatown.

Even while doing the hazardous work of blasting the railbed through the Rocky Mountains, the Chinese were discriminated against. The Anti-Asiatic Riots of 1907 stopped growth in Chinatown for 50 years, and immigration from China was discouraged by more and more restrictive policies, climaxing in a $500 head tax during the 1920s.

In the 1960s the city council was planning bulldozer urban renewal for Strathcona, the residential part of Chinatown, and freeway connections through the most historic blocks of Chinatown were charted. Fortunately, the plans were halted, and today Chinatown is an expanding, vital district fueled by investment from Vancouver's most notable newcomers—immigrants from Hong Kong. It is best to view the buildings in Chinatown from the south side of Pender Street, where the Chinese Cultural Center stands. From here you'll get a view of important details that adorn the upper stories. The style of architecture in Vancouver's Chinatown is patterned on that of Canton and won't be seen in any other Canadian cities.

19 The corner of Carrall and East Pender streets, now the western boundary of Chinatown, is one of the neighborhood's most historic spots. Standing at 8 West Pender Street is the **Sam Kee Building,** recognized by *Ripley's Believe It or Not!* as the narrowest building in the world. The 1913 structure still exists, with its bay windows overhanging the street and a basement that burrows under the sidewalk.

20 The **Chinese Freemasons Building** (1901) at 1 West Pender Street has two completely different styles of facades: The side facing Chinatown displays a fine example of Cantonese-imported recessed balconies; on the Carrall Street side, the standard Victorian style common throughout the British Empire is displayed. It was in this building that Dr. Sun Yat-sen hid for months from the agents of the Manchu dynasty while he raised funds for its overthrow, which he accomplished in 1911.

21 Directly across Carrall Street is the **Chinese Times Building,** constructed in 1902. Inside, there is a hidden mezzanine floor from which police officers could hear the clicking sounds of clandestine mah-jongg games played after sunset. Attempts by vice squads to enforce restrictive policies against the Chinese gamblers proved fruitless, because police were unable to find the players, who were hidden on the secret floor.

22 Planning for the **Chinese Cultural Center** and **Dr. Sun Yat-sen Gardens** (1980–87) began during the late 1960s; the first phase was designed by James Cheng, a former associate of Arthur Erickson. The cultural center has exhibition space, classrooms, and meeting rooms. The Dr. Sun Yat-sen Gardens, located behind the cultural center, were built by 52 artisans from Suzhou, the Garden City of the People's Republic. The gardens incorporate design elements and traditional materials from several of that city's centuries-old private gardens and are the first living classical Chinese gardens built outside China. As you walk through the gardens, remember that no power tools, screws, or nails were used in the construction. Free guided tours are offered throughout the day; telephone for times. *Dr. Sun Yat-sen Gardens. 578 Carrall St., tel. 604/689–7133. Ad-*

mission: $3.50 adults, $2.50 senior citizens and students, $7 families. Open May–Sept., daily 10–8; Oct.–Apr., daily 10–4:30.

Tour 2: Stanley Park

Numbers in the margin correspond to points of interest on the Tour 2: Stanley Park map.

A 1,000-acre wilderness park just blocks from the downtown section of a major city is a rarity but is one of Vancouver's major attractions. In the 1860s, due to a threat of American invasion, the area that is now Stanley Park was designated a military reserve (though it was never needed). When the city of Vancouver was incorporated in 1886, the council's first act was to request that the land be set aside for a park. In 1888 permission was granted and the grounds were named Stanley Park after Lord Stanley, then governor general of Canada (the same person after whom hockey's Stanley Cup is named).

An afternoon in Stanley Park gives you a capsule tour of Vancouver that includes beaches, the ocean, the harbor, Douglas fir and cedar forests, and a good look at the North Shore mountains. The park sits on a peninsula, and along the shore is a pathway 9 kilometers (5½ mi) long called the seawall. You can walk or bicycle all the way around or follow the shorter route suggested below.

Bicycles are for rent at the foot of Georgia Street near the park entrance. Cyclists must ride in a counterclockwise direction and stay on their side of the path. A good place for pedestrians
(23) to start is at the foot of Alberni Street beside **Lost Lagoon.** Go through the underpass and veer right to the seawall.

(24) The old wood structure that you pass is the **Vancouver Rowing Club,** a private athletic club (established 1903); a bit farther
(25) along is the **Royal Vancouver Yacht Club.**

(26) About ½ kilometer (⅓ mile) away is the causeway to **Deadman's Island,** a former burial ground for the local Salish Indians and the early settlers. It is now a small naval training base called the HMCS *Discovery* that is not open to the public. Just ahead
(27) is the **Nine O'Clock Gun,** a cannonlike apparatus that sits by the water's edge. Originally used to alert fishermen to a curfew ending weekend fishing, now it automatically signals every night at 9.

(28) Farther along is **Brockton Point** and its small but functional lighthouse and foghorn. The **totem poles,** which are situated more inland, make a popular photo spot for tourists. Totem poles were not carved in the Vancouver area; they were brought to the park from the north coast of British Columbia and were carved by the Kwakiutl and Haida peoples late in the last century. These cedar poles with carved animals, fish, birds, or mythological creatures were like family coats-of-arms or crests.

(29) At kilometer 3 (mile 2) is **Lumberman's Arch,** a huge log archway dedicated to the workers in Vancouver's first industry. Beside the arch is an asphalt path that leads back to Lost Lagoon, for those who want a shorter walk. (It's about a third of the dis-
(30) tance.) This path also leads to the **Vancouver Public Aquarium.** Also part of this attraction is the humid Amazon rain-forest

Tour 2: Stanley Park

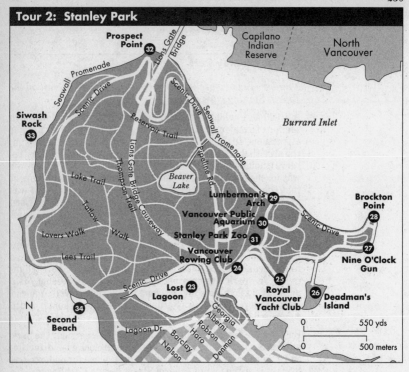

gallery, through which you can walk, with its piranhas, giant cockroaches, alligators, tropical birds, and jungle vegetation. Other displays show the underwater life of coastal British Columbia, the Canadian arctic, and other areas of the world. The Clamshell Gift Shop next to the aquarium is the best spot in town for high-quality souvenirs and gifts, most with an emphasis on natural history. *Aquarium, tel. 604/682–1118. Admission: $8.50 adults, $7.25 senior citizens and youths, $5.25 children 5–12. Open daily in summer 9:30–8; daily in winter 10–5:30. Clamshell open July–Labor Day, daily 9:30–8; rest of year, daily 10–5:30.*

31 Next to the aquarium is the **Stanley Park Zoo,** a friendly place, easily seen in an hour or two. Except for the polar bears, most of the animals are small—monkeys, seals, exotic birds, penguins, and playful otters.

32 About 1 kilometer (¾ mile) farther is the **Lions Gate Bridge—** the halfway point of the seawall. On the other side of the bridge is **Prospect Point,** where you can see cormorants in their seaweed nests on the ledges along the cliffs. The large black diving birds are recognized by their long necks and beaks; when not nesting, they often perch atop floating logs or boulders. Another remarkable bird found along the shore in the park is the beautiful great blue heron. Reaching up to 4 feet tall with a wing span of 6 feet, the heron preys on passing fish in the waters here. The oldest heron rookery in British Columbia is in the trees around the zoo.

㉝ Continuing around the seawall you will come to the **English Bay** side and the beginning of sandy beaches. The imposing rock just offshore is **Siwash Rock.** Legend tells of a young Indian who, about to become a father, bathed persistently to wash his sins away so that his son could be born pure; for his devotion he was blessed by the gods and immortalized in the shape of Siwash Rock. Two small rocks, said to be his wife and child, are just up on the cliff above the site.

Time Out   Along the seawall is one of Vancouver's best restaurants, the **Ferguson Point Teahouse.** Set on the great lawn among Douglas fir and cedar trees, the restaurant is the perfect stopover for a summer weekend lunch or brunch. If you want just a snack, a park concession stand is also at Ferguson Point.

㉞ The next attraction along the seawall is the large salt-water pool at **Second Beach.** In the summer it is a children's pool with lifeguards, but during winter the pool is drained and skateboarders perform stunts. At the pool you can take a shortcut back to Lost Lagoon. To take the shortcut, walk along the perpendicular road behind the pool, which cuts into the park. The wood footbridge that's ahead will lead you to a path along the south side of the lagoon and to your starting point at the foot of Alberni or Georgia street.

If you continue along the seawall, it will emerge out of the park into a high-rise residential neighborhood, the **West End.** You can walk back to Alberni Street along Denman Street, where there are plenty of places to stop for coffee, ice cream, or a drink.

Tour 3: Granville Island

Numbers in the margin correspond to points of interest on the Tour 3: Granville Island map.

Granville Island was just a sandbar until World War I, when the nearby creek was dredged for access to the sawmills that lined the shore. Sludge heaped on the sandbar gradually created the island that was then used to house supplies for the logging industry. In 1971 the federal government bought the island and used an imaginative plan to refurbish it and to introduce a public market, marine activities, and artisans' studios. The opposite shore of False Creek was the site of the 1986 World's Fair and is now part of the largest urban redevelopment plan in North America.

The small island is almost strictly commercial except for a small houseboat community. Most of the previously used industrial buildings and tin sheds have been retained but are painted in upbeat reds, yellows, and blues. The government regulates the types of businesses that settle on Granville Island; only businesses involving food, crafts, marine activities, and the arts are permitted here.

Access on foot to Granville Island starts with a 15-minute walk from downtown Vancouver to the south end of Thurlow Street. From a dock behind the Vancouver Aquatic Center, the Granville Island ferry leaves every six minutes for the short trip across False Creek to the Granville Island Public Market. These pudgy boats are a great way to see the sights on False Creek, but for a longer ride, go to the Maritime Museum (1905

Ogden St., tel. 604/737–2211). For more information, call Granville Island Ferries (tel. 604/684–7781).

Another option is to take a 20-minute ride on a BC Transit (tel. 604/261–5100) bus. Take a UBC, Granville, Arbutus, Cambie, or Oak bus from downtown to Granville and Broadway, and transfer to the Granville Island bus No. 51. Parking is limited, but if you must take a car, go early in the week and early in the day to avoid crowds. Parking is free for only three hours; an alternative is to use the pay parking buildings on the island if you can find a space.

35 The ferry to Granville Island will drop you off at the **Granville Island Public Market.** Although there are a few good food stores outside, most stalls are enclosed in the 50,000-square-foot building. Since the government allows no chain stores, each outlet is unique, and most are of good quality. You probably won't be able to leave the market without a snack, espresso, or fixings for a lunch out on the wharf. Don't miss the charcoal-grilled oysters from **Sea-kist,** fish chowder or bouillabaisse from the **Stock Market,** fresh fudge at **Olde World Fudge,** or smoked salmon from the **Salmon Shop.** In the summer you'll see mounds of raspberries, strawberries, blueberries, and even more exotic fruits like persimmons and lychees. On the water side of the market is lots of outdoor seating. *Public Market, tel. 604/666–5784. Open June–Aug., daily 9–6; closed Mon. Sept.– May except holidays.*

36 The **Granville Island Information Centre,** kitty-corner to the market, is a good place to get oriented to the island. Maps are available, and a slide show depicts the evolution of Granville Island. Ask here about special-events days; perhaps there's a boat show, outdoor symphony concert, dance performance, or some other happening. *1592 Johnston St., tel. 604/666–5784. Open daily 9–6.*

Continue walking south on Johnston Street, along a clockwise loop of the island. Next is **Ocean Cement,** one of the last of the island's former industries; its lease does not expire until the year 2004.

37 Next door is the **Emily Carr College of Art and Design.** Just inside the front door, to your right, is the **Charles H. Scott Gallery,** which hosts contemporary multimedia exhibits. *1399 Johnston St., tel. 604/687–2345. Open daily 11–5, Thurs. 11–8.*

Past the art school, on the left, is one of the only **houseboat communities** in Vancouver; others have been banned by the city because of problems with sewage and property taxes. The owners of this community appealed the ban and won special status. Take the boardwalk that starts at the houseboats and continues partway around the island.

As you circle around to Cartwright Street, stop in **Kakali** at number 1249, where you can watch the process of making fine handmade paper from all sorts of materials like bluejeans, herbs, and sequins. Another unusual artisan on the island is the glassblower at 1440 Old Bridge Street, around the corner.

The next two attractions will make any child's visit to Granville Island a thrill. First, on Cartwright Street, is the children's
38 **water park,** with a wading pool, sprinklers, and a fire hydrant made for children to shower one another. A bit farther down,
39 beside Isadora's restaurant, is the **Kids Only Market,** with two

Tour 3: Granville Island

floors of small shops selling toys, arts-and-crafts materials,
dolls, records and tapes, chemistry sets, and other sorts of kid
stuff. *Water park. 1318 Cartwright St., tel. 604/665–3425.
Admission free. Open June–Aug., daily 10–6. Kids Only Market. 1496 Cartwright St., tel. 604/689–8447. Open daily 10–6.*

40 At the **Granville Island Brewery,** next door, you can take a half-
hour tour every afternoon; at the end of the tour, sample the
Granville Island Lager that is produced here and sold locally in
most restaurants. *Tel. 604/688–9927. Admission free. Tours
daily at 1 and 3.*

Cross Anderson Street and walk down Duranleau Street. On
your left, the scuba diving pool in **Adrenalin Sports** marks the
41 start of the **Maritime Market,** a string of businesses all geared
to the sea. The first walkway to the left, Maritime Mews, leads
to marinas and dry docks. There are dozens of outfits in the
Maritime Market that charter boats (with or without skippers)
or run cruise-and-learn trips.

Another way to take to the water is by kayak. Take a lesson or
rent a kayak from **Ecomarine Ocean Kayak Center** (1668
Duranleau St., tel. 604/689–7575). Owner John Dowd is considered *the* expert on Pacific Northwest ocean kayaking.

Time Out | **Bridges** (1696 Duranleau St., tel. 604/687–4400), in the bright
yellow building across from the market, is a good spot to have
lunch, especially on a warm summer's day. Eat on the spacious
deck that looks out on the sailboats, fishing boats, and other
water activities.

The last place to explore on Granville Island is the blue building next to Ecomarine on Duranleau Street, the **Net Loft.** The loft is a collection of small, high-quality stores—good places to find a gift to take home: a bookstore, crafts store/gallery, kitchenware shop, postcard shop, custom-made hat shop, handmade paper store, British Columbian native Indian gallery, do-it-yourself jewelry store, and more reside here.

Behind Blackberry Books, in the Net Loft complex, is the **studio of Bill Reid,** British Columbia's most respected Haida Indian carver. His *The Raven and the First Men* (which took five carvers more than three years to complete) is in the Museum of Anthropology (*see* Other Museums, below). Reid's Pacific Northwest Coast Indian artworks are world renowned. Although you can't visit the studio, there are large windows through which you can look.

Since you have come full circle, you can either take the ferry back to downtown Vancouver or stay for dinner and catch a play at the **Arts Club** (tel. 604/687–1644) or the **Waterfront Theater** (tel. 604/685–6217).

Other Museums

The **Maritime Museum** traces the history of marine activities on the west coast. Permanent exhibits depict the port of Vancouver, the fishing industry, and early explorers; the model ships on display are a delight. Traveling exhibits vary but always have a maritime theme. Guided tours are led through the double-masted schooner *St. Roch,* the first ship to sail in both directions through the treacherous Northwest Passage. A changing variety of restored heritage boats from different cultures are moored behind the museum, and a huge Kwakiutl totem pole stands out front. *North foot of Cypress St., tel. 604/737–2211. Admission: $4 adults, $2.50 children, students, and senior citizens, $8 families. Open daily 10–5, closed Mon. in winter. Access available by the Granville Island Ferries.*

The **Museum of Anthropology,** focusing on the arts of the Pacific Northwest Indians, is Vancouver's most spectacular museum. Situated on the campus of the University of British Columbia, the museum is housed in an award-winning glass and concrete structure designed by Arthur Erickson. In the Great Hall are large and dramatic totem poles, ceremonial archways, and dugout canoes—all adorned with carvings of frogs, eagles, ravens, bears, and salmon. Also showcased are exquisite carvings of gold, silver, and argillite (a black stone found in the Queen Charlotte Islands). Masks, tools, and costumes from many other cultures are also displayed. A ceramics wing, housing 600 pieces from 15th- to 19th-century Europe, opened in 1990. *6393 N.W. Marine Dr., tel. 604/822–3825. Admission: $5 adults, $2.50 students 6–18 and senior citizens; free Tues. evenings. Open Tues. 11–9, Wed.–Sun. 11–5.*

Science World is in a gigantic shiny dome that was built for Expo 86 for an Omnimax Theater—the world's largest dome screen. Science World is not a traditional museum but is very much hands-on. Visitors are encouraged to touch and to participate in the theme exhibits. A special gallery, the Search Gallery, is aimed at younger children, as are the fun-filled demonstrations given in Center Stage. *1455 Quebec St., tel. 604/687–7832. Admission to Science World: $7 adults, $4.50* *senior citizens and children. Admission to Omnimax is the same; for admission to both you get a discount. Open weekdays 10–5, Saturday 10–9.*

Vancouver Museum displays permanent exhibits that focus on the city's early history and native art and culture. Life-size replicas of an 1897 Canadian Pacific Railway passenger car, a trading post, and a Victorian parlor, as well as a real dugout canoe are highlights. Also on the site are the Planetarium and Observatory (*see* Off the Beaten Track, below). *1100 Chestnut St., tel. 604/736–7736. Admission: $5 adults, $2.50 senior citizens and children. Open Tues.–Sun. 10–5 in winter, daily 10–5 in summer.*

Other Parks and Gardens

Nitobe Garden is a small (2.4-acre) garden that is considered the most authentic Japanese garden outside Japan. The circular path around the park symbolizes the cycle of life and provides a tranquil view from every direction. In April and May cherry blossoms are the highlight, and in June the irises are magnificent. *1903 West Mall, Univ. of B.C., tel. 604/822–4208. Admission: $2 adults, $1.25 senior citizens and students, free Wed. and every day Oct. 11–Mar. 17. Open daily 10–dusk in summer; Mon.–Fri. in winter; phone for specific closing times.*

Pacific Spirit Park (W. 16th Ave., tel. 604/224–5739) is a 1,000-acre park that is bigger and more rugged than Stanley Park. Pacific Spirit's only amenities are 30 miles of trails, a few washrooms, and a couple of signboard maps. Go for a wonderful walk in the west coast woods—it's hard to believe that you are only 15 minutes from downtown Vancouver.

Queen Elizabeth Park has lavish gardens and lots of grassy picnicking spots. Illuminated fountains; the botanical Bloedel Conservatory, with tropical and desert zones and 20 species of free-flying tropical birds; and other facilities including 20 tennis courts, lawn bowling, pitch and putt, and a restaurant are on the grounds. *Cambie St. and 25th Ave., tel. 604/872–5513. Admission to conservatory: $2.85 adults, $1.40 senior citizens and students, $5.70 families. Open May–Sept., weekdays 9–8, weekends 10–9; Oct.–Apr., daily 10–5.*

Van Dusen Botanical Garden was a 55-acre golf course but is now the grounds of one of the largest collections of ornamental plants in Canada. Native and exotic plant displays include the shrubbery maze and the rhododendrons in May and June. *5251 Oak St. at 37th Ave., tel. 604/266–7194. Admission: $4.50 adults, $2.25 senior citizens and children 13–18, $9 families; half-price off-season. Open 10–dusk.*

Vancouver for Free

Several public galleries and museums are free on certain days: The **Vancouver Art Gallery** (750 Hornby St., tel. 604/682–5621) is free on Thursday evenings; the **Museum of Anthropology** (6393 N.W. Marine Dr., tel. 604/822–3825) is free Tuesday evenings. The **Vancouver Museum** (1100 Chestnut St., tel. 604/736–7736) is free on the first Thursday evening of every month. It is also free every Tuesday for senior citizens.

The **University of British Columbia Botanical Garden** and **Nitobe Garden** (tel. 604/822–4208), a well-established Japanese garden also at UBC, are free on Wednesday and all winter.

What to See and Do with Children

Stanley Park Zoo (*see* Tour 2: Stanley Park, above).

The **miniature steam train** in Stanley Park, just five minutes northwest of the aquarium, is a big hit with children as it chugs through the forest.

Splashdown Park (Hwy. 17, just before the Tsawwassen Ferry causeway, tel. 604/943–2251), 38 kilometers (24 miles) outside Vancouver, is a giant waterslide park with 11 slides (for toddlers to adults), heated water, picnic tables, and minigolf.

Richmond Nature Park (No. 5 Rd. exit from Hwy. 99, tel. 604/273–7015), with its displays and games in the Nature House, is geared toward children. Guides answer questions and give tours. Since the park sits on a natural bog, rubber boots are recommended if it's been wet, but a boardwalk around the duck pond makes some of the park accessible to strollers and wheelchairs.

Maplewood Farms (405 Seymour River Pl., tel. 604/929–5610), a 20-minute drive from downtown Vancouver, is set up like a small farm, with all the barnyard animals for children to see and pet. Cows are milked every day at 1:15.

Kids Only Market (*see* Tour 3: Granville Island, above).

The Planetarium (1100 Chestnut St., tel. 604/736–3656), on the same site as the Vancouver Museum in Vanier Park, has astronomy shows each afternoon and evening, and laser rock music shows later in the night.

Science World (*see* Other Museums, above)

Off the Beaten Track

On the North Shore you can get a taste of the mountains and test your mettle at the **Lynn Canyon Suspension Bridge** (Lynn Headwaters Regional Park, North Vancouver, tel. 604/987–5922), which hangs 240 feet above Lynn Creek. Also on the North Shore is the **Capilano Fish Hatchery** in the Regional Park (4500 Capilano Park Rd., tel. 604/666–1790), with exhibits about salmon.

If the sky is clear, the telescope at the **Gordon Southam Observatory** (1100 Chestnut St., in Vanier Park, tel. 604/738–2855) will be focused on whatever stars or planets are worth watching that night. While you're there, visit the planetarium on the site. Open Friday, Saturday, Sunday, and holiday evenings.

The **Beatles Museum** (456 Seymour St., tel. 604/685–8841) exhibits memorabilia from the early years of the Fab Four. Admission is $3, and the museum is open daily 10–6, Sunday noon–6.

Shopping

Unlike many cities where suburban malls have taken over, Vancouver has a downtown area that is still lined with individual boutiques and specialty shops. Stores tend to be open every day and on Thursday and Friday nights.

Shopping Districts

The immense **Pacific Center Mall,** in the heart of downtown, connects Eaton's and The Bay department stores, which stand at opposite corners of Georgia and Granville streets. Pacific Center is on two levels and is mostly underground.

A new commercial center has developed around **Sinclair Center** (*see* Tour 1, above), which caters to sophisticated and upscale tastes.

On the opposite side of Pacific Center, stretching from Burrard to Bute streets, is **Robson Street**—the clothing place for the fashion conscious. Chockablock with small stores and cafés, it is Vancouver's liveliest street and provides many excellent corners for people watching.

Two other shopping districts, one on **West 41st Avenue** between West Boulevard and Larch Street in Kerrisdale and the other on **West 10th** from Discovery Street west, are both in upscale neighborhoods and have high-quality shops and restaurants.

Fourth Avenue, from Burrard to Balsam streets, offers an eclectic mix of stores (from sophisticated women's clothing to surfboards and Jams).

In addition to the Pacific Center Mall, **Oakridge Shopping Center** at Cambie Street and 41st Avenue has chic, expensive stores that are fun to browse.

Ethnic Districts **Chinatown** (*see* Tour 1, above)—centered on Pender and Main streets—is an exciting and animated place for restaurants, exotic foodstuffs, and distinctive architecture.

Commercial Drive (around East 1st Avenue) is the heart of the **Italian community,** here called Little Italy. You can sip cappuccino in coffee bars where you may be the only one speaking English or buy sun-dried tomatoes, real Parmesan, or an espresso machine.

The **East Indian shopping district** is on Main Street around 50th Avenue. Curry houses, sweet shops, grocery stores, and sari shops abound.

A small **Japantown** on Powell Street at Dunlevy Street is made up of grocery stores, fish stores, and a few restaurants.

Department Stores

The two biggest department stores in Vancouver, **Eaton's** and **The Bay,** are Canadian owned and located downtown and at most malls. The third, **Woodward's,** is a local chain and is found only in British Columbia and Alberta. The flagship store is in the Oakridge Shopping Center.

Flea Markets

A huge flea market (703 Terminal Ave., tel. 604/685–0666), with more than 300 stalls, is held Saturday, Sunday, and holidays from 8 to 4. It is easily accessible from downtown via SkyTrain.

Auctions

On Wednesday at noon and 7 PM, auctions are held at **Love's** (1635 W. Broadway, tel. 604/733–1157). **Maynard's** (415 W. 2nd Ave., tel. 604/876–6787) has home furnishings auctions on Wednesday at 7 PM. Phone for times of art and antiques auctions.

Specialty Stores

Antiques
A stretch of antiques stores runs along Main Street from 19th to 35th avenues. On 10th Avenue near Alma are a few antiques stores that specialize in Canadiana, including **Folkart Interiors** (3715 W. 10th Ave.) and **Old Country** (3720 W. 10th Ave.). Also try **Canada West** (3607 W. Broadway). For very refined antiques, see **Artemis** (321 Water St.) in Gastown. For Oriental rugs, go to Granville Street between 7th and 14th avenues.

Art Galleries
There are many private galleries throughout Vancouver. The best of them are **Bau-Xi** (3045 Granville St., tel. 604/733–7011), **Buschlen-Mowatt** (1445 W. Georgia St., tel. 604/682–1234), **Diane Farris** (1565 W. 7th Ave., tel. 604/737–2629), **Equinox** (2321 Granville St., tel. 604/736–2405), and the **Heffel Gallery** (2247 Granville St., tel. 604/732–6505).

Books
The best general bookstores are **Duthie's,** located downtown (919 Robson St.) and near the university (4444 W. 10th Ave.), and **Blackberry Books** (1663 Duranleau St.) on Granville Island.

Specialty bookstores include **The Travel Bug** (2667 W. Broadway) and **World Wide Books and Maps** (736 Granville St., downstairs) for travel books, **Vancouver Kidsbooks** (3083 W. Broadway), **Sportsbooks Plus** (230 W. Broadway), and **Pink Peppercorn** (2686 W. Broadway) for cookbooks, and **William McCarley** (213 Carrall St.) for design and architecture.

Most of the secondhand and antiquarian dealers, such as **William Hoffer** (60 Powell St.) and **Colophon Books** (407 W. Cordova St., upstairs), are in the Gastown area. A block or two away are **McLeod's** (455 W. Pender St. and around the corner at 432 Richards St.), **Ainsworth's** (321 W. Pender St.), and **Bond's** (319 W. Hastings St.). **Lawrence Books** (3591 W. 41st Ave.) is out of the way but is probably the best used-books bookstore in town.

Children's Stores
An unusual children's store worth checking out is **The Imagination Market** (528 Powell St.), an oddball warehouse-type store selling recycled industrial goods for arts and crafts materials: barrels of metallic plastic, feathers, fluorescent-colored paper, buttons, bits of Plexiglas, and other materials by the bagful.

Clothing
Men
Several high-quality men's clothing stores are in the business district: **Edward Chapman** (833 W. Pender St.) has conservative looks; **E.A. Lee** (466 Howe St.) is stylish; **Leone** (757 W. Hastings St.) is ultrachic.

A few blocks away, at Pacific Center, are **Harry Rosen, Eddie Bauer,** and **Holt Renfrew**. If your tastes are traditional, don't miss **George Straith** (900 W. Georgia St.) in the Hotel Vancouver.

On Robson Street, a more trendy shopping area, are **Boy's Co.** (No. 1080) and **Club Monaco** (No. 1153), for casual wear.

Outside downtown Vancouver there are two men's boutiques selling Italian imports: **Mondo Uomo** (2709 Granville St.) and **Boboli** (2776 Granville St.).

In Kerrisdale, three excellent men's clothing stores are **Finn's** (2159 W. 41st Ave.), **Hill's** (2125 W. 41st Ave.), and, across the street, **S. Lampman** (2126 W. 41st Ave.).

Women For women's fashions, visit **E.A. Lee** (466 Howe St.), **Wear Else?** (789 W. Pender St.), **Leone** (757 W. Hastings St.), and the more conservative **Chapy's** (833 W. Pender St.), all in the business district.

On Robson Street, look for **Margareta** (No. 948), **Alfred Sung** (No. 1143), **Club Monaco** (No. 1153), and a lingerie shop, **La Vie en Rose** (No. 1001). The two blocks between Burrard and Bute have six shoe stores.

Two expensive and very stylish import stores in South Granville are **Boboli** (2776 Granville St.) and **Bacci** (2788 Granville St.). Nearby, one of the largest and best shoe stores in town is **Freedman Shoes** (2867 Granville St.).

On the west side **Enda B.** (4346 W. 10th Ave.) and **Wear Else?** (2360 W. 4th Ave.) are the largest and best stores for high-quality fashions, but there's also **Bali Bali** for the more exotic (4462 W. 10th Ave.) and **Zig Zag** (4424 W. 10th Ave.) for fashion accessories.

Gifts Want something special to take home from British Columbia? The best places for good-quality souvenirs are the **Vancouver Art Gallery** (750 Hornby St.) and the **Clamshell Gift Shop** at the aquarium in Stanley Park. The **Salmon Shop** in the Granville Island Public Market will wrap smoked salmon for travel. In Gastown, Haida and Salish Indian art is available at **Images for a Canadian Heritage** (164 Water St.). Near Granville Island is **Leona Lattimer** (1590 W. 2nd Ave.), where the inside of her shop is built like an Indian longhouse and is full of Indian arts and crafts ranging from cheap to priceless.

Sports and Outdoor Activities

Participant Sports

Biking **Stanley Park** (*see* Tour 2 in Exploring Vancouver, above) is the most popular spot for family cycling. Rentals are available here from **Bayshore Bicycles** (745 Denman St., tel. 604/688–2453) or around the corner at **Stanley Park Rentals** (676 Chilco St., tel. 604/681–5581).

Another biking route is along the north or south shore of **False Creek**. Rent bikes at **Robson Cycles** (1840 Fir St., tel. 604/731–5552), near Granville Island.

Fishing   You can fish for salmon all year in coastal British Columbia. **Sewell's Landing Marina** (6695 Nelson St., Horseshoe Bay, tel. 604/921-7461) organizes a daily four-hour trip on Howe Sound or has hourly rates on U-drives. **Bayshore Yacht Charters** (1601 W. Georgia St., tel. 604/691-6936) has a daily five-hour fishing trip; boats are moored five minutes from downtown Vancouver. **Island Charters** (Duranleau St., Granville Island, tel. 604/688-6625) arranges charters or boat shares and supplies all gear.

Golf   Lower Mainland golf courses are open all year. **Fraserview Golf Course** (tel. 604/327-3717), a spacious course with fairways well defined by hills and mature conifers and deciduous trees, is the busiest course in the country. Fraserview is also the most central, about 20 minutes from downtown. **Seymour Golf and Country Club** (tel. 604/929-5491), on the south side of Mt. Seymour, on the North Shore, is a semiprivate club that is open to the public on Monday and Friday. One of the finest public courses in the country is **Peace Portal** (tel. 604/538-4818), near White Rock, a 45-minute drive from downtown.

Health and Fitness Clubs   Both the **YMCA** (955 Burrard St., tel. 604/681-0221) and the **YWCA** (580 Burrard St., tel. 604/683-2531) downtown have drop-in rates that let you participate in all activities for the day. Both have pools, weight rooms, and fitness classes; the YMCA has racquetball, squash, and handball courts. Two other recommended clubs are **Chancery Squash Club** (202-865 Hornby St., tel. 604/682-3752) and **Tower Courts Racquet and Fitness Club** (1055 Dunsmuir St., lower level, tel. 604/689-4424), both with racquetball courts, weight rooms, and aerobics.

Hiking   **Pacific Spirit Park** is a 1,000-acre wilderness park with 30 miles of hiking trails (*see* Parks and Gardens, above).

The **Capilano Regional Park** (*see* Off the Beaten Track, in Exploring Vancouver, above), on the North Shore, provides a scenic hike.

Jogging   The seawall around **Stanley Park** (*see* Tour 2 in Exploring Vancouver, above) is 9 kilometers (5½ miles) and gives an excellent minitour of the city. A shorter run of 4 kilometers (2½ miles) in the park is around **Lost Lagoon.**

Skiing   The best cross-country skiing is at **Hollyburn Ridge** in Cypress
Cross-country   Park (tel. 604/926-6007).

Downhill   Vancouver is two hours away from **Whistler/Blackcomb** (Whistler Resort Association, tel. 604/685-3650; snow report, tel. 604/687-7507), one of the top ski spots in North America.

There are three ski areas on the North Shore mountains, close to Vancouver, with night skiing. The snow is not as good as at Whistler, and the runs are generally used by novice, junior, and family skiers or those who want a quick ski after work. **Cypress Park** (tel. 604/926-5612; snow report, tel. 604/926-6007) has the most and the longest runs; **Grouse Mountain** (tel. 604/984-0661; snow report, tel. 604/986-6262) has extensive night skiing, restaurants, and bars; and **Mt. Seymour** (tel. 604/986-2261; snow report, tel. 604/986-3444) is the highest in the area, so the snow is a little better.

Water Sports   Rent a kayak from **Ecomarine** (tel. 604/689-7575) on Granville
Kayaking   Island (*see* Tour 3 in Exploring Vancouver, above).

Rafting The Thompson, the Chilliwack, and the Fraser are the principal rafting rivers in southwestern British Columbia. The Fraser River has whirlpools and big waves, but for frothing white water, try the Thompson and Chilliwack rivers. Trips range from three hours to several days. Some well-qualified outfitters that lead trips are **Kumsheen** (Lytton, tel. 604/455–2296; in British Columbia, tel. 800/482–2269), **Hyak** (Vancouver, tel. 604/734–8622), and **Canadian River Expeditions** (Vancouver, tel. 604/736–4449).

Sailing Several charter companies offer a cruise-and-learn vacation, usually to the Gulf Islands. The five-day trip is a crash course teaching the ins and outs of sailing. **Sea Wing** (Granville Island, tel. 604/669–0840), **Pacific Quest** (Granville Island, tel. 604/682–2205), and **Blue Orca** (Granville Island, tel. 604/687–4110) offer this package.

Windsurfing Boards can be rented at **Windsure** (Jericho Beach, tel. 604/224–0615) and **Windmaster** (English Bay Beach, tel. 604/685–7245).

Spectator Sports

The **Vancouver Canucks** (tel. 604/254–5141) of the National Hockey League play in the Coliseum October–April. The **Canadians** (tel. 604/872–5232) play baseball in an old-time outdoor stadium in the Pacific Coast League. Their season runs April–September. The **B.C. Lions** (tel. 604/585–3323) football team scrimmages at the B.C. Place Stadium downtown June–November. Tickets are available from Ticketmaster (tel. 604/280–4444).

Beaches

An almost continuous string of beaches runs from Stanley Park to the University of British Columbia. Children and hardy swimmers can take the cool water, but most others prefer to sunbathe; these beaches are sandy, with grassy areas running alongside. Note that liquor is prohibited in parks and on beaches. For information on beaches, call the **Parks Department of the City of Vancouver** (tel. 604/681–1141).

Kitsilano Beach. Kits Beach, with a lifeguard, is the busiest of them all—transistor radios, volleyball games, and sleek young people are ever present. The part of the beach nearest the Maritime Museum is the quietest. Facilities include a playground, tennis courts, heated salt-water pool (good for serious swimmers to toddlers), concession stands, and many nearby restaurants and cafés.

Point Grey Beaches. Jericho, Locarno, and Spanish Banks begin at the end of Point Grey Road. This string of beaches has a huge expanse of sand, especially in the summer and at low tide. The shallow water here is warmed slightly by the sun and the sand and so is best for swimming. Farther out, toward Spanish Banks, you'll find the beach becomes less crowded, but the last concession stand and washrooms are at Locarno. If you keep walking along the beach just past Point Grey, you'll hit Wreck Beach, Vancouver's nude beach. It is also accessible from Marine Drive at the university, but there is a fairly steep climb from the beach to the road.

West End Beaches. Second Beach and Third Beach, along Beach Drive in Stanley Park, are large family beaches. Second Beach has a guarded salt-water pool. Both have concession stands and washrooms. Farther along Beach Drive, at the foot of Jervis Street, is Sunset Beach, a surprisingly quiet beach considering the location. A lifeguard is on duty, but there are no facilities.

Dining

Among other allures, experiencing Vancouver's diverse gastronomical pleasures makes a visit to the city worthwhile. Restaurants appear throughout Vancouver—from the bustling downtown area to trendy beachside neighborhoods—making the diversity of the establishments' surroundings as enticing as the succulent cuisine they serve. A new wave of Chinese immigration and Japanese tourism has brought a proliferation of upscale Chinese and Japanese restaurants, offering dishes that would be at home in their own leading cities. Restaurants featuring Pacific Northwest fare—including homegrown regional favorites such as salmon and oysters, accompanied by British Columbia and Washington State wines—have become some of the city's leading attractions.

Highly recommended restaurants in each price category are indicated by a star ★.

Category	*Cost
Very Expensive	over $40
Expensive	$30—$40
Moderate	$20—$30
Inexpensive	under $20

*per person, including appetizer, entrée and dessert; excluding drinks, service, and sales tax

American **Isadora's.** Not only does Isadora's offer good coffee, a menu that ranges from samosas to lox and bagels, and children's specials, but there is also an inside play area packed with toys, and rest rooms with changing tables accommodate families. In the summer, the restaurant opens onto Granville Island's waterpark, so kids can entertain themselves. Service can be slow, but Isadora's staff is friendly. *1540 Old Bridge St., Granville Island, tel.604/681–8816. Reservations required for 6 or more. Dress: casual. Closed dinner Mon. Sept.–May. MC, V. Inexpensive.*

Nazarre BBQ Chicken. The best barbecued chicken in several hundred miles comes from this funky storefront on Commercial Drive. Owner Gerry Moutal massages his chickens for tenderness before he puts them on the rotisserie, then bastes them in a mixture of rum and spices. Chicken comes with roasted potatoes and a choice of mild, hot, extra hot, or hot garlic sauce. You can eat in, at one of four rickety tables, or take out. *1408 Commercial Dr., tel. 604/251–1844. No reservations. Dress: casual. No credit cards. Inexpensive.*

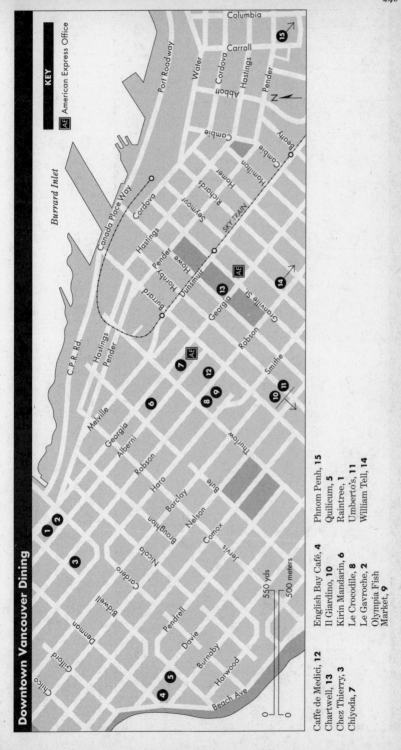

Downtown Vancouver Dining

Burrard Inlet

KEY

AE American Express Office

Caffe de Medici, **12**
Chartwell, **13**
Chez Thierry, **3**
Chiyoda, **7**

English Bay Café, **4**
Il Giardino, **10**
Kirin Mandarin, **6**
Le Crocodile, **8**
Le Gavroche, **2**
Olympia Fish
Market, **9**

Phnom Penh, **15**
Quilicum, **5**
Raintree, **1**
Umberto's, **11**
William Tell, **14**

550 yds

500 meters

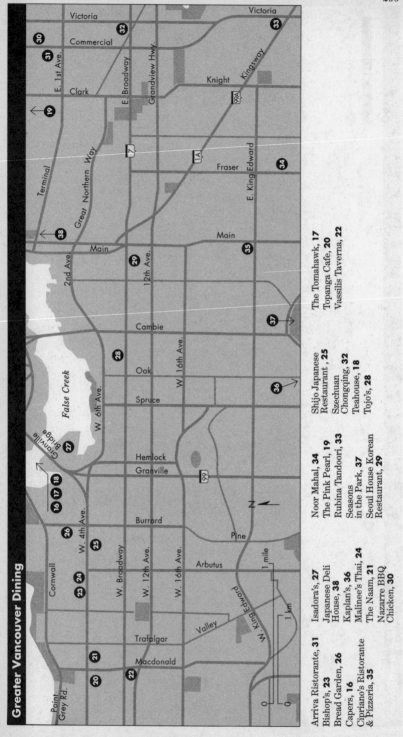

Greater Vancouver Dining

250

Arriva Ristorante, **31**
Bishop's, **23**
Bread Garden, **26**
Capers, **16**
Cipriano's Ristorante & Pizzeria, **35**

Isadora's, **27**
Japanese Deli House, **38**
Kaplan's, **36**
Malinee's Thai, **24**
The Naam, **21**
Nazarre BBQ Chicken, **30**

Noor Mahal, **34**
The Pink Pearl, **19**
Rubina Tandoori, **33**
Seasons in the Park, **37**
Seoul House Korean Restaurant, **29**

Shijo Japanese Restaurant, **25**
Szechuan Chongqing, **32**
Teahouse, **18**
Tojo's, **28**

The Tomahawk, **17**
Topanga Cafe, **20**
Vassilis Taverna, **22**

Cambodian/ Phnom Penh Restaurant. A block away from the bustle of
Vietnamese Keefer Street, the Phnom Penh is part of a small cluster of
★ Southeast Asian shops on the fringes of Chinatown. Simple,
pleasant decor abounds: arborite tables, potted plants, and
framed views of Ankor Wat on the walls. The hospitable staff
serves unusually robust Vietnamese fare, including crisp, peppery garlic prawns fried in the shell and slices of beef crusted
with ground salt and pepper mixed in the warm beef salad. The
decor in the new Broadway location is fancier and the food is
every bit as good as at East Georgia Street. *244 E. Georgia St.,
tel. 604/682–5777; 955 W. Broadway, tel. 604/734–8898. No reservations for lunch; reservations for 5 or more only for dinner.
Dress: casual. DC, MC. Closed Tues. Inexpensive.*

Chinese Kirin Mandarin Restaurant. Kirin, located two blocks from
★ most of the major downtown hotels, presents attentively
served Chinese food in posh, elegant surroundings. Live fish in
tanks set into the slate green walls remind one of aquariums
displayed in a lavishly decorated home. Drawn from a smattering of northern Chinese cuisines, dishes include Shanghai-style
smoked eel, Peking duck, and Szechuan hot-and-spicy scallops.
*1166 Alberni St., tel. 604/682–8833. Reservations advised.
Dress: neat but casual. AE, DC, MC, V. Moderate.*

★ **The Pink Pearl.** In the world of Cantonese restaurants, biggest
may very well be best: This 650-seat restaurant certainly wins
the prize in this city. The huge, noisy room features tanks of
live seafood—crab, shrimp, geoduck, oysters, abalone, rock
cod, lobsters, and scallops. Menu highlights include clams in
black bean sauce, crab sautéed with five spices (a spicy dish
sometimes translated as crab with peppery salt), and Pink
Pearl's version of crispy-skinned chicken. Arrive early for dim
sum on the weekend if you don't want to be caught in the lineup.
*1132 E. Hastings St., tel.604/253–4316. Reservations advised.
Dress: casual. AE, DC, MC, V. Inexpensive.*

Szechuan Chongqing. Although fancier Szechuan restaurants
can be found, the continued popularity of this unpretentious,
white tablecloth restaurant in a revamped fried chicken franchise speaks for itself. Try the Szechuan-style fried green
beans, steamed and tossed with spiced ground pork, or the
Chongqing chicken—a boneless chicken served on a bed of
spinach cooked in dry heat until crisp, giving it the texture of
dried seaweed and a salty, rich, and nutty taste. *2495 Victoria
Dr., tel. 604/254–7434. Reservations advised. Dress: casual.
AE, MC, V. Inexpensive.*

Continental Chartwell. Named after Sir Winston Churchill's country home
★ (a painting of which hangs over the green marble fireplace), the
flagship dining room at the Four Seasons Hotel (*see* Lodging,
below) looks like an upper-class British men's club. Floor-to-
ceiling dark wood paneling, deep leather chairs to sink back in
and sip claret, plus a quiet setting make this the city's top spot
for a power lunch. Chef Wolfgang von Weiser (formerly of the
Four Seasons in Toronto) cooks robust, inventive Continental
food. A salad of smoked loin of wild boar comes sprinkled with
hazelnuts; the seafood pot au feu is served with fennel bread
and aioli. Conclude the meal with port and Stilton. *791 W. Georgia St., tel. 604/689–9333. Reservations advised. Jacket
suggested. AE, DC, MC, V. Closed weekends for lunch.
Expensive.*

Seasons in the Park. Seasons has a commanding view over the
park gardens to the city lights and the mountains beyond. A

comfortable room with lots of light wood, white tablecloths, and deep-pile carpeting, this restaurant in Queen Elizabeth Park serves a conservative Continental menu with standards such as grilled salmon with fresh mint and roast duck with Bing cherry sauce. *Queen Elizabeth Park, tel. 604/874–8008. Reservations advised. Dress: neat but casual. AE, MC, V. Closed Christmas Day. Expensive.*

★ **The Teahouse Restaurant at Ferguson Point.** The best of the Stanley Park restaurants is perfectly poised for watching sunsets over the water, especially from its newer wing, a glassed-in room that conveys a conservatorylike ambience. Although the teahouse has a less innovative menu than its sister restaurant, Seasons in the Park, certain features, including the cream of carrot soup, duck in cassis, and the perfectly grilled fish, don't need any meddling. For dessert, there's baked Alaska—a natural for this restaurant. *Ferguson Point in Stanley Park, tel. 604/669–3281. Reservations required. Dress: neat but casual. AE, MC, V. Closed Christmas Day. Expensive.*

The William Tell. Silver underliners, embossed linen napkins, and a silver flower vase on each table set the tone of Swiss luxury. The William Tell's 28-year reputation for excellent Continental food continues at its quarters on the main floor of the Georgian Court Hotel, located 10 minutes from the central business district. Chef Pierre Dubrelle, a member of the gold medal–winning Canadian team at the 1988 Culinary Olympics, offers locally raised pheasant with glazed grapes and red wine sauce, sautéed veal sweetbreads with red onion marmalade and marsala sauce, and the Swiss specialty *Buendnerfleisch* (paper-thin slices of air-dried beef). Professional and discreet service contributes to the restaurant's excellence. *765 Beatty St., tel. 604/688–3504. Reservations advised. Jacket required at dinner. AE, DC, MC, V. Expensive.*

★ **English Bay Café.** Downstairs, the English Bay Café is a noisy bistro serving eggs Benedict, pasta, and fish specialties such as snapper or clam and sausage pasta. Upstairs, in the more serious dining room, you'll find the chef's fondness for venison and racks of lamb. Regardless of the level, however, when you look out the windows, it's all the same: With English Bay just two lanes of traffic away, you're guaranteed a glorious view of the sunset. Both bars are substantial; the bistro offers a large choice of imported beers. Valet parking is available and well worth the money. *1795 Beach Ave., tel. 604/669–2225. Reservations required. Dress: casual downstairs; neat but casual upstairs. AE, DC, MC, V. Moderate.*

Deli/Bakery **The Bread Garden Bakery, Café & Espresso Bar.** What began as a croissant bakery has taken over two neighboring stores and is now the ultimate Kitsilano 24-hour hangout. Salads, smoked salmon pizzas, quiches, elaborate cakes and pies, giant muffins, and cappuccino bring a steady stream of the young and fashionable. The Bread Garden To Go, next door, serves over-the-counter, but you may still be subjected to an irritatingly long wait in line; things just don't happen fast here. *1880 W. 1st Ave., tel. 604/ 738–6684; 812 Bute St., tel. 604/688–3213. No reservations. Dress: casual. MC, V. Inexpensive.*

★ **Kaplan's Deli, Restaurant and Bakery.** Tucked into a minimall on Oak Street (the road that leads to the Tsawwassen ferries and Seattle), Kaplan's is the traveler's last chance for authentic Jewish deli food before leaving town. Eat in at booths, or take your chopped liver, chopped herring, lox, and home-made corned beef with you. The bakery makes justly famous cinnamon buns. *5775 Oak St., tel. 604/263–2625. No reservations. Dress: casual. MC, V. Closed Jewish holidays. Inexpensive.*

East Indian **Rubina Tandoori.** If one must single out the best East Indian
★ food in the city, then Rubina Tandoori, 20 minutes from downtown, ranks as a top contender. The large menu spans most of the subcontinent's cuisines, and the especially popular *chevda* (East Indian salty snack) gets shipped to fans all over North America. Maître d' Shaffeen Jamal has a phenomenal memory for faces. Nonsmokers get the smaller, funkier back room with the paintings of coupling gods and goddesses; smokers get the big, upholstered banquettes in the new room. *1962 Kingsway, tel. 604/874–3621. Reservations advised on weekends. Dress: casual. MC, V. Closed lunch and Sun. Moderate.*

Noor Mahal. The only Lower Mainland restaurant that specializes in South Indian food, the Noor Mahal provides good-size portions at a reasonable price in authentic surroundings. The pink walls help to create the light and airy decor. Try a *dosa*—a lacy pancake made from bean, rice, and semolina flour, stuffed with curried potatoes, shrimp, or chicken—for lunch. Owners Susan and Paul Singh double as staff, so service can be slow and harried during busy periods. *4354 Fraser St., tel. 604/873–9263. Reservations advised on weekends. Dress: casual. AE, MC, V. Closed lunch. Inexpensive.*

French **Le Gavroche.** Time has stood still in this charming turn-of-the-
★ century house, where a woman dining with a man will be offered a menu without prices. Featuring classic French cooking, lightened—but by no means reduced—to nouvelle cuisine, Le Gavroche's menu also includes simple listings such as smoked salmon with blinis and sour cream. Other options may be as complex as smoked pheasant breast on a puree of celeriac, shallots, and wine with a light truffle sauce. The excellent wine list stresses Bordeaux. No reservations are necessary after 9:30, when the late-dessert menu is offered. Tables by the front window promise mountains and water views. *1616 Alberni St., tel. 604/685–3924. Reservations advised on weekends. Jacket and tie advised. AE, MC, V. Closed lunch, Sun., and holidays. Expensive.*

Chez Thierry. This cozy bistro on the Stanley Park end of Robson Street adds pizzazz to a celebration: Owner Thierry Damilano stylishly slashes open champagne bottles with a sword on request. The country-style French cooking emphasizes seafood. Try watercress and smoked salmon salad; fresh tuna grilled with artichokes, garlic, and tomatoes; and apple tarte Tatin for dessert. During the week the intimate dining room promises a relaxing meal; on the weekend, however, with every one of the 16 tables jammed, the restaurant gets noisy. *1674 Robson St., tel. 604/688–0919. Reservations required on weekends. Dress: casual. AE, DC, MC, V. Closed lunch and Dec. 24–26. Moderate.*

★ **Le Crocodile.** Why do people want to sit packed tighter than sardines in this tiny bistro? Because chef Michael Jacob serves extremely well cooked, simple food at very moderate prices. His Alsatian background shines with the caramelly, sweet onion tart. Anything that involves innards is superb, and even old standards such as duck à l'orange are worth ordering here. The one flaw? A small, overpriced wine list. *909 Burrard St., tel. 604/669–4298. Reservations required. Dress casual. AE, DC, MC, V. Closed Sat. lunch and Sun. Moderate.*

Greek **Vassilis Taverna.** The menu in this family-run restaurant, located in the heart of the city's small Greek community, is almost as conventional as the decor: checked tablecloths and mandatory paintings of white fishing villages and the blue Aegean Sea. At Vassilis, though, even standards become memorable due to the flawless preparation. The house specialty is a deceptively simple *kotopoulo* (a half-chicken, pounded flat, herbed, and charbroiled); the lamb fricassee with artichoke hearts and broad beans in an egg-lemon sauce is more complicated, though not necessarily better. Save room for a *navarino*, a creamy custard square topped with whipped cream and ground nuts. *2884 W. Broadway, tel. 604/733–3231. Reservations advised on weekends. Dress: casual. AE, DC, MC, V. Closed Mon. and lunch Sat. and Sun. Moderate.*

Health Food **Capers.** Hidden in the back of the most lavishly handsome
★ health food store in the Lower Mainland, Capers (open for breakfast, lunch, and dinner) drips with earth-mother chic: wood tables, potted plants, and heady smells from the store's bakery. Breakfast starts weekdays at 7:30, weekends at 8. Eggs and bacon? Sure, but Capers serves free-range eggs, as well as bacon without additives. Feather-light blueberry pancakes crammed with berries star here. The view of the water compensates for service that can be slow and forgetful. *2496 Marine Dr., W. Vancouver, tel. 604/925–3316. No reservations. Dress: casual. MC, V. Closed dinner Sun. Inexpensive.*
The Naam Restaurant. Vancouver's oldest alternative restaurant is now open 24 hours, so those needing to satisfy a late-night tofu burger craving, rest easy. The Naam has left its caffeine- and alcohol-free days behind and now serves wine, beer, cappuccino, and wicked chocolate desserts, along with the vegetarian stir-fries. Wood tables and kitchen chairs make for a homey atmosphere. On warm summer evenings, the outdoor courtyard at the back of the restaurant welcomes diners. *2724 W. 4th Ave., tel. 604/738–7151. Reservations required for 6 or more. Dress: casual. MC, V. Inexpensive.*

Italian **Caffe de Medici.** It takes shifting gears as you leave the stark
★ concrete walls of the Robson Galleria behind and step into this elegant restaurant with its ornate molded ceilings, rich green velvet curtains and chair coverings, and portraits of the de Medici family. But after a little wine, an evening's exposure to courtly waiters, and a superb meal, you may begin to wish the outside world conformed more closely to this peaceful environment. Although an enticing antipasto table sits in the center of the room, consider the *Bresaola* (air-dried beef marinated in olive oil, lemon, and pepper) as a worthwhile appetizer. Try the rack of lamb in a mint, mustard, and Martini & Rossi sauce. Any of the pastas is a safe bet. *1025 Robson St., tel. 604/669–9322. Reservations advised. Jacket advised. AE, DC, MC, V. Closed lunch Sat. and Sun. Expensive.*
Il Giardino di Umberto, Umberto's. First came Umberto's, a Florentine restaurant serving classic northern Italian food, installed in a century-old Vancouver home at the foot of Hornby Street. Then, next door, Umberto Menghi built Il Giardino, a sunny, light-splashed restaurant styled after a Tuscan house. This restaurant features braided breast of pheasant with polenta and reindeer fillet with crushed peppercorn sauce. Il Giardino attracts a regular young, moneyed crowd, while Umberto's is more quiet and sedate. Fish is treated either Italian style—rainbow trout grilled and served with sun-dried to-

matoes, black olives, and pine-nuts—or with a taste of the Far East, as in yellow-fin tuna grilled with wasabi butter. *Il Giardino, 1382 Hornby St., tel. 604/669–2422. Umberto's, 1380 Hornby St., tel. 604/687–6316. Reservations advised. Dress: neat but casual. AE, DC, MC, V. Umberto's closed lunch and Sun., Mon. Il Giardino closed lunch Sat. and Sun. Expensive.*

Arriva Ristorante. Commercial Drive Italian restaurants, like Chinese restaurants in Chinatown, are best looked at with a skeptical eye. The best of the breed are elsewhere, and what's left is often found cranking out North Americanized travesties of the home country's food. Arriva is one Little Italy restaurant that's worth the drive, and it's a welcome find if you've spent the day shopping in Italian groceries. There's a version of spaghetti and meatballs on the menu, ziti with spicy squid sauce, and a fusili with wild game—"Bambi and Bugs Bunny," as the waiters have affectionately coined it. The antipasto plate includes a heaping order of octopus, shrimp, roasted red peppers, cheese, sausage, and fat lima beans in an herby marinade. Don't miss the orange sherbet served in a hollowed-out orange for dessert. *1537 Commercial Dr., tel. 604/251–1177. Reservations advised. Dress: casual. AE, DC, MC, V. Closed lunch Sat. and Sun. Moderate.*

Cipriano's Ristorante & Pizzeria. Formerly a Greek pizza parlor, Cipriano's has been transformed into an Italian restaurant, with green-white-and-red walls representing the Italian flag, Mama-mia!—inexpensive and hearty Italian food is the mainstay here, including good pizza, even better pasta, and the "Pappa" lasagna. *3995 Main St., tel. 604/879–0020. Reservations accepted. Dress: casual. V. Closed lunch and Mon. Inexpensive.*

Japanese ★ **Tojo's.** Hidekazu Tojo is a sushi-making legend here. His handsome blond-wood tatami rooms, on the second floor of a new green-glass tower in the hospital district on West Broadway, provide proper ambience for intimate dining, but Tojo's 10-seat sushi bar stands as the centerpiece. With Tojo presiding, it is a convivial place for dinner and offers a ringside seat for watching the creation of edible art. Although tempura and teriyaki dinners will satisfy, the seasonal menu is more exciting. In October, ask for *dobbin mushi,* a soup made from pine mushrooms that's served in a teapot. In spring, try sushi made from scallops and pink cherry blossoms. *777 W. Broadway, No. 202, tel. 604/872–8050. Reservations advised on weekends. Dress: neat but casual. AE, DC, MC, V. Closed lunch and Sun.; Dec. 24–26. Expensive.*

Chiyoda. The robata bar curves like an oversize sushi bar through Chiyoda's main room: On one side are the customers and an array of flat baskets full of the day's offerings; on the other side are the robata chefs and grills. There are 35 choices of things to grill, from squid, snapper, and oysters to eggplant, mushrooms, onions, and potatoes. The finished dishes, dressed with sake, soy, or *ponzu* sauce, are dramatically passed over on the end of a long wooden paddle. If Japanese food means only sushi and tempura to you, check this out. *1050 Alberni St., tel. 604/688–5050. Reservations accepted. Dress: casual. AE, MC, V. Closed lunch Sat. and Sun.; closed Sun. off-season. Moderate.*

Shijo Japanese Restaurant. Shijo has an excellent and very large sushi bar, a smaller robata bar, tatami rooms, and a row of tables overlooking bustling Fourth Avenue. The epitome of modern urban Japanese chic is conveyed through the jazz music, handsome lamps with a patinated bronze finish, and lots of black wood. Count on creatively prepared sushi, eggplant *dengaku* topped with light and dark miso paste and broiled, and shiitake *foil yaki* (fresh shiitake mushrooms cooked in foil with *ponzu* sauce). *1926 W. 4th Ave., tel. 604/732–4676. Reservations advised. Dress: casual. AE, MC, V. Closed lunch, Sat. and Sun. Moderate.*

Japanese Deli House. The least expensive sushi in town is served in this high-ceilinged room on the main floor of a turn-of-the-century building on Powell Street, once the heart of Vancouver's Japantown. Along with the standard sushi-bar menu, Japanese Deli House makes a pungent but tender, hot ginger squid appetizer from baby squid caught off the Thai coast, and a geoduck appetizer in mayonnaise worth wandering off the beaten path for. The food is especially fresh and good if you can make it an early lunch: Nigiri sushi and sushi rolls are made at 11 AM for the 11:30 opening. *381 Powell St., tel. 604/681–6484. No reservations. Dress: casual. No credit cards. Closed lunch Mon. Inexpensive.*

Korean   **Seoul House Korean Restaurant.** The shining star in a desperately ugly section of East Broadway, Seoul House is a bright restaurant, decorated in Japanese style, that serves a full menu of Japanese and Korean food. The best bet is the Korean barbecue, which you cook at your table. A barbecue dinner of marinated beef, pork, chicken, or fish comes complete with a half dozen side dishes—*kim chee* (Korea's national pickle), salads, stir-fried rice, and pickled vegetables—as well as soup and rice. Service can be chaotic in this very popular restaurant. *36 E. Broadway, tel. 604/874–4131. Reservations advised. Dress: casual. MC, V. Closed lunch Sun. Inexpensive.*

Mexican   **Topanga Cafe.** Arrive before 6:30 or after 8 PM to avoid waiting in line for this 40-seat Kitsilano classic. The California-Mexican food hasn't changed much in the 15 years the Topanga has been dishing up fresh salsa and homemade tortilla chips. Quantities are still huge and prices are low. Kids can color blank menu covers while waiting for food; a hundred or more of the clientele's best efforts are framed and on the walls. *2904 4th Ave., tel. 604/ 733–3713. No reservations. Dress: casual. MC, V. Closed Sun. Inexpensive.*

Nouvelle   **Bishop's.** John Bishop established Vancouver's most influential
★   restaurant eight years ago, serving a variety of cuisines from northern Italian to nouvelle and East–West crossover. Penne with grilled eggplant, roasted peppers, and basil pasta cohabit the menu with marinated loin of lamb with ginger and sesame. The small white rooms—their only ornament some splashy, expressionist paintings—are favored by Pierre Trudeau and by Robert De Niro when he's on location in Vancouver. *2183 W. 4th Ave., tel. 604/738–2025. Reservations required. Dress: casual. AE, DC, MC, V. Closed 1st week in Jan., lunch Sat. and Sun. Expensive.*

Pacific Northwest   **Quilicum.** Only a few blocks from English Bay, this downstairs "longhouse" serves the original Northwest Coast cuisine: bannock bread, baked sweet potato with hazelnuts, alder-grilled salmon, and soap-berries for dessert. Try the authentic but odd dish—oolichan grease—that's prepared from candlefish. Native music is piped in, and Northwest Coast masks (for sale) peer out from the walls. *1724 Davie St., tel. 604/681–7044. Res-*

*ervations advised. Dress: casual. AE, MC, V. Closed lunch
Sat.–Tues. Moderate.*

★ **The Raintree.** This cool, spacious restaurant offers a local menu and wine list; the latter won a 1988 award from the *Wine Spectator* for its British Columbia, Washington, and Oregon choices. Raintree bakes its own bread, makes luxurious soups, and has pumped-up old favorites such as a slab of apple pie for dessert. With main courses, which change daily depending on market availability, the kitchen teeters between willfully eccentric and exceedingly simple. Specials could include either Queen Charlotte abalone and side-stripe shrimps stir-fried with scallions and spinach in chamomile essence, or grilled lamb chops with a mint and pear puree. Leon's Bar and Grill, on the ground floor, stocks local beers and a respectable number of single malt scotches. The pub-food menu, under the direction of chef Marion Dobson, includes organic-beef burgers and vegetarian chili. The $14 fixed-price Sunday brunch features ricotta and apple-stuffed French toast, sockeye salmon hash, and apricot-hazelnut pancakes, plus several other courses. *1630 Alberni St., tel. 604/688–5570. Reservations advised on weekends. Dress: casual. AE, DC, MC, V. Closed lunch Sat. and Dec. 24–26. Moderate.*

The Tomahawk. North Vancouver was mostly trees 66 years ago, when the Tomahawk first opened. Over the years, the original hamburger stand grew and mutated into part Northwest Coast Indian kitsch museum, part gift shop, and part restaurant. Renowned for its Yukon breakfast—five slices of back bacon, two eggs, hash browns, and toast—the Tomahawk also serves gigantic muffins, excellent French toast, and pancakes. The menu switches to oysters, trout, and burgers named after Indian chiefs for lunch and dinner. *1550 Philip Ave., tel. 604/988–2612. No reservations. Dress: casual. AE, MC, V. Inexpensive.*

Seafood **Olympia Fish Market and Oyster Co. Ltd.** Some of the city's best fish-and-chips are fried in this tiny shop located behind a fish store in the middle of the Robson Street shopping district. The choice is halibut, cod, prawns, calamari, and whatever's on special in the store, served with genuine—never frozen—french fries. *1094 Robson St., tel. 604/685–0716. No reservations. Dress: casual. DC, V. Inexpensive.*

Thai **Malinee's Thai.** The city's most consistently interesting Thai
★ food can be found in this typically Southeast Asian–style room, tapestries adorning the walls. The owners, two Canadians who lived several years in Thailand, can give you detailed descriptions of every dish on the menu. Steamed fish with ginger, pickled plums, and red chili sauce is on the regular menu; a steamed whole red snapper marinated in oyster sauce, ginger, cilantro, red pepper, and lime juice is a special worth ordering when available. *2153 W. 4th Ave., tel. 604/737–0097. Reservations advised. Dress: casual. AE, DC, MC, V. Closed lunch. Moderate.*

Lodging

Lodging has become a major business for Vancouver, a fairly young city that hosts a lot of Asian businesspeople who are used to an above-average level of service. Although by some standards pricey, properties here are highly competitive, and you can expect the service to reflect this trend.

Highly recommended lodgings in each price category are indicated by a star ★.

Category	Cost*
Very Expensive	over $180
Expensive	$120–$180
Moderate	$80–$119
Inexpensive	under $80

All prices are for a standard double room for two, excluding 10% provincial accommodation tax, 15% service charge, and 7% GST. Non-Canadians are eligible for a rebate on the GST paid for hotel accommodations.

Very Expensive   **Four Seasons.** This 28-story hotel is adjacent to the Vancouver Stock Exchange and is attached to the Pacific Centre shopping mall. Standard rooms are not large; corner deluxe or deluxe Four Seasons rooms are recommended. Expect tasteful and stylish decor in the rooms and hallways, providing a calm mood despite the bustling hotel. A huge sun deck and indoor-outdoor pool are part of the complete health club facilities. Service is outstanding, and the Four Seasons has all the amenities. The formal dining room, Chartwell (*see* Dining, above), is one of the best in the city. *791 W. Georgia St., V6C 2T4, tel. 604/689–9333; in Canada, 800/268–6282; in the U.S., 800/332–3442; fax 604/844–6744. 317 doubles, 68 suites. Facilities: restaurant, café, bars, indoor-outdoor pool, sun deck, weight room, aerobics classes, sauna, Jacuzzi, ping-pong. AE, DC, MC, V.*

★ **Le Meridien.** The Meridien feels more like an exclusive guest house than a large hotel. The lobby has sumptuously thick carpets, enormous displays of flowers, and a newsstand situated discreetly down the hall. The rooms are even better, furnished with rich, dark wood in a style that is reminiscent of 19th-century France. Despite the size of this hotel, the Meridien in Vancouver has achieved and maintained a level of intimacy and exclusivity. The **Café Fleuri** serves the best Sunday brunch in town (plus a chocolate buffet on Thursday, Friday, and Saturday evenings), and **Gerard,** a formal French restaurant, is a special-occasion place. The bar has lots of leather, dark wood, wingback chairs, and a fireplace. *845 Burrard St., V6Z 2K6, tel. 604/682–5511 or 800/543–4300, fax 604/682–2926. 350 doubles, 47 suites. Facilities: restaurant, café, bar, business center, rooms for the disabled, health club with pool, Jacuzzi, sauna, steam room, tanning bed, masseur, hairdresser, weights, exercise equipment, adjoining apartment hotel. AE, DC, MC, V.*

★ **Pan Pacific.** Canada Place sits on a pier right by the financial district and houses the luxurious Pan Pacific Hotel (built in 1986 for the Expo), the Vancouver Trade and Convention Centre, and a cruise ship terminal. The lobby has a dramatic three-

Vancouver Lodging

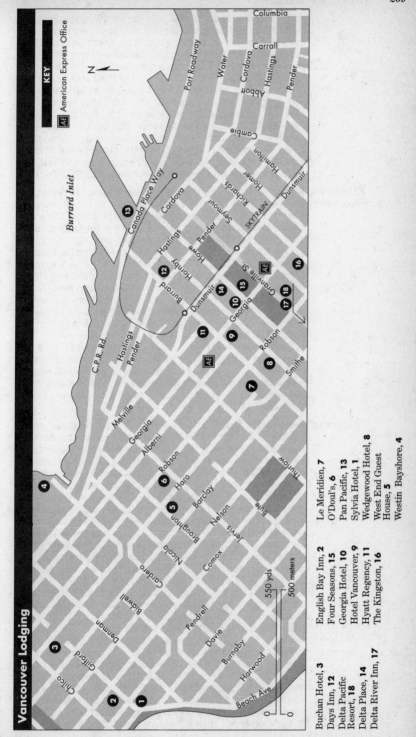

KEY

AE American Express Office

Burrard Inlet

Columbia

Carrall

Water

Cordova

Hastings

Pender

Abbott

Cambie

Hamilton

Port Roadway

Canada Place Way

Cordova

Homer

Richards

Dunsmuir

SKYTRAIN

Seymour

Hastings

Pender

Howe

Hornby

Dunsmuir

Granville St.

Georgia

Robson

Smithe

Burrard

C.P.R. Rd.

Hastings

Pender

Melville

Georgia

Alberni

Robson

Haro

Barclay

Nelson

Comox

Thurlow

Bute

Jervis

Broughton

Nicola

Cardero

Bidwell

Denman

Gilford

Chilco

Pendrell

Davie

Burnaby

Harwood

Beach Ave.

550 yds

500 meters

Buchan Hotel, **3**

Days Inn, **12**

Delta Pacific
Resort, **18**

Delta Place, **14**

Delta River Inn, **17**

English Bay Inn, **2**

Four Seasons, **15**

Georgia Hotel, **10**

Hotel Vancouver, **9**

Hyatt Regency, **11**

The Kingston, **16**

Le Meridien, **7**

O'Doul's, **6**

Pan Pacific, **13**

Sylvia Hotel, **1**

Wedgewood Hotel, **8**

West End Guest
House, **5**

Westin Bayshore, **4**

story atrium with a waterfall, and the lounge, restaurant, and café all have huge expanses of glass, so that you are rarely without a harbor view or mountain backdrop. Earthtones and Japanese detail give the rooms an understated elegance. Make sure you get a room that looks out on the water. The health club has a $15 fee that's well worth the price. The Pan Pacific is a grand, luxurious, busy hotel, but it is not a pick for an intimate weekend getaway. *300–999 Canada Pl., V6C 3B5, tel. 604/662–3223; in Canada, 800/663–1515; in the U.S., 800/937–1515; fax 604/685–8690. 468 doubles, 40 suites. Facilities: 3 restaurants, bar, health club with indoor track, sauna, steam room, state-of-the-art aerobics equipment, weights, massage and Shiatsu, sports lounge with wide-screen TV, squash, racquetball, and paddle-tennis courts, heated outdoor pool. AE, DC, MC, V.*

Expensive– Very Expensive **Westin Bayshore.** This hotel is the closest thing to a resort that you'll find in the downtown area. Because the Bayshore is perched right on the best part of the harbor, because it is a five-minute walk from Stanley Park, because of the truly fabulous view, and because of its huge outdoor pool, sun deck, and grassy areas, it is the perfect place to stay during the summer, especially for a family. The tower is the newer section, so rooms there are better furnished and larger and offer the best view of the water. The café is okay, but avoid the dining room, Trader Vic's; you can do much better at several neighborhood restaurants. People commuting from Seattle via Lake Union Air (downtown-to-downtown service) will find it handy that the floatplanes land at the Bayshore. *1601 W. Georgia St., V6G 2V4, tel. 604/682–3377 or 800/228–3000; fax 604/691–6959. 481 doubles, 38 suites, 2 floors for the disabled. Facilities: restaurant, café, bars, free shuttle service downtown, bicycle rentals, marina with fishing and sailing charters, health club with indoor and outdoor pools, Jacuzzi, sun deck, masseur, sauna, pool table. AE, DC, MC, V.*

Expensive **Delta Pacific Resort.** It's not a view or a shoreline that makes this place (five minutes from the airport) a resort, it's the facilities on the 12-acre site: three swimming pools (one indoor), four all-year tennis courts with a pro (matching list for partners), an outdoor fitness circuit, squash courts, aqua-exercise classes, outdoor volleyball nets, golf practice nets, a play center for children, summer camps for 5- to 12-year-olds, and a playground. In spite of the hotel's enormity, the atmosphere is casual and friendly. There are two guest-room towers and a few low-rise buildings for convention facilities. The rooms are nothing special, but all the extras and the hotel's proximity to the airport make it worthwhile. The Japanese restaurant is expensive and all show. *10251 St. Edwards Dr., V6X 2M9, tel. 604/278–9611; in Canada, 800/268–1133; in the U.S., 800/877–1133; fax 604/276–1122. 460 doubles, 4 suites. Facilities: restaurant, café, bar, shuttle to airport and shopping center, meeting rooms. AE, DC, MC, V.*

Delta Place. This 18-story hotel was built in 1985 by the luxurious Hong Kong Mandarin chain but was sold to Delta Hotels in 1987. The rates have gone down but the surroundings have not changed. The lobby is restrained and tasteful—one has to look for the registration desk. A slight Oriental theme is given to the deluxe furnishings, and dark, rich mahogany is everywhere. Most rooms have small balconies, and the studio suites are recommended since they are much roomier and only slightly more expensive than a standard room. The business center has secretarial services, workstations, cellular phones for rent, and small meeting rooms. The restaurant and bar are adequate and the location is perfect; the business and shopping district is a five-minute walk away. *645 Howe St., V6C 2Y9, tel. 604/687–1122; in Canada, 800/268–1133; in the U.S., 800/877–1133; fax 604/643–7267. 181 doubles, 16 suites. Facilities: restaurant, bar, squash and racquetball courts, lap pool, weight room. AE, DC, MC, V.*

Delta River Inn. This hotel, on the edge of the Fraser River, is two minutes from the airport. Rooms on the south side get the best view. Although renovations began in 1990, the River Inn still has a way to go to compete with others in the price range. The rooms do not have the style and pizzazz that some have. All the dark wood in the hotel gives it an out-of-date feel, but the hotel is convenient. The marina attached to the hotel organizes fishing charters. Food does not seem to be a priority with Delta. *3500 Cessena Dr., V7B 1C7, tel. 604/278–1241; in Canada, 800/268–1133; in the U.S., 800/877–1133; fax 604/276–1975. 410 doubles, 6 suites. Facilities: jogging route, outdoor pool, free shuttle to airport, shopping center, and extensive health club at the nearby Delta Pacific Resort. AE, DC, MC, V.*

★ **Hotel Vancouver.** The Hotel Vancouver, built in 1939 by the Canadian National Railway, is a grand old lady of the château-style hotels that appear in Canadian cities. It commands a regal position in the center of things across from the fountains of the art gallery. Standard rooms are nothing special but are decorated in a more classic style than those of the Hyatt or the Four Seasons. But the hotel has a category called Entré Gold: two floors with all the extra services and amenities. Entré Gold suites have a luxurious amount of space, French doors, graceful wingback chairs, and fine mahogany furniture. The style and elegance of the Hotel Vancouver leave their mark here. The hotel's restaurants and bars are adequate. *900 W. Georgia St., V6C 2W6, tel. 604/684–3131; in Ontario and Québec, 800/268–9420; rest of Canada, 800/268–9411; in the U.S., 800/828–7447; fax 604/662–1929. 466 doubles, 42 suites, rooms for the disabled. Facilities: 2 restaurants, 2 bars, two-line telephones, health club with lap pool, exercise machines, tanning bed, sun deck. AE, DC, MC, V.*

Hyatt Regency. The perfectly located, 18-year-old Hyatt has just completed an $11 million renovation. The Hyatt's standard rooms are the largest in the city and are decorated in deep, dramatic colors and dark wood. Ask for a corner room with a balcony on the north or west side. The lobby, however, can't escape the feel of a large convention hotel. For a small fee, the Regency Club gives you the exclusivity of three floors accessed by keyed elevators, your own concierge, a private lounge with a stereo and large TV, complimentary breakfast, 5 PM hors d'oeuvres, and evening pastries. Robes and special toiletries are also in the Regency Club rooms. For a hotel restaurant, Fish & Co. is unusual in that the room is casual, the atmosphere fun, and the food good. The Gallery Lounge is one of the most pleasant in town. Health club facilities are available, but they leave much to be desired. *655 Burrard St., V6C 2R7, tel. 604/687–6543 or 800/233–1234, fax 604/689–3707. 612 doubles, 34 suites. Facilities: restaurant, café, 2 bars, health club. AE, DC, MC, V.*

O'Doul's. Set on a lively street with loads of shops and restaurants, this hotel is a five-minute walk from either the heart of downtown or Stanley Park. It's a great location if you're traveling with teenagers who want time on their own. It was built in

1986 in a long, low style and feels like a very deluxe motel. The rooms are what you'd expect from any mid-range hotel, with modern decor and pastel color schemes, but the place is very well maintained. The deluxe rooms (with king-size beds) face Robson Street and are worth the price, especially offseason, when rates plummet. *1300 Robson St., V6E 1C5, tel. 604/684–8461 or 800/663–5491, fax 604/684–8326. 119 doubles, 11 suites. Facilities: 3 telephones in every room, pool, Jacuzzi, steam rooms, exercise machines. AE, DC, MC, V.*

★ **Wedgewood Hotel.** This hotel upholds its reputation for being a small, elegant hotel run by an owner who fervently cares about her guests. The intimate lobby is decorated in fine detail with polished brass, a fireplace, and tasteful artwork. All the extra touches are here, too: nightly turndown service, afternoon ice delivery, dark-out drapes, flowers growing on the balcony, terry-cloth robes, and morning newspaper. No tour groups or conventions stop here; the Wedgewood's clients are almost exclusively corporate, except on weekends, when the place turns into a honeymoon retreat. Health facilities are next door at the excellent Chancery Squash Club. The lounge and restaurant couldn't be better. It's a treasure. *845 Hornby St., V6Z 1V1, tel. 604/689–7777 or 800/663–0666, fax 604/688–3074. 60 doubles, 33 suites. Facilities: 2 restaurants, bar, use of the adjacent Chancery Squash Club with 7 squash courts, weight room, aerobics, sauna, and whirlpool. AE, DC, MC, V.*

Moderate **Days Inn.** For the businessperson looking for a bargain, this location is tops. The six-story, 72-year-old Days Inn (formerly the Abbotsford) is the only moderately priced hotel in the business core, and recent renovations of the guest rooms and the lobby have made this accommodation even more agreeable. This is a basic accommodation, but rooms are bright, clean, and functional. Standard rooms are very large, but there is no room service and few amenities. Suites 310, 410, 510, and 610 have a harbor view. The bar, the **Bombay Bicycle Club,** is a favorite with businesspeople. *921 W. Pender St., V6C 1M2, tel. 604/681–4335, fax 604/681–7808. 74 doubles, 11 suites. Facilities: restaurant, 2 bars, free overnight parking. AE, DC, MC, V.*

★ **English Bay Inn.** The English Bay Inn, in a newly renovated 1930s Tudor house, is one block from the ocean and Stanley Park in a quiet residential part of the West End. The five small guest rooms—each with private bath—have wonderful sleigh beds with matching armoires, Ralph Lauren linen, and alabaster lighting fixtures. The common areas are generous and elegantly furnished: The sophisticated but cozy parlor has wingback chairs, a fireplace, and French doors opening onto the front garden. A small, sunny English country garden graces the back of the inn. Breakfast is served in a rather formal dining room furnished with a Gothic dining room suite, a fireplace, and an 18th-century grandfather clock. *1968 Comox St., V6G 1R4, tel. 604/683–8002. 5 rooms. Facilities: off-street parking. AE, MC, V.*

★ **Georgia Hotel.** Across from the Four Seasons, the Georgia is a five-minute walk from the business district. This handsome 12-story hotel, built in 1927, has such Old World features as an oak-paneled lobby, ornate brass elevators, and a subdued, genteel atmosphere. Although it's lacking in special amenities, the Georgia is a reliable and satisfactory deal. Rooms are small but well furnished, with nothing worn around the edges. Executive rooms have an almost separate seating area. Rooms facing the art gallery have the best views. *801 W. Georgia St., V6C 1P7, tel. 604/682–5566 or 800/663–1111, fax 604/682–8192. 310 doubles, 4 suites. Facilities: restaurant, 3 bars. AE, DC, MC, V.*

★ **West End Guest House.** The bright-pink exterior of this delightful Victorian house may throw you: The gracious front parlor with its early 1900s furniture and fireplace is more indicative of the charm of the place. Most of the small but extraordinarily handsome rooms have high brass beds, antiques, gorgeous linen, and dozens of old framed pictures of Vancouver. Avoid the basement rooms. All rooms have phones, TVs, and new bathrooms. There's a veranda for people watching, and a back deck for sunbathing. A full breakfast is included and can be served in bed. The inn's genial host, Evan Penner, has learned that it is the little things that make the difference, including a predinner glass of sherry, duvets and feather mattress-pads, and a pantry where guests can help themselves to tea or snacks. The inn is in a residential neighborhood that is a 15-minute walk from downtown and Stanley Park and two minutes from Robson Street. This is a nonsmoking establishment. *1362 Haro St., V6E 1G2, tel. 604/681–2889, fax 604/688–8812. 7 rooms. Facilities: off-street parking. AE, MC, V.*

Inexpensive **Buchan Hotel.** This three-story 1930s building is conveniently
★ set in a tree-lined residential street a block from Stanley Park, a block from shops and restaurants on Denman Street, and a 15-minute walk from the liveliest part of Robson Street. The hallways appear a bit institutional, but the rooms are bright and clean. Furnishings, in good condition, consist of a color TV and a wood-grained arborite desk and chest of drawers. The rooms are small and the bathrooms tiny. None of the rooms have phones and you have to park on the street, but with this location you probably won't use your car much. Rooms on the east side are brightest and overlook a park; front corner rooms are the biggest. A popular restaurant with an eclectic menu is in the basement and is open for dinner. *1906 Haro St., V6G 1H7, tel. 604/685–5354, fax 604/685–5367. 60 rooms, 30 with private bath. Facilities: TV lounge, laundry room. AE, DC, MC, V.*

The Kingston. The Kingston is a small budget hotel in a location convenient for shopping. It is an old-style, four-story hotel, with no elevator—the type of establishment you'd find in Europe. The Spartan rooms are small and immaculate and share a bathroom down the hall. All rooms have phones but no TVs. Rooms on the south side are brighter. Continental breakfast is included. *757 Richards St., V6B 3A6, tel. 604/684–9024, fax 604/684–9917. 60 rooms, 7 with bath. Facilities: sauna, coin-op laundry, TV lounge, free nighttime parking. AE, MC, V.*

★ **Sylvia Hotel.** Perhaps the Sylvia Hotel is the best bargain in Vancouver, but don't count on staying here June–August unless you've booked six months ahead. What makes this hotel so popular are its low rates and near-perfect location: about 25 feet from the beach, 200 feet from Stanley Park, and a 20-minute walk from downtown. Vancouverites are particularly fond of the eight-story ivy-covered brick building—it was once the tallest building in the West End and the first to open a cocktail bar in the city, in 1954. It's part of the local history and was declared a protected heritage building in the 1970s. Rooms are unadorned and have basic plain furnishings that have probably been around for more than 20 years—not much to look at, but the view and price make it worthwhile. Suites are huge, and all have kitchens, making this a perfect family accommodation. There is little difference between the old and new wings. *1154 Gilford St., V6G 2P6, tel. 604/681–9321. 97 doubles, 18 suites. Facilities: restaurant, lounge, parking. AE, DC, MC, V.*

The Arts and Nightlife

For information on events, look in the entertainment section of the *Vancouver Sun;* also, Thursday's paper has complete listings in the **"What's On"** column, and there's the **Arts Hotline** (tel. 604/684–ARTS). For tickets to major events, book through **Ticketmaster** (tel. 604/280–3311).

The Arts

Theater The **Vancouver Playhouse** (Hamilton St., tel. 604/872–6622) is the most established venue in Vancouver. The **Arts Club Theatre** (tel. 604/687–1644), with two stages on Granville Island (1585 Johnston St.) and performances all year, is the most active. Both feature mainstream theatrical shows. **Carousel Theater** (tel. 604/669–3410), which performs off-off Broadway shows at the Waterfront Theatre (1405 Anderson St.) on Granville Island, and **Touchstone** (tel. 604/687–8737), at the Firehall Theater (280 E. Cordova St.), are smaller but lively companies. The **Back Alley Theatre** (751 Thurlow St., tel. 604/688–7013) hosts **Theatresports,** a hilarious improv event. The **Vancouver East Cultural Centre** (1895 Venables St., tel. 604/254–9578) is a multipurpose performance space that always hosts high-caliber shows.

Music The **Vancouver Symphony Orchestra** (tel. 604/684–9100) and the **CBC Orchestra** (tel. 604/662–6000) play at the restored **Orpheum Theatre** (601 Smithe St.). Choral groups like the **Bach Choir** (tel. 604/921–8012), the **Cantata Singers** (no tel.), and the **Vancouver Chamber Choir** (tel. 604/738–6822) play a major role in Vancouver's classical music scene. The **Early Music Society** (tel. 604/732–1610) performs medieval, renaissance, and baroque music throughout the year and hosts the summer concerts of the most important Early Music Festival in North America. Concerts by the **Friends of Chamber Music** (no tel.) and the **Vancouver Recital Society** (tel. 604/736–6034) are always of excellent quality.

Vancouver Opera (tel. 604/682–2871) stages four productions a year, usually in October, January, March, and May, at the **Queen Elizabeth Theatre** (600 Hamilton St.). Productions are high caliber with both local and imported talent.

Dance Watch for **Ballet BC's Dance Alive!** series, presenting visiting or local ballet companies (from the Kirov to Ballet BC). Most performances by these companies can be seen at the Orpheum or the Queen Elizabeth Theatre (*see* above). Local modern dance companies worth seeing are **Karen Jamison, Judith Marcuse,** and **JumpStart.**

Film Two theaters have distinguished themselves by avoiding the regular movie fare: **The Ridge** (3131 Arbutus St., tel. 604/738–6311), which generally plays foreign films and rerun double-bills, and **Pacific Cinématèque** (1131 Howe St., tel. 604/688–3456), which goes for even more esoteric foreign and art films. The **Vancouver International Film Festival** (tel. 604/685–0260) is held in September and October in several theaters around town.

Nightlife

Bars and Lounges The **Gérard Lounge** (845 Burrard St., tel. 604/682–5511) at Le Meridien Hotel is probably the nicest in the city because of its fireplaces, wingback chairs, dark wood, and leather. The **Bacchus Lounge** (845 Hornby St., tel. 604/689–7777) in the Wedgewood Hotel is stylish and sophisticated. The **Gallery Lounge** (655 Burrard St., tel. 604/687–6543) in the Hyatt is a genteel bar, with lots of windows letting in the sun and giving views of the action on the bustling street. The **Garden Lounge** (791 W. Georgia St., tel. 604/689–9333) in the Four Seasons is bright and airy with greenery and a waterfall, plus big soft chairs you won't want to get out of. For a more lively atmosphere, try **Joe Fortes** (777 Thurlow St., 604/669–1940), or **Night Court** (801 W. Georgia St., tel. 604/682–5566) in the Georgia Hotel.

The **English Bay Café** (1795 Beach Ave., tel. 604/669–2225) is the place to go to catch the sunset over English Bay. **La Bodega** (1277 Howe St., tel. 604/684–8815), beneath the Château Madrid, is a popular Spanish tapas bar.

Two bars on Granville Island catering to the after-work crowd are **Bridges** (tel. 604/687–4400), near the Public Market, and the upscale **Pelican Bay** (tel. 604/683–7373), in the Granville Island Hotel, at the other end of the island.

Music While discos come and go, lines still form every weekend at
Discos **Richard's on Richards** (1036 Richards St., tel. 604/687–6794) for live and taped Top-40 music.

Jazz A jazz and blues hotline (tel. 604/682–0706) gives you current information on concerts and clubs. **Carnegie's** (1619 W. Broadway, tel. 604/733–4141), **Café Django** (1184 Denman St., tel. 604/689–1184), and the **Alma Street Café** (2505 Alma St., tel. 604/222–2244), all restaurants, are traditional venues with good mainstream jazz. The **Glass Slipper** (185 E. 11th Ave., tel. 604/877–0066) has mainstream to contemporary jazz with a more underground atmosphere.

Rock The **Town Pump** (66 Water St., tel. 604/683–6695) is the main venue for local and touring rock bands. The **Soft Rock Café** (1925 W. 4th Ave., tel. 604/736–8480) is decidedly more upscale. There's live music with dinner. The **86th Street Music Hall** (750 Pacific Blvd., tel. 604/683–8687) serves up big-name bands.

Casinos A few casinos have been licensed recently in Vancouver, and proceeds go to local charities and arts groups. Downtown there are the **Royal Diamond Casino** (535 Davie St., tel. 604/685–2340) and the **Great Canadian Casino** (2477 Heather St., tel. 604/872–5543) in the Holiday Inn.

Comedy **Yuk Yuks** (750 Pacific Blvd., tel. 604/687–5233) is good for a few laughs.

Excursion: Mayne Island

The Gulf Islands lie in the Gulf of Georgia, between Vancouver and Victoria. The southern islands of Galiano, Mayne, Saturna, Pender, and Salt Spring (the most commercialized) are warmer, have half the rainfall of Vancouver, and are graced with smooth sandstone rocks and beaches. Marine birds are numerous, and unusual vegetation such as arbutus trees (a leafy evergreen with red peeling bark) and Garry oaks differentiate the islands from other areas around Vancouver. Writers, artists, craftspeople, weekend cottagers, and retirees take full advantage of the undeveloped islands.

For a first visit to the Gulf Islands, make a stopover on Mayne, the most agricultural of the group. In the 1930s and 1940s the island produced vegetables for Vancouver and Victoria until the Japanese farmers who worked the land were interned during World War II. Mayne's proximity to Vancouver and its manageable size (even if you're on a bicycle) make it accessible and feasible for a one- or two-day trip. A free map, published by the islanders, is available on the ferry or from any store on Mayne.

Arriving and Departing by Ferry

BC Ferry (tel. 604/685–1021 for recorded information; for reservations, 604/669–1211) runs frequent service from outside Vancouver and Victoria to the Gulf Islands. The trip to Mayne Island takes about 1½ hours, and a couple of sailings run each day. Call for a 24-hour recorded phone message about crossings. If you plan on taking a car, it is often necessary to make reservations a couple of weeks in advance, especially if you are traveling on the weekend. Go mid-week if possible.

Getting Around

By Bicycle Because Mayne Island is so small (20 square kilometers, or 8 square miles) and scenic, it is great territory for a vigorous bike ride, though the small hills make it not quite a piece of cake. Renting a bike in Vancouver is a good idea, unless the weather looks iffy; then it would be worth taking a car. Some bed-and-breakfasts have bicycles; ask for them to be set aside for you when making your reservation. A few bicycles are for rent at the island's only gas station (604/539–5411) at Miners Bay.

By Car The roads on Mayne Island are narrow and winding.

Exploring Mayne Island

Mayne Island saw its heyday around the turn of the century, when passenger ships traveling from Victoria and Vancouver stopped to enjoy Mayne's natural beauty. Late-19th-century wood houses, hotels, and a church still stand today among the newer A-frames, log cabins, and split-level homes. Although there is no real town on Mayne, except for a few commercial buildings and homes around Miners Bay, you will find eagles, herons, and rare ducks; sea lions and black-tail deer; quiet beaches, coves, and forest paths; and warm, dry weather in the summer.

Starting at the ferry dock at **Village Bay,** head toward Miners Bay via Village Bay Road. A small white sign on your left will indicate the way to **Helens Point,** previously an Indian reservation, which currently has no inhabitants. Indian middens at Village Bay show that the island had been inhabited for 5,000 years by Cowichan Indians from Vancouver Island who paddled to Mayne Island in dugout canoes. If you choose to go all the way to Helens Point (about a two-hour, round-trip walk), you can look north across **Active Pass** (named for the turbulent waters).

If you continue on Village Bay Road, head toward **Miners Bay,** a little town about 2 kilometers (1.2 miles) away. This commercial hub has a post office, restaurant, health-food store, gas station, bakery (with espresso), general store, and secondhand bookstore. Also, visit the **Plumbers Pass Lockup;** formerly a jail, it is now a minuscule museum with local history exhibits.

Time Out   Stop at the **Springwater Lodge** (tel. 604/539–5521), built in 1892 and the oldest operating hotel in British Columbia. The deck of the Springwater overlooks the bay and is a fine place for a cold soda or beer on a sunny day.

From Miners Bay head east on Georgina Point Road. About a mile away is **St. Mary Magdalene Church,** which doubles as an Anglican and United church. If Pastor Larry Grieg is around, he'll show you the century-old building, but the cemetery next to the church is even more interesting. Generations of islanders—the Bennetts, Georgesons, Maudes, and Deacons (whose names are all over the Mayne Island map)—are buried here. Across the road, a stairway leads down to the beach.

At the end of Georgina Point Road is the **Active Pass Lighthouse.** The grassy grounds, open to the public every day from 1 to 3, are great for picnicking. Bald eagles are often on the shore, along with many varieties of ducks (waterfowl is most abundant in spring and fall).

Head back down Georgina Point Road a short way, and turn left on Waugh Road, left on Porter Road, and right to the end of Edith Point Road. A path leads off into the woods to **Edith Point,** an hour's walk away. The path is a bit steep in parts—not recommended for small children—but the sunny, smooth sloping sandstone at the point is a real enticement. Many of the beaches on Mayne are on the north or east side, but at Edith Point you can take advantage of the full southern exposure. If the tide is out, beachcomb your way back to your car.

From Edith Point Road, go back along Waugh Road a short distance to Campbell Bay Road. Take this to Fernhill Road (which becomes Bennett Bay Road), heading east to **Bennett Bay,** the island's most popular beach. Just past the junction of Bennett Bay and Wilkes roads, beyond the Marisol Cottages, a small green sign on the right indicates beach access. The beach is wide and long and the bay is shallow, so the water warms up nicely. (Don't expect washrooms or concession stands in the Gulf Islands.) The mountain looming in the distance is Washington State's Mt. Baker. The nicest part of the beach is to your left if you are facing the water.

The last stop on the tour is **Mount Parke,** which was declared a wilderness park in 1989. Access is from Village Bay Road,

where you will see a timber archway naming Mt. Parke. Drive
up as far as you can until you see the sign that says "No Vehicles
Beyond This Point." It is then about a 15-minute walk to the
highest point on the island and a stunning, almost 360-degree
view of Vancouver, Active Pass, and Vancouver Island. You
may be face-to-face with eagles using the updraft to maintain
their cruising altitude.

Dining and Lodging

Dining **Mayne Mast.** A nautical theme in blues and grays is appropriate for the Mayne Mast, ensconced in a 1940s house with a
large, sunny deck facing Miners Bay. This family restaurant is
open every day for breakfast, lunch, and dinner. Fish-and-
chips made with red snapper is the most popular item on the
menu, followed closely by the steak, prawn, and scallop dinner.
Village Bay Rd., tel. 604/539–3056. MC, V. Moderate.

Dining and **Fernhill Lodge and Herb Farm.** The lodge has built its reputa-
Lodging tion on friendly service, distinctive rooms, and historical dinners. Odds are the chef and owner, Brian Crumblehume, will
be serving the Cleopatra, Chaucer, or Roman dinners. If you're
not staying at the lodge, you must make a dinner reservation
by 1 PM. Breakfasts are more traditional and are fabulous. They
feature fresh-squeezed orange juice, freshly baked buns and muffins, good coffee, and eggs and sausages. In the summer, reserve
in advance. You have a choice of seven rooms: the Jacobean, Oriental, Canadiana, Moroccan, East Indian, 18th-century French,
or Victorian. Two rooms have outdoor hot tubs. *Fernhill Rd.,
Box 140, V0N 2J0, tel. 604/539–2544. Facilities: bicycles, sauna under the trees, sun room, library, piano, herb garden. MC,
V. Moderate.*

Lodging **Oceanwood Country Inn.** Set in 10 wooded acres on the waterfront, the Oceanwood offers eight deluxe rooms. Seven of them
have a view of Navy Channel, which separates Mayne Island
from North Pender. All have a private bath and some have
whirlpools, French doors, fireplaces, or terraces. Each room is
individually decorated but features Canadian pine, Victorian
mahogany, and romantic chintzes. During the winter, theme
weekends are built around wine tastings, nature outings, mur-
der mysteries, and the like. Room rates include breakfast and
afternoon tea. The inn is open to the public daily for dinner and
Sunday brunch. The menu focuses on wines and seasonal foods
from the Pacific Northwest, such as grilled salmon and warm
scallop salad. No children or pets allowed. *630 Dinner Bay Rd.,
V0N 2J0, tel. 604/539–5074, fax 604/539–3002. Facilities: bicycles, sauna, hot tub, conference room, library, games room
with bridge tables. AE, MC, V. Expensive.*
Blue Vista Resort. The sizable '60s-style cabins, decorated with
rumpus room–style family furnishings and fireplaces, are
about 100 feet from the beach at Bennett Bay. This is the best
family accommodation on the island, because units are complete with kitchens and there are no restrictions on pets. Owners Gerry and Naomi Daignault can also provide bicycles,
barbecues, and a rowboat. *Arbutus Rd., V0N 2J0, tel. 604/539–
2463. MC, V. Inexpensive.*
Root Seller Inn. This warm and friendly country-style bed-and-
breakfast is in a 1924 clapboard house a mile from the ferry
dock. The location is popular with people getting around on
foot or by bicycle because it is in the heart of activity at Miners

Bay—within walking distance of stores and the pub. The four large rooms in this rustic house are furnished in old Canadiana oak and share two baths. The honeymoon suite has a fireplace, and the family room sleeps five people. Guest rooms on the south side overlook the huge front deck and Miners Bay. There are picnic facilities for guests in the shady backyard. The lounge has a TV and a VCR. Breakfast is served in the dining room at a long communal table. *Box 5, Village Bay Rd., V0N 2J0, tel. 604/539-2621. Closed Oct.–Mar. Inexpensive.*

7 British Columbia

by Ray Chatelin

Travel writer Ray Chatelin is a columnist for Province, *and contributing editor to* Business Travel Management Magazine. *His articles have appeared in a wide variety of travel and music publications worldwide.*

Updated by Melissa Rivers Victoria section updated by Cathy Slota

Canada's third-largest province (only Québec and Ontario are bigger), British Columbia occupies almost 10 percent of Canada's total surface area, stretching from the Pacific Ocean to the provinces of Alberta, Saskatchewan, and Manitoba, and from the U.S. border to the Yukon and Northwest Territories. It spans more than 360,000 square miles, making it larger than every American state except Alaska.

But size alone doesn't account for British Columbia's popularity as a vacation destination. Even easterners, content in the fact that Ontario and Québec form the industrial heartland of Canada, admit that British Columbia is the most spectacular part of the nation, with salmon-rich waters, abundant coastal scenery, and stretches of snow-capped peaks.

The region's natural splendor has ironically become the source of one of its more serious conflicts. For more than a century, logging companies have depended on the abundant supply of British Columbia wood, and whole towns are still centered on the industry. But environmentalists and many residents see the industry as a threat to the natural surroundings. Compromises have been achieved in recent years, but the issue is far from resolved.

The province used to be very British and predictable, reflecting its colonial heritage, but no longer. Vancouver, for example, has become an international city whose relaxed lifestyle is spiced by a rich and varied cultural scene embracing large Japanese, Chinese, Italian, and Greek communities. Even Victoria, which clings with restrained passion to British traditions and lifestyles, has undergone an international metamorphosis in recent years.

No matter how modern the province, evidence remains of the earliest settlers, Pacific Coast Indians (Haida, Kwakiutl, Nootka, Salish, and others), who occupied the land for more than 12,000 years before the first Europeans arrived en masse in the late 19th century.

But material proof of their heritage may not be enough for today's native Indians, who often face social barriers that have kept them from the mainstream of the province's rich economy. Although some have gained university educations and have fashioned careers, many are just now beginning to make demands on the nonnative population. In dispute are thousands of square miles of land claimed as aboriginal territory, some of which is located within major cities such as Vancouver, Prince George, and Prince Rupert.

Although the issue of ownership remains inconclusive, testimony of British Columbia's roots is apparent throughout the province, from small-town boutiques to big-city dining establishments. Native arts, such as wood-carved objects and silver-etched pendants, fetch top dollar from visitors and residents alike, and native Indian restaurants prepare authentic culinary delights from traditional recipes.

Essential Information

Important Addresses and Numbers

Tourist   For information concerning the province contact the **Ministry**
Information **of Tourism and Provincial Secretary** (Parliament Buildings,
Victoria V8V 1X4, tel. 604/387–1642 or 800/663–6000). More
than 140 communities in the province have **Travel Infocentres.**

The principal regional tourist offices are: **Tourism Association
of Southwestern B.C.** (304–828 W. 8th Ave., Vancouver V5Z
1E2, tel. 604/876–3088 or 800/667–3306 in the U.S., fax 604/
876–8916); **Tourism Association of Vancouver Island** (302–45
Bastion Sq., Victoria V8W 1J1, tel. 604/382–3551, fax 604/382–
3532); **Tourism Victoria** (812 Wharf St., Victoria V8W 1T3, tel.
604/382–2127 or 800/663–3883); **Okanagan–Similkameen Tourist Association** (104–515 Hwy. 97 S, Kelowna V1Z 3J2, tel. 604/
769–5959, fax 604/861–7493); **High Country Tourist Association**
(403–186 Victoria St., Box 962, Kamloops V2C 6H1, tel. 604/
372–7770, fax 604/828–4656); **North By Northwest Tourism**
(3840 Alfred Ave., Box 1030, Smithers V0J 2N0, tel. 604/847–
5227, fax 604/847–7585); **Rocky Mountain Visitors Association**
(495 Wallinger Ave., Box 10, Kimberley V1A 2Y5, tel. 604/427–
4838); **Prince Rupert Convention and Visitors Bureau** (100
McBride St., Box 669 CMG, Prince Rupert V8J 3S1, tel. 604/
624–5637); **Kootenay Country Tourist Association** (610 Railway
St., Nelson V1L 1H4, tel. 604/352–6033, fax 604/352–1656);
Cariboo Chilcotin Coast Tourist Association (190 Yorston St.,
Box 4900, Williams Lake V2G 2V8, tel. 604/392–2226 or 800/
663–5885, fax 604/392–2838); **Peace River Alaska Highway
Tourist Association** (106319–100th St., Box 6850, Fort St. John
V1J 4J3, tel. 604/785–2544, fax 604/785–4424).

For information on Whistler, contact the **Whistler Resort Association** (4010 Whistler Way, Whistler V0N 1B4; in Whistler,
tel. 604/932–3928; reservations, tel. 604/932–4222; in Vancouver, tel. 604/685–3650; in the U.S., tel. 800/634–9622). In Whistler Village an information booth at the front door of the
Conference Center is open 8:30–8.

A provincial government **Travel Infocentre** (tel. 604/932–5528)
is on the main highway, about a mile south of Whistler.

Emergencies   Dial **911** in Vancouver and Victoria; dial **0** elsewhere in the province for **police, ambulance,** or **poison control.**

Hospitals   British Columbia has hospitals in virtually every town, including: in Victoria, **Victoria General Hospital** (35 Helmcken St.,
tel. 604/727–4212); in Prince George, **Prince George Regional
Hospital** (2000 15th Ave., tel. 604/565–2000 or for emergencies,
604/565–2444); in Kamloops, **Royal Inland Hospital** (311 Columbia St., tel. 604/374–5111); in Kelowna, **Kelowna General Hospital** (2268 Pandosy St., tel. 604/862–4000).

Late-night   All-night pharmacies are unknown in British Columbia, even in
Pharmacies   the largest cities, although some pharmacies do offer after-
hours emergency numbers. Generally, emergency prescrip-
tions can be filled through major hospitals. The following is a
list of some pharmacies that could provide assistance: in Victoria, **McGill and Orme Pharmacies** (649 Fort St., tel. 604/384–
1195); in Prince George, **Hart Drugs** (3789 W. Austin Rd., tel.

604/962–9666); in Kamloops, **Kipp-Mallery I.D.A. Pharmacy** (273 Victoria St., tel. 604/372–2531).

Arriving and Departing by Plane

Airports and Airlines British Columbia is served by **Victoria International Airport** and **Vancouver International Airport**. Domestic airports are in most cities. **Air Canada** (tel. in Vancouver, 604/688–5515; in the U.S., 800/458–5811) and **Canadian Airlines International** (tel. in Vancouver, 604/279–6611; in the U.S., 800/426–7000) are the two dominant carriers. **Air B.C.** (tel. in Vancouver, 604/360–5515; in Victoria, 604/360–9074; in the U.S., 800/663–0522) is the major regional line and runs daily flights between Seattle and Victoria.

Arriving and Departing by Car, Bus, and Boat

By Car Driving time from Seattle to Vancouver is about 2½ hours. From other Canadian regions, there are three main routes leading into British Columbia: through Sparwood, in the south, take Highway 3; from Jasper and Banff, in the central region, travel on Route 1 (Trans-Canada) or Highway 5; and through Dawson Creek, in the north, follow Highways 2 and 97.

By Bus **Greyhound** (tel. in Vancouver, 604/662–3222; in Seattle, 206/624–3456) connects destinations throughout British Columbia with cities and towns throughout the Pacific North Coast.

By Boat There is year-round passenger service (closed Christmas) between Victoria and Seattle via the *Victoria Clipper* (tel. 800/888–2535).

Washington State Ferries (tel. in Victoria, 604/656–1551; in Seattle, 206/464–6400) cross daily, year-round, between Sidney, just north of Victoria, and Anacortes, WA. **Black Ball Transport** (tel. in Victoria, 604/386–2202; in Seattle, 206/622–2222) operates between Victoria and Port Angeles, WA.

Getting Around

By Air
Queen Charlotte Islands **Trans Provincial Airlines** (tel. in Prince Rupert, 604/627–1341; in Sandspit, 604/637–5355) runs scheduled floatplanes between Sandspit, Masset, Queen Charlotte City, and Prince Rupert daily except Christmas, December 26, and New Year's Day.

Air B.C. provides both airport-to-airport and harbor-to-harbor service from Vancouver to Victoria at least hourly. Both flights take about 35 minutes.

Vancouver Island **Helijet Airways** (tel. 604/273–1414 or 604/382–6222) helicopter service is available from downtown Vancouver to downtown Victoria.

By Car Major roads in B.C., and most secondary roads, are paved and well engineered. Mountain driving is slower but more scenic. There are no roads on the mainland coast once you leave the populated areas of the southwest corner near Vancouver.

Car Rentals Most major agencies, including **Avis, Budget,** and **Hertz,** service cities throughout the province (*see* Renting and Leasing Cars in Chapter 1).

By Bus **Greyhound Lines of Canada** (tel. 604/662–3222 or 604/388–5248) serves the area with hundreds of stops in the province.

North of   **Farwest Bus Lines** (tel. 604/624–6400) serves Prince Rupert,
Vancouver Island   Terrace, Kitimat, Stewart, and Smithers.

Vancouver Island   **Pacific Coach Lines** (tel. in Victoria, 604/385–4411 or 800/661–
1725) operates daily connecting service between Victoria and
Vancouver via B.C. Ferries. **Island Coach Lines** (tel. 604/385–
4411) serves the Vancouver Island area. **Maverick Coach Lines**
(tel. 604/255–1171) services Nanaimo from Vancouver, via B.C.
Ferries (*see* below).

Whistler   **Maverick Coach Lines** (tel. 604/255–1171) has buses leaving every couple of hours from the bus depot in downtown Vancouver.
The bus stops at Whistler Village and the fare is under $14 one
way. During ski season, the last bus leaves Whistler at 10 PM.

Perimiter Transportation (in B.C., tel. 800/663–4265; outside
B.C., tel. 604/261–2299) has daily service, November–May,
from Vancouver Airport to Whistler. Reservations are necessary; the ticket booth is on the arrivals level of the airport.

By Ferry   **B.C. Ferries** (tel. in Vancouver, 604/685–1021; in Victoria, 604/
656–0757; in Nanaimo, 604/753–6626) has an efficient cross-
strait ferry service from Tsawwassen and Horseshoe Bay (both
just outside of Vancouver) to Vancouver Island (Victoria and
Nanaimo), and the Gulf Islands. Ferries usually depart on the
hour 7 AM–9 PM and can carry about 360 cars and 1,500 passengers. Ferries also run from Powell River, Campbell River,
Comox, and Port McNeill to the Gulf Islands; from Port Hardy to
Prince Rupert; and from Prince Rupert to the Queen Charlotte
Islands, although schedules vary greatly. When traveling with a
car during summer months, expect a long line and delays. For
schedule information call the numbers above for a 24-hour recorded message.

Royal Sealink Express (tel. 604/687–6925) is a new passenger
service (no cars) that takes people by high-speed catamaran between downtown Victoria and downtown Vancouver in 2½
hours.

By Train   **BC Rail** (in Vancouver, tel. 604/984–5246 or 604/631–3500; in
Prince George, tel. 604/564–9080) travels from Vancouver to
Prince George, a 747-kilometer (463-mile route) including daily
service to Whistler. **Via Rail** (tel. in B.C., 800/561–8630) offers
service between Prince Rupert and Prince George.

Vancouver Island   **Esquimalt & Nanaimo Rail Liner** (450 Pandora Ave., Victoria
V8W 3L5, tel. 604/383–4324 or 800/561–8630 in B.C.), operated
by Via Rail, travels from Victoria to Courtenay and returns. It
leaves Victoria's Pandora Avenue Station daily at 8:15 AM, arrives in Courtenay by 12:50 PM, and departs 25 minutes later for a
5:45 PM return.

Guided Tours

Orientation   The following operators offer tours throughout the province:
Classic Holidays Tour & Travel (102–75 W. Broadway, Vancouver, B.C. V5Y 1P1, tel. 604/875–6377); **Klineburger Worldwide
Travel** (3627 1st Ave. S, Seattle, WA 98134, tel. 206/343–9699);
1311 W. 1st St., N. Vancouver, B.C. and **Sea to Sky** (1928 Nelson St., W. Vancouver, B.C., V7V 2P4, tel. 604/984–2224).

Special-interest   A few Vancouver Island–based companies that conduct whale-
Nature Tours   watching tours are: **Subtidal Adventures** (Box 253, Ucluelet
V0R 3A0, tel. 604/726–7336), **Inter-Island Excursions** (Box 393,

Tofino V0R 2Z0, tel. 604/725–3163), **Jamie's Whale Center** (Box 590, Tofino V0R 2Z0, tel. 604/725–3919), **Tofino Sea-Kayaking Company** (Box 620, Tofino, VOR 2Z0, tel. 604/725–4222), and, near Port Hardy, **Stubbs Island Charters** (Box 7, Telegraph Cove V0N 3J0, tel. 604/928–3185).

Ecosummer Expeditions (1516 Duranleau St., Vancouver V6H 3S4, tel. 604/669–7741) runs ecological tours of the Queen Charlotte Islands.

Exploring British Columbia

When traveling by car, keep in mind that more than three-quarters of British Columbia is mountainous terrain. Trips that appear relatively short may take longer, especially in the northern regions and along the coast, where roads are often narrow and winding. In certain areas—most of the uninhabited west coast of Vancouver Island, for example—roads do not exist.

Within British Columbia, there is a vast range of climates, largely a result of the province's size, its mountainous topography, and its border on the Pacific. Vancouver Island, surrounded by Pacific waters, experiences relatively mild winters and summers (usually above 32 degrees winter, below 80 degrees summer), although it rains a lot in the winter. Likewise, the northern coast around Prince Rupert and the Queen Charlotte Islands has wet winter months and few extremes in temperature. But as you move inland, and especially toward the Peace River region in the north, the climate becomes much colder. In the southern interior, the Okanagan Valley has an arid climate, with temperatures dropping below the freezing level in winter and sometimes reaching 90 degrees during the summer.

Highlights for First-time Visitors

Butchart Gardens, Victoria
Craigdarroch Castle, Victoria
Naikoon Provincial Park, Tour 3: North of Vancouver Island
O'Keefe Historic Ranch, Tour 4: Okanagan Valley
Pacific Rim National Park, Tour 2: Vancouver Island
Royal British Columbia Museum, Tour 1: Victoria

Vancouver Island

Vancouver Island, the largest island on the west coast, stretches 450 kilometers (280 miles) from Victoria in the south to Cape Scott, although 97% of the population live between Victoria and Campbell River (halfway up the island); 50% of them live in Victoria itself. Geographically, the differences between the east and west are impressive. The western side is wild, often inhospitable, with just a handful of small settlements. Virtually all of the island's human habitation is on the eastern coast, where the weather is gentler and the topography is low-lying.

The cultural heritage of the island is native Indian from the Kwakiutl, Nootka, and Coastal Salish groups. Native Indian art and cultural centers flourish throughout the region, especially in the lower section of the island. These centers enable visitors to catch a glimpse of contemporary Indian culture.

Mining, logging, and tourism are the important island industries. But environmental issues, such as logging practices by British Columbia's lumber companies, are becoming important to islanders—both native and nonnative. Residents are working to reach a happy coexistence with the island's wilderness and its economy, which is dependent on industrial development and tourism.

Victoria, originally Fort Victoria, was the first European settlement on Vancouver Island and is the oldest city on Canada's west coast. It was chosen in 1842 by James Douglas to be the Hudson's Bay Company's most western outpost, and it became the capital of British Columbia in 1868. Today it's a compact seaside town laced with tea shops and gardens. Though it's quite touristy during the high summer season, it's also at its prettiest, with flowers hanging from turn-of-the-century building posts and strollers feasting on the beauty of Victoria's natural harbor.

Tour 1: Exploring Victoria

Numbers in the margin correspond to points of interest on the Vancouver and Downtown Victoria maps.

The **BC Transit System** (tel. 604/382–6161) runs a fairly extensive service throughout Victoria and the surrounding areas, with an all-day pass that costs $4 for adults, $3 for students and senior citizens. Passes are sold at many outlets in downtown Victoria, including Eaton Centre and Harbour Square Ticket Centre.

❶ For the most part, **Victoria** is a walker's city; most of its main attractions are downtown or are a few blocks from the core. Attractions on the outskirts of downtown can easily be reached by bus or a short cab ride (though taxis can be alarmingly expensive). In the summer you have the added option of horse-drawn carriages, bicycle, boat, or double-decker bus tours.

❷ A logical place to begin this tour is at the **Visitors Information Centre,** located on the waterfront. *812 Wharf St., tel. 604/382–2127. Open July, Aug., daily 9–9; May, June, Sept., Oct., daily 9–7; Nov.–Apr., daily 9–5.*

❸ Just across the way is the recently renovated **Empress Hotel,** a symbol both of the city and of the Canadian Pacific Railway. Originally opened in 1908, the hotel was designed by Francis Rattenbury, whose works dot Victoria. The Empress is another of the great châteaus built by Canadian Pacific, the still-current owners who also built the Château Frontenac in Québec City, Château Laurier in Ottawa, and Château Lake Louise. The $55 million face-lift has been a hot topic of discussion in traditional Victoria, though not all of the comments have been positive; criticism aside, the ingredients that made the 488-room hotel a tourist attraction in the past are still alive. Stop in for high tea—served at hour-and-a-half intervals during the afternoon. *721 Government St., tel. 604/384–8111. Proper dress required; no jeans, shorts, or T-shirts.*

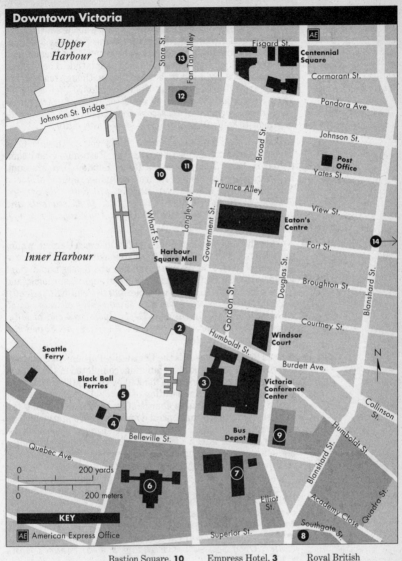

Downtown Victoria

Upper Harbour

Inner Harbour

Johnson St. Bridge

Store St.

Fan Tan Alley

Fisgard St.

Centennial Square

Cormorant St.

Pandora Ave.

Johnson St.

Broad St.

Post Office

Yates St.

Trounce Alley

View St.

Langley St.

Eaton's Centre

Fort St.

Wharf St.

Government St.

Harbour Square Mall

Broughton St.

Gordon St.

Douglas St.

Courtney St.

Blanshard St.

Humboldt St.

Windsor Court

Burdett Ave.

Victoria Conference Center

Collinson St.

Seattle Ferry

Black Ball Ferries

Belleville St.

N

Bus Depot

Humboldt St.

Blanshard St.

Quebec Ave.

0   200 yards
0   200 meters

Elliot St.

Academy Close

Quadra St.

KEY

Superior St.

Southgate St.

AE American Express Office

Bastion Square, **10**

Beacon Hill Park, **8**

Chinatown, **13**

Craigdarroch Castle, **14**

Crystal Gardens, **9**

Empress Hotel, **3**

Legislative/ Parliament Buildings, **6**

Maritime Museum, **11**

Market Square, **12**

Pacific Undersea Garden, **5**

Royal British Columbia Museum, **7**

Royal London Wax Museum, **4**

Visitors Information Centre, **2**

For contrast, take a pleasant stroll through the modern, elegantly designed **Victoria Conference Centre** at the south end of the Empress. Around the corner from the Empress is **Miniature World**, on Humboldt Street, where small replicas of people, trains, and historic events are displayed. The exhibit seems at times like a mix of fact and fiction, though many of the models are delicately laid out. *649 Humboldt St., tel. 604/385-9731. Admission: $6 adults, $5 children 12–17, $4 children 4–11, disabled persons with escort free. Open mid-June–mid-Sept., daily 8:30–10 PM; mid-Sept.–mid-June, daily 9–5.*

A short walk around the harbor leads you to the old CPR Steamship Terminal, also designed by Rattenbury and completed in 1924. Today it is the **Royal London Wax Museum,** housing more than 200 wax figures, including replicas of Queen Victoria, Elvis, and Marilyn Monroe. *470 Belleville St., tel. 604/388–4461. Admission: $6.25 adults, $5.25 students and senior citizens, $3 children 5–12. Open May–Aug., daily 9–9; Sept.–Apr., daily 9–5.*

Next to the wax museum is the **Pacific Undersea Garden,** where more than 5,000 marine specimens are on display in their natural habitat. You also get performing scuba divers and a giant Pacific octopus. Unfortunately, there are no washrooms, and the site is not wheelchair accessible. *490 Belleville St., tel. 604/382–5717. Admission: $6 adults, $5.50 senior citizens, $4.50 children 12–17, $2.75 children 5–11. Open Oct.–end of May, daily 10–5; summer, daily 9–9; closed Christmas. Shows run about every 45 minutes.*

Across Belleville Street is the **Legislative Parliament Buildings** complex. The stone-exterior building, completed in 1897, dominates the inner harbor-and is flanked by two statues: Sir James Douglas, who chose the location of Victoria, and Sir Matthew Baille Begbie, the man in charge of law and order during the gold-rush era. Atop the central dome is a gilded statue of Captain George Vancouver, who first sailed around Vancouver Island; a statue of Queen Victoria stands in front of the complex; and outlining the building at night are more than 3,000 lights. Another of Rattenbury's creations, the complex gives a good example of the rigid symmetry and European elegance that characterize much of the city's architecture. The public can watch the assembly, when it's in session, from the galleries overlooking the Legislative Chamber. *501 Belleville St., tel. 604/387–3046. Admission free. Tours run several times daily and are conducted in at least 4 languages in summer and 3 in winter. Open Sept.–June, weekdays 8:30–5; summer, daily 8:30–5:30.*

Follow Belleville Street one block east to reach the **Royal British Columbia Museum.** Adults and children can wander for hours through the centuries, back 12,000 years. In the prehistoric exhibit, you can actually smell the pines and hear the calls of mammoths and other ancient wildlife. Other exhibits allow you to explore a turn-of-the-century town, with trains rumbling past; in the Kwakiutl Indian Bighouse, the smell of cedar envelops you, while piped-in potlatch songs tell the origins of the genuine ceremonial house before you. *675 Belleville St., tel. 604/387–3014. Admission: Free Mon., Oct.–Apr.; otherwise $5 adults, $3 students and senior citizens, $2 children 6–18 and disabled persons. Open Oct.–Apr., daily 10–5:30; May–Sept., daily 9:30–7; closed Christmas.*

The **Newcombe Theatre** behind the museum presents slide talks and films. *Tel. 604/387–5822. Admission by donation.*

⑧ A walk east on Belleville Street to Douglas Street will lead you to **Beacon Hill Park,** a favorite place for joggers, walkers, and cyclists. The park's southern lawns offer one of the best views of the Olympic Mountains and the Strait of Juan de Fuca. There are also lakes, walking paths, abundant flowers, a wading pool, petting zoo, and an outdoor amphitheater for Sunday-afternoon concerts.

⑨ From the park, go north on Douglas Street and stop off at the **Crystal Gardens.** Opened in 1925 as the largest swimming pool in the British Empire, this glass-roof building—now owned by the provincial government—is home to flamingos, macaws, 75 varieties of other birds, hundreds of blooming flowers, penguins, and monkeys. At street level there are several boutiques and Rattenbury's Restaurant, one of Victoria's well-frequented establishments. *713 Douglas St., tel. 604/381–1213. Admission: $6 adults, $4 children 6–16 and senior citizens. Open Oct.–Apr., daily 10–5:30; summer, daily 9–9.*

⑩ From Crystal Gardens continue on Douglas Street going north to View Street, west to **Bastion Square,** with its gas lamps, restaurants, cobblestone streets, and small shops. This is the spot James Douglas chose as the original Fort Victoria in 1843 and the original Hudson's Bay Company trading post. Today fashion boutiques and restaurants occupy the old buildings. At the Wharf Street end of the square are some benches where you can rest your feet and catch a great view of the harbor. While you're here, you may want to stop in at what was Victoria's **⑪** original courthouse but is now the **Maritime Museum of British Columbia.** Dugout canoes, model ships, Royal Navy charts, photographs, uniforms, and ship's bells chronicle Victoria's seafaring history. A seldom-used 100-year-old cage lift, believed to be the oldest in North America, ascends to the third floor. *28 Bastion Sq., tel. 604/385–4222. Admission: $5 adults, $3 children 12–17, $2 children 6–11. Open Oct. 1–May 31, daily 9:30–4:30; June 1–Sept. 30, daily 9–6. Closed Christmas and New Year's Day.*

⑫ West of Government Street, between Pandora Avenue and Johnson Street, is **Market Square,** offering a variety of specialty shops and boutiques and considered one of the most picturesque shopping districts in the city. At the turn of the century this area—once part of Chinatown—provided everything a visitor desired: food, lodging, entertainment. Today the square has been restored to its original, pre-1900s character.

⑬ Just around the corner from Market Square is Fisgard Street, the heart of one of the oldest **Chinatowns** in Canada. It was the Chinese who were responsible for building much of the Canadian Pacific Railway in the 19th century, and their influences still mark the region. If you enter Chinatown from Government Street, you'll walk under the elaborate **Gate of Harmonious Interest,** made from Taiwanese ceramic tiles and decorative panels. Along the street, merchants display fragile paper lanterns, embroidered silks, imported fruits, and vegetables. **Fan Tan Alley,** situated just off Fisgard Street, holds claim not only to being the narrowest street in Canada but also to having been the gambling and opium center of Chinatown, where mah-jongg, fantan, and dominoes games were played.

A 15-minute walk or a short drive east on Fort Street will take you to Joan Crescent, where **Craigdarroch Castle** stands. This lavish mansion was built as the home of British Columbia's first millionaire, Robert Dunsmuir, who oversaw coal mining for the Hudson's Bay Company (he died before the castle's completion in about 1890). Recently converted into a museum depicting turn-of-the-century lifestyle, the castle is strikingly authentic, with elaborately framed landscape paintings, stained-glass windows, carved woodwork—precut in Chicago for Dunsmuir and sent by rail—and rooms for billiards and smoking. The location offers a wonderful view of downtown Victoria from the fifth-floor tower; guided tours are given. *1050 Joan Crescent, Victoria, tel. 604/592–5323. Admission: $5 adults, $4 students, children under 12 by donation. Open mid-June–Aug., daily 9– 7:30; Sept.–mid-June, daily 10–5.*

What to See and Do with Children

Anne Hathaway's Cottage, tucked away in a unique English-village complex, is a full-size replica of the original thatched home in Stratford-Upon-Avon, England. The building and the 16th-century antiques inside are typical of Shakespeare's era. The Olde England Inn, on the grounds, is a pleasant spot for tea or a traditional English-style meal. You can also stay ($68– $184; AE, DC, MC, V) in one of the 50 antiques-furnished rooms, some complete with four-poster beds. *429 Lampson St., Victoria, V9A 5Y9, tel. 604/388–4353. Admission: $5.75 adults, $3.50 senior citizens and children 8–17, children under 8 free. Open June–Sept., daily 9–9; rest of year, daily 10–4. Guided tours leave from the inn during the winter and directly from the cottage in summer. From downtown Victoria, take the Munro bus to the door.*

Dominion Astrophysical Observatory, maintained by the National Research Council of Canada, has a 72-inch telescope that transmits pictures of planets, star clusters, and nebulae. A museum display around the inside of the domed building provides a quick lesson in astrophysics, and video monitors are set up for visitors' easy viewing. *Off W. Saanich Rd. (Hwy. 17), 16 km (10 mi) from Victoria on Little Saanich Mt., tel. 604/363–0001. Admission free. Open Mon.–Fri. 9–4:30; Apr.–Oct., Mon.– Fri. 9–4:30, Sat. 8 PM–10 PM for telescope viewing.*

Swan Lake Christmas Hill Nature Sanctuary. This 23-acre lake, set within 110 acres of open fields and wetlands out Blanshard Street, is 10 minutes from downtown. From the 1½-mile chip trail and floating boardwalk, birders can spot a variety of waterfowl in winter and nesting birds in the tall grasses. Children will enjoy the displays and games in the nature house. *3873 Swan Lake Rd. (take the No. 70/No. 75 bus), tel. 604/479–0211. Admission free. Open year-round; nature House open Mon.– Fri. 8:30–4; weekends and holidays 12–4.*

Shopping

Shopping in Victoria is easy. Virtually everything can be found in the downtown area, beginning at the Empress and walking north along Government Street. In succession you'll hit **Roger's Chocolates** (tel. 604/384–7021), for fine chocolates; **George Straith Ltd.** (tel. 604/384–6912), for woolens; **Edinburgh Tartan Shop** (tel. 604/388–9312), for traditional Scottish clothing and accessories; **Gallery of the Arctic** (tel. 604/382–9012), for good-quality Inuit art; **Munro's Books** (tel. 604/382–2464), for the best selection of Victoriana in the city; and **Old Morris Tobacconist, Ltd.** (tel. 604/382–4811), for unusual pipe tobacco blends.

On the block of Douglas Street behind the Empress are shops like the exclusive **G. Gagliano of Florence,** with beautiful Italian leather goods; **LeJame Fashions,** with clothing designed and manufactured in Victoria, and the **Stephen Lowe Art Gallery.** Handy, also, is the **Currency Exchange,** which is open daily. The **Eaton's Centre** at Government and Fort streets is both a department store and a series of small boutiques, with a total of 140 shops and restaurants. Market Square, between Johnson and Pandora, has three stories of specialty shops.

At last count, Victoria had 60-plus **antiques shops** specializing in coins, stamps, estate jewelry, rare books, crystal, china, furniture, or paintings and other works of art. A short walk on Fort Street going away from the harbor will take you to **Antique Row** between Blanshard and Cook streets. **Waller Antiques** (tel. 604/388–6116) and **Newberry Antiques** (tel. 604/388–7732) offer a wide selection of furniture and collectibles. You will also find antiques on the west side of Government Street near the **Old Town.**

A 10-minute drive (or the No. 1/No. 2 bus) from downtown out Fort Street to Oak Bay Avenue will take you to one of the few residential shopping areas that is not a mall. The **Oak Bay Village** is great for browsing, buying, or an afternoon *cuppa'*. Start at the corner of Oak Bay and Foul Bay and work your way east toward the water.

Sports and Outdoor Activities

Golf   Though **Victoria Golf Club** (1110 Beach Dr., Victoria, tel. 604/598–4321) is private, it's open to other private-club members. This windy course is the oldest (built in 1893) in British Columbia and offers a spectacular view of the Strait of Juan de Fuca. **Uplands Golf Club** (3300 Cadboro Bay Rd., Victoria, tel. 604/592–1818) is a flat, semiprivate course (it becomes public after 2). **Cedar Hill Municipal** (1400 Derby Rd., Victoria, tel. 604/595–3103) is a public course with up-and-down terrain. **Royal Oak Golf Club** (4680 Elk Lake Dr., Victoria, tel. 604/658–1433) is the newest nine-hole course in the area. **Gorge Vale Golf Club** (1005 Craigflower Rd., Victoria, tel. 604/386–3401) is a semiprivate course but is open to the public. It has punitive traps and a deep gorge that eats up golf balls. **Glen Meadows Golf and Country Club** (1050 McTavish Rd., Sidney, tel. 604/656–3921), situated near the ferry terminal, is a semiprivate course that's open to the public at select times.

Dining and Lodging

See price charts for Vancouver, above.

Dining   **Chez Daniel.** One of Victoria's old standbys, Chez Daniel offers dishes that are rich, though the nouvelle influence has found its way into a few of the offerings. The interior, following a burgundy color scheme, seems to match the traditional rich, caloric cuisine. The wine list is varied, and the menu has a wide selection of basic dishes: rabbit, salmon, duck, steak. This is a restaurant where you linger for the evening in the romantic atmosphere. *2524 Estevan Ave., tel. 604/592–7424. Reservations advised. Jacket advised. AE, MC, V. Closed lunch and Sun.–Mon. Expensive.*

Chez Pierre. Established in 1973, this is the oldest French restaurant in Victoria, and the downtown location, combined with an intimate, rustic decor, creates a pleasant ambience. House specialties include *canard à l'orange* (duckling in orange sauce), rack of lamb, and British Columbia salmon. Although a tourist destination, this restaurant has managed to maintain its high quality over the years. *512 Yates, tel. 604/388–7711. Reservations advised. Dress: casual but neat. AE, MC, V. Closed lunch and Sun.–Mon. Moderate–Expensive.*

Camilles. This restaurant is romantic, intimate, and one of the few West Coast–cuisine restaurants in Victoria. House specialties such as chicken Napoli, papaya brochettes (prawns wrapped around chunks of papaya in a lime and jalapeño marinade), phyllo-wrapped salmon (fresh fillet of salmon in phyllo pastry) are all served in generous portions. Camilles also has an extensive wine cellar, uncommon in Victoria. *45 Bastion Sq., tel. 604/381–3433. Reservations advised. Dress: casual but neat. MC, V. Closed lunch and Sun.–Mon. Moderate.*

French Connection. Located in one of Victoria's Heritage homes, built in 1884, the restaurant has maintained the character of the time. From the outside, ornate details indicate the French tradition that you will find in the service and on the menu. The food is prepared with care, with an emphasis on the sauces. *512 Simcoe St., tel. 604/385–7014. Reservations required. Dress: casual. AE, MC, V. Closed Sat.–Mon. lunch and Sun. Moderate.*

★ **La Ville d'Is.** This seafood house is one of the best bargains in Victoria in terms of quality and price. Run by Michel Duteau, a Brittany native, the restaurant is cozy and friendly, with an outside café open May–October. An extensive, imaginative wine list features bottles from the Loire Valley that go well with the seafood, rabbit, lamb, and beef tenderloin specials. Try the *perche de la Nouvelle Zélande* (orange roughie in muscadet with herbs) or lobster soufflé for a unique taste. *26 Bastion Sq., tel. 604/388–9414. Reservations advised. Dress: casual but neat. AE, MC, V. Closed Sun. and Jan. Moderate.*

★ **Pagliacci's.** If you want Italian food, Pagliacci's is a must. Featured are dozens of pasta dishes, quiches, veal, and chicken in marsala sauce with fettuccine. The pastas are freshly made in-house. The orange-color walls are covered with photos of Hollywood stars, so there's always something to look at here. *1011 Broad St., tel. 604/386–1662. No reservations. Dress: casual. MC, V. Moderate.*

Le Petite Saigon. This is a small, intimate café-style restaurant, offering a quiet dining experience with beautifully presented meals and a fare that is primarily Vietnamese, with a touch of French. The crab, asparagus, and egg swirl soup is a specialty of the house, and combination meals are cheap and tasty. *1010 Langley St., tel. 604/386–1412. Dress: casual. AE, MC, V. Closed Sat. lunch and Sun. Inexpensive–Moderate.*

Cafe Mexico. This is a spacious, redbrick dining establishment just off the waterfront, serving hearty portions of Mexican food, such as *pollo chipolte* (grilled chicken with melted cheddar and spicy sauce, on a bed of rice). Bullfight ads and cactus plants decorate the restaurant, reinforcing its character and theme. *1425 Store St., tel. 604/386–5454. Reservations accepted. Dress: casual. AE, MC, V. Inexpensive.*

Periklis. Standard Greek cuisine is offered in this warm, taverna-style restaurant, but there are also steaks and ribs on the menu. On the weekends you can enjoy Greek and belly dancing, but be prepared for the hordes of people who come for the entertainment. *531 Yates St., tel. 604/386-3313. Reservations accepted. Dress: casual. Closed weekend lunch; during summer, open Sat. lunch. AE, MC, V. Inexpensive.*

★ **Six-Mile-House.** This 1855 carriage house is a Victoria landmark. The brass, carved oak moldings and stained glass set a festive mood for the evening. The menu is constantly changing but always features seafood selections and burgers. Try the cider or one of the many international beers offered. *494 Island Hwy., tel. 604/478-3121. Reservations accepted. Dress: casual. MC, V. Inexpensive.*

★ **Wah Lai Yuen.** Although Chinatown seems to be offering less-interesting restaurants than before, this one has managed to maintain its character. It's a small corner of authenticity, combining Cantonese cuisine with wonderful baked goods including pork and curry beef buns. The portions are enormous and the price is right. *560 Fisgard St., tel. 604/381-5355. Reservations accepted. Dress: casual. No credit cards. Closed Mon. Inexpensive.*

Lodging   **The Bedford Hotel.** This European-style hotel, located in the heart of downtown, is reminiscent of San Francisco's small hotels, with personalized service and strict attention to details. In keeping with the theme, rooms follow an earthen color scheme, and many have goose-down comforters, fireplaces, and Jacuzzis. Meeting rooms and small conference facilities are available also, making this a good businessperson's lodging. Gourmet breakfast is included in the room rate. *1140 Government St., V8W 1Y2, tel. 604/384-6835 or 800/665-6500; fax 604/386-8930. 40 rooms. Facilities: restaurant, pub. AE, MC, V. Very Expensive.*

★ **The Empress Hotel.** This is Victoria's dowager queen with a face-lift. First opened in 1908, it recently underwent a multi-million dollar renovation that has only enhanced its Victorian charm. In the renovation process, stained glass, carved archways, and hardwood floors were rediscovered and utilized effectively. Forty-six new rooms were added, and the others were brought up to modern standards, something the hotel desperately needed. A new entrance has been constructed, in addition to the new rooms and relandscaped grounds. The Empress dominates the inner-harbor area and is the city's primary meeting place for politicians, locals, and tourists. It is also one of Victoria's top tourist attractions, so don't expect quiet strolls through the lobby. *721 Government St., V8W 1W5, in Canada, tel. 604/384-8111 or 800/268-9411; in the U.S., 800/828-7447; fax 604/381-4334. 481 rooms. Facilities: 2 restaurants, café, 2 lounges, conference center, indoor pool, sauna, health club, in-room movies, cable TV, Christmas discount, family discount. AE, DC, MC, V. Very Expensive.*

★ **Hotel Grand Pacific.** This is a new hotel and one of Victoria's finest, with modern motifs and international service standards. Overlooking the harbor, and adjacent to the legislative buildings, the hotel accommodates business and vacationing people looking for comfort, convenience, and great scenery; all rooms have terraces, with views of either the harbor or the Olympic Mountains. The health club is elaborate, equipped with Nautilus, racquetball court, and sauna. *450 Québec St.,*

V8V 1W5, tel. 604/386–0450 or 800/663–7550; fax 604/383–7603. 149 rooms. Facilities: restaurant, lounge, sauna, whirlpool, fitness center, convention facilities, underground parking, indoor pool. AE, D, DC, MC, V. Very Expensive.

Ocean Pointe Resort. Set on the Inner Harbour on the site of an old shingle mill, this sparkling, new hotel has wonderful views of Old Town and the parliament buildings across the water, with the added bonus of a quiet location removed from the bustle of downtown Victoria. From stem to stern the property has every imaginable amenity, from soaring windows, in-house movies ($7.95) and minibars in the spacious guest rooms to hydrotherapy, aerobics, and beauty treatments in the spa. There are salads and sandwiches in the Boardwalk Cafe, steaks and seafood in the Boardwalk Brasserie, and Pacific Northwest and Continental cuisine in the Victorian Restaurant. *45 Songhees Rd., Victoria V9A 6T3, tel. 604/360–2999 or 800/667–4677; fax 604/360–1041. 213 rooms, 37 housekeeping suites. Facilities: 3 restaurants, lounge, 3 tennis courts, whirlpool, sauna, exercise room, indoor pool, squash and racquetball court, beauty parlor, supervised playroom. Reservations advised in restaurant. MC, V. Very Expensive.*

★ **Holland House Inn.** Two blocks from the inner harbor, legislative buildings, and ferry terminals, this nonsmoking hotel has a sense of casual elegance. Some of the individually designed rooms have original fine art created by the owner, and some have four-poster beds and fireplaces. All rooms have private baths, and all but two have their own balconies. A gourmet breakfast is served and included in room rates. You'll recognize the house by the picket fence around it. *595 Michigan St., V8V 1S7, tel. and fax 604/384–6644. 10 rooms. Facilities: lounge. AE, DC, MC, V. Expensive–Very Expensive.*

Victoria Regent Hotel. Originally built as an apartment, this is a posh, condo-living hotel that offers views of the harbor or city. The outside is plain, with a glass facade, but the interior is sumptuously decorated with warm earth tones and modern furnishings; each apartment has a living room, dining room, deck, kitchen, and one or two bedrooms with bath. *1234 Wharf St., V8W 3H9, tel. 604/386–2211 or 800/663–7472; fax 604/386–2622. 47 rooms. Facilities: restaurant, free parking, laundromat. AE, D, DC, MC, V. Expensive–Very Expensive.*

Captain's Palace Hotel and Restaurant. This is a unique lodging, contained within three Victorian-era mansions and located only one block from the legislative buildings. Once a one-bedroom bed-and-breakfast, it has expanded to 16 guest rooms and a restaurant. Rooms, decorated in florals and pastels, offer different extras: some have private baths with claw-foot tubs; others have balconies. Although the restaurant provides ample breakfasts—included in the room price—don't overlook offerings in the neighborhood for dinner. Ask about special honeymoon, holiday, and blossom-time packages. *309 Belleville St., V8V 1X2, tel. 604/388–9191; fax 604/388–7606. 16 rooms. Facilities: restaurant, money exchange, bicycles. AE, MC, V. Moderate–Very Expensive.*

Oak Bay Beach Hotel. This Tudor-style hotel in Oak Bay, on the southwest side of the Saanich Peninsula, is well removed from the bustle of downtown. There's a wonderful atmosphere here, though; the hotel, situated oceanside, overlooks the Haro Strait and catches the setting sun. The interior decor is as dreamy as the grounds, with antiques and flower prints decorating the rooms. The restaurant, Tudor Room by the Sea, is average, but the bar with its cozy fireplace is truly romantic. *1175 Beach Dr., V8S 2N2, tel. and fax 604/598–4556. 51 rooms. Facilities: restaurant, pub, yacht for cruises, access to health club. AE, DC, MC, V. Moderate–Very Expensive.*

★ **Abigail's.** A Tudor country inn with gardens and crystal chandeliers, Abigail's is not only posh but also conveniently located four blocks east of downtown. All guest rooms are lavishly detailed with a rose, peach, and mint color scheme. Down comforters, together with Jacuzzis and fireplaces in some, add to the luxurious atmosphere. There's a sense of elegant formality about the hotel, noticed especially in the guest library and sitting room, where you'll want to spend an hour or so relaxing in the evening. Breakfast, included in the room rate, is served from 8 to 9:30 in the downstairs dining room. *906 McClure St., V8V 3E7, tel. 604/388–5363; fax 604/361–1905. 16 rooms. MC, V. Expensive.*

★ **The Beaconsfield Inn.** Built in 1875 and restored in 1984, the Beaconsfield has a feel of Old World charm. Dark mahogany wood appears throughout the house; down comforters and some canopy beds and claw-foot tubs adorn the rooms, reinforcing the Victorian style of this residentially situated inn. Some of the rooms have fireplaces and Jacuzzis. An added plus is the guest library and conservatory/sun room. One block away, a new addition—the Humboldt House—offers three more romantic rooms. Full breakfast, with homemade muffins, and a cocktail hour (6–7 PM), with sherry, cheese, and fruit, are included in the room rates. *998 Humboldt St., V8V 2Z8, tel. 604/ 384–4044; fax 604/361–1908. 12 rooms. Facilities: library, Jacuzzi. MC, V. Expensive.*

Chateau Victoria. This 19-story hotel, situated across from Victoria's new Conference Centre, near the inner harbor and the Royal British Columbia Museum, promises wonderful views from its upper rooms and its rooftop restaurant. Following a Victorian motif, the rooms are warm and spacious, some with balconies or sitting areas and kitchenettes. *740 Burdett Ave., V8W 1B2, tel. 604/382–4221 or 800/663–5891; fax 604/380– 1950. 178 rooms. Facilities: restaurants, lounge, indoor pool, whirlpool, meeting rooms, courtesy vans to ferry, access to health club. AE, MC, V. Expensive.*

Dashwood Manor. One of those small, intimate places for which you're always on the lookout, Dashwood Manor is on the waterfront next to Beacon Hill Park and is truly a find. This Heritage Tudor mansion, built in 1912 on property once owned by Governor Sir James Douglas, offers panoramic views of the Strait of Juan de Fuca and the Olympic Mountains. Three rooms in this bed-and-breakfast have fireplaces. In the afternoon, join the other guests for sherry or brandy, or relax in the small library. *1 Cook St., V8V 3W6, tel. 604/385–5517. 14 rooms. AE, MC, V. Expensive.*

Admiral Motel. Located on the Victoria harbor and along the tourist strip, this motel is right where the action is, although it is relatively quiet in the evening. If you're looking for a basic, clean lodging, the Admiral is just that. The amicable owners take good care of the newly refurbished rooms, and small pets are permitted. *257 Belleville St., V8V 1X1, tel. 604/388–6267. 29 rooms, 23 with kitchens. Facilities: cable TV, free parking, laundry. AE, D, MC, V. Inexpensive–Moderate.*

★ **Craigmyle Guest House.** In the shade of Craigdarroch Castle, about 2 kilometers (1 mile) from the downtown core, this lodge, built in 1913, has a special view of the castle. The rooms are quietly elegant and simple, with decor reminiscent of Laura Ashley prints; most units have a private bath. The Edwardian touches are best felt in the main lounge, where you'll find high ceilings and a huge fireplace. A hearty English-style breakfast, with homemade preserves, porridge, and eggs, is a main attraction here. *1037 Craigdarroch Rd., V8S 2A5, tel. 604/595–5411, fax 604/370–5276. 19 rooms, 15 with private bath. MC, V. Inexpensive–Moderate.*

The Arts and Nightlife

The Arts   The **Art Gallery of Greater Victoria** is considered one of Cana-
Galleries   da's finest art museums and is home both to large collections of Chinese and Japanese ceramics and other art and to the only authentic Shinto shrine in North America. The gallery hosts about 40 different temporary exhibitions yearly. *1040 Moss St., Victoria, tel. 604/384–4101. Admission: $3 adults, $1.50 students and senior citizens, children under 12 free; free Thurs. after 5, though donations are accepted. Open Mon.–Wed. and Fri.–Sat. 10–5, Thurs. 10–9, Sun. 1–5.*

The **Emily Carr Gallery** (under the auspices of the Greater Victoria Gallery) presents the art of and films about this renowned artist, who was a contemporary of the Group of Seven. *1107 Wharf St., Victoria, tel. 604/384–3130.* Among the numerous commercial galleries, the **Fran Willis North Park Gallery** (200–1619 Store St., tel. 604/381–3422) is a good bet. In a gorgeously restored warehouse near the waterfront, it shows contemporary paintings and sculpture by local artists; music is performed from time to time. For a further look at what's going on in Victoria's art scene, try the **Winchester Galleries** (tel. 604/595–2777), the **Nunavut Gallery** (tel. 604/598–1344), and the **Barton Leir Gallery** (tel. 604/383–6477).

Music   The **Victoria Symphony** has a winter schedule and a summer season, playing in the recently refurbished **Royal Theatre** (805 Broughton St., Victoria, tel. 604/361–0820) and at the **University Centre Auditorium** (Finnerty Rd., Victoria, tel. 604/721–8480). The **Pacific Opera Victoria** performs three productions a year in the 800-seat **McPherson Playhouse** (3 Centennial Sq., tel. 604/386–6121), adjoining the Victoria City Hall. The **Victoria International Music Festival** (tel. 604/736–2119) features internationally acclaimed musicians, dancers, and singers each summer from the first week in July through late August.

The **Victoria Jazz Society** (tel. 604/388–4423) organizes an annual **JazzFest International** in late June, which in the past has featured jazz, blues, and world-beat artists, like Dizzy Gillespie, Frank Morgan, Ellis Marsalis, and Aster Aweke.

For listings of clubs and restaurants featuring jazz during the year, call **Jazz Hotline** (604/658–5255).

Theater   Live theater can be seen at the **Belfry Theatre** (1291 Gladstone Ave., Victoria, tel. 604/385–6815), **Phoenix Theatre** (Finnerty Rd., tel. 604/721–8000) at the University of Victoria, **Victoria Theatre Guild** (805 Langham Ct., tel. 604/384–2142), and **McPherson Playhouse** (3 Centennial Sq., tel. 604/386–6121).

Nightlife   After 8 PM, **Tudor House Hotel Pub** (533 Admirals Rd., tel. 604/389–9943) becomes a pub attracting the younger set. There's a dance floor and large screen for disco and video entertainment nightly.

Harpo's (15 Bastion Sq., tel. 604/385–5333) features live rock, blues, and jazz, with visits from internationally recognized bands.

Other Points of Interest

Butchart Gardens, situated on the 130-acre Butchart estate about 21 kilometers (13 miles) north of downtown Victoria, offers more than 700 varieties of flowers and includes Italian, Japanese, and English rose gardens. During the summer, many of the exhibits are illuminated at night. Once a limestone quarry, the grounds were transformed in 1904 when Canadian cement pioneer Robert Butchart began building bridges and walkways and planting shrubs and flowers on the 50-acre (20-hectare) site. Also on the premises is a gift shop, teahouse, and restaurants. *800 Benvenuto Ave., Victoria, tel. 604/652–5256. Admission: $9.50 adults, $5 children 12–17, $1 children under 12 excluding GST. Prices and schedules vary greatly depending on time of year; call ahead.*

A 15-minute drive northeast of downtown Victoria will take you to **Craigflower Farmhouse,** once the residence of Kenneth McKenzie, the overseer of one of the first farms established by the Hudson's Bay Company. The original structure—completed in 1856—and most of the furniture remain. While at the farmhouse, ask for a tour of the **Craigflower Schoolhouse,** constructed 1854–55 from lumber supplied by the sawmill at the farm and operated until 1911. Inside, the sloping door frames and tilting fireplace support the local legend that tells of drunken workers who built this one-room schoolhouse. *110 Island Hwy., tel. 604/387–4697. Schoolhouse: 2765 Admirals Rd. Admission: $3.25 adults, $2.75 students and senior citizens, $1.25 children over 6. Supplemental charge for schoolhouse. Open mid-May–June, Sept., Thurs.–Mon. 10–5; July, Aug., daily 10–5. Tours of the farmhouse are given upon request.*

Fable Cottage Estate, located 20 minutes from downtown Victoria, is 3½ acres of brightly flowered gardens with a 609-square-meter (2,000-square-foot) home, modeled on an English thatched cottage and offering spectacular ocean views. *5187 Cordova Bay, Victoria, tel. 604/658–5741. Admission: $7.50 adults, $6.50 senior citizens, $4 children 13–17, $3 children 5–12. Open early Mar.–late-Oct., daily 9–dusk.*

The Rest of the Island

Numbers in the margin correspond to points of interest on the Vancouver Island map.

15 Beginning your driving tour from Victoria, take Highway 14 west to **Sooke** (26 miles, or 42 kilometers, west of Victoria), a logging, fishing, and farming community. **East Sooke Park,** on the east side of the harbor, offers 3,500 acres of beaches, hiking trails, and meadows with wildflowers. You can also visit the **Sooke Region Museum and Travel Infocentre,** with Salish and Nootka crafts, artifacts from 19th-century Sooke, barbecued salmon, and strawberry shortcake on the front lawn during the summer, and plenty of information about the region. *2070 Phillips Rd., Box 774, V0S 1N0, tel. 604/642–6351. Admission free; donations accepted. Open summer, daily 9–6; winter, Tues.–*

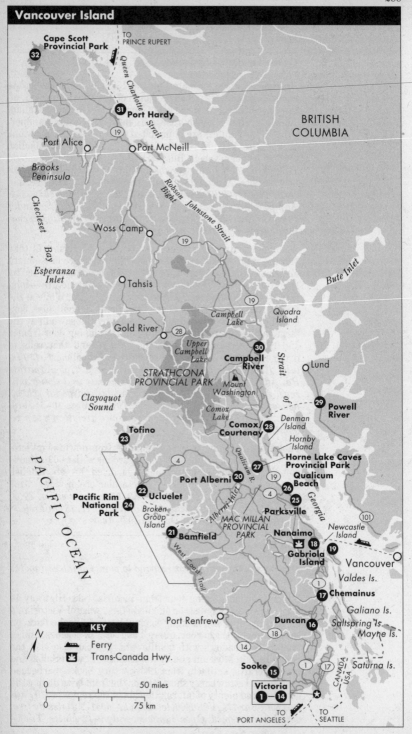

Vancouver Island

TO PRINCE RUPERT

Cape Scott Provincial Park 32

Queen Charlotte Strait

BRITISH COLUMBIA

31 **Port Hardy**

Port Alice 19 Port McNeill

Brooks Peninsula

Checleset Bay

Robson Johnstone Bight

Esperanza Inlet

Woss Camp 19

Bute Inlet

Tahsis

Campbell Lake

Quadra Island

Gold River 28 *Upper Campbell Lake*

30 **Campbell River**

Lund

Strait of

STRATHCONA PROVINCIAL PARK

▲ Mount Washington

Clayoquot Sound

Comox Lake

29 **Powell River**

Tofino 23

28 **Comox/ Courtenay**

Denman Island

Hornby Island

Horne Lake Caves Provincial Park

27 **Qualicum Beach**

Qualicum R.

Port Alberni 20

19

22 **Ucluelet**

Pacific Rim National Park 24

Broken Group Island

Alberni Inlet

26

4

25 **Parksville**

Georgia

101

21 **Bamfield**

MAC MILLAN PROVINCIAL PARK

Newcastle Island

Nanaimo 18

Gabriola Island

19 **Vancouver**

West Coast Trail

Valdes Is.

1 17 **Chemainus**

Port Renfrew

Duncan 16

Galiano Is.

Saltspring Is.

Mayhe Is.

18

1

17

Saturna Is.

14

Sooke 15

Victoria 1 — 14

★

CANADA USA

TO PORT ANGELES TO SEATTLE

KEY

⛴ Ferry

🍁 Trans-Canada Hwy.

N

PACIFIC OCEAN

0 — 50 miles
0 — 75 km

Sun. and holiday Mon., 9–5; closed Christmas and Boxing Day (Dec. 26).

Time Out **Seventeen Mile House** (5196 Sooke Rd., Victoria, tel. 604/642–5942) is on the road to Sooke from Victoria. Stop here for English pub fare, a beer, or fresh local seafood. Built as a hotel, the house is an education in turn-of-the-century island architecture, as well.

The adventurous can continue on Highway 14 west and pick up the logging road from Port Renfrew back to the east coast, although conditions on the gravel road may be hazardous, especially on weekdays with the trucks rolling by. The more reliable route backtracks to Victoria, then follows the Trans-Canada Highway up the eastern coast toward Nanaimo, the mid-island B.C. Ferries terminal point. On your way you'll pass

16 through the town of **Duncan** (about 60 kilometers, or 37 miles, north of Victoria), nicknamed City of Totems for the many totem poles that dot the small community. The two carvings behind the City Hall are worth a short trip off the main road. Duncan is also home to the **Native Heritage Centre.** Covering 13 acres of land on the banks of the Cowichan River, the center features a native big house, fantastic theater and interpretive dance presentations, an arts-and-crafts gallery that focuses on carvings and weaving traditions, and picnic meals of smoked salmon next to the river. *200 Cowichan Way, Duncan, tel. 604/746–8119. Admission: $5.50 adults, senior citizen and student rates, children 6 and under free. Open May–Sept., daily 10–9; Oct.–Apr., call for schedule.*

Also in Duncan is the **B.C. Forest Museum.** More a park than a museum, the attraction spans more than 40 hectares (100 acres), combining indoor and outdoor exhibits that focus on the history of forestry in British Columbia. You ride an original steam locomotive around the property and over an old wood trestle bridge. The exhibit feature logging and milling equipment. *RR 4 Trans-Canada Hwy., tel. 604/746–1251. Admission: $5 adults, $4 senior citizens and children 13–18, $2.50 children 6–12. Open late-Apr.–late-Sept., daily 9:30–6. For off-season visits, call for an appointment.*

17 Just north of Duncan, the small town of **Chemainus** has become known recently for the bold epic murals that decorate its landscape. Once dependent on the lumber industry, the town began to revitalize in the early 1980s when its mill closed down. Since then, more than 25 murals depicting local historical events have been painted around town by international artists. Restaurants, shops, cafés, and coffee bars have added to the town's growth. Footsteps on the sidewalk lead you on a self-guided tour of the murals.

18 **Nanaimo,** across the strait of Georgia from Vancouver, is about an hour's drive from Victoria. Throughout the Nanaimo region, petroglyphs (Indian rock carvings) representing humans, birds, wolves, lizards, sea monsters, and supernatural creatures can be found. The **Nanaimo Centennial Museum** (100 Cameron St., tel. 604/753–1821) will give you information about local carvings. Eight kilometers (5 miles) south of town is the **Petroglyph Provincial Park,** where designs estimated to have been carved thousands of years ago can be seen along the marked trails that begin at the parking lot.

⑲ Nanaimo is a convenient departure point for other island activities. A 20-minute ferry ride leaves from town for **Gabriola Island,** a rustic, rural island with lodging; and a 10-minute ferry takes you to **Newcastle Island,** where you can picnic, ride your bicycle, walk on trails leading past old mines and quarries, and wait for glimpses of deer, rabbits, and eagles.

⑳ As you continue north on Highway 19, you have the option of taking Highway 4 west to Port Alberni and the lower west-coast towns. **Port Alberni** is about an 80-kilometer (49-mile) drive from Nanaimo and is mainly a pulp-and-saw-mill town and a stopover for those on the way to Ucluelet and Tofino, though fishermen will want to take advantage of the salmon-rich waters. While you're there, consider taking a breathtaking trip down the Alberni Inlet to the open sea aboard the *Lady Rose*, a Scottish ship, built in 1937. The *Lady Rose* leaves the Argyle Street dock Tuesday, Thursday, and Saturday (and Sunday in July and August) for the four-hour cruise to **㉑** **Bamfield,** a remote village of about 200. Bamfield's seaside boardwalk affords an uninterrupted view of ships heading up the inlet to Port Alberni. Oddly, for a place this small, it is well equipped to handle overnight visitors. The west coast is invaded every summer by fishermen, kayakers, scuba divers, and hikers. Bamfield is also a good base from which to take boating trips to the Broken Group Islands and hikes along the West Coast Trail (*see* below). From early June to mid-September the *Lady Rose* and *Francis Barkley* sail for Ucluelet on Monday, Wednesday, and Friday. It's a unique trip and deserves all the accolades it receives. Most of the trips, to both Bamfield and Ucluelet, stop at the Broken Group Islands, but call ahead to make sure. *Argyle St. dock, tel. 604/723–8313. Bamfield fare: $31.50; Broken Group Islands fare: $33.60; Ucluelet fare: $36.75. Sailings depart daily at 8AM.*

㉒ North of Bamfield are Ucluelet and Tofino—the whale-watching capitals of Canada, if not of the whole west coast of North America. The two towns are quite different in character, though both are relaxed in the winter and swell to several times their sizes in summer. **Ucluelet,** which in the Indian language means "people with a safe landing place," is totally focused on the sea. Fishing, water tours, and whale-watching are the primary activities. Whale-watching is big business, with a variety of charter companies that take tourist boats to greet the 20,000 gray whales that pass within a short distance of Ucluelet on their migration to the Bering Sea every March–May.

㉓ **Tofino,** on the other hand, is more commercial, with beachfront resorts, motels, and several unique bed-and-breakfast establishments. But the surrounding area remains natural. You can walk along the beach discovering caves on the way, cruise around the ancient forests of Meares Island, or take an hour-long water taxi to the hot springs north of town.

㉔ Ucluelet and Tofino bookend the Long Beach section of the **Pacific Rim National Park** (Box 280, Ucluelet, V0R 3A0, tel. 604/726–7721), the first national marine park in Canada. The park itself comprises three separate areas—Long Beach, the Broken Group Islands, and the West Coast Trail. Each accommodates a specific interest.

The unit of **Long Beach** gets its name from an 11-kilometer (7-mile) strip of hard-packed white sand strewn with twisted driftwood, shells, and the occasional Japanese glass fishing float. The beach is a favorite spot during the summer, and you often have to fight heavy traffic along the twisting 85 kilometers (53 miles) of Highway 4 from Port Alberni.

The 100 islands of the **Broken Group Islands** can be reached only by boat. Many boating tours are available from Ucluelet, which rests at the southern end of Long Beach, and from Bamfield and Port Alberni. The 100 islands are alive with sea lions, seals, and whales. The sheltered lagoons of Gibraltar, Jacques, and Hand islands offer protection and good boating conditions, but go with a guide.

The third element of the park is the **West Coast Trail,** which stretches along the coast from Bamfield to Port Renfrew. It can be traveled only on foot and takes an average of six days to complete. A permit is necessary to hike this trail; reservations are available from March through September by calling 604/728–1282. The 77-kilometer (47-mile) trail is for experienced hikers and follows part of the coast dubbed the Graveyard of the Pacific, so called because of the large number of shipwrecks that occurred there. After the SS *Valencia* ran aground in 1906, killing all the crew and passengers, the Canadian government constructed a lifesaving trail to help future victims of shipwrecks reach safe ground. The trail remains, with demanding bogs, steep slopes and gullies, cliffs (with ladders), slippery boardwalks, and insects. Although it presents many obstacles for hikers, the rewards are the panoramic views of the sea, dense rain forest, sandstone cliffs with waterfalls, and wildlife that includes gray whales and seals. It's open from mid-May to late September.

Heading back to the east coast from Port Alberni, stop off at **Cathedral Grove,** located in MacMillan Provincial Park on Highway 4. Walking trails lead you past Douglas fir trees and western red cedars, some about 800 years old. Their remarkable height creates a spiritual effect, as though you were gazing at a cathedral ceiling. Another stop along the way is **Butterfly World** (Alberni Hwy., Coombs, B.C. V0R 1MO, tel. 604/248–7026), an enclosed tropical garden housing a massive collection of exotic, free-flying butterflies. At the junction of Highways 4

㉕ and 19 is **Parksville**—one of the east island's primary resort areas with lodges and waterfront motels catering to families, campers, and boaters. In **Rathtrevor Provincial Park,** 1½ kilometers (about 1 mile) south of Parksville, high tide brings ashore the warmest ocean water in British Columbia. Swimmers should time their visits accordingly.

㉖ Just 12 kilometers (7 miles) north of Parksville is **Qualicum Beach,** known largely for its salmon fishing and opportunities for beachcombing along the long, sandy beaches. The nonprofit **Old School House Gallery and Art Centre** (122 Fern Rd. W., tel. 604/752–6133), with nine working studios, shows and sells the work of local artists and artisans.

Continue north, then head west off the highway and follow signs for about 15 kilometers (9 miles) to Horne Lake and the **㉗** **Horne Lake Caves Provincial Park.** Three of the six caves are open at all times. If you decide to venture in, bring along a flashlight, warm clothes, and a hard hat, and be prepared to bend and even crawl. Riverbend Cave, spanning 383 meters (1,259 feet), requires ladders and ropes in some parts, and can only be explored with a guided tour. Spelunking lessons and tours are offered for all levels, from beginner to advanced. *Tel. 604/248-3931. Fees for tours vary depending on ability level. Reservations suggested for tours.*

Between the Horne Lakes turnoff and the twin cities of Comox and Courtenay is tiny Buckley Bay, where ferries leave for **Denman Island,** with connecting service to **Hornby Island.** Denman offers old-growth forests and long sandy beaches, while Hornby's spectacular beaches have earned it the nickname the Undiscovered Hawaii of British Columbia. Many artists have settled on the islands, establishing studios for pottery, jewelry, wood carving, and sculpture.

㉘ **Comox** and **Courtenay** are near **Strathcona Provincial Park** and are commonly used as a base for anyone skiing Mt. Washington in the winter. Strathcona, the largest provincial park on Vancouver Island, encompasses **Mt. Golden Hinde,** at 2,200 meters (7,218 feet) the island's highest mountain; and **Della Falls,** Canada's highest waterfall, reaching 440 meters (1,443 feet). The park's multitude of lakes and 161 campsites attract summer canoers, fishermen, and wilderness campers, and the **Strathcona Park Lodge and Outdoor Information Center,** well known for its wilderness-skills programs, provides information on the park's facilities. *Information Center, Hwy. 28, on Upper Campbell Lake, about 45 km (28 mi) west of Hwy. 19, Box 2160, Campbell River, V9W 5C9, tel. 604/286-3122.*

㉙ From Comox, you can take a 75-minute ferry east across the Strait of Georgia to **Powell River,** a city established around the MacMillan pulp-and-paper mill, which opened in 1912. Renowned as a year-round salmon-fishing destination, the Sunshine Coast town has 30 regional lakes that offer exceptional trout fishing, as well. For information contact **Powell River Travel Info Center** (6807 Wharf St., tel. 604/485-4701).

㉚ **Campbell River** is ringed by shopping centers that make it look like a free-zoned mess. But people don't come here for the aesthetics, they come for the fish; some of the biggest salmon ever caught on a line have been landed just off the coast at Campbell River. At the mouth of the town's namesake, you can try for membership in Campbell River's Tyee Club, which would allow you to fish in a specific area, and possibly land a giant chinook. Requirements for membership in the club include registering and landing a tyee (a spring salmon weighing 30 pounds or more). Coho salmon and cutthroat trout are also plentiful in the river. *Travel Information Center, 1235 Island Hwy., Box 400, Campbell River, V9W 5B6, tel. 604/287-4636. Open late-June–Labor Day, daily 8-6; rest of year, Mon.–Fri. 9-5.*

Pods of resident Orcas live nearby year-round in Johnstone Strait; and in Robson Bight they like using the beaches to rub against. Because of their presence, Robson Bight has been made into an ecological preserve: Whales must not be disturbed by human observers there. Some of the island's best whale-watching tours, however, are conducted nearby, out of Telegraph Cove, a village built on pilings over water.

㉛ Farther north is **Port Hardy,** the departure and arrival point for B.C. Ferries going through the Inside Passage to and from Prince Rupert, the coastal port serving the Queen Charlotte Islands. During the summer the town can be crowded, so book your accommodations well in advance. If you choose to continue

to the northernmost point on Vancouver Island, drive about 60
32 kilometers (about 37 miles) on logging roads to reach **Cape
Scott Provincial Park,** a wilderness camping region designed
for well-equipped and experienced hikers. At Sand Neck, a
strip of land that joins the cape to the mainland of the island,
you can see both the eastern and western shores at once.

Tour 2: North of Vancouver Island

*Numbers in the margin correspond to points of interest on the
British Columbia map.*

33 Cruising the 274-nautical-mile **Inside Passage,** between Port
Hardy on northern Vancouver Island and Prince Rupert, is a
sail through a sheltered marine highway that follows a series of
natural channels behind protective islands along the green-
and-blue shaded British Columbia coast. The undisturbed
landscape of rising mountains and humpbacked islands has a
prehistoric look that leaves an indelible impression.

After a short segment in the open ocean, the 410-foot MV
Queen of the North ducks in behind Calvert Island into Fitz
Hugh Sound. From there, its route is protected from ocean
swells all the way through Finlayson and Grenville channels,
which are flanked by high, densely wooded mountains that rise
steeply, in places, from narrow gorges. The *Queen of the North*
carries up to 800 passengers and 157 vehicles, and takes close to
an entire day to make the Port Hardy to Prince Rupert trip.
The ship has plenty of deck space plus lounge areas, a self-serve
cafeteria, and a satisfactory restaurant that offers a plentiful
buffet. Day-use cabins are available for an additional fee. Children can play in the Captain Kids Room. *British Columbia
Ferry Corporation, 1112 Fort St., Victoria V8V 4V2, tel. 604/
386–3431. Cost varies according to cabin, vehicle, and time of
season. Reservations required for the cruise and advised for
hotel accommodations at ports of call. Oct. 1–April 30 sailings
are once weekly; May 1–May 31 sailings twice-weekly; June 1–
Sept. 30 sailings daily, departing on alternate days from Port
Hardy and Prince Rupert; departure time 7:30 AM, arrival
time 10:30 PM. Schedule and fares subject to change.*

An alternative to the ferry cruise along the Inside Passage is
one of the more expensive luxury-liner cruises that sail along
the B.C. coast (*see* Chapter 1) from Vancouver to Alaska.

34 **Prince Rupert,** the final stop on the B.C. Ferries route through
the Inside Passage, is about 750 air kilometers (465 miles)
northwest of Vancouver, though it takes more than 20 hours to
drive the mountainous 1,500 kilometers (936 miles). Prince Rupert has a mild but wet climate, so take rain gear.

The town lives off fishing, fish processing, logging, saw- and
pulp-mill operations, and deep-sea shipping. A gondola ride to
the top of Mt. Hays, located just outside the downtown area,
offers magnificent views on a clear day of the industrial harbor,
the Queen Charlotte Islands, and the mountains of Alaska. You
can ski Mt. Hays during the winter and picnic in the summer.
Prince Rupert is also a place where British Columbia's cultural
heritage is quite evident. The **Museum of Northern British Columbia** has one of the finest collections throughout the province
of coastal Indian art, some artifacts dating back 10,000 years.
Native artisans carve totem poles in the carving shed and, dur-

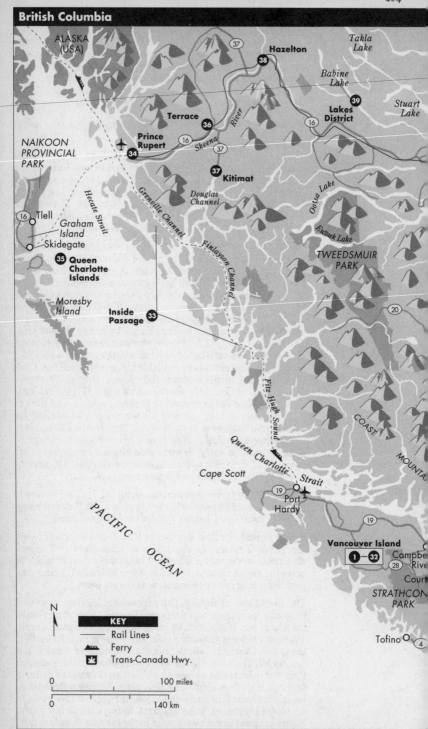

British Columbia

ALASKA
(USA)

*Takla
Lake*

37

Hazelton

38

*Babine
Lake*

Terrace

36

39

River

**Lakes
District**

*Stuart
Lake*

**Prince
Rupert**

16

34

16

Skeena

37

NAIKOON
PROVINCIAL
PARK

37

Kitimat

*Douglas
Channel*

Ootsa Lake

Grenville Channel

Hecate Strait

16 Tlell

*Graham
Island*

Skidegate

35 **Queen
Charlotte
Islands**

Eutsuk Lake

*TWEEDSMUIR
PARK*

Finlayson Channel

*Moresby
Island*

**Inside
Passage** 33

20

Fitz Hugh Sound

COAST

Queen Charlotte   **Strait**

Cape Scott

19

MOUNTA

**Port
Hardy**

19

PACIFIC   OCEAN

Vancouver Island

1 — 32

28 Campbell
River

Court

*STRATHCON
PARK*

Tofino 4

N

KEY
— Rail Lines
⛴ Ferry
🔱 Trans-Canada Hwy.

0   100 miles

0   140 km

ing the summer, the museum runs a 2½-hour boat tour of the harbor and Metlaktla Indian village. *1st Ave. and McBride St., Prince Rupert, tel. 604/624–3207. Admission: free; donations accepted. Open Sept–May, Mon.–Sat. 10–5; June–Aug., Mon–Sat. 9–9, Sun. 9–5.*

From Prince Rupert you can continue on to explore either the Alaskan Panhandle, the Queen Charlotte Islands, or interior British Columbia. If you wish to proceed north through the Alaskan waterways to Skagway, board the **Alaska Marine Highway System ferry** (tel. in Prince Rupert, 604/627–1744 or 800/642–0066), which docks alongside the *Queen of the North* in Prince Rupert. Alaska ferries travel this route four times a week in the summer, twice a week otherwise.

35 The popular vacation destination, the **Queen Charlotte Islands**, or misty islands, though once the remote preserve of the Haida Indians, is now easily accessible by ferry. Today the Haidas make up only one sixth of the population, but they continue to infuse the island with a sense of the Haida past and contribute to the logging and fishing industries, and to tourism, as well. Haida elders lead tours—an essential service if you want to reach the isolated, abandoned villages. Though the region has become a popular tourist destination, limited accommodations make it necessary to reserve guest rooms well in advance.

The *Queen of Prince Rupert* (tel. in Prince Rupert, 604/624–9627) sails four to five times a week between June and September, and can easily accommodate recreational vehicles. Crossing the Hecate Strait from Prince Rupert to Skidegate, near Queen Charlotte on Graham Island, takes about six hours. Schedules vary, so call ahead—a good idea anyway because the boat fills up quickly. The **MV Kwuna,** a B.C. Ferries ship, connects Skidegate Landing to Alliford Bay on Moresby Island, with 12 twenty-minute sailings daily. Access to smaller islands off Graham Island (the northernmost and largest of the group of 150) and Moresby Island is by boat or air, but plans should be made in advance through a travel agent.

In the Queen Charlottes, there are 150 kilometers (93 miles) of paved road, most of it on Graham Island, connecting Queen Charlotte in the south to Masset in the north. Some of the other islands are laced with gravel roads, most of which can be accessed with any sturdy car or RV. The rugged, rocky west coast of the archipelago faces the ocean; the east coast has many broad sandy beaches. Throughout, the mountains and shores are often shrouded in fog and rain-laden clouds, adding to the mysteriousness of the islands.

Naikoon Provincial Park (tel. 604/557–4390), in the northeast corner of Graham, preserves a large section of the unique wilderness found here, where low-lying swamps, pine and cedar forests, lakes, beaches, trails, and wildlife combine to create an intriguing environment. Take the 5-kilometer (3-mile) walk from the Tlell Picnic Site to the beach, and on to the bow section of the old wooden shipwreck of the *Pezuta*, a 1928 log-hauling vessel. On the southern end of Graham Island, the **Queen Charlotte Islands Museum** has a small but impressive display of Haida totem poles, masks, and carvings of both silver and argillite (a hard black slate). There is also a natural history exhibit, which gives interesting background on the wildlife of the islands. *Box RR1, 2nd Beach, Skidegate V0T 1S0, tel. 604/559–*

*4643. Admission: $2.25 adults, $1 senior citizens, children 12
and under free. Open Apr.–late-Oct., weekdays 9–5, weekends
1–5; winter, Tues.–Sun. 1–5.*

If you have time on Graham Island, drive up to Old Masset on
the northern coast, site of the **Ed Jones Haida Museum.** Exhibits here include totems and artifacts. Nearby, artists sell their
work from their homes. South of Graham, in and around South
Moresby National Park Reserve, lie most of the better-known
abandoned Haida villages, which are accessible by water. Visiting some of the villages requires at least several days, and lots
of planning for the wilderness. You (or your tour) need to contact the Skidegate Band Council and the Canadian Parks Services before you go.

For more information on the Queen Charlotte Islands, contact
the **Queen Charlotte Islands Travel Information Center** (Box
337, Queen Charlotte V0T 1S0, tel. 604/559–4742).

To see interior British Columbia, take Highway 16 east from
Prince Rupert. En route you'll pass through or near such communities as **Terrace,** with a hot springs complex at the Mt.
Layton Resort, skiing at Shames Mountain, and excellent fishing in the Skeena River; and **Kitimat** (on Highway 37, south of
Terrace), at the head of the Douglas Channel, where the fishing
is superb. At **Hazelton,** a town rich in the culture of the Gitksan
and Wet'suwet'en peoples you must visit **'Ksan,** just outside
town, a re-created Gitksan Indian village. The brightly painted
community of six longhouses is a replica of the one that stood on
the same site when the first explorers arrived in the last century. The **National Exhibition Centre and Museum** displays works
and artifacts from the Upper Skeena River region. A workshop, often used by 'Ksan artists, is open to the public, and
three other longhouses can be visited on a 45-minute tour: One
features contemporary masks and robes, another has song-
and-dance dramas in the summer. A gift shop and museum are
on the grounds. *Box 326, Hazelton, tel. 604/842–5544. Admission: $4.50 adults, $3 senior citizens, $2.50 students, $1.50
children 5–12. Open May–mid-Oct., daily 9–6; mid-Oct.–
Apr., Mon–Fri. 9–5. Tours given May–mid-Oct., on the hour.*

North of Highway 16 you pass by the serene **Lakes District,**
which is popular for camping, fishing, and water sports, before
coming to **Prince George** (Tourism Prince George, 1198 Victoria St., V2L 2L2, tel. 604/562–3700), British Columbia's third-
largest city. This provincial hub contains a regional historic
museum (tel. 604/562–1612), a railroad museum (tel. 604/563–
7351; open May–Labor Day), and the Prince George Native
Art Gallery (tel. 604/564–3568). From Prince George you can
turn south on Highway 97 for Kamloops and the Okanagan Valley (*see* Scenic Drives, below), or you can continue on Highway
16, then on 5 for a longer (some say even more spectacular)
route to the same place.

Tour 3: Okanagan Valley

The Okanagan Valley is part of a highland plateau between the
Cascade range of mountains on the west and the Monashee
mountains on the east. Dominating the valley is Okanagan
Lake, a vacation hot-spot for tourists from the west coast and
Alberta. In summer months it can be difficult to find rooms.

The largest towns along the lake are Vernon at the north end, Kelowna in the middle, and Penticton at the south. Between are the recreational and resort communities of **Summerland, Peachland, Westbank,** and **Oyama,** along the lake which are popular tourist destinations and have camping facilities, motels, and cabins. Favorite local lore attests to the legendary Ogopogo, a snakelike creature that inhabits the lake between Peachland and Summerland. Though small in size (only 3% of the province's total land mass), the area contains the interior's largest concentration of people.

The valley is the fruit-growing capital of Canada, producing apricots, cherries, pears, plums, apples, and peaches. A visit to the region from mid-April through early June promises to jolt your senses with the brightness and fragrance of the spring blossoms.

41 We arrive in the valley by way of **Kamloops,** which, though not officially a part of the Okanagan, is a convenient passageway from Fraser Canyon and Thompson Valley and a stop on the Canadian Pacific Railroad. The town is 50 minutes northeast of Vancouver by air and 425 kilometers (260 miles) by road and is surrounded by 500 lakes, providing an abundant source of trout, Dolly Varden, and kokanee. During late September and October, however, attention turns to the sockeye salmon, when thousands of these fish—intent on breeding—return home to their birth waters in Adams River (only 65 kilometers, or 40 miles, east of Kamloops off the Trans-Canada Highway).

Once every four years—the last time was 1990—the sockeye run reaches a massive scale, as more than a million salmon pack the waters and up to 500,000 visitors come to observe. The **Roderick Haig-Brown Conservation Area,** which protects the 11-kilometer (7-mile) stretch of Adams River, is the best place to watch.

Vernon, Kelowna, and Penticton, running south along Highway 97, like to believe each has a distinct personality, but local rivalries aside, the towns are actually one large unit. Okanagan Lake is their glue, offering recreation, lodging, and restaurants.

42 Of the three, **Vernon** is the least dependent on tourism, organized instead around forestry and agriculture. The city borders on two other lakes besides Okanagan, the most enticing of which is Kalamalka Lake. The Kalamalka Lake Provincial Park has warm waters, and some of the most scenic viewpoints and hiking trails in the region. Twelve kilometers (7.5 miles) north of Vernon, the **O'Keefe Historic Ranch** gives visitors a window on cattle-ranch life at the turn of the century. The O'Keefe house is a late-19th-century Victorian mansion opulently furnished with original antiques. On the grounds, which now are 50 acres (20 hectares), there are a Chinese cooks' house, St. Ann's Church, a blacksmith shop, a reconstructed general store, and a display of the old Shuswap and Okanagan Railroad. Also featured are a contemporary restaurant and gift shop. *9830 Hwy. 97, 12 km (8 mi) north of Vernon, tel. 604/542-7868. Admission: $4.50 adults, $3.50 senior citizens and children 13–18, $2.50 children 6–12; family and group rates available. Open mid-May–mid-Oct., daily 9–5.*

43 **Kelowna,** the largest city in the Okanagan, is home to **Father Pandosy's Mission** (tel. 604/860–8369), the first nonnative settlement in the region, founded in 1859. The city also offers the area's only tour of a fruit orchard; a covered wagon, pulled by a tractor, takes you on the hour-long narrated excursion. *2750 KLO Rd., East Kelowna, tel. 604/769–4719. Admission: $6.50 adults, $5.50 senior citizens, accompanied children free. Open July 1–early Sept., weekdays 10–4, weekends 10–12.*

Kelowna is the geographic center of the valley's wine industry, with **Calona Wineries** (1125 Richter St., tel. 604/762–9144), British Columbia's oldest and biggest winemaker. Also around Kelowna are smaller but more intimate wineries, including **Gray Monk Cellars** (1055 Camp Rd., 8 km, or 5 mi, west of Winfield, off Hwy. 97, tel. 604/766–3168), and **CedarCreek Estate Winery** (12 km, or 7.5 mi, south of Kelowna, off Hwy. 97 on the corner of Pandosy and Lakeshore Rds., tel. 604/764–8866).

④④ **Penticton** is the most tourist-oriented of the three. While its winter population is about 25,000, its population in summer nears 130,000. An 11-kilometer (5-mile) drive south on Highway 97 takes you to the **Okanagan Game Farm,** with more than 650 species of wild animals from around the world. Farther south, off Highway 3 and along the U.S. border, **Cathedral Provincial Park** (tel. 604/494–0321) features 82,000 acres (33,198 hectares) of lakes and rolling meadows, teeming with mule deer, mountain goats, and California bighorn sheep. To reach the main part of the park, either take the steep, eight-hour hike, or arrange (and pay in advance) for the Cathedral Lake Resort (in the park, tel. 604/499–5848) to transport you by four-wheel drive. There are 16 campsites in the park.

Tour 4: Whistler

④⑤ If you think of skiing when you hear mention of **Whistler,** British Columbia, you're thinking on track. Whistler and Blackcomb mountains, part of the Whistler Resort Association, are the two biggest ski mountains in North America; there's summer glacier skiing, the longest vertical drop in North America, and the most advanced lifts in the world. At the base of the mountains is Whistler Village—a small community of lodgings, restaurants, pubs, gift shops, and boutiques. With more than 28 hotels arranged within a five-minute walk between the mountains, the site is buzzing with activity. Culinary options within the village range from burgers to French, Japanese to deli cuisine; and nightly entertainment runs the gamut from sophisticated piano bars to casual pubs.

In the winter, the village buzzes with skiers taking to the slopes in vibrantly colored attire, but as the scenery changes from winter's snow-white to summer's lush-green landscapes, the mood of Whistler changes, too. Things seem to slow down a bit, and the resort sheds some of its competitive edge and welcomes a more relaxed, slower-paced environment. Even the local golf tournaments and the triathlon are interspersed with Mozart and bluegrass festivals.

Adjacent to the area is the 78,000-acre (31,579-hectare) **Garibaldi Provincial Park,** with dense mountainous forests splashed with hospitable lakes and streams. But even if you don't want to roam much farther than the village, there are five lakes for canoeing, fishing, swimming, and windsurfing, and many nearby hiking and mountain-bike trails.

No matter what the season, though, Whistler Village is very accessible to the pedestrian. Anywhere you want to go within the resort is at most five minutes away, and parking lots are just outside the village. The bases of Whistler and Blackcomb mountains are also just at the edge; in fact, you can ski right into the lower level of the Chateau Whistler Hotel, and all 1,220 of the village's hotel rooms are less than 1,000 feet (about 30 m) from the lifts.

If you are interested in a tour of the area, **Alpine Adventure Tours** (tel. 604/932–2705) has a Whistler history tour of the valley and a Squamish day trip.

Scenic Drives

From downtown Victoria, get on Dallas Road and follow the scenic route signs for a **marine drive around Victoria** that takes you past a residential area, along pebble beaches, and into the city's mansion area known locally as the Tweed Curtain, reflecting its house designs and residents' British lifestyles. The road continues past Beacon Hill Park (the street name changes to Beach Drive), Gonzales Point, through the township of Oak Bay, and past Uplands Park, with its stone-gate entrance leading to the huge estates of Uplands. After passing the east side of the University of Victoria, the route will eventually reach Sidney, from which you can take a ferry across to the mainland and head over to Vancouver.

The **Gold Rush Trail** is a 640-kilometer (400-mile) route along which the frontiersmen traveled in search of gold in the 19th and early 20th centuries. The interior British Columbia trail begins just below Prince George in the north, and extends to Lillooet in the south, but juts off at points in between. Following the route you can travel through Quesnel, Williams Lake, Wells, Barkerville, along the Fraser Canyon, and Cache Creek. Most towns and communities through which the trail passes have re-created villages, history museums, or historic sites that help to tell the story of the gold-rush era. For more information contact the **Cariboo Chilcotin Coast Tourist Association** (Box 4900, Williams Lake V2G 2V8, tel. 604/392–2226, or in U.S. 800/663–5885, fax 604/392–2838).

Completion of a new highway opened the **Coast Mountain Circle,** linking Vancouver to Cariboo Country. This 702-kilometer (435-mile) route takes in spectacular Howe Sound, the deepwater port of Squamish, Whistler Resort, and Pemberton Valley before heading back to Vancouver through scenic Fraser Canyon and Harrison Hot Springs. The loop makes a comfortable 2–3 day journey. For more information contact the **Tourism Association of Southwestern B.C.** (304–828 W. 8th Ave., Vancouver V52 1E2, tel. 604/876–3088 or 800/667–3306).

Shopping

Okanagan Valley The **Peter Flanagan Okanagan Pottery Studio** (tel. 604/767–2010), located on Highway 97 in Peachland, sells handcrafted ceramics.

Geert Maas Sculpture Gardens, Gallery, and Studio. World-class sculptor Geert Maas exhibits his art in an indoor gallery and a one-acre garden, in the hills above Kelowna. Maas, who works in bronze, stoneware, and mixed media, creates distinctive abstract figures with a round and fluid quality. He also sells medallions, original paintings, and etchings. *R.R. 1,250 Reynolds Rd., Kelowna, V1Y 7P9, tle. 604/860–7012. Admission free. Open year-round; call for exact hours.*

Prince Rupert Native art and other local crafts are available at **Studio 9** (516 3rd Ave. W, tel. 604/624–2366).

Queen Charlotte Islands The **Haida** Indians carve valuable figurines from the hard, black slate called argillite. The specific variety used by the Haidas is found only on the islands. Their works can be found at the **Adams Family House of Silver** (tel. 604/626–3215), in Old Masset, behind the Ed Jones Haida Museum, and at **Joy's Island Jewellers** (tel. 604/559–4742) in Queen Charlotte. Other island specialties are silk-screen prints and silver jewelry.

Vancouver Island Duncan is the home of Cowichan Indian wool sweaters, handknitted by the native Indians. A large selection is available from **Hills Indian Crafts** (tel. 604/746–6731) and **Big Foot Trading Post** (tel. 604/748–1153), both on the main highway, about 1½ kilometers (1 mi) south of Duncan. Also check out **Modeste Wool Carding** (2615 Modeste Rd., Duncan, tel. 604/748–8983), about a half mile off the highway in nearby Koksilah.

Sports and Outdoor Activities

Canoeing and Kayaking You'll see lots of canoes and kayaks at the many lakes and rivers near **Whistler.** If you want to get in on the fun, rentals are available at Alta Lake at both **Lakeside Park** and **Wayside Park.** Another spot that's perfect for canoeing is the **River of Golden Dreams,** either from Meadow Park to Green Lake or upstream to Twin Bridges. Kayakers looking for a thrill may want to try **Green River** from Green Lake to Pemberton. Call **Whistler Outdoor Experience** (tel. 604/932–3389) or **Whistler Kayak Adventures** (tel. 604/932–6615) for equipment or guided trips.

Fishing Miles of coastline and thousands of lakes, rivers, and streams bring more than 750,000 fishermen to British Columbia each year. The waters of the province hold 74 species of fish (25 of them sport fish), including Chinook salmon and rainbow trout. An annual fresh-water fishing license is about $19 for Canadians, $17 for B.C. residents. For a nonresident or non-Canadian, it's $10–$15 for six days, and $27 annually. A salt-water fishing license for one day costs $3.75 for Canadian residents and non-Canadians, and is available at virtually every fishing lodge and sporting-goods outlet along the coast. Annual licenses are about $11 for non-B.C. Canadians and $38 for non-Canadians.

For updated fishing information and regulations, contact the **B.C. Fish Branch** (Ministry of Environment, 810 Blanshard St., Victoria V8V 1X5, tel. 604/387–4573). For a guide to saltwater fishing, contact the **Department of Fisheries and Oceans** (Recreational Fisheries Div., Station 415, 555 W. Hastings St., Vancouver V6B 503, tel. 604/666–3271).

Whistler **Green River Fishing Guides** (tel. 604/932–3474) will take care of anything you need—equipment, guides, four-wheel-drive transportation. All five of the lakes around Whistler are stocked with trout, but the area around **Dream River Park** is one of the most popular fishing spots. Slightly farther afield, try **Cheakamus Lake, Daisy Lake,** and **Callaghan Lake.**

Golf
There are more than 200 golf courses in British Columbia and the figure is growing. The province is now an Official Golf Destination of the PGA Tour in Canada and of the American PGA tour. Greens fees are about $20–$35. The topography in British Columbia tends to be mountainous, and many courses have fine views as well as treacherous approaches to greens.

Okanagan Valley
The Okanagan has a central tee-time booking service for out-of-town golfers that lists all of the Okanagan/interior British Columbia courses below. *Box 342, Westbank V0H 2A0, tel. 604/768–7500, call collect. Open May 15–Oct. 15, Mon.–Fri. 9–5; leave message if no one is there.*

Gallaghers Canyon Golf Resort (4320 McCulloch Rd., Kelowna, tel. 604/861–4240) is one of the most challenging courses in British Columbia, with long, rolling and twisting fairways. **Kelowna Golf and Country Club** (1297 Glenmore Dr., Kelowna, tel. 604/763–2736) is a private club that favors straight drivers; visitors are welcome but advised to avoid weekends. **Osoyoos Golf and Country Club** (20th Ave., Osoyoos, tel. 604/495–7003) provides a green setting in the dry, parched hills; only two of the 12 par-fours on the course are under 350 yards. Visitors are welcome. **Penticton Golf and Country Club** (799 Eckhardt Ave. W, Penticton, tel. 604/492–8727) has 10 acres of water hazards, challenging traps, and bunkers; it is a semi-private club that welcomes visitors. **Rivershore Golf Club** (off Old Shuswap Rd., Kamloops, tel. 604/573–4622) is a Robert Trent Jones–designed course and is one of British Columbia's longest, at 7,007 yards. Visitors are welcome. **Salmon Arm Golf Course** (3400 Hwy. 97B, Salmon Arm, tel. 604/832–4727) welcomes visitors to its hilly terrain. **Shadow Ridge Golf Club** (3770 Bullman Rd., Kelowna, tel. 604/765–7777) is a relatively new course, set in a valley and surrounded by orchards. **Summerland Golf and Country Club** (2405 Mountain Rd., Summerland, tel. 604/494–9554) is slightly off the beaten track but has two distinctly different nines with the front nine clear and the back nine cut through a pine forest. **Twin Lakes Golf and Country Resort** (Hwy. 3A, Kaleden, tel. 604/497–5359) has an on-site RV park.

Whistler
Arnold Palmer designed the par-72 championship **Whistler Golf Course** (tel. 604/932–4544), which is said to be a "good four-iron shot from the village." The course is very scenic, fairly flat, and challenging for the experienced, but pleasant for beginners. The relatively new **Predator Ridge Golf Resort** (360 Commonage Rd., Vernon, tel. 604/542–3436) is a very challenging public course. The area's newest offering, the **Robert Trent Jones Jr. Golf Course** (4599 Chateau Blvd., tel. 604/938–8000), is equally scenic, nestled at the foot of the mountain on the opposite side of Whistler Village.

Hunting
All hunters for game—moose, bear, mountain goat and sheep, caribou, deer, birds—need licenses. Of the 112 species of mammals that dwell in British Columbia, 74 of them are peculiar only to this province. Nonresidents of Canada are required to be accompanied by a licensed guide while hunting big game in B.C. More than 300 outfitters provide the service. Prices vary depending on species and length of trip, but equipment, including a tent, food, and transportation, is usually part of the pack-

age. For more information contact the **B.C. Wildlife Branch** (780 Blanshard St., Victoria V8V 1X5, tel. 604/387–9737).

Skiing British Columbia has hundreds of kilometers of groomed cross-
Cross-country country (nordic) ski trails in the provincial parks and more than 40 cross-country resorts. Most downhill destinations have carved out nordic routes along the valleys, and there are literally thousands of more trails in unmanaged areas of British Columbia.

For cross-country enthusiasts, two of the finest in the province are **Lac le Jeune** (Box 3215, Kamloops V2C 6B8, tel. 604/732–2722), 30 kilometers (18 miles) southwest of Kamloops, and **Manning Park Resort** (Manning Park V0X 1R0, tel. 604/840–8822) en route to the Okanagan, about 200 kilometers (124 miles) east of Vancouver. Manning Park also has downhill facilities, which are just as popular as the nordic program. On Vancouver Island, **Mt. Washington** and **Mt. Cain Alpine Park** (*see* below) have nordic facilities, as do **Apex Alpine** and **Silver Star Mountain Resort** (*see* below) in the Okanagan Valley.

Downhill With more than half the province situated higher than 4,200 feet above sea level, new downhill courses are constantly opening. At the moment, more than 40 major resorts have downhill facilities.

On Vancouver Island, **Mt. Washington Ski Resort Ltd.** (Box 3069, Courtenay V9N 5N3, tel. 604/338–1386), with more than 30 runs and an elevation of 5,200 feet, is the largest ski area on Vancouver Island, and the third-largest in terms of visitors, in the province. Located in the Comox Valley, it's a modern, well-organized mountain with snowpack averaging 472 inches a year. It also has 30 kilometers (19 miles) of double trackset nordic trails. Other island ski areas are **Forbidden Plateau** (2050 Cliffe Ave., Courtenay V9N 2L3, tel. 604/334–4744), located near Mt. Washington, with 15 runs and a fall of 1,150 feet; and **Mt. Cain** (Box 1225, Port McNeill V0N 2R0, tel. 604/956–3849), on the northern part of the island near the community of Sayward off Highway 19, with 16 runs and a fall of 1,500 feet.

The Okanagan Valley region, four hours east by car from Vancouver, or one hour by air, offers some of the best ski bargains in the province. **Big White Ski Resort** (Box 2039, Station R, Kelowna V1X 4K5, tel. 604/765–3101) is the highest ski area in British Columbia, though Whistler has a longer free fall. The resort has more than 45 runs along with hotels, restaurants, and, like Whistler, is in the process of rapidly expanding. **Silver Star Mountain Resorts** (Box 2, Silver Star Mtn. V0E 1G0, tel. 604/542–0224), with more than 74 runs, offers well-lighted night skiing. The complete village at the base of the mountain has enough hotels to accommodate 650 people. **Apex Alpine** (275 Rosetown Ave., Penticton V2A 3J3, tel. 604/493–3200) has 44 runs and is the largest ski resort in South Okanagan. On-mountain condominiums—many for rent—can accommodate a total of 350.

Kootenay Country, a southeastern section of British Columbia that includes the Rockies, Purcells, Selkirks, and Monashees, features two major resorts: **Whitewater** (Box 60, Nelson V1L 5P7, tel. 604/354–4944), with more than 20 runs and a lot of powder skiing; and **Red Mountain Resorts** (Box 670, Rossland V0G 1Y0, tel. 604/362–7700), which spans two mountains and three mountain faces, and has 30 marked runs.

The resorts in the High Country reflect British Columbia's most diverse topographical area. At 3,100 feet of vertical drop, **Tod Mountain** (Box 869, Kamloops V2C 5M8, tel. 604/578–7222) has 47 runs. On-mountain accommodations are limited to private condominium rentals and a bed-and-breakfast that accommodates up to 32 people. **Mt. Mackenzie** (Box 1000, Revelstoke V0E 2S0, tel. 604/837–5268) has 20 runs and offers deep-powder skiing. Revelstoke, located 5 kilometers (3 miles) from the base, has a wide selection of lodging.

The vertical drops and elevation at **Blackcomb** and **Whistler** mountains are, perhaps, the most impressive features to skiers. Blackcomb has a 5,280-foot vertical drop (North America's longest); Whistler has a 5,020-foot drop. The top elevation is 7,494 feet on Blackcomb and 7,160 on Whistler. These mountains also have the most advanced ski-lift technology, with lift capacity on Blackcomb being 23,850 skiers per hour; on Whistler, 22,295 per hour. Blackcomb and Whistler have more than 100 marked trails each and receive an average of 450 inches of snow per year; Blackcomb is open June–August for summer glacier skiing.

Heli- and Snowcat Skiing Heli-skiing operators are often located at well-established resorts, taking clients into otherwise inaccessible deep-powder regions of the mountains. Others operate as independents and offer accommodations, dining, and recreational facilities in their deluxe lodges. Some companies offer Snowcat skiing, in which an enclosed all-terrain vehicle takes you into the wilderness areas.

In Kootenay Country, try **Kootenay Helicopter Skiing** (Box 717, Nakusp V0G 1R0, tel. 604/265–3121; in B.C., Alberta, and the U.S., 800/663–0100). With accommodations at Nakusp Lodge, they run seven-day packages to and from Kelowna, Spokane, WA, and Castlegar. **Selkirk Wilderness Skiing** (General Delivery, Meadow Creek V0G 1N0, tel. 604/366–4424) offers six-day packages (including remote lodging) to and from Nelson.

In the High Country, **Cat Powder Skiing** (Box 1479, Revelstoke V0E 2S0, tel. 604/837–9489) organizes two-, three-, and five-day, all-inclusive packages that run into the Selkirks and on the upper slopes of Mt. MacKenzie in Revelstoke.

In Whistler, **Canada Heli-Sports** (tel. 604/932–2070 or 604/932–3512), **Tyax Heli-Skiing** (tel. 604/932–7007), and **Whistler Heli-Skiing** (tel. 604/932–4105) have day trips with up to four glacier runs, or 12,000 vertical feet of skiing for experienced skiers; the cost is about $300.

Dining and Lodging

Dining

Throughout British Columbia you'll find a variety of cuisines, from Victoria's numerous French and Continental restaurants (*see* above) and Vancouver Island's seafood places to interior British Columbia's wild game–oriented menus. Prices vary from location to location, but ratings reflect the categories listed on the dining chart.

Category	Cost*
Very Expensive	over $35
Expensive	$25–$35
Moderate	$15–$25
Inexpensive	under $15

per person, excluding drinks, service, and 7% GST, in Canadian dollars

Highly recommended restaurants in each price category are indicated by a star ★.

Lodging

The lodging possibilities across the region are as diverse as the restaurant menus. Accommodations range from bed-and-breakfast inns and rustic cabins to deluxe chain hotels. In the cities, especially, there is an abundance of accommodations, but once you get off the beaten track, guest rooms are often a rare commodity and may require advance booking.

Prices below are quoted in Canadian dollars.

Category	Cost*
Very Expensive	over $125
Expensive	$90–$125
Moderate	$50–$90
Inexpensive	under $50

All prices are for a standard double room, excluding 7% GST. Prices are in Canadian dollars.

Highly recommended lodgings in each price category are indicated by a star ★.

North of Vancouver Island

Prince Rupert
Dining

Smile's Seafood Café. If you don't mind walking among the fish-processing plants by the railway, you'll find this place a real change of pace. It has been a mainstay of Prince Rupert since 1935 and has succeeded because it provides small-town friendly service along with its seafood menu. Favorites include the halibut cheeks and the fisherman's platter. *113 George Hills Way, tel. 604/624–3072. No reservations. Dress: casual. MC, V. Moderate.*

Lodging

Coast Highliner Inn. This modern high rise near the waterfront, in the heart of the downtown shopping district and one block from the airline terminal building, has a view of the harbor from some of the rooms' private balconies. *815 1st Ave. W, V8J 1B3, tel. 604/624–9060. 96 rooms; rooms available for the disabled. Facilities: restaurant, lounge, convention rooms, beauty salon, laundromat. AE, DC, MC, V. Moderate.*

Dining and Lodging
★

Crest Motor Hotel. It may surprise you to find a four-diamond AAA hotel in this small community, but this warm, modern hotel is probably the finest in the north. It's one block away from the two shopping centers but is situated on a bluff overlooking the harbor. The pleasantly decorated restaurant has brass rails, beam ceilings, and a waterfront view, and specializes in seafood; particularly outstanding are the salmon dishes. *222 1st Ave. W, V8J 3P6, tel. 604/624–6771 or in Canada, 800/663–8150; fax 604/627–7666. 103 rooms. Facilities: restaurant, lounge, coffee shop, convention-banquet facilities, cable TV, nightly entertainment. Reservations required for restaurant. Dress: casual but neat. AE, DC, MC, V. Moderate.*

Queen Charlotte Islands
Dining and Lodging

Tlell River House. The smell of fresh-cut wood welcomes you into this new, secluded lodge overlooking the Tlell River. From the property in the middle of the woods, it's only a few hundred feet to the beach (and the shipwreck of the *Pezuta*). The rooms feature all-wood paneling, floral curtains, and thick down comforters; many have views of the river. The restaurant serves excellent seafood and a variety of deliciously rich cheese cakes. *Beitush Rd., just south of the Tlell River Bridge on Hwy. 16, Tlell V0T 1Y0, tel. 604/557–4211, fax 604/557–4622. 10 rooms. Facilities: restaurant, lounge, meeting room, laundromat, boat rentals. MC, V. Moderate.*

Lodging

Alaska View Lodge. On a clear day, you can step onto your porch at this bed-and-breakfast and see the mountains of Alaska in the distance. The lodge is bordered by a long stretch of sandy beach on one side and by woods on the other. Eliane and Charly Feller, both European by origin, offer simple beach-house rooms with few of the amenities you're likely to find in a Hilton; but the private balconies more than compensate. For an additional cost, Eliane makes a three-course dinner, using classical recipes based on Queen Charlotte fare, such as home-smoked salmon, scallops, and Dungeness crab. *Tow Hill Rd., Box 227, Masett V0T 1M0, tel. 604/626–3333. 3 rooms. No credit cards. Moderate.*

Spruce Point Lodge. This cedar-sided building, encircled by a balcony, attracts families and couples because of its inexpensive rates and down-home feel. Like most Queen Charlotte accommodations, this one is more rustic than luxurious and features locally made pine furnishings that go with the northern-woods motif. For the money you get a Continental breakfast and an occasional seafood barbecue, with a menu that depends on the daily catch. Kayakers and hikers on a budget should ask about the bunk rooms, usually available at a low nightly rate. *609 6th Ave., Queen Charlotte V0T 1S0, tel. 604/559–8234. 7 rooms. DC, MC, V. Inexpensive.*

Okanagan Valley

Kamloops
Dining and Lodging
★

Lac le Jeune Resort. This is the property that locals use when they want to combine the outdoors and sophisticated, modern surroundings. With 160 kilometers (99 miles) of cross-country skiing, a lake stocked with trout, and a restaurant that serves robust helpings, this is a good choice for an accommodation. The rustic, self-sufficient cabins are perfect for families because of their ample size and amenities, and pets are permitted. There are also comfortable rooms in the main lodge. *Off Coquihala Hwy., 29 km (18 mi) southwest of Kamloops, Box 3215, Kamloops V2C 6B8, tel. 604/372–2722, fax 604/372–8755. 42 rooms. Facilities: restaurant, lounge, meeting room, gift shop, indoor whirlpool, sauna, boat rentals. AE, MC, V. Moderate.*

Kelowna **Papillon.** This contemporarily furnished restaurant features a
Dining Continental menu that offers pasta, seafood, and steak. While
seafood is not necessarily the specialty here, the prawns and
scallops Caribbean is superb and highly recommended. The
wine list includes a wide selection of imported and local wines
that work nicely with the meals. *375 Leon Ave., tel. 604/763–*
3833. Reservations advised. Dress: casual. AE, MC, V. Closed
weekend lunch. Expensive.

Dining and Lodging **Hotel Eldorado.** In 1989, the owners bought the old Eldorado
Arms, built in 1926, and floated it by barge to its present location. Shortly thereafter, the old property burned down, but a
new Eldorado has been built in its place, with much of the old-
style charm intact. Rooms tend to be small and cozy, with light
greens, floral patterns, and antique furnishings; many have
balconies affording superb views of Okanagan Lake. The restaurant has earned a fine reputation, serving fresh rack of lamb
and seafood dishes. Ask for a seat on the waterfront patio. *500*
Cook Rd., V1Y 9L5, tel. 604/763–7500. 20 rooms. Facilities:
restaurant, lounge, conference room, marina, Jacuzzi suite.
Dress: casual but neat. AE, MC, V. Expensive.

Dining and **Lake Okanagan Resort.** This Five-Star Resorts and Hotels
Lodging property is a popular, self-contained destination on the west
★ side of Okanagan Lake. All rooms have either kitchens or kitchenettes and range in size from one-room suites in the main hotel
to spacious three-room chalets situated around the 300 acres.
The resort shows some signs of age, particularly in the worn
floors; but functional, earthtone furnishings, wood-burning
fireplaces, and perfect views of the lake make this a good choice
of accommodations. *2751 Westside Rd., V1Y 8B2; tel. 604/769–*
3511 or 800/663–3273. 180 rooms. Facilities: restaurant, café,
poolside lounge, Jacuzzi and saunas, 3 pools, par-3 9-hole golf
course, 7 tennis courts, stables, marina. AE, DC, MC, V. Ex-
pensive.

Merritt **Corbett Lake Country Inn.** The locals want to keep this one a
Dining and Lodging secret, but not owner Peter McVey, a French-trained chef. His
★ restaurant offers a different fixed menu every night; favorites
include rack of lamb and chateaubriand. The six single cabins
(with extra beds) and two duplexes are comfortable, but not
plush, and there are also three rooms in the main lodge. Small
pets are allowed. *Off Hwy. 5A, 11 km (6.8 mi) south of Merritt,*
Box 327, V0K 2B0, tel. 604/378–4334. 8 cabins, 3 rooms. Facili-
ties: boat rentals, cross-country ski trails. Reservations re-
quired for restaurant. Dress: casual. No credit cards. Closed
Mar.–Apr., Oct. 15–Dec. 23. Moderate.

Penticton **Granny Bogner's.** The decor in this mostly Continental restau-
Dining rant is a bit contrived, with flowing lace curtains, Oriental
★ rugs, wood chairs, cloth-covered tables, and waitresses
adorned in long paisley skirts, conveying that this is a "homey"
place. But the food is excellent and prepared meticulously to
order. The poached halibut and roasted duck have contributed
to the widely held belief that this is the best restaurant in the
Okanagan. *302 Eckhardt Ave. W, tel. 604/493–2711. Reserva-*
tions advised. Dress: casual. AE, MC, V. Closed lunch; Sun.
and Mon.; Jan. Moderate–Expensive.

Lodging **Coast Lakeside Resort.** On the shore of Okanagan Lake, the inn
is both a peaceful retreat and right in the center of the action.
The waterfront offers relaxation, and the nearby Penticton

Golf and Country Club invites a competitive round of golf. Vancouver businesspeople love this place because it provides comfort and convention facilities. The newly renovated rooms are bright and airy, and many of them have lake views. *21 Lakeshore Dr. W, V2A 7M5, tel. 604/493–8221 or 800/663–9400; fax 604/493–0607. 204 rooms. Facilities: 2 restaurants, lounge, beauty salon, 2 tennis courts, volleyball, windsurfing, sailing, waterskiing, indoor pool, health club, sauna, Jacuzzi, games room. AE, DC, MC, V. Expensive.*

Riordan House. When John and Donna Ortiz bought and restored the former Tiffin Tea House/Riordan Restaurant for their residence, they didn't expect to give guided tours to the newly spiffed-up 1921 house. But people seemed to like the place, built by a Prohibition rum-runner and furnished now with family antiques, so the Ortizes bowed to the inevitable and opened it as a bed-and-breakfast. One bedroom has a fireplace and one a sitting area; all look out on the surrounding hills. The Continental breakfast stars house-baked croissants, scones, muffins, and a selection of seasonal fruit; box lunches are packed on request (and Granny Bogner's is 60 paces away). Lake Okanagan is only a short walk, and you can drift on a rubber raft down the canal that connects it with Skaha Lake. *689 Winnipeg St., V2A 5N1, tel. 604/493–5997. 3 rooms share 3 baths. Facilities: airport pickup, shuttle to lake beach, robes and slippers, fresh flowers. V., MC. Moderate.*

For bed-and-breakfast information contact **Okanagan Bed and Breakfast** (Box 5135, Kelowna V1Y 8T9, tel. 604/868–2700).

Vernon
Dining

Intermezzo. This intimate Italian restaurant combines dim lighting, high-backed chairs, olive-green wall paneling, and a lounge with a fireplace. The effect is formal and old European, although the service is anything but stiff. Owner Jean DeLisle offers standard veal, fish, and pasta dishes, and an excellent selection of wines, as displayed in the wood cabinet of the main dining room. *3206 34th Ave., Box 22, Vernon V1T 6M1, tel. 604/542–3853. Reservations accepted. Dress: casual but neat. AE, MC, V. Inexpensive.*

Lodging

Village Green Inn. This hotel offers access to four golf courses and to the Silver Star Ski Resort, just 22 kilometers (14 miles) away. The bright, pleasant decor and reasonable prices make this hotel a good alternative to the other accommodations that line Highway 97. The rooms are spacious and the service is personal and friendly. *4801 27th St., V1T 4Z1, tel. 604/542–3321; fax 604/549–4252. 138 rooms. Facilities: restaurant, coffee shop, lounge, night club, tennis courts, volleyball, indoor and outdoor pools, sauna, Jacuzzi. AE, D, DC, MC, V. Moderate.*

Vancouver Island

Campbell River
Dining

Royal Coachman Inn. This is another of those informal, blackboard-menu restaurants that dot the landscape of the island. The menu is surprisingly daring for what is essentially a high-end pub, and the inn draws crowds nightly, especially on Tuesday and Saturday (prime rib nights). The menu, however, changes daily, so if ribs aren't your favorite, try one of the other specials. Come early for both lunch and dinner to beat the crowds. *84 Dogwood St., tel. 604/286–0231. No reservations. Dress: casual. AE, MC, V. Inexpensive–Moderate.*

Lodging ★ **Painter's Lodge.** In business for more than 50 years, this is one of the region's major resorts. The wood-frame lodge was rebuilt in 1985 and is decorated with wood furnishings and old photos of award-winning catches. Most packages include guided fishing, but this resort, overlooking Discovery Passage, is appealing even to those who don't fish. *1625 MacDonald Rd., V9W 5C1, tel. 604/286–1102 or 800/663–7090; fax 604/ 286–0158. 80 rooms. Facilities: restaurant, lounge, pub, pool, Jacuzzis, gift shops, 2 golf courses in area, boats, fishing guides. Open late-Mar.–Oct. AE, MC, V. Moderate– Expensive.*

Dining and Lodging ★ **Tsa-Kwa-Luten Lodge.** This resort, operated by members of the Kwakiutl tribe, offers authentic Pacific Coast Indian food and cultural activities. It is located on a high bluff amid 1,100 acres of forest on Quadra Island, a 10-minute ferry ride from Campbell River. Each room in the main lodge has a sea view from a deck or patio; many have a fireplace and loft. There are also four beachfront cabins with fireplace, whirlpool tub, kitchen facilities, and private veranda. Guests are invited to take part in traditional dances in the resort's lounge, which resembles a longhouse, and to visit nearby Indian petroglyphs to make rubbings. *Box 460, Quathiaski Cove, V0P 1N0, tel. 604/ 285–2042, fax 604/285–2532. 26 rooms, 4 cabins. Facilities: restaurant, lounge, fitness room, sauna, Jacuzzi, mountain bikes, guided salmon fishing. AE, DC, MC, V. Very Expensive.*

Comox/Courtenay **Dining** **The Old House Restaurant.** This split-character restaurant offers both formal and casual dining, in a restored 1938 home with large cedar beams and a stone fireplace. Upstairs, among linen and fresh flowers, you select from an innovative Continental menu, with a delightful pepper steak leading as the house specialty. Downstairs, where it is decidedly more informal, you can get sandwiches, pastas, and salads. *1760 Riverside La., Courtenay, tel. 604/338–5406. Reservations advised upstairs; no reservations downstairs. Dress: casual but neat upstairs; casual downstairs. AE, DC, MC, V. Moderate.*

Lodging **The Greystone Manor.** This nonsmoking bed-and-breakfast, set in a 70-year-old house with period furnishings, looks right out on Comox Harbor, where a playful colony of seals is often visible from the house. The antiques, wood stove, and wood paneling add to the hospitable, cozy feel of this inn. Breakfast, which includes fresh fruit, muffins, fruit pancakes, or quiche, is enough to keep you filled most of the day. *4014 Haas Rd., Courtenay V9N 8H9, tel. 604/338–1422. 4 rooms. Facilities: garden, walking trails. No credit cards. Moderate.*

★ **The Kingfisher.** Situated among trees and set off the highway overlooking the Strait of Georgia, this hotel is five minutes south of Courtenay. The inn's solid furnishings, clean white-stucco walls, bright lobby with lots of greenery, and rooms with mountain and ocean views offer a nice change from the majority of plain accommodations lining the main drag. *Site 672, RR 6, Courtenay V9N 8H9, tel. 604/338–1323. 30 units. Facilities: restaurant, lounge, 2 tennis courts, outdoor pool, sauna, whirlpool. AE, DC, MC, V. Moderate.*

Malahat **Dining and Lodging** ★ **The Aerie.** The million-dollar view of Finlayson Arm and the Gulf Islands persuaded Austrians Leo and Maria Schuster to build their small, luxury resort. In this Mediterranean-style villa, some rooms have a patio; others have whirlpool tubs tucked into window nooks to take advantage of the scenery. The dining room is open to the public for stunning dinner views and outstanding cuisine. The maple-smoked salmon, pheasant consommé, medallions of venison in morel sauce, and crème brûlée with fruit sorbet are more than worth the short drive from Victoria. *600 Ebedona La., V0R 2L0, tel. 604/743–7115, fax 604/743–4766. 11 rooms, 5 suites. Facilities: restaurant, Jacuzzi, sauna, exercise room, library, heli-pad, nature trails. Reservations advised for restaurant. AE, MC, V. Expensive–Very Expensive.*

Nanaimo
Dining
★

Old Mahle House. This casually elegant place serves innovative Northwest cuisine, such as braised rabbit with Dijon mustard and red wine sauce. Twelve items adorn the regular menu, including a succulent carrot and ginger soup, and a catch of the day. Care to detail, an intimate setting, and a new addition to the three country-style rooms make this one of the finest dining experiences in the region. *Cedar and Heemer Rds., tel. 604/722–3621. Reservations advised. Dress: casual but neat. MC, V. Closed lunch and Mon.–Tues. Moderate.*

The Grotto. A perennial favorite, The Grotto is a Nanaimo institution that specializes in a variety of seafood. The restaurant is set against a waterfront background, and dining here is relaxed and casual. Try the spare ribs, gourmet pizzas, or the seafood platter—zum-zum—that's big enough for two. *1511 Stewart Ave., tel. 604/753–3303. Reservations accepted. Dress: casual. AE, MC, V. Closed lunch and Sun. Inexpensive–Moderate.*

Dining and Lodging
★

Yellow Point Lodge. Yellow Point is a spit of land south of Nanaimo, east of Ladysmith, that has a series of luxurious rustic lodges of which this is the finest example. Rebuilt in 1985 after a fire destroyed the original, the lodge lost almost nothing in ambience and gained a great deal: Larger rooms have better facilities (all have private baths). Situated on a rocky knoll overlooking the Stuart Channel, the hotel has nine lodge rooms (open year-round) and beach cabins, field cabins, a range of different-size cottages, and beach barracks (closed mid-October to mid-April) for the hardy (the summer-use cabins, cottages, and barracks have no running water and share a central bathhouse). Beach cabins can be private and include tree-trunk beds and wood-burning stoves; beach barracks are not as sound, and noises carry from unit to unit, but the location along the shore makes them popular. One hundred thirty-two acres of land allows for strolling and exploring. Three full meals and snacks are included in the tariff. *Yellow Point Rd., RR 3, Ladysmith V0R 2E0, tel. 604/245–7422. 50 rooms. Facilities: restaurant (for guests only), 2 tennis courts, seawater pool, hot tub, sauna, canoes, mountain bikes. MC, V. Expensive.*

Dining and Lodging

Dorchester Hotel. Upbeat Mediterranean tones of champagne, ochre, and teal replace the old drab blue exterior of the Dorchester. Once the Nanaimo Opera House, this elegant hotel overlooking the harbor has a distinctive character, with gold knockers on each of the doors, winding hallways, and a spacious library. The rooms are small but exceptionally comfortable, and most have views of the harbor. *70 Church St., V9R 5H4, tel. 604/754–6835; fax 604/754–2638. 70 rooms. Facilities: restaurant, meeting rooms, fitness room, hot tub, lounge, library, rooftop patio. AE, DC, MC, V. Moderate–Expensive.*

Dining and Lodging **La Coast Bastion Inn.** This hotel is conveniently located downtown near the ferry terminal, train, and bus stations. All rooms with balconies have views of the old Hudson's Bay fort and the ocean and are modernly furnished. The three eating/entertainment establishments located within the hotel make this a self-sufficient accommodation. *11 Bastion St., V9R 2Z9, tel. 604/753–6601, or 800/663–1144 in the U.S. 179 rooms. Facilities: restaurant, lounge, Irish deli/pub, gift shop, boutique, convention rooms, sauna, hot tub, gym. AE, DC, MC, V. Moderate–Expensive.*

Parksville **The Judge's Manor.** The interior of the judge's former home reflects his love for fine antiques and warm surroundings. Today, the family-run restaurant (with a glorious ocean view) still conveys kindness, from the service to the carefully prepared dishes. Local and organic produce, venison, rabbit, and other game highlight the eclectic menu. Other tasty choices include loin-of-lamb medallions. *193 Memorial Ave., tel. 604/248–2544. Reservations advised. Dress: casual but neat. AE, MC, V. Closed weekend lunch. Moderate.*

Dining and Lodging **Beach Acres Resort Hotel.** For a family vacation, this collection of cottages set in the woods facing the Georgia Strait is both charming and practical. Each unit has one or two bedrooms, living room, kitchen, fireplace, and storage areas. *1015 E. Island Hwy., V9P 2E4, tel. 604/248–3424; fax 604/248–6145. 60 cottages. Facilities: restaurant, indoor pool, sauna, whirlpool, playground, 3 tennis courts, health club. AE, DC, MC, V. 1-week minimum July–Aug. Very Expensive.*

Dining and Lodging **The Roadhouse Inn.** This Swiss chalet, set on three acres, is central to four of the region's golf courses. There are only a limited number of rooms, but all are comfortable. *1223 Smithers Rd., V9P 2C1, tel. 604/248–2912. 6 rooms. Facilities: restaurant. MC, V. Inexpensive.*

Port Hardy **Glen Lyon Inn.** All of the rooms have a full ocean view of Hardy
Dining and Lodging Bay and, like most area motels, have clean, modern amenities. Eagles are often on the premises, eyeing the water for fish to prey on. It's a short ride from the inn to the ferry terminal. *6345 Hardy Bay Rd., Box 103, V0N 2P0, tel. 604/949–7115; fax 604/949–7415. 29 rooms. Facilities: restaurant, lounge, nearby marina, boat launch. AE, DC, MC, V. Moderate.*

Sooke **Sooke Harbour House.** This original 1931 clapboard farmhouse
Dining and Lodging turned inn presents three suites, a 10-room addition, and a din-
★ ing room—all of which exude elegance. One of the finest restaurants in British Columbia, it is well worth the trip to Sooke, from Victoria. The fish is just-caught fresh, and the herbs, picked from some 200 varieties, are grown on the property. Four chefs sharing the kitchen guarantees an abundance of creative dishes. On a nice summer evening you may want to sit on the terrace, where you can catch a glimpse of the sea mammals that play by the spit of land in front of the restaurant. Equally exquisite are the romantic guest rooms, with natural-wood and white finishes adding to each unit's unique theme. Rooms range from the Herb Garden Room—decorated in shades of mint, with French doors opening onto a private patio—to the Longhouse Room, complete with Native American furnishings. All units, with fireplaces and either ocean or mountain views, come with fresh flowers, a decanter of port, and wet bars that include herbal teas and cookies. Breakfast and lunch

are included in your room rate. Hosts Frederica and Sinclair Philip have been paying attention to details here since 1979. *1528 Whiffen Spit Rd., RR 4, V0S 1N0, tel. 604/642–3421. 13 rooms. Facilities: restaurant; guest rooms and restaurant wheelchair accessible. Reservations strongly advised for restaurant. Closed lunch except for hotel guests. Dress: casual. AE, MC, V. Restaurant: Expensive–Very Expensive. Hotel: Very Expensive.*

Ucluelet/Tofino **Whale's Tale.** This is a no-frills, dark but warmly decorated the
Dining down-to-earth place where cooking and the rustic decor go hand-in-hand. The view isn't much, but the cedar-shingle building, set on pilings, shakes with a good gust of wind. The menu is highlighted by prime rib and a variety of local seafood. *1861 Peninsula Rd., Ucluelet, tel. 604/726–4621. Dress: casual. MC, V. Closed lunch and Nov.–Jan. Moderate.*

★ **The Wickaninnish Restaurant.** Before the Canadian government acquired this wonderful wood building for its interpretive center, it was a wonderful lodge. It is still a restaurant, with an ambience—the beach setting, combined with the building's glass exterior and stone-and-beam interior, accented by a stone fireplace—that cannot be matched anywhere else in the area. It is run by the same people who make Painter's Lodge in Campbell River (*see* above) such a delight. Seafood is the primary choice here—especially the West Coast chowder—but if you take the chicken-and-prawn stir-fry, you won't be disappointed. *On Long Beach, 16 km (11 mi) north of Ucluelet, tel. 604/726–7706. Reservations advised for 7 or more. Dress: casual. AE, MC, V. Closed mid-Oct.–mid-Mar. Moderate.*

Lodging **Chesterman's Beach Bed and Breakfast.** This is one of several
★ small, romantic bed-and-breakfasts located on the beach, but the front yard—which is the rolling ocean surf—makes this one unique. You can while away the hours just walking the beach, searching the tidal pools, or—from March to October—watching whales migrating by the front door. The self-contained suite in the main house and the separate Lookout Suite are romantic, cozy, and unique; both have comfortable beds and a view of the beach. The self-sufficient one-bedroom garden cottage offers no ocean view but accommodates up to four; it's a good option for a family vacation. Owner Joan Dublanko makes hot muffins every morning. *1345 Chesterman's Beach Rd., Tofino V0R 2Z0, tel. 604/725–3726. 3 suites. Facilities: bikes, surfboards, beach. V. Moderate–Expensive.*

Pacific Sands Beach Resort. Just a mile north of Pacific Rim National Park is this rustic resort with motel suites and individual two-bedroom cottages. The motel rooms are basic with modern furnishings, but fireplaces make them seem cozier. Some of the rooms in the new, three-story addition have Jacuzzi tubs. Pacific Sands is close to Long Beach golf course and is on the ocean. *1421 Pacific Rim Hwy., Box 237, Tofino V0R 2Z0, tel. 604/725–3322. 58 rooms. AE, MC, V. Moderate–Expensive.*

Canadian Princess Fishing Resort. If old ships are to your liking, book a berth on this converted survey ship which has 30 comfortable, but hardly opulent, staterooms. Each offers one to six berths, and all share washrooms; for something a bit more spacious, request the captain's cabin. Roomier than the ship cabins and complete with more contemporary furnishings are the resort's deluxe shoreside rooms. Promising an unusual experience, this Spartan resort provides the bare necessities—mostly to the many fishermen who flock here during the summer. *The Boat Basin, Box 939, Ucluelet V0R 3A0, tel. 604/726–7771 or 800/663–7090; fax 604/726–7121. 76 sleeping units. Facilities: 10 charter boats. AE, MC, V. Inexpensive–Moderate.*

Whistler

Dining **Florentyna's** When you've had your fill of the crowds and inflated prices of the village, head south to Florentyna's in Whistler Creek, where you'll find reasonably priced salad, pasta, seafood, and steak. Favorites include steamer clams or mussels in wine and herbs, sides of honey-and-garlic or barbecued pork ribs, and smoked-salmon fettuccine. A separate menu is available in the pub. *2129 Lake Placid Rd., Whistler, tel. 604/932–4424. Reservations recommended. Dress: casual. AE, DC, MC, V. Moderate.*

Il Caminetto Di Umberto; Trattoria di Umberto; The Grill. Umberto Menghi is Vancouver's best-known restaurateur because of his fabulously successful Italian restaurants. Now there are three in Whistler. Il Caminetto and the Trattoria are in the village, and The Grill is in Whistler Creek, a couple of miles south. Umberto offers home-style Italian cooking and specializes in pasta dishes like crab-stuffed cannelloni or a four-cheese lasagna that mix well with the relaxed atmosphere. The Trattoria has a Tuscan-style rotisserie, featuring a pasta dish served with a tray of chopped tomatoes, hot pepper, basil, olive oil, anchovies, and Parmesan so that you can mix it as spicy and flavorful as you like. The Grill's specialty is lean grilled beef and chicken, and Il Caminetto, perhaps the best restaurant in the Whistler area, is known for its veal, osso buco, and zabaglione. *Il Caminetto: 4242 Village Stroll, tel. 604/932–4442; Trattoria: Mountainside Lodge, tel. 604/932–5858; The Grill: Whistler Creek Lodge, tel. 604/932–3000. Reservations advised for dinner. Dress: neat but casual. AE, DC, MC, V. Expensive.*

★ **Les Deux Gros.** The name means "the two fat guys," which may explain the restaurant's motto, "Never trust a skinny chef." Portions of the country French cuisine are generous indeed. The spinach and warm duck salad, steak tartare, juicy rack of lamb, and salmon Wellington are all superbly crafted and presented, and the service is friendly but unobtrusive. Located just southwest of the village, this is the spot for that special romantic dinner; request one of the prime tables by the massive stone fireplace. *1200 Alta Lake Rd., tel. 604/932–4611. Dinner only. Reservations advised. Dress: neat but casual. AE, DC, MC, V. Expensive.*

The Wildflower Cafe. Although this is the main dining room of the Chateau Whistler, it's an informal, comfortable restaurant. Huge picture windows overlook the ski slopes and let in the bright sun reflected off the snow. The rustic effect of the Chateau Whistler lobby continues in the Wildflower—more than 100 antique wood birdhouses decorate the room, and chairs and tables have that farmhouse look. Although there is an à la carte menu that focuses on Pacific Northwest cuisine, the restaurant features terrific breakfast, lunch, and dinner buffets that may include fresh crepes and omelets, sweet potato–and–parsnip soup, barbecued salmon, smoked halibut, artichoke-and-mushroom salad, pepper salad, seafood pâté, pasta in a spicy tomato sauce, and cold meats. *Chateau Whistler Hotel, tel. 604/938–8000. Reservations advised for dinner. Dress: neat but casual. AE, DC, MC, V. Expensive.*

Dining and Lodging   Any accommodations, including pensions, can be booked through the Whistler Resort Association (tel. 604/932–4222). All pensions are outside the village, so if you don't have a car, pick one within walking distance.

Chateau Whistler. Whistler's most extravagant hotel is a large and friendly-looking fortress, just outside the village. It was built and run by Canadian Pacific Railway. It is the same style as the Banff Springs Hotel and the Jasper Park Lodge; the marvelous lobby is filled with rustic Canadiana, handmade Mennonite rugs, enormous fireplaces, and enticing overstuffed sofas. Floor-to-ceiling windows in the lounge, the health club, and the Wildflower Cafe overlook the base of Blackcomb Mountain. It's possible to schuss from there right into the basement of the hotel. The standard rooms are called premier and are fairly small, but the suites are fit for royalty, with specially commissioned quilts and artwork, and are complemented by antique furnishings. Both the Wildflower Cafe (*see* Dining, above) and La Fiesta, a tapas bar, are very good choices for a meal. Look for summer rates that drop by 50%. *4599 Chateau Blvd., Box 100, V0N 1B0, tel. 604/938–8000, fax 604/938–2020. 303 doubles, 40 suites, rooms for the disabled. Facilities: 2 restaurants, bar, indoor-outdoor pool, indoor and outdoor Jacuzzis, morning stretch classes for skiers, 3 covered tennis courts, golf course. AE, DC, MC, V. Very Expensive.*

★ **Le Chamois.** Sharing the prime ski-in, ski-out location at the base of the Blackcomb runs is this elegant, new luxury hotel. Of the 50 spacious guest rooms with convenience kitchens, the most popular are the studios with Jacuzzi tubs set in the living room in front of bay windows overlooking the slopes and lifts. Guests can keep an eye on the action also from the glass elevators and the heated outdoor pool. Parking in the underground lot is complimentary, an uncommon bonus in Whistler. *4557 Blackcomb Way, tel. 604/932–8700, fax 604/938–1888. 50 suites and studios, rooms for the disabled. Facilities: 2 restaurants, outdoor heated pool, Jacuzzi, fitness room, laundry room, complimentary valet ski locker, parking, shuttle to village. AE, DC, MC, V. Very Expensive.*

Pension Edelweiss. The Edelweiss is one of seven charming and very European bed-and-breakfasts around Whistler, and it's within walking distance of Whistler Village. Rooms have balconies and fireplaces and that crisp, northern European spic-and-span feel, in keeping with the Bavarian chalet style of the house. Each morning a different breakfast (included in room rate) is served: Scandinavian, American, French, German. For dinner, proprietor Ursula Morel serves fondue or raclette. Minimum stay in high season is three nights. *7162 Nancy Greene Way, Box 850, tel. 604/932–3641, fax 604/932–3776. 8 rooms, all with private bath. Facilities: sauna, Jacuzzi, transportation to lifts. MC, V. Moderate.*

8 The Canadian Rockies

by Peter Oliver

Peter Oliver is a New York writer whose articles have appeared in Backpacker, The New York Times, Skiing, Summit, *and many other publications. He is author of* The Insider's Guide to the Best Skiing in New England.

Comparing mountains is a subjective and imprecise business. Yet few would argue that the 640-kilometer (400-mile) stretch of the Canadian Rockies easily ranks as one of the most extravagantly beautiful ranges on earth. With little standing between the mountains and the Alberta prairie, the Rockies etch on the horizon an abrupt and stony line of chaotic grandeur that can be seen from 100 kilometers (60 miles) away to the east. Behind the prairie, granite walls rise thousands of feet above evergreen forests and glacially carved basins.

The peak that best epitomizes the character of the Canadian Rockies is Mt. Robson, which, at 3,954 meters (12,931 feet), is the highest of them all. A colossus of tumbling glaciers and cliff walls, usually shrouded in storm clouds, Mt. Robson creates its own irascible climate zone: The rush of avalanches down its flanks has triggered wind blasts well over 320 kilometers (200 miles) an hour.

The Canadian Rockies, about 60 million years old, are relatively young as mountains go. The parallel ranges of the Columbia Mountains, just west of the Rockies, were first formed about 180 million years ago. Measured against the U.S. Rockies, the Rockies of Canada are not exceptionally high; elevations generally average 600–900 meters (about 2,000–3,000 feet) lower than those in Colorado, for example. Still, the Canadian Rockies *seem* higher, primarily because the tree line—the approximate elevation above which trees generally can't grow—is lower. In the Canadian Rockies, the tree line is at about 2,000 meters (6,500 feet) compared with Colorado tree lines that usually start above 3,000 meters (9,750 feet).

But while glaciers in the United States have all but disappeared (except for those in Alaska and the Northern Cascades of Washington State), they remain a common sight in Canada—in Glacier National Park in the Columbias, for example, more than 400 glaciers cover 10% of the park's territory. The pale glacial blue strikes a dramatic balance against the blue-gray granite, the deep green of fir, spruce, and larch forests, and the panchromatic sweep of wildflowers. The glacial melt also feeds high-mountain lakes with mineral-rich silt deposits that tint the waters emerald green and cobalt blue, colors that change with the moods of the weather and the seasons.

Recognizing early the exceptional natural beauty of the region, the Canadian government began shielding the area from human development and resource exploitation in the 1880s. In 1885, the government created a park preserve around the Cave and Basin Hot Springs in Banff. Two years later, Canada's first national park, Rocky Mountain Park (later Banff National Park), was officially established. Lands that would later become Yoho National Park and Glacier National Park in the Columbias were first set aside in 1886.

Today, approximately 25,000 square kilometers (roughly 10,000 square miles)—an area larger than the state of New Hampshire—are protected in seven national parks in the Rockies and the Columbias. Because they were protected early on, the parks of the Rockies—Waterton Lakes, Banff, Kootenay, Yoho, and Jasper—have remained relatively untouched by human development. The only significant clusters of human settlement are the town centers of Banff, Jasper, and Waterton Lakes, and the area around Lake Louise. Several thousand more square kilometers are also protected as wilderness areas and provincial parks, most notably Mt. Robson and Mt. Assiniboine provincial parks and Kananaskis Country.

The establishment of parks was a boon to wildlife, and today, it is virtually impossible to visit the national parks and *not* spot elk, mule deer, or bighorn sheep, especially in fall and winter. The presence of two major roadways, Routes 1 and 93, as well as an extensive network of hiking trails and climbing routes, has made the wilderness of the Canadian Rockies remarkably accessible. Visitors taking advantage of easy wilderness access have made Banff the most visited of Canada's national parks. June, July, and August are the months when most visitors come to the parks; it's also the time when lodging prices double. But the changing colors of fall (especially when contrasted against the early snows) attract leaf lovers into mid-October. And winter snows, most abundant in the Columbias, keep skiers coming from December through April. Only the transitional months of April, May, late October, and November are quiet times.

Hikes of no more than 3 or 4 kilometers (about 2½ miles) can lead to secluded lakes and basins of pristine, high-alpine splendor. Roadside trailheads are plentiful, and a number of trails are wide and gentle enough for wheelchair access. Horses, helicopters, mountain bikes, canoes, skis in winter—the modes of transportation for exploring the mountain outback are many, as are equipment-rental and guide services as well as backcountry guide books. (*See* Sports and Outdoor Activities, below.)

Many, too, are the moods of the weather. Summer temperatures typically range between the 60s and 80s, although the temperature tends to drop 5 to 10 degrees with every 300 meters (1,000 feet) of elevation gain. Mid-winter temperatures typically range between the teens and low 30s. However, snow in July is not uncommon at higher elevations, and warm chinook winds that hit the eastern slopes in winter can raise temperatures into the 60s in January, as happened during the 1988 Winter Olympics. Even for summer months, it is advisable to pack a wool sweater, warm socks, and light gloves, especially if you plan to do much hiking, boating, cycling, or other outdoor activities. Weather can change quickly, and with it, temperatures. For half-day or longer hikes, it is always a good idea to pack a few light layers (e.g., a light sweater or sweatshirt) and a water-repellent windbreaker.

Essential Information

Important Addresses and Numbers

Tourist Information The three major sources of tourism information are **Alberta Tourism** (Main Level, City Centre, 10155 102 St., Edmonton, AB T5J 4L6, tel. 800/661–8888), **Tourism British Columbia** (Parliament Bldgs., Victoria, BC V8V 1X4, tel. 800/663–6000), and **Canadian Parks Service** (Information Services, Box 2989, Station M, Calgary, AB T2P 3H8, tel. 403/292–4401). Parks Canada information is also available at the **Parks Information Office** (Box 900, 224 Banff Ave., Banff, AB T0L 0C0, tel. 403/762–4256). Specify particular interests when requesting information; all the organizations have an extensive list of maps and publications.

For local information in Banff, contact the **Banff-Lake Louise Chamber of Commerce** (335 Beaver St., Banff, AB T0L 0C0, tel. 403/762–3777); in Jasper, **Jasper Park Chamber of Commerce** (Box 98, Jasper, AB T0E 1E0, tel. 403/852–3858); in Kananaskis Country, **Kananaskis Country** (Suite 100, 1011 Glenmore Trail SW, Calgary, AB T2V 4R6, tel. 403/297–3362); in Waterton Lakes, **Waterton Lakes National Park** (Superintendent, Waterton Park, AB T0K 2M0, tel. 403/859–2224) or **Waterton Park Chamber of Commerce** (Box 55, Waterton Park, AB T0K 2M0, tel. 403/859–2203); in Revelstoke and Glacier Parks, **Mount Revelstoke and Glacier National Parks** (Park Superintendent, Box 350, Revelstoke, BC V0E 2S0, tel. 604/837–5155); and in the British Columbia Rockies, the **Rocky Mountain Visitors Association** (Box 10, Kimberley, BC V1A 2Y5, tel. 604/427–3344).

Emergencies Throughout Alberta and British Columbia **911** is the number for **police** or **ambulance.** For any extended trip into the backcountry, always register with the nearest park warden's office.

Arriving and Departing by Plane

Calgary is the most common gateway for travelers arriving by plane. Those who plan to visit only Jasper and northern park regions may prefer to use Edmonton as a gateway city. Both cities have international airports served by several major carriers; the Calgary flight schedule is somewhat more extensive.

Airports and **Calgary International Airport** and **Edmonton International Air-**
Airlines **port** serve the British Columbia Rockies region. (For airline information, *see* Arriving and Departing by Plane in Chapter 9.)

Air Canada and **Canadian Air** have daily flights to and from Cranbrook's airport, in southern British Columbia; most of these flights connect with flights through Vancouver International Airport and the international airports in Calgary and Edmonton.

Arriving and Departing by Car, Train, and Bus

By Car Route 1, the Trans-Canada Highway, is the principal east–west route into the region. Banff is 128 kilometers (80 miles) west of Calgary on Route 1 and 858 kilometers (515 miles) east of Vancouver. The other major east–west routes are Route 16 to the north, the main highway between Edmonton and Jasper, and Route 3 to the south. The main routes from the south are Route 89, which enters Canada east of Waterton Lakes National Park from Montana, and Route 93, also from Montana, which provides access to the British Columbia Rockies.

By Train **Rocky Mountaineer Railtours** (tel. 800/665–7245) offers service connecting Vancouver, Kamloops, Banff, Jasper, Calgary, and Edmonton. **VIA Rail** (tel. 800/361–3677) offers overnight service connecting Toronto, Edmonton, and Vancouver. Call for schedules.

By Bus **Greyhound/Trailways** (call local listing) provides regular service to Calgary, Edmonton, and Vancouver, with connecting service to Jasper and Waterton Lakes. **Brewster Tours** (tel. 800/

661–1152) offers service between the Calgary International Airport and Banff, Jasper, and Lake Louise.

Getting Around

A fee is charged to all vehicles entering the national parks. A day pass is $4.25; a four-day pass, $9.50; and an annual pass, for any stay longer than four days, $26.75. You are permitted to leave and reenter the park for the duration of the pass without additional charge.

By Car Snow arrives early in fall and leaves late in spring. When traveling between October and April, stay informed of local road conditions, especially if you're traveling over mountain passes or along the Icefields Parkway (Route 93). A few roads, such as Route 40 over Highwood Pass in Kananaskis Country, are closed during the winter.

Rental Cars Car-rental outlets are located at the Calgary and Edmonton airports, as well as in Banff, Jasper, and Cranbrook. Daily rentals for sightseeing are available but should be reserved well ahead of time, especially in summer.

Guided Tours

Orientation **Brewster Transportation and Tours** (Box 1140, Banff, AB T0L
Bus Tours 0C0, tel. in Banff, 403/762–2241; in Lake Louise, 403/522–3544; in Jasper, 403/852–3332; or 800/661–1152) offers half-day and full-day sightseeing tours of the parks. Prices start at about $12.

Tauck Tours (11 Wilton Rd., Westport, CT 06881, tel. 203/226–6911) and **Holland American Westours** (300 Elliot Ave. W, Seattle, WA 98119, tel. 206/281–3535) feature multiday bus tours through the region. Some Tauck Tours include heli-hiking options.

Boat Tours **Minnewanka Boat Tours** (Box 2189, Banff, AB T0L 0C0, tel. 403/762–3473) offers summer tours on Lake Minnewanka, near Banff.

Maligne Lake Scenic Cruises (626 Connaught Dr., Jasper, AB T0E 1E0, tel. 403/852–3370) runs half-day tours on Maligne Lake, near Jasper, from mid-May through September.

Scenic Boat Cruises (Box 126, Waterton, AB T0K 2M0, tel. 403/859–2362) offers half-day and full-day cruises of Waterton Lake, some with hiking options.

Auto Tours Audiocassette tapes for self-guided auto tours of the parks are produced by **Inc. Auto Tape Tours** and **Rocky Mountain Tape Tours.** Tapes can be rented or purchased at news or gift shops in Banff, Lake Louise, and Jasper.

Special-interest **Challenge Enterprises** (1300 Railway Ave., Box 2008, Canmore,
Seasonal Tours AB T0L 0M0, tel. 403/678–2628) has a variety pack of tour options, including fishing, rafting, and cycling trips in summer, as well as snowmobiling, ice-fishing, and dogsledding tours in winter.

Kingmik Expeditions (Box 227, Lake Louise, AB T0L 1E0, tel. 604/344–7288) specializes in dogsledding tours, from half-day to five-day outings.

For hiking, mountaineering, or backcountry ski tours, **Banff Alpine Guides** (Box 1025, Banff, AB T0L 0C0, tel. 403/762–2791) organizes tours according to weather conditions. Bookings can be arranged for private groups. The **Canadian School of Mountaineering** (Box 723, Canmore, AB T0L 0M0, tel. 403/678–4134) offers tours and instruction for mountaineering (in summer and winter) and backcountry skiing. In the Jasper area, the **Jasper Climbing School and Mountaineering Service** (Box 452, Jasper, AB T0E 1E0, tel. 403/852–3964) has guided hiking and mountaineering trips, as well as ski tours in winter.

In Waterton Lakes National Park, **Russell Guide Service** (Box 68, Waterton Park, AB T0K 2M0, tel. 403/627–3241) runs fishing and hiking tours, focusing on regional flora and fauna.

Alberta Tourism's booklet, "Winter Vacationer's Guide," has listings and descriptions of more than 50 ski-tour operators that package trips to the region. Tours include downhill, heli-skiing, cross-country, and backcountry packages. The booklet is available from **Alberta Tourism** (*see* Essential Information, above).

Bicycle Tours Several operators offer guided on-road and off-road bicycle tours. **Rocky Mountain Cycle Tours** (Box 1987, Canmore, AB T0L 0M0, tel. 403/678–6770) features one- to seven-day tours, both in the Banff area and in British Columbia.

Exploring the Canadian Rockies

Most people who come to the Canadian Rockies arrive from the east, from Calgary, via Route 1. Because it is just more than an hour's drive west of Calgary, and because of the abundant lodging, dining, and shopping options, Banff is the logical first stop for most visitors. Many, however, continue on to Lake Louise, a half hour's drive north of Banff.

From Banff, the most popular excursion is the scenic drive north, along the Icefields Parkway (Route 93), to Jasper, 280 kilometers (180 miles) away. Excursions into Yoho and Kootenay parks are not as common, primarily because services, especially in Kootenay, are almost nonexistent.

A sensible and economical alternative to using Banff as a base camp is to stay in Canmore, 40 kilometers (25 miles) east, where lodging is generally less expensive. Canmore is an excellent stepping-off point for those interested in exploring Kananaskis Country, the mountain ranges that stretch south of Banff. With fewer restrictions than the national parks, Kananaskis Country is popular with sportsmen—horseback riders, hunters, snowmobilers, and the like.

Another economical option to staying in Banff is to find accommodations in the British Columbia Rockies. Inexpensive lodging is abundant in Radium Hot Springs, 128 kilometers (80 miles) southwest of Banff, at the southern edge of Kootenay National Park. Also, consider staying in Golden, on Route 1, 80 kilometers (50 miles) west of Lake Louise. These towns are good access points to the Columbia ranges as well as the Rockies, if not as scenic as the townsites within the parks.

Waterton Lakes National Park, 354 kilometers (220 miles) to the south, is a rare side trip from Banff, with much of the drive along a relatively undistinguished route (though no drive in this part of the world really lacks scenery). People who visit Waterton Lakes generally make it their principal destination or combine it with a vacation in Glacier National Park across the U.S. border in Montana.

Highlights for First-time Visitors

Banff Springs Hotel, Tour 1
Cave and Basin Hot Springs, Tour 1
Chateau Lake Louise, Tour 1
Icefields Parkway (between Bow Pass and Sunwapta Falls), Tour 2
Kananaskis Village, Tour 3
Kimberly, Tour 4
Maligne Lake, Tour 2

Tour 1: Banff and Lake Louise

Numbers in the margin correspond to points of interest on the Canadian Rockies and Banff maps.

❶ Banff is a town of unlikely contrasts: Amid the bustle of commercialism, elk regularly graze on the town common; tour-bus sightseers carrying souvenir-stuffed bags mix on Banff Avenue (the main drag) with rugged outdoorspeople, among them some of the world's most accomplished mountaineers. For almost all who come to the Canadian Rockies, Banff is the central depot in their Canadian Rockies travel. The reason is simple: Except for Jasper, the crossroads hamlet of Lake Louise, and tiny Field in Yoho, Banff is the only town in the four contiguous parks.

Banff, by far the largest of the four towns, straddles a thin line between mountain resort town and tourist trap. It is certainly not a quaint little western outpost; except for the oft-photographed Banff Springs Hotel, its architecture is mostly modern, simple, and undistinguished. Because of the limitations that park regulations have set on growth, Banff hasn't expanded in recent years but has instead compressed in on itself. This and the contrasting backdrop of surrounding wilderness make Banff the hub of hyperactivity during the summer.

The two points of reference that Banff explorers use are Banff Avenue and the Banff Springs Hotel. An amazing number of shops and restaurants have been crammed together on the
❷ short stretch of **Banff Avenue** that composes the core of downtown. Clustered together in about a half-dozen indoor malls are art galleries, clothing stores, photo stores, bookstores, and confectioners whose fudge and cookie output makes Banff Avenue a mine field for anyone with a sweet tooth. Items sold in the galleries range from trinkets to kitsch to genuine art. Except for a few stores in Jasper and a few boutiques in the Chateau Lake Louise and Samson Mall in Lake Louise, this is pretty much where shopping begins and ends in the national parks.

Heading south, Banff Avenue crosses the Bow River over a
❸ great stone bridge, ending in a T in front of the **Parks Information Office.** Here, you can pick up park trail maps and other

The Canadian Rockies

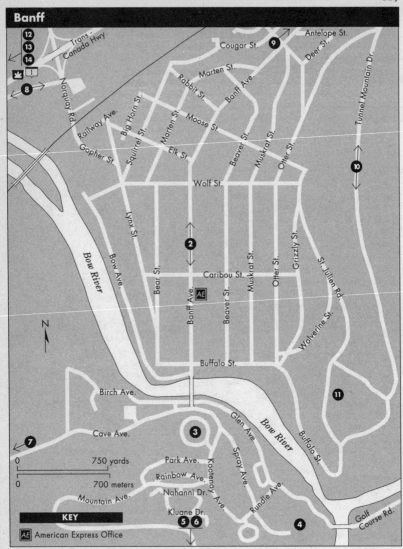

Banff

Antelope St.
Cougar St.
Marten St.
Rabbit St.
Banff Ave.
Moose St.
Big Horn St.
Marten St.
Squirrel St.
Elk St.
Beaver St.
Muskrat St.
Otter St.
Deer St.
Tunnel Mountain Dr.
Wolf St.
Railway Ave.
Gopher St.
Lynx St.
Bow Ave.
Bear St.
Banff Ave.
Caribou St.
Beaver St.
Muskrat St.
Otter St.
Grizzly St.
St. Julien Rd.
Wolverine St.
Bow River
Buffalo St.
Birch Ave.
Cave Ave.
Glen Ave.
Bow River
Buffalo St.
Park Ave.
Rainbow Ave.
Nahanni Dr.
Mountain Ave.
Kluane Dr.
Kootenay Ave.
Spray Ave.
Rundle Ave.
Golf Course Rd.
Trans-Canada Hwy.
Norquay Rd.
N

0   750 yards
0   700 meters

KEY

AE American Express Office

Banff Avenue, **2**
Banff Centre, **11**
Banff Springs Hotel, **4**
Buffalo Paddock, **9**
Cave and Basin Hot Springs, **7**
Chateau Lake Louise, **13**
Lake Louise Gondola, **12**
Moraine Lake, **14**
Parks Information Office, **3**
Sulphur Mountain Gondola, **6**
Tunnel Mountain Drive, **10**
Upper Hot Springs, **5**
Vermilion Lakes Drive, **8**

materials concerning the area. *224 Banff Ave., tel. 403/762–4256. Open daily 8 AM–10 PM.*

④ A left turn (about 2 kilometers, or 1 mile) leads to the **Banff Springs Hotel** (*see* Lodging, below), a year-round three-ring circus. Built in 1888, the hotel is easily recognized by its castlelike exterior; inside the visitor can expect to get lost in the crazy-quilt network of restaurants, shops, salons, and ballrooms. Even renovators got confused; evidently, the hotel has a hidden room—one that was accidentally sealed off by an over-zealous plasterer. It was left that way to add a chapter to the hotel lore.

South of the information office, take Kootenay Avenue to Mountain Avenue. Follow Mountain Avenue for one mile to ⑤ **Upper Hot Springs** (tel. 403/762–2056) for a dip, or to the ⑥ **Sulphur Mountain Gondola** for a vista. Views during the steep eight-minute ride to and from the summit are spectacular, but they are hardly private. The observation decks and short summit trails are well visited, especially in summer.

A right turn off Banff Avenue at the Parks Information Office leads to the **Cave and Basin Hot Springs.** Once considered sa-⑦ cred by the Stoney Indians, the springs were discovered by prospectors in 1883; they became the birthplace of the park system when they were given national park protection in 1885. Two interpretive trails provide good insight into the geology and plant life of the region.

The **Upper Hot Springs** and the **Cave and Basin Centre Pool** (Cave Ave., 2 km, or 1¼ mi, west of downtown Banff, tel. 403/762–4900) can be soothing, invigorating, or both. The Upper Hot Springs is more of a soak; Cave and Basin is more of a swim. Lockers, suits, and towels are available to rent at both. The Cave and Basin Centre is open June through September; the Upper Hot Springs is open year-round.

Several short excursions are possible from the town of Banff. ⑧ **Vermilion Lakes Drive,** just off the west Banff exit from Route 1, offers one of the best opportunities for wildlife sightings: elk, bighorn sheep, muskrat, and the very occasional moose. ⑨ During the summer, the **buffalo paddock,** near the east Banff exit from Route 1, is the place to go to see the animals.

⑩ Also on the eastern side of town, **Tunnel Mountain Drive** makes a scenic 4.8-kilometer (3-mile) loop. Two points of particular interest along the drive are the Hoodoos, fingerlike rock forma-⑪ tions caused by erosion, and the **Banff Centre** (St. Julien Rd., tel. 403/762–6300), *the* place in town and in the parks for the performing arts.

Most people traveling from Banff to Lake Louise take Route 1 for about 56 kilometers (35 miles) north along the Bow River. But if you aren't in a hurry, the two-lane Route 1A, running approximately parallel to Route 1, is the more scenic option.

⑫ The **Lake Louise Gondola,** which carries skiers to the ski-area summit in winter, is open for sightseeing rides in summer. The 2,034-meter (6,700-foot) summit of Mt. Whitehorn offers a good view of Lake Louise and the Victoria Glacier. Hiking trails—as well as ski trails that can be hiked—lead from the summit. *Lake Louise Gondola, exit Rte. 1 at Lake Louise, tel. 403/522–3555. Admission: $8 adults ($5.50 one-way hikers), $4 children 5–12. Open June–Sept.*

At the Lake Louise junction, a right turn leads to the Lake Louise ski area, one of the top three or four skiing sites in Canada. It was originally to be the site of the 1988 Olympic alpine skiing events, but concerns about the Olympic crowds' possible environmental impact on the park led instead to the development of Mt. Allen in Kananaskis Country as the main Olympic venue for alpine skiing.

A left turn at the junction leads to what ostensibly is the center of Lake Louise: a crossroads, a train crossing, a few hotels, and a small shopping center just off Route 1. Almost all visitors zip ⑬ through town barely noticing it on their way to **Chateau Lake Louise** (another 6 kilometers, or 3¾ miles), built in 1923, which overlooks the blue-green lake and the Victoria Glacier. The hotel's setting is as scenic as it is popular; camera shutters must certainly click thousands of times a day during the summer months. Canoe rentals are available at the boat house.

The chateau is also a departure point for several short, moderately strenuous, well-traveled hiking routes. The most popular hike (about 3.5 kilometers, or 2¼ miles) is to the small teahouse overlooking Lake Agnes. The tiny lake hangs on a mountain-surrounded shelf that opens to the east with a distant view of the Bow River valley.

Time Out The **Lake Agnes teahouse** is a one-room café tucked onto a ledge overlooking the small lake and the waterfall that descends steeply from it. Fresh baked goods and a variety of teas are a welcome reward for the short hike, and the view from the porch is fabulous.

A longer hike (about 6 kilometers, or 3¾ miles) leads to a larger teahouse-restaurant on the Plain of the Six Glaciers, at the edge of the Victoria Glacier moraine. This is a popular trail's end for day hikers—a great place for picnicking or basking in the sun on a warm day—as well as a starting point for more ambitious climbers headed for the high glacial ridges.

⑭ The other popular place to visit is **Moraine Lake,** 11 kilometers (7 miles) from the heart of Lake Louise. In an area dubbed the "Valley of the Ten Peaks," the lake reflects in deep blue the granite peaks that rise abruptly around it. Moraine Lake is one of the two main stops that tour buses make in Lake Louise (Lake Louise itself being the other).

Several moderate hiking trails lead from the lake into some spectacular country; a popular overnight hike is to trek over Sentinel Pass and through Paradise Valley to Lake Louise. For great views, the short (3-kilometer, or 1⅞-mile) but steep hike from Moraine Lake to Larch Valley is well worth the effort. Canoe rentals are available from the office of Moraine Lake Cabins. *Moraine Lake Cabin Office, Box 70, Lake Louise, AB T0L 1E0, tel. 403/522–3733. Open June 1–Sept. 30.*

Tour 2: North and West of Banff

Heading North Just north of Lake Louise, Routes 1 and 93 diverge. Route 93, the Icefields Parkway, continues northward for more than 230 kilometers (143 miles) to Jasper. Route 1 bears west over Kicking Horse Pass—named, according to local lore, after an unpleasant encounter between a pack animal and a member of an exploratory expedition in the mid-1800s—into Yoho National Park and British Columbia.

If possible, pick a clear day to drive the Icefields Parkway. Basically, the *only* thing to do along the parkway is to take in the scenery, whether through a car or bus window or from a hiking trail. As you drive north, the more dramatic scenery will be on your left. The peaks demarcate the Continental Divide; many of the great rivers of western Canada spring from the glaciers and ice fields along the divide. (Ice fields are essentially giant frozen lakes, while glaciers are the frozen rivers that extend from them.) There are several scenic overlooks and short, well-marked hiking trails along the highway, providing not only breathtaking mountain views but also firsthand lessons in glacial dynamics. Only experienced hikers or climbers should venture far onto the glacier without a guide. Hidden crevasses and other hazards can make a simple jaunt treacherous.

⑮ The parkway begins a steady climb from the intersection of Routes 1 and 93, to **Bow Pass,** which, at 2,088 meters (6,850 feet), may be covered with snow as late as May and as early as September. On the north side of the pass is Peyto Lake; on the south side is Bow Lake, source of the Bow River that flows through Banff. Above Bow Lake hangs the edge of Crowfoot Glacier; to the south, across the lake, is the beginning of the Waputik Icefield. Around the lake are stubbly pines and underbrush—the tree line ends here, and high-alpine country begins.

Time Out From Bow Pass, the road gradually descends past Peyto Lake to **Saskatchewan River Crossing.** Between Lake Louise and Jasper, this is the only place from fall to spring (except during the summer, when you can refuel at the Icefield Centre; *see* below) where you can get food and refuel. Stop for the gas, but you'll be wise to bring a picnic lunch; the cafeteria food is overpriced and unimpressive.

The road descends from the crossing into the North Saskatchewan River valley. Three river systems diverge here—the Saskatchewan, Howse, and Misaya rivers. From several overlooks you can see the three river valleys and the glaciers that reach from the giant ice fields ahead. The Parker Ridge trail—a 3-kilometer (1⅞-mile) loop north of the crossing—provides an excellent view of the Saskatchewan Glacier, whence the river of the same name begins.

Shortly, the road begins to climb again, in places along steep hairpin turns, toward Sunwapta Pass—the juncture of Banff and Jasper national parks. Wildlife abounds in this area and is most visible in spring and autumn after a snowfall, when herds of bighorn sheep come to the road to lick up the salt used to melt snow and ice. Drive cautiously.

After Sunwapta Pass, **Athabasca Glacier,** an extension of the Columbia Icefield, appears on your left. The Columbia Icefield, covering 325 square kilometers (125 square miles), is the largest mass of ice in subarctic North America. Well worthwhile is a trip onto the Athabasca Glacier, via buses (called snowcoaches) modified to drive on ice. Hikers can also walk onto the tongue of the glacier, but the going can be slow and chilly. *Bus tours: Brewster Tours, tel. 403/762-2241. Admission to buses May–mid-Oct.: $17.50 adults, $7 children, for 1½-hr tour.*

Walking tours: tel. 403/852–4242. $20 for 5-hr walk, $15 for 3-hr walk.

16 Across the highway, on your right, is the **Icefield Centre,** where you can get food, gas, and even lodging in the summer. The center also provides interpretive exhibits, including a model of the entire ice field, an audiovisual presentation, and guided walking tours. *125 km (75 mi) north of Lake Louise on Rte. 93, tel. 403/852–4242. Open Sept.–May, daily 9–5; June–Aug., daily 9–7.*

From Icefield Centre the highway descends gradually into Jasper National Park, leaving the glaciers, ice fields, and waterfalls behind. One point of interest along the way is **Athabasca Falls,** where the Athabasca River is squeezed through a narrow gorge. The site is especially dramatic in early summer, when the river is swollen by the snowmelt.

At Athabasca Falls there is a juncture: Route 93 continues ahead, while Route 93A bears left toward Mt. Edith Cavell, perhaps the most imposing peak in the park. From here you can pick up trails leading to Tonquin Valley, *the* most popular hiking area in the park, and Marmot Basin, which is particularly attractive to skiers. Twenty-four kilometers (15 miles) later the highways converge. Nearby, Route 93 joins Route 16, also called the Yellowhead Highway, which reaches east 360 kilometers (225 miles) to Edmonton.

The town of Jasper is at the edge of a broad, open valley where the Athabasca and Miette rivers converge. The modest but attractive town first came into being in 1911–1912, with the arrival of the railroad. As you enter the town from the south onto **18** **Connaught Drive,** the main drag, train tracks run parallel on the right.

On the left the stores, restaurants, and inexpensive motels line Connaught Drive. Unlike in Banff, the shopping and dining in Jasper are low-key matters, because most people who come here use the town as a base for traveling elsewhere in the park, rather than as a final destination.

Many people consider Jasper the preeminent backpacking area in North America. Multiday loops of more than 160 kilometers (100 miles) are possible on well-maintained trails. However, day trips are much more common, especially around Mt. Edith Cavell, Pyramid Lake, Jasper Park Lodge, and Maligne Lake.

19 Attractions nearest to the town are the **Jasper Tramway,** 3 kilometers (1⅞ miles) south of town off Route 93 on Whistlers Mountain Road. The tram rises 950 vertical meters (3,000 feet) on the steep flank of Whistlers Mountain, and you can take in stunning views from the summit of Mt. Robson (when clear) to the west and the Miette and Athabasca valleys, making the trip worth it. *Tel. 403/852–3093. Admission: $7.50 adults, $3.75 children. Open mid-Apr.–mid-Oct.; call for times; hours vary throughout season.*

Time Out At the summit of Whistler's, have a leisurely dinner on the glass-enclosed terrace of the **Tramway Restaurant** (Continental cuisine, fully licensed). After a sunset meal, a short after-dinner hike, and glorious views, take the 11 PM (summer) tram back down to the bottom.

⓴ Another short, popular excursion is to **Pyramid** and **Patricia lakes,** just 4 kilometers (2½ miles) from town. Different sorts of boats can be rented from Pyramid Lake Bungalows (*see* Lodging, below), including canoes, kayaks, catamarans, and motorized surfboards. *Pyramid Ave., tel. 403/852–3536. Open May–Oct., approximately 8 AM–10 PM. Boat rentals start at $10/hr per boat.*

A somewhat longer excursion will take you 30 kilometers (18 miles) to Maligne Lake, one of the largest glacier-fed lakes in the world. Follow Maligne Lake Road, which begins 3 kilometers (1⅞ miles) east of town, off Route 16. You'll pass Maligne Canyon, where the Maligne River cuts a deep, narrow gorge through limestone bedrock; it is an impressive site, but the 4-kilometer (2½-mile) trail along the canyon can be crowded, so it's best saved for evening, when the crowds thin out. The other point of interest along this road is **Medicine Lake,** whose water levels fluctuate dramatically at different times of year. At certain times, an underground drainage system completely empties the lake, leaving only a bed of glacial silt and residue.

㉑ **Maligne Lake,** 22 kilometers (14 miles) long, can be explored on a 1½-hour guided cruise or on a rented boat. Spirit Island, which earned its name because it elevates the spirit of those who witness the sight, is a small outcropping in the middle of the lake and is the main destination. Several hiking trails, some with brief, steep sections, lead to promontories offering panoramas of the lake and the surrounding mountain ranges. *Maligne Lake Tours, 626 Connaught Dr., tel. 403/852–3370. $26 adults, $13 children under 12. Open mid-May–Sept., daily 9–5, every hour on the hour.*

㉒ Eighty kilometers (50 miles) west of Jasper on Route 16 is towering **Mt. Robson.** First sighted by Hudson's Bay Company explorers about 1820, this peak was not successfully scaled until 1913, despite numerous attempts. Pick as clear a day as possible to go; Mt. Robson's weather is notoriously bad, and it is a rare day that the summit is not encircled by clouds. A favorite backpacking trip on the mountain is the strenuous 18-kilometer (11-mile) hike to Berg Lake, through the wonderfully named Valley of a Thousand Falls. Berg Lake is no tranquil body of water; the grunt and splash of chunks of ice calving from Robson's glaciers into the lake are regular sounds in summer. The 5-kilometer (3-mile) hike to Kinney Lake, along the Berg Lake trail, is a good option for day hikers.

㉓ For an entirely different experience, spend a day at **Miette Hot Springs,** 58 kilometers (36 miles) from Jasper. Visitors come here to soak in naturally heated mineral waters originating from three springs that are some of the warmest waters in the Canadian Rockies. *Tel. 403/866–3750. $2 adults, $1.25 children; suit, locker, and towel rentals available. Open mid-May–early Sept., daily 8:30 AM–10:30 PM.*

Driving east from Jasper, you will notice scenery that's different from that to the west. As the Athabasca River widens along the flat floodplain, notice how the trees begin to thin out, a sign that you're moving into the drier climate of the prairie.

West of Banff Smaller and less renowned than Banff and Jasper national parks are the less-visited siblings: Kootenay and Yoho national parks. **Kootenay National Park,** named after the Kootenai Indians who settled in the area, is 16 kilometers (10 miles) north-

㉔ west of Banff and is reached by bearing north on Route 1 and west on Route 93. The highway climbs steeply to **Vermilion Pass,** where Banff and Kootenay parks meet. The atmosphere is eerie here. In 1968, a huge forest fire swept over thousands of acres, leaving only charred spars in its wake. Regeneration has begun, though; amidst the skeletons left by the fire, new growths have reached heights of 2–3 meters (6–10 feet).

Just beyond the Vermilion Pass summit is the trailhead for the Stanley Glacier trail, one of the fine choices for a day hike in the park. The trail climbs easily for 4 kilometers (2½ miles), through fire remnants and new growth, across rock debris and glacial moraine, ending in the giant amphitheater of the Stanley Glacier basin.

From the Stanley Glacier trailhead, Route 93 turns south, and on the right, the high, rocky ridge—the park's most predominant feature—can be seen. Among the popular hiking destinations is **Floe Lake,** a 10-kilometer (6-mile) trek from the highway. The area surrounding the lake, a 1,000-meter-high (3,300-foot-high) dark limestone wall, characterizes the Kootenay terrain.

㉕

Along the 65-kilometer (40-mile) stretch from the intersection of Routes 1 and 93 to Radium Hot Springs (*see* Tour 4, below), the only service area is at Vermilion Crossing, the approximate halfway point. South of Vermilion Crossing, the mountains open up gradually, their flanks covered by thick stands of Douglas fir, as the Vermilion River joins with the wider Kootenay River. From there, the highway heads west, winding through the narrow limestone canyon cut by the Sinclair River before reaching the springs.

Farther north, along Route 1, **Yoho National Park** can be reached by continuing west on the highway at its intersection with the Icefields Parkway (Route 93), just north of Lake Louise. The park's name is an Indian word that translates, approximately, to "awesome." Indeed, the park is awesome, featuring some of the most outstanding scenery in the Canadian Rockies.

Yoho is divided into two parts—the northern half, which includes Emerald Lake and the Yoho River Valley, and the southern half, of which Lake O'Hara is the physical and spiritual epicenter.

㉖ The two main accesses to the northern half of Yoho are the Takakkaw Falls road and the Emerald Lake Lodge road. The **Takakkaw Falls,** 254 meters (833 feet) high, are spectacular especially in early summer, engorged by the runoff of melting snow and ice. (Also, the flow of the falls can increase during summer hot spells, which speed the melt of glacial ice.) But the falls are just a taste of what lies ahead for day hikers and backpackers. The Yoho River valley, leading toward the pyramid-capped Yoho glacier, is bound on one side by the peaks of the President Range and, on the other, by the distant Wapta Icefield.

㉗ Enthusiastic hikers can also reach points throughout the Yoho Valley from the vivid green **Emerald Lake** by taking well-marked trails. Otherwise, those who come to this corner of Yoho can take an easy stroll around the lake, rent a canoe, or have a cup of tea at the teahouse by the lodge.

(28) **Lake O'Hara,** Yoho's other half, is widely regarded as one of *the* places for outdoor enthusiasts to go in the Canadian Rockies. For summer, Lake O'Hara Lodge (*see* Lodging, below) is booked months in advance. You can take one of several moderately easy hikes from the lodge to high-alpine lakes above the tree line. The area is also popular among climbers. A lodge-run bus makes fast work of the several kilometers of forest-lined fire road between Route 1 and the lake, but the road makes the remote area more accessible to other people, too, therefore limiting your private wilderness experience.

(29) Also in Yoho, the **Burgess Shale site,** halfway between the Takakkaw Falls road and the Emerald Lake Lodge road, contains the fossilized remains of 120 marine species dating back 530 million years. Burgess Shale was designated a World Heritage Site in 1981; reservations for guided hikes through fossil sites can be made through the Yoho Park Information Centre (*Box 99, Field, BC V0A 1G0, tel. 604/343–6324*). The guided hikes are the only way to see the actual fossil sites, and they're popular, so reservations are recommended. The hikes are conducted July through mid-September, and the going is fairly strenuous; the round-trip distance is 20 kilometers (12 miles).

Three kilometers (1⅞ miles) west of the border between Alberta and British Columbia, you come to the observation deck for **(30)** the **Spiral Tunnels,** train tunnels that make figure-eight loops on each side of Route 1. These were the engineering answer to the problem of getting trains up and down the steep grade of the Rockies' western slope. The tunnels wind in circles through the mountainside, allowing trains to climb and descend more gradually, as if on spiral stairs. Many trains use the tunnels, and the Great Canadian Railtour Company (tel. 800/665–7245) and CPR provide schedules so you can time your arrival to the roadside observation deck off Route 1 for when a train is passing through. Without a train, the tunnels simply look like holes in the mountainside; but when a train goes through, its engine can be seen coming from one tunnel, while its caboose can be seen entering the other, almost directly above the engine.

Tour 3: South of Banff

Canmore and Kananaskis Country **(31) (32)** Until Calgary was awarded the Olympics in 1988, the area immediately south of Banff—the town of **Canmore** and **Kananaskis Country**—was generally the stomping ground of local folks from Calgary and Banff. Canmore, outside the park boundary, offered affordable housing for people living in Banff; Kananaskis Country, just an hour's drive from Calgary and with fewer restrictions on horseback riding, snowmobiling, and hunting, was a popular weekend locale for folks from the city.

Then came the Olympics. When logistical problems forced planners to look from Banff and Lake Louise to other possible sites for Olympic events, Canmore and Kananaskis Country popped into the limelight. The **Canmore Nordic Centre** (*see* Sports and Outdoor Activities, below), for nordic skiing events, was built. *Box 1979, Canmore, AB T0L 0M0, tel. 403/ 658–2400. No trail fee; rentals available. Open dawn to dusk, with lights until 9:00 PM.*

In Kananaskis Country, a half hour away, the Nakiska ski area on Mt. Allen was created, along with a nearby lodging complex—Kananaskis Village (*see* Lodging, below). Suddenly, Canmore and the 4,000-square-kilometer (1,600-square-mile) Kananaskis Country were on the international travel map. *Kananaskis Country, Suite 412, 1011 Glenmore Trail SW, Calgary, AB T2V 4R6, tel. 403/297-3362.*

The character of post-Olympic Canmore is not radically different from its pre-1988 incarnation. The former coal-mining outpost remains a bedroom community for Banff workers, although now more park visitors also save money by staying in Canmore's less expensive lodgings. The attractive, boutique-lined Main Street and several good restaurants are indications that Canmore is no longer strictly a locals' town; it's become the regional center for the active outdoor life—with streets full of young, robust types who live for climbing, hiking, and mountain-biking in the summer, cross-country and alpine skiing in winter. Several outfitters, climbing schools, and guide services make their base in Canmore.

This does not, however, add up to a town of historic or scenic attractions. You can get a good meal here, or a place to bed down at a reasonable price, and you can zip around the tracks of the nordic center. Generally, Canmore is a place to think of, as local people do, as a base camp for going into the parks or Kananaskis Country.

The main highway through Kananaskis Country is Route 40 (closed in winter about 20 kilometers, or 12 miles, south of Kananaskis Village), also known as the Kananaskis Trail. The highway begins 23 kilometers (14 miles) east of Canmore, off Route 1, and climbs past Kananaskis Village and Nakiska, which appear on the right at about the 20-kilometer (12-mile) point. The village, on a small plateau between the ski area and the twin 18-hole golf courses, is the only place in Kananaskis Country that offers hotel-style accommodations. Many visitors to the region stay at one of the several campgrounds, most of which can accommodate recreational vehicles.

The highway proceeds through **Peter Lougheed Provincial Park** (essentially a subsection of Kananaskis Country) and over Highwood Pass (2,208 meters, or 7,280 feet), the highest drivable pass in Canada. It then descends to join Route 541, east of Longview. Access to East Kananaskis Country, a popular area for horseback-riding trips, is via Route 66, which heads west from Priddis.

The climate in the mountains of Kananaskis Country is surprisingly different from that of the mountains in the neighboring parks. On the eastern slope of the Rockies, the Kananaskis mountains tend to get less precipitation, which often means snow-poor winters—a cause of controversy and occasional ridicule when Mt. Allen was chosen as the site for the Olympic ski area. Extensive snowmaking was the solution. Closer to the prairie, the Kananaskis mountains are also exposed to more wind, including the famed, warm chinooks, which have been known to sweep through in mid-winter, bearing temperatures exceeding 15°C (60°F).

Kananaskis Country has little of the glacial spectacle of the parks; its scenery is, in some ways, simpler, with thick pine forests and granite mountain peaks. Regularly modulating temperatures cause frequent snow and rock slides. Anyone interested in the power of sliding snow or rock should take a short drive on Route 40 south of Kananaskis Village, to see where the steep mountainsides are raked with one slide path after another.

As a multipurpose area run by the Alberta provincial government, Kananaskis Country offers advantages over the parks, but some disadvantages as well. On the plus side, there are more varieties of recreational activities in Kananaskis Country. For example, in its northeastern corner (take Route 68 east from Route 40), a large area has been set aside for motorcycles, all-terrain vehicles, and snowmobiles—all machinery that are anathema in the parks. East Kananaskis Country, where pine forests mix with stands of aspen, has been divvied up for use by licensed horse-pack outfitters. Also, the provincial government has made special efforts to accommodate disabled visitors. **William Watson Lodge,** near the Kananaskis Lakes, is one of the rare lodges designed exclusively for disabled people, as well as senior citizens. Access points have been built along Mt. Lorette Ponds north of Kananaskis Village to accommodate wheelchair fishermen, and many hiking trails near the village have been cut wide and gentle enough for wheelchair travel. *William Watson Lodge located 30 km (18 mi) south of Kananaskis Village on Rte. 40; for information write Kananaskis Country, Box 280, Cranmore, AB T0L 0M0, tel. 403/591–7227. Overnight and day-use facilities for senior citizens and disabled people open Mon.–Fri. 8:30–4:30; cabin reservations available year-round.*

On the down side, wildlife does not flourish in Kananaskis Country, as it does in the parks, primarily because hunting is permitted in season; animals are much more cautious about human interaction here than they are in protected areas.

Finally, Kananaskis Country is not all free-range land for recreational enthusiasts. Forestry, gas, and ranching operations may restrict backcountry travel in some areas.

Waterton Lakes National Park
㉝

Geologically, **Waterton Lakes National Park** is the meeting of two worlds—the flatlands of the prairie and the abrupt upthrust of the mountains. Chief Mountain, the squared-off peak on the eastern end of the stand of mountains seen as you drive from the north, juts up from the prairie, dominating the horizon from the north and east. In this juncture of worlds, the park squeezes into a relatively small arena (525 square kilometers, or 200 square miles) an unusual mix of wildlife, biota, and climate zones.

Take a drive up **Red Rock Canyon** (turning right before the town of Waterton), the bottom of which is covered with scrub pine and prairie grasses. Turn a few kilometers later, at the center of Waterton, onto the Akima Parkway, leading to **Cameron Lake,** and you'll find a land of high basins and glacially carved cirques, filled in summer with hundreds of varieties of alpine wildflowers, including about 22 varieties of wild orchids.

The common denominator in the park is wind. Although the mountains and canyon walls provide protection in some areas, the wind blows powerfully and regularly from the prairie, often at speeds of more than 50 kilometers (30 miles) an hour. Trees along the lakeside bear the evidence, as they grow at about an 80-degree angle, rather than straight up.

Politically, too, Waterton represents a meeting of worlds. Although the park was officially established in 1895, it was joined in 1932 with Glacier National Park in Montana to form Waterton/Glacier International Peace Park—a symbol of friendship and peaceful coexistence between Canada and the United States. In fact, some services in the park, including the Prince of Wales Hotel, are under Glacier Park management in the United States.

Whether it is a pervading spirit of international peace or the long driving distance from Calgary (especially compared with the short Calgary–Banff drive), Waterton is a decidedly low-key place. Hiking, horseback riding, and boating are the main activities. The park offers numerous short hikes for day-trippers and some longer treks for backpackers. Boats can be rented at the townsite for Upper Waterton Lakes or at Cameron Lake.

One of the most popular things to do is to take a two-hour cruise on Upper Waterton Lake from the townsite, south to **Goat Haunt,** where there are shelters, a ranger station, and a boat dock. From here, several short, easy hikes are possible before you return to Waterton; properly equipped overnighters can also camp out at Goat Haunt. (Because Goat Haunt is in the United States, travelers going to and from must clear customs.) *Shoreline Cruise Co., tel. 403/859–2362. Cruises run mid-May–mid-Sept.; call for schedules.*

Whatever the day's activity, turning in early is the order of things in Waterton. Except for reading and conversation, nightlife is virtually nonexistent. Most of Waterton turns in early for the season, too—from early October until mid-May, the park has all but closed up shop.

Because of Waterton's proximity to the U.S. border, and its bond with Glacier National Park, many visitors to the park come from the south. The common thing to do is to fly into Great Falls, Montana, and drive to Waterton via Routes 89, 17, and 6. Those who choose instead to drive the 264 kilometers (158 miles) from Calgary (via Routes 2, 3, and 6) have an interesting side trip worth considering.

Tour 4: The British Columbia Rockies

"British Columbia (B.C.) Rockies" is in part a misnomer, for it is a term often used to designate an area that includes the mountain ranges of the Columbias, which are not a part of the Rocky Mountain chain. Roughly, the British Columbia Rockies encompass the area of southeastern British Columbia immediately west of the four contiguous parks.

Keeping mountain ranges straight in this part of the world is a tricky business. In simple terms, southeastern British Columbia is defined by two main ranges: the Rockies to the east and the Columbias to the west. They are separated for most of their parallel run by the Columbia River valley—or "trench," as it is often called. Wide and flat, the valley has an elevation that's surprisingly low, only about 600 meters (2,000 feet) on average.

The mountain-range confusion is made even worse by the subdivision of the Columbias: To the north are the Cariboos, west of Jasper and Mt. Robson parks; reaching south like three long talons from the Cariboos are (west to east) the Monashees, the Selkirks, and the Purcells. Finally, perhaps the best-known mountains of all—the Bugaboos—are only a few dramatic peaks in the Purcells but are often thought of as encompassing the entire region.

In subtle and overt ways, the world of the British Columbia Rockies region is very different from that of the national parks. Perhaps the most obvious differences are the conspicuous lumber yards, mining pits, farms, and ranches—signs of development throughout the British Columbia Rockies that are not present in the industry-shielded parklands to the east. This physical evidence attests to minimally successful attempts made to mine gold, silver-lead ore, and other metals. The significant difference between the two ranges, however, is age. More than 100 million years older than the Rockies, the Columbias show the signs of their years: The effects of erosion are more in evidence, along with the more dramatic effects of upthrust and glaciation. This is not to suggest that the Columbias lack drama or beauty. The pyramidal peaks of Glacier National Park and the Bugaboo and Howser spires, rising in the Purcells like slender granite fingers from glacial beds, are sights as striking as anything in the four contiguous parks.

As the first ranges to capture storms moving from the west across the plains of interior British Columbia, the Columbias get much more rain and snow than do the Rockies. Annual precipitation in many areas exceeds 152 centimeters (60 inches), and in the Monashees, the most westerly of subranges, annual snowfalls have exceeded 2,032 centimeters (800 inches).

Such precipitation has helped to create the large, deep glaciers that add to the high-alpine beauty of the Columbias. Lower down, a rain-forest climate has contributed to a lush life of ferns, grasses, flowers, and shrubbery not found in the Rockies to the east. In winter, the deep snows have made the Columbias—particularly the Monashees—a must port-of-call for aficionados of deep-powder and helicopter skiing.

Of course, such extreme conditions can be hazardous, too. **34** **Rogers Pass,** the center of Canada's **Glacier National Park,** is a case in point. In the early 1900s avalanches claimed the lives of hundreds of railway-construction workers, and continued to be a threat during highway construction in the 1950s.

Today, the Rogers Pass war against avalanches is both active and passive. Heavy artillery—105mm howitzers—is used to shoot down snow buildups before they can become so severe as to threaten a major avalanche. (If traveling in the backcountry, be alert to unexploded howitzer shells that pose a potential hazard.) On the passive side, train tunnels and long snow sheds along the highway shield travelers from major slide paths.

The park's history is well documented at the **Rogers Pass Centre**—worth a visit whether you're staying in Glacier or just passing through. Open year-round, the center displays geology and wildlife and offers 30-minute movies on subjects ranging from avalanches to bears. *Tel. 604/837–6274, ext. 39. Admission free. Open daily 7 AM–9PM Oct.–Apr., Mon.–Fri. 9–4.*

Not all of the British Columbia Rockies region is inundated by rain and snow. Storms tend to exhaust themselves in the Columbias—the reason the Columbia River trench stays relatively dry. The annual precipitation in Golden is only about 500 millimeters (20 inches), less than half of what it is in Revelstoke, 148 kilometers (80 miles) west at the foot of the Monashees and the western extreme of the region discussed in this section.

For the most part, the towns of the Columbia River trench are 35 not beautiful, nor do they aspire to be. For example, **Golden**—a town best described as a service center—is the epitome of this plain-Jane character. Primarily a stopping-off point for anyone journeying elsewhere, Golden is a base for several river runners, outfitters, and guide services.

The 105 kilometers (63 miles) south from Golden to Radium Hot Springs, where Route 93 joins Route 95, across the rolling flood plain of the Columbia River, are relatively uneventful. To the right are the river and the Purcell Mountains; more immediately to the left are the Rockies, although the major peaks are hidden by the abrupt frontal ranges. Even though the landscape might not be as inspiring as in the parks, this is prime RV country. Resorts catering to RVs—hard to find in the parks—abound here. These include hotels and motels that offer RV hookups in addition to regular accommodations (*see* Lodging, below). Climbers and hikers should look for unpaved roads out of the towns of Spillimacheen and Brisco that lead to the 36 **Bugaboo Recreation Area.**

The Bugaboos are especially popular among experienced rock climbers. Granite "spires" that rise from glaciers like giant rocket cones are both dramatic to look at and challenging to climb. This is wild country: Except for the Bugaboo Lodge—reserved for heli-hiking and heli-skiing guests—and remote alpine huts, there are no facilities in this area.

For less adventurous tourists, the 90-kilometer (56-mile) 37 stretch of Route 93/95 from **Radium Hot Springs** to Kimberley is the main pod. The hot springs on Route 93, 2 kilometers (1¼ miles) northeast of the Routes 93 and 95 junction, are the town's longest-standing attraction, and the summer lifeblood for the numerous motels in the area. There is a large outdoor pool tucked beneath the walls of Sinclair Canyon. Lockers, towels, and suits are available to rent. *Jct. Rtes. 93 and 95, tel. 604/ 347–9615. Admission: Full day—$4 adults, $2.50 children 16 and under; half day—$2.50 adults, $1.25 children. Schedules vary with season; open 9 AM–11 PM mid-summer.*

However, sitting in the hot springs or hiking the short trails of Sinclair Canyon aren't the only things to do in this part of the world. Windermere and Columbia lakes—actually extrawide stretches of the Columbia River—are popular among boaters and boardsailers. Golf is becoming a growing attraction, with several fine courses between Radium Hot Springs and 38 **Fairmont Hot Springs.** And a right turn at the Invermere intersection leads to **Panorama** (*see* Lodging, below), the year-round resort known best for skiing in winter, and to the **Purcell Wilderness,** a large area devoted to backcountry hiking, camping, and fishing.

After traveling south for about 60 kilometers (36 miles), the road splits; Route 93/95 continues southeast to Fort Steele, and Route 95A leads to Kimberley. The two routes join again north of Cranbrook.

Fort Steele and Kimberley are historically significant because they were the home to many German and Swiss immigrants who arrived a century ago to work as miners and loggers. Southeastern British Columbia was not unlike the Tyrol region they had left, so it was easy to settle here. Later, a demand for experienced alpinists to guide and teach hikers, climbers, and skiers brought more settlers from the alpine countries, and Tyrolian influence is evident throughout southeastern British Columbia. Chalet-style buildings here are as common here as log cabin–style structures are in the national parks. Schnitzels and fondues appear on menus as often as burgers and fries.

39 **Fort Steele Heritage Town,** a reconstructed 19th-century mining outpost, is a step back to those silver-lead mining days. Its theater, milliner's, barbershop, and dry-goods store breathe authenticity, helping to preserve the 1890s lifestyle. Plan a half-day or more; there is enough here to hold the interest of adults as well as children. *Ft. Steele, 16 km (10 mi) northeast of Cranbrook on Rte. 93/95, tel. 604/426–6923. Admission for 2 consecutive days: $5 adults, $3 children 13–18 and senior citizens, $1 children 6–12, $10 families. Open mid-June–early Sept.; Old West shows performed in the summer months. Although buildings are closed in winter, the grounds are open to visitors free of charge.*

40 **Kimberley,** a cross between a quaint and a kitschy town, is rich with Tyrolian character. The Platzl ("small plaza," in German), a walking mall of shops and restaurants styled after a Bavarian village, is crowned by what is reputed to be the world's largest cuckoo clock. In the summer Kimberley plays its Bavarian theme to the hilt: Merchants dress up in lederhosen and dirndls, and promotional gimmicks abound.

Beyond Kimberley or Fort Steele, **Cranbrook** (28 kilometers, or 18 miles), primarily a service center, has an airport and offers moderately priced gas, lodging, and food.

Back at Golden, Route 1 continues west through Glacier and Mt. Revelstoke national parks. When the weather is clear, many of the glaciers can be seen from the highway. However, to fully appreciate Glacier, one must take to the trail. From the Illecillewaet Campground, a few kilometers west of the Rogers Pass Centre (off Route 1), several trails lead to good overlooks and glacier tongues, offering good day-hiking opportunities. One of the best, although fairly strenuous, is the Asulkan Valley trail. Its 13-kilometer (8-mile) round loop crosses brooks and moraine, passes waterfalls, and yields views of the Asulkan Glacier and three massifs, called the Ramparts, the Dome, and Mt. Jupiter. A much easier hike is the 1.6-kilometer (1-mile) Loop Brook trail (6 kilometers, or 3½ miles, west of the Rogers Pass Centre), with views of the glaciers of Mt. Bonney.

41 Conceived primarily as a day-use park, **Mt. Revelstoke National Park** covers just 260 square kilometers (100 square miles). The park's principal attraction is the 26-kilometer (15½-mile) Summit Road to the top of the mountain, at 1,938 meters (6,395 feet). The gravel road begins from Route 1, two kilometers (1¼ miles) before the turnoff to the town of Revelstoke, and its last few kilometers may be closed off by melting snows until well into July. There are several easy hikes to follow from the summit parking lot, taking you past small lakes, views of the Selkirk and Monashee ranges, and mountain meadows full of wild-flowers.

Shortly after the Summit Road turnoff is the junction with Route 23, which leads north to Mica Dam. Four kilometers (2½ miles) along this road is **Revelstoke Dam,** a large hydroelectric- and flood-control project. Lake Revelstoke, a reservoir created by the dam on the Columbia River, is a popular boating area in summer, primarily along its southern reaches. *Visitor Centre, tel. 604/837–6211. Self-guided tours free. Open March 14–July 14 and mid-Sept.–mid-Oct., daily 10–6; June 15–mid-Sept., daily 10–8.*

From Revelstoke Dam, Route 23 continues another 145 kilometers (90 miles) north to Mica Dam, the juncture of Revelstoke and Kinbasket lakes. Those who venture along this route are entering wild country—a world of wilderness canoeing, big fish, abandoned mining camps, and bears.

42 The town of **Revelstoke,** a skiers' headquarters in winter, is worth a brief side trip. In 1986, the town began to restore its downtown district, creating an attractive, authentic turn-of-the-century renovation that today houses modern shops, restaurants, and businesses.

What to See and Do with Children

Fort Steele Heritage Town (*see* Tour 4, above).

Rogers Pass Centre, Glacier National Park (*see* Tour 4, above).

The **Jasper-Yellowhead Museum** in Jasper (400 Pyramid Lake Rd., tel. 403/852–3013) features historical exhibits showing what life in the area was like when prospectors, surveyors, settlers, and the like arrived more than a century ago.

Another museum well worth a visit is the **Frank Slide Interpretive Centre** (*see* Off the Beaten Track, below).

The **Railway Museum** (1 Van Horne St. N, Canmore, tel. 604/489–3918), housed in restored Canadian Pacific Railway cars, presents a good picture of rail travel in the 1920s.

If you're visiting the Invermere area June through August, one of the best museums is the **Windermere Valley Pioneer Museum** (622 3rd St., tel. 604/342–9769), depicting the life of 19th-century pioneers.

Off the Beaten Track

A possible detour on the Calgary-Waterton trip is to continue for 60 kilometers (36 miles) on Route 3, past the turnoff for Route 6 to Waterton, until you reach **Crowsnest Pass.** In the early 1900s, Crowsnest Pass developed as a coal-mining community and was touted as "the Pittsburgh of Canada." From the outset, however, the coal-mining industry in Crowsnest Pass was ill-fated. In April of 1903, some 90 million tons of rock from Turtle Mountain buried a portion of the town of Frank, killing about 70 people. Then, in 1914, a massive mine explosion killed 189 people, and a few years later, with the uncertainties of an impending war, the coal-mining industry all but collapsed. The story of the slide, and the history of coal-mining in the region, is well recorded at the **Frank Slide Interpretive Center** (Crowsnest Pass, tel. 403/562–7388).

Head-Smashed-In Buffalo Jump is located 18 kilometers (11 miles) northwest of Ft. Macleod on Route 785 (off Route 2). It is considered one of the best-preserved examples of a site where Plains Indians herded buffalo to their death over a low cliff and later harvested the meat and fur from the carcasses. As an archaeological site, it is not especially inspiring; it is, simply, a ledge in the middle of the rolling prairie. However, the museum at the site provides not only a fascinating explanation of the buffalo jump tradition but also insight into the life and customs of the Plains Indians, particularly the Blackfoot. Guided walks and audiovisual exhibits are presented. *Tel. 403/553–2731. Admission: $5 adults, $2 children 7–17. Open summer, daily 9–8; Labor Day–May 15, daily 9–5.*

Shopping

When shopping in the Canadian Rockies, you'll find the best selection in Banff, although Canmore may offer better bargains. The **Banff Springs Hotel,** and shops on **Banff Avenue,** have the usual souvenirs, as well as native crafts, sporting gear, landscape paintings, woolens, and outdoor wear.

Native Crafts One of the most authentic places to shop for authentic articles is the **Banff Indian Trading Post** (Birch and Cave Aves., tel. 403/762–2456). Also, the **Lake Louise Trading Company** (Lake Louise Rd., tel. 403/522–2333) sells eclectic native items, from baked goods to twig furniture.

Local Crafts Of the numerous galleries and shops along Banff Avenue, perhaps the best for crafts and other art items, principally by Canadian craftspeople, is **The Quest for Handcrafts** (105 Banff Ave. tel. 403/762–2722).

Several galleries in Banff, Canmore, and Jasper offer arts and crafts, including handmade jewelry and watercolor paintings. Among those in Banff (with the widest selection) worth checking out are the **Canadian House Gallery** (Caribou and Bean Sts., tel. 403/762–3757) and the **Banff Indian Trading Post** (Birch and Cave Aves., tel. 403/762–2456).

Sporting Goods For sporting gear, **Mountain Magic** (224 Bear St., Banff, tel. 403/762–2591) has four floors of hiking, climbing, skiing, running, and biking equipment, and a 30-foot indoor climbing wall for gear testing.

Monod's (tel. 403/762–4571), with stores in Banff (111 Banff Ave.) and at the Chateau Lake Louise, also offers a wide array of sports equipment as well as clothing.

Sports and Outdoor Activities

Biking Around Banff, the **Vermilion Lakes loop** and the more strenuous **loop over Tunnel Mountain** are popular half-day bike tours. For a longer ride, **Route 1A** between Banff and Lake Louise is a good choice. Those seeking a rugged workout can test lungs and legs on the steep switchbacks leading up to **Mt. Norquay** ski area.

Mountain biking has become increasingly popular in the last few years. Although mountain bikes provide good access to the backcountry, they are restricted on many trails and in many areas. Check with the nearest park warden or bike store before heading off-road.

Bikes can be rented from **Park and Pedal Bike Shop** (229 Wolf St., tel. 403/762–3191) in Banff. Bikes can also be rented from **Freewheel Cycle** (off Miete St., between Patricia and Giekie Sts., tel. 403/852–5380) in Jasper; in Revelstoke try **Revelstoke Cycle Shop** (118 MacKenzie Ave., tel. 604/837–2648).

Guided bike tours, on-road and off-road, are also offered by several operators (*see* Guided Tours in Essential Information, above).

Camping   There are more than 40 public campgrounds within the national parks, not including backcountry sites for backpackers and climbers. Most operate on a first-come, first-served basis, though a few require reservations. The season generally runs from mid-May to October, although a few campgrounds are open year-round. Campground information is available from the **Canadian Parks Service** (Information Services, Box 2989, Station M, Calgary, AB T2P 3H8, tel. 403/859–2203) and from **Kananaskis Country** (Suite 412, 1011 Glenmore Trail SW, Calgary, AB T2V 4R6, tel. 403/297–3362).

Numerous privately run campgrounds, for which reservations usually can be made, offer sites outside park boundaries. Contact **Tourism British Columbia** for its "Super Camping" publication, which lists more than 25 campgrounds in the Canadian Rockies region, or contact the Canadian Parks Service or Alberta Tourism (*see* Important Addresses and Numbers in Essential Information, above).

Climbing   Except for Waterton Lakes, where the rock is generally crumbly, the Canadian Rockies is one of the world's great climbing regions. Among the ascents considered to be classics are **Mt. Assiniboine,** the oft-dubbed "Matterhorn of the Rockies"; glacier-cloaked **Mt. Athabasca,** near Sunwapta Pass; **Mt. Sir Donald,** in Glacier National Park; the daunting **Mt. Robson;** and, in the Purcells, the spires of the **Bugaboos.**

Climbing permits are required for activities within the parks and can be obtained at park warden offices. Except for very experienced mountaineers, guide and instruction services are essential for climbers in the Canadian Rockies.

The **Canadian School of Mountaineering** (629 10th St., Box 723, Canmore, AB T0L 0M0, tel. 403/678–4134) and **Banff Alpine Guides** (Box 1025, Banff, AB T0L 0C0, tel. 403/762–2791), catering to all ability levels, lead trips throughout the parks. Both organizations also conduct ski mountaineering tours in winter. Climbing gear can be rented at outdoor stores in Banff.

The **Lac des Arcs Climbing School** (1116 19th Ave. NW, Calgary, AB T2M 0Z9, tel. 403/240–6502) offers two- and four-day rock-climbing and mountaineering courses at moderate prices (starting at $125 per person). The school also leads caving groups in summer and backcountry ski tours in winter.

Climbers or backpackers interested in extended stays of more than three or four days might consider membership in the **Alpine Club of Canada** (Box 1026, Banff, AB T0L 0C0, tel. 403/

762–4481). The club maintains several mountain huts in the parks and leads hikes and climbs of varying difficulty.

Fishing The principal game fish in the Canadian Rockies is trout—cutthroat and rainbow being the most common varieties. The best fishing tends to be in streams, rivers, and lakes in the valleys, rather than in waters from glacial sources. The **Bow River** and the **lakes of British Columbia** are considered to have some of the best fishing in the region.

Fishing licenses are required and can be purchased at information centers and sports shops throughout the region. A sevenday license is $5; a yearly license, $10. For more information, contact the **Ministry of Environment & Parks** (Fish & Wildlife Branch, 780 Blanchard St., Victoria, BC V8V 1X4, tel. 604/387–4573). Separate licenses for fishing outside the parks are required and can be purchased at sporting goods stores, tackle shops, and marinas. A British Columbia license is good only in British Columbia; an Alberta license is good only in Alberta.

Alberta Tourism and Tourism British Columbia (*see* Important Addresses and Numbers in Essential Information, above) can provide lists of outfitters and guides who offer half-day to week-long fly-in adventure services.

Golf The golf season is short, running from about mid-May through mid-October. Given the abundance of water in the region, golf courses are generally in excellent playing condition, with lush grasses and well-kept greens. If hole lengths seem long, keep in mind that at the elevation of Canadian Rockies courses (above 1,200 meters, or 4,000 feet), a golf ball tends to travel 10% farther than at sea level.

Canadian Rockies courses, situated on the relatively flat valley floors, are not difficult to walk for those so inclined; the mountains simply provide dramatic backdrops. However, all courses listed below offer full pro-shop services, including cart rentals. Most courses enforce a standard dress code, requiring shirts with collars and Bermuda-length shorts or long pants.

Greens fees range from $20 to $40 for 18 holes. Cart rentals range from $15 to $30.

Within the parks, the **Banff Springs Hotel** (tel. 403/762–2211, ext. 162) and the **Jasper Park Lodge** (tel. 403/852–3301) each have an 18-hole course. **Kananaskis Village** (tel. 403/591–7070) has two 18-hole courses.

The area between Golden and Kimberley in British Columbia is growing as a golfing hotbed: Golfers here can now choose from ten 18-hole courses and two 9-hole courses. Arrangements for golfing can be made through **Fairmont Hot Springs Resort** (tel. 604/345–6311 or 800/663–4979), with two courses on site; **Radium Hot Springs Resort** (tel. 604/347–9311), with one course on site; and **Panorama** (tel. 604/342–6941). All offer multicourse, multiday packages.

Hiking The four contiguous parks (Banff, Jasper, Kootenay, and Yoho) have 2,900 kilometers (1,750 miles) of hiking trails. In Waterton Lakes there are 183 kilometers (114 miles) of trails, with further access to more than 1,200 kilometers (750 miles) of trails in adjacent Glacier National Park in the United States. Kananaskis Country offers numerous hiking and backpacking opportunities (although water can be in short supply, especially in late summer and fall), while Revelstoke and Glacier parks in British Columbia are generally best for shorter day hikes.

The hiking season runs from mid-May to early November, depending on the latitude and elevation of the trail. Trails along the Icefields Parkway, where elevations are generally highest, tend to be passable only between June and September. The hiking season in Waterton Lakes Park, far to the south, tends to be longest. Though most trails are restricted to foot traffic, horses and mountain bikes are permitted in some areas. Check with the park warden for selected trails.

Backpackers are required to register with the nearest park warden for permits. This is principally for safety reasons—so that you can be tracked down in case of emergency—as well as for trail-usage records. There is generally no fee for the use of backcountry campsites, although there is a fee for reservations, which can be made by contacting the park superintendent up to three weeks in advance. The park warden's office can also supply trail and topographical maps and information on current trail status.

Anyone interested in hiking or backpacking should obtain one of several good books that describe various routes and route combinations. One of the best, *The Canada Rockies: Trail Guide,* by Brian Patton and Bart Robinson (Summerthought Ltd., $14.95), is available in most bookstores in Banff, Lake Louise, and Jasper.

Banff The trails of Banff tend to get the most traffic, especially in summer. Although there are several trails within and leading from Banff townsite, more interesting hikes tend to be north of town. The most popular day-hiking areas, both accessible and scenic, are around **Lake Louise** and **Moraine Lake.**

Jasper **Jasper,** with the most extensive trail network (nearly 1,000 kilometers, or 600 miles), is popular for hikers seeking to get deep into the wilderness for several days at a time. **Tonquin Valley,** near Mt. Edith Cavell, is considered one of Canada's classic backpacking routes. Its high mountain lakes, bounded by a series of steep, rocky peaks known as the Ramparts, receive many visitors in the height of summer. One drawback: Some trails in this area are open to horse-pack trips. Good day-hiking areas in Jasper are around **Maligne Lake** and **Mt. Edith Cavell.**

Kootenay The trail that best characterizes the hiking in Kootenay is the strenuous **Rockwall trail,** which runs along the series of steep rock facades that are the predominant feature of the park. **Floe Lake,** sitting at the base of a sheer, 1,000-meter (3,300-foot) wall, is a trail highlight. Several long day-hike spurs connect the trail with Route 93.

Yoho Yoho is divided into two parts: the popular hiking arena around **Lake O'Hara,** dotted with high-alpine lakes, and the less-traveled **Yoho River valley,** terminating at the Yoho Glacier. Access to the Lake O'Hara region is somewhat restricted by the long, rather uneventful fire road from Route 1. Most hikers and climbers take the Lake O'Hara Lodge shuttle bus (*see* Lodging, below). Entry into the Yoho River valley is more immediate, either from Takakkaw Falls or from Emerald Lake.

Heli-hiking Another way to experience high-alpine hiking is by heli-hiking, a summer offspring of heli-skiing. Most of the climbing is done by the helicopter; the hiking itself tends to be flat or even downslope. **Canadian Mountain Holidays** (CMH, Box 1660, Banff, AB T0L 0C0, tel. 403/762–4531), in conjunction with **Tauck Tours** (11 Wilton Rd., Westport, CT 06881, tel. 203/226–6911), offers heli-hiking tours for three to nine days, using CMH's relatively luxurious remote lodges in the Cariboo and Purcell ranges.

Horseback Riding   One of the most popular ways to experience the Canadian Rockies is on horseback. Horses are restricted from many trails within the national parks, but there are still some opportunities; among the most popular areas for pack trips within the parks is Tonquin Valley in Jasper. Restrictions are far fewer in Kananaskis Country, the provincial parks, and the British Columbia Rockies region.

Arrangements for hourly or daily rides, as well as riding instruction, can be made through the sports desks at the **Banff Springs Hotel, Chateau Lake Louise, Emerald Lake Lodge,** and **Jasper Park Lodge** (*see* Lodging, below). Other stables in the region include **Alpine Stables** (Box 53, Waterton Park, AB T0K 2M0, tel. 403/859–2462), **Boundary Stables** (Box 44, Kananaskis Village, AB T0L 2H0, tel. 403/591–7171), **Brewster Stables** (Box 2280, Banff, AB T0L 0C0, tel. 403/762–2832), and **Pyramid Riding Stables** (Box 787, Jasper, AB T0E 1E0, tel. 403/852–3562).

Alberta Tourism and Tourism British Columbia can provide listings of pack-trip outfitters and guest ranchers, which proliferate the fringes of the national parks. In British Columbia, further information is also available from the **Guide-Outfitters Association** (Box 769, 100 Mile House, BC V0K 2E0, tel. 604/395–2438).

Rafting   Rafting opportunities range from gentle floats along the Bow River near Banff to rollicking white-water rides on the Kicking Horse River near Golden. Most trips are half-day or full-day. For those seeking white water at its frothiest, June is the best month, when rivers are still swollen with the snow melt but not dangerously so.

In the Banff area, **Rocky Mountain Raft Tours** (Box 1771, Banff, AB T0L 0C0, tel. 403/762–3632) features trips on the Bow River and others. In the Jasper area, **Jasper Raft Tours** (Box 398, Jasper, AB T0E 1E0, tel. 403/852–3613) offers half-day float trips on the Athabasca. **Maligne River Adventures** (626 Connaught Dr., Jasper, AB T0E 1E0, tel. 403/852–3370) offers half-day white-water trips on the Maligne.

Alpine Rafting Company (Box 1409, Golden, BC V0A 1H0, tel. 604/344–5016) offers a variety of trips on the Kicking Horse and the Illecillewaet, between Glacier National Park and Revelstoke.

Skiing   There are 11 lift-serviced ski areas in the region, five of which are within an hour's drive of Banff; daily lift tickets cost between $22 and $36. Cross-country opportunities are also plentiful, and many backcountry lodges are winterized and offer guide services for backcountry touring. Numerous tour operators—based both in the region and elsewhere—feature ski packages; Alberta Tourism or Tourism British Columbia can assist you in choosing a tour that best suits your interests, abilities, and budget.

Cross-Country **The Canmore Nordic Centre** (Box 1979, Canmore, AB T0L 0M0, tel. 403/678–2400) was the site of most 1988 Olympic nordic events. With 56 kilometers (36 miles) of groomed trails, the center features the most extensive, groomed cross-country network in the region. Some trails are lit for night skiing, and, best of all, there is no trail fee. Some trails are even open in summer for roller-skiing. Other groomed trails (and rental equipment) can be found near the **Banff Springs Hotel, Chateau Lake Louise, Jasper Park Lodge, Fairmont Hot Springs Resort,** and **Mt. Engadine Lodge** (*see* Lodging, below).

Lake O'Hara Lodge, Mt. Assiniboine Lodge, and **Skoki Lodge** (*see* Lodging, below) are among several lodges that offer guided backcountry ski touring. In Jasper, reservations for backcountry huts in Tonquin Valley can be made through **Tonquin Valley Ski Tours** (Box 520, Jasper, AB T0E 1E0, tel. 403/852–5337). The **Canadian School of Mountaineering** (Box 723, Canmore, AB T0L 0M0, tel. 403/678–4134) and **Banff Alpine Guides** (Box 1025, Banff, AB T0L 0C0, tel. 403/762–2791) also lead backcountry ski tours.

Downhill The three ski areas in the immediate Banff vicinity are **Lake Louise** (Box 5, Lake Louise, AB T0L 1E0, tel. 403/522–3555), **Mt. Norquay** (Box 1258, Banff, AB T0L 0C0, tel. 403/762–4421), and **Sunshine Village** (Box 1510, Banff, AB T0L 0C0, tel. 403/762–6500 or 800/661–1363). Lake Louise's terrain is large and varied; Mt. Norquay's is generally short and steep; Sunshine Village's terrain is mostly intermediate and above the tree line.

Nakiska (Box 1988, Kananaskis Village, AB T0L 0M0, tel. 403/591–7777), about 45 minutes southeast of Banff, was the sight of the 1988 Olympic alpine events and features wide-trail intermediate skiing. **Marmot Basin** (Box 1300, Jasper, AB T0E 1E0, tel. 403/852–3816), near Jasper, has a wide mix of terrain.

In the British Columbia Rockies, **Panorama** (Panorama, BC V0A 1T0, tel. 604/342–6941 or 800/663–2929) has the largest lift-serviced vertical rise (1,156 meters, or 3,800 feet) of any ski area in the region. **Fernie Snow Valley** (Box 788, Fernie, BC V0A 1M0, tel. 604/423–4655) and **Kimberley Ski Resort** (Box 40, Kimberley, BC V1A 2Y5, tel. 604/427–4881) have vertical rises of more than 600 meters (2,000 feet). Sunshine Village, Nakiska, Panorama, Fernie Snow Valley, and Kimberley have on-mountain lodging and resort facilities.

Heli-skiing Heli-skiing has become increasingly popular in the region, and tours can be arranged through several operators on a daily or weekly basis. Daily tours start above $250 per person, and weekly packages (including meals and lodging but not airfare) begin at about $2,500.

The original, and by far the largest, heli-skiing operator in the region is **Canadian Mountain Holidays** (*see* Heli-hiking, above). Perhaps the best known of the CMH permit areas is the Bugaboos, a subrange of the Purcells, where the whole heli-skiing business started in the mid-'60s. The Bugaboos, however, is now just one of nine areas in which CMH operates, each with 1,500 to 3,000 square kilometers (580 to 1,160 square miles) of skiable terrain. Skiers are housed mostly in remote mountain lodges. CMH runs only weekly tours, and reservations should be made several months in advance. Other weekly operators include **Mike Wiegele Helicopter Skiing** (Box 249, Banff, AB T0L 0C0, tel. 403/762–5548 or 800/661–9170), which operates out of Blue River in British Columbia, and **Selkirk Tangiers Heli-Skiing** (Box 1409, Golden, BC V0A 1H0, tel. 604/344–5016). Selkirk Tangiers also offers daily tours. **R.K. Heli-Ski** (Box 695, Invermere, BC V0A 1K0, tel. 604/342–6494), based at the Panorama ski area, offers daily tours as well as multiday packages that combine heli-skiing with lift-serviced skiing.

Water Sports With an abundance of lakes and rivers in the region, watersport opportunities abound. However, the glacier-fed waters of the Canadian Rockies tend to be cold, even in midsummer. Whether you're waterskiing, board sailing, boating, or swimming, know the conditions and wear proper gear.

Boat and canoe rentals are available at **Lake Louise** and **Moraine Lake** in Banff National Park, at **Emerald Lake** and **Lake O'Hara** in Yoho, and at **Pyramid Lake** in Jasper. However, the main centers of boating activity within the four contiguous parks are Lake Minnewanka in Banff and Maligne Lake in Jasper. In Banff, **Minnewanka Boat Tours** (Box 2189, Banff, AB T0L 0C0, tel. 403/762–3473) offers boat and canoe rentals; **Monod Sports** (111 Banff Ave., tel. 403/762–4571) offers sailboard rental and instruction. Boat rentals on Maligne Lake are available at the boat house by the **Maligne Lake Chalet** and through **Maligne Lake Scenic Cruises** (626 Connaught Dr., Jasper, AB T0E 1E0, tel. 403/852–3370).

Spray Lakes reservoir and Kananaskis Lake are the main sites of boating activity in Kananaskis Country, and boat rentals are available through **Peregrin Sports** (Kananaskis Village, T0L 2H0, tel. 403/591–7555). Lake Invermere, in British Columbia, is popular among sailors, board sailors, and waterskiers and is warm enough for swimming in the midsummer months. For information and equipment rentals, contact the **Invermere Information Centre** (Box 2605, Invermere on the Lake, BC V0A 1K0, tel. 604/342–6316). To the north, the long, dam-controlled Kinbasket and Revelstoke lakes give boaters, canoeists, and fishermen more of a wilderness experience. There are several boat ramps on the lakes but few services.

For sailors and board sailers who like strong winds, Waterton Lakes, with winds from the Alberta prairies often exceeding 50 kilometers (30 miles) per hour, is the place to be. The **Athabasca, Bow, Kicking Horse,** and **Maligne rivers** provide various levels of river-running challenges for canoeists and kayakers—from relatively still water to white water (*see* Rafting, above).

Dining and Lodging

Dining

Dining in the Canadian Rockies is, for the most part, a casual affair. Given the general mix of travelers to the region—families and active outdoorspeople—emphasis is on good food served in large quantities, at moderate prices. This is not the place for the traveler who expects haute service and cuisine; there is only a handful of top-caliber restaurants in the region. However, people who like fresh game and fish will not be disappointed. Trout, venison, elk, moose, quail, and other game are items that even modest dining establishments feature on their menus.

Highly recommended restaurants are indicated by a star ★.

Category	Cost*
Very Expensive	over $30
Expensive	$20–$30
Moderate	$10–$20
Inexpensive	under $10

*per person, excluding drinks, service, and sales tax

Lodging

The hotels, inns, and lodges of the Canadian Rockies compose an eclectic list, ranging from rustic, backcountry lodges without electricity or running water to standard roadside motels to hotels of supreme luxury. With just a few exceptions, however, they share one common trait—room rates that are considerably higher in the summer than during the rest of the year. The week between Christmas and New Year's often commands a higher rate as well. For this reason, flexibility in travel planning can mean considerable savings—a room that goes for $100 a night on September 15 may well drop to $50 on September 16. Lodgings are categorized according to their off-peak rates. High-season rate increases, if any, are noted within each listing.

Highly recommended lodgings are indicated by a star ★.

Category	Cost*
Very Expensive	over $120
Expensive	$80–$120
Moderate	$50–$79
Inexpensive	under $50

*All prices are for a standard double room (or an equivalent, where not applicable), are in Canadian dollars, and do not include a 5% room tax in Alberta, an 8% room tax in British Columbia, and in some areas, a small municipal tax.

Banff
Dining
★

Le Beaujolais. Elegantly decorated in a neoclassical style, this restaurant is strikingly out of place in casual Banff. The color scheme is a rich velvety red, and horse-scene oil paintings adorn the walls. The most successful menu items are traditional French specialties: chateaubriand and trout fillets with fresh herbs. The wine cellar is lavishly and imaginatively stocked. *212 Buffalo St. at Banff Ave., tel. 403/762–2712. Reservations required. Jacket and tie required. AE, MC, V. Dinner only. Very Expensive.*

Banff Springs Hotel. This hotel (*see* Lodging, below) houses 18 bars and lounges of varying formality and cuisine, from coffee-houses to a grand dining room. Samurai, a Japanese restaurant, may have the best food—its standards must be high enough to satisfy the hotel's large Japanese clientele. The best overall dining experience may be at the Waldhaus, where a Bavarian-style meal is often followed by a Bavarian-style singalong. The Grapes Wine Bar, which serves a light-fare menu, including salads and cheeses, is tucked away in a small, quiet room on the mezzanine level. Big windows make for nice views here. The Alhambra, open in summer only, specializes in Spanish-style cuisine and flambé in a grottolike setting. In the Rob Roy Supper Club, waiters negotiate flambé carts around guests who come here to dance to live music. A hotel highlight in summer is the barbecue on the Red Terrace. The flavor of the traditional barbecue fare—steaks, corn on the cob, roast potatoes—seems greatly enhanced by the view of Rundle Mountain, the Bow River, and the hotel golf course. *Spray Ave., tel. 403/762-2211. Dining hours, dress codes, and reservation policies vary among restaurants. Dinner reservations in summer required at most restaurants. AE, DC, MC, V. Moderate–Very Expensive.*

Caboose. Situated in the railway depot, the Caboose is reminiscent of the bygone train era. Old train-engine, rail-car, and train-depot paraphernalia fills the dining room; dim lighting adds to the spirit of nostalgia. The Continental dishes, served with salad, are good but basic: simply prepared prime rib, crab legs, beef, and salmon steaks. *Elk and Lynx Sts., tel. 403/762-3622. Dinner only. Reservations advised. Dress: neat but casual. AE, MC, V. Expensive.*

Buffalo Mountain Lodge. An exposed, rough-hewn post-and-beam interior gives the dining room a comfortable likeness to a converted barn. This is a woodcrafter's showcase, highlighted by the large polished wine cabinet that divides the dining and bar areas. The menu features fish, meat, and game dishes with sweet-tasting nouvelle sauces and is supplemented by hearty soups and fresh-baked breads. *Tunnel Mountain Rd., tel. 403/762-2400. Open 7 AM–11 PM. Reservations advised. Dress: neat but casual. AE, MC, V. Moderate–Expensive.*

★ **Giorgio's.** This is two restaurants in one: **La Pasta,** a casual spot, is located downstairs; **La Casa,** the more formal dining room, is upstairs. La Casa serves classic Italian fare with a romantic, dinner-under-the-eaves atmosphere. La Pasta, appealing to the local crowd, serves pizzas and pasta dishes in the dimly lit, tavernlike room. *219 Banff Ave., tel. 403/762-5116 (La Casa); 403/762-5114 (La Pasta). Dinner only. Reservations advised for La Casa. Dress for La Casa: neat but casual; La Pasta, casual. AE, MC, V. Moderate (La Pasta)–Expensive (La Casa).*

Balkan Restaurant. The bright blue-and-white decor, with tile trim, cane-back chairs, and plants, evokes the Mediterranean. The menu offers classic Greek dishes, such as moussaka and souvlakia, as well as creative ethnic mixes, such as Greek chow mein (rice and veggies with feta cheese). Lunchtime can attract a crowd. *120 Banff Ave., tel. 403/762-3454. Reservations accepted. Dress: casual. AE, DC, MC, V. Moderate.*

Melissa's Missteak. Behind an ersatz German-beerhaus facade is an ersatz log-cabin interior. Upstairs, the lounge is true roadside-America, with popcorn, video games, and TV monitors. The restaurant serves decent food at fair prices, three meals daily, and the video games serve as a great diversion for children. Steaks are the predominant dinner-menu item, although deep-dish pizza is a house specialty. *218 Lynx St., tel. 403/762-5511. Reservations advised for dinner. Dress: casual. AE, MC. Moderate.*

★ **Barbary Coast.** This sports-theme restaurant with neo-California cuisine is a local favorite. The plant-filled, skylighted dining room is littered with paraphernalia from all manner of sport, baseball to bobsledding. Pizzas with pesto sauce are a house specialty, along with oddities such as the Einstein Theory salad (chicken, bananas, sprouts, etc., in a curry dressing). Live rock and blues bands play in the bar after 9 PM. *119 Banff Ave., upstairs, tel. 403/762–4616. Reservations for parties of 6 or more only. Dress: casual. AE, DC, MC, V. Inexpensive–Moderate.*

★ **Joe Btfsplk's Diner.** It's either fun, camp, or overbearing, depending on your tastes. This restaurant is a re-created '50s-style diner, with red vinyl banquettes, chrome-trimmed tables, and waitresses dressed in vintage '50s attire. The menu is taken straight from a true-Americana cookbook: meat loaf and hash for lunch or dinner, eggs and biscuits for breakfast. Fresh-baked cookies and muffins, available for take-out, are the culinary highlight. *221 Banff Ave., tel. 403/762–5529. No reservations. Dress: casual. AE, MC, V. Inexpensive.*

Lodging **Banff Springs Hotel.** Built in 1888, this castlelike hotel was the beginning of Banff's tourism boom. The massive, stone-walled hotel has a seemingly endless maze of hallways and stairwells, huge sitting areas, and banquet rooms, complemented by lots of dark wood furnishings and chandeliers. The complexity of the hotel's floor plan, however, can be disorienting, and the lobby is surprisingly small—contributing to traffic jams during checkout time. The 829 guest rooms come in all shapes and sizes, with such old-hotel characteristics as high ceilings, rattling windows, and layers of cream-color paint. Refurbished bathrooms are a plus. The hotel caters to tour groups and conventioneers—a $23 million convention center being the hotel's most recent major addition—making this ever-active lodge anything but a getaway mountain retreat. Rooms are not soundproof, and often the noises carry. *Spray Ave., Box 960, T0L 0C0, tel. 403/762–2211 or 800/268–9411. 760 rooms, 69 suites. Facilities: 18 restaurants and pubs, 24-hr room service, cable TV, shops, health club, 5 tennis courts, riding stables, golf course. Premium rates mid-May–mid-Oct. AE, DC, MC, V. Very Expensive.*

Banff Park Lodge. The high, slanted ceiling and dark-cedar paneling, in addition to the lean, modern, and unembellished style, exude a Scandinavian feeling. On a quiet street in downtown Banff, the lodge is within walking distance of shops and restaurants. The rooms are bright, with lots of beige and ecru. A few have large, in-room Jacuzzis, two giant steps from bedside. *217 Lynx St., Box 2200, T0L 0C0, tel. 403/762–4433 or 800/661–9266. 211 rooms, some with steam showers and Jacuzzis. Facilities: 2 restaurants, room service, whirlpool, sauna, indoor pool, shops, cable TV. Premium rates June–Sept. AE, DC, MC, V. Expensive.*

Banff Rocky Mountain Resort. Five kilometers (3 miles) east of Banff, this resort, with chalet-style buildings and numerous outdoor facilities, is the place for active people. Inside, rooms are bright, with white walls, wall-to-wall carpeting, and lots of blond-wood trim. Many rooms have fireplaces and kitchens with microwave ovens. *Banff Ave. and Tunnel Mountain Rd., Box 100, T0L 0C0, tel. 403/762–5531 or 800/661–9563. 170 studio, 1-bedroom, and 2-bedroom units. Facilities: cable TV, 2 tennis courts, squash courts, weight room, games room, indoor pool complex, video service on premises, shuttle-bus service to and from Banff. Approximate 35% to 50% rate increase* *mid-June–mid-Sept. and late-Dec.–early-Jan. AE, DC, MC, V. Expensive.*

★ **Buffalo Mountain Lodge.** Part of the Canadian Rocky Mountain Resorts group, along with Emerald Lake Lodge in Yoho and Deer Lodge in Lake Louise, this lodge is similar in ambience and style. The lobby area, with lots of polished pine and exposed rough-hewn beams, is dominated by a large stone hearth with a buffalo head over the mantel. There is a main lodge, with lobby and restaurant; a new hotel-condo cluster built in 1987; and an older group of chalet buildings. Newer rooms are dressed in pastel shades and have small fireplaces, wicker chairs, and pine cabinetry. Older chalet units are larger, with two bedrooms, and are similarly decorated. Although the lodge sits high atop the road, on the outskirts of Banff, few rooms have views. *Tunnel Mountain Rd., Box 1326, T0L 0C0, tel. 403/762–2400 or 800/661–1367. 85 units, including hotel rooms, and 2-bedroom condos. Facilities: cable TV, hot tub, steam room. Approximately 60% rate increase mid-June–mid-Sept. and Christmas week. AE, MC, V. Expensive.*

Cascade Inn. A recent renovation has turned this establishment, formerly the town dive, into one of Banff's nicer hotels. You wouldn't know it from the unpretentious exterior, which looks like an extension of the neighboring (and more modest) Mount Royal Hotel. Rooms are tastefully furnished in an executive-suite motif, with lots of dark, polished wood. Financial difficulties, unfortunately, forced a recent—and temporary—closing, but the hotel expects to be in full operation for 1993. *124 Banff Ave., Box 790, Banff, AB T0L 0C0, tel. 403/762–3311. Facilities: 58 rooms and suites, some with wet bars and in-room Jacuzzis. Cable TV. Restaurant. AE, DC, MC, V. Moderate–Expensive.*

★ **Storm Mountain Lodge.** This is one of the original Canadian Pacific Railway backcountry lodges, built in 1922. Not nearly as back-country today, it is on Route 93, just east of Vermilion Pass. The sitting area of the main, log cabin–style lodge is dominated by a large fireplace that is crowned by the head of a big-horn sheep. The dining area embodies the elegance of simplicity: straight-back wood chairs and white tablecloths on an enclosed porch with big glass windows overlooking the pass. Sleeping cabins, tucked in the woods, are smallish but cozy, made so by fireplaces, old lamps, and down comforters. *Rte. 93, 4.8 km (3 mi) west of Rte. 1 interchange. Box 670, T0L 0C0, tel. 403/762–4155. 12 cabins. Facilities: restaurant, lounge, hiking trails. Closed mid-Sept.–late-May. AE, MC, V. Moderate–Expensive.*

Castle Mountain Village. The Village, about halfway between Banff and Lake Louise, consists of three different chalet styles. The smallest—about 3½ by 4¼ meters (12 by 14 feet)—have kitchens, bathrooms, and sleeping areas with fireplaces. Although cramped and on the dark side, they are also clean and quiet. Larger and newer pine-log chalets have two bedrooms and can sleep as many as six. For four people, the large chalets are a comfortable, economic choice. Request a cabin with a view of Castle Mountain. *Rte. 1A between Banff and Lake Louise, Box 1655, T0L 0C0, tel. 403/762–3868. 21 chalets. Facilities: satellite TV, convenience store, barbecue facilities. 35%–40% rate increases June–Oct. and Christmas week. Pets $10 extra. MC, V. Moderate.*

High Country Inn. There is nothing fancy here—just clean,

simple, comfortable motel rooms. The units are slightly more
spacious than those in the Red Carpet Inn next door, wood-
veneer furnishings are a little newer, and cedar-covered walls
give some rooms a touch of regional character. Ask for a room in
the back, away from heavy traffic running along Banff Avenue.
419 Banff Ave., Box 700, T0L 0C0, tel. 403/762–2236 or 800/
661–1244. 71 rooms. Facilities: restaurant, satellite TV, whirl-
pool, heated parking. Premium rates May–mid-Sept. AE,
MC, V. Moderate.

Red Carpet Inn. Under the same management as the High
Country Inn next door, Red Carpet offers one of the few moderately priced lodging options in downtown Banff. Like its neighbor, this motel is basically no-frills; the lobby is modestly
adorned with a desk, an office, and a postcard stand. Motel-
style rooms are small, but by Banff standards so are the prices,
which are slightly below those of the High Country Inn. Rooms
in the front, on Banff Avenue, get traffic noise. *425 Banff Ave.,*
Box 1800, T0L 0C0, tel. 403/762–4184. 46 rooms. Facilities: sat-
ellite TV, indoor pool, whirlpool. Premium rates May–mid-
Sept. AE, MC, V. Moderate.

Canmore **Pepper Mill.** The small dining room is simply adorned with off-
Dining white walls, brown tablecloths, and cloth-covered hanging
★ lamps. Reputed for its pepper steak, the restaurant offers well-
prepared pasta dishes as well. In summer, meals are also
served on a deck in front, alongside a quiet Canmore side
street. *726 9th St., tel. 403/678–2292. Reservations advised.*
Dress: neat but casual. AE, MC, V. Dinner only. Moderate–
Expensive.

Faro's. Colorful drawings of Canmore hung against white walls
and blond-wood tabletops lend to a bright, casual environment.
The menu is eclectic, offering barbecued dishes, pizzas, and
steaks, but such Greek entrées as souvlakia are the house specialties. *8th St. and 8th Ave., tel. 403/678–2234. Reservations*
recommended after 5 PM. Open 11 AM–10 PM. Dress: casual. AE,
MC, V. Moderate.

Lodging **Bow Valley Motel.** Located in the center of Canmore, this two-
story, few-frills motel is enhanced by the friendliness of its
management and its proximity to town. For those who put a
premium on being able to walk to dining and shopping, this is
the place to stay. Rooms are simply furnished with a wood-veneer bed, a dresser, a 12-inch TV, and not much more. Five
rooms have kitchens. *610 8th St., Box 231, T0L 0M0, tel. 403/*
678–5085. 25 rooms. Facilities: cable TV. Premium rates
June–Sept. AE, DC, MC, V. Moderate.

Skiland Motel. In terms of facilities and prices, several motels
in Canmore are pretty much interchangeable as lower-price alternatives to Banff accommodations. Of these, the Skiland
might be a notch above the rest. The newer section (built in
1987) of this two-part motel is certainly more attractive than
the older section. Slanting, exposed wood-and-beam ceilings
give a chaletlike feel to otherwise simple motel rooms. Rooms
in the older section have kitchenettes, but the decor is more
'60s American than Swiss-chalet. *Highway 1A, Box 696,*
Canmore, AB TOL ONO, tel. 403/678–5445 or 800/661–1249.
Facilities: 45 rooms, 23 with kitchenette. Steam room, exercise
room, playground, cable TV. Premium rates June–Sept. MC,
V. Moderate.

★ **Mt. Engadine Lodge.** Hiking and cross-country skiing trails begin out the back door of this backcountry-style lodge, where

the mountains and lakes of Kananaskis Country are an immediate presence. The surroundings draw young and old, and most of the clientele come here to enjoy the outdoors. Wood is the lodge's main design feature, with cedar walls on the exterior and white-pine ceilings and furnishings inside. Rooms (dormitory-style as well as private) have a scrubbed simplicity to them, as do the common areas. Meals, served family-style, are included in the rate. The lodge operators are also backcountry guides, and hiking or skiing packages are available. *At Mt. Shark turn off on Spray Trail, 38 km (22 mi) south of Canmore. Box 1679, Canmore T0L 0M0, tel. 403/678–4080. Lodging for 28 persons in dorm-style, shared, and private rooms, all with shared baths. Facilities: restaurant, sun deck. Winter rates slightly higher than in summer. MC, V. Inexpensive–Moderate.*

Cranbrook
Dining

City Cafe. If you find yourself stuck for lunch in the fast-food world of Cranbrook, City Cafe will be a breath of fresh air. The flowered tablecloths, low ceilings, and pine banquettes give the small dining room a French-country-bistro air, especially in the morning, when breakfast is served. Sandwiches served on fresh, crusty French bread are tasty and very reasonably priced. *1015 Baker St., tel. 604/489–5413. Reservations advised. Dress: casual. MC, V. Inexpensive–Moderate.*

Fairmont Hot Springs
Lodging

Fairmont Hot Springs Resort. With an extensive selection of activities from golf to heli-hiking, a vacation at this resort is like being at camp. In addition to the recreational facilities, Fairmont also has hot springs, a spa, and an airport. Rooms, available in condo villas and the main lodge, are familiarly furnished with contemporary decor, and many are wood-paneled. The low-slung, bungalow-style architecture is attractive. Some rooms are equipped with kitchens and have balconies or patios. *Rte. 93/95, Box 10, Fairmont Hot Springs V0B 1L0, tel. 604/ 345–6311 or 800/663–4979. 140 lodge rooms and 194 villa units, some with kitchens, patios, and/or balconies. Also 265 RV sites. Facilities: 7 restaurants, lounge, snack bar, 2 golf courses, 10 tennis courts, heli-hiking, 4 pools, hot springs, spa, airport. Golf, ski, and spa packages. AE, MC, V. Expensive.*

Glacier National Park
Lodging

Glacier Park Lodge. This modern, two-floor motel at the top of Rogers Pass offers ambience in the familiar Best Western format: wood-veneer tables and chairs, maroon wall-to-wall carpeting, and undecorated walls. The steep-sloping A-frame roof is a design concession to the heavy winter snows. Since this is the only lodging within Glacier National Park boundaries, the location is the main attraction. Situated on Highway 1, the lodge accommodates long-distance travelers with its 24-hour service station, 24-hour coffee shop, and gift shop. *The Summit, Rogers Pass, BC V0E 2S0, tel. 604/837–2126 or 800/528– 1234. 51 motel-style rooms. Facilities: restaurant, 24-hr coffee shop, heated outdoor pool. AE, MC, V. Moderate.*

Golden
Lodging

Swiss Village. This is a combination motel and campground lodging, with a little more modern polish than some of its Golden neighbors. There is nothing special here, just basic motel rooms—bed, bathroom, TV—at a fair price. The RV sites have electrical set-ups and water. *Off Rte. 1, west end of Golden. Box 765, V0A 1H0, tel. 604/344–2276. 40 motel rooms, 10 RV sites. Facilities: satellite TV, whirlpool. AE, MC, V. Inexpensive.*

Invermere   **Chalet Edelweis.** This cute little chalet really looks as if it could
Dining   have been plucked and transplanted from a hillock in the Swiss
★   countryside. The interior is refreshingly simple—a few blond-
wood tables, scrubbed white walls, and a small bar. The atmosphere inspires you to try the fondue, but schnitzels and
fettuccine are also good. *934 7th Ave., tel. 604/342–3525. Reservations advised. Dress: casual. MC, V. Dinner only. Moderate–Expensive.*

Lodging   **Delphine Lodge.** This is the sort of place for those seeking an
★   out-of-the-way cubbyhole. Originally built in 1899, this hotel
has been restored to its present bed-and-breakfast status. Big,
lace-curtained windows shed lots of light on a living/dining area
that is distinguished by its polished, wide-board floors, huge
stone hearth, and antique straight-back chairs and wicker
rockers. Handcrafted pine furnishings and down comforters fill
the smallish, pastel-shaded bedrooms. Full breakfast is served
every morning. *Main St., 5 km (3 mi) from Invermere, Box
2797, V0A 1K0, tel. 604/342–6851. 6 rooms, 1 with private bath,
5 sharing 2 baths. V. Inexpensive.*

Jasper   **Beauvert Room** and **Moose Nook.** For fancy dining and a wide-
Dining   ranging Continental menu, the Beauvert Room is the place to
go around Jasper. The huge dining room, whose main decor is
stone pillars and hard angles, conveys a big-hotel-style ambience. Moose Nook, more intimate but retaining a modernistic
coolness, has an imaginative, game-oriented menu that includes pheasant, reindeer, and buffalo steaks, although the
quality can be uneven. Both restaurants are open for breakfast.
*Jasper Park Lodge, 4 km (2½ mi) northeast of Jasper, off Rte.
16, tel. 403/852–3301. Reservations required. Jacket advised
for dinner. AE, MC, V. Very Expensive.*

★   **Le Beauvallon.** When Jasperites go out for a special meal, this
is often where they go. Upholstered chairs, blue tablecloths,
and wood-trimmed crimson walls bring an air of elegance to
this dining room. The menu has some seafood items, but meat
dishes are featured, including lamb in pesto sauce and an elk,
beef, and pork mélange. The giant Sunday-brunch buffet has
epic feast potential for active outdoorspeople. Try Le
Beauvallon for breakfast, too. *Chateau Jasper, 96 Giekie St.,
tel. 403/852–5644. Dinner reservations advised. Dress: neat
but casual; jacket advised for dinner. AE, MC, V. Expensive–
Very Expensive.*

★   **L'Auberge.** French cuisine is offered in this small mountain-
lodge retreat with panoramic views of the Athabasca River.
Weather permitting, meals are served on the porch in front, but
traffic noise from nearby Route 93 may make indoor dining
preferable. The menu is creatively assembled from French
classics; highlights are brie baked in puff pastry (appetizer)
and veal with wild mushrooms (entrée). Though no lunch is
served, breakfast begins at 8 AM. *Near Becker's Chalets, 5 mi
south of Jasper on Rte. 93, tel. 403/852–3535. Reservations advised for dinner. Dress: casual. AE, MC, V. Closed lunch and
mid-Oct.–Apr. Expensive.*

L & W. Plants adorning the sloping greenhouse roof bring life
to this otherwise ordinary hotel coffee shop. The menu is all
over the lot—pizzas, Greek dishes, barbecued ribs—the common denominator being a salad bar. Dishes are adequately prepared, and the simplest—burgers and pizzas—are the best
choices. Families come here for a decent meal at a reasonable

price. Take-out and delivery service are available. *Hazel and Patricia Sts., tel. 403/852-4114. No reservations. Dress: casual. AE, MC, V. Moderate.*

The Palisades. A surprisingly rich Greek streak runs through Jasper, and this restaurant is a good place to get a feel for it. Bright-white walls, a greenhouse ceiling over part of the dining room, and numerous plants evoke a sunny Mediterranean mood. Moussaka and souvlakia, along with baklava for dessert, are the characteristic Greek items, although pizzas are available, too. *Cedar Ave., near Connaught Dr., tel. 403/852-5222. Dinner reservations accepted. Dress: casual. AE, MC, V. Moderate.*

Mountain Foods. This is a good place to pick up a morning cup of coffee or sandwiches for a picnic lunch. The café has a health-food store in the back and a deli counter up front. Though the emphasis is on health foods, you can still get an old-fashioned three-meat hero to eat in or take out. The tabbouleh salad is especially good. Browse through the store's book rack while waiting for your sandwich to be made. *606 Connaught St., tel. 403/852-4050. No reservations. Dress: casual. MC, V. Inexpensive.*

Lodging **Jasper Park Lodge.** Jasper's original resort, a lakeside compound northeast of town, hums with on-site recreational amenities, including guided activities. The main lodge, with a large window overlooking Beauvert Lake and the mountains, features polished-stone floors, carved totem-pole pillars, and high ceilings that convey a cool, open-warehouse atmosphere. The rooms vary: Some are in a modern, hotel-room style; others have an exposed-log, rustic character, with fireplaces; but most are arranged in one-story cottages, and all have brightly patterned down comforters on all the beds, and a porch, patio, or balcony. Breakfast and dinner at the lodge's restaurants, the Beauvert Room and Moose Nook (*see* Dining, above), are included in most room rates. *4 km (2½ mi) northeast of Jasper, off Rte. 16, Box 40, T0E 1E0, tel. 403/852-3301; in the U.S., 800/828-7747. 419 rooms. Facilities: 3 restaurants, satellite TV, golf course, 2 tennis courts, boating, bicycling, horseback riding, fishing. 40%-50% rate increase June-Sept. AE, DC, MC, V. Very Expensive.*

Chateau Jasper. Big wood beams cantilevered over the front door of this two-story inn suggest a Scandinavian interior, but rooms are of the American motel style with Colonial motif, most notable in the Colonial-style headboards. Burgundy carpets and low ceilings add coziness to largish rooms; some units have kitchen areas, though they are spare and in need of a facelift. The hotel's restaurant, Le Beauvallon, is excellent (*see* Dining, above). *96 Giekie St., T0E 1E0, St., tel. 403/852-5644. 119 rooms, 6 with kitchen. Facilities: satellite TV, heated indoor parking, indoor pool, whirlpool, roof-top sun deck. Premium rates June-Sept. AE, DC, MC, V. Expensive.*

Jasper Inn. A modern interpretation of chalet-style architec-7ture, this inn has lots of oblique angles and hard edges, with sleek, low-slung furniture to match. This angular coolness is warmed by slanted cedar ceilings and red brick. During breakfast, the skylighted dining area is as bright as the beach on a sunny day. Accommodations are arranged in a variety of ways, but living areas in condo-style units are particularly spacious. Most units have kitchenettes and fireplaces. *Giekie St. and Bonhomme Ave., Box 879, T0E 1E0, tel. 403/852-4461 or 800/*

661–1933. 141 rooms, including 14 new suites. Facilities: satellite TV, indoor pool, sauna, whirlpool, steam bath. Approximately 40% rate increase June–Sept. Children under 12 stay free in parents' room. AE, DC, MC, V. Moderate–Expensive.

Pyramid Lake Bungalows. Situated on the shores of active Pyramid Lake, this lodging is a great place for those who enjoy hiking, boating, horseback riding, and marvelous sunrises, or cross-country skiing and ice skating in winter. The 16 units built in 1988 in two log-cabin chalets are preferable to the older bungalows that are closer to the lake but more run-down. All units have kitchenettes. The restaurant is fair, but Jasper, a few kilometers down the road, has much to offer. *Pyramid Lake Rd., 5.6 km (4 mi) from Jasper. Box 388, T0E 1E0, tel. 403/852–3536. 42 units in 10 bungalows and 2 chalets. Facilities: satellite TV; beach with boat, canoe, and sailboard rentals; 16 units have whirlpools. MC, V. Moderate.*

★ **Alpine Village.** Located just south of town, this is one of Jasper's bargains. Logs in many cabins are left exposed on interior walls, adding to the warm, rustic feeling of this family-run operation. Furnishings are garage-sale eclectic, and frilly throw cushions abound. Most units, including 12 recently built log-cabin chalets, have fireplaces and sun decks; two-bedroom cabins have full kitchens. The Athabasca River and a view of distant Mt. Edith Cavell are just out front, although a small road must be crossed to get to the river. *Rte. 93A, 1 km (⅔ mi) south of Jasper. Box 610, T0E 1E0, tel. 403/852–3285. 42 units, including 1-room sleeping cabins and 2-bedroom cabins. 25%–35% rate increase mid-June–mid-Dec. DC, V. Closed mid-Oct.–Apr. Inexpensive–Moderate.*

Kananaskis Country Dining

L'Escapade. In the evening, the atmosphere in L'Escapade is tastefully elegant and romantic, with such fine details as white tablecloths, real silver, and candlelight. The menu is French-influenced and features such items as lamb Niçoise, duck breast, and lobster linguine. Together, the fare and ambience make this restaurant the most elegant in all the village. Breakfast is served. *Hotel Kananaskis, Kananaskis Village, Hwy. 40, tel. 403/591–7711. Reservations advised for dinner. Dress: neat but casual; jacket advised for dinner. AE, DC, MC, V. Very Expensive.*

Lodging

Kananaskis Village. This is the lodging village built for the 1988 Olympics, as the look attests. This full-service resort, sandwiched on a small plateau between the Nakiska ski area and two 18-hole golf courses, is tastefully designed and decorated. Accommodations are in three facilities—the Inn, the Lodge, and the Hotel. All surround an attractively landscaped, artificial pond that provides a nice lounging spot on a summer day. Of the three, the Inn is the most moderately priced, with log pillars and a redwood exterior inviting you into the motel-style rooms, some with private balconies (balconies facing west get the best sun), kitchenettes, or fireplaces. Larger and more lavish, some rooms in the Lodge and Hotel have rosewood furnishings, ceramic-base lamps, and rustic wood armoires to hide TV sets. The hotel throws in special amenities, such as bathrobes and hair dryers, and some rooms have fireplaces and Jacuzzis. Several restaurants, skewed toward high-end elegance, offer food ranging from sushi to haute cuisine. The Peaks dining room in the Lodge, with floor-to-ceiling windows casting light on a dark wood motif, may have the nicest atmosphere for those seeking a fancy meal. *Hwy. 40, 28 km (17 mi) south of Rte. 1.*

Kananaskis Village T0L 2H0, tel. 403/591–7711 or 800/828–7447. Inn: 96 rooms. Lodge: 253 rooms and suites. Hotel: 68 rooms and suites. Facilities: 5 restaurants, satellite TV, indoor pool, sauna, whirlpool, health club, ski area, two 18-hole golf courses, stables nearby, shops, post office, heated indoor parking for the Lodge and Hotel. Lodge and Hotel: AE, DC, MC, V; Inn: AE, MC, V. Expensive–Very Expensive.

Kimberley
Dining

Gasthas am Platzl. With individually lit wood booths and waitresses dressed in dirndls, the restaurant is a none-too-subtle re-creation of a German bierstube. The menu goes right along with the furnishings: Schnitzels and wursts are served, but non-German pasta dishes are also listed. *240 Spokane St., tel. 604/427–4851. Reservations advised. Dress: casual. AE, MC, V. Moderate–Expensive.*

★ **Chef Bernard's Kitchen.** Dining in this small, homey storefront on the Kimberley pedestrian mall is like dining in someone's pantry. The decor is alpine—with goat horns, cowbells, and photos adorning the walls. The menu is small but widely varied, including pastas and fondues. Breakfast is served in summer. *170 Spokane St., tel. 604/427–4820. Reservations advised. Dress: neat but casual. MC, V. Moderate.*

Lodging

Inn of the Rockies. In keeping with downtown Kimberley's Bavarian theme, the hotel's exterior is very German, with exposed-wood beams and stucco, and tinted, blown-glass windows. (The hotel's former name, Rhinekastle, is still used by many Kimberley locals.) Large rooms have a small sitting area and are plainly furnished with dark brown wood-veneer furniture, including a bed, bureau, and TV. The restaurant serves good, reasonably priced food. Just a block from the Platzl, this is *the* hotel in Kimberley. *300 Wallinger Ave., V1A 1Z4, tel. 604/427–2266 or 800/661–7559. 41 hotel rooms. Facilities: restaurant, lounge, cable TV. AE, MC, V. Moderate.*

Lake Louise
Dining
★

Post Hotel. Here is one of the true epicurean experiences in the Canadian Rockies. The restaurant receives numerous commendations and awards, and with good reason. A low, exposed-beam ceiling and a stone hearth in the corner lend a warm, in-from-the-cold atmosphere; white tablecloths and fanned napkins provide an elegant touch. Venison and veal are specialties, and sauces and garnishes are Alpine-influenced. Homemade pastries and desserts cap off the meal; you can also order them for tea in the hotel lobby (*see* Lodging, below). Breakfast is served. While the food is excellent, service can be stuffy. *200 Pipestone St., tel. 403/522–3989. Reservations advised. Jacket advised for dinner. AE, MC, V. Very Expensive.*

Chateau Lake Louise. Several restaurants and pubs in this hotel (*see* Lodging, below) present an array of options, from light snacking in the Alpine Lounge to night-on-the-town elegance in the Edelweiss Dining Room. Regardless of choice, dining inevitably defers to the view, brought into play by arced, 10-foot-high windows. The size of the Victoria Dining Room, with seating for more than 300, is nicely toned down by plush carpeting, upholstered chairs, and standing plants. The food and atmosphere are European hotel–style—croissants and jam for breakfast, Continental fare for lunch and dinner—with white cotton tablecloths, and polished silver. For simpler, less expensive, coffee shop–style eating throughout the day, there is the Poppy Room. Afternoon tea in the Lakeside Lounge is a culinary highlight that usually includes fresh scones, pastries, or croissants—along with coffee and tea—served on high-tea silver. *Lake Louise Dr., tel. 403/522–3511, ext. 52. Dinner reservations required in summer for most restaurants. Dress: casual; jacket required for dinner in Edelweiss Dining Room. AE, DC, MC, V. Moderate (Poppy Room)–Very Expensive (Edelweiss and Victoria dining rooms).*

Laggan's Mountain Bakery and Deli. This six-table coffee shop is where the local work crews, mountain guides, and park wardens come for an early-morning muffin and a cup of coffee. Laggan's, in Sampson Mall, has excellent baked goods, especially the poppy-seed sweet breads. You might want to pick up a sandwich here for your drive north on the Icefields Parkway. *Samson Mall, off Rte. 1, tel. 403/522–2017. No reservations. Dress: casual. No credit cards. Inexpensive.*

Lodging **Chateau Lake Louise.** There's a good chance that no hotel—
★ anywhere—has a more dramatic view out its back door than this chateau. Terraces and lawns reach to the famous aquamarine lake, backed up by the Victoria Glacier. The impressive turn-of-the-century stone facade opens to a similarly grand interior, with lobby and sitting areas that convey a stadiumlike sense of spaciousness. A $60 million renovation, completed in 1991, has been tastefully done. In the public areas, off-white walls, polished wood and brass, and burgundy carpeting blend well with the lake view, seen through large, horseshoe-shaped windows. Guest rooms feature bright, floral-pattern wallpaper, neo-Colonial furnishings, and terraces. In spite of all the space, though, the hotel can become very crowded with bus tours, hikers, day-trippers from Banff, and hotel guests. *Lake Louise, AB T0L 1E0, tel. 403/522–3511 or 800/828–7447. 540 rooms and suites. Facilities: 6 restaurants, indoor pool, canoeing, riding stables, sauna, whirlpool, shops. AE, DC, MC, V. Very Expensive.*

★ **Post Hotel.** The location, next to the small shopping mall just off Highway 1, is rather ordinary, but the hotel makes up for it in other ways. A gold-colored wood dominates the decor, giving the hotel an atmosphere of muted elegance—a modern interpretation of the country-lodge concept. Rooms come in 13 different configurations, from standard doubles to units with sleeping lofts, kitchens, balconies, and fireplaces. The wood theme extends to the furniture, made of solid Canadian pine. Bathrooms are large, most equipped with whirlpool tubs. Two recently renovated, stream-side log cabins—each intended for two people—date back to the original Post Hotel, built in 1938, and evoke a mood of old-fashioned, in-the-mountains romance. The restaurant (*see* Dining, above) is regularly rated as one of the best in the Canadian Rockies. *Box 69, T0L 1E0, tel. 403/522–3989 or 800/661–1586. 93 units. Facilities: cable TV, indoor pool, steam bath, whirlpool. 25%–35% rate increase mid-May–mid-Sept. and Christmas week. AE, MC, V. Expensive.*

Lake Louise Inn. This five-building complex offers a variety of accommodations, from motel rooms to two-bedroom condo units. A three-story building, completed in early 1991, with 12 one-room suites and 24 motel-style rooms, adds to the wide array of lodging options here. Catch the morning sun in the recently renovated lobby, with its wood and stone-wall decor. For economy-minded travelers, the Pinery, a separate 56-room building, offers spare but comfortable accommodations. *210 Village Rd., Box 209, T0L 1E0, tel. 403/522–3791 or 800/661–9237. 222 rooms and condo units, many with balconies, fire-*

You've Let Your Imagination Go, Now Get Up And Follow Your Dreams.

For The Vacation You're Dreaming Of, Call American Express® Travel Agency At 1-800-YES-AMEX.*

American Express will send more than your imagination soaring. We'll fly you, sail you, drive you to any Fodor's destination and beyond. Because American Express believes the best vacations happen from Europe to the Orient, Walt Disney®World to Hawaii and everywhere in between.

For dependable service, expert advice, and value wherever your dreams take you, call on American Express. After all, the best traveling companion is a trustworthy friend.

AMERICAN EXPRESS **Travel Agency**

It's easy to recognize a good place when you see one.

American Express Cardmembers have been doing it for years.

The secret? Instead of just relying on what they see in the window, they look at the door. If there's an American Express Blue Box on it, they know they've found an establishment that cares about high standards.

Whether it's a place to eat, to sleep, to shop, or simply meet, they know they will be warmly welcomed.

So much so, they're rarely taken in by anything else.

Always a good sign.

places, and/or kitchenettes. Facilities: restaurant, pub, cable TV, indoor pool, sauna, whirlpool, exercise room, ski-area shuttle-bus service, multiday ski packages. AE, D, DC, MC, V. Moderate.

Paradise Lodge & Bungalows. This lodge is only 2 kilometers (1¼ miles) down the access road from the lake, and this location and the moderate prices are what attract guests. Six small rooms share baths upstairs in the log-cabin main lodge. The bungalows, or log-sided cabins (some with kitchenettes), are more rustic from the outside than from the inside. As the lodge is set in a spruce and pine grove, rooms can be somewhat dark and cramped but are well maintained. *Box 7, T0L 1E0, tel. 403/ 522–3595 (summer), 403/522–3987 (winter). 6 lodge rooms with shared bath, 21 1- and 2-room cottages. Facilities: barbecue facilities, playground. Closed mid-Oct.–mid-May. MC, V. Moderate.*

Panorama
Lodging

Panorama Resort. The resort, at the edge of the Purcell Wilderness, has a wide variety of accommodations and activities. The lodge at the base of the ski lifts is more casual and conveys a college-dorm atmosphere, with its long hallways and doors that look as though they've been kicked a few times with ski boots. Inside, rooms are large, with yellow walls and lots of mirrors. The other accommodations are in condo villas that look to be part of a mountainside suburb. Attractively decorated, the villa rooms follow a light-brown-and-beige color scheme, and many rooms have fireplaces, patios, or balconies. Originally conceived as a winter resort, Panorama has a fine ski area and is adding other amenities that will appeal to summer visitors, such as tennis, swimming, and hiking. *18 km (11 mi) west of Invermere. Box 7000, Panorama V0A 1T0, tel. 604/342– 6941 or 800/663–2929. 355 lodge and condo units. Facilities: satellite TV, sauna, indoor and outdoor whirlpools, outdoor pool, tennis courts, skiing, heli-skiing. AE, MC, V. Expensive.*

Dining

Toby Creek Lodge. The restaurant, part of a 1960s-era ski lodge, has cedar walls, lighting fixtures that look like upside-down buttercups, a slant-roof ceiling, and—in winter—a big roaring fire in the central fireplace. In the summer, the outside deck offers fresh air, though not much of a view. The food, alas, is fairly ordinary Continental fare. Toby Creek is open for breakfast, too. *Panorama Resort, 18 km (11 mi) west of Invermere, tel. 604/342–6941. Dinner reservations advised during ski season. Dress: neat but casual. AE, MC, V. Expensive.*

Radium Hot Springs
Dining

Alte Liebe. The main cuisine is German, but it comes with an unusual twist—a touch of Japanese. This might be the only restaurant with Wiener schnitzel and salmon sushi on the same menu. The dining room has a German decor, but the place to sit on a nice evening is on the outdoor deck, with a panoramic view of the Radium Valley under the setting sun. *Madsen Rd. (turn off .5 km, or ⅓ mi, east of Rtes. 93 and 95 junction), tel. 604/ 347–9548. Reservations advised. Dress: neat but casual. No credit cards. Closed lunch and mid-Sept.–March. Moderate– Expensive.*

Lodging

Radium Hot Springs Resort. Although the architecture and style of this resort are undistinguished, the recreational facilities and activities bring to life this otherwise basic Best Western property. Rooms, decorated with bright colors and modern furnishings, are simple but functional; some have kitchens and wet bars. Breakfast in the main dining room is a good way to start the day, as the morning sun shines brightly through the big windows. *Off Rte. 93, south of Radium Hot Springs. Box 310, V0A 1M0, tel. 604/347-9311 or 800/655-3585. 119 hotel and condo units. Facilities: indoor pool, hot tub, sauna, whirlpool, exercise room, 2 tennis courts, squash and racquetball court, golf, cross-country skiing, cable TV. Golf and ski packages available. 25% rate increase May-mid-Oct. and Christmas week. AE, MC, V. Moderate-Expensive.*

The Chalet. In a town where ordinary, interchangeable motels abound, the Chalet is a cut above—figuratively and literally. The hotel sits on a crest above town and has several rooms with expansive views of the Columbia River valley, though these units come at a premium. The decor is nothing special—lots of browns, navy blue, and wood veneer—but each room comes with a sitting area and minikitchen (microwave, refrigerator, sink), and many have balconies. This is a good, economical choice for a family with one or two small children. *Madsen Rd., Box 456, V0A 1M0, tel. 604/347-9305. 17 studios. Facilities: cable TV, sauna, whirlpool, games room. 35% rate increase June-Aug. $8 additional for young children. AE, DC, MC, V. Moderate.*

Revelstoke
Dining
★

One-Twelve. Housed in the Regent Inn (*see* Lodging, below), this restaurant is the real star of the British Columbia Rockies, where dinner is usually an ordinary affair. Lots of cedar, low ceilings, and an abundance of historic photos lend a warm atmosphere. Continental dishes, such as salmon, chicken Cordon Bleu, and beef brochette, are the basic fare, but the unrivaled king of the menu is the lamb broiled with rosemary and red wine. *Regent Hotel, 112 1st St. E, tel. 604/837-2107. Reservations advised. Lunch and dinner. Dress: neat but casual. AE, DC, MC, V. Expensive.*

Lodging

Regent Inn. The newly renovated inn mixes many styles: colonial, with its brick-arcade facade; true Canadian, in its pine-trimmed lobby area and restaurant; and Scandinavian, in the angular, low-slung wood furnishings of the guest rooms. Rooms are on the large side but have no spectacular views. The hotel is located downtown, in a revitalized, two-block area of Revelstoke, and is near several boutiques and restaurants. The hotel's own restaurant, One-Twelve, is the best of all (*see* Dining, above). *112 Victoria Rd., Box 450, V0E 2S0, tel. 604/837-2107. 43 rooms. Facilities: restaurant, club with live entertainment, cable TV, whirlpool. AE, MC, V. Moderate.*

Waterton Lakes
Lodging

Bayshore Inn. As the name suggests, the two-story inn is on the lakeside, and rooms with balconies take full advantage of the setting. Indeed, the setting is the thing; otherwise, the inn's common areas and motel-style rooms are rather ordinary, although some have balconies and kitchenettes. A distinctive touch is the heart-shaped tubs in the three honeymoon suites. When the usual Waterton wind is mellow, the lakeside patio is a great spot for light meals and drinks. *Main St., Box 38, Waterton Park, AB T0K 2M0, tel. 403/859-2211. 70 rooms, including 2-bedroom and honeymoon suites. Facilities: restaurant, coffee shop, satellite TV, gift shop. AE, MC, V. Closed Oct.-Apr. Moderate-Expensive.*

★ **Prince of Wales Hotel.** Situated between two lakes, this property has a breathtaking view of a mountain backdrop from one direction, and a lake-and-prairie setting from another. Eaves, balconies, and turrets fantastically adorn this hotel, and it's crowned by a high steeple. The baronial, dark-paneled interior evokes the feeling of a royal Scottish hunting lodge. Expect creaks and rattles at night—the old hotel (built in the 1920s) is exposed to rough winds. *Waterton townsite. Write to: Mail Station 5570, Phoenix, AZ 85078, tel. 602/248–6000. 81 rooms. Facilities: restaurant. Children under 12 stay free in parents' room. MC, V. Closed mid-Sept.–May. Moderate–Expensive.*

★ **Kilmorey Lodge.** The 60-year-old inn with a log-cabin facade sits at the edge of the Waterton Lakes townsite. Rooms are steeped in country-cottage atmosphere, with pine-wood walls, Indian rug wall hangings, sloped floors, and homespun antique furnishings. Some rooms have additional sleeping or sitting areas. There is a decent full restaurant that serves three meals a day. This is the only lodging in Waterton Lakes that's open year round. *Box 100, Waterton Park, T0K 2M0, tel. 403/859–2334 or 800/661–8069. 25 rooms. Facilities: restaurant. AE, MC, V. Moderate.*

Yoho
Dining and Lodging
★
Emerald Lake Lodge. This is an enchanted place, set at the edge of a secluded, glacier-fed lake in Yoho National Park. It's a great spot for canoeing on the lake, hiking, and cross-country skiing through miles of trails in the park. A sitting area in the main lodge has overstuffed chairs and small tables and offers light meals served around a large stone hearth. Cottages surround the log-cabin main lodge. Guest rooms have fireplaces, and many have balconies with lake views. Sound-proofing is the one amenity lacking—you can hear your neighbors. The dining room is a glass-enclosed terrace, with views of the lake through tall stands of evergreens. The furnishings are eclectic, some tables with upholstered chairs, some straight-backs, but all evoking an old-lodge atmosphere. Also eclectic is the menu, which mixes traditional Canadian and American fare—steaks, game, and fish—with nouvelle sauces like ginger-tangerine glaze. Excellent pastas and hamburgers are also available. For those who want a light meal in a more casual setting, salads, quiches, and baked cheeses are served around a giant stone hearth in the lounge area. The lodge serves breakfast also. *9.5 km (6 mi) north of Field, BC. Box 10, Field, BC V0A 1G0, tel. 604/343–6321 or 800/663–6336. 85 units in 2- and 4-room cottages. Facilities: restaurant, teahouse, bar, exercise room, sauna, outdoor hot tub, boat rentals. AE, MC, V. Expensive.*

Backcountry Lodges and Guest Ranches

Backcountry lodges have been an integral part of Canadian Rockies travel since the '20s. They vary considerably in terms of accommodations and accessibility: At the luxurious end are lodges with private rooms, private baths, full electricity, telephones, and restaurant-style dining; at the rugged extreme are lodges with bunk beds and kerosene lamps for evening light. A few are accessible by car in the summer, some can be reached only by hiking or by skiing in winter, and still others can be reached only by helicopter.

Surprisingly—given the difficulty of getting supplies to remote locations—meals served at most backcountry lodges tend to be excellent, no doubt improved by the fresh mountain air and appetites swelled by the active life of the backcountry. The lodges and ranches listed below are a sampling. Both Alberta

Tourism and Tourism B.C. can provide more complete lodge and ranch listings as well as descriptions (*see* Important Addresses and Numbers in Essential Information, above.)

Backcountry Lodges

Lake O'Hara Lodge. Secluded in the heart of one of the most scenic and popular hiking and climbing regions in the Canadian Rockies, this lodge is situated just west of Lake Louise. In summer, guests are ferried by a lodge-operated bus along an 11.25-kilometer (7-mile) fire road between Highway 1 and the grounds. In winter, guests must ski the distance. The lodge and lakeside cabins offer fairly luxurious backcountry living, including private rooms with baths and a restaurant that serves three meals a day (included in room rates). *Off Hwy. 1 in Yoho National Park. Box 55, Lake Louise, AB T0L 1E0, tel. 604/343–6418 or 403/762–2118. 23 units in lodge and cabins. Facilities: hiking, climbing, canoeing. Reservations for high season should be booked several months in advance. Closed May, Oct., Nov., Dec. MC, V. Moderate–Expensive.*

Mt. Assiniboine Lodge. Built by the Canadian Pacific Railroad in 1928, the handsome, log-sided main lodge appears to have changed little in more than 60 years. The lodge's setting is classically alpine—at the edge of mile-long Lake Magog, with the rocky pyramid of Mt. Assiniboine as a backdrop. Guests can hike in from Sunshine Village or hike (or ski) in from Spray Lakes Reservoir, the distance ranging between 20 and 30 kilometers (12 and 18 miles) depending on the route chosen. Many guests choose to fly in by helicopter from Canmore, saving their hiking legs for high-country jaunts from the lodge. Among the lodge's noteworthy amenities are large down comforters on the beds and hearty meals served family-style. The lodge has some electricity and running water, but guests should be prepared to use outhouses. *Box 1527, Canmore, AB T0L ON0, tel. 403/678–2883. 6 rooms in main lodge, plus 6 cabins sleeping 2–4 people. Room rates include all meals and hiking (or skiing) guide service. Guided hiking in summer; guided backcountry skiing in winter. No credit cards. Moderate.*

Skoki Lodge. An 11-kilometer (6½-mile) hike or ski from the Lake Louise ski area, Skoki is the kind of backcountry lodge you must work to get to. The high-alpine scenery of Skoki Valley makes the travel well worthwhile, as does the small log-cabin lodge itself, built in 1930. The log walls, big stone fireplace, and mantel cluttered with old ski gear make Skoki seem the epitome of backcountry coziness. So, too, do the rooms upstairs in the main lodge, with beds tucked tightly under the wood eaves. Don't expect such luxuries as private baths, running water, or electricity, but meals are included in the rates. *Box 5, Lake Louise, AB T0L 1E0, tel. 403/522–3555. Lodging in 22 guest rooms and cabins with wood-burning stoves and outdoor washrooms. Reservations must be made in advance. AE, MC, V. Inexpensive–Moderate.*

Guest Ranches

Homeplace Ranch. Just east of the Kananaskis Country foothills, the ranch is just as its name suggests: homey. It is secluded, several miles along gravel roads, surrounded by other working ranches. Bedrooms have tiny, private baths (unusual for ranch accommodations), and the small living/dining area is cluttered with books and magazines that provide good nightly reading, the principal evening activity. During the day, the activity is riding over the rolling land, aspen groves, and open meadows near the ranch. Also available are extended, multiday pack trips into Kananaskis Country. Meals, included in the guest rate, are served family-style, and such is the homey atmosphere that you might find yourself wanting to pitch in and help with the cooking or the dishes. *Off Rte. 2, 10 km (6 mi) west of Priddis. R.R. 1, Box 6, Priddis, AB T0L 1W0, tel. 403/ 931-3245. Lodging for 12 in private rooms in ranch house. Packages, including pack trips, available. Moderate–Expensive.*

Kananaskis Guest Ranch. Set near the Bow River at the edge of Kananaskis Country, a main lodge with restaurant and lounge is surrounded by cabins and larger "chalets." Cedar walls and, in some units, cedar-beamed ceilings give a rustic flavor to two otherwise plain, double-bed bedrooms. The Donut Tent—a log-and-wood-roofed "tent" with a large hole in the middle, where bonfires are built for family-style barbecues—is the ranch's claim to fame. In addition to the obligatory horseback riding, the ranch also offers jet-boat trips on the Bow River. *Ranch office on Ranch Rd., from the Seebe-Exshaw exit on Rte. 1 east of Canmore, General Delivery, Seebe AB T0L 1X0, tel. 403/673-3737. Lodging for 50 in cabins and chalets. Facilities: dining room, lounge, souvenir shop, whirlpool. AE, MC, V. Closed Nov.–Apr. Inexpensive–Moderate.*

The Arts and Nightlife

The Arts

Most of the cultural activity in the Canadian Rockies is in and around Banff. Unquestionably, the hub of cultural activity is the **Banff Centre** (St. Julien Rd., tel. 403/762-6300). Presenting a performing-arts grab bag throughout the year, with pop and classical music, theater, dance, and film, the center peaks in summer with the two-month Banff Festival of the Arts.

Galleries and Museums

Housed in Banff Centre is the **Walter J. Philips Gallery,** which focuses principally on works by Canadian artists and artists at the Banff Centre School of Fine Arts. *Tel. 403/762-6253. Admission free. Open noon–5.*

Also in Banff, the **Whyte Museum** features art, photography, historical artifacts, and exhibits about life in the Canadian Rockies. *111 Bear St., tel. 403/762-2291. Admission: $2, children free. Open mid-May–mid-Oct., daily 10–6; off-season hours vary.*

The **Banff Park Museum** features wildlife displays, wildlife art, and a library on natural history. *93 Banff Ave., tel. 403/ 762-3324. Admission free. Open 10–6.*

The **Jasper-Yellowhead Museum** features exhibits on the history of the Jasper area. *400 Pyramid Lake Rd., Jasper, AB T0L 1E0, tel. 403/852-3013. Donations requested. Open Memorial Day through Labor Day 10–4:30; off-season, Sun.–Wed. 1:30– 4:30.*

Performing Arts

The **Jasper Activity Centre** (303 Pyramid Ave., tel. 403/852- 3381) hosts local troupes presenting theater, music, and dance productions throughout the year.

The **Jasper Summer Theatre** (Giekie and Miette Sts., tel. 403/ 852-5325) performs shows from June through August, at the Anglican Church Hall.

At the **Wild Horse Theater** (Fort Steele, BC V0B 1N0, tel. 604/426–6923), in Fort Steele, college presentations are staged from late June to mid-September.

Music During the summer months, Bavarian bands in Kimberley strike up with oompah music on the Platzl, especially when festivals are in swing. The **Old Time Accordion Championships,** in early July, is a Kimberley musical highlight.

In late summer, the Royal Canadian Mounted Police perform their precision **Musical Ride at Fort Steele** (tel. 604/426–6923).

Nightlife

Like many activities in the Canadian Rockies, nightlife, too, is an outdoor event. In summer darkness doesn't fall until after 10 PM, so an after-dinner hike, sail, or even nine holes of golf is possible.

For cocktails and socializing, the big hotels—the **Banff Springs Hotel, Chateau Lake Louise, Jasper Park Lodge,** and the **Lodge at Kananaskis**—have lounges or dining rooms with entertainment and dancing (*see* Lodging, above).

The **Works** (tel. 403/762–3311), a record-spinning discotheque at the Banff Springs Hotel, is a lively, jam-packed hot spot.

In Canmore, local folk kick back at **Sherwood House** (738 8th St., tel. 403/678–5211), which occasionally has live bands on weekends.

In Jasper, the **Athabasca Hotel's** nightclub (510 Patricia St., tel. 403/852–3386) features dancing to Top-40 music and live bands.

9 Manitoba Saskatchewan Alberta

by Theodore Fischer

Updated by Mac Mackay

Between the wilds of western Ontario and the eastern slopes of the Rockies lie Canada's three prairie provinces—Manitoba, Saskatchewan, and Alberta. This is Canada's heartland: the principal source of such solid commodities as wheat, oil, and beef. These provinces are also the home of a rich stew of ethnic communities that make the flat plains unexpectedly colorful and cosmopolitan.

The northern sectors (about two-thirds of Manitoba, one-third of Saskatchewan, and the northeast corner of Alberta) are part of the Canadian Shield—sparsely inhabited expanses of lakes and forests atop a foundation of Precambrian rock. To the south lie the prairies, vast plains of fertile soil mostly covered with fields of wheat. Some consider the landscape boring; we'll concede that it's monotonous but also stipulate that it's soothing, inspiring, and brimming with subtle variations in topography, agronomy, and rural architecture.

Certain historical threads are common to all three provinces: Dinosaurs roamed what was semitropical swampland 75 million years ago, and the first human settlers crossed the Bering Strait from Asia 12,000 years ago. European fur traders began arriving in the 17th century, and in 1670 the British Crown granted the Hudson's Bay Company administrative and trading rights to "Rupert's Land," a patch that incorporated the vast territory whose waters drained into Hudson Bay. A hundred years later, the North West Company went into direct competition by building outposts throughout the area. The fur trade produced a new group of people called the Métis, French-speaking offspring of Indian women and European traders who followed the Roman Catholic religion but adhered to a traditional Indian lifestyle.

The North West Mounted Police was established in 1873, six years after the formation of the Canadian government and three years after the Hudson's Bay Company had sold its western holdings to the new government. The Mounties' first chores included resolving conflicts between the Indians and American whiskey traders and overseeing the orderly distribution of the free homesteads granted by the Dominion Lands Act of 1872. The Mounties ultimately had to suppress the North West Rebellion—a revolt by Métis, who feared that incorporation into Canada threatened their traditions and freedom. Although the Métis eventually succumbed, and their leader, Louis Riel, was hanged in 1885, Riel is now hailed as a martyr of French-language rights and provincial autonomy, and a statue of him stands on the grounds of Manitoba's Legislature Building.

Railroads arrived in the 1880s and with them a torrent of immigrants seeking free government land. An influx of farmers from the British Isles, Scandinavia, Holland, Germany, Eastern Europe, and Russia (and especially the Ukraine), plus persecuted religious groups, such as the Mennonites, Hutterites, Mormons, and Jews, transformed the prairies into a rich wheat-growing breadbasket and cultural mosaic, if never exactly a melting pot, that is still very much in evidence today. Alberta and southwest Saskatchewan offered rich opportunities to cattle ranchers after the treaties were signed with the native Indians in the 1870s. In 1947, a big oil strike transformed Edmonton and Calgary into gleaming metropolises full of "blue-eyed Arabs."

The people of the prairie provinces are relaxed, reserved, and irascibly independent. They maintain equal suspicion toward "Ottawa" (big government) and "Toronto" (big media and big business). To visitors, the people of this region convey a combination of Western openness and Canadian-style courtesy: no fawning, but no rudeness. Visitors also find exceptional outdoor recreational facilities—a spectrum of historical attractions that focuses on Mounties, Métis, dinosaurs, and railroads; excellent accommodations and cuisine at reasonable (but not low) prices; and quiet, crowdless expanses of extraordinarily wide open spaces.

Essential Information

Important Addresses and Numbers

Tourist Information **Manitoba**
Travel Manitoba (Dept. 9036, 7th floor, 155 Carlton St., Winnipeg, Man., R3C 3H8, tel. 204/945–3777 or 800/665–0040) distributes a free road map and several useful brochures. The office is open weekdays 8:30–4:30.

Manitoba Travel Information Centers are located just inside the Manitoba border along major routes. The centers are open mid-May through early September from 8 AM to 9 PM.

Saskatchewan
Tourism Saskatchewan (Saskatchewan Trade & Convention Centre, 1919 Saskatchewan Dr., Regina, Sask. S4P 3V7, tel. in Sask., 800/667–7538) can provide you with brochures and maps of attractions, accommodations, and parks inside and outside the province. The main office is open weekdays 8–7, Saturday 10–4.

Information centers are located in cities throughout the province, and in the summer along the Trans-Canada Highway.

Alberta
Alberta Tourism (City Centre Bldg., 10155 102nd St., 3rd Floor Vacation Counselling, Edmonton, Alberta T5J 4L6, tel. 403/427–4321, Edmonton; 800/661–8888, Alberta; 800/222–6501 in U.S. and Canada) distributes extremely comprehensive and useful free promotional literature. The office is open weekdays 9–4:30.

Arriving and Departing by Plane, Bus, and Train

By Plane
Air Canada has direct or connecting service from Boston, New York, Chicago, San Francisco, and Los Angeles to Winnipeg, Regina, Saskatoon, Calgary, and Edmonton. Commuter affiliates serve other U.S. and Canadian destinations. U.S. airlines serving the prairie provinces include **Northwest** to Winnipeg; **America West, American, Continental, Delta,** and **United** to Calgary; **America West, American, Delta,** and **Northwest** to Edmonton.

By Bus
Greyhound (consult local directory) and local bus companies provide service from the United States, other parts of Canada, and throughout the prairie provinces.

By Train
There is no rail service between the United States and the prairie provinces.

Via Rail trains (tel. 800/361–3677 from New York and Connecticut; 800/561–3949 from the Atlantic seaboard; 800/387–1144 from the Midwest; 800/665–0200 from the western U.S.) connect eastern Canada and the west coast through Winnipeg–Saskatoon–Edmonton.

Getting Around

By Car Two main east–west highways link the major cities of the prairie provinces. The Trans-Canada Highway (Route 1), mostly a four-lane divided freeway, runs through Winnipeg, Regina, and Calgary on its nationwide course. The two-lane Yellowhead Highway (Route 16) branches off the Trans-Canada Highway west of Winnipeg and heads northwest toward Saskatoon, Saskatchewan, and Edmonton, Alberta. Traveling north–south, four-lane divided freeways connect Saskatoon–Regina (Route 11) and Edmonton–Calgary (Route 2).

From the United States, interstate highways cross the Canadian border, and two-lane highways continue on to major prairie province cities. From Minneapolis, I–94 and then I–29 connect to Highway 75 at the Manitoba border south of Winnipeg. Driving distance between Minneapolis and Winnipeg is 691 kilometers (432 miles). A main route to Alberta is I–15 north of Helena, Montana, which connects to Highways 4, 3, and 2 to Calgary. Calgary is 690 kilometers (425 miles) from Helena; it's also 670 kilometers (419 miles) from Seattle, via the Trans-Canada Highway.

Winnipeg

With a population of just more than 600,000, Winnipeg ranks as Canada's seventh-largest city and the largest population center between Toronto and Calgary. Though geographically isolated, this provincial capital has become a center for both commerce and culture, boasting a symphony orchestra, ballet and opera companies, a lively theater scene, and a thriving community of local and native artists.

The first stop on the great Canadian land rush of the late-19th century, Winnipeg is still home to descendants of the original French and British settlers, and it has distinct neighborhoods of Ukrainians, Jews, Italians, Mennonites, Hungarians, Portuguese, Poles, and Chinese. Unlike the boom-and-bust towns farther west, Winnipeg has enjoyed steady growth, with a diversified economy based on manufacturing, banking, transportation, and agriculture. Winnipeg looks like the cosmopolitan centers of midwest America—Minneapolis, Milwaukee, Chicago—with a downtown area filled with cast-iron buildings and established neighborhoods of older homes along curving, tree-lined streets.

Originally, buffalo-hunting Plains Indians were the only inhabitants of the area that was franchised by the British Crown to the Hudson's Bay Company. That was until Pierre Gaultier de Varennes established in 1738 a North West Company fur-trading post at the junction of the Red and Assiniboine rivers. Lord Selkirk, a Scot, brought a permanent agricultural settlement in 1812; Winnipeg was incorporated as a city in 1873; and soon after, in 1886, the Canadian Pacific Railroad arrived, bringing a rush of European immigrants. Winnipeg boomed as a railroad hub, a center of the livestock and grain industries, and the principal market city of central Canada.

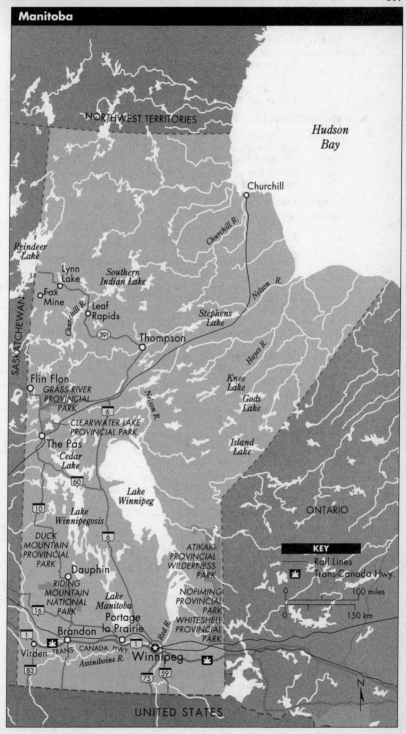

Manitoba

NORTHWEST TERRITORIES

Hudson Bay

Churchill

Reindeer Lake

Churchill R.

Nelson R.

Lynn Lake

Southern Indian Lake

Fox Mine

Churchill R.

Leaf Rapids

391

Stephens Lake

Thompson

Hayes R.

Flin Flon

GRASS RIVER PROVINCIAL PARK

Knee Lake

Gods Lake

6

Nelson R.

CLEARWATER LAKE PROVINCIAL PARK

Island Lake

The Pas

Cedar Lake

60

Lake Winnipeg

10

Lake Winnipegosis

6

ONTARIO

DUCK MOUNTAIN PROVINCIAL PARK

ATIKAKI PROVINCIAL WILDERNESS PARK

Dauphin

RIDING MOUNTAIN NATIONAL PARK

Lake Manitoba

NOPIMING PROVINCIAL PARK

16

Portage la Prairie

WHITESHELL PROVINCIAL PARK

KEY

— Rail Lines

Trans-Canada Hwy.

0   100 miles

0   150 km

1

Brandon

Red R.

TRANS. CANADA Hwy

1

Virden

83

Assiniboine R.

Winnipeg

75   59

N

UNITED STATES

SASKATCHEWAN

Important Addresses and Numbers

Tourist Information The **Government Tourist Reception Office** (Broadway and Osborne St., tel. 204/945–3777 or 800/665–0040), housed in the Manitoba Legislative Building, is open May–Labor Day, daily 8:30 AM–9 PM; Labor Day–April, weekdays 8:30–4:30. **Tourism Winnipeg** (375 York Ave., 2nd floor, tel. 204/943–1970) is open weekdays 8:30–4:30.

Emergencies Dial 911 for **fire, police, ambulance,** or **poison control.**

Hospital Emergency rooms are located at the **Health Services Centre** (820 Sherbrook St., tel. 204/787–3167 general emergency; tel. 204/787–2306 children's emergency), **Winnipeg Municipal Hospital** (1 Morley Ave., tel. 204/452–3411), and **Misericordia General Hospital** (99 Cornish Ave., tel. 204/788–8188).

Late-night Pharmacy **Nieman Pharmacies** (905 Corydon Ave., tel. 204/453–8331) is open until 11:30 PM.

Arriving and Departing by Plane

Winnipeg International Airport is served by Northwest, Air Canada, Canadian Airlines International, and several commuter airlines. Because the airport is only about 8 kilometers (5 miles) away, taxi fare downtown runs about $10. Some airport-area hotels provide complimentary airport shuttles.

Getting Around

By Bus The **City of Winnipeg Transit System** (tel. 204/284–7190) operates an extensive network of buses throughout the city and metropolitan area. Adult fare is $1.15 exact change for adults, 60¢ for senior citizens and children; transfers are free.

Free **Downtown Area Shuttle** (DASH) buses loop downtown and around the warehouse area weekdays 11–3: Look for DASH bus stops along Broadway, Main Street, Graham Avenue, King Street, and elsewhere.

By Taxi Taxis—relatively expensive by U.S. standards—can be found outside downtown hotels or summoned by phone. Car services are **Unicity** (tel. 204/947–6611) and **Duffy's Taxi** (tel. 204/775–0101).

Guided Tours

Boat Tours Several lines ply the Red and Assiniboine rivers between May and mid-October. The **MS *Lady Winnipeg*** and **MS *River Rouge*** (tel. 204/669–2824) offer a variety of cruises (dining, dinner-dance, evening) from a dock at 312 Nairn Avenue, beside the Louise Bridge. The 179-foot **MS *Lord Selkirk*** (tel. 204/582–2331) has daily dinner and dance cruises, as well as Sunday-afternoon excursions from Redwood Bridge, Redwood Avenue, and Main Street. The **MS *Paddlewheel Queen*** and **MS *Paddlewheel Princess*** (tel. 204/942–4500) combine cruises with double-decker bus tours from docks at 2285 Main Street.

Train Tours The **Prairie Dog Central Steam Train** (tel. 204/832–5259) plies a 58-kilometer (36-mile) route from the CNR St. James Station (1661 Portage Ave.) to Gross Isle on Sunday, June–September.

Walking Tours Walking tours of the turn-of-the-century **Exchange District** begin at the Manitoba Museum of Man & Nature (190 Rupert Ave., tel. 204/774–3514) during July and August.

Exploring Downtown Winnipeg

Numbers in the margin correspond to points of interest on the Downtown Winnipeg map.

It's somewhat difficult to get one's bearings in Winnipeg. The downtown area is located just north of the junction of the Red and Assiniboine rivers, and its streets interconnect at skewed angles with the curving rivers, creating diagonal streets in all directions. Much of downtown Winnipeg is linked by a network of enclosed overhead pedestrian overpasses and underground concourses. The intersection of Portage Avenue and Main Street is the focal point of the city, with Portage Avenue (Hwy. 1) the principal artery heading west and Main Street (Hwy. 52) heading north. South of Winnipeg, the main drag is Pembina Highway (Hwy. 42). Streets in St. Boniface, east of the Red River, are labeled in French—evidence of the community's ethnic heritage.

Begin at the southeast corner of downtown Winnipeg at the tourist information center (*see* Important Addresses and Numbers, above), housed in the **Legislative Building.** The classic Greek–style structure made of local Tyndall stone contains the offices of Manitoba's premier and members of the cabinet, as well as the chamber where the legislature meets. The 240-foot dome supports Manitoba's symbol, Golden Boy—a gold-sheathed statue with a sheaf of wheat under his left arm and the torch of progress in his right hand. Along the grounds and gardens surrounding the riverside stand statues that celebrate Manitoba's ethnic diversity, including Scotland's Robert Burns, Iceland's Jon Sigurdson, Ukrainian poet Taras Ahevchenko, and Métis leader and "Father of Manitoba" Louis Riel.

❷ Walk east on Broadway and south on Carlton Street to **Dalnavert,** a Victorian gingerbread-style house built in 1895 for Hugh John MacDonald, the son of Canada's first prime minister. Costumed guides escort visitors around the premises. *61 Carlton St., tel. 204/943–2835. Admission: $3 adults, $2 senior citizens, $1.50 students, $1 children 5–12. Open June–Aug., Tues.–Thurs. and weekends 10–6; Sept.–May, Tues.–Thurs. and weekends noon–5; Jan.–Feb., weekends noon–5.*

Back at the Legislature, head north on Osborne Street past the stately The Bay store (the legacy of the Hudson's Bay Company) to the **Winnipeg Art Gallery.** The gallery, which owns the world's largest collection of Inuit sculpture and art, also houses contemporary Canadian art and sculpture. *300 Memorial Blvd., tel. 204/786–6641. Admission free. Open Tues., Fri., and weekends 11–5; Wed., Thurs. 11–9; closed Mon.*

Turn east at the north end of the Winnipeg Art Gallery to Portage Avenue. The north side of Portage between Balmoral and Carlton streets is occupied by sprawling **Portage Place,** an indoor mall encompassing 150 stores (*see* Shopping, below).

Time Out Winnipeg's oldest restaurant, the 1918 **Chocolate Shop** (268 Portage Ave., tel. 204/942–4855), serves generous sandwiches

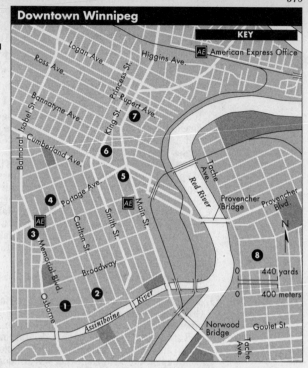

Downtown Winnipeg

for lunch and more ambitious entrées at dinnertime. Teacups and tarot cards are read from 1 to 9.

Continue east on Portage Avenue to Main Street and what's reputed to be the windiest intersection in the world. Five floors above the breeze, visit the **Winnipeg Commodity Exchange** and observe the controlled chaos of wild men (and a few women) involved in the buying and selling of grains, cooking oils, gold, and silver. *360 Main St., tel. 204/949–0495. Open weekdays 9:30–1:15.*

Below-ground is **Winnipeg Square,** an underground concourse with shops and fast-food stores. Emerge to street level on the north side of Portage Avenue and into the **Exchange District**—a concentration of renovated warehouses, banks, and insurance companies that were built during Winnipeg's turn-of-the-century boom period but now stand as a thriving nightlife spot. On Sunday, May–October, attention focuses on **Old Market Square Park** (King St. and Bannatyne Ave.), a new marketplace bursting with fresh produce, fish, crafts, and street performers.

Continue north on Main Street to Rupert Avenue and **Centennial Centre,** site of a concert hall, the **Manitoba Museum of Man and Nature,** and the dazzling **Manitoba Planetarium.** Exhibits at the museum focus on prehistoric Manitoba, local wildlife, the native peoples of the region, and the exploration of Hudson Bay. Downstairs, the planetarium presents a variety of cosmic adventures in the multimedia **Star Theater;** 60 interactive multisensory exhibits in Touch the Universe explain laws of nature. *190 Rupert Ave., tel. 204/943–3139 (museum), tel. 204/943–3142 (planetarium). Admission: museum $3.50, planetarium $4, Touch the Universe $2.50, all three $7.50 adults; $2.50, $2.50, $2, $5.50 students; $2.50, $2.50, $2.75, $4.50 senior citizens and children 4–12. Open mid-June–Sept. 2, daily 10–8; Sept. 3–mid-June, Tues.–Thurs. 10–5, weekends noon–6, closed Mon.*

St. Boniface, about 2.5 kilometers (1½ miles) away, can be reached by crossing the Provencher Bridge and turning right onto Avenue Tache. The largest French community in western Canada was founded as Fort Rouge in 1783 and became an important fur-trading outpost for the North West Company. Upon the arrival of Roman Catholic priests, the settlement was renamed St. Boniface. Remnants of a 1908 basilica that survived a 1968 fire can be seen outside the perimeter of the present **St. Boniface Cathedral** (av. de la Cathedral and av. Tache, tel. 204/233–7304), built in 1972. The grave of Louis Riel, the St. Boniface native son who led the Métis rebellion, is in the churchyard.

Housed in the oldest (1846) structure in Winnipeg and the largest oak log building in North America, the **St. Boniface Museum** tells the French and Métis side of Manitoba history. Artifacts include an altar crafted from papier-mâché, the first church bell in western Canada, and a host of innovative household gadgets. *494 av. Tache, tel. 204/237–4500. Admission free. Open mid-May–Sept., daily 9–9; Sept.–mid-May, weekdays 9–5, weekends and holidays 10–5.*

You can see Canadian and foreign coins rolling off the presses at the **Royal Canadian Mint,** 6.4 kilometers (4 miles) southeast of downtown off Highway 1 or by bus No. 50, available on the east side of Fort Street between Portage and Graham avenues on weekdays. Tours are available, 9–3:30. *520 Lagimodière Blvd. (at the Trans-Canada Hwy.), Winnipeg, R2J 3E7, tel. 204/257–3359. Admission: $2.*

Other Points of Interest

About 48 kilometers (30 miles) southeast of Winnipeg is the town of **Steinbach,** populated with nearly 10,000 pious and austere descendants of Mennonites who fled religious persecution in the Ukraine in 1874. Note the large number of automobile dealerships: Manitoban car buyers flock here because of the Mennonite reputation for making square deals.

In the **Mennonite Heritage Village,** a 20-building complex, museum guides demonstrate blacksmithing, wheat grinding, and old-time housekeeping chores while conversing in the Mennonite Low German dialect. During the Pioneer Days festival in early August, everyone wears costumes and demonstrates homespun crafts. An authentic and extremely low-priced restaurant serves Mennonite specialties, such as borscht, pirogies, and *ukrenky* (cheese or potato torte). *Hwy. 12, 2 km (1¼ mi) north of Steinbach, tel. 204/326–9661. Admission: $2 adults, $1 students and senior citizens, 75¢ children grades 1–6. Open May and Sept., Mon.–Sat. 10–5, Sun. noon–5; June–Aug., Mon.–Sat. 9–7, Sun. noon–7.*

Lower Fort Garry, built in 1830, is the oldest stone fort remaining from the Hudson's Bay Company fur-trading days. Nowadays, costumed employees describe daily tasks and recount thrilling journeys by York boat, the "boat that won the west." Beaver, raccoon, fox, and wolf pelts hang in the fur loft as a reminder of the bygone days. *Hwy. 9, 32 km (20 mi) north of Winnipeg, tel. in Winnipeg, 204/983–6341; in Selkirk, 204/482–6483. Admission: $3.25 adults, $1.50 children 5–16. Grounds open year-round in daylight hours. Buildings open mid-May–Sept. 2, daily 10–6; Sept., weekends 10–6.*

Gimli, the largest Icelandic community outside the homeland, was once the center of the independent state of New Iceland. A giant Viking statue proclaims allegiance to the far-off island; the **Gimli Historical Museum,** on the Gimli harbor waterfront, preserves the ethnic heritage of early Ukrainian and Icelandic settlers and records the history of the Lake Winnipeg commercial fishing industry. *Hwy. 9, Gimli harbor area, tel. 204/642–5317. Admission: $1.25 adults, 75¢ children, $3 families, senior citizens free.*

National and Provincial Parks

Opening and closing times vary from park to park, although admission fees are generally uniform within the province. Unless otherwise noted, the daily rate is $3 per vehicle per day, $12 per vehicle per year.

Assiniboine Park, situated in Winnipeg along the river of the same name, encompasses 376 acres of cycling paths, picnic areas, playgrounds, a miniature railway, formal English and French gardens, a conservatory, and a cricket pitch. **Assiniboine Zoo,** also on the grounds, houses more than 1,200 species in reasonably natural settings. *Assiniboine Park and Zoo, tel. 204/889–0007. Admission free. Open year-round daily 10 AM–dusk.*

The Forks National Historic Site, at the junction of the Red and Assiniboine rivers, is where Winnipeg began 6,000 years ago. Today, the 56 acres host a playground, riverside promenade, small boat dock, amphitheater, and archaeological excavations. The promenade has recently been extended, and interpretive programs are available. *At the confluence of the Red and Assiniboine rivers, tel. 204/983–2007.*

Grand Beach Provincial Park is on the eastern shore of Lake Winnipeg, the seventh-largest lake in North America. On summer weekends, crowds flock here from Winnipeg for the white powder sand, the grass-crowned 30-foot dunes, and a lagoon that makes bird-watchers' dreams come true. **Grand Marais** is the service area at the southern portal to the park. *Hwy. 12, 87 km (54 mi) northwest of Winnipeg, tel. 204/754–2212. Open May–Sept.*

Hecla Provincial Park, about a 2½-hour drive from Winnipeg, is a densely wooded archipelago named for the Icelandic volcano that drove the area's original settlers to Canada. The park is located on the central North American flyway, and 50,000 waterfowl summer here. **Moose Tower** is a good spot in the early morning and evening to view moose and other wildlife. The original 1880s Hecla Icelandic Fishing Village is restored near **Gull Harbour,** the tourist center of the park and site of the luxurious **Gull Harbour Resort** (tel. 204/475–2354), complete with a marina, hiking trails, and a devilishly difficult golf course.

Helca Provincial Park, Hwy. 8, 175 km (109 mi) north of Winnipeg, tel. 204/378–2945. Open May–Sept.

Spruce Woods Provincial Heritage Park encompasses, among rolling hills of spruce and basswood, the desertlike Spirit Sands, a 16-square-kilometer (10-square-mile) tract of cactus-filled sand dunes. Walk the self-guided trail through the dunes, but keep your eyes peeled for lizards and snakes! Your final destination will be **Devil's Punch Bowl,** a dramatic pit dug out by an underground stream. You can also tour the park in a horse-drawn covered wagon. *Hwy. 5, 180 km (114 mi) west of Winnipeg, tel. 204/827–2543. Open May–Sept.*

Whiteshell Provincial Park, a 2,590-square-kilometer (1,550-square-mile) tract on the edge of the Canadian Shield, encompasses 200 lakes that offer some of the best northern pike, perch, walleye, and lake trout fishing in western Canada. The **Falcon Lake** area has a shopping center, a golf course, tennis courts, a very good beach, a sailing club, and top-grade accommodations in the 35-room **Falcon Lake Resort & Club** (tel. 204/349–8400). **Beaver Creek** trail is a short walk to wilderness denizens like beaver and deer. Farther on, **West Hawk Lake** (or Crater Lake)—formed a few thousand years ago by a falling meteor—is 111 meters (365 feet) deep and full of feisty small-mouth bass. Scuba divers love it. *Whiteshell Provincial Park, Hwy. 1E, 143 km (89 mi) from Winnipeg. Open daily 8 AM–11 PM.*

What to See and Do with Children

Assiniboine Park and Zoo (*see* National and Provincial Parks, above).

Fort Whyte Center for Environmental Education (1961 McCreary Rd., Winnipeg, tel. 204/895–7001) makes use of several cement quarries and the 200 acres of land around them to re-create the natural habitats of Manitoba's lakes and rivers. Self-guided nature trails and an interpretive center explain all.

Fun Mountain Water Slide Park (Rte. 1, east at Murdock Rd., Winnipeg, tel. 204/255–3910), located about 13 kilometers (8 miles) east of downtown, includes bumper boats, a mammoth hot tub, rides, and a playground.

Manitoba Children's Museum (109 Pacific Ave., Winnipeg, tel. 204/957–0005) is western Canada's first hands-on museum for children, and it shows them how to operate a grain elevator, put on a circus, understand their senses, and much more.

Manitoba Museum of Man and Nature/Planetarium (*see* Exploring Downtown Winnipeg, above).

Skinner's Wet n' Wild Waterslide Park (Hwy. 44, Lockport, tel. in Winnipeg, 204/477–0676; in Lockport, 204/757–2623) has four big slides, two kiddie slides, and many other damp attractions.

Shopping

Malls and Shopping Districts Downtown shopping is dominated by **Portage Place** (Portage Ave. between Balmoral and Carlton Sts.) and **Eaton Place** (bounded by Graham Ave., Hargrave St., St. Mary Ave., and

Donald St.), two malls with numerous stores, fast-food joints, and movie theaters.

Across the Assiniboine River, the **Osborne Village** area (Osborne St. between River and Corydon Aves.) has 150 trendy boutiques and specialty shops, cafés, restaurants, and crafts shops.

Art and Crafts The **Crafts Guild of Manitoba** (183 Kennedy St., tel. 204/943–1190) features works by Manitoba carvers, weavers, and jewelers. **Northern Images** (Portage Pl., tel. 204/942–5501; Airport Executive Centre, 1780 Wellington Ave., tel. 204/788–4806) markets the work of the Inuit and Dene members of the NWT Co-operative, which owns the stores. For more Indian art, check out the **Great Canadian Indian Gallery** (75 Albert St., tel. 204/942–1002) or **The Upstairs Gallery** (266 Edmonton St., tel. 204/943–2734) for prints, drawings, wall hangings, and sculpture.

Sports

Participant Sports
Bicycling and Jogging Most public parks in Manitoba have marked biking and jogging paths. For routes, pick up maps from **Travel Manitoba** (*see* Important Addresses and Numbers in Essential Information, above).

Health and Fitness Clubs Drop-in rates and a full slate of classes and equipment are available at **Body Options** (1604 St. Mary's Rd., Winnipeg, tel. 204/255–6600) and **Bodyworks** (2 Donald St., Winnipeg, tel. 204/477–1691).

Spectator Sports
Hockey The **Winnipeg Jets** confront National Hockey League opposition between October and April at the **Winnipeg Arena** (1430 Maroons Rd., Winnipeg, tel. 204/773–5387).

Horse Racing **Assiniboia Downs** (3975 Portage Ave. at Perimeter Hwy. W, Winnipeg, tel. 204/885–3330) hosts Thoroughbred racing May–October; trotters November–April.

Soccer The **Winnipeg Fury** of the Canadian Soccer League play a May–September schedule at **Winnipeg Stadium** (1465 Maroons Rd., Winnipeg, tel. 204/786–3879).

Dining and Lodging

Dining Although places specializing in generous helpings of Canadian beef still dominate the scene, restaurants throughout the prairie provinces now tastily reflect the region's ethnic make-up and offer a wide variety of cuisine to fit every price range.

Highly recommended restaurants in each price category are indicated by a star ★.

Category	Cost*
Very Expensive	over $25
Expensive	$20–$25
Moderate	$15–$19
Inexpensive	under $15

*three-course dinner, per person, excluding drinks, service, and 7% sales tax

Lodging Highly recommended lodgings in each price category are indicated by a star ★.

Category	Cost*
Very Expensive	over $150
Expensive	$75–$150
Moderate	$50–$74
Inexpensive	under $50

All prices are for a standard double room, excluding 5%–7% service charge.

Dining **Restaurant Dubrovnik.** The setting is a romantic Victorian town house, with seating on an enclosed veranda overlooking the Assiniboine River. An extensive menu blends Continental specialties, such as rack of lamb, breast of duck, and pheasant, with southern Yugoslavian dishes. Two good dishes to try are the *gibanica* (feta cheese in phyllo pastry) and the *muckalica* (pork, lamb, chicken, and sausage casserole). A lengthy wine list is available. *390 Assiniboine Ave., tel. 204/944–0594. Reservations advised. Jacket required. AE, DC, MC, V. Closed Sun. Very Expensive.*

★ **Victor's.** Before Osborne Village was a fashionable locale, Winnipeg's power restaurant had already taken over the ground floors of a renovated apartment house. Downstairs, the natural brick walls and bentwood chairs offer an understated setting for such Continental specialties as breast of pheasant, bouillabaisse, and pepper steak. Upstairs, Joanna's is a more casual spot for drinks and some of Victor's dishes at greatly reduced prices. On either level, Joanna's poppyseed cake is a must for dessert. *100 Osborne St., tel. 204/284–2339. Reservations advised. Jacket advised. AE, DC, MC, V. Closed Sun. Very Expensive.*

Amici. The sophisticated and posh downtown *ristorante* is the local avatar of *cucina nuova*, the Italian version of nouvelle cuisine. Clever pastas and such dishes as roast quail on radicchio and chicken stuffed with goat cheese are served in a second-floor dining room that's divided by partitions of frosted glass. Downstairs, the Bombolini Wine Bar serves many of the simpler dishes at lower prices. *326 Broadway, tel. 204/943–4997. Reservations advised. Jacket advised for Amici; casual for Bombolini. AE, DC, MC, V. Closed Sun. Expensive.*

★ **Le Beaujolais.** This sophisticated, bright spot in the French St. Boniface district presents waiters in black tie; a softly lit ambience with French blue, coral, and burgundy decor; fresh-cut flowers; and a menu that combines classic French with lighter nouvelle cuisine. Salmon with basil or monkfish in red wine is the recommended seafood; tournedos with five peppers and rack of lamb are other entrée suggestions. Save room for dessert; after-theater menu served from 10 PM. *131 Provencher Blvd., tel. 204/237–6306. Reservations advised. Jacket advised. AE, DC, MC, V. Expensive.*

★ **Bistro Dansk.** Wood tables, bright red chairs, and strains of classical music convey a cozy European air. Dinner entrée selections mingle Danish specialties like *frikadeller* (meat patties) and more-expected Continental dishes like roast chicken. A less expensive lunch menu features a vast variety of open-face sandwiches. *63 Sherbrook St., tel. 204/775–5662. Reservations advised. Dress: casual. DC, V. Closed Sun. Moderate.*

Homer's. This unpretentious, good-time downtown place has been one of the city's favorite Greek restaurants for more than 20 years, with Ionic columns and hanging grapevines setting the mood. Stick to modern Greek standards: souvlaki, moussaka, and excellent Greek desserts. Non-Greek dishes, served with french fries, are also available. *520 Ellice Ave., tel. 204/788–4858. Reservations advised. Dress: casual. AE, DC, MC, V. Moderate.*

Mandarin. The Sargent Avenue Mandarin is a crowded, 12-table west-side place with unique and reasonably exotic northern Chinese dishes. Complete "Gourmet Delight Dinners" include soup, dumplings, entrées, and dessert. Wine is the only alcohol served. The River Mandarin, a spin-off, has a slightly different menu, a calmer pace, and a full liquor license. *Mandarin, 613 Sargent Ave., tel. 204/775–7819; River Mandarin, 252 River Ave., tel. 204/284–8963. Reservations advised. Dress: casual. V. Moderate.*

Picasso's. It may be named after a Spanish painter, but this is a Portuguese restaurant, featuring outstanding seafood. On the street level it's a bustling neighborhood café; upstairs there's a subdued atmosphere where white tablecloths, candlelight, and soft music prevail. Try the salmon or Arctic char; Portuguese favorites are paella, octopus stew, and steak Picasso. *615 Sargent Ave., tel. 204/775–2469. Reservations advised. Dress: casual. AE, DC, MC, V. Moderate.*

★ **d'8 Schtove.** The name is Mennonite for "the eating room," and, true to its name, the menu features heavyweight servings of soup, salads, and Mennonite concoctions, usually involving meat, potatoes, onions, and vegetables. Try the *klopz* (ground-beef-and-pork meatballs) or *wrenikje* (cottage-cheese pierogies). The new south-side location is bright and immaculately clean, and it looks spacious, although you may still have to wait for a table. Service is quick and friendly. *1842 Pembina Hwy., tel. 204/275–2294. No reservations. Dress: casual. AE, MC, V. Inexpensive.*

Kelekis. This north-end shrine has purveyed legendary burgers, hot dogs, fries, and onion rings for more than 60 years. Decor includes a photo montage of family history and autographed celebrities' photos. Breakfast is served daily. *1100 Main St., tel. 204/582–1786. No reservations. Dress: casual. No credit cards. Inexpensive.*

Osborne's Cafe. This crowded little basement spot in swinging Osborne Village features borscht and other hearty soups, an array of salads, and diverse dishes from around the globe, including Siberian *pelmeni* (dumplings), Danish quiche, and Greek moussaka. Beer and a brief list of wines from France, Hungary, and Canada are available. *106 Osborne St., tel. 204/475–9599. No reservations. Dress: casual. MC, V. Inexpensive.*

Lodging **Holiday Inn.** Winnipeg's largest hotel, this Holiday Inn is 17 stories high and connects to the Convention Centre. Rooms, having recently undergone a major renovation, are decorated in pastels and have pleasant modern furnishings; some rooms overlook the skylighted pool. Ticker's lobby bar is a lively spot for a rendezvous. *350 St. Mary Ave., R3C 3J2, tel. 204/942–0551 or 800/465–4329. 409 rooms, including nonsmoking rooms. Facilities: 3 restaurants, lounge, cabaret, indoor and* *outdoor pools, sauna, whirlpool, exercise room. AE, DC, MC, V. Very Expensive.*

★ **Westin Hotel.** The top luxury hotel is located near Winnipeg's hub—Portage and Main streets—and is connected by the skywalk to office buildings and North Portage Mall. Large, newly restored rooms feature striking colonial-style furniture. The 21st-floor rooftop indoor pool makes a dramatic setting for a swim. Chimes offers a contemporary setting for light meals and dinner theater. *2 Lombard Pl., R3B 0Y3, tel. 204/957–1350 or 800/228–3000. 350 rooms; nonsmoking rooms available. Facilities: 3 restaurants, 2 lounges, dinner theater, indoor pool, sauna, whirlpool, fitness center. AE, DC, MC, V. Very Expensive.*

Birchwood Inn. This bright and sumptuous modern property is located on the Trans-Canada Highway's western approach to Winnipeg, near the airport, race track, and shopping areas. Rooms are large, with modern earthtone furnishings. Executive suites, decorated in blue and green, are a bit fancier than standard units. The atrium is a lush setting for a pool and poolside lounge. *2520 Portage Ave., R3J 3T6, tel. 204/885–4478 or 800/665–0352. 230 rooms. Facilities: 2 restaurants, lounge, indoor pool, sauna, exercise room. AE, DC, MC, V. Expensive.*

Hotel Fort Garry. Built in 1913 and known far and wide as the Grand Castle, the old railroad hotel has been resuscitated from near bankruptcy and has resumed its role as one of Winnipeg's gathering places. Located on the south edge of downtown, near Union Station, the hotel and its hushed spacious lobby are furnished with inviting armchairs and original marble, brass, and crystal finishes. Large guest rooms still have classic dark-wood furnishings and floral wallpapers. *222 Broadway, R3C 0R3, tel. 204/942–8251 or 800/665–8088. 270 rooms. Facilities: 2 restaurants, lounge, cabaret. AE, DC, MC, V. Expensive.*

★ **Place Louis Riel.** This luxury-class bargain is a converted apartment building that has 250 contemporary suites with living rooms, dining areas, and fully equipped kitchens. Though all rooms are up-to-date, the suites on the upper floors facing west are preferred because of their view of the Parliament Building. The supreme downtown location—adjacent to Eaton Place mall—is only one of the hotel's highlights. *190 Smith St., R3C 1J8, tel. 204/947–6961; in Canada, 800/665–0569. 250 suites. Facilities: restaurant/lounge, free parking. AE, DC, MC, V. Expensive.*

Relax Plaza. Positioned at the low end of the expensive range, this high-rise venture of Canada's oldest budget chain is in a strategically desirable location, next to the bus depot and adjacent to The Bay and Winnipeg Art Gallery. Rooms on the south side look out on the Legislative Building, and north-side rooms overlook the city. Guest rooms have subdued modern furnishings in either neutral or pastel colors. *360 Colony St., R3B 2P3, tel. 204/786–7011 or 800/661–9563. 157 rooms, including nonsmoking rooms. Facilities: restaurant, indoor pool, whirlpool. AE, DC, MC, V. Expensive.*

★ **Charter House.** Half the refurbished rooms in this five-story low-rise on the south side of downtown have balconies. Furnishings are contemporary motel style, and the atmosphere is quite friendly. The Rib Room is a popular; moderately priced place for dinner. *330 York Ave., R3C 0N9, tel. 204/942–0101, in Manitoba, 204/942–0101 or 800/782–0175. 90 rooms. Facilities: 2 restaurants, lounge, outdoor pool. AE, MC, V. Moderate.*

Gordon Downtowner. There's nothing fancy here, but it's a good deal on the edge of downtown a block from the Portage Place mall. Most rooms are decorated in dusty rose with gray carpeting. Two-room suites, modernly furnished, are the best bargains. *330 Kennedy St., R3B 2M6, tel. 204/943–5581. 40 rooms. Facilities: restaurant, pub, free parking. AE, DC, MC, V. Moderate.*

Marlborough Inn. The rooms of this ornate old (1914) Gothic structure in the Financial District are large, but furnishings could use refreshing. Try to avoid rooms facing the unsightly inner core. Flander's Cafe has vaulted ceilings, a stained-glass window, and acceptable breakfasts and lunches. *331 Smith St., R3B 2G9, tel. 204/942–6411 or 800/667–7666. 147 rooms. Facilities: 2 restaurants, lounge. AE, DC, MC, V. Moderate.*

Assiniboine Gordon Inn on the Park. This two-story hotel and motor inn is adjacent to a park on the west side, not far from the airport. Rooms are modern and large, albeit somewhat over-wrought with masculine dark wood and bold designs. *1975 Portage Ave., R3J 0J9, tel. 204/888–4806. 48 rooms. Facilities: restaurant, lounge, disco. AE, DC, MC, V. Inexpensive.*

Journey's End. This is a reliable choice for an inexpensive, south-side lodging. The rooms are an adequate size and are furnished in contemporary style, with rose or beige carpets and either dusty-rose or earthtone accessories. There's no charge for local phone calls, and morning coffee is free. *3109 Pembina Hwy., R3T 4R6, tel. 204/269–7390 or 800/268–0405. 80 rooms. AE, MC, V. Inexpensive.*

Arts and Nightlife

The Arts Theater One of Canada's most acclaimed regional theaters, the **Manitoba Theatre Centre,** produces serious plays from many sources on the 785-seat **Mainstage** (164 Market Ave., Winnipeg, tel. 204/942–6537) and more experimental work in the **MTC Warehouse Theatre** (140 Rupert Ave., Winnipeg, tel. 204/942–6537). The **Prairie Theatre Exchange** focuses on local playwrights in an attractive facility in the Portage Place mall (Portage Ave. and Carlton St., Winnipeg, tel. 204/942–5483).

Music and Dance Winnipeg's principal venue for serious music, dance, and pop concerts is the magnificent 2,263-seat Centennial Concert Hall in the **Manitoba Centennial Centre** (555 Main St., Winnipeg, tel. 204/956–1360). From September to mid-May it is the home of the **Winnipeg Symphony Orchestra** (tel. 204/947–1148); the **Royal Winnipeg Ballet** (tel. 204/956–0183) performs there in October, December, March, and May; and the **Manitoba Opera Association** (tel. 204/942–7479) presents three operas a year—in November, February, and May. Throughout the year, pop concerts use the center.

The **Winnipeg Art Gallery** (300 Memorial Blvd., tel. 204/786–6641) features jazz, blues, chamber music, and contemporary groups. The **Westend Cultural Centre** (586 Ellice Ave., tel. 204/775–1055) is a downtown venue for blues, folk music, and dance. For contemporary dance and new music, check out **Le Rendez-Vous** (768 av. Tache, tel. 204/452–0229) in St. Boniface. Other performance spaces include **Pantages Playhouse Theatre** (180 Market Ave. E, tel. 204/986–3003) and the **Winnipeg Convention Centre** (375 York Ave., tel. 204/956–1720).

Film In Winnipeg, the best places to find imports, art films, oldies, and midnight cult classics are at **Cinémathèque** (100 Arthur

St., Winnipeg, tel. 204/942–6795) and **Cinema 3** (585 Ellice Ave., Winnipeg, tel. 204/783–1097). The **WAG** (Winnipeg Art Gallery, 300 Memorial Blvd., Winnipeg, tel. 204/786–6641) also has a cinema series.

Nightlife **Hy's Steak Loft** (216 Kennedy St., Winnipeg, tel. 204/942–
Bars and Clubs 1000) is convenient for cocktails and has a late-evening piano bar. The **Rorie Street Marble Club** (65 Rorie St., Winnipeg, tel. 204/943–4222) is the contemporary hot spot of the young crowd. A most convincingly British pub in the Exchange District is **The King's Head** (120 King St., Winnipeg, tel. 204/957–1479).

Casinos Play blackjack, baccarat, la boule, and roulette at the **Crystal Casino** (7th floor, Hotel Fort Garry, 222 Broadway Ave., Winnipeg, tel. 204/957–2600) daily except Sunday.

Comedy **Yuk Yuk's** (108 Osborne St., tel. 204/475–YUKS), in a large Osborne Village basement, in Winnipeg, presents raunchy comedy, certain to offend everyone. Try also **Rumors Comedy Club** (2025 Croydon Ave., Winnipeg, tel. 204/488–4520) or the **Comedy Oasis** (531 St. Mary's Rd., Winnipeg, tel. 204/231–1463), just for laughs.

Music Country-and-western music fans flock to Winnipeg's **Golden Nugget** (1155 Main St., Winnipeg, tel. 204/589–6308) and the **Palomino Club** (1133 Portage Ave., Winnipeg, tel. 204/772–0454). The hardest-rocking places in town are the **Circuit** (611 rue Archibald, Winnipeg, tel. 204/231–2111), the **Spectrum** (176 Fort St., Winnipeg, tel. 204/943–6487), and the **Albert** (48 Albert St., Winnipeg, tel. 204/943–8750). Good rock-and-roll dancing can be found at **DeSoto's** (171 McDermott Ave., Winnipeg, tel. 204/943–4444). A more sedate dance floor comes alive after 9 PM in **Windows Lounge** in the Sheraton Winnipeg (161 Donald St., Winnipeg, tel. 204/942–5300).

Regina

Originally named Pile O'Bones, in reference to the remnants left by buffalo-hunting native tribes centuries ago, Regina was named after the Latin title of former Queen Victoria, the reigning monarch in 1882. It was at this time, when the railroad arrived, that the city became the capital of the North West Territories, and the Mounties made it their headquarters. When the province of Saskatchewan was formed in 1905, Regina was chosen as its capital. At the beginning of the 20th century, immigrants from the British Isles, Eastern Europe, and the Far East rushed in to claim parcels of the river-fed prairie land for $1 per lot. Oil and potash were discovered in the 1950s and 1960s, and Regina became a major agricultural and industrial distribution center as well as the location of the world's largest grain-handling cooperative.

Although situated on 109 square kilometers (42 square miles) of undistinguished, dry flatlands, Regina has relieved the monotony with Wascana Centre. It was created by expanding meager Wascana Creek into the broad Wascana Lake and surrounding it with 2,300 acres of parkland. This unique multipurpose site contains the city's major museums, the Saskatchewan legislature, the University of Regina campus, and all the amenities of a big-city park and bucolic forest preserve.

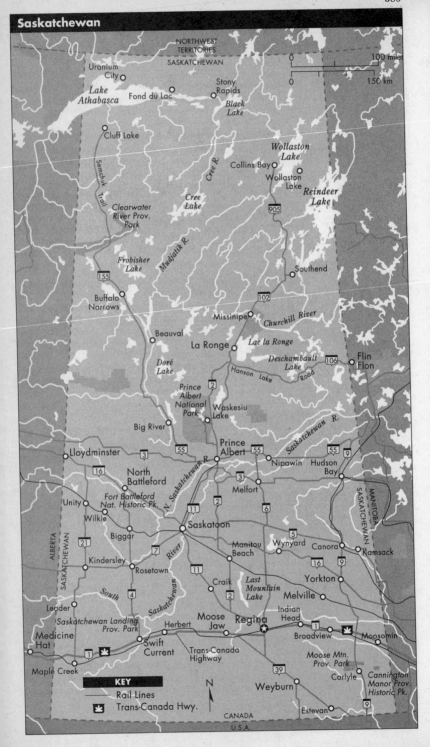

380

Saskatchewan

NORTHWEST
TERRITORIES
SASKATCHEWAN

0   100 miles
0   150 km

Uranium
City
*Lake
Athabasca*   Fond du Lac
Stony
Rapids
*Black
Lake*

Cluff Lake

*Wollaston
Lake*
Collins Bay
Wollaston
Lake
*Reindeer
Lake*

*Semchuk
Trail*

Cree R.

*Clearwater
River Prov.
Park*

*Cree
Lake*

905

*Frobisher
Lake*

Mudjatik R.

155

Southend

Buffalo
Narrows

102

Missinipe
Churchill River

Beauval

La Ronge   *Lac la Ronge*

*Doré
Lake*

*Deschambault
Lake*

106

Flin
Flon

Hanson Lake   Road

*Prince
Albert
National
Park*

2

Waskesiu
Lake

Big River

Prince
Albert

Saskatchewan R.

55

Lloydminster

3

55

55

9

16

N. Saskatchewan R.

Nipawin   Hudson
Bay

North
Battleford

3

*Fort Battleford
Nat. Historic Pk.*

Melfort

Unity

11

2

6

Wilkie

Biggar

Saskatoon

ALBERTA

21

River

7

Manitou
Beach

Wynyard

5

Canora

Kamsack

MANITOBA

SASKATCHEWAN

Kindersley

Rosetown

11

16

9

Yorkton

South

4

Craik

2

*Last
Mountain
Lake*

Melville

Leader

*Saskatchewan Landing
Prov. Park*

Saskatchewan

Moose
Jaw

Regina

Indian
Head

Medicine
Hat

Herbert

1

Broadview

Moosomin

1

Swift
Current

*Trans-Canada
Highway*

*Moose Mtn.
Prov. Park*

Maple Creek

39

Carlyle

*Cannington
Manor Prov.
Historic Pk.*

KEY

— Rail Lines

N

Weyburn

9

Trans-Canada Hwy.

CANADA

Estevan

U.S.A.

Important Addresses and Numbers

Tourist Information — **Tourism Regina** (Box 3355, Regina, Sask. S4P 3H1, tel. 306/789–5099) has an information center on the Trans-Canada Highway (Rte. 1) on the eastern approach to the city and is open weekdays 8–8; Saturday, Sunday, and holidays 10–6. The **Tourism Saskatchewan** information center (Saskatchewan Dr. and Rose St., tel. 306/787–2300) is open weekdays 8–7, Saturday 10–4.

Emergencies — Dial 911 for emergency **fire, police,** or **ambulance service.**

Hospitals — Emergency rooms are located at **Regina General Hospital** (1140 14th Ave., tel. 306/359–4444) and **Pasqua Hospital** (4101 Dewdney Ave., tel. 306/359–2222).

Late-night Pharmacy — **Pinders Drugs** (2160 Broad St., tel. 306/757–9665; 3992 Albert St. S, tel. 306/584–2284) is open until midnight.

Arriving and Departing by Plane

Regina Airport, located 8 kilometers (5 miles) southwest of downtown, is served by Air Canada, Canadian Airlines International, and several Canadian commuter airlines. Cabs charge about $7 for the 10- to 15-minute ride downtown.

Getting Around

By Bus — **Regina Transit's** (tel. 306/777–7433) 19 bus routes serve the metropolitan area daily except Sunday. The fare is $1.10 for adults, 65¢ for students, 55¢ for children 5–14.

By Taxi — Taxis are relatively expensive but easy to find outside major hotels or to summon by phone. Call **Regina Cabs** (tel. 306/543–3333) or **Capital Cab** (tel. 306/781–7777).

Guided Tours

Double Decker Bus Tours (tel. 306/522–3661) offers 45-minute tours of Wascana Centre that depart from Wascana Place (2900 Wascana Dr.) on the hour, between noon and 7 on weekends and holidays from May to September 2. **Ferry Boat Tours** (306/525–8494) from the Wascana Marina are also available.

Exploring Regina

Numbers in the margin correspond to points of interest on the Regina map.

Streets in Regina run north–south; avenues, east–west. The most important north–south artery is Albert Street (Rte. 6); Victoria Avenue is the main east–west thoroughfare. The Trans-Canada Highway (Route 1) bypasses the city to the south and east.

❶ Begin at the northwest corner of **Wascana Centre,** at the **Saskatchewan Museum of Natural History.** A time line traces local history from prehistory through the dinosaur era to today. Vivid dioramas depict the area's animal life in natural, sometimes violently realistic, settings. The **Native Peoples Gallery** highlights all aspects of native life with displays, tapes of Indian dances, holograms, and live performances. *College Ave. and*

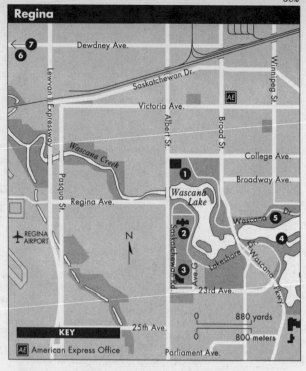

Albert St., tel. 306/787–2815. Admission free. Open May–Sept. 2, daily 9–8:30; Sept. 3–Apr., daily 9–4:30.

Continue south on Albert Street past **Speakers Corner,** where, as in London's Hyde Park, free speech is volubly expressed. Turn left on Legislative Drive, to the quasi-Versailles–style
② Legislative Building. "The Ledge" was built in 1908–12, with local Tyndall stone on the exterior and an interior composed of 34 types of marble from all over the world. As you tour the Legislative Assembly Chamber, note the huge picture of Queen Elizabeth—a reminder that Canada retains a technical allegiance to the British Crown. *Legislature Dr., tel. 306/787–5357. Admission free. Open May 20–Sept. 2, daily 8–9; winter, daily 8–5. Free tours leave on the half hour.*

Take Saskatchewan Road (west of the Legislature) south to the
③ new location of the **Mackenzie Art Gallery,** which displays American and European works from the mid-19th century to the present. The popular Prairie Artists Series allows emerging Saskatchewan artists to display recent work. On Thursday, Friday, and Saturday nights in August, a stage becomes the courtroom setting for "The Trial of Louis Riel." Riel led rebellions of the Métis against the new Canadian government in the 1870s and 1880s and was tried here (and ultimately hanged) for treason. *3475 Albert St., tel. 306/522–4242. Admission free. Open Mon., Tues., Fri., and weekends 11–6; Wed. and Thurs. 11–10.*

Continuing along Saskatchewan Road, turn north on Avenue G
④ and then east on Lakeshore Drive to the **Wascana Waterfowl**

Park Display Ponds, a boardwalk constructed over a marsh and accompanied by display panels that help identify the more than 60 breeds of migrating waterfowl found here. *Lakeshore Dr., tel. 306/522–3661. Admission free. Open year-round daily 9–9; guided tours available (if there is a group) June–Sept. at 3.*

Return to Broad Street (Wascana Parkway), cross the bridge to Wascana Drive, and head toward Winnipeg Street and the new

5 **Saskatchewan Science Centre,** now housed in the old SaskPower powerhouse. Hands-on exhibits encourage visitors to build bubbles, juggle hot-air balloons, make voice prints, and take apart human bodies; demonstrations of biological, geological, and astronomical phenomena take place on the hour. *Winnipeg St. and Wascana Dr., tel. 306/352–5811. Admission: $5.50 adults, $3.50 senior citizens, students, and children. Open Tues., Wed., Fri. 10–6 (in winter 10–5); Sat., Sun., holiday Mon. noon–6; Thurs. 10–8 (in winter 10–5); closed nonholiday Mon.*

Time Out   **In Vision** at the Science Centre comprises an appropriately high-tech setting for old-fashioned sandwiches, tasty salads, pastries, beer, and wine. Museum admission is not necessary for access.

A car or bike will be necessary to continue the tour. Return to Broad Street and take it north to Dewdney Avenue, then head

6 west to the **Government House.** Between 1891 and 1945 this was the lavish home of Saskatchewan's lieutenant governors. *4607 Dewdney Ave., tel. 306/787–5726. Admission free. Open Sept.–June, Tues.–Sat. 1–4, Sun. 1–5; July–Aug., Tues.–Sun. 1–5.*

7 Continue west on Dewdney Avenue to the **Royal Canadian Mounted Police Academy,** the Mounties' only training center. Visitors can tour the grounds and nondenominational RCMP Chapel, a converted cookhouse originally built in 1883 and considered Regina's oldest building. Try to arrive about 12:45 weekdays for the stirring Sergeant Major's parade on Parade Square (in Drill Hall during winter and inclement weather). On the grounds is the **Centennial Museum,** featuring exhibits and mementos of the Mounties (originally the North West Mounted Police). The order's proud history is revealed by weaponry, uniforms, photos, and oddities, such as Sitting Bull's rifle case and tobacco pouch. A minitheater screens *Rose-Marie, Saskatchewan,* and other Mountie-theme flicks. *Dewdney Ave. W, tel. 306/780–5358. Admission free. Open June–Sept. 15, daily 8 AM–8:45 PM; Sept. 16–May, daily 8–4:45.*

Other Points of Interest

Cannington Manor Historic Park, just south of Moose Mountain Provincial Park (*see* National and Provincial Parks, below), preserves the 1880s lifestyles of this experimental aristocratic Victorian settlement. Abandoned after 15 years, what remains to be seen are the original manor house, a church, shops, and a museum housed in the original schoolhouse. *Hwy. 603, 16 km (10 mi) northeast of Manor, tel. 306/787–9573. Donations requested. Open late-May–Sept. 2, daily 10–6.*

Moose Jaw, Saskatchewan's third-largest city (population 35,000), is a prosperous railroad and industrial center, renowned as a wide-open Roaring '20s haven for American gangsters. It is said that Al Capone visited here from Chicago, on the old Soo Line train. Today, Moose Jaw's most prominent citizen is Mac the Moose, an immense sculpture that greets travelers alongside the visitor information center (Rte. 1 east of Rte. 2, tel. 306/692–6414) on the Trans-Canada Highway.

A stop at the information center can direct you to other Moose Jaw attractions, including the **Moose Jaw Wild Animal Park** (7th Ave. SW, tel. 306/691–0111), a log fortress that combines a zoo with an amusement park; the **Western Development Museum** (50 Diefenbaker Dr., tel. 306/693–6556), focusing on air, land, water, and rail transportation; and **the Moose Jaw Art Museum** (Crescent Park, Athabasca St. and Langdon Crescent, tel. 306/692–3144), which features Indian art and small farm implements. While there, pick up *A Walking Tour of Downtown Moose Jaw* ($1.50), a guide to the city's notable and notorious landmarks.

National and Provincial Parks

Canada's newest national park, **Grasslands National Park,** is located between Val Marie and Killdeer in the southwest corner of Saskatchewan. Colonies of black-tailed prairie dogs still live in their natural habitat of mixed-grass prairie. Interpretive and visitor services are limited at this time. *Box 150, Val Marie, Sask. S0N 2T0, tel. 306/298–2257. Open (park office) June–Aug., daily; Sept.–May, weekdays 8–4:30.*

Moose Mountain Provincial Park is 401 square kilometers (155 square miles) of rolling poplar and birch forest that forms a natural refuge for moose and elk and a wide variety of birds. A 24-kilometer (15-mile) gravel road accesses moose and elk grazing areas (best times: early morning and early evening). The park supplements wildlife experiences with beaches, golf, tennis, and riding horses. The Kenosee Inn (Kenosee Village, S0C 2S0, tel. 306/577–2099) is a 30-room accommodation on the park grounds. *Hwys. 9 and 209, tel. 306/577–2131. Admission: $5/day per car, senior-citizen drivers free. Open year-round.*

A 50-kilometer (31-mile) drive north on Highway 4, from Swift Current, will bring you to **Saskatchewan Landing Provincial Park** (tel. 306/375–2434). The 54-square-kilometer (21-square-mile) natural preserve is situated at the point where Indians and pioneers forded the South Saskatchewan River en route to northern Saskatchewan. The hills are full of Indian grave sites and tepee rings. Campsites, picnic facilities, and an interpretive center are on hand. *Hwy. 4, tel. 306/375–2434. Admission: $5/day per car, senior-citizen drivers free. Open year-round.*

What to See and Do with Children

RCMP Academy & Centennial Museum (*see* Exploring Regina, above).

Saskatchewan Museum of Natural History (*see* Exploring Regina, above).

Saskatchewan Science Centre (*see* Exploring Regina, above).

Tee Off Park (3310 Pasqua St., Regina, tel. 306/586–4585). This is a family-fun complex with year-round indoor miniature golf and, between June and September, a walk-through maze and kiddieland rides.

Shopping

Malls **Cornwall Centre** (11th Ave. and Saskatchewan Dr.), located downtown, is an indoor mall with more than 100 shops, including Eaton's and Sears. Indoor passages connect to the **Galleria** (11th Ave. and Saskatchewan Dr.), an indoor mall with more than 50 stores. Other major malls include **Northgate Mall** (Albert St. N and 9th Ave. N), with more than 80 stores, and **Southland Mall** (Albert St. S and Gordon Rd.), which also has more than 80 stores.

Art and Antiques The **Strathdee Shoppes** (Dewdney Ave. and Cornwall St.) consist of arts, crafts, antiques, and specialty stores—plus a food court. The **Antique Mall** (1175 Rose St., tel. 306/525–9688) encompasses 28 antiques, art, and collectibles sellers. Also featuring arts and crafts are **Patchworks** (3026 13th Ave., tel. 306/522–0664), **Sarah's Corner** (1853 Hamilton St., tel. 306/565–2200), and **Saskatchewan Indian Arts & Crafts Corp.** (2431 8th Ave., tel. 306/522–5669).

Sports

Participant Sports Wascana Place (2900 Wascana Dr., Regina, tel. 306/522–3661) *Bicycling and* provides maps of the many jogging, biking, and hiking trails in *Jogging* **Wascana Centre.** Rent bikes within Wascana Centre at the **Wascana Pool** (2211 College Ave., Regina, tel. 306/777–7921).

Health and The **Regina Sportplex** (1717 Elphinstone St., Regina, tel. 306/ *Fitness Clubs* 777–7156 for fieldhouse; tel. 306/777–7323 for aquatic center) encompasses a pool and diving well, a 200-meter track, tennis and badminton courts, weight rooms, a sauna, a whirlpool, and drop-in aerobic and aquacize sessions.

Spectator Sports Check out this incredibly popular local sport at the **Curlodrome** *Curling* (Exhibition Park, Lewvan Expwy. and 11th Ave., Regina, tel. 306/352–9809).

Hockey The **Regina Pats** play other Canadian Hockey League (minor league) teams in the **Agridome** (Exhibition Park, Lewvan Expwy. and 11th Ave., Regina, tel. 306/522–5604).

Horse Racing **Queensbury Downs Raceway** (Exhibition Park, Lewvan Expwy. and 11th Ave., Regina, tel. 306/781–9310) hosts Thoroughbred or Standardbred racing year-round.

Dining and Lodging

For price categories, *see* Winnipeg Dining and Lodging, above.

Dining **Jules for Dining.** This bright, cheerful, and very sophisticated art deco spot in the Landmark Inn features European cuisine with a regional touch. Menu specialties include lobster; steak Diane; fillet de boeuf Madagascar; and a lamb dish, *carré d'agneau canadien.* The wine list is diverse and reasonably priced. *4150 Albert St., tel. 306/585–1880. Reservations advised. Jacket advised. AE, DC, MC, V. Closed lunch and Sun. Very Expensive.*

C.C. Lloyd's. Locals esteem the fine service and casual elegance of the dining room in the downtown Chelton Inn. The decor evokes the atmosphere of Manhattan circa 1930, and the menu features international classics like veal Oscar, fillet of beef Madeira, shrimp Provençal, and a variety of tasty steaks. *1907*

11th Ave., tel. 306/569–4650. Reservations advised. Jacket advised. AE, MC, V. Expensive.

★ **Mieka's.** Chef Mieka Wiens learned her craft at the Cordon Bleu; her art-filled walls and sleek contemporary furniture certainly reflect outside influence. The menus of this downtown café change with the season but always include imaginative combinations of fresh seafood and meat, local produce, spices, and liquors. There are also creative sandwiches, unusual salads, and a terrific cheesecake. A cookware shop is located on the premises. *1810 Smith St., tel. 306/522–6700. Reservations advised. Dress: casual. AE, MC, V. Closed Sun. Expensive.*

Bartleby's. This good-time downtown "dining emporium and gathering place" is a veritable museum of western memorabilia, musical instruments, and old-time carnival games. Victorian lampshades and heavy leather armchairs further convey the whimsical tone. The menu features big sandwiches, western beef, and a local specialty, Saskatchewan pickerel. *1920 Broad St., tel. 306/565–0040. Reservations suggested. Dress: casual. AE, MC, V. Closed Sun. dinner. Moderate.*

Bukovina. A nondescript space alongside the Trans-Canada Highway is the setting for hearty meals from Saskatchewan's significant Ukrainian community. Specialties include *koubisi* pork and perogies, but lunch and dinner buffets offer a sampling of everything. The wine list is small but modestly priced. *1840 Victoria Ave. E, tel. 306/789–1822. No reservations. Dress: casual. MC, V. Moderate.*

Brewsters. The copper kettle and shiny fermentation tanks are proudly prominent in Saskatchewan's first brew pub. Three home brews are always available, as is a large selection of imports and domestic beers. Menu consists of "pub grub" snacks, sandwiches, salads, and fish-and-chips. *Victoria East Plaza, 1832 Victoria Ave. E, tel. 306/761–1500. No reservations. Dress: casual. AE, MC, V. Inexpensive.*

Lodging **Ramada Renaissance.** The tallest building in Saskatchewan, Regina's newest and most luxurious hotel rises 25 stories over the city and is attached to the Saskatchewan Trade & Convention Centre. Rooms are furnished in subtle pastels and have modern amenities. The pool has a three-story waterslide, and there's a Tourism Saskatchewan information center in the lobby. *1919 Saskatchewan Dr., S4P 4H2, tel. 306/525–5255 or 800/268–8998. 256 rooms, including nonsmoking rooms. Facilities: 2 restaurants, 2 lounges, indoor pool, waterslide, whirlpool. AE, DC, MC, V. Very Expensive.*

Regina Inn. A plant-filled lobby with a soothing fountain welcomes you into this modern downtown hotel. Most rooms, decorated with blues, grays, and browns, have balconies, and the local hot spot, the Original California Club discotheque, is on the ground floor. *1975 Broad St. at Victoria Ave., S4P 1Y2, tel. 306/525–6767 or 800/667–8162. 237 rooms. Facilities: 2 restaurants, 2 lounges, indoor parking, indoor pool, sauna, whirlpool. AE, MC, V. Expensive.*

★ **Sheraton Centre.** This modern downtown property has a dramatic multilevel, sun-filled lobby that's graced by abundant foliage and a charming waterfall. A second-floor Oasis is the perfect setting for water-theme pastimes, such as a soothing soak in the whirlpool or, for the children, a dip in either the kiddie or standard pool. Rooms are airy and modernly furnished in light colors and dusty rose. *1818 Victoria Ave., S4P 0R1, tel. 306/569–1666 or 800/325–3535. 251 rooms. Facilities: 2 restau-*

rants, *lounge, pub, underground heated parking, indoor pool, sauna, whirlpool, games room. AE, DC, MC, V. Expensive.*

Chelton Inn. A bargain situated in the heart of downtown, Chelton Inn is an older property where rooms are modernized and downright huge, with contemporary, light-wood furnishings to match earthtones. Service is particularly friendly, and the cuisine in C.C. Lloyd's (*see* Dining, above) is among the best in town. *1907 11th Ave., S4P 0J2, tel. 306/569–4600; in Saskatchewan, 800/667–9922. 56 rooms. Facilities: restaurant, coffee shop, lounge. AE, MC, V. Moderate.*

★ **Landmark Inn.** This locally owned three-story property, on the south side, has large, modern rooms and a unique indoor-outdoor waterslide. Rooms, decorated in pastel greens and white, are light and airy and have modern furnishings. Jules (*see* Dining, above), a top restaurant, is on the premises. *4150 Albert St. (Hwy. 6), S4S 3R8, tel. 306/586–5363; in Saskatchewan 800/667–9811; elsewhere in Canada 800/667–8191. 188 rooms, including nonsmoking rooms. Facilities: 2 restaurants, lounge, pub, indoor pool, waterslide, sauna, whirlpool, games room. AE, DC, MC, V. Moderate.*

Journey's End. One of Canada's largest budget chains operates a tidy modern roadside property on the eastern edge of town. Earthtones, contemporary furnishings, and basic amenities make this a comfortable place to stay. Not many frills, but freebies include morning coffee, newspaper, and local phone calls. *3221 E. Eastgate Dr., S4N 0T0, tel. 306/789–5522 or 800/668–4200. 100 rooms. AE, DC, MC, V. Inexpensive.*

★ **Sandman Inn.** This easternmost outpost of a Vancouver-based budget chain has a mock-Tudor facade; average-size, well-furnished rooms; and Saskatchewan's largest private indoor pool. The poolside Showboat lounge offers dining and dancing to music of the '50s. *4025 Albert St. (Hwy. 6), S4S 3R6, tel. 306/586–2663 or 800/663–6900. 184 rooms. Facilities: 2 restaurants, lounge, indoor pool, whirlpool. AE, DC, MC, V. Inexpensive.*

Arts and Nightlife

The Arts Theater On a theater-in-the-round stage inside the old Regina City Hall, the **Globe Theatre** (1801 Scarth St., Regina, tel. 306/525–9553) offers classics and contemporary Saskatchewan works from October to April. **Theatre Regina** (Performing Arts Centre, 1077 Angus St., Regina, tel. 306/565–2277) presents lighthearted original productions.

Music and Dance Two theaters in the **Saskatchewan Centre of the Arts** (Wascana Centre, 200 Lakeshore Dr., Regina, tel. 306/565–0404) are venues for the Regina Symphony, pop concerts, dance performances, and Broadway musicals and plays. **Dance Works Regina** (1077 Angus St., Regina, tel. 306/359–3181) presents contemporary productions.

Nightlife Bars and Clubs **Caper's,** in the Ramada Renaissance (1919 Saskatchewan Dr., Regina, tel. 306/525–5255), is where local movers and shakers mingle with visitors from the convention center next door.

Music The **Original California Club** (Regina Inn, Victoria Ave. and Broad St., Regina, tel. 306/525–6767) is the city's liveliest discotheque. **W.H. Shooters** (2075 Broad St., Regina, tel. 306/525–3525) features Canadian and American country-and-western bands. Relax English-style with darts and ale and music at

Formerly's, in the Hotel Saskatchewan (2125 Victoria Ave., Regina, tel. 306/522–7691).

Excursion from Regina: Swift Current to Cypress Hills Provincial Park

West of Regina, the Canadian West begins as the square townships and straight roads of the grain-belt prairie farms gradually give way to the arid rolling hills of the upland plains ranches.

The Trans-Canada Highway skirts the edge of the Missouri Coteau—glacial hills that divide the prairie from the dry western plain—on its way west to **Swift Current** (174 kilometers, or 108 miles). The West begins at Swift Current (population 16,000), which cultivates the image during Frontier Days Stampede and rodeo (*see* Festivals and Seasonal Events in Chapter 1). Further depicting Swift are the exhibits at the **Swift Current Museum,** where pioneer and Indian artifacts and exhibits of local natural history are displayed. *105 Chaplin St., tel. 306/778–2775. Admission free. Open July–Aug., daily 2–5, 7–9; June and Sept.–Oct. 15, weekends and Mon. 2–5, Tues.–Fri. 7–9; Oct. 16–May, Sun. and Mon. 2–5.*

Along the next 128-kilometer (80-mile) stretch of the Trans-Canada Highway, the road skirts the southern edge of **the Great Sand Hills.** These desertlike remnants of a huge glacial lake now abound with such native wildlife as pronghorn antelope, mule deer, coyote, jackrabbit, and kangaroo rats. Heading south on Highway 21 will bring you into **Maple Creek,** a self-styled "old cow town," with a number of preserved Old West storefronts. Saskatchewan's oldest museum, the **Old Timer's Museum,** features pictures and artifacts of Mounties, early ranchers, and Indians. *218 Jasper St., tel. 306/662–2474. Admission: $2 adults, $1 seniors, 50¢ children. Open daily 10–5.*

Time Out It doesn't look like much from the outside, but inside the **Commercial Hotel** (Pacific Ave., tel. 306/662–2673) is a haphazardly preserved specimen of an Old West hotel and saloon. The bar, restaurant, and lobby are adorned with trophies of local game. This is a class joint, or so indicates the sign that warns "Your Shoes Must Be Cleaned" for admittance to the hotel.

Drive south on Highway 21 for another 27 kilometers (17 miles) to **Cypress Hills Provincial Park.** Cypress Hills consists of two sections, a Centre Block and a West Block, which are about 25 kilometers (16 miles) apart and separated by nonpark land. The larger West Block abuts the border with Alberta and is connected to Alberta's Cypress Hills Provincial Park (*see* Excursion from Calgary, below). Within the Centre Block, the Cypress Hills plateau, rising more than 4,000 feet above sea level, is covered with spruce, aspen, and lodgepole pines that were erroneously identified as cypress by early European explorers. From Lookout Point you have a 50-mile-range view of Maple Creek and the Great Sand Hills beyond. In addition to the wildlife and flora that abound in the park, there is Cypress Four Seasons (*see* Lodging, below) resort, complete with a golf course, tennis courts, campgrounds, riding stables, and a full complement of winter sports. Maps are available at the Administrative Building near the park entrance. *Cypress Hills Pro-*

This trip
we found a
road less
traveled.
And the
perfect way
to see it.

Vacation Cars. Vacation Prices. Wherever you travel,

Budget offers you a wide selection of quality cars – from economy models to roomy minivans and even convertibles. You'll find them all at competitively low rates that include unlimited mileage. At over 1500 locations in the U.S. and Canada. For information and reservations, call your travel consultant or Budget at **800-527-0700**. In Canada, call **800-268-8900**.

Budget

THE SMART MONEY IS ON BUDGET.®

We feature Lincoln-Mercury and other fine cars.   *A system of corporate and licensee owned locations.*

No matter what your travel style, the best trips start with **Fodor's**

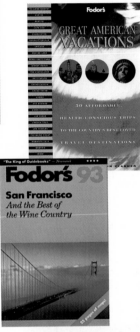

vincial Park, Hwy. 21, tel. 306/662–4411. Admission: $5/day per car, senior-citizen drivers free. Open year-round.

A rough gravel road connects the Cypress Hills Centre Block plateau with the West Block plateau. During wet weather, take Highway 21 north to Maple Creek and Highway 271 southwest to the West Block.

The two blocks share the same plant life, animal life, and scenic vistas, but the West Block also encompasses **Fort Walsh National Historic Park.** The original fort was built by the Mounties in 1875 to establish order between the "wolfers" (whiskey traders) and the Assiniboine Indians. Fort Walsh remained the center of local commerce until its abandonment in 1883. Today, free bus service is available between the **Visitor Reception Centre** and the reconstructed fort itself, Farwell's Trading Post, and a picnic area. No private vehicles are permitted beyond the parking area. *Ft. Walsh, Hwy. 271, 55 km (34 mi) southwest of Maple Creek, tel. 306/662–2645. Admission free. Open mid-May–mid-Oct., daily 9–6.*

Dining For rates, *see* Dining and Lodging chart, above.

Cypress Hills **Cypress Four Seasons Resort.** Located within the Centre Block of Cypress Hills Provincial Park, the restaurant of the resort is a bright and woodsy place with picture windows overlooking the forest. The standard Canadian fare is more successful than the Chinese dishes on the menu. *Box 1480, Maple Creek, tel. 306/662–4477. No reservations. Dress: casual. MC, V. Moderate.*

Swift Current **Wong's Kitchen.** This longtime area favorite features fine Canadian food and an even better Oriental menu: Dry garlic ribs are the star attraction. Count on live entertainment nightly. *Hwy. 1, S. Service Rd., tel. 306/773–6244. Reservations advised. Dress: casual. AE, MC, V. Expensive.*

Lodging **Cypress Four Seasons Resort.** It's not part of the Four Seasons
Cypress Hills chain, but the rooms here are new, comfortable, modern, and right in the middle of a lodgepole pine forest. Either pastels or earthtones adorn the rooms that are contemporary with basic amenities. *Box 1480, Maple Creek, S0N 1N0, tel. 306/662–4477. 35 rooms; cabins and condos. Facilities: restaurant, lounge, indoor pool, whirlpool. MC, V. Moderate.*

Swift Current **Horseshoe Lodge.** It's conveniently situated along the Trans-Canada Highway service road, yet the rooms still have fine views of the surrounding countryside. The cocktail lounge is a popular meeting spot, and the restaurant features solid Canadian cooking. *Mobile Rte. 35 Hwy. 1E, S9H 3X6, tel. 306/773–4643. 49 rooms. Facilities: 2 restaurants, lounge, outdoor pool. AE, DC, MC, V. Inexpensive.*

Saskatoon

Saskatchewan's largest city, Saskatoon (population 185,000) is nicknamed "City of Bridges" because seven spans cross the undeveloped riverfront that cuts the town in half diagonally. Saskatoon was founded in 1882 when a group of Ontario Methodists were granted 200,000 acres to form a temperance colony. Teetotaling Methodists controlled only half the land, however, and eventually the influence of the other "half" turned the town "wet." The coming of the railroad in 1890 made it the major regional transportation hub, but during the 20th century it became known for its three major resources: potash, oil, and wheat. One of Canada's fastest-growing cities, Saskatoon today is the high-tech hub of Saskatchewan's agricultural industry and is also home to the University of Saskatchewan—a major presence in all aspects of local life.

Important Addresses and Numbers

Tourist Information
The **Saskatoon Visitor & Convention Bureau** (310 Idylwyld Dr. N, Box 369, Saskatoon, Sask. S7K 3L3, tel. 306/242–1206) is open weekdays 8:30–4:30 year-round. In summer, information booths are set up at various points along the highway. **Tourism Saskatchewan** (122 3rd Ave. N, tel. 306/664–6240) is open weekdays 9–5:30.

Emergencies
Dial 911 for **police, fire, ambulance, poison,** and **emergency** services.

Hospitals
Emergency rooms include **City Hospital** (Queen St. and 6th Ave. N, tel. 306/242–6681) and **St. Paul's Hospital** (1702 20th St. W, tel. 306/382–3220).

Late-night Pharmacy
Pinders Drug stores (2410 22nd St. W, tel. 306/382–5005; 610 Taylor St. E, at Broadway Ave., tel. 306/343–1608) are open until midnight.

Arriving and Departing by Plane

Saskatoon Airport, 7 kilometers (4½ miles) northwest of downtown, is served by Canadian Airlines International, Air Canada, and Canadian commuter carriers. Taxis to the downtown area cost about $9.

Getting Around

By Bus
Saskatoon Transit (tel. 306/975–3100) buses offer convenient service to points around the city. The fare is $1 for adults, 60¢ for students, 50¢ for children 5–12.

By Taxi
Taxis are plentiful, especially outside downtown hotels, but they are fairly expensive. For service, call **United Yellow Cab** (tel. 306/652–2222) or **Saskatoon Radio Cab** (tel. 306/242–1221).

Guided Tours

Heritage Tours (tel. 306/382–1911) offers guided bus tours of the city and outlying areas mid-May–August. **W.W. Northcote River Cruises** depart on the hour for 11-kilometer (7-mile) tours of the **South Saskatchewan River** (tel. 306/665–1818; tours run May–Sept., weekends 1–4; June–Aug., daily 1–8).

Exploring Saskatoon

Numbers in the margin correspond with points of interest on the Saskatoon map.

Reasonably compact for a Western city, Saskatoon proper is easily accessible to drivers and cyclists. Idylwyld Drive divides the city into east and west; 22nd Street divides the city into north and south. The downtown area and the Spadina Crescent are located on the west side of the South Saskatchewan River.

❶ Begin exploring at **Meewasin Valley Centre,** a small museum that traces Saskatoon history back to temperance-colony days. Meewasin is Cree for "beautiful valley," and this is a fitting place to embark upon the **Meewasin Valley Trail,** a 15-kilometer (9-mile) biking and hiking trail along both banks of the beautiful South Saskatchewan River. *Meewasin Valley Centre, 402 3rd Ave. S, tel. 306/665–6888. Admission free. Open weekdays 9–5, weekends 10:30–6.*

Follow Spadina Crescent north along the river and past the

❷ **Hotel Bessborough** (*see* Lodging, below), the most prominent old building in the Saskatoon skyline. A few blocks farther

❸ north is the **Ukrainian Museum of Canada,** which celebrates—through photos, costumes, textiles, and of course the famous *pysanky* (Easter eggs)—the rich history of the Ukrainian peoples, who make up 10% of Saskatchewan's population. *910 Spadina Crescent E, tel. 306/244–3800. Admission: $2 adults, $1 senior citizens, 50¢ children. Open mid-June–Aug., weekdays 10–4:30, Sat. 1–5, Sun. 1–8; Sept.–mid-June, 1–4:30, closed Sat. and Mon.*

From Spadina Crescent, head east over the river via the Uni-

❹ versity Bridge to the **University of Saskatchewan,** which occupies a 2,550-acre site overlooking the river. Turn left into the campus at Bottomley Avenue and look for the **Place Riel Campus Centre** (Campus Dr., tel. 306/966–6988). Here, you can pick up a map that will help to orient you to the whereabouts of the **Biology Museum, Museum of Natural Sciences, Museum of Antiquities, Observatory,** and **Diefenbaker Centre** (tel. 306/966–8382), an art museum commemorating the Saskatchewan-bred (though Ontario-native) Canadian prime minister John G. Diefenbaker. Continue on Campus Drive to **University Farm.** Note the 1909 stone barn, purported to be the most photographed building in Saskatchewan.

Exit the campus, head west on College Drive, and then pick up University Drive, lined with grand old homes. University

❺ Drive eventually becomes **Broadway Avenue,** the city's oldest business district and location of more than 150 shops, restaurants, and a cinema.

Time Out | Unpretentious and entirely too small, **Calories** (721 Broadway Ave., tel. 306/665–7991) is a crowded but delicious place to stop for cheesecakes and pastries, ice cream, sandwiches, and superb coffee.

Take Broadway Avenue south to 8th Street; then head west to

❻ Lorne Avenue and south to the **Western Development Museum.** One of Saskatchewan's four such museums, the Saskatoon branch is called "1910 Boomtown" and re-creates early 20th-century life in the Canadian west. *2610 Lorne Ave. S, tel. 306/931–1910. Admission: $3.50 adults, $3 senior citizens, $1.50 children 5–12. Open mid-May–mid-Sept., daily 9–9; winter, weekdays 9–5, weekends noon–5.*

❼ The museum is part of the **Saskatoon Prairieland Exhibition Grounds** (tel. 206/931–7149), a vast plot that encompasses space for agricultural shows and rodeos, horse races, and Diefenbaker Park by the river.

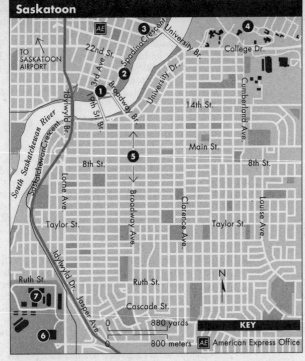

To return to downtown Saskatoon, take the scenic route: Head
north on Lorne Avenue, then east on Ruth Street to the river.
Follow Henry Avenue, Taylor Street, and Saskatchewan Crescent past the fine old homes that overlook one of the prettier
stretches of the South Saskatchewan River. Cross over the
Idylwyld Bridge.

Other Points of Interest

Wanuskewin Heritage Park, just a few kilometers north of Saskatoon, is a relatively new complex. Its visitor center, exhibit
hall, and walking trails focus on the 19 archaeological sites
where native Indians encamped for 6,000 years. The sites include a medicine wheel, tipi rings, bison kills and pounds, habitation sites, and stone cairns. *R.R. 4, Saskatoon, S7K 3J7, tel.
306/931–6767. Admission: $5 adult $4.25 senior citizens, $2
children 5–12, $12 families.*

Prince Albert, 141 kilometers (88 miles) north of Saskatoon, is
Saskatchewan's fourth-largest city (population 34,000), the
center of the lumber industry, and the self-proclaimed "Gateway to the North." It's a prosperous modern city straddling the
North Saskatchewan River, and the most interesting attractions are downtown. Pick up a walking-tours pamphlet at the
Prince Albert Historical Museum, housed in an old firehouse.
*River St. and Central Ave., tel. 306/764–2992. Admission: $1
adults, 50¢ senior citizens and students. Open daily 10–6.*

The **Western Development Museum** in North Battleford, 138
kilometers (86 miles) northwest of Saskatoon, presents a re-

created 1920s farming village, complete with homes, offices, churches, and a Mountie post. The museum also exhibits vintage farming tools and provides demonstrations of agricultural skills used. *Hwys. 16 and 40, tel. 306/445–8033. Admission: $3 adults, $2.50 senior citizens, $1 children under 13. Open May 1–Oct. 31, daily 9–6.*

For a refreshing, revitalizing 24-kilometer (77-mile) getaway from Saskatoon, take Routes 16 and 365 southeast, to **Manitou Beach.** Fifty years ago the town of Manitou Beach was a world-famous spa nicknamed the "Carlsbad of Canada." The mineral water in Little Manitou Lake is said to be three times saltier than the ocean and dense enough to make anyone float. Today, **Manitou Springs Mineral Spa** (open year-round) attracts vacationers, as well as sufferers of arthritis, rheumatism, and skin disorders, to the healing facility. *Hwy. 365, Manitou Beach, tel. 306/946–3949.*

National and Provincial Parks

Fort Battleford National Historic Park, established at Battleford in 1876 by the North West Mounted Police, originated as a post to make the land safe for farming from local Indians and white fur traders. Costumed guides explain day-to-day life at the post, and an interpretive center displays weapons, vehicles, and souvenirs of the fur trade. *Central Ave., tel. 306/937–2621. Admission free. Open May–mid-Oct., daily 10–6; other times, Mon.–Sat. 9–5, Sun. and holidays 10–6.*

Prince Albert National Park, 220 kilometers (137 miles) north of Saskatoon, encompasses nearly a million acres of wilderness and waterways and is divided into three landscapes: wide-open fescue grassland, rolling wooded parkland, and dense arboreal forest.

In addition to hiking trails, the park has three major campgrounds, with more than 500 sites, plus rustic campgrounds and primitive sites in the backcountry. Pick up maps and information at the visitor center in **Waskesiu Lake,** a townsite with restaurants, motels, and stores within the park.

The **Nature Centre,** located inside the visitor center, can help to orient you to the plant and animal life of the area. Hiking along the marked trails, you have a good chance of spotting moose, deer, bear, elk, and red fox. Canoes, rowboats, and powerboats can be rented from Waskesiu Lake Marina. Lodging in Waskesiu Lake includes the Lakeview Hotel (Lakeview Dr., Box 26, S0J 2Y0, tel. 306/663–5311), a year-round accommodation. *Prince Albert National Park, off Hwy. 2, tel. 306/663–5322. Admission: $3/day per car; $6 for 4 days. Open year-round. Waskesiu Lake Visitor Center, Rtes. 263 and 264, tel. 306/663–5322. Open May–Sept., daily 8 AM–10 PM; Oct.–Apr., weekdays 8–4:30.*

What to See and Do with Children

Battlefords Superslide (King Hill, off Railway Ave., N. Battleford, tel. 306/445–0000) is a massive water park with 11 waterslides, pools, a hot tub, and a games area.

Forestry Farm Park and Zoo (off Attridge Dr. in NE Saskatoon, tel. 306/975–3382) spotlights cold-weather denizens like deer, bear, and wolves. The park encompasses barbecue areas, nature displays, cross-country ski trails, and sports fields.

Kinsmen Park (Spadina Crescent and 25th St., Saskatoon, tel. 306/975–7529) is a riverside amusement park and a children's play village.

Western Development Museum (*see* Exploring Saskatoon, above).

Shopping

Malls and Shopping Districts
Midtown Plaza (22nd St. and 1st Ave., tel. 306/652–9366) and **Scotia Centre Mall** (123 2nd Ave., tel. 306/665–6120) are enclosed malls located downtown. The area around **Broadway Avenue,** between 8th and 12th streets east of the river, has 150 boutiques and services.

Specialty Stores
Trading Post Limited (226 2nd Ave. S, tel. 306/653–1769) carries an extensive and reasonably priced selection of Inuit and Indian crafts and Canadian foodstuffs—including Saskatoon berry products. Local crafts are also available at **Handmade House** (710 Broadway Ave., tel. 306/665–5542) and the **Homespun Craft Emporium** (212 3rd Ave. S, tel. 306/652–3585).

Sports

Participant Sports
Bicycling and Jogging
The **Meewasin Valley Trail** (tel. 306/665–6887) is a gorgeous 15.35-kilometer (9½-mile) biking and jogging trail along both banks of the South Saskatchewan River in Saskatoon.

Health and Fitness Clubs
The **Courtyard Racquet & Fitness Centre** (322 Saguenay Dr., Saskatoon, tel. 306/242–0010) has racquetball and squash courts, a weight room, aerobics classes, minigolf, and beach volleyball in summer. The **Saskatoon Field House** (University of Alberta, 2020 College Dr., Saskatoon, tel. 306/975–3354) has tennis courts, a weight room, a gymnastics area, an indoor track, a fitness dance area, and drop-in fitness classes.

Spectator Sports
Hockey
The **Saskatoon Blades** play Canadian Hockey League (minor league) matches at **Saskatchewan Place** (3515 Thatcher Ave., Saskatoon, tel. 306/242–1000).

Horse Racing
Marquis Downs Racetrack (Prairieland Exhibition Centre, enter on Ruth St., Saskatoon, tel. 306/242–6100) has Thoroughbred and harness racing early May–mid-October.

Dining and Lodging

For price categories, *see* Winnipeg Dining and Lodging, above.

Dining
R.J. Willoughby's. The lush, tropical, pink-and-green color scheme of the Holiday Inn's main dining room is enhanced by copious groves of bamboo and foliage. The menu features Continental preparations plus "Sizzling Stone Cooking" of meat, fish, and veggies on a hot slab of granite. Entrées labeled with hearts have been approved by the Canadian Heart Foundation; breakfast augments the regular menu with a healthful "Fruit & Fibre Buffet." *Holiday Inn, 90 22nd St. E, tel. 306/665–7576. Reservations advised. Jacket advised. AE, DC, MC, V. Very Expensive.*
St. Tropez Bistro. This sophisticated dining establishment features intimate French-bistro decor, with blue-and-pink florals,

candle-lit tables, an outdoor café, and imaginative preparations that change daily. Veal, fish, pasta, quiche, crepes—and outstanding homemade bread are often offered. For dessert, the chocolate fondue is aces. The bistro is a short stroll from downtown hotels. *243 3rd Ave. S, tel. 306/652–1250. Reservations advised. Dress: casual. AE, MC, V. Closed Sun. Expensive.*

Lydia's. Lydia's, occupying the main rooms in an old house on Broadway Avenue, has a split personality. The front room is an unpretentious setting for Ukrainian specialties like *nalysnyky* (crepes), *varenyky* (mashed potato and cheddar cheese boiled with butter and served with sour cream), and smoked sausage; the back room is the oak and stained-glass white-tablecloth venue for such exotic concoctions as "A Night in Hungary" (pork Tokany), "Ascent to the Carpathians" (Dijon veal), and "A Visit to Bulgaria" (beef Gulyas). The wine list is small but inexpensive. *650 Broadway Ave., tel. 306/652–8595. Reservations advised. Dress: casual. MC, V. Moderate.*

Saskatoon Station Place. The station is newly built, but the railroad cars and decorative antiques are fascinatingly authentic. The newspaper-style menu headlines Canadian prime rib and steaks, seafood, and Greek specialties, such as Greek ribs and souvlakia. *221 Idylwyld Dr. N, tel. 306/244–7777. Reservations advised. Dress: casual. AE, DC, MC, V. Moderate.*

★ **Adonis.** By day such Middle Eastern dishes as falafel, hummus, and donair are served cafeteria-style. At night, tablecloths and candles transform the room into a romantic setting for couscous, dolmades, steak Andalousia, and other Mediterranean delights. It's one of Saskatoon's few outdoor cafés and a great place for breakfast. *101 3rd Ave. S, tel. 306/652–9598. No reservations. Dress: casual. AE, DC, MC, V. Inexpensive.*

Taunte Maria's. This is a Mennonite restaurant, which is to suggest a menu of hearty soups, huge farmer's sausages, coleslaw, potato salad, homemade bread, and noodles steeped in gravy. The decor, too, reflects the Mennonite tradition: simple, functional, and comfortable. *Try* to save room for Ho-Ho Cake (chocolate cake with chocolate icing) or bread-and-butter pudding. Taunte Maria's is convenient to the airport. *51st St. and Faithfull Ave., tel. 306/931–3212. No reservations. Dress: casual. MC, V. Closed Sun. Inexpensive.*

Lodging **Ramada Renaissance.** Saskatoon's newest luxurious property has a prime riverfront/downtown location and 18 floors of classically styled, ample-size rooms (request a river view). Units are large, and the peach, gray, and pastel colors make them bright and airy. The elaborate Waterworks Recreation Complex encompasses an indoor pool, whirlpool, sauna, and two 3-story water slides. *405 20th St. E, S7K 6X6, tel. 306/665–3322 or 800/268–8998. 295 rooms, including nonsmoking rooms. Facilities: 2 restaurants, lounge, indoor pool, sauna, whirlpool, waterslides. AE, DC, MC, V. Very Expensive.*

★ **Hotel Bessborough.** Saskatoon's grand old landmark, opened in 1935, looks like a French château and dominates the skyline from its riverfront setting. Rooms have quirky shapes and antique furniture but are complete with modern amenities. Front rooms are larger; rear rooms have river views. Delta Hotels acquired it in 1989, promising a major (and much-needed) facelift. What won't change are the gold-leaf details in the public areas, the gardens, or "The Castle's" role as Saskatoon's meeting place. *601 Spadina Crescent E, S7K 3G8, tel. 306/244–5521 or 800/667–8788. 230 rooms, including nonsmoking rooms. Fa-*

cilities: 2 restaurants, 2 lounges, indoor and outdoor pools, sauna, whirlpool. AE, DC, MC, V. Expensive.

Sheraton Cavalier. Located downtown opposite Kiwanis Park, this eight-story property features unusually large mauve-and-blue rooms that face either the city or the river, and an elaborate water-sports complex. The Top of the Inn is one of Saskatoon's top discotheques; the Barley Bin is a sophisticated but chummy pub. *612 Spadina Crescent E, S7K 3G9, tel. 306/652–6770 or 800/325–3535. 250 rooms, including nonsmoking rooms. Facilities: 2 restaurants, pub, disco, 2 indoor pools, waterslides, sauna, whirlpool, exercise room, games room. AE, DC, MC, V. Expensive.*

Travelodge. This sprawling property near the airport has themed its decor around the two flora-filled indoor pool complexes. Rooms come in a great variety of sizes and shapes; many have balconies overlooking the pool. The Aloha Gardens offers poolside dining; the Heritage Dining Room has medieval feasts. *106 Circle Dr. W, S7L 4L6, tel. 306/242–8881 or 800/255–3050. 219 rooms, including nonsmoking rooms. Facilities: 2 restaurants, lounge, pub, 2 indoor pools, waterslides, sauna, whirlpools, games room. AE, DC, MC, V. Moderate.*

Colonial Square Motel. This pink-stucco, two-story motel opened in 1989 east of the river, along a fast-food strip. Rooms are furnished in pastel colors and have two queen-size beds or a double bed plus pullout sofa. Across the parking lot is the Venice Pizza House and Lounge. *1301 8th St. E, S7H 0S7, tel. 306/343–1676 or 800/667–3939. 80 rooms, including nonsmoking rooms. Facilities: restaurant, lounge. AE, MC, V. Inexpensive.*

★ **King George.** Situated in the center of downtown, opposite the transit mall, this older hotel welcomes senior citizens and anyone else looking for a bargain. Earthtone rooms are large but a bit dreary; suites—some with wet bars—are terrific deals. Senior citizens get 30% off rooms and 15% off meals in several restaurants, including the entertaining Karl's Schnitzel Haus. *157 2nd Ave. N, S7K 2A9, tel. 306/244–6133 or 800/667–1234. 104 rooms. Facilities: 2 restaurants, 2 lounges, bowling alley. AE, DC, MC, V. Inexpensive.*

The Arts and Nightlife

The Arts

Theater

Saskatoon's oldest professional theater, **25th Street Theatre Centre** (420 Duchess St., Saskatoon, tel. 306/664–2239) produces mostly works by Canadian playwrights during its October–May season. **Persephone Theatre** (2802 Rusholme Rd., Saskatoon, tel. 306/384–7727) presents six plays and musicals a year. **Gateway Players** (709 Cumberland St., Saskatoon, tel. 306/653–1200) presents five productions October–April. **Nightcap Productions** (tel. 306/653–2300) offers "Shakespeare on the Saskatchewan" in a riverside tent in July and August, as well as midnight improvisational comedy at the Broadway Theatre (715 Broadway Ave., Saskatoon, tel. 306/652–6556).

Music and Dance

The **Saskatoon Symphony** (tel. 306/665–6414) performs an October–April season at **Saskatoon Centennial Auditorium** (35 22nd St. E, Saskatoon, tel. 306/644–9777). When the symphony isn't in concert, the 2,003-seat auditorium hosts ballet, rock and pop concerts, comedians, musical comedies, and opera. The **Mendel Art Gallery** (950 Spadina Crescent E, Saskatoon, tel. 306/975–7610) has a regular concert program, and the **Sas-**

katoon Jazz Society performs in its permanent space, **The Bassment** (245 3rd Ave. S, Saskatoon, tel. 306/652–1421).

Nightlife
Bars and Clubs

One Up (410 22nd St. E, Saskatoon, tel. 306/244–0955) is a civilized rooftop place with great river views. Saskatoon's businesspeople interface with traveling executives at **Caper's Lounge** (405 20th St. E, Saskatoon, tel. 306/665–3322) in the Ramada Renaissance.

Comedy

Saskatoon's **Yuk Yuk's** (806 Idylwyld Dr. N, tel. 306/244–9857) presents cutting-edge comedy.

Literature

Literary readings by candlelight take place at the **Victorian Dining Room** (243 21st St. E, Saskatoon, tel. 306/244–0060).

Music

See top rock groups at **Bud's On Broadway** (817 Broadway Ave., Saskatoon, tel. 306/244–4155) and **Amigos** (632 10th St. E, Saskatoon, tel. 306/652–4912). **Top of the Inn** (612 Spadina Crescent, Saskatoon, tel. 306/652–6770), atop the Sheraton Cavalier, has great river views and the city's hottest dance floor. The **Artful Dodger** (100–119 4th Ave. S, Saskatoon, tel. 306/653–2577) is a pub with live entertainment. Go out to **Texas T** (3331 8th St. E, Saskatoon, tel. 306/373–8080) for country sights and sounds around the city's largest dance floor.

Calgary

With the eastern face of the Rockies as its backdrop, Calgary's crisp concrete-and-steel skyline seems to rise from flat plains as if by sheer force of will. In fact, all the elements in the great saga of the Canadian West—Mounties, Indians, railroads, cowboys, oil—have converged to create a city with a brand-new face and a surprisingly traditional soul.

Calgary, Gaelic for "preserved pasture at the harbor," was founded in 1875 at the junction of the Bow and Elbow rivers as a North West Mounted Police post. The Canadian Pacific Railroad arrived in 1883, and ranchers established major spreads on the plains surrounding the town. Incorporated as a city in 1885, Calgary grew quickly, and by 1911 its population had reached 43,000.

Oil was first discovered in 1914, but it wasn't until the late 1960s that the industry exploded, with about 80% of Canada's oil companies and subsidiaries establishing headquarters here. Today, Calgary is a city of more than 712,000 that combines Wild West geography with a mild West disposition. People are easygoing, slowtalking, and downright neighborly. Downtown is still evolving but Calgary ("Cal-gree" to locals) makes life nice by connecting most of the buildings with Plus 15, a network of enclosed walkways 15 feet above street level.

Important Addresses and Numbers

Tourist Information

The main **Calgary Convention & Visitors Bureau** (237 8th Ave. S.E. T2G 0K8, tel. 403/263–8510 or 800/661–1678) is open daily 8 AM–9 PM in summer, varying hours the rest of the year. There are also walk-in Visitor Service Centres at the base of the Calgary Tower and at Canada Olympic Park.

Emergencies

Dial 911 for all emergencies; **police,** tel. 403/266–1234; **poison center,** tel. 403/670–1414.

Alberta

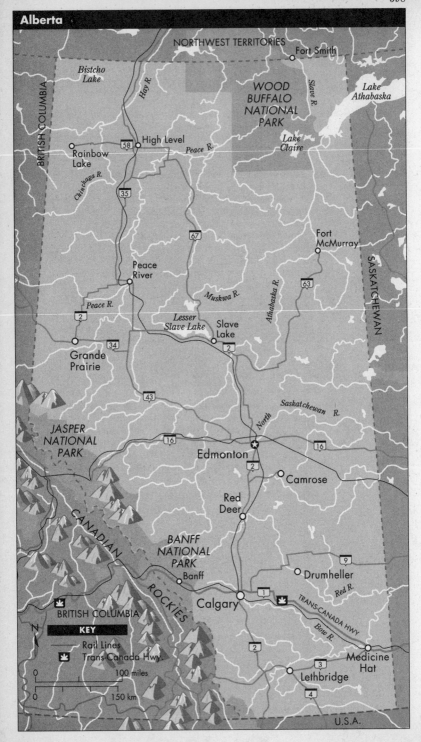

NORTHWEST TERRITORIES

Fort Smith

Bistcho Lake

Hay R.

WOOD BUFFALO NATIONAL PARK

Slave R.

Lake Athabaska

BRITISH COLUMBIA

58 High Level

Peace R.

Lake Claire

Rainbow Lake

Chinchaga R.

35

Fort McMurray

67

Peace River

Peace R.

Muskwa R.

Athabaska R.

63

2

34

Lesser Slave Lake

Slave Lake

2

Grande Prairie

SASKATCHEWAN

43

Saskatchewan R.

North

JASPER NATIONAL PARK

16

Edmonton

16

2

Camrose

Red Deer

CANADIAN

BANFF NATIONAL PARK

Banff

9

Drumheller

Red R.

ROCKIES

Calgary

1

TRANS-CANADA HWY

BRITISH COLUMBIA

Bone R.

KEY

N

— Rail Lines

⚑ Trans-Canada Hwy.

0   100 miles

0   150 km

2

Medicine Hat

3

Lethbridge

4

U.S.A.

Hospitals Emergency rooms are located at **General Hospital** (841 Centre Ave. E, tel. 403/268–9111), **Foothills Hospital** (1403 29th St. NW, tel. 403/670–1110), and **Alberta Children's Hospital** (1820 Richmond Rd. SW, tel. 403/229–7211). **Rocky View Hospital** (7007 14th St. SW, tel. 403/541–3450).

Late-night The **Super Drug Mart** (504 Elbow Dr. SW, tel. 403/228–3338) is
Pharmacy open daily until midnight.

Arriving and Departing by Plane

Calgary International Airport is located 8 kilometers (5 miles) northeast of the city. Along with Air Canada and Canadian Airlines International, Calgary is served by the U.S. carriers American, Delta, Horizon Airlines, and United. Taxis make the 30-minute trip for about $16.

Getting Around

By Car Although many attractions are located in the downtown area, a car is advisable for visiting outlying attractions. Visitors can obtain a three-day **Visitor Car Park** permit offering "hassle-free" parking at city meters. The permit is free at **Convention & Visitors Bureau** (*see* above).

By Bus/LRT Calgary Transit (206 7th Ave. SW, tel. 403/276–7801) operates a comprehensive bus system and light rail transit system (the **"C-Train"** or **"LRT"**) throughout the area. Fares are $1.50 for adults, 90¢ for children over 6. Books of 10 children's tickets are $8.50; 10 adults' tickets $12. A CT Day Pass good for unlimited rides costs $3.50 for adults, $2 for children. The C-Train has lines running northwest (Brentwood), northeast (Whitehorn), and south (Anderson) from downtown.

By Taxi Taxis are fairly expensive, at $2.05 for the "drop" and about $1.90 for each additional mile. Major taxi services are **Aero** (tel. 403/250–8800), **Checker** (tel. 403/299–9999), and **Yellow Cab** (tel. 403/250–8311).

Guided Tours

White Stetson Tours (tel. 403/274–2281) conducts City of Calgary Tours (plus tours to Banff, Lake Louise, Dinosaur Valley, and West Edmonton Mall) with pickup by small vans and buses. **Brewster Transportation & Tours** (tel. 403/221–8242 or 800/332–1419) offers tours of Calgary and environs.

Exploring Calgary

Numbers in the margin correspond to points of interest on the Downtown Calgary and Greater Calgary maps.

In the Calgary grid pattern, numbered streets run north–south in both directions from Centre Street, and numbered avenues run east–west in both directions from Centre Avenue.

❶ Begin your downtown walking tour at **Calgary Tower,** a 190-meter (626-foot), scepter-shape edifice that affords great views of the city's layout, the surrounding plains, and the face of the Rockies rising 80 kilometers (50 miles) west. A flame on top is lit for special occasions; the revolving **Panorama Dining Room** and **Sky's Rotisserie & Wine Bar** provide refreshment. *9th Ave.*

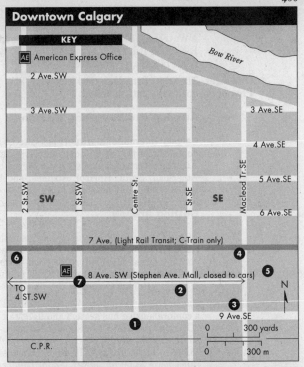

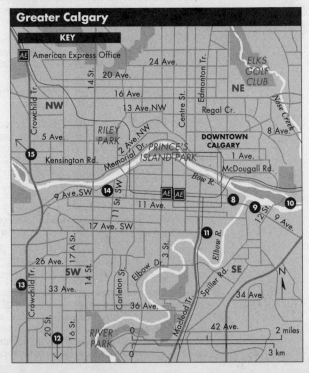

and Centre St. S, tel. 403/266-7171. Admission: $3.75 adults, $2.50 senior citizens and children 13–17, $1.75 children 6–12. Open weekdays and Sat. 7:30 AM–11:30 PM, Sun. 7:30 AM–10:30 PM.

② Take the "plus 15 walkway" (it is 15 feet above street level) over 9th Avenue Southwest to **Glenbow Museum,** Calgary's premier showcase of both art and history. Along with traveling exhibits, the Glenbow has comprehensive displays devoted to Alberta's native (Indian and Inuit) inhabitants, early European settlers, and later-day pioneers. The mineralogy collection and cache of arms and armor are superb. *130 9th Ave. SE, tel. 403/264-8300; tel. 403/237-8988 for exhibit information. Admission: $3 adults, $2 students 13–17, $1 senior citizens. Sat. free. Open daily 10–6. Closed Mon.*

③ Take the pedway over 1st Street Southeast to the **Calgary Centre for the Performing Arts** (tel. 403/294-7444), a complex of three theater spaces, a concert hall, and shopping area. The center was pieced together with the historic Calgary Public Building (1930) and the Burns Building (1913). Come at night for a performance (*see* The Arts and Nightlife, below), or take a one-hour walking tour at noon most weekdays.

④ Step outside into **Olympic Plaza** (7th Ave. SE and Macleod Trail SE), site of the Olympic medals presentation. Now, during lunchtime, it's a popular park space full of governmental brown-baggers; at night, there's a full slate of entertainment.

⑤ You're not likely to overlook the **Municipal Building** (8th Ave. SE and Macleod Trail), an angular mirror-walled structure that reflects city landmarks. One of the most stunning reflections is **City Hall,** a stately 1911 sandstone building that still houses the mayor's office and some city offices.

Seventh Avenue Southeast is closed to cars to make room for the C-Train, Calgary's light rail system. Hop on for a free ride (along 7th Avenue downtown only) to the center of the downtown shopping district. Literally, the top attraction of the area **⑥** is **Devonian Gardens,** above Toronto Dominion Square. The 2½-acre enclosed roof garden has 20,000 mostly tropical plants, nearly a mile of lush walkways, a sculpture court, and playground. Accessed by a glass-enclosed elevator just inside the 8th Avenue door, the Gardens has a reflecting pool that turns into a skating rink in winter and a small stage for musical performances year-round. *Between 2nd and 3rd Sts., and 7th and 8th Aves. SW. Admission free. Open daily 9–9.*

Seventh Avenue Southeast, between Macleod Trail and 4th Street Southwest, is a pedestrian-only shopping area called **⑦** **Stephen Avenue Mall.** Shops, nightclubs, and restaurants occupy the ground floors of Calgary's oldest structures, mostly sandstone buildings erected after an 1886 fire destroyed almost everything older. To learn more about old Calgary, check out the historical photographs on display at the **Alberta Historical Resources Foundation** and pick up the pamphlet. *Stephen (8th) Ave. Mall walking tour. 102 8th Ave. SE, tel. 403/297-7320. Open weekdays 8:30–4:30.*

Time Out **The Prospector** (205 8th Ave. SW, tel. 403/263-4909) provides an excellent breakfast/lunch/supper with basic pork, lamb, chicken, seafood, steak, salads, hot sandwiches, and burgers at reasonable prices. Try the chocolate pecan pie. It's at street level on Stephen Avenue Mall and provides a good location for people-watching.

---

❽ You'll need a car to continue from here. Head on to **Fort Calgary,** at the confluence of the Bow and Elbow rivers, established in 1875 by the North West Mounted Police to subdue local whiskey traders who were raising havoc among the Indians. In the 40-acre park in the valley occupied by Fort Calgary, a line of stumps traces the outline of the original post, and an ultracontemporary interpretive center traces the history of area Indi- **❾** ans, Mounties, and white settlers. The **Deane House** (809 9th Ave. SE, tel. 403/269-7747), situated directly across the 9th Avenue Bridge, is the renovated 1906 post commander's house; it has free tours and a tearoom serving light meals. *Ft. Calgary Interpretive Centre, 750 9th Ave. SE, tel. 403/290-1875. Admission free. Open daily 9-5.*

Continue east on 9th Avenue, turn north on 12th Street, and **❿** cross the bridge to St. George's Island and the **Calgary Zoo,** with more than 1,400 animals, including 388 rare and endangered species, in plausibly natural settings. Polar bears and seals cavorting underwater are perennial crowd pleasers. The **Kinsmen's Children's Zoo,** part of the larger site, offers hands-on experiences with baby animals, and the adjacent Prehistoric Park displays dinosaur replicas in a bygone natural habitat. *1300 Zoo Rd. NE, tel. 403/232-9372. Admission: $7.50 adults, $4.75 senior citizens, $3.75 children 2-15; $5 adults and senior citizens free on Tues. Open 9 AM, closing times seasonally adjusted.*

⓫ Head south and east to Olympic Way and **Stampede Park** (17th Ave. and 2nd St. SE, tel. 403/261-0101), the focus each July of the world-famous Calgary Exhibition and Stampede (*see* Festivals and Seasonal Events in Chapter 1). Throughout the year the Roundup Centre, Big Four Building, and Agriculture Building host trade shows; the Olympic Saddledome has concerts and Calgary Flames hockey games; and the Grandstand is the site of thoroughbred and harness racing (*see* Sports, below). Visitors can wander the grounds, take free one-hour tours of the **Saddledome** (tel. 403/261-0400), and visit the free **Grain Academy** in Roundup Centre, an interesting little museum that proudly proclaims itself "Canada's only grain interpretive centre." *Grain Academy in Stampede Park, tel. 403/263-4594. Admission free. Open weekdays 10-4, Sat. noon-4.*

Follow Macleod Trail past a strip of fast-food outlets, motels, and shopping centers and go west on Heritage Drive to **⓬** **Heritage Park,** where more than 100 authentic structures from all over western Canada have been collected in a parklike setting beside Glenmore Reservoir. The "neighborhoods," inhabited by costumed staff, range from an 1850s fur-trading post to a 1910-era town. Steam trains, horse-drawn buses, and paddlewheel steamers provide transportation, and North America's only antique amusement park re-creates bygone thrills. Theme snacks—sasparilla, beef jerky, fresh apple pie—abound. *1900 Heritage Dr. SW, tel. 403/259-1900. Admission: $6 adults, $5 senior citizens, $3 children 3-16. Open late-May-June, weekdays 10-4, weekends 10-6; July-Sept. 2, daily 10-6; Sept. 3-early Oct., weekends and holidays 10-5.*

East across Glenmore Reservoir, turn north on Crowchild Trail
⑬ to reach the **Canadian Forces Currie Barracks** (4225 Crowchild
Trail SW), site of two military museums in one building: **Lord
Strathconas (Royal Canadian) Horse Museum** (tel. 403/242–
6610) features an extensive collection of medals and weapons;
Princess Patricia's Canadian Light Infantry (tel. 403/240–7901)
displays memorabilia of a distinguished old regiment (founded
in 1914) that fought in both world wars and joined with the
United Nations peacekeeping forces. Note: Both museums are
free, but you may need to show identification to enter the military base. *Bldg. B6, Currie Barracks, 4225 Crowchild Trail
SW. Admission free. Horse Museum open weekdays 9–4, weekends 10–4; Infantry Museum open Tues.–Fri. and Sun. 10–4.*

Continuing north on Crowchild Trail, turn east on 9th Avenue
Southwest and then north again on 11th Street Southwest to
⑭ the **Alberta Science Centre/Planetarium.** The Science Centre
in the lower chamber has more than 35 hands-on exhibits of
scientific marvels, such as holograms, frozen shadows, and
laser beams; user-friendly demonstrations are given Friday–
Sunday. Up in the planetarium, the 360-degree Star Chamber
presents educational Star Shows with children's matinees on
weekends, Laser Shows on Friday–Sunday nights. Imaginative combinations of special effects, magic tricks, and old-time
show-biz make performances fascinating for all ages. *701 11th
St. SW, tel. 403/221–3700. Admission: Science Centre, $2.25
adults and senior citizens, $1.75 children, free with Star Show
ticket; Star Shows, $5.75 adults, $1.75 senior citizens and children; Laser Shows, $5. Open 1:30–9.*

Follow Crowchild Trail north to 16th Avenue Northwest (Rte.
⑮ 1) and then head west about 8 kilometers (5 miles) to **Canada
Olympic Park,** site of the 1988 Winter Olympics and a year-
round attraction. A one-hour bus tour goes over, under,
around, and through the 70- and 90-meter ski jumps, bobsled,
and luge tracks (in summer you have the option of walking
down the slopes). In winter the slopes are open to the public
(lessons available). Visitors can experience Olympic-size
thrills on the one-minute Tourist Bobsleigh Ride ($100) and
slightly briefer Tourist Luge Ride ($10); safety equipment is
provided. Premises include a Calgary Visitor Information Centre, a day lodge with a cafeteria, and the **Olympic Hall of Fame,**
a collection of Olympic memorabilia and video displays. The
highlight here is the scarifying 4-man bobsled simulator.
*Trans-Canada Hwy. W (Rte. 1) at Bowfort Rd. NW, tel. 403/
286–2632. Admission: Bus or self-guided tour, $6.50 adults,
$3.50 senior citizens, students, and children. Hall of Fame,
$3.50 adults, $2.50 senior citizens, students, and children.
Tour and Hall of Fame, $8.50 adults, $4.50 senior citizens, students, and children. Park open mid-June–Sept. 2, daily 7
AM–9 PM; Sept. 3–mid-June, daily 10–5; Hall of Fame open daily
8–8.*

What to See and Do with Children

Calaway Park (Rte. 1, 10 km, or 6 mi, west of Calgary, tel. 403/
240–3822). The 20-ride amusement park supplements thrills
with rock and children's shows, a petting farm, and 18 fast-food
outlets.

Calgary Zoo (*see* Exploring Calgary, above).

Canada Olympic Park (*see* Exploring Calgary, above).

Heritage Park (*see* Exploring Calgary, above).

Off the Beaten Track

Museum of Movie Art. Far north of Hollywood, the mazelike museum claims to possess the world's largest collection (4,000) of movie posters. There are continuous video movies and a well-stocked poster shop. *#9, 3600 21st St. NE, tel. 403/250–7588. Admission: $1. Open Tues.–Fri. 9:30–5:30, Sat. 11–5.*

Shopping

Malls and Shopping Districts Calgary's premier shopping areas are located in the center of the downtown area. **Centre Four** consists of an interconnected network of department stores and malls, with more than 300 stores located along the 7th Avenue Southwest transit way between 1st and 5th streets Southwest. Directly to the south, the six-block stretch of 8th Avenue Southwest between 3rd Street Southwest and Macleod Trail Southeast has been turned into the traffic-free Stephen Avenue Mall.

Specialty Stores **Western Outfitters** (128 8th Ave. SE, tel. 403/266–3656) and **Boot & Jean** (235 8th Ave. SE, tel. 403/264–4775, and Westbrook Mall, 1200 37th St. SW, tel. 403/240–0990) carries a full line of Western clothing. The **Alberta Boot Co.** factory outlet (614 10th Ave. SW, tel. 403/263–4623) specializes in footwear. **Cottage Craft Gifts** (6503 Elbow Drive SW, tel. 403/252–3797) has a large stock of authentic Indian and Inuit sculpture, carvings, and prints.

Sports

Participant Sports
Bicycling and Jogging Calgary has about 120 kilometers (75 miles) of bicycling and jogging paths, most of which wind along rivers and through city parks. Maps are available at **Visitor Information Centres** (*see* Important Addresses and Numbers in Calgary, above) and bike shops. Rent bikes at **The Bike Shop** (1321 1st St. SW, Calgary, tel. 403/264–0735) and **Sports Rent** (4424 16th Ave. NW, Calgary, tel. 403/292–0077).

Health and Fitness Clubs Three **Leisure Centre** waterparks in Calgary have wave pools and waterslides, plus gymnasiums and training facilities; Southland and Family have racquetball and squash courts. *Village Square Leisure Centre, 2623 56th St. NE, tel. 403/280–9714; Family Leisure Centre, 11150 Bonaventure Dr. SE, tel. 403/278–7542; Southland Leisure Centre, 2000 Southland Dr. SW, tel. 403/251–3505. Rates and hours vary.*

Just south of downtown, the striking white-dome **Lindsay Park Sports Centre** (2225 Macleod Trail SW, Calgary, tel. 403/233–8619) encompasses a 50-meter natatorium, a 200-meter track, racquetball and squash courts, and a weight room.

Spectator Sports
Hockey The **Calgary Flames** play National Hockey League matches October–April at the **Olympic Saddledome** (17th Ave. and 2nd St. SE, Calgary, tel. 403/261–0475) in Stampede Park.

Horse Racing There's racing year-round (except March) in **Stampede Park** (17th Ave. and 2nd St. SE, Calgary, tel. 403/261–0101); Thoroughbreds race April–May and September–November; trotters May–September and December–February. **Spruce**

Meadows (just south and west of the Calgary city boundary, tel. 403/254–3200) is one of the world's finest show jumping facilities, with major competitions held June–Sept.

Dining and Lodging

For price categories, *see* Winnipeg Dining and Lodging, above.

Dining **Hy's Steak House.** This is where Calgary (and Edmonton, Winnipeg, Toronto, and elsewhere in Canada) goes for immense portions of charcoal-broiled steaks, fresh seafood, chicken, and a huge selection of wines. Wood paneling and earthy decor are evidence of the sedate Victorian ambience. *316 4th Ave. SW, tel. 403/263–2222. Reservations advised. Jacket advised. AE, DC, MC, V. Closed Sun. Very Expensive.*

★ **Owl's Nest.** Plush armchairs and dark-wood booths express the subdued confidence of a restaurant long proclaimed the best in town. Standards are maintained, and all dishes are served with impeccable Continental flair. Alberta beef entrées are still ample and tender; British Columbia salmon is memorably fresh; the wine list is still exhaustive. *Westin Hotel, 320 4th Ave. SW, tel. 403/266–1611. Reservations advised. Jacket advised. AE, DC, MC, V. Very Expensive.*

Green Street Café. This lively and unpretentious spot serves French, Italian, and Cajun specialties in a three-level setting that's loaded with greenery inside and out. Menu highlights include veal medallions Danny Kaye and a panfried oyster dish with pecan pie for dessert. Come to the café for Sunday brunch, too. Upstairs bar features live jazz. *815 7th Ave. SW, tel. 403/266–1551. Reservations advised. Jacket advised. AE, MC, V. Closed Sat. lunch, Sun. Expensive.*

Mama's. Just what you'd expect from a place called Mama's: cheery red-and-white-check tablecloths; warm, friendly service; and large portions of tasty Italian food. The antipasto buffet—marinated eggplant, scallops, shrimp, squid, quail eggs, plus much more—is excellent. Veal dishes are the best entrée choices, and the wine list emphasizes Italian. *320 16th Ave. NW, tel. 403/276–9744. Reservations required. Jacket advised. AE, MC, V. Closed Sun. Expensive.*

Santorini Greek Taverna. This restaurant has an open patio that chimes with music and chatter. The northside spot transplants the Mediterranean to the northern plains. Stick with classic Greek specialties, such as moussaka, calamari, *taramasalata* (roe), *dolmades* (stuffed grape leaves), and *soutzoukakia* (beef sausage). Or order *mezethes*, and get a taste of a lot of things. *1502 Centre St. N, tel. 403/276–8363. No reservations. Dress: casual. AE, DC, MC, V. Moderate.*

★ **Buzzards Cafe.** This lively European-style downtown café serves 70 wines by the bottle or glass and the exclusive home brew, Buzzard Breath Ale. Wine-theme prints and posters adorning the walls remind you of the tour original attraction to this place. However, fine food selections include various species of eight-ounce Alberta beef Buzzard Burgers, pub grub, and low-priced entrées, such as teriyaki chicken and fettuccine Alfredo. In summer, dine out on the patio. *140 10th Ave. SW, tel. 403/264–6959. No reservations. Dress: casual. AE, DC, MC, V. Inexpensive.*

Silver Dragon. A Chinatown institution for more than 20 years, the huge L-shape dining room is mellowed out by soft carpeting and delicate Chinese paintings. The menu includes standard beef, pork, and poultry dishes but shines on concoctions of rock cod, crab, abalone, cuttlefish, and other seafood. Dim sum lunch is featured daily. *106 3rd Ave. SE, tel. 403/264–5326. No reservations. Dress: casual. AE, DC, MC, V. Inexpensive.*

Lodging **Delta Bow Valley.** The bright, new 24-story high rise occupies a relatively quiet street on the southern edge of downtown. The pinkish lobby is sunny and full of lush foliage. Decent-size contemporary rooms, with rose-and-green furnishings, have good views on upper floors. For the brightest and most colorful units, request a room with a northern exposure. *209 4th Ave. SE, T2G 0C6, tel. 403/266–1980 or 800/268–1133. 400 rooms. Facilities: 2 restaurants, 2 lounges, indoor pool, saunas, exercise room, nonsmoking floors. AE, DC, MC, V. Very Expensive.*

Skyline Plaza Hotel. This is a business-class hotel with an incredibly convenient location in the heart of downtown. The warm, inviting lobby works well with the clean pastel-and-maroon-toned rooms. Surrounded by and connected to the convention center, Glenbow Museum, and the Calgary Centre for Performing Arts, the hotel appeals to executive and leisure travelers. *110 9th Ave., T2G 5A6, tel. 403/266–7331 or 800/648–7200. 387 rooms. Facilities: 2 restaurants, 2 lounges, indoor pool, sauna, fitness club, racquetball arrangements at nearby club, nonsmoking floors. AE, DC, MC, V. Very Expensive.*

★ **Westin Hotel.** The luxury high rise in the midst of downtown connects to most other important structures via Calgary's Plus 15 pedway system. Renovated in 1987, the rooms—especially those in the Tower Section—are large and furnished with tasteful contemporary furniture and are dominated by pastel peach tones and neutrals. Rooftop pool, poolside buffet, and sauna offer great city views and light breakfasts. Owl's Nest (*see* Dining, above) is among the best in town, and Lobby Court features Fitness Buffet breakfasts. *320 4th Ave. SW, T2P 2S6, tel. 403/266–1611 or 800/228–3000. 525 rooms, including nonsmoking rooms. Facilities: 2 restaurants, 2 lounges, indoor pool, fitness club, sauna. AE, DC, MC, V. Very Expensive.*

★ **Palliser.** The downtown area of every Canadian city has a grand old railroad hotel, and the Canadian Pacific Palliser (opened 1914) is Calgary's. The enormous lobby is paneled in dark wood and festooned with twinkling chandeliers. Guest rooms may have quirky shapes, but all are newly renovated with classic furnishings, ornate moldings, and high ceilings. *133 9th Ave. SW, T2P 2M3, tel. 403/262–1234 or 800/828–7447. 404 rooms. Facilities: restaurant, bar, exercise room, nonsmoking floor. AE, DC, MC, V. Expensive.*

Carriage House. Located about 9.7 kilometers (6 miles) south of City Centre, this unique, locally owned property has a lobby with fish tanks, caged songbirds, and a waterfall. Room decor is comfortably mismatched. Nighttime entertainment options include a disco/rock club, country-and-western saloon, and English pub. Guests get discounts at nearby Family Leisure Centre (*see* Sports, above). *9030 Macleod Trail S, T2H 0M4, tel. in U.S. call collect, 403/253–1101; or 800/661–9566. 175 rooms, including nonsmoking rooms. Facilities: 3 restaurants, 3 bars, outdoor pool, sauna. AE, DC, MC, V. Moderate.*

Prince Royal Inn. This 28-story high rise has quite a lot going for it: downtown location, all-suite (studios, one- and two-bedrooms) accommodations with fully equipped kitchens, free parking, free Continental breakfast, and health club. Large rooms with kitchens make it a great deal for families. *618 5th Ave. SW, T2P 0M7, tel. 403/263–0520; in Canada 800/661–1592. 300 suites. Facilities: restaurant, bar, health club with sauna, exercise equipment, convenience store, florist, dry cleaner, nonsmoking floors. AE, DC, MC, V. Moderate.*

Ramada Inn. This convenient and comfortable property is located on the northeast side of town a few minutes from Calgary International Airport. Bright rooms are large, have standard furnishings, and are tastefully decorated with a rose-and-mauve scheme. *1250 McKinnon Dr. NE, T2E 7T7, tel. 403/230–1999 or 800/228–5151. 168 rooms, including nonsmoking rooms. Facilities: restaurant, bar, indoor pool, sauna, sun deck. AE, DC, MC, V. Moderate.*

Relax Inns. Like most units of Canada's first economy chain, the two Calgary properties have clean, efficient rooms, indoor pools, family-style restaurants, and suburban locations. The design exudes taste and warmth; blues and maroons enhance the appeal of the modern furnishings. *Calgary Airport: 2750 Sunridge Blvd. NE, T1Y 3C2, tel. 403/291–1260 or 800/661–9563. 203 rooms; nonsmoking rooms available. Facilities: restaurant, indoor pool, games room. AE, DC, MC, V. Inexpensive. Calgary South: 9206 Macleod Trail S, T2J 0P5, tel. 403/253–7070 or 800/661–9563. 260 rooms. Facilities: restaurant, indoor pool, games arcade. AE, DC, MC, V. Inexpensive.*

The Arts and Nightlife

Tickets for events at the Calgary Centre for the Performing Arts, Jubilee Auditorium, and Olympic Saddledome are available at BASS ticket outlets at Calgary Centre box office, The Bay, Sears, or by telecharge (tel. 403/270–6700 or 403/266–8888).

The Arts Calgary's showcase theater facility is the **Calgary Centre for**
Theater **the Performing Arts** (205 8th Ave. SE, Calgary, tel. 403/294–7455), with three modern auditoriums in two contiguous historic buildings. Productions by resident Alberta Theatre Projects (ATP) of principally Canadian playwrights are highly recommended. More than 20 local companies use the stage of the **Pumphouse Theatre** (2140 9th Ave. SW, Calgary, tel. 403/263–0079). The **University of Calgary Theatre** (Reeve Theatre, 2500 University Drive NW, Calgary, tel. 403/220–4900) features classic and contemporary works.

Music and Dance **Calgary Philharmonic Orchestra** (tel. 403/294–7420) concerts, chamber groups, and a broad spectrum of music and dance shows are performed in the 1,755-seat Jack Singer Concert Hall in the **Calgary Centre for the Performing Arts** (205 8th Ave. SE, Calgary, tel. 403/294–7455). The larger **Jubilee Auditorium** (1415 14th Ave. NW, Calgary, tel. 403/297–8000) hosts the Alberta Ballet company and a variety of classical music, opera, dance, pop, and rock concerts. Concerts are also performed at **University of Calgary Theatres** (2500 University Dr. NW, Calgary, tel. 403/220–4900).

Nightlife **Loose Moose** (2003 McKnight Blvd. NE, Calgary, tel. 403/291–
Bars and Clubs 5682) features competitive "Theatresports" and all sorts of fun and games.

Casinos In Calgary, play blackjack, roulette, and wheel of fortune at **River Park Casino** (1919 Macleod Trail S, Calgary, tel. 403/269–

6771), **Cash Casino Place** (4040B Blackfoot Trail SE, Calgary,
tel. 403/287–1635), **Tower Casino** in Tower Centre, and **Frontier
Casino** at the top of Big Four in Stampede Park.

Comedy The Calgary outpost of **Yuk Yuk's** (Blackfoot Inn, 5940 Blackfoot Trail, Calgary, tel. 403/258–2028), Canada's comedy chain,
has name performers from Canada and the United States. **Jest-
er's** (239 10th Ave. SE, Calgary, tel. 403/269–6669) has comedians and Wednesday-night open mikes.

Music Calgary's **Sparky's Diner** (1006 11th Ave. SW, Calgary, tel.
403/244–4888) presents a pleasing array of blues, rock, folk,
and big-band performers. The Casablanca-style **Cafe Calabash**
(107 10A St. NW, Calgary, tel. 403/270–2266) has live jazz every night but Sunday. **Cover to Cover** (738 11th Ave. SW, Calgary, tel. 403/262–1933) also features jazz musicians. For
Western sights and sounds, head for **Ranchman's** (9615 Macleod Trail S, Calgary, tel. 403/253–1100) or the **Longhorn Restaurant & Dance Hall** (9631 Macleod Trail S, Calgary, tel. 403/
258–0528). The **Rocking Horse Saloon** (24 7400 Macleod Trail
Trail S, Calgary, tel. 403/255–4646) also features country music every night but Sunday. Dance to Top-40 high-tech at **Raf-
fles** (5940 Blackfoot Trail SE, Calgary, tel. 403/252–2253).

Excursion from Calgary: Southern Alberta

Head east on the Trans-Canada Highway (Route 1) out of Calgary and enter the vast Canadian prairie of seemingly endless
expanses of flat country in every direction. About 30 kilometers (19 miles) east of Calgary, turn north on Highway 9 and
drive 70 kilometers (43 miles) to **Drumheller,** a town that mined
coal until oil and natural gas were discovered in the late 1940s.
The small town is situated in the rugged valley of the Red Deer
River, where millions of years of wind and water erosion exposed the "strike" that produced what amounts to present-day
Drumheller's major industry: dinosaurs.

The barren lunar landscape of stark badlands and eerie rock
cylinders (called hoodoos) may seem an ideal setting for the
herds of dinosaurs that stalked the countryside 75 million years
ago, but in fact, when the dinosaurs were here the area had a
semitropical climate and verdant marshlands not unlike the
Florida Everglades. You learn this and more geological and paleontological history of Alberta at the **Tyrell Museum of Paleontology.** Participate in hands-on exhibits and meet the local
hero, Albertosaurus, a smaller, fiercer version of Tyrannosaurus rex that was the first dino discovered around here.
*Hwy. 838, 6 km (4 mi) northwest of Drumheller, tel. 403/823–
7707; in Calgary, 403/294–1992. Admission: $5 adults; $2 children 5 and over. Tues. free. Open mid-May–early Sept., daily
9–9; mid-Sept.–mid-May, Tues.–Sun. 10–5.*

Capitalizing on its rich paleontological past, Drumheller has a
number of dinosaur-related businesses. **Reptile World** (Hwy. 9,
tel. 403/823–TOAD) boasts a crowd-pleasing collection of poi-
sonous snakes; the **Homestead Antique Museum** (Hwy. 838, tel.
403/823–2600) packs 4,000 Indian artifacts, medical instruments, period clothing, and other items of Canadiana into a
roadside quonset hut; **Ollie's Rock & Fossil Shop** (off Hwy. 575,
tel. 403/823–6144) depicts life-size dinosaurs in a badlands setting and sells a vast selection of fossils, bones, rocks, and petri-
fied wood. No visit to Drumheller is complete without a family

portrait beside the comic-book Tyrannosaurus rex guarding the Highway 9 bridge over the Red Deer River.

Continuing the dinosaur tour of Alberta requires a 142-kilometer (90-mile) drive south from Drumheller on Highway 56. Go east on the Trans-Canada Highway (Route 1), north at Brooks on Highway 873, east on Highway 544, and follow the signs to **Dinosaur Provincial Park,** a 15,000-acre park encompassing Canada's baddest badlands. Soft sedimentary rock was deposited by 72-million-year-old rivers and sculpted into starkly fascinating shapes by melting waters of the Ice Age that occurred a mere 14,000 years ago. Incessant wind, water, and frost erosion have exposed one of the world's most important collections of fossilized bones. Roads access some *in situ* fossil sites; two looped interpretive trails lead to more, with guided tours on weekends. During summer, 90-minute bus tours explore backcountry areas from which visitors are otherwise restricted. The cacti bloom from June through August. The **Tyrell Museum of Paleontology Field Station** in the park offers a concise orientation to the prehistoric world. Note: Since concessions are limited, bring a lunch to eat in one of the picnic areas. *Hwy. 551, Patricia, 48 km (30 mi) northeast of Brooks, tel. 403/378–4587. Admission: $1.50. Tyrell Field Station open May 20–Sept. 2, daily 9–9 winter, Wed.–Sun. 10–5.*

Time Out   Throughout the year the **Patricia Water Hole** (Main St., tel. 403/378–4647) in the Patricia Hotel is the renowned Wild West setting for Alberta beefsteak, with all the trimmings and 100% buffalo burgers (buffalo steaks available with 24-hour notice).

Medicine Hat lies about 95 kilometers (60 miles) southeast of Patricia on the Trans-Canada Highway. Roadside views consist of small well pumps and storage tanks amid endless expanses of "prairie wool," principally spear and blue grama grass. There is much local lore concerning the origin of the name Medicine Hat, but one legend tells of a battle waged between Cree and Blackfoot Indians; the Cree fought bravely until their medicine man deserted, losing his headdress in the South Saskatchewan River. The site's name, "Saamis," meaning "medicine man's hat," was later translated by white settlers into Medicine Hat.

Medicine Hat is a prosperous and scenic city built on high banks overlooking the South Saskatchewan River. Alberta's fifth-largest city's wealth derives from vast deposits of natural gas below, some of which gets piped up to fuel quaint gas lamps in the turn-of-the-century downtown area. Prosperity is similarly communicated by the striking glass-sided **Medicine Hat City Hall.** *1st St. SE and 6th Ave. SE, tel. 403/529–8100. Open weekdays 8:30–4:30. Guided group and self-guided tours available.*

But Medicine Hat's greatest achievement was turning the land alongside the South Saskatchewan River and Seven Persons Creek into parkland and environmental preserves interconnected by 15 kilometers (9⅓ miles) of walking, biking, and cross-country ski trails. Detailed trail maps are available at the **Tourist Information Centre** (8 Gehring Rd. SW, tel. 403/527–6422). Other Medicine Hat attractions include a half-mile of falling water at **Riverside Waterslide** (Hwy. 1 and Power House Rd., tel. 403/529–6218) and **Echo Dale Regional Park** (Holsom Rd. off Hwy. 3, tel. 403/529–6225), the riverside setting for swimming, boating, fishing, a 1900s farm, and an historic coal mine.

For a side trip out of Medicine Hat, take Highway 1 east and Highway 41 south for the 70-kilometer (43-mile) drive to **Cypress Hills Provincial Park.** Alberta's second-largest provincial park, Cypress Hills is a 200-square-kilometer (77-square-mile) oasis of hills and tall lodgepole pines. Elkwater Townsite provides a full complement of services. The park is contiguous to Cypress Hills Provincial Park, Saskatchewan (*see* Excursion from Regina, above), which also has accommodations and visitor amenities. *Visitor Centre, Elkwater Townsite, tel. 403/893-3833. Open late June–Sept. 2. Administration Bldg., tel. 403/893-3777. Open weekdays 8:15–4:30.*

Head west out of Medicine Hat toward **Lethbridge** on Crowsnest Highway (Rte. 3). Lethbridge, Alberta's third-largest city, is an 1870s coal boomtown that is now the center of agriculture, oil, and gas. The main attraction, **Fort Whoop-Up,** part of the **Indian Battle Park,** is a reconstruction of a southern Alberta whiskey fort. Along with weapons, relics, and a 15-minute audiovisual historical presentation, Fort Whoop-Up has wagon-train tours of the river valley and other points of local historical interest. *Indian Battle Park, Whoop-Up Dr. and Oldman River, tel. 403/329-0444. Fort Whoop-Up admission free. Open late May–Labor Day, daily 10–8; Labor Day–late May weekdays, noon–4, weekends noon–5.*

Henderson Lake Park, 3 kilometers (2 miles) east on the other side of downtown Lethbridge, is filled with lush trees, a golf course, baseball stadium, tennis courts, a swimming pool, and a 60-acre man-made lake. Alongside the lake, **Nikka Yuko Japanese Gardens** is a tranquil setting for manicured trees and shrubs, miniature pools and waterfalls, a teahouse, and pebble designs constructed in Japan and reassembled alongside Henderson Lake. *Henderson Lake Park, Mayor Magrath Dr. and S. Parkside Dr., tel. 403/320-3020; Gardens, tel. 403/328-3511. Admission: $2 adults, $1 senior citizens and students 12 and over. Open mid-May–mid-June, daily 9–5; mid-June–Aug., daily 9–8; Sept.–early Oct., daily 9–5.*

Travel west along Highway 3 for 50 kilometers (31 miles) to **Fort Macleod.** Southern Alberta's oldest settlement, the installation was founded by the Mounties in 1874 to maintain order among the farmers, Indians, whiskey vendors, and ranchers beginning to settle here. The wood-frame buildings (pre-1900) and the more recent sandstone-and-brick buildings have established this as Alberta's first historic area. For information about guided and self-guided tours, visit the information booth (tel. 403/553-2500) beside Fort Macleod Museum. An authentic reconstruction of the 1874 fort, **Fort Macleod Museum** grants almost equal exhibitory weight to settlers, Indians, old North West Mounted Police, and today's Royal Canadian Mounted Police. *25th St., tel. 403/553-4703. Admission: $3 adults, $2.50 seniors, $1 students 13–18, 50¢ children 6–12. Open May–June 14 and Sept. 3–Oct. 15, daily 9–5; June 15–Sept. 2, daily 9–7.*

Dining For rates, *see* Winnipeg Dining and Lodging, above.

Lethbridge **Cafe Martinique.** Located in the El Rancho Motor Hotel, this locally renowned fine dining spot puts the emphasis on aged steaks and chateaubriand made with tender Alberta beef. Live music and dancing take place most nights. Try the El Rancho coffee shop for less expensive, more informal meals. *526 Mayor Magrath Dr., tel. 403/327–5701. Reservations advised. Jacket advised. AE, DC, MC, V. Expensive.*

Sven Eriksen's Family Restaurant. The homey, colonial-style place features hearty and tasty versions of Canadian prairie standards like chicken, seafood, and an especially good prime rib. "Family Restaurant" label notwithstanding, there's a full bar. *1715 Mayor Magrath Dr., tel. 403/328–7756. Reservations advised, especially on weekends. Dress: casual. AE, MC, V. Moderate.*

Lodging
Lethbridge

Lethbridge Lodge Hotel. This modern-day lodge has great Oldman River views and a pleasant tropical courtyard. *320 Scenic Dr., T1J 4B4, tel. 800/661–1232 or 403/328–1123. 190 rooms, including nonsmoking rooms. Facilities: restaurant, lounge, indoor pool, whirlpool. AE, MC, V. Moderate.*

Parkside Inn. This comfortable hotel is a good bargain within walking distance of Henderson Lake Park. *1009 Mayor Magrath Dr., T1K 2P7, tel. 403/328–2366. 64 rooms, including nonsmoking rooms. Facilities: restaurant, lounge. AE, MC, V. Inexpensive.*

Medicine Hat

Medicine Hat Lodge. Situated on the edge of town adjacent to a shopping mall, this hotel has several rooms with inward views of the indoor pool, whirlpool, and huge, curving waterslide. The Atrium Dining Room serves fine Continental meals. J.D.'s is a hotel country-and-western spot. *1051 Glen Dr. SE, T1B 3T8, tel. 403/529–2222 or 800/661–8095. 190 rooms, including nonsmoking rooms. Facilities: 2 restaurants, 2 lounges, indoor pool, whirlpool, waterslide, steam room. AE, DC, MC, V. Moderate.*

Edmonton

Lucky Edmonton is a recidivist boomtown that never seems to go bust. The first boom arrived in 1795, when the North West Company and Hudson's Bay Company both established fur-trading posts in the area. Boom II came in 1897, when Edmonton became principal outfitter on the overland "All Canadian Route" to the Yukon goldfields; as a result, Edmonton was named capital when the province of Alberta was formed in 1905. The latest and greatest of booms began on February 13, 1947, when oil was discovered in Leduc, 40 kilometers (25 miles) to the southwest. More than 10,000 wells were eventually drilled within 100 kilometers (62 miles) of the city and with them fields of refineries and supply depots. By 1965 Edmonton had solidified its role as the "Oil Capital of Canada."

More interesting is how wisely Edmonton has spread the wealth to create a beautiful and livable city. Shunning the uncontrolled development of some other oil boomtowns, Edmonton turned its great natural resource, the North Saskatchewan River Valley, into a 27-kilometer (17-mile) greenbelt of parks and recreational facilities. With a population of 850,000, Edmonton is the largest northerly city in the Americas and the fourth-largest city in Canada. It is also Canada's largest city in land area—681 hectares (270 square miles). As the seat of the Alberta government and home to the University of Alberta, Edmonton has an unusually sophisticated atmosphere that has generated many fine restaurants and a thriving arts community. Its premier attraction, the West

Edmonton Mall, is a year-round drawing card for shoppers and families, complete with facilities ranging from Fantasyland shopping center to a hotel, from a cinema complex to a water park.

Important Addresses and Numbers

Tourist Information The main office of the **Edmonton Convention and Tourism Authority Visitor Information Centre** (97th St. and Jasper Ave., tel. 403/988–5455 or 403/422–5505) is located downtown at the Edmonton Convention Centre. The office is open mid-May–September, daily 8:30–4:30; September–mid-May, weekdays 8:30–4:30. Other offices are open around Edmonton; for locations and times call the main office.

Emergencies Dial 911 for **police, fire, ambulance,** and **poison center.**

Hospitals Emergency rooms are located at the **Royal Alexandra Hospital** (10240 Kingsway Ave., tel. 403/477–4111) and **University of Alberta Hospitals** (8440 112th St., tel. 403/492–8822).

Dentists For 24-hour dental care, contact **Tridont Dental Service** (472 Southgate Shopping Centre, 111th St. and 51st Ave., tel. 403/434–9566.

Late-night Pharmacy **Mid-Niter Drugs** (11408 Jasper Ave., tel. 403/482–1011) is open until midnight.

Arriving and Departing by Plane

Edmonton has two airports, though most international flights and long-haul domestic flights use **Edmonton International Airport.** Short-haul flights, mainly to neighboring provinces, use **Edmonton Municipal Airport,** just north of downtown. Along with the major Canadian airlines (Air Canada, Canadian Airlines International), Edmonton is served by American, America West, Delta, and Northwest.

Taxi rides from Edmonton International can be costly, but The Grey Goose Airporter (tel. 403/463–7520) provides frequent service between the airport and major downtown hotels. Fare is $9 one way, $16 round-trip. Grey Goose also provides service between Edmonton International and Edmonton Municipal Airport or West Edmonton Mall ($10 one way, $16 round-trip).

Getting Around

By Bus/LRT Edmonton Transit (tel. 403/421–INFO) operates a comprehensive system of buses throughout the area and a light rail transit (**LRT**) line from downtown to the northeast side of the city. The fare is $1.35 for adults, 80¢ for senior citizens and children 6–16; transfers are free. Adult fares are $1.60 during weekday rush hours. Buses operate from 5:30 AM to 2 AM. The LRT is free in the downtown area (between Churchill and Grandin stations) weekdays 9–3 and Saturday 9–6. The **Downtown Information Centre** above Central LRT Station (100A St. and Jasper Ave.) provides free information, timetables, and maps, weekdays 9–5.

By Taxi Taxis tend to be costly: $1.90 for the first 125 meters (¹⁄₁₅ mile) and 10¢ for each additional 125 meters. Cabs may be hailed on the street, but phoning is recommended. Call **Alberta Co-op**

Taxi (tel. 403/425–8310), **Checker** (tel. 403/455–2211), or **Yellow** (tel. 403/462–3456).

Guided Tours

From early May to early October three **Royal Tours** (tel. 403/ 424–8687) itineraries hit the high points of Edmonton. Day tours of the Alberta countryside are also offered. **Klondike Jet Boats** (tel. 403/451–4263) ply the North Saskatchewan River, May–October. **Landing Trail House** (tel. 403/931–3370 or 403/ 450–0267) offers customized horse-drawn carriage tours for $60 per hour.

Exploring Downtown Edmonton

Numbers in the margin correspond to points of interest on the Downtown Edmonton map.

The Edmonton street system is a straight grid with numbered streets running north–south and numbered avenues running east–west. Meeting at the center are 100th Street and 100th Avenue; Edmontonians often use the last digit or two as shorthand for the complete number: the Inn on 7th is on 107th Street; the 9th Street Bistro can be found on 109th Street. Edmonton's "Main Drag" is Jasper Avenue, which runs east–west through the center of downtown.

The city's striking physical feature, where most recreational facilities are located, is the broad green valley of the North Saskatchewan River, running diagonally northeast–southwest through the city center. The downtown area lies just north of the river, between 95th and 109th streets.

❶ Start exploring downtown Edmonton from the top: at **Vista 33,** the 33rd floor of the **Alberta Government Telephone** (AGT) corporate headquarters. It's not the tallest building in town (that honor goes to ManuLife Place at 34 stories), but it's high enough for you to appreciate the South Saskatchewan River and to overlook 4,000 square kilometers (2,500 square miles) of (mostly flat) Alberta countryside. In addition to the view, Vista 33 includes the **AGT Man and Telecommunications Museum,** which traces the history of the telephone. *10020 100th St., tel. 403/493–3333. Admission: 50¢ adults and children, senior citizens and preschoolers free. Open daily 10–8.*

Walk north on 100th Street and turn right on Jasper beside the MacDonald Hotel, a grand old railroad hotel that had been closed since 1983 for major renovations but reopened in mid-**❷** 1991. Walk two blocks to the **Edmonton Convention Centre** (9797 Jasper Ave., tel. 403/421–9797), a most unconventional building filled with surprises. On street level the building houses the **Edmonton Tourism Visitor Information Centre** (*see* Important Addresses and Numbers, above), a repository of useful brochures and advice. It's all literally downhill from there, since the Centre has been built onto a slope with various terraced levels accessed by glass-enclosed escalators with great views of the North Saskatchewan River valley. The Pedway Level houses **Canada's Aviation Hall of Fame,** with exhibits and artifacts from Canada's flying past. On Exhibition Level check out the **Canadian Country Music Hall of Honor,** actually a wall filled with plaques memorializing good old boys like Hank Snow, Wilf Carter, and Orval "The Canadian Plow-

Downtown Edmonton

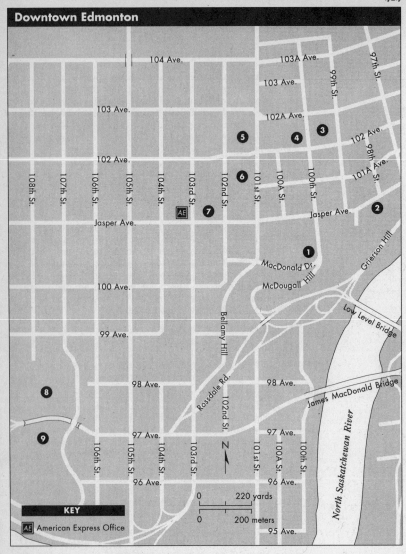

104 Ave.
103A Ave.
97th St.
103 Ave.
99th St.
103 Ave.
102A Ave.
5
4
3
102 Ave.
102 Ave.
98th St.
101A Ave.
108th St.
107th St.
106th St.
105th St.
104th St.
103rd St.
102nd St.
6
101st St.
100A St.
100th St.
Jasper Ave.
2
AE
7
Jasper Ave.
1
MacDonald Dr.
Grierson Hill
McDougall Hill
100 Ave.
Low Level Bridge
Bellamy Hill
99 Ave.
98 Ave.
98 Ave.
Rossdale Rd.
James MacDonald Bridge
8
102nd St.
97 Ave.
97 Ave.
9
N
106th St.
105th St.
104th St.
103rd St.
101st St.
100A St.
100th St.
96 Ave.
96 Ave.

North Saskatchewan River

0   220 yards
0   200 meters

95 Ave.

KEY

AE American Express Office

Alberta Government
Centre, **8**
Alberta Legislature
Building, **9**
The Bay, **7**
Eaton Centre, **5**

Edmonton Convention
Centre, **2**
Edmonton Square, **4**
ManuLife Place, **6**
Sir Winston Churchill
Square, **3**
Vista 33, **1**

boy" Prophet. *Hall of Fame, tel. 403/424–2458. Admission: $3 adults, $1 senior citizens, 50¢ students, $7 families. Open Tues.–Thurs. 10–5, Fri. 10–8, weekends noon–5.*

Return to 99th Street and turn north to the **Civic Centre,** a six-block area that incorporates many of Edmonton's major institutions; Civic Centre structures surround **Sir Winston Churchill Square.** The largest theater complex in Canada, the **Citadel Theatre** (*see* The Arts and Nightlife, below) houses five different theaters (plus workshops and classrooms) and an indoor garden with waterfall. Across 99th Street the **Edmonton Public Library** (7 Sir Winston Churchill Sq., tel. 403/423–2331) augments books and art exhibits with a lively round of activities in the Children's Art Department.

As you cross 102nd Avenue, glance east at **Chinatown Gate,** a symbol of friendship between Edmonton and sister city Harbin, China; it spans the portal to Edmonton's meager Chinatown. A new city hall was recently constructed across the square from the **Edmonton Art Gallery,** site of more than 30 yearly exhibits of classical and contemporary art from Canada and the rest of the world. *2 Sir Winston Churchill Sq., tel. 403/ 422–6223. Admission: $3 adults, $1.50 senior citizens and youths, children 12 and under free. Open Mon.–Wed. 10:30–5, Thur. and Fri. 10:30–8, weekends and holidays 11–5; free Thurs. after 4.*

Directly west of Churchill Square begins a maze of multilevel shopping malls, department stores, cinemas, and office buildings—all climatically controlled and interconnected by a network of tunnels and second-floor pedways. Cross 100th Street to enter **Edmonton Square;** head west to **Eaton Centre,** with a miniature golf course in the middle of the mall; south of 102nd Avenue are the shops of **ManuLife Place;** and on 102nd Street you'll find the domain of one of Canada's most powerful institutions, **The Bay,** contemporary retail descendant of the Hudson's Bay Company (*see* Shopping, below).

Time Out For a change of scenery, exit briefly to **Boardwalk Market** (102nd Ave. and 103rd St., tel. 403/424–6297). The bright and airy renovated historic block encompasses an indoor-outdoor market with everything from Mongolian beef to steamed clams and pastries, all accompanied by a lively assemblage of street entertainers.

Emerging from The Bay on Jasper Avenue, enter the LRT station at 103rd or 104th Street for the ride to Grandin Station and the seat of the Alberta government. The **Alberta Government Centre** (109th St. and 97th Ave.) encompasses several hectares of carefully manicured gardens and fountains highlighted by the Government Greenhouse (tel. 403/427–7445). The **Alberta Legislature Building** is a stately 1912 Edwardian structure overlooking the river on the site of an early trading post. Frequent free tours of the building help to explain the intricacies of the Albertan and Canadian systems of government. *109th St. and 97th Ave., tel. 403/427–7362. Admission and tours free. Open May 20–Sept. 2, weekdays 9–8:30, weekends 9–4:30.*

Other Points of Interest

The **Muttart Conservatory** is one of the most important botanical facilities in North America. Separate greenhouses each contain flora of a different climate: arid, tropical, temperate. A show pavilion features special seasonal floral displays. *9626 96A St., tel. 403/428–5226. Admission: $4 adults, $3 senior citizens and youths 13–18, $2 children. Open June–Aug., daily 11–9; Sept.–May, Sun. Wed. 11–9, Thur.–Sat. 11–6.*

The **Old Strathcona Historic Area** (the area surrounding 104th Street and 82nd Avenue) is a district of restored houses and shops built mainly when Strathcona Town amalgamated with Edmonton, in 1912. The low buildings and wide streets have a decidedly Old West air, and Old Strathcona is a good place to get out and wander. For a more determined exploration, pick up a walking tour map at the Old Strathcona Foundation. *8331 104th St., tel. 403/433–5866. Open weekdays 8:30–4:30.*

The **Provincial Museum of Alberta** hosts exhibits concerning paleontology, geological evolution, native crafts and life, and pioneer settlement. Displays of Canadian wildlife in near-natural settings are especially informative. *12845 102nd Ave., tel. 403/453–9100. Suggested donation: $2 adults, $5 families, senior citizens and children free. Open May 20–Sept. 2, daily 9–8; Sept. 3–May 19, Tues.–Sun. 9–5, Wed. 9–8, closed Mon.*

The **Edmonton Space Sciences Centre** explores the heavens with a stunning variety of high-tech techniques. Standing exhibits and a fascinating science shop are always of interest, but the star attractions include laser-light concerts and IMAX films of an appropriately celestial nature. *11211 142nd St., tel. 403/451–7722. Admission: exhibits free; IMAX or Star Theatre shows, $5.50 adults, $4.25 senior citizens and children over 12, $3.25 children 3–12; Laser Show, $5.50 adults, $4.25 senior citizens and children over 12, $3.25 children 3–12; 2-theater package, $8.50 adults, $3.50 senior citizens and children. Open late June–Sept. 2, Sun.–Thurs. 10–10, Fri. and Sat. 10–10:30; Sept. 3–late June, Tues.–Sat. 10–10, Sun. noon–10, closed Mon.*

Fort Edmonton Park is home to an authentic re-creation of several periods in Edmonton history. There are a fur press and re-enactments of shooting matches from the old Fort Edmonton days; blacksmith shops, saloons, and jails along 1885 Street; photo studios and a firehouse on 1905 Street; and relatively modern conveniences on 1920 Street. Horsewagon, streetcar, stagecoach, and pony rides are available; a farmers' market operates on summer Sundays. *Whitemud and Fox Drs., tel. 403/ 435–0755. Admission: $6 adults, $4.50 senior citizens and youths 13–17, $2.75 children 12 and under, $17.50 families. Open mid-May–June, weekdays 9:30–4, weekends 10–6; July 1–Sept. 2, daily 10–6; Sept. 3–Thanksgiving (second Mon. in Oct.), Sun. and holidays 11–5; closed Thanksgiving–mid-May.*

West Edmonton Mall, acclaimed by the *Guinness Book of World Records* as the world's largest mall, is Edmonton's preeminent attraction. Its sheer magnitude and variety transform it from a mere shopping center to an indoor city with high-rent districts, blue-collar strips, and hidden byways waiting to be discovered. The credentials shout for themselves. There are 800 stores, including 11 major department stores, 19 movie theaters, and 110 places to eat, but the mall also contains a Fantasyland amusement park; an ice-skating rink; a replica of Columbus's ship the *Santa Maria;* an 18-hole miniature-golf course; the Deep Sea Adventure submarine ride and dolphin show; the five-acre World Waterpark water amusement park; a luxury hotel (*see* Lodging, below); auto dealerships; a playhouse; a bingo parlor; a chapel; and much more. If you don't feel like walking the Mall, rent an electric scooter or hitch a ride on a rickshaw. *8770 170th St., tel. 403/444–5200. Attraction costs: Fantasyland, day pass—$18.95 adults, $7.95 senior citizens, $15.95 children under 46 inches, $49.95 families of up to 5, individual ride tickets 80¢ with rides costing 1–7 tickets. World Waterpark, day pass—$18.95 adults, $15.95 senior citizens and children 3–10, $49.95 families of up to 5. Deep Sea Adventure, $11.50 adults, senior citizens, children 3–10, $36.95 families. Open mid-June–Sept. 2, Mon.–Sat. 10–10, Sun. noon–8; Sept. 3–mid-June, Sun.–Thurs. noon–8, Fri. and Sat. 10–10.*

What to See and Do with Children

Edmonton Space Sciences Centre (*see* Other Points of Interest, above).

Fort Edmonton Park (*see* Other Points of Interest, above).

Old Strathcona Model and Toy Museum (8603 104th St., tel. 403/ 433–4512) features playthings from the past.

Valley Zoo (134th St. and Buena Vista Rd., tel. 403/483–5511) is a small but imaginative zoo in riverside Laurier Park that uses well-known storybook settings with exotic species.

William Hawrelak Park (off Groat Rd., just south of North Saskatchewan River, tel. 403/428–3559) invites children only—or adults in their company—to fish in this rainbow trout–stocked pond. Park includes paddleboats and adventure playground.

West Edmonton Mall (*see* Other Points of Interest, above).

Whitemud Drive Amusement Park (7411 51st Ave., tel. 403/ 465–1190) features go-carts, bumper-boats, miniature golf, and batting cages.

Wild Waters Waterslide Park (21415 103rd Ave., tel. 403/447– 3900) offers lots of wet fun on the western edge of the city.

Shopping

Malls and Shopping Districts   In the heart of **downtown,** between 100th and 103rd streets, is a complex of shopping centers (Eaton Centre, 120 stores; ManuLife Place, 65 stores; Edmonton Centre, 140 stores), and department stores (The Bay, Eaton's, Woodward's) connected by tunnels or second-level pedways. **West Edmonton Mall** (87th Ave. and 170th St.; *see* Other Points of Interest, above) has 800 retail establishments, including such department stores as Sears, The Bay, Eaton's, Woodward's, Zeller's, Ikea (furniture), and Canadian Tire. **Strathcona Square** (8150 105th St., tel. 403/424–6060) in the Old Strathcona Town (*see* Other Points of Interest, above) 1913-era post office has been converted into a cheerful market filled with restaurants, food stalls, and enticing boutiques. **High Street/124th Street** (along 124th and 125th streets between 102nd and 109th avenues) is an outdoor shopping area full of boutiques, bistros, bookstores, and galleries.

Sports

Participant Sports
Bicycling and Jogging
The North Saskatchewan River valley is the longest stretch of urban parkland in Canada. For information about jogging and cycling trails call the **River Valley Outdoor Centre** (10125 97th Ave., Edmonton, tel. 403/428–3033).

Health and Fitness Clubs
The **Kinsmen Sports Centre** (9100 Walterdale Rd., Edmonton, tel. 403/428–5350) and **Mill Woods Recreation Centre** (7207 28th Ave., Edmonton, tel. 403/428–2888) have swimming pools and a variety of facilities for the entire family.

Spectator Sports
Hockey
The **Edmonton Oilers** play National Hockey League hockey October–April at the **Northlands Coliseum** (118th Ave. and 74th St., Edmonton, tel. 403/471–2191).

Horse Racing
Northlands Park (112th Ave. and 74th St., Edmonton, tel. 403/471–7378) hosts harness racing from early March to mid-May and from mid-September through November. Thoroughbred racing occupies the summer months, mid-May through early September.

Dining and Lodging

For price categories, *see* Winnipeg Dining and Lodging, above.

Dining
La Boheme. On the historic east side Gibbard Block, this restaurant is fittingly splendid. The cuisine is classic French, prepared with invention and served with solicitous care. The setting features Edwardian pressed-tin ceilings and a French provincial fireplace surrounded by Voltaire chairs. Specialties include lamb sausages, pâté maison, and daily concoctions of fresh fish. *6427 112th Ave., tel. 403/474–5693. Reservations advised. Jacket advised. AE, MC, V. Very Expensive.*

★ **Unheardof Dining Lounge.** Hardly "unheard of" any longer, this is an extremely popular restaurant in an antiques-filled old house. The seven-course prix-fixe dinner changes weekly but is likely to feature game in autumn, poultry or beef the rest of the year. Dinners begin with a light pâté and are punctuated by surprising salads and refreshing sorbets. Desserts, especially the Danish cream-cheese cheesecake, are light and delicious. *9602 82nd Ave., tel. 403/432–0480. Reservations required, often far in advance. Jacket advised. AE, MC, V. Closed lunch Tues.–Sat. Very Expensive.*

Walden's. Dine romantically outside in the sunny garden or within the raw cedar confines of the cozy dining room. The Continental menu spotlights flavorful Alberta beef—try it raw with seed mustard and black pepper—and fresh fish flown in daily from British Columbia. Other good bets include Alberta rabbit, lamb with mustard and garlic, and marinated salmon. The wine list features California; desserts are so-so. *10245 104th St., tel. 403/420–6363. Reservations advised for dinner. Jacket advised. AE, MC, V. Very Expensive.*

Bistro Praha. The decor of table lamps and paintings of Praha (Prague) street scenes makes this European-style café feel as homey as Grandma's living room. Background music is classical, clientele mainly urban young professional. The menu features Eastern European favorites such as cabbage soup, Wiener schnitzel, and *natur schnitzel* (no breading). A rich selection of desserts and a choice from 12 brands of tea makes it perfect for snacks. *10168 100A St. at Jasper Ave., tel. 403/424–4218. No reservations. Dress: casual. AE, DC, MC, V. Expensive.*

La Spiga. Admirable Northern Italian cuisine is served in a flower-filled 1913 home that feels more like Montréal than the western plains. Menu highlights include rack of lamb with grappa, breast of chicken with fresh tomato, and various renditions of veal. Portions are large and accompanied by fettuccine; the wine list is long. *10133 125 St. at 102nd Ave., tel. 403/482–3100. Reservations advised. Jacket advised. AE, MC, V. Closed lunch and Sun. Expensive.*

Bourbon Street. This is actually an assemblage of moderately priced restaurants situated around a cul-de-sac on the main floor of West Edmonton Mall. "Exterior" decor features New Orleans street lamps and wrought-iron balconies. **Café Orleans** serves Cajun/Creole dishes such as jambalaya and oysters. **Sherlock Holmes** is an English pub with imported draft beer and dishes like Mrs. Hudson's Home Made Pies. **Albert's** has deli fare including the Montréal favorite, smoked meat. Other spots include **Zambelli's Pizza & Steak House, Pacific Fish Co.** (*see* below), and, for belly-up-to-the-bar drinking, the **Bourbon Street Saloon.** *West Edmonton Mall, 8770 170th St., Entrance 6. No reservations. Dress: casual. AE, MC, V. Moderate.*

Pacific Fish Company. Three locations satisfy landlocked Edmonton's appetite for fresh seafood with daily fly-ins. Order oysters Rockefeller and whiskey shrimp as appetizers, and anything charbroiled over mesquite turns out fine. Decor varies slightly, but count on the deck flooring, corrugated walls, and nets dangling overhead. *10020 101A Ave., tel. 403/422–0282; Argyll Plaza, 6258 99th St., tel. 403/437–7472; West Edmonton Mall, Bourbon St., Entrance 6, tel. 403/444–1905. Reservations advised. Dress: casual. AE, MC, V. Moderate.*

Vi's. In summer, this old house has outdoor seating on a deck overlooking the river; in winter, tables are warmed by a blazing fire. All year the menu emphasizes the basics: hearty soups, fresh salads, extravagant sandwiches, and desserts—with special mention for chocolate pecan pie. Try Vi's for Sunday champagne brunch. *9712 111th St., tel. 403/482–6402. No reservations. Dress: casual. AE, MC, V. Moderate.*

★ **Chianti.** This extremely popular spot occupies part of the main floor of Strathcona Square, a converted post office in the lively Old Strathcona District. A mostly young crowd gathers for square meals featuring tasty shellfish appetizers, more than 20 varieties of pasta, a couple dozen veal dishes, and a discriminating selection of desserts. Be prepared to wait for seating on weekend evenings. *10501 82nd Ave. S, tel. 403/439–9829. No reservations. Dress: casual. AE, MC, V. Inexpensive.*

Mongolian Food Experience. The "experience" is selecting from a vast buffet of raw meat (lamb, beef, turkey), vegetables (mushrooms, scallions, sprouts, cabbage), and exotic sauces and then having the chef barbecue it for you. Non-"experience" dishes, such as Szechuan beef, lemon chicken, and moo shoo pork, are also available. Decor is bright and unpretentious. *10160 100A St., tel. 403/426–6806; 12520 102nd Ave., tel. 403/452–7367. Reservations advised. Dress: casual. AE, MC, V. Inexpensive.*

Lodging   **Fantasyland Hotel & Resort.** This important component of massive West Edmonton Mall (*see* Other Points of Interest, above) has regular and theme rooms; the latter include Victorian Coach Rooms, where guests sleep in hackney cabs; Roman Rooms, with classic round beds; Truck Rooms, where the bed is the back of a pickup; and Polynesian Rooms, with catamaran beds and waterfalls. All theme rooms have Jacuzzis, and nontheme quarters are comfortable and tidy. *17700 87th Ave., T5T 4V4, tel. 403/444–3000 or 800/661–6454. 354 rooms, 125 theme rooms. Facilities: 3 restaurants; attached to shopping mall with 5-acre water park, miniature golf course, indoor amusement park, 800 shops. AE, DC, MC, V. Very Expensive.*

★ **Hilton International Edmonton.** Formerly the Four Seasons, and a Hilton International property since 1988, this financial-district luxury high rise connects by second-level passageways to five major office buildings and two shopping centers. Rooms, all with bay windows, convey sophistication, with marble table-tops, walnut furniture, and accents of brass—all complimented by the blue-and-gray color scheme. Mezzanine-level Patisserie serves a bargain Loonie Breakfast (coffee and muffin for a buck), and The Rose and Crown is an authentic English pub, perfect for throwing darts and drinking draft beers. *10235 101st St., T5J 3E9, tel. 403/428–7111 or 800/268–9275. 314 rooms. Facilities: 4 restaurants, 2 lounges, indoor pool, whirlpool, saunas, access to exercise room and squash and racquetball courts, nonsmoking floors. AE, DC, MC, V. Very Expensive.*

Westin Hotel. The stunning, brown block structure in the heart of downtown has large, comfortable rooms that are tastefully decorated with attractive artwork. The atrium lobby, with a decorative mobile, trees, and plants, conveys comfort and luxury; beige-and-pastel rooms, in keeping with the hotel's outward appearance, are equally sophisticated, down to the Caswell and Massey toiletries. The experienced staff speaks a total of 29 languages. The Carvery serves some of the finest beef in the downtown area. *10135 100th St., T5J 0Z1, tel. 403/426–3636 or 800/228–3000. 420 rooms. Facilities: 2 restaurants, 2 lounges, indoor pool, sauna, whirlpool, nonsmoking floors. AE, DC, MC, V. Very Expensive.*

★ **Edmonton House.** The cylindrical design creates oddly shaped but large and comfortable one- and two-bedroom suites. All units have balconies with views of the skyline or river valley, and kitchens are fully equipped (down to a toaster). A small mezzanine-level convenience store supplies basic essentials. Free Continental breakfast is provided every morning. Weekend and long-term rates are available. *10205 100th Ave., T5J 4B5, tel. 403/424–5555 or 800/661–6562. 283 suites. Facilities: restaurant, lounge, indoor parking, shuttle service to mall, indoor pool, sauna, fitness center, games room, nonsmoking floors. AE, MC, V. Expensive.*

Sheraton Plaza Edmonton. The renovated property on a quiet street a few blocks from downtown features a lobby and fair-size guest rooms with old-style flair: richly appointed cherry-wood furniture and a warm, cozy ambience. Some rooms have balconies, and almost all have MovieBars—a unit that includes TV, VCR, minibar, and snacks. A selection of videotapes is for rent in the lobby. Room rates include breakfast buffet. *10010 104th St., T5J 0Z1, tel. 403/423–2450 or 800/325–3535. 138 rooms. Facilities: restaurant, lounge, indoor pool, sauna, exercise room, nonsmoking floors. AE, DC, MC, V. Expensive.*

Inn on 7th. Edmonton shorthand provides the name for this cheerful property on 107th Street. The foliage-filled lobby features Paul Bunyan–size easy chairs. A former Holiday Inn now run by the Courtyard Inn chain, this hotel caters to tourists, government employees, and Pacific Coast League baseball teams who play in nearby John Ducey Park. Rooms are comfortably modern; the location is convenient but not stressful. *10001 107th St., T5J 1J1, tel. 403/429–2861 or 800/661–7327. 190 rooms. Facilities: restaurant, lounge, nonsmoking floors. AE, MC, V. Moderate.*

West Harvest Inn. One of Edmonton's newest lodging establishments, this clean, modern three-story hotel catering to the family is on the western edge of town and is only five minutes away from West Edmonton Mall. Rooms in the new wing are slightly larger and more expensive than those in the older wing, but all are comfortable. Grainfield's family restaurant is located on the premises; Yian Chinese restaurant is next door. *17803 Stony Plain Rd. (Rte. 16), T5S 1B4, tel. 403/484–8000 or 800/661–6993. 162 rooms. Facilities: restaurant, lounge. AE, DC, MC, V. Moderate.*

Relax Inn. Canada's home-grown budget chain operates two clean and functional motels (plus the spiffier, moderately priced Relax Inn–Edmonton International Airport). Relax Inn–West is located on the edge of town, not far from West Edmonton Mall; Relax Inn–South is on the road to the airport. *18320 Stony Plain Rd., T5S 1A7, tel. 403/483–6031 or 800/661–9563, 227 rooms including nonsmoking rooms. 10320 45th Ave. S, T6H 5K3, tel. 403/436–9770, 222 rooms including nonsmoking rooms. Facilities: restaurant, lounge, indoor pool, whirlpool. AE, DC, MC, V. Inexpensive.*

YMCA of Edmonton. This Y is in an outstanding location: in the heart of downtown next door to the Hilton International and adjacent to Edmonton Centre shopping mall. Rooms are small and spare but carpeted and cheerfully furnished. Women and couples welcome; rates are $20–$30 a room. All facilities are available to overnight guests. *10030 102A Ave., T5J 0G5, tel. 403/421–9622. 113 rooms, 30 with bath. Facilities: cafeteria, indoor pool, fitness center, weight room, running track, racquetball courts. MC, V. Inexpensive.*

The Arts and Nightlife

Tickets for events in Edmonton are available from BASS ticket outlets, located in Edmonton Centre, Citadel Theatre box office, Champions in West Edmonton Mall, and Sears stores, or call 403/451–8000 to telecharge tickets to most events.

The Arts
Theater
Edmonton has 13 professional theater companies. The paramount facility is the glass-clad downtown **Citadel Theatre Complex** (99th St. and 101A Ave., Edmonton, tel. 403/425–1820), where four theaters mingle esoteric works and classics. **Northern Light Theater** (Kaasa Theatre, Jubilee Auditorium, 118th Ave. and 74th St., Edmonton, tel. 403/471–1586) takes chances that usually succeed.

Music and Dance
The **Edmonton Opera** (tel. 403/482–7030), **Edmonton Symphony Orchestra** (tel. 403/428–1414), and **Alberta Ballet Company** (tel. 403/438–4350) all perform in the **Northern Alberta Jubilee Auditorium** at the University of Alberta (87th Ave. and 114th St., Edmonton, tel. 403/427–9622).

Film
Edmonton's **Metro Cinema** (NFB Theatre, Canada Place, 9700 Jasper Ave., Edmonton, tel. 403/425–9212) presents classics,

imports, and brave new films on weekend nights. The **Edmonton Film Society** screens an ambitious program at a theater in the **Provincial Museum of Alberta** (12845 102nd Ave., Edmonton, tel. 403/427–1730). The **Princess Theatre** (10337 Whyte Ave., Edmonton, tel. 403/433–5785), an old-time movie house in Old Strathcona district, presents revivals, experiments, and foreign films.

Nightlife
Bars and Clubs

The **Rose & Crown** English-style pub in the Hilton International (10235 101st St., Edmonton, tel. 403/428–7111) is a popular downtown gathering place with dart boards and a huge selection of beers. **Elephant & Castle Pubs** are pleasant watering holes in downtown Edmonton's Eaton Centre (tel. 403/424–4555) and the West Edmonton Mall (tel. 403/444–3555).

Casinos

Roulette, blackjack, and wheel of fortune action usually takes place in Edmonton between noon and midnight daily except Sunday at the **Casino ABS Downtown** (10161 112th St., Edmonton, tel. 403/428–6679), **Casino ABS South** (7055 Argyll Rd., Edmonton, tel. 403/466–0199), and at the **Mayfair Hotel** (10815 Jasper Ave., Edmonton, tel. 403/484–0821).

Comedy

Edmonton boasts two branches of **Yuk Yuk's** (7103 78th Ave., tel. 403/466–2131).

Music

The **Sidetrack Cafe** (10333 112th St., Edmonton, tel. 403/421–1326) features top-name entertainers, big-screen telecasts of sports events, Variety Night on Sunday, and the Monday-night Comedy Bowl. **Yardbird Suite** (10206 86th Ave., Edmonton, tel. 403/432–0328) is Edmonton's premier jazz showcase. **Club Malibu** (10310 85th Ave., Edmonton, tel. 403/432–7300) blasts out Top-40 hits in a converted armory. **Goose Loonies** (6250 99th St., Edmonton, tel. 403/438–5571) has two levels of lights, lasers, and loudness. **Cook County Saloon** (8010 103rd St., Edmonton, tel. 403/432–0177) has mellow honky-tonk ambience and country-and-western music.

10 Province of Ontario

David E. Scott

David E. Scott is author of the best-selling The Ontario Getaway Guidebook, A Taste of Ontario Country Inns, and Ontario for Free.

Ontario is an Iroquoian word variously interpreted as: beautiful lake, beautiful water, or rocks standing high beside the water (the last an apparent reference to Niagara Falls). Ontario is Canada's second-largest province—from east to west the traveler will cross 2,080 kilometers (1,300 miles) and one time zone. However, only 10 million people live in this vast area, and 90% of them are within a narrow strip just north of the U.S. border.

Ontario is Canada's most urbanized province; half of its population lives in four cities whose boundaries have spread to such an extent that they almost adjoin. Metropolitan Toronto has more than 3 million people. To the east, Oshawa has a population of 125,000 and heavily populated suburbs. South and west of Toronto are Hamilton with 560,000 people and St. Catharines with 345,000. Half of Ontario's population is British, but the province contains the largest settlement of Finns outside Finland, at Thunder Bay. Toronto has half a million Italians, the largest Chinese community in Canada, and the biggest Portuguese colony in North America.

The towns and cities of northern Ontario are strung along the railway lines that brought them into being. And the discovery of immense deposits of gold, silver, uranium, and other minerals by railway construction gangs sparked mining booms that established communities such as Sudbury, Cobalt, and Kirkland Lake, which continue to owe their existence to mining.

Ontario has the most varied landscape of any Canadian province. The most conspicuous topographical feature is the Niagara Escarpment, which runs from Niagara to Tobermory at the tip of the Bruce Peninsula in Lake Huron. The northern 90% of Ontario is covered by the Canadian Shield, worn-down mountain ranges of the world's oldest rock, reaching only 682 meters (2,183 feet) above sea level at their highest point. On James Bay January temperatures range from –14C to –28C (7F to –15F).

East of Hamilton toward Niagara Falls is a narrow strip along the south shore of Lake Ontario in a partial rain shadow of the Niagara Escarpment. The climate, moderated in winter by Lakes Ontario and Erie, allows the growing of tender fruits and grapes, making it Canada's largest wine-producing area.

You could spend a lifetime exploring this enormous province and still not see it all. But by using three cities—Ottawa, Sault Ste. Marie, and Toronto—as bases for one- and two-day excursions, you can see all the major sights and some special little corners that even many Ontarians don't know about.

Essential Information

Important Addresses and Numbers

Tourist Information *Ontario* Ontario has a wealth of excellent and free tourist information. From within Canada or the continental United States (except Yukon, Northwest Territories, and Alaska) dial 800/668–2746, 8–8 daily, mid-May–Labor Day, and 8–4:30 weekdays the rest of the year. Or write to the **Ministry of Tourism and Recreation** (77 Bloor St. W, Toronto, Ont. M7A 2R9). When requesting information, specify your areas of interest: antiquing, boating, camping, fishing, dining, hiking, etc. There is literature available on the entire province. Free booklets on accommodations, camping, country inns, marinas, cruises, antiques markets, etc., can all be obtained.

This same information is also available at Travel Information Centers at every major entry point by road and at dozens of Regional Travel Information Centers province-wide.

Hamilton For information on Hamilton, contact the **Greater Hamilton, Regional Municipality of Hamilton–Wentworth** (1 James St. S, 3rd floor, Hamilton, Ont. L8P 4R5, tel. 416/546–4222 or 800/263–8590; fax 416/546–4107).

Kingston Contact the **Kingston District Chamber of Commerce** (209 Wellington St., Kingston, Ont. K7K 2Y6, tel. 613/548–4453).

Kitchener Contact the **Kitchener Chamber of Commerce** (Box 2367, 67 King St. E, Kitchener, Ont. N2H 6L4, tel. 519/742–4760).

Midland Contact **Midland Chamber of Commerce** (Box 158, Midland, Ont. L4R 4K8, tel. 705/526–7884).

Niagara Falls Contact **Niagara Falls, Canada Visitor and Convention Bureau** (4673 Ontario Ave., Niagara Falls, Ont. L2E 3R1, tel. 416/356–6061).

Ottawa For information on Ottawa, contact **Ottawa and Hull Tourism Inc.** (Ottawa–Carleton Centre, 2nd floor, 111 Lisgar St., Ottawa, Ont. K2P 2L7, tel. 613/237–5150).

Peterborough Contact **Greater Peterborough Chamber of Commerce** (135 George St. N, Peterborough, Ont. K9J 3G6, tel. 705/748–9771).

Sault Ste. Marie Contact **Hospitality & Travel** (99 Foster Dr., 3rd floor, Sault Ste. Marie, Ont. P6A 5X6, tel. 705/942–4001).

Windsor Contact **Convention and Visitors Bureau of Windsor, Essex County, and Pelee Island** (80 Chatham St. E, Windsor, Ont. N9A 2W1, tel. 519/255–6530).

Emergencies Dial 911 for **police, fire,** or **ambulance** anywhere in Ontario. The main hospitals in Ottawa are **Ottawa General Hospital** (tel. 613/737–7777) and **Ottawa Civic Hospital** (tel. 613/761–4000). **Shoppers Drug Mart** (1460 Merivale Rd., tel. 613/224–7270) is open 24 hours a day. The main hospitals in Sault Ste. Marie are **General Hospital** (tel. 705/759–3333) and **Plummer Memorial Public Hospital** (tel. 705/759–3800). Also available for emergency service is **Group Health Centre** (240 McNabb St. tel. 705/759–1234). There are no 24-hour pharmacies in Sault Ste. Marie, but **Shoppers Drug Mart** in the Cambrian Mall is open seven days a week.

Arriving and Departing by Plane

Airports and Airlines Toronto, the area's major city, is served by most major international airlines. *See* Chapter 3 for details.

Ottawa International Airport (tel. 613/998–3151), 18 kilometers (12 miles) from downtown, is served by **Air Canada** (tel. 800/776–3000), **First Air** (tel. 800/468–8292), **City Express** (tel. 800/387–2664), **Air France** (tel. 800/237–2747), **Canadian Airlines** (tel. 800/426–7000), **KLM** (tel. 800/777–5553), **Lufthansa** (tel. 800/645–3880), **Intair** (tel. 613/233–6062), **US Air** (tel. 800/428–4322), and **Nation Air** (tel. 613/737–4202).

Arriving and Departing by Car, Train, and Bus

By Car   The **Macdonald–Cartier Freeway,** known as Highway 401, is Ontario's major highway link. It runs from Windsor in the southwest through Toronto, along the north shore of Lake Ontario, and along the north shore of the St. Lawrence River to the Québec border west of Montréal. The **Trans-Canada Highway** follows the west bank of the Ottawa River from Montréal to Ottawa and on to North Bay. From North Bay to Nipigon at the northern tip of Lake Superior, there are two Trans-Canada highways, and from just west of Thunder Bay to Kenora, near the Manitoba border, another two. For 24-hour road condition information anywhere in Ontario, tel. 416/235–1110.

By Train   Ontario is served by cross-Canada **Via Rail** (tel. 800/361–3677) service and connects with **Amtrak** (tel. 800/872–7245) service at Windsor (Detroit) and Fort Erie (Buffalo). Via Rail operates frequent trains on the Windsor–London–Toronto–Kingston–Montréal corridor and the Ottawa rail station at the southeastern end of town (200 Tremblay Rd., tel. 613/238–8289, or in Canada, tel. 800/361–5390).

By Bus   **Voyageur Colonial Bus Lines** (265 Catherine St. tel. 613/238–5900) offers frequent service from Montréal and Toronto to Ottawa, including some express buses.

Getting Around

By Taxi   Major cab companies such as **Blue Line** (tel. 613/238–1111) and **Diamond** (tel. 613/235–1821) operate in and around Ottawa.

By Bus   **OC Transpo** serves the metropolitan region of Ottawa–Carleton on the Ontario side of the Ottawa River. It operates buses on city streets and on the Transitway, a system of bus-only roads. All bus routes in downtown Ottawa meet at the Rideau Centre (Rideau St. between Nicholas and Sussex and the Mackenzie King Bridge). From mid-June to September 2, 9 AM to 6 PM, a Visipass is available on a loop route through Ottawa and Hull that passes 22 of the major tourist attractions in both cities. You can get on and off as many times as you wish on the loop for $3 a day or $7 for a family pass (tel. 613/239–5000).

By Car   A valid driver's licence from any country is good in Ontario for up to three months. Ontario is a no-fault province, and minimum liability insurance is $200,000. Driving motorized vehicles (including boats, all-terrain vehicles, and motor bikes) while impaired by alcohol is taken seriously in Ontario and results in heavy fines or imprisonment, or both. You can be convicted for refusing to take a breathalyzer test. Radar warning devices are not permitted in Ontario even if they are turned off and are just in transit to other provinces. Police can seize them on the spot, and heavy fines may be imposed. Seat belts must be worn by adults and children over 18 kg (40 lb) if the car is designed with them; infants from birth to 9 kg (20 lb) must travel in a rear-facing child restraint system; children 9–18 kg (20–40 lb) must travel in a safety seat.

Studded tires and window coatings that do not allow a clear view of the vehicle interior are forbidden in Ontario. Right turns on red lights are permitted unless otherwise noted.

Guided Tours

Ottawa
City Tours

The **Gray Line** (tel. 613/748–4426) operates frequent, two-hour, 50-kilometer (31-mile) orientation tours from mid-April through October. **Picadilly Bus Tours** (tel. 613/235–7674) has a regular schedule of 1¾-hour tours in double-decker London buses to Ottawa's major sites, May through mid-October.

Boat Tours

Paul's Boat Lines Limited (office, tel. 613/733–5186; boat dock, tel. 613/235–8409) offers seven 75-minute cruises daily on the Rideau Canal and four 90-minute cruises daily on the Ottawa River from mid-May to mid-October. Canal boats dock across from the National Arts Centre; river cruise boats dock at the Bytown Museum at the foot of the Ottawa Locks on the Rideau Canal. **Ottawa Riverboat Company** (tel. 613/232–4888) operates two-hour sightseeing tours on the Ottawa River from May through October. The SS *Bytown Pumper* (tel. 613/226–8737) is a wood-burning steamboat that offers tours on the Rideau River from mid-May to mid-October. It has an 1897 engine in a 1903 hull. Cruises depart daily at 10, noon, 2, and 4 from Hog's Back Marina Park; dinner cruises are available (call ahead because the boat is sometimes chartered for the evening).

Niagara Falls
City Tours

Double Deck Tours (tel. 416/295–3051) touches all the bases in its 4½- to 5-hour tours in double-decker English buses, which include most of the major sights of Niagara Falls. The tours operate daily from mid-June through September and on weekends only from May to mid-June and in October and November. The fare of $34.25 for adults and $19.25 for children 6–12 includes admissions to Table Rock Scenic Tunnels, Great Gorge Adventure, Maid of the Mist, and a trip in the Niagara Spanish Aero Car. A shorter tour does not stop at attractions to which admission is charged and costs $15 for adults and $8.50 for children. **Gray Line Motor Tours** (tel. 416/354–4524) operates a variety of tours of Niagara Falls and the surrounding area year-round in motor coaches. **Honeymoon City Tours** (tel. 416/357–4330) provides private tours in air-conditioned limousines. The **Niagara Parks Commission** operates People Mover System, consisting of semiarticulated air-conditioned buses, on a loop route between its public parking lot above the falls at Rapids View Terminal (well signposted) and the Niagara Spanish Aero Car parking lot about 8 kilometers (5 miles) downriver. With a day's pass (available at any booth on the system: $3 adults, $1.50 children 6–12) you can get on and off as many times as you wish at the well-marked stops along the route.

Boat Tours

Maid of the Mist Steamboat Company Ltd. (tel. 416/358–5781) operates small cruise boats that pass so near the American and Horseshoe Falls that passengers are outfitted with hooded rain slickers. The boats sail frequently between mid-May and the third week in October. *Admission: $8.30 adults, $4.70 children 6–12.*

Air Tours

Niagara Helicopters Ltd. (tel. 416/357–5672) takes you over the Giant Whirlpool, up the Niagara Gorge, and past the American Falls and then banks around the curve of the Horseshoe Falls for a never-to-be-forgotten thrill—if you can keep your eyes open! *$61 one adult, $107 two adults, $15 children 2–12.*

Sault Ste. Marie
City Tours

Hiawathaland Tours (tel. 705/759–6200) operates three city tours by double-decker bus and three wilderness tours by minivan to Wawa, Aubrey Falls, or St. Joseph's Island from

June 15 to October 15. A 75-minute evening tour is also available.

Boat Tours **Lock Tours Canada** runs two-hour excursions through the 21-foot-high Soo Locks, the 16th and final lift for ships bound for Lake Superior from the St. Lawrence River. Tours aboard the 200-passenger MV *Chief Shingwauk* or 156-passenger MV *Bon Soo* leave from the Norgoma Dock just downriver from the Holiday Inn May 15–October 15 and up to eight times daily July 1–Labor Day. *$14 adults, $7 children 5–12, $10.50, 13–18.*

Train Tours The **Agawa Canyon Train** or the **Snow Train** (tel. 705/254–4331)—the name varies with the seasons—runs from Sault Ste. Marie to Mile 114 (182 km) in summer, and to Mile 120 (192 km) in winter. Trains operate daily June 5–October 15 and on Saturday and Sunday only January–March. Trains leave Sault Ste. Marie at 8 AM in summer and 8:30 AM in winter and return at 5 PM. *$42.75 adults, $21.40 children.*

The **Choo-Choo Steam Train Company** runs a 75-minute excursion along the Gatineau River between Hull and Wakefield, in Quebec (*see* Chapter 11, Guided Tours, below).

Exploring Ontario

Highlights for First-time Visitors

Canada's best bird/butterfly-watching, Tour 4: Fort Erie–Windsor
Changing of the Guard in front of the Parliament Buildings, Tour 1: Ottawa
Fort Wellington, Tour 2: Ottawa–Kawartha Lakes
Hamilton's Castle, Tour 5: Niagara Falls–London
Mennonite country, Tour 5: Niagara Falls–London
Niagara's Horseshoe Falls, Tour 5: Niagara Falls–London
Old Fort Henry, Tour 2: Ottawa–Kawartha Lakes
Ontario's grand canyons, Tour 6: Sault Ste. Marie–Thunder Bay
Polar Bear Express to the Gateway to the Arctic, Tour 8: Moosonee and Moose Factory Island
Shaw Festival, Tour 5: Niagara Falls–London
Stratford's Shakespearean Festival, Tour 5: Niagara Falls–London
Upper Canada Village, Tour 2: Ottawa–Kawartha Lakes

Tour 1: Ottawa

Numbers in the margin correspond to points of interest on the Lower Ontario Province, Downtown Ottawa, and Greater Ottawa and Hull maps.

Canadians are taught in school that it was Queen Victoria's fault their capital is inconveniently situated off the main east–west corridor along the U.S. border. But the facts are that politicians of the day were no more capable of making an unpopular decision than many who have followed them. They dithered from 1841 to 1857 trying to decide among five possible sites, including Québec City, Montréal, Cobourg, Kingston, and Ottawa. In 1857 they passed the buck to Buckingham Palace, and Queen Victoria got them off the hook.

She chose Ottawa for five reasons, all valid at the time: The site was politically acceptable to both Canada east and Canada west. It was also centrally located, reassuringly remote from the hostile United States, and industrially prosperous. And it had a naturally beautiful setting at the confluence of the Ottawa and Rideau rivers.

Three decades earlier, when Colonel John By and his Royal Engineers arrived to build a canal from Ottawa to Kingston, there were only a few scattered settlers at what is now Ottawa. The waterway was to ensure a protected supply route from Montréal to the Great Lakes in the event of a repeat of the War of 1812 against the Americans. Between 1826 and 1832 the canal was hacked through 200 kilometers (125 miles) of swamp, rock, and lakes whose different levels were overcome by locks.

By established his canal headquarters at what is now Ottawa, and the population growth was immediate as men arrived with their families, seeking employment on the biggest construction project on the continent. The settlement, then called Bytown, grew rapidly and fast became a rowdy, rough-and-tumble backwoods town. The Ottawa River then was used for floating timber to Montréal—each spring lumberjacks tied their rafts of timber to the shore and celebrated their release from isolated lumber camps in the taverns and brothels of Bytown.

By 1837, when its population had reached 2,400, Bytown was declared by the attorney general of Upper Canada to be a town. Government moved slowly even then, and it was not legally incorporated until 1850. Five years later, when the population had reached 10,000, Bytown became a city and was farsightedly given the name Ottawa, an Indian name meaning "a place for buying and selling."

Construction started on the Parliament Buildings in 1859. The buildings are magnificent, but their location in the mid-1850s earned Ottawa the nickname "Westminster in the Wilderness." More recently, perhaps because of their neo-Gothic towers and spires—or possibly because of legislation passed inside them— some refer to Parliament Hill as "Disneyland on the Rideau."

As early as 1899, federal politicians were concerned with more than just the grounds around the Parliament Buildings, known as "The Hill." A variety of commissions and committees and plans have become today's National Capital Commission (NCC). The NCC works with all municipalities within the 1,800-square-mile National Capital Region, which includes neighboring Hull and a big chunk of Québec, to coordinate development in the best interests of the region. The result is a profusion of beautiful parks, bicycle paths, jogging trails, and the world's longest skating rink, a 6-kilometer (4-mile) stretch of the Rideau Canal kept cleared and smooth and provided with heated huts, food concessions, and skate-sharpening and rental services.

Ottawa's population is only 303,000, but parking is at a premium. This is also a tricky city for the first-time visitor to negotiate by car: One wrong turn, it seems, and you're on one of five bridges across the Ottawa River to Hull.

❶ Much of your **Ottawa** sightseeing will be on foot. Begin at the **❷ Parliament Buildings.** Like London's Buckingham Palace, these striking buildings will be passed by visitors moving

Lower Ontario Province

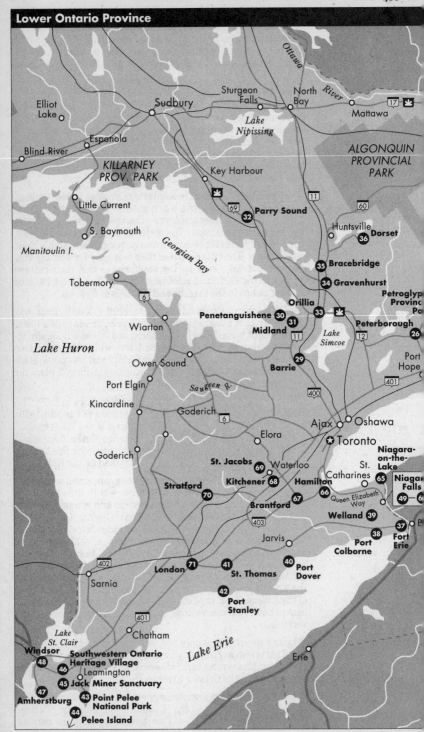

Elliot Lake

Blind River

Espanola

Sudbury

Sturgeon Falls

North Bay

Ottawa River

Mattawa

17

Lake Nipissing

KILLARNEY PROV. PARK

Key Harbour

ALGONQUIN PROVINCIAL PARK

Little Current

S. Baymouth

69

32 Parry Sound

11

60

Huntsville

36 Dorset

Manitoulin I.

Georgian Bay

35 Bracebridge

34 Gravenhurst

Petroglyp Provinc Pa

Tobermory

6

Wiarton

Penetanguishene 30

31

33 Orillia

Lake Simcoe

12

Peterborough

26

Lake Huron

Owen Sound

Midland

11

29 Barrie

Port Hope

Port Elgin

Saugeen R.

400

401

Kincardine

Goderich

6

Ajax

Oshawa

Goderich

Elora

Toronto

Niagara-on-the-Lake

St. Jacobs

69

Waterloo

St. Catharines

65

Stratford

Kitchener

68

Hamilton

66

Niaga Falls

70

Brantford

67

Queen Elizabeth Way

49

403

Welland 39

37

Jarvis

38

Port Colborne

Fort Erie

London

71

41

St. Thomas

40 Port Dover

P

402

Sarnia

42 Port Stanley

401

Chatham

Lake Erie

Lake St. Clair

Windsor 48

46

Southwestern Ontario Heritage Village

Leamington

Erie

47

45 Jack Miner Sanctuary

Amherstburg

43 Point Pelee National Park

44 Pelee Island

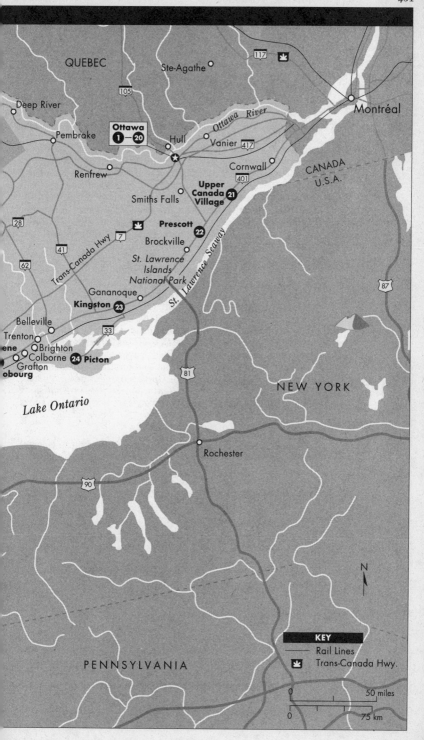

QUEBEC

Ste-Agathe

Deep River

Pembroke

105

117

Ottawa River

Montréal

Ottawa 1—20

Hull

Vanier 417

Renfrew

Cornwall

CANADA

U.S.A.

Smiths Falls

401

Upper Canada Village 21

28

Trans-Canada Hwy 7

Prescott 22

Brockville

St. Lawrence Islands National Park

St. Lawrence Seaway

87

41

62

Gananoque

Kingston 23

Belleville

33

Trenton

ene Brighton

Colborne 24 Picton

Grafton

obourg

NEW YORK

81

Lake Ontario

Rochester

90

N

PENNSYLVANIA

KEY

—— Rail Lines

Trans-Canada Hwy.

0   50 miles

0   75 km

around Ottawa whether they plan to visit them or not. What you see on The Hill is similar to what opened in 1867, but the only part not destroyed by fire in 1916 was the 1876 Library of Parliament behind the Centre Block and the northwest wing. There are three massive buildings on a promontory overlooking the Ottawa River, though none face it. The **Centre Block** is where the Senate and House of Commons, the two houses of Parliament, work to shape the laws of the land. The central **Peace Tower** houses a Memorial Chamber with an Altar of Sacrifice, which records the names of 66,651 Canadians killed during active service in World War I and 44,895 Canadians who died in World War II. There is also a 53-bell carillon whose bells range from 10 pounds to 11 tons. (Call 613/992–4793 for information on concerts given by the **Dominion Carillonneur**.) North (toward the river) of the Centre Block and reached from it is the **Library of Parliament,** which escaped the fire of 1916 but was damaged in its own fire in 1952. A statue of a young Queen Victoria is the centerpiece of the many-sided chamber, whose walls are lined with books, many of them priceless, and carved wooden galleries restored from the 1952 fire. In front of, and to either side of, the Parliament Buildings are the **East Block** and **West Block.** The East Block has four historic rooms open to the public: the original Governor General's office restored to the period of Lord Dufferin, 1872–1878; the offices of Sir John A. Macdonald and Sir George-Étienne Cartier, Fathers of the Confederation in 1867; and the Privy Council Chamber. The West Block, originally designed to house the civil service, has been converted to offices for parliamentarians and is not open to the public. The Parliament Buildings are surrounded by 29 acres of lawns that contain statues of famous Canadians. *Tel. 613/992–4793. Open summer, daily 9–8:30; winter, daily 9–4:30. Free 40-min. tours given in English or French. To avoid waiting in the busy summer period, visitors may make same-day reservations for tours at the white Infotent just east of the Centre Block.*

There's lots of room to stand and no charge for the colorful **Changing of the Guard ceremony** that takes place in front of the Peace Tower at 10 AM daily, June 22–August 25, weather permitting. The Ceremonial Guard brings together two of Canada's most historic regiments, the Canadian Grenadier Guards and the Governor General's Foot Guards.

Against the backdrop of the imposing Parliament Buildings, a half-hour **Sound and Light Show** highlights Canada's history. There's bleacher seating, and the shows are free. Shows are daily from early July through Labor Day and four nights a week from early May through June and in September. In summer there are two shows daily, English first, followed by French. Check dates and times with the Public Information Office (tel. 613/992–4793).

❸ Turn right onto Wellington Street and walk past Bank Street to the **Bank of Canada** inside which is the **Currency Museum.** The ancestors of the credit card are all here: bracelets made from elephant hair, cowrie shells, whale's teeth, and what is believed to be the world's largest coin. Here, too, of course, is the most complete collection of Canadian notes and coins. *245 Sparks St., tel. 613/782–8914. Admission free. Open May–Sept., Mon–Sat. 10:30–5, Sun. 1–5; Sept.–May, Tues.–Sat. 10:30–5, Sun. 1–5.*

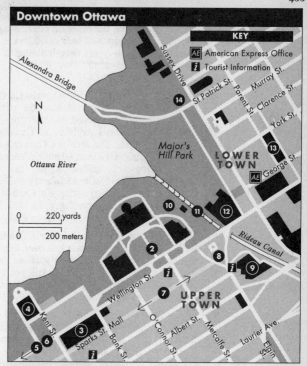

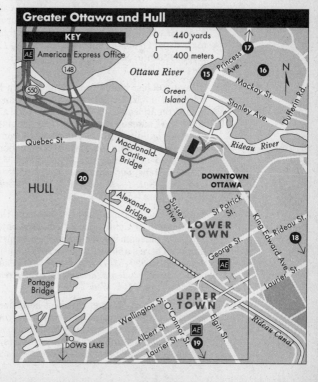

4 Turn right onto Kent Street to the **Supreme Court.** Established in 1875, it became the ultimate court of appeal in the land in 1949. The nine judges sit only in Ottawa in three sessions each year in their stately art deco building. *Kent and Wellington Sts., tel. 613/995–4330. Free tours May–Aug., daily 9–5; Sept.–Apr., weekdays 9–5.*

5 At the end of Wellington Street is the **Garden of the Provinces,** which commemorates confederation with the emblems of Canada's 10 provinces and two territories. Across from the **6** park is the **National Archives of Canada** and the **National Library of Canada.** The archives, Canada's oldest cultural institution, contains more than 60 million manuscripts and government records, 1 million maps, and about 11 million photographs. The National Library collects, preserves, and promotes the published heritage of Canada and exhibits books, paintings, maps, and photographs. *395 Wellington St., tel. 613/992–3052. Admission free. Open daily 9–9.*

7 Return toward Parliament Hill via **Sparks Street Pedestrian Mall,** where the automobile has been banished and browsers wander among fountains, rock gardens, sculptures, and out-**8** door cafés. Emerging from the mall, you'll face **Confederation Square** and the **National War Memorial** honoring the 66,655 Canadian dead of World War I.

9 Adjacent to the square stands the complex of the **National Arts Centre,** a huge theater complex designed around the repetitive motif of the hexagon. It includes an opera hall, a theater, a studio theater, and a salon for readings and concerts. The center has its own orchestra, and touring companies offer more than 900 performances a year. Its canal-side café, Le Cafe, spills outside in warm weather and is popular for a meal or drink. *53 Elgin St., tel. 613/996–5051. Admission free. 30- to 40-minute tours depart from the main lobby at noon, 1:30, and 3, May 1– Aug. 31, daily; Sept.–Apr., Tues., Thurs., and Sat. (Sun. to the end of Oct.).*

10 Ottawa's oldest building, now the **Bytown Museum,** houses a collection of 3,500 artifacts of Colonel By and Ottawa memora-**11** bilia at the **Rideau Locks** between The Hill and Ottawa's grand **12** hotel, the **Château Laurier Hotel** (*see* Lodging, below). By built the stone building in 1826, and it was his commissariat for payroll monies and supplies during construction of the canal. *Tel. 613/234–4570. Admission: $2.25 adults, $1.10 students and senior citizens, 50¢ children. Open mid-May–mid-Oct., Mon. and Wed.–Sat. 10–4, Sun. 2–5; Apr. 1–mid-May, mid-Oct.– Nov. 30, Mon.–Fri. 10–4.*

Between the Chateau Laurier Hotel and the Rideau Canal is the **Museum of Contemporary Photography,** which opened in 1992. The museum has 158,000 images, shown in changing exhibitions. There's a 50-seat theater and a boutique. *1 Rideau Canal, tel. 613/990–8257. Admission: $2.50 adults, $1.25 senior citizens and students, under 12 free. Free on Thurs. Open Thurs.–Tues. 11–6, Wed. 4–8.*

There has been a farmer's market here since 1840 with fresh produce, maple products, and flowers; surrounding the market stalls are permanent specialty food shops, some well over 100 **13** years old. In **By Ward Market** there are cafés, restaurants, patios, boutiques, and bars, and the area hops day and night.

(14) The **National Gallery of Canada,** a magnificent glass-towered temple to art, reflects the Parliament Buildings in its modern mirror and granite facade. The gallery contains the most comprehensive collection of Canadian art. Inside is the reconstructed Rideau Convent Chapel, a classic example of 19th-century French Canadian architecture with the only neo-Gothic fan-vaulted ceiling on the continent. The building has three restaurants and a large bookstore with publications on the arts. *380 Sussex Drive, tel. 613/990–1985. Admission: $5 adults, $3 senior citizens and students, under 16 free. Thurs. free. Closed Mon. and holidays in winter.*

It's best to continue the tour by car or bicycle as Sussex Drive skirts the Ottawa River above limestone bluffs. An address known to most Canadians, 24 Sussex Drive is the official (15) **residence of the prime minister.** Don't try parking near the mansion; security is tight. The best way to view the mansion is by slowing down in your car as you pass the gates, though all you'll get is a glimpse of a couple of roof gables and some expensive landscaping.

(16) Government House, also known as **Rideau Hall,** has been the official residence of the governor general of Canada since 1865. Visiting heads of state, royal visitors, and the monarch stay here while on official visits. The 1830 mansion has a ballroom, and there are a skating rink and a cricket pitch. Sentries of the Canadian Grenadier Guards and the Governor General's Foot Guards are posted outside the main gate of Rideau Hall from late June through August. Free walking tours of the grounds are conducted year-round, but days and times change frequently according to season. *1 Sussex Dr., tel. 613/993–0311.*

Follow Sussex Drive past Rideau Hall to the Rockcliffe Driveway and then signs that say 4 kilometers (2.5 miles) to the (17) **National Aviation Museum** at Rockcliffe Airport. There are more than 100 aircraft in this collection, from a replica of the Silver Dart that made the first powered flight in Canada through World War I Sopwiths. *Tel. 613/993–2010. Admission: $4.28 adults, $3.50 students and senior citizens, $1.50 children 6–15, under 6 free, $9 families. Free Thurs. Open May–Aug., Wed.–Fri. 9–8, Sat.–Tues. 9–6; Sept.–Apr., Tues.–Sun. 9–5, Thurs. 9–8. Closed Mon. except public holidays.*

(18) Don't plan on scampering through the **National Museum of Science and Technology** collections in half an hour. There are static displays of printing presses, antique cars, steam locomotives, and agricultural machinery, and there are ever-changing exhibits, many of which are hands-on, or "minds-on." Take the St. Laurent Boulevard South exit from the Queensway. The entrance is 1.6 kilometers (1 mile) south off Lancaster Road. *1867 St. Laurent Blvd., tel. 613/991–3044. Admission: $4.28 adults, $3.50 senior citizens and students, $1.50 children 6–15, $9 families. Free on Thurs. 5–9. Open May–Aug., Wed.–Fri. 9–8, Sat.–Tues. 9–6; Sept.–Apr., Tues.–Sun. 9–5, Thurs. 9–9. Closed Mon. except holidays.*

(19) **The Canadian Museum of Nature** collection used to be called the National Museum of Natural Sciences, and some of the collection has gone across the river to Hull to help fill galleries in the enormous Canadian Museum of Civilization (*see* below). But there's lots of interest left in this grand old building that was briefly the seat of government in 1916 after the Parliament

Buildings burned. The dinosaur collection is fabulous, and so are the stuffed birds and animals in simulated habitats. *Mc-Leod St. at Metcalfe, tel. 613/996–3102. Admission: $2 adults, $1.50 students and senior citizens, $1 children 6–16, free on Thurs. Open May 1–Aug., daily 9:30–5, Thurs. 9:30–8; Sept.–Apr., daily 10–5, Thurs. 10–8.*

⓴ Although the **Canadian Museum of Civilization** is not in Ontario, it is definitely considered part of the Ottawa scene, literally, because visitors can see it on the other side of the Ottawa River from behind the Parliament Buildings on The Hill. This immense, modernistic building on the Québec shore of the Ottawa River features galleries, displays, films, lectures, theaters, and exhibitions chronicling thousands of years of Canadian history. In the Grand Hall, six native longhouses, towering totem poles, and life-size reconstructions of Canadian historic scenes help you travel through time. Special exhibitions throughout the year are offered for an additional admission fee at Cineplus, the first theater to project either Imax or Omnimax, both larger than life size. *100 Laurier St., Hull, tel. 613/776–7000. Admission to the museum: $4.50 adults, $3 students and senior citizens, children 15 and under free, free 5–8 Thurs.; Cineplus: $7 adults, $5 students and senior citizens, and children. Open May–Sept., daily 9–5, Thurs. 9–8; Sept.–Apr., Tues.–Sun. Closed Christmas and New Year's Day.*

Tour 2: Heritage Highway

From Ottawa, Highway 31 runs southeast about 75 kilometers (46 miles) to scenic Highway 2 at Morrisburg. One of the province's major tourist attractions is 11 kilometers (7 miles) west by Highway 2 or Highway 401. Eight villages disappeared under rising waters when the St. Lawrence Seaway opened in 1959, but their best historic buildings were moved to a new vil-
⓴ lage called **Upper Canada Village,** a faithful re-creation of an Ontario community from the 1800s. The village occupies 66 acres of the 2,000-acre **Crysler's Farm Battlefield Memorial Park,** a site that figured prominently in the War of 1812. New-fangled gadgets such as radios, walkie-talkies, and tape players are banned in this throwback to the days of the United Empire Loyalists. The village has three mills, two farms, two churches, two hotels, and 25 other buildings. A leisurely tour takes three to four hours. There are more than 150 staff people on the site, all in early 1800s costume, to answer questions. The Village Store is open year-round and sells Canadian crafts and village-made bread, cheese, and flour. At Willard's Hotel, licensed for beer and wine, lunches, full-course meals, and teas are served. Two-day passes are available (at reduced rates). *Hwy. 2 E, tel. 613/543–3704. Admission: $9 ($13.75) adults, $6 ($9) students, $5.25 ($7.75) senior citizens, $3.75 ($5.75) children 6–12. Open mid-May–mid-Oct., daily 9:30–5; in winter, special events only.*

Head west on Highway 2 about 40 kilometers (25 miles) to
⓴ **Prescott** and its second fort, Fort Wellington, built by the British in 1813 to protect goods and troops moving between Montréal and Upper Canada after the outbreak of the War of 1812. The fort was never attacked and was completed in 1814, the year the war ended. The Ottawa–Kingston Rideau Canal eliminated its need and it was abandoned. In 1837 rebellion broke out in Upper and Lower Canada, and the British built a new and

stronger Fort Wellington on the site. The buildings are furnished in the 1846 period. *370 Vankoughnet St., tel. 613/925–2896. Admission free. Open mid-May–Aug., daily 10–6; Sept.–mid-Oct., daily 10–5; mid-Oct–mid-May by reservation only.*

Ontario's oldest barracks building is one block west of Fort Wellington at 356 East Street and open daily in July and August as both a museum and luncheon facility. Lunches at **Stockade Barracks and Hospital Museum** feature historical menus. By prior arrangement, groups can have five- or six-course dinners of 1812-style dishes served by mess waiters in military uniform. *Tel. 613/925–4894.*

㉓ Kingston's imposing architecture has been impressing visitors since 1673, when LaSalle chose the location as the site for a meeting between Governor Frontenac and the Iroquois. Before the meeting, Frontenac built a stockaded fort to impress the Indians and thus tap into the fur trade. Thanks to misguided American strategy, Kingston survived the War of 1812 almost totally unscathed. Many of its beautiful limestone buildings remain in mint condition today. From 1841 to 1844, Kingston was the capital of the province of Canada; today the gorgeous, cut-limestone city hall building dominates the city's downtown core, facing a riverfront park. Tours are given weekdays in the summer, but visitors can wander through the lobby area any time of the year.

The city occupied a strategic site at the junction of the St. Lawrence River and Rideau Canal system, and four Martello towers still guard the harbor. The **Royal Military College of Canada** features a museum in Fort Frederick, the largest of the Martello towers. The museum contains the internationally renowned Douglas Arms Collection, which includes the small-arms collection of General Porfirio Díaz, president of Mexico from 1886 to 1912. *Off Hwy. 2 just east of Kingston, tel. 613/541–6663 or 613/541–6665. Admission free. Open last weekend in June–Labor Day, daily 10–5.*

The massive **Fort Henry** was built during the War of 1812 to repel a possible American invasion, which never came. Students in period military costume guide visitors through, hold parades, and re-create the pomp and pageantry of an era past. *Hwys. 2 and 15, tel. 613/542–7388. Admission: late May to Thanksgiving, $8.75 adults, $5 senior citizens, $5.75 students, $3.75 children 6–12; Thanksgiving to mid-May, $3.25 adults, $1.65 senior citizens, students and children. Open daily.*

Locals nicknamed it Tea Caddy Castle, Molasses Hall, and Pekoe Pagoda, but Canada's first prime minister, Sir John A. Macdonald, who lived in the house for a year, called it **Bellevue** because of its view over the St. Lawrence River. Today the 1840 house is a National Historic Park site restored and furnished to the 1848 period when Macdonald lived there. *35 Centre St., tel. 613/545–8666. Admission free. Open May–Nov., daily 9–6, Dec.–Apr., daily 10–5.*

All you ever wanted to know about steam engines and their history—and then some—is on display in the **Pump House Steam Museum** (23 Ontario St., tel. 613/546–4696), the restored Victorian-style 1849 municipal water-pumping station. All the exhibits run on steam (only between mid-May and Labor Day), and the collection is believed to be the largest in the world.

Models range from miniatures to an 1897-model Toronto-built engine with a 9-ton flywheel. The **Marine Museum of the Great Lakes at Kingston** (55 Ontario St., tel. 613/542–2261), under the same management, features a rambling display area at the historic former Kingston Drydock that traces Great Lakes shipping since 1678. The 3,000-ton, 210-foot retired icebreaker, the *Alexander Henry*, is also on tour from mid-May to mid-October. Summer visitors can rent a stateroom and sleep aboard. Tickets are available for one, two, or all three of these attractions. *Admission: $3.25, $4.75, $6.25 adults, $2.25, $3.75, $5.25 senior citizens and children. Both museums open daily Apr.–Dec., 10–5. Jan.–Mar., open weekdays 10–4.*

Kingston is the birthplace of organized hockey—the first league game was played in the city in 1885. So it seems fitting that the city is also home to the **International Hockey Hall of Fame,** the shrine to puck-chasing. *York and Alfred Sts., 1 block north of Princess St. (Hwy. 2), tel. 613/544–2355. Admission: $2.14 adults, $1.61 senior citizens and students, $4.28 families, children under 12 free. Open mid-June–mid-Sept., daily 10–5; weekends the rest of the year, or by appointment.*

Highway 2 or 401 will take you to **Belleville,** but consider Highway 33, which will take you past Kingston's Gothic penitentiary at Collins Bay to Picton in the island county of Prince Edward. A free, 10-minute ferry ride (service every 15 minutes in summer) lands you at Glenora on the island, and it's 9 kilometers (6 miles) to Picton, the county seat.

㉔ Picton is a serene town of 4,000 with fine old buildings and strong associations with Sir John A. Macdonald, Canada's first prime minister, who practiced law at the 1834 county courthouse that is still in use. Tours are available during summer by prior arrangement and may include a visit to the jail at the rear, where a double gallows is kept handy (although it hasn't been used since 1884). *Tel. 613/476–3833.*

New Englanders wandering the island might find themselves wondering if they had ever left home—so similar are the scenery and the pages of history that brought both regions into being. The island was one of the earliest parts of Ontario to be settled after the American Revolution, and the Loyalist influence remained dominant for generations. The first of these settlers landed at Adolphustown Reach from Bateaux on June 16, 1784, and village locals nicknamed the landing area the Plymouth Rock of Ontario. The earliest burial ground in the district is located here, and the Loyalist church erected in 1822 is still used as a parish meeting hall.

About an hour west of Belleville, or 90 minutes from Picton, are **㉕** the towns of **Cobourg** and **Port Hope,** both richly endowed with mansions originally built as summer homes by Americans. Again, the traveler has the choice of the four-lane Highway 401 or Highway 2, which is closer to the shore of Lake Ontario and wanders through the pretty communities of **Brighton, Colborne,** and **Grafton.** Cobourg is another community that expected to be chosen as the provincial capital. It was passed over, but not before the town just about bankrupted itself building the magnificent **Victoria Hall,** officially opened in 1860 by the young Prince of Wales, later King Edward VII. The hall was used for town council meetings, formal balls, and concerts on the second floor; a courtroom modeled after London's Old

Bailey was located on the ground floor. Today's visitor can take a free tour of some of the 41 rooms in the building. *55 King St. W, tel. 416/372–5831. Admission free. Guided tours in summer or by prior arrangement.*

From Port Hope, take Highway 28 for about 40 kilometers (25 miles) into the Kawartha lakes region to reach the small city of
26 **Peterborough,** home of Trent University and 61,000 people. High notes in Peterborough are the signature lift locks on the Trent-Severn Waterway, which are the world's highest, and Centennial Fountain in Little Lake, which at 250 feet is the highest jet fountain in Canada. The lift lock on the Trent Canal system was built in 1904. In less than 10 minutes it lifts boats, and the water they're floating in, 65 feet straight up. The lock and the Trent Canal operate mid-May–mid-October; slides and films at a visitor center explain their mechanism. *Tel. 705/742– 9267. Admission free. Open mid-May–mid-Oct., daily; in winter, Wed.–Sun.*

27 Southeast of Peterborough, around the town of **Keene,** are several attractions. **Serpent Mounds Provincial Park** is 13 kilometers (9 miles) southeast of Peterborough on the shores of Rice Lake. About 2,000 years ago a nomadic native tribe buried its dead in nine earth mounds, the largest of which is shaped like a 200-foot-long serpent. An interpretation center explains the site and displays artifacts. *Tel. 705/295–6879. Admission: $5 per vehicle. Open mid-May–Thanksgiving, daily.*

On the way to the park, about 3 kilometers (2 miles) north of the village of Keene, **Lang Pioneer Village** has a museum and 26 pioneer buildings. There are displays and demonstrations of pioneer arts and crafts in the summer. *Tel. 705/295–6694. Admission, including GST: $5.50 adults, $4.50 senior citizens and students, $2.75 children under 14, $12.50 families. Open mid-May–mid-Oct., weekdays 11–5, Sat. 1–5, Sun. 1–6; museum gallery open daily except Christmas, 1–5 PM.*

Canada's largest concentration of native rock carvings was found at the east end of Stoney Lake, outside the hamlet of Stonyridge, in 1954. The site, 50 kilometers (31 miles) north-
28 west of Peterborough, is now within **Petroglyphs Provincial Park.** The well-preserved symbols and figures, which are carved on a flat expanse of white marble almost 70 feet wide, are encased in a protective building. The more than 900 carvings are believed to be of Algonkin spirit figures. *East of Hwy. 28 on Northey's Bay Rd., tel. 705/877–2552. Admission: $5 per vehicle. Open mid-May–Thanksgiving, daily.*

Tour 3: North of Toronto to the Lakes

29 **Barrie,** a city of 50,000 on the shores of Lake Simcoe, is about 75 kilometers (46 miles) north of Toronto on the four-lane Highway 400. A winter carnival attracts ice fishermen, dogsled racers, and ice motorcyclists. From late June through Labor Day, there's straw-hat theater in Gryphon Theatre at Georgian College and harness racing at Barrie Raceway.

From just north of Barrie, take Highways 400 and 93 about 50
30 kilometers (30 miles) to the towns of **Penetanguishene** (known
31 locally as Penetang) and **Midland** in a small corner of northern Simcoe County known as Huronia. This 30- by 60-kilometer (20- by 40-mile) area was the scene of some of the most grisly

episodes in North American history. Each town sits on a snug, safe harbor at the foot of two bays that lead out to Georgian Bay.

Just 5 kilometers (3 miles) east of Midland on Highway 12, visitors can explore a complete reconstruction of **Sainte-Marie among the Hurons.** Jesuit missionaries built the Sainte-Marie mission at this spot in 1639. The Jesuits preached Christianity, and the Hurons—also called Wendat—taught the French settlers how to survive in the harsh climate. By 1648 the mission was home to one-fifth of the European population of New France. The villagers built Ontario's first hospital, farm, school, and social service center here and constructed a canal from the Wye River. A combination of disease and Iroquois attacks led to the mission's demise. Twenty-two structures, faithfully reproduced from a scientific excavation, including an Indian longhouse and wigwam, can now be toured. The canal is working again; staff in period costume saw timber, repair shoes, sew clothes, and grow vegetables. *Tel. 705/526–7838. Admission: $5.75 adults, $3.50 students, $3.25 senior citizens, children under 6 free. Open daily mid-May to Labor Day and some weekends in winter.*

On a hill overlooking Sainte-Marie is **Martyr's Shrine,** a twin-spired stone cathedral built in 1926 to honor the eight missionaries who died in Huronia (the name given to the area originally); in 1930 five of the priests were canonized by the Roman Catholic Church. The grounds include a theater, souvenir shop, cafeteria, and picnic area, all open daily Victoria Day through Thanksgiving weekend. *Tel. 705/526–3788.*

The best artifacts from several hundred archaeological digs in the area are displayed at **Huronia Museum and Gallery of Historic Huronia** in Little Lake Park in Midland. Behind the museum and gallery building is **Huron Indian Village,** a full-scale replica of a 16th-century Huron Indian village. *Little Lake Park, tel. 705/526–2844. Admission to museum and village: $4.75 adults, $4.25 senior citizens, $3.50 students. Open Jan.– late May, Mon.–Fri. 9–5; late May–Thanksgiving, Mon.– Sat. 9–5, Sun. 10–5.*

Cruises leave from the town docks of both Midland and Penetang to explore the 30,000 Island region of Georgian Bay from mid-June to Labor Day. From Midland the 215-passenger MS *Miss Midland* offers 2½-hour sightseeing cruises (tel. 705/ 526–0161, from Ontario 800/461–1767). From Penetang, the 200-passenger MS *Georgian Queen* takes passengers on three-hour tours of the islands (tel. 705/549–7795).

❸❷ From Penetang to Midland, it's 110 kilometers (68 miles) by Highways 12 and 69 to **Parry Sound.** Here Canada's largest sightseeing cruise ship, the *Island Queen*, offers a more extensive three-hour cruise of Georgian Bay. *9 Bay St., tel. 705/746–2311. Free parking at the town dock. Operates June–Thanksgiving.*

From mid-July to mid-August, Festival of the Sound is held. Jazz and popular music concerts are featured in the auditorium of Parry Sound High School and aboard the *Island Queen* (tel. 705/746–2410).

❸❸ **Orillia,** about 35 kilometers (21 miles) north of Barrie on Highway 11 at the junction of Highway 12, will be recognized by readers of Canada's greatest humorist, Stephen Leacock, as Mariposa, the "little town" he described in *Sunshine Sketches of a Little Town.* The writer's former summer home is now a museum, the Stephen Leacock Memorial Home. In the Mariposa Room, characters from the book are matched with the Orillia residents who inspired them. *Off Hwy. 12B in the east end of Orillia, well signposted (tel. 705/326–9357). Admission: $3 adults, $1 high school students and senior citizens. Open mid-Apr.–mid-June and Labor Day–mid-Dec., 10–2 and by appointment; mid-June to Labor Day, daily 10–5. Closed Dec. 15–Apr. 15.*

North along Highway 11, rolling farmland suddenly changes to pine trees amid granite outcrops of the Canadian Shield. This region, called Muskoka, is the playground of folks who live in the highly urbanized areas in and on either side of Toronto. **④ Gravenhurst,** 39 kilometers (24 miles) north of Orillia, is a town of 10,000 and the birthplace of Canada's least-known hero—least known in Canada, that is. In China, Norman Bethune's name is as well known as Wayne Gretzky's is in Canada. Bethune is remembered for his heroic work in China as a field surgeon and medical educator. The **Bethune Memorial House,** an 1880-vintage frame home, has become a shrine of sorts to Chinese diplomats visiting North America. *235 John St., tel. 705/687–4262. Admission free. Open June–Labor Day, daily 10–6; the rest of the year 10–5. Closed on holidays in winter.*

The RMS *Segwun* (the initials stand for Royal Mail Ship) is the sole survivor of a fleet of steamships that once provided transportation through the Muskoka Lakes. The 128-foot boat, built in Scotland and assembled in Gravenhurst in 1887, carries 99 passengers on cruises from early June to early October. Cruises range from 90 minutes to two days in length (passengers dine aboard but sleep in one of Muskoka's grand resorts). Reservations are strongly recommended. *Muskoka Lakes Navigation and Hotel Company Limited, Box 68, Gravenhurst, Ont. P0C 1G0, tel. 705/687–6667.*

Just 11 kilometers (8 miles) north of Gravenhurst outside **⑤ Bracebridge** is **Santa's Village.** After letting Santa know what they'd like to find under the Christmas tree, youngsters can delight in the Kris Kringle Riverboat, the Candy Cane Express Train, minibikes, bumper boats, paddleboats, or pony rides, to name a few. *Just west of Bracebridge, well signposted, tel. 705/ 645–2512. Admission: $8 children 2–4, $14 children and adults 5 and over, $10 senior citizens; unlimited use of rides all day. Open mid-June–Labor Day, daily 10–6.*

⑥ Dorset is a pretty village on a narrows between two bays of the Lake of Bays, about 40 kilometers (25 miles) east of Huntsville by Highways 60 and 35. The village is home to **Robinson's General Store** (tel. 705/766–2415), which makes the modest claim "Voted Canada's Best Country Store." (Voting was by the editors of *Canadian Living* magazine, but visitors are not likely to question the choice.) With the exception of the World War II years, the store, established in 1921, has been open continuously and operated by a Robinson. You'll find everything here from moose-fur hats to stoves and pine furniture. You can circle back to Toronto on scenic Highway 35 or make Dorset a circle tour from Huntsville around the Lake of Bays.

Tour 4: Fort Erie and West to Windsor

㊲ **Fort Erie** is at the extreme southeast tip of the Niagara Peninsula, 155 kilometers (95 miles) south of Toronto and just across the International Peace Bridge over the Niagara River from Buffalo, New York. It's a drab, boom-or-bust town of chain fast-food restaurants, taverns, and gas stations whose profits rise or fall with the exchange rate between Canadian and U.S. dollars. The heavy American influx to the area is not without historic irony; the last American presence on Canadian soil took place here at the end of the War of 1812.

Old Fort Erie, reconstructed as it existed before it was destroyed at the end of the War of 1812, has a colorful and bloody history. Thousands of soldiers lost their lives within sight of the earthworks, drawbridges, and palisades. The fort itself was destroyed in 1779 and again in 1803 by spectacular storms that drove masses of ice ashore at the foot of Lake Erie. Visitors are conducted through the display rooms by guards in period uniforms of the British army. During summer the guards stand sentry duty, fire the cannon, and demonstrate drill and musket practice. *Tel. 416/871–0540. Admission: $3.50 adult, $3.15 seniors, $1.75 students, $9 family. Open mid-May–mid-Sept.*

The town's other major attraction, the **Fort Erie Race Track,** opened in 1897, but it is one of the most modern—and picturesque—tracks in North America. Glass-enclosed dining lounges overlook a one-mile dirt track and a seven-furlong turf course. *Tel. 416/871–3200.*

㊳ The Lake Erie port of **Port Colborne,** or "The Ports," is about 30 kilometers (20 miles) west of Fort Erie by Highway 3 (at the south end of the Welland Canal—*see* Tour 5, below). There's no admission charge to **Port Colborne Historical and Marine Museum,** a six-building complex where afternoon tea is served (at a price) from Arabella's Tea Room. *200 King St., tel. 416/834–7604. Open May–Dec., noon–5.*

㊴ About 10 kilometers (6 miles) north of Port Colborne is the industrial city of **Welland.** For years the city was bypassed by the 14–16 million tourists who visit Niagara Falls annually, so in 1988 Welland initiated its Festival of Arts Murals. There now are 27 giant murals on downtown buildings; the longest is 130 feet, and the tallest is three stories high. Visitors can pick up a free mural tour map and drive around. *Festival of Arts, 800 Niagara St. N, tel. 416/788–3000.*

㊵ From Welland, Highway 3 wanders west through rolling farm country occasionally slashed by a river emptying into Lake Erie. At **Jarvis,** 80 kilometers (50 miles) west, turn south on Highway 6 to **Port Dover,** home of the world's largest fleet of freshwater fishing boats. It's a pretty beach resort town where freshwater fish is served up steamy and golden at a number of restaurants.

㊶ Take Highway 24 north to Simcoe to rejoin Highway 3 westbound. **St. Thomas's** first buildings went up in 1810, over a decade and a half ahead of the first building in London, 28 kilometers (17 miles) north. For all its premature cosmopolitanism, its population has leveled at 29,000, while London's has hit the 300,000 mark. Note the **statue of Jumbo,** the Barnum and Bailey circus elephant, killed there in a freak railway acci-

dent in 1885. The monument is a 10%-larger-than-life-size statue of the largest elephant ever in captivity. Adjacent to the
Jumbo monument is a railway caboose, summer office of the St.
Thomas Chamber of Commerce, and a gift shop for Jumbo
kitsch. *Tel. 519/631–8188. Chamber office open in summer,
daily 9–9.*

About 15 kilometers (10 miles) south of St. Thomas is the sum-
(42) mer resort town of **Port Stanley,** with a fine brown sand beach
and the boutiques, snack bars, and kitsch stands that live off
vacationers following the sun.

It isn't hauled by a steam engine anymore, but the London and
Port Stanley Railroad (L&PS) still packs in travelers. The operation has proven so popular the little train now runs year-
round and its trackage has been doubled. The railroad was built
in 1856 between London and Port Stanley and intended as a
main trade link between Canada and the United States. The
trade didn't materialize, but the railroad survived on excursion
traffic until 1957. Railroad buffs restored some passenger cars
and repaired the line to Union, in 1992 extending it to St. Thomas. You can take a 45-minute excursion to Union year-round, or
a two-hour round trip to St. Thomas (June–Oct.) *Port Stanley
Railway Station, tel. 519/782–9993. Round-trip fares to Union: $5.50 adults, $4.75 senior citizens, $2.75 children under
12, all plus tax; to St. Thomas: $10 adults, $9 seniors, $5 chil-
dren, tax included.*

From Port Stanley/St. Thomas the fastest way to cover the 150
kilometers (95 miles) to the extreme southwest corner of Ontario is on Highway 401, but it's a flat, straight, and deadly dull
trip. The two-lane Highway 3 is a better choice—it follows the
shore of Lake Erie and passes through a number of towns and
villages. In summer and fall, vegetable stands sprout like
mushrooms along this route, offering fresh locally grown fruits
and vegetables.

Point Pelee juts into Lake Erie, serving as a rest stop for migrating birds and butterflies. The southern tip of the point,
(43) **Point Pelee National Park,** has the smallest dry land area of any
Canadian national park, yet it manages to draw more than half
a million visitors every year. There's no overnight camping, and
there are a lot of other rules and regulations to observe because
the park is home to a number of endangered species of plants
and reptiles. Drive slowly to the visitor center, 5 kilometers (3
miles) inside the park, where there are exhibits, slide shows,
and a keen, knowledgeable staff to answer questions. Seven
hundred kinds of plants and 347 species of birds have been recorded here. A propane-powered, open-sided train operates
from the center to the tip of Point Pelee, the southernmost part
of the Canadian mainland. September in Pelee is the best time
to see monarch butterflies resting before they head 3,350 kilometers (2,100 miles) south to winter in the Sierra Madre of
Mexico. It is also the best location in North American for bird-
watching, especially during spring and fall migrations. In September, groups of birders bedecked with camera lenses the
size of rocket launchers and clanking with binoculars, tape re-
corders, video equipment, and even CB radios converge on the
park and on the hotels, highways, motels, and restaurants of
this otherwise quiet town of 13,000. *Tel. 519/322-2365. Admission: $5 per vehicle Apr.–Labor Day, free rest of the year. Open
daily 10–6.*

44 **Pelee Island** is a small, flat island, roughly 8 by 4 miles (13 by 6 km), at the west end of Lake Erie served spring through fall by ferry boats that link it with Kingsville and Leamington in Ontario and Sandusky in Ohio. In winter there are scheduled flights from Windsor. Ferries land at either West Dock or Scudder Dock, the main communities on the island. The permanent population is 300, but in summer that quadruples as vacationers, mostly from Ohio, cram into 200 private cottages. At the end of October and beginning of November 700 hunters arrive to fill 18,000 pheasants with buckshot. The island has raised pheasants for hunters since 1932, a business that helps reduce taxes. There's usually someone to show visitors around the island's biggest industry, the pheasant farm in the middle of the island, and explain why the chicks wear what look like sunglasses. (It's so they can't peck one anothers' eyes out.) Pelee Island is not the most southerly place in Canada—that honor belongs to neighboring Little Middle Island—but Pelee *is* south; it's on the same latitude as northern California and northern Spain.

From the community of **West Dock** you can see **Perry's Victory and International Peace Monument,** a 352-foot-high monument commemorating American commander Captain Oliver Hazard Perry, who won control of Lake Erie at Put-in-Bay Island, Ohio, in 1813 by sailing straight into the British fleet while firing broadside, succinctly reporting: "We have met the enemy and they are ours."

From Leamington, take Highway 18 west to Kingsville and then follow Division Road north to Essex County Road 29. The
45 road to **Jack Miner's Bird Sanctuary** is well signposted. Jack Miner was an avid hunter who realized no species could survive both its natural enemies *and* man. In 1904 he dug ponds, planted trees, and introduced four Canada geese with clipped wings to the ponds. That number grew to the 50,000 that now winter here. From 1910 to 1940 Miner lectured on conservation and convinced kings and presidents of its need, thus earning him the Order of the British Empire in 1943. His former home is now a trust, open year-round except Sundays. No admission is charged and nothing is sold on the grounds. A two-story museum in the former stables has a wealth of Miner memorabilia, and at a pond beside the house you can feed far-from-shy geese and ducks with free feed. At 3 and 4 PM daily, including Sunday, the birds are flushed for "air shows," circling wildly overhead until they feel it's safe to land. The best times to view migrations are late March, October, and November. *On Essex County Rd. 29, 5 km (3 mi) north of Kingsville. Admission free. Open year-round, daily. Museum closed on Sun.*

The **John R. Park Homestead and Conservation Area,** 8 kilometers (5 miles) west of Kingsville, is a pioneer village anchored by one of Ontario's few examples of American Greek Revival architecture, an 1842 home. The 10 buildings include the house of John R. Park, a shed built with no nails, a smokehouse, icehouse, outhouse, blacksmith shop, sawmill, and livestock stable. *County Rd. 50 at Iler Rd., tel. 519/738–2029. Open July 1–Labor Day, daily 10–5; Oct.–mid-May, Mon.–Fri., and on Sun. when special events are held, 10–4.*

46 The turn-of-the-century **Southwestern Ontario Heritage Village** has 20 historic buildings on 54 wooded acres. Volunteers in period dress show visitors how pioneers baked, operated weaving looms, and dipped candles. The Transportation Museum of the Historic Vehicle Society of Ontario, Windsor Branch, features a fine collection of travel artifacts, from snowshoes to buggies to vintage automobiles. The gem of the collection is the world's only 1893 Shamrock. This adorable two-seater was the second effort at a workable prototype built by the Mira Brothers. When this one didn't run properly, either, the brothers abandoned their brief career as auto manufacturers. *About halfway bet. Kingsville and Essex on County Rd. 23, tel. 519/ 776–6909. Open Apr.–Nov., Wed.–Sun. 11–5; July–Aug., daily 11–5.*

47 The riverside parks in the quiet town of **Amherstburg** are great places from which to watch the procession of Great Lakes shipping. **Navy Yard Park,** with flower beds ringed by old anchor chains, has benches overlooking Bois Blanc Island and the narrow, main shipping channel.

Fort Malden was the British base in the War of 1812, when Detroit was captured, though its history goes back to 1727, when a Jesuit mission began occupying lands in the area. Now the fort is an 11-acre National Historic Park, which includes remains of the original earthworks, restored barracks, a military pensioner's cottage, two exhibit buildings, and picnic facilities. *Tel. 519/736–5416. Admission free. Open in winter, daily 10–5; June–Labor Day, daily 10–6.*

The **North American Black Historical Museum** tells of daring escapes by U.S. slaves and the Underground Railroad system many used to flee to Canada. Between 1800 and 1860, 30,000–50,000 slaves made the pilgrimage to Canada, the Promised Land, and many of those crossed the Detroit River at Amherstburg because it was the narrowest point. An 1848-vintage church and log cabin contain exhibits, artifacts, and biographies. *227 King St., tel. 519/736–5433. Admission free. Open Wed.–Fri. 10–5, Sat.–Sun. 1–5.*

48 **Windsor,** long an unattractive industrial city that hosted Ford, General Motors, and Chrysler manufacturing plants, has become an attractive place to visit. The riverfront has pretty parks, some with fountains and statues, all overlooking the spectacular Detroit skyline. The cities are linked by the Ambassador Bridge and the Windsor–Detroit Tunnel. If you're traveling by car, start your visit at the Convention and Visitors Bureau (80 Chatham Street East), where you can get a free date-stamped parking pass for use during your stay.

The **Art Gallery of Windsor** features changing displays of contemporary and historic Canadian and foreign art. *445 Riverside Drive W, tel. 519/258–7111. Admission free. Open Tues.–Sun.*

The **Hiram Walker Historical Museum** is a collection of area artifacts displayed in the 1812 Francois Baby House where the Battle of Windsor, the final incident in the Upper Canada Rebellion, was fought in 1838. *254 Pitt St., tel. 519/253–1812. Admission free. Open Tues.–Sun.*

Farmers, butchers, and bakers from southwestern Ontario sell their fresh produce at **Windsor City Market,** which offers more than 100 permanent vendors. *Chatham St. E. bet. MacDougall and Market Sts., tel. 519/255–6260. Open Wed.–Thurs. 7–4, Fri. 7–6, Sat. from 5 AM. Some stalls open Mon. and Tues.*

Willistead Manor is the former home of Edward Chandler Walker, second son of Hiram, who founded Walker's Distillery in 1858. The 15-acre estate is now a city park. Work on the mansion was completed in 1906, and no expense was spared building the 36-room spread designed in the 16th-century Tudor-Jacobean style of an English manor house. *1899 Niagara St., tel. 519/255–6545 or 519/255–6270. Admission free. Tours available. Open Sept.–Nov., daily.*

Since 1959, Windsor and Detroit have combined their national birthday parties (Canada Day, July 1; and Independence Day, July 4) into a massive bash called **International Freedom Festival.** The two-week party includes nonstop entertainment with more than 100 special events on both sides of the river and a spectacular fireworks display, billed as the largest in North America. *Tel. 519/255–6530.*

Tour 5: Niagara and West to London

49 There is probably no natural attraction exploited as thoroughly as the falls at **Niagara.** You can go over the falls in a helicopter; get almost directly underneath them by boat; go around them on bridges; or go behind them in a tunnel. The first travel writer to visit Niagara Falls more than 300 years ago wrote, "The universe does not afford its parallel. The roar of them can be heard 15 leagues away" (a distance of 72 kilometers, or 45 miles). And explorer and missionary Father Louis Hennepin described their height as 600 feet—when in fact they are 176 feet high. When Europeans read Hennepin's 1678 accounts, they ranked Niagara among the Seven Wonders of the World. Despite Hennepin's gross exaggerations, few have ever been disappointed by a visit to the falls. About 12 million tourists visit each year. And daredevils have been drawn to the falls since 1828. Eight people have survived plunging over them in a variety of contraptions, and the list of those who perished in the attempt is a long one. Fines for performing illegal stunts on property owned by the Niagara Parks Commission (NPC) have been raised to $10,000, but the stunt-lovers keep on coming.

Numbers in the margin correspond to points of interest on the Niagara Falls map.

The NPC was formed in 1885 to preserve the area around the falls. Beginning with a small block of land, the NPC has gradually acquired most of the land fronting on the Canadian side of the Niagara River, from Niagara-on-the-Lake to Fort Erie. This 56-kilometer (35-mile) riverside drive is a 3,000-acre ribbon of parkland lined with parking areas, picnic tables, and barbecue pits, and the public is welcome to use the facilities at **50** no charge. The NPC's **Greenhouse and Plant Conservatory,** just south of the Horseshoe Falls, is open year-round daily.

51 Visitors are also welcome at the NPC **School of Horticulture** several miles north of (downriver from) the falls, on the Niagara Parkway. The school has been graduating professional gardeners since 1936, and students display their expertise with flowers and shrubbery.

52 From the school it's a short distance (downriver) to one of the world's largest **floral clocks.** Its 40-foot-wide "living" face is planted in a different design each year.

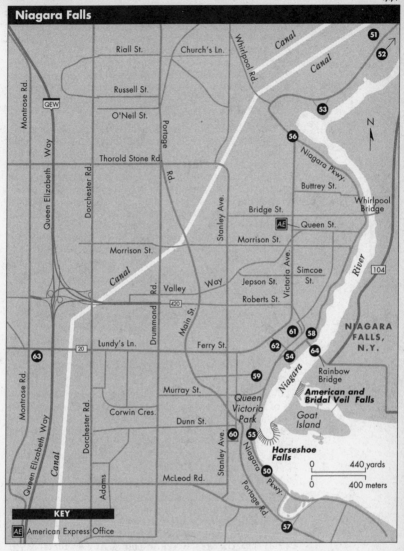

Niagara Falls

Riall St.
Church's Ln.
Whirlpool Rd.
Canal
Canal

Russell St.

Montrose Rd.
QEW

O'Neil St.

Queen Elizabeth Way

Portage Rd.

Thorold Stone Rd.

Niagara Pkwy.

Dorchester Rd.

Buttrey St.

Whirlpool Bridge

Stanley Ave.

Bridge St.

AE Queen St.

Morrison St.
Morrison St.

Canal

River

104

Valley
Way

Victoria Ave.

Simcoe St.

Drummond Rd.

420

Jepson St.

Roberts St.

Main St.

NIAGARA FALLS, N.Y.

Lundy's Ln.
20

Ferry St.

63

Montrose Rd.

Murray St.

Dorchester Rd.

Corwin Cres.

Dunn St.

Niagara

Rainbow Bridge

American and Bridal Veil Falls

Queen Victoria Park

Goat Island

Stanley Ave.

Adams

McLeod Rd.

Niagara Pkwy.

Portage Rd.

Horseshoe Falls

0 — 440 yards
0 — 400 meters

N

KEY

AE American Express Office

Clifton Hill, **62**
Floral Clock, **52**
Greenhouse and Plant Conservatory, **50**
Maid of the Mist, **54**
Maple Leaf Village, **61**
Marineland, **57**
Minolta Tower, **60**

Niagara Falls Museum, **58**
Niagara Glen , **53**
NPC(Niagara Parks) School of Horticulture, **51**
Niagara Spanish Aero Car, **56**
Ride Niagara, **64**
Skylon Tower, **59**

Table Rock Scenic Tunnels, **55**
White Water Water Park, **63**

53 Heading back upriver, there are trails maintained by the NPC in the **Niagara Glen.** A **bicycle trail** that parallels the Niagara Parkway from Fort Erie to Niagara-on-the-Lake winds between beautiful homes on one side and the river, with its abundant bird life, on the other. There are free band concerts on summer Sundays at **Queenston Heights Park, Queen Victoria Park,** and **Old Fort Erie** (*see* Tour 4, above) as well as **Rainbow Bridge Carillon** recitals. And don't forget to catch the free colored illumination of the falls 365 nights a year.

The **Festival of Lights** runs from the end of November to the third week of February. It started in Niagara Falls, Ontario, in 1981, and now stretches the length of the Niagara Parkway between Fort Erie and Niagara-on-the-Lake. The city claims a lot of superlatives during this period: world's largest Christmas tree (the Skylon Tower), world's largest gift (Your Host Motor Inn decorated to look like a giant gift-wrapped box), world's largest candle (the Minolta Tower), etc. The festival started with massive corporate displays, but the idea caught on with smaller businesses and private residents. There are now so many displays that tours are offered ranging from 2½ to 3½ hours.

54 *Maid of the Mist* boats have been operating since 1846, when they were wooden-hulled, coal-fired steamboats. Nowadays, passengers are issued hooded rain slickers for the 30-minute trip because the three modern boats get so close to both falls that the spray is heavy. *Boats leave from the foot of Clifton Hill, tel. 416/358–5781. Admission: $8.30 adults, $4.70 children 6–12. Open mid-May–late Oct., daily. Late June–Labor Day, boats leave as often as every 15 min. from 9:45 to 7:45; off-season, boats leave every 30 minutes weekdays from 9:45.*

55 At **Table Rock Scenic Tunnels** your admission ticket includes use of rubber boots and a hooded rain slicker. You walk to an observation plaza just under the lip of the falls, and from there a tunnel takes you almost to the middle of the falls and behind the wall of crashing water. *Tours begin at Table Rock House in Queen Victoria Park, tel. 416/354–1551. Admission: $5 adults, $4.50 senior citizens, $2.50 children 6–12. Open mid-June–Labor Day, 9–11; 9–5 the rest of the year. Closed Dec. 25.*

56 The **Niagara Spanish Aero Car,** a cable car that crosses the Whirlpool Basin in the Niagara Gorge, has been operating since 1918. This trip is not for the fainthearted; when you're swinging high above the roiling whirlpool, those cables seem awfully thin. **The Great Gorge Adventure.** An elevator takes you to the bottom of the Niagara Gorge where you can walk a boardwalk beside the roaring torrent of the Niagara River as it is forced between sheer cliffs and enters the Giant Whirlpool. *On River Rd., 3 km (2 mi) north of the falls, tel. 416/354–5711. AeroCar Admission: $4.25 adults, $3.85 senior citizens, $2.15 children 6–12. Adventure Admission: $4 adults, $3.60 senior citizens, $2 children. Open June–Labor Day, 9–9; shorter hours until mid-October, weather permitting.*

57 **Marineland,** a year-round marine park, game farm, and theme park, is located 1.5 kilometers (1 mile) south of the falls. The daily marine show includes the world's largest troupe of performing dolphins, killer whales, clowns, and trained seals. Children can pet and feed a herd of 500 deer, get nose-to-nose with exotic fish, and meet cartoon characters. Among the many rides is the world's largest steel roller coaster. Marineland is signposted from Niagara Parkway or reached from the Queen Elizabeth Way by exiting at McLeod Road (Exit 27). *7657 Portage Rd., tel. 416/356-9565. Admission: $17.95 adults, $14.95 children 4-9 and senior citizens. In winter the rides are closed and prices drop to less than half. Open mid-June-Labor Day, weekdays 10-5, weekends 10-6; winter, 10-4:30.*

58 The **Niagara Falls Museum** claims to be North America's oldest museum and is chockablock with everything from stuffed birds to an excellent display of Egyptian mummies. It houses the Daredevil Hall of Fame and displays barrels and other contraptions in which people have gone over the falls. There are 26 galleries on four floors and 700,000 exhibits, so gauge your time accordingly—this museum is well worth two hours of browsing. *5651 River Rd., tel. 416/356-2151. Admission: $5.75 adults, $5 senior citizens, $3.75 students, $2.75 children 5-10. Open summer, 8:30-11 daily; winter, 10-5.*

Three towers and a huge Ferris wheel offer **panoramic views** of the falls and area, as does Niagara Helicopters Ltd. (*see* Guided Tours, above). The view of the Horseshoe Falls is best from the **59 60 61** **Skylon** or **Minolta** tower, but the **Kodak Tower at Maple Leaf Village** has the best view over the American Falls, Niagara Gorge, and the rapids above the falls. You can also get a good look over all the falls from atop North America's largest Ferris wheel at **Maple Leaf Village Amusement Park.**

Skylon Tower, 520 feet above ground level, 5200 Robinson St. (directly above the Horseshoe Falls), tel. 416/356-2651. Admission: $5.95 adults, $4.95 senior citizens, $3.50 children 6-12, $16.95 families (2 adults, 2 children). For dining, elevator rate is $1.50 adults, $1 children and senior citizens. Open mid-June-Labor Day, 8-1; 10-9 rest of the year.

Minolta Tower, 325 feet above ground level, 6732 Oakes Dr., tel. 416/356-1501. At the base of the tower, there is an aquarium and reptile display. Admission to tower only: $4.95 adult, $3.50 students 5-18 and senior citizens. Admission to tower and aquarium and reptile exhibit: $6.95 adults, $5.95 students and senior citizens. Open in summer, 9-midnight; in winter, 9-9.

Maple Leaf Village and Kodak Tower: The tower is 360 feet above ground level; the top of the Ferris wheel is 175 feet above ground level; 5685 Falls Ave., tel. 416/357-3090. Admission to the village is free. Admission to tower and daredevil exhibit: $5.50 adults, $3.50 senior citizens, $1.50 children under 12. Single ride on Ferris wheel: $3.30, children under 3 free. Open mid-May-mid-Oct., daily 10:30-4; summer, 10-6:30.

62 **Clifton Hill,** almost directly opposite the American falls, is probably the most touristy corner of Niagara Falls. Sometimes referred to as "Museum Alley," this area encompasses the Guinness World of Records Museum, Ripley's Believe It Or Not Museum, Louis Tussaud's Waxworks Museum, The Haunted House, The Funhouse, The House of Frankenstein and Super Star Recording (where you can record the musical number of your choice), Movieland Wax Museum, Criminals Hall of Fame Wax Museum, The Elvis Presley Museum, and the That's Incredible Museum.

Ⓧ **White Water Water Park** offers just about every means of getting wet there is, including Canada's biggest waterslide. *7430 Lundy's La., tel. 416/357–3380. Open June–Labor Day, daily.*

Ⓧ **Ride Niagara** is a new attraction opened in 1991 by the NPC. It's located near the falls and simulates riding a barrel over the falls. *5755 River Rd., tel. 416/374–7433. Admission: $7.95 adults, $6.95 senior citizens, $3.95 children 3–12. Not recommended for children under 3. Open year-round.*

Some of the Niagara Peninsula's 13 **wineries** are on the Niagara Parkway between Niagara Falls and Niagara-on-the-Lake (*see* below), or on Highway 55 from the Queen Elizabeth Way. All offer tours, and the product may be sampled and bought, though never on Sunday! For exact times, call ahead: **Chateau des Charmes Wines Ltd.** (tel. 416/262–4219), **Hillebrand Estates Winery** (tel. 416/468–7123), **Iniskillin Wines** (tel. 416/468–3554), **Konzelmann Winery** (tel. 416/935–2866), **Reif Winery** (tel. 416/468–7738), and **Willowbank Estate Wines** (tel. 416/468–4219).

Numbers in the margin correspond to points of interest on the Lower Ontario Province map.

Ⓧ The Victorian town of **Niagara-on-the-Lake,** 15 kilometers (10 miles) north of Niagara Falls (downriver), is one of Ontario's showplaces. Stately homes sit back from tree-shaded streets, well apart from their neighbors. Though most are at least a century old, their modern-day owners keep rose trellises painted and brass door knockers gleaming. A dozen lovely inns here, some of which were built for that purpose a century and a half ago, make this a perfect getaway for Torontorians and tourists worn down by the neon of this village's southern neighbor. Any proposed new business is screened by the village council to ensure that no chrome, glass, or neon-girdled atrocity will mar its Victorian character. There's no room on these tiny roads for the invasion of motor homes, campers, and buses that occurs here each summer, so be prepared for long traffic snarls. The best way to experience the town at any time of year is to stroll.

Don't miss the **Niagara Apothecary,** a pharmacy museum on the main street, across from the 1848 courthouse, which replicates the pharmacy that first opened here in 1866. The serving counters are solid planks of walnut, and the crystal chandeliers are reproductions of original gasoliers. *5 Queen St. Admission free. Open mid-May–Labor Day, daily noon–6.*

The **Niagara Historical Society Museum,** built in 1906, houses a collection of artifacts from native times through the arrival of the Loyalists and the War of 1812. *43 Castlereagh St., tel. 416/468–3912. Admission: $2 adults, $1 students, 50¢ children under 12. Open May–Oct., daily 10–5; Jan.–Feb., weekends only 1–5; Mar.–Apr. and Nov.–Dec., daily 1–5.*

The British **Fort George** was fully restored in 1939. Today soldiers in period dress perform drills and musical programs on the parade square. *Niagara Pky. (tel. 416/468–4257). Open daily mid-May–Oct.*

The event that has really put Niagara-on-the-Lake on the map is the **Shaw Festival** (*see* The Arts and Nightlife, below, for details).

The **Niagara Peninsula** is Ontario's fruit basket. From mid-summer to late fall, fruit and vegetable stands proliferate along the highways and byways. There are several farmers' markets along the Queen Elizabeth Way. One of the best displays of fruits and vegetables is on Lincoln County Road 55 between Niagara-on-the-Lake and the Queen Elizabeth Way, the route you'll take to Hamilton. **Harvest Barn Market,** marked by a red-and-white-striped awning, not only features regional fruits and vegetables but also tempts with a bakery offering sausage rolls, tiny loaves of bread, and fruit pies. You can test the market's wares at the picnic tables, where knowledgeable locals have lunch.

66 **Hamilton** is Canada's steel capital—the Dofasco and Stelco mills produce 60% of Canada's iron and steel. This isn't the sort of city where you'd expect to find 2,700 acres of gardens and exotic plants, a symphony orchestra, a modern and active theater, 45 parks, a 100-voice choir, and an opera. But they're all here in Ontario's second-largest city and Canada's third-busiest port.

The city's downtown is on a plain between the harbor and the base of "the mountain," a 250-foot-high section of the Niagara Escarpment. Downtown Hamilton is a potpourri of glass-walled high rises, century-old mansions, a convention center, coliseum, and shopping complex. Hamilton is also home to Canada's largest indoor farmers' market—176 stalls spread over more than 20,000 square feet—started in 1837. Its new home adjoins Jackson Square and the new Eaton Centre. *Tel. 416/546-2096. Open Tues., Thurs., and Sat. 7–6, Fri. 9–6.*

The 50-year-old **Royal Botanical Gardens** encompass five major gardens and 48 kilometers (30 miles) of trails that wind across marshes and ravines, past the world's largest collection of lilac, two acres of roses, and all manner of shrubs, trees, plants, hedges, and flowers. Two teahouses are open May 1–Thanksgiving. *Plains Rd. (Hwy. 2) in Burlington, accessible from the Queen Elizabeth Way and Hwys. 6 and 403, tel. 416/527–1158; in Ontario and Quebec, 800/668–9449.*

Sir Allan Napier MacNab, War of 1812 hero and Upper Canada's pre-Confederation prime minister, built a 35-room mansion called **Dundurn Castle** in 1832–35. It has been furnished to reflect the opulence in which MacNab lived at the height of his political career. *Dundurn Park at York Blvd., tel. 416/522–5313. Open June–Labor Day, daily 11–4, rest of the year 1–4. Closed Christmas and New Year's Day.*

Flamboro Downs harness racing track, just west of Hamilton, has matinee and evening races year-round, though not on a daily basis. The clubhouse has two dining areas that overlook the track. *Hwy. 5., tel. 416/627–3561.*

67 **Brantford,** 40 kilometers (25 miles) west of Hamilton on Highway 403, is named after Joseph Brant, the Loyalist Mohawk chief who brought members of the Six Nations Confederacy into Canada after the American Revolution.

King George III showed gratitude to Chief Brant and his loyal Indian subjects by building the **Mohawk Church.** In 1904, by Royal assent, it was given the name His Majesty's Chapel of the Mohawks (now changed to Her Majesty's). It is the oldest Protestant church in Ontario and the only one that may include Royal in its name. The simple, white-painted frame building has eight stained-glass windows depicting the colorful history of the Six Nations people. *291 Mohawk St., tel. 519/445–4528. Admission free. A guide is available. Open July–Aug., daily 10–6; the rest of the year, Wed.–Sat. 10–6, Sun. 1–5.*

Woodland Indian Cultural Educational Centre is a museum of sorts that aims to preserve and promote the culture and heritage of the native people of the First Nation. The modern building contains displays and exhibits showing early Woodland Indian culture. *184 Mohawk St., near the Mohawk Chapel., tel. 519/759–2650. Open year-round, daily.*

Although the city is the hometown of hockey star Wayne Gretzky, it is better known as "The Telephone City" because Alexander Graham Bell invented the device here and made the first long-distance call from his parents' home to nearby Paris in 1874. The **Bell Homestead** is now a National Historic Site. Next door is the house of the Reverend Thomas Henderson, a Baptist minister who left the church when he recognized the profit potential in telephones. His home was the first telephone office and now is a museum of telephone artifacts and displays. *94 Tutela Heights Rd., tel. 519/756–6220. Admission free. Guides available. Open daily except Mon.*

About 27 kilometers (18 miles) north of Brantford by Highway 24 are the cities of **Kitchener** and **Waterloo,** which merge into each another and are usually referred to as K–W. The region was settled around 1800 by Swiss-German Mennonites from Pennsylvania. The German origins remain obvious: There's a huge glockenspiel downtown by Speakers' Corner, and each October since 1967 the city has hosted Oktoberfest. The event now draws more than 600,000 people who swarm to 21 festival halls where they dance, gorge on German-style food, listen to oom-pah bands, and drink with a fervor that seems driven by a fear that all Canadian breweries are about to go on strike.

There are farmers' markets all over Ontario, but the **Kitchener Market** is particularly well known. It isn't the oldest or biggest, but it's been around since 1869 and since 1986 has been housed in spacious quarters at Market Square. The block-long complex is wrapped in green-tinted glass and contains 70 shops and snack bars and an Eaton's department store. *Cor. Frederick and Duke Sts., tel. 519/741–2287. Open Sat. 5 AM–2 PM; mid-May–mid-Oct., Wed. 7 AM–2 PM.*

William Lyon Mackenzie King, who was prime minister of Canada for 22 of the years between 1821 and 1948, spent his teenage years in a rented 10-room house called Woodside, now **Woodside National Historic Park.** There's no particular imprint here of the bachelor prime minister whose diaries reveal his belief in mysticism, portents, and communications with the dead, but the house has been furnished to reflect the period of the King family occupancy. *528 Wellington St., tel. 519/742–5273. Admission free. Open daily 10–5. Closed holidays in winter.*

The **Seagram Museum** is a shrine to booze, and every exhibit in the enormous former barrel warehouses and new exhibition building relates to the product. Tour guides are available, and for those who develop a powerful thirst while browsing, there's a specialty liquor store that sells Seagram products and gift items. *57 Erb St. W, tel. 519/746–1673. Open Tues.–Fri. 11–8, Sat.–Sun. 11–5. Closed Mon.*

Doon Heritage Crossroads is a complete pioneer village just north of Highway 401, a few kilometers south and west of Kitchener. The village tranquilly recalls the lifestyle of a people who lived near the main highway of the early 1800s, the Huron Road. Visitors wander tree-shaded roadways where neither automobiles nor the noises of the urban complex to the north intrude. Staff at the village wear period costumes, and some work at the old-time crafts. *Tel. 519/748–1914. Open May–Labor Day, 10–4:30; Labor Day–Dec., 1:30–4:30. Closed Jan.–Apr.*

69 The villages of **St. Jacobs** and **Elmira**, a few kilometers north of K–W, are in the heart of Mennonite and Hutterite country. These are peaceful people who live off the land, refuse to participate in wars, and have a strict moral code. They also resist modern conveniences, like cars, electricity, and the internal combustion engine. The region is a shopper's paradise, with many shops selling all manner of fresh and preserved foods and gift items handcrafted by the Mennonites. **Brox's Olde Town Village** (tel. 519/669–5121) at the main intersection in Elmira is a massive shopping complex all under one roof.

70 The **City of Stratford** is 46 kilometers (28 miles) west of Kitchener by Highways 7 and 8. It was named by homesick English settlers; all that the town would have had in common with England's Stratford was a river called Avon meandering through rolling countryside—and not even particularly similar countryside.

The **Stratford Festival** hosts music, opera, and drama annually for more than 400,000 people. (*See* The Arts and Nightlife, below, for details.)

71 To reach **London** from Stratford, take Highway 7 west and turn south on Highway 4 at Elginfield. This will bring you into the city's north end and past the entrance to the University of Western Ontario. London is a quiet, provincial city where old money rules the arts and development projects. Its nickname is The Forest City—it has more than 50,000 trees on city property and 1,500 acres of parks, including 1,000 acres along the Thames River. This low-key city has been called a microcosm of Canadian life; it is so "typically Canadian," it's often used as a test market for new products—if something will sell in London, it will probably sell anywhere in Canada.

The easiest way to get an overview of the town is to take a tour on a big, red, double-decker—what else?—London bus. They operate from City Hall at 10 and 2, July 1 to Labor Day. From June through October you can get another view of London by cruising on the Thames River in a 60-passenger boat. Afternoon cruises depart every hour, June through August, from Storybook Gardens (696 Headley Dr., tel. 519/473–0363).

Because **Storybook Gardens** is owned and operated by the city's Public Utility Commission, this is one of the least expensive children's theme parks in the country. It's on the Thames River in 281-acre Springbank Park. You'll see a castle, storybook characters, and a zoo with foreign and indigenous animals, including those from Old MacDonald's Farm. Children can slide down Jack and Jill's hill and the throat of Willie the Whale. *Tel. 519/661–5770. Admission: $3 adults, $1 children. Open early May–Labor Day.*

London Regional Art Gallery is as interesting from the outside as its exhibits are on the inside. The gallery is contained in six joined, glass-covered structures whose ends are the shape of croquet hoops. *At The Forks of the Thames, tel. 519/672–4580. Open year-round, Tues.–Sat.*

The **Museum of Indian Archaeology** houses more than 40,000 Indian artifacts and a gallery of artists' conceptions of the lives of the Attawandaron Indians, who lived on the museum site some 500 years ago. Nearby is a reconstructed multifamily longhouse on its original site. *Wonderland Rd., south of Hwy. 22., tel. 519/473–1360. Open year-round, daily.*

London's oldest building is also one of its most impressive. The wrecker's ball came awfully close to the **Old Courthouse Building,** and it got one wall of the former Middlesex County Gaol. But a citizens' group prevailed, and in 1981, after a $2.5 million face-lift, the Old Courthouse, modeled after Malahide Castle in England, reopened as the home of Middlesex County Council. On weekday afternoons free tours are available. *Tel. 519/434–7321.*

On the grounds of **Labatt's Brewery** is a well-researched replica of the 1828 London Brewery, which became Labatt's Brewery in 1853. *150 Simcoe Street. Admission free. Open June–Labor Day, Mon.–Sat. 11–5. No samples.*

Tour 6: Sault Ste. Marie and West to Thunder Bay

Numbers in the margin correspond to points of interest on the Upper Ontario Province map.

72 **Sault Ste. Marie** has always been a natural meeting place and cultural melting pot. Long before Etienne Brule "discovered" the rapids in 1622, Ojibwa tribes gathered here. Whitefish, their staple food, could easily be caught year-round, and the rapids in the St. Marys River linking Lakes Huron and Superior were often the only open water for miles during the winter. When Father Jacques Marquette opened a mission in 1668, he named it Sainte Marie de Sault. Today everybody but tourists calls it simply "The Sault," and the smaller city across the river in Michigan is called "The Soo." Different spelling, identical pronunciation.

The elegant **Ermatinger Stone House** was built by Montréal fur trader Charles Oakes Ermatinger in 1814 and is the oldest building in Canada west of Toronto. Ermatinger married Charlotte, a daughter of influential Indian chief Katawebeda, a move that didn't hurt his business. Today, costumed interpreters show visitors through the house and demonstrate cooking, baking, and crafts. *831 Queen St. E, tel. 705/759–5443. Admission: donation. Open Apr.–May 31, weekdays 10–5; June–Sept. 30, daily 10–5; Oct.–Nov. 30, daily 1–5.*

One of The Sault's most-touted sights is a boat tour through the **Soo Locks,** the 16th and final lift for ships bound for Lake Superior from the St. Lawrence River, 600 feet lower and 3,200 kilometers (2,000 miles) downstream. Your cruise boat will be lifted only 21 feet through one of the four locks on the U.S. side, but if you haven't been through a lock before it's an interesting experience. Two-hour tours aboard the **MV *Chief Shingwauk*** or the **MV *Bon Soo*** leave the Norgoma Dock near the Holiday

Upper Ontario Province

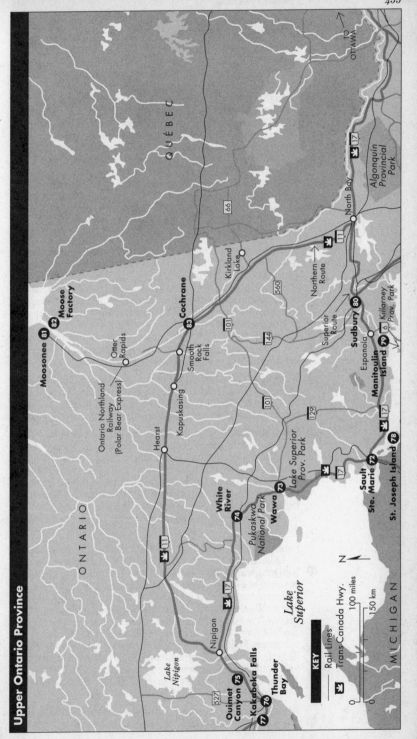

QUÉBEC

TO OTTAWA →

ONTARIO

Moosonee **81**

Moose Factory **82**

Otter Rapids

Ontario Northland Railway
(Polar Bear Express)

Cochrane **83**

Smooth Rock Falls

Kapuskasing

Hearst

Kirkland Lake

North Bay

Algonquin Provincial Park

Northern Route

Superior Route

Sudbury **80**

Killarney Prov. Park

Espanola

Manitoulin Island **79**

Lake Superior Prov. Park

White River **74**

Wawa **73**

Pukaskwa National Park

Sault Ste. Marie **72**

St. Joseph Island **78**

MICHIGAN

Lake Superior

Lake Nipigon

Nipigon

Ouimet Canyon **75**

Kakabeka Falls **76**

Thunder Bay **77**

KEY
Rail Lines
Trans-Canada Hwy.

N

0   100 miles
0   150 km

Inn mid-May to mid-October, and up to eight times daily July to Labor Day. *Tel. 705/253–9850.*

The Algoma Central Railway (129 Bay St., tel. 705/254–4331) not only operates main line track between The Sault and iron mines at Hearst and Michipicoten Harbor but also runs a lucrative sideline of tour trains to and from scenic Agawa Canyon, through which their main line passes. From spring through fall the **Agawa Canyon Train Tour** runs from The Sault to Mile 114 (182 kilometers). In winter, the **Snow Train** goes to Mile 120 (192 kilometers). In summer the train stops for two hours in **Agawa Canyon,** a deep valley 19 kilometers (12 miles) long with cliff walls up to 800 feet high through which the Agawa River flows. During the stopover, passengers can lunch in a park, hike to their choice of three waterfalls, or climb to a lookout 250 feet above the train. Tour trains run daily June 5 to mid-October and on Saturday and Sunday only, January through March. Trains depart at 8 AM in summer and 8:30 AM in winter and return at 5 PM. Dining car service is continuous 7 AM–3:45 PM.

Gas up in The Sault before you head north on Highway 17, **The Great North Road.** There is some spectacular scenery along this route. The highway climbs through high hills, and from the top of headlands there are vistas across wide bays in Lake Superior. At the crossings of the Batchawana, Montreal, Agawa, and Michipicoten rivers, south of **Wawa** there are picnic spots. It's 225 kilometers (131 miles) from The Sault to Wawa; the last 80 kilometers (50 miles) is through **Lake Superior Provincial Park.** If you're going to Thunder Bay, 690 kilometers (400 miles) northwest, plan to stop at **Wawa** or **White River.**

73 **Wawa** is an Ojibwa word meaning "wild goose," and the 4,000 residents of Wawa have erected a massive goose monument at the entrance to town from Highway 17. Next door is the town's new log-cabin tourist information office.

74 **White River,** 90 kilometers (56 miles) north on Highway 17, is marked by a huge thermometer indicating 72 degrees below zero and a sign that advises: "White River—coldest place in Canada." Mayor Ollie Chapman says she'd love to see the thermometer torn down and have a large statue of Winnie-the-Pooh erected in its place to honor the black bear from White River immortalized in Christopher Robin children's stories by British author A.A. Milne. The town is trying to raise half a million dollars for it.

Continue west on the Trans-Canada Highway, around the top of Lake Superior. Just past the town of Hurkett, west of
75 Nipigon, watch for signs to **Ouimet Canyon.** This geological anomaly is a midget compared to Agawa Canyon but, because of the vantage point, it is more spectacular. At Ouimet, the visitor strolls a wide path and suddenly comes to the edge of the canyon. Viewing platforms extend over the edge so you can look straight down 329 feet. The far wall is only 492 feet away, and the chasm is only 2.4 kilometers (1.5 miles) long. Geologists believe the canyon could be a gigantic fault in the world's surface, or it could have been carved by a glacier. *The turnoff to Ouimet Park is 67 km (42 mi) northeast of Thunder Bay. Admission: free. Open mid-May–Thanksgiving.*

Although they amalgamated into one city of 120,000 in 1970,
76 there is still a **Port Arthur** section of **Thunder Bay** and a **Fort**

William section. The city is the world's largest grain-handling center and Canada's second-largest port. It has an extraordinary ethnic mix, with 42 nationalities clearly represented, 110 churches, and the largest Finnish population outside Finland. The area has Ontario's best skiing and longest ski season, superb fishing and hunting, unlimited canoe and boating routes, and even mountain climbing. The city has an art gallery, hundreds of restaurants, nine shopping malls, and **Old Fort William,** a reconstructed fur-trading fort with 42 historic buildings on a 125-acre site (tel. 807/577–8461).

The double-decker cruise ship *Welcome* carries visitors on harbor tours and to and from Old Fort William. The harbor cruises get the visitor closer to the giant grain elevators, the ships servicing them, and the nearby islands. Visitors can take the *Welcome* to the fort and return on the cruise company's bus. In mid-summer there are three harbor tours daily, including an evening cruise. *467 Parkwood Dr., tel. 807/344–2512. Mid-May to early Oct.*

If legend is to be believed, wearing an amethyst will protect you from hangovers. Ontario's gemstone is an imperfect quartz, tinted violet or purple by the impurity of iron atoms mixing with the original liquid rock. There are five amethyst mines between Sleeping Giant Provincial Park and Ouimet Canyon, a distance of 50 kilometers (31 miles) along Highways 11 and 17 east of Thunder Bay. All are signposted from the highway, and each offers the opportunity to hand-pick some samples (you pay for them by the pound). If you don't want to drive to a mine, the stone is sold in jewelry stores, and several of the mines have shops in the city. **Thunder Bay Amethyst Mine Panorama** (tel. 807/622–6908) is closest to the city and claims to be North America's largest. Follow Loon Lake Road from Highways 11 and 17, east of Thunder Bay. *Closed Sun.*

⓱ **Kakabeka Falls** on the Kaministikwia River, 40 kilometers (25 miles) northwest of Thunder Bay, drop 154 feet over a limestone ledge into a deep gorge. The falls can be seen from either side and there are large, free parking lots.

Tour 7: East along Georgian Bay and South to Manitoulin Island

⓲ **St. Joseph Island** is a sparsely settled island about 24 by 30 kilometers (16 by 20 miles) in the mouth of the St. Mary's River, 40 kilometers (25 miles) southeast of The Sault and connected by causeway and bridge to the mainland. In spring the island is a scented riot of wild lilac, and you're likely to see moose and deer along the quiet side roads. In fur-trading days, Fort St. Joseph was a British fort at the southeast tip of the island that guarded the trade route from Montréal to the upper Great Lakes. Today's visitor can wander the rounded peninsula on which the fort and commercial buildings once stood and see the outlines and a few above-ground stone ruins of the 42 building sites that have been identified. Get a free walking-tour booklet at the visitor center. *Tel. 705/246–2664. Open late May–Thanksgiving, daily.*

East of St. Joseph Island and south of **Espanola,** along Route 6, the world's largest freshwater island sits at the top of Lake **⓳** Huron plugging the mouth of Georgian Bay. **Manitoulin Island** is 160 kilometers (100 miles) long and varies in width from 3 to

64 kilometers (2 to 40 miles). The island is pretty and rugged, with granite outcrops, forests, meadows, rivers, and rolling countryside. Only 20% of the land is arable, and much of the rest is used for grazing sheep and cattle. Yachtsmen rate the waters around the islands among the best in the world, and hunters and fishermen have taken advantage of the island's riches for generations. Hikes and exploration could easily turn this "side trip" into a week-long stay. This is a place that for the most part has been unravaged by time. Archaeological digs on Manitoulin Island have produced traces of human habitation that are more than 30,000 years old, making them the oldest on the North American continent. There is no interim record of people living on the island until explorer Samuel de Champlain met some island residents in 1650.

Little Current–Howland Centennial Museum, about 18 kilometers (12 miles) south of **Little Current,** in the village of Sheguiandah on Highway 6, displays native and pioneer artifacts. *Tel. 705/368–2367. Open mid-May–mid-Sept., daily 10–4:30.*

The extreme eastern end of the island is **Wikwemikong,** 484 square kilometers (300 square miles). One of Manitoulin's most colorful events is the Wikwemikong Pow Wow, held on Civic Holiday weekend. Dancers accompanied by drummers and singers compete for prizes while performing the steps of their ancestors.

Back on the mainland, about 60 kilometers (40 miles) east of Espanola, is the mining town of **Sudbury,** which used to bear the brunt of a lot of unkind jokes. After all, didn't the U.S. astronauts go there to train in the type of terrain they were likely to encounter on the moon? Today, the Greening of Sudbury, a student planting project, and other renovations have given this clean city of 90,000 a face-lift. New, imaginatively designed buildings, well-lighted streets, and a downtown anchored by a spiffy Civic Square Provincial Tower invite visitors. There are concerts in the park, art centers, and a cruise on Lake Ramsey, the largest freshwater lake inside city limits in North America.

Northern Ontario's biggest tourism magnet, **Science North,** opened in 1984. This hands-on science museum is housed in two snowflake-shaped buildings that cling to a rocky ledge of the shore of Lake Ramsey. Lie on a bed of nails, create a soapstone carving, or make your own hurricane or snowstorm. At every turn there are eager museum staff to answer questions and encourage participation in the dozens of laboratories. *100 Ramsey Lake Rd., tel. 705/522–3701. Open daily spring and fall, 9–5; in winter, 10–4; late June–Labor Day, 9–7.*

The Big Nickel, a 30-foot replica of the Canadian 1951 commemorative coin, has been synonymous with Sudbury for almost three decades. It is the largest coin in the world and stands on a barren hillside on the west side of the city, overlooking the smokestacks of the International Nickel Company (INCO). Near the Big Nickel is the entrance to **The Big Nickel Mine.** At 23 meters (73 feet), it is one of the shallowest mines in the area. Science North (*see* above) offers tours of the mine in summer. Visitors are given hard hats, coats, and boots and lowered into the mine shaft in a "cage" elevator. In the 400-meter-long (437-yard-long) drifts, or tunnels, miners demonstrate mining techniques. *At Hwy. 17 and Big Nickel Mine Rd., tel. 705/673–5659* *or 705/522–3701. Tour runs daily, May–June 25, 9–5; June 26–Labor Day, 9–7; Labor Day–Oct. 9, 9–5.*

The 2½-hour **Path of Discovery Tour** bus leaves from The Big Nickel and Science North several times daily. Visitors are taken to the spot where a railroad worker discovered copper and nickel ores 4 kilometers (2.5 miles) west of the townsite in 1884. The tour also goes to the edge of the Sudbury Basin, a massive indentation in the landscape created 2 billion years ago by a meteorite, a volcanic eruption, or a combination of the two. The event created an elliptical depression 59 kilometers (40 miles) long and 27 kilometers (18 miles) wide. The tour visits Sudbury's oldest mine, historic sites in Copper Cliff, and the smelter and super stack at INCO, the world's largest integrated nickel mining, smelting, and refining complex. *Tel. 705/673–5659 or 705/522–3701.*

Tour 8: From Cochrane to Moosonee and Moose Factory Island

③① ③② **Moosonee** and **Moose Factory** are considered Ontario's gateway to the Arctic. Although you can fly to Moosonee (Air Creebac, tel. 705/264–9521, has service from Timmins), Ontario Northland's **Polar Bear Express** train is the more popular and the more nostalgia-inducing option. The Polar Bear makes a round-

③③ trip from **Cochrane,** 300 kilometers (200 miles) south, every day of the week except Friday, from late June to Labor Day. There's train service to Cochrane from Toronto or North Bay. The Polar Bear Express leaves Cochrane at 8:30 AM and arrives at Moosonee just before 1 PM. It departs Moosonee at 5:15 PM and returns to Cochrane by 9:20 PM. Meals, light lunches, and snacks are available in the restaurant/snack car.

Moose Factory Island, one of a number in the delta of the Moose River, is 8 kilometers (5 miles) long and just over a kilometer wide. It's a 20-minute boat ride from Moosonee. Passengers then transfer to a bus or van. The island was the site of the second Hudson's Bay Company trading post, established in 1672 on what was then called Hayes Island, 24 kilometers (16 miles) up the Moose River from James Bay. It was captured by the French in 1686 and renamed Fort St. Louis. Contrary to popular myth, the holes in the floor of **St. Thomas Anglican Church** are to let floodwater *out* and to ventilate the foundation. When the church was being built in 1864, the foundation floated a short distance in a spring flood, but the church itself has never floated anywhere. The altar cloths and lectern hangings are of moose hide decorated with beads. The Hudson's Bay Post is a modern building, and the company now goes by the name of Northern Stores. Beside it is the 1850 staff house in which are sold animal pelts, carvings, snowshoes, gloves, slippers, and beadwork. Some guidebooks will tell you the **Blacksmith's Shop** in Centennial Park on Moose Factory Island is the oldest wooden building in Ontario. It isn't, but the stone forge inside it may be the oldest "structure" in the province. The original shop was built in the late 1600s but moved back from the riverbank in 1820. Because the forge stones had been transported a long distance, they were disassembled and rebuilt at the present location. In summer an apprentice smithy runs the forge and explains its operation.

Moosonee is Ontario's only tidal port and, even though it's almost 20 kilometers (14 miles) from James Bay, summer tides
average 5 feet. The community came into existence only in
1903, when the Revillon Freres Trading Company of France established a post to compete with the Hudson's Bay Company. It
wasn't until the Ontario Northland Railway arrived in 1932
that the region's population began to catch up to that of Moose
Factory. The Moosonee visitor center is in a small, one-floor office building on First Street. Next door is a theater in which
free videos on wildlife and natural and cultural history are
shown (tel. 705/336–2480). Opposite the dock on Revillon Road,
a small, two-story frame house has displays and artifacts recall-
ing the heyday of the area's fur trade. Farther down Revillon
Road is the modern Ministry of Natural Resources Interpretive
Centre, offering exhibits of regional wildlife and of the area's
geological and geographical history. During tourist season
there are stalls on Revillon Road where natives sell handcrafts
ranging from moccasins and buckskin vests to trinkets, beadwork, and wood and stone carvings.

For more information about the area, or if you're interested in
an overnight stay, contact **Ontario Northland** (65 Front St. W,
Toronto, Ont. M5J 1E6, tel. 416/965–4268).

What to See and Do with Children

African Lion Safari, Rockton, near Hamilton. Lions, tigers,
cheetahs, elephants, and zebras abound in this wildlife park.
You can drive your own car or take an air-conditioned tram over
a 9-kilometer (6-mile) safari trail. *Off Hwy. 8, south of Cambridge, tel. 519/623–2620. Call for admission fees. Open mid-
Apr.–late Oct., daily.*

Doon Heritage Crossroads, near Kitchener (*see* Tour 5).

Maple Leaf Village, Niagara Falls (*see* Tour 5).

Marineland, Niagara Falls (*see* Tour 5).

National Museum of Science and Technology, Ottawa (*see* Tour
1).

Old Fort William, Thunder Bay (*see* Tour 6).

Sainte Marie among the Hurons, Midland (*see* Tour 3).

Santa's Village, Bracebridge (*see* Tour 3).

Science North (*see* Tour 7).

Storybook Gardens, London (*see* Tour 5).

Upper Canada Village, Morrisburg (*see* Tour 2).

Shopping

Native Crafts

Ottawa, Sault Ste. Marie, Midland, and Thunder Bay have museum shops and galleries that specialize in native and Inuit
crafts. In Thunder Bay, **The North West Company Inc.** (413 Victoria Ave. E, tel. 807/623–2241) has Inuit soapstone carvings,
fossilized ivory, and Hudson's Bay point blankets and coats.

Antiques

John Coles at the **Astrolabe Gallery** (90 Sparks St., tel. 613/234–
2348) is a good source for 19th-century prints of Ottawa scenes
or antique maps of North America. Some of the best antiques

can be found at small shops in **Bayfield, Cobourg, Meaford, Peterborough, Shakespeare,** and **St. Jacobs.** Sunday flea markets in **Aberfoyle, Burlington, Grand Bend,** and **Hamilton** can be another good source of antiques.

Shopping Centers and Malls

Rideau Centre at Rideau and Sussex streets in Ottawa has more than 200 stores, including The Bay, Ogilvy's, and Eaton department stores.

In Hamilton, **Hess Village** is a small area crammed with interesting boutiques, cafés, and pubs.

Windsor draws shoppers from nearby Michigan seeking British imports of china and woolens.

In Paris, try **Halls's** on the main street for Irish linens.

Sports and Outdoor Activities

Bicycling

Ottawa has 114 kilometers (65 miles) of **bicycle paths.** On Sunday, **Queen Elizabeth Drive** and **Colonel By Drive** are closed to traffic until noon for cyclists. The NPC operates 55 kilometers (30 miles) of bicycle trail **along the Niagara River between Fort Erie and Niagara-on-the-Lake.** The city of **Brantford** is protected by a flood-control dam on top of which is a bicycle trail that passes most of the city's many interesting tourist attractions. **London's Springbank Park** has miles of pretty bicycle trails.

Hiking

The 680-kilometer (430-mile) **Bruce Trail** stretches along the limestone Niagara Escarpment from the orchards of the Niagara Peninsula to the cliffs and bluffs at Tobermory, at the end of the Bruce Peninsula. Contact the Bruce Trail Association (Box 857, Hamilton, Ont. L8N 3N9). The **Grand Valley Trail** runs 128 kilometers (80 miles) between Elora and Brantford. Contact the Grand Valley Trail Association (Box 1233, Kitchener, Ont. N2G 4G8). The **Rideau Trail** runs 406 kilometers (241 miles) along the Rideau Canal from Kingston to Ottawa. Access points from the highway are marked with orange triangles. Contact Rideau Trail Association (Box 15, Kingston, K7L 4V6).

Skiing

Ontario has hundreds of slopes for downhill skiing, although most are under 200 feet in vertical drop. The highest are **Candy Mountain Resort** (tel. 807/475–5633) and **Loch Lomond** (tel. 807/475–7787), both just outside Thunder Bay and both with 235 feet of vertical. **Blue Mountain** (tel. 416/869–3799), near Collingwood north of Toronto, is the most extensively developed and heavily trafficked and has a vertical drop of 216 feet. **Calabogie Peaks** ski area (tel. 416/752–2720), west of Ottawa, has a vertical drop of 228 feet. Cross-country ski trails exist anywhere in the province where there is snow and accommodations for skiers. In the Toronto area, try **Caledon Ski Club** in Caledon (tel. 416/453–7404), **Glen Eden Ski Area** near Milton (tel. 416/878–5011), and **Hockley Valley Resort** near Orangeville (tel. 519/942–0754). **Horseshoe Valley** (tel. 705/835–2790) is near Barrie, and **Hidden Valley** (tel. 705/789–2301) is near Huntsville.

Dining and Lodging

Dining

While the golden arches of McDonald's and the cardboard buckets of Colonel Sanders—and every other fast-food franchise of the Western world—have staked claims in all corners of the province, so has a backlash spread. Entrepreneurs have gambled that there still exist customers prepared to pay for real food hospitably served in historic or otherwise interesting surroundings. With a vengeance they have converted abandoned stone grist and woolen mills, brick schoolhouses and churches, and wooden pioneers' homes into quaint dining spots. Where no suitable building existed for such a purpose, they have designed new ones that look old and furnished their interiors with dusty fishnets, rusted ploughshares, and all the other Canadiana that assures the patron he or she has chosen a chic place in which to dine.

In Ontario, as in most population centers of any size, the diner has a global choice of ethnic restaurants. Highly recommended restaurants in each price category are indicated by a star ★.

Category	Cost*
Very Expensive	over $50
Expensive	$35–$50
Moderate	$15–$35
Inexpensive	under $15

per person, excluding drinks, service, 7% GST, 8% food tax, and 10% bar tax

Lodging

Reservations are strongly recommended anywhere in Ontario during summer months. Without them, you can get stuck in some of the most unlikely places. If all the rooms are gone in one town, for whatever reason, the odds are good that this will be the case in nearby towns as well. Many communities hold special weekends or festivals during the summer and fall months, which draw more visitors than usual. For unsuspecting tourists, this can mean another hour's drive when they are already tired and ready to call it a day.

Generally you get what you pay for at Ontario hotels and motels, though rates are often double those charged in the United States for comparable accommodation. The reason is not so much that Canadian owners are trying to cash in on a short tourist season, but that Canadian hoteliers' operating costs are so high—the hotel-motel industry is subject to many federal, provincial, and municipal taxes and the regulations of numerous government agencies at all levels.

Bed-and-breakfast associations exist in most cities, but many of those rates exceed what you'd pay for a good hotel or motel room south of the border.

In **Niagara Falls,** the closer the hotel is to the falls, or the better the view is of them, the higher the rate.

Highly recommended lodgings in each price category are indicated by a star ★.

Category	Cost*
Very Expensive	over $100
Expensive	$75–$100
Moderate	$35–$75
Inexpensive	under $35

All prices are for a standard double room, excluding 10% service charge.

Alton
Dining and Lodging
★

The Millcroft Inn. About 80 kilometers (50 miles) northwest of Toronto, this 19th-century stone knitting mill has been converted to an exquisite full-service country inn beside the millpond. It is one of Canada's finest hostelries and a member of the Relais & Chateaux Association. The dining room is a stage for the Millcroft's executive chef, Fredy Stamm, who changes the menus monthly but with advance notice will prepare any guest's favorite dish. *John St., L0N 1A0, tel. 519/941–8111. 42 rooms and suites, some with fireplaces. Reservations advised for restaurant. Dress: casual. AE, DC, MC, V. Very Expensive.*

Bracebridge
Dining and Lodging
★

Inn at the Falls. Recently redone by professional new owners, this Victorian inn and its annex of motel-style rooms command a magnificent view of the pretty Bracebridge Falls on the Muskoka River. The main dining room and pub-lounge offer food and live entertainment; there's an outdoor patio for dining and sipping as well. The innkeepers live up to their boast of "the best steak-and-kidney pie this side of the Atlantic." *17 Dominion St., Box 1139, P0B 1C0, tel. 705/645–2245. 17 rooms, 6 with fireplaces. Facilities: dining room, pub, dining patio, parlor, outdoor heated pool. Reservations advised for restaurant. Dress: casual. AE, MC, V. Expensive.*

Cambridge
Dining and Lodging
★

Langdon Hall. This magnificent colonial-revival-style mansion on 40 landscaped acres has grand public rooms and huge fireplaces. It was built in 1898 as a summer home for a great-grandson of John Jacob Astor and has been sensitively converted to a grand country hotel with 13 guest rooms in the original building and 28 in a modern annex. The chef, Nigel Didcock, has trained in a number of prestigious kitchens in France, and his menu offers variations on French and Continental dishes. *Take Exit 275 from Hwy. 401 west of Kitchener, travel south on Fountain St./Homer Watson Blvd., to Blair Rd. Go through the village of Blair to Langdon Rd. Turn at the first driveway on the left and follow the lane to Langdon Hall, RR3,*

N3H 4R8, tel. 519/740–2100. Facilities: meeting rooms, conservatory and drawing room, outdoor heated pool, sauna, whirlpool, exercise equipment, billiard room, card room, canoes (for the nearby Grand River), ballooning, tennis, croquet, 24-hour room service. Jacket recommended in dining room. AE, MC, V. Very Expensive.

Cochrane
Dining and Lodging

If you plan to take the *Polar Bear Express* train, you'll probably need to stay over in Cochrane. There are seven motels in and around Cochrane, ranging in size from seven to 42 units. Only two have restaurant facilities, but all are geared to early wakeup calls for guests taking the *Polar Bear Express* and late check-ins for those returning from the excursion. The four largest are **Westway Motor Motel,** 21 First St., tel. 705/272–4285; **First Canada Inns,** 200 Railway St., tel. 705/272–3500; **Motel Cochrane,** R.R. 2, tel. 705/272–4253; and **Chimo Motel,** Box 2326, tel. 705/272–6555. The postal code for all four is P0L 1C0.

Elora
Dining and Lodging
★

Elora Mill. This is one of Canada's few remaining five-story gristmills, which has been converted to luxury accommodations and offers superb dining. There are 16 guest rooms in the 1859 mill building and 16 more rooms in four other historic stone buildings in the immediate vicinity of the mill. The inn is in the heart of a village with historic stone buildings that could have been lifted from England's Cotswolds or southern France. The cuisine is a mix of imaginative Canadian and European dishes. *77 Mill St. W, tel 519/846–5356. Reservations advised for dining room. Dress: casual. AE, MC, V. Expensive.*

Goderich
Dining
★

La Brassine. The kitchen in this large farm home–cum–country inn produces some of the finest French cuisine west of the Québec border. It's available only to those few who have booked ahead at least 24 hours for Wednesday–Saturday dinners or daily for residents of the five double guest rooms in the inn. Everything served is created in-house; the linen-covered tables are set with crystal and silver. *Off Hwy. 21, midway between Bayfield and Goderich; turn toward Lake Huron on Kitchigami Rd., RR2, N7A 3X8, tel. 519/524–6300. Dress: casual; no shorts or T-shirts. Cash or personal check preferred to major credit cards. Note: no license for beer, wine, or liquor. Moderate.*

Hamilton
Dining

Ancaster Old Mill. This historic mill is just outside Hamilton and worth the trip if only to sample the bread, baked daily with flour made at the mill on millstones installed in 1863. The dining rooms are light and bright and have hanging plants. Try to get a table overlooking the mill stream and a waterfall. *548 Old Dundas Rd., Ancaster, L9G 3J4 (from Hwy. 403 west of Hamilton take Mohawk Road W exit to Wilson St. in Ancaster. Turn right to Montgomery Dr., turn left and follow signs), tel. 416/648–1827. AE, DC, MC, V. Moderate.*

Dining and Lodging

The Royal Connaught Hotel. The venerable Royal Connaught Hotel in the heart of downtown Hamilton was built in 1914 and is one of those grand old places complete with ballroom. The lobby and seventh floor have recently been renovated. The indoor swimming pool has one of Canada's longest waterslides. The Grill is the hotel's very popular dining room. Meat is broiled over an open fire of mesquite. There's a marble floor, and after you've eaten—or while you're waiting for your entrée to be flamed—you can dance in the gazebo. *112 King St. E, L8N 1A8, tel. 416/546–8111 or 800/263–8558; fax 416/546–8144. 207*

rooms, 21 suites. Facilities: restaurant, lounge, comedy cabaret, sauna, whirlpool. Dress: casual. AE, MC, V. Expensive.

Kingston
Dining and Lodging

The Prince George Hotel and the **Canoe Club Bar and Grill.** Located just down the street from the city's magnificent town
hall, this hotel, built in 1809, is also one of the city's historic
showplaces. The Canoe Club (which gets its name from the 60-
foot-long rowing scull built for Olympic rowers in 1950 and
hanging from the ceiling) is a popular dining spot with an eclectic menu. And the hotel is a cozy charmer. Rooms are decorated
in Victorian style and overlook a park and Lake Ontario. Continental breakfast is included with the room rate. *200 Ontario
St., K7L 2Y9, tel. 613/549–5440. 30 rooms, 2 suites. AE, MC,
V. Hotel: Moderate. Restaurant: Inexpensive.*

Kitchener
Dining and Lodging

Valhalla Inn. This modern hotel has a major sports complex in
its basement and is connected by a glassed-in skywalk to the
Market Square shopping mall and Farmers' Market. *105 King
St. E, N2G 3W9, tel. 519/744–4141. 203 rooms. Facilities: dining room, lounge, restaurant, banquet room, fitness center
with indoor pool, sauna, whirlpool, miniature golf. AE, MC,
V. Expensive.*

Walper Terrace Hotel. This rejuvenated 1893 hotel sustains a
Kitchener tradition started in 1820 by Phineas Varnum, who
leased land from Joseph Schneider (of packing-house fame) to
build what was then called the Varnum Inn. It now features at
least one piece of period cherry-wood furniture in each of the
guest rooms. The wooden-trim moldings, carved marble pillars, and the ornate brass bannister of the main staircase have
been preserved. The Terrace Cafe has an art deco floor,
vaulted ceilings, marble pillars, stained glass windows, and a
view of one of the city's major intersections. The setting is romantic, and meals are moderately priced. *1 King St. W, N2G
1A1, tel. 519/745–4321. 90 rooms, 12 suites. Facilities: restaurant, lounge, mini shopping mall, ballroom. AE, MC, V. Expensive.*

London
Dining

Marienbad and Chaucer's Pub. Reasonably priced Czechoslova-
kian fare is served in surroundings that will remind you of your
Eastern European vacation (if you had one). Great goulash,
schnitzels, and sauerbraten are among the choices. *122 Carling
St., N6A 1H6, tel. 519/679–9940. Dress: casual. AE, MC, V.
Moderate.*

Michael's on the Thames. This popular lunch and dinner spot
overlooking the Thames River offers flambéed dishes and has a
maître d', Jack DiCarlo, who has become something of a local
celebrity with his impromptu song-and-dance acts. The Canadian and Continental cuisine includes fresh seafood, chateaubriand, and flaming desserts and coffees. *1 York St. at the
Thames River, N6A 1A1, tel. 519/672–0111. Reservations advised. Dress: casual. AE, MC, V. Moderate.*

Lodging

Idlewylde Inn. Though an elevator was installed in this converted 1878 mansion, the architects succeeded in keeping many
original features in the 25 luxurious guest rooms and suites and
in the public rooms. Complimentary breakfast and snacks are
included in the rate. *36 Grand Ave., N6C 1L1, tel. 519/433–
2891. AE, DC, MC, V. Very Expensive.*

Sheraton Armouries Hotel. This 20-story silver-mirrored tower
rises from the center of the 1905 London Armoury. The lobby is
a greenhouse of vines, trees, plants, and fountains wrapped in
marble and accented by rich woods and old yellow brick. The

architects left as much of the original armory intact as possible. A set of steps through manicured jungle takes you to the indoor swimming pool, sauna, and whirlpool. Guest rooms are spacious and decorated in pastel shades. Suites vary in size and grandeur—for example, the Middlesex Suite has a grand piano. *325 Dundas St., N6B 1T9, tel. 519/679–6111 or 800/325–3535. 250 rooms and suites. Facilities: racquetball and squash courts, pool, sauna, whirlpool, entertainment, sushi restaurant, dining room. AE, MC, V. Expensive.*

London also has a strip of motels on Wellington Road north of Highway 401 and on Dundas Street East, out toward the airport.

Midland
Dining and Lodging

The Highland Inn. This is a completely self-contained year-round hotel/motel/resort, most of which is contained in an enormous atrium. Sunday brunches by the pool in the Garden Cafe are popular. There are four dining areas, honeymoon suites with heart-shaped tubs or sunken Jacuzzis, meeting rooms, a tanning room, exercise and weight rooms, and a full-time fitness director. *King St. and Hwy. 12, Box 515, L4R 4L3, tel. 705/526–9307; 800/461–4265 for reservations. 150 rooms and suites. AE, MC, V. Moderate.*

Moosonee
Dining and Lodging

In Moosonee you can choose either the 30-room **Polar Bear Lodge** (tel. 705/336–2345), or the 21-room **Moosonee Lodge** (tel. 705/336–2351), both of which are on Revillon Street facing the Moose River. Rates are high for the caliber of accommodation, but if you want to stay, these are your choices. Both hotels serve meals, but alcohol is served only during the dinner hour, and then only to those dining at the hotel. The mailing address for both Moosonee hotels is: 65 Enterprise Rd., Rexdale, Ont. M9W 1C4.

Niagara Falls
Dining

Every North American fast-food franchise appears to be represented in or near this city, and there are outlets for every known form of junk food. There are no true gourmet restaurants on the Canadian side, but some places come close.

Capri Restaurant. Soft chairs and a softly tinkling piano create an elegant mood here. The combination of good steak, seafood, and Italian dishes makes this one of the better Niagara dining spots. *5438 Ferry St., tel. 416/354–7519. Dress: casual. AE, MC, V. Moderate.*

Queenston Heights Restaurant. This is one of four restaurants operated by the NPC, which ensures good food at fair prices. Queenston Heights Restaurant is a few kilometers north of (downriver from) the falls, and you can have a relaxed lunch or dinner overlooking a golf course or, if you're lucky, the Niagara Gorge. *Tel. 416/262–4274. Dress: casual. AE, DC, MC, V. Moderate.*

Skylon Tower's Revolving Dining Room and Summit Suite Restaurant. If you have just one night for dining at the falls, make a reservation at the Skylon Tower's Revolving Dining Room. It makes a full circle every hour, and the view of the illuminated falls at night—at any time of the year—is a sight long remembered. The Canadian and Continental cuisine is usually excellent. The Skylon's Summit Suite Restaurant serves buffet breakfasts, plus lunch and dinner, and it has dancing, but it doesn't revolve. *Skylon Tower, tel. 416/356–2651. Dress: casual. AE, DC, MC, V. Moderate.*

Lodging   **Skyline Brock Hotel, Skyline Foxhead Hotel, Skyline Village Hotel.** The former Sheraton-Foxhead Hotel is now the 232-room Skyline Brock Hotel, the 395-room Skyline Foxhead Hotel, and the 208-room Skyline Village Hotel, and all are located at 5685 Falls Avenue. The most distinguishing characteristic of these hotels is the price. The Foxhead rates start lower than those at the other two but climb to as high at $209 for some rooms. Many guest room windows overlook the falls; some have particularly splendid views, and rates are based to some extent on the view. The hotels have bars, lounges, restaurants, coffee shops, dining rooms. *5685 Falls Ave., L2E 6W7, tel. (for all 3) 416/374–4444. AE, MC, V. Expensive.*

Michael's Inn. If you're on a first, second, third, or even fourth honeymoon, consider something fun and romantic. Michael's Inn has a number of theme rooms, all of which overlook the American falls and the gorge. Carry your mate across the threshold into deepest Africa, the Old South, or the Orient. The "Midnight at the Oasis" room has a Jacuzzi for two surrounded by mirrors, a 2-meter-high (6 ½-foot-high) stuffed tiger, palm-leaf wallpaper, and bamboo trees. *5599 River Rd., L2E 3H3, tel. 416/354–2727. 130 rooms. Facilities: indoor swimming pool with slide, sauna, whirlpool, gift shop, lounge, and The Embers dining room. AE, MC, V. Moderate.*

Niagara-on-the-Lake
Dining and Lodging
★

Prince of Wales. This hotel is a family affair. The Wiens family has been doling out its gracious hospitality since 1975, turning a 16-room inn into a 105-room hotel. The original section of the inn was built as Long's Hotel in 1864. The additions over the years now make the hotel a block long, but the changes (inside and out) have been so sensitively wrought that only an expert could guess where most of the changes were made. One obvious exception is the Patio Restaurant, where tables are under a canopy of hanging plants and behind glass walls overlooking the main street. Guest rooms are furnished in reproduction French provincial or traditional English furniture. Guests may dine in the Dining Room, the Queen's Royal Lounge, or the Greenhouse Patio Restaurant, particularly popular with the local lunch crowd. *6 Picton St., L0S 1J0, tel. 416/468–3246; within the 416 area code, 800/263–2452. 106 rooms and suites with bath, some with fireplaces. Facilities: 3 dining areas, lounge, indoor swimming pool, sauna, whirlpool, health club, tennis. AE, MC, V. Very Expensive.*

Oban Inn. This elegant, historic country inn is centrally located and has a view of Lake Ontario. The respected dining room offers standard treatments of beef, duck, lobster, and steak. *160 Front St., L0S 1J0, tel. 416/468–2165. 23 rooms, some with fireplaces. Facilities: dining room, lounge, lap pool, indoor pool, whirlpool, exercise room. AE, DC, MC, V. Expensive.*

★ **Queen's Landing.** Also called the Inn at Niagara-on-the-Lake, this remarkable property is a welcome addition to an old town that has had no new places in a long while. The owner—who also runs the Pillar & Post—has obtained antique furnishings and installed fireplaces in 78 rooms and Jacuzzis in 44 rooms. Located at the mouth of the Niagara River, right across from historic Fort Niagara, the hotel has knockout views. And, unlike other century-old country inns of this lovely town, Queen's Landing has a superb indoor swimming pool, lap pool, and even a fully equipped exercise room. The dining room has recently won some acclaim. The views, too, make for a romantic night out. *Cnr. Melville and Bryon Sts., Box 1180, L0S 1J0, tel. 416/*

468–2195. 137 rooms. Facilities: dining room, lounge, lap pool, indoor pool, whirlpool, exercise facilities, baby-sitting service, 24-hour room service, tennis and golf nearby. AE, DC, MC, V. Expensive.

Ottawa
Dining

Flippers. As the name suggests, this is a seafood restaurant, and the specialties change almost daily as different kinds of fresh fish and seafoods are available. Part of the decor in the old building on Bank Street is marine artifacts and model ships. *823 Bank St. on the 2nd floor, tel. 613/232–2703. Reservations recommended. Dress: casual. AE, MC, V. Expensive.*

Grenville's. This is one of Ottawa's finest dining establishments, located in an old house on Somerset Street between Banks and O'Connor. The cuisine is North American, and there's a nice touch for those having difficulty deciding which of the tempting appetizers or desserts they wish. The kitchen will put together a sampler of either course—a half order of each of your two choices. *315 Somerset St. W, tel. 613/235–0369. Reservations recommended. Dress: casual. AE, MC, V. Expensive.*

Chequers. In this three-story, Gothic-style 1868 country inn 25 kilometers (16 miles) southwest of Ottawa, the specialties are French and Spanish haute cuisine. The service is European and so is the decor. *5816 Hazeldean Rd., Stittsville K0A 3G0 (from the Queensway, take Terry Fox Dr. south to Hazeldean Rd.— old Hwy. 7), tel. 613/836–1665. Reservations required. Dress: casual. AE, MC, V. Moderate.*

Courtyard Restaurant. Fine French cuisine is served in this lovely, historic limestone building on a quiet cul-de-sac near By Ward Market, a five-minute stroll from the Parliament Buildings. The forerunner of today's elegant dining establishment was a log tavern built in 1827, likely inspired by construction of the nearby Rideau Canal. The humble log tavern was replaced by the limestone Ottawa Hotel a decade later. Extensive renovations created Courtyard Restaurant, and its cuisine and ambience established a dedicated following. *21 George St., tel. 519/565–2611. Reservations recommended. Dress: informal. AE, MC, V. Moderate.*

Lodging

Château Laurier Hotel. Ottawa has all kinds of posh new hotels with great service and food, but this hotel is an institution. It's one of Canada's great railroad hotels, built in 1916. It now has 480 large, airy rooms; an indoor pool; a variety of dining rooms, lounges, and bars; and indoor parking. The Château, as it's known, is part of the Ottawa experience; it's also smack dab in the middle of the must-see list for Ottawa. *1 Rideau St., K1N 8S7, tel. 613/232–6411. AE, MC, V. Very Expensive.*

Minto Place Suite Hotel. One- and two-bedroom suites in this 31-story hotel, which overlooks the capitol and is within strolling distance of Sparks Street Mall, have full kitchen and laundry facilities. The hotel has a sauna, indoor pool, whirlpool, health spa, indoor parking, licensed lounge, and dining room. *433 Laurier Ave., W K1R 7Y1, tel. 613/232–2200. AE, MC, V. Expensive–Very Expensive.*

O'Connor House Bed and Breakfast. In the heart of downtown Ottawa, this former hotel has 34 guest rooms and family suites. Ice skates and bicycles are available to guests along with a lounge, 24-hour snacks, and a full breakfast. *172 O'Connor St., K2P 1T5, tel. 613/236–4221. AE, MC, V. Moderate.*

Peterborough
Dining and Lodging

Stel Red Oak Inn. This 183-room hotel has an indoor swimming pool, sauna, and whirlpool, and it's connected to the city's largest downtown indoor shopping complex. Guest rooms are comfortably furnished. Sir William's Dining Room offers Continental fare and lighter meals, and snacks are served at the Garden Cafe in the pool area. There is free underground parking. *100 Charlotte St., K9J 7L4, tel. 705/743–7272. AE, D, MC, V. Expensive.*

Picton
Dining and Lodging

Isaiah Tubbs Resort. A dozen kilometers west of Picton, this posh 58-room property has rooms and suites with fireplaces, indoor and outdoor swimming pools, saunas and whirlpool, 12 cottages, and 35 housekeeping cottages. There's fine dining in The Restaurant on the Knoll Overlooking the Sandbanks at West Lake. (That's the correct name of the restaurant and that's what it overlooks!) *RR 1, K0K 2T0, tel. 613/393–2090 or 800/267–0525. AE, MC, V. Moderate.*

Lodging

Merrill Inn. This beautiful 1870 home is a short stroll from the heart of downtown Picton. It has been converted to a cozy 15-room inn by the same folks who created Idlewyld Inn at London (*see* above). The refrigerator is stocked with soft drinks and the sideboard with croissants, muffins, tea, and coffee 24 hours a day, but no meals are served. *343 Main St. E, K0K 2T0, tel. 613/476–7451. MC, V. Expensive.*

Port Stanley
Dining and Lodging
★

Kettle Creek Inn. This small, elegant, full-service country inn features fine food and a friendly pub ambience. Two new suites with balconies, fireplaces, and whirlpools and five new rooms with baths were installed in the original inn in 1992, and in 1990 eight rooms, three suites, and full facilities for small business meetings were added in a cleverly designed annex. Some of the new rooms have whirlpool baths and gas fireplaces. There are other nice touches, such as old-fashioned pedestal sinks, interesting local artwork, and views from all the rooms and suites of a landscaped courtyard and gazebo. Continental breakfast is included in room rates. The three dining rooms in the original inn offer daily specials, including fresh Lake Erie fish just brought ashore by the local fishing fleet. Fresh Ontario lamb and pork tenderloin are also featured. *Main St., N0L 2A0, tel. 519/782–3388, fax 519/782–4747. 10 rooms, 5 suites. AE, D, DC, MC, V. Moderate–Expensive.*

Rossport
Dining and Lodging

Rossport Inn. The hamlet of Rossport on a harbor off Lake Superior is about as close as you can get to an outport on the Great Lakes. The inn was built in 1884 as a railroad hotel and now has six small guest rooms sharing two bathrooms. This is one of the nicest country inns in the province. It's cozy and down-home— the nightlife consists of swapping lies with the innkeepers and other guests about fish that got away. Breakfast is included in the room rate. The dining room's home-style cooking of locally caught fish, as well as of steak, chicken, pork chops, and lobster is irresistible. *On Rossport Loop, ½ mile from Trans-Canada Hwy., Bowman St., P0T 2R0, tel. 807/824–3213. MC, V. Closed Nov.–May. Moderate.*

St. Jacobs
Dining and Lodging

Benjamins. This is a lovely re-creation of the original 1852 Farmer's Inn. Nine guest rooms on the second floor are furnished in antiques, and every bed is covered with a locally made Mennonite quilt. The licensed restaurant has pine ceiling beams, an open-hearth fireplace, lots of greenery, and imaginative French cuisine. *17 King St., N0B 2N0, tel. 519/664–3731. AE, MC, V. Expensive.*

Sault Ste. Marie
Dining and Lodging

Quality Inn Bayfront. If you're planning to take the Agawa Canyon Snow Train, try to get a room at this popular hotel. The 110 rooms (including 18 suites) are clean and modern with many creature comforts, including a sauna and in-house movies. Most important—because the train leaves at 8 AM and you should be at the station by 7:30 AM at the latest—the hotel is directly across the street from the Algoma Central Railroad station. That means you can enjoy a room-service or dining-room breakfast, stroll across the street, and leave your car parked at the hotel. When you return at night, the hotel's swimming pool and dining room await you. Blossoms Bistro in the hotel offers good prices, friendly service . . . and edible floral garnishes! The dining area is bright and airy with lots of brass and greenery, and reservations are suggested. *180 Bay St., P6A 6S2, tel. 705/945–9264. 82 rooms, 18 suites. Facilities: indoor pool, sauna, whirlpool, exercise room. AE, MC, V. Expensive.*

Stratford
Dining and Lodging

The Queen's Inn at Stratford. In this beautifully restored 1853 hotel, guests can enjoy traditional Canadian food in the dining room while listening to tinkling music from a baby grand piano. Light fare is served in one half of the divided room, and there are also a popular pub-lounge and two function rooms. *161 Ontario St., N5A 3H3, tel. 519/271–1400, fax 519/271–7373. 30 rooms with bath. Facilities: restaurant, lounge. AE, MC, V. Expensive.*

Woods Villa Bed and Breakfast. Owner Ken Vinen has restored this elegant 1875 home of a wealthy magistrate to its original grandeur, and some of the five rooms have fireplaces. Vinen uses the public rooms to display an astonishing collection of vintage juke boxes, music boxes, and player pianos he has restored to mint condition. If he doesn't have the old favorite you want to hear, he'll sit down at one of the pianos and pound it out for you. In summer, breakfast is served on an outside patio beside an enormous, ceramic-tiled swimming pool. Woods Villa does not accept children or pets; the latter might ruffle the feathers of Vinen's three pet macaws. *62 John St. N, Stratford, N5A 6K7, tel. 519/271–4576. 5 rooms. Major credit cards accepted, but cash preferred. Moderate.*

Windsor
Dining

Brigantino's. This popular establishment is outstanding for home-style Italian cooking and melt-in-your-mouth pasta. *851 Erie St. E, tel. 519/254–7041. Reservations advised. Dress: casual. AE, D, DC, MC, V. Moderate.*

The Old Fish Market. A wonderful ambience is created here with hanging plants and brass railings and lots of lovely woodwork. The menu lives up to the name and is heavy on seafoods. It has a deserved reputation of excellence. *156 Chatham St. W, tel. 519/253–7417. Weekend reservations advised. Dress: casual. AE, DC, MC, V. Moderate.*

Lodging

Hilton International Windsor. Each of the 314 guest rooms in this 22-story, downtown riverbank hotel has a view of Detroit's impressive skyline and the shipping activity on the world's busiest inland waterway. The Park Terrace Restaurant and Lounge offers a wide menu and spectacular river view. In the River Runner Bar and Grill, there's music and dancing. *277 Riverside Dr. W, N9A 5K4, tel. 519/973–5555. Facilities: indoor pool, sauna, whirlpool, meeting facilities, room service. AE, MC, V. Very Expensive.*

The Arts and Nightlife

Hamilton   Opera Hamilton holds performances in the Great Hall of Hamilton Place September through April (Summers Lane, opposite the Art Gallery of Hamilton, tel. 416/527–7627).

The Shaw Festival   A stage-struck Toronto lawyer's dream in 1961 now has an impressive track record and a world-class reputation. Brian Doherty started the festival in 1961 with a few Shaw plays produced on weekends in the old town courthouse. The performances were well received, and the company drew continuing support, mainly from Toronto. Government kicked in most of the $3 million needed to build the 863-seat Shaw Festival Theatre, which opened in 1973. Shaw Festival is the only theater group in the world specializing in the works of George Bernard Shaw and his contemporaries. The festival starts at the end of April and runs through mid-November. *Tel. 416/468–2172.*

The Stratford Festival   It all started in 1953, in a massive tent, with Sir Alec Guiness playing Richard III. The next year, musical programs were added to augment Shakespeare's plays. The venture was a huge success, and the 1957 season opened in a permanent home with 2,262 seats, none of which is more than 65 feet from the stage. The 1901-vintage, 1,107-seat Avon Theatre became a partner in the festival in 1967, and The Third Stage, seating 410, opened in 1971. Stratford Festival now starts in late April and runs into November. *For information: Stratford and Area Visitors and Convention Bureau, 38 Albert St., Stratford, Ont. N5A 3K3, tel. 519/271–5361; box office, tel. 519/273–1600.*

Nightlife   The brochure says **Lulu's Roadhouse** has a "warm, casual atmosphere" but doesn't try to suggest it's "cozy" or "intimate." This unique play spot, located in a former K-Mart store just south of Kitchener, is Canada's largest bar. It can seat 2,000 customers at 450 tables and on bar stools, and there's room for another 1,000 standing along the longest and second-longest bars in the world. (The world's longest bar is 333 feet; the second-longest is 310 feet.) Since Lulu's opened in 1984, it's been packing 'em in to watch performances by big-name rock-and-roll entertainers. *4263 King St. E (Hwy. 8), tel. 519/653–8333 or 800/265–6782. Cover charge varies with entertainment. Open Thurs.–Sat. 4:30 PM–1 AM, sometimes Wed. for special concerts. Jeans not permitted.*

11 Province of Québec

by Dorothy Guinan

Dorothy Guinan is a political researcher for the Montréal Gazette *and is a freelance writer.*

Among the provinces of Canada, Québec is set apart by its strong French heritage, a matter not only of language but of customs, religion, and political structure. Québec covers a vast area—almost one-sixth of Canada's total—although the upper three-quarters is only sparsely inhabited. Most of the population lives in the southern cities, especially Montréal (*see* Chapter 4) and Québec City (*see* Chapter 5). Outside the cities, however, you'll find serenity and natural beauty in the province's innumerable lakes, streams, and rivers, in its farmlands and villages, in its great mountains and deep forests, and in its rugged coastline along the Gulf of St. Lawrence. Though the winters are long, there are plenty of winter sports to while away the cold months, especially in the Laurentians, with its many ski resorts.

Québec's recent threats to secede from the Canadian union are part of a long-standing tradition of independence. The first European to arrive in Québec was French explorer Jacques Cartier, in 1534; another Frenchman, Samuel de Champlain, arrived in 1603, determined to build French settlements in the region, and Jesuit missionaries followed in due course. Louis XIV of France proclaimed Canada a crown colony in 1663, and the land was allotted to French aristocrats in large grants called *seigneuries*. As tenants, known as *habitants*, settled upon farms in Québec, the Roman Catholic Church took on an importance that went beyond religion. Priests and nuns also acted as doctors, educators, and overseers of business arrangements between the habitants and between French-speaking fur traders and English-speaking merchants. An important doctrine of the church in Québec was *survivance*, the survival of the French people and their culture. Couples were told to have large families, and they did—families of 10 or 12 children were the norm.

Although the British won control of Canada in the French and Indian War, in 1763, Parliament passed the Quebec Act in 1774, which ensured the continuation of French law in Québec and left provincial authority in the hands of the Roman Catholic Church. In general, the law preserved the traditional Québecois way of life. Tensions between Québec and English-speaking Canada accelerated throughout the 20th century, however, and in 1974 the province defiantly proclaimed French its national language. In 1990 a three-year attempt by the Canadian government to add Québec's signature to the Canadian Constitution failed. Québec had been willing to sign provided that it received special status to promote its French language and culture. However, two of the 10 provinces would not agree to Québec's request. The incident became known as Meech Lake. If Québec and Canada did not reach an agreement before the end of 1992, the provincial government was to hold a vote, allowing the people of Québec to decide their future.

Being able to speak French can make your visit to the province more pleasant—many locals do not speak English. If you don't speak French, arm yourself with a phrase book or at least a knowledge of some basic phrases. It's also worth your while to sample the hearty traditional Québecois cuisine, for this is a province where food is taken seriously.

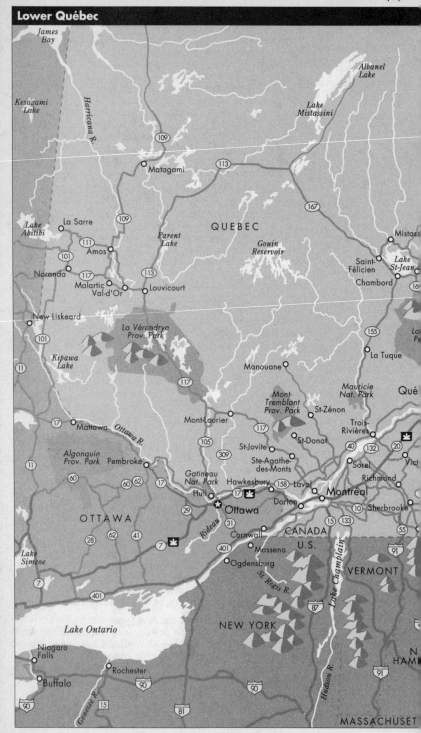

Lower Québec

James Bay

Kesagami Lake

Harricana R.

109

○ Matagami

113

Albanel Lake

Lake Mistassini

167

QUEBEC

Parent Lake

Gouin Reservoir

Mistass

Lake Abitibi

La Sarre ○

109

111

Amos ○

101

113

Noranda ○

117

Malartic ○

Val-d'Or

○ Louvicourt

Saint-Félicien

Lake St-Jean

Chambord ○

16

New Liskeard ○

101

La Vérendrye Prov. Park

155

La ○ P.

○ La Tuque

11

Kipawa Lake

117

Manouane ○

Mauricie Nat. Park

Qué

17

○ Mattawa

Ottawa R.

Algonquin Prov. Park

Pembroke ○

11

60

Mont-Tremblant Prov. Park

St-Zénon ○

Mont-Laurier ○

117

○ St-Donat

Trois-Rivières ○

40

132

20

Vict

60 62

17

Gatineau Nat. Park

105

309

St-Jovite ○

Ste-Agathe-des-Monts ○

○ Sorel

Richmond ○

29

Hull ○

Hawkesbury ○

158

Laval ○

○ Montréal

OTTAWA

★ Ottawa

17

Dorion ○

10 ○ Sherbrooke

28

62 41

31

Cornwall ○

Rideau

CANADA

15 133

55

7

Lake Simcoe

401

○ Massena

U.S.

91

7

Ogdensburg ○

St. Regis R.

VERMONT

401

Lake Ontario

NEW YORK

87

Lake Champlain

Hudson R.

N HAM

Niagara Falls ○

○ Rochester

90

Buffalo ○

90

Genesee R.

15

81

90

MASSACHUSET

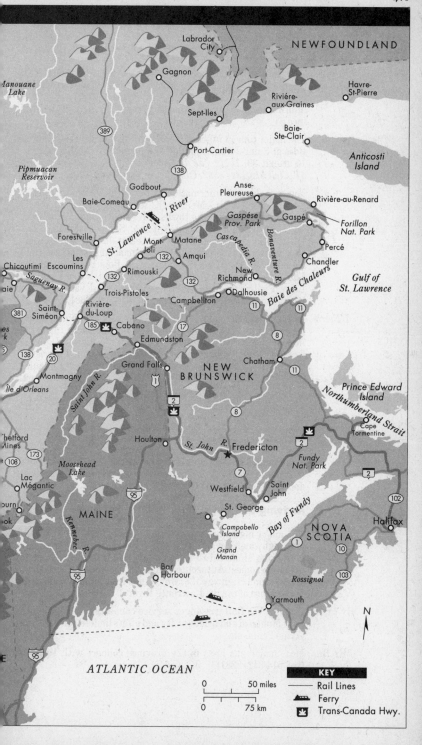

NEWFOUNDLAND

Manouane Lake

Labrador City

Gagnon

Rivière-aux-Graines

Sept-Iles

Havre-St-Pierre

Baie-Ste-Clair

Anticosti Island

389

Pipmuacan Reservoir

138

Port-Cartier

Godbout

138

St. Lawrence River

Baie-Comeau

Anse-Pleureuse

Rivière-au-Renard

Gaspé

Forestville

Gaspése Prov. Park

Forillon Nat. Park

Mont-Joli

Matane

Cascapedia R.

Bonaventure R.

Percé

Chicoutimi

Escoumins

132

Rimouski

Amqui

132

New Richmond

Chandler

Saguenay R.

aie

381

Trois-Pistoles

Dalhousie

Gulf of St. Lawrence

Campbellton

Baie des Chaleurs

Saint-Siméon

Rivière-du-Loup

11

11

s k

138

20

185

Cabano

17

8

Montmagny

Edmundston

Chatham

Prince Edward Island

Île d'Orléans

Saint John R.

Grand Falls

NEW BRUNSWICK

11

Northumberland Strait

1

hetford Aines

108

173

2

8

Cape Tormentine

Houlton

St. John R. Fredericton

2

Lac Mégantic

Moosehead Lake

7

Fundy Nat. Park

2

ourn

95

Westfield

Saint John

102

ok

MAINE

St. George

Campobello Island

Bay of Fundy

NOVA SCOTIA

Halifax

Kennebec R.

Grand Manan

1

10

Rossignol

103

Bar Harbour

Yarmouth

95

N

ATLANTIC OCEAN

E

95

KEY

0   50 miles

0   75 km

—— Rail Lines

Ferry

Trans-Canada Hwy.

Essential Information

Important Addresses and Numbers

Tourist
Information
Québec

Tourism Québec (Case Postale 20000, Québec City G1K 7X2, tel. 514/873–2015, toll-free from the Montréal area; from Québec, Canada, or the United States, 800/363–7777) can provide information on provincial tourist bureaus throughout the province.

The Laurentians

The major tourist office is the **Maison du Tourisme des Laurentides** at Saint-Jérôme, just off the Autoroute des Laurentides 15 at exit 39. *14142 rue de Lachapelle, RR 1, St-Jérôme J7Z 5T4, tel. 514/436–8532. Open year-round, daily 9–5.*

You can also get information in person at **Infotouriste** (1001 Square Dorchester, Montréal). Year-round regional tourist offices are located in the towns of L'Annociation, Mont Laurier, Mont Tremblant, Saint-Antoine, Saint-Eustache, Saint-Faustin, Saint-Sauveur-des-Monts, Saint-Jovite, Sainte-Adèle, and Sainte-Agathe-des-Monts. Seasonal tourist offices (mid-June–Labor Day) are also located in Bois Briand, Labelle, Lachute, Sainte-Marguerite-du-Lac-Masson, Notre-Dame-du-Laus, Piedmont, Saint-Adolphe-Howard, and Val David. For information about ski conditions, tel. 514/766–5631.

L'Estrie

In Montréal, information about l'Estrie is available at **Infotouriste** (*see* above). Year-round regional provincial tourist offices are located in the towns of Bromont, Coaticook, Danville, Granby, Magog, Sherbrooke, and Sutton. Seasonal tourist offices (June–Labor Day) are also located in Ascot, Beaulac, Knowlton, La Patrie, Lac-Mégantic, Masonville, and North Hatley. For lodging information, contact **Association Touristique de l'Estrie** (25 Brocage, Sherbrooke, J1L 2J4, tel. 819/565–5469).

Arriving and Departing by Plane

Most airline arrivals will be into either of Montréal's airports (Mirabel or Dorval) or Québec City's airport (*see* Chapters 4 and 5).

Arriving and Departing by Car, Train, and Bus

By Car

The major highways are Autoroute des Laurentides 15, a six-lane highway from Montréal to the Laurentians; Autoroute 10 East from Montréal to l'Estrie; U.S. 91 from New England, which becomes Autoroute 55 as it crosses the border to l'Estrie; and Highway 138, which runs from Montréal along the north shore of the St. Lawrence River.

By Train

Regular **Via Rail** passenger service connects all the provinces with Montréal and Québec City and offers limited service to the Gaspé Peninsula.

By Bus

Most major bus lines in the province connect with **Voyageur** (tel. 514/842–2281).

Getting Around

Québec Province
By Car
The province has fine roads, along which drivers insist on speeding. Free road maps are available at any of the numerous seasonal or permanent Québec Tourist Offices (call 800/363–7777 for the nearest location). Major entry points are Ottawa/Hull, U.S. 87 from New York State south of Montréal, U.S. 91 from Vermont into l'Estrie area, and the Trans-Canada Highway just west of Montréal.

By Bus
Most bus traffic to the outer reaches of the province begins at the bus terminal in downtown Québec City (225 boul. Charest E, tel. 418/524–4692).

The Laurentians
By Car
Autoroute des Laurentides 15, a six-lane highway, and the slower but more scenic secondary road, Route 117, lead to this resort country. Try to avoid traveling to and from the region on Friday evenings or Sunday afternoons, as you're likely to sit for hours in bumper-to-bumper traffic.

By Bus
Frequent bus service is available from the Terminus Voyageur (505 boul. de Maisonneuve E, tel. 514/842–2281) in downtown Montréal. **Limocar Laurentides'** service (tel. 514/435–8899) departs regularly for Sainte-Adèle, Sainte-Agathe-des-Monts, Saint-Jovite, and Mont Tremblant, among other stops en route. Limocar also has a service to the Basses Laurentides (Lower Laurentians) region, departing from the Laval bus terminal at the Métro Henri-Bourassa stop in north Montréal, stopping in many towns, and ending in Saint-Jérôme.

L'Estrie
By Car
Take Autoroute 10 East from Montréal or from New England on U.S. 91, which becomes Autoroute 55 as it crosses the border at Rock Island.

By Bus
Buses depart daily from the Terminus Voyageur in Montréal (505 boul. de Maisonneuve E, tel. 514/842–2281), to Granby, Lac-Mégantic, Magog, Sherbrooke, and Thetford Mines.

Guided Tours

Special-interest
Whale-watching
The St. Lawrence estuary is a habitat for 10 whale species, from white belugas that stay year-round to 140-ton blue whales that arrive late in May. Graduate-student marine biologists assigned to Montréal's Zoological Society accompany weekend trips from Montréal, one in July and two in August. Contact **Montréal Zoological Society** (2055 rue Peel, Montréal H3A 1V4, tel. 514/845–8317).

Croisières Navimex Canada, Inc. (25 Pl. Marché Champlain, Suite 101, Québec City G1K 4H2, tel. 418/692–4643), offers three-hour whale-watching cruises ($35 for adults) and 4½-hour dinner cruises on the Saguenay Fjord ($46 for adults, children under 14 half-price). Cruises depart from either Baie-Ste-Catherine or Tadoussac.

Train Tours
The **Choo-Choo Steam Train Company** (819/778–7246) runs 75-minute scenic excursions along the Gatineau River from Hull to Wakefield and back, daily or on weekends, depending on season. There's room for 70, and the train makes an hour's stopover in Wakefield, where there's a museum, a gristmill, and a crafts shop. Fares range from $16 (Mon.–Wed.) to $24 (week-

ends) for adults, $12–$17 for ages 6–11, and $6–$10 for those
under 11.

Exploring Québec

There are two major attractions beyond the city limits of Montréal: l'Estrie (formerly the Eastern Townships), where city
folk retreat in summer, and Les Laurentides (the Laurentians), where they escape in winter. Les Laurentides are characterized by thousands of miles of unspoiled wilderness and
world-famous ski resorts, while l'Estrie has rolling hills and
farmland. As major vacation areas in both winter and summer,
they offer outdoor activities on ski slopes and lakes and in their
provincial parks. The two other regions worth exploring are
Charlevoix, often called the Switzerland of Québec because of
its landscape, and the knobby Gaspé Peninsula, where the St.
Lawrence River meets the Gulf of St. Lawrence.

Highlights for First-time Visitors

Basilica of Ste-Anne-de-Beaupré, Ste-Anne-de-Beaupré, Tour
3: Charlevoix
Bonaventure Island and its gannet colony, off Perce, Tour 4: The
Gaspé Peninsula
Cross-country skiing in Les Laurentides, Tour 1: Les Lauren-
tides
Jardin Zoologique de Granby, Granby, Tour 2: L'Estrie
"Sugaring off" at a sugar shack in Les Laurentides, Dining
Théâtre du lac Brome, Knowlton, Tour 2: L'Estrie
Whale-watching in the St. Lawrence Seaway, Guided Tours and
Tour 3: Charlevoix

Tour 1: Les Laurentides

Avid skiers might call Montréal a bedroom community for the
Laurentians; just 56 kilometers (35 miles) to the north, they are
home to some of North America's best-known ski resorts. The
Laurentian range is ancient, dating to the Precambrian era
(more than 600 million years ago). These rocky hills are relatively low, worn down by glacial activity, but they include
eminently skiable hills, with a few peaks above 2,500 feet.
World-famous Mont Tremblant, at 3,150 feet, is the tallest.

The **P'tit Train du Nord** made it possible to easily transport settlers and cargo to the Upper Laurentians. It also opened them
up to skiing by the turn of the century. Before long, trainloads
of skiers replaced settlers and cargo as the railway's major
trade. The Upper Laurentians soon became known worldwide
as the number-one ski center in North America—a position
that they still hold today. Initially a winter weekend getaway
for Montréalers who stayed at boardinghouses and fledgling resorts while skiing its hills, the Upper Laurentians began attracting an international clientele, especially with the advent
of the Canadian National Railway's special skiers' train, begun
in 1928. (Its competitor, the Canadian Pacific Railway, jumped
on the bandwagon soon after, doubling the number of train
runs bringing skiers to the area.)

Soon, points north of Saint-Jérôme began to develop as resort
areas: Saint-Sauveur-des-Monts, Saint-Jovite, Sainte-Agathe-

des-Monts, Mont Tremblant, and points in between became major ski centers. The Upper Laurentians also began to grow as a winter haven for prominent Montréalers, who traveled as far north as Sainte-Agathe-des-Monts to establish private family ski lodges. A number of these properties continue to be preserved in their rustic turn-of-the-century wilderness settings.

Accessible only by train until the 1930s, when the highway was built, these were used primarily as winter ski lodges. But once the road opened up, cottages became year-round family retreats. Today, there is an uneasy alliance between the longtime cottagers and resort-driven entrepreneurs. Both recognize the other's historic role in developing the Upper Laurentians, but neither espouses the other's cause. At the moment, commercial development seems to be winning out. A number of large hotels have added indoor pools and spa facilities, and efficient highways have brought the country closer to the city—45 minutes to Saint-Saveur, 1½–2 hours to Mont Tremblant. Montréalers can drive up to enjoy the fall foliage or engage in spring skiing and still get home before dark. The only slow periods are early October, when there is not much to do, and June, when there is plenty to do but the area is beset by blackflies.

Les Basses Laurentides The Laurentians are actually divided into two major regions—les Basses Laurentides (the Lower Laurentians) and les Hautes Laurentides (the Upper Laurentians). But don't be fooled by the designations; they don't signify great driving distances.

The Lower Laurentians start almost immediately outside Montréal. Considered the birthplace of the Laurentians, this area is rich in historic and architectural landmarks. Beginning in the mid-17th century, the governors of New France, as Québec was then called, gave large concessions of land to its administrators, priests, and top-ranking military, who became known as *seigneurs*. In the Lower Laurentians, towns like Terrebonne, Saint-Eustache, Lac-des-Deux-Montagnes, and Oka are home to the manors, mills, churches, and public buildings these seigneurs had built for themselves and their *habitants*—the inhabitants of these quasi-feudal villages.

Numbers in the margin correspond to points of interest on the Laurentians map.

① Two of the most famous seigneuries are within an hour of Montréal: **La Seigneurie de Terrebonne,** on l'Île-des-Moulins, is about 20 minutes from Montréal; La Seigneurie du Lac-des-Deux-Montagnes, in St-Scholastique, is 40 minutes from Montréal. You reach Terrebonne by taking boulevard Pie-IX in Montréal to the bridge of the same name. From the bridge take Highway 25 North. Exit at Terrebonne to Highway 440.

Governor Frontenac gave the land to Sieur André Daulier in 1673. Terrebonne was maintained by a succession of seigneurs until 1832, when Joseph Masson, the first French Canadian millionaire, bought it. He and his family were the last seigneurs de Terrebonne; their reign ended in 1883.

Today, Terrebonne offers visitors a bona fide glimpse of the past. Now run by the Corporation de l'Île-des-Moulins rather than a French aristocrat, the seigneurie's mansions, manors, and buildings have all been restored. Take a walk through Terrebonne's historical center and then stop at the **Centre**

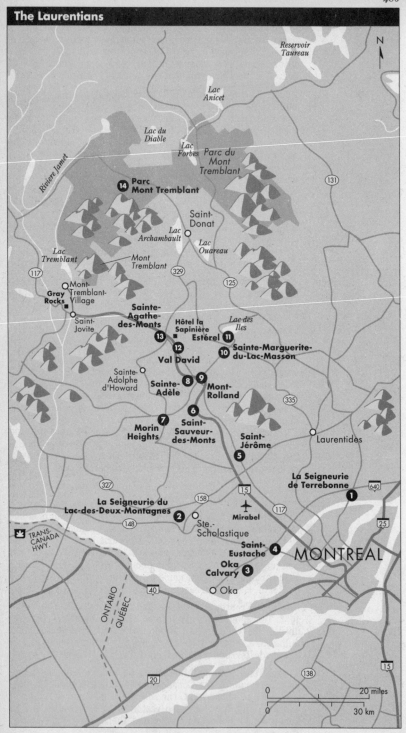

The Laurentians

d'Interprétation Historique de Terrebonne Museum. It features three exhibits: the Seigneurial Regime; the water, saw, flour, and wool mills of the region that gave the island its name; and the beginning of the Industrial Revolution in Terrebonne. The Île-des-Moulins art gallery hosts exhibitions of works by local artists, and a theater presents plays in French as well as musical matinees and outdoor summer shows. Most activities are free. *Cnr. boul. des Braves and rue St-Pierre, tel. 514/471–0619. Admission free. Open mid-May–June, Tues.–Sun. 10–5; July–Aug., Tues.–Sun. 10–8.*

❷ La Seigneurie du Lac-des-Deux-Montagnes was allotted to the Sulpician priests in 1717. Already appointed the seigneurs of the entire island of Montréal, the priests used this as the base from which to establish an Amerindian mission. To reach this mission, take Highway 13 or 15 North out of Montréal to Highway 640 West. Exit from Highway 640 West at Highway 148. Take this road into the town of Saint-Scholastique. A highlight of the seigneurie is the Sulpicians' seignorial manor on rue Belle-Rivière, erected between 1802 and 1808 in the village of Saint-Scholastique. The manor was used as part of the set for the late Claude Jutra's acclaimed film, *Kamouraska*, based on the novel by Québec's prize-winning author Anne Hébert.

❸ To promote piety among the Amerindians, the Sulpicians erected the **Oka Calvary (Stations of the Cross)** between 1740 and 1742. Three of the seven chapels are still maintained, and every September 14 since 1870, Québecois pilgrims have congregated here from across the province to participate in the half-hour ceremony that proceeds on foot to the Calvary's summit. A sense of the divine is inspired as much by the magnificent view of Lac-des-Deux-Montagnes as by religious fervor.

In 1887, the Sulpicians gave about 865 acres of their property located near the Oka Calvary to the Trappist monks, who had arrived in New France in 1880 from the Bellefontaine Abbey in France. Within 10 years they had built their monastery, the **Abbaye Cistercienne d'Oka,** and they transformed this land into one of the most beautiful domains in Québec. The abbey is one of the oldest in North America. Famous for creating Oka cheese, the Trappists established the Oka School of Agriculture, which operated until 1960. Today, the monastery is a noted prayer retreat. Tour the miller's modest home, where the Trappists stayed when they first arrived here, and visit the gardens and the chapel. *1600 chemin d'Oka, tel. 514/479–8361. Admission free. Chapel open daily 8–8; gardens and boutique open Mon.–Fri. 9:30–11:30 and 1–4:30, Sat. 9–4:30.*

Close by is the **Ferme Avicole d'Oka,** one of Québec's largest poultry farms, also developed by the Trappists. Tours of the breeding grounds for exotic pheasant, partridge, and guinea-hen fowl, as well as for the ordinary variety, are given, and there is a slide show of the transition from farm to table—an interesting encounter for city children. Fresh eggs and fowl can be bought on site. *1525 chemin d'Oka, tel. 514/479–8394. Store open Mon.–Fri. 9–noon and 1–5, Sat. 9–5, Sun. 1–5.*

Kanestake, a Mohawk Indian reserve near Oka, made the headlines during the summer of 1990 when a 78-day armed standoff between Mohawk Warriors (the reserve's self-proclaimed peacekeeping force) and Canadian and provincial authorities took place. The Mohawks of Kanestake opposed the expansion of the Oka golf course, claiming the land was stolen from them 273 years before. When the standoff ended, the golf course was not expanded, although territorial discussions were still in progress.

④ Nearby **Saint-Eustache** is another must for history buffs. One of the most important and tragic scenes in Canadian history took place here: the 1837 Rebellion. Since the British conquest of 1760, French Canadians had been confined to preexisting territories while the new townships were allotted exclusively to the English. Adding to this insult was the government's decision to tax all imported products from England, which made them prohibitively expensive. The result? In 1834, the French Canadian Patriot party defeated the British party locally. Lower Canada, as it was then known, became a hotbed of tension between the French and English, with French resistance to the British government reaching an all-time high. Rumors of rebellion were rife, and in December 1837, some 2,000 English soldiers led by General Colborne were sent in to put down the "army" of North Shore patriots by surrounding the village of Saint-Eustache. Jean-Olivier Chénier and his 200 Patriots took refuge in the local church, which Colborne's cannons bombed and set afire. Chénier and 80 of his comrades were killed during the battle, and more than 100 of the town's houses and buildings erected during the seignorial regime were looted and burned down by Colborne's soldiers. Even today, traces of the bullets fired by the English army cannons are visible on the facade of Saint-Eustache's church at 123 rue St-Louis. Most of the town's period buildings are open to the public. Note especially **Manoir Globenski** and **Moulin Légaré,** the only water mill still in operation in Canada. For a guided tour or for a free brochure that gives a good walking-tour guide, visit the town's Arts and Cultural Services Center (235 rue St-Eustache, tel. 514/472–4440).

Time Out   Before heading north, stop at **Pâtisserie Grande-Côte** (367A chemin de la Grande-Côte, tel. 514/473–7307) to sample the wares of St-Eustache's most famous bakery and pastry shop.

Les Hautes   Rivaling Saint-Eustache in Québec's historic folklore is **Saint-**
Laurentides   **Jérôme,** founded in 1830. Today a thriving economic center and
⑤   cultural hub off Route 117, it first gained prominence in 1868 when Curé Antoine Labelle became pastor of this parish on the shores of Rivière du Nord. Curé Labelle devoted himself to opening up northern Québec to French Canadians. Between 1868 and 1890, he founded 20 parish towns—an impressive achievement given the harsh conditions of this vast wilderness. But his most important legacy was the famous P'tit Train du Nord railway line, which he persuaded the government to build in order to open Saint-Jérôme to travel and trade.

Follow Saint-Jérôme's **promenade,** a 4-kilometer-long (2½-mile) boardwalk alongside the Rivière du Nord from rue de Martigny bridge to rue St-Joseph bridge for a walk through the town's history. Descriptive plaques en route highlight episodes of the Battle of 1837. The **Centre d'Exposition du Vieux-Palais** housed in St-Jérôme's old courthouse has temporary exhibits of contemporary art, featuring mostly Québec artists. A music hall next door hosts concerts. *185 rue du Palais, tel. 514/ 432–7171. Admission free. Open Tues.–Fri. noon–5, Sun. 1–5.*

Saint-Jérôme's **Parc Régional de la Rivière-du-Nord** (1051 boul. International, tel. 514/431–1676) was created as a nature retreat. Paths throughout the park lead to the spectacular Wilson Falls (*"chutes,", en français*). Rain or shine, the Pavillon Marie-Victorin is open daily, with summer weekend displays and workshops devoted to nature, culture, and history.

The resort vacation area truly begins at Saint-Sauveur-des-Monts (Exit 60) and extends as far north as Mont Tremblant, where it turns into a wilderness of lakes and forests best visited with an outfitter. Laurentian guides planning fishing and hunting trips are concentrated around Saint-Donat near Parc Mont Tremblant.

To the first-time visitor, the hills and resorts around Saint-Sauveur, Sainte-Marguerite Station, Morin Heights, Val Morin, and Val David, up to Sainte-Agathe, form a pleasant hodgepodge of villages, hotels, and inns that seem to blend one into another.

❻ Saint-Sauveur-des-Monts, exit 60 off the Autoroute, is the focal point for area resorts. It has gone from a 1970s sleepy Laurentian village of 4,000 residents that didn't even have a traffic light to a thriving year-round town attracting some 30,000 cottagers and visitors on weekends. Its main street, rue Principale, once dotted with quaint French restaurants, now boasts *brochetteries* and sushi bars, and the narrow strip is so choked in summertime by cars and tourists that it has earned the sobriquet "Crescent Street of the North," borrowing its name from the well-known, action-filled street in Montréal. Residents here once won the battle against a McDonald's opening. Now the parking lots of major franchise fast-food eateries are always packed. Despite all this development, Saint-Sauveur has managed to maintain some of its charming, rural character.

The gleaming white spires of **Saint-Sauveur Church** still dominate rue Principale, but **Saint Francis of the Birds** has not been so lucky. Built in 1951 with support from Montréal's Molson family, this sturdy, rustic log church with its fine stained-glass-window portraits of the Laurentian countryside no longer offers the worshiper or visitor a secluded and peaceful spiritual retreat. Where only a few years ago its immediate neighbors were modest chalets dotting the forest, today the empty, bankrupt Delta Hotel complex sits in the church's backyard. However, classical concerts can still be heard in the church every second Saturday evening during September and October (tel. 514/227–2423).

But for those who like their vacations—winter or summer—lively and activity-filled, Saint-Sauveur is *the* place where the action rolls nonstop. In winter, skiing is the main thing. (Mont-Saint-Sauveur, Mont Avila, Mont Gabriel, and Mont Olympia all offer special season passes and programs, and some ski-center passes can be used at more than one center in the region.) From Mont-Saint-Sauveur to Mont Tremblant, the area's ski centers (most situated in or near Saint-Sauveur, Sainte-Adèle, Sainte-Agathe, and Saint-Jovite) offer night skiing. All boast ski instructors—many are members of the Canadian Ski Patrol Association.

Just outside Saint-Sauveur, the $7 million Mont-Saint-Sauveur **Aquatic Park** and tourist center (exit 58 or 60) will keep children happy with slides, wave pools, snack bars, and more. Its latest attraction is the $1.7 million man-made "Colorado" rafting river, which follows the natural contours of the steep hills. The nine-minute ride requires about 12,000 gallons of water to be pumped per minute. In winter, the "Colorado River" becomes a giant ice slide. *Rue Saint-Denis, Saint-Sauveur-des-Monts, tel. 514/871-0101 or 800/363-2426. Open mid-June-Aug., daily 10-7. Admission: full day—$20.75 adults, $15 children 3 and over; half day (after 3 PM)—$17 adults, $13 children 3 and over; evening (after 5 PM)—$13 adults, $10 children 3 and over. Sept.-mid-June, telephone for schedule. Admission: full day—$17 adults, $12 children 3 and over; half day (after 3 PM)—$14 adults, $11 children 3 and over.*

7 Nearby in **Morin Heights,** there's a new spin on an old sport at **Ski Morin Heights** (exit 60, Autoroute 15 N, tel. 514/226-1333 or 800/363-2527), where snowboarding is the latest craze. Likened to surfing a big wave, riding a skateboard down a hill, or windsurfing on a white-capped lake, snowboarding demands similar skills and dexterity, not to mention the fearlessness of the lionhearted. Nonetheless, it is carefully supervised by Ski Morin Heights' instructors. Although it doesn't have overnight accommodations, Ski Morin Heights boasts a 44,000-square-foot chalet with a full range of hospitality services and sports-related facilities, eateries, après-ski activities, pubs, a health club, and a day-care center. There's also a large nursery on-site and special ski-lesson programs for children ages 2 and up.

The town's architecture and population reflect its English settlers' origins. Most residents are English-speaking. Morin Heights has escaped the overdevelopment of Saint-Sauveur but still offers the visitor a good range of restaurants, bookstores, boutiques, and crafts shops to explore. During the summer months, windsurfing, swimming, and canoeing on the area's two lakes are popular pastimes. The most recent addition, now entering its fifth season to popular and critical acclaim, is **Théâtre Morin Heights** (tel. 514/226-5863), whose "professional amateur" productions are presented at Ski Morin Heights during the summer months. Popular musicals, lighthearted comedies, mysteries, and children's plays are in the repertoire. A dinnershow package costs about $32 per person. Reservations are a must.

In the summer, holiday goers head for the region's golf courses (two of the more pleasant are 18-hole links at Sainte-Adèle and Mont Gabriel), campgrounds at Val David, Lacs Claude and Lafontaine, and beaches; in the fall and winter, they come for the foliage as well as alpine and nordic skiing.

8 The busy town of **Sainte-Adèle** is full of gift and Québec-crafts shops, boutiques, and restaurants. It also has an active nightlife, including a few discos.

Just as much of a rave with adults and children are the **Super Splash** ice slides, which are converted to waterslides in the summer. *1791 boul. Ste-Adèle, tel. 514/229-2909. 2 giant ice slides for adults, 3 for children. Admission to ice slide: $15 adults, $10 children. Open Dec.-Mar., 9 AM-10 PM. Admission to waterslide: $15 adults, $10 children, $37 families. Open June 15-Sept. 2, 9 AM-10 PM.*

A couple of miles north on Highway 117, the reconstructed **Village de Seraphin's** 20 small homes, grand country house,

general store, and church recall the settlers who came to
Sainte-Adèle in the 1840s. This award-winning historic town
also features a train tour through the woods. *Tel. 514/229–
4777. Admission: $8.25 adults, $6 children 12–17, $4.50 chil-
dren 5–11. Open May 15–June 24, Sat.–Wed. 10–6; June 25–
Aug., daily 10–6; Sept.–Oct. 16, Sat.–Wed. 10–6.*

9 In **Mont Rolland, Station Touristique de Mont Gabriel** offers superb skiing, primarily for intermediate and advanced skiers.
The on-site lodge, **Auberge Mont Gabriel** (*see* Lodging, below),
has week-long and weekend packages. *Autoroute 15, exit 64,
Mont Rolland J0R 1G0, tel. 514/229–3547.*

10 Neighboring community **Sainte-Marguerite-du-Lac-Masson**
celebrated its 125th anniversary in 1990. The town's Service
des Loisirs (tel. 514/228–2545) is the place to call for details
about events, as well as cruises and skating on Lac-Masson.

11 The permanent population of the town of **Estérel** is a mere 80
souls. But visitors to **Ville d'Estérel,** a 135-room resort at
Autoroute 69, near Sainte-Marguerite Station, swell that number into the thousands. Founded in 1959 on the shores of Lac
Dupuis, this 5,000-acre domain was bought by Fridolin Simard
from Baron Louis Empain. Named Estérel by the baron because it evoked memories of his native village in Provence, Ville
d'Estérel soon became a household word for holiday vacationers in search of a first-class resort area. (For more details, *see*
Lodging, below.)

12 Children know **Val David** for its **Santa Claus Village.** *987 rue
Morin, Val David, tel. 819/322–2146. Open mid-May–mid-
June, weekends only 10–6; mid-June–Aug., daily 10–6. Ad-
mission: $7 adults, $5.50 children 2–12.*

Val David is a rendezvous for mountain climbers, ice scalers,
dogsledders, hikers, and summer or winter campers. For
equipment rentals and other information, contact the Maison
du Tourisme des Laurentides (tel. 514/436–8532).

Val David is also a haven for artists, many of whose studios are
open to the public. Most of their work is for sale. **Les Créateurs
Associés** (2495 rue d'Église, tel. 819/322–2043) boutique and
art gallery features a wide range of artisan handcrafts. **Atelier
Bernard Chaudron, Inc.** (2449 chemin de l'Île, tel. 819/322–
3944), sells hand-shaped and hammered lead-free pewter objets d'art.

About 96 kilometers (60 miles) from Montréal, overlooking Lac
13 des Sables, is **Sainte-Agathe-des-Monts,** the largest commercial
center for ski communities farther north. This lively resort
area attracts campers to its spacious **Camping Ste-Agathe** (Rte.
329, C.P. 156, Sainte-Agathe-des-Monts J8C 3A3, tel. 819/
326–5577), bathers to its municipal beach, and sailors to its lake
cruises on the *Alouette* (tel. 819/326–2282) touring launch. Sailing is the favorite summer sport, especially during the "24
Heures de la Voile" sailing competition (tel. 819/326–0457) each
Canada Day weekend in July.

Skin diving is also popular here. The **Centre de plongée
sousmarine** (124 rue Principale, tel. 819/326–4464) will refill air
tanks and provide information about equipment rentals, etc.

But mountain climbing may be one of the best ways to view the
scenery of the Upper Laurentians. The **Fédération Québécoise**

de la Montagne (4545 rue Pierre-de-Coubertin, C.P. 1000, Succursale M, Montréal H1V 3R2, tel. 514/252–3004) can give you information about this, as can the region's tourist offices.

About 1 kilometer (½ mile) north of Sainte-Agathe-des-Monts is the **Village du Mont-Castor,** an attractive re-creation of a turn-of-the-century Québecois village; more than 100 new homes have been built here in the traditional fashion of full-length logs set *pièce sur pièce* (one upon the other).

Farther north lie two of Québec's best-known ski resorts— Gray Rocks and Mont Tremblant Lodge, now part of Station Touristique de Mont Tremblant (*see* Lodging, below). Mont Tremblant is also car-racing country. Racing champion Jackie Stewart has called Mont Tremblant "the most beautiful race-track in the world." The **Formula 2000 "Jim Russell Championships"** of the Canadian Car Championships (tel. 819/425–2739) take place here on weekends in June, July, August, September, and October.

The mountain and the hundreds of square miles of wilderness beyond it constitute **Parc Mont Tremblant.** Created in 1894, this was once the home of the Algonquin Indians, who called this area Manitonga Soutana, meaning "mountain of the spirits." Today it is a vast wildlife sanctuary of more than 500 lakes and rivers protecting some 230 species of birds and animals, including moose, deer, bear, and beaver. In the winter, its trails are used by cross-country skiers, snowshoers, and snowmobile enthusiasts. Moose hunting is allowed in season, and camping and canoeing are the main summer activities.

Tour 2: L'Estrie

Numbers in the margin correspond to points of interest on the L'Estrie map.

L'Estrie (also known as the Eastern Townships) refers to the area in the southeast corner of the province of Québec, bordering Vermont and New York State. Its northern Appalachian hills, rolling down to placid lakeshores, were first home to the Abenaki Indians, long before "summer people" built their cottages and horse paddocks here. The Indians are gone, but the names they gave to the region's recreational lakes remain— Memphremagog, Massawippi, Mégantic.

L'Estrie was initially populated by United Empire Loyalists fleeing the American War of Independence and, later, the newly created United States of America, to continue living under the English king in British North America. It's not surprising that l'Estrie is reminiscent of New England with its covered bridges, village greens, white church steeples, and country inns. The Loyalists were followed, around 1820, by the first wave of Irish immigrants—ironically, Catholics fleeing their country's union with Protestant England. Some 20 years later the potato famine sent more Irish pioneers to the townships.

The area became more Gallic after 1850, as French Canadians moved in to work on the railroad and in the lumber industry, and later to mine asbestos at Thetford. Around the turn of the century, English families from Montréal and Americans from the border states discovered the region and began summering at cottages along the lakes. During the Prohibition era, the area attracted even more cottagers from the United States. Lac

Massawippi became a favorite summer resort of wealthy families whose homes have since been converted into gracious inns, including the Manoir Hovey and the Hatley Inn.

Today the summer communities fill up with equal parts French and English visitors, though the year-round residents are primarily French. Nevertheless, the locals are proud of both their Loyalist heritage and Québec roots. They boast of "Loyalist tours" and Victorian gingerbread homes and in the next breath direct visitors to the snowmobile museum in Valcourt, where, in 1937, native son Joseph-Armand Bombardier built the first *moto-neige* (snowmobile) in his garage. (Bombardier's inventions were the basis of one of Canada's biggest industries, supplying New York City and Mexico City with subway cars and other rolling stock.)

Over the past two decades, l'Estrie has developed from a series of quiet farm communities and wood-frame summer homes to a thriving all-season resort area. In winter, skiers flock to nine downhill centers and 26 cross-country trails. By early spring, the sugar huts are busy with the new maple syrup. L'Estrie's southerly location makes this the balmiest corner of Québec, notable for its spring skiing. In summer, boating, swimming, sailing, golfing, and bike riding take over. And every fall the inns are booked solid with "leaf peepers" eager to take in the brilliant foliage.

⑮ Granby, about 80 kilometers (50 miles) from Montréal, is considered to be the gateway to l'Estrie. This town is best known for its zoo, the **Jardin Zoologique de Granby.** It houses some 800 animals from 225 species. Two rare snow leopards on loan from Chicago's Lincoln Park Zoo and New York's Bronx Zoo recently became parents. The Granby pair have won the zoo recognition from the International Union for the Conservation of Nature. The young snow leopard is the zoo favorite. The complex includes amusement park rides and souvenir shops as well as a playground and picnic area. *347 rue Bourget, tel. 514/372–9113. Admission: $14 adults, $12 senior citizens, $7 children 5–17, $4 children 1–4. Open June–Aug., daily 10–5.*

Granby is also gaining repute as the townships' gastronomic capital. Each October, the month-long Festival Gastronomique attracts more than 10,000 *gastronomes* who use the festival's "gastronomic passport" to sample the cuisines at several dining rooms. To reserve a passport, contact: Festival Gastronomique de Granby et Région, 650 rue Principle, Granby J2G 8L4. *Tel. 514/378–7272.*

The **Yamaska** recreation center on the outskirts of town features sailboarding, swimming, and picnicking all summer, and cross-country skiing and snowshoeing in winter.

In the past two decades, l'Estrie has developed into a scenic and increasingly popular ski center. Although it is still less crowded and commercialized than the Laurentians, it boasts ski hills on four mountains that dwarf anything the Laurentians have to offer, with the exception of lofty Mont Tremblant. And, compared with those in Vermont, ski-pass rates are still a bargain.

⑯ Bromont, closest to Montréal, is as lively at night as during the day. It offers the only night skiing in l'Estrie and a slope-side disco, **Le Débarque,** where the action continues into the night

488

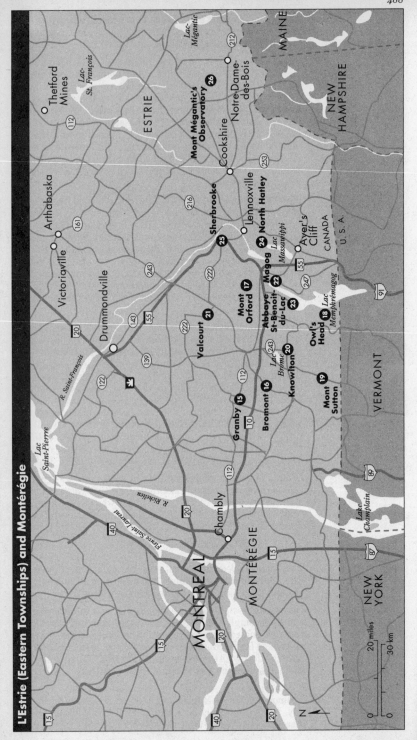

L'Estrie (Eastern Townships) and Montérégie

⑰ après-ski. **Mont Orford,** located at the center of a provincial
park, offers plenty of challenges for alpine and cross-country
⑱ skiers, from novices to veterans. **Owl's Head** has become a mecca for skiers looking for fewer crowds on the hills. It also boasts
a 4-kilometer (2.4-mile) intermediate run, the longest in
l'Estrie. Aside from superb skiing, Owl's Head offers tremen-
dous scenery. From the trails you can see nearby Vermont and
Lac Memphremagog. (You might even see the lake's legendary
sea dragon, said to have been sighted some 90 times since
⑲ 1816.) As it has for decades, **Mont Sutton** attracts the same diehard crowd of mostly Anglophone skiers from Québec. It's also
one of the area's largest resorts, with trails that plunge and
wander through pine, maple, and birch trees slope-side. **Sutton**
itself is a well-established community with crafts shops, cozy
eateries, and bars (La Paimpolaise is a favorite among skiers).

Bromont and Orford are *stations touristiques* (tourist centers),
meaning that they offer a wide range of activities in all seasons—boating, camping, golf, horseback riding, swimming,
tennis, water parks, trail biking, canoeing, fishing, hiking,
cross-country and downhill skiing, snowshoeing, etc. A waterslide park (tel. 514/534–2200)—take exit 78 off Autoroute 10—
and a large flea market (weekends from May to mid-November)
offer pleasant additions to horseback riding.

⑳ Along the shore of Lac Brome is the village of **Knowlton,** a
pleasant place to shop for antiques and gifts. In summer check
to see what's playing at Knowlton's popular **Théâtre Lac Brome**
(*see* The Arts, below). In winter many Montréalers come here
to ski at **Glen Mountain** (off Route 243, tel. 514/243–6142).

㉑ **Valcourt** is the birthplace of the inventor of the snowmobile, so
it follows that this is a world center for the sport, with more
than 1,500 kilometers (1,000-plus miles) of paths cutting
through the woods and meadows. The **Musée Joseph-Armand
Bombardier** displays this innovator's many inventions year-
round. *1001 boul. Joseph-Armand Bombardier, tel. 514/532–
2258. Admission: $5 adults, $3 students and senior citizens,
children under 5 free. Open June 24–Aug., daily 10–5:30;
Sept.–June 23, Tues.–Sun. 10–5.*

South of Mont Orford at the northern tip of Lac Memphremagog, a large body of water reaching into northern Vermont, lies
㉒ the bustling resort town of **Magog,** which celebrated its cente-
nary in 1988. A once sleepy village, the town has grown into a
four-season resort destination. Two sandy beaches, great bed-
and-breakfasts, hotels and restaurants, boating, ferry rides,
bird-watching, sailboarding, aerobics, horseback riding, and
snowmobiling are just some of the activities offered.

Stroll along Magog's **rue Principale** for a look at boutiques, art
galleries, and crafts shops with local artisans' work. Other
shops are spread throughout the town's downtown, where the
streets are lined with century-old homes and churches, some of
which have been converted into storefronts, galleries, and theaters.

Magog is lively after dark, with a variety of bars, cafés, bistros,
and great restaurants to suit every taste and pocketbook. **La
Lanterne** (tel. 819/843–7205) is a popular hangout. The more
sedentary may find **La Source's** (tel. 819/843–0319) array of
cheeses, pâtés, and Swiss chocolates irresistible.

㉓ Near Magog is the **Abbaye St-Benoît-du-Lac**. To reach St-Benoît from Magog, take the road to Austin and then follow the signs for the side road to the abbey. This abbey's slender bell tower juts up above the trees like a fairy-tale castle. Built on a wooded peninsula in 1912 by the Benedictines, the abbey is home to some 60 monks, who sell apples and apple cider from their orchards as well as distinctive cheeses: Ermite, St-Benoît, and ricotta. Gregorian masses are held daily. Check for those open to the public (tel. 819/843–4080). The abbey is also known as a favorite retreat for some of Québec's best-known politicians; they abandon the thrust-and-cut of their secular concerns for spiritual rejuvenation.

㉔ One of the pastimes of **North Hatley** crosses language barriers easily. The town on the tip of Lac Massawippi is home to **The Pilsen,** Québec's earliest microbrewery. Although the beer is no longer brewed on-site, the Pilsen (tel. 819/842–2971) still serves Massawippi pale and dark ales on tap. For those who ask, proprietor Gilles Peloquin will arrange a visit to the famous brewery, now located in nearby Lennoxville. The pub also has great food, loads of atmosphere, and a convivial crowd year-round. The avant-garde **Piggery** theater is based in North Hatley (*see* the Arts, below).

㉕ The region's unofficial capital and largest city is **Sherbrooke,** named in 1818 for Canadian Governor General Sir John Coape Sherbrooke. Founded by Loyalists in the 1790s, and located along the St-François River, it boasts a number of art galleries, the **Musée des Beaux-Arts de Sherbrooke** (174 rue Palais, tel. 819/821–2115; admission free; open Tues.–Sun. 1–5), and the historic **Domaine Howard** (tel. 819/564–8331) headquarters of the townships' historic society, which conducts city tours from this site from June 24 through August. Reservations are recommended.

㉖ For a more cosmic experience, continue from Sherbrooke along Route 212 to **Mont Mégantic's Observatory.** Both amateur stargazers and serious astronomers are drawn to this site, located in a beautifully wild and mountainous part of l'Estrie. The observatory is at the summit of l'Estrie's second-highest mountain (3,601 feet), whose northern face records annual snowfalls rivaling any in North America. The observatory is a joint venture by l'Université de Montréal and l'Université Laval. Its powerful telescope allows resident scientists to observe celestial bodies 10 million times smaller than the human eye can detect. There's a welcome center on the mountain's base, where amateur stargazers can get information about the evening celestial sweep sessions, Thursday through Saturday. *Notre-Dame-des-Bois, tel. 819/888–2822. Open June 24–Labor Day, daily 10–5.*

Tour 3: Charlevoix

Numbers in the margin correspond to points of interest on the Charlevoix map.

Stretching along the St. Lawrence River's north shore east of Québec City from Sainte-Anne-de-Beaupré to the Saguenay River, Charlevoix embraces mountains rising from the sea and a succession of valleys, plateaus, and cliffs cut by waterfalls, brooks, and streams. The roads wind into villages of picturesque houses and huge tin-roof churches.

New France's first historian, the Jesuit priest François-Xavier de Charlevoix, gave his name to the region. Charlevoix (Sharle-vwah) was first explored by Jacques Cartier, who landed in 1535, although the first colonists didn't arrive until well into the 17th century. They developed a thriving shipbuilding industry, specializing in the sturdy schooner they called a *goelette*, which they used to haul everything from logs to lobsters up and down the coast in the days before rail and paved roads. Shipbuilding has been a vital part of the provincial economy until recent times, though wrecked and forgotten goelettes are visible from many beaches in the region.

㉗ Charlevoix begins about 33 kilometers (20 miles) east of Québec City, in the tiny town of **Sainte-Anne-de-Beaupré**. Each year more than a million pilgrims visit the region's most famous religious site, the **Basilica of Sainte-Anne-de-Beaupré** (Québec's patron saint), which is dedicated to the mother of the Virgin Mary (*see* Chapter 5).

㉘ Only 8 kilometers (5 miles) beyond the pilgrimage center is the **Cap Tourmente Wildlife Reserve**, where more than 100,000 greater snow geese gather every October and May. Other parts of the region offer whale-watching cruises, and you can often spot whales, seals, and dolphins, on occasion, from ferries and on land, so nature-lovers are encouraged to bring their binoculars. *St-Joachim G0A 3X0, tel. 418/827-3776.*

In fact, the region is a haven for anyone who enjoys being active in the outdoors, including hikers, joggers, cyclists, and, in particular, skiers. Charlevoix has three main ski areas, with excellent facilities for both the downhill and cross-country skier.
㉙ **Parc du Mont-Sainte-Anne**, outside Québec City, is on the
㉚ World Cup downhill ski circuit; **Mont Grand Fonds** has 13 slopes
㉛ and 135 kilometers (84 miles) of cross-country trails; and **Le Massif** is a three-peak ski resort that boasts the province's highest vertical drop (762 meters, or 2,500 feet). At Le Massif, you take a 30-minute bus ride to the top, and a guide leads you through powder snow to the beginning of your run. *For information on Parc du Mont-Ste-Anne, see Chapter 5; Mont Grand Fonds, 1000 chemin des Loisirs, La Malbaie, tel. 418/665-4405; Le Massif, Rte. 138, tel. 418/435-3593.*

㉜ **Baie-St-Paul,** Charlevoix's earliest settlement after Beaupré, is popular with hang-gliding fans and artists. You will find artisans working in old habitant houses. Here, the high hills circle a wide plain holding the village beside the sea. Many of Québec's greatest landscapists portray the area, and their work is on display year-round at the **Centre d'Art Baie-St-Paul** (4 boul. Faford, tel. 418/435-3681). Recently the center has garnered a reputation in North America as a major regional arts center promoting the area's own talent, as well as providing those just starting out with wider exposure while they study their crafts. At town-center, **Auberge la Maison Otis,** an 1858 stone house, has been converted into what many consider the area's finest inn-restaurant (*see* Lodging, below).

From Baie-St-Paul, you can take the open, scenic coastal drive (Rte. 362) or the faster Route 138 to **Pointe-au-Pic, La Malbaie,** and **Cap-à-l'Aigle.** This section of Route 362 has memorable views of rolling hills—green, white, or ablaze with fiery hues, depending on the season—meeting the broad expanse of the "sea" as the locals like to call the St. Lawrence estuary.

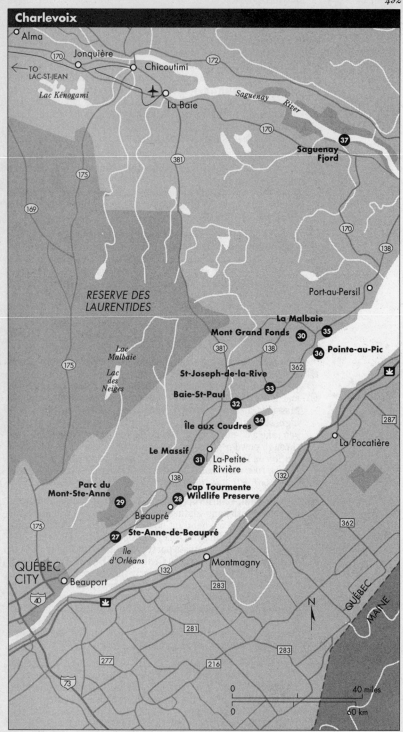

Charlevoix

Alma

Jonquière
Chicoutimi

170

TO
LAC-ST-JEAN

172

Lac Kénogami

La Baie

Saguenay River

170

Saguenay Fjord 37

381

175

169

170

138

Port-au-Persil

RESERVE DES LAURENTIDES

La Malbaie

Mont Grand Fonds 30 35

381 138

Pointe-au-Pic 36

Lac Malbaie

362

175

Lac des Neiges

St-Joseph-de-la-Rive

33

Baie-St-Paul

32

287

Île aux Coudres 34

Le Massif

La Pocatière

31 **La-Petite-Rivière**

138

132

Parc du Mont-Ste-Anne

29

Cap Tourmente Wildlife Preserve

28

362

Beaupré

27 **Ste-Anne-de-Beaupré**

175

QUÉBEC CITY

Beauport

Île d'Orléans

Montmagny

40

132

283

N

QUÉBEC

MAINE

281

277

216

283

73

| 0 | | 40 miles |
| 0 | | 60 km |

③ A secondary road leads sharply down into **St-Joseph-de-la-Rive**, with its line of old houses hugging the mountain base on the narrow shore road. The town is host to peaceful inns and inviting restaurants, such as l'Auberge sous les Pins, which means "inn under the pines." Nearby Papeterie St-Gilles produces unusual handcrafted stationery, using a 17th-century process. The small **Charlevoix Musée** commemorates the days of the St. Lawrence goelettes. From St-Joseph you can catch a ferry to

③ **Île aux Coudres,** an island where Jacques Cartier's men gathered *les coudres* (hazelnuts) in 1535. Since then, the island has produced many a goelette, and former captains now run several small inns. Larger inns feature folk-dance evenings. Many visitors like to bike around the 16-kilometer (10-mile) island taking in inns, windmills, and old schooners, as well as boutiques selling paintings and local handcrafts, such as household linen.

Continuing on Route 362, you will come to one of the most elegant and historically interesting resorts in the entire province.

③ **La Malbaie** was known as Murray Bay in an earlier era when wealthy Anglophones summered here and in the neighboring villages of Pointe-au-Pic and Cap-à-l'Aigle. The regional museum—**Musée de Charlevoix**—traces its history as a vacation spot in a series of exhibits and is developing an excellent collection of local paintings and folk art. *1 rue du Havre, Pointe-au-Pic, tel. 418/665–4411.*

Once called the "summer White House," this area became popular with both American and Canadian politicians in the late 1800s when Ottawa Liberals and Washington Republicans partied decorously through the summer with members of the Québec judiciary. William Howard Taft built the first of three

③ summer residences in **Pointe-au-Pic** in 1894, when he was the American civil governor of the Philippines. He became the 27th president of the United States in 1908, and later chief justice of the Supreme Court. Locals still fondly remember the Tafts and the parties they threw in their elegant summer homes.

Now many Taft-era homes serve as handsome inns, guaranteeing an old-fashioned coddling, with extras like breakfast in bed, gourmet meals, whirlpools, and free shuttles to the ski areas in winter. Many serve lunch and dinner to nonresidents, so you can tour the area going from one gourmet's delight to the next. The cuisine, as elsewhere in Québec, is genuine French, rather than a hybrid invented for North Americans.

The road, the views, and the villages continue all the way up to Baie-Ste-Catherine, which shares the view up the magnificent

③ **Saguenay Fjord** with the small town of **Tadoussac.** Jacques Cartier made a stop at this point in 1535, and it became an important meeting site for fur traders in the French Territory until the mid-19th century. Whale-watching excursions and cruises of the fjord now depart from Tadoussac, as well as from Chicoutimi, farther up the deep fjord. As the Saguenay River flows from Lake St-Jean south toward the St. Lawrence, it has a dual character: Between Alma and Chicoutimi, the once rapidly flowing river has been turned into hydroelectric power; in its lower section, it becomes wider and deeper and flows by steep mountains and cliffs, en route to the St. Lawrence. The white beluga whale breeds in the lower portion of the Saguenay in summer, and in the confluence of the fjord and the seaway are many marine species, which attract other whales, such as pilot, finback, humpback, and blues. Sadly, the beluga is an endangered species, and the estimated 400 left, along with 27 species of mammals and birds and 17 species of fish, are being threatened by pollution from the St. Lawrence River. This has inspired a $100 million project funded by both the federal and provincial governments. An 800-square-kilometer (496 sq. mi) marine park at the confluence of the Saguenay and St. Lawrence rivers has been created to protect its fragile ecosystem in hope of reversing some of the damage already done. Full-day and half-day cruises from Chicoutimi operate daily June–September (tel. 418/543–7630); other trips leave from Hotel Tadoussac (tel. 418/235–4421) from May through mid-October.

Tour 4: The Gaspé Peninsula

Numbers in the margin correspond to points of interest on the Gaspé Peninsula map.

Jutting into the stormy Gulf of St. Lawrence like the battered prow of a ship, the Gaspé Peninsula remains an isolated region of unsurpassed wild beauty, an area where the land ends. Sheer cliffs tower above broad beaches, and tiny coastal fishing communities cling to the shoreline. Inland rise the Chic-Choc Mountains, eastern Canada's highest, the realm of woodland caribou, black bear, and moose. Townspeople in some Gaspé areas speak mainly English, though *Gaspésiens* speak slightly Acadian-accented French.

Jacques Cartier landed on the Gaspé in 1534, but it wasn't until the early 1800s that the first settlers arrived. Today, the area still seems unspoiled and timeless, a blessing for travelers dipping and soaring along the spectacular coastal highways or venturing on river-valley roads to the interior. Geographically, the peninsula is among the oldest lands on earth. A vast, mainly uninhabited forest covers the hilly hinterland. Local tourist officials can be helpful in locating outfitters and guides to fish and hunt large and small game. The Gaspé's four major parks—**Port Daniel, Forillon, Causapscal,** and **Gaspé Park**—cover a total of 2,292 square kilometers (885 square miles).

Take the Trans-Canada Highway northeast along the southern shore of the St. Lawrence River to just south of Rivière-du-Loup, where you pick up the 270-kilometer (150-mile) Route 132, which hugs the dramatic coastline. At Ste-Flavie, follow the southern leg of Route 132. Windsurfers and sailors enjoy the breezes around the Gaspé; there are windsurfing marathons in **Baie des Chaleurs** (at Carleton) each summer.

The Gaspé was on Jacques Cartier's itinerary—he first stepped ashore in North America in the town of Gaspé—but Vikings, Basques, and Portuguese fisherfolk had come long before. The area's history is told in countless towns en route. Acadians, displaced by the British from New Brunswick in 1755, settled **Bonaventure; Paspébiac** still has a gunpowder shed built in the 1770s to help defend the peninsula from American ships; and United Empire Loyalists settled **New Carlisle** in 1784.

The largest colony of gannets in the world summers on the Gaspé's **Bonaventure Island,** off Percé. The most famous sight in the region is the huge fossil-embedded rock off the town of **Percé** that the sea "pierced" thousands of years ago.

Gaspé Peninsula

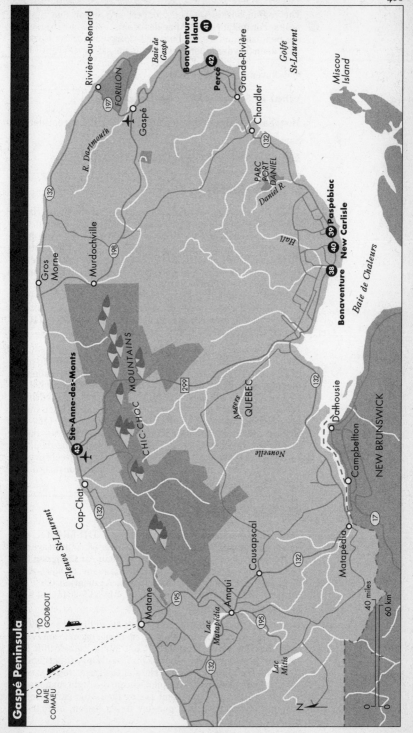

TO BAIE COMEAU

TO GODBOUT

Fleuve St-Laurent

Matane

195

Cap-Chat

132

Ste-Anne-des-Monts 43

CHIC-CHOC MOUNTAINS

299

Gros Morne

Murdochville

198

132

FORILLON

R. Dartmouth

Gaspé

197

Rivière-au-Renard

Baie de Gaspé

Bonaventure Island 41

42 Percé

Grande-Rivière

Golfe St-Laurent

Miscou Island

Chandler

132

PARC PORT DANIEL

Daniel R.

Hall

Angers

Nouelle

QUEBEC

39 Paspébiac

40 New Carlisle

38 Bonaventure

Baie de Chaleurs

132

Dalhousie

Campbellton

NEW BRUNSWICK

17

Matapédia

132

Causapscal

Amqui

195

Lac Matapédia

Lac Mitis

132

N

0

0

40 miles

60 km

43 The region boasts Québec's longest ski season and highest peaks. For instance, **Ste-Anne-des-Monts,** on the north shore of the peninsula, offers the only heli-skiing east of the Rockies, with deep powder, open bowl, and glade skiing clear into June on peaks that rise to 2,700 feet. Other centers operate from mid-November through May.

What to See and Do with Children

Mont Saint-Sauveur Aquatic Park, Tour 1, Les Laurentides

Santa Claus Village, Tour 1, Les Laurentides

Jardin Zoologique de Granby, Tour 2, L'Estrie

Shopping

When in the Laurentians, consider a stroll along Saint-Sauveur-des-Monts' rue Principale amid shops, fashion boutiques, and outdoor café terraces decorated with bright awnings and flowers. Housed in a former bank, **La Voute Boutique** (239B rue Principale, tel. 514/227–4144) carries such international labels as Byblos and an up-to-the-minute all-season selection of coordinates in cotton, knits, suede, and leather, plus sequined dresses, sweaters, pants, jackets, and suits from France, Italy, and Spain. If you are hungry, have a bite at **Jardin des Oliviers** (239 rue Principale, tel. 514/227–2110), a popular, moderately priced French restaurant in the middle of town.

Magog's rue Principale, in l'Estrie, is another interesting place to browse. The street is dotted with boutiques, art galleries, and crafts shops with local artisan's work. **Amandine** (499 rue Principale O, tel. 819/847–1346) is a lovely gift shop with unusual dishes, stemware, luxury bath items, and Belgian chocolate. When you want a rest, drop by **La Source** (420 rue Principale O, tel. 819/843–0319) for an array of cheeses, pâtés, and Swiss chocolates. Other shops are spread throughout the town's downtown, where the streets are lined with century-old homes and churches, some of which have been converted into storefronts, galleries, and theaters.

Sports and Fitness

Bicycling **Estrie à Bicyclette** (C.P. 772, Sherbrooke, J1H 5K7, tel. 819/346–6795) sells a cycling guide of Estrie for $8. Guides are sold at most bicycle rental shops. **Base de Plein Air Davignon** (319 chemin Gale, Bromont, tel. 514/534–2277 or 800/363–8952) rents bicycles, and the **Sutton Tourist Association** (20 Place Sutton, C.P. 418, Sutton J0E 2K0, tel. 514/538–2646) has a list of places to rent bicycles in the region.

Deltaplaning If white-water rafting isn't adventure enough, there is always deltaplaning, in which man and machine become one. The **Vélidelta Free-Flying School** (C.P. 631, Mont Rolland J0R 1J0, tel. 514/229–6887) offers lessons on free-flying, flight simulation, and the more advanced tricks of the trade you'll need to earn the required deltaplane pilot's license—flight maneuvers, speed, and turns. Equipment is provided. You can choose a half-day initiation lesson, one-day flying lesson, or four-day course.

Fishing and Hunting There are more than 60 outfitters (a.k.a. innkeepers) in the northern Laurentians area, where provincial parks and game sanctuaries abound. Pike, walleye, lake and speckled trout, moose, deer, partridge, and rabbit are plentiful just a three-hour drive north of Montréal. Outfitters provide the dedicated hunter or angler with accommodations and every service wildlife and wilderness enthusiasts could possibly require. Open year-round in most cases, their lodging facilities range from the most luxurious first-class resort to the log-camp type "back of beyond." As well as supplying trained guides, all offer services and equipment to allow neophytes or experts the best possible hunting and fishing in addition to boating, swimming, river rafting, windsurfing, ice-fishing, cross-country skiing, hiking, or just relaxing amid the splendor of this still spectacularly unspoiled region.

Outfitters recommended by the Laurentian tourist association include **Pourvoirie des 100 Lacs Nords** (tel. 514/444–4441), run by Claude Lavigne; **Club de Chasse et Pêche du Lac Beauregard** (tel. 819/425–7722) in Saint-Jovite; and **Club des Guides** (tel. 819/597–2486) at Lac-du-Cerf, run by Raymond Webster. Before setting off into the wilds, consult the Fédération des Pourvoyeurs du Québec (Québec Outfitters Federation, 2485 boul. Hamel, Québec G1P 2H9, tel. 418/527–5191) or ask for its list of outfitters available through tourist offices.

Don't forget: Hunting—which is strictly regulated, particularly for moose and deer—and fishing require a permit, available from the regional offices of the Ministère du Loisir, de la Chasse et de la Pêche (6255 13ième av., Montréal H1X 3E6, tel. 514/374–2417), or inquire at any Laurentians sporting-goods store displaying an "authorized agent" sticker.

Golf **Club de Golf Chantecler Sainte-Adèle** is an 18-hole golf course in the Laurentians. *Exit 67, 2520 chemin du Golf, Ste-Adèle, tel. 514/229–3742.*

Les Rochers Bleus is an 18-hole golf course in Sutton, located in Estrie. Reservations must be made in advance. *Rte. 139, Sutton, tel. 514/538–2324.*

When in the Charlevoix region, you may want to try the 18-hole course in Pointe-au-Pic, **Club de Golf de Manoir Richelieu**. *181 ave. Richelieu, Pointe-au-Pic, tel. 418/665–3703 or 800/463–2613.*

Horseback Riding As the former Olympic equestrian site, **Bromont** is horse country, and every year, in late June and early July, it holds a riding festival (tel. 514/534–3255).

Mountain Climbing Mountain climbing is one of the best ways to view the scenery of the Upper Laurentians. For information, contact the **Fédération Québécoise de la Montagne**. *4545 rue Pierre-de-Coubertin, C.P. 1000, Succ. M, Montréal H1V 3R2, tel. 514/252–3004.*

River Rafting The Rivière Rouge in the Laurentians rates as one of the best in North America, according to expert river rafters, so it's not surprising that this river has spawned a miniboom in the sport. Just an hour's drive north of Montréal, the Rouge cuts across the rugged Laurentians through rapids, canyons, and alongside beaches. From April through October, the adventurous can experience what traversing the region must have meant in the days of the voyageurs and *coureurs du bois*, though today's trip, by comparison, is much safer and more comfortable.

Four companies specializing in white-water rafting are on-site at the trip's departure point near Calumet. (Take Rte. 148 past Calumet; turn onto chemin de la Rivière Rouge until you see the signs for the access road to each rafter's headquarters.) **Aventures en Eau Vive** (tel. 819/242–6084), **Nouveau Monde** (tel. 819/242–7238), **Propulsion** (tel. 514/953–3300), and **W-3 Rafting** (tel. 514/334–0889) all offer four- to five-hour rafting trips. All provide transportation to and from the river site, as well as guides, helmets, life jackets, and, at the end of the trip, a much-anticipated meal. Most have facilities on-site or nearby for dining, drinking, camping, bathing, swimming, hiking, and horseback riding.

Skiing
Les Laurentides

With the longest vertical drop (2,131 feet) in eastern Canada, **Mont Tremblant** (tel. 819/425–8711) offers a wide range of ski trails. Beginners favor the 5-kilometer (3-mile) Nansen trail; intermediate skiers head for the steeply sloped Flying Mile and Beauchemin runs. Experts choose the challenging Duncan and Expo runs on the mountain's north side. The Vancouver-based developers who bought the resort in 1991 promised to invest $47 million over the next five years in order to turn Mont Tremblant into a world-class ski and four-season resort. The new and fast Duncan Express, a quadruple chair lift, is only a beginning.

Ski Mont Gabriel (tel. 514/229–3547) in Mont Rolland has 16 downhill trails primarily for intermediate and advanced skiers. The most popular runs are the Tamarack and the O'Connell trails for advanced skiers and Obergurgl for intermediates. Mont Gabriel is also the site for the annual Free-Style World Cup Championships every January.

For something different, try **Ski Morin Heights** (*see* Tour 1, Les Laurentides, above), where snowboarding is the latest craze.

L'Estrie

In l'Estrie the larger downhill slopes include **Mont Bromé** (tel. 514/534–2200) in Bromont (site of the 1986 World Cup) with 23 trails, **Mont Orford** (tel. 819/843–6548) with 33, **Owl's Head** (tel. 514/292–3342) with 26, and **Mont Sutton** (tel. 514/538–2339), where you pay to ski by the hour, with 53. The steepest drop, one of 853 meters (2,800 feet), is at Orford. All four resorts feature interchangeable lift tickets so skiers can test out all the major runs in the area. Call Ski East, tel. 819/820–2020.

L'Estrie's 26 cross-country trails are peaceful getaways. Trails at Bromont crisscross the site of the 1976 Olympic equestrian center. Three inns—Le Manoir Hovey, Auberge Hatley, and the Ripplecove Inn (*see* Dining and Lodging, below)—offer the **Skiwippi**, a week-long package of cross-country treks from one inn to another. The network covers some 32 kilometers (20 miles) of l'Estrie.

Snowmobile

Point de Vue Canada offers snowmobilers tours in the Laurentians, in Charlevoix, and as far north as the James Bay region. The group also has such adventure packages as "Winter Passion," a five-night, six-day tour featuring ice-fishing, water rafting, skiing, and trapping, accompanied by Montagnais Indians. Another tour, "The Magic of the Nunavik Arctic," is a week-long adventure in Québec's Grand Nord, where participants spend one night in an igloo, travel on dogsleds, and ice-fish. *1227 av. St-Hubert, Suite 200, Montréal H2L 3Y8, tel. 819/595–8005.*

Dining

Whether you enjoy a croissant and espresso at a sidewalk café or order *poutine* (a streetwise mix of homemade french fries—*frites*—from a fast-food emporium), you won't soon forget your meals in Québec. There is no such thing as simply "eating out" in the province, as restaurants are an integral slice of Québec life.

Outside of Montréal and Québec City, you can find both good value and classic cuisine. Cooking in the province tends to be hearty, with such fare as cassoulet, *tourtières* (meat pies), onion soup, and apple pie heading up menus. In the Laurentians, chefs at some of the finer inns have attracted international followings. Local blueberries and maple syrup find their way into a surprising number of dishes.

Early reservations are essential. Monday or Tuesday is not too soon to book weekend tables at the best provincial restaurants. If you have any doubt about acceptable dress at a restaurant, call ahead. Jacket and tie are still the rule at many first-rate restaurants, even in summer.

Granby and its environs is one of Québec's foremost regions for traditional Québecois cuisine, here called *la fine cuisine estrienne*. Specialties include mixed-game meat pies like *cipaille* and sweet, salty dishes like ham and maple syrup. Actually, maple syrup—on everything and in all its forms—is a mainstay of Québecois dishes. L'Estrie is one of Québec's main maple-sugaring regions.

In addition to maple sugar, cloves, nutmeg, cinnamon, and pepper—the same spices used by the first settlers—have never gone out of fashion here, and local restaurants make good use of them in their distinctive dishes. The full country experience of l'Estrie includes warm hospitality at lodges and inns in the area as well.

Highly recommended restaurants in each price category are indicated by a star ★.

Category	Cost*
Very Expensive	over $35
Expensive	$25–$35
Moderate	$15–$25
Inexpensive	under $15

per person, excluding drinks, service, 7% federal tax, and 7% provincial tax

Les Laurentides

Ste-Adèle **La Clef des Champs.** This family-owned hillside restaurant, well known for its gourmet French cuisine, is a charming alternative to even the most superbly prepared hotel fare. The restaurant, hidden among trees and facing a mountain, offers elegant dishes in a cozy, romantic atmosphere. Try the *noisette d'agneau en feuilleté* (lamb in pastry) or fresh poached salmon in red wine sauce. Top off your meal with the *gâteau aux deux* *chocolats* (a two-chocolate cake). *875 chemin Ste-Marguerite, tel. 514/229–2857. Reservations advised. Dress: casual. AE, DC, MC, V. Closed 2 weeks after Easter; Mon. in November and January–April. Very Expensive.*

★ **L'Eau à la Bouche.** A consistent award winner in gastronomic circles, the restaurant picked up Québec's 1988 *Ordre du Mérite de la Restauration,* the top award among the Laurentians region's auberge/restaurants for its superb marriage of nouvelle cuisine and traditional Québec dishes. L'Eau à la Bouche is also distinguished as one of the region's most expensive restaurants. However, the care and inventiveness of chef-proprietor Anne Desjardins, who opened the Bavarian-style restaurant a decade ago with her husband, Pierre Audette, is extraordinary. Such dishes as goat cheese tart, saddle of rabbit with onions, *baluchon* of lobster and scallops, roast partridge stuffed with oyster mushrooms and cream sauce, *pavé* of dark chocolate with English cream, and *cachette* of rhubarb and strawberries leave dinner guests clamoring for more. *3041 boul. Ste-Adèle, Rte. 117, tel. 514/229–2991. Reservations required. Dress: casual but neat. AE, MC, V. Very Expensive.*

Ste-Agathe **Chatel Vienna.** Run by Eberhards Rado and his wife, who is
★ also the chef, this moderately priced Austrian restaurant offers Viennese and other Continental dishes served up in a lakeside setting. You may want to try the prize-winning home-smoked trout, served with an herb and spice butter, and garden fresh vegetables. Also offered are a variety of schnitzels (veal dishes), a sauerkraut plate, and venison. Meals are accompanied by hot spiced wine, Czech pilsner beer, or dry Austrian and other international white wines. A Sunday buffet-brunch with about 30 dishes is served from 11:30 until 2 for about $17.95. *6 rue Ste-Lucie, tel. 819/326–1485. Reservations accepted. Dress: casual. MC, V. Moderate–Expensive.*

Chez Girard. This restaurant serves up moderately priced, excellent French cuisine in an auberge on the shores of Lac des Sables. The airy dining room has windows facing the lake and pastel colors that create a soft, romantic atmosphere. Some of the house specialties include *saumon au champagne* (salmon with champagne), lamb with cream of garlic sauce, caribou, *feuilleté d'escargots et de pleurotes* (escargots and mushroom pastry). Tarte Girard, a coffee-iced pie, is a must. A Sunday brunch is offered for $16.95. *18 rue Principale O, tel. 819/326–0922. Reservations advised. Dress: casual. AE, MC, V. Moderate.*

St-Sauveur- **Auberge Saint-Denis.** This classic Québec inn has earned the ti-
des-Monts tle "Relais Gourmand" for its fine French cuisine. Specializing in game, the artfully presented dishes are served in one of three dining rooms with a huge stone fireplace, and pastel colors creating a warm atmosphere. Try the *arrivage de gibier,* an assortment of wild game served with an exotic fruit sauce. *61 St-Denis, tel. 514/227–4602. Reservations advised for dinner. Dress: casual but neat. AE, DC, MC, V. Very Expensive.*

Estrie

Ayer's Cliff **The Ripplecove Inn.** This inn vies with the Hatley and Hovey inns (*see* Lodging, below) for best in the region. Its dining, accommodations, and service are consistently excellent. Ripplecove's dining room is an award winner. Its English-pub style dining offers a combination of classical and nouvelle cuisine with such dishes as *confit de canard Lac Brome* (preserved duck) followed by *rable de lapin* (rabbit served with honey sauce), topped off with a sublime dessert such as *mousse au chocolat arabica* (a mousse laced with coffee flavor). *700 chemin Ripplecove, C.P. 246, tel. 819/838–4296. Reservations advised Fri. and Sat. nights. Dress: casual. AE, MC, V. Expensive.*

Magog **Auberge de l'Étoile.** This popular restaurant serves three meals a day in casual surroundings. Its somber interior, decorated in dark colors, is brightened by the windows facing Lac Memphé-Magog. Its specialties include wild game and Swiss fondue. *1150 rue Principale O, 819/843–6521. Reservations advised. Dress: casual. AE, DC, MC, V. Moderate.*

Notre-Dame- **Aux Berges de l'Aurore.** This tiny bed-and-breakfast is situated
des-Bois at the foot of Mont Mégantic. The draw here is the inn's cuisine. The four-star restaurant features a five-course meal with ingredients supplied from the inn's huge fruit, vegetable, and herb garden, as well as wild game from the surrounding area: boar, fish, hare, and quail. It has been attractively furnished by its owners, Michel Martin and Daniel Pepin, and is closed from January 2 until April 1. *51 chemin de l'Observatoire, tel. 819/888–2715. Reservations advised. Dress: casual. MC, V. Expensive.*

Sherbrooke **Restaurant au P'tit Sabot.** This restaurant recently won an award for the best local-style eatery in the region. Among the many provincial dishes are wild boar, quail, and bison. *1410 rue King O, tel. 819/563–0262. Reservations advised. Dress: casual. AE, MC, V. Moderate.*

Charlevoix

Baie-St-Paul **Auberge la Maison Otis.** Québec-oriented French cuisine is how chef Bernard Paten describes his cuisine. The restaurant is a 150-year-old Norman-style house, elegantly decorated in pink pastel, centered on a huge stone fireplace. This four-star restaurant's menu continually changes, always adapting to the region and the season. *Ballotine de faisan* (pheasant), stuffed with quail and served in a venison sauce, is an example of the chef's creativity. Finish your meal with either an assortment of cheese or one of many delicious desserts. *23 rue St-Jean-Baptiste, tel. 418/435–2255. Reservations advised. Dress: casual but neat. MC, V. Expensive.*

Mouton Noir. This restaurant offers French cuisine amid flowers on the terrace in the summer or in a cozy rustic setting in the winter. You'll always find a varied menu, with pasta, fish, and meat, for a very reasonable price. This restaurant comes highly recommended from the locals. *43 rue Ste-Anne, tel. 418/435–3075. Reservations accepted. Dress: casual. AE, DC, MC, V. Closed Nov. Inexpensive–Moderate.*

La Malbaie **Auberge sur la Côte.** Fine French cuisine is served here in a rustic setting. The simple, white tablecloths complement the natural wood and stone walls. A house specialty is *agneau de Charlevoix*, lamb seasoned with lemon and thyme, served with fresh vegetables. Lunch is served in summer only, but the dining room is open in the evening year-round. *205 chemin des Falaises, tel. 418/665–3972. Reservations advised. Dress: casual. AE, MC, V. Expensive.*

Pointe-au-Pic **Auberge des 3 Canards.** This inn has made a name for itself in the region, not only for its accommodations but also for its award-winning, four-star restaurant. Nouvelle cuisine, with a varied menu including game, fish, and meat is elegantly presented in a rustic setting. The warmth of the natural wood contrasts with the pale and deep blue touches throughout. *49 côte Bellevue, tel. 418/665–3761. Reservations advised. Dress: casual. AE, MC, V. Very Expensive.*

Gaspé Peninsula

Gaspé **La Belle Hélène.** This restaurant evokes a feeling of warmth, with natural wood blending harmoniously with the forest-green floral wallpaper. Large windows face the bay and the busy fishing boats. The menu specializes in regional cuisine, namely seafood and game. In the summer, the restaurant features *crêpes bretonnes*, thin pancakes with a variety of fillings and toppings. *135A rue de la Reine, tel. 418/368–1455. Reservations in summer advised. Dress: casual. MC, V. Moderate–Expensive.*

La Brise-Bise Bistro. This chic bistro-bar, overlooking the Gaspé Bay, offers deluxe fast food, such as sauerkraut and sausages, a variety of imported beer, and live entertainment. *2 côte Carter, tel. 418/368–1456. Reservations accepted. Dress: casual. MC, V. Inexpensive.*

Pabos Mills **La Sieur de Pabos.** This rustic restaurant overlooks Pabos Bay, just outside of Chandler. La Sieur de Pabos specializes in seafood and boasts the best in the province. The chef suggests *crêpe de la signeurie*, a seafood crepe with a delicately seasoned white sauce. *325 Rte. 132, tel. 418/689–2281. Reservations accepted. AE, MC, V. Inexpensive–Moderate.*

Sugar Huts

Every March the combination of sunny days and cold nights causes the sap to run in the maple trees. Sugar huts (*cabanes à sucre*) go into operation boiling the sap collected from the trees in buckets (now, at some places, complicated tubing and vats do the job). The many commercial shacks scattered over the area host "sugaring offs" and tours of the operation, including the tapping of maple trees, the boiling vats, and *tire sur la neige*, when hot syrup is poured over cold snow to give it a taffy consistency just right for "pulling" and eating. A number of cabanes offer hearty meals of ham, baked beans, and pancakes, all drowned in maple syrup. It's best to call before visiting these cabanes: **Erablière Patoine**, 1105 chemin Beauvoir, in Fleurimont, near Sherbrooke, tel. 819/563–7455, and **Bolduc** in Cookshire, 525 chemin Lower, tel. 819/875–3022.

Lodging

Weary travelers have a full spectrum of accommodation options in Québec: from large resort hotels in the Laurentians and Relais et Châteaux properties in l'Estrie to shared dormitory space in rustic youth hostels near the heart of Gaspé. For information on camping in the province's private trailer parks and campgrounds, write for the free publication "Québec Camping," available from Tourisme Québec, Box 20,000, Québec City, G1K 7X2, tel. 418/643–2280. Inquiries about camping in

Québec's three national parks should be directed to Parks Canada, Information Services, 3 Buade St., Box 6060, Haute Ville, Québec City, G1R 4V7, tel. 418/648–4177. **Agricotours** (4545 av. Pierre de Couberten, Montréal H1V 3R2, tel. 514/252–3138), the Québec farm-vacation association, can provide lists of guest farms in the province.

Highly recommended lodgings in each price category are indicated by a star ★.

Category	Cost*
Very Expensive	over $125
Expensive	$90–$125
Moderate	$50–$90
Inexpensive	under $50

Prices are for a standard double room, excluding 10% service charge, 7% federal tax, and 7% provincial tax, unless Modified American Plan (MAP) is indicated. MAP charges apply to each guest and include all meals, service charges, and taxes.

Charlevoix

Baie-St-Paul
★
Auberge la Maison Otis. Situated in the center of the village, this inn offers calm and romantic accommodations in three buildings, including an old stone house. Chef Bernard Paten specializes in nouvelle "Québec" cuisine—nouvelle cuisine with a regional twist—and summer lunches are served amid flowers on an outdoor terrace. Some of the 30 country-style rooms have whirlpools, fireplaces, and antique furnishings; all are air-conditioned and have private bath, TV, and radio. Skiing and ice-skating are nearby. *23 rue St-Jean-Baptiste, G0A 1B0, tel. 418/435–2255. 30 rooms, 3 suites. Facilities: restaurant, piano bar, lounge, indoor pool, health center, and sauna. MAP optional. MC, V. Expensive–Very Expensive.*

Cap-à-l'Aigle
★
Auberge la Pinsonnière. The Pinsonnière is a member of the French association of fine country hotels, the Relais & Châteaux. Some even classify this small inn as a resort. Rooms offer a commanding view of Murray Bay on the St. Lawrence River. An atmosphere of country luxury prevails. Each room is decorated differently, some featuring fireplaces, whirlpools, and king-size four-poster beds. The weary traveler may relax in one of the three lounges throughout the auberge. *124 rue St-Raphael, G0T 1B0, tel. 418/665–4431. 22 rooms, 6 suites. Facilities: 2 restaurants, tennis court, indoor pool, sauna, private beach, and horseback riding. MAP. AE, MC, V. Very Expensive.*

Île aux Coudres
★
Hôtel Cap-aux-Pièrres. Located on Coudres Island in the St. Lawrence River, this hotel provides top-notch accommodations in both a traditionally Canadian main building and a motel section (open summer only). About a third of the rooms afford river views, and all have color TV and telephones. The restaurant serves a mix of Québec standards and nouvelle cuisine, and entertainment includes folk dancing on Saturday evening. *246 rue Principale, La Baleine, G0A 2A0, tel. 418/438–2711 or 800/463–5250. 98 rooms. Facilities: restaurant, bar, indoor and outdoor heated pools. MAP. AE, DC, MC, V. Expensive.*

Pointe-au-Pic **Hôtel Manoir Richelieu.** The Manoir Richelieu, an imposing castle nestled amid trees on a cliff overlooking the St. Lawrence River, has been offering first-class accommodations to vacationers for centuries, literally. Founded in 1776, it was once a haven for wealthy travelers. Although still rich in elegance and charm, the resort has adapted to the needs of today's traveler and is now an affordable vacation spot. Guests can swim in the hotel's indoor and outdoor swimming pools and enjoy horseback riding, golf, and cross-country and downhill skiing. Whale-watching and snowmobile packages are available. *181 rue Richelieu, G0T 1M0, tel. 418/665–3703 or 800/463–2613. 391 rooms. Facilities: restaurant, indoor and outdoor pools, golf course, cross-country skiing, tennis, exercise room, sauna, snowmobiling. AE, DC, MC, V. Very Expensive.*

St-Irenée **Les Studios du Domaine.** This unique retreat, located at the foot of the Charlevoix Mountains facing the St. Lawrence River, is an artists' colony in the summer but is open to tourists during the winter season. Studio apartments, each with one bedroom, bathroom, and living area with fully equipped kitchenette, are available for a rather reasonable price. Although its workshops and studios make this a great setting for artists, it's also a good base for sports lovers: Golf and cross-country and downhill skiing are all nearby. *398 rue les Bains, G0T 1V0, tel. 418/452–3535. 30 apartments. Facilities: 5 artists' workshops. MC, V. Open Sept.–May. Moderate.*

Gaspé Peninsula

Matane **Auberge des Gouverneurs.** Built in 1975, this seaside motor inn is well equipped with recreational facilities and offers many rooms with an ocean view. The rooms are not fancy, but all are comfortable, with whirlpool baths. Located near the dock of the ferry for Baie Comeau, it's a good choice for visitors who have come to ski, fish, or hunt. All rooms have telephone and color TV. *250 av. du Phare E, G4W 3N4, tel. 418/566–2651. 72 rooms, 2 suites. Facilities: restaurant, lounge, outdoor pool, tennis court, sauna, exercise room, parking. AE, DC, MC, V. Moderate.*

Percé **La Normandie Hotel/Motel.** All but four rooms of this decade-old split-level motel face the ocean, with views of Percé Rock and Bonaventure Island. The location in the center of town puts shops and restaurants within walking distance. The new third floor has larger rooms done in pastel colors. A more rustic, piney style prevails on lower floors. *Rte. 132, C.P. 129, G0C 2L0, tel. 418/782–2112 or 800/463–0820. 45 rooms. Facilities: restaurant, lounge, exercise room, sauna, beach and municipal pool nearby. AE, DC, MC, V. Open May–Oct. Moderate–Expensive.*

La Bonaventure-sur-Mer Hotel. Though the decor is motel-standard, the waterfront location with views of Percé Rock and Bonaventure Island makes this place stand out. The older section is a big hotel building renovated a few years ago. Some motel units offer kitchenettes. *Rte. 132, C.P. 339, G0C 2L0, tel. 418/782–2166. 90 rooms. Facilities: dining room, solarium, private beach, water sports, parking. AE, MC, V. Open June–Oct. Moderate.*

La Côte Surprise Motor Hotel. Most of the rooms of this recently renovated motel have views of Percé Rock and the village. Decor is the same motel-standard style in motel and second-floor hotel units, but the private balconies and terraces are a plus. *Rte. 132, C.P. 339, tel. 418/782–2166. 36 rooms. Facilities: dining rooms, snack bar, lounge, private beach, water sports, parking. AE, MC, V. Open June–Oct. Moderate.*

Les Laurentides

Coeur du Québec
★
L'Auberge du Lac Saint-Pierre. This modern small hotel on the lake near Trois Rivières, halfway between Montréal and Québec City, was built in 1988 and has quickly gained the highest ratings for cuisine and accommodations. The luxurious rooms are done in soothing pearl grays, peach, and beige, with television, telephones, and many whirlpool baths. The views to the lake from the dining room, the conservatory, and many of the guest rooms, add to the tranquillity, but the food is, on the other hand, exciting. It's an ideal stop on a tour of southern Québec. *1911 rue Notre-Dame (Rte. 138) Box 10, Pointe-du-Lac GOX 1ZO, tel. 819/377–5971, fax 819/377–5579. 30 rooms. Facilities: Restaurant, heated pool, tennis court, meeting rooms for 40 and 15, business equipment rentals. AE, MC, V. Expensive–Very Expensive.*

Estérel
Ville d'Estérel. If this all-inclusive resort were in the Caribbean, it would probably be run by Club Med, given the nonstop activities. The hotel features a private 18-hole golf course, beach, marina, downhill skiing facilities, 87 kilometers of cross-country ski trails, outdoor skating rink, and sports complex. Comfortable rooms offer a view of either the lake or the beautiful flower gardens. *Boul. Fridolin Simard, JOT 1E0, tel. 514/228–2571 or 800/363–3623. 135 rooms. Facilities: restaurant, disco, indoor pool, tennis courts, and gym. MAP optional. AE, DC, MC, V. Expensive–Very Expensive.*

Mont Rolland
Auberge Mont Gabriel. This resort is worth a stay—overnight or for longer. Relax in one of the spacious, modern rooms with a view of the valley, or be close to nature in one of the cozy log cabins with fireplaces to keep you warm. This deluxe resort, located on a 1,200-acre estate, offers superb dining. Tennis, golf, and ski-week and -weekend packages are available. *Autoroute 15, exit 64, JOR 1G0, tel. 514/229–3547. 120 rooms, 10 suites. Facilities: restaurant, 18-hole golf course, indoor and outdoor pools, tennis court. MAP optional. AE, MC, V. Moderate.*

Mont Tremblant
Club Tremblant. Across the lake from Mont Tremblant Lodge, this hotel and condominium complex uses the mountain for its skiing. Built as a private retreat in the 1930s by a wealthy American, the original large log-cabin lodge is furnished in colonial style, with wooden staircases and huge stone fireplaces. The rustic but comfortable main lodge has excellent facilities and a dining room with four-star gourmet cuisine. Both the main lodge and the deluxe condominium complex (fireplaces, private balconies, kitchenettes, and split-level design de rigueur), built just up the hill from the lodge, offer magnificent views of Mont Tremblant and its ski hills. At this hotel bordering Lac Tremblant, summer activities include swimming, fishing, boating, tennis, and golf. *Chemin Lac Tremblant N, JOT 1Z0, tel. 819/425–2731. 150 rooms. Facilities: restaurant, indoor pool, exercise room. AE, MC, V. Expensive–Very Expensive.*
Auberge Villa Bellevue. This equally venerable and less expen-

sive alternative to Gray Rocks (*see* below) is on Lac Ouimet.
Run by the Dubois family for more than three generations, this
inn has made its reputation as a family resort. In the summer,
children under 18 who share a room with their parents stay
free of charge and pay only for meals. In winter, weekend packages include transportation to nearby Mont Tremblant, baby-
sitting services, and a full program of children's activities.
Accommodations range from hotel rooms to chalets and condominiums. In summer, special tennis-school packages for adults
and children are available. Sailing, windsurfing, water-skiing,
and lounging about on the outdoor lakeside terrace are other
possible pastimes at Villa Bellevue. The indoor swimming pool
and fitness center offer nonskiers plenty of physical activity
during the winter without stepping outdoors. *845 rue
Principale, J0T 1Z0, tel. 819/425-2734 or 800/567-6763. 98
rooms, 14 suites. Facilities: restaurant, indoor pool, gym, tennis courts, private beach, exercise room, marina. MAP optional. AE, DC, MC, V. Expensive.*

★ **Station Mont Tremblant Lodge.** Only 90 minutes from Montréal, on 14-kilometer-long (9-mile-long) long Lac Tremblant, this
is the northernmost resort that is easily accessible in the Upper
Laurentians. Accommodations include modern condo units
with kitchenettes, a rustic lodge, and individual cabins. The
partying is lively in the winter, with lots of après-ski bars in
the hotel and the immediate area. In the summer, guests swim,
windsurf, and sail. *3005 chemin Principale, Lac Tremblant,
J0T 1Z0, tel. 819/425-8711 or 800/461-8711. Facilities: restaurant, bar, disco, outdoor pool, golf course, tennis courts, horseback riding, private beach. MAP optional. MC, V. Expensive.*

Auberge du Coq de Montagne. This auberge, situated on Lac
Moore, has earned a favorable reputation for its owners, Nino
and Kay Faragalli. Moderately priced, this cozy family-run inn
is touted for its friendly service, great hospitality, and modern
accommodations. Kudos have also been garnered for the great
Italian cuisine served up nightly, which also draws a local
crowd, making reservations a must. Year-round facilities and
activities on-site or close by include canoeing, kayaking, sailboarding, fishing, badminton, tennis, horseback riding, skating, and skiing. *2151 chemin Principale, C.P. 208, Lac Moore,
J0T 1Z0, tel. 819/425-3380. 26 rooms. Facilities: restaurant,
exercise room, sauna, private beach. MC, V. Moderate.*

Morin Heights **The Auberge Swiss Inn.** Less than 4 kilometers (3 miles) from
Ski Morin Heights, this moderately priced inn is a bargain. The
authentic Swiss-style chalet exudes coziness, from the wood
paneling and fireplace lounge to the individually decorated
rooms. *796 Rte. St-Adolphe J0R 1H0, tel. 514/226-2009. 10
rooms. Facilities: restaurant, canoeing, cross-country skiing,
lounge with live entertainment. MC, V. Moderate.*

Ste-Adèle **Le Chantecler.** This Montréaler favorite on Lac Rond is nestled
at the base of a mountain with 22 downhill ski runs. Skiing is
the obvious draw—trails begin almost at the hotel entrance.
(It's the official training site of the National Alpine Ski Teams.)
The condominium units, hotel rooms, and chalets all have a rustic appeal, furnished with Canadian pine. Summer activities include tennis, golf, and boating. An indoor pool and spa, as well
as a beach, make swimming a year-round possibility. *1474
chemin Chantecler, C.P. 1048, J0R 1L0, tel. 514/229-3555;
elsewhere in Quebec, 800/363-2420. 365 rooms, 20 suites. Facil-*

ities: *restaurant, indoor pool, spa, private beach, golf course. MAP optional. AE, DC, MC, V. Very Expensive.*

L'Eau à la Bouche. This 26-room auberge has received commendations for superb service, luxurious appointments, and first-class status as an intimately scaled resort, perfect for weekend getaways or business retreats. Its restaurant is a draw in itself (*see* Dining, above). The auberge faces Le Chantecler's ski slopes, so skiing is literally at the door. Tennis, sailing, horseback riding, and a golf course are nearby. Package rates are available. Some suites with fireplaces. *3003 boul. Ste-Adèle, J0R 1L0, tel. 514/229–2991. 26 rooms. Facilities: restaurant, outdoor pool, whirlpool, flower garden terrace, wine cellar, facilities for the disabled. MAP optional. AE, MC, V. Expensive–Very Expensive.*

Auberge aux Croissants. Situated at the foot of the Laurentian Mountains, this inn is only a five-minute drive from Mont-Saint-Sauveur. Although rooms have no TV or telephone, such conveniences are found in one of the two cozy lounges, and an impressive brunch is included with the price of the room. *750 chemin Ste-Marguerite, J0R 1L3. 14 rooms with private bath. MC, V. Inexpensive–Moderate.*

Ste-Agathe **Auberge du Lac des Sables.** A favorite with couples, this inn offers a quiet, relaxed atmosphere in a country setting with a magnificent view of Lac des Sables. Enjoy the view from your balcony or from the dining room. All rooms have contemporary decor, with queen-size beds and color TVs. A complimentary breakfast is served. *230 St-Venant, C.P. 151, J8C 3A3, tel. 819/326–3994. 19 rooms. Facilities: dining room, whirlpool, fireplace. AE, MC, V. Expensive.*

Ste-Jovite **Gray Rocks.** The oldest ski resort in the Laurentians, it was founded by the Wheeler family more than three generations ago. A sprawling wood hotel with modern chalets and units, it overlooks Lac Ouimet. Gray Rocks has its own private mountain ribboned by 20 ski runs. The winter ski weeks and weekends, including cross-country, are good value for the money, as are the summer tennis packages. Gray Rocks also runs the more intimate Auberge le Château with 36 rooms farther along Route 327 North. *Rte. 327 N, J0T 2H0, tel. 819/425–2771 or 800/567–6767. 175 rooms, 13 with shared bath. Facilities: restaurant, 22 clay tennis courts, tennis school, riding stables, marina, La Spa fitness center with hot tubs, indoor swimming pool, sports-medicine clinic, children's activity programs, private airstrip and seaplane anchorage. MAP optional. Ski packages available. AE, MC, V. Moderate–Expensive.*

Ste-Marguerite Station **Alpin Inn.** This has a log-cabin main house with separate chalets for rent. Surrounded by rolling ski hills and manicured grounds, it features good dining, golf (CPGA pro for lessons), a putting green, outdoor swimming pool, and one of the Laurentians' most scenic cross-country ski trails. The social director organizes folksy summer barbecues around the pool, and there are two-night packages available. *Chemin Ste-Marguerite, J0T 2K0, tel. 514/229–3516 or 800/363–2577. 102 rooms. Facilities: restaurant, outdoor swimming pool, private 9-hole golf course, cross-country ski trails. MAP optional. AE, DC, MC, V. Moderate–Expensive.*

Val David **Hôtel La Sapinière.** Canada's first member of the French association of fine country hotels, the Relais & Châteaux, this homey, dark-brown frame hotel with its bright country flowers provides comfortable accommodations but is best known for its fine dining room and wine cellar. *1244 chemin de la Sapinière, J0T 2N0, tel. 819/322-2020 or 800/567-6635. 70 rooms. MAP. AE, DC, MC, V. Very Expensive.*

L'Estrie

Bromont **Le Château Bromont Resort Spa.** This European-style resort spa offers massages, algotherapy, electropuncture, algae wraps, facials, and aroma therapy. The Atrium houses an indoor pool, hot tubs, and a sauna. There are also outdoor hot tubs, squash, racquetball, and access to tennis courts. After your workout, head for the château's dining room, Les Quatres Canards, where "cuisine sauvage" is created by chef Daniel Guay. (There is also a special spa menu offered.) Its L'Equestre Bar, named for Bromont's equestrian interests, features a cocktail hour and live entertainment. *90 rue Stanstead, J0E 1L0, tel. 514/534-3433. 147 rooms. Facilities: restaurant, bar, spa, indoor pool, sauna. MAP optional. AE, DC, MC, V. Very Expensive.*

Eastman **Centre de Santé Eastman.** This four-season resort offers respite to the bone-weary and bruised skier. The 20 country-style rooms are located in three separate houses: the rustic Maison Canadienne, the country-style Volet Bleu, and the modern Pavillon Kaufman. Holistic spa treatments include massage (Swedish and shiatsu) and gentle gymnastic workouts. Top off an already healthy day with fine vegetarian cuisine offered in the dining room. *712 chemin Diligence, J0E 1P0, tel. 514/297-3009. 20 rooms. Facilities: restaurant, whirlpool baths. MAP. AE, MC, V. Expensive.*

Lennoxville **Bishop's University.** If you are on a budget, this is a great place to stay. The prices can't be beat, and the location near Sherbrooke is good for touring. The university's grounds are lovely, with a river cutting through the campus and its golf course. Much of the architecture is reminiscent of stately New England campuses. Visit the university's 134-year-old chapel, and also look for the butternut tree, an endangered species in l' Estrie. Reservations for summer guests are accepted as early as September, so it's a good idea to book in advance. *Rue College, J1M 1Z7, tel. 819/822-9651. 513 beds. Facilities: sports complex with Olympic-size indoor pool, 4 outdoor tennis courts. No credit cards. Open May 15-Aug. Inexpensive.*

Magog **Club Azur.** This is a Club Med-type condo facility that is perfect for family ski trips. Each unit has a fireplace and fully equipped kitchenette so you can warm up with some hot cocoa after a full day of skiing. There are activities for children, as well as tennis courts and indoor and outdoor pools. For the summertime, it is a convenient two-minute walk from the beach. *81 Desjardins, J1X 5R9, tel. 819/847-2131 or 800/567-3535. 160 units. Facilities: restaurant, bistro, sauna, tennis courts, recreation complex, day-care service. AE, MC, V. Expensive-Very Expensive.*

O'Berge du Village. Half of this condo complex is on a timeshare basis, and the other condos are run like a hotel. Rustic Canadian pine furniture and fireplaces are scattered throughout. The condos, accommodating from two to eight people, all have both a balcony facing the lake and a fully equipped kitchenette. However, if you don't feel like cooking, try the bistro.

For those with something more elaborate in mind, enjoy dinner in the formal dining room. *261 rue Merry S, J1X 3L2, tel. 819/843–6566 or 800/567–6073. 119 rooms. Facilities: restaurant, bistro, wine bar, indoor and outdoor pools, gym, marina, aquatic sports, day-care service, daily activities. AE, MC, V. Moderate–Expensive.*

North Hatley **Auberge Hatley.** Gourmet cuisine is the main attraction at this country inn. Its dining room was named the top restaurant in Québec in the third annual Ordre du Mérite de la Restauration awards in 1988. A member of the Relais & Châteaux, it is home to chef Alain Labrie. After eating one of his fine meals, guests sleep it off in one of the 25 charmingly decorated rooms in this 1903 country manor. *C.P. 330, J0B 2C0, tel. 819/842–2451. 25 rooms, some with Jacuzzi and fireplace. Facilities: 4-star restaurant. MAP. MC, V. Closed last 2 wks in Nov. Very Expensive.*

★ **Le Manoir Hovey.** This inn is acclaimed for its gastronomic delights as well as for its accommodations. It is a former private estate dating to 1899. Reserve ahead for the dining room, where you can expect such dishes as scallop mousseline with essence of clam and tarragon, or lamb trilogy, three cuts of lamb braised with a light sauce of *morilles* (morels). Its rooms are elegantly furnished, many featuring four-poster beds and fireplaces. The grounds are exceptionally handsome, with English gardens and a view of Lac Missawippi. *C.P. 60, J0B 2C0, tel. 819/842–2421. 35 rooms. Facilities: dining room, bar, heated outdoor pool, tennis courts, 2 private beaches, aquatic sports. MAP. AE, DC, MC, V. Very Expensive.*

Orford **Auberge Estrimont.** An exclusive complex in cedar combining hotel rooms, condos, and larger chalets, it is close to ski hills, riding stables, and golf courses. Every room, whether in the hotel or in an adjoining condo unit, has a fireplace and a private balcony. *44 av. de l'Auberge, C.P. 98, Orford-Magog, J1X 3W7, tel. 819/843–1616 or 800/567–7320. 76 rooms, 7 suites. Facilities: restaurant, bar, indoor and outdoor pools, 4 tennis courts, exercise room, sauna, Jacuzzi, cross-country ski trails. AE, DC, MC, V. Expensive.*

Sutton **Auberge la Paimpolaise.** This auberge is located right on Mont Sutton, 50 feet from the ski trails. Although it offers nothing fancy, its location is hard to beat. Rooms are simple, comfortable, and clean, with a certain woodsy appeal. All-inclusive weekend ski packages are available. A complimentary breakfast is always served. *615 rue Maple, J0E 2K0, tel. 514/538–3213. 29 rooms. MAP optional. AE, MC, V. Moderate.*

Auberge Schweizer. This lodge operates year-round and is the perfect place to relax. It has its own farm, and guests feast on home-cooked meals with vegetables straight from the garden. Nearby is a pond for swimming as well as some hiking trails. Ski trails are nearby. In addition to the standard accommodations, the auberge has a three-bedroom apartment with bath and living room; a two-bedroom chalet, each with private bath and powder room; and a three-bedroom chalet with one bath and a playroom. All the chalets have kitchens as well as washers and dryers. *357 chemin Schweizer, J0E 2K0, tel. 514/538–2129. 11 rooms, 2 chalets with fireplace. V. Moderate.*

Auberge le Refuge. In contrast to the area's many resorts, this small inn, only a three-minute drive from Mont Sutton, operates as a bed-and-breakfast during the winter season. This

19th-century home was built about 100 years ago. Rooms are simple and clean, but the piney surroundings add a homey touch. *33 rue Maple, J0E 2K0, tel. 514/538–3802. 12 rooms. MAP available. AE, MC, V. Inexpensive.*

Montérégiê

St-Marc-sur-Richelieu
★

Hostellerie Les Trois Tilleuls. This romantic little place, a Relais et Châteaux member on a quiet country road, is a perfect spot to hole up in and investigate the surrounding Montérégie region or to return to after a hard day exploring the big city (Montréal is 20 minutes away). The rooms are modern, conveniently arranged, and well equipped (with hair dryers and magnifying mirrors), and each has a balcony or terrace facing the lovely Rivière Richelieu just outside. Packages are available for hunters, summer-theater goers, and cross-country skiers, among others. Montréalers come to savor the cuisine of chef Roger Robin—and in the hopes of taking home one of his recipes. *290 rue Richelieu, Saint-Marc-sur-Richelieu, Que. J0L 2E0, tel. 514/584–2231, fax 514/584–3146. 24 rooms with bath. Facilities: restaurant, bar, pool, 2 tennis courts, boating, 5 meeting rooms. AE, DC, MC, V. Expensive–Very Expensive.*

The Arts and Nightlife

The Arts

Lac Brome **Théâtre Lac Brome** (tel. 514/243–0361) is an English-language theater company that presents staged productions of classic Broadway and West End hits. The 175-seat, air-conditioned theater is located behind Knowlton's popular pub of the same name.

Lac Massawippi **L'Association du Festival du Lac Massawippi** presents an annual antiques and folk-arts show (tel. 819/842–2637) each July. The association also sponsors concerts, exhibitions, and poetry readings at various venues throughout the town from late April until the end of June.

Lennoxville Lennoxville's **Centennial Theatre and Consolidated-Bathurst Theatre** at Bishop's University (tel. 819/822–9692) presents a roster of international, Canadian, and Québecois jazz, classical, and rock concerts, as well as dance, mime, and children's theater. Jazz greats Gary Burton, Carla Bley, and Larry Coryell have appeared here, as have classical artists like the Amsterdam Guitar Trio and the Allegri String Quartet.

Magog **Théâtre le Vieux Clocher** (64 rue Merry N, tel. 819/847–0470) presents summer pop and rock concerts, as well as French plays.

North Hatley **The Piggery** reigns supreme in l'Estrie cultural life. Housed in a former pig barn in North Hatley on the shores of Lac Massawippi, the Piggery is renowned for its risk taking, often presenting new plays by Canadian playwrights and even experimenting with bilingual productions. An attractive on-site restaurant serves country suppers and picnic fare indoors and out before the 8:30 PM curtain. *Box 390, North Hatley J0B 2C0, tel. 819/842–2432 or 819/842–2431. Reservations required. Season runs June 21–Aug. 24.*

Orford Orford's regional park is the site of an annual arts festival highlighting classical music, pops, and chamber orchestra concerts. For the past 42 summers, some 300 students have come to the **Orford Arts Center** to study and perform classical music. Canada's internationally celebrated Orford String Quartet originated here. Lately, Festival Orford has expanded to include jazz and folk music. Budding musicians rub shoulders and trade notes at master classes and in public performances with such big-name artists as jazz pianist Oliver Jones and the inimitable folksinging duo Kate and Anna McGarrigle. The center also welcomes artisans during its summer art exhibitions. Musicians give concerts in the gracefully designed concert hall or in the park, where they often practice while seated among the outdoor sculptures. *Orford Arts Center, Box 280, Magog J1X 3W8, tel. 819/843–3981 or, in Canada from May to Aug., 800/567–6155.*

Sutton Sutton is also home to the visual and performing arts. **Arts Sutton** (7 rue Academy, tel. 514/538–2563) is a long-established mecca for the visual arts. Aside from exhibitions of work by renowned Québec artists, the center also runs summer workshop sessions in several media, with many of the seasonal instructors drawn from the Saidye Bronfman Centre's faculty members.

Nightlife

The Laurentians and l'Estrie are your best bets when looking for nightlife in Québec's outlying regions. Après-ski bars, bistros, and cafés are spread throughout the Laurentians. In Piedmont, **La Nuit Blanche** (762 rue Principale, tel. 514/227–5419) is a popular dancing spot. If live music is what you want, head to **Bourbon Street** (2045 rte. 117, tel. 514/229–2905) in Mont Rolland. **Les Vieilles Portes** (185 rue Principale, tel. 514/227–2662) in Saint-Sauveur is a popular pub where you can relax, order your favorite beer, and if you are hungry, have a bite to eat.

If you are looking for action in l'Estrie, visit Magog, a village that comes to life after dark. **La Lanterne** (70 rue du Lac, tel. 819/843–7205) is a popular restaurant-bar that often hosts theme nights. For information, tune in to the local radio station. **La Grosse Pomme** (276 rue Principale O, tel. 819/843–9365) is also a popular place. This multilevel complex considers itself a cinema-bar, with huge video screens, dance floors, and restaurant service. An outdoor summer terrace has live entertainment. **The Auberge Orford** (20 rue Merry S, tel. 819/843–9361) is another outdoor summer terrace that doesn't stop. Here you can enjoy live entertainment nightly.

12 Nova Scotia

by Colleen
Whitney
Thompson

Colleen Whitney
Thompson is the
author of New
Brunswick Inside
Out and the
coauthor of Slow
Men Working in
Trees (a humorous
Fredericton
dictionary). She
writes a weekly
travel column for
the Saint John
Telegraph Journal
and contributes
regularly to
dozens of other
travel
publications.

Nova Scotia's not really an island—it's attached by a narrow neck of land to New Brunswick—but it has that mystical island feeling. It's often said that it resembles a lobster in shape. That's totally in keeping with its image as a kingdom of the sea.

A lot of its charm is the effect of two different geographical areas. West of Halifax, the lobster body is a land of apple blossoms, legends of Evangeline, sturdy little shipbuilding towns, photogenic fishing villages, and the sandy beaches of the south shore. East of Halifax, the real island part of the province, Cape Breton, is a giant claw with precipitous highland cliffs and roads that roll merrily and often from scenic height down to hidden coves, making it one of the most attractive drives of the east coast. To the north the other claw reaches back toward New Brunswick, its Northumberland Strait beaches warm and inviting, its small towns offering everything from harness racing to coal-mine exploring.

Sprinkle all this with good restaurants, abundant seafood, unique history, and you'll find yourself in a magical land of giants, giantesses, and fortresses, bagpipes and Gaelic, lobster and inventors, enticing mountain resorts, bustling Acadian or Loyalist villages by the sea, and a lively, cosmopolitan capital that is one of Canada's prettiest.

Pleasure sailors often settle here. They're lured by the fact that no part of the province is farther than 35 miles from the sea and a good part of the coast is protected by Prince Edward Island and New Brunswick, not to mention large inland lakes and the lovely, deeply indented coastline.

Nova Scotia's reputation as a vacation paradise is richly deserved. Good roads lead from Maine and Québec through New Brunswick to the Nova Scotia border. Large car-carrying ferries operate from Digby in Saint John, New Brunswick, and from Bar Harbor and Portland, Maine, directly to Nova Scotia's shores.

For years tourism has been big business. For some families it has freed younger members from following the hard coal-mining life of their fathers, although, as in other maritime provinces, the flow of young people to richer provinces with higher pay scales has been intense. Still, despite the influx of visitors each summer, Nova Scotia has remained miraculously unspoiled. Genuine "old salts" haunt the wharves at Lunenburg. Honest-to-goodness fishermen man lobster boats at Cheticamp, and even in Halifax, a city of convention centers and posh hotels, the people in all facets of the hospitality industry are refreshing and amiable.

Nova Scotians also have access to some of the finest educational opportunities in the Atlantic provinces with several universities of note, Dalhousie Medical School and the Bedford Institute of Oceanography among them.

Residents are mainly well educated, well traveled, and gregarious. Still, in a thriving capital like Halifax, it is often surprising to open the largest daily paper of the province to find front-page coverage of local road construction or a new sewage system on a Halifax street while you have to search for news of the world. But that's part of its charm.

Essential Information

Important Addresses and Numbers

Tourist Information The **Nova Scotia Department of Tourism and Culture** (Box 456, Halifax, NS B3J 2R5, tel. 902/424–5000; in Canada, 800/565–0000; in continental U.S. except Maine, 800/341–6096; in Maine, 800/492–0643) can provide information on sights, accommodations, and transportation.

Halifax The **Nova Scotia Tourism Information Centre** (Old Red Store at Historic Properties, tel. 902/424–4247), and **Tourism Halifax** (Old City Hall, Duke and Barrington Sts., tel. 902/421–8736) are open mid-June–Labor Day daily 9–6, and sometimes later, rest of the year, weekdays 9–4:30.

Emergencies Dial O for operator in emergencies or check front of local phone book. Victoria General (tel. 902/428–2110) is Halifax's major **hospital**.

Arriving and Departing

By Plane **Air Canada** (tel. 800/872–0487) provides regular, daily service to Halifax and Sydney, Nova Scotia, from New York, Boston, Toronto, Montréal, and St. John's, Newfoundland. **Canadian Airlines International** (tel. 800/527–8499) has service to Halifax via Toronto and Montréal. **Air Nova** and **Air Atlantic** provide regional service with flights to Toronto, Montréal, and Boston.

The **Halifax International Airport** is 40 kilometers (25 miles) northeast of downtown Halifax (tel. 902/426–1223 for the Nova Scotia Tourism information desk). Airport bus service to most downtown hotels costs $18 round-trip, $11 one way. Taxi fare is $33 each way. *See* Rental Cars, below. The trip takes 30–40 minutes.

By Car The Trans-Canada Highway (Route 104) will lead you to Nova Scotia by the overland route, through New Brunswick, entering the province at Amherst; to reach Halifax pick up Route 2/102 at Truro. Most highways in the province lead to Halifax/Dartmouth. Highways 3/103, 7, 2/102, and 1/101 terminate in the twin cities.

To get to Cape Breton Island from mainland Nova Scotia, drive across the Canso Causeway, which is part of the Trans-Canada Highway.

By Ferry You can reach Nova Scotia by one of six car-ferry connections from Maine, New Brunswick, Prince Edward Island, and Newfoundland. **Marine Atlantic** (tel. 800/341–7981) sails from Bar Harbor, Maine, and **Prince of Funday Cruises** (tel. 800/341–7540) sails from Portland, Maine; both arrive in Yarmouth. From Saint John, New Brunswick, to Digby, Nova Scotia, ferry service is provided by **Marine Atlantic** (in New Brunswick, tel. 800/565–9470).

By Train **Via Rail** provides service from Montréal to Halifax via Moncton and Saint John in New Brunswick and Amherst and Truro in Nova Scotia. **Amtrak** from New York City makes connections in Montréal. For information and reservations, contact any Via Rail ticket office (tel. 800/561–3949) in Canada or Amtrak (tel. 800/USA–RAIL) in the United States.

By Bus   **Greyhound** (consult telephone directory for local number) from New York, and **Voyageur Inc.** (tel. 613/238–5900) from Montréal, connect with **SMT** (tel. 506/458–6000) in New Brunswick. From there service is on **Acadian Lines Limited** (tel. 902/454–8279) in Nova Scotia.

Getting Around Halifax

Walking and biking are excellent ways to get around and see the city, especially on weekdays, when parking in the downtown area can be a problem.

Rental Cars   **Avis,** 5600 Sackville St., tel. 902/423–6303; airport, tel. 902/873–3523. **Budget,** 1558 Hollis St., tel. 902/421–1242; airport, tel. 902/873–3509. **Hertz,** at the Halifax Sheraton, tel. 902/421–1763; airport, tel. 902/873–3700. **Thrifty,** 6930 Lady Hammond, tel. 902/422–4455; airport, tel. 902/873–3527. **Tilden,** 1130 Hollis St., tel. 902/422–4433; airport, tel. 902/873–3505.

By Taxi   Rates begin at about $2.40 and increase based on the mileage and time engaged. A crosstown trip should be $4–$5 depending on traffic. Hailing a taxi on the street can be difficult, so the best bet is to call a taxi service.

By Bus   The **Metropolitan Transit Commission** (tel. 902/421–6600) bus system covers the entire Halifax/Dartmouth area. The base fare is $1.10, and exact change is necessary.

By Ferry   The **Dartmouth Ferry Commission** (tel. 902/464–2336) runs two passenger ferries from the George Street terminal in Halifax to the Portland Street terminal in Dartmouth from 6 AM to midnight on an hourly and half-hourly schedule. The fare for a single crossing is 65¢.

Guided Tours

City Tours   Both **Gray Line Sightseeing** (tel. 902/454–8279) and **Cabana Tours** (tel. 902/423–6066) have coach tours of Halifax/Dartmouth and Peggy's Cove. **Halifax Double Decker Tours** (tel. 902/420–1155) offers two-hour tours on a double-decker English-style bus, leaving daily from Historic Properties. You can also charter a bus from the **Metropolitan Transit Commission** (tel. 902/421–6600) for a narrated tour.

Boat Tours   **Halifax Water Tours** (tel. 902/425–1271) operates an excellent two-hour, narrated cruise of Halifax Harbor and the Northwest Arm from mid-June through October. Tours leave from Privateer's Wharf up to four times a day in the height of the season and cost $10 for adults, $9 for senior citizens, $6.75 for youths, and $5 for children.

A 143-foot replica of the famous Nova Scotia sailing schooner *Bluenose II* (tel. 902/422–2678 or 902/424–5000) departs from Privateer's Wharf three times daily on a two-hour harbor sail in summer whenever the traveling schooner is in Halifax. Fares (subject to change) are $14 adults, $7 senior citizens and children.

Exploring Nova Scotia

Highlights for First-time Visitors

Cape Breton Highlands National Park, Tour 7: Cabot Trail
Evangeline Trail, Tour 2: Evangeline Trail
Fortress Louisbourg National Historic Park, Tour 8: Marconi Trail
Halifax Citadel National Historic Park, Tour 1: Halifax and Dartmouth
Historic Properties, Tour 1: Halifax and Dartmouth
Peggy's Cove, Tour 3: Lighthouse Route
Pictou's Scottish heritage, Tour 5: Sunrise Trail
Sherbrooke Village, Tour 6: Marine Drive

Tour 1: Halifax and Dartmouth

Numbers in the margin correspond to points of interest on the Nova Scotia and Halifax maps.

1 Pretty and cosmopolitan, **Halifax** is one of Canada's jolliest cities as well as the largest in the maritime provinces. The Nova Scotian capital is built on a peninsula, and it's a city where you're always aware of the sea. From the hilly, downtown streets, you can smell the sea and, on misty days, hear the moan of foghorns; along the waterfront you can sit on a bench on the boardwalk and watch freighters, yachts, tugboats, warships, sailboats, and ferries come and go in the harbor. The waterfront is a great place for walking, as is the rest of the city. Spring Garden Road is said to have the highest pedestrian count east of Montréal. The downtown area is small enough to explore comfortably on foot, and although it offers big-city shopping and dining, it manages to keep a leisurely maritime pace. Drivers are remarkably courteous, and residents are warm and helpful to strangers. The Old Town clock, located at the base of Citadel Hill and donated by time-conscious Prince Edward, son of King George III, in 1803, serves to remind Halifax workers that there is work to be done. So does the ear-splitting cannon blast that reverberates from the hill each day at noon.

2 We begin our tour where the city itself began—at the **Citadel,** the star-shaped fort first built in 1749 by Lord Cornwallis as a military base to protect the British colony. Set on a hill overlooking the Halifax peninsula and the harbor beyond, the Citadel is now a national historic park containing the fourth fortress built on this site, in 1861. Kilted soldiers drill on the grounds, and the **Army Museum** on-site depicts the history of colonial warfare. *Halifax Defense Complex, Box 1480, North Postal Station, Halifax B3K 5H7, tel. 902/426–5080. Admission: $2 adults, $1 children, senior citizens free. Open mid-June–early Sept., daily 9–6; mid-Sept.–early June, grounds open 9–5 (admission free).*

3 Beside the Citadel on Summer Street is the **Nova Scotia Museum,** whose exhibits focus on the social and natural history of Nova Scotia. "Touch and feel" exhibits make this a good place to bring kids. *1747 Summer St., tel. 902/429–4610. Admission free. Open mid-May–Oct., Mon., Tues., Thurs., Sat. 9:30–*

5:30, Wed. 9:30–8, Sun. 1–5:30; Nov.–early May, Tues., Thurs., Sat. 9:30–5, Wed. 9:30–8, Sun. 1–5.

④ The **Halifax Public Gardens,** 45 hectares (18 acres) of color in the heart of the city, is a favorite spot for relaxation for visitors and Haligonians. Landscaped originally in 1753, these gardens are among the oldest on the continent. In addition to trees and shrubs from every corner of the globe, there are fountains, a bandstand, and a large pond with various water birds. One corner has been set aside as a children's area. *Open mid-May–mid-Nov., 8–sundown.*

If you turn right on Spring Garden Road you can visit the cam-
⑤ pus of **Dalhousie University,** which has a fine art gallery and performing-arts center (the Rebecca Cohn Auditorium, tel. 902/424–2646). If you turn left on Spring Garden Road from the gardens, you'll head downhill toward the harbor. At Barring-
⑥ ton Street you'll pass **St. Mary's Basilica,** reputed to have the highest granite spire in the world. Turn left on Barrington
⑦ Street to see **St. Paul's Church,** the oldest surviving building in Halifax (built 1749) and the oldest Protestant church in Cana-
⑧ da. One block east, on Granville Street, you'll find **Province House,** the oldest existing legislative building in Canada (built 1819). Charles Dickens called it "a gem of Georgian architecture." Nova Scotia's legislature still meets here. *Tel. 902/424–5982. Admission free. Open July–Aug., weekdays 9–6, Sat. 9–4, Sun. 10–4; Sept.–June, weekdays 9–4.*

⑨ Across the street is the **Art Gallery of Nova Scotia,** which features work by Canadian and Nova Scotian artists. *1741 Hollis St., tel. 902/424–7542. Admission: $2. Open Tues., Wed., Fri., Sat. 10–5:30; Thurs. 10–9; Sun. 12–5:30. Closed Mon.*

Proceed up Granville Street past Duke Street. On your left will
⑩ be **Scotia Square,** an ultramodern shopping-office-apartment-
⑪ hotel complex. On your right, you'll enter the **Historic Properties** area, whose cobblestone streets give you an idea of what Halifax looked like in the 1800s. Shops, restaurants, and offices are housed today in 12 restored buildings, which have interesting nooks and crannies, arches and odd-shape windows, stucco and wood beams.

The block of North American Renaissance buildings on Granville Street's pedestrian mall north of Duke Street was constructed after the great Halifax fire of 1859, which razed the area. Designed by Toronto architect William Thomas, the buildings were not built at the same time, but all exhibit a common theme and exterior format. Some of the storefronts that remain were fabricated of cast iron and were probably designed by James Bogardus, an American inventor known for his work with cast iron. Although many of the extravagant architectural details of the 1870s have been obliterated by time, the original elegance may still be seen in the tall windows and storefront designs. This part of Granville Street is now a pedestrian area.

The **Privateer's Warehouse** is a stone building (now a three-layered restaurant—*see* Dining, below) that housed the cargoes captured by Nova Scotia schooners serving as privateers; captured ships and cargoes were auctioned off by the Admiralty. **Privateer's Wharf,** on the waterfront at the south end of the Historic Properties, is the docking place for the schooner
⑫ *Bluenose II,* which carries passengers into the harbor whenev-

Nova Scotia

NEW BRUNSWICK

Borden

Cape Torme

PRINC

Northumberl

Pugwash

Amherst

Oxford

Trans-Canada

Joggins

28 **Springhill**

Ba

Chignecto Game
Sanctuary

2

Parrsboro

27

2

Great
Village

Deb

104

Advocate
Harbour

Cape
Split

18 **Cape**
Blomidon

Cobequid Bay

25

St. John

(358)

Minas
Basin

Maitland

Bay of Fundy

Minas Channel

Wolfville

Hantsport

Sh

Mount
Uniacke

Evangeline Trail

Berwick

1

Windsor

1

17

Annapolis
Royal

Kingston

101

19

Middleton

Three
Mile Plains

101

102

Lower
Sackvi

Port Royal

Bridgetown

Ross
Farm **21**

Upper Sackville

Middle Sackville

12

103

St.
Margarets
Bay

Dart

Ea

Digby Neck

Digby

1

Bear
River

KEJIMKUJIK
NATIONAL PARK

Mahone
Bay

Chester

20

Herring
Cove

Tiverton

Westport

Brier
Island

Evangeline Trail

101

TOBEATIC
WILDLIFE
MANAGEMENT AREA

Lake
Rossignol

3

22

Mahone
Bay

Peggy's
Cove

Lunenburg

Halifax

1 — **16**

La Have

TO
BAR HARBOR
(MAINE)

1

Milton

103

Brooklyn

ATLA

24

Liverpool

TO
PORTLAND
(MAINE)

Yarmouth
County Museum
and Archives

Shelburne

103

3

Lockeport

Woods
Harbour

23

Barrington Woolen
Mill Museum

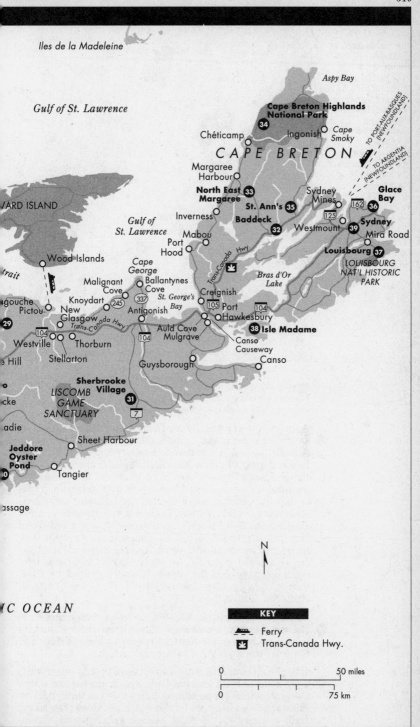

Iles de la Madeleine

Gulf of St. Lawrence

Aspy Bay

Cape Breton Highlands
National Park
34

Chéticamp

Ingonish

Cape
Smoky

C A P E   B R E T O N

TO PORT-AUX-BASQUES
(NEWFOUNDLAND)

TO ARGENTIA
(NEWFOUNDLAND)

Margaree
Harbour

**North East
Margaree**
33

St. Ann's
35

Sydney
Mines

**Glace
Bay**
36

WARD ISLAND

Gulf of
St. Lawrence

Inverness

Baddeck

32

162

125

Westmount

39

Sydney

Mabou

Mira Road

Wood Islands

Port
Hood

Trans-Canada Hwy.

Bras d'Or
Lake

Louisbourg
37

*LOUISBOURG
NAT'L HISTORIC
PARK*

trait

Cape
George

Ballantynes
Cove

Creignish

agouche

Malignant
Cove

337

*St. George's
Bay*

105

104

Pictou

Knoydart

245

Port
Hawkesbury

38 **Isle Madame**

29

New
Glasgow

Antigonish

104

Trans-Canada Hwy.

Auld Cove
Mulgrave

Canso
Causeway

Canso

Westville

104

Thorburn

Stellarton

Guysborough

e Hill

Sheet Harbour

ke

**Sherbrooke
Village**

*LISCOMB
GAME
SANCTUARY*

31

7

adie

**Jeddore
Oyster
Pond**

Tangier

IC OCEAN

assage

N

KEY

Ferry
Trans-Canada Hwy.

0   50 miles

0   75 km

Art Gallery of
Nova Scotia, **9**

Bluenose II, **12**

Brewery Market, **14**

Dalhousie
University, **5**

Fort Needham
Memorial Park, **16**

Halifax Citadel
National Historic
Park, **2**

Halifax Public
Gardens, **4**

Historic Properties, **11**

Maritime Museum of
the Atlantic, **13**

Nova Scotia
Museum, **3**

Point Pleasant
Park, **15**

Province House, **8**

St. Mary's Basilica, **6**

St. Paul's Church, **7**

Scotia Square, **10**

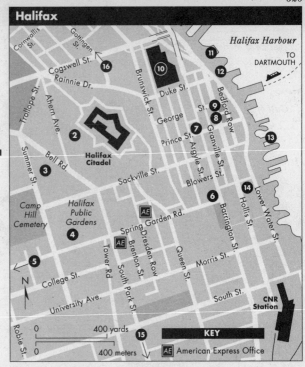

Halifax

er the schooner is in port during the summer months for three
two-hour sailings daily. *Tel. 902/422–2678. Fares (subject to
change): $14 adults, $7 children and senior citizens.*

⑬ A couple of blocks south, along Lower Water Street, is a waterfront development that includes the **Maritime Museum of the
Atlantic,** housed in a restored chandlery and dockside warehouse. Displays describe Nova Scotia's golden age of sail, when
the province's flag was seen in ports around the world. The
main display is docked outside, however: a 900-ton hydrograph-
ic ship, the *Acadia*, which charted the Labrador and Arctic
coasts early in this century. Docked at the opposite wharf is
HMCS *Sackville*, Canada's naval memorial, a restored World
War II convoy escort corvette. Adjacent to the *Sackville* is
an interpretation center with displays on the Battle of the Atlantic. *1675 Lower Water St., tel. 902/429–8210. Admission free.
Open mid-May–mid-Oct., Mon., Wed.–Sat. 9:30–5:30, Tues.
9:30–8, Sun. 1–5:30; late-Oct.–early May, Tues. 9:30–8,
Wed.–Sat. 9:30–5, Sun. 1–5.*

⑭ South of the Maritime Museum, on lower Water Street, is
Brewery Market, a collection of boutiques and restaurants
housed in the restored Keith's Brewery building. Friday and
Saturday mornings there's a farmers' market.

⑮ If you head toward the southernmost tip of the city's peninsula,
you'll come to **Point Pleasant Park,** a natural woodland where
automobile traffic is prohibited. Surrounded on three sides by
salt water, it's a fine place for ship watching. Along the walking
trails you may spot Scottish heather growing wild, sprung

from seeds shaken out of mattresses by British sailors many decades ago. Among the partially ruined fortifications in the park is the **Prince of Wales Martello Tower,** a stout stone tower built at the end of the 18th century as part of the harbor defense that is now a National Historic Site open in summer.

For another excellent view venture north from downtown up **⑯** Gottingen Street 20 blocks or so to **Fort Needham,** a hilltop memorial park that offers a panoramic view of the area devastated in the Great Halifax Explosion, on December 6, 1917. The explosion, the largest single man-made blast prior to the atomic bomb, was caused when a munitions ship collided with another vessel in the harbor. Two thousand fatalities were recorded, 10,000 more people suffered serious injuries, 25,000 were left homeless, and the shock wave was felt in the town of Truro, more than 60 miles away.

Time Out   If you happen to be strolling down Spring Garden Road at noontime, you'll see crowds of office workers, students, and shoppers perched on the stone wall in front of the library. They're probably snacking on fish-and-chips sold from one of the trucks that park on the street here every day in summer. **Bud the Spud** is a perennial favorite. For sweet treats, try the **Silver Spoon,** at 1813 Granville Street, near the waterfront. It has a dazzling display of tortes (the white chocolate rum buttercream is quite a mouthful), cheese cakes, and truffles.

Tour 2: Evangeline Trail

The 278-kilometer (189-mile) drive from Mount Uniacke, near Halifax, to Yarmouth, along the Fundy Coast, takes about 3½ hours (eight hours with two excursions). This route is clearly posted with trailway markers, as are the other routes described below; Route 101 is the quickest route, with little scenic value. The time you'll add by taking detours to Route 1 will **⑰** be worth it. Starting at **Mount Uniacke,** you'll come upon **Uniacke House,** 1812–1815. With an imposing veranda and most of its furniture original to the house, the building is a grand example of late-Georgian architecture. *Rte. 1, tel. 902/ 866–2560. Admission free. Open mid-May–Oct. 31, Mon.–Sat. 9:30–5:30, Sun. 1–5:30.*

En route from Windsor to Digby (through the apple-orchard-dotted **Annapolis Valley** where some of the earliest French settlements flourished), be sure to drive through pretty little **Wolfville,** a town of Victorian charm, and see the Georgian buildings of Acadia University and the harbor views. Then take **⑱** a detour north from Route 1 on Route 358 to **Cape Blomidon** for a view of four counties from the bluff. At the end of the road is one of Nova Scotia's most popular hiking trails, which extends for 13 kilometers (8 miles) to the cliffs of **Cape Split.** The view from the trail extends for miles in three directions. Return to Route 1 and continue west toward Annapolis Royal. Turn right just before crossing the Annapolis Causeway, to reach **Port Royal National Historic Site,** the first permanent European settlement north of the Gulf of Mexico. Here, in 1605, French explorers Samuel de Champlain and Sieur de Monts established their *habitation,* or trading post, which stood until Virginia raiders scattered the French and leveled the buildings in 1613. The rebuilt compound is an exact replica, constructed without nails. *Tel. 902/532–2898. Admission free. Park open year-round; buildings open mid-May–mid-Oct., daily 9–6.*

Drive east to Route 1 and cross the causeway into **Annapolis Royal,** where you should stop to see **Fort Anne,** the scene of continuing French-British conflict for supremacy over the province. The 18th-century officers' quarters are reconstructed, although the earthworks and stone powder-magazine are original. *Tel. 902/532–2397. Admission free. Open mid-May–mid-Oct., daily 9–6; mid-Oct.–mid-May, weekdays 9–5. Closed holidays.*

Here also is the **Annapolis Royal Historic Gardens,** a 10-acre site, with a rose garden, a Victorian one, and other theme gardens, overlooking a marsh of the Allain River. There are also a gift shop and a tearoom. *Tel. 902/532–7108. Admission: $3.50 adults, $2.75 seniors and children under 12. Open mid-May–mid-Oct. 8–dusk.*

A second excursion, along Digby Neck on Route 217, with two ferries, is to **Westport,** on Brier Island, one of the richest grounds for whale-watching in the North Atlantic. Brier Island is also a good spot for bird-watching; many species of sea and land birds rest here during migrations.

Just east of Digby, and 6 kilometers (4 miles) off Route 101, is **Bear River,** an antique jewel of a village surrounded by hills, with 19th-century houses tucked behind the trees that line the terraced slopes. The village is noted for its many resident artists and craftspeople.

Tour 3: Lighthouse Route

This rugged coastal tour along the South Shore, from Halifax to Yarmouth, covers 470 kilometers (275 miles) and takes up to seven hours to drive, depending on whether you take the fast Route 103 or hug the winding shore on Route 3 and take side excursions. Early fishing and shipbuilding ports abound, but none is more picturesque than **Peggy's Cove,** near Halifax, one of the most photographed villages in Canada. It possesses one of the dozen or so lighthouses to be seen on this route and has North America's only post-office lighthouse (open Apr.–Nov.). Its postal cancellation shows an image of—what else?—a lighthouse. On windy days, the surf crashes onto the granite rocks below the lighthouse with spectacular fury. Exploring the rocks too close to the shoreline can be dangerous. For a snack or a full-course meal while you're in the village, stop at the **Sou-'wester** restaurant (tel. 902/823–2561) near the lighthouse for good seafood chowder and gingerbread.

Continue west through **Chester,** a favorite summer resort town with back and front harbors, go on to Chester Basin, turning north on Route 12 for a short excursion. You'll soon reach **Ross Farm,** a living museum illustrating advances in agriculture from 1600 to 1925. Wear comfortable shoes or boots and old clothes. *Rte. 12, New Ross, tel. 902/689–2210. Admission: $2 adults, 50¢ children 5–16, $5 families. Open mid-May–mid-Oct., daily 9:30–5:30; late-Oct.–early May by appointment.*

Returning along Route 12, back to the Lighthouse Route, you'll drive through **Mahone Bay,** which is easily recognized by the famous view of three churches standing side by side at the head of the harbor. In the historic buildings near the waterfront, you

can find good antiques and crafts shops, including one selling
②② locally made pewter. Stop at **Lunenburg,** whose **Fisheries Museum of the Atlantic** is located on the waterfront. Three floors
of exhibits tell the story of Atlantic fishing, and tied at the
wharf are two "floating" exhibits, the *Theresa E. Connor,* last
of the salt-bankers, and *Cape Sable,* a steel-hulled stern trawler. *Tel. 902/634–4794. Admission: $2 adults, 50¢ children.
Open daily, May 15–June and Sept.–Oct. daily 9:30–5:30;
July–Aug. 9:30–7.*

Built on a peninsula with a front and back harbor, Lunenburg
was first settled by French, German, and Swiss pioneers, and
the town's architecture, surnames, and traditions still show a
European influence. Older residents still have a distinctive accent. This is where the famous *Bluenose I* and *Bluenose II*
schooners were built. (The *Bluenose I* is the ship you see on the
Canadian dime.) The town hosts a crafts festival every July, a
folk-music festival on the waterfront in August, and a fisheries
exhibition in August, with an international dory race, scallop-
shucking contest, and ox-pulls. Privately run sailing tours of
Lunenburg Harbour aboard the *Timberwind,* a 35-foot gaff-rig
schooner, operate from the museum mid-June to Labor Day.
*Bluenose Dr., tel. 902/634–4794. Admission: $2 adults, 50¢
school-age children. Tours: $1.50. Open mid-May–July and
Sept.–Oct., 9:30–5:30; July–Aug. 9:30–7.*

Driving south, you'll come to **La Have,** where you can visit the
Fort Point Museum, a former lighthouse-keeper's house (admission free; open June–Aug., daily 10–6; Sept., weekends
1–5). Farther down the coast you pass through **Shelburne,** settled by Loyalists escaping from the American Revolution.
Some of the world's greatest yachts have been built here. (You
can charter your own sailboat, large or humble, with or without
crew, along this route.)

②③ On the southern tip of Nova Scotia stop at the **Barrington Woolen Mill Museum,** where you will be shown how wool is woven
into bolts of twills and flannels, blankets, and suitings. *Rte. 3,
tel. 902/637–2185. Admission free. Open mid-June–Sept. 30,
Mon.–Sat. 9:30–5:30, Sun. 1:30–5:30.*

Along the western coast, you drive through a stretch of countryside known as the **French Shore.** In many places, you'll see
the Acadian flag, a tri-color with one gold star. The Acadians in
this region are descendants of settlers who came here in 1767.
Their main industry is fishing.

②④ An appropriate ending to this marine tour is the **Yarmouth County Museum and Archives,** with its outstanding collection of
19th-century portraits of merchant ships built locally or commanded by Yarmouth sailors. *22 Collins St., tel. 902/742–5539.
Admission: $1 adults, 50¢ students, 25¢ children under 14,
$2.50 family. Open June–mid-Oct., Mon.–Sat. 9–5, Sun. 1–5;
mid-Oct.–June, Tues.–Sat. 2–5.*

Tour 4: Glooscap Trail

Starting at the historic town of Windsor, this 394-kilometer
(246-mile) trail, named after the Micmac Indian warrior god,
runs along the Minas Basin and Bay of Fundy to Amherst, just
across the border from New Brunswick. This 7½-hour drive encircles the site of the world's highest tides. Take Route 215

from Windsor east around Cobequid Bay. An early landmark is
㉕ the **William Lawrence House** in **Maitland.** The Victorian house,
designed for a prosperous shipbuilder in 1870, overlooks the
site where the largest clipper ship ever built in Canada was
launched, in 1874. *Rte. 215, tel. 902/261–2628. Admission free.
Open mid-May–mid-Oct., Mon.–Sat. 9:30–5:30, Sun. 1–5:30.*

Proceed to South Maitland and then join Route 102 toward
㉖ **Truro.** For one of the best vantage points from which to view
the twice-daily Bay of Fundy tidal bore (the first gushing wave
of the incoming high tide), follow Tidal Bore Road off Route 102
to the Palliser Restaurant, in the Tideview Motel. (Call 902/
426–5494 for a schedule of high tides at Truro and other locations in the province.) The water level quickly rises after the
bore, reaching the highest point about an hour later.

Following the northern shore of Minas Basin brings you to
㉗ **Parrsboro,** where the **Geological Mineral and Gem Museum** displays local fossils and the agate, amethyst, and other minerals
that are found on nearby beaches. **Partridge Island,** just south
of Parrsboro, is a prime spot for mineral gathering. *Geological
Museum, 1 Eastern Ave., tel. 902/254–3814. Admission free.
Open mid-May–mid-Oct., daily 9–9.*

㉘ A branch of the trail runs north to **Springhill,** the site of several
tragic mining disasters: Descend into a mine shaft at the
Springhill Miners' Museum. *Tel. 902/597–3449. Admission: $3
adults, $2 children. Open June, daily 10–5; July–Aug., daily
9–8; Sept.–mid-Oct., daily 10–4.*

Also in Springhill, the **Anne Murray Centre** documents the life
and career of the Springhill-born country singer, with gold records, awards, and other memorabilia. *Main St., tel. 902/597–
8614. Admission: $4.50 adults, $3.50 senior citizens, $3 stu-
dents, $2 children. Open mid-May–mid-Oct., daily 10–7.*

From Parrsboro, continue west to the village of **Advocate Harbour.** The road climbs and falls along the coastline through
breathtakingly beautiful terrain. Advocate Harbour is an excellent spot for clam-digging and collecting interesting rocks.
The final leg of the trail follows Chignecto Bay to Amherst,
along scenic Route 209, taking you through **Joggins,** where you
can see fossilized palm trees in the cliffs. **The Joggins Fossil
Center** has a large collection of fossils and conducts guided
tours to the cliffs. *Museum admission: $2.20 adults, $1.10 students; tours: $6.60 adults, $2.20 students. Open June–Sept. 9–
6:30.*

Tour 5: Sunrise Trail

This 208-kilometer (129-mile) route along the Northumberland
Strait from Amherst east to Mulgrave takes you through a fog-
free playland of rolling hills and sandy beaches (65% of Nova
Scotia's beaches are here). This shore is the warmest in the
province: The water reaches 80°F in summer. The area retains
a strong Scottish influence; **Pictou** (where the first Scottish
settlers arrived, in 1773) and **Antigonish** host week-long Highland festivals every summer, and **Pugwash** has bilingual—English and Gaelic—street signs.

㉙ Around the middle of the four-hour drive, head south off the
trail at Tatamagouche onto Route 311 to **Balmoral Grist Mill** at
Balmoral Mills. One of the oldest operating mills in the prov-

ince, dating from 1860, it produces stone-ground flours and meals that visitors may purchase. A picnic ground overlooks the millpond and falls. *Tel. 902/657–3016. Admission free. Open mid-May–mid-Oct., Mon.–Sat. 9:30–5:30, Sun. 1–5:30.*

Rejoining the trail, you'll go through Pictou and New Glasgow. Just north of Pictou at Caribou, ferries provide frequent service across the Northumberland Strait to Prince Edward Island (except in winter months). Route 245 leads to a mountainous drive known as the **Mini-Cabot Trail.** It winds along the coast from Malignant Cove to the tip of **Cape George** and south to **Antigonish,** 53 kilometers (33 miles) away. At **Knoydart,** on a windswept headland facing the open sea, there's a cairn commemorating the Highland veterans who fought for Bonnie Prince Charlie at Culloden and fled here for sanctuary.

Ballantynes Cove, a fishing village with a lighthouse 300 meters (1,000 feet) above **St. George's Bay,** is beloved by artists and photographers. Approaching Mulgrave you'll skirt **Canso Causeway,** the gateway to Cape Breton Island, which passes over one of the deepest man-made, ice-free ports in the world.

Tour 6: Marine Drive

This 400-kilometer (250-mile) drive from Dartmouth to Canso follows the Atlantic coast, twisting and turning with every bend of the south shore as it passes thick inland forests and tiny fishing villages. This is an important area for fishing and fish processing, with **Canso** the closest mainland point to the North Atlantic fishing grounds. This is largely unspoiled country, not nearly as highly developed as the coastline west of Halifax, and there aren't a lot of tourist facilities. But the route skirts some of the best beaches, trout-fishing waters, and canoe-kayak paddling regions in Nova Scotia. **Lawrencetown,** a few minutes' drive from Dartmouth, is a mecca for surfers. Some days, 2.75-meter (9-foot-high) swells roar onto the rocky headlands. Surfing is especially fine in winter (surfers don wetsuits), when the storms at sea are most intense. **Martinique Beach,** a dramatic, 13-kilometer (8-mile) sweep of sand and surf backed by large sand dunes, is about a half-hour drive from Dartmouth. The views of the ocean—and the dozens of uninhabited islands that shelter the coastline—are spectacular all along this curvy drive; allow 10–11 hours for the trip.

For an introduction to the life of a typical Nova Scotia inshore fisherman from 1890 to 1920, visit the **Fisherman's Life Museum** at **Jeddore Oyster Pond,** just east of Dartmouth. *Tel. 902/ 889–2053. Admission free. Open mid-May–mid-Oct., Mon.– Sat. 9:30–5:30, Sun. 1–5:30.*

At **Jeddore Oyster Pond,** you can stop for a snack at **Golden Coast Seafoods,** a cheery, bright roadside diner overlooking the ocean. The fish-and-chips are excellent. So is the fresh, hot gingerbread.

Farther east on Route 7 is **Tangier,** where you can tour Willy Krauch's internationally renowned salmon-smoking plant and buy smoked salmon, trout, and eel.

Time Out   At Liscomb, on Spanish Ship Bay, you should stop at the **Island View Restaurant,** in a gleaming white lighthouse with spanking red trim, for a delicious sandwich or snack. This spotless place has a small crafts shop and is a licensed premises.

About two-thirds of the way to Canso, follow the markers inland to **Sherbrooke Village,** on Route 7, a restoration of a 19th-century lumbering-and-gold-mining community. All of the buildings are staffed by costumed residents working at their trade. There are 25 buildings on their original sites, including a doctor's house and office, and a hotel that now functions as a restaurant. *Rte. 7, tel. 902/522–2400. Admission: $2 adults, 50¢ children. Open mid-May–mid-Oct., daily 9:30–5:30.*

The salmon and trout fishing is excellent in the rivers and streams of the forests along Marine Drive, especially in **St. Mary's River** near Sherbrooke. Some of the best smoked salmon in North America can be purchased here on the Atlantic coast.

Tour 7: Cabot Trail

Considered one of the greatest scenic marine drives in the world, this 294-kilometer (184-mile) trail, one of four on Cape Breton Island, loops through the Cape Breton Highlands, starting and ending at Baddeck, on the north shore of Bras d'Or Lake, a vast interior sea. The trip takes five hours.

Baddeck is the resort town Alexander Graham Bell chose for his summer home, and he is buried here. Although the estate is still used by the family and is not open to the public, you can spot it from the roof garden of the **Alexander Graham Bell Museum** nearby. Bell's genius went beyond inventing the telephone, and the museum documents all his experiments: in sound, aeronautics, medical technology, even sea transportation. He also invented the hydrofoil, and the remains of the original vessel are on display. *Chebucto St., tel. 902/295–2069. Admission free. Open July–Sept., daily 9–9; Oct.–June, daily 9–5.*

Many drivers prefer to follow the trail in a clockwise direction. Proceeding from Baddeck, stop at **North East Margaree,** where the **Margaree Salmon Museum** explores the remarkable life cycle of the Atlantic salmon and houses a collection of fishing paraphernalia used on the Margaree River in search of the fighting fish. *Tel. 902/248–2848. Admission: 50¢ adults, 25¢ children. Open mid-June–mid-Oct., daily 9–5.*

Continue to the Acadian community of **Chéticamp,** notable for locally made hooked rugs and other handwork. The area is also noted for its fine traditional fiddlers. On Saturday afternoons, fiddlers and stepdancers from throughout Cape Breton perform at the **Doryman Tavern.** The place is usually packed.

The trail rings the northern and eastern boundaries of the forests of **Cape Breton Highlands National Park,** with its sheer cliffs dropping into the sea. Outstanding panoramas abound, especially overlooking Aspy Bay; heading south after Black Brook Cove to Ingonish; and going down Cape Smoky. The park is 950 square kilometers (376 square miles), with numerous rivers providing good fishing, excellent hiking and nature trails, camping (including a trailer park), and an 18-hole championship golf course ($17 per day, $85 weekly). A number of beaches on the eastern coast offer excellent swimming. *Tel. in winter 902/285–2270, in summer 902/285–2535. Admission: $4 per ve-*

hicle per day, $9 for 4-day pass, $25 for annual pass. No charge for vehicles passing through on Cabot Trail. Camping fee: $8.50–$13 per day.

After Cape Smoky the trail skirts the Gaelic Coast, past several Scottish fishing villages. Stop to visit the **Gaelic College** at
③⑤ **St. Ann's** (tel. 902/295–3411), where the Scottish language and arts are taught and preserved. During the summer, students perform at regularly scheduled daytime and evening *ceilidh* (*kay*-lee), or entertainments. The college also hosts special festivals, and visitors may sit in on practice sessions of traditional Scottish music.

Tour 8: Marconi Trail

The 55-kilometer (34-mile) coastal route from Glace Bay to Louisbourg takes an hour to drive without stopping, but Fortress Louisbourg requires at least half a day to visit.

Mining coal has long been a way of life in Cape Breton. Part of
③⑥ the Three Mine Tour in the **Glace Bay** area, the **Miners Museum** displays a 200-year history of mining in the area. Visitors can walk into the Ocean Deeps Colliery, and the adjoining Miner's Village has a replica of the company store and housing. *Quarry Point, tel. 902/849–4522. Admission including mine tour: $4.50 adults, $2.75 children, $2.25 students. Open June–Labor Day, daily 10–6; mid-Sept.–May, weekdays 9–4.*

Also in Glace Bay, the **Marconi Museum** is situated on the spot where in 1902 Guglielmo Marconi transmitted the first transatlantic wireless message. *Timmerman St., tel. 902/564–2730. Admission free. Open mid-June–Labor Day, daily 10–6.*

③⑦ The trail culminates in **Fortress Louisbourg,** the most ambitious restoration project ever undertaken in Canada. The original fortress, constructed by the French between 1720 and 1745, was the focal point of the struggle between the French and English until its total destruction by the English in 1760. Buildings open to the public within the garrison (including the quarters of the governor, officers, and soldiers stationed here) are occupied by "animators" in period costume, who also roam the complex. Furnishings are either original to the period or are meticulously researched copies. A park bus takes visitors from the interpretive center to the fortress proper. *Rte. 22, Louisbourg, tel. 902/733–2280. Admission June–Sept.: $6 adults, $3 children 5 and over, senior citizens free, $15 families. Open July–Aug. 9–6; June, Sept. 9:30–5; May, Oct., three tours daily, at 10, 1 (in French), and 2.*

Tour 9: Fleur-de-lis Trail

This 160-kilometer (100-mile) drive takes 3½ hours to complete, starting at Port Hawkesbury, on Cape Breton Island near the Strait of Canso, and ending at the industrial city of Sydney. About 60% of the trail takes you along the low, curvy eastern coast of the island, through some of the oldest fishing villages in North America. Soon after leaving Port Hawkes-
③⑧ bury on Route 4, the trail crosses the bridge to **Isle Madame,** an Acadian area for 400 years. **Little Anse** is a particularly picturesque fishing village. In **Arichat,** another Isle Madame village, you can visit **Le Noir Forge,** a restored 18th-century stone blacksmith shop with working forge. *Tel. 902/226–2800. Ad-*

mission free. Open mid-June–mid-Sept., weekdays 9–5, Sat. 10–3.

Back on Cape Breton Island proper take Route 104 east, and you'll soon come upon **St. Peters Canal**, dug in 1854 to link Bras d'Or Lake with the Atlantic. A park on the east side overlooks the canal and is a perfect spot for picnicking as you watch the pleasure craft negotiate the locks. After Fourchu on the Atlantic coast, the trail cuts north, inland past Gabarus Lake, to
㊴ Marion Bridge and into **Sydney**. Stop by the **Cossitt House**, built in 1787, which is the oldest house in the city. *75 Charlotte St., tel. 902/539–1572. Admission free. Open mid-May–Oct., Mon.–Sat. 9:30–5:30, Sun. 1–5:30.*

Tour 10: Ceilidh Trail

This 107-kilometer (67-mile) drive goes along the west coast of Cape Breton Island from Port Hastings, at the Canso Causeway, to Margaree Harbour. Along the shoreline, which in summer is washed in warm water, are 17 sandy beaches. A pretty introduction to the highlands of Cape Breton, the route takes 1½–2 hours to drive.

Soon after leaving Port Hastings you'll pass through **Creignish**, on St. George's Bay, one of several traditional Scottish villages on the trail. **Port Hood** and **Mabou** are charming fishing ports and were well-known shipbuilding centers in the 19th century. The scenery becomes more dramatic as you climb the coastal cliffs of the **Mabou Highlands** perched over the Northumberland Strait. The trail connects with the Cabot Trail at **Margaree Harbour.** This part of Cape Breton is especially rich in traditional culture. It has many fine traditional singers, stepdancers, and fiddlers, including the nationally known Rankin Family, from Mabou. You're likely to get a chance to see them at Scottish concerts and festivals throughout the summer; one of the best is an all-day, outdoor concert at Broad Cove in late July. Some country halls have old-fashioned square dances every weekend, with a fiddler or two in attendance.

Shopping

You may claim a refund of Nova Scotia's 10% sales tax (nonrefundable on accommodations, meals, and alcohol) paid on goods you transport home. Refund claims must be filed within 90 days of leaving Nova Scotia and must be in excess of $15. (Refunds of the national Goods and Services Tax must be applied for separately; *see* Highlights '93, above). (For refund forms and information contact the Provincial Tax Commission, Tax Refund Unit, Box 755, Halifax, NS B3J 2V4, tel. 902/424–5946 or, toll free in NS, 1–424–6708.)

Halifax The Spring Garden Road area has two new, stylish shopping malls, with shops selling everything from designer clothing to fresh pasta. **Jennifers of Nova Scotia**, (5635 Spring Garden Rd.) sells the work of more than 120 Nova Scotia craftspeople, including jewelry, pottery, wool sweaters, and soaps. You can also find fine crafts in the oldest part of Halifax—**Historic Properties** and the **Barrington Inn complex** near the waterfront—at such shops as **Pewter House** and the **Stornoway.** The **Plaid Place** (1903 Barrington Pl.) has a dazzling array of tartans and Highland accessories. The **Wool Sweater Outlet** (1870 Hollis St.) offers wool and cotton sweaters at good prices.

Yarmouth If you hope to make a kilt or anything else out of Nova Scotian tartan, stop at **Yarmouth Wool Shoppe** (352 Main St., tel. 902/742–2255) near the ferry.

Elsewhere in Nova Scotia Nova Scotia's shopping centers tend to be uninspiring and not all that different from those in other parts of Canada or in the United States. The two largest malls in the province are the **MicMac Mall** in Dartmouth, off the A. Murray Mackay Bridge, and the **Halifax Shopping Centre** on Mumford Road. On Route 4 in Sydney you'll find the Mayflower Mall, on the way to Glace Bay.

Antiques stores proliferate all over the province, especially in **Cape Breton.** And in the shops of craftspeople throughout the province you'll find everything from blacksmithing in East Dover and silversmithing in Waverly, to leaded glass hanging ornaments in Purcells Cove, hooked rugs in Chéticamp, wood toys in Middletown, pewter in Wolfville, pottery in Arichat, and apple dolls in Halifax. To help you sort out the various crafts and their regions, request a copy of the "Buyers Guide to Art and Crafts in Nova Scotia" from the Department of Tourism (*see* Important Addresses and Numbers in Essential Information, above).

Sports and Fitness

Bird-Watching Nova Scotia is located on the Atlantic "flyway" and is an important staging point for migrating species. One of the highest concentrations of bald eagles in North America—about 250 nesting pairs—is located in Cape Breton, along the **Bras d'Or Lake region** or in **Cape Breton Highlands National Park.** July and August are the best eagle-watching times. **MacNabs Island,** in the middle of Halifax harbor, has a large osprey population. **The Bird Islands,** off the coast of Cape Breton, are home to a variety of sea birds, including the rare Atlantic puffin. A bird-watching boat tour from Big Bras d'Or makes regular trips around the islands from June through September.

Canoeing Canoe route information is available from the Nova Scotia Government Bookstore (Box 637, 1 Government Pl., Halifax, NS D3J 2T3). The publication *Canoe Routes of Nova Scotia* is available from Canoe Nova Scotia (Box 3010 South, 5516 Spring Garden Rd., Halifax B3J 3G6, tel. 902/425–5450) for $9.25.

Cycling **Bicycle Nova Scotia** (5516 Spring Garden Rd., Box 3010, Halifax B3J 3G6, tel. 902/425–5450) conducts a variety of two-wheeling excursions around the province.

Fishing Nova Scotia has more than 9,000 lakes and 100 brooks; practically all lakes and streams are open to visitors. The catch includes Atlantic salmon (the season is most of June through September), brook and sea trout, rainbow trout, and shad. You can get a nonresident fishing license from any Department of Natural Resources in the province and at most sporting-goods stores.

Golf Nova Scotia and Cape Breton have 38 golf courses as well as driving ranges and miniature golf courses. One of Canada's finest courses is at the **Digby Pines Resort,** in Digby (*see* Lodging, below).

Hiking The province has a wide variety of trails, along the rugged coastline and inland through forest glades. The trails let you experience scenery, wildlife, and vegetation not accessible any other way. Maps of Nova Scotia trails are available through the Canadian Hostelling Association (5516 Spring Garden Rd., Box 3010, Halifax B3J 3G6).

Windsurfing Wind and water conditions are often excellent for windsurfing, the fastest-growing aquatic summer sport in Nova Scotia. Lessons and equipment rentals are available from retail outlets throughout the province.

Beaches

The province is one big seashore: The warmest beaches are found on the Northumberland Strait shore and include **Heather Beach, Caribou,** and **Melmerby,** all in provincial parks.

National Parks

Nova Scotia has two national parks: **Cape Breton Highlands National Park** (*see* Tour 7, above) and **Kejimkujik National Park,** in the interior of the western part of the province. Essentially a wilderness area with many lakes, Kejimkujik offers well-marked canoe routes into the interior with primitive campsites. Nature trails are marked for hikers, boat rentals are available, and there's freshwater swimming. One precaution: Check for ticks after hiking in the deep woods. *Box 36, Maitland Bridge, B0T 1N0, take Hwy. 8 from Liverpool or Annapolis Royal, tel. 902/682–2770. Admission: $4 per vehicle per day, $9 for 4-day pass, $25 for annual pass. Camping fee: $8.50–$13 per day.*

Dining and Lodging

Dining

Many of Halifax's restaurants are set in refurbished historic homes or other restored quarters. The menu almost always centers on seafood, including Malpeque oysters, Fundy lobster, and Digby scallops, though considering the city's proximity to some of the world's best fishing grounds, there should be more high-quality fish available. Only in expensive restaurants will a jacket be required; dress elsewhere is casual.

Highly recommended restaurants in each price category are indicated by a star ★.

Category	Cost*
Very Expensive	over $50
Expensive	$35–$50
Moderate	$15–$35
Inexpensive	under $15

*per person, excluding drinks, service, 7% GST, and 10% sales tax on meals more than $3

Lodging

Accommodations in Halifax/Dartmouth are generally comfortable, and reservations are necessary year-round. Reservations can be made by calling the Check-In Service at the toll-free numbers of the Nova Scotia Department of Tourism (*see* Important Addresses and Numbers in Essential Information, above). Expect to pay quite a bit more in the capital district than elsewhere in the province. For those on a budget, look into a hostel or bed-and-breakfast.

Highly recommended lodgings in each price category are indicated by a star ★.

Category	Cost*
Very Expensive	over $80
Expensive	$65–$80
Moderate	$45–$65
Inexpensive	under $40

All prices are for a standard double room, excluding 10% service charge.

Halifax/Dartmouth

Dining
★
Clipper Cay. This restaurant gets the prize for the best location in the city: overlooking Privateer's Wharf and the entire harbor. Request a table with a window view and order smoked salmon. The downstairs eatery, The Cay Side, serves lunch—seafood, of course—outside on the wharf in the summer. *1869 Upper Water St., Halifax, tel. 902/432–6818. Reservations advised. AE, DC, MC, V. Expensive.*

Ryan Duffy's. Steaks are the specialty at this spot in the Spring Garden Place shopping mall. From upstairs corner windows you can watch the world walk by; brass and wood paneling and a green and burgundy color scheme add to the old-time atmosphere. You can select your own steak by the ounce or choose seafood, lamb, or other entrées. *5640 Spring Garden Rd., Halifax, tel. 902/421–1116. Reservations advised for dining room but not necessary for grill. AE, MC, V. Moderate–Expensive.*

Daily Catch. Don't be fooled by appearances. This small, nondescript neighborhood restaurant in a working-class section of town serves fabulous food. The menu, scribbled on a blackboard on the wall, features Italian seafood. Try the lobster Fra Diavolo—lobster, squid, mussels, shrimp, clams, and scallops served over linguini, in a cast-iron skillet. *2590 Agricola St., Halifax, tel. 902/429–2223. AE, MC, V. Reservations advised. Moderate.*

Da Maurizio is a popular North Italian restaurant in the Brewery Center, with an adjoining wine bar, **Baccus**, under the same management. Chef-owner Maurizio serves pastas with olive oil, ravioli stuffed with duck or rabbit, liver Veneziano, veal, beef, duck, rabbit, grilled fish and meats, and the only risotto in town. The brewery's enormously high ceilings—15 and 20 feet—and its stone and brick walls are warmed by fresh flowers, gleaming silver and linen, and a Venetian carnival theme, with paintings and masks on the walls. There's a wide wine selection by the bottle and by the glass, and food is served

in the wine bar too. *1496 Lower Water St., tel. 902/423–0859.
Reservations recommended. AE, MC, V. Closed, Sun., Mon.,
and Sat. lunch. Moderate.*

★ **Old Man Morias.** Authentic Greek specialties at this turn-of-
the-century Halifax town house include lamb on a spit and
moussaka. Greek music, tapestries, and archways set the mood
for traditional, full-flavored dishes. Try a sampling of the fried
squid and Greek fried cheese appetizers. *1150 Barrington St.,
Halifax, tel. 902/422–7960. Reservations advised. AE, DC,
MC, V. Closed Sun. Moderate.*

Scanway. Scandanavian dishes are the specialty of this bright,
pretty restaurant, decorated with pine wood and orange-and-
yellow drapes. Try the *sjokreps* (Danish scampi with garlic and
parsley butter). The dessert menu alone makes Scanway worth
a visit: homemade ice cream, King Olav's cake (chocolate truffle torte), marzipan cake filled with fresh fruit. *1569 Dresden
Row, Halifax, tel. 902/422–3733. Reservations advised. AE,
MC, V. Moderate.*

Privateer's Warehouse contains three restaurants, all sharing
the early 18th-century stone walls and hewn beams, and serving meals in descending order of elegance. **Bradley's Upper
Deck,** a comfortably elegant place with great views of the harbor, specializes in regional Nova Scotia cooking, with fresh ingredients and lots of seafood (reservations advised; moderate;
closed lunch Sat. and Sun.). The **Middle Deck** is a bistro-style
casual place serving panfried haddock and barbecued ribs till
10 PM and snacks till midnight; on Thursday, Friday, and Saturday maritime folk music fills the air (inexpensive; closed Sun.).
The **Lower Deck** is a boisterous pub with long trestle tables, a
patio, beer mugs for thumping, and lots of holding hands and
singing of traditional maritime, Irish, and Scottish songs (inexpensive; closed Sun.). *Privateer's Wharf, Historic Properties,
tel. 902/422–1289. AE, DC, MC, V.*

Satisfaction Feast. This small, vegetarian restaurant and bake-
ry is informal, friendly, and usually packed at lunchtime. The
food is simple and wholesome, with a truly homemade flavor.
Try the fresh wholewheat bread and one of the daily curries.
No smoking. *1581 Grafton St., Halifax, tel. 902/422–3540. MC,
V. Inexpensive.*

Lodging **Chateau Halifax.** This central first-class Canadian Pacific hotel
offers large, pretty rooms in a perfect location, near Scotia
Square and Historic Properties. There's a good dining room
and a lively bar. *1990 Barrington St., Scotia Sq., Scotia Sq.,
Halifax B3J 1P2, tel. 902/425–6700. 279 rooms, 21 suites. Facilities: restaurant, coffee shop, lounge with live entertainment, pool, sauna. AE, DC, MC, V. Very Expensive.*

Citadel Halifax. Situated at the base of Citadel Hill, but still
within walking distance of the action, this property attracts a
business clientele. Rooms with a harbor view are recommended, though they will cost more than those without. It offers free parking, which is an asset in car-clogged Halifax. *1960
Brunswick St., Halifax B3J 2G7, tel. 902/422–1391. 261 rooms,
6 suites. Facilities: restaurant; cable TV; indoor pool; fitness
center with sauna, whirlpool, and exercise room. AE, DC, MC,
V. Very Expensive.*

Delta Barrington. This traditional-style hotel was built in 1979
using the original granite from the facade of an entire city
block. It has a prime downtown location, and the rooms are spacious. All-weather walkways connect the hotel to Scotia Square

shops. *1875 Barrington St., Halifax B3J 3L6, tel. 902/429–7410. 200 rooms, 1 suite. Facilities: restaurant, lounge, piano bar, sauna, whirlpool, and pool. AE, DC, MC, V. Very Expensive.*

The Halifax Hilton. This wonderful, spacious old hotel, which used to be the Nova Scotian, was recently bought by Hilton International and totally renovated. It's down by the river near the end of Lower Water Street, within walking distance of the Brewery Market and other places of interest. There's ample parking, a tennis court, and a newly installed roof terrace, where you can sit in the evening looking over the city. Renowned for its business facilities, it has 13 conference rooms and a lavish breakfast buffet to fuel you up for the day. *1181 Hollis St., Halifax B3H 2P6, tel. 902/423–7231 or 800/445–8667; fax 902/422–9465. 307 rooms. Facilities: 2 restaurants, indoor pool, sauna, ballroom, tennis court, roof terrace. AE, D, DC, MC, V. Very Expensive.*

Holiday Inn–Halifax Centre. This first-class property overlooks Halifax Commons, 1 kilometer (½ mile) from Scotia Square. *1980 Robie St., Halifax B3H 3G5, tel. 902/423–1161. 228 rooms, 3 suites. Facilities: restaurant, piano bar, pool, sauna, whirlpool, gift shop, free parking. AE, DC, MC, V. Very Expensive.*

Prince George Hotel. Connected by underground tunnel to the World Trade and Convention Center, the Prince George is a luxurious addition to the downtown accommodations roster. It is near the harbor and business districts. *1725 Market St., Halifax B3J 3N9, tel. 902/425–1986 or 800/565–1567. 208 rooms, 3 suites. Facilities: restaurant, café, 2 lounges, pub, pool, whirlpool, fitness center, concierge, children's playroom, roof deck and gardens. AE, DC, MC, V. Very Expensive.*

Sheraton Halifax. Located in the charming Historic Properties in the heart of the business and shopping district, this elegant Sheraton on the waterfront features the Café Maritime restaurant and has an indoor pool with a summer sun deck, whirlpool, sauna, exercise room, and docking space for yachts. In summer you can sit on an outdoor terrace, eat lobster, and watch the ships go by. *1919 Upper Water St., Halifax B3J 3J5, tel. 902/421–1700 or 800/325–3535. 332 rooms, 24 suites. Facilities: 24-hr room service, concierge, shops, meeting facilities, skywalk to shopping and office complexes. AE, DC, MC, V. Very Expensive.*

Holiday Inn. There are no surprises at this chain hotel, but the location is convenient: next to the Angus Macdonald Bridge in Dartmouth. All rooms are air-conditioned and have color TV with movies; some have minibars. *99 Wyse Rd. at MacDonald Bridge, Dartmouth B3A 1L9, tel. 902/463–1100. 197 rooms, 6 suites. Facilities: restaurant, lounge, gym, sauna, outdoor pool, parking. AE, DC, MC, V. Moderate.*

Journey's End Motel. Located on the main highway on the Dartmouth side of the Narrows, this new chain motel offers clean, modern, no-frills rooms. *456 Windmill Rd. (Rte. 7), Dartmouth B3A 1J7, tel. 902/463–9900. 81 rooms. AE, DC, MC, V. Moderate.*

Martin House Bed and Breakfast. This modest house, furnished with antiques, overlooks the harbor and the Halifax skyline. *62 Pleasant St., Dartmouth B2Y 3P5, tel. 902/469–1896. 3 rooms, 1½ baths. No smoking indoors. No credit cards. Moderate.*

Waken'n Eggs B&B. This small operation, across the common from the citadel, is in an 1873 Victorian house that was built as a side-by-side duplex. It serves a lavish full breakfast. *2114 Windsor St., Halifax B3K 5B4, tel. 902/422–4737. 3 rooms with 1 private, 1 shared bath. No credit cards. Moderate.*

Wandlyn Motels. This is a chain of basic, family-oriented places in eastern Canada. They all have restaurants, some have pools, and they are clean and reliable. *In Amhurst, Dartmouth, Halifax, Sydney and other locations. Tel. 800/561–0006. AE, DC, MC, V. Moderate.*

Around the Mainland

Annapolis Royal
Lodging

Royal Anne Motel. Rebuilt in 1989 to accommodate more clientele and to upgrade facilities, this modern, no-frills motel offers clean rooms at reasonable prices. Enjoy the pleasant quiet country setting by taking a walk on the motel's 20 acres of land. *400 Annapolis Royal, B0S 1A0, tel. 902/532–2323. 30 rooms. Facilities: whirlpool, sauna, conference room. AE, DC, MC, V. Moderate.*

Antigonish
Dining

Lobster Treat Restaurant. Located on the Trans-Canada Highway, this restaurant is a converted two-room schoolhouse, cozily decorated with brick, pine, and stained glass. The menu features fresh seafood and vegetables year-round, as well as bread and pies baked on the premises. Because of a relaxed atmosphere and a varied menu, including a separate one for the children, families like to frequent this restaurant. *241 Post Rd., tel. 902/863–5465. Reservations advised in summer. AE, DC, MC, V. Closed Jan. Moderate.*

Chester
Dining

The Galley. Decked out in nautical bric-a-brac and providing a spectacular view of the ocean, this restaurant has a menu that features seafood. Smoked salmon and mussel dishes are the local favorites, but save room for the homemade blueberry pie. *Hwy. 3, on the Marina, tel. 902/275–4700. Reservations advised. AE, MC, V. Closed Dec. 16–St. Patrick's Day. Inexpensive.*

Debert
Lodging

Shady Maple Inn B&B. Take a look at a working dairy farm where you can breakfast on fresh eggs, the farm's own maple syrup, jams, and jellies. Enjoy the smoke-free rooms and sundried linen, and take a dip in the pool. One of the three rooms is a deluxe suite with a water bed. *RR 1, B0M 1G0, tel. 902/662–3565. MC, V. Moderate–Expensive.*

Digby
Dining and Lodging

The Pines Resort Hotel. An elegant resort with fireplaces, sitting rooms, a colossal dining room, and a view of Digby harbor, this hotel offers myriad amenities. Seafood with a French touch is served daily, and there is live entertainment in the lounge nightly. *Box 70, Shore Rd., B0V 1A0, tel. 902/245–2511. 90 rooms in main lodge, 60 in cottages. Facilities: restaurant, lounge, tennis, outdoor pool, golf. AE, DC, MC, V. Closed Oct. 15–May 30. Expensive.*

Lorneville
Dining and Lodging

Amherst Shore Country Inn. Located at Lorneville, 20 miles from Amherst on Route 366, this superb inn has five rooms in-house and two seaside cottages with fireplaces. The food is incredible; four-course dinners are served in one daily seating, at 7:30 PM (reservations required). *RR2, Amherst, B4H 3X9, tel. 902/667–4800. 7 rooms. Facilities: restaurant. AE, DC, MC, V. Closed winter. Expensive.*

Lunenburg
Lodging

Bluenose Lodge. This 126-year-old mansion has nine large bedrooms and offers a full complimentary breakfast, featuring treats such as freshly baked muffins, stewed rhubarb, and quiche. You can also partake of deep-sea fishing excursions, arranged by the lodge. *Box 339, 10 Falkland St., B0J 2C0, tel. 902/634–8851. 9 rooms. MC, V. Closed Nov.–Apr. Expensive.*

New Glasgow
Lodging

Peter Pan Motel. Clean rooms and good hospitality keep people coming back to this motel. One of the few lodgings in the area that stay open all year, this motel is a good buy. *390 Marsh St., B2H 4S6, tel. 902/752–8327. 52 rooms. Facilities: dining room, bar, outdoor pool. AE, DC, MC, V. Moderate.*

Pictou

The Walker Inn. A hospitable and energetic Swiss couple run this downtown inn in their brick Georgian-style town house built in 1865. Every room is different, the dining room is fully licensed, and there's a new library/conference room. A Continental breakfast buffet is included in the rate. *34 Coleraine St., Box 629, B0K 1H0, tel. 902/485–1433. 10 rooms with bath. Facilities: restaurant, meeting room. AE, MC, V. Moderate.*

Salmon River

Salmon River House. About 35 minutes east of Dartmouth, where Route 7 crosses the Salmon River, there's an unpretentious white-frame inn on 30 acres, with a glorious view. It has a licensed dining room, a sun room, a room accessible to wheelchairs, and one equipped with a water bed and whirlpool bath. *RR 2, Head of Jeddore, B0J 1P0, tel. 902/889–3353 or 800/341–6096. 6 rooms with bath or shower. Facilities: dining room, canoe and boat rentals, hunting and fishing arranged. MC, V. Moderate–Expensive.*

Wolfville
Dining and Lodging

Blomidon Inn. Rooms at this elegant 19th-century sea-captain's mansion, restored in 1981, are uniquely decorated in authentic colonial and Victorian fashion. The inn is located on a hectare (2½ acres) of terraced land shaded by century-old elms, chestnuts, and maples. The dining room serves local cuisine cooked in traditional style, using fresh seasonal produce. Complimentary tea is served every day at 4 PM. *127 Main St., B0P 1X0, tel. 902/542–2291. 27 rooms. Facilities: dining room, conference room, tennis court. MC, V. Closed Dec. 24–26. Expensive.*

Yarmouth
Dining and Lodging

Manor Inn. With superior rooms and good food in pleasant surroundings, this colonial mansion on Highway 1 is a nice find. There are three settings to choose from: a lakeside cottage, the main estate, or the more secluded side wing. Steak and lobster are the specialties in the dining room. *Box 56, Hebron, B0W 1X0, tel. 902/742–2487. 54 rooms. Facilities: 2 dining rooms, 2 bars, whirlpool, heated pool, tennis court, fireplaces. Reservations required for restaurant. AE, DC, MC, V. Moderate.*

Cape Breton Island

Baddeck
Lodging

Inverary Inn Resort. These pleasant accommodations, in a 100-year-old inn, 3 housekeeping cottages, motel units, and duplex cabins are in a waterfront complex on the island's scenic central drive. The property offers boating and swimming and the nearby village will keep you busy, yet the resort is tranquil. Families will appreciate the on-site children's playground, and everyone likes the wharfside restaurant. The main lodge with its paneled walls, stone fireplace, and polished horse brasses, has a strong Scottish flavor. *Box 190, B0E 1B0, tel. 902/295–2674. 137 rooms. Facilities: restaurant, chapel, indoor and* *outdoor pools, fitness and games room, tennis, sauna. AE, MC, V. Very Expensive.*

Iona
Dining

Highland Heights Inn. The rural surroundings, the Scottish home-style cooking served near the dining room's huge stone fireplace, and the unspoiled view of the lake are nice substitutes for being in the Scottish Highlands. The inn is located on a hillside beside the NS Highland Village museum and overlooking the village of Iona, where some residents still speak the Gaelic language of their ancestors. Enjoy the salmon (or any fish in season), fresh-baked oat cakes, and homemade desserts. *Box 19, Iona, tel. 902/725-2360. AE, MC, V. Closed mid-Oct.– mid-May. Moderate.*

Margaree Valley
Lodging

Normaway Inn. This secluded, 1920s inn is nestled in the hills of the river valley, on a 250-acre property. Many of the cabins have wood-burning stoves. Take advantage of the recreation barn and the nightly traditional entertainment—square dances and the like. The inn is known for its country gourmet food, all prepared on the premises. The owners will organize salmon-fishing trips. *Box 326, Margaree Valley, B0E 2C0, tel. 902/248-2987. 9 rooms, 17 cabins. Facilities: restaurant, tennis, bicycles. AE, MC, V. Closed Oct. 16–mid-June. Moderate.*

Northeast Margaree
Lodging

Heart of Hart's Tourist Farm. This 100-year-old rural farmhouse on Cabot Trail is within walking distance of the village. Hot homemade oatmeal and Red River cereal are a favorite part of the full breakfast that is included in the room rate. Salmon- and trout-fishing trips can be arranged. *Northeast Margaree, B0E 2H0, tel. 902/248-2765. 5 rooms. No credit cards. Inexpensive.*

Sydney
Dining

Joe's Warehouse. For excellent food in the heart of town, stop here, where the specialties include local seafood and prime rib. The porridge rolls and homemade scones also win rave reviews. In summer, when the patio is open, the restaurant seats 200 people. Dress is casual and the atmosphere fun. After dinner head downstairs for live music and dancing at Smooth Herman's. *424 Charlotte St., tel. 902/539-6686. AE, DC, MC, V. Moderate.*

Lodging

Sydney Mariner Hotel. This hotel is excellently situated, on the bay beside the yacht club and close to the center of town. The attractively decorated guest rooms have all the amenities, and each has a view of the harbor. The intimate dining room specializes in seafood and Continental cuisine. *300 Esplanade, B1P 6J4, tel. 902/562-7500. 152 rooms. Facilities: restaurant, lounge, indoor pool, sauna, fitness center. AE, DC, MC, V. Expensive.*

The Arts and Nightlife

The Arts

Theater
Halifax's premier professional theater group performs at the **Neptune Theatre** (Sackville St., tel. 902/429-7300). The **Mulgrave Road Co-Op Theatre** (tel. 902/533-2092) is a small but active professional company performing all over the maritime provinces, producing original plays based on local history.

Among the best of Nova Scotia's thriving amateur companies are the **Kipawa Show Boat Company** (tel. 902/542-3500), which performs in Wolfville on summer weekends, and **Theatre Antigonish** (tel. 902/867–3954), which performs in Antigonish.

Parrsboro's professional **Ship's Company Theatre** offers a summer season of plays based on historical events of the region, performed aboard the MV *Kipawo*, a former Minas Basin ferry. Dinner theaters in Halifax include the **Historic Feast Company** (tel. 902/420–1840), which presents shows set in the 19th century at Historic Properties Thursday, Friday, and Saturday evenings. At the **Grafton Street Dinner Theatre** (tel. 902/425–1961), shows run Wednesday through Saturday.

Music Live concerts and musical presentations are held in Halifax at the **Rebecca Cohn Auditorium** (6101 University Ave., tel. 902/494–2646) and the **Metro Centre** (Brunswick and Duke Sts., tel. 902/451–1202).

Talented musicians abound in Nova Scotia, especially traditional fiddlers, singers, pipers, and dancers. In the summer, there's a festival or concert almost every day of the week somewhere in the area. Some of the most popular events include the annual Nova Scotia Bluegrass and Oldtime Music Festival in Ardoise the last weekend in July; the International Festival of Scottish Fiddling at St. Ann's in mid-August; and the Nova Scotia Gaelic Mod at St. Ann's, the first week of August.

Nightlife

The multilevel entertainment center in Historic Properties, **Privateer's Warehouse** (tel. 902/422–1289), is a popular nighttime hangout. At the ground-level Lower Deck tavern you can quaff a beer to Celtic music or enjoy jazz riffs at the Middle Deck on the second floor. There is a cover for both decks, and they are packed on weekends, so get there early.

Other popular Halifax night spots include **Cheers** (1743 Grafton St., tel. 902/421–1655), with bands and entertainment nightly; **O'Carroll's** (1860 Upper Water St., tel. 902/423–4405), a restaurant, oyster bar, and lounge where you can hear live Irish music nightly; the **Flamingo Cafe and Lounge** (1505 Barrington St., tel. 902/420–1051), featuring a wide variety of live entertainment (Mondays are open-mike nights); and **Le Bistro Café** (South Park St., tel. 902/423–8428 or 902/423–8024), where you can listen to classical guitar.

13 Prince Edward Island

by Marian Bruce

Updated by
Colleen Whitney
Thompson

Cradled on the waves of the Gulf of St. Lawrence, off the coasts of New Brunswick and Nova Scotia, Prince Edward Island has enchanted people for nearly 2,000 years. From about AD 100, the Micmac Indians canoed from the mainland across Northumberland Strait for summers of fishing. French explorer Jacques Cartier, on sighting Prince Edward Island in 1534, called it "the fairest land 'tis possible to see!" When the British took possession more than 200 years later, Edward, duke of Kent, was impressed enough to give it his name. But those who live there and visit it know it simply (and fondly) as "the Island."

The island is naturally beautiful. The red sandstone cliffs of the southern coastline, topped by fields in brilliant shades of green, give visitors arriving by ferry across the Northumberland Strait their first impressions of the beauty of the province. The north shore, with its white, silky sand beaches, and the immaculate communities that form part of the gently rolling inland landscape, provide a contrasting beauty.

Prince Edward Island offers visitors a broad range of activities and attractions. Not surprisingly, many of them relate to water. There is sportfishing, windsurfing, and boating on inland and coastal waters. The salt-water coastline offers hundreds of kilometers of first-class beaches, huge sand dunes, and some of the warmest salt water north of Florida.

What the visitor will find most distinctive are the historic and personal elements: the French Acadian and Micmac settlements, the respect for tradition, the importance placed on family ties and community spirit, and the enduring Scottish and Irish influence on music, food, and speech patterns. Vacation farms offer visitors the experience of sharing accommodations with their farm family hosts; homes and studios of the many local craftsmen give travelers a chance to watch artisans at work and buy their products. Above all there is a sense of peace and innocence that sets Prince Edward Island apart from similar but more commercial destinations.

Essential Information

Important Addresses and Numbers

Tourist Information

For prices and information before your trip, contact the **Prince Edward Island Department of Tourism and Parks,** Visitor Service Division (Box 940, Charlottetown, PEI C1A 7M5, tel. 800/565–0267). To call for reservations from inside the maritime provinces, tel. 800/565–7421; from the rest of North America, tel. 902/368–5555. The province maintains 10 **Visitor Information Centres** (VICs) on the Island and two on the mainland—one at Aulac, New Brunswick, and one at Caribou, Nova Scotia. The main VIC, open year-round, is in **Charlottetown** (Oak Tree Place, University Ave., tel. 902/368–4444). It is open daily mid-May through October; weekdays November to mid-May.

Emergencies **Police** and **fire,** dial 0.

Hospitals **Queen Elizabeth Hospital,** Charlottetown, tel. 902/566–6200.

Arriving and Departing by Plane

Charlottetown Airport is 5 kilometers (3 miles) north of town. **Air Canada** (tel. 800/776–3000) and **Canadian Airlines International** (902/892–3581) offer daily service to major cities in eastern Canada and the United States.

Arriving and Departing by Ferry

Two car-ferry services operate regularly between Prince Edward Island and the mainland: **Marine Atlantic Ferries** (tel. 902/794–5700) sails between Cape Tormentine, New Brunswick, and Borden, Prince Edward Island. There are regular daily crossings year-round between 6:30 AM and 1 AM. The crossing takes about 45 minutes and costs $17 per car round-trip (payable on leaving the island), and $6.50 per adult. The second service, **Northumberland Ferries** (tel. 800/565–0201), sails between Caribou, Nova Scotia, and Wood Islands, Prince Edward Island, from May to mid-December. The crossing takes about 75 minutes, and the round-trip costs $24.50 per automobile and $7.50 per person (reduced price for senior citizens and children). For both ferries, plan to arrive early and expect long lines leaving Prince Edward Island during the peak summer season. Neither service takes reservations.

Getting Around

By Car There are more than 3,700 kilometers (2,294 miles) of paved road in the province, including the three scenic coastal drives called Lady Slipper Drive, Blue Heron Drive, and Kings Byway.

Guided Tours

The island has about 20 sightseeing tours to choose from, including double-decker bus tours, cycling tours, harbor cruises, and walking tours. Most tour companies are located in Charlottetown and offer excursions around the city and to the beaches.

Exploring Prince Edward Island

The tours here divide Prince Edward Island into central Queens County, Kings County in the northeast, and finally Prince County at the western end of the island. Tour 1 is primarily a walking tour, while tours 2, 3, and 4 follow the major scenic highways—Blue Heron Drive, Kings Byway, and Lady Slipper Drive. There are plenty of chances to get out of the car, go fishing, hit the beach, collect wildflowers, or just watch the sea roll in.

Highlights for First-time Visitors

Anne of Green Gables **farmhouse,** Tour 2: Blue Heron Drive
around Souris, Tour 3: Kings Byway
Orwell Corner Pioneer Village, Tour 3: Kings Byway
Province House, Tour 1: Charlottetown

Seascapes and July's wild lupins near Sorris, Tour 3: Kings By-way

Tour 1: Charlottetown

Sheltered on an arm of the Northumberland Strait, Prince Edward Island's only city is named for the stylish consort of King George III. Charlottetown is a small city (population 15,800) with generous, gingerbread-clad clapboard Victorian houses and tree-shaded squares. It is often called "the Cradle of Confederation," a reference to the 1864 conference held here that led to the uniting of Nova Scotia, New Brunswick, Ontario, and Québec in 1867.

Charlottetown's main activities center on government, tourism, and private commerce. While new suburbs were springing up around it, the core of Charlottetown remained unchanged and the waterfront was restored to recapture the flavor of earlier eras. Today the waterfront includes the Prince Edward Hotel and Convention Centre, several informal restaurants, and handcraft and retail shops. You can easily explore the downtown by foot in a couple of hours.

Numbers in the margin correspond to points of interest on the Prince Edward Island and Charlottetown maps.

1 2 **Charlottetown's** historic redbrick core is the setting for the modern concrete **Confederation Centre of the Arts,** opened in 1964 as a tribute to the Fathers of Confederation. The Confederation Centre houses a 1,100-seat theater, an art gallery, a library, a children's theater, a memorial hall, and a gift shop with an assortment of Canadian crafts. From June to September the center's **Charlottetown Festival** offers excellent professional theater, including the annual musical adaptation of *Anne of Green Gables. Queen St., bet. Grafton and Richmond Sts., tel. 902/566–2464; box office 902/566–1267. Open July–Sept., daily 8 AM–9 PM; rest of the year, Mon.–Sat. 9–6, Sun. 2–5.*

3 Next door, on Richmond Street, is the Georgian-style **Province House,** the meeting place of the provincial legislature. The three-story sandstone building, completed in 1847, contains the Confederation Chamber, where representatives of the 19th-century provinces met to forge a union. The room, restored to its 1864 condition, and the legislative chamber are open to the public. Displays and a slide presentation portray the historic meeting. *Richmond St., tel. 902/566–7626. Admission free. Open July–Labor Day, daily 9–8; June and Labor Day–mid-Oct., daily 9–5; mid-Oct.–May, weekdays 9–5. Note: When provincial legislature is in session, certain rooms are closed to the public.*

4 5 Two churches near Province House are noteworthy. **St. Paul's Anglican Church** (east of Province House) was erected in 1747, making it the oldest Protestant church on the island. **St. Dunstan's Basilica,** south of Province House on Great George Street, is the seat of the Roman Catholic diocese on the island. Known for its twin Gothic spires and fine Italian carvings, it is one of Canada's largest churches.

Time Out   **The Strawberry Patch** (104 Water St., tel. 903/368–3840), located in a Victorian home in the old section of town near the waterfront, is a cozy spot for a light lunch or a late-afternoon tea.

Prince Edward Island

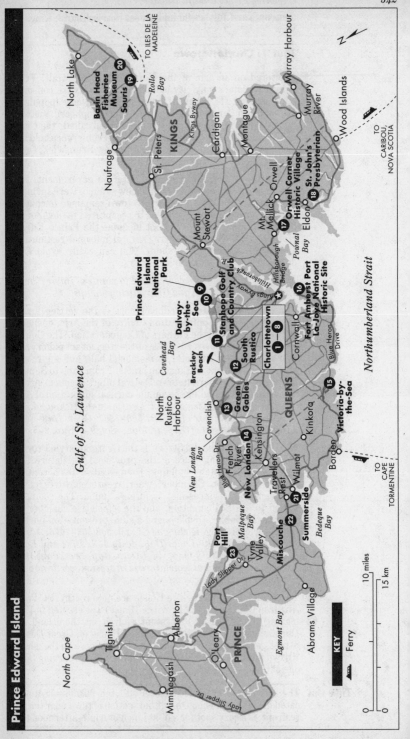

Gulf of St. Lawrence

TO ÎLES DE LA MADELEINE

North Lake

Basin Head
Fisheries
Museum **20**
Souris **19**

Rollo Bay

Naufrage

St. Peters

KINGS

Cardigan

Montague

Kings Byway

Murray Harbour

Murray River

Wood Islands

TO
CARIBOU,
NOVA SCOTIA

Mount
Stewart

Orwell

Mt.
Mellick

Orwell Corner **17**
Historic Village

Eldon

St. John's **18**
Presbyterian

Prince Edward
Island National
Park

9
10 Stanhope Golf
and Country Club

Delvay-
by-the-
Sea

11

Brackley Beach

Coveheod Bay

North Rustico Harbour

South
Rustico

12

Pownal Bay

Hillsborough
Bridge

Kings Byway

Charlottetown

1–8

Cornwall

Fort Amherst
Port
La-Joye National
Historic Site **16**

Blue Heron Drive

15 Victoria-by-
the-Sea

QUEENS

Green
Gables **13**

Cavendish

New London **14**

Kensington

Kinkora

New London Bay

Blue Heron Dr.

French
River

Travellers
Rest

Wilmot

21

Borden

TO
CAPE
TORMENTINE

Summerside

22

Miscouche

Bedeque Bay

Port
Hill **23**

Tyne Valley

Malpeque Bay

Lady Slipper Dr.

PRINCE

Alberton

O'Leary

Egmont Bay

Abrams Village

North Cape

Tignish

Miminegash

Lady Slipper Dr.

Northumberland Strait

KEY
Ferry

0   10 miles
0   15 km

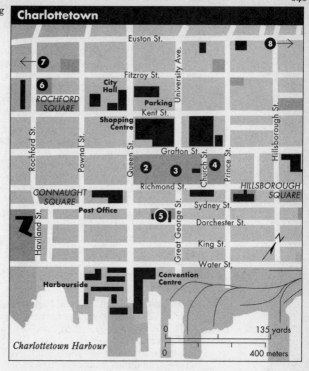

Charlottetown

Charlottetown Harbour

⑥ A few blocks northeast of Province House, on Rochford Square, is **St. Peter's Cathedral.** It contains murals by Robert Harris, the famous Canadian portrait painter. The chapel was designed in 1888 by his brother W. C. Harris.

⑦ At the southern tip of the city is the beautiful 40-acre **Victoria Park,** overlooking the Charlottetown Harbour. Next to the park, on a hill between groves of white birches, is the white colonial **Government House,** built in 1835 as the official residence of the province's lieutenant-governors. Near the park entrance, **Beaconsfield,** a gracious Victorian mansion designed by W. C. Harris, contains the offices of the PEI Museum and Heritage Foundation, a genealogical research center, and a bookstore featuring publications about the island. *Park open year-round, daily sunrise–sunset.*

⑧ At the eastern end of the city is the **Charlottetown Driving Park** on Kensington Road, home of a sport that is dear to the hearts of islanders—harness racing. Standardbred horses are raised on farms throughout the island, and harness racing on the ice and on country tracks has been popular for generations. In fact, there are more horses per capita on the island than in any other province of Canada. *Races are held year-round twice a week from Jan. to May; three nights a week in June, July, and most of Aug.; and twice daily (except Sun.) during Old Home Week in mid-Aug. On Kensington Road, tel. 902/892–6823. Admission: $2 adults, 50¢ children.*

Tour 2: Blue Heron Drive

Circling the island's center segment and roughly outlining Queens County, Blue Heron Drive is 190 kilometers (114 miles) long. It takes its name from the great blue heron, a stately water bird that migrates to Prince Edward Island every spring to nest in the shallow bays and marshes. You are likely to see several herons along the route. The highway marker is a white square with a blue border and a blue heron in the center.

From Charlottetown, Blue Heron Drive follows Route 15 north to the north shore, then winds along Route 6 through the north-shore fishing villages, the spectacular white sand beaches of Prince Edward Island National Park and Cabot Provincial Park, through Anne of Green Gables country, and finally along the south shore with its red sandstone seascapes and historic sites. This drive circles some of the most beautiful landscapes on the island and its best beaches, but its north shore, ironically around picturesque Cavendish and the Green Gables farmhouse, is also cluttered with tourist traps. If you're looking for unspoiled beauty, you'll have to look beyond the fried chicken joints, the tacky gift shops, King Tut's Tomb, and Ripley's Believe It Or Not, and try to keep in your mind's eye the island's simpler days.

9 **Prince Edward Island National Park** stretches for about 40 kilometers (25 miles) along the north shore of the island on the Gulf of St. Lawrence. Follow the shore road for views of the beaches and bluffs—especially Orby Head, with red sandstone cliffs up to 30 meters (33 yards) high. At Brackley Beach, you can see sand dunes 18 meters (19½ yards) high. The park has several hiking trails; the longest, about 8 kilometers (5 miles), starts near the Cavendish Campground. Among more than 200 species of birds are the northern phalarope, Swainson's thrush, and the protected piping plover. The park **Visitor Centre** in Cavendish provides a slide presentation and exhibit. The 56-acre campground has toilets, showers, electrical hookups, and a laundromat. *24 km (15 mi) north of Charlottetown, tel. 902/672–2211. Park open daily; Visitor Centre open June–Oct., daily 9–8.*

10 At the eastern end of the park is **Dalvay-by-the-Sea,** built in the 1890s as a summer home by an oil magnate. The park now operates the hotel as a resort lodge (*see* Lodging, below).

Time Out The dining room of **Dalvay-by-the-Sea** (tel. 902/672–2048) specializes in fresh seafood and homegrown vegetables; it's known for a traditional dessert called blueberry grunt.

11 A few kilometers west of Dalvay, off Route 6, along beautiful Covehead Bay, is the **Stanhope Golf and Country Club.** The course is among the island's longest, most challenging, and most scenic.

12 Moving west, you pass Brackley Beach and then come to **South Rustico,** on Route 243. The town sits on a peninsula on Rustico Bay, with a collection of Victorian houses gathered around a dainty church. One of Canada's first cooperative banks—now a National Historic Site and museum—was founded here.

13 Continue along the shore road and follow the signs to **Green Gables,** the green and white farmhouse that is the setting for Lucy

Maud Montgomery's first and most famous novel, *Anne of Green Gables*. Published in 1908, it became one of the most popular children's books ever written. It is the story of a young orphan girl adopted by a strict but kindly brother and sister who live on a Prince Edward Island farm. The story has so caught the imagination of readers that thousands from around the world visit Green Gables every summer. The house, once owned by Montgomery's cousins, is organized to reflect the story. *Near Cavendish, in Prince Edward Island National Park, tel. 902/963-2675. Open May 15-June 28, daily 9-5, June 29-Aug. 31, daily 9-8; Sept. 1-Nov. 1, daily 9-5.*

⓮ In **New London,** east of Cavendish on Route 6, is the modest white house where Lucy Maud Montgomery was born in 1874. Among memorabilia on display are the author's wedding dress and personal scrapbooks. *In New London, on Route 6, tel. 902/886-2596. Admission: $1 adults, 50¢ children. Open June 1-30 and Sept. 1-15, daily 9-6; July-Aug., 9-8; Sept. 16-Oct. 12, 10-5.*

The Blue Heron Drive follows the coastline south, through rolling farmland to the other side of the Island. At **Carleton,** Route 1 leads to **Borden,** the terminal for ferries crossing the Northumberland Strait to New Brunswick. **Victoria,** a picturesque
⓯ fishing village, also has antiques, art galleries, handcraft shops, and live summer theater in the historic Victoria Playhouse. *Tel. 902/566-4267 for ticket information and reservations.*

⓰ Completing the circle of Queen County, you can visit **Fort Amherst Port-La-Joye National Historic Site.** This pretty spot, with its lighthouses and view of the Charlottetown Harbour, is the location of the first settlement on the island, established in 1720 during French rule. You can picnic on the site while watching sailboats and cruise ships sail into the harbor. *32 km (20 mi) south of Charlottetown on Rte. 19 at Rocky Point, tel. 902/675-2220. Open June-Labor Day, daily 10-6.*

Tour 3: Kings Byway

The Kings Byway, named after Kings County, follows the coastline for 375 kilometers (225 miles) on the eastern end of the island. The route passes patchwork-quilt farms, pretty fishing villages, and historic sites in this green and tranquil section of the province. Starting at Charlottetown, take Route 1 east and follow Kings Byway counter-clockwise.

⓱ **The Orwell Corner Historic Village** re-creates a 19th-century rural settlement in the form of a living farm museum. Farming is done by methods used by Scottish settlers in the 19th century, including the use of handsome draft horses. The village contains a beautifully restored store and post office, school, church, farmhouse, and barns. Musical evenings (ceilidhs) in the village feature traditional Scottish music by local musicians. *Tel. 902/651-2013. Admission: $3 adults, children under 12 free. Open late June-Labor Day, daily 9-5; mid-May-late June and Labor Day-late Oct., Mon.-Fri. 10-3.*

⓲ One of the island's most historic churches, **St. John's Presbyterian,** in Belfast, is just off Route 1 on Route 207. Located on a hill against a backdrop of trees, this pretty white church was built by settlers from the Isle of Skye who were brought to the island in 1803 by Lord Selkirk.

Continuing south on Route 1, you go through **Wood Islands,** where a car-ferry crosses to Nova Scotia about seven months of the year.

The eastern coastline is dotted with fishing villages and pleasant, uncrowded beaches. In early summer, you can see whole fields of blue, white, pink, and purple wild lupins sloping down to red cliffs and blue sea. The view from the hill overlooking the **⑲** town of **Souris,** on the northeastern coast, is especially lovely. At Souris, a car-ferry links the islands with the Québec-owned Magdalen Islands. The Souris area is noted for its fine traditional musicians: An outdoor Scottish concert at Rollo Bay in July, featuring fiddling and step-dancing, attracts thousands every year.

⑳ North of Souris, the **Basin Head Fisheries Museum** is located on a bluff overlooking the Atlantic Ocean. Just over the bluff, past a little fishing settlement, is an exquisite, silvery beach surrounded by rolling sand dunes where you can experience the "singing sands" (so called because the sand squeaks loudly when you walk on it). Displays include a boat shed, an aquarium, a smokehouse, a fish-box factory, and fishermen's sheds. *Box 248, Souris, tel. 902/357–2966. Admission: $3 adults, children under 12 free. Open mid-June–Labor Day, daily 9–5; Labor Day–Sept. 30, weekdays 9–5.*

Tour 4: Lady Slipper Drive

Taking its name from the delicate lady slipper orchid, the province's official flower, this drive winds along the coast of the narrow indented western end of the island through some of the very old and very small villages that still adhere to a more traditional way of life. This region is the home of the island's Acadians, descendants of the original French settlers. The area is known for potato farms—half the province's potato crop is grown here—as well as for oysters and Irish moss.

㉑ From Charlottetown, take Route 2 to **Summerside,** the second-largest community on the island. The eight-day Summerside Lobster Carnival, held every July, includes livestock exhibitions, harness racing, fiddling contests, and lobster suppers.

From Summerside, follow the Lady Slipper signs on Route 1A **㉒** to St. Eleanors, then turn west on Route 2 to the **Miscouche** and the **Acadian Museum of Prince Edward Island.** The artifacts predate the 19th century and include household and farm implements. *Tel. 902/436–6237. Admission: $2 adults, $1 children 6–17. Open Sept. 8–June 11, weekdays 9:30–4; June 12–Sept. 7, weekdays 9:30–4, Sun. 1–5.*

About 35 kilometers (22 miles) north and west of Summerside, **㉓** in **Port Hill,** you'll find the **Green Park Shipbuilding Museum** and **Historic House.** Originally the home of James Yeo, Jr., this 19th-century mansion, restored and open to visitors, is topped by a cupola, from which Yeo observed his nearby shipyard through a spyglass. The modern museum building on the site details the history of the shipbuilder's craft. *Rte. 12, Port Hill, tel. 902/831–2206. Admission: $2.50 adults, children under 12 free. Open mid-June–Labor Day, daily 9–5.*

Shopping

Prince Edward Islanders have been making beautiful home-made items since colonial days, when crafts were necessities of life. Island craftspeople excel at quilting, rug-hooking, weaving, knitting, and pottery, to name a few of the crafts. Full information on outlets and types of crafts is provided by the **PEI Crafts Council** (156 Richmond St., Charlottetown, PEI C1A 1H9, tel. 902/892–5152). There are more than 100 crafts outlets throughout the island.

The **Island Craft Shop** (156 Richmond St., Charlottetown) has a wide selection of weaving, pottery, woodwork and other items. It is open July and August, Monday–Saturday 9–8, Sunday 11–4; September–June, Monday–Saturday 10–5:30. The **Wood Islands Handcraft Co-op Association Ltd.** in Murray River, in southeastern Kings County, sells a large number of knitted and crocheted items and other crafts. It is open daily June through September 30; 9–6 in July and August, 9–5 the rest of the year. Along Lady Slipper Drive look for turned bird's-eye maple-wood products at the **Leavitts' Maple Tree Craft Shop** in Alberton (open Mon.–Sat. 8–5), and **Shoreline Sweaters,** sometimes known as **Tyne Valley Studios,** in Tyne Valley, where Lesley Dubey sells handmade sweaters and local crafts (open mid-May–Sept., daily 9:30–5:30).

You can buy fresh, canned, or frozen lobsters and other seafood at numerous processing plants and retail stores throughout the island. Some, such as **Crabby's Seafood** in Wood Islands (tel. 902/962–3228), will pack for travel.

Sports and Outdoor Activities

Bicycling Prince Edward Island is popular with bike touring companies for its moderately hilly and always stunning scenery. Most of the island offers level areas, especially east of Charlottetown to Montague and along the north shore. However, the shoulderless, narrow roads and summer's car traffic can be dismal for cyclists. An 8.7-kilometer (5.4-mile) path near Cavendish campground loops around marsh, woodland, and farmland.

Fishing The brook trout fishing is some of the best in eastern Canada, as is deep-sea fishing off the island's northeast coast. Charter boats leave from fishing ports like Cove Head, North Lake, and North Rustico daily in summer for very elusive tuna and rich mackerel fishing, and there are more than 20 boat charters to choose from.

Clam digging is possible in many less-populated coastal areas around the island.

Golf Golf isn't a popular pastime of islanders, but it is with tourists. **Stanhope Golf Course** (*see* Tour 2) is considered one of the more challenging courses on the island. In the western end, **Mill River Provincial Golf Course** in Mill River Provincial Park, 57 kilometers (35 miles) west of Summerside, is the most scenic and challenging course in eastern Canada. **Brudenell River Provincial Golf Course** at the east end of the island has hosted four national championships and three CPGAs.

Dining

On Prince Edward Island, plain, wholesome, home-cooked fare is a matter of course. The service is friendly—though a little pokey at times—and the setting is informal everywhere but in a few restaurants in Charlottetown. Seafood is generally good anywhere on the island, with top honors being given to lobster and any dish using local produce. Unless noted, there is no need to wear a jacket and tie.

The lobster supper, offered both commercially and by church and civic groups, is an island tradition and should be sought out when touring the province. Likely places to find these meals featuring lobster, rolls, salad, and mountains of sweet, home-baked goodies, are New London, New Glasgow, St. Ann's Church in Hope River, and Fisherman's Wharf in North Rustico. Check the local papers or the bulletin boards of the local grocery stores.

Highly recommended restaurants in each price category are indicated by a star ★.

Category	Cost*
Very Expensive	over $35
Expensive	$25–$35
Moderate	$15–$24
Inexpensive	under $15

per person, excluding drinks, service, 10% sales tax, and 7% GST

Brackley Beach
Expensive
★

Shaw's Hotel and Cottages. This family-oriented hotel dating from the 1860s offers fine home cooking in an elegant, country setting. Lobster is served twice weekly, and the grand Sunday-night buffets draw people from near and far to sample fresh salmon, seafood casserole, home-baked breads, and a variety of popular desserts, such as cheese cake and fresh berries in season. Lunch is not served. *Rte. 15, tel. 902/672–2022. Reservations advised. AE, MC, V. Closed Oct.–May.*

Cavendish
Inexpensive

Fiddles 'n Vittles. Here's a great place to take the family for dinner. Lively, friendly, and rustic marine, with fishnets decorating the dining room, the restaurant specializes in fresh-fried seafood. *Bay Vista Motor Inn, RR1, Breadalbane, tel. 902/963–3003. AE, DC, MC, V. Closed mid-Sept.–mid-June.*

Charlottetown
Moderate–Expensive
★

Claddagh Room Restaurant. You'll find some of the best seafood in Charlottetown here. The "Galway Bay Delight," one of the Irish owner's specialties, is a savory combination of fresh scallops and shrimp sautéed with onions and mushrooms, flambéed in Irish Mist, and doused with fresh cream. A pub upstairs features live Irish entertainment every night in summer and on weekends in winter. *131 Sydney St., tel. 902/892–9661. AE, DC, MC, V.*

★ **The Griffin Room.** This cozy dining room of the Dundee Arms Motel and Inn has a working fireplace and is filled with antiques, copper, and brass. It's a comfortable and elegant place to enjoy French Continental cuisine; the restaurant prides itself in using no artificial preservatives or additives and in cooking only with fresh and natural ingredients. Fresh seafood is served year-round, and salmon, scallops, and crab are available all winter. Specialties include rack of lamb, chateaubriand, and poached or grilled fillet of salmon in a light lime-dill sauce. *Dundee Arms Motel and Inn, 200 Pownal St., tel. 902/892–2496. MC, V.*

Moderate **Off Broadway.** This attractive, cozy spot near the Confederation Centre of the Arts is popular with Charlottetown's young professional set. It began modestly as a crepe and soup joint, and indeed, you can still make a meal of the lobster or chicken crepe and the spinach or Caesar salad that's served with it. But the restaurant also has a fairly inventive menu of Continental entrées such as the hearty mussel chowder, fillets, and salmon. The old-fashioned private booths won't reveal your indiscretions—including your penchant for one of the many desserts. *125 Sydney St., tel. 902/566–4620. AE, MC, V.*

Queen Street Cafe. Soft recordings of the music of Ella Fitzgerald and Louis Armstrong add to the intimacy of this small, colorful restaurant. The changing menu is unusually fine for Charlottetown and features whatever ingredients are fresh and in season. Chicken breasts, seafood salad with mustard vinaigrette, and rum-raisin tart are among the favorites, and the seafood chowder is rumored to be the best on the island. Try any of the baked desserts. *52 Queen St., tel. 902/566–5520. DC, MC, V.*

Inexpensive **Captain Scott's.** The fish-and-chips served at this spot in the Confederation Court Mall rival England's. *Cor. of Grafton and Queen Sts., tel. 902/892–2097. No credit cards. Closed Sun.*

Cornwall **Bonnie Brae.** Welcoming and comfortable, this modern restauModerate rant offers fresh seafood and steaks, as well as Swiss specialties created by the Swiss owner-chef. Summer's nightly all-you-can-eat lobster buffet is guaranteed to satisfy any appetite—but leave room for desserts such as Black Forest cake and raspberry cheese cake. *Trans-Canada Hwy., tel. 902/566–2241. AE, DC, MC, V.*

Grand Tracadie **Dalvay-by-the-Sea.** Choose a table by the island-stone fireplace
Expensive or dine with a lake view on the enclosed terrace. The menu of this elegant Victorian dining room includes island lobster, curried scallops, poached halibut, peppercorn steak, and filet Mignon—all served with fresh vegetables. Desserts are baked on the premises by the restaurant's pastry chef; blueberry grunt, a sweet dumpling with blueberry sauce, is the Dalvay's own traditional specialty dessert and should not be missed. *Rte. 6, near Dalvay Beach, tel. 902/672–2048. Reservations advised. AE, MC, V.*

★ **Shady Lady Restaurant.** This restaurant is located in a log house built by the chef-owners—twin sisters—who financed the project by working as cooks in the Yukon. It's a warm and charming place decorated in Victorian style—each table setting is different, with linens and fine china collected by the owners. The cuisine is basically French, with an emphasis on steaks and seafood. All desserts are made on the premises, including the unforgettable Hawaiian tropical fruit-almond cake, made with fruit soaked in brandy for 30 days. *Rte. 6, tel. 902/672–2003. MC, V. Open daily mid-May–Oct., weekends the rest of the year.*

Lodging

Prince Edward Island offers a variety of accommodations at a variety of prices, from luxury hotels to moderately priced motels, cottages, and lodges, to farms that take guests. Lodgings on the north coast in summer should be booked early, especially if you're planning a long stay.

Highly recommended lodgings in each price category are indicated by a star ★.

Category	Cost*
Very Expensive	over $75
Expensive	$55–$75
Moderate	$40–$54
Inexpensive	under $40

All prices are for a standard double room, excluding 10% provincial sales tax and 7% GST.

Brackley Beach
Very Expensive
★

Shaw's Hotel and Cottages. Each room is unique in this 1860s hotel, with antique furnishings, floral-print wallpapers, and hardwood floors. Half the cottages have fireplaces. This country elegance doesn't come cheap—Shaw's is one of the most expensive hotels on the island. Guests can choose to include in their room rate a home-cooked breakfast and dinner in the Shaw's dining room (*see* Dining, above). *Rte. 15, C0A 2H0, tel. 902/672–2022. 40 units, including 18 cottages and 2 suites. Facilities: cocktail bar, sailboats, windsurfing, beach nearby. AE, MC, V. Closed late-Sept.–May.*

Cavendish
Expensive

Bay Vista Inn. This clean, friendly motel caters to families. Parents can sit on the outdoor deck and admire the New London Bay panorama while keeping an eye on their children in the motel's large playground. Almost all of the rooms have views of the bay. Fiddles 'n Vittles is a great place to eat with the family (*see* Dining, above). *RR1, Breadalbane, C0A 1E0; in winter, RR1, North Wiltshire, C0A 1Y0, tel. 902/963–2225. 30 units, including 2 motel efficiencies. Facilities: restaurant, outdoor heated pool, playground, boating, deep-sea fishing, golf nearby. AE, MC, V. Closed late Sept.–mid-June.*

Charlottetown
Very Expensive

Best Western MacLauchlan's Motel. This is one of the many good motels in the Best Western chain. Two convenient apartment suites have a bedroom, living room, kitchen, and bathroom. *238 Grafton St., C1A 1L5, tel. 902/892–2461. 149 units, including 2 suites. Facilities: dining room, lounge, indoor pool, sauna, Jacuzzi, laundry facilities. AE, DC, MC, V.*

★ **The Charlottetown.** This classic five-story, redbrick hotel with white pillars and a circular driveway is just two blocks from the center of Charlottetown. The rooms and public areas offer the latest amenities but retain the hotel's old-fashioned flavor, with well-detailed, antique-reproduction furnishings. *Kent and Pownal Sts., C1A 7K4, tel. 902/894–7371. 109 rooms, including 2 suites. Facilities: dining room, lounge with entertainment, indoor pool, sauna, whirlpool, parking. AE, DC, MC, V.*

Dundee Arms Motel and Inn. Depending on your mood, you can choose to stay in either a 1960s motel or a 1904 inn. The motel is simple, modern, and neat; the inn is homey and furnished with brass and antiques. The Griffin Room, the inn's dining room, serves fine French cuisine (*see* Dining, above). Continental breakfast is included in motel and inn rates. *200 Pownal St., C1A 3W8, tel. 902/892–2496. 18 rooms, including 2 suites. Facilities: restaurant, pub. MC, V.*

Inn on the Hill. This hotel is comfortable and convenient: Rooms are contemporary and spacious, and the inn is near the center of Charlottetown. *150 Euston St., Box 1720, C1A 7N4, tel. 902/894–8572. 48 units, including 8 suites. Facilities: dining room, lounge, parking. AE, DC, MC, V.*

★ **Prince Edward Hotel and Convention Centre.** Two-thirds of the rooms in this 10-story hotel overlook the newly developed Charlottetown waterfront. Part of the Canadian Pacific chain of hotels and resorts, the Prince Edward has all the comforts and luxuries of a first-rate hotel and conference center—from Jacuzzis in some suites to a grand ballroom. Guest rooms are modern and decorated in warm pastels. The lobby is a bright, open, two-story atrium complete with a waterfall above the front desk. *18 Queen St., Box 2170, C1A 8B9, tel. 902/566–2222 or 800/828–7447. 211 rooms, including 33 suites. Facilities: 3 restaurants, lounge with nightly entertainment, heated indoor pool, whirlpool, sauna, Nautilus equipment. AE, DC, MC, V.*

Moderate **Duchess of Kent Inn.** This turreted Victorian bed-and-breakfast is packed with antiques, even in the bedrooms. It's within walking distance of Charlottetown's major sites including the Convention Centre where *Anne of Green Gables*—usually just known as "Anne"—is put on every year. *218 Kent St., Charlottetown, C1A 1P2, tel. 902/566–5826. 8 rooms share 5 baths. Facilities: guest kitchen, bicycle storage. MC, V. Closed Dec.–May.*

Inexpensive **Court Bed and Breakfast.** In a residential area 2 kilometers (1.2 miles) from the center of town, this two-story bed-and-breakfast with a welcoming red door offers truly reasonable rates. You get a large, simple, comfortable room and a full, hearty breakfast, including ham, eggs, bacon, muffins, and fresh fruits in season. *68 Hutchinson Ct., Charlottetown, C1A 8H7, tel. 902/894–5871. 2 rooms with shared bath. No credit cards. Closed early Sept.–May 1.*

Sherwood Motel. This is a small, clean, family-oriented motel about 5 kilometers (3.1 mi) north of downtown Charlottetown on Rte. 15. The friendly owners offer help in reserving tickets and planning day trips. Don't be daunted by the Sherwood's proximity to the airport—it sees very little traffic. *RR 1, Winslow C0A 2H0, tel. 902/892–2622. 30 rooms with bath; animals accepted. Facilities: kitchenettes (22 rooms), cable TV. MC, V.*

Southport Motel. This motel has cozy cabins in addition to the regular motel building. There's nothing fancy about the Southport, but rooms are clean and quiet. Most have a pleasant view of the Hillsboro River and Charlottetown. *20 Stratford Rd., Charlottetown C1A 7B7, tel. 902/569–2287. 32 rooms with bath, 26 have kitchenettes. 6 small cabins each with 2 double beds, and 3 larger cabins with 2 full bedrooms each. Facilities: playground, private beach on river, trailer park with 84 hookups. MC, V.*

Grand Tracadie **Dalvay-by-the-Sea.** Just within the borders of the Prince
Very Expensive Edward Island National Park, this Victorian house was built in
★ 1896 as a private summer home. Now a popular inn and restau-

rant, Dalvay-by-the-Sea offers elegant but homey rooms furnished with original antiques and reproductions. Guests can sip drinks or tea on the porch while admiring the inn's gardens, Dalvay Lake, or the nearby beach. Breakfasts and dinners in the dining room, included in the room rates, are exceptional (*see* Dining, above). *Rte. 6, near Dalvay Beach. Box 8, York, C0A 1P0, tel. 902/672–2048, or 902/672–2546 in winter. 31 rooms in main house and 2 cottages. Facilities: restaurant, lounge, 2 tennis courts, driving range, canoes, rowboats, windsurfing. AE, MC, V. Closed mid-Sept.–mid-June.*

Montague
Moderate

Lobster Shanty North. With roses growing outside the windows of its weathered-wood facade, and old fishnets draped around the barn-board walls of the dining room, this hotel is truly charming. All rooms have picture windows and open onto a deck overlooking the wandering Montague River. *Main St., Montague, Box 158, C0A 1R0, tel. 902/838–2463. 11 rooms. Facilities: restaurant, lounge, golf, clam-digging, swimming nearby. AE, MC, V.*

O'Leary
Very Expensive

Rodd's Mill River Resort and Conference Centre. With activities ranging from night skiing and tobogganing to golfing, this is truly an all-season resort. With so much to do here, don't forget to sightsee. Ask about family-package weekends, offered year-round. *Box 399, C0B 1V0, tel. 902/859–3555. 90 rooms including 3 suites. Facilities: dining room, 2 bars, 2 heated indoor pools, golf course, pro shop, tennis court, 2 squash courts, fitness center with whirlpool and sauna, games room, gift shop, canoeing, windsurfing, bike rental, ice-skating rink, toboggan run, cross-country skiing. AE, MC, V. Closed Nov.–early Dec., Apr.*

Summerside
Expensive–
Very Expensive

Best Western Linkletter Inn. This motel with standard modern comforts is conveniently located within walking distance of Summerside's shops and beaches. *311 Market St., C1N 1K8, tel. 902/436–2157. 107 rooms, including 2 suites. Facilities: restaurant, lounge, golf, tennis, beach nearby. AE, DC, D, MC, V.*

Moderate–Expensive

Quality Inn Garden of the Gulf. Close to downtown Summerside, this motel is a clean and convenient place to stay. The nine-hole golf course on the property slopes to Bedeque Bay. *618 Water St. E, C1N 2V5, tel. 902/436–2295. 83 rooms, including 6 suites. Facilities: restaurant, coffee shop, lounge, heated outdoor pool, 9-hole golf course. AE, DC, MC, V.*

Moderate

Glade Motor Inn and Cottages. Conveniently located 10 minutes from the Borden Ferry Terminal, this property has comfortable if generic motel rooms as well as one- and two-bedroom cottages and one four-bedroom "house" that can accommodate up to eight people. What's different about the place is that it is set on a 300-acre farm, with horseback riding and nature trails. Kids get free rides in the corral. *Box 1387, C1N 4K2, tel. 902/436–5564. 33 units. Facilities: restaurant, lounge, heated outdoor pool, horseback riding, nature trails. AE, MC, V. Closed late-Sept.–mid-June.*

The Arts

The highlights of the island's theater season are the productions of the **Charlottetown Festival,** which take place from June through October at the Confederation Centre of the Arts. The perennial favorite is *Anne of Green Gables*. Special art exhibitions are presented in the center's gallery, one of Canada's premier museums. The permanent collection features the country's largest assemblage of paintings by Robert Harris (1848–1919), Canada's foremost portrait artist. For information and tickets to the festival, contact the Confederation Centre of the Arts (Box 848, Charlottetown, PEI C1A 7L9, tel. 902/566–2464; box office, 902/566–1267).

The **King's Playhouse** (tel. 902/652–2053) in Georgetown, 50 kilometers (30 miles) east of Charlottetown, offers professional repertory theater from June through early September, as does the **Victoria Playhouse** (tel. 902/566–4267) in Victoria, a half hour's drive west of Charlottetown.

Concerts and musical festivals abound on the island, especially in summer. Live traditional Celtic music, with fiddling and step-dancing, can be heard almost any day of the week. Best bets: the outdoor fiddle festival at Rollo Bay in late July (tel. 902/368–5555), Monday night ceilidhs at the Benevolent Irish Hall (tel. 902/892–2367) in Charlottetown, and the Sunday concerts of classical, sacred, and traditional music at St. Mary's Church (tel. 902/836–3733) in Indian River, between Charlottetown and Summerside.

14 New Brunswick

*by Colleen
Whitney
Thompson*

New Brunswick is where the great Canadian forest, sliced by sweeping river valleys and modern highways, meets the sea. It's an old place in New World terms, and the remains of a turbulent past are still in evidence in some of its quiet nooks. Near Moncton, for instance, bees gather nectar and wild strawberries perfume the air of the grassy slopes of Fort Beausejour, where, in 1755, one of the last battles for possession of Acadia took place—the English finally overcoming the French. The dual heritage of New Brunswick (35% of its population is Acadian French) provides added spice. If you decide to stay in both Acadian and Loyalist regions, a trip to New Brunswick can seem like two vacations in one.

More than half the province is surrounded by coastline—the rest nestles into Québec and Maine, creating slightly schizophrenic attitudes in border towns. The dramatic Bay of Fundy, which has the highest tides in the world, sweeps up the coast of Maine, around the enchanting Fundy Isles at the southern tip of New Brunswick and on up the province's rough and intriguing south coast. To the north and east, the gentle, warm Gulf Stream washes quiet beaches.

New Brunswick is still largely unsettled—85 percent of the province is forested lands. Inhabitants have chosen the easily accessible area around rivers, ocean, and lakes, leaving most of the interior to the pulp companies. For years this Cinderella province has been virtually ignored by tourists who whiz through to better known Atlantic destinations. New Brunswick's residents can't seem to decide whether this makes them unhappy. Money is important in the economically depressed maritime area where younger generations have traditionally left home for higher-paying jobs in Ontario and "The West." But no one wishes to lose the special characteristics of this still unspoiled province by the sea.

This attitude is a blessing in disguise to motorists who leave major highways to explore 2,240 kilometers (1,400 miles) of spectacular seacoast, pure inland streams, pretty towns and historical cities. The custom of hospitality is so much a part of New Brunswick nature that tourists are perceived more as welcome visitors than paying guests. Even cities often retain a bit of naiveté. It makes for a charming vacation, but don't be deceived by ingenuous attitudes. Most residents are products of excellent school and university systems, generally travel widely, live in modern cities, and are well versed in world affairs.

Essential Information

Important Addresses and Numbers

Tourist
Information

Department of Economic Development and Tourism (Box 12345, Fredericton E3B 5C3, tel. 506/453–3984 or 800/561–0123; in New Brunswick, 800/442–4422) can provide information on the 15 provincial tourist bureaus and municipal information centers throughout the province. Also helpful are information services of major cities: **Fredericton** (tel. 506/452–9500); **Moncton** (tel. 506/853–3333); and **Saint John** (tel. 506/658–2990).

Emergencies

Dial 911 for medical emergencies and police.

Hospital **Dr. Everett Chalmers Hospital** (Priestman St., Fredericton, tel. 506/452–5400); **Moncton City Hospital** (135 Macbeath Ave., Moncton, tel. 506/857–5111); **Dr. Georges Dumont Hospital**, (330 Archibald St., Moncton, tel. 506/858–3232); **Saint John Regional Hospital** (Tucker Park Rd., Saint John, tel. 506/648–6000).

Arriving and Departing by Plane

Canadian Airlines International (tel. 800/426–7000) and **Air Canada** (tel. 800/776–3000) both have flights into Saint John, Fredericton, and Moncton. **Air Nova** and **Air Atlantic** are regional carriers that fly between Montréal, Toronto, and Boston, and within the Atlantic provinces.

Arriving and Departing

By Car Ferry There are car ferries from Prince Edward Island and Nova Scotia. **Marine Atlantic** (tel. 902/794–7203) has a car-and-passenger ferry from Digby, Nova Scotia, which takes 2½ hours. For reservations in the United States, call 800/341–7981; in Maine, tel. 800/432–7344.

By Train Regular **Via Rail** passenger service from Moncton to Montréal and Halifax connects via ferry to Prince Edward Island and Newfoundland. The rail line does not pass through Fredericton, but buses take passengers from Fredericton Junction the last 30 miles to the city.

By Bus **SMT** (tel. 506/458–6009) within the province connects with most major bus lines.

Getting Around

By Car New Brunswick has an excellent highway system with numerous facilities. The only map you'll need is the free one given out at the tourist information centers listed above. Major entry points are at St. Stephen, Houlton, Edmundston, and Cape Tormentine from Prince Edward Island, and Aulac from Nova Scotia.

Guided Tours

Boat Tours Harbor tours are offered in Saint John by **Partridge Island Tours** (tel. 506/693–2598) and **DMK Marine Tours** (tel. 506/672–3944).

In Fredericton **Pioneer Princess** (tel. 506/488–5588) embarks on riverboat tours and dinner cruises from the Lighthouse.

City Tours **Heritage Tour Guide Service** (856 George St., Fredericton E3B 1K7, tel. 506/459–5950) provides step-on guides for bus tours of Fredericton.

The **Calithumpians** theater company offers guides dressed in 18th-century costumes for free historical walks from City Hall (Queen St., tel. 506/459–1975).

In Saint John free guided walking tours begin in Market Square at Barbours General Store. For information call the Saint John Tourist and Convention Center (tel. 506/658–2990).

Special-interest   More than 240 species of seabirds nest on Grand Manan Island, and the island is a paradise for painters, nature photographers, and hikers, not to mention whale-watchers. Any of these activities can be arranged by calling **Tourism New Brunswick** at 800/561–0123. **Covered Bridge Bicycle Tours** (Box 693, Main Post Office, Saint John E2L 4B3, tel. 506/849–9028) offers bike tours. **East Coast Adventures** (Box 6713, Station A, Saint John, E2L 4S2, tel. 506/648–9462) offers guided hiking in the Fundy area.

Exploring New Brunswick

Our exploration of New Brunswick is broken down into four areas: a tour of the city of Fredericton, a tour of the Saint John Valley ending at the city of Saint John, a tour of the Fundy Coast, and a jog north to the sunny Acadian Peninsula.

Highlights for First-time Visitors

Acadian Village, Grand Anse, Tour 4: Moncton and the Acadian Peninsula

Beaverbrook Art Gallery, Tour 1: Fredericton

Campobello Island, Tour 3: The Fundy Coast

Fundy National Park, Tour 3: The Fundy Coast

Kings Landing, Prince William, Tour 1: Fredericton

Kouchibouquac National Park, Acadian Peninsula, Tour 4: The Acadian Peninsula

Market Square and Market Slip, Saint John, Tour 2: Saint John River Valley

Moncton's Tidal Bore and Magnetic Hill, Tour 4: Moncton and the Acadian Peninsula

Tour 1: Fredericton

Numbers in the margin correspond to points of interest on the New Brunswick and Fredericton maps.

The small inland city of Fredericton spreads itself on a broad point of land jutting into the Saint John River. Its predecessor, the early French settlement of Ste-Anne's Point, was established in 1642, during the reign of the French governor, Villebon, who made his headquarters at the junction of the Nashwaak and the Saint John rivers. Settled by Loyalists and named for Frederick, second son of George III, the city serves as the seat of government for New Brunswick's 710,900 residents. From the first town plan, the wealthy and scholarly Loyalists set out to create a gracious and beautiful place, and thus even before the establishment of the University of New Brunswick, in 1785, the town served as a center for "liberal arts and sciences."

Fredericton's streets are shaded by leafy plumes of ancient elms. Downtown Queen Street runs parallel with the river, and its blocks enclose historic sites and attractions. Most major sites are within walking distance.

❶ The **Military Compound** (including officer's quarters, parade grounds, guardhouse, and enlisted men's barracks) extends two blocks along Queen Street. The buildings have been restored and are partly open to the public. Redcoats stand guard and act as guides; in summer a changing-of-the-guard ceremony takes place at 11 and 7. *Queen St. at Carleton St., tel. 506/*

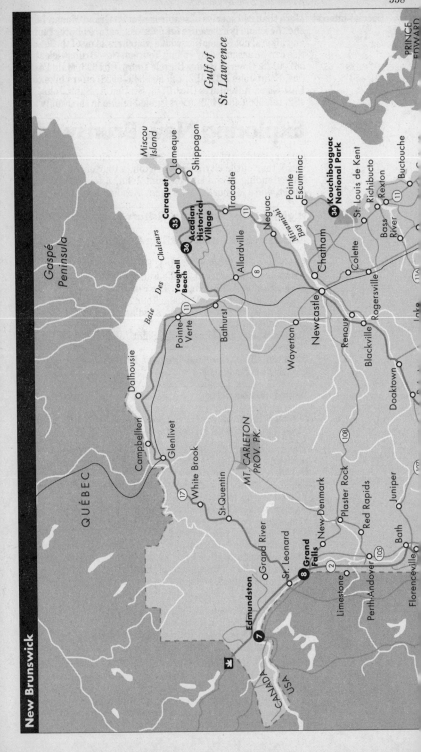

New Brunswick

Gulf of
St. Lawrence

PRINCE
EDWARD

Miscou
Island

Lameque
Shippagon

Caraquet

35

36 Acadian
Historical
Village

Tracadie

Neguac

Pointe
Escuminac

34 Kouchibouguac
National Park

St. Louis de Kent
Richibucto

Rexton

Buctouche

Youghall
Beach

Allardville

(8)

Miramichi
Bay

Chatham

Colette

Bass
River

(11)

Baie

Des

Chaleurs

Pointe-
Verte

(11)

Bathurst

Newcastle

Rogersville

Gaspé
Peninsula

Dalhousie

Wayerton

Renous

Blackville

Lake

(11)

Campbellton

Glenlivet

White Brook

MT. CARLETON
PROV. PK.

Doaktown

(108)

QUÉBEC

St-Quentin

(17)

New-Denmark

Plaster Rock

Red Rapids

Juniper

Grand River

St. Leonard

8 Grand
Falls

(2)

Edmundston

7

Limestone

Perth-Andover

Bath

(105)

Florenceville

CANADA

USA

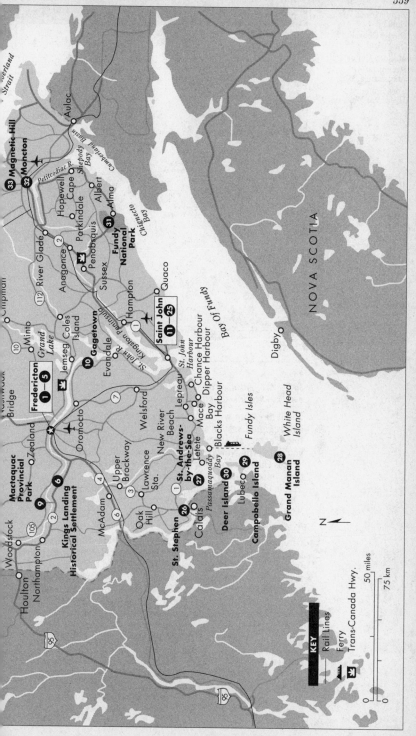

KEY

Rail Lines

Ferry

Trans-Canada Hwy.

N

NOVA SCOTIA

Bay Of Fundy

Fundy National Park

Mactaquac Provincial Park

Kings Landing Historical Settlement

Saint John 11—25

Fredericton 1—5

Gagetown 10

St. Andrews-by-the-Sea 27

St. Stephen 26

Deer Island 30

Campobello Island 29

Grand Manan Island 28

White Head Island

Fundy Isles

Passamaquoddy Bay

Digby

Magnetic Hill 33

Moncton 32

Aulac

Hopewell Cape 31

Parkindale

Albert

Alma

Petitcodiac R.

Shepody Bay

Cumberland Basin

Chignecto Bay

Sussex

Anagance

Penobsquis

River Glade

Chipman

Minto

Grand Lake

Coles Island

Jemseg

Evandale

Welsford

Hampton

Quaco

Lepreau

Mace

Chance Harbour

Dipper Harbour

Blacks Harbour

Beaver Harbour

Pennfield

New River Beach

Lawrence Sta.

Upper Brockway

Oak Hill

Calais

Lubec

McAdam

Zealand

Oromocto

Woodstock

Houlton

Northampton

Hartland Bridge

Kingston Peninsula

St. John R.

St. John Harbour

Norwood

Petitcodiac

Westmorland Strait

50 miles

75 km

0

0

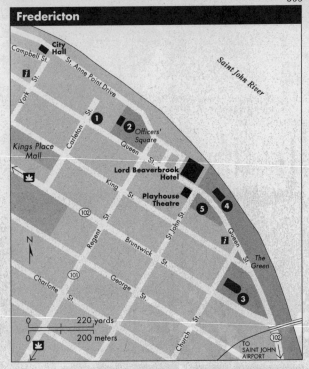

453–3747. Admission free. Open June 15–Sept. 4, daily 10–5, Fri. 10–9. Closed Sept. 5–June 14.

You'll have fun with the scintillating displays of works of local and regional artists and artisans in the small **National Exhibition Center,** also located in the Military Compound. Upstairs you'll find the New Brunswick Sports Hall of Fame, which celebrates the surprising array of locals who have made sports history, most notably, Ron Turcotte, who won horse racing's Triple Crown on the immortal Secretariate. *503 Queen St., tel. 506/453–3747. Admission free. Both museums open May 1– Sept. 10, daily 10–5, Fri. 10–9; Sept. 3–Apr. 30, Tues.–Fri. noon–4:30; Sat. 10–5, Sun. 1–5.*

❷ Officer's Quarters houses the **York-Sunbury Historical Museum,** displaying mementos of the past, including Indian artifacts (the local tribes were the Micmacs and the Malicetes) and replicas of early Acadian rooms, 19th-century Fredericton homes, and area history. It also contains the shellacked remains of one of Fredericton's legends, the puzzling Coleman Frog. This giant frog, allegedly discovered in nearby Killarney Lake by late hotelier Fred Coleman, supposedly weighed 42 pounds soaking wet at the time of its death (by a dynamite charge set by unorthodox fishermen). Coleman had the frog stuffed and displayed it for years in the lobby of his hotel. Take a look and judge for yourself—the frog just keeps on smiling. *Officer's Sq., Queen St., tel. 506/455–6041. Admission: $1 adults, 50¢ senior citizens and students, $2.50 families. Open*

May–Oct., Mon., Wed., Fri., and weekends 10–6, Tues. and Thurs. 10–9; in winter, Mon., Wed., Fri. 11–3.

Just a block or so east along the same street, at the intersection where Queen Street becomes Waterloo Row, you'll come to the **❸** **Christ Church Cathedral,** one of Fredericton's prides. Completed in 1853, the gray stone building is an excellent example of decorated Gothic architecture and the first new cathedral foundation built on British soil since the Norman Conquest. Inside you'll see a clock known as "Big Ben's little brother," the test-run for London's famous timepiece, designed by Lord Grimthorpe.

The late Lord Beaverbrook, former New Brunswick resident and multimillionaire British peer and newspaper magnate, showered gifts upon his native province. Near the cathedral **❹** you'll find the **Beaverbrook Art Gallery,** displaying works by many of New Brunswick's noted artists. Salvador Dali's gigantic canvas *Santiago el Grande* is worth more than a passing glance. There are also canvases by Reynolds, Turner, Hogarth, Gainsborough, the Canadian Group of Seven, and even Andy Warhol. The gallery has the largest collection in any institution of the works of Cornelius Krieghoff, famed Canadian landscape painter of the early 1800s. *703 Queen St., tel. 506/ 458–8545. Admission: $3 adults, $2 senior citizens, $1 students. Open Sun., Mon. noon–8, Tues., Wed. 10–8, Thurs., Fri., Sat. 10–5; in fall and winter, Tues.–Sat. 10–5, Sun.– Mon, noon–5.*

Beside the gallery sits **The Playhouse** (686 Queen St., tel. 506/ 458–8344), a gift of the Beaverbrook and Dunn Foundation to the city and province. It is the home of the professional **Theatre New Brunswick,** whose major season runs from September through May.

Directly across the street from the gallery is the 1880 **❺** **Provincial Legislature.** In its library, past the freestanding spiral staircase, you'll find a rare copy of the Domesday Book, the Western world's first census, commissioned by William the Conquerer in 1085. Also to be found here is a four-volume 1834 set of the priceless king-size Audubon bird books, more than 3 feet high, containing 435 hand-colored pictures. *Queen St., tel. 506/453–2527. Admission free. Open June 15–Labor Day, daily 9–9; Sept. 3–June 14, Mon.–Fri. 9–4.*

Continue east on Waterloo Row (Rte. 102), turn south at University Avenue, and you'll arrive at the **University of New Brunswick** campus. Be prepared to climb—the buildings are scattered over a fairly steep hill. Established in 1783, and thus ancient by Canadian standards, it was originally called the College of New Brunswick, and later Kings College.

Tour 2: The Saint John River Valley to Saint John

To understand New Brunswick's background and history, visit **❻** **Kings Landing,** located about 23 miles west of Fredericton on the Trans-Canada Highway. This reconstructed village—55 buildings, including homes, inn, forge, store, church, school, working farms, and sawmill—illustrates life in the central Saint John River valley between 1790 and 1870. Winding country lanes, creaking wagons, old houses, and freshly baked bread pull you back a century or more. The costumed staff is friendly and informative. The Tap Room of Kings Head Inn is a congenial spot to try a draft of cold beer or a mug of frosty cider; the restaurant upstairs serves tasty, old-fashioned traveler's fare. After lunch you can head for the barn that houses the Kings Theatre, which mounts lighthearted entertainment from "mellerdrama" to a humorous take-off on Chekhov. *Box 522, Fredericton, tel. 506/363–5805. Admission: $7 adults, $5 senior citizens, $4 students, $14 families. Open June–Aug., daily 10–6; Sept.–mid-Oct., daily 10–5.*

The Saint John River forms 75 miles of the border with Maine and rolls down to Saint John, New Brunswick's largest and Canada's oldest city. Gentle hills of rich farmland and the blue sweep of the water make this a pretty drive. The Trans-Canada Highway (Highway 2) follows the banks of the river for most of its winding, 403-kilometer (250-mile) course.

At the northern end of the valley, near the border with Québec, you will find yourself in the mythical Republic of Madawaska. In the early 1800s the narrow wedge of land was coveted by Québec on one side and New Brunswick on the other; the United States claimed it as well. Seeking to retain it for New Brunswick, Governor Sir Thomas Carleton found it easy to settle with Québec. He rolled dice all night with the governor of British North America at Québec, who happened to be his brother. Sir Thomas won at dawn—by one point. Settling with the Americans was more difficult. The border had always been disputed, and even the lumbermen engaged in combat. Finally, in 1842, the British flag was hoisted over Madawaska county. One old-timer, tired of being asked to which country he belonged, replied, "I am a citizen of the Republic of Madawaska." So began the republic, which exists today with its own flag (an independent eagle on a field of white) and a coat of arms.

7 **Edmundston,** the unofficial capital of Madawaska, has always depended on the wealth of the deep forest around it. Even today, Edmundston looks to the Fraser Company paper mill as the major source of employment. It was in these woods that the legend of Paul Bunyan was born. Tales spread to Maine and even to the West Coast. The Foire Brayonne festival (which includes lumberjack competitions, folk dancing, handcraft exhibits, and pancake-eating contests) is a popular event, held annually, during the last week of July. In winter the whole province enjoys skiing on the slopes of Mt. Farlagne.

8 About 50 kilometers (30 miles) downriver, at **Grand Falls,** the Saint John throws itself over a high cliff, squeezes through a narrow rocky gorge, and emerges as a wider river. The result is a magnificent cascade, whose force has worn strange round wells in the rocky bed—some as much as 16 feet in circumference and 30 feet deep. Take the Gorge Walk ($2 charge) where you'll see the holes and the magnificent stream up close. According to Indian legend, a young maiden named Malabeam led her Iroquois captors to their deaths over the foaming cataract rather than guide them to her village. Local history is depicted at the **Grand Falls Historical Museum.** *209 Sheriff St., tel. 506/ 473–3667. Admission free. Open July–Aug., Mon.–Sat. 9–5, Sun. 2–5; Sept.–June, by appointment.*

Although Grand Falls is largely French-speaking, English becomes more prevalent as you move down the Saint John River valley. Stop in **Florenceville** for a look at the small but reputable Andrew and Laura McCain Gallery, which has launched the career of many a New Brunswick artist.

The Trans-Canada Highway is intriguingly scenic, but if you're looking for less-crowded highways and typical small communities cross the river to Route 105 at Hartland, via the **longest covered bridge** in the world—1,282 feet in length.

If you prefer to stay on the Trans-Canada Highway you'll come to quiet **Woodstock** (population 5,068), home of bluegrass festivals, not rock concerts. Named for a novel by Sir Walter Scott, the town is most lively during its Old Home Week celebrations, in July, although harness racing at Connell Park, with pari-mutuel betting, is a big draw all summer. The **Old Courthouse** (built in 1833)—once a coaching stop, a social hall, a political meeting place, and the seat of justice for the area—has been carefully restored.

Time Out   Between Woodstock and Meductic, look for good German food at **Heino's Restaurant,** in the John Gyles Motel (junction Route 2 and Trans-Canada Highway).

❾ Mactaquac Provincial Park. Mactaquac is a pond created by the flooding of the upper Saint John River as far up as Woodstock, due to the building of the hydroelectric dam. Although there are several privately owned campgrounds in the area, cars line up sometimes all night to claim an empty site in the morning. *Hwy. 105 and Mactaquac Dam, tel. 506/363–3011. 300 campsites, supervised recreation, 2 beaches, 2 marinas, 18-hole golf course, and lodge with dining room. Admission: $3 per vehicle summer, free in off-season. Open May 15–Sept. 2, 24 hrs; Sept. 2–Nov. 30, 8–6; Dec. 1–May 14, 8–11.*

From Fredericton to Saint John you have a choice of two routes. Route 7 cuts away from the river to run straight south for its fast 68 miles. Route 102 leads along the Saint John River through engaging communities. You make your decision at **Oromocto,** the site of the Canadian Armed Forces Base, **Camp Gagetown** (not to be confused with the pretty town of Gagetown farther down river), the largest military base in Canada (Prince Charles completed his helicopter training here). An interesting military museum within the base is open to the public. *Tel. 506/422–2630. Admission free. Open July 1– Aug. 30, weekdays 9–5, weekends 12–5; Sept. 1–June 30, weekdays 8:30–4, closed weekends.*

❿ Gagetown, one of New Brunswick's pleasant historic communities, bustles with artisans' studios and the summer sailors who tie up at the marina. The gingerbread-trimmed **Tilley House** takes you back to Canada's beginnings. Once the home of Sir Leonard Tilley, one of the Fathers of Confederation, it is now a museum. *Front St., tel. 506/488–2966. Admission: $1 adults, 25¢ students. Open June–Sept. 15, daily 10–5.*

From Gagetown you can ferry to Jemseg and continue to **Grand Lake Provincial Park** (tel. 506/385–2919), which offers freshwater swimming off sandy beaches. At Evandale you can ferry to Belleisle Bay and the beautiful **Kingston Peninsula,** with its mossy Loyalist graveyards and pretty churches.

As you travel south you'll begin to get a feeling for how old New ⓫ Brunswick really is, and nowhere more so than in **Saint John.** It

was the first incorporated city in Canada and has that weather–
beaten quality common to so many antique seaport communities. Although sometimes termed a blue-collar town because so
many of its residents work for Irving Oil, its genteel Loyalist
heritage lingers; you sense it in its grand old buildings, the ladies' teas at the old Union Club, and the beautifully restored
downtown harbor district.

The city has spawned many of the province's major artists—
Jack Humphrey, Millar Brittain, Fred Ross—along with such
Hollywood notables as Louis B. Mayer, Donald Sutherland,
and Walter Pidgeon. There's also a large Irish population that
emerges in a jubilant Irish Festival every March. In July costumed residents re-enact the landing of the Loyalists during
Saint John's Loyalist Days.

In 1604 two Frenchmen, Samuel de Champlain and Sieur de
Monts, landed here on St. John the Baptist Day to trade with
the natives. Nearly two centuries later, in May of 1785, 3,000
Loyalists escaping from the Revolutionary War poured off a
ship to found a city amid the rocks and forests. From those beginnings Saint John has emerged as a thriving industrial port.

Up until a few years ago the buildings around Saint John's waterfront huddled together in forlorn dilapidation, their facades
crumbling and blurred by a century of grime. A recent surge of
civic pride sparked a major renovation project that reclaimed
old warehouses as part of an enchanting waterfront development.

*Numbers in the margin correspond to points of interest on the
Downtown Saint John and Greater Saint John maps.*

⑫ You can easily explore Saint John's town center and harbor area
on foot. Get your bearings on **King Street,** the town's old main
street, whose sidewalks are paved with red brick and lit with
⑬ old-fashioned lamps. King Street connects **Market Slip** on the
waterfront with King Square at the center of town.

At Market Slip, where the Loyalists landed in 1783, and the ad-
⑭ joining **Market Square** you can while away a morning among the
shops, historic displays, and cafés (some with outdoor dining in
summer). Market Slip is the site of **Barbour's General Store**
(tel. 506/658–2939), a fully stocked 19th-century shop redolent
of the past: Inside the scents of tobacco, pickles, smoked fish,
and peppermint sticks mingle with the tangy, unforgettable
aroma of dulse, the edible seaweed. Beside the store is a 19th-
century red school house, now a tourist information center, and
over toward Market Square is the *Ocean Hawk II,* an old tug-
boat whose deck is great for watching sunsets. Skywalks and
underground passages lead from Market Square to City Hall,
the new Delta Hotel, and Brunswick Square, an adjoining
shopping mall.

Stroll up King Street to Germain Street, turn left, and walk up
⑮ to the block-long **Old City Market,** built in 1876, which offers a
variety of temptations, including red fresh-cooked lobster,
great cheeses, dulse, and other inexpensive snacking along
with much friendly chatter.

⑯ The imposing **Old Loyalist House,** built in 1810 by Daniel David
Merritt, a wealthy Loyalist merchant, is distinguished by its
authentic period furniture and eight fireplaces. *120 Union St.,*

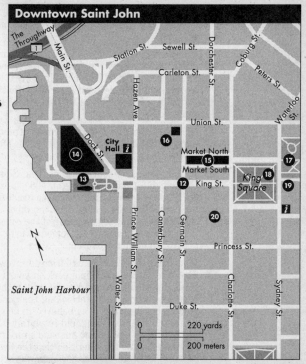

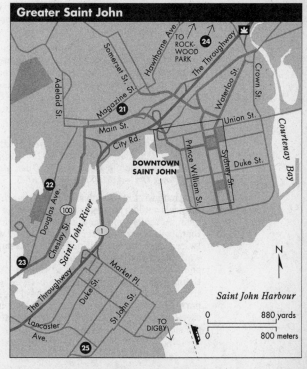

*tel. 506/652–3590. Admission: $2 adults, 25¢ children. Open
Mon.–Sat. 10–5, Sun. 2–5, or by appointment.*

Follow Union Street away from the harbor to Sydney Street
❶❼ and turn right to visit the **Old Loyalist Burial Grounds.** At one
❶❽ corner, in adjacent **King Square,** you'll find a strange mass of
metal on the ground. It is actually a great lump of melted stock
from a neighboring hardware store that was demolished in
Saint John's Great Fire of 1877, in which 115 buildings were destroyed.

❶❾ At the corner of King and Sydney streets is the **Old Courthouse.** Its spiral staircase, built of tons of unsupported stone,
ascends seemingly by miracle for three stories.

❷⓿ Walk around the south side of King Square to visit **Trinity
Church** (115 Charlotte St., tel. 506/693–8558). It dates from
1877, when it was rebuilt after the great fire. Inside, over the
west door, note the coat of arms, a symbol of the monarchy, rescued from the council chamber of the colony at Massachusetts
Bay. The coat of arms was deemed a worthy refugee and given a
place of honor in the church.

If you have a car, drive north from downtown on Prince William
❷❶ Street to Main Street; in a park on your right you'll find **Fort
Howe** (Rockland Rd. and Magazine St.). The reconstructed fortress sits atop a cliff overlooking the harbor and affords fine
views from its walls. It is believed to be near the site of Fort
LaTour, a French stronghold resolutely defended by Madame
La Tour from her absent husband's fur-trading rival. Finally
surrendering on the condition that the lives of her men would
be spared, the unfortunate woman was betrayed and forced to
watch them all put to death. She died shortly after, of a broken
heart it is said—a romantic fate befitting her former profession
as star of the Paris stage.

Main Street soon crosses Douglas Avenue; turn left to reach
❷❷ two of the city's most notable attractions. First is the **New
Brunswick Museum.** The first museum to be built in Canada, it
is still recognized as one of the best of its size. You'll see the
figurehead from the bad-luck ship built in Saint John's famous
shipyards—a ship that is said to have killed a man on every voyage. Along with impressive artifacts, there are costumes, a collection of dolls, some Egyptian relics, an impressive art
gallery, and native animals displayed in natural surroundings.
*277 Douglas Ave., tel. 506/693–1196. Admission: $2 adults,
50¢ students, senior citizens free. Open May–mid-Oct., daily
10–5; mid-Oct.–Apr., Tues.–Sun. 10–5.*

❷❸ Continue west on Douglas Avenue to reach the **Reversing Falls
Rapids,** touted by all tourist brochures as a sight no one should
miss. Actually, you *should* see it, though less for its beauty
than its interest: It's a series of rapids and whirlpools at which,
twice a day, the strong Fundy Tides attempt to push the river
water back upstream. When the tide ebbs, the river once again
pours over the rock ledges and the rapids appear to reverse
themselves. A pulp mill on the bank is less scenic, and the
stench it occasionally sends out is one of the less-than-charming
parts of a visit. To learn more about the phenomenon, see the
excellent free film shown in the tourist information center on
the site.

㉔ Cherry Brook Zoo, at the very northern tip of Rockwood Park, houses Siberian tigers, camels, and other exotic species. Tel. 506/634-1440. *Open daily 10–dusk. $2 adults, $1.50 senior citizens and students.*

Cross the river on Bridge Road to **West Saint John.** Make a right on Lancaster Avenue and proceed to Charlotte Street, where ㉕ you can't miss the **Carleton Martello Tower.** Like Fort Howe, this is a great place to survey the harbor. The tower was built in 1810 as a precaution against American attack. Costumed guides point out 8-foot-thick walls and pose for photographs. *Charlotte Ext. W, tel. 506/636-4011. Admission free. Open July–Aug., 9–8; Sept.–June, 9–6.*

Tour 3: The Fundy Coast

Numbers in the margin correspond to points of interest on the New Brunswick map.

Bordering the chilly and powerfully tidal Bay of Fundy is some of New Brunswick's loveliest coastline. A tour of the region will take you from the border town of St. Stephen, through tiny fishing villages and past rocky coves, to Fundy National Park, where the world's most extreme tides rise and fall twice daily.
㉖ **St. Stephen,** on the Maine border, is a mecca for chocoholics, who converge on the small town during the Chocolate Festival held the first week in August. Choctails and chocolate puddings, cakes, and complete meals should come as no surprise when you realize that it was here that the chocolate bar was invented. Sample Ganong's famed hand-dipped chocolates at the factory store, **The Chocolatière.** *73 Milltown Blvd., tel. 506/466-6437. Open July 1–Aug. 31, weekdays 9–8, Sat. 9–5, Sun. noon–5; Sept. 1–June 30, daily 9–5. Closed Dec. 25, Jan. 1.*

A small side trip along Ledge Road will take you to **Crocker Hill Gardens,** a tranquil oasis of herbs, dried flowers, irresistible potpourris, carved decoys, and comfortable garden seats. From here you can shout across the St. Croix River to friends in Maine. *209 Sheriff St., tel. 506/466-4251. Admission free. Open July–Aug., Mon.–Sat. 9–5, Sun. 2–5; Sept.–June, by appointment.*

㉗ Take Route 127 off Route 1 to **St. Andrews,** one of North America's prettiest and least spoiled resort towns. Long the summer place of the affluent (mansions ring the town), St. Andrews retains its population of fishermen, and little has changed in the past two centuries. Of the town's 550 buildings 280 were erected before 1880; 14 have survived from the 1700s. Some Loyalists brought their homes with them piece by piece from Castine, Maine, across the bay, when the war didn't go their way.

Pick up a walking-tour map at the tourist information center on Water Street and follow it through the pleasant streets. Particular gems are the **Court House** and **Greenock Church.** The church owes its existence to a remark someone made at an 1822 dinner party about the "poor" Presbyterians not having a church of their own. Captain Christopher Scott, who took exception to the slur, spared no expense on the building, which is decorated with a carving of a green oak tree in honor of Scott's birthplace, Greenock, Scotland. Also along Water Street are numerous antiques shops and artists' studios. The porch of the hiretown Inn (218 Water St., tel. 506/529–8877) is a perfect place for a snack and a view.

The **Ross Memorial Museum** features a fine antiques collection. *188 Montague St., tel. 506/529–3906. Admission free. Open June 15–Sept. 30, Mon.–Sat. 10–4, Sun. 1:30–4:30; Oct. 2– June 14, by appointment.*

A drive up Joe's Point Road takes you to the **Huntsman Marine Museum,** which houses marine life and displays. *Brandy Cove Rd., tel. 506/529–8895. Admission: $3.50 adults, $3 senior citizens, $2.50 children under 17. Open May–June, daily 10–4:30; July–Aug., daily 10–6; Sept.–Oct. 7, daily 10–4:30. Closed Oct. 8–Apr. 30.*

Back on Route 1 is **St. George,** a pretty town with some excellent bed-and-breakfasts, one of the oldest Protestant graveyards in Canada, and a fish ladder running up the side of a dam.

The Fundy Isles—Grand Manan, Deer Island, and Campobello—are havens of peace that have lured harried mainlanders for generations. **Grand Manan Island,** largest of the three, is also farthest away (about two hours by car–ferry from Black's Harbour); you might see spouting whales, sunning seals, or a rare puffin on the way. Circular herring weirs dot the coastal water, and fish sheds and smokehouses lie beside long wharfs that reach out to bobbing fishing boats. Place names are romantic—Swallowtail, Southern Head, Seven Days Work, and Dark Harbour. It's easy to get around—only about 20 miles of road lead from the lighthouse at Southern Head to the one at Northern Head. A living encyclopedia of birds, Grand Manan attracted John James Audubon in 1831. The puffin is the island's symbol. Whale-watching expeditions can be booked at the Marathon Hotel and the Compass Rose, and scuba diving to old wrecks is popular.

Connected to Lubec, Maine, by an international bridge, **Campobello Island** may be approached from the other side by toll ferry from Deer Island. Neatly manicured, preening itself in the bay, Campobello Island has always had a special appeal to the wealthy and the famous. It was here that the Roosevelt family spent their summers. The home of Franklin Delano Roosevelt, former president of the United States, is now maintained as a lovely museum in his honor. Located in the center of Roosevelt International Park, a joint project of the Canadian and American governments, **President Roosevelt's home** was the setting for the movie *Sunrise at Campobello. Roosevelt Park Rd., tel. 506/752–2922. Admission free. Open May 15– Oct. 15, daily 10–6. Closed Oct. 16–May 14.*

The island's **Herring Cove Provincial Park** has camping facilities and a nine-hole golf course.

An easy, 20-minute, free ferry ride from Letete near St. George brings you to **Deer Island** for a relaxing visit. You'll enjoy exploring the fishing wharves such as those at **Chocolate Cove.** The world's largest lobster pound is at **Northern Harbour,** and you can walk through a small nature park at **Deer Point** while waiting for the toll ferry to nearby Campobello. If you listen carefully, you may be able to hear the sighing and snorting of "the Old Sow," the second largest whirlpool in the world. If you can't hear it, you'll be able to see it, just a few feet offshore. Exploring the island takes only a few hours; it's 12 kilometers (7½ miles) long, varying in width from 3 miles to a few hundred feet at some points.

After returning from the Fundy Isles to the mainland, proceed east along coastal Route 1. If you have the time, dip down to the peaceful, hidden fishing villages of **Maces Bay, Dipper,** and **Chance Harbour,** all much the same as they have been for centuries. At Dipper Harbour, you can rent sea kayaks (Fundy Marine, tel. 506/634–1530) or buy a lobster roll to munch on the long sun-warmed wharf.

Drive east through Saint John along a scenic stretch of Route 1 to Route 114, which angles south to the 80-square-mile **Fundy National Park.** Stand on a sandstone ledge above a dark-sand beach and watch the bay's phenomenal tide rise or fall. *Box 40, Alma E0A 1B0, tel. 506/887–2000. Admission: June 26–Labor Day, $4.25 per car; rest of the year, free.*

Alma is the small seaside town that services the national park. Here you'll find great lobster and the local specialty, sticky buns. Past Alma, the coast road to Moncton winds by covered bridges and along rocky coasts, past photogenic spots such as the wild driftwood-cluttered beach at **Cape Enragé** and **Hopewell Cape,** home of the famous giant flowerpots, rock formations carved by the Fundy Tides.

Tour 4: Moncton and the Acadian Peninsula

A friendly town, often called the Gateway to Acadia because of its mix of English and French and its proximity to the Acadian shore, **Moncton** has a pretty downtown where wisely placed malls do a booming business.

This city has long touted two natural attractions, the Tidal Bore and the Magnetic Hill. You may be disappointed if you've read too much tourist hype. In days gone by, before the harbor mouth filled with silt, the **Tidal Bore** was indeed an incredible sight, a high wall of water that surged in through the narrow opening of the river to fill red-mud banks to the brim. It still moves up the river, and the moving wave is worth waiting for, but it's nowhere near as lofty as it used to be, except sometimes in the spring when the tides are very high. Bore Park on Main Street is the best vantage point; viewing times are posted there.

Magnetic Hill, north of town just off the Trans-Canada Highway, creates a bizarre optical illusion. If you park your car in neutral at the designated spot, you'll seem to be coasting up hill without power. An excellent family water theme park, **Magic Mountain,** is adjacent to the hill. *On Magnetic Hill, tel. 506/857–9283. Admission: $16 adults, $9.50 half-day; $11.75 children under 12 and senior citizens, $8 half-day; $49.25 for a family of 4 for a full day. Open June 15–28, 10–6; June 29–Aug. 18, 10–8; Aug. 19–Sept. 2, 10–6.*

Among Moncton's notable man-made attractions is the **Acadian Museum,** at the University of Moncton, whose remarkable collection of artifacts reflects 300 years of Acadian life in New Brunswick. *Clement Cormier Building, University of Moncton campus, tel. 506/858–4088. Admission free. Open June 1–Sept. 30, weekdays 10–5, weekends 1–5; Oct. 1–May 31, Tues.–Fri. 1–4:30, weekends 1–4. Closed Mon., holidays.*

Turn northeast along the coast from Moncton to the salty shores of unique Acadian communities such as **Shediac, Cocagne, Buctouche,** and **Rexton,** where you'll find long warm sand dunes, lobster feeds, lighthouses, weathered wharves, and sea-stained churches. The friendliness of the Acadians makes this trip a joy, and the white, dune-edged beaches of

㉞ **Kouchibouguac National Park** are among the finest on the continent. *Kouchibouguac National Park E0A 2A0, tel. 506/876–2443. Admission: $4 per vehicle. Open daily 8–8.*

Route 11 continues north to the Miramichi River and the fabled **Miramichi region** of lumberjacks, fishermen, and "come all ye's." Celebrated for its salmon rivers and the ebullient nature of its residents (Scottish, English, Irish, and a smattering of French and Indian), this is a land of stories, folklore, and lumber kings. Pleasant towns and villages of sturdy wood homes dot the banks of Miramichi Bay at **Chatham** and **Newcastle** (where the politician and British media mogul Lord Beaverbrook grew up and is buried). At **Doaktown** (south of Newcastle on Route 8), the **Miramichi Salmon Museum** (tel. 506/365–7787) provides a look at the endangered Atlantic salmon and at life in noted fishing camps along the rivers.

The **Woodmen's Museum** of Boiestown (in the exact center of the province) is housed in what looks like two giant logs, and portrays a lumberman's life. *Rte 8, Boiestown, tel. 506/369–7214. Closed winter.*

Return to Newcastle and swing north and east on Route 11 to

㉟ **Caraquet,** on the Acadian Peninsula. The town is perched along the Baie des Chaleurs, with Québec's Gaspé Peninsula beckoning across the inlet.

The *pièce de résistance* of the Acadian Peninsula is, without

㊱ doubt, the **Acadian Historical Village,** 10 kilometers (6 miles) west of Caraquet on Route 11, near Grand Anse. As Kings Landing depicts the early English settlement, this village recreates an early Acadian community between 1780 and 1890. Summer days are wonderfully peaceful. A chapel bell tolls, ducks waddle and quack under a footbridge, wagons creak, and the smell of hearty cooking wafts from cottage doors. Costumed staff act as guides, and a restaurant serves old-Acadian dishes. *Tel. 506/727–3467. Admission: $7 adults, $4.25 children, $15 families. Open June–mid-Sept., daily 10–6.*

Shopping

New Brunswick is famous for its crafts, and the *Directory of New Brunswick Craftsmen & Craft Shops* provides comprehensive listings of potters, weavers, glassblowers, jewelers, and carvers throughout the province. Get a copy from Tourism New Brunswick (Box 12345, Fredericton, E3B 5A6, tel. 800/561–0123).

Fredericton Mammoth crafts markets are held occasionally in town and every Labor Day weekend in Mactaquac Park. **Aitkens Pewter** (81 Regent St.) and **Pewtercraft** (582 Brunswick St.) offer beautiful pewter hollowware, goblets, belt buckles, jewelry, and authentic reproductions of ancient folk dishes. **Shades of Light Studio and Gift Shop** (28 Regent St.) features stained glass and other local crafts. **Mulhouse Country Classics,** about 2 kilometers (1 mile) from downtown in Lower St. Marys across the river on the north side, is a gem for crafts and handmade furniture.

Excellent men's shoes can be bought at **Hartt's Shoe Factory** (York St.); **The Linen Closet** (King St.) sells laces, exquisite bedding, and Victorian nightgowns.

Gagetown **Flo Grieg's** on Front Street carries superior pottery. **Claremont House B&B,** on Tilley Road, displays unusual batik items and copper engravings. **Loomcrafters,** just off Main St., is a good choice for hand-woven items.

Moncton Five spacious malls and numerous pockets of shops in downtown Moncton make it one of the best places to shop in New Brunswick. Among the crafts to look for are the whimsically designed hats at **Et Cetera** (corner of Main and Botsford Sts.) and the yarn portraits of La Sagouine, "the old sage" of Buctouche. The sayings of the old Acadian woman as she does her daily chores were made famous in Antonine Maillet's novel *La Sagouine.*

St-Andrews-by-the-Sea This "veddy British" town has many places to buy English and New Brunswick woolens, English bone china, and marvelous wool yarn, among them **The Sea Captain's Loft** (Water St.), and **Cottage Craft** (Town Sq.). Antiques, and rare and out-of-print books are sold at the **Pansy Patch** (Carleton St.), a stunning old home across from the Algonquin Hotel. On Water Street, the main shopping strip, head to **Tom Smith's Studio** (Water St.), for highly regarded oriental Raku pottery.

Saint John The little antiques stores and crafts shops sprinkled around the downtown area provide the best shopping in Saint John. **Prince William Street** has interesting browsing in antiques shops and crafts boutiques; **House of Tara** (72 Prince William St.) is wonderful for fine Irish linens and woolens. Airy **Brunswick Square** and **Market Square** in the new harborfront have many top-quality boutiques. **Old City Market,** between Charlotte and Germaine streets, bustles six days a week and always stocks delicious local specialties, such as maple syrup and lobster.

St. Leonard A visit to the studio and store of the **Madawaska Weavers** (Main St.), whose handwoven items are known the world over, is a must. Handsome skirts, stoles, and ties are some of the items on sale.

Sports and Fitness

Bicycling Byroads, lanes, and rolling secondary highways run through small towns, along the ocean, and into the forest. Set out on your own; or try a guided adventure with a specialist tour operator such as **Covered Bridge Bicycle Tours** (Box 693, Main Post Office, Saint John, E2L 4B3, tel. 506/849–9028). For bicycle rentals contact **Bennett's Bicycle Shop** (Bathurst, tel. 506/564–6280) and **Mike's Bike Shop** (Shediac, tel. 506/532–4999). In addition, bed-and-breakfasts frequently have bicycles for hire. The Department of Economic Development and Tourism has listings and free cycling maps (*See* Important Addresses and Numbers, above). Information on competitive cycling and races is available from **Velo New Brunswick** (Box 1856, Sussex, E0E 1P0).

Fishing Dotted with freshwater lakes, crisscrossed with fish-laden rivers, and bordered by 700 miles of seacoast, this province is one of Canada's natural treasures. Sportspeople are drawn by the excellent bass fishing and the world-famous salmon rivers such as the Miramichi, the Restigouche, and the Nashwaak. Commercial fishermen often take visitors line fishing for ground fish. An annual freshwater fishing license for out-of-province visitors costs $25 for three days; $50 for seven days; $100 for the season. For more information, call New Brunswick Fish and Wildlife (tel. 506/453–2440).

Golf There are 36 excellent golf courses in New Brunswick—many, such as the **Algonquin Golf Club** in St. Andrews and the **Gowan Brae Golf and Country Club** in Bathurst, with sparkling views of the sea. The **Fundy National Park Golf Club** at Alma is nestled near cliffs overlooking the restless Bay of Fundy; deer grazing on the course are one of its hazards. Greens fees run about $20–$25, $15 for some nine-hole courses; and visitors are generally welcome. For a list of golf courses, ask for the free "New Brunswick Travel Guide" from the Department of Economic Development and Tourism (Box 12345, Fredericton, E3B 5C3).

Hiking Rocky coastline and inland highland trails offer hiking opportunities for both experienced and casual trekkers. **East Coast Adventures** (Box 6713, Station A, Saint John, E2L 4S2, tel. 506/648–9462) and **Miramichi Four Seasons Outfitters** (Box 705, RR 2, Newcastle, E1V 3L9, tel. 506/622–0089) offer guided hiking tours. For trail information, call Eric Hadley, the president of New Brunswick Trails Club (tel. 506/453–2730).

Hunting More than 75% of New Brunswick is forested, so deer hunting is excellent. Moose hunting is restricted to residents. Licenses are required for bear and deer hunting and are available at registered outlets around the province as well as from the Department of Natural Resources (Box 6000, Fredericton, E3B 5H1). A list of fishing and hunting outfitters is available from the Department of Tourism, Recreation and Heritage (Box 12345, Fredericton, E3B 5C3).

Skiing A perfect province for cross-country skiing, New Brunswick
Cross-country offers groomed trails at provincial and national parks such as Mactaquac Provincial Park near Fredericton, Fundy National Park in Alma, and Kouchibouguac National Park near Bathurst. Many communities and small hotels offer groomed trails. It's also possible to set off on your own in almost every section of the province.

Downhill New Brunswick downhill ski areas usually operate from mid-December through April. They include **Crabbe Mountain Winter Park** (tel. 506/463–2686) in Lower Hainesville (near Fredericton); **Sugarloaf Provincial Park** (tel. 506/789–2366) in Campbelleton, northern New Brunswick; **Mont Farlagne** (tel. 506/735–8401) in St. Jacques, near Edmundston; **Poley Mountain Ski Area** (tel. 506/433–2201) in Sussex; and **Silverwood Winter Park** (tel. 506/450–3380) in Fredericton.

Tennis Courts are available in most city and town parks. Most are free. Many resorts and hotels have courts.

Water Sports Sailboats can be chartered in many areas: **Fundy Yacht Sales**
Sailing **and Charter** (Dipper Harbour, Rte. 2, Lepreau, E0G 2H0, tel. 506/659–2769); **Sailboat** (Box 27, Rte. 3, Site 4, Fredericton, E3B 4X4, tel. 506/459–6089). Information is also available from **Sailing Association** (71 la Salle Crescent, Moncton, E1A 5Z8,

tel. 506/854–9280) or **Lower Saint John River Promotion Association** (Gagetown, E0G 1V0, in New Brunswick, tel. 800/561–0123; outside the province, tel. 800/442–4442).

Canoeing and Kayaking Kayaking along the coasts of Fundy and Chaleur has become very popular. A list of canoe and kayak liveries is available from Department of Economic Development and Tourism (Box 12345, Fredericton, E3B 5C3). For canoes, try **A to Z Rentals** in Fredericton (128 Prospect St., tel. 506/452–9758), and St. John (535 Rothesay, tel. 506/633–1919). Outfitters such as **Fundy Marine** (Brunswick Square, Saint John, tel. 506/634–1530) offer single and double kayaks, lessons, and tours.

Rowing Shells can be rented at the **Kennebecasis Club** in Rothesay (tel. 506/849–9910) and the **Aquatic Center** (tel. 506/458–5513) in Fredericton.

Whale-watching One New Brunswick experience that is difficult to forget is the sighting of a huge humpback, right whale, finback, or minke. Whale-watching tours are available from a number of operators such as **Ocean Search** (Marathon Inn, North Head, Grand Manan, E0G 2M0, tel. 506/662–8144) and **West Isles World** (Lambertville, Deer Island, E0G 2E0, tel. 506/747–2946). **Cline Marine Tours,** (tel. 506/747–2287) and **Chaleur Phantom** in Dahlousie (tel. 506/648–4722) have scenic tours to observe marine life in the calmer waters around the islands as well.

Dining and Lodging

Dining

Although there are not a lot of choices for fine dining in New Brunswick, a few good restaurants exist, and families will find plenty of quality food in many outlets. A number of gourmet restaurants have popped up in Saint John in recent years—so there is hope that the dining scene will improve throughout the province.

In the spring, once the ice has left streams and rivers, a provincial delicacy, the fiddlehead fern, is picked from the shores. Eaten as a vegetable (boiled, drenched with lemon, butter, salt, and pepper), fiddleheads have something of an artichoke taste and go well with spring's bony fish, shad, and gaspereaux. Silver salmon, once a spring staple when set nets were allowed, is still available but quite costly. Most salmon served in restaurants is farm reared. Lobster, a favorite maritime dish, is available in most restaurants, but is not always cheap. The custom of the residents is to buy it fresh from the fishermen or shore outlets and devour it in huge quantities. Because of the cool waters, shellfish is especially tasty. Look for oysters, scallops, clams, crab, and mussels. And be sure to try the purple seaweed called dulse that the residents eat like potato chips. To be truly authentic, accompany any New Brunswick–style feast with hearty Moosehead beer, brewed in Saint John and one of the province's well-known exports.

Dress is casual everywhere except at the Expensive and Very Expensive listings, and, unless noted, no reservations are needed.

Highly recommended restaurants in each price category are indicated by a star ★.

Category	Cost*
Very Expensive	over $40
Expensive	$20–$40
Moderate	$10–$19
Inexpensive	under $10

per person, excluding drinks, service, and 11% sales tax

Lodging

New Brunswick has a number of officially designated Heritage Inns—historically significant establishments built in the last century. Many have antique china and furnishings or other charming touches, and their accommodations run the gamut from elegant to homey.

Hotels and motels in and around Saint John and Fredericton are adequate and friendly. Accommodations in Saint John are at a premium in summer, so reserve ahead to ensure a place to stay.

Highly recommended lodgings in each price category are indicated by a star ★.

Category	Cost*
Expensive	over $60
Moderate	$45–$60
Inexpensive	under $40

All prices are for a standard double room, excluding 10% service charge.

Campbelltown
Dining and Lodging
★
Aylesford Inn. Truly a find, this friendly inn housed in a Victorian mansion near the Québec border and Sugarloaf Provincial Park has guest rooms handsomely furnished with Eastlake and Canadian-pine antiques. Large gardens and verandas offer views of the Restigouche River. Excellent dinners are served to guests (quail and frogs' legs are featured entrées), and full breakfasts are included in the room rate. Nonguests are welcome for afternoon tea. *8 MacMillan Ave., E3N 1E9, tel. 506/ 759-7672. 7 rooms, 1 with bath. Facilities: dining room, croquet. AE, MC, V. Moderate.*

Campobello Island
Lodging
★
Owen House. Mellow with history, this 200-year-old home was built by Admiral Owen, who fancied himself ruler of the island. Its gracious old rooms have hosted such luminaries as actress Greer Garson, who stayed here (in a room with a fireplace in the bathroom) when filming *Sunrise at Campobello*. Breakfasts are wonderful—pancakes come topped with local berries. *Welshpool, E0G 3H0, tel. 506/752-2977. 9 rooms. No credit cards. Moderate.*

Island Club Lodge. Originally a vacation home built by the Adams family (friends of the Roosevelts) around the turn of the century, these three attractive log buildings built on a bluff overlooking the Bay of Fundy have been converted into a modern guest lodge. The 12 available rooms occupy two of the cabins; the third houses the dining room, which specializes in simple but well-prepared local seafood. *Box 16, Welshpool, NB*

EOG 3HO, tel. 506/752–2487. 12 rooms. Facilities: restaurant. MC, V. Moderate.

Caraquet
Dining and Lodging

Hotel Paulin. The word *quaint* really fits this property. There are pretty rooms, a bathroom down the hall, and an excellent small dining room specializing in fresh fish cooked perfectly. *143 Blvd. St. Pierre, tel. 506/727–9981. 10 rooms with shared bath. Facilities: restaurant. MC, V. Inexpensive.*

Deer Island
Dining and Lodging

45th Parallel Motel and Restaurant. Deer Island has only one motel, and it's clean and comfortable. A full breakfast is included, and everything from lobster to pizza is available at the informal restaurant. Pets are welcome. *Fairhaven, Deer Island E0G 1R0, tel. 506/747–2231. 10 rooms, 3 with kitchenette. Facilities: restaurant. V. Moderate.*

West Isles World B&B. This white frame house overlooks the cove and offers three snug rooms with an informal country feel; the big upstairs bedroom has a water view. The owners will arrange whale-watching cruises for you. A full breakfast is included in the room rate, and other meals are served on request. *Lord's Cove, E0G 2J0, tel. 506/747–2946. 4 rooms, 1 with bath. No credit cards. Moderate.*

Fredericton
Dining

Benoit's. Fredericton's top-of-the-line restaurant features excellent French cuisine served in an art deco dining room. JC is the genial host, and seafood (try the "feast for two") is well prepared. *536 Queen St., tel. 506/459–3666. AE, DC, MC, V. No lunch Sat.; closed Sun. Expensive.*

Luna Steakhouse. Specialties include huge Caesar salad, garlic bread, escargots, and brochettes. In fine weather you can dine on an outdoor terrace. *168 Dundonald St., tel. 506/455–4020. AE, DC, MC, V. Moderate.*

Bar B Q Barn. Special children's menus and barbecued ribs and chicken are the standards; the blackboard lists plenty of other daily dinner specials, such as salmon, scallops, and chili. This is a popular, attractive spot, great for winding down, and the bar serves fine martinis. *540 Queen St., tel. 506/455–2742. AE, MC, V. Inexpensive–Moderate.*

Pink Pearl. This restaurant features tasty Cantonese food, with exceptional wontons and daily buffets. *343 Queen St., tel. 506/450–8997. MC, V. Inexpensive.*

Lodging

Howard Johnson Motor Lodge. This Hojo's, located on the north side of the river and at the north end of the Princess Margaret Bridge, has a terrace bar in a pleasant interior courtyard overlooked by balconies from all the rooms. Guest-room decor is standard for the chain. *Trans-Canada Highway, Box 1414, tel. 506/472–0480. 117 rooms. Facilities: restaurant, bar, indoor pool. AE, DC, MC, V. Expensive.*

Lord Beaverbrook Hotel. A central location is this modern, seven-story hotel's main attraction, although 1991 renovations spruced things up a bit. Some rooms have Jacuzzis or minibars. The food in the main dining room is forgettable. There are a couple of lively bars downstairs. *659 Queen St., E3B 5G2, tel. 506/455–3371. 175 rooms. Facilities: 3 restaurants, bar, indoor pool, nonsmoking rooms. AE, D, DC, MC, V. Expensive.*

Sheraton Inn Fredericton. Brand-new and within walking distance of downtown, this big hotel offers modern rooms with sunset views over the river. *225 Woodstock Rd. Fredericton, E3B 2H8, tel. 506/457–7000. 223 rooms, some with minibars. Facilities: restaurant with outdoor terrace, bar, indoor and outdoor pools. AE, DC, MC, V. Expensive.*

Auberge Wandlyn Inn. Just off the Trans-Canada Highway, this hotel is away from the downtown area but close to three shopping malls, many restaurants, and theaters. The guest rooms are no-frills, but the family-oriented dining room is pretty, and there's a cozy bar. *58 Prospect St. W, Box 214, E3B 4Y9, tel. 506/452–8937. 116 rooms. Facilities: restaurant, bar, pool. AE, DC, MC, V. Moderate.*

Carriage House Bed and Breakfast. This heritage mansion has lovely bedrooms. Breakfast is served in a sunny, glass-walled room. *230 University Ave., E3B 4H7, tel. 506/452–9924. 7 rooms, 2 with bath. MC, V. Moderate.*

Happy Apple Acres Bed and Breakfast. This B&B offers friendly atmosphere in a country setting. Besides the full breakfast that is included in the room rate, dinner can be arranged for guests, and the cooking is excellent. *Highway 105 (7 mi north of Fredericton), Rte. 4, E3B 1A1, tel. 506/472–1819. 3 rooms with bath. MC, V. Inexpensive–Moderate.*

Grand Manan Island
Lodging

Compass Rose. Lovely guest rooms are available in the two old houses that have been combined into this small inn. It's conveniently near the ferry landing, and whale-watching tours can be arranged. Breakfast is included in the room rate. *North Head, E0G 3K0, tel. 506/662–8570. V. Moderate.*

The Marathon Inn. Perched on a hill overlooking the harbor, this gracious mansion built by a sea captain offers guest rooms furnished with antiques. Meals are served in the restaurant (breakfast and dinner are included in the room rate), and whale- and bird-watching cruises can be arranged. The active bar is noisy, so book a room farthest from the fray. *Box 129, North Head, E0G 2M0, tel. 506/662–8144. 28 rooms, 15 with bath. Facilities: restaurant, bar, pool, tennis. MC, V. Moderate.*

Ludlow
Lodging

Pond's Chalet Resort. You'll get a traditional fishing-camp experience here, in a lodge and chalets set among trees overlooking a salmon river. *Ludlow (near Boiestown), E0C 1N0, tel. 506/369–2612. 10 rooms in lodge, 8 camps. Facilities: dining room. AE, DC, MC, V. Moderate.*

Moncton
Dining
★

Cy's Seafood Restaurant. This favorite for seafood, decorated in dark wood and brass, has been serving generous portions for decades. Though renowned for its seafood casserole, the restaurant also offers reliable scallop, shrimp, and lobster dishes. You can see the Tidal Bore from the windows. *170 Main St., tel. 506/857–0032. AE, DC, MC, V. Moderate.*

Fisherman's Paradise. In spite of the enormous dining area (more than 350 tables), this restaurant serves memorable à la carte seafood dishes, in an atmosphere of candlelight and wood furnishings. The children's menu and down-home specials such as lobster bake make this a good spot for families. *375 Dieppe Blvd., tel. 506/859–4388. AE, MC, V. Moderate.*

Lodging
★

Hotel Beausejour. Moncton's finest hotel is decorated in Acadian style. The downtown location is convenient. Besides the standard guest rooms, there are some luxury concierge rooms. Staff in 18th-century costume lend a pleasant ambience to the main dining room, L'Auberge; the other restaurant is more formal. *750 Main St., tel. 506/854–4344. 317 rooms. Facilities: 2 restaurants, bar, outdoor pool, access to health club. AE, MC, V. Expensive.*

The Crystal Palace. Moncton's newest hotel is unique: There are theme rooms (want to be Ali Baba for a night?) and, for families, an indoor pool and a miniature wonderland of rides, midway stalls, coin games, food booths, and boutiques. Champlain Mall is across the street. *499 Paul St., tel. 506/858–8584. 119 rooms. Facilities: restaurant, indoor pool. AE, DC, MC, V. Moderate–Expensive.*

Newcastle **Wharf Inn.** Here in Miramichi country, the staff is friendly and
Lodging the restaurant serves excellent salmon dinners. This low-rise modern building has two wings; guest rooms in the executive wing have extra amenities. *Jane St., tel. 506/622–0302. 70 rooms. Facilities: restaurant, patio lounge, indoor pool. AE, DC, MC, V. Moderate.*

Sackville **Marshlands Inn.** In this white clapboard inn, a welcoming
Lodging double living room with fireplace sets the informal, country
★ atmosphere. Bedrooms are furnished with sleigh beds or four-posters, but they also have modern touches such as air-conditioning and in-room telephones. *Box 1440, E0A 3C0, tel. 506/536–0170. 21 rooms, 14 with bath. Facilities: restaurant. AE, DC, MC, V. Moderate–Expensive.*

St. Andrews **Algonquin Hotel.** The wraparound veranda of this grand old ho-
Lodging tel overlooks wide lawns. Bellmen wear kilts. The dining room is noted for its buffets, and meals can be pleasant here if the staff is in the mood. *Rte. 127, E0G 2X0, tel. 506/529–8823. 193 rooms. Facilities: restaurant, bar, pool, golf, tennis. AE, MC, V. Closed winter. Expensive.*

L'Europe. You may be amused by the cheerful decor in this intimate restaurant, in particular the whimsical objets d'art reflecting the tastes of the German owners. The food is Continental—some German dishes, French, and so on, with particular attention given to seafood. All meals are served with delicious homemade Black Forest bread and pâté. *48 King St., St. Andrews, E0G 2X0, tel. 506/529–3818. Reservations advised. Open mid-May–September. V. Expensive.*

★ **Pansy Patch B & B.** Across the street from the Algonquin Hotel is this Norman-style farmhouse, built in 1912, distinguished by a turret and steep roofs. The guest rooms are appointed with antiques and have views of the water. The owners also operate an antiques shop and bookshop on the property. Full breakfast is included in the room rate. *59 Carleton St., E0G 2X0, tel. 506/ 529–3834. 4 rooms with shared bath. AE, MC, V. Closed mid-Oct.–mid-May. Expensive.*

St. George **Granite Town Hotel.** Although this hotel was just built in 1991,
Lodging it nevertheless has an old-country-inn feeling to it. The decor is subtle, with pine and washed-birch woodwork prominent. Light blues and pinks dominate in the rooms. A restaurant is in the works that should be open for the 1993 season. The scenery is pleasant: one side of the building overlooking an apple orchard, the other just atop the bank of the Maguadavic River. A Continental breakfast is served but is not included in the room rate. During the week a full, made-to-order "manager's breakfast" is also available. *15 Main St., St. George E0G 2Y0, tel. 506/755–6415. 32 rooms, some with Jacuzzi. AE, DC, MC, V. Expensive.*

Saint John **La Belle Vie.** At one of the province's best restaurants, you'll
Dining dine in the drawing rooms of a lovely Second Empire–style
★ mansion, where 19th-century examples of trompe l'oeil adorn the ceilings and fine art graces the walls. The cooking is traditional French; try the lobster bisque. *325 Lancaster Ave., tel.*

506/635–1155. Reservations advised. AE, DC, MC, V. Expensive.

Turn of the Tide. Overlooking the harbor, this large hotel dining room is decorated with antiques. Although the dining is pleasant at all times, the best meal of the week is the Sunday buffet, with a long table full of dishes from the exotic to the tried-and-true. Fill your own crepes for dessert. *Hilton Hotel, Market Sq., tel. 506/693–8484. Reservations advised. AE, DC, MC, V. No lunch Sat. Expensive.*

Mexicali Rosa's. For a franchise, this restaurant has a lot of character. The decor is essentially Santa Fe–style with adobe arches and so forth. The specialty is "Cali-Mex" food, which is heavy on sauces, as opposed to "Tex-Mex," which concentrates more on meats. Guests waiting to be seated can order one of the fine margaritas in the large lounge. The fried chimichangas are with good reason the most popular dish. *88 Prince William St., tel. 506/652–5252. AE, DC, MC, V. Moderate.*

Grannan's. Seafood is featured in this nautically decorated restaurant, and the desserts here are memorable. Dining spills over onto the sidewalk in summer, and there are three lively bars connected to the restaurant. *Market Sq., tel. 506/634–1555. AE, DC, MC, V. No lunch Sun. Inexpensive–Moderate.*

Incredible Edibles. Here you can enjoy down-to-earth food—biscuits, garlic-laden hummus, salads, pastas, and desserts—in cozy rooms or, in summer, on the outdoor terrace. They also serve a good cup of coffee. *42 Princess St., tel. 506/633–7554. AE, MC, V. Closed Sun. Inexpensive–Moderate.*

Reggie's. This popular spot near Brunswick Square begins serving breakfast at 6 AM. Later in the day specialties include chowders, bagel burgers, and lobster rolls. The restaurant closes at 6 or 7 PM, so come early if you want dinner. *26 Germain St., tel. 506/657–6270. MC, V. Inexpensive.*

Lodging **Delta Brunswick Inn.** This lively new hotel atop Brunswick Square has a good, moderately priced dining room and banquet-and-convention facilities. *39 King St., E2L 4W3, tel. 506/648–1981. 255 rooms. Facilities: restaurant, bar, pool, children's center. AE, DC, MC, V. Expensive.*

Saint John Hilton. Part of the Market Square complex, the smallest Hilton in the world is furnished in Loyalist decor; guest rooms overlook the harbor or the town. Mellow antiques furnish corners of the dining room and the medieval-style Great Hall, which hosts banquets. Adjoining the 12-story property are shops, restaurants, bars, and a library. *1 Market Sq., E2L 4Z6, tel. 506/693–8484 or 800/361–6140. 197 rooms. Facilities: restaurant, bar, pool. AE, DC, MC, V. Expensive.*

★ **Shadow Lawn Country Inn.** This charming village inn is located in an affluent suburb with tree-lined streets and palatial houses, 10 minutes from Saint John. Tennis, golf, horseback riding, and a yacht club are nearby. The inn has eight old-fashioned bedrooms, some with fireplaces. Besides breakfast for guests (not included in the room rate), the dining room is open to the public for a set-menu dinner by reservation only; specialties include beef Wellington and seafood brioches. Pre-dinner sherry is served in the mahogany-paneled bar. *Box 41, Rothesay Rd., E0G 2W0, tel. 506/847–7539. 8 rooms with bath. DC, MC, V. Moderate–Expensive.*

Shediac **Chez Françoise.** This lovely old mansion with a wraparound ve-
Dining and Lodging randa has been decorated in Victorian style, with hardwood
★ floors and antiques; an annex across the street contains several

guest rooms as well. Front rooms have water views. The dining room, open to the public for lunch and dinner, serves excellent traditional French cuisine with an emphasis on seafood. *93 Main St., tel. 506/532–4233. 10 rooms in main house, 6 with bath; 10 rooms in annex, 4 with bath. Facilities: restaurant. AE, MC, V. Closed Jan. 1–Easter. Inexpensive–Moderate.*

The Arts and Nightlife

The Arts

Theatre New Brunswick performs in the Playhouse in Fredericton (686 Queen St., tel. 506/458–8344) and tours the province. Top musical groups, noted professional singers, and other performers usually appear at the **Aitken Center** on the University of New Brunswick campus, at **Colosseum** in Moncton, and at the **Hilton Trade Center** in Saint John.

Beaverbrook Art Gallery in Fredericton is the province's major gallery, but art exhibitions are also held at the **Aitken Bicentennial Exhibition Center** (ABEC) in Saint John, at **Moncton City Hall,** and at the University of Moncton's **Acadian Museum.**

Nightlife

Fredericton   The **Cosmopolitan Club** (King St.) sometimes presents great jazz and also has a back room where a younger crowd hangs out. The **Chestnut Inn,** on York Street, has dining and live country or folk music. Try **The Lunar Rogue** (King St.) for Irish folk music and the **Hilltop** (Prospect St.) for good pub food. Jazz and blues bands occasionally play at **Rye's Deli** (415 King St.), which also features hot-wings and popular Montréal smoked-meat sandwiches.

Saint John   Taverns and lounges, usually with music of some kind, provide a lively nightlife. For quiet conversation with a "Play it, Sam" background, try the **Brigantine,** in the Hilton. Lively **Grannans,** in Market Square, has several bars and theme nights during summer. **O'Leary's,** on Princess Street, is good for Saint John Irish fun; **Checkers,** in Keddy's Motel, is the place for dancing; go to **Sherlock's,** at the foot of King Street, for a young, congenial crowd.

15 Newfoundland and Labrador

by Margaret M. Kearney

Margaret M. Kearney is a native Newfoundler and a freelance writer. She has worked in broadcasting and was promotions manager for the Newfoundland Department of Tourism.

Newfoundland is Canada's youngest province. "Discovered" by John Cabot in 1497, and claimed for England in 1583 by Sir Humphrey Gilbert, it only became a part of modern Canada in 1949. Indeed, its capital, St. John's, is one of the oldest cities in North America—business was being conducted here on Water Street as early as 1627. The Province of Newfoundland and Labrador incorporates the huge land mass of Labrador on the mainland of North America adjacent to Québec and the insular land mass of Newfoundland to the southeast of it, which is the 10th largest island in the world.

Not only did Newfoundland bring her rich resources of fishing and mining into Canadian Confederation, she also brought the rich history, culture, and lifestyle that make this province different from any other in Canada. Visitors to Newfoundland often find themselves straddling the centuries. The language and customs of Newfoundland's forbears remain in small towns and seaside villages while the progress of the 20th century infiltrates the region's two major cities, St. John's on the east coast and Corner Brook on the west coast. It is only the people themselves who make the juxtaposition of old and new less jarring—often classified as the friendliest people in North America, they welcome visitors to their province with genuine warmth and affection and when they greet a visitor with "hello, how are you?" they really mean it.

Before even English-speaking visitors can shoot the breeze, though, they must get used to the language. It's English alright, but provincial dialects are strong and they vary from area to area. In general, Newfoundlanders speak quickly, and Newfoundland is the only province in Canada with its own dictionary. On the east coast of Newfoundland, the Irish heritage is so strong that in certain parts of the Southern Avalon peninsula you would swear you were on O'Connell Bridge in the middle of Dublin. In Bonavista, site of Cabot's landing in 1497, the language and heritage more particularly reflect that of Plymouth and Devon where Cabot recruited most of his crew. On the west coast, French and Scottish influences can be felt, and as you journey north up the west coast and into Labrador, the native cultures of the Innu and Inuit, who have lived in Labrador for thousands of years, survive and intrigue.

Second only to the charm and friendliness of the people is the uniqueness of many of the outport fishing villages that run along the coastline. It is in these villages that you witness the great influence of the sea on the history and architecture of this province. Each seaside village has been able to maintain its special character over the centuries. Some were built into the lee of the land to be protected from the elements; others were built right out on the headlands to defy nature.

Depending on the time of year you visit the province, the scenery can be dramatically different. In spring the strong, steep cliffs and huge rock escarpments are evident, and it is not unusual to see icebergs in the harbor. Summer hides the dramatic landscape in leaf and green, and in the fall, particularly on the west coast, it looks as though hundreds of colored lights have been turned on. The climate of Newfoundland varies considerably from place to place. However, because Newfoundland has no pollution, fine days are just that—beautiful sunshine, free of smog or haze. The temperature in late June, July, August and early September is 75–85 degrees with a gentle cooling-off in the evening so that one can get a good night's sleep.

Newfoundlanders cherish their culture and history and any occasion at all is an excuse for a "time." During the tourist season from June through September, the province is awash with festivals, fairs, concerts, plays, and craft shows.

Because of the lack of pollution, fishing in the waters off Newfoundland and Labrador is relaxing, carefree, and rewarding. In some areas, the streams are so plentiful that you can literally stop by the side of the road, drop a line into a stream, and be assured of a fish supper that evening.

For the naturalist, Newfoundland offers easily accessible seabird sanctuaries, where one can see thousands of nesting seabirds, including the gannet and the comical puffin. En route to these sanctuaries, by tour boat, the visitor can marvel at the antics of the many species of whales that inhabit these waters. Many arctic plants grow in Newfoundland, and the province is host to a large variety of wild orchids. Labrador is the land of the wild, although newly developed roads continue to open up this province's untouched inlands to car travel.

Essential Information

Important Addresses and Numbers

Tourist Information **Department of Development, Tourism Branch** (Confederation Building, West Block, St. John's, NF A1B 4J6, tel. 709/576–2830 or 800/563–6353) distributes brochures and maps. The province also maintains a tourism information line (tel. 800/563–6353), which operates year-round, 24 hours a day.

From June until Labor Day, a network of **Visitor Information Centers,** open 9–9, are dotted throughout the province. These centers all have up-to-date information on events, accommodations, shopping, and craft stores in their area.

Emergencies Dial 911 for medical emergencies and police.

Hospitals **St. Clare's Mercy Hospital,** 154 La Marchant Rd., tel. 709/778–3111; **Grace Hospital,** 241 La Marchant Rd., tel. 709/778–6222; **General Hospital,** 300 Prince Philip Dr., tel. 709/737–6300, in St. Johns; **George B. Cross Hospital,** tel. 709/466–3411, in Clarenville; **James Paton,** tel. 709/651–2500, in Gander; **Western Memorial,** tel. 709/637–5000, in Corner Brook; **Charles S. Curtis Memorial Hospital,** tel. 709/454–3333, in St. Anthony; and **Captain William Jackman,** 410 Booth Ave., tel. 709/944–2632, in Labrador City.

Arriving and Departing by Plane, Car Ferry, and Train

By Plane The major airport for the province for connections from all major North American and European destinations is **St. John's. Canadian Airlines International** and **Air Canada** fly into Newfoundland. **Air Nova** and **Air Atlantic** are regional connectors. Airports in Newfoundland are at Stephenville, Deer Lake, St. Anthony, Gander, St. John's, and Goose Bay; airports in Labrador are located in Wabush and Churchill Falls.

By Car Ferry **Marine Atlantic** operates a car ferry from North Sydney, Nova Scotia, to Port-aux-Basques, Newfoundland; crossing time is 6 hours, and from June through October from North Sydney to Argentia, twice a week, crossing time 12–14 hours. In all cases, reservations are required. Contact **Marine Atlantic** (Box 250, North Sydney, NS B2A 3M3, tel. 902/562–9470, in the U.S. 800/341–7981, fax 902/564–3439; hearing-impaired 902/794–8109 or call TDD operator and request collect call). For information about getting to Labrador, *see* Exploring, Tour 6, below.

By Train Rail service is provided between Sept Isles, Québec, and Labrador City by Iron Ore Canada's Quebec North Shore and Labrador Railways. For information, call 514/871–1331. For more information about this train, *see* Exploring, Tour 6. There is no train on the Island.

Getting Around Newfoundland

By Bus **Terra Transport** runs a transisland bus service. Call 709/737–5912.

By Car Newfoundland has an excellent highway system, all part of the Trans-Canada Highway. One of the most pleasurable aspects of traveling throughout the island portion of the province is the relatively uncrowded roads. Traveling time from St. John's to Port-aux-Basques is about 13 hours, with time out for a meal in either Gander or Grand Falls. The trip from Corner Brook to St. Anthony, the tip of the island, takes about five hours and from St. John's to Grand Bank on the Burin Peninsula is about four hours.

In winter some highways may close during and after severe snowstorms. For winter road conditions call the **Department of Works, Services, and Transportation** at: 709/635–2162, Deer Lake; 709/292–4300, Grand Falls; 709/466–7953, Clarenville; 709/576–2391, St. John's.

Getting Around Labrador

See Tour 6 in Exploring Newfoundland and Labrador, below.

Guided Tours

Boat Tours **Harbour Charters** (tel. 709/754–1672) offers cod jigging and whale-watching out of St. John's. **Bird Island Charters** (tel. 709/753–4850 or 709/334–2355) offers whale-watching and visits to bird sanctuaries. **Gatherall's Boat Charters** (tel. 709/334–2887) also is recommended for whale-watching and visits to bird sanctuaries. **SPM Tours** (tel. 709/722–3892) leads trips to the French Islands of St. Pierre and Miquelon. **Ocean Watch Tours** (tel. 709/535–2801) operates out of Terra Nova National Park for whale-watching, wildlife, and cod-jigging tours.

Bus Tours **McCarthy's Party**, in St. John's, offers bus tours with guides across Newfoundland, from May through October (tel. 709/781–2244, fax 709/781–2233). **Fleetline Motorcoach Tours** (Main St., Holyrood, NF, tel. 709/722–2608, fax 709/722–2608) leads tours of Newfoundland.

Exploring Newfoundland and Labrador

The tours here divide the province into the island of Newfoundland, beginning with St. John's and the Avalon Peninsula and moving west. Labrador is considered as a whole, with suggested driving and train excursions.

Tour 1: St. John's and the Avalon Peninsula

Numbers in the margin correspond to points of interest on the Newfoundland and Labrador map.

When Sir Humphrey Gilbert sailed into St. John's harbor to establish British colonial rule for Queen Elizabeth, he found Spanish, French, and Portuguese fishermen already settled. For many years, the British tried to discourage settlement in St. John's because of the rich fish resources off its shores, but this proved futile, and as early as 1627, Water Street in St. John's was doing a thriving business.

St. John's

❶ True early birds can get their tour of this area started by getting their host or hotelier to supply them with a thermos of coffee and some muffins, and driving on Route 11 to **Cape Spear** at daybreak to be some of the first people to watch the sun come up over North America. In the dim light of day, the "chit chit" of the small birds in the pigeon wheat moss, and the whales below whooshing and blowing as the sun slowly rises over the eastern horizon will make this an unforgettable day.

❷ The less adventurous may begin their "walk-about" of **St. John's** a little later in the day, say about 10, from the Tourist Chalet on the waterfront. This is a converted old railway caboose, staffed from May through October.

From here, turn right, and you can see historic **Signal Hill**. Gaze at **Gibbet Hill**, where unfortunates could be hanged and left as a message to those entering the harbor that even the smallest offence would not be tolerated by the ruling fishing admiral of the day. A walk or a drive up the steep Signal Hill takes you back into history. Here Dutch pirates tried to gain supremacy in the 1600s. Bloody battles raged between the French and the British in the 1600s and 1700s. Stand on the top of the hill and look down—it's a 500-foot drop to the narrow entrance of the harbor, which is said to be shaped like a sheep's stomach.

Signal Hill is a National Historic Park, and Parks Canada has established an interesting Interpretation Centre (tel. 709/772–5367) that provides the visitor with the history and the evolution of St. John's. Here also, at the top of the hill, is **Cabot Tower.** It was from here in 1901, in the shadow of the tower, that Marconi received the first transatlantic wireless message from Cornwall in England—beginning a series of events in communication that would change the world forever.

Come down from Signal Hill, make a right turn at Quidi Vidi Road, go into Forest Road and right down into **Quidi Vidi** village, an authentic fishing village, whose history goes back to the beginning of St. John's.

While in the area, continue on and walk around **Quidi Vidi Lake.** This lovely body of water has become the place for walkers and joggers, in all kinds of weather, and in all seasons. It is also the site of the **St. John's Annual Regatta**—the oldest continuing sporting event in North America—on the first Wednesday in August. It's popular with natives and tourists alike; if you're in town, don't miss it.

Walking around St. John's, it's difficult not to notice the architecture. The city boasts some of the finest examples of 18th- and 19th-century wooden homes. Its churches, too, are rich in architectural history. The **Roman Catholic Basilica,** with a commanding position on a height on Military Road, looks out over the whole of the older section of the city and the harbor. The land was granted to the church by the young Queen Victoria, and the edifice was built with stones from both Ireland and Newfoundland. From here you can also see the **Anglican Cathedral** on Church Hill, one of the earliest examples of Gothic architecture in North America. Nearby, **Gower Street United Church** is very imposing, with its redbrick facade and green turrets. At the bottom of Military Road, adjacent to Hotel Newfoundland, is the old **Anglican Garrison Church,** where the English soldiers used to worship in the early and mid-1800s. Nearby is **Commissariat House,** restored to the way it appeared in the 1830s.

Memorial University Botanical Gardens is worth a whole afternoon's visit. Located at Oxen Pond on Mt. Scio Road, this 100-acre nature reserve has five attractive trails, an English cottage garden, Newfoundland heritage plants, and heather beds. It is also one of two butterfly farms in North America and is home to nesting ospreys.

The Avalon Peninsula From St. John's take the northern seashore route that wraps around the top of the peninsula. Small hamlets and fishing villages hug the shore right out to **Bay de Verde.** At the very end, connected by roadway, is **Baccalieu Island,** where it's possible to see whales feed offshore. Many of the homes in the fishing villages have been turned into bed-and-breakfast establishments and offer visitors an opportunity to experience the culture and lifestyle of the seaside first-hand. For information about B&Bs, contact the Department of Development (Tourism Branch, tel. 709/576–2830 or 800/563–6353).

The south side of the peninsula is less populated than the north. You can continue your circular loop, heading south on Route 100, or if you are using St. John's as your base, you can continue south from there on Route 10. Either way, there are a couple of things you shouldn't miss while exploring South Avalon. The ❺ **Salmonier Nature Park,** along Route 90, is well worth a visit. This wilderness reserve offers visitors a place to see many of the animal species that are indigenous to the province. *Rte. 90, 12 km (7½ mi) off Rte. 1. Admission 50¢ adults, 25¢ children, senior citizens free. Open June 6–Labor Day, Thur.–Mon., 12–7.*

❻ From **Trepassey** on Route 10, take a chance on seeing the wild caribou herds that roam back and forth across the highway.

❼ On Route 100 visit the **Cape St. Mary's Bird Sanctuary,** where, among the many other nesting birds, are included about 50,000 pairs of garnets.

Newfoundland and Labrador

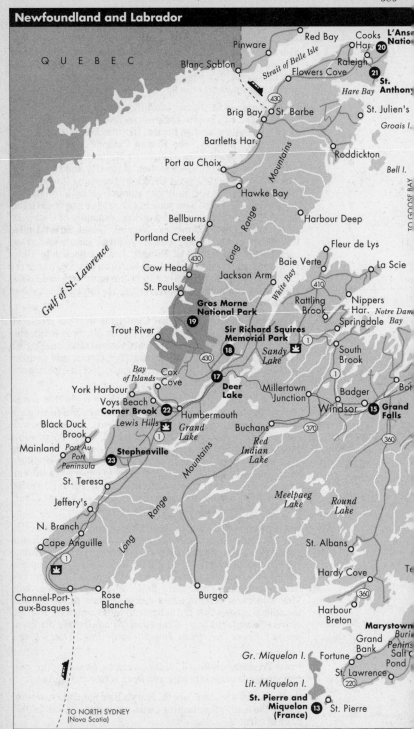

QUEBEC

Pinware

Red Bay

Cooks Har.

L'Anse Natio

20

Blanc Sablon

Strait of Belle Isle

Raleigh

21

Flowers Cove

St. Anthony

Hare Bay

Brig Bay

St. Barbe

St. Julien's

430

Groais I.

Bartletts Har.

Mountains

Roddickton

Port au Choix

Bell I.

Hawke Bay

Bellburns

Harbour Deep

TO GOOSE BAY

Portland Creek

Long

Fleur de Lys

430

Cow Head

Range

Baie Verte

La Scie

Jackson Arm

410

St. Pauls

White Bay

Rattling Brook

Nippers Har.

Notre Dam

Gros Morne National Park

Springdale

Bay

19

Sir Richard Squires Memorial Park

Sandy Lake

South Brook

Trout River

18

430

1

1

Bay of Islands

Cox Cove

17

Deer Lake

Millertown Junction

Badger

Bot

York Harbour

Windsor

15 **Grand Falls**

Voys Beach

Corner Brook

22

Humbermouth

Lewis Hills

Grand Lake

Buchans

360

Black Duck Brook

370

Mainland

Port Au Port Peninsula

Port

Stephenville

Red Indian Lake

23

Mountains

St. Teresa

Meelpaeg Lake

Round Lake

Jeffery's

Long

N. Branch

St. Albans

Cape Anguille

Range

Hardy Cove

1

360

Te

Channel-Port-aux-Basques

Rose Blanche

Burgeo

Harbour Breton

Marystown

Buri Penins

Grand Bank

Salr Pond

Gr. Miquelon I.

Fortune

St. Lawrence

220

Lit. Miquelon I.

St. Pierre and Miquelon (France)

13

St. Pierre

TO NORTH SYDNEY
(Nova Scotia)

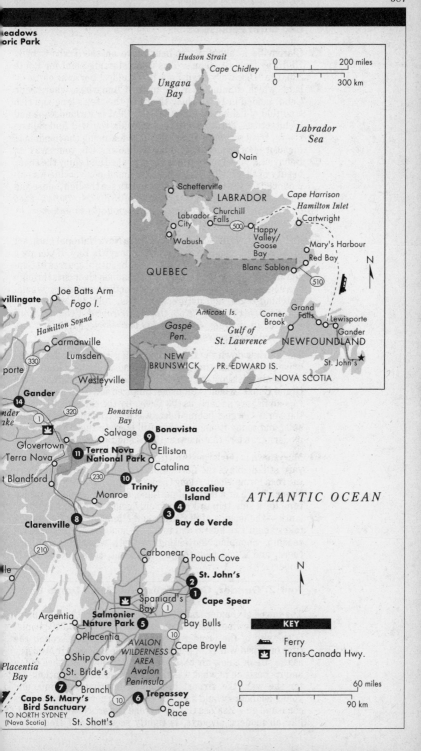

eadows
oric Park

Hudson Strait
Cape Chidley

0   200 miles
0   300 km

Ungava
Bay

Labrador
Sea

Nain

Scheffervile

LABRADOR

Cape Harrison
Hamilton Inlet

Labrador
City

Churchill
Falls

(500)

Cartwright

Wabush

Happy
Valley/
Goose
Bay

Mary's Harbour
Red Bay

Blanc Sablon

QUEBEC

(510)

N

Anticosti Is.

Gaspé
Pen.

Gulf of
St. Lawrence

Corner
Brook

Grand
Falls

Lewisporte

NEWFOUNDLAND

Gander

NEW
BRUNSWICK

PR. EDWARD IS.

NOVA SCOTIA

St. John's ★

villingate

Joe Batts Arm
Fogo I.

Hamilton Sound

Carmanville

Lumsden

porte

(330)

Wesleyville

Gander

(14)

nder
ake

(1)

(320)

Bonavista
Bay

Salvage

Bonavista

(9)

Glovertown

Terra Nova

(11)

Terra Nova
National Park

Elliston

Catalina

t Blandford

(230)

(10)

Trinity

Monroe

Baccalieu
Island

(4)

Clarenville

(8)

Bay de Verde

ATLANTIC OCEAN

(210)

Carbonear

Pouch Cove

lle

St. John's

(2)

(1)

Spaniard's
Bay

(1)

Cape Spear

Argentia

Salmonier
Nature Park

(5)

Bay Bulls

(10)

Cape Broyle

Placentia

AVALON
WILDERNESS
AREA

KEY

Ship Cove

Avalon
Peninsula

Ferry
Trans-Canada Hwy.

Placentia
Bay

St. Bride's

Branch

(7)

Cape St. Mary's
Bird Sanctuary

TO NORTH SYDNEY
(Nova Scotia)

(10)

Trepassey

(6)

Cape
Race

St. Shott's

0   60 miles
0   90 km

Tour 2: Clarenville and the Bonavista and Burin Peninsulas

8 **Clarenville** is about a two-hour drive on the Trans-Canada Highway from St. John's. This is the starting point for Route 230, the "Discovery Trail," one of the oldest portions of the is-
9 land, which culminates in the town of **Bonavista,** where John Cabot landed in 1497. Along the road, the area's long and rich tradition of fishing and farming is evident in its landscape and architecture. Throughout this peninsula you will find salmon rivers, trout streams, and craft shops featuring the handmade furniture for which this area is known. On your way to
10 Bonavista, visit **Trinity** to see the boat shed and enjoy the sheer beauty of this little town, where the small-pox vaccine was in-troduced for the first time. In Bonavista see the lighthouse and the museum, furnished in the period of 1870. *Tel. 709/729–2460 or 709/468–7444. Admission free. Open daily in summer, by appointment in winter.*

11 Back in Clarenville, drive west to **Terra Nova National Park,** set in the rugged coastline that adjoins Bonavista Bay. If you are a golfer, you can play on one of the most beautiful courses in Can-ada and the only one where a licensed salmon river cuts through the course. The park also offers attractive campsites, whale-watching tours, and nature walks. *Tel. 709/533–2801 or 709/ 533–2358, fax 709/533–2706. Open year-round. Vehicle permit required in summer: $4.25 per day per vehicle, $9.50 for 4-day pass, $26.75 for seasonal pass.*

The journey down the **Burin Peninsula** is a three- to four-hour drive through sometimes incredible landscape along Route 210. The peninsula's history is tied to the rich fishing grounds of the Grand Banks, which established this area as a center of the Eu-ropean fishery as early as the 1500s. By the early 1900s, one of the world's largest fishing fleets was based on the Burin Penin-sula, and today its inhabitants still operate the fishery in the modern trawlers that harvest the Grand Banks.

12 **Marystown** is the largest town on the peninsula. Its busy ship-yard still displays the fierce industry of this town. From here the road forms a loop. Along the way, if you have an inkling for a French lunch or a bottle of perfume, consider stopping at For-tune for a side-trip to France's only colonies in the North At-
13 lantic—the islands of **St. Pierre** and **Miquelon.** The ferry ride takes about two hours, and tourists should carry proof of citi-zenship. Shopping and eating are both wonderful pastimes there, and if you plan to stay overnight, consider the Hotel Robert.

Tour 3: Gander, Grand Falls, and Notre Dame Bay

The towns of Gander and Grand Falls are really the focal point
14 of central Newfoundland. **Gander,** a busy town of 15,000 people, is the site of the Gander International Airport. Around the time of World War II, it was chosen by the British Air Ministry as the site of a new air base because of its low incidence of fog and its position in what was then a fairly isolated location. Af-ter the war, the airport became an international hub, and young islanders would hang around the airport to see the stars come and go—Zsa Zsa Gabor, Tyrone Power. Now the airport, like all modern airports, is tightly secured, and Hollywood

stars have found new playgrounds. But Gander still makes a good base for your travels here. The Aviation Exhibition Provincial Exhibit, located in the airport's Domestic Passenger's Lounge, traces Newfoundland's role in the history of air travel. *Tel. 709/729-2460. Open daily.*

⓯ Grand Falls, 50 minutes west of Gander along the Trans-Canada Highway, is a paper town. The Mary March Regional Museum depicts the lives of the Boethuck Indians before they were exterminated by the white man. The museum is named for 23-year-old Demasduit (Mary March), one of the last Beothuks, who was captured in 1819. *St. Catherine St., off Rte. 1, tel. 709/489-9331. Admission free. Open weekdays 9-4:45, weekends and holidays, 10-5:45.*

Using either Route 330 from Gander on the Trans-Canada Highway or Route 340 from Grand Falls, wander north through wooded countryside and small villages to **Twillingate.** The in-
⓰ habitants of this charming old fishing village make their entire living from the sea and have been doing so for nearly two centuries. On the last weekend in July, every year, the town hosts the "Fish, Fun and Folk Festival," where every kind of fish is cooked in every kind of way. Twillingate is also one of the best places on the island to see icebergs—and is known to the locals as "Iceberg Alley." These majestic and dangerous mountains of ice are fascinating to watch and photograph while they're grounded in early summer.

You might also be interested in taking a ferry ride to either **Fogo** or **Change islands.** Branch off Route 340 to Route 335 and catch the ferry to either of the islands, located in Notre Dame Bay. These islands give one the impression of a place frozen in time. Interesting clapboard homes are precariously perched on rocks or built on small lots, surrounded by vegetable gardens. All along these roads, watch out for moose and herds of wild Newfoundland ponies who spend their summers grazing and enjoying the warm breeze off the ocean.

Tour 4: Deer Lake and the Great Northern Peninsula to St. Anthony

⓱ Deer Lake was once just another small town on the Trans-Canada Highway, but the opening of Gros Morne National Park and a first-class paved highway right through to St. Anthony changed all that in the late '60s. Today, with an airport and car rentals available, Deer Lake is a good starting point for a fly-drive vacation.

⓲ Head north out of Deer Lake on Route 430 to Route 422 to **Sir Richard Squires Memorial Park.** This drive will take you through Cormack, which is the first-class farming area of the island. The park remains natural and unspoiled, and it contains one of the most interesting salmon fishing areas in Newfoundland. At Big Falls here, the salmon can be seen jumping and scaling the falls in the summer to spawn in the river above. You really feel for them as they struggle upward, only to fall back, again and again. Nearby, fishermen in waders and boats try their luck with rod and reel.

Return to Route 430, and in a short while you are on the **Viking**
⓳ Trail leading into **Gros Morne National Park.** Because of its geological uniqueness and immense splendor, this park has been

named a UNESCO World Heritage Site. Among the more breathtaking sights are the expanses of wild orchids in springtime. There is an excellent visitor center (called Interpretation Centre, tel. 709/458–2066), which has displays, films, and videos about the park. Camping and hiking are also available. Just a brisk walk to the edge of Western Brook Pond, you can board a boat that will take you right up the gorge where the cliffs rise 300 to 400 feet on either side. Sometimes moose and bears can be seen on the shores, and nesting bald eagles fly overhead.

Farther up the highway, stop at the **Arches.** This is a geological wonder where the pounding sea has cut through a bed of dolomite. Whether the sea is rough or gentle, it is worth your while to stop here and breathe in the marvelous clean, fresh sea air. A sunset here is unforgettable.

As you drive north, parallel to the Gulf of St. Lawrence River, small villages are interspersed with rivers where salmon and trout get to be real "liar" size. All along here, too, are the remains of the Maritime Archaic Indians, and there is a most interesting Interpretation Centre at Port aux Choix (tel. 709/623–2601) that tells their story and that of the Dorset Eskimo.

❷⓪ Continuing on Route 430, turn onto Route 436 to **L'Anse aux Meadows National Historic Park.** This tourist site wins the vote as the least likely to be considered a tourist trap. Uncovered by a Norwegian team, Helge and Anne Stine Ingstad, in 1960, this is believed to have been the site of the Norseman Lief Erikson's colony in the New World around AD 1000. Parks Canada has established a marvelous Interpretation Centre (tel. 709/623–2601) and has meticulously restored some of the sod huts. With fires burning inside and sheepskins about, one does get a sense of centuries past. The authenticity can be as eerie as it is wonderful. *Rte. 436, 48 km (30 mi) from St. Anthony, tel. 709/623–2601 or 709/623–2608. Admission free. Visitor center open mid-June–Labor Day, daily 9–8.*

❷① Back on Route 430, you will come to **St. Anthony,** at the tip of what is known as "the Great Northern Peninsula." This is the home of the **Grenfell Mission.** The huge hospital attests to the work done here by Sir Wilfred Grenfell, who established nursing stations and cooperatives and provided medical services to the scattered villages of northern Newfoundland and the south coast of Labrador in the early 1900s. The main foyer of the hospital is filled with historic murals done in tiles and is worth a visit. The **Grenfell House,** the home of Sir Wilfred and Lady Grenfell, has been restored to period condition and can also be visited. *On the west side of St. Anthony on a hill overlooking the harbor, adjacent to Charles S. Curtis Memorial Hospital, tel. 709/454–3333. Admission: $1 adults; 50¢ students, children under 5 and senior citizens free. Open daily.*

St. Anthony, settled around a natural harbor, is a beautiful town. Take a trip out to the lighthouse—you may see an iceberg or two floating by.

Don't leave without visiting the **Grenfell Handcraft** store (tel. 709/454–3576). Importing craftspeople to train the villagers to become self-sufficient in a harsh environment, was one of Grenfell's aims. A windproof cloth that villagers turned into well-made parkas came to be known as Grenfell cloth. Beautiful clothes fashioned out of Grenfell cloth of a quality and style of work not found anywhere else are available for sale here. Return to Deer Lake along Route 430.

Tour 5: Corner Brook and the West Coast

② **Corner Brook** is Newfoundland's second city and the hub of the west coast of the island. With mountains on three sides and a beautiful view of the harbor and the Bay of Islands, Corner Brook is home to one of the largest paper mills in the world. Every July it hosts the Hangashore Folk Festival, where you can go to hear some great traditional Canadian and Newfoundland music. Corner Brook is also a good place to stay if you plan to explore the west coast. It is only three hours from the Port aux Basques ferry, and it's an attractive and active city. Here, superb wooden houses are set beside tall birch trees. The town enjoys more clearly defined seasons than most of the rest of the island, and in summer there are many pretty gardens to view and enjoy.

The north and south shores of the **Bay of Islands** have fine paved roads—**Route 440** on the north shore, and **Route 450** on the south—and both offer a pleasant and scenic drive, each of a morning or afternoon duration. On both roads, farming and fishing communities exist side by side. Take a camera on these drives—the scenery is breathtaking, with farms, mountains, and beautiful pockets of brilliant wildflowers.

Another day, drive farther west on the Trans-Canada Highway and turn off at Route 460. Spend some time on the **Port au Port**
② **Peninsula,** stopping at **Stephenville,** home of the old Harmon Air Force Base, and now home every year to the Stephenville Arts Festival. The peninsula itself was largely settled by the French who brought their way of life and language to this small corner of Newfoundland.

As you move farther down the Trans-Canada Highway toward Port aux Basques, Routes 404, 405, 406, and 407 will bring you into the small Scottish communities where you might be lucky enough to hear some Gaelic. Nestled among the farms here are some of the finest salmon rivers and some of the most pastoral land in the province, all of this against the backdrop of the Long Range Mountains and the Lewis Hills, from which gales strong enough to stop traffic hurl themselves along the coast.

Tour 6: Labrador

Isolated from the rest of the continent, Labrador has remained one of the world's truly wild places, and yet its two main centers of Labrador City–Wabush, and Happy Valley/Goose Bay offer all the amenities available in larger, urban centers.

Labrador is steeped in history, a place where the past invades the present and life evolves as it did many years ago, a composite of natural phenomena, wilderness adventure, history, and culture.

English is the main language, but you will hear it spoken with many charming lilts and dialects of the British Isles, Germany, Norway, France, and Spain. The intriguing language of the Inuit and Innu, as well as French, are also heard in various parts of Labrador.

Labrador's vast landscape—294,330 square kilometers (113,204 square miles) of land and 8,000 kilometers (5,000 miles) of coastline—is home to a small but richly diverse population with a history that in some areas stretches back thousands of years and in others, like the mining towns of Labrador West, covers less than 40 years.

Getting There From the island of Newfoundland, you can fly to Labrador from St. John's, Gander, Deer Lake, or Stephenville. In summer, you can also make your way here by car ferry. **Marine Atlantic** (tel. 709/535-6876 in Lewisporte, Newfoundland; 709/896-0041 in Goose Bay, Labrador; or 800/341-7981 in the U.S.) travels from Lewisporte in Newfoundland to Cartwright, on the coast of Labrador, and then through the Hamilton inlet to Happy Valley/Goose Bay. To explore the south coast of Labrador, catch the ferry at St. Barbe on Route 430 in Newfoundland to Blanc Sablon, Quebec. From here you can drive into Labrador along Route 510.

If you plan on doing any extensive driving in Labrador, you should contact the Department of Tourism (tel. 709/729-2830 or 800/563-6353) for advice on the best routes and road conditions.

The South Coast The trip from Blanc Sablon to Red Bay on Route 510 will take you through the small fishing communities of L'Anse au Clair, Forteau, and L'Anse au Loup. In **L'Anse au Clair,** you can walk the "Doctor's Path," where long ago a Dr. Marcoux would search out herbs and medicinal plants in the days when hospitals and nursing stations were few and far between. Anglers can try their luck for trout and salmon of immense size. As you drive, be on the lookout for burial sites of the Maritime Archaic Indians, some estimated to be 9,000 years old. Visit the Point Amour lighthouse, one of the few truly ancient working structures, and for the adventuresome few, climb the steps to the top—the view is breathtaking. It is the second-tallest lighthouse in Canada.

At the end of Route 510 is **Red Bay,** the site of the 16th-century Basque whaling station. Research teams are working here every day from June through October, and visitors are welcome on the site to see the artifacts—some four centuries old—that have been lifted from the cold waters off the Labrador coast.

Coastal Labrador You can tour coastal Labrador aboard Marine Atlantic's car ferry from Lewisporte, Newfoundland, to Cartwright and Goose Bay. It operates from mid-June to mid-September and is the main carrier of all food and goods for people living along the coast. Passenger space is extremely limited, and you must make your reservations from within the province. The trip takes 33 hours one-way, and two regularly scheduled return trips are made weekly (*see* Getting There, above). Each ferry takes two weeks to complete the trip. Because this is the provider boat, you'll put in at a number of coastal communities before your arrival at **Happy Valley/Goose Bay,** considered the hub for coastal Labrador. From its origins as a transatlantic air ferry stop during the war, Happy Valley/Goose Bay is now a thriving community. As well as being an alternate stop for aircraft flying the Atlantic, it is also the low-level flying training base for the British, Dutch, and German airforces.

Labrador West Labrador West's subarctic landscape is challenging and unforgettable. The area offers some of the world's best angling and both downhill and cross-country skiing. Hikers are spell-bound by the beauty of the **Torngat Mountains.** And mining communities, forged out of the rugged landscape, are still vibrant. The simple lifestyle and the unique folklore of the Innuit people that date back thousands of years can still be felt.

The best way to see this area is by taking the **Québec North Shore and Labrador Railway** (tel. 709/944–8205), which leaves Sept Isles, Québec, twice weekly. The 10-hour trip takes you through 419 kilometers (260 miles) of virgin forest, spectacular waterfalls, and majestic mountains. The refurbished vintage dome car is ideal for an expanded view of this breathtaking panorama. The train, though, is more than a pleasure ride—it carries iron ore from Wabush and Labrador City (site of the largest open-pit mining operation in the world) to various distribution points in Québec.

The modern towns of Wabush and Labrador City have all of the amenities of larger, urban centers, including accommodations, sports and recreational facilities, good shopping, live theater, and some of the finest hospitality you will find anywhere. Nearby are the **Smokey Mountain Alpine Skiing Center** (open mid-November to early May, tel. 709/944–3505) and the **Menihek Nordic Ski Club** (tel. 709/944–6339 or 709/944–2154), with trails and slopes for both beginners and advanced skiers.

Shopping

The main centers of Newfoundland and Labrador—St. John's, Clarenville, Gander, Grand Falls, Corner Brook, Labrador West—all have modern shopping centers. However, the smaller communities often offer interesting crafts and native wares. Wander about—each town and village has its own country store and crafts store or general store. There are even some stores where packages are still being wrapped in brown paper and tied with twine—it almost reminds one of Dickens's England.

Nonia (Newfoundland Outport Nurses Industrial Association), at 286 Water Street in St. John's, was started in 1923 to give Newfoundland women an opportunity to earn extra money. Throughout history, the women of Newfoundland had earned a reputation for turning homespun wool into exquisite clothing. In 1923 Jubilee Guilds supplied these outport women with wool of all kinds and colors, and in this shop on Water Street, even today, you can buy their well-made knitware.

Other fine crafts stores in St. John's are the Salt Box, The Cod Jigger and the Newfoundland Weavery. For antiques, Murray's Antiques and Livyers are well worth a visit.

At St. Anthony, on the northern tip of Newfoundland, browse in the Grenfell Handcraft Store (*see* Exploring, above).

Sports and Fitness

All Provincial and National Parks in Newfoundland have hiking and nature trails. Gros Morne on the west coast has opportunities for mountain climbing and nature walks. St. John's has an aquarena, and visitors can join the residents of St. John's as they walk around Quidi Vidi Lake. There are also windsurfing and small-boat sailing on the lake. Most cities and towns of any size have walking trails, and because of its geography, most parts of the island offer great opportunities for hiking and nature walks.

For the rod-and-reel fishermen, Newfoundland has 105 salmon rivers and trout streams, and angling in these unpolluted waters is a fisherman's dream. Information must be obtained from the **Department of Development**, Tourism Branch (tel. 800/563–6353) regarding license fees and scheduled rivers.

In the major centers, visitors can access fitness programs offered by the YM–YWCA, private fitness centers, and community groups.

Dining and Lodging

Dining

John Cabot and Sir Humphrey Gilbert raved about our "waters teeming with fish." Today our fish are still considered some of the best in the world; and one of the best bargains you will find, especially in the smaller centers. In season you will be treated to local delicacies such as panfried, baked, or poached cod, cod tongues, salt cod, fish and brewis (cod of course!). You'll find that in Newfoundland if you ask for "fish," you will always get cod. Fresh lobster (always cooked in sea water) and Atlantic salmon are also good choices in season.

Other foods you shouldn't leave without trying are the partridgeberries and, for the lucky ones who get to northern Newfoundland and into Labrador in late August, the bakeapples. This marvelous low-growing berry that looks like a raspberry with jaundice and tastes heavenly is known in the Scandinavian countries as the "cloud berry." You may also hear Newfoundlanders talk about the herb they call summer savory. Newfoundlanders are so partial to this herb that they refuse to eat roast chicken or turkey without it. Growers in the province ship the product all over the world, and any Newfoundlander visiting relatives living outside the province is always asked to "bring the savory."

The large urban centers across the province, especially St. John's and Corner Brook, offer a number of gourmet choices. But visitors shouldn't be shy about trying some of the excellent meals offered in the expanding network of "hospitality homes" across the province, where "home cooking" goes hand in hand with the warm welcome for which Newfoundlanders are famous.

Dress is casual everywhere except at the very expensive listings.

Highly recommended restaurants and lodging in each price category are indicated by a star ★.

Category	Cost*
Very Expensive	over $50
Expensive	$35–$50

Moderate	$20–$35
Inexpensive	under $20

per person, excluding drinks, service, and 11% sales tax

Lodging

Newfoundland and Labrador offer lodging that ranges from the modestly priced "hospitality homes" to luxury accommodations. In between, visitors can choose from affordable, basic lodging and mid-priced hotels. In the remote areas, visitors should be prepared to find very basic lodgings. However, the lack of urban amenities is more than made up for by home-cooked meals and the great hospitality that you'll find wherever you go in Newfoundland and Labrador. Life is definitely more relaxed here—if you are expected at a "hospitality home," even in St. John's, and you are running late, your host or hostess will leave your room key with a welcome note in the mailbox!

Highly recommended lodgings in each price category are indicated by a star ★.

Category	Cost*
Expensive	over $100
Moderate	$60–$90
Inexpensive	under $50

Clarenville
Dining and Lodging

Holiday Inn. There are no surprises at this chain member. Rooms are standard Holiday Inn fare. The daily buffet is plentiful and well worth the drive. *Box 967, Clarenville, A0E 1J0, tel. 709/466–7911, fax 709/466–3854. 64 rooms. AE, MC, V. Moderate.*

Corner Brook
Dining and Lodging
★

The Glynmill Inn. This charming inn has the feel of old England. The inn was once the staff house for the visiting top brass of the mill. Rooms are cozy and the dining room serves basic and well-prepared Newfoundland seafood, soups, and speciality desserts made with Newfoundland partridgeberries. *Cobb La., Box 550, Corner Brook, A2H 6E6, tel. 709/634–5106, fax 709/634–5106. 90 rooms. AE, MC, V. Moderate.*

Holiday Inn. Again, there's nothing extraordinary here, aside from the convenience of being located right in town. The rooms were completely remodeled in 1991, so there are none of the '70s-style oranges and browns. The restaurant is average but has good seasonal fish dishes. *48 West St., Corner Brook A2H 2Z2 tel. 709/634–5381. 103 rooms. Facilities: lounge, restaurant, cable TV, minibars in some rooms, heated swimming pool. Pets allowed. AE, D, DC, MC, V. Moderate.*

Journey's End Motel. This is a comfortable, modern motel (built in 1988) with an attractive interior (the dominating colors are dusty rose and blue) and beautiful views on either the city or the Bay of Islands. *Box 1142, Corner Brook A2H 6T2 (on Rte. 1), tel. 709/639–1980. 81 rooms with color TV, pets allowed. AE, MC, DC, V. Moderate.*

★ **Mamateek Inn.** Rooms are more modern than at the Glynmill Inn. The dining room, which serves good Newfoundland home-cooked food, is known for its exquisite view looking out over the whole city. Come here at sunset. *Rt. 1, Box 787, Corner Brook, A2H 6G7, tel. 709/639–8901, fax 709/639–7567. 55 rooms. AE, MC, V. Moderate.*

Deer Lake
Dining and Lodging

Deer Lake Motel. The guest rooms here are clean and comfortable, and the food is basic, home-cooked fare. This is a popular trucker's spot, so you can expect some of the best coffee on the Trans-Canada Highway here. *Box 820, Deer Lake, A0K 2E0, tel. 709/635–2108, fax 709/635–3842. 54 rooms, 2 suites. AE, MC, V. Moderate.*

Gander
Dining and Lodging
★

Albatross Motel. This newly renovated motel has earned its reputation as a great place to stop off for a meal. Try the cod au gratin—you won't find it this good anywhere else. Rooms are basic and clean. *Box 450, Gander, A1V 1W8, tel. 709/256–3956, fax 709/651–2692. 107 rooms, 4 suites. AE, MC, V. Moderate.*

Grand Falls
Dining and Lodging

Mount Peyton Hotel. The rooms aren't sound-proof here, but they are clean and comfortable. And the excellent Newfoundland menu makes this a great place to break your journey across the island. *214 Lincoln Rd., Grand Falls, A2A 1P8, tel. 709/489–2251. 150 rooms. AE, MC, V. Moderate.*

L'Anse aux Meadows
Lodging

Valhalla Lodge Bed & Breakfast. Located adjacent to the Viking site at L'Anse aux Meadows, this is the only game in town, but that doesn't make it any less comfortable and inviting. Note the interesting fossils in the rock fireplace in the dining room. Hot breakfasts are available, and extra meals can be had on request. *Gunner's Cove, Griquet A0K 2X0, tel. 709/623–2018 (summer), 709/896–5476 (winter). 6 rooms. V. Inexpensive.*

Port aux Basques
Dining and Lodging

St. Christopher's Hotel. This clean, comfortable hotel is a new addition in Port aux Basque that offers quiet, air-conditioned rooms and good food. *Caribou Rd., Box 2049, Port aux Basques, A0M 1C0, tel. 709/695–7034, fax 709/695–9841. 58 rooms. Facilities: banquet room, restaurant (reservations not necessary, dress casual), conference room, satellite TV. AE, MC, V. Moderate.*

St. John's
Dining
★

The Cellar. This restaurant situated in a historic building on the waterfront gets rave reviews for its innovative Continental cuisine. Menu selections include Creole chicken and tiramisu for dessert. *Baird's Cove, between Harbour and Water Sts., St. John's, tel. 709/579–8900. Reservations advised. No jeans or sweatshirts. AE, MC, V. Very Expensive.*

★ **The Flake House.** Situated in a working fishing village within St. John's, this restaurant has already won international awards for its cuisine. It features all species of Newfoundland seafood, as well as Canadian cuisine. *16 Barrows Rd., Quidi Vidi Village, St. John's, tel. 709/576–7518. Reservations advised. AE, MC, V. Expensive.*

★ **Stone House.** Situated in one of St. John's most historic buildings—an old restored Elizabethan stone cottage—this dining room features nouvelle cuisine and Newfoundland specialties. *8 Kennas Hill, St. John's, tel. 709/753–2380. Reservations advised. Dress: casual. AE, MC, V. Moderate–Expensive.*

Dining and Lodging
★

Hotel Newfoundland. This hotel replaces the old hotel that stood on this site for many years. St. John's residents gather here for all their special occasions. Noted for its buffets, its charming rooms that overlook St. John's harbor, its atrium, and the exquisite cuisine at the Cabot Club, this is one of St.

John's finest dining establishments. *Box 5637, St. John's A1C 5W8, tel. 709/726–4980, fax 709/726–2025. 288 rooms, 14 suites. AE, MC, V. Expensive.*

★ **Radisson Plaza Hotel.** In this new convention hotel in downtown St. John's, rooms overlook the harbor and the city. It offers two great dining rooms: Brazil Square, noted for its noon buffets, and Newman's, for its small, quiet secluded dining room serving international and Newfoundland cuisine. *120 New Gower St., St. John's A1C 1J3, tel. 709/739–6404. 276 rooms, 9 suites. AE, MC, V. Expensive.*

Journey's End Motel. This is the newest member of this hotel chain and it overlooks St. John's harbor. Like other Journey's Ends, it offers clean, comfortable rooms at a reasonable price. The hotel has one of St. John's newest and most popular restaurants, Rumplestiltskins, serving great Canadian food with fast, efficient service. *Hill O'Chips, St. John's A1C 6B1, tel. 709/754–7788. 164 rooms. AE, MC, V. Moderate.*

Lodging **Compton House Bed & Breakfast.** Housed in a charming, re-
★ stored historic St. John's residence in the west end of the city, this inn is beautifully decorated. Twelve-foot ceilings and wide halls give the place a majestic feeling, and rooms done in pastels and chintzes add an air of coziness. The location, within easy walking distance of downtown St. John's, is ideal. *26 Waterford Bridge Rd., St. John's A1E 1C6, tel. 709/739–5789. 4 rooms, 2 suites. AE, MC, V. Moderate.*

The Arts and Nightlife

It is claimed that St. John's has more bars per mile than any other city in North America. However, each has its own personality. Irish music, in particular, can be heard at Erin's Pub, Water Street, and a mix of traditional folk songs and Irish music can be had at Bridgett's, Cookstown Road, St. John's.

George Street, in downtown St. John's, is a street of pubs and restaurants that has been beautifully restored. Open-air concerts can be heard here during the popular annual George Street Festival.

Newfoundlanders love a party, and from the cities to the smallest towns they celebrate their history and unique culture in colorful pageant, story, and song throughout a summer of festivals and events. Two of note are the award-winning Newfoundland and Labrador Folk Arts Festival, held in St. John's every summer, and The Stephenville Festival of the Arts (live theater), held annually in that west coast town.

The province has a very active arts community, and live theater has become very popular in the larger centers. Most major towns have an Arts and Culture Center that offers traveling art shows, live theater presentations, ballet, and excellent concerts by local, national, and international artists.

16 Wilderness Canada

by Mac Mackay

Mac Mackay is a Calgary-based writer, editor, and publisher whose nonfiction has appeared in a variety of U.S. and Canadian publications.

Canada's northern wilderness is big—bigger than Alaska, Texas, New Mexico, Arizona, and California combined. Together, the Northwest Territories and Yukon contain 3,909,770 square kilometers (1,536,900 square miles), or 39% of the area of the entire country, yet fewer than 85,000 people live here. This vast area is filled with unmatched sights and experiences: the rugged beauty of the natural wilderness, with its unique birds, animals, and sea life; the endless horizon; the midnight sun; and the meeting of three distinct cultures—Inuit, Dene (native Indian), and European.

The first residents of this area came from Asia about 30,000 years ago over a land bridge that spanned the Bering Sea. Those early adventurers who traveled east were the Inuit; those who journeyed south became the Dene. It wasn't until the 1500s that the first Europeans arrived, spurred on by the dreams of eastern riches. Martin Frobisher, Henry Hudson, John Franklin, Samuel Hearne, and Alexander Mackenzie explored and mapped the rugged land and waterways, and most lost their lives doing so. In 1670, the Hudson's Bay Company (now Canada's oldest corporation) was given title to what is now Canada's northern wilderness. Over the next 150 years the Hudson's Bay and the North West companies competed for the fur-trading revenues that drove them into the northwest. They eventually joined forces in 1821.

In August 1896, three prospectors stumbled upon gold at Rabbit Creek in the Klondike River Valley in Yukon. When news broke in the south more than a quarter of a million people—Canadians, Americans, and others from around the world—left their homes for the valley, making it the greatest gold rush in North American history. By 1900 the rush was virtually over.

Yukon became a separate territory in 1896. In 1905, the provinces of Alberta and Saskatchewan were carved out of the Northwest Territories, and later additional lands were granted to Manitoba, Ontario, and Québec. By 1912, the Northwest Territories had shrunk to its present-day boundaries.

Furs and fish were the only resources of value in the north in the early 20th century. But the building of the Alaska Highway in 1942; the opening of lead-zinc mines at Pine Point, Northwest Territories, and Faro, Yukon; and the discovery of significant oil and natural gas deposits in the Mackenzie Delta brought about many changes, particularly to the native people and to the fragile ecosystems of the north.

The population of Yukon today is 28,000; the Northwest Territories is home to 55,000. Both areas are administered by a commissioner appointed by the federal government in Ottawa and governed by an elected legislative assembly, headed by a government leader. Unlike provinces of Canada, the territories have only limited control over their natural resources and crown (or public) land and limited powers of taxation.

Life here fosters a spirit of independence, and you'll find the people friendly, helpful, and always willing to aid a newcomer. Ancient traditions live on in northern Canada: Dene and Inuit still hunt, fish, and trap furs for a living. But modern life is not far behind: Many of the native communities have recognized the detrimental effects of social drinking and banned alcohol in their neighborhoods. Your tolerance of these activities and situations will help to ensure your warm welcome among north-erners.

Temperatures rise to 30°C (86°F) on the hottest days, but in spring and fall the evenings can be sweater weather. In the winter, daylight is a rare commodity here; consider yourself fortunate if you see the sun for a few hours. And –40°C (–40°F) is a common daytime temperature.

The north country is too vast to see in one visit. You'll have to decide what to focus on and discover the best mode of transportation to get you there: car, chartered plane or commercial airline, or boat.

Essential Information

Important Addresses and Numbers

Tourist **TravelArctic** (Box 1320, Yellowknife, X1A 2L9, tel. 403/873–
Information 7200 or 800/661–0788) distributes a free map, explorers' guide,
Northwest and several useful brochures. Office hours are 8:30–4:30 week-
Territories days. **Tourist Information Centres** are located in most communi-ties, and the NWT government operates highway information centers at the Alberta border on the Mackenzie Highway (mid-May through mid-Sept., 8AM to midnight), Nitainlaii Territorial Park, on the Dempster Highway (June-mid-Sept.) near Fort Mc-Pherson, and at Blackstone Territorial Park 147 kilometers (92 miles) north of the British Columbia border on the Liard High-way. Regional tourism associations provide more precise infor-mation on the many diverse communities. If the towns of Coppermine, Bathurst Inlet, Gjoa Haven, Pelly Bay, Spence Bay, Cambridge Bay, and Holman Island intrigue you, write **Arctic Coast Tourist Association** (Box 91, Cambridge Bay, X0E 0C0, tel. 403/983–2224). If Baffin and Ellesmere islands and Auyuittuq National Park beckon, contact **Baffin Tourism Asso-ciation** (Box 820, Iqaluit, X0A 0H0, tel. 819/979–6551). The up-per Mackenzie River, the southern shore of Great Slave Lake, and Wood Buffalo National Park are served by **Big River Tour-ism Association** (Box 185, Hay River, X0E 0R0, tel. 403/874–2422). **Delta-Beaufort Tourism Association** (Box 2759, Inuvik, X0E 0T0, tel. 403/979–4321) can tell you about the Mackenzie Delta, the Dempster Highway, and Banks Island. Information about Keewatin, on the western coast of Hudson Bay to the barrens is available from **Travel Keewatin** (Box 328, Rankin In-let, X0C 0G0, tel. 819/645–2618). Nahanni National Park infor-mation is available from **Nahanni-Ram Tourism Association** (Box 177, Fort Simpson, X0E 0N0, tel. 403/695–3182). Yellow-knife and Great Slave Lake are located in the jurisdiction of **Northern Frontier Visitors' Association** (Box 1107, Yellow-knife, X1A 2N8, tel. 403/873–3131). The **Sahtu Tourism Associ-ation** (Box 115, Norman Wells, X0E 0V0, tel. 403/587–2054) serves the Mackenzie River valley and Great Bear Lake.

Yukon **Tourism Yukon** (Box 2703, Whitehorse, Y1A 2C6, tel. 403/667–5340) can provide you with brochures and maps of attractions throughout the territory. Six **Visitor Reception Centres** oper-ate during the summer from mid-May to mid-September: **Wat-son Lake** (Alaska Highway Interpretive Centre, junction of Campbell and Alaska Hwys., tel. 403/536–7469); **Carcross** (tel. 403/821–4431); **Whitehorse** (302 Steele St., tel. 403/667–2915);

Haines Junction (located in Kluane National Park headquarters, tel. 403/634–2345); **Beaver Creek** (at road marker "Mile 1,202; kilometer 1,934" on) Alaska Hwy., tel. 403/862–7321); and **Dawson City** (at the corner of Front and King Sts., tel. 403/ 993–5566). For additional information on the Whitehorse area, write **Whitehorse Visitor Reception Centre** (102–302 Steele St., Whitehorse, Y1A 2C5, tel. 403/667–2915. Open May–Sept., daily 8–8; Oct.–Apr., 8:30–5. For a Dawson City and region update, contact **Klondike Visitors Association** (Box 389, Dawson City, Y0B 1G0, tel. 403/993–5575).

Emergencies For emergency services in either Yukon or the Northwest Territories, travelers should dial "0" for the operator and explain the nature of the emergency. The operator will connect you with the police, ambulance, fire company, or medical help, as needed.

The Royal Canadian Mounted Police patrol Yukon and the Northwest Territories.

Hospitals and Medical services are available at the nursing station in every
Clinics small community. Air ambulance service is also available to the
Northwest nearest hospital, located in the larger centers. **Fort Simpson:**
Territories Fort Simpson Hospital, tel. 403/695–2291. **Fort Smith:** Fort Smith Health Centre, tel. 403/872–2713; Fort Smith Dental Clinic, tel. 403/872–2004. **Hay River:** Hay River Dental Clinic, tel. 403/874–6663; H.H. Williams Memorial Hospital, tel. 403/ 874–6512. **Inuvik:** Clark Dental Clinic, 22 Reliance St., tel. 403/ 979–3008; Inuvik General Hospital, tel. 403/979–2955. **Igaluit:** Baffin Regional Hospital, tel. 819/979–5231. **Norman Wells:** Norman Wells Dental Clinic, tel. 403/587–2629. **Pine Point:** H.H. Williams Hospital, tel. 403/393–2281. **Yellowknife:** Adam Dental Clinic, 5209 Franklin Ave., tel. 403/873–2775; Mackenzie Dental Clinic, 5103–50 St., tel. 403/873–8505; Stanton Yellowknife Hospital, tel. 403/920–4111; Yellowknife Dental Clinic, 5014–48 St., tel. 403/873–2450.

Yukon Medical facilities in Whitehorse, Watson Lake, and Dawson City are staffed 24 hours daily; the remaining communities have a nurse on call 24 hours a day. **Dawson City:** Dawson Medical Clinic, tel. 403/993–5744. **Watson Lake:** Watson Lake Cottage Hospital, tel. 403/536–2541. **Whitehorse:** Whitehorse General Hospital, 5 Hospital Rd., tel. 403/667–8700; Branigan Clinic, 106 Lambert St., tel. 403/667–6491; Klondyke Medical Clinic, 2–3089–3rd Ave., tel. 403/668–4060; Whitehorse Medical Clinic, 406 Lambert St., tel. 403/667–6444; Pine Medical Centre, 5110–5th Ave., tel. 403/668–4353.

Pharmacies There are no late-night services in the Northwest Territories.
Northwest After hours, call the local hospital or nursing station. **Fort**
Territories **Smith:** Wally's Drugs, 65 Breynat St., tel. 403/872–2134. **Hay River:** Ring's Drug Store, 6 Capital Cr., tel. 403/874–6744. **Inuvik:** Inuvik Rexall Drugs, 123 Mackenzie Rd., tel. 403/979–2266. **Yellowknife:** Shopper's Drug Mart, Panda II Mall, tel. 403/873–4055, Sutherland's Drugs, 50 Ave. & 50 St., tel. 403/ 873–4555.

Yukon There are no late-night services in Yukon. After hours, call the local hospital or nursing station. **Dawson City:** Arctic Drugs, Front St., tel. 403/993–5331. **Whitehorse:** Medicine Chest, 406 Lambert St., tel. 403/668–7000; Shopper's Drug Mart, 211 Main St., tel. 403/667–2485 and 2–303 Ogilvie St., tel. 403/667–6757.

Arriving and Departing by Plane

Airports and Airlines **Whitehorse International Airport** is the major airport for Yukon. It lies alongside the Alaska Highway, 200 feet above the Yukon River and downtown Whitehorse. Look for the unique DC-3 windvane beside the entrance. **Yellowknife Airport** is 5 kilometers (3 miles) northeast of the center of Yellowknife.

The gateway cities in Canada are Vancouver, Edmonton, Winnipeg, Ottawa, and Montréal, and many U.S. airlines fly to these centers. **Canadian Airlines International** (tel. 403/498–3800; in Eastern Arctic, 800/361–7413; in Keewatin, 800/665–1430; in Western Arctic, 800/661–1505; in the U.S., 800/427–7000) and **Air BC** (tel. 604/273–2464; from BC and western U.S., 800/663–0522) fly from Vancouver to Whitehorse. **Canadian** also flies from Edmonton to Yellowknife and from Montréal to Iqaluit. **First Air** (tel. 613/839–3340 or 800/267–1247) offers flights from Ottawa and Montréal to many eastern Arctic communities as well as connecting flights to Yellowknife. **NWT Air** (tel. 403/920–2500 or 800/661–0789) connects Yellowknife, Edmonton, and Winnipeg; and **Calm Air** (tel. 204/778–6471 or 204/778–7327) serves the Keewatin communities from Thompson and Churchill in Manitoba.

Between the Airports and Center City *Whitehorse* **Yellow Cabs** (tel. 403/668–4811) operates an airport limousine service to the downtown Whitehorse hotels for $4. Taxi fare from the airport to downtown will cost about $7.50. Cab fares start at $2.25; each additional tenth of a kilometer costs 12¢ (about $1.90 per mile). Other cab companies in Whitehorse are **Co-Op Cabs** (tel. 403/668–2121) and **5th Ave Taxi** (tel. 403/668–4111).

Yellowknife **City Cab** (tel. 403/873–4444) will take you from Yellowknife Airport to city center for $3 (airport limousine service) or $10 in a taxi. Taxi rates start at $2.15; each additional tenth of a kilometer costs 10¢ (about $1.60 per mile).

Taxi rates in the north are high, but drivers are courteous and the cars reliable.

Arriving and Departing by Car, Train, and Bus

By Car The most direct route north from Great Falls, Montana, is by taking I–15 188 kilometers (116 miles) to the Canadian border. Another 320 kilometers (198 miles) via Highways 4, 3, and 2 will bring you to Calgary. You'll want to continue on Highway 2 290 kilometers (180 miles) to Edmonton. If your destination is Yellowknife and the Northwest Territories, take Highways 16, 43, 34, and 2 to Grimshaw, Alberta, where the Mackenzie Highway begins. From Grimshaw, it's 475 kilometers (295 miles) to the NWT border. If the Alaska Highway is your goal, drive to Dawson Creek, British Columbia, where it starts. The route from Edmonton is Highways 16, 43, 34, and 2, a distance of 590 kilometers (366 miles). From Seattle or Vancouver, British Columbia, your route is to Dawson Creek via Cache Creek and Prince George on Highways 1 and 97. The distance is 1,150 kilometers (715 miles) from Vancouver to Dawson Creek. Once you're on the Alaska Highway, you're bound for Yukon and Alaska. At Fort Nelson, 465 kilometers (288 miles) to the north you'll have one last chance to change your mind and head for the Northwest Territories. The Liard Highway from Fort Nelson snakes northeast through poplar muskeg to the NWT border (257 kilometers, or 160 miles) and Fort Simpson (415 kilometers, or 257 miles). However, if you head due northwest you'll reach the Yukon border near Watson Lake after 1,021 kilometers (634 miles).

For more information about driving in Yukon and the Northwest Territories, *see* Getting Around, below.

By Train There is no rail service into Yukon or Northwest Territories.

By Bus **Greyhound Lines of Canada Ltd.** (10324 103rd St., Edmonton, AB T5J 0Y9, tel. 403/421–4211) provides service from Edmonton north to Hay River, Northwest Territories, daily except Saturday. Greyhound will also take you from Vancouver or Edmonton to Whitehorse in Yukon along the Alaska Highway.

Getting Around

By Car Regardless of what you may have heard, road travel in the Yukon and Northwest Territories is becoming easier each year. The Alaska, Klondike, Dempster, and Mackenzie highways are hard-packed gravel roads with ever-increasing paved sections. You won't go quite as fast as you would on the superhighways of the south, but with the exception of the Dempster, there are few stretches in excess of 160 kilometers (100 miles) between services. A little advance preparation for driving in the north is a good idea. You should have good tires, including a good spare, plus an extra fan belt. Plastic headlight protectors are a must, especially on the graveled sections of the highways, where you may encounter flying stones. Roads are being constantly upgraded, so be on the watch for heavy equipment working in your lane. Ensure that your windshield washers are filled, and drive with your headlights on. During the summer, the roads are watered to keep dust down, and therefore can be slippery. The use of seat belts is recommended. Winter driving requires extra preparation: Take along emergency survival gear, such as an ax, shovel, matches, sleeping bag, paper kindling, sensible outdoor clothing, and food. Your vehicle should be properly winterized, with light oil in the engine and transmission, a block heater, antifreeze, and tire chains.

Car and Boat Rentals Most of the larger centers in Yukon and the western Northwest Territories have outlets for renting a variety of vehicles—cars, trucks, campers, motorhomes, all-terrain vehicles (ATVs), boats, and canoes—that allow you to abandon the beaten path for the countryside. In Whitehorse and Yellowknife, car rental agencies are located at the airports.

Dawson City, YT **Dawson Trading Post** (5th Ave., Box 889, Dawson City, Y0B 1G0, tel. 403/993–5316) offers canoe rentals.

Whitehorse, YT **Access Yukon** (3089 3rd Ave., Y1A 5B3, tel. 403/668–5598) has canoes, campers, and 4×4s. **Ambassador Motorhome & Recreational Services Ltd.** (Mile 912 Alaska Hwy., Y1A 3S9, tel. 403/667–4130) rents motorhomes, trucks, campers, and 4×4s. One-way rentals available between Vancouver and Terrace, BC, to and from Whitehorse. **Budget Rent-A-Car** (4178 4th Ave., Y1A 1J6, tel. 403/667–6200 or 403/667–6220) offers car, truck, and 4×4 rentals. **Hertz Rent A Car** (4158 4th Ave., Y1A 1J2, tel. 403/667–2505) leases out cars, trucks, 4×4s, and mini-vans. **Kanoe People** (Box 5152, Y1A 4S3, tel. 403/668–4899) offers boat and motor rentals; river guidebooks available. **Klondike**

Recreational Rentals Ltd. (108 Industrial Rd., Box 5156, Y1A 4S3, tel. 403/668–2200; in winter, 604/675–4911) rents vans, motorhomes, trucks, and campers. **Listers Rentals Ltd.** (3209 3rd Ave., Y1A 5J5, tel. 403/668–2776) has canoes, boats, motors, and ATV rentals. **Thrifty Car Rental** (tel. 9038 Quartz Rd., Y1A 5L8, tel. 403/667–7936 or 800/FOR-CARS) offers a full range of vehicle rentals. **Tatshenshini Expediting** (1602 Alder St., Y1A 3W8, tel. 403/633–2742) has complete rental packages of canoes and rafts including waterproof gear bags for clothing. **Wasa Wasa Adventures Ltd.** (RR 2, Site 19, Comp. 16, Y1A 5A5, tel. 403/633–4562) is the place for canoes. **Yukon Tours** (200–307 Jarvis St., Y1A 2H3, tel. 403/667–7790) rents canoes, as does **Yukon Whitewater Recreation** (6 Koidern Ave., Y1A 3N8, tel. 403/667–6071).

Yellowknife, NWT **Avis Rent-A-Car** (Box 400, X1A 2N3, tel. 403/873–5648); **Budget Rent-A-Car** (Yellowknife Airport, Box 2464, X1A 2P8, tel. 403/873–3366); and **Hertz Rent-A-Car** (Yellowknife Airport, Box 9000, X1A 2R3, tel. 403/873–5043) offer a full line of car rentals. **NARWAL Northern Adventures** (Box 1175, X1A 2N8, tel. 403/873–6443) and **Overlander Sports** (Box 964, X1A 2N7, tel. 403/873–2474) rent canoes. **Rent-A-Relic** (Box 751, X1A 2N6, tel. 403/873–3400) and **Tilden Rent-A-Car** (5118 50th St., Box 162, X1A 2N2, tel. 403/873–2911, 403/920–2970, or 800/387–4747) offer vehicle rentals.

By Bus If you've taken the Greyhound to Hay River and you want to continue on to Yellowknife, contact **Frontier Coachlines** (Box 1860, Yellowknife, NWT X1A 2P4, tel. 403/873–4892), which has a connecting schedule. **North of 60 Bus Lines** (Box 748, Fort Smith, NWT X0E 0P0, tel. 403/872–2467) also connects with Greyhound if your destination is east from Hay River to Pine Point, Fort Resolution, or Fort Smith (and Wood Buffalo National Park). In Whitehorse, **Norline Coaches** (2191 2nd Ave., Whitehorse, YT Y1A 4B4, tel. 403/668–3355) has scheduled service to Carmacks, Mayo, and Dawson City. **Alaskon Express** (208G Steele St., Whitehorse, YT Y1A 2C4, tel. 403/668–3225) provides service from Whitehorse northwest on the Alaska Highway to Tok, Fairbanks, and Anchorage in Alaska and south on the Klondike Highway to Skagway, Alaska. From mid-May through September, **Dempster Highway Bus Service** (Box 960, Dawson City, YT Y0B 1G0, tel. 403/993–5175) offers twice-weekly trips between Dawson City and Inuvik, NWT, on the Dempster Highway.

By Plane Chartering an aircraft in the north can be as easy as calling a taxi in the south. Not only is it a good way to get out and view the countryside; it is the only way to reach the more remote areas in the territories, such as Baffin Island. In Whitehorse, call **Action Aviation** (tel. 403/633–3343), **Air North** (tel. 403/668–2228), **Alkan Air** (tel. 403/668–2107), or **Trans North Air** (tel. 403/668–2177) for reliable service. In Yellowknife, **Adlair Aviation** (tel. 403/873–5161), **Air Tindi** (tel. 403/920–4177), **Latham Island Airways** (tel. 403/920–2891), **Ptarmigan Airways** (tel. 403/873–4461), and **Spur Aviation** (tel. 403/873–3626) are recommended.

Guided Tours

Package Tours General tours usually originate from major centers in Canada and the United States, are all-inclusive, and offer cruises, motorcoach trips, and flights to a wide range of Yukon and Northwest Territories destinations. The following tour operators have guided travelers for many years to these areas. These tours will normally be booked months in advance, so be sure to inquire early. Most tours are offered May through August.

Adventure Canada (c/o Worldwide Adventures, 1159 West Broadway, Vancouver, BC V6H 1G1, tel. 604/736–7447 or 800/387–1483) has tours from Toronto in April. Play a round of golf at the North Pole, and tour Ellesmere and the High Arctic islands. **Adventure Network** (1676 Duranleau St., Suite 200, Vancouver, BC V6H 3S5, tel. 604/683–8033) offers tours to the North Pole and Lake Hazen. **Canada North Outfitting Inc.** (Box 3100, 87 Mills St., Almonte, ON K0A 1A0, tel. 613/256–4057) gives travelers the chance to experience modern and traditional Inuit communities on Baffin Island; to visit the North Pole via Resolute; to see the subarctic from Yellowknife to Hay River to Fort Smith at the gateway to Wood Buffalo National Park; and more. **Canadian Motor Coach Travel Ltd.** (10324 103 St., Edmonton, AB T5J 0Y9, tel. 403/448–1188) offers 10-day trips from Edmonton with tours of Wood Buffalo, Hay River, Yellowknife, Fort Simpson, and the Alaska Highway. **Horizon Holidays** (160 John St., Toronto, ON M5V 2X8, tel. 800/387–2977) conducts an escorted tour and cruise aboard the *Island Princess* up the British Columbia coast stopping at Inuvik, Tuktoyaktuk, and Yellowknife. **Polar Adventures Inc.** (Box 75218, White Rock, BC V4A 9N4, tel. 604/535–2424) lets you "plant your flag" at the North Pole or stay in Inuit communities. **Rainbow Tours** (3089 3rd Ave., Whitehorse, YT Y1A 5B3, tel. 403/668–5598) offers a comprehensive network of overland tours throughout Yukon and western Arctic. **Society Expeditions Cruises, Inc.** (700–3131 Elliott Ave., Seattle, WA 98121, tel. 206/285–9400) tours the Canadian Arctic and Hudson Bay. **Special Interestours** (Box 37E, Medina, WA 98039, tel. 206/455–1960) has guided expeditions leaving from Ottawa that cross the sea ice of Hudson Strait and offer photo opportunities of the migratory birds and caribou from Cape Dorset. **Swiftsure Tours Ltd.** (1241 Broad St., Victoria, BC V8W 2A4, tel. 604/388–4227) offers escorted cultural, natural history tours from Whitehorse to Inuvik and beyond; fly across the Mackenzie Delta, photograph big game, wildflowers, birds, and scenery. **Wells Gray Tours** (250 Landsdowne St., Kamloops, BC V2C 1X7, tel. 604/374–0831) runs an escorted motorcoach tour that includes Hay River, Fort Smith, and a flight to Virginia Falls.

Guides and Outfitters If trekking through the tundra without a guide isn't for you, many professional guides and outfitters will help you with activities such as fishing, water sports, exploring parks, stalking wildlife, bird-watching, camping, or hunting—and even photo safaris, horseback riding, and river trips.

Northwest Territories Nonresident hunters in the Northwest Territories require an outfitter to hunt big game. Outfitters provide licensed guides for the hunters they serve. Each of the following Class A outfitters is assigned a specific area of the Mackenzie Mountains in the western region of the Northwest Territories. Class B outfitters are required to hunt barrenground caribou, wolf, wolverine, black bear, and barrenground grizzly bear. Only Hunters' and Trappers' Associations (HTAs) and Clubs (HTCs) may act as outfitters for grizzly bear. Class C outfitters are required to hunt musk-ox and polar bear. Total harvest for both species is limited by quotas allocated to local HTAs. Only HTAs may act as outfitters of musk-ox and polar bear. For information about seasons, bag limits, fees, and hunting regulations, contact Conservation Education/Resource Development, Department of Renewable Resources, Government of NWT, Box 1320, Yellowknife, NWT X1A 2L9, tel. 403/920–8716.

Arctic Red River Outfitters Ltd. (Box 1457, Lloydminster, AB S9V 1K4, tel. 403/875–0560) is a Class A outfitter, tracking Dall sheep and mountain caribou (July 15–Sept. 30) and offering recreational adventures June 1–Aug. 30. **Arctic Safaris** (Box 1294, Yellowknife, NWT X1A 2N9, tel. 403/873–3212 or 403/873–5522) is a Class B outfitter. They hunt central barrenground caribou, wolf, and wolverine and offer trophy fishing (Aug.–Sept.). **Bill Tait High Arctic Hunting Adventures** (Box 2435, Yellowknife, NWT X1A 2P8, tel. 403/920–2196) is a Class B outfitter and booking agent for Class C outfitters. **Canada North Outfitting** (Box 3100, 87 Mill St., Almonte, ON K0A 1A0, tel. 613/256–4057) is also a booking agent for Class C outfitters. **Ekaloktotiak HTA** (Cambridge Bay, NWT X0E 0C0, tel. 819/983–2426) is a Class B outfitter. **Gana River Outfitters Ltd.** (Box 4659, Quesnel, BC V2J 3J8, tel. 604/992–8639) is a Class A outfitter providing backpack horseback hunts (rifle or bow) for Dall sheep, mountain caribou, moose, wolf, and wolverine. **Mackenzie Mountain Outfitters Ltd.** (Box 124, Norman Wells, NWT X0E 0V0, tel. 403/587–2255) is a Class A outfitter providing guided hunts for Dall sheep, mountain caribou in Mackenzie Mountains, moose, wolf, and wolverine. Twelve-day hunts are conducted July–October. **Nahanni Butte Outfitters Ltd.** (Box 879, Nanton, AB T0L 1R0, tel. 403/645–5768) is a Class A outfitter offering hunts for Dall sheep, caribou, and moose and backpack hunts using pack dogs. **Peterson's Point Lake Camp** (Box 447, Yellowknife, NWT X1A 2N3, tel. 403/920–4654) is a Class B outfitter conducting guided caribou hunts in the barrenlands. **Qaivvik Limited** (Box 1538, Yellowknife, NWT X1A 2P2, tel. 403/873–3303) is a Class B outfitter and booking agent for Class C outfitters. **Rabesca Company Outfitters** (Rae–Edzo, NWT X0E 0N0, tel. 403/392–6920) is a Class B outfitter for barrenlands caribou hunting (mid-Aug.–late-Sept.). Guides, tent camp, accommodation, meals, and equipment are provided. **Redstone Mountain Trophy Hunts** (Box 608, Banff, AB T0L 0C0, tel. 403/762–5241 or 403/388–2117) is a Class A outfitter for hunting sheep, wolf, caribou, and moose (July–Sept.). **South Nahanni Outfitters Ltd.** (Box 586, Cardston, AB T0K 0K0, tel. 403/653–2562) is a Class A outfitter. **True North Safaris** (3919 School Draw Ave., Yellowknife, NWT X1A 2J7, tel. 403/873–8533) and **Webb and Freeland** (2260 Sumneytown Pike, Harleysville, PA 19438, tel. 215/256–1118; or Box 1538, Yellowknife, NWT X1A 2P2, tel. 403/873–3303) are Class B outfitters.

Yukon Hunters in Yukon require the services of a registered outfitter to hunt caribou, wolf, moose, mountain sheep, mountain goat, black and grizzly bear, wolverine, and coyote. Each experienced outfitter/guide has a registered hunting territory and knows the area well. For current information on hunting regulations and license fees, contact **Fish and Wildlife Branch** (Government of Yukon, Box 2703, Whitehorse, YT Y1A 2C6, tel. 403/667–5221).

Although the outfitters listed here are primarily used by hunters, those listed as offering "other activities" may be hired by hikers and wilderness photographers as well.

Bonnet-Plume Outfitters Ltd. (Box 5963, Whitehorse, YT Y1A 5L7, tel. 403/633–3366) and **Caesar Lake Outfitters** (Box 484, Watson Lake, YT Y0A 1C0, tel. 403/536–2174) offer other activities. **Pete Jensen** (58 Alsek Rd., Whitehorse, YT Y1A 3K4, tel. 403/667–2030). **Koser Outfitters** (Ross River, YT Y0B 1S0, tel. 403/969–2210) offers big-game hunting, fishing and photo safaris. **Kusawa Outfitters Ltd.** (28 Alsek Rd., Whitehorse, YT Y1A 3K2, tel. 403/667–2755) and **MacMillan River Outfitters** (Box 5088, Whitehorse, YT Y1A 4S3, tel. 403/667–6345) offer other activities, as do **Nisutlin Bay Outfitters Ltd.** (Teslin, YT Y0A 1B0, tel. 403/390–2557), **Ostashek Outfitting Ltd.** (Box 4132, Whitehorse, YT Y1A 3S9, tel. 403/668–7886), and **Pelly Mountain Outfitters Ltd.** (Box 4492, Whitehorse, YT Y1A 2R8, tel. 403/633–6606). **Richie Outfitters Ltd.** (Box 5480, Whitehorse, YT Y1A 5H4, tel. 403/668–2217). **Rogue River Outfitters** (Box 5602, Whitehorse, YT Y1A 5H4, tel. 403/633–2472). **Ruby Range Outfitters** (Box 3995, Whitehorse, YT Y1A 5M6, tel. 403/668–4500) offers other activities. **Widrig Outfitters Ltd.** (Box 5390, Whitehorse, YT Y1A 4Z2, tel. 403/668–2752) has guided backpack trips in the Mackenzie and Wernecke mountains. **Yukon Hunting & Guiding Ltd.** (25–5 Klondike Rd., Whitehorse, YT Y1A 3L7, tel. 403/667–7182). **Yukon Outfitting** (Box 5364, Whitehorse, YT Y1A 4Z2, tel. 403/667–2712) runs summer horseback trips, hiking, wildlife-viewing, photography, winter dog-sled trips.

Exploring Wilderness Canada

Due to the size of Wilderness Canada, one could not hope to see it all in one trip. The tours that follow focus on various cities and driving tours. Tour 1 covers Whitehorse and the sites around it. Tour 2 takes you from Whitehorse south along the Alaska Highway, giving you a good feel for the Yukon Territory. Tour 3 is a walking tour of Dawson City, while Tour 4 charts a common loop through Dawson City and along the Dempster Highway to Inuvik in the Northwest Territories' Mackenzie Delta. Tour 5 concludes with the sites of Yellowknife and Great Slave Lake, via the Mackenzie Highway. Above all, Wilderness Canada appeals to the hearty adventurer and nature worshiper—consider these tours, but also look beyond them. For instance, Iqaluit and Pangnirtung on Baffin Island are reached by air (*see* Getting Around, by Plane, above), and the Keewatin area on the west coast of Hudson Bay contains some unique communities and some of the best fishing in the north. So if you have the time, plan on a fishing or hunting trip at one of the many lodges in the territories (*see* Guides and Outfitters, above, and Fishing in Sports and Outdoor Activities, below), or a hiking and camping expedition at one of the scenic national parks (*see* National and Territorial Parks, below).

Highlights for First-time Visitors

Bison and whooping cranes in Wood Buffalo National Park, National and Territorial Parks

The Discovery Claim and the view from the Dome at Dawson City, Tour 3: Dawson City

The Frantic Follies and the S.S. Klondike National Historic Site, Tour 1: Whitehorse

Ice caps in the Penny Highlands on Baffin Island, National and Territorial Parks

Kaskawulsh Glacier in Kluane, National and Territorial Parks

Signpost Forest at Watson Lake, What to See and Do with Children

Victoria Falls in Nahanni, National and Territorial Parks

Tour 1: Whitehorse

Whitehorse began as an encampment beside the Yukon River's White Horse Rapids when Klondikers were forced to portage the river on their way to the goldfields in 1898. The rapids are submerged now below Schwatka Lake, but the encampment grew thanks, in part, to the construction of the White Pass and Yukon Route (WP&YR) railway, the building of the Alaska Highway and, in 1953, the moving of the territorial government seat here from Dawson City. Today this city of 20,700 serves as the transportation and communications center of Yukon Territory.

Begin your tour at the **Whitehorse Visitor Reception Centre** in the T.C. Richards Building at 302 Steele Street, one block north of Main Street. Information is available here on hotels, restaurants, stores, attractions, and local events. Audio-visual presentations at the Centre highlight the Alaska Highway, Dawson City, and other Yukon sites. *Tel. 403/667–2915. Open mid-May–mid-Sept., daily 8–8.*

Upon leaving, turn right and right again on 4th Avenue. You're heading north to **Yukon Native Products,** across from McDonald's, just past the Yukon Inn. On your way, you'll pass Qwanlin Mall on your right, the city's largest shopping center. At Yukon Native Products, you can take a tour of this specialized garment factory and see how the stylish double-shell Yukon Parka and anorak are manufactured by native craftspeople. *4230 4th Ave., tel. 403/668–5955. Open in summer, 7:30AM–8PM; in winter, 9–5:30.*

Next, retrace your steps on 4th Avenue, but turn east on Wood Street. You'll pass the Andrew Phillipsen Law Centre, the Yukon News newspaper office, the Westmark Whitehorse Hotel, and the city's main Fire Hall (at 2nd Avenue). Turn right at 1st Avenue and you're at the **MacBride Museum.** Exhibits feature profiles of native cultures, the 1898 gold rush, early exploration and the fur trade, and post–gold rush development. The natural history section, with exhibits on prehistoric mammals and other subjects, is superb. An Alaska Highway construction exhibit was added in 1992. Look out the back door and you'll see the original cabin of local folk hero Sam McGee. *1st Ave. and Wood St., tel. 403/667–2709. Gift shop and RV parking. Admission: $3.25 adults, $2.25 senior citizens, 50¢ children 6–12, $7.50 families. Open mid-May–Sept. 30, daily; Oct.–mid-May, Sun. 1–4.*

Back on 1st Avenue, turn right to Main Street. On your left is the **WP&YR station,** a hub of activity until 1982, when the line shut down. Along your stroll, you may encounter students dressed in gold rush–era uniforms of the North West Mounted Police. They are there to answer your questions and will be more than happy to pose for photos.

Time Out For a light lunch or a Swiss pastry, visit **The Pot Belly** at 106–100 Main Street. Located at street level, this small restaurant will give you breakfast, sandwiches, a salad, or just a fabulous dessert.

Turn up Main Street to 2nd Avenue and head south to the Yukon Territorial Government complex just past Hanson Street. Beside the old archives building is the Whitehorse Public Library, which houses the **Territorial Art Gallery** with its exhibits by local artists and shows from other parts of Canada. *Tel. 403/667–5239. Admission free. Open Mon.–Fri., 10–9; Sat., 10–6; Sun., 1–9.* Beside the library is the main YTG building. In the foyer is the **Yukon Permanent Art Collection,** a selection of northern landscapes and lifestyles (with an emphasis on Yukon art). *Tel. 403/667–5239. Admission free. Open weekdays 8:30–5.*

After leaving the YTG buildings, continue on and you'll see the **S.S. Klondike National Historic Site** in the distance just past Rotary Park on the other side of 2nd Avenue. This 71.6-meter (235-foot) sternwheeler was built in 1929, sank in 1936, and was rebuilt in 1937. The largest ever to ply the Yukon River between Whitehorse and Dawson City, it has been drydocked and restored to reflect its 1930s origins. *Admission free. Daily tours, mid-May–mid-Sept.*

It's time to head back downtown on the west side of 2nd Avenue. Turn left at Lambert Street and you'll pass by the log skyscraper. A right on 3rd Avenue will bring you to the **Old Log Church Museum.** Built in 1900, it remained in service until 1960. Exhibits show the history of Yukon with special emphasis on the role of the Christian church in the North. *3rd Ave. & Elliott St., tel. 403/668–2555. Admission: $2 adults, $1 children 6–12, $5 families. Open June–Aug., Mon.–Sat. 9–8, Sun noon–4.*

Following 3rd Avenue to Wood Street brings you back to the Westmark Whitehorse Hotel, site of the **Frantic Follies Vaudeville Show.** Created in 1969, this summer live show features gold-rush songs and skits, cancan dancers, and the poetry of Robert Service. *211 Wood St., tel. 403/668–3161. Admission: $16.35 adults, $8.20 chidren under 12. Daily performances: late May–mid-June, 9:15 PM; mid-June–mid-Aug., 7 PM and 9:15 PM; mid-Aug.–mid-Sept., 9:15 PM.*

Cruise historic Miles Canyon on board the **MV *Schwatka*** over the White Horse rapids. *Schwatka Lake Dock, tel. 403/668–3161. Early June, 2 PM daily; mid-June to mid-Aug., 2 and 7 PM daily; mid-Aug.–mid-Sept., 2 PM daily. Admission: $20 adults (from downtown), $13 (from the dock); $10 children under 12 (from downtown), $6.50 (from the dock).*

At the end of Nisutlin Drive in the suburb of Riverdale is the **Whitehorse Rapids Dam and Fish Ladder.** The ladder allows

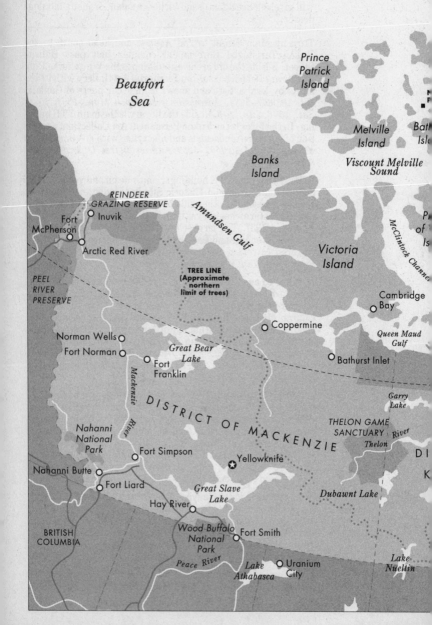

ARCTIC OCEAN

Beaufort
Sea

Prince
Patrick
Island

Melville
Island

Bat
Isl

Banks
Island

Viscount Melville
Sound

REINDEER
GRAZING RESERVE

Inuvik

Fort
McPherson

Arctic Red River

Amundsen Gulf

Victoria
Island

McClintock Channel

P
of
Is

PEEL
RIVER
PRESERVE

TREE LINE
(Approximate
northern
limit of trees)

Cambridge
Bay

Coppermine

Norman Wells

Fort Norman

Great Bear
Lake

Fort
Franklin

Queen Maud
Gulf

Bathurst Inlet

Mackenzie

DISTRICT OF MACKENZIE

Garry
Lake

THELON GAME
SANCTUARY

River

Thelon

D

Nahanni
National
Park

River

Fort Simpson

Yellowknife

Nahanni Butte

Fort Liard

Great Slave
Lake

Dubawnt Lake

K

Hay River

BRITISH
COLUMBIA

Wood Buffalo
National
Park

Fort Smith

Peace River

Lake
Athabasca

Uranium
City

Lake
Nuelin

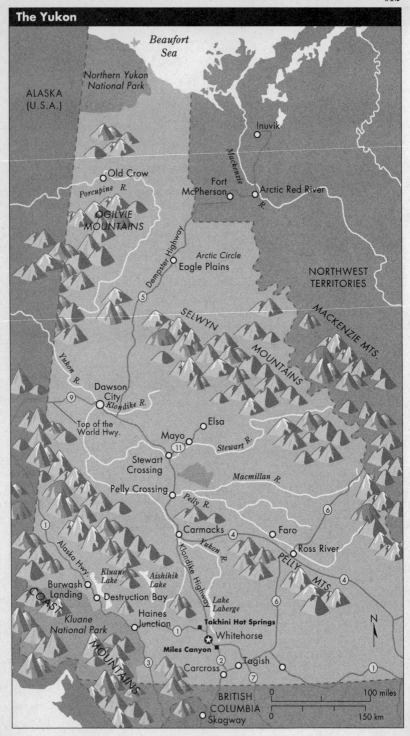

The Yukon

Beaufort Sea

ALASKA (U.S.A.)

Northern Yukon National Park

Old Crow

Porcupine R.

OGILVIE MOUNTAINS

Inuvik

Fort McPherson

Arctic Red River

Mackenzie R.

Dempster Highway

Arctic Circle
Eagle Plains

⑤

NORTHWEST TERRITORIES

SELWYN MOUNTAINS

MACKENZIE MTS.

Yukon R.

⑨

Dawson City

Klondike R.

Top of the World Hwy.

Elsa

Mayo

⑪

Stewart R.

Stewart Crossing

Macmillan R.

Pelly Crossing

Pelly R.

⑥

Carmacks

④

Faro

Ross River

Yukon R.

①

Alaska Hwy.

Kluane Lake

Aishihik Lake

Klondike Highway

PELLY MTS.

④

Burwash Landing

Destruction Bay

Lake Laberge

⑥

COAST

Kluane National Park

Haines Junction

①

Takhini Hot Springs

Whitehorse

MOUNTAINS

Miles Canyon

③

②

Carcross

Tagish

⑦

①

BRITISH COLUMBIA

Skagway

N

0   100 miles

0   150 km

spawning salmon to bypass the dam. This is the longest migration of the Chinook. *Open mid-July–mid-Sept., daily 8–10.*

Tour 2: Whitehorse to Carcross

This driving tour culminates at Fraser Station, 127 kilometers (80 miles) south on the Klondike Highway. Leave the downtown area of Whitehorse and head up the South Access road to the Alaska Highway. At the highway, you'll find **Yukon Gardens,** with its large displays of wild plants, vegetables, trees, and commercial flowers. *Box 5059, Whitehorse, tel. 403/668–7972. Open mid-May–mid-Sept., daily 9–9. Admission: $5.75 adults, $5 senior citizens, $3.75 students, $2 children.*

Continue south. After 14 kilometers (9 miles) you'll turn right on the southern leg of the Klondike. After 15 kilometers (9 miles), you'll pass the **Robinson Roadhouse,** the historic remains of an old 1900s townsite. If you like golf, try the **Annie Lake Golf Course,** a picturesque 18-hole course with sand greens 2 kilometers farther (open May–Sept.; greens fee $2). At the end of the curve around Emerald Lake, there's **Spirit Lake Lodge.** Check out the ice cream. It's top-notch. The **Museum of Yukon Natural History** and **Frontierland Theme Park** are side by side 6 kilometers (4 miles) farther on. The museum offers a wide variety of mounted Yukon wildlife in authentic dioramas. *Museum open mid-May–mid-Sept., daily 9–6. Admission: $3 adults, $1.50 children under 12, $8 families.*

The theme park contains live stone sheep and a mounted sabretooth tiger. Pan for gold or have a doughnut. *Admission: $6 adults, $4 children under 12, $20 families. Open mid-May–Sept., daily 8–7.*

As you pass the Yukon's only desert, you'll see **Carcross** in the distance. Located on the shores of Bennett Lake, Carcross was at one time a major depot for the WP&YR until it closed in 1982. Visit **Matthew Watson's General Store** in downtown Carcross across from the old **Train Depot,** now a gift shop with a café.

Continuing south, you'll view the historic remains of **Venus Mine,** an active gold and silver producer in the early 1900s. You'll cross the British Columbia border before you reach Fraser Station, the northern terminus of the *White Pass,* now a summer-only excursion train running out of Skagway, Alaska. *White Pass & Yukon Route Rail Depot, Box 435, Skagway, AK 99840, tel. 907/983–2217; in the U.S., 800/343–7373; in BC, Yukon, NWT, 800/478–7373.*

Both trains and buses connect at Fraser, and there is access to the Chilkoot Trail at Bennett, British Columbia. From here you can continue on to Skagway or return to Whitehorse.

Tour 3: Dawson City

Dawson City sprang to prominence in the days of the Klondike gold rush, boasting a population of 30,000, the largest west of Chicago and north of San Francisco. Today there are about 1,700 residents. Many of the original buildings have been restored to their early splendor, and attractions have been created to interest the Klondike visitor.

Start your tour at the **Palace Grand Theatre,** home of the **Gaslight Follies,** a Klondike-style variety show performed with music, songs, dances, and colorful costumes. *For info. call Klondike Visitors Association tel. 403/993–5575. Admission: $13 adults, $5.50 children under 12. Shows Wed.–Mon. 8PM June–mid-Sept.*

Across the street is the **1901 Post Office,** and up on 4th Avenue and Queen Street is **Diamond Tooth Gertie's Gambling Hall,** an adult entertainment reminiscent of the gold rush. Blackjack, roulette, crown and anchor, and a licensed bar highlight the activities. *Tel. 403/993–5575. Admission: $4.50. Open mid-May– mid-Sept., Mon.–Sat. 8PM–2AM.*

Up on 8th Avenue, within a block of each other, are the **residences of two writers,** the poet Robert Service, who penned such ballads as *The Cremation of Sam McGee* and *The Shooting of Dan McGrew,* and the novelist Jack London. *Robert Service cabin, tel. 403/993–5462. Admission free. Daily recitals at 10 AM and 3 PM. Open June–mid-Sept., daily 9–5. Jack London cabin, tel. 403/933–5575. Admission free. Readings from London's work daily at 1 PM. Open June–mid-Sept., daily 9–5.*

Back on 5th Avenue, at Church Street, sits the **Dawson City Museum,** housed in the former Territorial Administration Building. Exhibits range from the history of the Klondike era to native history and contemporary displays. There are also a slide presentation on the Dempster Highway and historic silent films unearthed during a construction project in 1978. The Klondike reference center provides assistance to historical and genealogy researchers. *Tel. 403/993–5291. Admission: $3 adults, $2 senior citizens and students, children under 6 free, $7 families. Open June 1–Sept. 3, daily 10–6.*

Back down on Front Street, you'll find the **SS *Keno,*** one of the last riverboats to travel the Yukon and Stewart rivers. There were more than 200 such riverboats on the Yukon waterways until the mid-1950s.

The *Yukon Queen* leaves the dock on Front Street bound for Eagle, Alaska, 173 kilometers (108 miles) and seven hours west down the Yukon River. *Tel. 403/993–5599 or 403/993–5482; to book the excursion as part of a 5- or 11-day package tour, 800/ 544–2206. Fares: $80 adult one-way, $40 children; $125 adult round-trip, $62.50 children. Open June–Sept.*

Also from the dock, you can enjoy a leisurely 1½-hour cruise down the river aboard the *Yukon Lou* to Pleasure Island, 5 kilometers (3 miles) away, for a salmon barbecue. *Box 859, Dawson City, YT Y0B 1G0, tel. 403/993–5482. Reservations required. Fares: $28 adults, $14 children. Open June–Aug., daily at 1 PM.*

No visit to Dawson City is complete without a tour up King Street through the wooded slopes to the **Midnight Dome.** The summit offers a panoramic view of the Klondike and Yukon River valleys, Dawson City, and the Ogilvie Mountains. This is the place to be at midnight on June 21 when the sun sets into the Ogilvies and immediately begins its ascent again.

Tour 4: Dempster Highway from Dawson City to Inuvik

The **Dempster Highway** begins 40 kilometers (25 miles) east of Dawson City at its junction with the Klondike Highway. From here to Inuvik, Northwest Territories, is a 740-kilometer (460-mile) gravel road with stretches of clay surface that can be slippery. There are not many services on the highway, but gas, food, and lodging are available at Eagle Plains Hotel (tel. 403/979–4187, open year-round, rooms run about $100 a night; call well in advance for reservations), about halfway to Inuvik. You should see lots of wildlife: bear, wolves, foxes, moose, ptarmigan, owls, and grouse. The porcupine caribou herd migrates through the area in October and in June. The Dempster is the traditional home of the Kutchin, or Loucheux Dene, who traded west to Alaska for centuries. Each part of the summer season has its own appeal. In May and June birds arrive from wintering areas to the south. Migrating caribou can sometimes be seen in June. Wildflowers are at their height in July, along with mosquitoes. In late August, the whole Dempster area changes from green to shades of mauve and pink. By September, snow may again cover the road as the caribou head back to wintering areas in the mountains. Taking it easy, you can cover the entire trip in about 20 hours.

Weather, even in summer, can be changeable, and visitors can run into high winds, blizzards, or heavy rains. There are two ferry crossings on the Dempster, one at Peel River and one at Arctic Red River. They operate on demand from early June to late October. The equipment is owned by the government of the Northwest Territories, and crews must meet Canadian Coast Guard standards. In spring and fall, ferry service is not available. In winter, the rivers are crossed on ice bridges maintained by highway crews. For information on road conditions, ask at hotels and information centers along the way. Highway bulletins can be heard on CBC AM radio: 560 Dawson City, 680 Fort McPherson, and 860 Inuvik, or tel. 800/661–0752.

Tour 5: Yellowknife

You can drive or walk through Yellowknife or take one of a variety of tours offered. **Raven Tours** (Box 2345, Yellowknife, NWT X1A 2P8, tel. 403/873–4776) and **North Star Tours** (Box 447, Yellowknife, NWT X1A 2N3, tel. 403/920–4654) are good ones. Or try flightseeing with **Air Tindi** (Box 1693, Yellowknife, NWT X1A 2N2, tel. 403/920–4177).

At the entrance to the city the **Bristol Monument,** a freight plane, sits prominently on an outcropping of rock. A veteran of World War II, this freighter made history when Wardair pilot Don Braun touched it down on the North Pole, the first wheeled aircraft to do so. It spent most of its working years freighting construction materials, including bulldozers.

Walk through **Old Town,** on the peninsula where in the 1930s shacks fought for space on the bare rocks. Today, the **Bush Pilot's Monument** is perched on one of these rocks. From the top, 80 steps from the base, you can see a panorama of Yellowknife and the surrounding area including the float planes in the bays. The monument salutes the daring men who opened Canada's north, and the modern bush pilots who use the city as their base.

Time Out While in Old Town, visit the **Wildcat Cafe,** a legendary squat log building rebuilt to match the original 1930s version, the early spirit of early Yellowknife. Try some of the local delicacies: caribou, whitefish, char, or muskox.

The **Prince of Wales Northern Heritage Centre** on the shore of Frame Lake is just a few minutes from downtown. It houses extensive displays of northern artifacts ranging from Inuit carvings to dioramas of northern wildlife. It has a piece of *Cosmos 954*, the Soviet satellite that crashed 480 kilometers (298 miles) east of Yellowknife in 1978; a reconstructed Fox Moth; and a large moosehide boat. *On Frame Lake opposite City Hall. Admission free. Open June–Aug., daily 10:30–5:30, Sept.–May, Tues.–Fri., weekends, hol. 10–5.*

The 33-foot **MV** *Naocha* tours the waterfront, the oldest goldmine of the area and Detah village. The two-hour trip leaves in the evenings from Latham Island. A four-hour trip to Great Slave Island is also offered, which includes a northern-style barbecue of whitefish or trout. *Sail North, Box 2497, Yellowknife, NWT X1A 2P8, tel. 403/873–8019.*

What to See and Do with Children

On the Klondike Highway, 10 kilometers (6 miles) north of Whitehorse, is the **Takhini Hot Springs.** Swimming is the highlight; suits and towels may be rented. There are 17 serviced and 75 unserviced campsites, a picnic area, laundromat, dump site, duck pond, and guided horseback trail rides. *Tel. 403/633–2706. Open in summer 7AM–10PM.*

Along the Alaska and Klondike highways, there are many opportunities to **pan for gold.** For example, at Guggieville Gold Panning on Bonanza Creek, miners will show you the correct panning methods used to extract those valuable "colors." You're guaranteed to come away with some gold in your poke and a touch of that well-known Yukon ailment—gold fever.

Try to find a sign from your hometown at the Watson Lake **Signpost Forest.** In 1942, a homesick U.S. Army soldier, who was working on the construction of the Alaska Highway, erected the first sign stating the mileage and direction to his hometown. Others followed, and in 1990 there were more than 10,000 signs in the Signpost Forest.

Shopping

Whitehorse and Yellowknife have a selection of conventional goods and foodstuffs that you'd find in any city of similar size.

Specialties in the territories include native crafts, Inuit carvings, and books on northern subjects. Each of the smaller communities will have a general store and a crafts shop. And don't leave Yukon and the Northwest Territories without a gold nugget souvenir. You can buy gold in a variety of forms, from well-crafted jewelry to funny little pill vials filled with the precious flakes.

Dawson City, YT	Have your picture taken with "Max" the stuffed moose at **Maximilian's Gold Rush Emporium** (Front and Queen Sts., tel. 403/993–5486). It has an excellent variety of books, gifts, and souvenirs. **The Raven's Nook** (2nd Ave. and Queen St., tel. 403/993–5530) sells unique gold nugget jewelry.
Inuvik, NWT	**Boreal Bookstore** (181 Mackenzie Rd., tel. 403/979–3748) is the place for northern books, Holman hangings, and NWT posters.
Whitehorse, YT	**Books on Main** (203 Main St., tel. 403/668–2434) and **Mac's Fireweed Books** (305B Main St., tel. 403/667–2358) have the widest selection of northern books. **Murdoch's Gem Shop** (207 Main St., tel. 403/667–7403) is Yukon's largest manufacturer of gold nugget jewelry. There are Murdoch's outlets in Watson Lake, Faro, and Dawson City. **Yukon Native Products** (4230–4th Ave., tel. 403/668–5955) has exclusive distribution of the original Yukon Parka. It has an outlet in Dawson City on Front St. (tel. 403/993–5115). **Indian Craft Shop** (102 Main St. & 504 Main St., tel. 403/667–7216) is your source for mukluks, moccasins, and gold nugget jewelry. **Yukon Gallery** (2093–2nd Ave., tel. 403/667–2391) carries carvings, moosehair tuftings, pottery, cards, and posters.
Yellowknife, NWT	Books can be found in **The Book Cellar** (Panda II Mall, tel. 403/920–2220). **Yellowknife Trading Post** (4 Lessard Dr., tel. 403/873–3020) is the store for Inuit and Dene arts and crafts, caribou tuftings, soapstone carvings, and Dene beading. Moosehair tuftings and other crafts are available from **Treeline Trappings** (50 Ave. & 52 St., tel. 403/920–2854).

Sports and Outdoor Activities

Camping	Waking up to the crisp, clean, and clear morning air in a campground nestled on the shores of a majestic lake or a gurgling stream is an exhilarating experience. Territorial campgrounds are found along all roads in the north and most are open from spring thaw to freeze up, though this can vary from year to year. These campgrounds provide a wilderness setting for the road traveler, and visitors are asked to keep the sites clean as a courtesy to the next party. Most have drinking water, fireplaces, and outdoor privies. For your protection, however, you should boil any water for 10 minutes prior to drinking. Territorial campgrounds in the Northwest Territories are free of charge, but there are few of them. Privately owned campgrounds, however, do charge where they are available in the western Northwest Territories (and also in Yukon). Yukon Territory campsites along the Alaska and Klondike highways charge $5 per night; either pay an attendant or use the honor box.
Canoeing	The north is a veritable latticework of wilderness rivers waiting to be explored. The Yukon and Mackenzie rivers and their tributaries for the most part are fast-flowing flat waters with a few rough sections. Topographic maps are available at most bookstores. If you are on your own, it's a good idea to leave your itinerary with the local RCMP detachment. And don't forget to advise them when you have completed your voyage. If you don't want to canoe on your own, there are outfitters who will pro-

vide competent guides and handle the logistics (*see* Getting Around, above).

The following specialize in water travel/day trips on rafts and other water vehicles: **East Wind Arctic Tours & Outfitters** (Box 2728A, Yellowknife, NWT X1A 2R1, tel. 403/873–2170); **Whitewolf Adventure Expeditions** (2565 W. 2nd Ave., Vancouver, BC V6K 1J7, tel. 604/736–0664); **Northwinds Arctic Adventures** (Iqaluit, NWT X0A 0H0, tel. 819/979–0551); **Nahanni River Adventures** (Box 8368, Station F, Edmonton, AB T6W 4W6, tel. 403/439–1316); and **Mountain River Outfitters** (Box 449, Norman Wells, NWT X0E 0V0, tel. 403/587–2324).

Fishing The north is home to a variety of fish, including lake trout, rainbow and cutthroat trout, Arctic grayling, whitefish, inconnu, walleye, and northern pike. Few fishermen on the roads and highways will pass up a chance to cast or fly-fish the streams along the way. In the Arctic waters, near Inuvik, you can try for Arctic char, some of which weigh up to 30 pounds. Lake trout and northern pike are common at that size and are abundant throughout the Mackenzie River drainage systems. Chinook salmon enter the Canadian section of the Yukon River in mid-July and August in their migration to its headwaters, and small numbers of coho salmon ascend the Porcupine River system in September and October. Fishing licenses are required in both Yukon and the Northwest Territories and are available from hardware and sporting-goods stores, department stores, and highway lodges. A special license is required to fish in Canada's national parks (children 16 and under don't need licenses). Lodges and outpost fishing camps are scattered throughout the north, and some of their operators charter their own aircraft from major southern points.

Northwest **Blachford Lake Lodge** (Box 1568, Yellowknife, NWT X1A 2P2,
Territories tel. 403/873–3303). Lake trout, northern pike, Arctic grayling, walleye, whitefish. Boats, motors, ice house; guests provide food, sleeping bags, tackle. On Blachford Lake, east of Yellowknife. May–Sept. **Brabant Lodge** (Box 1095, Hay River, NWT X0E 0R0, tel. 403/874–2600). Lake trout, Arctic grayling, northern pike, walleye, whitefish. On Brabant Island in Mackenzie River, 51 kilometers (32 miles) by air from Hay River. Lounge, dining room, boats, motors, storage, guides, tackle. June 20–Sept. 30. **Bransons Lodge** (17346 W. Kirkwood Dr., Muskego, WI 53150, tel. 414/679–9644). Lake trout, Arctic grayling, northern pike, whitefish. Sidetrips for Arctic char. On east side of Great Bear Lake at Cameron Bay. Meals, guides, boats, freezer, tackle. All-inclusive from Edmonton. July–Aug. **Drum Lake Lodge** (Fort Norman, NWT X0E 0K0, tel. 403/588–3161). Lake trout, Arctic grayling, Dolly Varden. Licenses, boats, motors, guides, meals. On Wrigley Lake 132 kilometers (82 miles) southwest of Fort Norman. Mid-June–Oct. **Frontier Fishing Lodge** (5515 82nd Ave., Edmonton, AB T6B 2J6, tel. 403/465–6843). Lake trout, Arctic grayling, whitefish, northern pike. On the East Arm of Great Slave Lake near Snowdrift. Boats, motors, guides, private 701-meter (2,300-foot) airstrip, tackle. Mid-June–mid-Sept. **High Arctic Lodge** (Box 280, Penticton, BC V2A 6K4, tel. 604/493–3300). Arctic char, lake trout. On Merkley Lake, Victoria Island. Boats, motors, guides, meals. Mid-July–Sept. **Indian Mountain Fishing Lodge** (176 West Courtney Lane, Tempe, AZ 85284, tel. 602/829–6200). Lake trout, Arctic grayling. At Mc-

Leod Bay on Great Slave Lake. Boats, motors, guides on request. July–Aug. **Koluctoo Bay Sports Fishing Camp** (Pond Inlet, NWT X0A 0S0, tel. 819/899–8912). Arctic char. On Baffin Island near Pond Inlet. Boats, motors, guides. Aug.–mid-Sept. **Nonacho Lake Fishing Camp** (Box 510, Hay River, NWT X0E 0R0, tel. 403/874–2281). Lake trout, northern pike, Arctic grayling, whitefish. On Nonacho Lake 321 kilometers (200 miles) east of Hay River. Cabin accommodation. Licensed facilities, boats, motors, gas, oil, freezer. Store sells tackle and basic necessities. Round-trips from Hay River. Mid-June–mid-Sept. **North of Sixty Fishing Lodges** (1381 Erin St., Winnipeg, MB R3E 2S7, tel. 204/786–6054). Northern pike, Arctic grayling, lake trout, whitefish. Camps located in the Dubawnt and Kazan River areas. Direct flights from Winnipeg. Mid-June–Sept. **Plummer's Great Bear Lake Lodge** and **Plummer's Great Slave Lake Lodge** (950 Bradford St., Winnipeg, MB R3H 0N5, tel. 204/774–5775 or 800/665–0240). Lake trout, Arctic grayling. Boats, motors, guides, licensed dining room. Fly direct from Winnipeg or Yellowknife. Great Slave Lake: June–mid-Sept.; Great Bear Lake: July–Aug. **Prelude Lake Lodge** (Box 2548, Yellowknife, NWT X1A 2P8, tel. 403/873–8511). Lake trout, walleye, northern pike, whitefish. On Prelude Lake, 25 minutes by road from Yellowknife. Boats, motors, licenses, tackle, café. Mid-May–Sept. **Rutledge Lake Lodge** (Box 342, Hay River, NWT X0E 0R0, tel. 403/874–2571). Lake trout, northern pike, whitefish. On Rutledge Lake northeast of Hay River. Boats, motors. Guests bring tackle and food. June–Sept. **Sitidgi Lake Fishing Lodge** (Box 1332, Inuvik, NWT X0E 0T0, tel. 403/979–3349). Lake trout, Arctic grayling, whitefish, northern pike. 52 kilometers (32 miles) east of Inuvik. Boats, licenses. Mid-June–mid-Sept. **Thubun Lake Lodge** (Box 480, Hay River, NWT X0E 0R0, tel. 403/874–2950 or 403/874–6416). Lake trout, northern pike, walleye. Fly-in resort northeast of Hay River. Boats, motors, guides, meals. June–Sept. **Tongait Arctic Sports Fishing Camp** (Box 3100, Almonte, ON K0A 1A0, tel. 613/256–4057). Arctic char. At Kingnait Fiord on Baffin Island. Boats, motors, guides, meals. July–Aug. **Watta Lake Lodge** (Box 806, Yellowknife, NWT X1A 2N6, tel. 403/873–3626 or 403/873–4036). Lake trout, Arctic grayling, whitefish, northern pike. Boats, motors, licenses, guides. All-inclusive from Yellowknife. Mid-June–Sept.

Yukon **Brooklands Wilderness Fishing Camp** (Box 299, Atlin, BC V0W 1A0). Lake trout, Arctic grayling, northern pike. Meals, guides. **Kluane Lake Tours** (Mile 1,083 Alaska Highway, Destruction Bay, YT Y0B 1H0, tel. 403/841–4411). Specializes in sport and trophy fishing on Kluane Lake. Drive or fly to other remote lakes. Trips range from half-day excursions to 14-day packages. **Kluane Wilderness Lodge** (Box 75, Tappen, BC V0E 2X0, tel. 604/835–8640). Lake trout, Arctic grayling, northern pike. Fly in to Wellesley Lake. All-inclusive from Whitehorse. **Peacock's Yukon Camps** (77 Alsek Rd., Whitehorse, YT Y1A 3K5, tel. 403/667–2846). Lake trout, northern pike, Arctic grayling. Housekeeping camps on lakes 97 to 185 kilometers (60 to 115 miles) north of Whitehorse. **Takhini River Guiding** (Box 5147, Whitehorse, YT Y1A 4S3). Lake trout, northern pike, Arctic grayling. Specializes in fly fishing on southwest Yukon rivers. **Tina Lakes Wilderness Resort** (Box 5221, Whitehorse, YT Y1A 4Z1, tel. 403/668–4059). Lake trout, Arctic grayling, northern pike. **Toobally Lakes Fishing Camps** (Box 7,

Watson Lake, YT Y0A 0C0). Northern pike, lake trout, Arctic grayling, Dolly Varden. Specializes in fly-in fishing in the southeast corner of Yukon. **Wolf Lake Wilderness Camp** (12–528 Cedar Cr., SW, Calgary, AB T3C 2Y8, tel. 403/249–4949). Lake trout, Arctic grayling, northern pike. Meals, boats, tackle.

National and Territorial Parks

Auyuittuq National Park has special treats for those seeking an exciting Arctic experience. Lying 2,400 kilometers (1,500 miles) northeast of Montréal, Auyuittuq covers 21,470 square kilometers (8,290 square miles) of Baffin Island. The Penny Highlands dominate the park, rising 2,135 meters (7,000 feet) above sea level, and carry on their peaks the Penny Ice Cap, 3,550 square kilometers (2,200 square miles) of solid ice—a remnant of the last ice age. Glaciers, spawned by the ice cap, flow majestically into the surrounding valleys. The park can be reached by flying directly to Pangnirtung. Here you will find wonderful camping spots and first-class opportunities to climb, fish, hike, read rocks, study nature, and take pictures.

Most visitors come here to hike. Difficult terrain and changeable weather demand considerable outdoor experience, careful selection of equipment, and adequate planning. The best time to hike is from late June to early August, when the valleys are clear of snow. Pangnirtung Pass has all the ingredients for a great hiking challenge—gravel flats, boulder-strewn morraines, glacial tongues, and icy streams to ford. Overlord Campground is located on the Weasal River Delta, some 32 kilometers (20 miles) from Pangnirtung, very close to the boundary of the park. From here, it is possible to walk to Summit Lake. *Auyuittuq National Park, Pangnirtung, NWT X0A 0R0, tel. 819/473–8828.*

Kluane National Park, in the southwestern corner of the Yukon, offers spectacular scenery in the form of alpine meadows, glaciers, mountain lakes, and many varieties of flora and fauna. There are moose, Dall's sheep (which can be seen from the Alaska Highway), mountain goats, caribou, grizzly and black bears, and a variety of smaller mammals. Kluane's best-known feature is the St. Elias mountain range, of which Canada's highest peak, Mount Logan (5,954 meters, or 19,520 feet), is a part. For hikers, the park offers a number of old mining roads, trails, and creekside paths. One route leads to the Kaskawulsh glacier, one of the few that may be reached on foot. *Kluane National Park, Haines Junction, YT Y0B 1L0, tel. 403/634–2251.*

Nahanni National Park is the land of legend and mystery. Centered along the South Nahanni and Flat rivers, the park is a magnificent wilderness corridor with deep canyons, rapids, waterfalls, hot springs, alpine prairie, and rugged mountains. White-water canoeists, hikers, photographers, and naturelovers from all over the world thrill to the adventure available here in the heart of the Mackenzie Mountains. At Virginia Falls, the South Nahanni takes a spectacular plunge of 98 meters (321 feet). If you travel on your own, keep in mind that the Nahanni is wilderness and help is not always readily available. The park can be reached by air from Fort Simpson and Fort

Liard. *Nahanni National Park, Bag 300, Fort Simpson, NWT X0E 0N0, tel. 403/695–3151.*

Northern Yukon National Park (also known as the Reindeer Grazing Reserve) encompasses 10,000 square kilometers (3,861 square miles) in the northwest corner of the territory. Barren ground caribou, grizzly bear, Dall sheep and Arctic fox inhabit this magnificent tundra. The porcupine caribou herd of more than 150,000 animals is the prominent wildlife feature. As there is no road access, you will have to charter a small aircraft to get to the park. Aircraft landings require approval from the park office, and access is restricted only to a few locations. *Northern Yukon National Park, Inuvik, NWT X0E 0T0, tel. 403/979–3248.*

Wood Buffalo National Park, on the border of Alberta and the Northwest Territories, is the second-largest park in the world and is accessible from Fort Smith. The park is home to 3,500 bison, 200 species of birds, and large populations of beaver and muskrat. The park also contains the last nesting grounds of the rare whooping crane. Only 100 or so of these magnificent birds exist, and visitors are not allowed near the nesting sites. Most of the park remains in its natural wilderness state, but there are areas for camping, picnicking, boating, and swimming. Private outfitters will take visitors on overnight hikes and boating tours in the summer and skiing and dogsledding trips in the winter. *Wood Buffalo National Park, Box 750, Fort Smith, NWT X0E 0P0, tel. 403/872–2349.*

Dining and Lodging

Dining

Your best bet for dining out is to stick to the dining facilities in your hotel, or ask your hosts for their recommendations. In the larger centers, there are some good restaurants featuring some of the local delicacies, such as caribou and moose. Though the north isn't a gastronomic paradise, the restaurants listed here are reliably good. Highly recommended restaurants are indicated by a star ★.

Category	Cost*
Very Expensive	over $20
Expensive	$15–$20
Moderate	$10–$15
Inexpensive	under $10

per person, excluding drinks, service, and 7% GST

Lodging

Accommodation in Wilderness Canada is not like the hotel-motel lodgings in the southern part of the country. You won't find many of the amenities common to the lodgings of the major metropolitan centers: Montréal, Toronto, or Vancouver. The main criteria used here are that the hotels are relatively quiet and safe and that guest rooms are at least clean and comfortable.

These basic hotel rooms are decorated in a traditional style, and for the most part, they have telephones and access to satellite TV. The majority now have private baths and/or showers. Your hosts will usually be amiable and well informed about the area you have chosen to visit—you can often rely on their expertise to guide you through your stay. Because of the very heavy tourist flow to the north during the summer, you should make reservations early in the year. Accommodations are relatively expensive during the summer season but can be as much as 70% cheaper during the off-season. Most places accept major credit cards, but you should call ahead to check if you plan to pay this way.

Category	Cost*
Very Expensive	over $150
Expensive	$120–$150
Moderate	$90–$120
Inexpensive	under $90

All prices are for a standard double room (or an equivalent, where not applicable), excluding gratuities and 7% GST.

Northwest Territories

Fort Smith
Lodging

Pelican Rapids Inn. This modern motel offers all the conveniences in the heart of downtown Fort Smith. There are a restaurant and laundromat across the street. *152 McDougal Rd., Box 52, X0E 0P0, tel. 403/872–2789. 50 rooms with private bath, including 6 kitchenettes. Facilities: telephone, TV. AE, MC, V. Open year-round. Inexpensive.*

Hay River
Lodging

Ptarmigan Inn. This hotel has just about every convenience at your fingertips. Guests have access to the swimming pool and fitness center across the street. The rooms are modern and equipped with double beds, and there are five nonsmoking units. In 1990, the dining lounge and bar were renovated. This is value. *17 Capital Cr., Box 1000, X0E 0R0, tel. 403/874–6781. 41 units with private bath. Facilities: TV, telephone, laundry, hair salon, bank, gift shop, women's apparel shop, tennis courts close by. AE, MC, V. Open year-round. Moderate.*

Migrator Motel. Built in 1973, this quiet motel just north of downtown Hay River is one of the few that accepts pets. The rooms are clean and modern despite this. It's an ideal family stop and just a half-block walk to two restaurants. Special senior citizen rates are available. *807 Mackenzie Dr., Box 1847, X0E 0R0, tel. 403/874–6792. 24 units with private bath, including 6 kitchenettes. Facilities: TV, telephones. AE, MC, V. Open year-round. Inexpensive.*

Inuvik
Dining and Lodging

Finto Motor Inn. A quiet atmosphere is the drawing card at this hotel located at the Marine Bypass and Mackenzie Road junction, just a five-minute walk from downtown. The 1985 expansion doubled the number of clean, bright rooms, tastefully decorated. The Peppermill Restaurant features caribou and char in addition to a wide range of western food. *Box 1925, X0E 0T0, tel. 403/979–2647. 52 rooms with private bath; 6 with shower only, 1 suite. Facilities: telephone, TV, laundry, room* service by prior arrangement. MC, V. Closed Christmas–New Year's Day. Expensive.

Eskimo Inn. Located right downtown on Mackenzie Road, this modern hotel with a newly renovated lobby provides a clean, neat home away from home for the traveler. Stained-glass windows in the Nanook Lounge and musk-ox steaks served in the Caribou Dining Room are just two of the features. It's close to everything in Inuvik. *Box 1740, X0E 0T0, tel. 403/979–2801. 75 rooms with private bath. Facilities: telephone, TV. AE, MC, V. Open year-round. Moderate.*

Iqaluit
Dining and Lodging

Discovery Lodge Hotel. Situated between the airport and downtown Iqaluit, this hotel underwent extensive renovations in 1989–90. The installation of skylights did much to brighten the lobby area, and some of the rooms feature trapezoidal beds, wider at the top than at the bottom. This is one of the cleaner, more cheerful hotels in town, and the Granite Dining Room features caribou brochettes and caribou rouladen along with poached char. Each table is a slab of granite. *Box 387, X0A 0H0, tel. 819/979–4433. 38 rooms with private bath; 1 suite. Facilities: laundry, airport shuttle, telephones, TV. AE, DC, MC, V. Closed Christmas–New Year's Day. Very Expensive.*

Frobisher Inn. The front rooms of this hotel located on Astro Hill afford the best view of downtown Iqaluit and Frobisher Bay. Major renovations took place in 1990–91 to thoroughly modernize the hotel; all guest rooms feature queen-size beds, some with extralong beds and sofas. A recent name change to Hotel Iqaluit was short-lived. *Box 610, X0A 0H0, tel. 819/979–2222. 50 rooms with private bath. Facilities: telephone, laundry, TV, access to a neighboring indoor pool. AE, MC, V. Open year-round. Expensive.*

Yellowknife
Dining

Factor's Club. Located in the Explorer Hotel (*see below*), this convivial dining room looks out over Back Bay, a picturesque view in either summer or winter. The Continental cuisine is complemented by northern dishes that feature caribou, Arctic char, and a marinated musk-ox reputed to be the best in the north. The fireplace warms diners on cool evenings. *49th St. & 48th Ave., tel. 403/873–3531. Reservations advised. Jacket and tie suggested. AE, MC, V. Closed Sun. Expensive.*

The Red Apple. Located in the Discovery Inn next to the Legion, the Red Apple serves up traditional, home-cooked western fare in a friendly atmosphere. *4701 Franklin Ave., tel. 403/873–2324. Reservations suggested. Dress: casual. AE, MC, V. Moderate.*

Lodging

Explorer Hotel. This modern and well-equipped eight-story hotel is in the heart of downtown at 49th Street and 49th Avenue. Guest rooms on the east side have the best view. Polaris Lounge features live entertainment. *Postal Service 7000, X1A 2R3, tel. 403/873–3531. 125 rooms with private bath, including 2 suites. Facilities: gift shop, courtesy airport van, TV, telephones, central air-conditioning, room service. AE, MC, V. Open year-round. Very Expensive.*

Yellowknife Inn. This is Yellowknife's other major hotel besides the Explorer and offers equally fine accommodations and facilities. Sit in on the Legislative Assembly of the NWT; it's right next door. You're likely to see some of these folks in the inn's lobby as well; this is a popular home-away-from-home for business and government people. Following a recent trend, the hotel has set aside the fourth floor for nonsmokers. *Box 490, X1A*

2N4, tel. 403/873–2601 or 403/873–2600 (collect). 150 rooms
with private bath including 4 suites. Facilities: café, lounge,
dining room, tavern, gift shop, telephones, TV, free airport
bus. AE, DC, MC, V. Very Expensive.

Igloo Inn. Known as the Twin Pine Motor Inn until 1991, the
Igloo Inn offers basic modern accommodations; most rooms are
equipped with kitchenettes. There is a good view of Back Bay
on one side and Yellowknife's Old Town on the other. It is located between Old Town and city center at 4115 Franklin Ave.
Box 596, X1A 2N4, tel. 403/873–8511. 44 rooms with private
bath, including 33 with kitchenettes. Facilities: telephones,
TV. AE, MC, V. Open year-round. Moderate.

Yukon Territory

Dawson City
Dining and Lodging

Downtown Hotel. Located at 2nd Avenue and Queen Street,
this hotel is just one block from Diamond Tooth Gertie's and the
Palace Grand Theatre. The Jack London Grill provides a great
meal for your dollar; or you can relax in the Sourdough Saloon
and take in the local color. Box 780, Y0B 1G0, tel. 403/993–5346.
60 units with private bath including 2 suites. Facilities: TV,
telephone, airport limousine, Jacuzzi. AE, DC, MC, V. Open
year-round. Moderate.

Eldorado Hotel. The draws at this hotel, at 3rd Avenue and
Princess Street, are its Bonanza Dining Room and Sluice Box
lounge. A few of the rooms have kitchenettes, which are convenient for guests planning longer stays. Box 338, Y0B 1G0, tel.
403/993–5451; in Alaska, 800/764–3536. 54 units with private
bath including 6 kitchenettes and 4 suites. Facilities: complimentary airport service, TV, telephones, coin laundromat,
limited-menu room service in summer season. AE, DC, MC,
V. Open year-round. Moderate.

★ **Westmark Inn Dawson City.** Major additions in 1990 and 1991
have increased this hotel from 90 rooms to 131. Belinda's Cafe
features a bright courtyard deck and regular salmon barbecues, and the Keno Lounge is the home of the legendary
Sourtoe Cocktail. 5th Ave. & Harper St., Box 420, Y0B 1G0,
tel. 403/993–5542; in Canada, 800/999–2570; in U.S., 800/544–
0970. 131 units with private bath including 4 suites. Room
service on request. Facilities: access for the disabled, gift shop,
TV, telephones on request. AE, D, DC, MC, V. Open mid-
May–mid-Sept. Moderate.

Haines Junction
Lodging

Kluane Park Inn. New curtains and carpeting and a general refurbishment of guest rooms brightened this inn in 1990. The
inn is located on the left side of the Alaska Highway just before
the Haines Highway cutoff. There's no restaurant, but sandwiches are served in the lounge. Box 5400, Y0B 1L0, tel. 403/
634–2261. 16 rooms with private bath; 2 rooms with showers; 2
rooms with kitchenettes. Facilities: satellite TV. AE, DC, MC,
V. Open year-round. Inexpensive.

Watson Lake
Dining and Lodging
★

Belvedere Hotel. The lobby of this midsize hotel was renovated
in 1990. There's a lounge, restaurant, and coffee shop on the
premises. This is the first hotel as you come into Watson Lake
from the south, on the left side of the Alaska Highway. Box
288, Y0A 1C0, tel. 403/536–7712. 48 units with private bath.
Facilities: access for the disabled, TV, telephones in 21 rooms,
Jacuzzi in 1 room. AE, DC, MC, V. Open year-round. Moderate.

Gateway Motor Inn. Located on the south side of the Alaska

Highway across from the post office, the Gateway underwent extensive renovations to the lobby and restaurant (the Gateway Garter) in 1991, and both are now larger. *Box 560, Y0A 1C0, tel. 403/536–7744. 53 units with private bath, including 1 suite and 3 kitchenettes. Facilities: TV, telephones. AE, MC, V. Open year-round. Moderate.*

Watson Lake Hotel. Located on the north side of the Alaska Highway on the western edge of Watson Lake, this hotel provides basic services, and guest rooms are clean and neat. The dining room is licensed, and there's a café and lounge. *Box 370, Y0A 1C0, tel. 403/536–7781. 48 units with private bath, including 3 kitchenettes and 1 suite. Facilities: TV, telephones, sauna, coin laundromat. AE, DC, MC, V. Open year-round. Inexpensive.*

Whitehorse
Dining
★

Charlie's Dining Room. Named after the legendary Arizona Charlie Meadows, this restaurant is set in an authentic 1898 atmosphere. The menu features fine Continental cuisine. House specialties include pepper steak, rack of lamb, and Caeser salad. Try the gin tomato soup. *2288 2nd Ave., tel. 403/668–4747. Reservations advised. Dress: casual. AE, DC, MC, V. No lunch weekends. Very Expensive.*

The Cellar. The specialties here are prime rib, king crab, lobster, prawns, and chicken. Completely remodeled in 1990, The Cellar is appropriately located downstairs in the Edgewater Hotel. There's no view. *101 Main St., tel. 403/667–2572. Reservations suggested. Dress: casual but neat. AE, MC, V. Open year-round. Expensive.*

Panda's. In the heart of downtown, Panda's provides a nostalgic, Klondike setting for its French cuisine. It's a romantic spot that's ideal for that special night out. And it's one of the few places in Wilderness Canada where you'll find escargots—perfectly prepared. *212 Main St., tel. 403/667–2632. Reservations advised. Jacket and tie suggested. AE, MC, V. Open evenings only. Closed Jan. Expensive.*

Lodging

Westmark Klondike Inn. Most of this hotel's guest rooms and Trapper, the night club, were completely renovated in 1990. Charlie's (*see* above), the restaurant, is reason enough to stay here. Located at the edge of the downtown area at the bottom of Two-Mile Hill. *2288 Second Ave., Y1A 1C8, tel. 403/668–4747 or 800/999–2570. 98 units with private bath, including 3 suites. Facilities: TV, telephones, access for the disabled, nonsmoking rooms, coin laundromat, hair salon, gift shop, sauna, dining room, coffee shop, lounge, cabaret. AE, DC, MC, V. Open year-round. Expensive.*

★ **Westmark Whitehorse Hotel.** Formerly known as the Sheffield and before that, the Travelodge, this is Whitehorse's premier hotel located right downtown on Wood Street at 2nd Avenue. It has more facilities than most hotels in the territory, and the Frantic Follies (*see* Exploring, Tour 1, above) liven this spot at night—this is as good as it gets in Yukon. *Box 4250, Y1A 3T3, tel. 403/668–4700, 800/478–1111, or 800/999–2570. 181 units with private bath, including 5 suites. Facilities: lounge, restaurant, TV, telephones, access for the disabled, nonsmoking rooms, gift shop, barber shop, art gallery, beauty salon, travel agency. AE, DC, MC, V. Open year-round. Expensive.*

Yukon Inn. There's nothing fancy about this inn, but the kitchenettes are welcome by travelers on a budget. *4220 4th Ave., Y1A 1K1, tel. 403/667–2527 or 800/661–0454. 97 units with private bath including 25 kitchenettes and 2 suites. Facilities: gift* *shop, hair salon, café, dining room, restaurant, Jacuzzi, TV, telephones. AE, MC, V. Open year-round. Moderate.*

The Arts and Nightlife

The Arts

Theater and music are very much a part of the life of the northerner, though the caliber of entertainment may not be equal to that enjoyed in the south. In **Dawson City,** the show at the Palace Grand, **Gaslight Follies** (*see* Exploring, Tour 3, above) is a good one; and you're sure to enjoy the readings at the Jack London and Robert Service Cabins. The **Dawson City Music Festival** (DCMF Association, Box 456, Dawson City, YT Y0B 1G0, tel. 403/993–5584) is held each July.

In **Whitehorse** the **Frantic Follies Vaudeville Show** (*see* Exploring, Tour 1, above) is excellent, and the **Eldorado Musical Revue** (411 Main St., tel. 403/668–6472) is a similar presentation held June–September. Plays and musical events are held at the **Guild Hall** (tel. 403/633–5351) in Porter Creek subdivision throughout the year. The **Frostbite Music Society** (tel. 403/668–4921) presents a summer concert series. For information call the ArtsLine, tel. 403/667–ARTS.

Folk on the Rocks (SENT, Box 326, Yellowknife, NWT X1A 2N3, tel. 403/873–4923) takes place each July in **Yellowknife.** This open-air concert features artists from all over the north, Canada, and the United States. During the summer, the **Northern Arts and Cultural Centre** (Box 1025, Yellowknife, NWT X1A 2N7, tel. 403/837–3840) schedules a number of productions.

Nightlife

In the north, the bars and lounges of the better hotels tend toward country-and-western entertainment and can be the center of activity during the long winter season. Stick with the recommendations of your hosts before venturing out. Favorite stops in Whitehorse are **Cheers** in the Taku Hotel, the **Kopper King** on the Alaska Highway west of the airport, **Trappers** in the Westmark Klondike Inn, and the **Shannon Lounge** in the Whitehorse Center Motor Inn. Yellowknife's most popular nightspots are the **Polaris Lounge** in the Explorer Hotel, and **Mackenzie Lounge** in the Yellowknife Inn. For rock-and-roll, check out **RJ's Bar** in the Discovery Inn.

Index

WHEREVER YOU TRAVEL, *H*ELP IS NEVER FAR AWAY.

From planning your trip to providing travel assistance along the way, American Express® Travel Service Offices* are always there to help.

Alberta
BANFF
403-762-3207

CALGARY
403-261-5982

EDMONTON
403-421-0608

British Columbia
PRINCE GEORGE
604-564-7000

PRINCE RUPERT
604-627-1266

VANCOUVER
604-669-2813
604-687-7686

VICTORIA
604-385-8731

Manitoba
WINNIPEG
204-949-9349
204-786-5671

Northwest Territories
YELLOWKNIFE
403-873-2121

Nova Scotia
HALIFAX
902-423-3900
902-455-9676

Ontario
OTTAWA
613-563-0231

THUNDER BAY
807-623-7473

TORONTO
416-868-1044
416-967-3411
416-963-6060

Quebec
MONTREAL
514-284-3300

QUEBEC CITY
418-627-2580

Saskatchewan
REGINA
306-352-8685

SASKATOON
306-665-3300

Over 1500 Great Weekend Escapes...

in Six Fabulous Fodor's Guides to
Bed & Breakfasts, Country Inns, Cottages,
and Other Weekend Pleasures!

Fodor's
★★★★
Bed &
Breakfasts,
Country
Inns,
and Other
Weekend
Pleasures
MID-
ATLANTIC
REGION

The
Mid-Atlantic
Region

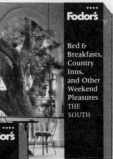

Fodor's
★★★★
Bed &
Breakfasts,
Country
Inns,
and Other
Weekend
Pleasures
THE SOUTH

The
South

Fodor's
★★★★
Bed &
Breakfasts,
Country
Inns,
and Other
Weekend
Pleasures
THE WEST
COAST

New
England

Fodor's
★★★★
Bed &
Breakfasts
and
Country
Inns
**New
England**
and other
weekend
pleasures

The
West Coast

Fodor's
★★★★
Canada's
Great
Country
Inns
*The Best in
Food and
Lodging*
by Anita
Stewart

Fodor's
★★★★
Cottages,
B&Bs and
Country
Inns of
England
and Wales
*Staying Off
the Beaten
Track*
by Elizabeth
Gundrey

England
and
Wales

Canada

Fodor's
Where the best memories begin

Fodor's Travel Guides

U.S. Guides

Alaska

Arizona

Boston

California

Cape Cod, Martha's
Vineyard, Nantucket

The Carolinas & the
Georgia Coast

Chicago

Disney World & the
Orlando Area

Florida

Hawaii

Las Vegas, Reno,
Tahoe

Los Angeles

Maine, Vermont,
New Hampshire

Maui

Miami & the Keys

New England

New Orleans

New York City

Pacific North Coast

Philadelphia & the
Pennsylvania Dutch
Country

San Diego

San Francisco

Santa Fe, Taos,
Albuquerque

Seattle & Vancouver

The South

The U.S. & British
Virgin Islands

The Upper Great
Lakes Region

USA

Vacations in New York
State

Vacations on the
Jersey Shore

Virginia & Maryland

Waikiki

Washington, D.C.

Foreign Guides

Acapulco, Ixtapa,
Zihuatanejo

Australia & New
Zealand

Austria

The Bahamas

Baja & Mexico's
Pacific Coast Resorts

Barbados

Berlin

Bermuda

Brazil

Budapest

Budget Europe

Canada

Cancun, Cozumel,
Yucatan Penisula

Caribbean

Central America

China

Costa Rica, Belize,
Guatemala

Czechoslovakia

Eastern Europe

Egypt

Euro Disney

Europe

Europe's Great Cities

France

Germany

Great Britain

Greece

The Himalayan
Countries

Hong Kong

India

Ireland

Israel

Italy

Italy's Great Cities

Japan

Kenya & Tanzania

Korea

London

Madrid & Barcelona

Mexico

Montreal &
Quebec City

Morocco

The Netherlands
Belgium &
Luxembourg

New Zealand

Norway

Nova Scotia, Prince
Edward Island &
New Brunswick

Paris

Portugal

Rome

Russia & the Baltic
Countries

Scandinavia

Scotland

Singapore

South America

Southeast Asia

South Pacific

Spain

Sweden

Switzerland

Thailand

Tokyo

Toronto

Turkey

Vienna & the Danube
Valley

Yugoslavia

CNN TRAVEL GUIDE

PASSPORT TO THE WORLD

Join host Valerie Voss for an entertaining and informative program that takes you to the four corners of the earth. With expert advice from Michael Spring, Fodor's Editorial Director, *CNN Travel Guide* is the perfect companion for anyone planning a trip or just interested in travel.

Drawing on CNN's vast network of international correspondents, you'll discover an exciting variety of new destinations from the most exotic locales to some well-kept secrets just a short trip away. You'll also find helpful tips on everything from hotels and restaurants to packing and planning. So tune in to *CNN Travel Guide*. And make it your first stop on any trip.

SUNDAY 1:00AM ET   **SUNDAY 8:30AM** ET